Preface

As the official handbook of the Federal Government, *The United States Government Manual* provides comprehensive information on the agencies of the legislative, judicial, and executive branches. The *Manual* also includes information on quasi-official agencies; international organizations in which the United States participates; and boards, commissions, and committees.

A typical agency description includes a list of principal officials, a summary statement of the agency's purpose and role in the Federal Government, a brief history of the agency, including its legislative or executive authority, a description of its programs and activities, and a "Sources of Information" section. This last section provides information on consumer activities, contracts and grants, employment, publications, and many other areas of public interest.

The *Manual* is also available and periodically updated on its own website. The U.S. Government Manual website (usgovernmentmanual.gov) is jointly administered by the Office of the Federal Register (OFR)/Government Printing Office (GPO) partnership. The website offers three ways to and information about Government agencies and organizations by entering a term in the keyword search box, browsing categories, or using "The Government of the United States" site map for an overview of the Government. For more information and to view The *Manual* online, go to *www.usgovernmentmanual.gov*.

The 2014 *Manual* was prepared by the Presidential and Legislative Publications Unit, Office of the Federal Register. Alfred W. Jones was Team Leader; Joseph Frankovic was Managing Editor; assisted by Lois Davis, Joshua Liberatore, Joseph Vetter, Edgar G. Gibbs, Ryan R. Nolan, and Todd Goodman.

THE FEDERAL REGISTER AND ITS SPECIAL EDITIONS

The *Manual* is published as a special edition of the *Federal Register* (see 1 CFR 9.1). Its focus is on programs and activities. Persons interested in detailed organizational structure, the regulatory documents of an agency, or Presidential documents should refer to the Federal Register or one of its other special editions, described below. Issued each Federal working day, the *Federal Register* provides a uniform system for publishing Presidential documents, regulatory documents with general applicability and legal effect, proposed rules, notices, and documents required to be published by statute. For more information and to look at the Federal Register online, go to *www.federalregister.gov*.

The Code of Federal Regulations is an annual codification of the general and permanent rules published in the Federal Register. The Code is divided into 50 titles that represent broad areas subject to Federal regulation. The Code is kept up to date by the individual issues of the Federal Register. For more information and to look at the Code of Federal Regulations online, go to *www.gpo.gov/fdsys/browse/collectionCfr.action?collectionCode=CFR*.

The *Compilation of Presidential Documents* serves as a timely, up-to-date reference source for the public policies and activities of the President. It contains remarks, news conferences, messages, statements, and other Presidential material of a public nature issued by the White House. The *Compilation of Presidential Documents* collection is composed of the *Daily Compilation of Presidential Documents* and its predecessor, the *Weekly Compilation of Presidential Documents*. For more information and to look at the Presidential documents online, go to *www.gpo.gov/fdsys/browse/collection. action?collectionCode=CPD*. The Compilation of Presidential Documents now has a free mobile application at *www.gpo.gov/mobile*.

A companion publication to the Compilation of Presidential Documents is the Public Papers of the Presidents, which contains public Presidential documents and speeches in convenient book form. Volumes of the Public Papers have been published for every President since Herbert Hoover, with the exception of Franklin D. Roosevelt, whose papers were published privately. For more information and to view the Public Papers online, go to *www.gpo.gov/fdsys/browse/collection.action? collectionCode=PPP*.

OTHER OFFICE OF THE FEDERAL REGISTER PUBLICATIONS

The Office of the Federal Register publishes slip laws, which are pamphlet prints of each public and private law enacted by Congress. Slip laws are compiled annually as the *United States Statutes at Large*. For more information and to look at the slip laws online, go to *www.gpo.gov/fdsys/browse/collection.action?collectionCode=PLAW*. The *Statutes* at Large volumes contain all public and private laws and concurrent resolutions enacted during a session of Congress; recommendations for executive, legislative, and judicial salaries; reorganization plans; proposed and ratified amendments to the Constitution; and Presidential proclamations. Included with many of these documents are sidenotes, *U.S. Code* and statutes citations, and a summary of their legislative histories. For more information and to look at the Statutes at Large online, go to *www.gpo.gov/fdsys/browse/collection.action?collectionCode=STATUTE*.

ELECTRONIC SERVICES

The Office of the Federal Register maintains an Internet site for the Federal Register's public inspection list, and information on the Office and its activities at *www.ofr.gov*. This site also contains links to the texts of *The United States Government Manual*, public laws, the *Compilation of Presidential Documents*, the *Federal Register*, and the *Code of Federal Regulations* (both as officially published on a quarterly basis and an unofficial, daily updated version, the e-CFR) in electronic format through the GPO's Federal Digital System (FDsys) at *www.fdsys.gov*. For more information, contact the GPO Customer Contact Center, U.S. Government Printing Office. Phone, 202–512–1800, or 866–512–1800 (toll-free). Email, gpo@custhelp.com, Online, *www.gpo.gov/askgpo*.

INQUIRIES

For inquiries concerning *The United States Government Manual* and other publications of the Office of the Federal Register, call 202–741–6000, write to the Director, Office of the Federal Register, National Archives and Records Administration, Washington, DC 20408, or email fedreg.info@nara.gov.

SALES

The publications of the Office of the Federal Register are available for sale by writing to the Superintendent of Documents, P.O. Box 371954, Pittsburgh, PA 15250–7954. Publications are also available for sale through the GPO's online bookstore at *http://bookstore.gpo.gov*, the GPO bookstore located in Washington, DC, and the retail sales outlet in Laurel, MD. Telephone inquiries should be directed to 202–512–1800, 866–512–1800 (toll-free), or 202–512–2104 (fax).

The United States Government Manual 2014

Revised July 1, 2014

Charles A. Barth,
Director of the Federal Register.

David S. Ferriero,
Archivist of the United States.

Contents

EXECUTIVE BRANCH: INDEPENDENT AGENCIES AND GOVERNMENT CORPORATIONS

Declaration of Independence

Action of Second Continental Congress, July 4, 1776

IN CONGRESS, JULY 4, 1776.

THE UNANIMOUS DECLARATION of the thirteen united STATES OF AMERICA,

WHEN in the Course of human events, it becomes necessary for one people to dissolve the political bands which have connected them with another, and to assume among the powers of the earth, the separate and equal station to which the Laws of Nature and of Nature's God entitle them, a decent respect to the opinions of mankind requires that they should declare the causes which impel them to the separation.

We hold these truths to be self-evident, that all men are created equal, that they are endowed by their Creator with certain unalienable Rights, that among these are Life, Liberty and the pursuit of Happiness.—That to secure these rights, Governments are instituted among Men, deriving their just powers from the consent of the governed,— That whenever any Form of Government becomes destructive of these ends, it is the Right of the People to alter or to abolish it, and to institute new Government, laying its foundation on such principles and organizing its powers in such form, as to them shall seem most likely to effect their Safety and Happiness. Prudence, indeed, will dictate that Governments long established should not be changed for light and transient causes; and accordingly all experience hath shewn, that mankind are more disposed to suffer, while evils are sufferable, than to right themselves by abolishing the forms to which they are accustomed. But when a long train of abuses and usurpations, pursuing invariably the same Object evinces a design to reduce them under absolute Despotism, it is their right, it is their duty, to throw off such Government, and to provide new Guards for their future security.—Such has been the patient sufferance of these Colonies; and such is now the necessity which constrains them to alter their former Systems of Government. The history of the present King of Great Britain is a history of repeated injuries and usurpations, all having in direct object the establishment of an absolute Tyranny over these States. To prove this, let Facts be submitted to a candid world.—He has refused his Assent to Laws, the most wholesome and necessary for the public good.—He has forbidden his Governors to pass Laws of immediate and pressing importance, unless suspended in their operation till his Assent should be obtained; and when so suspended, he has utterly neglected to attend to them.—He has refused to pass other Laws for the accommodation of large districts of people, unless those people would relinquish the right of Representation in the Legislature, a right inestimable to them and formidable to tyrants only.—He has called together legislative bodies at places unusual, uncomfortable, and distant from the depository of their public Records, for the sole purpose of fatiguing them into compliance with his measures.—He has dissolved Representative Houses repeatedly, for opposing with manly firmness his invasions on the rights of the people.—He has refused for a long time, after such dissolutions, to cause others to be elected; whereby the Legislative powers, incapable of Annihilation, have returned to the People at large for their exercise; the State remaining in the mean time exposed to all the dangers of invasion from without, and convulsions within.—He has endeavoured to prevent the population of these States; for that purpose obstructing the Laws for Naturalization of Foreigners; refusing to pass others to encourage their migrations hither, and raising the conditions of new Appropriations of Lands.—He has obstructed the Administration of Justice, by refusing his Assent to Laws for establishing Judiciary powers.—He has made Judges dependent on his Will alone, for the tenure of their offices, and the amount and payment of their salaries.—He has erected a multitude of New Offices, and sent hither swarms of Officers to harrass our people, and eat out their substance.—He has kept among us, in times of peace, Standing Armies without the Consent of our legislatures.—He has affected to render the Military independent of and superior to the Civil power.—He has combined with others to subject us to a jurisdiction foreign to our constitution, and unacknowledged by our laws; giving his Assent to their Acts of pretended Legislation:—For Quartering large bodies of armed troops among us:—For protecting them, by a mock Trial, from punishment for any Murders which they should commit on the Inhabitants of these States:—For cutting off our Trade with all parts of the world:—For imposing Taxes on us without our Consent:—For depriving us in many cases, of the benefits of Trial by Jury:—For transporting us beyond Seas to be tried for pretended offences—For abolishing the free System of English Laws in a neighbouring Province, establishing therein an Arbitrary government, and enlarging its Boundaries so as to render it at once an example and fit instrument for introducing the same absolute rule into these Colonies:—For taking away our Charters, abolishing our most valuable Laws, and altering fundamentally the Forms of our Governments:—For suspending our own Legislatures, and declaring themselves invested with power to legislate for us in all cases whatsoever.—He has abdicated Government here, by declaring us out of his Protection and waging War against us.—He has plundered our seas, ravaged our Coasts, burnt our towns, and destroyed the lives of our people.—He is at this time transporting large Armies of foreign Mercenaries to compleat the works of death, desolation and tyranny, already begun with circumstances of Cruelty & perfidy scarcely paralleled in the most barbarous ages, and totally unworthy the Head of a civilized nation.—He has constrained our fellow Citizens taken Captive on the high Seas to bear Arms against their Country, to become the executioners of their friends and Brethren, or to fall themselves by their Hands.—He has excited domestic insurrections amongst us, and has endeavoured to bring on the inhabitants of our frontiers, the merciless Indian Savages, whose known rule of warfare, is an undistinguished destruction of all ages, sexes and conditions.—In every stage of these Oppressions We have Petitioned for Redress in the most humble terms: Our repeated Petitions have been answered only by repeated injury. A Prince whose character is thus marked by every act which may define a Tyrant, is unfit to be the ruler of a free people.—Nor have We been wanting in attentions to our Brittish brethren. We have warned them from time to time of attempts by their legislature to extend an unwarrantable jurisdiction over us. We have reminded them of the circumstances of our emigration and settlement here. We have appealed to their native justice and magnanimity, and we have conjured them by the ties of our common kindred to disavow these usurpations, which, would inevitably interrupt our connections and correspondence. They too have been deaf to the voice of justice and of consanguinity. We must, therefore, acquiesce in the necessity, which denounces our Separation, and hold them, as we hold the rest of mankind, Enemies in War, in Peace Friends.

WE, THEREFORE, the Representatives of the UNITED STATES OF AMERICA, in General Congress, Assembled, appealing to the Supreme Judge of the world for the rectitude of our intentions, do, in the Name, and by Authority of the good People of these Colonies, solemnly publish and declare, That these United Colonies are, and of Right ought to be FREE AND INDEPENDENT STATES; that they are Absolved from all Allegiance to the British Crown, and that all political connection between them and the State of Great Britain, is and ought to be totally dissolved; and that as Free and Independent

States, they have full Power to levy War, conclude Peace, contract Alliances, establish Commerce, and to do all other Acts and Things which Independent States may of right do. And for the support of this Declaration, with a firm reliance on the protection of divine Providence, we mutually pledge to each other our Lives, our Fortunes and our sacred Honor.

The 56 signatures on the Declaration appear in the positions indicated:

Column 1

Georgia:
Button Gwinnett
Lyman Hall
George Walton

Column 2

North Carolina:
William Hooper
Joseph Hewes
John Penn

South Carolina:
Edward Rutledge
Thomas Heyward, Jr.
Thomas Lynch, Jr.
Arthur Middleton

Column 3

Massachusetts:
John Hancock

Maryland:
Samuel Chase
William Paca
Thomas Stone
Charles Carroll of
Carrollton

Virginia:
George Wythe
Richard Henry Lee
Thomas Jefferson
Benjamin Harrison
Thomas Nelson, Jr.
Francis Lightfoot Lee
Carter Braxton

Column 4

Pennsylvania:
Robert Morris
Benjamin Rush
Benjamin Franklin
John Morton
George Clymer
James Smith
George Taylor
James Wilson
George Ross

Delaware:
Caesar Rodney
George Read
Thomas McKean

Column 5

New York:
William Floyd
Philip Livingston
Francis Lewis
Lewis Morris

New Jersey:
Richard Stockton
John Witherspoon
Francis Hopkinson
John Hart
Abraham Clark

Column 6

New Hampshire:
Josiah Bartlett
William Whipple

Massachusetts:
Samuel Adams
John Adams
Robert Treat Paine
Elbridge Gerry

Rhode Island:
Stephen Hopkins
William Ellery

Connecticut:
Roger Sherman
Samuel Huntington
William Williams
Oliver Wolcott

New Hampshire:
Matthew Thornton

For more information on the Declaration of Independence and the Charters of Freedom, see http://archives.gov/exhibits/charters/declaration.html

Constitution of the United States

Note: The following text is a transcription of the Constitution in its original form. Items that are underlined have since been amended or superseded.

Preamble

WE THE PEOPLE of the United States, in order to form a more perfect union, establish justice, insure domestic tranquility, provide for the common defense, promote the general welfare, and secure the blessings of liberty to ourselves and our posterity, do ordain and establish this Constitution for the United States of America.

Article I

Section 1. All legislative powers herein granted shall be vested in a Congress of the United States, which shall consist of a Senate and House of Representatives.

Section 2. The House of Representatives shall be composed of members chosen every second year by the people of the several states, and the electors in each state shall have the qualifications requisite for electors of the most numerous branch of the state legislature.

No person shall be a Representative who shall not have attained to the age of twenty five years, and been seven years a citizen of the United States, and who shall not, when elected, be an inhabitant of that state in which he shall be chosen.

Representatives and direct taxes shall be apportioned among the several states which may be included within this union, according to their respective numbers, which shall be determined by adding to the whole number of free persons, including those bound to service for a term of years, and excluding Indians not taxed, three fifths of all other Persons. The actual Enumeration shall be made within three years after the first meeting of the Congress of the United States, and within every subsequent term of ten years, in such manner as they shall by law direct. The number of Representatives shall not exceed one for every thirty thousand, but each state shall have at least one Representative; and until such enumeration shall be made, the state of New Hampshire shall be entitled to chuse three, Massachusetts eight, Rhode Island and Providence Plantations one, Connecticut five, New York six, New Jersey four, Pennsylvania eight, Delaware one, Maryland six, Virginia ten, North Carolina five, South Carolina five, and Georgia three.

When vacancies happen in the Representation from any state, the executive authority thereof shall issue writs of election to fill such vacancies.

The House of Representatives shall choose their speaker and other officers; and shall have the sole power of impeachment.

Section 3. The Senate of the United States shall be composed of two Senators from each state, chosen by the legislature thereof, for six years; and each Senator shall have one vote.

Immediately after they shall be assembled in consequence of the first election, they shall be divided as equally as may be into three classes. The seats of the Senators of the first class shall be vacated at the expiration of the second year, of the second class at the expiration of the fourth year, and the third class at the expiration of the sixth year, so that one third may be chosen every second year; and if vacancies happen by resignation, or otherwise, during the recess of the legislature of any state, the executive thereof may make temporary appointments until the next meeting of the legislature, which shall then fill such vacancies.

No person shall be a Senator who shall not have attained to the age of thirty years, and been nine years a citizen of the United States and who shall not, when elected, be an inhabitant of that state for which he shall be chosen.

The Vice President of the United States shall be President of the Senate, but shall have no vote, unless they be equally divided.

The Senate shall choose their other officers, and also a President pro tempore, in the absence of the Vice President, or when he shall exercise the office of President of the United States.

The Senate shall have the sole power to try all impeachments. When sitting for that purpose, they shall be on oath or affirmation. When the President of the United States is tried, the Chief Justice shall preside: And no person shall be convicted without the concurrence of two thirds of the members present.

Judgment in cases of impeachment shall not extend further than to removal from office, and disqualification to hold and enjoy any office of honor, trust or profit under the United States: but the party convicted shall nevertheless be liable and subject to indictment, trial, judgment and punishment, according to law.

Section 4. The times, places and manner of holding elections for Senators and Representatives, shall be prescribed in each state by the legislature thereof; but the Congress may at any time by law make or alter such regulations, except as to the places of choosing Senators.

The Congress shall assemble at least once in every year, and such meeting shall be on the first Monday in December, unless they shall by law appoint a different day.

Section 5. Each House shall be the judge of the elections, returns and qualifications of its own members, and a majority of each shall constitute a quorum to do business; but a smaller number may adjourn from day to day, and may be authorized to compel the attendance of absent members, in such manner, and under such penalties as each House may provide.

Each House may determine the rules of its proceedings, punish its members for disorderly behavior, and, with the concurrence of two thirds, expel a member.

Each House shall keep a journal of its proceedings, and from time to time publish the same, excepting such parts as may in their judgment require secrecy; and the yeas and nays of the members of either House on any question shall, at the desire of one fifth of those present, be entered on the journal.

Neither House, during the session of Congress, shall, without the consent of the other, adjourn for more than three days, nor to any other place than that in which the two Houses shall be sitting.

Section 6. The Senators and Representatives shall receive a compensation for their services, to be ascertained by law, and paid out of the treasury of the United States. They shall in all cases, except treason, felony and breach of the peace, be privileged from arrest during their attendance at the session of their respective Houses, and in going to and returning from the same; and for any speech or debate in either House, they shall not be questioned in any other place.

No Senator or Representative shall, during the time for which he was elected, be appointed to any civil office under the authority of the United States, which shall have been created, or the emoluments whereof shall have been increased during such time: and no person holding any office under the United States, shall be a member of either House during his continuance in office.

Section 7. All bills for raising revenue shall originate in the House of Representatives; but the Senate may propose or concur with amendments as on other Bills.

Every bill which shall have passed the House of Representatives and the Senate, shall, before it become a law, be presented to the President of the United States; if he approve he shall sign it, but if not he shall return it, with his objections to that House in which it shall have originated, who shall enter the objections at large on their journal, and proceed to reconsider it. If after such reconsideration two thirds of that House shall agree to pass the bill, it shall be sent, together with the objections, to the other House, by which it shall likewise be reconsidered, and if approved by two thirds of that House, it shall become a law. But in all such cases the votes of both Houses shall be determined by yeas and nays, and the names of the persons voting for and against the bill shall be entered on the journal of each House respectively. If any bill shall not be returned by the President within ten days (Sundays excepted) after it shall have been presented to him, the same shall be a law, in like manner as if he had signed it, unless the Congress by their adjournment prevent its return, in which case it shall not be a law.

Every order, resolution, or vote to which the concurrence of the Senate and House of Representatives may be necessary (except on a question of adjournment) shall be presented to the President of the United States; and before the same shall take effect, shall be approved by him, or being disapproved by him, shall be repassed by two thirds of the Senate and House of Representatives, according to the rules and limitations prescribed in the case of a bill.

Section 8. The Congress shall have power to lay and collect taxes, duties, imposts and excises, to pay the debts and provide for the common defense and general welfare of the United States; but all duties, imposts and excises shall be uniform throughout the United States;

To borrow money on the credit of the United States;

To regulate commerce with foreign nations, and among the several states, and with the Indian tribes;

To establish a uniform rule of naturalization, and uniform laws on the subject of bankruptcies throughout the United States;

To coin money, regulate the value thereof, and of foreign coin, and fix the standard of weights and measures;

To provide for the punishment of counterfeiting the securities and current coin of the United States;

To establish post offices and post roads;

To promote the progress of science and useful arts, by securing for limited times to authors and inventors the exclusive right to their respective writings and discoveries;

To constitute tribunals inferior to the Supreme Court;

To define and punish piracies and felonies committed on the high seas, and offenses against the law of nations;

To declare war, grant letters of marque and reprisal, and make rules concerning captures on land and water;

To raise and support armies, but no appropriation of money to that use shall be for a longer term than two years;

To provide and maintain a navy;

To make rules for the government and regulation of the land and naval forces;

To provide for calling forth the militia to execute the laws of the union, suppress insurrections and repel invasions;

To provide for organizing, arming, and disciplining, the militia, and for governing such part of them as may be employed in the service of the United States, reserving to the states respectively, the appointment of the officers, and the authority of training the militia according to the discipline prescribed by Congress;

To exercise exclusive legislation in all cases whatsoever, over such District (not exceeding ten miles square) as may, by cession of particular states, and the acceptance of Congress, become the seat of the government of the United States, and to exercise like authority over all places purchased by the consent of the legislature of the state in which the same shall be, for the erection of forts, magazines, arsenals, dockyards, and other needful buildings;—And

To make all laws which shall be necessary and proper for carrying into execution the foregoing powers, and all other powers vested by this Constitution in the government of the United States, or in any department or officer thereof.

Section 9. The migration or importation of such persons as any of the states now existing shall think proper to admit, shall not be prohibited by the Congress prior to the year one thousand eight hundred and eight, but a tax or duty may be imposed on such importation, not exceeding ten dollars for each person.

The privilege of the writ of habeas corpus shall not be suspended, unless when in cases of rebellion or invasion the public safety may require it.

No bill of attainder or ex post facto Law shall be passed.

No capitation, or other direct, tax shall be laid, unless in proportion to the census or enumeration herein before directed to be taken.

No tax or duty shall be laid on articles exported from any state.

No preference shall be given by any regulation of commerce or revenue to the ports of one state over those of another: nor shall vessels bound to, or from, one state, be obliged to enter, clear or pay duties in another.

No money shall be drawn from the treasury, but in consequence of appropriations made by law; and a regular statement and account of receipts and expenditures of all public money shall be published from time to time.

No title of nobility shall be granted by the United States: and no person holding any office of profit or trust under them, shall, without the consent of the Congress, accept of any present, emolument, office, or title, of any kind whatever, from any king, prince, or foreign state.

Section 10. No state shall enter into any treaty, alliance, or confederation; grant letters of marque and reprisal; coin money; emit bills of credit; make anything but gold and silver coin a tender in payment of debts; pass any bill of attainder, ex post facto law, or law impairing the obligation of contracts, or grant any title of nobility.

No state shall, without the consent of the Congress, lay any imposts or duties on imports or exports, except what may be absolutely necessary for executing it's inspection laws: and the net produce of all duties and imposts, laid by any state on imports or exports, shall be for the use of the treasury of the United States; and all such laws shall be subject to the revision and control of the Congress.

No state shall, without the consent of Congress, lay any duty of tonnage, keep troops, or ships of war in time of peace, enter into any agreement or compact with another state, or with a foreign power, or engage in war, unless actually invaded, or in such imminent danger as will not admit of delay.

Article II

Section 1. The executive power shall be vested in a President of the United States of America. He shall hold his office during the term of four years, and, together with the Vice President, chosen for the same term, be elected, as follows:

Each state shall appoint, in such manner as the Legislature thereof may direct, a number of electors, equal to the whole number of Senators and Representatives to which the State may be entitled in the Congress: but no Senator or Representative, or person holding an office of trust or profit under the United States, shall be appointed an elector.

The electors shall meet in their respective states, and vote by ballot for two persons, of whom one at least shall not be an inhabitant of the same state with themselves. And they shall make a list of all the persons voted for, and of the number of votes for each; which list they shall sign and certify, and transmit sealed to the seat of the government of the United States, directed to the President of the Senate. The President of the Senate shall, in the presence of the Senate and House of Representatives, open all the certificates, and the votes shall then be counted. The person having the greatest number of votes shall be the President, if such number be a majority of the whole number of electors appointed; and if there be more than one who have such majority, and have an equal number of votes, then the House of Representatives shall immediately choose by ballot one of them for President; and if no person have a majority, then from the five highest on the list the said House shall in like manner choose the President. But in choosing the President, the votes shall be taken by States, the representation from each state having one vote; A quorum for this purpose shall consist of a member or members from two thirds of the states, and a majority of all the states shall be necessary to a choice. In every case, after the choice of the President, the person having the greatest number of votes of the electors shall be the Vice President. But if there should remain two or more who have equal votes, the Senate shall choose from them by ballot the Vice President.

The Congress may determine the time of choosing the electors, and the day on which they shall give their votes; which day shall be the same throughout the United States.

No person except a natural born citizen, or a citizen of the United States, at the time of the adoption of this Constitution, shall be eligible to the office of President; neither shall any person be eligible to that office who shall not have attained to the age of thirty five years, and been fourteen Years a resident within the United States.

In case of the removal of the President from office, or of his death, resignation, or inability to discharge the powers and duties of the said office, the same shall devolve on the Vice President, and the Congress may by law provide for the case of removal, death, resignation or inability, both of the President and Vice President, declaring what officer shall then act as President, and such officer shall act accordingly, until the disability be removed, or a President shall be elected.

The President shall, at stated times, receive for his services, a compensation, which shall neither be increased nor diminished during the period for which he shall have been elected, and he shall not receive within that period any other emolument from the United States, or any of them.

Before he enter on the execution of his office, he shall take the following oath or affirmation:—"I do solemnly swear (or affirm) that I will faithfully execute the office of President of the United States, and will to the best of my ability, preserve, protect and defend the Constitution of the United States."

Section 2. The President shall be commander in chief of the Army and Navy of the United States, and of the militia of the several states, when called into the actual service of the United States; he may require the opinion, in writing, of the principal officer in each of the executive departments, upon any subject relating to the duties of their respective offices, and he shall have power to grant reprieves and pardons for offenses against the United States, except in cases of impeachment.

He shall have power, by and with the advice and consent of the Senate, to make treaties, provided two thirds of the Senators present concur; and he shall nominate, and by and with the advice and consent of the Senate, shall appoint ambassadors, other public ministers and consuls, judges of the Supreme Court, and all other officers of the United States, whose appointments are not herein otherwise provided for, and which shall be established by law: but the Congress may by law vest the appointment of such inferior officers, as they think proper, in the President alone, in the courts of law, or in the heads of departments.

The President shall have power to fill up all vacancies that may happen during the recess of the Senate, by granting commissions which shall expire at the end of their next session.

Section 3. He shall from time to time give to the Congress information of the state of the union, and recommend to their consideration such measures as he shall judge necessary and expedient; he may, on extraordinary occasions, convene both Houses, or either of them, and in case of disagreement between them, with respect to the time of adjournment, he may adjourn them to such time as he shall think proper; he shall receive ambassadors and other public ministers; he shall take care that the laws be faithfully executed, and shall commission all the officers of the United States.

Section 4. The President, Vice President and all civil officers of the United States, shall be removed from office on impeachment for, and conviction of, treason, bribery, or other high crimes and misdemeanors.

Article III

Section 1. The judicial power of the United States, shall be vested in one Supreme Court, and in such inferior courts as the Congress may from time to time ordain and establish. The judges, both of the supreme and inferior courts, shall hold their offices during good behaviour, and shall, at stated times, receive for their services, a compensation, which shall not be diminished during their continuance in office.

Section 2. The judicial power shall extend to all cases, in law and equity, arising under this Constitution, the laws of the United States, and treaties made, or which shall be made, under their authority;—to all cases affecting ambassadors, other public ministers and consuls;—to all cases of admiralty and maritime jurisdiction;—to controversies to which the United States shall be a party;—to controversies between two or more states;—between a state and citizens of another state;—between citizens of different states;—between citizens of the same state claiming lands under grants of different states, and between a state, or the citizens thereof, and foreign states, citizens or subjects.

In all cases affecting ambassadors, other public ministers and consuls, and those in which a state shall be party, the Supreme Court shall have original jurisdiction. In all the other cases before mentioned, the Supreme Court shall have appellate jurisdiction, both as to law and fact, with such exceptions, and under such regulations as the Congress shall make.

The trial of all crimes, except in cases of impeachment, shall be by jury; and such trial shall be held in the state where the said crimes shall have been committed; but when not committed within any state, the trial shall be at such place or places as the Congress may by law have directed.

Section 3. Treason against the United States, shall consist only in levying war against them, or in adhering to their enemies, giving them aid and comfort. No person shall be convicted of treason unless on the testimony of two witnesses to the same overt act, or on confession in open court.

The Congress shall have power to declare the punishment of treason, but no attainder of treason shall work corruption of blood, or forfeiture except during the life of the person attainted.

Article IV

Section 1. Full faith and credit shall be given in each state to the public acts, records, and judicial proceedings of every other state. And the Congress may by general laws prescribe the manner in which such acts, records, and proceedings shall be proved, and the effect thereof.

Section 2. The citizens of each state shall be entitled to all privileges and immunities of citizens in the several states.

A person charged in any state with treason, felony, or other crime, who shall flee from justice, and be found in another state, shall on demand of the executive authority of the state from which he fled, be delivered up, to be removed to the state having jurisdiction of the crime.

No person held to service or labor in one state, under the laws thereof, escaping into another, shall, in consequence of any law or regulation therein, be discharged from such service or labor, but shall be delivered up on claim of the party to whom such service or labor may be due.

Section 3. New states may be admitted by the Congress into this union; but no new states shall be formed or erected within the jurisdiction of any other state; nor any state be formed by the junction of two or more states, or parts of states, without the consent of the legislatures of the states concerned as well as of the Congress.

The Congress shall have power to dispose of and make all needful rules and regulations respecting the territory or other property belonging to the United States; and nothing in this Constitution shall be so construed as to prejudice any claims of the United States, or of any particular state.

Section 4. The United States shall guarantee to every state in this union a republican form of government, and shall protect each of them against invasion; and on application of the legislature, or of the executive (when the legislature cannot be convened) against domestic violence.

Article V

The Congress, whenever two thirds of both houses shall deem it necessary, shall propose amendments to this Constitution, or, on the application of the legislatures of two thirds of the several states, shall call a convention for proposing amendments, which, in either case, shall be valid to all intents and purposes, as part of this Constitution, when ratified by the legislatures of three fourths of the several states, or by conventions in three fourths thereof, as the one or the other mode of ratification may be proposed by the Congress; provided that no amendment which may be made prior to the year one thousand eight hundred and eight shall in any manner affect the first and fourth clauses in the ninth section of the first article; and that no state, without its consent, shall be deprived of its equal suffrage in the Senate.

Article VI

All debts contracted and engagements entered into, before the adoption of this Constitution, shall be as valid against the United States under this Constitution, as under the Confederation.

This Constitution, and the laws of the United States which shall be made in pursuance thereof; and all treaties made, or which shall be made, under the authority of the United States, shall be the supreme law of the land; and the judges in every state shall be bound thereby, anything in the Constitution or laws of any State to the contrary notwithstanding.

The Senators and Representatives before mentioned, and the members of the several state legislatures, and all executive and judicial officers, both of the United States and of the several states, shall be bound by oath or affirmation, to support this Constitution; but no religious test shall ever be required as a qualification to any office or public trust under the United States.

Article VII

The ratification of the conventions of nine states, shall be sufficient for the establishment of this Constitution between the states so ratifying the same.

Signers

Done in convention by the unanimous consent of the states present the seventeenth day of September in the year of our Lord one thousand seven hundred and eighty seven and of the independence of the United States of America the twelfth. *In witness whereof We have hereunto subscribed our Names,*

G⁰ Washington—Presid^t
and deputy from Virginia

New Hampshire	John Langdon
	Nicholas Gilman
Massachusetts	Nathaniel Gorham
	Rufus King
Connecticut	W^m: Saml Johnson
	Roger Sherman
New York	Alexander Hamilton
New Jersey	Wil: Livingston
	David Brearly
	Wm Paterson
	Jona: Dayton
Pennsylvania	B. Franklin
	Thomas Mifflin
	Robt Morris
	Geo. Clymer

Thos FitzSimons
Jared Ingersoll
James Wilson
Gouv Morris

Delaware	Geo: Read
	Gunning Bedford jun
	John Dickinson
	Richard Bassett
	Jaco: Broom
Maryland	James McHenry
	Dan of St Thos Jenifer
	Danl Carroll
Virginia	John Blair—
	James Madison Jr.
North Carolina	Wm Blount
	Richd Dobbs Spaight
	Hu Williamson
South Carolina	J. Rutledge
	Charles Cotesworth Pinckney
	Charles Pinckney
	Pierce Butler
Georgia	William Few
	Abr Baldwin

Amendments

Note: The first ten Amendments were ratified December 15, 1791, and form what is known as the Bill of Rights.

Amendment 1

Congress shall make no law respecting an establishment of religion, or prohibiting the free exercise thereof; or abridging the freedom of speech, or of the press; or the right of the people peaceably to assemble, and to petition the government for a redress of grievances.

Amendment 2

A well regulated militia, being necessary to the security of a free state, the right of the people to keep and bear arms, shall not be infringed.

Amendment 3

No soldier shall, in time of peace be quartered in any house, without the consent of the owner, nor in time of war, but in a manner to be prescribed by law.

Amendment 4

The right of the people to be secure in their persons, houses, papers, and effects, against unreasonable searches and seizures, shall not be violated, and no warrants shall issue, but upon probable cause, supported by oath or affirmation, and particularly describing the place to be searched, and the persons or things to be seized.

Amendment 5

No person shall be held to answer for a capital, or otherwise infamous crime, unless on a presentment or indictment of a grand jury, except in cases arising in the land or naval forces, or in the militia, when in actual service in time of war or public danger; nor shall any person be subject for the same offense to be twice put in jeopardy of life or limb; nor shall be compelled in any criminal case to be a witness against himself, nor be deprived of life, liberty, or property, without due process of law; nor shall private property be taken for public use, without just compensation.

Amendment 6

In all criminal prosecutions, the accused shall enjoy the right to a speedy and public trial, by an impartial jury of the state and district wherein the crime shall have been committed, which district shall have been previously ascertained by law, and to be informed of the nature and cause of the accusation; to be confronted with the witnesses against him; to have compulsory process for obtaining witnesses in his favor, and to have the assistance of counsel for his defense.

Amendment 7

In suits at common law, where the value in controversy shall exceed twenty dollars, the right of trial by jury shall be preserved, and no fact tried by a jury, shall be otherwise reexamined in any court of the United States, than according to the rules of the common law.

Amendment 8

Excessive bail shall not be required, nor excessive fines imposed, nor cruel and unusual punishments inflicted.

Amendment 9

The enumeration in the Constitution, of certain rights, shall not be construed to deny or disparage others retained by the people.

Amendment 10

The powers not delegated to the United States by the Constitution, nor prohibited by it to the states, are reserved to the states respectively, or to the people.

Amendment 11

(Ratified February 7, 1795)

The judicial power of the United States shall not be construed to extend to any suit in law or equity, commenced or prosecuted against one of the United States by citizens of another state, or by citizens or subjects of any foreign state.

Amendment 12

(Ratified July 27, 1804)

The electors shall meet in their respective states and vote by ballot for President and Vice-President, one of whom, at least, shall not be an inhabitant of the same state with themselves; they shall name in their ballots the person voted for as President, and in distinct ballots the person voted for as Vice-President, and they shall make distinct lists of all persons voted for as President, and of all persons voted for as Vice-President, and of the number of votes for each, which lists they shall sign and certify, and transmit sealed to the seat of the government of the United States, directed to the President of the Senate;—The President of the Senate shall, in the presence of the Senate and House of Representatives, open all the certificates and the votes shall then be counted;—the person having the greatest number of votes for President, shall be the President, if such number be a majority of the whole number of electors appointed; and if no person have such majority, then from the persons having the highest numbers not exceeding three on the list of those voted for as President, the House of Representatives shall choose immediately, by ballot, the President. But in choosing the President, the votes shall be taken by states, the representation from each state having one vote; a quorum for this purpose shall consist of a member or members from two-thirds of the states, and a majority of all the states shall be necessary to a choice. And if the House of Representatives shall not choose a President whenever the right of choice shall devolve upon them, before the fourth day of March next following, then the Vice-President shall act as President, as in the case of the death or other constitutional disability of the President. The person having the greatest number of votes as Vice-President, shall be the Vice-President, if such number be a majority of the whole number of electors appointed, and if no person have a majority, then from the two highest numbers on the list, the Senate shall choose the Vice-President; a quorum for the purpose shall consist of two-thirds of the whole number of Senators, and a majority of the whole number shall be necessary to a choice. But no person constitutionally ineligible to the office of President shall be eligible to that of Vice-President of the United States.

Amendment 13

(Ratified December 6, 1865)

Section 1. Neither slavery nor involuntary servitude, except as a punishment for crime whereof the party shall have been duly convicted, shall exist within the United States, or any place subject to their jurisdiction.

Section 2. Congress shall have power to enforce this article by appropriate legislation.

Amendment 14

(Ratified July 9, 1868)

Section 1. All persons born or naturalized in the United States, and subject to the jurisdiction thereof, are citizens of the United States and of the state wherein they reside. No state shall make or enforce any law which shall abridge the privileges or immunities of citizens of the United States; nor shall any state deprive any person of life, liberty, or property, without due process of law; nor deny to any person within its jurisdiction the equal protection of the laws.

Section 2. Representatives shall be apportioned among the several states according to their respective numbers, counting the whole number of persons in each state, excluding Indians not taxed. But when the right to vote at any election for the choice of electors for President and Vice President of the United States, Representatives in Congress, the executive and judicial officers of a state, or the members of the legislature thereof, is denied to any of the male inhabitants of such state, being twenty-one years of age, and citizens of the United States, or in any way abridged, except for participation in rebellion, or other crime, the basis of representation therein shall be reduced in the proportion which the number of such male citizens shall bear to the whole number of male citizens twenty-one years of age in such state.

Section 3. No person shall be a Senator or Representative in Congress, or elector of President and Vice President, or hold any office, civil or military, under the United States, or under any state, who, having previously taken an oath, as a member of Congress, or as an officer of the United States, or as a member of any state legislature, or as an executive or judicial officer of any state, to support the Constitution of the United States, shall have engaged in insurrection or rebellion against the same, or given aid or comfort to the enemies thereof. But Congress may by a vote of two-thirds of each House, remove such disability.

Section 4. The validity of the public debt of the United States, authorized by law, including debts incurred for payment of pensions and bounties for services in suppressing insurrection or rebellion, shall not be questioned. But neither the United States nor any state shall assume or pay any debt or obligation incurred in aid of insurrection or rebellion against the United States, or any claim for the loss or emancipation of any slave; but all such debts, obligations and claims shall be held illegal and void.

Section 5. The Congress shall have power to enforce, by appropriate legislation, the provisions of this article.

Amendment 15

(Ratified February 3, 1870)

Section 1. The right of citizens of the United States to vote shall not be denied or abridged by the United States or by any state on account of race, color, or previous condition of servitude.

Section 2. The Congress shall have power to enforce this article by appropriate legislation.

Amendment 16

(Ratified February 3, 1913)

The Congress shall have power to lay and collect taxes on incomes, from whatever source derived, without apportionment among the several states, and without regard to any census or enumeration.

Amendment 17

(Ratified April 8, 1913)

The Senate of the United States shall be composed of two Senators from each state, elected by the people thereof, for six years; and each Senator shall have one vote. The electors in each state shall have the qualifications requisite for electors of the most numerous branch of the state legislatures.

When vacancies happen in the representation of any state in the Senate, the executive authority of such state shall issue writs of election to fill such vacancies: Provided, that the legislature of any state may empower the executive thereof to make temporary appointments until the people fill the vacancies by election as the legislature may direct.

This amendment shall not be so construed as to affect the election or term of any Senator chosen before it becomes valid as part of the Constitution.

Amendment 18

(Ratified January 16, 1919. Repealed December 5, 1933 by Amendment 21)

Section 1. After one year from the ratification of this article the manufacture, sale, or transportation of intoxicating liquors within, the importation thereof into, or the exportation thereof from the United States and all territory subject to the jurisdiction thereof for beverage purposes is hereby prohibited.

Section 2. The Congress and the several states shall have concurrent power to enforce this article by appropriate legislation.

Section 3. This article shall be inoperative unless it shall have been ratified as an amendment to the Constitution by the legislatures of the several states, as provided in the Constitution, within seven years from the date of the submission hereof to the states by the Congress.

Amendment 19

(Ratified August 18, 1920)

The right of citizens of the United States to vote shall not be denied or abridged by the United States or by any state on account of sex.

Congress shall have power to enforce this article by appropriate legislation.

Amendment 20

(Ratified January 23, 1933)

Section 1. The terms of the President and Vice President shall end at noon on the 20th day of January, and the terms of Senators and Representatives at noon on the 3d day of January, of the years in which such terms would have ended if this article had not been ratified; and the terms of their successors shall then begin.

Section 2. The Congress shall assemble at least once in every year, and such meeting shall begin at noon on the 3d day of January, unless they shall by law appoint a different day.

Section 3. If, at the time fixed for the beginning of the term of the President, the President elect shall have died, the Vice President elect shall become President. If a President shall not have been chosen before the time fixed for the beginning of his term, or if the President elect shall have failed to qualify, then the Vice President elect shall act as President until a President shall have qualified; and the Congress may by law provide for the case wherein neither a President elect nor a Vice President elect shall have qualified, declaring who shall then act as President, or the manner in which one who is to act shall be selected, and such person shall act accordingly until a President or Vice President shall have qualified.

Section 4. The Congress may by law provide for the case of the death of any of the persons from whom the House of Representatives may choose a President whenever the right of choice shall have devolved upon them, and for the case of the death of any of the persons from whom the Senate may choose a Vice President whenever the right of choice shall have devolved upon them.

Section 5. Sections 1 and 2 shall take effect on the 15th day of October following the ratification of this article.

Section 6. This article shall be inoperative unless it shall have been ratified as an amendment to the Constitution by the legislatures of three-fourths of the several states within seven years from the date of its submission.

Amendment 21

(Ratified December 5, 1933)

Section 1. The eighteenth article of amendment to the Constitution of the United States is hereby repealed.

Section 2. The transportation or importation into any state, territory, or possession of the United States for delivery or use therein of intoxicating liquors, in violation of the laws thereof, is hereby prohibited.

Section 3. This article shall be inoperative unless it shall have been ratified as an amendment to the Constitution by conventions in the several states, as provided in the Constitution, within seven years from the date of the submission hereof to the states by the Congress.

Amendment 22

(Ratified February 27, 1951)

Section 1. No person shall be elected to the office of the President more than twice, and no person who has held the office of President, or acted as President, for more than two years of a term to which some other person was elected President shall be elected to the office of the President more than once. But this article shall not apply to any person holding the office of President when this article was proposed by the Congress, and shall not prevent any person who may be holding the office of President, or acting as President, during the term within which this article becomes operative from holding the office of President or acting as President during the remainder of such term.

Section 2. This article shall be inoperative unless it shall have been ratified as an amendment to the Constitution by the legislatures of three-fourths of the several states within seven years from the date of its submission to the states by the Congress.

Amendment 23

(Ratified March 29, 1961)

Section 1. The District constituting the seat of government of the United States shall appoint in such manner as the Congress may direct:
   A number of electors of President and Vice President equal to the whole number of Senators and Representatives in Congress to which the District would be entitled if it were a state, but in no event more than the least populous state; they shall be in addition to those appointed by the states, but they shall be considered, for the purposes of the election of President and Vice President, to be electors appointed by a state; and they shall meet in the District and perform such duties as provided by the twelfth article of amendment.

Section 2. The Congress shall have power to enforce this article by appropriate legislation.

Amendment 24

(Ratified January 23, 1964)

Section 1. The right of citizens of the United States to vote in any primary or other election for President or Vice President, for electors for President or Vice President, or for Senator or Representative in Congress, shall not be denied or abridged by the United States or any state by reason of failure to pay any poll tax or other tax.

Section 2. The Congress shall have power to enforce this article by appropriate legislation.

Amendment 25

(Ratified February 10, 1967)

Section 1. In case of the removal of the President from office or of his death or resignation, the Vice President shall become President.

Section 2. Whenever there is a vacancy in the office of the Vice President, the President shall nominate a Vice President who shall take office upon confirmation by a majority vote of both Houses of Congress.

Section 3. Whenever the President transmits to the President pro tempore of the Senate and the Speaker of the House of Representatives his written declaration that he is unable to discharge the powers and duties of his office, and until he transmits to them a written declaration to the contrary, such powers and duties shall be discharged by the Vice President as Acting President.

Section 4. Whenever the Vice President and a majority of either the principal officers of the executive departments or of such other body as Congress may by law provide, transmit to the President pro tempore of the Senate and the Speaker of the House of Representatives their written declaration that the President is unable to discharge the powers and duties of his office, the Vice President shall immediately assume the powers and duties of the office as Acting President.

Thereafter, when the President transmits to the President pro tempore of the Senate and the Speaker of the House of Representatives his written declaration that no inability exists, he shall resume the powers and duties of his office unless the Vice President and a majority of either the principal officers of the executive department or of such other body as Congress may by law provide, transmit within four days to the President pro tempore of the Senate and the Speaker of the House of Representatives their written declaration that the President is unable to discharge the powers and duties of his office. Thereupon Congress shall decide the issue, assembling within forty-eight hours for that purpose if not in session. If the Congress, within twenty-one days after receipt of the latter written declaration, or, if Congress is not in session, within twenty-one days after Congress is required to assemble, determines by two-thirds vote of both Houses that the President is unable to discharge the powers and duties of his office, the Vice President shall continue to discharge the same as Acting President; otherwise, the President shall resume the powers and duties of his office.

Amendment 26

(Ratified July 1, 1971)

Section 1. The right of citizens of the United States, who are 18 years of age or older, to vote, shall not be denied or abridged by the United States or any state on account of age.

Section 2. The Congress shall have the power to enforce this article by appropriate legislation.

Amendment 27

(Ratified May 7, 1992)

No law, varying the compensation for the services of the Senators and Representatives, shall take effect, until an election of Representatives shall have intervened.

For more information on the Constitution of the United States and the Charters of Freedom, see http://archives.gov/exhibits/charters/constitution.html

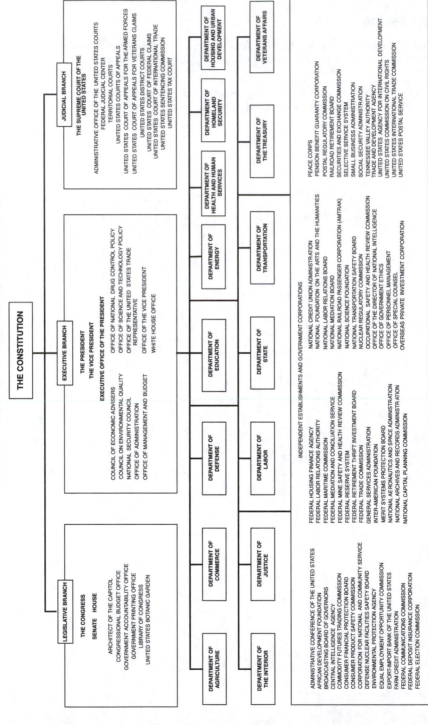

THE GOVERNMENT OF THE UNITED STATES

Legislative Branch

LEGISLATIVE BRANCH

CONGRESS

One Hundred and Thirteenth Congress, Second Session

The Congress of the United States was created by Article I, section 1, of the Constitution, adopted by the Constitutional Convention on September 17, 1787, providing that "All legislative Powers herein granted shall be vested in a Congress of the United States, which shall consist of a Senate and House of Representatives."

The first Congress under the Constitution met on March 4, 1789, in the Federal Hall in New York City. The membership then consisted of 20 Senators and 59 Representatives.[1]

Congressional Record Proceedings of Congress are published in the Congressional Record, which is issued each day when Congress is in session. Publication of the Record began March 4, 1873. It was the first record of debate officially reported, printed, and published directly by the Federal Government. The Daily Digest of the Congressional Record, printed in the back of each issue of the Record, summarizes the proceedings of that day in each House and each of their committees and subcommittees, respectively. The Digest also presents the legislative program for each day and, at the end of the week, gives the program for the following week. Its publication was begun March 17, 1947.

Sessions Section 4 of Article I of the Constitution makes it mandatory that "The Congress shall assemble at least once in every Year. . . ." Under this provision, also, the date for convening Congress was designated originally as the first Monday in December, "unless they shall by Law appoint a different Day." Eighteen acts were passed, up to 1820, providing for the meeting of Congress on other days of the year. From 1820 to 1934, however, Congress met regularly on the first Monday in December. In 1934 the 20th amendment changed the convening of Congress to January 3, unless Congress "shall by law appoint a different day." In addition, the President, according to Article II, section 3, of the Constitution "may, on extraordinary Occasions, convene both Houses, or either of them, and in Case of Disagreement between them, with Respect to the Time of Adjournment, he may adjourn them to such Time as he shall think proper. . . ."

Powers of Congress Article I, section 8, of the Constitution defines the powers of Congress. Included are the powers to assess and collect taxes—called the chief power; to regulate commerce, both interstate and foreign; to coin money; to establish post offices and post roads; to establish courts inferior to the Supreme Court; to declare war; and to raise and maintain an army and navy. Congress is further empowered "To provide for calling forth the Militia to execute the Laws of the Union, suppress Insurrections and repel Invasions;" and "To make all Laws which shall be necessary and proper for carrying into Execution the foregoing Powers, and all other Powers

---

[1] New York ratified the Constitution on July 26, 1788, but did not elect its Senators until July 15 and 16, 1789. North Carolina did not ratify the Constitution until November 21, 1789; Rhode Island ratified it on May 29, 1790.

vested by this Constitution in the Government of the United States, or in any Department or Officer thereof."

Amendments to the Constitution Another power vested in the Congress is the right to propose amendments to the Constitution, whenever two-thirds of both Houses shall deem it necessary. Should two-thirds of the State legislatures demand changes in the Constitution, it is the duty of Congress to call a constitutional convention. Proposed amendments shall be valid as part of the Constitution when ratified by the legislatures or by conventions of three-fourths of the States, as one or the other mode of ratification may be proposed by Congress.

Prohibitions Upon Congress Section 9 of Article I of the Constitution also imposes prohibitions upon Congress. "The Privilege of the Writ of Habeas Corpus shall not be suspended, unless when in Cases of Rebellion or Invasion the public Safety may require it." A bill of attainder or an ex post facto law cannot be passed. No export duty can be imposed. Ports of one State cannot be given preference over those of another State. "No money shall be drawn from the Treasury, but in Consequence of Appropriations made by Law. . . ." No title of nobility may be granted.

Rights of Members According to section 6 of Article I, Members of Congress are granted certain privileges. In no case, except in treason, felony, and breach of the peace, can Members be arrested while attending sessions of Congress "and in going to and returning from the same. . . ." Furthermore, the Members cannot be questioned in any other place for remarks made in Congress. Each House may expel a Member of its body by a two-thirds vote.

Enactment of Laws In order to become law, all bills and joint resolutions, except those proposing a constitutional amendment, must pass both the House of Representatives and the Senate and either be signed by the President or be passed over the President's veto by a two-thirds vote of both Houses of Congress. Section 7 of Article I states: "If any Bill shall not be returned by the President within ten Days (Sundays excepted) after it shall have been presented to him, the Same shall be a Law, in like Manner as if he had signed it, unless the Congress by their Adjournment prevent its Return, in which Case it shall not be a Law." When a bill or joint resolution is introduced in the House, the usual procedure for its enactment into law is as follows: assignment to House committee having jurisdiction; if favorably considered, it is reported to the House either in its original form or with recommended amendments; if the bill or resolution is passed by the House, it is messaged to the Senate and referred to the committee having jurisdiction; in the Senate committee the bill, if favorably considered, may be reported in the form as received from the House, or with recommended amendments; the approved bill or resolution is reported to the Senate, and if passed by that body, is returned to the House; if one body does not accept the amendments to a bill by the other body, a conference committee comprised of Members of both bodies is usually appointed to effect a compromise; when the bill or joint resolution is finally approved by both Houses, it is signed by the Speaker (or Speaker pro tempore) and the Vice President (or President pro tempore or acting President pro tempore) and is presented to the President; and once the President's signature is affixed, the measure becomes a law. If the President vetoes the bill, it cannot become a law unless it is re-passed by a two-thirds vote of both Houses.

The Senate

The Capitol, Washington, DC 20510
Phone, 202–224–3121. Internet, http://www.senate.gov.

President of the Senate (Vice President of the United States)	JOSEPH R. BIDEN, JR.
President pro tempore	PATRICK J. LEAHY
Majority Leader	HARRY REID
Minority Leader	MITCH MCCONNELL
Secretary of the Senate	NANCY ERICKSON
Sergeant at Arms	TERRANCE W. GAINER
Secretary for the Majority	GARY MYRICK
Secretary for the Minority	LAURA DOVE
Chaplain	BARRY C. BLACK

The Senate is composed of 100 Members, 2 from each State, who are elected to serve for a term of 6 years. Senators were originally chosen by the State legislatures. This procedure was changed by the 17th amendment to the Constitution, adopted in 1913, which made the election of Senators a function of the people. There are three classes of Senators, and a new class is elected every 2 years.

Senators must be residents of the State from which they are chosen. In addition, a Senator must be at least 30 years of age and must have been a citizen of the United States for at least 9 years.

Officers   The Vice President of the United States is the Presiding Officer of the Senate. In the Vice President's absence, the duties are taken over by a President pro tempore, elected by that body, or someone designated by the President pro tempore.

The positions of Senate Majority and Minority Leader have been in existence only since the early years of the 20th century. Leaders are elected at the beginning of each new Congress by a majority vote of the Senators in their political party. In cooperation with their party organizations, Leaders are responsible for the design and achievement of a legislative program. This involves managing the flow of legislation, expediting noncontroversial measures, and keeping Members informed regarding proposed action on pending business. Each Leader serves as an ex officio member of his party's policymaking and organizational bodies and is aided by an assistant floor leader (whip) and a party secretary.

The Secretary of the Senate, elected by vote of the Senate, performs the duties of the Presiding Officer of the Senate in the absence of the Vice President and pending the election of a President pro tempore. The Secretary is the custodian of the seal of the Senate, draws requisitions on the Secretary of the Treasury for moneys appropriated for the compensation of Senators, officers, and employees, and for the contingent expenses of the Senate, and is empowered to administer oaths to any officer of the Senate and to any witness produced before it. The Secretary's executive duties include certification of extracts from the Journal of the Senate; the attestation of bills and joint, concurrent, and Senate resolutions; in impeachment trials, issuance, under the authority of the Presiding Officer, of all orders, mandates, writs, and precepts authorized by the Senate; and certification to the President of the United States of the advice and consent of the Senate to ratification of treaties and the names of persons confirmed or rejected upon the nomination of the President.

The Sergeant at Arms, elected by vote of the Senate, serves as the executive, chief law enforcement, and protocol officer and is the principal administrative manager for most support services in the Senate. As executive officer, the Sergeant

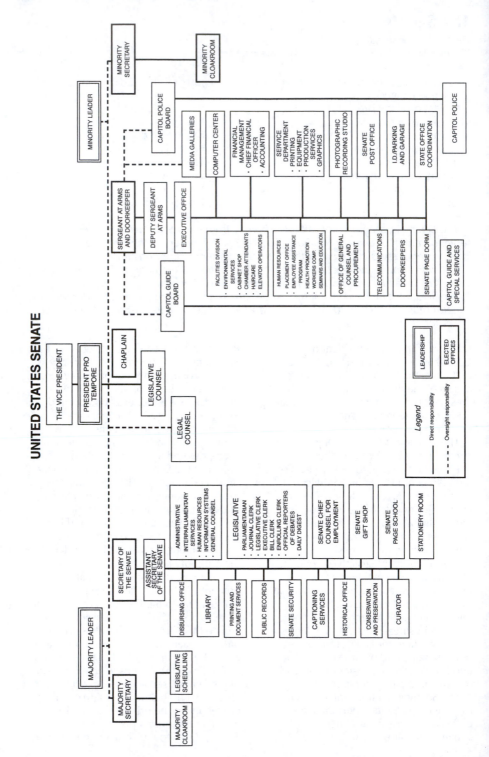

UNITED STATES SENATE

at Arms has custody of the Senate gavel; enforces Senate rules and regulations as they pertain to the Senate Chamber, the Senate wing of the Capitol, and the Senate office buildings; and subject to the Presiding Officer, maintains order on the Senate floor, Chamber, and galleries. As chief law enforcement officer of the Senate, the Sergeant at Arms is authorized to maintain security in the Capitol and all Senate buildings, as well as to protect Senators; to arrest and detain any person violating Senate rules; and to locate absentee Senators for a quorum. The Sergeant at Arms serves as a member of the Capitol Police Board and as its chairman each odd year. As protocol officer, the Sergeant at Arms escorts the President and other heads of state or official guests of the Senate who are attending official functions in the Capitol; makes arrangements for funerals of Senators who die in office; and assists in planning the inauguration of the President and organizing the swearing-in and orientation programs for newly elected Senators.

Committees The work of preparing and considering legislation is done largely by committees of both Houses of Congress. There are 16 standing committees in the Senate. The standing committees of the Senate are shown in the list below. In addition, there are two select committees in each House and various congressional commissions and joint committees composed of Members of both Houses. Each House may also appoint special investigating committees. The membership of the standing committees of each House is chosen by a vote of the entire body; members of other committees are appointed under the provisions of the measure establishing them.

Each bill and resolution is usually referred to the appropriate committee, which may report a bill out in its original form, favorably or unfavorably, recommend amendments, report original measures, or allow the proposed legislation to die in committee without action.

Standing Committees of the Senate

Senate Commitee	Room*
Agriculture, Nutrition, and Forestry	SR328A
Appropriations	S128
Armed Services	SR228
Banking, Housing, and Urban Affairs	SD534
Budget	SD624
Commerce, Science, and Transportation	SR254
Energy and Natural Resources	SD304
Environment and Public Works	SD410
Finance	SD219
Foreign Relations	SD444
Health, Education, Labor, and Pensions	SD428
Homeland Security and Governmental Affairs	SD340
Judiciary	SD224
Rules and Administration	SR305
Small Business and Entrepreneurship	SR428A
Veterans' Affairs	SR412

*Room numbers preceded by S are in the Senate wing of the Capitol Building; those preceded by SD are in the Dirksen Office Building; and those preceded by SR are in the Russell Office Building.

Special Powers of the Senate Under the Constitution, the Senate is granted certain powers not accorded to the House of Representatives. The Senate approves or disapproves certain Presidential appointments by majority vote, and treaties must be concurred in by a two-thirds vote.

Senators

[Democrats (53); Republicans (45); Independents (2); total, 100]. Room numbers preceded by SD are in the Dirksen Office Building (First Street and Constitution Avenue); those preceded by SH are in the Hart Office Building (Second and C Streets); and those preceded by SR are in the Russell Office Building (Delaware and Constitution Avenues). Members' offices may be reached by phone at 202–224–3121. The most current listing of Senators can be found on the Internet at http://www.senate.gov.

Name	State	Room
Alexander, Lamar (R)	Tennessee	SD455
Ayotte, Kelly A. (R)	New Hampshire	SR144
Baldwin, Tammy (D)	Wisconsin	SH717
Barrasso, John A. (R)	Wyoming	SD307
Begich, Mark (D)	Alaska	SR111
Bennet, Michael F. (D)	Colorado	SR458
Blumenthal, Richard (D)	Connecticut	SH724
Blunt, Roy (R)	Missouri	SR260
Booker, Cory A. (D)	New Jersey	SH141
Boozman, John (R)	Arkansas	SH320
Boxer, Barbara (D)	California	SH112
Brown, Sherrod (D)	Ohio	SH713
Burr, Richard (R)	North Carolina	SR217
Cantwell, Maria (D)	Washington	SH311
Cardin, Benjamin L. (D)	Maryland	SH509
Carper, Thomas R. (D)	Delaware	SH513
Casey, Robert P., Jr. (D)	Pennsylvania	SR393
Chambliss, Saxby (R)	Georgia	SR416
Coats, Daniel (R)	Indiana	SR493
Coburn, Tom (R)	Oklahoma	SR172
Cochran, Thad (R)	Mississippi	SD113
Collins, Susan M. (R)	Maine	SD413
Coons, Christopher A. (D)	Delaware	SR127A
Corker, Bob (R)	Tennessee	SD425
Cornyn, John (R)	Texas	SH517
Crapo, Mike (R)	Idaho	SD239
Cruz, Ted (R)	Texas	SD185
Donnelly, Joe (D)	Indiana	SH720
Durbin, Richard J. (D)	Illinois	SH711
Enzi, Michael B. (R)	Wyoming	SR379A
Feinstein, Dianne (D)	California	SH331
Fischer, Deb (R)	Nebraska	SR383
Flake, Jeff (R)	Arizona	SR368
Franken, Al (D)	Minnesota	SH309
Gillibrand, Kristen E. (D)	New York	SH702
Graham, Lindsey (R)	South Carolina	SR290
Grassley, Chuck (R)	Iowa	SH135
Hagan, Kay (D)	North Carolina	SD521
Harkin, Tom (D)	Iowa	SH731
Hatch, Orrin G. (R)	Utah	SH104
Heinrich, Martin (D)	New Mexico	SH702
Heitkamp, Heidi (D)	North Dakota	SH502
Heller, Dean (R)	Nevada	SH324
Hirono, Mazie K. (D)	Hawaii	SH330
Hoeven, John (R)	North Dakota	SR338
Inhofe, James M. (R)	Oklahoma	SR205
Isakson, Johnny (R)	Georgia	SR131
Johanns, Mike (R)	Nebraska	SR404
Johnson, Ron (R)	Wisconsin	SH328
Johnson, Tim (D)	South Dakota	SH136
Kaine, Tim (D)	Virginia	SR388
King, Angus S., Jr. (I)	Maine	SD359

Senators—Continued

[Democrats (53); Republicans (45); Independents (2); total, 100]. Room numbers preceded by SD are in the Dirksen Office Building (First Street and Constitution Avenue); those preceded by SH are in the Hart Office Building (Second and C Streets); and those preceded by SR are in the Russell Office Building (Delaware and Constitution Avenues). Members' offices may be reached by phone at 202–224–3121. The most current listing of Senators can be found on the Internet at http://www.senate.gov.

Name	State	Room
Kirk, Mark S. (R)	Illinois	SH524
Klobuchar, Amy (D)	Minnesota	SH302
Landrieu, Mary (D)	Louisiana	SH703
Leahy, Patrick J. (D)	Vermont	SR437
Lee, Michael S. (R)	Utah	SH316
Levin, Carl (D)	Michigan	SR269
Manchin, Joe, III (D)	West Virginia	SH306
Markey, Edward J. (D)	Massachusetts	SR218
McCain, John (R)	Arizona	SR241
McCaskill, Claire (D)	Missouri	SH506
McConnell, Mitch (R)	Kentucky	SR317
Menendez, Robert (D)	New Jersey	SH528
Merkley, Jeff (D)	Oregon	SH313
Mikulski, Barbara A. (D)	Maryland	SH503
Moran, Jerry (R)	Kansas	SR361A
Murkowski, Lisa (R)	Alaska	SH709
Murphy, Christopher (D)	Connecticut	SH303
Murray, Patty (D)	Washington	SR154
Nelson, Bill (D)	Florida	SH716
Paul, Rand (R)	Kentucky	SR124
Portman, Rob (R)	Ohio	SR448
Pryor, Mark (D)	Arkansas	SD255
Reed, Jack (D)	Rhode Island	SH728
Reid, Harry (D)	Nevada	SH522
Risch, James E. (R)	Idaho	SR483
Roberts, Pat (R)	Kansas	SH109
Rockefeller, John D., IV (D)	West Virginia	SH531
Rubio, Marco (R)	Florida	SR284
Sanders, Bernard (I)	Vermont	SD332
Schatz, Brian (D)	Hawaii	SH722
Schumer, Charles E. (D)	New York	SH322
Scott, Tim (R)	South Carolina	SR167
Sessions, Jeff (R)	Alabama	SR326
Shaheen, Jeanne (D)	New Hampshire	SH520
Shelby, Richard C. (R)	Alabama	SR304
Stabenow, Debbie (D)	Michigan	SH133
Tester, Jon (D)	Montana	SH706
Thune, John (R)	South Dakota	SD511
Toomey, Pat (R)	Pennsylvania	SR248
Udall, Mark E. (D)	Colorado	SH730
Udall, Tom (D)	New Mexico	SH110
Vitter, David (R)	Louisiana	SH516
Walsh, John E. (D)	Montana	SRC2
Warner, Mark R. (D)	Virginia	SR475
Warren, Elizabeth (D)	Masschusetts	SH317
Whitehouse, Sheldon (D)	Rhode Island	SH530
Wicker, Roger F. (R)	Mississippi	SD555
Wyden, Ron (D)	Oregon	SD221

Sources of Information

Electronic Access   Specific information and legislation can be found on the Internet at http://thomas.loc.gov or www.senate.gov.

Publications   The Congressional Directory, the Senate Manual, and telephone directory for the U.S. Senate may be obtained from the Superintendent of Documents, Government Printing Office, Washington, DC 20402. Internet, http://www.gpo.gov/fdsys/browse/collectiontab.action.

For further information, contact the Secretary of the Senate, The Capitol, Washington, DC 20510. Phone, 202–224–2115. Internet, http://www.senate.gov.

The House of Representatives

The Capitol, Washington, DC 20515
Phone, 202–225–3121. Internet, http://www.house.gov.

The Speaker	JOHN A. BOEHNER
Clerk	KAREN L. HAAS
Sergeant at Arms	PAUL D. IRVING
Chief Administrative Officer	ED CASSIDY
Chaplain	PATRICK J. CONROY

The House of Representatives comprises 435 Representatives. The number representing each State is determined by population, but every State is entitled to at least one Representative. Members are elected by the people for 2-year terms, all terms running for the same period. Representatives must be residents of the State from which they are chosen. In addition, a Representative must be at least 25 years of age and must have been a citizen for at least 7 years.

A Resident Commissioner from Puerto Rico (elected for a 4-year term) and Delegates from American Samoa, the District of Columbia, Guam, and the Virgin Islands complete the composition of the Congress of the United States. Delegates are elected for a term of 2 years. The Resident Commissioner and Delegates may take part in the floor discussions but have no vote in the full House. They do, however, vote in the committees to which they are assigned and in the Committee of the Whole House on the State of the Union.

Officers   The Presiding Officer of the House of Representatives, the Speaker, is elected by the House. The Speaker may designate any Member of the House to act in the Speaker's absence.

The House leadership is structured essentially the same as the Senate, with the Members in the political parties responsible for the election of their respective leader and whips.

The elected officers of the House of Representatives include the Clerk, the Sergeant at Arms, the Chief Administrative Officer, and the Chaplain.

The Clerk is custodian of the seal of the House and administers the primary legislative activities of the House. These duties include accepting the credentials of the Members-elect and calling the Members to order at the commencement of the first session of each Congress; keeping the Journal; taking all votes and certifying the passage of bills; and processing all legislation. Through various departments, the Clerk is also responsible for floor and committee reporting services; legislative information and reference services; the administration of House reports pursuant to House rules and certain legislation including the Ethics in Government Act and the Lobbying Disclosure Act of 1995; the distribution of House documents; and administration of the House Page Program. The Clerk is also charged with supervision of the offices vacated by Members due to death, resignation, or expulsion.

HOUSE OF REPRESENTATIVES

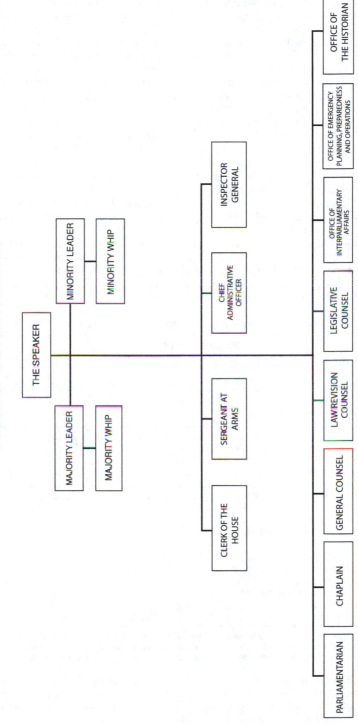

The Sergeant at Arms maintains the order of the House under the direction of the Speaker and is the keeper of the Mace. As a member of the U.S. Capitol Police Board, the Sergeant at Arms is the chief law enforcement officer for the House and serves as Board Chairman each even year. The ceremonial and protocol duties parallel those of the Senate Sergeant at Arms and include arranging the inauguration of the President of the United States, Joint Sessions of Congress, visits to the House of heads of state, and funerals of Members of Congress. The Sergeant at Arms enforces the rules relating to the privileges of the Hall of the House, including admission to the galleries, oversees garage and parking security of the House, and distributes all House staff identification cards.

Committees   The work of preparing and considering legislation is done largely by committees of both Houses of Congress.

There are 19 standing committees in the House of Representatives. The standing committees of the House of Representatives are shown in the list below. In addition, there are two select committees in the House and various congressional commissions and joint committees composed of Members of both Houses. Each House may also appoint special investigating committees. The membership of the standing committees of each House is chosen by a vote of the entire body; members of other committees are appointed under the provisions of the measure establishing them.

Each bill and resolution is usually referred to the appropriate committee, which may report a bill out in its original form, favorably or unfavorably, recommend amendments, report original measures, or allow the proposed legislation to die in committee without action.

Standing Committees of the House of Representatives

House Committee	Room*
Agriculture	1301
Appropriations	H307
Armed Services	2120
Budget	207
Education and the Workforce	2181
Energy and Commerce	2125
Ethics	1015
Financial Services	2129
Foreign Affairs	2170
Homeland Security	H2–176
House Administration	1309
House Administration (Franking Office)	1313
Judiciary	2138
Natural Resources	1324
Oversight and Government Reform	2157
Rules	H312
Rules (Minority)	1627
Science, Space, and Technology	2321
Small Business	2361
Transportation and Infrastructure	2165
Veterans' Affairs	335
Ways and Means	1102

*Room numbers with three digits are in the Cannon House Office Building, four digits beginning with 1 are in the Longworth House Office Building, and four digits beginning with 2 are in the Rayburn House Office Building. Room numbers preceded by H or HT are in the House wing of the Capitol Building.

Special Powers of the House of Representatives   The House of Representatives is granted the power of originating all bills for the raising of revenue. Both Houses of Congress act in impeachment proceedings, which, according to the Constitution, may be instituted against the President, Vice President, and all civil officers of the United States. The House of

Representatives has the sole power of impeachment, and the Senate has the sole power to try impeachments.

Representatives, Delegates, and Resident Commissioners

[Republicans (233); Democrats (200); vacancies (2); total, 435 Members; 5 Delegates; 1 Resident Commissioner]. Members who have died or resigned appear in bold brackets [ ]. Room numbers with three digits are in the Cannon House Office Building (New Jersey and Independence Avenues), four digits beginning with 1 are in the Longworth House Office Building (between South Capitol Street and New Jersey Avenue on Independence Avenue), and four digits beginning with 2 are in the Rayburn House Office Building (between First and South Capitol Streets on Independence Avenue). Members' offices may be reached by phone at 202–225–3121. The most current listing of House Members can be found on the Internet at http://clerk.house.gov.

Name	State (District) / Territory	Room
Aderholt, Robert B. (R)	Alabama (4)	2369
Amash, Justin (R)	Michigan (3)	114
Amodei, Mark E. (R)	Nevada (2)	222
[Andrews, Robert E.] (D)	New Jersey (1)	2265
Bachmann, Michele (R)	Minnesota (6)	2417
Bachus, Spencer (R)	Alabama (6)	2246
Barber, Ron (D)	Arizona (2)	1029
Barletta, Lou (R)	Pennsylvania (11)	115
Barr, Andy (R)	Kentucky (6)	1432
Barrow, John (D)	Georgia (12)	2202
Barton, Joe (R)	Texas (6)	2107
Bass, Karen (D)	California (37)	408
Beatty, Joyce (D)	Ohio (3)	417
Becerra, Xavier (D)	California (34)	1226
Benishek, Dan (R)	Michigan (1)	514
Bentivolio, Kerry L. (R)	Michigan (11)	226
Bera, Ami (D)	California (7)	1408
Bilirakis, Gus M. (R)	Florida (12)	2313
Bishop, Rob (R)	Utah (1)	123
Bishop, Sanford D., Jr. (D)	Georgia (2)	2429
Bishop, Timothy H. (D)	New York (1)	306
Black, Diane (R)	Tennessee (6)	1531
Blackburn, Marsha (R)	Tennessee (7)	217
Blumenauer, Earl (D)	Oregon (3)	1111
Boehner, John A. (R)	Ohio (8)	1011
Bonamici, Suzanne (D)	Oregon (1)	439
Bordallo, Madeleine Z. (D)	Guam (Delegate)	2441
Boustany, Charles W., Jr. (R)	Louisiana (3)	1431
Brady, Kevin (R)	Texas (8)	301
Brady, Robert A. (D)	Pennsylvania (1)	102
Braley, Bruce L. (D)	Iowa (1)	2263
Bridenstine, Jim (R)	Oklahoma (1)	216
Brooks, Mo (R)	Alabama (5)	1230
Brooks, Susan W. (R)	Indiana (5)	1505
Broun, Paul C. (R)	Georgia (10)	2437
Brown, Corrine (D)	Florida (5)	2111
Brownley, Julia (D)	California (26)	1019
Buchanan, Vern (R)	Florida (16)	2104
Bucshon, Larry (R)	Indiana (8)	1005
Burgess, Michael C. (R)	Texas (26)	2336
Bustos, Cheri (D)	Illinois (17)	1009
Butterfield, G. K. (D)	North Carolina (1)	2305
Byrne, Bradley (R)	Alabama (1)	2236
Calvert, Ken (R)	California (42)	2269

Representatives, Delegates, and Resident Commissioners—Continued

[Republicans (233); Democrats (200); vacancies (2); total, 435 Members; 5 Delegates; 1 Resident Commissioner]. Members who have died or resigned appear in bold brackets [ ]. Room numbers with three digits are in the Cannon House Office Building (New Jersey and Independence Avenues), four digits beginning with 1 are in the Longworth House Office Building (between South Capitol Street and New Jersey Avenue on Independence Avenue), and four digits beginning with 2 are in the Rayburn House Office Building (between First and South Capitol Streets on Independence Avenue). Members' offices may be reached by phone at 202–225–3121. The most current listing of House Members can be found on the Internet at http://clerk.house.gov.

Name	State (District) / Territory	Room
Camp, Dave (R)	Michigan (4)	341
Campbell, John (R)	California (45)	2331
[Cantor, Eric] (R)	Virginia (7)	303
Capito, Shelley Moore (R)	West Virginia (2)	2366
Capps, Lois (D)	California (24)	2231
Capuano, Michael E. (D)	Massachusetts (7)	1414
Cárdenas, Tony (D)	California (29)	1508
Carney, John C., Jr. (D)	Delaware (At Large)	1406
Carson, Andre (D)	Indiana (7)	2453
Carter, John R. (R)	Texas (31)	409
Cartwright, Matt (D)	Pennsylvania (17)	1419
Cassidy, Bill (R)	Louisiana (6)	1131
Castor, Kathy (D)	Florida (14)	205
Castro, Joaquin (D)	Texas (20)	212
Chabot, Steve (R)	Ohio (1)	2371
Chaffetz, Jason (R)	Utah (3)	2464
Christensen, Donna M. (D)	Virgin Islands (Delegate)	1510
Chu, Judy (D)	California (27)	1520
Cicilline, David N. (D)	Rhode Island (1)	128
Clark, Katherine M. (D)	Massachusetts (5)	2108
Clarke, Yvette D. (D)	New York (9)	2351
Clawson, Curt (R)	Florida (19)	1123
Clay, William Lacy (D)	Missouri (1)	2418
Cleaver, Emanuel (D)	Missouri (5)	2335
Clyburn, James E. (D)	South Carolina (6)	242
Coble, Howard (R)	North Carolina (6)	2188
Coffman, Mike (R)	Colorado (6)	2443
Cohen, Steve (D)	Tennessee (9)	2404
Cole, Tom (R)	Oklahoma (4)	2458
Collins, Chris (R)	New York (27)	1117
Collins, Doug (R)	Georgia (9)	513
Conaway, K. Michael (R)	Texas (11)	2430
Connolly, Gerald E. (D)	Virginia (11)	424
Conyers, John, Jr. (D)	Michigan (13)	2426
Cook, Paul (R)	California (8)	1222
Cooper, Jim (D)	Tennessee (5)	1536
Costa, Jim (D)	California (16)	1314
Cotton, Tom (R)	Arkansas (4)	415
Courtney, Joe (D)	Connecticut (2)	2348
Cramer, Kevin (R)	North Dakota (At Large)	1032
Crawford, Rick (R)	Arkansas (1)	1711
Crenshaw, Ander (R)	Florida (4)	440
Crowley, Joseph (D)	New York (14)	1436
Cuellar, Henry (D)	Texas (28)	2431
Culberson, John Abney (R)	Texas (7)	2352
Cummings, Elijah E. (D)	Maryland (7)	2235
Daines, Steve (R)	Montana (At Large)	206
Davis, Danny K. (D)	Illinois (7)	2159
Davis, Rodney (R)	Illinois (13)	1740

Representatives, Delegates, and Resident Commissioners—Continued

[Republicans (233); Democrats (200); vacancies (2); total, 435 Members; 5 Delegates; 1 Resident Commissioner]. Members who have died or resigned appear in bold brackets [ ]. Room numbers with three digits are in the Cannon House Office Building (New Jersey and Independence Avenues), four digits beginning with 1 are in the Longworth House Office Building (between South Capitol Street and New Jersey Avenue on Independence Avenue), and four digits beginning with 2 are in the Rayburn House Office Building (between First and South Capitol Streets on Independence Avenue). Members' offices may be reached by phone at 202–225–3121. The most current listing of House Members can be found on the Internet at http://clerk.house.gov.

Name	State (District) / Territory	Room
Davis, Susan A. (D)	California (53)	1526
DeFazio, Peter A. (D)	Oregon (4)	2134
DeGette, Diana (D)	Colorado (1)	2368
Delaney, John K. (D)	Maryland (6)	1632
DeLauro, Rosa L. (D)	Connecticut (3)	2413
DelBene, Suzan K. (D)	Washington (1)	318
Denham, Jeff (R)	California (10)	1730
Dent, Charles W. (R)	Pennsylvania (15)	2455
DeSantis, Ron (R)	Florida (6)	427
DesJarlais, Scott (R)	Tennessee (4)	413
Deutch, Theodore E. (D)	Florida (21)	1024
Diaz-Balart, Mario (R)	Florida (25)	436
Dingell, John D. (D)	Michigan (12)	2328
Doggett, Lloyd (D)	Texas (35)	201
Doyle, Michael F. (D)	Pennsylvania (14)	239
Duckworth, Tammy (D)	Illinois (8)	104
Duffy, Sean P. (R)	Wisconsin (7)	1208
Duncan, Jeff (R)	South Carolina (3)	116
Duncan, John J., Jr. (R)	Tennessee (2)	2207
Edwards, Donna F. (D)	Maryland (4)	2445
Ellison, Keith (D)	Minnesota (5)	2244
Ellmers, Renee L. (R)	North Carolina (2)	426
Engel, Eliot L. (D)	New York (16)	2161
Enyart, William L. (D)	Illinois (12)	1722
Eshoo, Anna G. (D)	California (18)	241
Esty, Elizabeth H. (D)	Connecticut (5)	509
Faleomavaega, Eni F. H. (D)	American Samoa (Delegate)	2422
Farenthold, Blake (R)	Texas (27)	117
Farr, Sam (D)	California (20)	1126
Fattah, Chaka (D)	Pennsylvania (2)	2301
Fincher, Stephen Lee (R)	Tennessee (8)	1118
Fitzpatrick, Michael G. (R)	Pennsylvania (8)	2400
Fleischmann, Chuck (R)	Tennessee (3)	230
Fleming, John (R)	Louisiana (4)	416
Flores, Bill (R)	Texas (17)	1030
Forbes, J. Randy (R)	Virginia (4)	2135
Fortenberry, Jeff (R)	Nebraska (1)	1514
Foster, Bill (D)	Illinois (11)	1224
Foxx, Virginia (R)	North Carolina (5)	2350
Frankel, Lois (D)	Florida (22)	1037
Franks, Trent (R)	Arizona (8)	2435
Frelinghuysen, Rodney P. (R)	New Jersey (11)	2306
Fudge, Marcia L. (D)	Ohio (11)	2344
Gabbard, Tulsi (D)	Hawaii (2)	502
Gallego, Pete P. (D)	Texas (23)	431
Garamendi, John (D)	California (3)	2438
Garcia, Joe (D)	Florida (26)	1440
Gardner, Cory (R)	Colorado (4)	213
Garrett, Scott (R)	New Jersey (5)	2232

Representatives, Delegates, and Resident Commissioners—Continued

[Republicans (233); Democrats (200); vacancies (2); total, 435 Members; 5 Delegates; 1 Resident Commissioner]. Members who have died or resigned appear in bold brackets [ ]. Room numbers with three digits are in the Cannon House Office Building (New Jersey and Independence Avenues), four digits beginning with 1 are in the Longworth House Office Building (between South Capitol Street and New Jersey Avenue on Independence Avenue), and four digits beginning with 2 are in the Rayburn House Office Building (between First and South Capitol Streets on Independence Avenue). Members' offices may be reached by phone at 202–225–3121. The most current listing of House Members can be found on the Internet at http://clerk. house.gov.

Name	State (District) / Territory	Room
Gerlach, Jim (R)	Pennsylvania (6)	2442
Gibbs, Bob (R)	Ohio (7)	329
Gibson, Christopher P. (R)	New York (19)	1708
Gingrey, Phil (R)	Georgia (11)	442
Gohmert, Louie (R)	Texas (1)	2243
Goodlatte, Bob (R)	Virginia (6)	2309
Gosar, Paul A. (R)	Arizona (4)	504
Gowdy, Trey (R)	South Carolina (4)	1404
Granger, Kay (R)	Texas (12)	1026
Graves, Sam (R)	Missouri (6)	1415
Graves, Tom (R)	Georgia (14)	432
Grayson, Alan (D)	Florida (9)	430
Green, Al (D)	Texas (9)	2201
Green, Gene (D)	Texas (29)	2470
Griffin, Tim (R)	Arkansas (2)	1232
Griffith, H. Morgan (R)	Virginia (9)	1108
Grijalva, Raul (D)	Arizona (3)	1511
Grimm, Michael (R)	New York (11)	512
Guthrie, Brett (R)	Kentucky (2)	308
Gutiérrez, Luis (D)	Illinois (4)	2408
Hahn, Janice (D)	California (44)	404
Hall, Ralph M. (R)	Texas (4)	2405
Hanabusa, Colleen W. (D)	Hawaii (1)	238
Hanna, Richard L. (R)	New York (22)	319
Harper, Gregg (R)	Mississippi (3)	307
Harris, Andy (R)	Maryland (1)	1533
Hartzler, Vicky (R)	Missouri (4)	1023
Hastings, Alcee L. (D)	Florida (20)	2353
Hastings, Doc (R)	Washington (4)	1203
Heck, Denny (D)	Washington (10)	425
Heck, Joseph J. (R)	Nevada (3)	132
Hensarling, Jeb (R)	Texas (5)	2228
Herrera Beutler, Jaime (R)	Washington (3)	1130
Higgins, Brian (D)	New York (26)	2459
Himes, James (D)	Connecticut (4)	119
Hinojosa, Ruben (D)	Texas (15)	2262
Holding, George (R)	North Carolina (13)	507
Holt, Rush (D)	New Jersey (12)	1214
Honda, Michael (D)	California (17)	1713
Horsford, Steven (D)	Nevada (4)	1330
Hoyer, Steny (D)	Maryland (5)	1705
Hudson, Richard (R)	North Carolina (8)	429
Huelskamp, Tim (R)	Kansas (1)	129
Huffman, Jared (D)	California (2)	1630
Huizenga, Bill (R)	Michigan (2)	1217
Hultgren, Randy (R)	Illinois (14)	332
Hunter, Duncan (R)	California (50)	223
Hurt, Robert (R)	Virginia (5)	125
Israel, Steve (D)	New York (3)	2457

Representatives, Delegates, and Resident Commissioners—Continued

[Republicans (233); Democrats (200); vacancies (2); total, 435 Members; 5 Delegates; 1 Resident Commissioner]. Members who have died or resigned appear in bold brackets [ ]. Room numbers with three digits are in the Cannon House Office Building (New Jersey and Independence Avenues), four digits beginning with 1 are in the Longworth House Office Building (between South Capitol Street and New Jersey Avenue on Independence Avenue), and four digits beginning with 2 are in the Rayburn House Office Building (between First and South Capitol Streets on Independence Avenue). Members' offices may be reached by phone at 202–225–3121. The most current listing of House Members can be found on the Internet at http://clerk.house.gov.

Name	State (District) / Territory	Room
Issa, Darrell E. (R)	California (49)	2347
Jackson Lee, Sheila (D)	Texas (18)	2160
Jeffries, Hakeem S. (D)	New York (8)	1339
Jenkins, Lynn (R)	Kansas (2)	1027
Johnson, Bill (R)	Ohio (6)	1710
Johnson, Eddie Bernice (D)	Texas (30)	2468
Johnson, Hank (D)	Georgia (4)	2240
Johnson, Sam (R)	Texas (3)	1211
Jolly, David W. (R)	Florida (13)	2407
Jones, Walter B. (R)	North Carolina (3)	2333
Jordan, Jim (R)	Ohio (4)	1524
Joyce, David P. (R)	Ohio (14)	1535
Kaptur, Marcy (D)	Ohio (9)	2186
Keating, William R. (D)	Massachusetts (9)	315
Kelly, Mike (R)	Pennsylvania (3)	1519
Kelly, Robin L. (D)	Illinois (2)	2419
Kennedy, Joseph P., III (D)	Massachusetts (4)	1218
Kildee, Daniel T. (D)	Michigan (5)	327
Kilmer, Derek (D)	Washington (6)	1429
Kind, Ron (D)	Wisconsin (3)	1502
King, Peter T. (R)	New York (2)	339
King, Steve (R)	Iowa (4)	2210
Kingston, Jack (R)	Georgia (1)	2372
Kinzinger, Adam (R)	Illinois (16)	1221
Kirkpatrick, Ann (D)	Arizona (1)	330
Kline, John (R)	Minnesota (2)	2439
Kuster, Ann M. (D)	New Hampshire (2)	137
Labrador, Raul R. (R)	Idaho (1)	1523
LaMalfa, Doug (R)	California (1)	506
Lamborn, Doug (R)	Colorado (5)	2402
Lance, Leonard (R)	New Jersey (7)	133
Langevin, James R. (D)	Rhode Island (2)	109
Lankford, James (R)	Oklahoma (5)	228
Larsen, Rick (D)	Washington (2)	2113
Larson, John B. (D)	Connecticut (1)	1501
Latham, Tom (R)	Iowa (3)	2217
Latta, Robert E. (R)	Ohio (5)	2448
Lee, Barbara (D)	California (13)	2267
Levin, Sander M. (D)	Michigan (9)	1236
Lewis, John (D)	Georgia (5)	343
Lipinski, Daniel (D)	Illinois (3)	1717
LoBiondo, Frank A. (R)	New Jersey (2)	2427
Loebsack, David (D)	Iowa (2)	1527
Lofgren, Zoe (D)	California (19)	1401
Long, Billy (R)	Missouri (7)	1541
Lowenthal, Alan S. (D)	California (47)	515
Lowey, Nita M. (D)	New York (17)	2365
Lucas, Frank D. (R)	Oklahoma (3)	2311
Luetkemeyer, Blaine (R)	Missouri (3)	2440

Representatives, Delegates, and Resident Commissioners—Continued

[Republicans (233); Democrats (200); vacancies (2); total, 435 Members; 5 Delegates; 1 Resident Commissioner]. Members who have died or resigned appear in bold brackets [ ]. Room numbers with three digits are in the Cannon House Office Building (New Jersey and Independence Avenues), four digits beginning with 1 are in the Longworth House Office Building (between South Capitol Street and New Jersey Avenue on Independence Avenue), and four digits beginning with 2 are in the Rayburn House Office Building (between First and South Capitol Streets on Independence Avenue). Members' offices may be reached by phone at 202–225–3121. The most current listing of House Members can be found on the Internet at http://clerk.house.gov.

Name	State (District) / Territory	Room
Luján, Ben Ray (D)	New Mexico (3)	2446
Lujan Grisham, Michelle (D)	New Mexico (1)	214
Lummis, Cynthia M. (R)	Wyoming (At Large)	113
Lynch, Stephen F. (D)	Massachusetts (8)	2133
Maffei, Daniel B. (D)	New York (24)	422
Maloney, Carolyn B. (D)	New York (12)	2308
Maloney, Sean Patrick (D)	New York (18)	1529
Marchant, Kenny (R)	Texas (24)	1110
Marino, Tom (R)	Pennsylvania (10)	410
Massie, Thomas (R)	Kentucky (4)	314
Matheson, Jim (D)	Utah (4)	2211
Matsui, Doris O. (D)	California (6)	2434
McAllister, Vance M. (R)	Louisiana (5)	316
McCarthy, Carolyn (D)	New York (4)	2346
McCarthy, Kevin (R)	California (23)	2421
McCaul, Michael T. (R)	Texas (10)	131
McClintock, Tom (R)	California (4)	434
McCollum, Betty (D)	Minnesota (4)	1714
McDermott, Jim (D)	Washington (7)	1035
McGovern, James P. (D)	Massachusetts (2)	438
McHenry, Patrick T. (R)	North Carolina (10)	2334
McIntyre, Mike (D)	North Carolina (7)	2428
McKeon, Buck (R)	California (25)	2310
McKinley, David B. (R)	West Virginia (1)	412
McMorris Rodgers, Cathy (R)	Washington (5)	203
McNerney, Jerry (D)	California (9)	1210
Meadows, Mark (R)	North Carolina (11)	1516
Meehan, Patrick (R)	Pennsylvania (7)	204
Meeks, Gregory W. (D)	New York (5)	2234
Meng, Grace (D)	New York (6)	1317
Messer, Luke (R)	Indiana (6)	508
Mica, John L. (R)	Florida (7)	2187
Michaud, Michael H. (D)	Maine (2)	1724
Miller, Candice S. (R)	Michigan (10)	320
Miller, Gary G. (R)	California (31)	2467
Miller, George (D)	California (11)	2205
Miller, Jeff (R)	Florida (1)	336
Moore, Gwen (D)	Wisconsin (4)	2245
Moran, James P. (D)	Virginia (8)	2252
Mullin, Markwayne (R)	Oklahoma (2)	1113
Mulvaney, Mick (R)	South Carolina (5)	1207
Murphy, Patrick (D)	Florida (18)	1517
Murphy, Tim (R)	Pennsylvania (18)	2332
Nadler, Jerrold (D)	New York (10)	2110
Napolitano, Grace F. (D)	California (32)	1610
Neal, Richard E. (D)	Massachusetts (1)	2208
Negrete McLeod, Gloria (D)	California (35)	1641
Neugebauer, Randy (R)	Texas (19)	1424
Noem, Kristi L. (R)	South Dakota (At Large)	1323

Representatives, Delegates, and Resident Commissioners—Continued

[Republicans (233); Democrats (200); vacancies (2); total, 435 Members; 5 Delegates; 1 Resident Commissioner]. Members who have died or resigned appear in bold brackets [ ]. Room numbers with three digits are in the Cannon House Office Building (New Jersey and Independence Avenues), four digits beginning with 1 are in the Longworth House Office Building (between South Capitol Street and New Jersey Avenue on Independence Avenue), and four digits beginning with 2 are in the Rayburn House Office Building (between First and South Capitol Streets on Independence Avenue). Members' offices may be reached by phone at 202–225–3121. The most current listing of House Members can be found on the Internet at http://clerk.house.gov.

Name	State (District) / Territory	Room
Nolan, Richard M. (D)	Minnesota (8)	2447
Norton, Eleanor Holmes (D)	District of Columbia (Delegate)	2136
Nugent, Richard B. (R)	Florida (11)	1727
Nunes, Devin (R)	California (22)	1013
Nunnelee, Alan (R)	Mississippi (1)	1427
Olson, Pete (R)	Texas (22)	312
O'Rourke, Beto (D)	Texas (16)	1721
Owens, William L. (D)	New York (21)	405
Palazzo, Steven M. (R)	Mississippi (4)	331
Pallone, Frank, Jr. (D)	New Jersey (6)	237
Pascrell, Bill, Jr. (D)	New Jersey (9)	2370
Pastor, Ed (D)	Arizona (7)	2465
Paulsen, Erik (R)	Minnesota (3)	127
Payne, Donald M., Jr. (D)	New Jersey (10)	103
Pearce, Stevan (R)	New Mexico (2)	2432
Pelosi, Nancy (D)	California (12)	235
Perlmutter, Ed (D)	Colorado (7)	1410
Perry, Scott (R)	Pennsylvania (4)	126
Peters, Gary C. (D)	Michigan (14)	1609
Peters, Scott H. (D)	California (52)	2410
Peterson, Collin C. (D)	Minnesota (7)	2109
Petri, Thomas E. (R)	Wisconsin (6)	2462
Pierluisi, Pedro R. (D)	Puerto Rico (Resident Commissioner)	1213
Pingree, Chellie (D)	Maine (1)	1318
Pittenger, Robert (R)	North Carolina (9)	224
Pitts, Joseph R. (R)	Pennsylvania (16)	420
Pocan, Mark (D)	Wisconsin (2)	313
Poe, Ted (R)	Texas (2)	2412
Polis, Jared (D)	Colorado (2)	1433
Pompeo, Mike (R)	Kansas (4)	107
Posey, Bill (R)	Florida (8)	120
Price, David E. (D)	North Carolina (4)	2162
Price, Tom (R)	Georgia (6)	100
Quigley, Mike (D)	Illinois (5)	1124
Rahall, Nick J., II (D)	West Virginia (3)	2307
Rangel, Charles B. (D)	New York (13)	2354
Reed, Tom (R)	New York (23)	1504
Reichert, David G. (R)	Washington (8)	1127
Renacci, James B. (R)	Ohio (16)	130
Ribble, Reid J. (R)	Wisconsin (8)	1513
Rice, Tom (R)	South Carolina (7)	325
Richmond, Cedric L. (D)	Louisiana (2)	240
Rigell, E. Scott (R)	Virginia (2)	418
Roby, Martha (R)	Alabama (2)	428
Roe, David P. (R)	Tennessee (1)	407
Rogers, Harold (R)	Kentucky (5)	2406
Rogers, Mike (R)	Alabama (3)	324
Rogers, Mike (R)	Michigan (8)	2112
Rohrabacher, Dana (R)	California (48)	2300

Representatives, Delegates, and Resident Commissioners—Continued

[Republicans (233); Democrats (200); vacancies (2); total, 435 Members; 5 Delegates; 1 Resident Commissioner]. Members who have died or resigned appear in bold brackets [ ]. Room numbers with three digits are in the Cannon House Office Building (New Jersey and Independence Avenues), four digits beginning with 1 are in the Longworth House Office Building (between South Capitol Street and New Jersey Avenue on Independence Avenue), and four digits beginning with 2 are in the Rayburn House Office Building (between First and South Capitol Streets on Independence Avenue). Members' offices may be reached by phone at 202–225–3121. The most current listing of House Members can be found on the Internet at http://clerk.house.gov.

Name	State (District) / Territory	Room
Rokita, Todd (R)	Indiana (4)	236
Rooney, Thomas J. (R)	Florida (17)	221
Roskam, Peter J. (R)	Illinois (6)	227
Ros-Lehtinen, Ileana (R)	Florida (27)	2206
Ross, Dennis A. (R)	Florida (15)	229
Rothfus, Keith J. (R)	Pennsylvania (12)	503
Roybal-Allard, Lucille (D)	California (40)	2330
Royce, Edward R. (R)	California (39)	2185
Ruiz, Raul (D)	California (36)	1319
Runyan, Jon (R)	New Jersey (3)	1239
Ruppersberger, C. A. Dutch (D)	Maryland (2)	2416
Rush, Bobby L. (D)	Illinois (1)	2268
Ryan, Paul (R)	Wisconsin (1)	1233
Ryan, Tim (D)	Ohio (13)	1421
Sablan, Gregorio Kilili Camacho (D)	Northern Mariana Islands (Delegate)	423
Salmon, Matt (R)	Arizona (5)	2349
Sánchez, Linda T. (D)	California (38)	2423
Sanchez, Loretta (D)	California (46)	1114
Sanford, Mark (R)	South Carolina (1)	322
Sarbanes, John P. (D)	Maryland (3)	2444
Scalise, Steve (R)	Louisiana (1)	2338
Schakowsky, Janice D. (D)	Illinois (9)	2367
Schiff, Adam B. (D)	California (28)	2411
Schneider, Bradley S. (D)	Illinois (10)	317
Schock, Aaron (R)	Illinois (18)	328
Schrader, Kurt (D)	Oregon (5)	108
Schwartz, Allyson Y. (D)	Pennsylvania (13)	1227
Schweikert, David (R)	Arizona (6)	1205
Scott, Austin (R)	Georgia (8)	516
Scott, Bobby (D)	Virginia (3)	1201
Scott, David (D)	Georgia (13)	225
Sensenbrenner, F. James, Jr. (R)	Wisconsin (5)	2449
Serrano, Jose E. (D)	New York (15)	2227
Sessions, Pete (R)	Texas (32)	2233
Sewell, Terri A. (D)	Alabama (7)	1133
Shea-Porter, Carol (D)	New Hampshire (1)	1530
Sherman, Brad (D)	California (30)	2242
Shimkus, John (R)	Illinois (15)	2452
Shuster, Bill (R)	Pennsylvania (9)	2209
Simpson, Michael K. (R)	Idaho (2)	2312
Sinema, Kyrsten (D)	Arizona (9)	1237
Sires, Albio (D)	New Jersey (8)	2342
Slaughter, Louise McIntosh (D)	New York (25)	2469
Smith, Adam (D)	Washington (9)	2264
Smith, Adrian (R)	Nebraska (3)	2241
Smith, Christopher H. (R)	New Jersey (4)	2373
Smith, Jason T. (R)	Missouri (8)	2230
Smith, Lamar (R)	Texas (21)	2409
Southerland, Steve, II (R)	Florida (2)	1229

Representatives, Delegates, and Resident Commissioners—Continued

[Republicans (233); Democrats (200); vacancies (2); total, 435 Members; 5 Delegates; 1 Resident Commissioner]. Members who have died or resigned appear in bold brackets [ ]. Room numbers with three digits are in the Cannon House Office Building (New Jersey and Independence Avenues), four digits beginning with 1 are in the Longworth House Office Building (between South Capitol Street and New Jersey Avenue on Independence Avenue), and four digits beginning with 2 are in the Rayburn House Office Building (between First and South Capitol Streets on Independence Avenue). Members' offices may be reached by phone at 202–225–3121. The most current listing of House Members can be found on the Internet at http://clerk. house.gov.

Name	State (District) / Territory	Room
Speier, Jackie (D)	California (14)	211
Stewart, Chris (R)	Utah (2)	323
Stivers, Steve (R)	Ohio (15)	1022
Stockman, Steve (R)	Texas (36)	326
Stutzman, Marlin A. (R)	Indiana (3)	1728
Swalwell, Eric (D)	California (15)	501
Takano, Mark (D)	California (41)	1507
Terry, Lee (R)	Nebraska (2)	2266
Thompson, Bennie G. (D)	Mississippi (2)	2466
Thompson, Glenn (R)	Pennsylvania (5)	124
Thompson, Mike (D)	California (5)	231
Thornberry, Mac (R)	Texas (13)	2329
Tiberi, Patrick J. (R)	Ohio (12)	106
Tierney, John F. (D)	Massachusetts (6)	2238
Tipton, Scott R. (R)	Colorado (3)	218
Titus, Dina (D)	Nevada (1)	401
Tonko, Paul (D)	New York (20)	2463
Tsongas, Niki (D)	Massachusetts (3)	1607
Turner, Michael R. (R)	Ohio (10)	2239
Upton, Fred (R)	Michigan (6)	2183
Valadao, David G. (R)	California (21)	1004
Van Hollen, Chris (D)	Maryland (8)	1707
Vargas, Juan (D)	California (51)	1605
Veasey, Marc A. (D)	Texas (33)	414
Vela, Filemon (D)	Texas (34)	437
Velázquez, Nydia M. (D)	New York (7)	2302
Visclosky, Peter J. (D)	Indiana (1)	2256
Wagner, Ann (R)	Missouri (2)	435
Walberg, Tim (R)	Michigan (7)	2436
Walden, Greg (R)	Oregon (2)	2182
Walorski, Jackie (R)	Indiana (2)	419
Walz, Timothy J. (D)	Minnesota (1)	1034
Wasserman Schultz, Debbie (D)	Florida (23)	118
Waters, Maxine (D)	California (43)	2221
[Watt, Melvin L.] (D)	North Carolina (12)	2304
Waxman, Henry A. (D)	California (33)	2204
Weber, Randy K., Sr. (R)	Texas (14)	510
Webster, Daniel (R)	Florida (10)	1039
Welch, Peter (D)	Vermont (At Large)	2303
Wenstrup, Brad R. (R)	Ohio (2)	1223
Westmoreland, Lynn A. (R)	Georgia (3)	2433
Whitfield, Ed (R)	Kentucky (1)	2184
Williams, Roger (R)	Texas (25)	1122
Wilson, Frederica S. (D)	Florida (24)	208
Wilson, Joe (R)	South Carolina (2)	2229
Wittman, Robert J. (R)	Virginia (1)	2454
Wolf, Frank R. (R)	Virginia (10)	233
Womack, Steve (R)	Arkansas (3)	1119
Woodall, Rob (R)	Georgia (7)	1725

Representatives, Delegates, and Resident Commissioners—Continued

[Republicans (233); Democrats (200); vacancies (2); total, 435 Members; 5 Delegates; 1 Resident Commissioner]. Members who have died or resigned appear in bold brackets [ ]. Room numbers with three digits are in the Cannon House Office Building (New Jersey and Independence Avenues), four digits beginning with 1 are in the Longworth House Office Building (between South Capitol Street and New Jersey Avenue on Independence Avenue), and four digits beginning with 2 are in the Rayburn House Office Building (between First and South Capitol Streets on Independence Avenue). Members' offices may be reached by phone at 202–225–3121. The most current listing of House Members can be found on the Internet at http://clerk.house.gov.

Name	State (District) / Territory	Room
Yarmuth, John A. (D)	Kentucky (3)	403
Yoder, Kevin (R)	Kansas (3)	215
Yoho, Ted S. (R)	Florida (3)	511
Young, Don (R)	Alaska (At Large)	2314
Young, Todd C. (R)	Indiana (9)	1007

Sources of Information

Electronic Access Specific information and legislation can be found on the Internet at http://thomas.loc.gov or http://clerk.house.gov.
Publications The Congressional Directory, telephone directories for the House of Representatives, and the House Rules and Manual may be obtained from the Superintendent of Documents, Government Printing Office, Washington, DC 20402. Internet, http://www.gpo.gov/fdsys/browse/collectiontab.action.

For further information, contact the Clerk, The Capitol, Washington, DC 20515. Phone, 202–225–7000. Internet, http://clerk.house.gov.

ARCHITECT OF THE CAPITOL

U.S. Capitol Building, Washington, DC 20515
Phone, 202–228–1793. Internet, http://www.aoc.gov.

Architect of the Capitol	STEPHEN T. AYERS
Chief Operating Officer	CHRISTINE A. MERDON
Assistant Architect of the Capitol	MICHAEL G. TURNBULL
General Counsel	JASON BALTIMORE
Inspector General	KEVIN MULSHINE
Chief Administrative Officer	DAVID FERGUSON
Chief Executive Officer, Visitor Services	BETH PLEMMONS
Chief Financial Officer	THOMAS CARROLL
Director, Communications and Congressional Relations	MIKE CULVER
Director, Planning and Project Management	ANNA FRANZ
Director, Safety, Fire and Environmental Programs	SUSAN ADAMS
Director, Security Programs	KENNETH EADS
Director, U.S. Botanic Garden	ARI NOVY, *Acting*
Director, Utilities and Power Plant Operations	CHRISTOPHER POTTER
Facility Manager, Supreme Court Buildings and Grounds	TRENT WOLFERSBERGER
Superintendent, Capitol Building	CARLOS ELIAS
Superintendent, Capitol Grounds	TED BECHTOL
Superintendent, House Office Buildings	WILLIAM WEIDEMEYER

Superintendent, Library Buildings and Grounds	LARRY BROWN
Superintendent, Senate Office Buildings	TAKIS TZAMARAS

The Architect of the Capitol maintains the U.S. Capitol and the buildings and grounds of the Capitol complex.

In addition to the Capitol, the Architect is responsible for the upkeep of all of the congressional office buildings, the Library of Congress buildings, the U.S. Supreme Court building, the Thurgood Marshall Federal Judiciary Building, the Capitol Power Plant, the Capitol Police headquarters, and the Robert A. Taft Memorial. The Architect performs his duties in connection with the Senate side of the Capitol and the Senate office buildings subject to the approval of the Senate Committee on Rules and Administration. In matters of general policy in connection with the House office buildings, his activities are subject to the approval and direction of the House Office Building Commission. The Architect is under the direction of the Speaker in matters concerning the House side of the Capitol. He is subject to the oversight of the Committee on House Administration with respect to many administrative matters affecting operations on the House side of the Capitol complex. In addition, the Architect of the Capitol serves as the Acting Director of the U.S. Botanic Garden under the Joint Committee on the Library.

The position of Architect of the Capitol was historically filled by Presidential appointment for an indefinite term. Legislation enacted in 1989 provides that the Architect is to be appointed for a term of 10 years by the President, with the advice and consent of the Senate, from a list of three candidates recommended by a congressional commission. Upon confirmation by the Senate, the Architect becomes an official of the legislative branch as an officer of Congress. He is eligible for reappointment after completion of his term.

Projects carried out by the Architect of the Capitol include operating the Capitol Visitor Center; conservation of murals, statuary, and decorative paintings in the Capitol; improvement of life-safety and fire-protection systems in the Capitol and congressional office buildings; security and accessibility improvements within the Capitol complex; renovation, restoration, and modification of the interiors and exteriors of the Thomas Jefferson and John Adams Buildings of the Library of Congress; and facility management of the Thurgood Marshall Federal Judiciary Building.

For further information, contact the Office of the Architect of the Capitol, U.S. Capitol Building, Washington, DC 20515. Phone, 202–228–1793. Internet, http://www.aoc.gov.

UNITED STATES BOTANIC GARDEN

Office of Executive Director, 245 First Street SW., Washington, DC 20024
Phone, 202–225–6670. Internet, http://www.usbg.gov.
Conservatory, 100 Maryland Avenue SW., Washington, DC 20001
Phone, 202–226–8333.
Production Facility, 4700 Shepherd Parkway SW., Washington, DC 20032
Phone, 202–226–4780.

Director (Architect of the Capitol)	STEPHEN T. AYERS, *Acting*
Executive Director	HOLLY H. SHIMIZU

The United States Botanic Garden informs visitors about the importance and value of plants to the well-being of humankind and earth's ecosystems.

The United States Botanic Garden (USBG) is one of the oldest botanic gardens in North America. The Garden highlights the diversity of plants worldwide, as well as their aesthetic, cultural, economic, therapeutic, and ecological significance. The USBG encourages plant appreciation and the growth of botanical knowledge through artistic plant displays, exhibits, educational programs, and curation of a large collection of plants. It fosters plant conservation by serving as a repository for endangered species. Uniquely situated at the heart of the U.S. Government, the Garden seeks to promote the exchange of ideas and information relevant to its mission among national and international visitors and policymakers.

The Garden's collections include orchids, epiphytes, bromeliads, carnivorous plants, ferns, cycads, cacti, succulents, medicinal plants, rare and endangered plants, and plants valued as sources of food, beverages, fibers, cosmetics, and industrial products.

The USBG's facilities include the Conservatory, the National Garden, Bartholdi Park, an administration building, and an off-site production facility. The Conservatory, one of the largest structures of its kind in this country, reopened on December 11, 2001, after undergoing major renovation that required more than 4 years to complete. In addition to upgraded amenities for visitors, it features 12 exhibit and plant display areas.

The National Garden opened on October 1, 2006. Located on three acres adjacent to the west side of the Conservatory, the National Garden comprises a First Ladies Water Garden, a Butterfly Garden, a Rose Garden celebrating our national flower, a Lawn Terrace, a Regional Garden of native Mid-Atlantic plants, and an amphitheater where visitors may relax and enjoy the stunning views of the U.S. Capitol.

Outdoor plantings are also showcased in Bartholdi Park, a home-landscape demonstration area located across from the Conservatory. Each of the displays is sized and scaled for suitability in an urban or suburban setting. The gardens display ornamental plants that perform well in this region arrayed in a variety of styles and themes. Also located in this park is Bartholdi Fountain, created by Frederic Auguste Bartholdi (1834–1904), sculptor of the Statue of Liberty. After undergoing extensive restoration and modifications to save both energy and water, Bartholdi Fountain was re-installed in 2010.

The USBG's staff is organized into horticulture, operations, administration, and public programs divisions. Programs for the public are listed in a quarterly calendar of events and also on the Garden's Web site. A horticultural hotline and email address are available to answer questions from the public.

The USBG was founded in 1820 under the auspices of the Columbian Institute for the Promotion of Arts and Sciences, an organization that was the outgrowth of an association known as the Metropolitan Society, which received its charter from Congress on April 20, 1818. The Garden continued under the direction of the Institute until 1837, when the Institute ceased to exist as an active organization.

In June 1842, the U.S. Exploring Expedition under the command of Captain Charles Wilkes returned from its 4-year voyage with a wealth of information, artifacts, pressed-plant specimens, and living plants from around the world. The living plants were temporarily placed on exhibit on a lot behind the old Patent Office under the care of William D. Brackenridge, the Expedition's botanist. By November 1842, the plants were moved into a greenhouse built there with funds appropriated by Congress. Subsequently, the greenhouse was expanded with two additions and a small growing area to care for the burgeoning collection. In 1843, stewardship of the collection was placed under the direction and control of the Joint Committee on the Library, which had also assumed responsibility for publication of the results of the Expedition. Expansion of the Patent Office in 1849 necessitated finding a new location for the botanical collections.

The act of May 15, 1850 (9 Stat. 427), provided for the relocation of the Botanic Garden under the direction of the Joint Committee on the Library. The site selected was on the National Mall at the west end of the Capitol Grounds, practically the same site the Garden occupied during the period it functioned under the Columbian Institute. This site was later enlarged, and the main area continued to serve as the principal Garden site from 1850 to 1933, when the Garden was relocated to its present site.

Although the Government had assumed responsibility for the maintenance and stewardship of the plant collection in 1842, the two functions were divided between the Commissioner of Public Buildings and the Joint Committee on the Library, respectively. In 1856, in recognition of their increasing stature, the collections and their associated operations and facilities were officially named the United States Botanic Garden, and the Joint Committee on the Library assumed jurisdiction over both its direction and maintenance (11 Stat. 104). An annual appropriation has been provided by Congress since 1856.

Presently, the Joint Committee on the Library has supervision over the USBG through the Architect of the Capitol, who has held the title of Acting Director since 1934.

For further information concerning the United States Botanic Garden, contact the Public Program Division, 245 First Street SW., Washington, DC 20024. Phone, 202–225–8333. Plant Hotline, 202–226–4785. Email, usbg@aoc.gov. Internet, http://www.usbg.gov.

EDITORIAL NOTE: The Government Accountability Office did not meet the publication deadline for submitting updated information of its activities, functions, and sources of information as required by the automatic disclosure provisions of the Freedom of Information Act (5 U.S.C. 552(a)(1)(A)).

GOVERNMENT ACCOUNTABILITY OFFICE

441 G Street NW., Washington, DC 20548
Phone, 202–512–3000. Internet, http://www.gao.gov.

Comptroller General of the United States	GENE L. DODARO
Chief Operating Officer	PATRICIA DALTON
Chief Administrative Officer/Chief Financial Officer	KARL MASCHINO
Deputy Chief Administrative Officer	CHERYL WHITAKER
General Counsel	SUSAN POLING
Inspector General	ADAM TRZECIAK
Chief Human Capital Officer	CAROLYN TAYLOR
Chief Information Officer	HOWARD WILLIAMS
Financial Management and Business Operations	WILLIAM ANDERSON
Chief Quality Officer, Audit Policy and Quality Assurance	TIMOTHY P. BOWLING
Managing Director, Acquisition and Sourcing Management	PAUL L. FRANCIS
Managing Director, Applied Research and Methods	NANCY KINGSBURY
Managing Director, Continuous Process Improvement Office	THOMAS WILLIAMS
Managing Director, Defense Capabilities and Management	CATHLEEN BERRICK
Managing Director, Congressional Relations	KATHERINE SIGGERUD
Managing Director, Education, Workforce, and Income Security	BARBARA D. BOVBJERG
Managing Director, Field Offices	DENISE HUNTER
Managing Director, Financial Management and Assurance	STEVE SEBASTIAN
Managing Director, Forensic Audits and Investigative Service	STEPHEN LORD
Managing Director, Financial Markets and Community Investments	ORICE WILLIAMS BROWN
Managing Director, Health Care	CYNTHIA A. BASCETTA
Managing Director, Homeland Security and Justice	GEORGE SCOTT
Managing Director, International Affairs and Trade	LOREN YAGER
Managing Director, Information Technology	JOEL WILLEMSSEN
Managing Director, Infrastructure Operations	TERRELL DORN
Managing Director, Natural Resources and Environment	MARK GAFFIGAN
Managing Director, Opportunity and Inclusiveness	REGINALD E. JONES
Managing Director, Physical Infrastructure	PHIL HERR

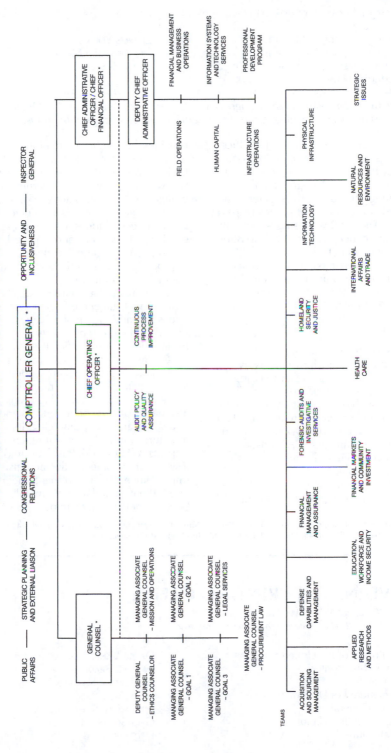

GOVERNMENT ACCOUNTABILITY OFFICE

* THE EXECUTIVE COMMITTEE

--- INDICATES A SUPPORT OR ADVISORY RELATIONSHIP WITH THE TEAMS/UNITS RATHER THAN A DIRECT REPORTING RELATIONSHIP

Managing Director, Professional Development Program	Denise Hunter
Managing Director, Public Affairs	Charles Young
Managing Director, Strategic Issues	J. Christopher Mihm
Managing Director, Strategic Planning and External Liaison	Helen Hsing

---

As the investigative arm of the Congress, the Government Accountability Office examines all matters relating to the receipt and disbursement of public funds.

The Government Accountability Office (GAO) is an independent, nonpartisan Agency that works for Congress. GAO is often called the "congressional watchdog" because it investigates how the Federal Government spends taxpayer dollars. The GAO was established as the General Accounting Office by the Budget Accounting Act of 1921 (31 U.S.C. 702). It was renamed the Government Accountability Office pursuant to the GAO Capital Reform Act of 2004 (31 U.S.C. 702 note).

Activities

GAO gathers information to help Congress determine how effectively executive branch agencies are doing their jobs. GAO's work routinely answers such basic questions as whether Government programs are meeting their objectives or providing good service to the public. Ultimately, GAO ensures that Government is accountable to the American people.

To help Senators and Representatives arrive at informed policy decisions, GAO provides them with information that is accurate, timely, and balanced. The Office supports congressional oversight by evaluating how well Government policies and programs are working; auditing Agency operations to determine whether Federal funds are being spent efficiently, effectively, and appropriately; investigating allegation of illegal and improper activities; and issuing legal decisions and opinions.

With virtually the entire Federal Government subject to its review, GAO issues a steady stream of products, including hundreds of reports and testimonies by GAO officials each year. GAO's familiar "blue book" reports meet short-term immediate needs for information on a wide range of Government operations. These reports also help Congress better understand issues that are newly emerging, long term in nature, and with more far-reaching impacts. GAO's work translates into a wide variety of legislative actions, improvements in Government operations, and billions of dollars in financial benefits for the American people.

For further information, contact the Office of Public Affairs, Government Accountability Office, 441 G Street NW., Washington, DC 20548. Phone, 202–512–4800. Internet, http://www.gao.gov.

GOVERNMENT PRINTING OFFICE

732 North Capitol Street NW., Washington, DC 20401
Phone, 202–512–1800. Internet, http://www.gpo.gov.

Public Printer of the United States	Davita Vance-Cooks
Deputy Public Printer	James C. Bradley
Chief of Staff	Andrew M. Sherman
Superintendent of Documents	Mary Alice Baish
Inspector General	Michael A. Raponi
Manager, Public Relations	Gary Somerset
General Counsel	Drew Spalding

Chief Administrative Officer	HERBERT H. JACKSON
Chief Financial Officer	STEVEN T. SHEDD
Chief Human Capital Officer	GINGER THOMAS
Chief Information Officer	CHUCK RIDDLE
Chief Technology Officer, Programs, Strategy and Technology	RICHARD G. DAVIS
Director, Acquisitions Services	DAMON MCCLURE
Director, Equal Employment Opportunity	JUANITA FLORES
Director, Labor Relations	MELISSA HATFIELD
Director, Security Services	LAMONT VERNON
Managing Director, Customer Services	BRUCE SEGER
Managing Director, Library Services and Content Management	JANE SANCHEZ
Managing Director, Official Journals of Government	LYLE GREEN
Managing Director, Plant Operations	JOHN CRAWFORD
Managing Director, Security and Intelligent Documents	STEPHEN G. LEBLANC

The Government Printing Office produces, procures, and disseminates printed and electronic publications of the Congress, executive departments, and Federal agencies and establishments.

The Government Printing Office (GPO) was created on June 23, 1860, by Congressional Joint Resolution 25. It opened for business on March 4, 1861. GPO's duties are defined in title 44 of the U.S. Code. The Public Printer, who serves as the head of GPO, is appointed by the President and confirmed by the Senate.

Activities

Headquartered in Washington, DC, with a total employment of approximately 1,900, GPO is responsible for the production and distribution of information products and services for all three branches of the Federal Government. GPO is the Federal Government's primary centralized resource for producing, procuring, cataloging, indexing, authenticating, disseminating, and preserving the official information products of the U.S. Government in digital and tangible forms.

While many of our Nation's most important products, such as the "Congressional Record" and "Federal Register," are produced at GPO's main plant, the majority of the Government's printing needs are met through a longstanding partnership with America's printing industry. GPO procures 75

percent of all printing orders through private sector vendors across the country, competitively buying products and services from thousands of private sector companies in all 50 States. The contracts cover the entire spectrum of printing and publishing services and are available to fit almost any firm from the largest to the smallest.

GPO disseminates Federal information products through a sales program, distribution network of more than 1,200 Federal libraries nationwide, and via GPO's Federal Digital System (FDsys). More than 800,000 Federal Government document titles are available to the public at www.fdsys.gov.

Printed copies of many documents, ranging from Supreme Court opinions to reports from the Bureau of Labor Statistics, may also be purchased as follows:

To order in person, please visit the GPO Main Bookstore at 710 North Capitol Street NW., Washington, DC, (corner of North Capitol and H Streets) from 8 a.m. to 4 p.m., eastern standard time. To order online, visit the GPO Online Bookstore at bookstore.gpo. gov. To order by phone or inquire about an order, call 866–512–1800 or, in the Washington, DC, metro area, call

GOVERNMENT PRINTING OFFICE

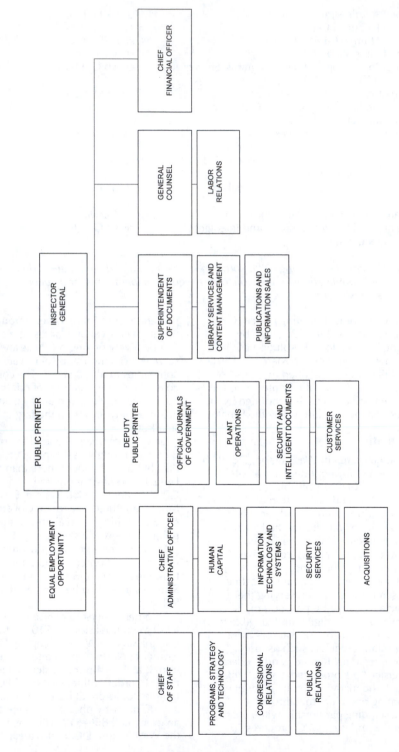

202–512–1800 from 8 a.m. to 5:30 p.m., eastern standard time. To order by fax, dial 202–512–2104. To order by email, send inquiries to contactcenter@gpo.gov. To order by mail, write to Superintendent of Documents, P.O. Box 979050, St. Louis, MO 63197–9000. All orders require prepayment by VISA, MasterCard, American Express, or Discover/NOVUS credit cards, check, or SOD deposit account.

Sources of Information

Congressional Relations Phone, 202–512–1991. Fax, 202–512–1293.

Public Relations Phone, 202–512–1957. Fax, 202–512–1998.

Contracts Commercial printers interested in contract opportunities should contact Customer Services, Government Printing Office, Washington, DC 20401. Phone, 202–512–0526. Internet, http://www.gpo.gov/customers/print.htm.

FDsys User Support Phone, 866–512–1800. In the Washington, DC, metropolitan area, call 202–512–1800.

Regional Offices A complete list of GPO's regional offices is available on the Agency's Web site. Internet, http://www.gpo.gov/customers/offices.htm.

For further information, contact Public Relations, Government Printing Office, 732 North Capitol Street NW., Washington, DC 20401. Phone, 202–512–1957. Fax, 202–512–1998. Internet, http://www.gpo.gov.

LIBRARY OF CONGRESS

101 Independence Avenue SE., Washington, DC 20540
Phone, 202–707–5000. Internet, http://www.loc.gov.

Librarian of Congress	JAMES H. BILLINGTON
Deputy Librarian	ROBERT DIZARD, JR.
Chief, Support Operations	LUCY D. SUDDRETH
Associate Librarian for Library Services	ROBERTA I. SHAFFER
Associate Librarian for Human Resources Services	DENNIS HANRATTY
Register of Copyrights	MARIA A. PALLANTE
Law Librarian	DAVID MAO
General Counsel	ELIZABETH PUGH
Inspector General	KURT W. HYDE, *Acting*
Library of Congress Trust Fund Board	
Chairman (Librarian of Congress)	JAMES H. BILLINGTON
(Secretary of the Treasury)	JACOB J. LEW
(Chairman, Joint Committee on the Library)	GREGG HARPER
(Vice Chairman, Joint Committee on the Library)	CHARLES E. SCHUMER
Members	KATHLEEN L. CASEY, J. RICHARD FREDERICKS, THOMAS GIRARDI, BARBARA GUGGENHEIM, JOAN W. HARRIS, JAMES V. KIMSEY, CHRISTOPHER G. LONG, SALLY SUSSMAN, ELAINE WYNN, (VACANCY)

The Library of Congress is the national library of the United States, offering diverse materials for research including the world's most extensive collections in many areas such as American history, music, and law.

The Library of Congress was established by Act of April 24, 1800 (2 Stat. 56), appropriating $5,000 "for the purchase of such books as may be necessary for the use of Congress . . . ." The Library's scope of responsibility has been widened by subsequent legislation (2 U.S.C. 131–168d). The Librarian, appointed by the President with the advice and consent of the Senate, directs the Library.

The Library's first responsibility is service to Congress. As the Library has developed, its range of service has expanded to include the entire governmental establishment and the public at large, making it a national library for the United States and a global resource through its Web site at www. loc.gov.

Activities

Collections   The Library's extensive collections are universal in scope. They include books, serials, and pamphlets on every subject and in a multitude of languages and research materials in many formats, including maps, photographs, manuscripts, motion pictures, and sound recordings. Among them are the most comprehensive collections of Chinese, Japanese, and Russian language books outside Asia and the former Soviet Union; volumes relating to science and legal materials outstanding for American and foreign law; the world's largest collection of published aeronautical literature; and the most extensive collection in the Western Hemisphere of books printed before 1501 A.D.

The manuscript collections relate to manifold aspects of American history and civilization and include the personal papers of most of the Presidents from George Washington through Calvin Coolidge. The music collections contain volumes and pieces—manuscript and published—from classic works to the newest popular compositions. Other materials available for research include maps and views; photographic records from the daguerreotype to the latest news photo; recordings, including folksongs and other music, speeches, and poetry readings; prints, drawings, and posters; government documents, newspapers, and periodicals from all over the world; and motion pictures, microforms, audio and video tapes, and digital products.

Reference Resources   Admission to the various research facilities of the Library is free. No introduction or credentials are required for persons over high school age. Readers must register by presenting valid photo identification with a current address, and for certain collections there are additional requirements. While priority is given to inquiries pertaining to its holdings of special materials or to subjects in which its resources are unique, the Library does attempt to provide helpful responses to all inquirers. Online reference service is also available through the "Ask a Librarian" site, at www.loc.gov/rr/askalib.

Copyrights   With the enactment of the second general revision of the U.S. copyright law by Act of July 8, 1870 (16 Stat. 212–217), all activities relating to copyright, including deposit and registration, were centralized in the Library of Congress. The Copyright Act of 1976 (90 Stat. 2541) brought all forms of copyrightable authorship, both published and unpublished, under a single statutory system which gives authors protection immediately upon creation of their works. Exclusive rights granted to authors under the statute include the right to reproduce and prepare derivative works, distribute copies or phonorecords, perform and display the work publicly, and in the case of sound recordings, to perform the work publicly by means of a digital audio transmission. Works eligible for copyright include literary works (books and periodicals), musical works, dramatic works, pantomimes and choreographic works, pictorial, graphic, and sculptural works, motion pictures, sound recordings, vessel hull designs, mask works, and architectural works. Serving in its capacity as a national registry for creative works, the Copyright Office registers more than 500,000 claims to copyright annually (representing more than 800,000 works) and is a major source of acquisitions for the universal collections of the Library of Congress. Most of the information available on paper is also accessible online, at www.loc.gov/copyright.

Extension of Service   The Library extends its service through the following:

LIBRARY OF CONGRESS

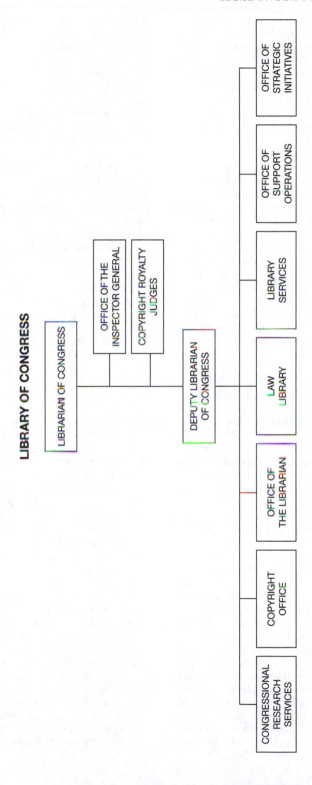

LIBRARIAN OF CONGRESS

OFFICE OF THE INSPECTOR GENERAL

COPYRIGHT ROYALTY JUDGES

DEPUTY LIBRARIAN OF CONGRESS

CONGRESSIONAL RESEARCH SERVICES

COPYRIGHT OFFICE

OFFICE OF THE LIBRARIAN

LAW LIBRARY

LIBRARY SERVICES

OFFICE OF SUPPORT OPERATIONS

OFFICE OF STRATEGIC INITIATIVES

an interlibrary loan system; duplication services, at reasonable cost, of books, manuscripts, maps, newspapers, and prints in its collections; the sale of sound recordings, which are released by its Recording Laboratory; the exchange of duplicates with other institutions; the sale of CD–ROM cataloging tools and magnetic tapes and the publication in book format or microform of cumulative catalogs, which make available the results of the expert bibliographical and cataloging work of its technical personnel; a centralized cataloging program whereby the Library of Congress acquires material published all over the world, catalogs it promptly, and distributes cataloging information in machine-readable form and other means to the Nation's libraries; a cooperative cataloging program whereby the cataloging of data, by name authority and bibliographic records, prepared by other libraries becomes part of the Library of Congress database and is distributed through Cataloging Services; a cataloging-in-publication program in cooperation with American publishers for printing cataloging information in current books; the National Serials Data Program, a national center that maintains a record of serial titles to which International Standard Serial Numbers have been assigned and serves, with this file, as the United States Register; and the development of general schemes of classification (Library of Congress and Dewey Decimal), subject headings, and cataloging, embracing the entire field of printed matter.

Furthermore, the Library provides for the following: the preparation of bibliographical lists responsive to the needs of Government and research; the maintenance and the publication of cooperative publications; the publication of catalogs, bibliographical guides, and lists, and of texts of original manuscripts and rare books in the Library of Congress; the circulation in traveling exhibitions of items from the Library's collections; the provision of books in Braille, electronic access to Braille books on the Internet, "talking books," and books on tape for the blind and the physically handicapped

through more than 100 cooperating libraries throughout the Nation; the distribution of its electronic materials via the Internet; and the provision of research and analytical services on a fee-for-service basis to agencies in the executive and judicial branches.

American Folklife Center   The Center was established in the Library of Congress by Act of January 2, 1976 (20 U.S.C. 2102 et seq.). It supports, preserves, and presents American folklife by receiving and maintaining folklife collections, scholarly research, field projects, performances, exhibitions, festivals, workshops, publications, and audiovisual presentations. The Center has conducted projects in many locations across the country, such as the ethnic communities of Chicago, IL; southern Georgia; a ranching community in northern Nevada; the Blue Ridge Parkway in southern Virginia and northern North Carolina; and the States of New Jersey, Rhode Island, and Montana. The projects have provided large collections of recordings and photographs for the Archive of Folk Culture. The Center administers the Federal Cylinder Project, which is charged with preserving and disseminating music and oral traditions recorded on wax cylinders dating from the late 1800s to the early 1940s. A cultural conservation study was developed at the Center, in cooperation with the Department of the Interior, pursuant to a congressional mandate. Various conferences, workshops, and symposia are given throughout the year.

The American Folklife Center maintains and administers the Archive of Folk Culture, an extensive collection of ethnographic materials from this country and around the world. It is the national repository for folk-related recordings, manuscripts, and other unpublished materials. The Center administers the Veterans History Project, which records and preserves the first-person accounts of war veterans. It also participates in StoryCorps, a program to record and collect oral histories from people from all walks of life. This collection also resides in the American Folklife Center. The Center's reading room contains over

3,500 books and periodicals; a sizable collection of magazines, newsletters, unpublished theses, and dissertations; field notes; and many textual and some musical transcriptions and recordings.

The Folklife Center News, a quarterly newsletter, and other informational publications are available upon request. Many Center publications and a number of collections are available online through the Internet, at www.loc.gov/folklife.

For further information, call 202–707–5510.

Center for the Book   The Center was established in the Library of Congress by an Act of October 13, 1977 (2 U.S.C. 171 et seq.), to stimulate public interest in books, reading, and libraries, and to encourage the study of books and print culture. The Center is a catalyst for promoting and exploring the vital role of books, reading, and libraries, nationally and internationally. As a partnership between the Government and the private sector, the Center for the Book depends on tax-deductible contributions from individuals and corporations to support its programs.

The Center's activities are directed toward the general public and scholars. The overall program includes reading promotion projects with television and radio networks, symposia, lectures, exhibitions, special events, and publications. More than 80 national educational and civic organizations participate in the Center's annual reading promotion campaign.

The Center provides leadership for 52 affiliated State centers for the book (including the District of Columbia and the U.S. Virgin Islands) and nonprofit reading-promotion partners. It oversees the Library's Read.gov Web site, administers the Library's Young Readers Center, and plays a key role in the Library's annual National Book Festival. The Center also administers the position of the National Ambassador for Young People's Literature in collaboration with the Children's Book Council. For more information on the Center and the Library's literacy promotion activities, go to www.Read.gov.

For further information, contact the Center for the Book. Phone, 202–707–5221. Fax, 202–707–0269. Email, cfbook@loc.gov.

National Film Preservation Board   The National Film Preservation Board, established by the National Film Preservation Act of 1992 (2 U.S.C. 179) and reauthorized by the National Film Preservation Act of 2005 (2 U.S.C. 179n), serves as a public advisory group to the Librarian of Congress. The Board works to ensure the survival, conservation, and increased public availability of America's film heritage, including advising the Librarian on the annual selection of films to the National Film Registry and counseling the Librarian on development and implementation of the national film preservation plan. Key publications are Film Preservation 1993: A Study of the Current State of American Film Preservation; Redefining Film Preservation: A National Plan; and Television and Video Preservation 1997: A Study of the Current State of American Television and Video Preservation.

For further information, call 202–707–5912.

National Sound Recording Preservation Board   The National Sound Recording Preservation Board, established by the National Recording Preservation Act of 2000 (2 U.S.C. 1701 note), includes three major components: a National Recording Preservation Advisory Board, which brings together experts in the field, a National Recording Registry, and a fundraising foundation, all of which are conducted under the auspices of the Library of Congress. The Board implements a national plan for the long-term preservation and accessibility of the Nation's audio heritage. It also advises the Librarian on the selection of culturally, aesthetically, or historically significant sound recordings to be included on the National Recording Registry. The national recording preservation program sets standards for future private and public preservation efforts and will be conducted in conjunction with the Library's Packard Campus for Audio Visual Conservation in Culpeper, VA.

For further information, call 202–707–5856.

Preservation   The Library provides technical information related to the preservation of library and archival material. The Library's Preservation Directorate includes three preservation science laboratories, a Center for the Library's Analytical Science Samples, and a Collections Recovery Room. Information on various preservation and conservation topics is available at www.loc.gov/preservation. General information and publications are available from the Office of the Director for Preservation, Library of Congress, Washington, DC 20540–4500.

For further information, call 202–707–1840.

Sources of Information

Books for the Blind and Physically Handicapped   Talking and Braille books and magazines are distributed through more than 100 regional and subregional libraries to blind and physically handicapped residents of the United States and its territories. Qualified users can also register for Web-Braille, an Internet-based service. Information is available at public libraries throughout the United States and from the headquarters office, National Library Service for the Blind and Physically Handicapped, Library of Congress, 1291 Taylor Street NW., Washington, DC 20542–4960. Phone, 202–707–5100.

Cataloging Data Distribution   Cataloging and bibliographic information in the form of microfiche catalogs, book catalogs, magnetic tapes, CD–ROM cataloging tools, bibliographies, and other technical publications is distributed to libraries and other institutions. Information about ordering materials is available from the Cataloging Distribution Service, Library of Congress, Washington, DC 20541–4910. Phone, 202–707–6100. TDD, 202–707–0012. Fax, 202–707–1334. Email, cdsinfo@mail.loc.gov. Card numbers for new publications and Electronic Preassigned Control Numbers for publishers are available from the Cataloging in Publication Division, Library of Congress, Washington, DC 20541–4910. Phone, 202–707–6345.

Contracts   Persons seeking information on conducting business with the Library of Congress should visit the Library's Web site. Internet, http://www.loc.gov/about/business.

Copyright Services   Information about the copyright law (title 17 of the U.S. Code), the method of securing copyright, and copyright registration procedures may be obtained by writing to the Copyright Office, Library of Congress, 101 Independence Avenue SE., Washington, DC 20559–6000. Phone, 202–707–3000. Copyright information is also available through the Internet at www.loc.gov/copyright. Registration application forms may be ordered by calling the forms hotline at 202–707–9100. Copyright records may be researched and reported by the Copyright Office for a fee; for an estimate, call 202–707–6850. Members of the public may use the copyright card catalog in the Copyright Office without charge. The database of Copyright Office records cataloged from January 1, 1978, to the present is available through the Internet at www.loc.gov/copyright/rb.html. The Copyright Information Office is located in Room LM–401, James Madison Memorial Building, 101 Independence Avenue SE., Washington, DC 20559–6000. It is open to the public Monday through Friday, 8:30 a.m. to 5 p.m., except for Federal holidays.

Employment   Employment inquiries should be directed to Human Resources Services, Library of Congress, 101 Independence Avenue SE., Washington, DC 20540–2200. Vacancy announcements and applications are also available from the Employment Office, Room LM–107, 101 Independence Avenue SE., Washington, DC 20540. Phone, 202–707–4315. Internet, www.loc.gov/hr/employment.

Duplication Services   Copies of manuscripts, prints, photographs, maps, and book material not subject to copyright and other restrictions are available for a fee. Order forms for photo reproduction and price schedules are available from Duplication Services, Library of Congress, 101 Independence

Avenue SE., Washington, DC 20540–4570. Phone, 202–707–5640.

Exhibitions Throughout the year, the Library offers free exhibitions featuring items from its collections. Library exhibitions may be viewed Monday through Saturday, 8:30 a.m. to 4:30 p.m., in the Thomas Jefferson Building. For more information, call 202–707–4604. To view current and past exhibitions online, use the link below. Internet, http://www.loc.gov/exhibits.

Publications Library of Congress publications are available through the Internet at www.loc.gov/shop. The Library of Congress Magazine (LCM) is published 6 times a year and may be viewed online at www.loc.gov/loc/lcm/. The calendar of public events is also available online at www.loc.gov/loc/events and is available by mail to persons within 100 miles of Washington, DC. To be added to the calendar mailing list, send requests to Office Systems Services, Mail and Distribution Management Section, Library of Congress, 101 Independence Avenue SE., Washington, DC 20540–9441 or email pao@loc.gov.

Reference and Bibliographic Services Guidance is offered to readers in identifying and using the material in the Library's collections, and reference service is provided to those with inquiries who have exhausted local, State, and regional resources. Persons requiring services that cannot be performed by the Library staff can be supplied with names of private researchers who work on a fee-for-service basis. Requests for information should be directed to the Reference Referral Service, Library of Congress, 101 Independence Avenue SE., Washington, DC 20540–4720. Phone, 202–707–5522.

Fax, 202–707–1389. They may also be submitted online through "Ask a Librarian," www.loc.gov/rr/askalib/.

Research and Reference Services in Science and Technology Reference specialists in the Science, Technology, and Business Division provide a free service in answering brief technical inquiries entailing a bibliographic response. Requests for reference services should be directed to the Science, Technology, and Business Division, Library of Congress, Science Reference Section, 101 Independence Avenue SE., Washington, DC 20540–4750. Phone, 202–707–5639. Internet, www.loc.gov/rr/scitech.

Research Services in General Topics Federal Government agencies can procure directed research and analytical products on foreign and domestic topics using the collections of the Library of Congress through the Federal Research Division. Science, technology, humanities, and social science topics of research are conducted by staff specialists exclusively on behalf of Federal agencies on a fee-for-service basis. Requests for service should be directed to the Federal Research Division, Marketing Office, Library of Congress, Washington, DC 20540–4840. Phone, 202–707–9133. Fax, 202–707–3920.

Visiting the Library of Congress Guided tours of the Library are offered to the public Monday through Friday at 10:30 and 11:30 a.m. and 1:30, 2:30, and 3:30 p.m. and on Saturday at 10:30 and 11:30 a.m. and 1:30 and 2:30 p.m. For more information about scheduling tours for groups of 10 or more, contact the Visitor Services Office at 202–707–0919.

For further information, contact the Public Affairs Office, Library of Congress, 101 Independence Avenue SE., Washington, DC 20540–8610. Phone, 202–707–2905. Fax, 202–707–2905. Fax, 202–707–9199. Email, pao@loc.gov. Internet, http://www.loc.gov.

Congressional Research Service

101 Independence Avenue SE., Washington, DC 20540
Phone, 202–707–5000. Internet, http://www.loc.gov/crsinfo.

Director, Congressional Research Service   MARY B. MAZANEC

The Congressional Research Service (CRS) provides comprehensive research and analysis on all legislative and oversight issues of interest to Congress. CRS assists Congress by responding to specific questions and by preparing reports on legislative issues in anticipation of questions and emerging issues. CRS works with Members, committees, and congressional staff to objectively, authoritatively, and confidentially identify and clarify policy problems, assess the implications of proposed policy alternatives, and provide timely responses to meet immediate and long-term needs.

For further information, call 202–707–5700.

CONGRESSIONAL BUDGET OFFICE

Director	DOUGLAS W. ELMENDORF
Deputy Director	ROBERT A. SUNSHINE
Associate Director for Communications	DEBORAH KILROE
Associate Director for Economic Analysis	JEFFREY KLING
Associate Director for Legislative Affairs	EDWARD DAVIS
General Counsel	MARK P. HADLEY
Assistant Director for Budget Analysis	PETER H. FONTAINE
Assistant Director for Financial Analysis	DAMIEN MOORE
Assistant Director for Health, Retirement, and Long-Term Analysis	LINDA BILHEIMER
Assistant Director for Macroeconomic Analysis	WENDY EDELBERG
Chief Administrative Officer for Management, Business, and Information Services	JOSEPH E. EVANS, JR.
Assistant Director for Microeconomic Studies	JOSEPH KILE
Assistant Director for National Security	DAVID MOSHER
Assistant Director for Tax Analysis	DAVID WEINER

The Congressional Budget Office produces independent analyses of budgetary and economic issues to support the congressional budget process.

The Congressional Budget Office (CBO) was established by the Congressional Budget Act of 1974 (2 U.S.C. 601), which also created a procedure by which the Congress considers and acts upon the annual Federal budget. This process enables the Congress to have an overview of the Federal budget and to make overall decisions regarding spending and taxing levels and the deficit or surplus these levels incur.

Activities

The CBO assists the congressional budget committees with drafting and enforcing the annual budget resolution, which serves as a blueprint for total levels of Government spending and revenues in a fiscal year. Once completed, the budget resolution guides the action of other congressional committees in drafting subsequent spending and revenue legislation within their jurisdiction.

To support this process, the CBO makes budgetary and economic projections, analyzes the proposals set forth in the President's budget request, and details alternative spending and revenue options for lawmakers to consider. The CBO also provides cost estimates of bills approved by congressional committees and tracks the progress of spending and revenue legislation in a scorekeeping system. The CBO's cost estimates and scorekeeping system help the budget committees determine whether the budgetary effects of individual proposals are consistent with the most recent spending and revenue targets.

CONGRESSIONAL BUDGET OFFICE

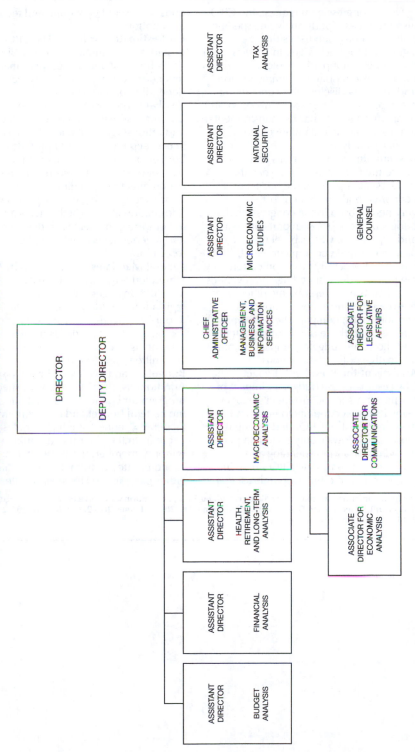

Upon congressional request, the CBO also produces reports analyzing specific policy and program issues that are significant for the budget. In keeping with the agency's nonpartisan role, its analyses do not present policy recommendations and routinely disclose their underlying assumptions and methods. This open and nonpartisan stance has been instrumental in preserving the credibility of the agency's analyses.

Baseline Budget Projections and Economic Forecasts   Each year, the CBO issues reports on the budget and economic outlook that cover the 10-year period used in the congressional budget process. Those reports present and explain the CBO's baseline budget projections and economic forecast, which are generally based on current law regarding Federal spending and revenues. The reports also describe the differences between the current projections and previous ones, compare the economic forecast with those of other forecasters, and show the budgetary impact of some alternative policy assumptions.

Analysis of the President's Budget   The CBO estimates the budgetary impact of the proposals in the President's budget using its own economic forecast and assumptions. The CBO's independent reestimate allows Congress to compare the administration's spending and revenue proposals with CBO's baseline projections and other proposals using a consistent set of economic and technical assumptions.

Cost Estimates for Bills   The CBO provides cost estimates of every bill to show how it would affect spending or revenues over the next 5 or 10 years, depending on the type of spending involved. The CBO also provides informal estimates at the committee level and other stages in the legislative process.

Scorekeeping   The CBO provides the budget and appropriations committees with frequent tabulations of congressional action affecting spending and revenues. Those scorekeeping reports provide information about whether legislative actions are consistent with the spending and revenue levels set by the budget resolution.

Federal Mandates   As required by the Unfunded Mandates Reform Act of 1995, the CBO analyzes the costs that proposed legislation would impose on State, local, and tribal governments and on the private sector. The CBO produces mandate statements with its cost estimates for each committee-approved bill.

Budgetary and Economic Policy Issues   Additionally, the CBO analyzes specific program and policy issues that affect the Federal budget and the economy. Generally, requests for these analyses come from the chairman or ranking minority member of a committee or subcommittee or from the leadership of either party in the House or Senate.

For further information, contact the Management, Business, and Information Services Division, Congressional Budget Office, Second and D Streets SW., Washington, DC 20515. Phone, 202–226–2600. Fax, 202–226–2714. Internet, http://www.cbo.gov.

Judicial Branch

JUDICIAL BRANCH

THE SUPREME COURT OF THE UNITED STATES

Members

Chief Justice of the United States	JOHN G. ROBERTS, JR.
Associate Justices	ANTONIN SCALIA, ANTHONY M. KENNEDY, CLARENCE THOMAS, RUTH BADER GINSBURG, STEPHEN G. BREYER, SAMUEL A. ALITO, JR., SONIA M. SOTOMAYOR, ELENA KAGAN

Officers

Counselor to the Chief Justice	JEFFREY P. MINEAR
Clerk	SCOTT S. HARRIS
Legal Officer	ETHAN TORREY
Curator	CATHERINE E. FITTS
Director of Information Technology	ROBERT J. HAWKINS
Librarian	LINDA MASLOW
Marshal	PAMELA TALKIN
Public Information Officer	KATHLEEN L. ARBERG
Reporter of Decisions	CHRISTINE L. FALLON

Article III, section 1, of the Constitution of the United States provides that "[t]he judicial Power of the United States, shall be vested in one supreme Court, and in such inferior Courts as the Congress may from time to time ordain and establish."

The Supreme Court of the United States was created in accordance with this provision and by authority of the Judiciary Act of September 24, 1789 (1 Stat. 73). It was organized on February 2, 1790. Article III, section 2, of the Constitution defines the jurisdiction of the Supreme Court.

The Supreme Court is comprised of the Chief Justice of the United States and such number of Associate Justices as may be fixed by Congress, which is currently fixed at eight (28 U.S.C. 1). The President nominates the Justices with the advice and consent of the Senate. Article III, section 1, of the Constitution further provides that "[t]he Judges, both of the supreme and inferior Courts, shall hold their Offices during good Behaviour, and shall, at stated Times, receive for their Services, a Compensation, which shall not be diminished during their Continuance in Office."

Court officers assist the Court in the performance of its functions. They include the Counselor to the Chief Justice, the Clerk, the Reporter of Decisions, the Librarian, the Marshal, the Legal Officer, the Curator, the Director of Information Technology, and the Public Information Officer.

Appellate Jurisdiction Appellate jurisdiction has been conferred upon the Supreme Court by various statutes under the authority given Congress by the Constitution. The basic statute effective at this time in conferring and controlling jurisdiction of the Supreme Court may be found in 28 U.S.C. 1251, 1253, 1254, 1257–1259, and various special statutes.

Congress has no authority to change the original jurisdiction of this Court.

Rulemaking Power   Congress has from time to time conferred upon the Supreme Court power to prescribe rules of procedure to be followed by the lower courts of the United States.

Court Term   The term of the Court begins on the first Monday in October and lasts until the first Monday in October of the next year. Approximately 8,000–10,000 cases are filed with the Court in the course of a term, and some 1,000 applications of various kinds are filed each year that can be acted upon by a single Justice.

Access to Facilities   The Supreme Court is open to the public from 9 a.m. to 4:30 p.m., Monday through Friday, except on Federal holidays. Unless the Court or Chief Justice orders otherwise, the Clerk's office is open from 9 a.m. to 5 p.m., Monday through Friday, except on Federal holidays. The library is open to members of the bar of the Court, attorneys for the various Federal departments and agencies, and Members of Congress.

For further information concerning the Supreme Court, contact the Public Information Office, United States Supreme Court Building, One First Street NE., Washington, DC 20543. Phone, 202–479–3211. Internet, http://www.supremecourt.gov.

LOWER COURTS

Article III of the Constitution declares, in section 1, that the judicial power of the United States shall be invested in one Supreme Court and in "such inferior Courts as the Congress may from time to time ordain and establish." The Supreme Court has held that these constitutional courts ". . . share in the exercise of the judicial power defined in that section, can be invested with no other jurisdiction, and have judges who hold office during good behavior, with no power in Congress to provide otherwise."

United States Courts of Appeals

The courts of appeals are intermediate appellate courts created by act of March 3, 1891 (28 U.S.C. ch. 3), to relieve the Supreme Court of considering all appeals in cases originally decided by the Federal trial courts. They are empowered to review all final decisions and certain interlocutory decisions (18 U.S.C. 3731; 28 U.S.C. 1291, 1292) of district courts. They also are empowered to review and enforce orders of many Federal administrative bodies. The decisions of the courts of appeals are final except as they are subject to review on writ of certiorari by the Supreme Court.

The United States is divided geographically into 12 judicial circuits, including the District of Columbia. Each circuit has a court of appeals (28 U.S.C. 41, 1294). Each of the 50 States is assigned to one of the circuits. The territories and the Commonwealth of Puerto Rico are assigned variously to the first, third, and ninth circuits. There is also a Court of Appeals for the Federal Circuit, which has nationwide jurisdiction defined by subject matter. At present each court of appeals has from 6 to 28 permanent circuit judgeships (179 in all), depending upon the amount of judicial work in the circuit. Circuit judges hold their offices during good behavior as provided by Article III, section 1, of the Constitution. The judge senior in commission who is under 70 years of age (65 at inception of term), has been in office at least 1 year, and has not previously been chief judge, serves as the chief judge of the circuit for a 7-year term. One of the Justices of the Supreme Court is assigned as circuit justice for each of the 13 judicial circuits. Each court of appeals normally hears cases in panels consisting of three judges but may sit en banc with all judges present.

The judges of each circuit (except the Federal Circuit) by vote determine the size of the judicial council for the circuit, which consists of the chief judge and an equal number of circuit and district judges. The council considers the state of Federal judicial business in the circuit and may "make all necessary and appropriate orders for [its] effective and expeditious administration . . ." (28 U.S.C. 332).

The chief judge of each circuit may summon periodically a judicial conference of all judges of the circuit, including members of the bar, to discuss the business of the Federal courts of the circuit (28 U.S.C. 333). The chief judge of each circuit and a district judge elected from each of the 12 geographical circuits, together with the chief judge of the Court of International Trade, serve as members of the Judicial Conference of the United States, over which the Chief Justice of the United States presides. This is the governing body for the administration of the Federal judicial system as a whole (28 U.S.C. 331).

To obtain a complete list of judges, court officials, and official stations of the United States Courts of Appeals for the Federal Circuit, as well as information on opinions and cases before the court, consult the Judicial Circuit Web sites listed below.

List of Judicial Circuit Web Sites—United States Courts of Appeals

Circuit	URL
District of Columbia Circuit	http://www.cadc.uscourts.gov
First Circuit	http://www.ca1.uscourts.gov
Second Circuit	http://www.ca2.uscourts.gov
Third Circuit	http://www.ca3.uscourts.gov
Fourth Circuit	http://www.ca4.uscourts.gov
Fifth Circuit	http://www.ca5.uscourts.gov
Sixth Circuit	http://www.ca6.uscourts.gov
Seventh Circuit	http://www.ca7.uscourts.gov
Eighth Circuit	http://www.ca8.uscourts.gov
Ninth Circuit	http://www.ca9.uscourts.gov
Tenth Circuit	http://www.ca10.uscourts.gov/
Eleventh Circuit	http://www.ca11.uscourts.gov/

United States Court of Appeals for the Federal Circuit

This court was established under Article III of the Constitution pursuant to the Federal Courts Improvement Act of 1982 (28 U.S.C. 41, 44, 48), as successor to the former United States Court of Customs and Patent Appeals and the United States Court of Claims. The jurisdiction of the court is nationwide (as provided by 28 U.S.C. 1295) and includes appeals from the district courts in patent cases; appeals from the district courts in contract, and certain other civil actions in which the United States is a defendant; and appeals from final decisions of the U.S. Court of International Trade, the U.S. Court of Federal Claims, and the U.S. Court of Appeals for Veterans Claims. The jurisdiction of the court also includes the review of administrative rulings by the Patent and Trademark Office, U.S. International Trade Commission, Secretary of Commerce, agency boards of contract appeals, and the Merit Systems Protection Board, as well as rulemaking of the Department of Veterans Affairs; review of decisions of the U.S. Senate Committee on Ethics concerning discrimination claims of Senate employees; and review of a final order of an entity to be designated by the President concerning discrimination claims of Presidential appointees.

The court consists of 12 circuit judges. It sits in panels of three or more on each case and may also hear or rehear a case en banc. The court sits principally in Washington, DC, and may hold court wherever any court of appeals sits (28 U.S.C. 48).

To obtain a complete list of judges and court officials of the United States Courts of Appeals for the Federal Circuit, as well as information on opinions and cases before the court, consult the following Web site: http://www.cafc.uscourts.gov.

United States District Courts

The district courts are the trial courts of general Federal jurisdiction. Each State has at least one district court, while the larger States have as many as four. There are 89 district courts in the 50 States, plus the one in the District of Columbia. In addition, the Commonwealth of Puerto Rico has a district court with jurisdiction corresponding to that of district courts in the various States.

At present, each district court has from 2 to 28 Federal district judgeships, depending upon the amount of judicial work within its territory. Only one judge is usually required to hear and decide a case in a district court, but in some limited cases it is required that three judges be called together to comprise the court (28 U.S.C. 2284). The judge senior in commission who is under 70 years of age (65 at inception of term), has been in office for at least 1 year, and has not previously been chief judge, serves as chief judge for a 7-year term. There are 645 permanent district judgeships in the 50 States and 15 in the District of Columbia. There are seven district judgeships in Puerto Rico. District judges hold their offices during good behavior as provided by Article III, section 1, of the Constitution. However, Congress may temporary judgeships for a court with the provision that when a future vacancy occurs in that district, such vacancy shall not be filled. Each district court has one or more United States magistrate judges and bankruptcy judges, a clerk, a United States attorney, a United States marshal, probation officers, court reporters, and their staffs. The jurisdiction of the district courts is set forth in title 28, chapter 85, of the United States Code and at 18 U.S.C. 3231.

Cases from the district courts are reviewable on appeal by the applicable court of appeals.

Territorial Courts

Pursuant to its authority to govern the Territories (Art. IV, sec. 3, clause 2, of the Constitution), Congress has established district courts in the territories of Guam and the Virgin Islands. The District Court of the Canal Zone was abolished on April 1, 1982, pursuant to the Panama Canal Act of 1979 (22 U.S.C. 3601 note). Congress has also established a district court in the Northern Mariana Islands, which presently is administered by the United States under a trusteeship agreement with the United Nations. These Territorial courts have jurisdiction not only over the subjects described in the judicial article of the Constitution but also over many local matters that, within the States, are decided in State courts. The District Court of Puerto Rico, by contrast, is established under Article III, is classified like other "district courts," and is called a "court of the United States" (28 U.S.C. 451). There is one judge each in Guam and the Northern Mariana Islands, and two in the Virgin Islands. The judges in these courts are appointed for terms of 10 years.

For further information concerning the lower courts, contact the Administrative Office of the United States Courts, Thurgood Marshall Federal Judiciary Building, One Columbus Circle NE., Washington, DC 20544. Phone, 202–502–2600.

United States Court of International Trade

This court was originally established as the Board of United States General Appraisers by act of June 10, 1890, which conferred upon it jurisdiction theretofore held by the district and circuit courts in actions arising under the tariff acts (19 U.S.C. ch. 4). The act of May 28, 1926 (19 U.S.C. 405a), created the United States Customs Court to supersede the Board; by acts of August 7, 1939, and June 25, 1948 (28 U.S.C. 1582, 1583), the court was integrated into the United States court structure, organization, and procedure. The act of July 14, 1956 (28 U.S.C. 251), established the court as a court of record of the United States under Article III of the Constitution. The Customs Court Act of 1980 (28 U.S.C. 251) constituted the court as the United States Court of International Trade.

The Court of International Trade has jurisdiction over any civil action against the United States arising from Federal laws governing import transactions. This includes classification and valuation cases, as well as authority to review certain agency determinations under the Trade Agreements Act of 1979 (19 U.S.C. 2501) involving antidumping and countervailing duty matters. In addition, it has exclusive jurisdiction of civil actions to review determinations as to the eligibility of workers, firms, and communities for adjustment assistance under the Trade Act of 1974 (19 U.S.C. 2101). Civil actions commenced by the United States to recover customs duties, to recover on a customs bond, or for certain civil penalties alleging fraud or negligence are also within the exclusive jurisdiction of the court.

The court is composed of a chief judge and eight judges, not more than five of whom may belong to any one political party. Any of its judges may be temporarily designated and assigned by the Chief Justice of the United States to sit as a court of appeals or district court judge in any circuit or district. The court has a clerk and deputy clerks, a librarian, court reporters, and other supporting personnel. Cases before the court may be tried before a jury. Under the Federal Courts Improvement Act of 1982 (28 U.S.C. 1295), appeals are taken to the U.S. Court of Appeals for the Federal Circuit, and ultimately review may be sought in appropriate cases in the Supreme Court of the United States.

The principal offices are located in New York, NY, but the court is empowered to hear and determine cases arising at any port or place within the jurisdiction of the United States.

For further information, contact the Clerk, United States Court of International Trade, One Federal Plaza, New York, NY 10278–0001. Phone, 212–264–2814.

Judicial Panel on Multidistrict Litigation

The Panel, created by act of April 29, 1968 (28 U.S.C. 1407), and consisting of seven Federal judges designated by the Chief Justice from the courts of appeals and district courts, is authorized to temporarily transfer to a single district, for coordinated or consolidated pretrial proceedings, civil actions pending in different districts that involve one or more common questions of fact.

For further information, contact the Clerk, Judicial Panel on Multidistrict Litigation, Room G–255, Thurgood Marshall Federal Judiciary Building, One Columbus Circle NE., Washington, DC 20002–8041. Phone, 202–502–2800.

SPECIAL COURTS

United States Court of Appeals for the Armed Forces

This court was established under Article I of the Constitution of the United States pursuant to act of May 5, 1950, as amended (10 U.S.C. 867). Subject only to certiorari review by the Supreme Court of the United States in a limited number of cases, the court serves as the final appellate tribunal to review court-martial convictions of all the Armed Forces. It is exclusively an appellate criminal court, consisting of five civilian judges who are appointed for 15-year terms by the President with the advice and consent of the Senate.

The court is called upon to exercise jurisdiction to review the record in all cases extending to death; certified to the court by a Judge Advocate General of one of the Armed Forces; or petitioned by accused who have received a sentence of confinement for 1 year or more and/or a punitive discharge.

The court also exercises authority under the All Writs Act (28 U.S.C. 1651(a)).

In addition, the judges of the court are required by law to work jointly with the senior uniformed lawyer from each of the Armed Forces and two members of the public appointed by the Secretary of Defense to make an annual comprehensive survey, to report annually to the Congress on the operation and progress of the military justice system under the Uniform Code of Military Justice, and to recommend improvements wherever necessary.

For further information, contact the Clerk, United States Court of Appeals for the Armed Forces, 450 E Street NW., Washington, DC 20442–0001. Phone, 202–761–1448. Fax, 202–761–4672. Internet, http://www. armfor.uscourts.gov.

United States Court of Appeals for Veterans Claims

The United States Court of Appeals for Veterans Claims, a court of record under Article I of the Constitution, was established on November 18, 1988 (38 U.S.C. 7251) and given exclusive jurisdiction to review decisions of the Board of Veterans' Appeals. Appeals concern veteran disability benefits, dependent educational assistance, survivor benefits, and pension benefits claims. In addition to its review authority, the Court has contempt authority, as well as the authority to compel action by the Secretary of Veterans Affairs, the authority to grant a petition for extraordinary relief under the All Writs Act (28 U.S.C. 1651), and the authority to make attorney fee determinations under the Equal Access to Justice Act (28 U.S.C. 2412). Decisions of the Court of Appeals for Veterans Claims are subject to review by the United States Court of Appeals for the Federal Circuit on questions of law and on writ of certiorari by the United States Supreme Court.

The Court consists of nine judges appointed by the President, with the advice and consent of the Senate, for 15-year terms. One of the judges serves as chief judge.

The Chief Judge generally conducts a judicial conference every 2 years. The primary purpose of the conference, which involves the active participation of members of the legal community, attorneys, and practitioners admitted to practice before the Court, is to consider the business of the Court and to recommend means of improving the administration of justice within the Court's jurisdiction.

The Court is located in Washington, DC, but it is a court of national jurisdiction and may sit at any location within the United States.

Opinions issued by the Court, case information, and a current list of judges and officials of the United States Court of Appeals for Veterans Claims are available at www.uscourts.cavc.gov.

For further information, contact the Clerk, United States Court of Appeals for Veterans Claims, Suite 900, 625 Indiana Avenue NW., Washington, DC 20004–2950. Phone, 202–501–5970. Fax, 202–501–5848 Internet, http://www.uscourts.cavc.gov.

United States Court of Federal Claims

The United States Court of Federal Claims has jurisdiction over claims seeking money judgments against the United States. A claim must be founded upon the Constitution, an act of Congress, an Executive order, a contract with the United States, or Federal regulations. Judges are appointed by the President for 15-year terms, subject to Senate confirmation. Appeals are to the U.S. Court of Appeals for the Federal Circuit.

For further information, contact the Clerk's Office, United States Court of Federal Claims, 717 Madison Place NW., Washington, DC 20439. Phone, 202–357–6400. Internet, http://www.uscfc.uscourts.gov.

EDITORIAL NOTE: The United States Tax Court did not meet the publication deadline for submitting updated information of its activities, functions, and sources of information as required by the automatic disclosure provisions of the Freedom of Information Act (5 U.S.C. 552(a)(1)(A)).

United States Tax Court

The United States Tax Court is a court of record under Article I of the Constitution of the United States (26 U.S.C. 7441). The Court was created as the United States Board of Tax Appeals by the Revenue Act of 1924 (43 Stat. 336). The name was changed to the Tax Court of the United States by the Revenue Act of 1942 (56 Stat. 957). The Tax Reform Act of 1969 (83 Stat. 730) established the court under Article I and then changed its name to the United States Tax Court.

The Court comprises 19 judges who are appointed by the President to 15-year terms and subject to Senate confirmation. The court also has varying numbers of both senior judges (who may be recalled by the chief judge to perform further judicial duties) and special trial judges (who are appointed by the chief judge and may hear and decide a variety of cases). The Court's jurisdiction is set forth in various sections of title 26 of the U.S. Code.

The offices of the Court and its judges are in Washington, DC. However, the Court has national jurisdiction and schedules trial sessions in more than 70 cities in the United States. Each trial session is conducted by one judge, senior judge, or special trial judge. Court proceedings are open to the public and are conducted in accordance with the Court's Rules of Practice and Procedure and the rules of evidence applicable in trials without a jury in the U.S. District Court for the District of Columbia. A fee of $60 is charged for the filing of a petition. Practice before the Court is limited to practitioners admitted under the court's Rules of Practice and Procedure.

Decisions entered by the Court, other than decisions in small tax cases, may be appealed to the regional courts of appeals and, thereafter, upon the granting of a writ of certiorari, to the Supreme Court of the United States. At the option of petitioners, simplified procedures may be used in small tax cases. Small tax cases are final and not subject to review by any Court.

For further information, contact the Office of the Clerk of the Court, United States Tax Court, 400 Second Street NW., Washington, DC 20217–0002. Phone, 202–521–0700. Internet, http://www.ustaxcourt.gov.

ADMINISTRATIVE OFFICE OF THE UNITED STATES COURTS

Director	JOHN D. BATES
Deputy Director	JILL C. SAYENGA
General Counsel	ROBERT K. LOESCHE
Judicial Conference Secretariat Officer	JEFFREY A. HENNEMUTH
Legislative Affairs Officer	CORDIA A. STROM
Public Affairs Officer	DAVID A. SELLERS
Associate Director, Department of Program Services	LAURA C. MINOR
Associate Director, Department of Administrative Services	GEORGE H. SCHAFER

Associate Director, Department of Technology Services   JOSEPH R. PETERS, JR.

The Administrative Office of the United States Courts supports and serves the nonjudicial, administrative business of the United States Courts.

The Administrative Office of the United States Courts was created by act of August 7, 1939 (28 U.S.C. 601). It was established November 6, 1939. The Chief Justice of the United States, after consultation with the Judicial Conference, appoints the Director and Deputy Director of the Administrative Office.

Administering the Courts   The Director is the administrative officer of the courts of the United States (except the Supreme Court). Under the guidance of the Judicial Conference of the United States, the Director is required to supervise all administrative matters relating to the offices of clerks and other clerical and administrative personnel of the courts; to examine the state of the dockets of the courts, secure information as to the courts' need of assistance, and prepare and transmit statistical data and reports each quarter to the chief judges of the circuits; to submit to the annual meeting of the Judicial Conference of the United States an activities report of the Administrative Office and the courts' state of business; to fix the compensation of court employees whose compensation is not otherwise fixed by law; to regulate and pay annuities to widows and surviving dependent children of judges; to disburse moneys appropriated for the maintenance and operation of the courts; to examine accounts of court officers; to regulate travel of judicial personnel; to provide accommodations and supplies for the courts and their clerical and administrative personnel; to establish and maintain programs for the certification and utilization of court interpreters and the provision of special interpretation services in the courts; and to perform such other duties as may be assigned by the Supreme Court or the Judicial Conference of the United States.

The Director also is responsible for the preparation and submission of the budget of the courts, which the Office of Management and Budget transmits to Congress without change.

Probation Officers   The Administrative Office exercises general supervision of the accounts and practices of the Federal probation offices, which are subject to primary control by the respective district courts that they serve. The Administrative Office publishes quarterly, in cooperation with the Department of Justice's Bureau of Prisons, the electronically accessible "Federal Probation Journal," whose content centers on current thought, research, and practice in corrections and criminal justice.

The Director also has the responsibility to establish pretrial services in the district courts under the Pretrial Services Act of 1982 (18 U.S.C. 3152). The offices of these district courts report information concerning pretrial release of persons charged with Federal offenses and supervise such persons who are released to their custody.

Bankruptcy   According to the Bankruptcy Amendments and Federal Judgeship Act of 1984 (28 U.S.C. 151), the bankruptcy judges for each judicial district constitute a unit of the district court known as the bankruptcy court. The courts of appeals appoint bankruptcy judges in such numbers as authorized by Congress. These judges serve for a term of 14 years as judicial officers of the district courts.

This act placed jurisdiction in the district courts over all cases under title 11, United States Code, and all proceedings arising in or related to cases under that title (28 U.S.C. 1334). The district court may refer such cases and proceedings to its bankruptcy judges (as authorized by 28 U.S.C. 157).

The Director of the Administrative Office recommends to the Judicial Conference the duty stations of bankruptcy judges and the places they hold court, surveys the need for additional bankruptcy judgeships to

ADMINISTRATIVE OFFICE OF THE UNITED STATES COURTS

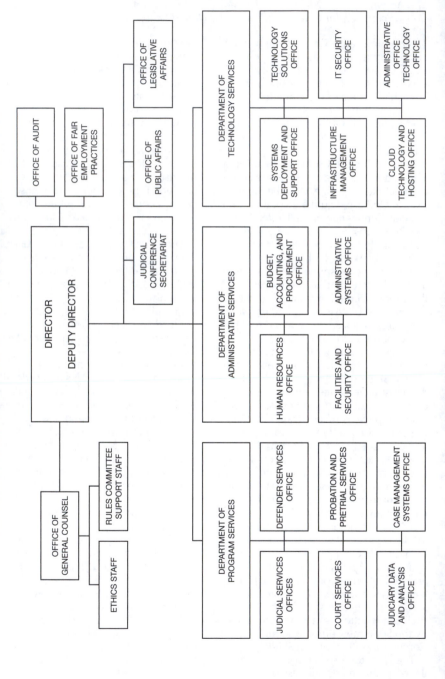

be recommended to Congress, and determines the staff needs of bankruptcy judges and the clerks of the bankruptcy courts.

Federal Magistrate Judges The Director of the Administrative Office exercises general supervision over administrative matters in offices of U.S. magistrate judges, compiles and evaluates statistical data relating to such offices, and submits reports thereon to the Judicial Conference. The Director reports annually to Congress on the business that has come before U.S. magistrate judges and also prepares legal and administrative manuals for the magistrate judges. In compliance with the act, the Administrative Office conducts surveys of the conditions in the judicial districts to make recommendations as to the number, location, and salaries of magistrate judges. The Judicial Conference then determines their number, location, and salaries, subject to the availability of appropriated funds.

Federal Defenders The Criminal Justice Act (18 U.S.C. 3006A) establishes the procedure for the appointment of private panel attorneys in Federal criminal cases for individuals who are unable to afford adequate representation, under plans adopted by each district court. The act also permits the establishment of Federal public defender or Federal community defender organizations by the district courts in districts where at least 200 persons annually require the appointment of counsel. Two adjacent districts may be combined to reach this total.

Each defender organization submits to the Director of the Administrative Office an annual report of its activities along with a proposed budget or, in the case of community defender organizations, a proposed grant for the coming year. The Director is responsible for the submission of the proposed budgets and grants to the Judicial Conference for approval. The Director also makes payments to the defender organizations out of appropriations in accordance with the approved budgets and grants, as well as compensating private counsel appointed to defend criminal cases in the United States courts.

Sources of Information

Budget, Accounting, and Procurement Office. Phone, 202–502–2000.
Court Services Office. Phone, 202–502–1500.
Defender Services Office. Phone, 202–502–3030.
General Counsel Office. Phone, 202–502–1100.
Human Resources Office. Phone, 202–502–3100.
Judicial Conference Executive Secretariat. Phone, 202–502–2400.
Judicial Services Office. Phone, 202–502–1800.
Judiciary Reporting and Analysis Division. Phone, 202–502–1440.
Legislative Affairs Office. Phone, 202–502–1700.
Probation and Pretrial Services Office. Phone, 202–502–1600.
Public Affairs Office. Phone, 202–502–2600.

For further information, contact the Administrative Office of the United States Courts, Thurgood Marshall Federal Judiciary Building, One Columbus Circle NE., Washington, DC 20544. Phone, 202–502–2600. Internet, http://www.uscourts.gov.

FEDERAL JUDICIAL CENTER

Director	JEREMY D. FOGEL
Deputy Director	JOHN S. COOKE
Director, Education Division	BRUCE M. CLARKE
Director, Information Technology Office	ESTHER DEVRIES
Director, Research Division	JAMES B. EAGLIN
Director, Interjudicial Relations Office	MIRA GUR-ARIE

| Director, Federal Judicial History Office | BRUCE A. RAGSDALE |
| Director, Editorial and Information Services Office | SYLVAN A. SOBEL |

The Federal Judicial Center is the judicial branch's agency for policy research and continuing education.

The Federal Judicial Center was created by act of December 20, 1967 (28 U.S.C. 620), to further the development and adoption of improved judicial administration in the courts of the United States.

The Center's basic policies and activities are determined by its Board, which is composed of the Chief Justice of the United States, who is permanent Chair of the Board by statute, and two judges of the U.S. courts of appeals, three judges of the U.S. district courts, one bankruptcy judge, and one magistrate judge, all of whom are elected for 4-year terms by the Judicial Conference of the United States. The Director of the Administrative Office of the United States Courts is also a permanent member of the Board.

The Center develops and administers orientation and continuing education programs for Federal judges and defenders and nonjudicial court personnel, including probation officers, pretrial services officers, and clerks' office employees. It conducts research and evaluation on the Federal judicial processes, court management, and sentencing and its consequences. The Center produces research reports, training manuals, video programs, computer-based training, and periodicals about the Federal courts; provides guidance and advice and maintains data and records relevant for documenting and conserving the history of the Federal courts; and cooperates with and assists other agencies and organizations in providing advice to improve the administration of justice in foreign courts.

Sources of Information

For general information about the Federal Judicial Center, including a directory of telephone and fax numbers for its component offices and divisions, visit www.fjc.gov/public/home.nsf/pages/104.
Electronic Access   Selected Federal Judicial Center publications, Federal judicial history databases, and various educational resources are available at www.fjc.gov.
Publications   Single copies of most Federal Judicial Center publications are available free of charge. Phone, 202–502–4153. Fax, 202–502–4077.

For further information, contact the Federal Judicial Center, Thurgood Marshall Federal Judiciary Building, One Columbus Circle NE., Washington, DC 20002–8003. Phone, 202–502–4000. Internet, http://www.fjc. gov.

UNITED STATES SENTENCING COMMISSION

Suite 2–500, One Columbus Circle NE., Washington, DC 20002–8002
Phone, 202–502–4500. Internet, http://www.ussc.gov.

Chair	PATTI B. SARIS
Vice Chairs	CHARLES R. BREYER, RICARDO H. HINOJOSA, KETANJI BROWN JACKSON
Commissioners	RACHEL E. BARKOW, DABNEY L. FRIEDRICH, WIILIAM H. PRYOR, JR.
Commissioner (ex officio)s	ISAAC FULWOOD, JR., JONATHAN J. WROBLEWSKI
Staff Director	KENNETH P. COHEN

General Counsel	KATHLEEN C. GRILLI
Public Affairs Officer	JEANNE DOHERTY
Director of Administration and Planning	SUSAN M. BRAZEL
Director and Chief Counsel of Training	PAMELA G. MONTGOMERY
Director of Legislative and Public Affairs	NOAH BOOKBINDER
Director of Research and Data	GLENN R. SCHMITT

The United States Sentencing Commission develops sentencing guidelines and policies for the Federal court system.

The United States Sentencing Commission was established as an independent agency in the judicial branch of the Federal Government by the Sentencing Reform Act of 1984 (28 U.S.C. 991 et seq. and 18 U.S.C. 3551 et seq.). The Commission establishes sentencing guidelines and policies for the Federal courts, advising them of the appropriate form and severity of punishment for offenders convicted of Federal crimes.

The Commission is composed of seven voting members appointed by the President with the advice and consent of the Senate for 6-year terms, and two nonvoting members. One of the voting members is appointed Chairperson.

The Commission evaluates the effects of the sentencing guidelines on the criminal justice system, advises Congress regarding the modification or enactment of statutes relating to criminal law and sentencing matters, establishes a research and development program on sentencing issues, and performs other related duties.

In executing its duties, the Commission promulgates and distributes to Federal courts and to the U.S. probation system guidelines to be consulted in determining sentences to be imposed in criminal cases, general policy statements regarding the application of guidelines, and policy statements on the appropriate use of probation and supervised release revocation provisions. These sentencing guidelines and policy statements are designed to further the purposes of just punishment, deterrence, incapacitation, and rehabilitation; provide fairness in meeting the purposes of sentencing; avoid unwarranted disparity; and reflect advancement in the knowledge of human behavior as it relates to the criminal justice process.

In addition, the Commission provides training, conducts research on sentencing-related issues, and serves as an information resource for Congress, criminal justice practitioners, and the public.

Sources of Information

Electronic Access Commission information and materials may be accessed online. Internet, http://www.ussc.gov.
Guideline Application Assistance Helpline Phone, 202–502–4545.
Public Information Information concerning Commission activities is available from the Office of Publishing and Public Affairs. Phone, 202–502–4590.

For further information, contact the Office of Publishing and Public Affairs, United States Sentencing Commission, Suite 2–500, One Columbus Circle NE., Washington, DC 20002–8002. Phone, 202–502–4590. Internet, http://www.ussc.gov.

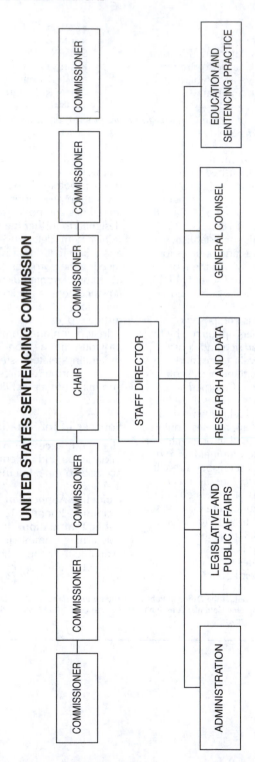

UNITED STATES SENTENCING COMMISSION

Executive Branch

EXECUTIVE BRANCH: THE PRESIDENT

THE PRESIDENT

The President of the United States

Article II, section 1, of the Constitution provides that "[t]he executive Power shall be vested in a President of the United States of America. He shall hold his Office during the Term of four Years, . . . together with the Vice President, chosen for the same Term . . . ." In addition to the powers set forth in the Constitution, the statutes have conferred upon the President specific authority and responsibility covering a wide range of matters (United States Code Index).

The President is the administrative head of the executive branch of the Government, which includes numerous agencies, both temporary and permanent, as well as the 15 executive departments.

The Cabinet The Cabinet, a creation of custom and tradition dating back to George Washington's administration, functions at the pleasure of the President. Its purpose is to advise the President upon any subject, relating to the duties

BARACK OBAMA

of the respective offices, on which he requests information (pursuant to Article II, section 2, of the Constitution).

The Cabinet is composed of the Vice President and the heads of the 15 executive departments—the Secretaries of Agriculture, Commerce, Defense, Education, Energy, Health and Human Services, Homeland Security, Housing and Urban Development, Interior, Labor, State, Transportation, Treasury, and Veterans Affairs, and the Attorney General. Additionally, in the Obama administration, Cabinet-level rank has been accorded to the Chief of Staff to the President; the Administrator, Environmental Protection Agency; the Chair, Council of Economic Advisers; the Director, Office of Management and Budget; the U.S. Permanent Representative to the United Nations; and the U.S. Trade Representative.

THE VICE PRESIDENT

The Vice President

Article II, section 1, of the Constitution provides that the President "shall hold his Office during the Term of four Years, . . . together with the Vice President . . . ." In addition to his role as President of the Senate, the Vice President is empowered to succeed to the Presidency, pursuant

JOSEPH R. BIDEN, JR.

to Article II and the 20th and 25th amendments to the Constitution.

The executive functions of the Vice President include participation in Cabinet meetings and, by statute, membership on the National Security Council and the Board of Regents of the Smithsonian Institution.

THE EXECUTIVE OFFICE OF THE PRESIDENT

Under authority of the Reorganization Act of 1939 (5 U.S.C. 133–133r, 133t note), various agencies were transferred to the Executive Office of the President by the President's Reorganization Plans I and II of 1939 (5 U.S.C. app.), effective July 1, 1939. Executive Order 8248 of September 8, 1939, established the divisions of the Executive Office and defined their functions. Subsequently, Presidents have used Executive orders, reorganization plans, and legislative initiatives to reorganize the Executive Office to make its composition compatible with the goals of their administrations.

White House Office

1600 Pennsylvania Avenue NW., Washington, DC 20500
Phone, 202–456–1414. Internet, http://www.whitehouse.gov.

Assistant to the President and Chief of Staff	DENIS R. MCDONOUGH
Assistant to the President and Deputy Chief of Staff for Operations	ANITA DECKER BRECKENRIDGE
Assistant to the President and Deputy Chief of Staff for Implementation	KRISTIE A. CANEGALLO
Counselor to the President	JOHN D. PODESTA
Senior Advisor and Assistant to the President for Intergovernmental Affairs and Public Engagement	VALERIE B. JARRETT
Senior Adviser and Assistant to the President for Strategy and Communications	DANIEL H. PFEIFFER
Assistant to the President and National Security Adviser	SUSAN E. RICE
Assistant to the President and Deputy National Security Adviser	ANTONY J. BLINKEN
Assistant to the President and Deputy National Security Adviser, Strategic Communications and Speechwriting	BENJAMIN J. RHODES
Assistant to the President and Cabinet Secretary	BRODERICK D. JOHNSON
Assistant to the President and Counsel to the President	WARREN N. EGGLESTON
Assistant to the President and Director of Communications	JENNIFER M. PALMIERI
Assistant to the President and Director of Presidential Personnel	JONATHAN D. MCBRIDE
Assistant to the President and Director of Legislative Affairs	KATHERINE B. FALLON
Assistant to the President and Director of Scheduling and Advance	DANIELLE M. WHITE
Assistant to the President and Director of Political Strategy and Outreach	DAVID M. SIMAS
Assistant to the President and Director of Speechwriting	CODY S. KEENAN
Assistant to the President and Director of White House Military Office	EMMETT S. BELIVEAU
Assistant to the President and Press Secretary	JOSHUA R. EARNEST
Assistant to the President for Homeland Security and Counterterrorism	LISA O. MONACO

Assistant to the President for Management and Administration	KATY A. KALE
Assistant to the President and Chief of Staff to the First Lady	CHRISTINA M. TCHEN

The White House Office serves the President in the performance of the many detailed activities incident to his immediate office.

The President's staff facilitates and maintains communication with the Congress, the heads of executive agencies, the press and other information media, and the general public. The various Assistants to the President aid the President in such matters as he may direct.

Office of the Vice President

Eisenhower Executive Office Building, Washington, DC 20501
Phone, 202–456–7549.

Assistant to the President and Chief of Staff to the Vice President	STEVE RICCHETTI
Deputy Assistant to the President and Deputy Chief of Staff to the Vice President	SHAILAGH MURRAY
Deputy Assistant to the President and Chief of Staff to Dr. Jill Biden	SHEILA NIX
Deputy Assistant to the President and National Security Advisor to the Vice President	JAKE SULLIVAN
Deputy Assistant to the President and Director of Economic and Domestic Policy to the Vice President	SARAH BIANCHI
Counsel to the Vice President	DEMETRA LAMBROS
Special Assistant to the President and Senior Advisor to the Vice President	GREG SCHULTZ
Special Assistant to the President and Assistant to the Vice President for Intergovernmental Affairs, Public Engagement, and Correspondence	LISE CLAVEL
Special Assistant to the President and Senior Personal Aide to the Vice President	FRAN PERSON
Special Assistant to the President and Deputy Chief of Staff to Dr. Jill Biden	ANTHONY BERNAL
Special Assistant to the President and Director of Speechwriting for the Vice President	SEAN O'BRIEN
Director of Administration to the Vice President	FAISAL AMIN
Director of Advance to the Vice President	CHAD BOLDUC
Director of Legislative Affairs to the Vice President	TONYA WILLIAMS
Director of Scheduling to the Vice President	ALEX HORNBROOK
Assistant to the Vice President	KATHY CHUNG

The Office of the Vice President serves the Vice President in the performance of the many detailed activities incident to his immediate office.

Council of Economic Advisers

Seventeenth and Pennsylvania Avenue NW., Washington, DC 20502
Phone, 202–395–5084. Internet, http://www.whitehouse.gov/cea.

Chairman	JASON L. FURMAN
Members	BETSEY A. STEVENSON, JAMES H. STOCK

The Council of Economic Advisers performs an analysis and appraisal of the national economy for the purpose of providing policy recommendations to the President.

The Council of Economic Advisers (CEA) was established in the Executive Office of the President by the Employment Act of 1946 (15 U.S.C. 1023). It now functions under that statute and Reorganization Plan No. 9 of 1953 (5 U.S.C. app.), effective August 1, 1953.

The Chairman and two Members govern the Council. The Chairman is appointed by the President and confirmed by the United States Senate. The Members are appointed by the President.

The Council analyzes the national economy and its various segments; advises the President on economic developments; appraises the economic programs and policies of the Federal Government; recommends to the President policies for economic growth and stability; assists in the preparation of the economic reports of the President to the Congress; and prepares the Annual Report of the Council of Economic Advisers.

For further information, contact the Council of Economic Advisers, Seventeenth and Pennsylvania Avenue NW., Washington, DC 20502. Phone, 202–395–5084. Internet, http://www.whitehouse.gov/cea.

Council on Environmental Quality

722 Jackson Place NW., Washington, DC 20503
Phone, 202–395–5750 or 202–456–6224. Fax, 202–456–2710. Internet, http://www.whitehouse.gov/administration/eop/ceq.

Chair	MICHAEL J. BOOTS, *Acting*
General Counsel	BRENDA MALLORY
Chief of Staff	LOWRY CROOK
Associate Director for Energy and Climate Change	RICHARD D. DUKE
Associate Director for Communications	TARYN L. TUSS
Associate Director for Lands and Water Ecosystems	JAY JENSEN
Associate Director for Legislative Affairs	TRENT BAUSERMAN
Associate Director for NEPA Oversight	HORST GRECZMIEL
Associate Director for Public Engagement	ROHAN PATEL

The Council on Environmental Quality formulates and recommends national policies and initiatives to improve the environment.

The Council on Environmental Quality (CEQ) was established within the Executive Office of the President by the National Environmental Policy Act of 1969 (NEPA) (42 U.S.C. 4321 et seq.). The Environmental Quality Improvement

Act of 1970 (42 U.S.C. 4371 et seq.) established the Office of Environmental Quality (OEQ) to provide professional and administrative support for the Council. The Council and OEQ are collectively referred to as the Council on Environmental Quality, and the CEQ Chair, who is appointed by the President and confirmed by the Senate, serves as the Director of OEQ.

The Council develops policies which bring together the Nation's social, economic, and environmental priorities, with the goal of improving

Federal decisionmaking. As required by NEPA, CEQ evaluates, coordinates, and mediates Federal activities. It advises and assists the President on both national and international environmental policy matters. CEQ also oversees Federal agency and department implementation of NEPA.

For further information, contact the Information Office, Council on Environmental Quality, 722 Jackson Place NW., Washington, DC 20503. Phone, 202–395–5750. Fax, 202–456–2710. Internet, http://www. whitehouse.gov/administration/eop/ceq.

National Security Council

Eisenhower Executive Office Building, Washington, DC 20504
Phone, 202–456–1414. Internet, http://www.whitehouse.gov/nsc.

Members
The President	BARACK OBAMA
The Vice President	JOSEPH R. BIDEN, JR.
The Secretary of State	JOHN F. KERRY
The Secretary of Defense	CHARLES T. HAGEL

Statutory Advisers
Director of National Intelligence	JAMES R. CLAPPER
Chairman, Joint Chiefs of Staff	GEN. MARTIN E. DEMPSEY, USA

Standing Participants
The Secretary of the Treasury	JACOB J. LEW
Chief of Staff to the President	DENIS R. MCDONOUGH
Counsel to the President	WARREN N. EGGLESTON
National Security Adviser	SUSAN E. RICE
Assistant to the President for Economic Policy	JEFFREY D. ZIENTS

Officials
Assistant to the President for National Security Affairs	SUSAN E. RICE
Assistant to the President for National Security Affairs and Deputy National Security Adviser	ANTONY J. BLINKEN

The National Security Council was established by the National Security Act of 1947, as amended (50 U.S.C. 402). The Council was placed in the Executive Office of the President by Reorganization Plan No. 4 of 1949 (5 U.S.C. app.).

The National Security Council is chaired by the President. Its statutory members, in addition to the President, are the Vice President and the Secretaries of State and Defense. The Chairman of the Joint Chiefs of Staff is the statutory military adviser to the Council, and the Director of National Intelligence is its intelligence adviser. The Secretary of the Treasury, the U.S. Representative to

the United Nations, the Assistant to the President for National Security Affairs, the Assistant to the President for Economic Policy, and the Chief of Staff to the President are invited to all meetings of the Council. The Attorney General and the Director of National Drug Control Policy are invited to attend meetings pertaining to their jurisdictions; other officials are invited, as appropriate.

The Council advises and assists the President in integrating all aspects of national security policy as it affects the United States—domestic, foreign, military, intelligence, and economic—in conjunction with the National Economic Council.

For further information, contact the National Security Council, Eisenhower Executive Office Building, Washington, DC 20504. Phone, 202–456–1414. Internet, http://www.whitehouse.gov/nsc.

Office of Administration

Eisenhower Executive Office Building, 1650 Pennsylvania Avenue, NW., Washington, DC 20503 Phone, 202–456–2861. Internet, http://www.whitehouse.gov/oa.

Director	ELIZABETH JONES
Chief Administrative Officer	KRISTIE MARK
Chief Financial Officer	CATHERINE SOLOMON
Chief Information Officer	KAREN G. BRITTON
Chief Procurement and Contract Management Officer	ALTHEA KIREILIS
Chief of Operations Services	(VACANCY)
Director for Equal Employment Opportunity	CLARA M. PATTERSON
General Counsel	HUGH BRADY

The Office of Administration was formally established within the Executive Office of the President by Executive Order 12028 of December 12, 1977. The Office provides administrative support services to all units within the Executive Office of the President. The services provided include information, personnel, technology, and financial management; data processing; library and research services; security; legislative liaisons; and general office operations such as mail, messenger, printing, procurement, and supply services.

For further information, contact the Office of the Director, Office of Administration, Washington, DC 20503. Phone, 202–456–2861. Internet, http://www.whitehouse.gov/oa.

Office of Management and Budget

New Executive Office Building, Washington, DC 20503 Phone, 202–395–3080. Internet, http://www.whitehouse.gov/omb.

Director	SHAUN L.S. DONOVAN
Deputy Director	BRIAN C. DEESE
Deputy Director for Management	BETH COBERT
Associate Director for Management and Operations	JULIE MILLER
Administrator, Office of Federal Procurement Policy	LESLEY FIELD, *Acting*
Administrator, Office of Information and Regulatory Affairs	HOWARD A. SHELANSKI
Assistant Director for Management and Operations	LAUREN E. WRIGHT
Assistant Director for Budget	COURTNEY TIMBERLAKE
Assistant Director for Legislative Reference	MATTHEW VAETH
Associate Director for Communications	STEVEN POSNER
Associate Director for Economic Policy	AVIVA ARON-DINE
Associate Director for Education, Income Maintenance and Labor	MARTHA COVEN

Associate Director for General Government Programs	ANDREW MAYOCK
Associate Director for Information Technology and E–Government	STEVEN VANROEKEL
Associate Director for Legislative Affairs	KRISTEN SARRI
Associate Director for National Security Programs	STEVE KOSIAK
Associate Director for Natural Resource Programs	SALLY ERICSSON
Controller, Office of Federal Financial Management	DAVID ARTHUR MADER
General Counsel	GEOVETTE WASHINGTON
Associate Director for Health	JULIAN HARRIS
Executive Associate Director	(VACANCY)
Associate Director for Performance Management	LISA DANZIG
Intellectual Property Enforcement Coordinator	HOWARD SHELANSKI, *Acting*

The Office of Management and Budget evaluates, formulates, and coordinates management procedures and program objectives within and among Federal departments and agencies. It also controls the administration of the Federal budget, while routinely providing the President with recommendations regarding budget proposals and relevant legislative enactments.

The Office of Management and Budget (OMB), formerly the Bureau of the Budget, was established in the Executive Office of the President pursuant to Reorganization Plan No. 1 of 1939 (5 U.S.C. app.).

The Office's primary functions are: to assist the President in developing and maintaining effective government by reviewing the organizational structure and management procedures of the executive branch to ensure that the intended results are achieved; to assist in developing efficient coordinating mechanisms to implement Government activities and to expand interagency cooperation; to assist the President in preparing the budget and in formulating the Government's fiscal program; to supervise and control the administration of the budget; to assist the President by clearing and coordinating departmental advice on proposed legislation and by making recommendations effecting Presidential action on legislative enactments, in accordance with past practice; to assist in developing regulatory reform proposals and programs for paperwork reduction, especially reporting burdens of the public; to assist in considering, clearing, and,

where necessary, preparing proposed Executive orders and proclamations; to plan and develop information systems that provide the President with program performance data; to plan, conduct, and promote evaluation efforts that assist the President in assessing program objectives, performance, and efficiency; to keep the President informed of the progress of activities by Government agencies with respect to work proposed, initiated, and completed, together with the relative timing of work between the several agencies of the Government, all to the end that the work programs of the several agencies of the executive branch of the Government may be coordinated and that the moneys appropriated by the Congress may be expended in the most economical manner, barring overlapping and duplication of effort; and to improve the economy, efficiency, and effectiveness of the procurement processes by providing overall direction of procurement policies, regulations, procedures, and forms.

Sources of Information

Employment Delegated examining is used for filling positions, such

OFFICE OF MANAGEMENT AND BUDGET

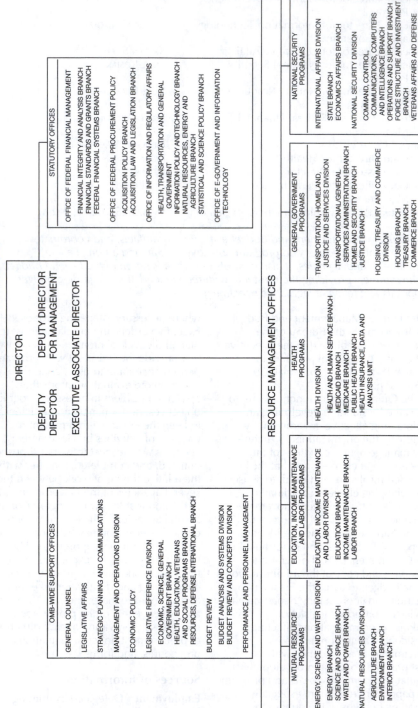

DIRECTOR
DEPUTY DIRECTOR

DEPUTY DIRECTOR
DEPUTY DIRECTOR FOR MANAGEMENT
EXECUTIVE ASSOCIATE DIRECTOR

STATUTORY OFFICES

OFFICE OF FEDERAL FINANCIAL MANAGEMENT
FINANCIAL INTEGRITY AND ANALYSIS BRANCH
FINANCIAL STANDARDS AND GRANTS BRANCH
FEDERAL FINANCIAL SYSTEMS BRANCH

OFFICE OF FEDERAL PROCUREMENT POLICY
ACQUISITION POLICY BRANCH
ACQUISITION LAW AND LEGISLATION BRANCH

OFFICE OF INFORMATION AND REGULATORY AFFAIRS
HEALTH, TRANSPORTATION AND GENERAL
GOVERNMENT
INFORMATION POLICY AND TECHNOLOGY BRANCH
NATURAL RESOURCES, ENERGY AND
AGRICULTURE BRANCH
STATISTICAL AND SCIENCE POLICY BRANCH

OFFICE OF E-GOVERNMENT AND INFORMATION
TECHNOLOGY

OMB-WIDE SUPPORT OFFICES

GENERAL COUNSEL

LEGISLATIVE AFFAIRS

STRATEGIC PLANNING AND COMMUNICATIONS

MANAGEMENT AND OPERATIONS DIVISION

ECONOMIC POLICY

LEGISLATIVE REFERENCE DIVISION
ECONOMIC, SCIENCE, GENERAL
GOVERNMENT BRANCH
HEALTH, EDUCATION, VETERANS
AND SOCIAL PROGRAMS BRANCH
RESOURCES, DEFENSE, INTERNATIONAL BRANCH

BUDGET REVIEW
BUDGET ANALYSIS AND SYSTEMS DIVISION
BUDGET REVIEW AND CONCEPTS DIVISION

PERFORMANCE AND PERSONNEL MANAGEMENT

RESOURCE MANAGEMENT OFFICES

NATURAL RESOURCE PROGRAMS

ENERGY, SCIENCE AND WATER DIVISION
ENERGY BRANCH
SCIENCE AND SPACE BRANCH
WATER AND POWER BRANCH

NATURAL RESOURCES DIVISION
AGRICULTURE BRANCH
ENVIRONMENT BRANCH
INTERIOR BRANCH

EDUCATION, INCOME MAINTENANCE AND LABOR PROGRAMS

EDUCATION, INCOME MAINTENANCE
AND LABOR DIVISION
EDUCATION BRANCH
INCOME MAINTENANCE BRANCH
LABOR BRANCH

HEALTH PROGRAMS

HEALTH DIVISION
HEALTH AND HUMAN SERVICE BRANCH
MEDICAID BRANCH
MEDICARE BRANCH
PUBLIC HEALTH BRANCH
HEALTH INSURANCE, DATA AND
ANALYSIS UNIT

GENERAL GOVERNMENT PROGRAMS

TRANSPORTATION, HOMELAND,
JUSTICE AND SERVICES DIVISION
TRANSPORTATIONAL/GENERAL
SERVICES ADMINISTRATION BRANCH
HOMELAND SECURITY BRANCH
JUSTICE BRANCH

HOUSING, TREASURY AND COMMERCE
DIVISION
HOUSING BRANCH
TREASURY BRANCH
COMMERCE BRANCH

NATIONAL SECURITY PROGRAMS

INTERNATIONAL AFFAIRS DIVISION
STATE BRANCH
ECONOMICS AFFAIRS BRANCH

NATIONAL SECURITY DIVISION
COMMAND, CONTROL,
COMMUNICATIONS, COMPUTERS
AND INTELLIGENCE BRANCH
OPERATIONS AND SUPPORT BRANCH
FORCE STRUCTURE AND INVESTMENT
BRANCH
VETERANS AFFAIRS AND DEFENSE
HEALTH BRANCH

as economist, program examiners, and program analyst. Inquiries on employment should be directed to the Human Resources Division, Office of Administration, Washington, DC 20500. Phone, 202–395–1088.

Inquiries   Contact the Management and Operations Division, Office of Management and Budget, New Executive Office Building, Washington, DC 20503.

Phone, 202–395–3080. Fax, 202–395–3504. Internet, http://www.whitehouse.gov/omb/contact.

Publications   The Budget of the U.S. Government and The Budget System and Concepts are available for sale by the Superintendent of Documents, Government Printing Office, Washington, DC 20402.

For further information, contact the Office of Management and Budget, New Executive Office Building, Washington, DC 20503. Phone, 202–395–3080. Internet, http://www.whitehouse.gov/omb.

Office of National Drug Control Policy

Executive Office of the President, Washington, DC 20503
Phone, 202–395–6700. Fax, 202–395–6708. Internet, http://www.ondcp.gov.

Director	MICHAEL P. BOTTICELLI, *Acting*
Senior Policy Adviser	RENÉ N. HANNA
Correspondence Manager	VIRLENA COOPER-BRISCOE
Deputy Director	MICHAEL P. BOTTICELLI
Chief of Staff	REGINA M. LABELLE
Deputy Chief of Staff	JON E. RICE, *Acting*
Deputy Director for Demand Reduction	DAVID K. MINETA
Assistant Deputy Director for Demand Reduction	JUNE S. SIVILLI
Deputy Director for State, Local, and Tribal Affairs	BENJAMIN B. TUCKER
Staff Director for State, Local, and Tribal Affairs	MARY F. HYLAND
Director, High Intensity Drug Trafficking Area (HIDTA) Program	MICHAEL GOTTLIEB
Drug-Free Communities Grants Program Administrator	(VACANCY)
Deputy Director for Supply Reduction	MARILYN A. QUAGLIOTTI
Assistant Deputy Director for Supply Reduction	GERARD K. BURNS, *Acting*
Associate Director for Performance and Budget	JON E. RICE
Associate Director for Legislative Affairs	(VACANCY)
Program Support Specialist for Legislative Affairs	(VACANCY)
Associate Director for Public Affairs	RAFAEL E. LEMAITRE
Associate Director for Management and Administration	MICHELE C. MARX
General Counsel	JEFFREY J. TEITZ
Associate Director for Research/Data Analysis	TERRY E. ZOBECK
Associate Director for Intergovernmental Public Affairs	KATHRYN A. GREENE

The Office of National Drug Control Policy assists the President in establishing policies, priorities, and objectives in the National Drug Control Strategy. It also provides budget, program, and policy recommendations on the efforts of National Drug Control Program agencies.

The Office of National Drug Control Policy was established by the National Narcotics Leadership Act of 1988 (21 U.S.C. 1501 et seq.), effective January 29, 1989, reauthorized through the Office of National Drug Control Policy Reauthorization Act of 1988 (21 U.S.C. 1701 et seq.), and again reauthorized through the Office of National Drug Control Policy Reauthorization Act of 2006 (21 U.S.C. 1701 et seq.).

The Director of National Drug Control Policy is appointed by the President with the advice and consent of the Senate. The Director is assisted by five statutorily-recognized Presidential appointees: a Deputy Director, a Deputy Director for Demand Reduction, a Deputy Director for Supply Reduction, and a Deputy Director for State, Local, and Tribal Affairs.

The Director is responsible for establishing policies, objectives, priorities, and performance measurements for the National Drug Control Program, as well as for annually promulgating the President's National Drug Control Strategy, other related drug control strategies, supporting reports, and a program budget, which the President submits to Congress. The Director advises the President regarding necessary changes in the organization, management, budgeting, and personnel allocation of Federal agencies monitoring drug activities. The Director also notifies Federal agencies if their policies do not comply with their responsibilities under the National Drug Control Strategy. Additionally, the Office has direct programmatic responsibility for the Drug-Free Communities Support Program and the High Intensity Drug Trafficking Areas Program.

Sources of Information

Employment   Inquiries regarding employment should be directed to the Personnel Section, Office of National Drug Control Policy. Phone, 202–395–6695.
Publications   To receive publications on drugs and crime control policies, access specific drug-related data, obtain customized bibliographic searches, and learn more about data availability and other information resources, visit the ONDCP Web site.

For further information, contact the Office of National Drug Control Policy, Executive Office of the President, Washington, DC 20503. Phone, 202–395–6700. Fax, 202–395–6708. Internet, http://www. whitehouse.gov/ondcp.

Office of Policy Development

The Office of Policy Development is comprised of the Domestic Policy Council and the National Economic Council, which are responsible for advising and assisting the President in the formulation, coordination, and implementation of domestic and economic policy. The Office of Policy Development also provides support for other policy development and implementation activities as directed by the President.

Domestic Policy Council

Room 469, Eisenhower Executive Office Building, Washington, DC 20502
Phone, 202–456–5594. Internet, http://www.whitehouse.gov/dpc.

Assistant to the President and Director of the   Cecilia Munoz
    Domestic Policy Council

The Domestic Policy Council was established August 16, 1993, by Executive Order 12859. The Council oversees development and implementation of the President's domestic policy agenda and ensures coordination and communication among the heads of relevant Federal offices and agencies.

National Economic Council

Room 235, Eisenhower Executive Office Building, Washington, DC 20502
Phone, 202–456–2800. Internet, http://www.whitehouse.gov/nec.

Assistant to the President for Economic Policy and Director of the National Economic Council	JEFFREY D. ZIENTS

The National Economic Council was created January 25, 1993, by Executive Order 12835, to coordinate the economic policymaking process and provide economic policy advice to the President. The Council also ensures that economic policy decisions and programs are consistent with the President's stated goals, and monitors the implementation of the President's economic goals.

Office of Science and Technology Policy

Eisenhower Executive Office Building, 1650 Pennsylvania Avenue NW., Washington, DC 20504
Phone, 202–456–7116. Fax, 202–456–6021. Internet, http://www.ostp.gov.

Director	JOHN P. HOLDREN
Chief of Staff	RICK SIGER
Deputy Chief of Staff and Assistant Director	TED WACKLER
General Counsel	RACHAEL LEONARD
Operations Manager/Security Officer	STACY MURPHY
Assistant Director, Federal Research and Development	KEI KOIZUMI
Assistant Director, Legislative Affairs	DONNA PIGNATELLI
Assistant Director, Strategic Communications	KRISTIN LEE
Chief Technology Officer	TODD PARK
Deputy Chief Technology Officers	NICK SINAI, JENNIFER PAHLKA, NICOLE WONG
Deputy Chief Technology Officer, Telecommunications	TOM POWER
Associate Director for Environment and Energy	(VACANCY)
Principal Assistant Director for Environment and Energy	TAMMY DICKINSON
Assistant Director, Clean Energy and Materials Research and Development	CYRUS WADIA
Assistant Director, Environmental Information	PETER COLOHAN
Assistant Director, Ocean Sciences	BRADLEY MORAN
Assistant Director, Environmental Health	BRUCE RODAN
Assistant Director, Polar Sciences	BRENDAN KELLY
Associate Director, National Security and International Affairs	PATRICIA FALCONE
NSIA Staff Director and Assistant Director for Defense Programs	REED SKAGGS
Assistant Director, Biological and Chemical Threats	ANDREW HEBBELER
Assistant Director, Nuclear Matters	CINDY ATKINS-DUFFIN
Assistant Director, Intelligence Programs	MICHAEL JOHNSON
Assistant Director, Cybersecurity	TIM POLK
Associate Director for Science	JO EMILY HANDELSMAN

Principal Assistant Director for Science and Assistant Director for Social, Behavioral, and Economic Sciences	PHILIP RUBIN
Assistant Director, Biotechnology	MIKE STEBBINS
Assistant Director, Forensic Science	TANIA SIMONCELLI
Assistant Director, Nanotechnology	ALTAF CARIM
Assistant Director, Physical Sciences	GERALD BLAZEY
Deputy Director for Technology and Innovation	TOM KALIL
Assistant Director, Grand Challenges	CRISTIN DORGELO
Assistant Director, Robotics and Cyber-Physical Systems	RICHARD VOYLES
Assistant Director, Space and Aeronautics	RICHARD DALBELLO
Assistant Director, Global Health	ROBYNN STEFFEN
Assistant Director, Learning and Innovation	KUMAR GARG
Assistant Director, Telecommunications	NICK MAYNARD
Assistant Director, Entrepreneurship	DOUGLAS RAND
Executive Director, President's Council of Advisers on Science and Technology	MARJORY BLUMENTHAL
Executive Director, National Science and Technology Council	JAYNE MORROW
Director, Nanotechnology National Coordination Office	LLOYD WHITMAN
Director, Networking and Information Technology Research and Development National Coordination Office	GEORGE STRAWN
Director, United States Global Change Research Program National Coordination Office	THOMAS ARMSTRONG

The Office of Science and Technology Policy was established within the Executive Office of the President by the National Science and Technology Policy, Organization, and Priorities Act of 1976 (42 U.S.C. 6611).

The Office supports the President by serving as a source of scientific, engineering, and technological analysis and judgment on major policies, plans, and programs of the Federal Government. In carrying out its mission, the Office advises the President of scientific and technological considerations involved in areas of national concern, including the economy, national security, health, foreign relations, and the environment; evaluates the scale, quality, and effectiveness of the Federal effort in science and technology; provides advice and assistance to the President, the Office of Management and Budget, and Federal agencies throughout the Federal budget development process; and assists the President in providing leadership and coordination for the Federal Government's research and development programs.

For further information, contact the Office of Science and Technology Policy, Eisenhower Executive Office Building, 1650 Pennsylvania Avenue NW., Washington, DC 20504. Phone, 202–456–4444. Fax, 202–456–6021. Internet, http://www.ostp.gov.

Office of the United States Trade Representative

600 Seventeenth Street NW., Washington, DC 20508
Phone, 202–395–3230. Internet, http://www.ustr.gov.

United States Trade Representative	MICHAEL FROMAN
Deputy U.S. Trade Representatives (Washington)	WENDY CUTLER, *Acting,* (VACANCY)
Deputy U.S. Trade Representative (Geneva)	MICHAEL PUNKE
Chief of Staff	MATTHEW VOGEL

General Counsel	TIMOTHY REIF
Chief Agricultural Negotiator	(VACANCY)
Assistant U.S. Trade Representative for Administration	FRED AMES
Assistant U.S. Trade Representative for Agricultural Affairs	SHARON BOMER LAURITSEN
Assistant U.S. Trade Representative for Southeast Asia and the Pacific	BARBARA WEISEL
Assistant U.S. Trade Representative for Congressional Affairs	HUN QUACH
Assistant U.S. Trade Representative for Trade Policy and Economic Affairs	DOUGLAS BELL
Assistant U.S. Trade Representative for Environment and Natural Resources	JENNIFER PRESCOTT
Assistant U.S. Trade Representative for Europe and the Middle East	DANIEL MULLANEY
Assistant U.S. Trade Representative for Small Business, Market Access and Industrial Competitiveness	JAMES SANFORD
Assistant U.S. Trade Representative for Intergovernmental Affairs and Public Engagement	JEWEL JAMES
Assistant U.S. Trade Representative for Japan, Korea, and Asia Pacific Economic Cooperation Affairs	WENDY CUTLER
Assistant U.S. Trade Representative for China Affairs	CLAIRE READE
Assistant U.S. Trade Representative for Central and South Asian Affairs	MICHAEL DELANEY
Assistant U.S. Trade Representative for Monitoring and Enforcement	JUAN MILLAN, *Acting*
Director for Interagency Trade Enforcement Center	BRADFORD WARD
Assistant U.S. Trade Representative for Africa	FLORIZELLE LISER
Assistant U.S. Trade Representative for Services and Investment	CHRISTINE BLISS
Assistant U.S. Trade Representative for Intellectual Property and Innovation	PROBIR MEHTA, *Acting*
Assistant U.S. Trade Representative for Labor	LEWIS KARESH
Assistant U.S. Trade Representative for World Trade Organization (WTO) and Multilateral Affairs	MARK LINSCOTT
Assistant U.S. Trade Representative for the Western Hemisphere	JOHN MELLE
Assistant U.S. Trade Representative for Public and Media Affairs	MATTHEW MCALVANAH
Assistant U.S. Trade Representative for Textiles	GAIL STRICKLER
Deputy Chief of Mission (Geneva)	CHRIS WILSON

The United States Trade Representative is responsible for directing all trade negotiations of and formulating trade policy for the United States.

The Office of the United States Trade Representative was created as the Office of the Special Representative for Trade Negotiations by Executive Order 11075 of January 15, 1963. The Trade Act of 1974 (19 U.S.C. 2171) established the

OFFICE OF THE UNITED STATES TRADE REPRESENTATIVE

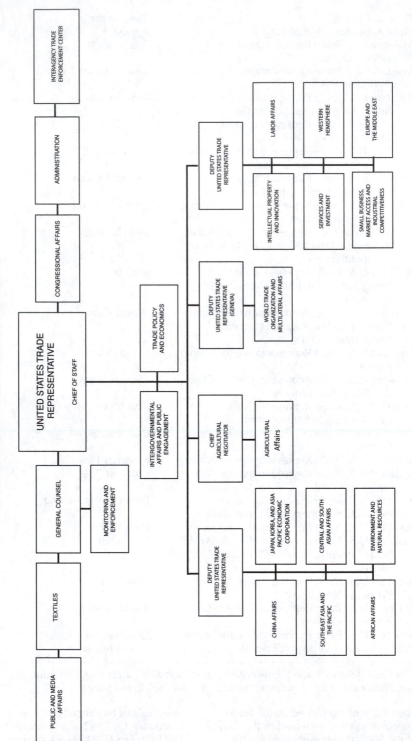

Office as an agency of the Executive Office of the President charged with administering the trade agreements program.

The Office is responsible for setting and administering overall trade policy. It also provides that the United States Trade Representative shall be chief representative of the United States for the following: all activities concerning the General Agreement on Tariffs and Trade; discussions, meetings, and negotiations in the Organization for Economic Cooperation and Development when such activities deal primarily with trade and commodity issues; negotiations in the U.N. Conference on Trade and Development and other multilateral institutions when such negotiations deal primarily with trade and commodity issues; other bilateral and multilateral negotiations when trade, including East-West trade, or commodities is the primary issue; negotiations under sections 704 and 734 of the Tariff Act of 1930 (19 U.S.C. 1671c and 1673c); and negotiations concerning direct investment incentives and disincentives and bilateral investment issues concerning barriers to investment.

The Omnibus Trade and Competitiveness Act of 1988 codified these prior authorities and added additional authority, including the implementation of section 301 actions (regarding enforcement of U.S. rights under international trade agreements).

The Office is headed by the United States Trade Representative, a Cabinet-level official with the rank of Ambassador, who is directly responsible to the President. There are three Deputy United States Trade Representatives, who also hold the rank of Ambassador, two located in Washington and one in Geneva. The Chief Agricultural Negotiator also holds the rank of Ambassador.

The United States Trade Representative serves as an ex officio member of the Boards of Directors of the Export-Import Bank and the Overseas Private Investment Corporation and serves on the National Advisory Council for International Monetary and Financial Policy.

For further information, contact the Office of Public Affairs, Office of the United States Trade Representative, 600 Seventeenth Street NW., Washington, DC 20506. Phone, 202–395–3230. Internet, http://www.ustr.gov.

EXECUTIVE BRANCH: DEPARTMENTS

DEPARTMENT OF AGRICULTURE

1400 Independence Avenue SW., Washington, DC 20250
Phone, 202–720–4623. Internet, http://www.usda.gov.

Secretary of Agriculture	THOMAS J. VILSACK
Deputy Secretary	KRYSTA L. HARDEN
Director, Office of Communications	MATT PAUL
Inspector General	PHYLLIS K. FONG
General Counsel	RAMONA ROMERO
Assistant Secretary for Congressional Relations	TODD A. BATTA
Assistant Secretary for Administration	GREGORY PARHAM
Assistant Secretary for Civil Rights	JOE LEONARD
Chief Information Officer	CHERYL COOK
Chief Financial Officer	JON HOLLADAY, *Acting*
Chief Economist	JOSEPH GLAUBER
Director, Office of Budget and Program Analysis	MIKE YOUNG
Under Secretary for Natural Resources and Environment	ROBERT BONNIE
Chief, Forest Service	THOMAS TIDWELL
Chief, Natural Resources Conservation Service	JASON WELLER
Under Secretary for Farm and Foreign Agricultural Services	MICHAEL SCUSE
Administrator, Farm Service Agency	JUAN GARCIA
Administrator, Foreign Agricultural Service	PHIL KARSTING
Administrator, Risk Management Agency	BRANDON WILLIS
Under Secretary for Rural Development	DOUG O'BRIEN, *Acting*
Administrator, Rural Business-Cooperative Service	LILLIAN SALERNO
Administrator, Rural Housing Service	TONY HERNANDEZ
Administrator, Rural Utilities Service	JOHN C. PADALINO
Under Secretary for Food, Nutrition, and Consumer Services	KEVIN CONCANNON
Administrator, Food and Nutrition Service	AUDREY ROWE
Director, Center for Nutrition Policy and Promotion	JACKIE HAVEN
Under Secretary for Food Safety	BRIAN RONHOLM, *Acting*
Administrator, Food Safety and Inspection Service	ALFRED V. ALMANZA
Under Secretary for Research, Education, and Economics	CATHERINE WOTEKI
Administrator, Agricultural Research Service	CHAVONDA JACOBS-YOUNG

a source of capital that promotes job growth and economic development.

Rural Business Enterprise Grant Program The Rural Business Enterprise Grant Program (RBEG) provides grants for rural projects that fund and facilitate the development of small and emerging businesses, business incubators, employment, and related adult education programs. Eligible organizations include rural public entities (towns, communities, State agencies, and authorities), Native American tribes, and nonprofit corporations.

Rural Economic Development Loan and Grant Program The REDLoan program provides zero-interest loans to local utilities, which the utilities provide to local businesses (ultimate recipients) for projects that will create and retain employment in rural areas. The ultimate recipients repay the lending utility directly, and the utility repays the loan to the agency.

The REDGrant program provides grant funds to local utility organizations, which they use to establish revolving loan funds. Each utility provides loans through a revolving loan fund for projects that will create or retain rural jobs.

Rural Microenterprise Assistance Program This program supports the development and ongoing success of rural microentrepreneurs and microenterprises by providing loans and grants to Micro Development Organizations (MDOs). MDOs use the loan funds to establish or recapitalize a Rural Microloan Revolving Fund and grants funds to provide training and technical assistance to support the development of new microenterprises and successful continuing operation and growth of rural microenterprises.

Organizations eligible to become MDOs are nonprofit entities, Native American tribes, and public institutions of higher education that have a record of successfully delivering such services or that have a credible plan to develop an effective program to deliver them.

Biorefinery Assistance Program This program provides loan guarantees for the development, construction, and retrofitting of new and emerging technologies for the development of advanced biofuels.

Internet, http://www.rurdev.usda.gov/BCP_Biorefinery.html.

Repowering Assistance Program This program provides payments to biorefineries in existence as of June 18, 2008. These biorefineries use renewable biomass to replace the fossil fuel used to produce heat or power biorefineries.

Advanced Biofuel Repayment Program The program provides payments to producers to support and expand production of advanced biofuels refined from sources other than corn kernel starch.

Rural Energy for America Program The Rural Energy for America Program (REAP) provides loan guarantees and grants to agricultural producers and rural small businesses so they can install renewable energy systems, make energy efficiency improvements, conduct energy audits, provide renewable energy development assistance, and conduct feasibility studies for renewable energy systems.

Delta Health Care Services Grant Program This program provides financial assistance to address the continued unmet health needs in 252 counties and parishes in parts of 8 States through cooperation among health care professionals, institutions of higher education, research institutions, and other entities in the Delta Region.

Internet, http://www.rurdev.usda.gov/BCP_DeltaHealthCare.html.

Rural Business Opportunity Grant Program This program promotes sustainable economic development in rural communities with exceptional needs. Recipients use the grants to fund community- and technology-based economic development projects, feasibility studies, leadership and entrepreneur training, rural business incubators, and long-term business strategic planning.

Rural Cooperative Development Grant Program This program provides grants to public, nonprofit organizations and institutions of higher learning so they

Director, National Institute of Food and Agriculture	SONNY RAMASWAMY
Administrator, Economic Research Service	MARY BOHMAN
Director, National Agricultural Library	SIMON Y. LIU
Administrator, National Agricultural Statistics Service	JOE REILLY
Under Secretary for Marketing and Regulatory Programs	EDWARD M. AVALOS
Administrator, Agricultural Marketing Service	ANNE ALONZO
Administrator, Animal and Plant Health Inspection Service	KEVIN SHEA
Administrator, Grain Inspection, Packers, and Stockyards Administration	LARRY MITCHELL
Chief Judge, Administrative Law Judges	PETER DAVENPORT

[For the Department of Agriculture statement of organization, see the Code of Federal Regulations, Title 7, Part 2]

The Department of Agriculture develops agricultural markets, fights hunger and malnutrition, conserves natural resources, and ensures standards of food quality through safeguards and inspections.

The Department of Agriculture (USDA) was created by an act of Congress on May 15, 1862 (7 U.S.C. 2201). In carrying out its work in the program mission areas, USDA relies on the support of departmental administration staff, as well as the Office of the Chief Financial Officer, Office of the Chief Information Officer, Office of Communications, Office of Congressional and Intergovernmental Relations, Office of the Inspector General, and the Office of the General Counsel.

Rural Development

USDA's rural development mission is to increase the economic opportunities of rural Americans and improve their quality of life. To accomplish this, USDA works to foster new cooperative relationships among Government, industry, and communities. As a capital investment bank, USDA provides financing for rural housing and community facilities, business and cooperative development, telephone and high-speed Internet access, electric, water, and sewer infrastructure. Approximately 800 Rural Development field offices, staffed by 7,000 employees, provide frontline delivery of rural development loan and grant programs at the local level.

Rural Business-Cooperative Service To meet business credit needs in underserved rural areas, USDA's Rural Business-Cooperative Service provides loan guarantees, direct loans, and grants to rural businesses, cooperatives, farmers, and ranchers, often in partnership with private sector lenders. The following is a list and description of USDA's Rural Development business and cooperative programs.

Business and Industry Guaranteed Loan Program This program creates jobs and stimulates the rural economy by providing financial backing to rural businesses. Borrowers use loan proceeds for working capital, machinery and equipment, buildings, real estate, and certain types of debt refinancing. A borrower may be a cooperative organization, corporation, partnership, nonprofit corporation, Native American tribe, federally recognized tribal group, public body, or individual.

Intermediary Relending Program This program provides capital to rural areas through low-interest and direct loans made to nonprofit corporations, public agencies, Native American groups, and certain corporations (intermediaries). These intermediaries establish revolving loan funds so they can relend the money to businesses in economically and socially disadvantaged rural communities. The process creates

DEPARTMENT OF AGRICULTURE

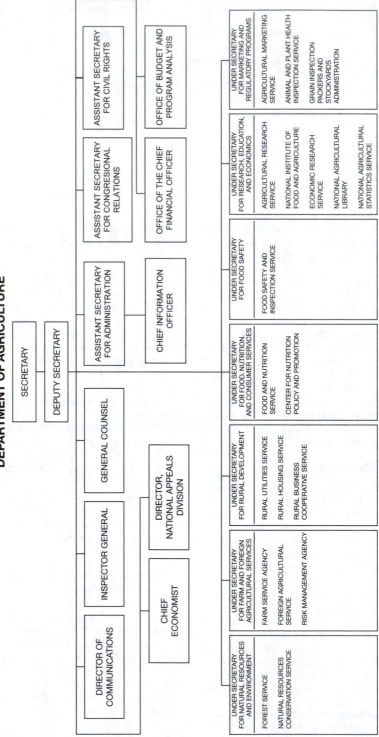

can establish and operate centers for cooperative development.

Small Socially-Disadvantaged Producer Grant Program This program provides technical assistance to small socially-disadvantaged agricultural producers in rural areas.

Value-Added Producer Grant Program The Value-Added Producer Grant program encourages independent agricultural producers to refine or enhance their raw products into marketable goods, which increases the value of the product and the returns to producers.

Cooperative Programs Cooperative Programs research helps farmers and rural communities become self-reliant through the use of cooperative organizations. Studies support cooperatives that market farm products, purchase production supplies, and perform related business services. These studies concentrate on the financial, organizational, legal, social, and economic aspects of cooperative activity. Technical assistance and research help businesses effectively improve cooperative performance by organizing new cooperatives, merging existing cooperatives, changing business structures, and developing strategies for growth. Applied research gives farmers and rural communities expert assistance pertaining to their cooperatives.

The Cooperative Programs research staff collects and publishes statistics on cooperative activity in U.S. agriculture and provides research for USDA/Rural Development's "Rural Cooperatives," a bimonthly magazine on developments and research in the field of cooperative management.

Rural Housing Programs Rural Development provides affordable rental housing, homeownership opportunities, and essential community facilities to rural Americans through a broad array of direct loan, guarantee, and grant programs. Rural residents and communities may inquire about any of these programs through local and State rural development offices. It provides assistance that enables low- and very low-income rural Americans to live in safe and decent rental housing. It also provides financial and management assistance through the following services: guaranteed single-family housing (SFH) loans that guarantee loans made by commercial lenders to moderate-income rural residents with sufficient income and acceptable credit, who may lack the down payment to secure a loan without assistance; direct SFH loans made available to people with incomes less than 80 percent of area median, to build, purchase, and repair rural homes; home improvement and repair loans and grants for owner-occupants to remove health and safety hazards from a home; mutual self-help housing technical assistance grants for nonprofit organizations and public bodies to help groups of six to eight lower income families to build their own homes by providing "sweat equity," which reduces the families' mortgages; rural housing site loans for private or public nonprofit organizations to purchase sites for the development of housing for lower income families; direct and guaranteed multifamily housing loans for private nonprofit corporations, consumer cooperatives, State or local public agencies, and individuals or organizations operating on a nonprofit or limited profit basis to provide rental or cooperative housing in rural areas for persons of very low, low, and moderate income; farm labor housing loans and grants enabling farmers, public or private nonprofit organizations, or units of local government to build, buy, or rehabilitate farm labor housing; housing preservation grants made to a public body or public or private nonprofit organization to provide assistance to homeowners and landlords to repair and rehabilitate housing for lower income families in rural areas; housing for the homeless, SFH real estate-owned (REO) property to nonprofit organizations or public bodies for transitional housing for the homeless and to the Federal Emergency Management Agency to house families affected by natural disasters; and community program loans, direct and guaranteed loans, and grants for public and quasi-public bodies, nonprofit associations, and Indian tribes for essential community facilities such as health care centers, public safety buildings and vehicles, and childcare centers.

Internet, http://www.rurdev.usda.gov/LP_Subject_ HousingAndCommunityAssistance.html.

Rural Utilities Programs   Rural Development helps rural electric and telecommunications utilities in obtaining financing and administers a nationwide water and waste loan and grant program to improve the quality of life and promote economic development in rural America. A total of 890 rural electric and 800 rural telecommunications utilities in 47 States, Puerto Rico, the Virgin Islands, Guam, the Republic of the Marshall Islands, the Northern Mariana Islands, and the Federated States of Micronesia have received financial assistance. It also provides assistance through the programs that are mentioned here. The electric program provides loans for furnishing and improving electric service to persons in rural areas, including construction of electric generating plants, transmission and distribution lines, on- and off-grid renewable energy systems, and conservation and energy efficiency improvements to provide reliable electric service. The telecommunications program provides loans and grants to improve telecommunications service and high-speed Internet access in rural areas. The water and waste direct and guaranteed loan program provides assistance to develop water and wastewater systems, including solid waste disposal and storm drainage in rural areas, cities, and towns. Water and waste disposal grants assist in reducing water and waste disposal costs to a reasonable level for users of the system. Emergency community water assistance grants provide assistance to rural communities experiencing a significant decline in quantity or quality of drinking water. Technical assistance and training grants are available to nonprofit organizations to provide rural water and waste system officials with technical assistance and training on a wide range of issues relating to the delivery of water and waste service to rural residents. Solid waste management grants are available for nonprofit organizations and public

bodies to provide technical assistance and training to rural areas and towns to reduce or eliminate pollution of water resources and improve planning and management of solid waste facilities. The rural water circuit rider technical assistance program provides technical assistance to rural water systems to solve operational, financial, and management challenges. The distance learning and telemedicine program provides financing to help rural schools and health care providers purchase or improve telecommunications facilities and equipment to bring educational and medical resources to rural areas that otherwise might be unavailable. Rural Development also guarantees loans from the Department of the Treasury's Federal Financing Bank (FFB), which lends to borrowers, primarily for large-scale electric and telecommunication facilities. It may also guarantee electric and telecommunications loans from private sources.

For further information, contact the Rural Development Legislative and Public Affairs Staff, Department of Agriculture, Stop 0705, 1400 Independence Avenue SW., Washington, DC 20250–0320. Phone, 202–720–4323. Internet, http://www. rurdev.usda.gov/Utilities_Assistance.html.

Marketing and Regulatory Programs

This mission area includes marketing and regulatory programs other than those concerned with food safety.

Agricultural Marketing Service The Agricultural Marketing Service was established by the Secretary of Agriculture on April 2, 1972, under the authority of Reorganization Plan No. 2 of 1953 (5 U.S.C. app.) and other authorities. The Service administers standardization, auditing, grading, certification, market news, marketing orders, research and promotion, and regulatory programs.

Audit Services   The Service provides a wide range of voluntary, user-fee audit-based programs that facilitate the global marketing of agricultural products. The Service develops and maintains audit programs, conducts direct and indirect audits, and serves as third-party unbiased contract auditors to verify specified product, process, or system requirements, such as production, processing, and handling requirements for the agricultural industry.

Market News The Service provides current, unbiased information to producers, processors, distributors, and others to assist them in the orderly marketing and distribution of farm commodities. Information is collected on supplies, shipments, prices, location, quality, condition, and other market data on farm products in specific markets and marketing areas. The data is disseminated globally via the Internet and other electronic means. The Service also assists other countries in developing their own marketing information systems.

Standardization, Grading, and Classing Nearly 600 grade standards have been established for some 230 agricultural commodities to help buyers and sellers trade on agreed-upon quality levels. Standards are developed with assistance from individuals outside the Department, particularly from those involved with the industries directly affected. The Service also participates in developing international commodity standards to facilitate trade. Grading and classing services are provided to certify the grade and quality of products. These grading services are provided to buyers and sellers of live cattle, swine, sheep, meat, poultry, eggs, rabbits, fruits, vegetables, tree nuts, peanuts, dairy products, tobacco, and other miscellaneous food products. Classing services are provided to buyers and sellers of cotton and cotton products. These services are mainly voluntary and are provided upon request and for a fee. The Service is also responsible for testing seed.

Laboratory Testing and Laboratory Approval Services The Service provides microbiological, chemical, and other scientific laboratory support to its commodity and food procurement programs, testing peanuts for aflatoxin and seeds for germination and purity. The Service also carries out quality assurance and safety oversight activities for its milk market laboratories, resident grading programs, and State and private laboratory programs. The Service also develops and establishes specific laboratory approval programs for private laboratories that test for a specific analyte in agriculture commodities for various industries or stakeholders.

Food Quality Assurance Under a Governmentwide quality assurance program, the Service is responsible for the development and revision of specifications used by Federal agencies in procuring food for military and civilian uses. The Service coordinates and approves certification programs designed to ensure that purchased products conform to the specification requirements.

Internet, http://www.ams.usda.gov/AMSv1.0/ standards.

Regulatory Programs The Service administers several regulatory programs designed collectively to protect producers, handlers, and consumers of agricultural commodities from financial loss or personal injury resulting from careless, deceptive, or fraudulent marketing practices. Such regulatory programs encourage fair trading practices in the marketing of fruits and vegetables and require truth in seed labeling and in advertising. The Service also monitors the disposition of restricted shell eggs.

Marketing Agreements and Orders The Service administers marketing agreements and orders to establish and maintain orderly marketing conditions for certain commodities. Milk marketing orders establish minimum prices that handlers or distributors are required to pay producers. Programs for fruits, vegetables, and related specialty crops like nuts and spearmint oil promote product quality control and help stabilize supplies and market prices. In some cases, they also authorize research and market development activities, including advertising supported by assessments that handlers pay. Through the orderly marketing of commodities facilitated by these programs, the interests of both producers and consumers are protected.

Plant Variety Protection Program The Service administers a program that provides for the issuance of certificates of plant variety protection. These certificates afford developers of novel varieties of sexually reproduced plants exclusive rights to sell, reproduce, import, or export such varieties, or use them in the production of hybrids or different varieties for a period of 20 years for nonwoody plants and 25 years for woody plants.

Research and Promotion Programs
The Service monitors certain industry-sponsored research, promotion, and information programs authorized by Federal laws. These programs provide farmers and processors with a means to finance and operate various research, promotion, and information activities for agricultural products, including cotton, potatoes, soybeans, sorghum, peanuts, popcorn, mushrooms, blueberries, processed raspberries, avocados, mangoes, watermelon, honey, eggs, milk and dairy products, beef, pork, lamb, and softwood lumber.

Transportation Programs   The Service provides insightful information and analysis on the transportation of agricultural products. Work products are used by agricultural shippers to make better decisions and thereby improve farm income, expand exports, and better utilize the transportation system to meet the growing needs of rural America. Analysis is provided to Federal, State, and local decisionmakers and to agricultural shippers on policy matters related to agricultural and rural transportation. The program also provides technical assistance and information on agricultural and food transportation for producers, shippers, rural communities, carriers, Government agencies, and universities.

National Organic Program   Through the National Organic Program, the Service develops, implements, and administers national production, handling, and labeling standards for organic food production. Organic production integrates cultural, biological, and mechanical practices to foster cycling of resources, promote ecological balance, and conserve biodiversity.

Internet, http://www.ams.usda.gov/AMSv1.0/NOP.

Farmers Markets and Local Food Marketing   The Service helps improve

marketing and distribution opportunities for U.S. agricultural products through a combination of applied research, marketing grants, and technical services, such as designing marketing facilities, conducting infrastructure assessments, feasibility studies, and providing information to States, municipalities, and others regarding funding and business resources for strengthening local and regional food enterprises.

Pesticide Data Program   The Service also administers the Pesticide Data Program, which, in cooperation with States, samples and analyzes over 30 agricultural commodities in the U.S. food supply for pesticide residue. It shares residue test results with the Environmental Protection Agency and other public agencies.

Pesticide Recordkeeping Program   The Service manages the Pesticide Recordkeeping Program in coordination with State agencies and the Environmental Protection Agency. The Service has developed educational programs and works with State agencies in inspecting applicator records.

For further information, contact the Public Affairs Staff, Agricultural Marketing Service, Department of Agriculture, Room 2532, South Agriculture Building, Stop 0273, 1400 Independence Ave, SW., Washington, DC 20250. Phone, 202–720–8998.

Animal and Plant Health Inspection Service   [For the Animal and Plant Health Inspection Service statement of organization, see the Code of Federal Regulations, Title 7, Part 371]

The Animal and Plant Health Inspection Service (APHIS) was reestablished by the Secretary of Agriculture on March 14, 1977, pursuant to authority contained in 5 U.S.C. 301 and Reorganization Plan No. 2 of 1953 (5 U.S.C. app.). APHIS was established to conduct regulatory and control programs to protect and improve animal and plant health for the benefit of agriculture and the environment. In cooperation with State governments, industry stakeholders, and other Federal agencies, APHIS works to prevent the entry and establishment of foreign animal and plant pests. APHIS also regulates certain genetically engineered organisms and works to support healthy international agricultural trade and exports of U.S. agricultural products. In addition, the Agency enforces regulations to ensure the humane treatment of certain animals and carries out research and operational activities to reduce crop and livestock depredation caused by birds, rodents, and predators.

Biotechnology Regulatory Services Biotechnology regulatory officials are responsible for regulating the importation, movement, and field release of genetically engineered plants and certain other genetically engineered organisms that may pose a risk to plant health.

Biotechnology regulations are designed to ensure that genetically engineered organisms, such as herbicide-tolerant or drought-resistant crops, are as safe for agriculture and the environment as traditionally bred crop varieties. In regulating biotechnology, APHIS works in concert with the Environmental Protection Agency and the Food and Drug Administration, agencies that also play important roles in protecting agriculture, a safe food supply, and the environment. APHIS's involvement begins when a person or organization wishes to import, move across a State line, or field-test a genetically engineered plant. These activities are subject to the Agency's permitting and notification system.

Plant Protection and Quarantine Plant protection officials are responsible for programs to control or eradicate damaging foreign plant pests and diseases. These programs are carried out in cooperation with the States involved, other Federal agencies, farmers, and private organizations. Pest control programs use a single tool or a combination of pest control techniques, both chemical and nonchemical, which are both effective and safe. Plant protection officials develop Federal regulations and policies that prohibit or restrict the entry into the United States of foreign pests and plants, plant products, and other materials that may harbor pests, diseases, or noxious weeds. They also manage programs for

overseas preclearance—agricultural inspection—of commodities, passengers, and U.S. military activities. These efforts help protect the health and value of U.S. agricultural production and natural resources.

Veterinary Services Animal health officials are responsible for programs to protect and improve the health, quality, and marketability of U.S. animals and animal products. The programs are carried out through cooperative links with States, foreign governments, livestock producers, and other Federal agencies.

APHIS officials conduct exclusion and quarantine activities for animal pests and diseases, carry out eradication and control programs for certain diseases, provide laboratory diagnostic services, and conduct animal health monitoring and surveillance. They also certify as to the health status of animals and animal products being exported to other countries and respond to animal disease incursions or epidemics that threaten the health status of U.S. livestock and poultry. Because human health is closely linked to veterinary health, APHIS animal health officials cooperate with other agencies and organizations to manage effectively the intersection between wildlife, veterinary, and human health issues. APHIS also administers a Federal law intended to ensure that all veterinary biological products used in the diagnosis, prevention, and treatment of animal disease are safe, pure, potent, and effective.

Animal Care APHIS administers the Animal Welfare Act, which establishes standards for the humane care and handling of certain warmblooded animals bought, sold, and transported in commerce and used or intended for use as pets at the wholesale level or used or intended for use in exhibitions or for research purposes. The Agency also enforces the Horse Protection Act of 1970, which prohibits the soring of horses at shows and sales.

International Services APHIS activities in the international arena include conducting cooperative plant and animal pest and disease control, eradication, and surveillance programs in foreign countries. These programs provide a first line of defense for the United States against threats such as screwworm, Mediterranean fruit fly, and other exotic pests and diseases. APHIS also provides international representation concerning sanitary and phytosanitary technical trade issues and conducts capacity building activities to help develop the animal and plant health competencies and infrastructure of international counterparts.

Wildlife Services   Wildlife Services officials provide assistance, upon request, to States, counties, local communities, and agricultural producer groups to reduce crop and livestock depredations caused by birds, rodents, and predators. Using methods and techniques that are biologically sound, environmentally acceptable, and economically feasible, they educate and advise farmers and ranchers on proper uses of control methods and techniques; suppress serious nuisances and threats to public health and safety caused by birds, rodents, and other wildlife in urban and rural communities; and work with airport managers to reduce risks of bird strikes. Wildlife Services officials also assist in the recovery of endangered and threatened species and monitor wildlife across the country for diseases to help protect animal and human health. In addition, they conduct research into predator-prey relationships, new control methods such as wildlife contraception, and more efficient and safe uses of existing methods such as toxicants, repellants and attractants, biological controls, scare devices, and habitat alteration.

For further information, contact Legislative and Public Affairs, Animal and Plant Health Inspection Service, Department of Agriculture, 1400 Independence Avenue SW., Washington, DC 20250. Phone, 202–799–7030. Internet, http://www.aphis. usda.gov.

Grain Inspection, Packers, and Stockyards Administration   The Grain Inspection, Packers, and Stockyards Administration (GIPSA) was established in 1994, to facilitate the marketing of livestock, poultry, meat, cereals, oilseeds, and related agricultural products, and

to promote fair and competitive trading practices for the overall benefit of consumers and American agriculture. GIPSA's Packers and Stockyards Program protects fair trade practices, financial integrity, and competitive markets for livestock, meat, and poultry. GIPSA's Federal Grain Inspection Service facilitates the marketing of U.S. grains, oilseeds, and related agricultural products through its world-renowned grain inspection and weighing system, and it maintains the integrity of the grain marketing system by developing unbiased grading standards and methods for assessing grain quality.

Internet, http://www.gipsa.usda.gov/.

Inspection   The United States Grain Standards Act requires most U.S. export grain to be officially inspected. At export port locations, inspection is performed by GIPSA or by State agencies that have been delegated export inspection authority by the Administrator. For domestic grain marketed at inland locations, the Administrator designates private and State agencies to provide official inspection services upon request. Both export and domestic services are provided on a fee-for-service basis.

Weighing   Official weighing of U.S. export grain is performed at port locations by GIPSA or by State agencies that have been delegated export weighing authority by the Administrator. For domestic grain marketed at inland locations, the weighing services may be provided by GIPSA or by designated private or State agencies. Upon request, weighing services are provided on a fee-for-service basis.

Standardization   GIPSA is responsible for establishing, maintaining, and revising official U.S. standards for corn, wheat, rye, oats, barley, flaxseed, sorghum, soybeans, triticale, sunflower seed, canola, and mixed grain. It is authorized to perform applied research to develop methods to improve accuracy and uniformity in grading grain. It is also responsible for standardization and inspection activities for rice, dry beans, peas, lentils, hay, straw, hops, and related processed grain commodities. Although standards no longer exist for hay, straw, and hops, GIPSA maintains inspection procedures for, and retains authority to inspect, these commodities.

Methods Development GIPSA's methods development activities include applied research or tests to produce new or improved techniques for measuring grain quality. Examples include knowledge gained through the study of how to establish real-time grain inspection, develop reference methods in order to maintain consistency and standardization in the grain inspection system, as well as the comparison of different techniques for evaluation of end-use quality in wheat.

Packers and Stockyards Activities Through the administration of the Packers and Stockyards Act, GIPSA prohibits unfair, deceptive, and unjust discriminatory practices by market agencies, dealers, stockyards, packers, swine contractors, and live poultry dealers in the livestock, meat packing, and poultry industries. GIPSA fosters fair competition and ensures payment protection for growers and farmers. To this end, GIPSA performs various regulatory functions, including investigating alleged violations of the Act, auditing regulated entities, verifying the accuracy of scales, and monitoring industry trends to protect consumers and members of the livestock, meat, and poultry industries.

GIPSA is also responsible for the Truth-in-Lending Act and the Fair Credit Reporting Act as each relates to persons and firms subject to the Act. GIPSA carries out the Secretary's responsibilities under section 1324 of the Food Security Act of 1985 pertaining to State-established central filing systems to prenotify buyers, commission merchants, and selling agents of security interests against farm products. GIPSA administers the section of the statute commonly referred to as the "Clear Title" provision and certifies qualifying State systems.

For further information, contact the Grain Inspection, Packers, and Stockyards Administration, Department of Agriculture, 1400 Independence Avenue SW., Washington, DC 20250. Phone, 202–720–0219. Internet, http://www.gipsa.usda.gov/psp.html.

Food Safety

Food Safety and Inspection Service
The Food Safety and Inspection Service (FSIS) was established by the Secretary of Agriculture on June 17, 1981, pursuant to authority contained in 5 U.S.C. 301 and Reorganization Plan No. 2 of 1953 (5 U.S.C. app.). FSIS is responsible for monitoring the Nation's commercial supply of meat, poultry, and processed egg products.

Meat, Poultry, and Processed Egg Products Inspection FSIS is the public health regulatory agency in the U.S. Department of Agriculture that ensures meat, poultry, and processed egg products are safe, wholesome, accurately labeled, and properly packaged. FSIS enforces the Federal Meat Inspection Act (FMIA), the Poultry Products Inspection Act (PPIA), and the Egg Products Inspection Act (EPIA), which require Federal inspection and regulation of meat, poultry, and processed egg products prepared for distribution in commerce for use as human food. FSIS is also responsible for administering the Humane Methods of Slaughter Act, which requires that livestock are handled and slaughtered humanely at the FSIS-inspected establishment.

FSIS administers FMIA, PPIA, and EPIA by developing and implementing data-driven regulations, including inspection, testing, and enforcement activities for the products under FSIS's jurisdiction. In addition to mandatory inspection of meat, poultry, and processed egg products, FSIS tests samples of these products for microbial and chemical residues to monitor trends for enforcement purposes and to understand, predict, and prevent contamination. FSIS also ensures that only meat, poultry, and processed egg products that meet U.S. requirements are imported into the United States, and it certifies meat, poultry, and processed egg products for export.

FSIS also monitors meat, poultry, and processed egg products throughout storage, distribution, and retail channels, and it ensures regulatory compliance to protect the public, including detention of products, voluntary product recalls, court-ordered seizures of products, administrative suspension and withdrawal of inspection, and referral of violations for criminal and civil prosecution. To protect against intentional contamination, the Agency conducts food defense activities, as well.

FSIS maintains a toll-free Meat and Poultry Hotline (phone, 888–674–6854; TTY, 800–256–7072) and chat feature to answer questions in English and Spanish about the safe handling of meat, poultry, and egg products. The Hotline's hours are weekdays, from 10 a.m. to 4 p.m., EST, year round. An extensive selection of food safety messages in English and Spanish is available at the same number at all hours of the day. Questions can also be submitted anytime to MPHotline.fsis@usda.gov.

"Ask Karen," an online virtual representative, provides answers to consumer questions on preventing foodborne illness, safe food handling and storage, and safe preparation of meat, poultry, and egg products (http://www.fsis.usda.gov/wps/portal/informational/askkaren).

For further information, contact the Assistant Administrator, Office of Public Affairs and Consumer Education, Department of Agriculture, 1400 Independence Avenue SW., Washington, DC 20250. Phone, 202–720–3884. Internet, http://www.fsis.usda.gov.

Food, Nutrition, and Consumer Services

The mission of Food, Nutrition, and Consumer Services is to reduce hunger and food insecurity, in partnership with cooperating organizations, by providing access to food, a healthful diet, and nutrition education to children and needy people in a manner that supports American agriculture.

Food and Nutrition Service   The Food and Nutrition Service (FNS) administers the USDA domestic food assistance programs. These programs, which serve one in four Americans in the course of a year, represent our Nation's commitment to the principle that no one in this country should fear hunger. They provide a Federal safety net to people in need. The goals of the programs are to provide low-income families and individuals with access to a more nutritious diet, to improve the eating habits of the Nation's children, and to help provide America's farmers with an expanded customer base.

FNS works in partnership with the States in all its programs. State and local agencies determine most administrative details regarding distribution of nutrition benefits and eligibility of participants, and FNS provides commodities and funding for additional food and to cover administrative costs. FNS administers the following nutrition assistance programs:

The Supplemental Nutrition Assistance Program (SNAP) provides nutrition benefits through State and local agencies to low-income families and individuals to increase their food purchasing power. The benefits are used by program participants to buy food in retail stores approved by the FNS to accept and redeem the benefits.

The Special Supplemental Nutrition Program for Women, Infants, and Children (WIC) improves the health of low-income pregnant and postpartum women, infants and children up to 5 years of age by providing them with specific nutritious foods, nutrition education, and health care referrals. The WIC and Seniors' Farmers' Market Nutrition Programs (FMNP and SFMNP) provide WIC participants and senior citizens with increased access to fresh produce. WIC participants receive coupons to purchase fresh fruits and vegetables from authorized farmers.

The Commodity Supplemental Food Program provides a package of foods monthly to low-income pregnant, postpartum, and breastfeeding women, their children under age 6, and the elderly. Nutrition education is also provided through this program.

The National School Lunch Program supports nonprofit food services in elementary and secondary schools and in residential childcare institutions. Almost 70 percent of the meals served through these institutions are free or at reduced cost.

The School Breakfast Program provides needy children with free or low-cost breakfasts that meet established nutritional standards.

The Special Milk Program for Children provides milk for children in those schools, summer camps, and childcare institutions that have no federally supported meal programs.

The Child and Adult Care Food Program provides cash and commodities for meals for preschool- and school-age children in childcare facilities and for functionally impaired adults in facilities that provide nonresidential care for such individuals.

The Summer Food Service Program helps various organizations get nutritious meals to needy preschool- and school-age children during the summer months.

The Emergency Food Assistance Program provides State agencies with commodities for distribution to food banks, food pantries, soup kitchens, and other charitable institutions throughout the country, with administrative funds to assist in distribution.

The Food Distribution Program on Indian Reservations and the Trust Territories provides an extensive package of commodities monthly to low-income households on or near Indian reservations in lieu of SNAP benefits. This program is administered at the local level by Indian tribal organizations.

The Nutrition Assistance Programs for Puerto Rico and the Northern Marianas are block grant programs that replace the Supplemental Nutrition Assistance Program in these two territories and provide food coupons to resident participants.

For further information, contact the Public Information Officer, Food and Nutrition Service, Department of Agriculture, 3101 Park Center Drive, Alexandria, VA 22302. Phone, 703–305–2286. Internet, http://www.usda.gov.

Center for Nutrition Policy and Promotion The Center coordinates nutrition policy in USDA and provides overall leadership in nutrition education for the American public. It also coordinates with the Department of Health and Human Services in the review, revision, and dissemination of the Dietary Guidelines for Americans, the Federal Government's statement of nutrition policy formed by a consensus of scientific and medical professionals.

For further information, contact the Office of Public Information, Center for Nutrition Policy and Promotion, Suite 200, 1120 20th Street NW., Washington, DC 20036–3406. Phone, 202–418–2312. Internet, http://www.cnpp.usda.gov.

Farm and Foreign Agricultural Services

Farm Service Agency The Farm Service Agency (FSA) administers farm commodity, disaster, and conservation programs for farmers and ranchers, and makes and guarantees farm emergency, ownership, and operating loans through a network of State and county offices.

Farm Commodity Programs FSA manages commodity programs such as the direct and countercyclical program, commodity and livestock disaster programs, marketing assistance loan programs, noninsured crop disaster assistance programs, and the tobacco transition payment program. It administers commodity loan programs for wheat, rice, corn, grain sorghum, barley, oats, oilseeds, peanuts, upland and extra-long-staple cotton, and sugar. FSA provides operating personnel for the Commodity Credit Corporation (CCC), a Government-owned and -operated organization. CCC provides short-term loans using the commodity as collateral. These loans provide farmers with interim financing and facilitate orderly marketing of farm commodities throughout the year.

Farm Loan Programs FSA makes and guarantees loans to family farmers and ranchers to purchase farmland and finance agricultural production. These programs help farmers who are temporarily unable to obtain private commercial credit. These may be beginning farmers who have insufficient net worth to qualify for commercial credit, who have suffered financial setbacks from natural disasters, or who have limited resources with which to establish and maintain profitable farming operations.

Noninsured Crop Disaster Assistance Program (NAP) NAP provides catastrophic crop loss protection for crops not covered by Federal crop insurance. Crops that are eligible include commercial crops grown for food and fiber, floriculture, ornamental nursery products, Christmas tree crops, turfgrass sod, seed crops, aquaculture (including ornamental fish such as goldfish), and industrial crops. Losses resulting from natural disasters not covered by the crop insurance policy may also be eligible for NAP assistance. NAP does not include trees grown for wood, paper, or pulp products.

Other Emergency Assistance   There are FSA programs to assist farmers who encounter natural disasters from drought, flood, freeze, tornadoes, and other calamities. Eligible producers can be compensated for crop losses, livestock feed losses, and tree damage and for the cost of rehabilitating eligible farmlands damaged by natural disaster. Low-interest loans for eligible farmers can help cover production and physical losses in counties declared disaster areas.

The largest component of USDA disaster assistance is the Crop Disaster Program (CDP), which has provided more than $3 billion in financial relief to farmers, ranchers, foresters, and other agricultural producers who incurred losses because of recent adverse weather conditions.

Conservation Programs   FSA's conservation programs include enhancement of wildlife habitat and water and air quality. The Conservation Reserve Program is the Federal Government's single-largest environmental improvement program on private lands. It safeguards millions of acres of topsoil from erosion, improves air quality, increases wildlife habitat, and protects ground and surface water by reducing water runoff and sedimentation. In return for planting a protective cover of grass or trees on vulnerable property, the owner receives a rental payment each year of a multiyear contract. Cost-share payments are also available to help establish permanent areas of grass, legumes, trees, windbreaks, or plants that improve water quality and give shelter and food to wildlife.

Internet, http://www.fsa.usda.gov/FSA/ webapp?area=home&subject=copr&topic=landing.

Commodity Operations   FSA's commodity operations system

facilitates the storage, management, and disposition of commodities used to meet humanitarian needs abroad. It administers the United States Warehouse Act (USWA), which authorizes the Secretary of Agriculture to license warehouse operators who store agricultural products. Warehouse operators that apply must meet the USDA standards established within the USWA and its regulations. Under the milk price support program, the Commodity Credit Corporation buys surplus butter, cheese, and nonfat dry milk from processors at announced prices to support the price of milk. These purchases help maintain market prices at the legislated support level, and the surplus commodities are used for hunger relief both domestically and internationally. FSA's commodity operations system also coordinates with other Government agencies to provide surplus commodities for various programs and also purchases commodities for the National School Lunch Program and other domestic feeding programs.

For further information, contact the Public Affairs Branch, Farm Service Agency, Department of Agriculture, Stop 0506, 1400 Independence Avenue SW., Washington, DC 20250. Phone, 202–720–5237. Internet, http://www.fsa.usda.gov/FSA/ webapp?area=home&subject=coop&topic=landing.

Commodity Credit Corporation   The Commodity Credit Corporation (CCC) stabilizes, supports, and protects farm income and prices, assists in maintaining balanced and adequate supplies of agricultural commodities and their products, and facilitates the orderly distribution of commodities.

CCC carries out assigned foreign assistance activities, such as guaranteeing the credit sale of U.S. agricultural commodities abroad. Major emphasis is also being directed toward meeting the needs of developing nations. Agricultural commodities are supplied and exported to combat hunger and malnutrition and to encourage economic development in developing countries. In addition, under the Food for Progress Program, CCC supplies commodities to provide assistance to developing democracies.

For further information, contact the Information Division, Foreign Agricultural Service, Department of Agriculture, Stop 1004, 1400 Independence Avenue SW., Washington, DC 20250. Phone, 202–720–7115. Fax, 202–720–1727. Internet, http://www.fsa.usda.gov/FSA/webapp?area=about&subject=landing&topic=sao-cc.

Risk Management Agency   The Risk Management Agency (RMA), via the Federal Crop Insurance Corporation (FCIC), oversees and administers the Federal crop insurance program under the Federal Crop Insurance Act.

Federal crop insurance is offered to qualifying producers through 18 private sector crop insurance companies. Under the Standard Reinsurance Agreement (SRA), RMA provides reinsurance, pays premium subsidies, reimburses insurers for administrative and operating expenses, and oversees the financial integrity and operational performance of the delivery system. RMA bears much of the noncommercial insurance risk under the SRA, allowing insurers to retain commercial insurance risks or reinsure those risks in the private market.

In 2006, the Federal crop insurance program provided producers with more than $44 billion in protection on approximately 246 million acres through about 1.2 million policies. There were 22 insurance plans available and 26 active pilot programs in various stages of development. Today, there are 350 plans of insurance, 1.2 million premium earning policies covering approximately 282 million acres of land, and 23 pilot programs in various stages of development.

RMA also works closely with the private sector to find new and innovative ways to provide expanded coverage. This includes risk protection for specialty crops, livestock and forage, and rangeland and pasture. Thus, RMA is able to reduce the need for ad hoc disaster assistance while providing valuable coverage for production declines that result from extended drought in many areas.

Additional information about RMA can be found on its Web site, www.rma.usda.gov. The Web site features agency news, State profiles, publications, and announcements on current issues. It also features summaries of insurance sales, pilot programs, downloadable crop policies, and agency-sponsored events. Online tools, calculators, and applications are also available on the Web site.

For further information, contact the Office of the Administrator, Risk Management Agency, Department of Agriculture, Stop 0801, 1400 Independence Avenue SW., Washington, DC 20250. Phone, 202–690–2803. Internet, http://www.rma.usda.gov.

Foreign Agricultural Service   The Foreign Agricultural Service (FAS) works to improve foreign market access for U.S. products, to build new markets, to improve the competitive position of U.S. agriculture in the global marketplace, and to provide food aid and technical assistance to foreign countries.

FAS has the primary responsibility for USDA's activities in the areas of international marketing, trade agreements and negotiations, and the collection and analysis of international statistics and market information. It also administers the USDA's export credit guarantee and food aid programs. FAS helps increase income and food availability in developing nations by mobilizing expertise for agriculturally led economic growth.

FAS also enhances U.S. agricultural competitiveness through a global network of agricultural economists, marketing experts, negotiators, and other specialists. FAS agricultural counselors, attaches, trade officers, and locally employed staff are stationed in over 90 countries to support U.S. agricultural interests and cover 140 countries.

In addition to agricultural affairs offices in U.S. embassies, agricultural trade offices also have been established in a number of key foreign markets and function as service centers for U.S. exporters and foreign buyers seeking market information.

Reports prepared by our overseas offices cover changes in policies and other developments that could affect U.S. agricultural exports. FAS staff in U.S. Embassies around the world assess U.S. export marketing opportunities and respond to the daily informational needs of those who develop, initiate, monitor, and evaluate U.S. food and agricultural policies and programs.

In addition to data collection, FAS also maintains a worldwide agricultural reporting system based on information from U.S. agricultural traders, remote sensing systems, and other sources. Analysts in Washington, DC, prepare production forecasts, assess export marketing opportunities, and track changes in policies affecting U.S. agricultural exports and imports.

FAS programs help U.S. exporters develop and maintain markets for hundreds of food and agricultural products, from bulk commodities to brand-name items. Formal market promotion activities are carried out chiefly in cooperation with agricultural trade associations, State-regional trade groups, small businesses, and cooperatives that plan, manage, and contribute staff resources and funds to support these efforts. FAS also provides guidance to help exporters locate buyers and provides assistance through a variety of other methods. This includes supporting U.S. participation in several major trade shows and a number of single-industry exhibitions each year.

For further information, contact the Public Affairs Division, Foreign Agricultural Service, Stop 1004, 1400 Independence Avenue SW., Department of Agriculture, Washington, DC 20250–1004. Phone, 202–720–7115. Fax, 202–720–1727. Internet, http://www.fas.usda.gov.

Research, Education, and Economics

This mission area's main focus is to create, apply, and transfer knowledge and technology to provide affordable food and fiber, ensure food safety and nutrition, and support rural development and natural resource needs of people by conducting integrated national and international research, information, education, and statistical programs and services that are in the national interest.

Agricultural Research Service   The Agricultural Research Service (ARS) conducts research to develop and transfer solutions to agricultural problems of high national priority. It provides information access and dissemination to ensure high-quality safe food and other agricultural products; assess the nutritional needs of Americans; sustain a competitive agricultural economy; enhance the natural resource base and the environment; and provide economic opportunities for rural citizens, communities, and society as a whole.

Research activities are carried out at 103 domestic locations (including Puerto Rico and the U.S. Virgin Islands) and 5 overseas locations. Much of this research is conducted in cooperation with partners in State universities and experiment stations, other Federal agencies, and private organizations. National Programs, headquartered in Beltsville, MD, is the focal point in the overall planning and coordination of ARS's research programs. Day-to-day management of the respective programs for specific field locations is assigned to eight area offices.

ARS also includes the National Agricultural Library (NAL), which is the primary resource in the United States for information about food, agriculture, and natural resources and serves as an electronic gateway to a widening array of scientific literature, printed text, and agricultural images. NAL serves USDA and a broad customer base including policymakers, agricultural specialists, research scientists, and the general public. NAL works with other agricultural libraries and institutions to advance open and democratic access to information about agriculture and the Nation's agricultural knowledge.

For further information, contact the Agricultural Research Service, Department of Agriculture, 1400 Independence Avenue SW., Washington, DC 20250. Phone, 202–720–3656. Fax, 202–720–5427. Internet, http://www.ars.usda.gov.

The National Institute of Food and Agriculture   The National Institute of Food and Agriculture (NIFA) links the research and education resources and activities of USDA and works with academic and land-grant institutions throughout the Nation. In cooperation with its partners and customers, NIFA advances a global system of research, extension, and higher education in the food and agricultural sciences and related environmental and human sciences to benefit people, communities, and the Nation.

NIFA's programs increase and provide access to scientific knowledge; strengthen the capabilities of land-grant and other institutions in research, extension, and higher education; increase access to and use of improved communication and network systems; and promote informed decisionmaking by producers, consumers, families, and community leaders to improve social conditions in the United States and around the world. These conditions include improved agricultural and other economic enterprises; safer and cleaner water, food, and air; enhanced stewardship and management of natural resources; more responsible, productive, and healthy individuals, families, and communities; and a stable, secure, diverse, and affordable national food supply.

NIFA provides research, extension, and education leadership through programs in plant and animal systems; natural resources and environment; economic and community systems; families, 4–H, and nutrition; competitive research and integrated research, education, and extension programs and awards management; science and education resources development; and information systems and technology management.

NIFA's partnership with the land-grant universities is critical to the effective shared planning, delivery, and accountability for research, higher education, and extension programs to support a growing and thriving American economy.

For further information, contact the Communications Staff, The National Institute of Food and Agriculture , Department of Agriculture, 1400 Independence Avenue SW., Washington, DC 20250–2207. Phone, 202–720–4651. Fax, 202–690–0289. Internet, http://www.csrees.usda.gov/index.html.

Economic Research Service   The mission of the Economic Research Service (ERS) is to inform and enhance public and private decisionmaking on economic and policy issues related to agriculture, food, the environment, and rural development.

Activities to support this mission and the following goals involve research and development of economic and statistical indicators on a broad range of topics including, but not limited to, global agricultural market conditions, trade restrictions, agribusiness concentration, farm and retail food prices, foodborne illnesses, food labeling, nutrition, food assistance programs, worker safety, agrichemical usage, livestock waste management, conservation, sustainability, genetic diversity, technology transfer, rural infrastructure, and rural employment.

Research results and economic indicators on such important agricultural, food, natural resource, and rural issues are fully disseminated to public and private decisionmakers through published and electronic reports and articles; special staff analyses, briefings, presentations, and papers; databases; and individual contacts. Through such activities, ERS provides public and private decisionmakers with economic and related social science information and analysis in support of the Department's goals of enhancing economic opportunities for agricultural producers; supporting economic opportunities and quality of life in rural America; enhancing the protection and safety of U.S. agriculture and food; improving U.S. nutrition and health; and enhancing the natural resource base and environment. More information on ERS's program is available online.

For further information, contact the Information Services Division, Economic Research Service, Department of Agriculture, 1400 Independence Avenue SW., Washington, DC 20250. Phone, 202–694–5100. Fax, 202–245–4781. Internet, http://www.ers.usda.gov.

National Agricultural Statistics Service   The National Agricultural Statistics Service (NASS) prepares estimates and reports on production, supply, price, chemical use, and other items necessary for the orderly operation of the U.S. agricultural economy.

The reports include statistics on field crops, fruits and vegetables, dairy, cattle, hogs, sheep, poultry, aquaculture, and related commodities or processed products. Other estimates concern farm numbers, farm production expenditures, agricultural chemical use, prices received by farmers for products sold, prices paid for commodities and services, indexes of prices received and paid, parity prices, farm employment, and farm wage rates.

NASS prepares these estimates through a complex system of sample surveys of producers, processors, buyers, and others associated with agriculture. Information is gathered by mail, electronic data reporting, telephone, and personal interviews.

NASS is responsible for conducting the Census of Agriculture. The Census of Agriculture is taken every 5 years and provides comprehensive data on the agricultural economy down to the county level. Follow-on studies are also conducted on aquaculture, irrigation, horticultural energy, and organic agriculture.

NASS also performs reimbursable survey work and statistical consulting services for other Federal and State agencies and provides technical assistance for developing agricultural data systems in other countries.

For further information, contact the Executive Assistant to the Administrator, National Agricultural Statistics Service, Department of Agriculture, 1400 Independence Avenue SW., Washington, DC 20250–2000. Phone, 202–720–2707. Fax, 202–720–9013. Internet, http://www.nass.usda.gov/.

Natural Resources and Environment

This mission area is responsible for fostering sound stewardship of 75 percent of the Nation's total land area. Ecosystems are the underpinning for the Department's operating philosophy in this area in order to maximize stewardship of our natural resources. This approach ensures that products, values, services, and uses desired by people are produced in ways that sustain healthy, productive ecosystems.

Forest Service   [For the Forest Service statement of organization, see the Code of Federal Regulations, Title 36, Part 200.1]

The Forest Service was created by the Transfer Act of February 1, 1905 (16 U.S.C. 472), which transferred the Federal forest reserves and the responsibility for their management from the Department of the Interior to the Department of Agriculture. The mission of the Forest Service is to achieve quality land management under the sustainable, multiple-use management concept to meet the diverse needs of people. Its objectives include the following: advocating a conservation ethic in promoting the health, productivity, diversity, and beauty of forests and associated lands; listening to people and responding to their diverse needs in making decisions; protecting and managing the National Forests and Grasslands to best demonstrate the sustainable, multiple-use management concept; providing technical and financial assistance to State and private forest landowners, encouraging them toward active stewardship and quality land management in meeting their specific objectives; providing technical and financial assistance to cities and communities to improve their natural environment by planting trees and caring for their forests; providing international technical assistance and scientific exchanges to sustain and enhance global resources and to encourage quality land management; assisting States and communities in using the forests wisely to promote rural economic development and a quality rural environment; developing and providing scientific and technical knowledge, improving our capability to protect, manage, and use forests and rangelands; and providing work, training, and education to the unemployed, underemployed, elderly, youth, and the disadvantaged.

Internet, http://www.fs.fed.us/.

National Forest System   The Service manages 155 National Forests, 20 National Grasslands, 1 tall grass prairie, and 5 land utilization projects on over 193 million acres in 44 States, the Virgin Islands, and Puerto Rico under the principles of multiple-use and sustained yield. The Nation's tremendous need for wood and paper products is balanced with the other vital, renewable resources or benefits that the National Forests and Grasslands provide: recreation and natural beauty, wildlife habitat, livestock forage, and water supplies. The guiding principle is the greatest good to the greatest number in the long run.

These lands are protected as much as possible from wildfire, epidemics of disease and insect pests, erosion, floods, and water and air pollution. Burned areas get emergency seeding treatment to prevent massive erosion and stream siltation. Roads and trails are built where needed to give the public access to outdoor recreation areas and provide scenic drives and hikes. Picnic, camping, water sports, skiing, and other areas are provided with facilities for public convenience and enjoyment. Vegetative management methods are used to protect the land and streams, ensure rapid renewal of the forest, provide food and cover for wildlife and fish, and have minimum impact on scenic and recreation values. Local communities benefit from activities that occur on National Forest lands. These lands also provide needed oil, gas, and minerals. Rangelands are improved for millions of livestock and game animals. The National Forests provide a refuge for many species of endangered birds, animals, and fish. Some 34.6 million acres are set aside as wilderness and 175,000 acres as primitive areas where timber will not be harvested.

Internet, http://www.fs.fed.us/managing-land/national-forests-grasslands.

Forest Research   The Forest Service performs basic and applied research to develop the scientific information and technology needed to protect, manage, use, and sustain the natural resources of the Nation's forests and rangelands. The Forest Service's forest research strategy focuses on three major program components: understanding the structure and functions of forest and range ecosystems; understanding how people perceive and value the protection, management, and use of natural resources; and determining which protection, management, and utilization practices are most suitable for sustainable

production and use of the world's natural resources.

For further information on the Forest Service or State and private forestry areas, visit the Forest Service's Web site. Internet, http://www.fs.fed.us/research/research-topics/.

Natural Resources Conservation Service   [For the Natural Resources Conservation Service statement of organization, see the Code of Federal Regulations, Title 7, Parts 600 and 601]

Internet, http://www.nrcs.usda.gov/wps/portal/nrcs/site/national/home/.

The Natural Resources Conservation Service (NRCS), formerly the Soil Conservation Service, has national responsibility for helping America's farmers, ranchers, and other private landowners develop and carry out voluntary efforts to conserve and protect our natural resources.

Conservation Technical Assistance This is the foundation program of NRCS. Under this program, NRCS provides technical assistance to land users and units of government for the purpose of sustaining agricultural productivity and protecting and enhancing the natural resource base. This assistance is based on the voluntary cooperation of private landowners and involves comprehensive approaches to reduce soil erosion; improve soil and water quantity and quality; improve and conserve wetlands; enhance fish and wildlife habitat; improve air quality; improve pasture and range condition; reduce upstream flooding; and improve woodlands.

Internet, http://www.nrcs.usda.gov/wps/portal/nrcs/main/national/programs/technical/.

Emergency Watershed Protection Program   This program provides emergency assistance to safeguard lives and property in jeopardy due to sudden watershed impairment by natural disasters. Emergency work includes quickly establishing a protective plant cover on denuded land and stream banks; opening dangerously restricted channels; and repairing diversions and levees. An emergency area need not be declared a national disaster area to be eligible for help under this program.

Internet, http://www.nrcs.usda.gov/wps/portal/
nrcs/detail/national/programs/landscape/
ewpp/?cid=nrcs143_008263.

**Environmental Quality Incentive
Program**   This program assists producers
with environmental and natural resource
conservation improvements on their
agricultural lands. Half of the available
funds are for conservation activities
related to livestock production. Technical
assistance, cost-share payments,
incentive payments, and education focus
on priority areas and natural resource
concerns identified in cooperation with
State technical committees, including
such areas as nutrient management,
pest management, and grazing land
management.

Internet, http://www.nrcs.usda.gov/wps/portal/nrcs/
main/national/programs/financial/eqip/.

Forestry Incentives Program   This
program helps to increase the Nation's
supply of products from nonindustrial
private forest lands. This also ensures
more effective use of existing forest lands
and, over time, helps to prevent shortages
and price increases for forest products.
The program shares the cost incurred
by landowners for tree planting and
timberstand improvement.

Internet, http://www.nrcs.usda.gov/wps/portal/nrcs/
main/national/programs/easements/forests/.

National Cooperative Soil Survey
The National Cooperative Soil
Survey provides the public with local
information on the uses and capabilities
of their soils. The published soil survey
for a county or other designated area
includes maps and interpretations that
are the foundation for farm planning and
other private land use decisions as well
as for resource planning and policy by
Federal, State, and local governments.
The surveys are conducted cooperatively
with other Federal, State, and local
agencies and land-grant universities. The
Service is the national and world leader
in soil classification and soil mapping,
and is now expanding its work in soil
quality.

Internet, http://www.nrcs.usda.gov/wps/portal/nrcs/
site/soils/home/.

Plant Materials Program   At 26 plant
materials centers across the country,
NRCS tests, selects, and ensures the
commercial availability of new and
improved conservation plants for erosion
reduction, wetland restoration, water
quality improvement, streambank and
riparian area protection, coastal dune
stabilization, biomass production, carbon
sequestration, and other needs. The
Plant Materials Program is a cooperative
effort with conservation districts, other
Federal and State agencies, commercial
businesses, and seed and nursery
associations.

Internet, http://www.nrcs.usda.gov/wps/portal/nrcs/
main/plantmaterials/pmc/.

**Resource Conservation and
Development Program**   This is a locally
driven program, an opportunity for
civic-oriented groups to work together
sharing knowledge and resources in
solving common problems facing
their region. The program offers aid in
balancing the environmental, economic,
and social needs of an area. USDA
coordinators help resource conservation
and development councils plan, develop,
and carry out programs for resource
conservation, water management,
community development, and
environmental enhancement.

Rural Abandoned Mine Program   This
program helps protect people and the
environment from the adverse effects
of past coal mining practices and
promotes the development of soil and
water resources on unreclaimed mine
land. It provides technical and financial
assistance to land users who voluntarily
enter into 5- to 10-year contracts for the
reclamation of eligible land and water.

Small Watersheds Program   The
program helps local sponsoring groups
to voluntarily plan and install watershed
protection projects on private lands.
These projects include flood prevention,
water quality improvement, soil erosion
and sediment reduction, rural and
municipal water supply, irrigation water
management, fish and wildlife habitat
enhancement, and wetlands restoration.
The Service helps local community
groups, government entities, and private

landowners working together using an integrated, comprehensive watershed approach to natural resource planning.

Snow Survey and Water Supply Forecasting Program This program collects snowpack moisture data and forecasts seasonal water supplies for streams that derive most of their water from snowmelt. It helps farm operators, rural communities, and municipalities manage water resources through water supply forecasts. It also provides hydrometeorological data for regulating reservoir storage and managing streamflow. The Snow Supply Program is conducted in the Western States and Alaska.

Internet, http://www.nrcs.usda.gov/wps/ portal/nrcs/detail/national/programs/ alphabetical/?cid=stelprdb1044181.

Watershed Surveys and Planning This program assists Federal, State, and local agencies and tribal governments in protecting watersheds from damage caused by erosion, floodwater, and sediment, and it conserves and develops water and land resources. Resource concerns addressed by the program include water quality, water conservation, wetland and water storage capacity, agricultural drought problems, rural development, municipal and industrial water needs, upstream flood damages, and water needs for fish, wildlife, and forest-based industries. Types of surveys and plans include watershed plans, river basin surveys and studies, flood hazard analysis, and flood plain management assistance. The focus of these plans is to identify solutions that use land treatment and nonstructural measures to solve resource problems.

Internet, http://www.nrcs.usda.gov/wps/portal/nrcs/ main/national/programs/landscape/wsp/.

Sources of Information

Consumer Activities Educational, organizational, and financial assistance is offered to consumers and their families in such areas as rural housing and farm operating programs, as well as improved nutrition, family living and recreation, food stamp, school lunch, donated foods, and other food programs.

Contracts and Small-Business Activities To obtain information about contracting or subcontracting opportunities, attending small-business outreach activities, or how to do business with USDA, contact the Office of Small and Disadvantaged Business Utilization. Phone, 202–720–7117. Internet, http://www.dm.usda.gov/osdbu/index.php.

Employment Most jobs in the Department are in the competitive service and are filled by applicants who have established eligibility under an appropriate examination administered by the Office of Personnel Management or Department Special Examining Units. General employment information is available online at USAJOBS. Internet, http://www.usda.gov/wps/portal/usda/usdahome?navid=CAREERS.

Whistleblower Hotline Persons wishing to register complaints of alleged improprieties concerning the Department should contact one of the regional offices or the Inspector General's whistleblower hotline. Phone, 800–424–9121 (toll free, outside Washington, DC); 202–690–1622 (within the Washington, DC, metropolitan area); or 202–690–1202 (TDD). Fax, 202–690–2474. Internet, http://www.usda.gov/oig/hotline.htm.

Reading Rooms Reading Rooms are located at the headquarters of each USDA agency. Use the contact information provided in the "For further information" sections in the program description text above to inquire about locations, hours, and availability.

Speakers Contact the nearest Department of Agriculture office or county extension agent. In the District of Columbia, contact the Office of Public Liaison, Office of Communications, Department of Agriculture, 1400 Independence Avenue SW., Washington, DC 20250. Phone, 202–720–2798.

For further information concerning the Department of Agriculture, contact the Office of Communications, Department of Agriculture, 1400 Independence Avenue SW., Washington, DC 20250. Phone, 202–720–4623. Internet, http://www.usda.gov/wps/portal/usda/usdahome?contentid=OC_Splash.xml&contentidonly=true.

DEPARTMENT OF COMMERCE

Fourteenth Street and Constitution Avenue NW., Washington, DC 20230
Phone, 202–482–2000. Internet, http://www.doc.gov.

Secretary of Commerce	PENNY S. PRITZKER
Deputy Secretary	BRUCE H. ANDREWS
Assistant Secretary for Legislative and Intergovernmental Affairs	MARGARET LOUISE CUMMISKY
Chief Financial Officer and Assistant Secretary for Administration	ELLEN C. HERBST
Chief Information Officer	SIMON SZYKMAN
General Counsel	KELLY R. WELSH
Inspector General	TODD J. ZINSER
Director, Office of Business Liaison	MATTHEW T. MCGUIRE
Director, Office of Policy and Strategic Planning	(VACANCY)
Director, Office of Public Affairs	CIARAN CLAYTON, *Acting*
Director, Executive Secretariat	CHRISTINE L. TURNER
Director, Office of White House Liaison	THEODORE JONSTON

The Department of Commerce promotes the Nation's domestic and international trade, economic growth, and technological advancement by fostering a globally competitive free enterprise system, supporting fair trade practices, compiling social and economic statistics, protecting Earth's physical and oceanic resources, granting patents and registering trademarks, and providing assistance to small and minority-owned businesses.

The Department was designated as such by act of March 4, 1913 (15 U.S.C. 1501), which reorganized the Department of Commerce and Labor, created by act of February 14, 1903 (15 U.S.C. 1501), by transferring all labor activities into a new, separate Department of Labor.

Office of the Secretary

Secretary The Secretary is responsible for the administration of all functions and authorities assigned to the Department of Commerce and for advising the President on Federal policy and programs affecting the industrial and commercial segments of the national economy. The Secretary is served by the offices of Deputy Secretary, Inspector General, General Counsel, and the Assistant Secretaries of Administration, Legislative and Intergovernmental Affairs, and Public Affairs. Other offices whose public purposes are widely administered are detailed below.

Business Liaison The Office of Business Liaison directs the business community to the offices and policy experts who can best respond to their needs by promoting proactive, responsive, and effective outreach programs and relationships with the business community. It also informs the Secretary and Department officials of the critical issues facing the business community, informs the business community of Department and administration initiatives and priorities, as well as information regarding Department resources, policies, and programs, and provides general assistance to the business community.

For further information, call 202–482–1360.

DEPARTMENT OF COMMERCE

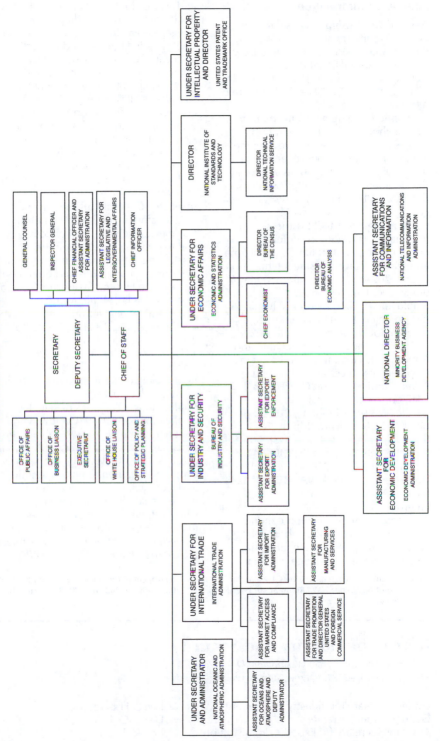

SECRETARY

DEPUTY SECRETARY

CHIEF OF STAFF

GENERAL COUNSEL

INSPECTOR GENERAL

CHIEF FINANCIAL OFFICER AND ASSISTANT SECRETARY FOR ADMINISTRATION

ASSISTANT SECRETARY FOR LEGISLATIVE AND INTERGOVERNMENTAL AFFAIRS

CHIEF INFORMATION OFFICER

OFFICE OF PUBLIC AFFAIRS

OFFICE OF BUSINESS LIAISON

EXECUTIVE SECRETARIAT

OFFICE OF WHITE HOUSE LIAISON

OFFICE OF POLICY AND STRATEGIC PLANNING

UNDER SECRETARY FOR INTELLECTUAL PROPERTY AND DIRECTOR
UNITED STATES PATENT AND TRADEMARK OFFICE

DIRECTOR
NATIONAL INSTITUTE OF STANDARDS AND TECHNOLOGY

DIRECTOR
NATIONAL TECHNICAL INFORMATION SERVICE

UNDER SECRETARY FOR ECONOMIC AFFAIRS
ECONOMIC AND STATISTICS ADMINISTRATION

DIRECTOR
BUREAU OF THE CENSUS

CHIEF ECONOMIST

DIRECTOR
BUREAU OF ECONOMIC ANALYSIS

ASSISTANT SECRETARY FOR COMMUNICATIONS AND INFORMATION
NATIONAL TELECOMMUNICATIONS AND INFORMATION ADMINISTRATION

NATIONAL DIRECTOR
MINORITY BUSINESS DEVELOPMENT AGENCY

ASSISTANT SECRETARY FOR ECONOMIC DEVELOPMENT
ECONOMIC DEVELOPMENT ADMINISTRATION

UNDER SECRETARY FOR INDUSTRY AND SECURITY
BUREAU OF INDUSTRY AND SECURITY

ASSISTANT SECRETARY FOR EXPORT ENFORCEMENT

ASSISTANT SECRETARY FOR EXPORT ADMINISTRATION

UNDER SECRETARY FOR INTERNATIONAL TRADE
INTERNATIONAL TRADE ADMINISTRATION

ASSISTANT SECRETARY FOR IMPORT ADMINISTRATION

ASSISTANT SECRETARY FOR MANUFACTURING AND SERVICES

ASSISTANT SECRETARY FOR MARKET ACCESS AND COMPLIANCE

ASSISTANT SECRETARY FOR TRADE PROMOTION AND DIRECTOR GENERAL UNITED STATES AND FOREIGN COMMERCIAL SERVICE

UNDER SECRETARY AND ADMINISTRATOR
NATIONAL OCEANIC AND ATMOSPHERIC ADMINISTRATION

ASSISTANT SECRETARY FOR OCEANS AND ATMOSPHERE AND DEPUTY ADMINISTRATOR

Sources of Information

Age and Citizenship   Age search and citizenship information is available from the Personal Census Search Unit, Bureau of the Census, National Processing Center, P.O. Box 1545, Jeffersonville, IN 47131. Phone, 812–218–3046. Internet, http://www.eda.gov.

Economic Development Information Clearinghouse   The EDA will host on its Web site the Economic Development Information Clearinghouse, an online depository of information on economic development. Internet, http://www.osec.doc.gov/osdbu. Internet, http://www.eda.gov.

Contracting and Small Business   For information regarding contract opportunities, contact the Office of Small and Disadvantaged Business Utilization. Phone, 202–482–1472. Internet, http://www.osec.doc.gov/osdbu.

Employment   Information is available electronically through the Internet, at www.doc.gov/ohrm. Phone, 202–482–5138. The National Oceanic and Atmospheric Administration has field employment offices at the Western Administrative Support Center, Bin C15700, 7600 Sand Point Way NE., Seattle, WA 98115 (phone, 206–526–6294); 325 Broadway, Boulder, CO 80303 (phone, 303–497–6332); 601 East Twelfth Street, Kansas City, MO 64106 (phone, 816–426–2056); and 200 World Trade Center, Norfolk, VA 23510–1624 (phone, 757–441–6516).

Environment   The National Oceanic and Atmospheric Administration conducts research and gathers data about the oceans, atmosphere, space, and Sun, and applies this knowledge to science and service in ways that touch the lives of all Americans, including warning of dangerous weather, charting seas and skies, guiding our use and protection of ocean and coastal resources, and improving our understanding and stewardship of the environment which sustains us all. For further information, contact the Office of Communications, National Oceanic and Atmospheric Administration, Room 6013, Fourteenth Street and Constitution Avenue NW., Washington, DC 20230. Phone, 202–482–6090. Fax, 202–482–3154. Internet, http://www.noaa.gov.

Inspector General Hotline   The Office of Inspector General works to promote economy, efficiency, and effectiveness and to prevent and detect fraud, waste, abuse, and mismanagement in departmental programs and operations. Contact the Hotline, Inspector General, Complaint Intake Unit, Mail Stop 7886, 1401 Constitution Avenue, NW, Washington, DC 20230. Phone, 202–482–2495 or 800–424–5197 (toll free). TTD, 202–482–5923 or 856–860–6950 (toll free). Fax, 855–569–9235. Email, hotline@oig.doc.gov. Internet, http://www.oig.doc.gov.

Publications   The titles of selected publications are printed below with the operating units responsible for their issuance. These and other publications dealing with a wide range of business, economic, environmental, scientific, and technical matters are announced in the weekly Business Service Checklist, which may be purchased from the Superintendent of Documents, Government Printing Office, Washington, DC 20402. Phone, 202–512–1800.

For further information, contact the Office of Public Affairs, Department of Commerce, Fourteenth Street and Constitution Avenue NW., Room 5040, Washington, DC 20230. Phone, 202–482–3263. Internet, http://www.doc.gov.

Bureau of Industry and Security

Department of Commerce, Washington, DC 20230
Phone, 202–482–2721. Internet, http://www.bis.doc.gov.

Under Secretary for Industry and Security	ERIC L. HIRSCHHORN
Deputy Under Secretary	DANIEL O. HILL
Assistant Secretary for Export Administration	KEVIN J. WOLF

Assistant Secretary for Export Enforcement   Davɪᴅ W. Mɪʟʟs

[For the Bureau of Industry and Security statement of organization, see the Federal Registers of June 7, 1988, 53 FR 20881, and April 26, 2002, 67 FR 20630]

The Bureau of Industry and Security (BIS) is to advance U.S. national security, foreign policy, and economic objectives by ensuring an effective export control and treaty compliance system and promoting continued U.S. strategic technology leadership. BIS activities include regulating the export of sensitive goods and technologies in an effective and efficient manner; enforcing export control, antiboycott, and public safety laws; cooperating with and assisting other countries on export control and strategic trade issues; assisting U.S. industry to comply with international arms control agreements; monitoring the viability of the U.S. defense industrial base; evaluating the effects on national security of foreign investments in U.S. companies; and supporting continued U.S. technology leadership in industries that are essential to national security.

Export Administration The Office of the Assistant Secretary for Export Administration is responsible for export licenses, treaty compliance, treaty obligations relating to weapons of mass destruction, and the defense industrial and technology base. The Office regulates the export of dual-use items requiring licenses for national security, nonproliferation, foreign policy, and short supply; ensures that approval or denial of license applications is consistent with economic and security concerns; promotes an understanding of export control regulations within the business community; represents the Department in interagency and international forums relating to export controls, particularly in multilateral regimes; monitors the availability of industrial resources of national defense; analyzes the impact of export controls on strategic industries; and assesses the security consequences of certain foreign investments.

Export Enforcement The Office of the Assistant Secretary for Export Enforcement enforces dual-use export controls. This enables exporters to take advantage of legal export opportunities while ensuring that illegal exports will be detected and either prevented or investigated and sanctioned. The Office also ensures prompt, aggressive action against restrictive trade practices; reviews visa applications of foreign nationals to prevent illegal technology transfers; and conducts cooperative enforcement activities on an international basis.

For information on the Export Enforcement field offices, visit our Web site at www.bis.doc.gov/about/programoffices.htm.

Management and Policy Coordination
The Management and Policy Coordination (MPC) unit establishes and evaluates the Bureau's overall policy agenda, priorities, goals, unit objectives, and key metrics. MPC performs oversight of program operations and expenditures; executes or supervises the President's Management Agenda; and adjudicates appeals of licensing and enforcement decisions as part of an extended legal process involving administrative law judges and the Office of General Counsel. MPC provides guidance and coordination for the Bureau's participation in the Export Control and Related Border Security Assistance Program, which provides technical assistance to strengthen the export and transit control systems of nations that are identified as potential locations for the exporting of weapons of mass destruction, missile delivery systems, or the commodities, technologies, and equipment that can be used to design and build them.

Sources of Information

Business Information Information for the U.S. business community, including export news, updates to Export Administration regulations, export license and enforcement information, compliance and training information, Bureau program information, e-FOIA information, export seminar event schedules, and information on the Denied Persons List, can be found on the Bureau's Web site. Internet, http://www. bis.doc.gov.

Enforcement   For enforcement-related questions, contact the partnership-in-security hotline. Phone, 800–424–2980.

Outreach and Educational Services   The Outreach and Educational Services Division has offices in Washington, DC

(phone, 202–482–4811; fax, 202–482–2927) and on the West Coast (phone, 949–660–0144 or 408–998–8806; fax, 949–660–9347 or 408–998–8677).

Publications   Publications available on the Bureau's Web site include the Bureau's annual report, the foreign policy export controls report, and the Exporter User Manual and Licensing FAQ.

For further information, contact the Office of Public Affairs, Bureau of Industry and Security, Room 3895, Fourteenth Street and Constitution Avenue NW., Washington, DC 20230. Phone, 202–482–2721. Internet, http://www.bis.doc.gov.

Economic Development Administration

Department of Commerce, Washington, DC 20230
Phone, 202–482–2309. Internet, http://www.eda.gov.

Assistant Secretary for Economic Development	ROY K.J. WILLIAMS
Deputy Assistant Secretary for Economic Development	MATTHEW ERSKINE

The Economic Development Administration (EDA) was created in 1965 under the Public Works and Economic Development Act (42 U.S.C. 3121) as part of an effort to target Federal resources to economically distressed areas and to help develop local economies in the United States. It was mandated to assist rural and urban communities that were outside the mainstream economy and that lagged in economic development, industrial growth, and personal income.

EDA provides grants to States, regions, and communities across the Nation to help wealth and minimize poverty by promoting a favorable business environment to attract private capital investment and higher skill, higher wage jobs through capacity building, planning, infrastructure, research grants, and strategic initiatives. Through its grant program, EDA utilizes public sector resources to facilitate an environment where the private sector risks capital and job opportunities are created.

Public works and development facilities grants support infrastructure projects that foster the establishment or expansion of industrial and commercial

businesses, supporting the retention and creation of jobs.

Planning grants support the design and implementation of effective economic development policies and programs, by local development organizations, in States and communities. EDA funds a network of over 350 planning districts throughout the country.

Technical assistance provides for local feasibility and industry studies, management and operational assistance, natural resource development, and export promotion. In addition, EDA funds a network of university centers that provides technical assistance.

Research, evaluation, and demonstration funds are used to support studies about the causes of economic distress and to seek solutions to counteract and prevent such problems.

Economic adjustment grants help communities adjust to a gradual erosion or sudden dislocation of their local economic structure. This assistance provides funding for both planning and implementation to address economic change.

The Trade Adjustment Assistance program helps U.S. firms and industries injured as the result of economic globalization. A nationwide network of Trade Adjustment Assistance Centers offers low-cost, effective professional assistance to certified firms to develop and implement recovery strategies.

For information on the EDA's regional offices, visit http://www.eda.gov/AboutEDA/Regions.xml.

For further information, contact the Economic Development Administration, Department of Commerce, Washington, DC 20230. Phone, 202–482–5081. Fax, 202–273–4781. Internet, http://www.eda.gov.

Economics and Statistics Administration
Department of Commerce, Washington, DC 20230
Phone, 202–482–3727. Internet, http://www.esa.doc.gov.

Under Secretary for Economic Affairs	MARK E. DOMS
Deputy Under Secretary	(VACANCY)
Chief Economist	SUSAN R. HELPER
Director, Bureau of the Census	JOHN H. THOMPSON
Director, Bureau of Economic Analysis	J. STEVEN LANDEFELD

The Economics and Statistics Administration (ESA), headed by the Under Secretary for Economic Affairs, has three principal components: the Office of the Chief Economist, the Bureau of the Census, and the Bureau of Economic Analysis (BEA). ESA develops policy options, analyzes economic developments, manages economic data systems, and produces a major share of U.S. economic and demographic statistics, including the national economic indicators. The Under Secretary is the chief economic adviser to the Secretary and provides leadership and executive management of the Bureau of the Census and BEA.

Office of the Chief Economist

The expert economists and analysts of the Office of the Chief Economist analyze domestic and international economic developments and produce in-depth reports, fact sheets, briefings, and social media postings. These tools cover policy issues and current economic events, as well as economic and demographic trends. Department of Commerce and White House policymakers rely on these tools, as do American businesses, State and local governments, and news organizations around the world.

Bureau of the Census

[For the Bureau of the Census statement of organization, see the Federal Register of Sept. 16, 1975, 40 FR 42765]

The Bureau of the Census was established as a permanent office by act of March 6, 1902 (32 Stat. 51). The major functions of the Census Bureau are authorized by the Constitution, which provides that a census of population shall be taken every 10 years, and by laws codified as title 13 of the United States Code. The law also provides that the information collected by the Census Bureau from individual persons, households, or establishments be kept strictly confidential and be used only for statistical purposes.

The Census Bureau is responsible for the decennial censuses of population and housing; the quinquennial censuses of State and local governments, manufacturers, mineral industries, distributive trades, construction industries, and transportation; current surveys that provide information on many of the subjects covered in the censuses at monthly, quarterly, annual, or other intervals; compilation of current statistics on U.S. foreign trade, including data on imports, exports, and shipping; special censuses at the request and expense of State and local government units; publication of estimates and projections of the population; publication of current data on population and housing characteristics; and current reports on manufacturing, retail and wholesale trade, services, construction, imports and exports, State and local government finances and employment, and other subjects.

The Census Bureau makes available statistical results of its censuses, surveys, and other programs to the public through the Internet, mobile applications, and other media. The Bureau also prepares special tabulations sponsored and paid for by data users. It also produces statistical compendia, catalogs, guides, and directories that are useful in locating information on specific subjects. Upon request, the Bureau makes searches of decennial census records and furnishes certificates to individuals for use as evidence of age, relationship, or place of birth. A fee is charged for searches.

Internet, http://www.census.gov.

For information on the Census Bureau regional offices, visit http://www.census.gov/regions.

For further information, contact the Public Information Office, Bureau of the Census, Department of Commerce, Washington, DC 20233. Phone, 301–763–3030. Fax, 301–763–3762. Email, PIO@census.gov. Internet, http://www.census.gov.

Bureau of Economic Analysis

[For the Bureau of Economic Analysis statement of organization, see the Federal Register of Dec. 29, 1980, 45 FR 85496]

The Bureau of Economic Analysis (BEA) promotes a better understanding of the U.S. economy by providing the most timely, relevant, and accurate economic accounts data in an objective and cost-effective manner. BEA's economic statistics are closely watched and provide a comprehensive picture of the U.S. economy. BEA prepares national,

regional, industry, and international accounts that present essential information on such issues in the world economy.

BEA's national economic statistics provide a comprehensive look at U.S. production, consumption, investment, exports and imports, and income and saving. The international transactions accounts provide information on trade in goods and services (including the balance of payments and trade), investment income, and government and private finances. In addition, the accounts measure the value of U.S. international assets and liabilities and direct investment by multinational companies.

The regional accounts provide data on total and per capita personal income by region, State, metropolitan area, and county, and on gross State product. The industry economic account provides a detailed view of the interrelationships between U.S. producers and users and the contribution to production across industries.

For further information, contact the Public Information Office, Bureau of Economic Analysis, Department of Commerce, Washington, DC 20230. Phone, 202–606–9900. Fax, 202–606–5310. Email, customerservice@bea.gov. Internet, http://www.bea.gov.

Sources of Information

Economic Analysis Publications   The monthly journal Survey of Current Business is available from the Government Printing Office. Current and historical estimates, general information, and employment opportunities are available on BEA's Web site at www.bea.gov. For more information, contact the Public Information Office. Phone, 202–606–9900. Email, webmaster@bea.gov.

For further information, contact the Economics and Statistics Administration, Department of Commerce, Washington, DC 20230. Phone, 202–482–3727. Internet, http://www.esa.doc.gov.

International Trade Administration

Department of Commerce, Washington, DC 20230
Phone, 202–482–3917. Internet, http://www.trade.gov.

Under Secretary for International Trade	STEFAN M. SELIG
Deputy Under Secretary	KEN HYATT
Assistant Secretary for Enforcement and Compliance	PAUL PIQUADO
Assistant Secretary for Industries and Analysis	MAUREEN SMITH, *Acting*
Assistant Secretary for Trade Promotion and Director General of the U.S. and Foreign Commercial Service	ARUN M. KUMAR

[For the International Trade Administration statement of organization, see the Federal Register of Jan. 25, 1980, 45 FR 6148]

The International Trade Administration (ITA) was established on January 2, 1980, by the Secretary of Commerce to promote world trade and to strengthen the international trade and investment position of the United States.

ITA is headed by the Under Secretary for International Trade, who coordinates all issues concerning trade promotion, international commercial policy, market access, and trade law enforcement. The Administration is responsible for nonagricultural trade operations of the U.S. Government and supports the trade policy negotiation efforts of the U.S. Trade Representative.

Import Administration   The Office of Import Administration defends American industry against injurious and unfair trade practices by administering efficiently, fairly, and in a manner consistent with U.S. international trade obligations the antidumping and countervailing duty laws of the United States. The Office ensures the proper administration of foreign trade zones and advises the Secretary on establishment of new zones; oversees the administration of the Department's textiles program; and administers programs governing watch assemblies, and other statutory import programs.

Market Access and Compliance
The Office of Market Access and Compliance advises on the analysis, formulation, and implementation of U.S. international economic policies and carries out programs to promote international trade, improve access by

U.S. companies to overseas markets, and strengthen the international trade and investment position of the United States. The Office analyzes and develops recommendations for region- and country-specific international economic, trade, and investment policy strategies and objectives. In addition, the Office is responsible for implementing, monitoring, and enforcing foreign compliance with bilateral and multilateral trade agreements.

Manufacturing and Services   The Manufacturing and Services unit advises on domestic and international trade and investment policies affecting the competitiveness of U.S. industry and carries on a program of research and analysis on manufacturing and services. Based on this analysis and interaction with U.S. industry, the unit Secretary develops strategies, policies, and programs to strengthen the competitive position of U.S. industries in the United States and world markets. The unit manages an integrated program that includes both industry and economic analysis, trade policy development and multilateral, regional, and bilateral trade agreements for manufactured goods and services; administers trade arrangements (other than those involving AD/CVD proceedings) with foreign governments in product and service areas; and develops and provides business information and assistance to the United States on its rights and opportunities under multilateral and other agreements.

Trade Promotion and U.S. and Foreign Commercial Service The Trade Promotion and U.S. and Foreign Commercial Service unit directs ITA's export promotion programs, develops and implements a unified goal-setting and evaluation process to increase trade assistance to small- and medium-sized businesses, directs a program of international trade events, market research, and export-related trade information products and services; and directs programs to aid U.S. firms to compete successfully for major projects and procurements worldwide. ITA provides a comprehensive platform of export assistance services to support U.S. firms who enter or expand their presence in overseas markets, including counseling, trade events, and outreach services through 109 export assistance centers located in the United States and 158 posts located in 83 countries throughout the world. For a complete listing of ITA's export assistance centers, both in the United States and abroad, consult the Web site at www.export.gov/eac or call the Trade Information Center at 1–800–872–8723.

Sources of Information

Electronic Access The Administration maintains a Web site, (Internet, www.trade.gov) which offers the single best place for individuals or firms seeking reports, documents, import case/regulations, texts of international agreements like NAFTA and GATT, market research, and points of contact for assistance in exporting, obtaining remedies from unfair trading practices, or receiving help with market access problems. Customers are able to review comprehensive information on how to export, search for trade information by either industry or by country, learn how to petition against unfairly priced imports, and obtain information on a number of useful international trade-related products like overseas trade leads and agent distributor reports. The Web site also features email addresses and locations for trade contacts in Washington, overseas, in major exporting centers in the United States, and in other parts of the Federal Government.

For further information, contact the International Trade Administration, Department of Commerce, Washington, DC 20230. Phone, 202–482–3917. Internet, http://www.trade.gov.

Minority Business Development Agency

Department of Commerce, Washington, DC 20230
Phone, 202–482–2332. Internet, http://www.mbda.gov.

National Director, Minority Business   Alejandrea Castillo
    Development Agency

[For the Minority Business Development Agency statement of organization, see the Federal Register of Mar. 17, 1972, 37 FR 5650, as amended]

The Minority Business Development Agency was established by Executive order in 1969. The Agency develops and coordinates a national program for minority business enterprise.

The Agency was created to assist minority businesses in achieving effective and equitable participation in the American free enterprise system and in overcoming social and economic disadvantages that have limited their participation in the past. The

Agency provides national policies and leadership in forming and strengthening a partnership of business, industry, and government with the Nation's minority businesses.

Business development services are provided to the minority business community through three vehicles: the minority business opportunity committees, which disseminate information on business opportunities; the minority business development centers, which provide management and technical assistance and other business development services; and electronic commerce, which includes a Web site that shows how to start a business and use the service to find contract opportunities.

The Agency promotes and coordinates the efforts of other Federal agencies in assisting or providing market opportunities for minority business. It coordinates opportunities for minority firms in the private sector. Through such public and private cooperative activities, the Agency promotes the participation of Federal, State, and local governments, and business and industry in directing resources for the development of strong minority businesses.

Sources of Information

Electronic Access Comprehensive information about programs, policy, centers, and access to the job matching database is available through the Internet at www.mbda.gov.

Publications Copies of Minority Business Today and the BDC Directory may be obtained by contacting the Office of Business Development. Phone, 202–482–6022.

For further information, contact the Office of the National Director, Minority Business Development Agency, Department of Commerce, Washington, DC 20230. Phone, 202–482–5061. Internet, http://www.mbda.gov.

National Oceanic and Atmospheric Administration

Department of Commerce, Washington, DC 20230
Phone, 202–482–2985. Internet, http://www.noaa.gov.

Under Secretary, Oceans and Atmosphere and Administrator	KATHRYN D. SULLIVAN
Assistant Secretary, Conservation and Management and Deputy Administrator	MARK SCHAEFER
Assistant Secretary, Environmental Observation and Prediction and Deputy Administrator	(VACANCY)

[For the National Oceanic and Atmospheric Administration statement of organization, see the Federal Register of Feb. 13, 1978, 43 FR 6128]

The National Oceanic and Atmospheric Administration (NOAA) was formed on October 3, 1970, by Reorganization Plan No. 4 of 1970 (5 U.S.C. app.).

NOAA's mission centers on environmental assessment, prediction, and stewardship. It is dedicated to monitoring and assessing the state of the environment in order to make accurate and timely forecasts to protect life, property, and natural resources, as well as to promote the economic well-being of the United States and to enhance its environmental security. NOAA is committed to protecting America's ocean, coastal, and living marine resources while promoting sustainable economic development.

A complete listing of NOAA facilities and activities in your State or Territory is available online.

Internet, http://www.legislative.noaa.gov/NIYS/index.html.

National Weather Service The National Weather Service (NWS) provides weather, water and climate warnings, forecasts and data for the United States, its Territories, adjacent waters, and ocean areas. NWS data and products form a national information database and infrastructure used by Government agencies, the private sector, the public, and the global community to protect life and property and to enhance the national economy. Working with partners in Government, academic and research institutions, and private industry, NWS offers products and services that are responsive to the needs of the American public. NWS data and information services support aviation and marine activities, wildfire suppression, and many other sectors of the economy.

NWS supports national security efforts with long- and short-range forecasts, air quality and cloud dispersion forecasts, and broadcasts of warnings and critical information over the 800-station NOAA Weather Radio network.

For further information, contact the National Weather Service, 1325 East-West Highway, Silver Spring, MD 20910–3283. Phone, 301–713–0675. Fax, 301–713–0049. Internet, http://www.nws.noaa. gov.

National Environmental Satellite, Data, and Information Service   The National Environmental Satellite, Data, and Information Service (NESDIS) operates the Nation's civilian geostationary and polar-orbiting environmental satellites. It also manages the largest collection of atmospheric, climatic, geophysical, and oceanographic data in the world. From these sources, NESDIS develops and provides, through various media, environmental data for forecasts, national security, and weather warnings to protect life and property. These data are also used to assist in energy distribution, the development of global food supplies, the management of natural resources, and in the recovery of downed pilots and mariners in distress.

For further information, contact the National Environmental Satellite, Data, and Information Service, 1335 East-West Highway, Silver Spring, MD 20910–3283. Phone, 301–713–3578. Fax, 301–713–1249. Internet, http://www.nesdis.noaa. gov/about_nesdis.html.

National Marine Fisheries Service   The National Marine Fisheries Service (NMFS) supports the management, conservation, and sustainable development of domestic and international living marine resources and the protection and restoration of healthy ecosystems. NMFS is involved in the stock assessment of the Nation's multibillion dollar marine fisheries. It protects marine mammals and threatened species, conserves habitats, assists trade and industry, and is active in fishery enforcement.

For further information, contact the National Marine Fisheries Service, 1315 East-West Highway, Silver Spring, MD 20910. Phone, 301–713–2239. Fax, 301–713–2258. Internet, http://www.nmfs.noaa.gov.

National Ocean Service   The National Ocean Service (NOS) works to balance the Nation's use of coastal resources through research, management, and policy. NOS monitors the health of U.S. coasts by examining how human use and natural events impact coastal ecosystems. Coastal communities rely on NOS for information on natural hazards so they can more effectively reduce or eliminate the destructive effects of coastal hazards. NOS assesses the damage caused by hazardous material spills and works to restore or replace the affected coastal resources. Through varied programs, NOS protects wetlands, water quality, beaches, and wildlife. NOS also provides a wide range of navigational products and data that assist vessels' safe movement through U.S. waters. It provides the basic set of information that establishes the latitude, longitude, and elevation framework necessary for the Nation's surveying, navigation, positioning, and mapping activities.

For further information, contact the National Ocean Service, Room 13231, SSMC 4, 1305 East-West Highway, Silver Spring, MD 20910. Phone, 301–713–3070. Fax, 301–713–4307. Internet, http://www.nos.noaa.gov.

Office of Oceanic and Atmospheric Research   The Office of Oceanic and Atmospheric Research (OAR) carries out research on weather, air quality and composition, climate variability and change, and ocean, coastal, and Great Lakes ecosystems. OAR conducts and directs its research programs in coastal, marine, atmospheric, and space sciences through its own laboratories and offices, as well as through networks of university-based programs across the country.

For further information, contact the Office of Oceanic and Atmospheric Research, Room 11458, 1315 East-West Highway, Silver Spring, MD 20910. Phone, 301–713–2458. Fax, 301–713–0163. Internet, http://www.oar.noaa.gov.

Office of Marine and Aviation Operations   The Office of Marine and Aviation Operations maintains a fleet of ships and aircraft, and manages several safety programs. Ships and aircraft are used for operational data collection and research in support of NOAA's mission, the Global Earth Observation System, and the Integrated Ocean Observing System. Its activities include flying "hurricane hunter" aircraft into nature's most turbulent storms to collect data critical to hurricane research.

For further information, contact Office of Marine and Aviation Operations, Suite 500, 8403 Colesville Rd., Silver Spring, MD 20910. Phone, 301–713–1045. Internet, http://www.omao.noaa.gov/about.html.

Sources of Information

Publications and Resources The Administration provides technical

For further information, contact the Office of Communications and External Affairs, National Oceanic and Atmospheric Administration, Department of Commerce, Washington, DC 20230. Phone, 202–482–6090. Internet, http://www.noaa.gov.

memoranda, technical reports, monographs, nautical and aeronautical charts, coastal zone maps, data tapes, and a wide variety of raw and processed environmental data. Information on NOAA products is available online. Contact the Office of Communications and External Affairs, Fourteenth Street and Constitution Avenue NW., Washington, DC 20230. Phone, 202–482–6090. Fax, 202–482–3154. Internet, http://www.noaa.gov/media.html.

National Telecommunications and Information Administration

Department of Commerce, Washington, DC 20230
Phone, 202–428–1840. Internet, http://www.ntia.doc.gov.

Assistant Secretary for Communications and Information and Administrator

LAWRENCE E. STRICKLING

[For the National Telecommunications and Information Administration statement of organization, see the Federal Register of June 5, 1978, 43 FR 24348]

The National Telecommunications and Information Administration (NTIA) was established in 1978 by Reorganization Plan No. 1 of 1977 (5 U.S.C. app.) and Executive Order 12046 of March 27, 1978 (3 CFR, 1978 Comp., p. 158), by combining the Office of Telecommunications Policy of the Executive Office of the President and the Office of Telecommunications of the Department of Commerce to form a new agency reporting to the Secretary of Commerce. NTIA operates under the authority of the National Telecommunications and Information Administration Organization Act (47 U.S.C. 901).

NTIA's principal responsibilities and functions include serving as the principal executive branch adviser to the President on telecommunications and information policy; developing and presenting U.S. plans and policies at international communications conferences and related meetings; prescribing policies for and managing Federal use of the radio frequency

spectrum; serving as the principal Federal telecommunications research and engineering laboratory, through NTIA's Institute for Telecommunication Sciences, headquartered in Boulder, CO; administering Federal programs to assist telecommunication facilities, public safety organizations, and the general public with the transition to digital broadcasting; providing grants through the Broadband Technology Opportunities Program to increase broadband accessibility in underserved areas of the United States; and providing grants through the Public Telecommunications Facilities Program to extend delivery or public telecommunications services to U.S. citizens, to increase ownership and management by women and minorities, and to strengthen the capabilities of existing public broadcasting stations to provide telecommunications services.

Sources of Information

Publications Since 1970, several hundred technical reports and memoranda, special publications, contractor reports, and other information products have been published by NTIA or its predecessor agency. The publications are available from the National Telecommunications and Information Administration, Department of Commerce, Washington, DC 20230 (phone, 202–482–1551); or the National Telecommunications and Information Administration, Institute for Telecommunication Sciences, Department of Commerce, Boulder, CO 80302 (phone, 303–497–3572). More information can be obtained by visiting the Web site at www.ntia.doc.gov.

For further information, contact the National Telecommunications and Information Administration, Department of Commerce, Washington, DC 20230. Phone, 202–482–1551. Internet, http://www.ntia.doc. gov.

National Institute of Standards and Technology

100 Bureau Drive, Gaithersburg, MD 20899
Phone, 301–975–2000. TTY, 800–877–8339. Internet, http://www.nist.gov.

Under Secretary for Standards and Technology and Director	Patrick D. Gallagher

The National Institute of Standards and Technology (NIST) operates under the authority of the National Institute of Standards and Technology Act (15 U.S.C. 271), which amends the Organic Act of March 3, 1901 (ch. 872), that created the National Bureau of Standards (NBS) in 1901. In 1988, Congress renamed NBS as NIST and expanded its activities and responsibilities.

NIST is a nonregulatory Federal agency within the Commerce Department. Its mission is to promote measurement science, standards, and technology to enhance productivity, facilitate trade, and improve the quality of life. NIST carries out its mission through the NIST laboratories, which conduct research to advance the U.S. technological infrastructure; the Baldrige National Quality Program, which helps U.S. businesses and other organizations improve the performance and quality of their operations; the Hollings Manufacturing Extension Partnership, which helps smaller firms adopt new manufacturing and management technologies; and the Technology Innovative Program, which provides cost-shared awards to industry and other institutions for high-risk, high-reward research in areas of critical national need.

Sources of Information

Publications Journal of Research of the National Institute of Standards and Technology and other publications are available on the NIST publications portal at http://www.nist.gov/publication-portal. cfm.

For further information, contact the National Institute of Standards and Technology, 100 Bureau Drive, Mail Stop 1070, Gaithersburg, MD 20899. Phone, 301–975–6478. Fax, 301–926–1630. Email, inquiries@nist.gov. Internet, http://www.nist.gov.

National Technical Information Service

5301 Shawnee Road, Alexandria, VA 22312
Phone, 703–605–6050; 888–584–8332. Internet, http://www.ntis.gov.

Director	Bruce Borzino

The National Technical Information Service (NTIS) serves as the largest central resource for Government-funded scientific, technical, engineering, and business-related information available today. For more than 60 years, the

Service has assured businesses, universities, Government, and the public timely access to approximately 3 million publications covering over 350 subject areas. The Service supports the Department of Commerce mission to promote the Nation's economic growth by providing access to information that stimulates innovation and discovery. It receives no appropriations; it is mandated to recover its costs through fees charged for its products and services.

NTIS collects scientific and technical information; catalogs, abstracts, indexes, and permanently archives the information; disseminates information through electronic and other media; and provides information processing services to other Federal agencies. Printed and electronic versions of NTIS technical reports are available online through the NTIS Bibliographic Database at www.ntis.gov. NTIS information is also available electronically by subscribing to the National Technical Reports Library. In 2011, the Service established its Federal Science Repository Service,

which provides additional access to Federally-funded scientific, technical, and engineering information. In addition, the Service provides Web services for Federal Government agencies, and it works closely with them to assist in implementing and maintaining their training, systems, and applications.

Sources of Information

Products and Services For general inquiries or to place a telephone order, contact the National Technical Information Service's Customer Contact Center from 8 a.m. to 6 p.m., eastern standard time. Phone, 800–553–6847; TDD, 703–487–4639; Fax, 703–605–6900; Email, info@ntis.gov.

To inquire about the Service's information services for other Federal agencies, call its Office of Federal Services at 703–605–6800, or send an email to obdinfo@ntis.gov. In addition, the National Technical Information Service can be followed on Twitter, Facebook, and YouTube.

For further information, contact the National Technical Information Service Administration, 5301 Shawnee Road, Arlington, VA 22312. Phone, 703–605–6000, or 800–553–6847. Internet, http://www.ntis.gov.

United States Patent and Trademark Office

600 Dulany Street, Arlington, VA 22313
Phone, 571–272–8700. Internet, http://www.uspto.gov.

Under Secretary for Intellectual Property and Director	(VACANCY)
Deputy Under Secretary for Intellectual Property and Deputy Director	MICHELLE K. LEE

[For the Patent and Trademark Office statement of organization, see the Federal Register of Apr. 14, 1975, 40 FR 16707]

The United States Patent and Trademark Office (USPTO) was established by the act of July 19, 1952 (35 U.S.C. 1) to promote the progress of science and the useful arts by securing for limited times to inventors the exclusive right to their respective discoveries for a certain period of time (Article I, Section 8 of the United States Constitution). The registration of trademarks is based on the commerce clause of the U.S. Constitution.

USPTO examines and issues patents. There are three major patent categories: utility patents, design patents, and plant patents. USPTO also issues statutory invention registrations and processes international patent applications.

Through the registration of trademarks, USPTO assists businesses in protecting their investments, promoting goods and services, and safeguarding consumers against confusion and deception in the marketplace. A trademark includes any distinctive word, name, symbol, device, or any combination thereof adopted and used or intended to be used by a manufacturer or merchant to identify his goods or services and distinguish them from those manufactured or sold by others. Trademarks are examined by the Office for compliance with various statutory requirements to prevent unfair competition and consumer deception.

In addition to the examination of patent and trademark applications, issuance of patents, and registration of trademarks, USPTO advises and assists government agencies and officials in matters involving all domestic and global aspects of intellectual property. USPTO also promotes an understanding of intellectual property protection.

USPTO provides public access to patent, trademark, and related scientific and technical information. Patents and trademarks may be freely reviewed and searched online at www.uspto.gov or at designated Patent and Trademark Depository Libraries. There are 80 Patent and Trademark Depository Libraries located within the United States and the territory of Puerto Rico. Additionally, USPTO's Scientific and Technical Information Center in Alexandria, VA, houses over 120,000 volumes of scientific and technical books in various languages; 90,000 bound volumes of periodicals devoted to science and technology; the official journals of 77 foreign patent organizations; and over 40 million foreign patents on paper, microfilm, microfiche, and CD–ROM.

Sources of Information

General Information   Information and publications concerning patents, trademarks, attorneys and agents registered to practice before the USPTO, and USPTO satellite offices is available online at www.uspto.gov. Phone, 571–272–1000 or 800–786–9199. TTY, 571–272–9950.

Patents   The United States Patent and Trademark Office has priority programs for advancement of examination of certain patent applications where the invention could materially enhance the quality of the environment of mankind. For further information, contact the Commissioner for Patents, Office of Petitions, Washington, DC 20231. Phone, 571–272–3282.

Publications   The Official Gazette of the USPTO and other publications can be found online at www.uspto.gov.

For further information, contact the Office of the Chief Communications Officer, United States Patent and Trademark Office, 600 Dulany Street, Alexandria, VA 22314. Phone, 571–272–8400. Internet, http://www.uspto.gov.

DEPARTMENT OF DEFENSE

Office of the Secretary, The Pentagon, Washington, DC 20301–1155
Phone, 703–545–6700. Internet, http://www.defense.gov.

Secretary of Defense	CHARLES T. HAGEL
Deputy Secretary of Defense	ROBERT O. WORK
Under Secretary of Defense for Acquisition, Technology and Logistics	FRANK KENDALL
Under Secretary of Defense Comptroller and Chief Financial Officer	MIKE MCCORD
Under Secretary of Defense for Intelligence	MICHAEL G. VICKERS
Under Secretary of Defense for Personnel and Readiness	LAURA JUNOR
Under Secretary of Defense for Policy	CHRISTINE E. WORMUTH
Principal Deputy Under Secretary of Defense for Acquisition, Technology and Logistics	ALAN ESTEVEZ
Principal Deputy Under Secretary of Defense Comptroller and Chief Financial Officer	(VACANCY)
Principal Under Secretary of Defense for Intelligence	MARCEL LETTRE
Principal Under Secretary of Defense for Personnel and Readiness	JESSICA GARFOLA WRIGHT
Principal Under Secretary of Defense for Policy	BRIAN P. MCKEON
Assistant Secretary of Defense for Acquisition	KATRINA G. MCFARLAND
Assistant Secretary of Asian and Pacific Security Affairs	DAVID B. SHEAR
Assistant Secretary of Defense for Global Strategic Affairs	MADELYN CREEDON
Assistant Secretary of Defense for Health Affairs	JONATHAN WOODSON
Assistant Secretary of Defense for Homeland Defense and America's Security Affairs	ERIC ROSENBACH
Assistant Secretary of Defense for International Security Affairs	DEREK CHOLLET
Assistant Secretary of Defense for Legislative Affairs	ELIZABETH L. KING
Assistant Secretary of Defense for Logistics & Materiel Readiness	PAUL D. PETERS
Assistant Secretary of Defense for Nuclear, Chemical, and Biological Defense Programs	ANDREW C. WEBER
Assistant Secretary of Defense for Operational Energy Plans and Programs	(VACANCY)
Assistant to the Secretary of Defense for Public Affairs	BRENT COLBURN
Assistant Secretary of Defense for Readiness and Force Management	(VACANCY)
Assistant to the Secretary of Defense for Research and Engineering	(VACANCY)

Assistant Secretary of Defense for Reserve Affairs	RICHARD O. WIGHTMAN JR., *Acting*
Assistant Secretary of Defense for Special Operations/Low-Intensity Conflict	MICHAEL D. LUMPKIN
Assistant to the Secretary of Defense for Intelligence Oversight	MICHAEL GOODROE, *Acting*
Chief Information Officer	TERRY HALVORSEN, *Acting*
Chief Operating Officer	ANTHONY A. ALDWELL
General Counsel	STEPHEN W. PRESTON
Inspector General	JON T. RYMER
Director, Administration and Management	MICHAEL L. RHODES
Director, Cost Assessment and Program Evaluation	JAMIE MICHAEL MORIN
Director, Operational Test and Evaluation	J. MICHAEL GILMORE

Joint Chiefs of Staff

Chairman	GEN. MARTIN E. DEMPSEY, USA
Vice Chairman	ADM. JAMES A. WINNEFELD, JR., USN
Chief of Staff, Army	GEN. RAYMOND T. ODIERNO, USA
Chief of Naval Operations	ADM. JONATHAN W. GREENERT, USN
Chief of Staff, Air Force	GEN. MARK A. WELSH, III, USAF
Commandant, Marine Corps	GEN. JAMES F. AMOS, USMC
Senior Enlisted Advisor to the Chairman	SGT. MAJ. BRYAN B. BATTAGLIA, USMC

[For the Department of Defense statement of organization, see the Code of Federal Regulations, Title 32, Chapter I, Subchapter R]

The Department of Defense provides the military forces needed to deter war and protect our Nation's security and interests. The major elements of these forces are the Army, Navy, Marine Corps, and Air Force. They are backed, in case of emergency, by members of the Reserve and National Guard. Hundreds of thousands of civilians also work in the Defense Department. Under the President, who is also Commander in Chief, the Secretary of Defense exercises authority, direction, and control over the Department, which comprises the separately organized military departments of the Army, Navy, and Air Force; the Joint Chiefs of Staff; the combatant commands; and defense agencies and field activities established for specific purposes.

The National Security Act Amendments of 1949 redesignated the National Military Establishment as the Department of Defense (DOD) and established it as an executive department (10 U.S.C. 111) headed by the Secretary of Defense.

Structure The Department of Defense is composed of the Office of the Secretary of Defense; the military departments and the military services within those departments; the Chairman of the Joint Chiefs of Staff and the Joint Staff; the combatant commands; the defense agencies; DOD field activities; and such other offices, agencies, activities, and commands as may be established or designated by law or by the President or the Secretary of Defense.

Each military department is separately organized under its own Secretary and functions under the authority, direction, and control of the Secretary of Defense. The Secretary of each military department is responsible to the Secretary of Defense for the operation and efficiency of his department. Orders to the military departments are issued through the Secretaries of these departments or their designees, by the Secretary of Defense, or under authority specifically delegated in writing by the Secretary of Defense or provided by law.

The commanders of the combatant commands are responsible to the President and the Secretary of Defense for accomplishing the military missions assigned to them and exercising

DEPARTMENT OF DEFENSE

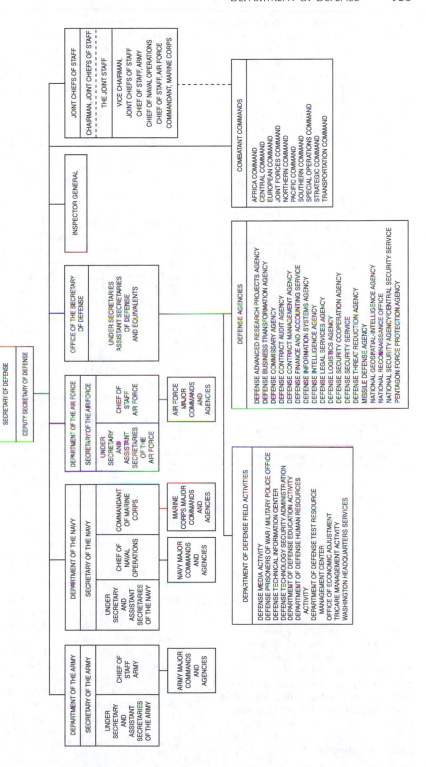

SECRETARY OF DEFENSE

DEPUTY SECRETARY OF DEFENSE

DEPARTMENT OF THE ARMY

SECRETARY OF THE ARMY

UNDER SECRETARY AND ASSISTANT SECRETARIES OF THE ARMY

CHIEF OF STAFF ARMY

ARMY MAJOR COMMANDS AND AGENCIES

DEPARTMENT OF THE NAVY

SECRETARY OF THE NAVY

UNDER SECRETARY AND ASSISTANT SECRETARIES OF THE NAVY

CHIEF OF NAVAL OPERATIONS

COMMANDANT OF MARINE CORPS

NAVY MAJOR COMMANDS AND AGENCIES

MARINE CORPS MAJOR COMMANDS AND AGENCIES

DEPARTMENT OF THE AIR FORCE

SECRETARY OF THE AIR FORCE

UNDER SECRETARY AND ASSISTANT SECRETARIES OF THE AIR FORCE

CHIEF OF STAFF AIR FORCE

AIR FORCE MAJOR COMMANDS AND AGENCIES

OFFICE OF THE SECRETARY OF DEFENSE

UNDER SECRETARIES ASSISTANT SECRETARIES OF DEFENSE AND EQUIVALENTS

INSPECTOR GENERAL

JOINT CHIEFS OF STAFF

CHAIRMAN, JOINT CHIEFS OF STAFF

THE JOINT STAFF

VICE CHAIRMAN, JOINT CHIEFS OF STAFF
CHIEF OF STAFF, ARMY
CHIEF OF NAVAL OPERATIONS
CHIEF OF STAFF, AIR FORCE
COMMANDANT, MARINE CORPS

DEPARTMENT OF DEFENSE FIELD ACTIVITIES

DEFENSE MEDIA ACTIVITY
DEFENSE PRISONERS OF WAR / MILITARY POLICE OFFICE
DEFENSE TECHNICAL INFORMATION CENTER
DEFENSE TECHNOLOGY SECURITY ADMINISTRATION
DEPARTMENT OF DEFENSE EDUCATION ACTIVITY
DEPARTMENT OF DEFENSE HUMAN RESOURCES ACTIVITY
DEPARTMENT OF DEFENSE TEST RESOURCE MANAGEMENT CENTER
OFFICE OF ECONOMIC ADJUSTMENT
TRICARE MANAGEMENT ACTIVITY
WASHINGTON HEADQUARTERS SERVICES

DEFENSE AGENCIES

DEFENSE ADVANCED RESEARCH PROJECTS AGENCY
DEFENSE BUSINESS TRANSFORMATION AGENCY
DEFENSE COMMISSARY AGENCY
DEFENSE CONTRACT AUDIT AGENCY
DEFENSE CONTRACT MANAGEMENT AGENCY
DEFENSE FINANCE AND ACCOUNTING SERVICE
DEFENSE INFORMATION SYSTEMS AGENCY
DEFENSE INTELLIGENCE AGENCY
DEFENSE LEGAL SERVICES AGENCY
DEFENSE LOGISTICS AGENCY
DEFENSE SECURITY COOPERATION AGENCY
DEFENSE SECURITY SERVICE
DEFENSE THREAT REDUCTION AGENCY
MISSILE DEFENSE AGENCY
NATIONAL GEOSPATIAL-INTELLIGENCE AGENCY
NATIONAL RECONNAISSANCE OFFICE
NATIONAL SECURITY AGENCY/CENTRAL SECURITY SERVICE
PENTAGON FORCE PROTECTION AGENCY

COMBATANT COMMANDS

AFRICA COMMAND
CENTRAL COMMAND
EUROPEAN COMMAND
JOINT FORCES COMMAND
NORTHERN COMMAND
PACIFIC COMMAND
SOUTHERN COMMAND
SPECIAL OPERATIONS COMMAND
STRATEGIC COMMAND
TRANSPORTATION COMMAND

command authority over forces assigned to them. The operational chain of command runs from the President to the Secretary of Defense to the commanders of the combatant commands. The Chairman of the Joint Chiefs of Staff functions within the chain of command by transmitting the orders of the President or the Secretary of Defense to the commanders of the combatant commands.

Office of the Secretary of Defense

Secretary of Defense The Secretary of Defense is the principal defense policy adviser to the President and is responsible for the formulation of general defense policy and policy related to DOD and for the execution of approved policy. Under the direction of the President, the Secretary exercises authority, direction, and control over the Department of Defense.

Acquisition, Technology, and Logistics The Under Secretary of Defense for Acquisition, Technology, and Logistics is the principal staff assistant and adviser to the Secretary of Defense for all matters relating to the DOD Acquisition System; research and development; modeling and simulation; systems engineering; advanced technology; developmental test and evaluation; production; systems integration; logistics; installation management; military construction; procurement; environment, safety, and occupational health management; utilities and energy management; business management modernization; document services; and nuclear, chemical, and biological defense programs.

Intelligence The Under Secretary of Defense for Intelligence is the principal staff assistant and adviser to the Secretary and Deputy Secretary of Defense for intelligence, intelligence-related matters, counterintelligence, and security. The Under Secretary of Defense for Intelligence supervises all intelligence and intelligence-related affairs of DOD.

Networks and Information Integration The Assistant Secretary of Defense (Networks and Information Integration) is the principal staff assistant and adviser to the Secretary and Deputy Secretary of Defense for achieving and maintaining information superiority in support of DOD missions, while exploiting or denying an adversary's ability to do the same. The Assistant Secretary of Defense also serves as the Chief Information Officer.

Personnel and Readiness The Under Secretary of Defense for Personnel and Readiness is the principal staff assistant and adviser to the Secretary of Defense for policy matters relating to the structure and readiness of the total force. Functional areas include readiness; civilian and military personnel policies, programs, and systems; civilian and military equal opportunity programs; health policies, programs, and activities; Reserve component programs, policies, and activities; family policy, dependents' education, and personnel support programs; mobilization planning and requirements; language capabilities and programs; and the Federal Voting Assistance Program. The Under Secretary of Defense (Personnel and Readiness) also serves as the Chief Human Capital Officer.

Policy The Under Secretary of Defense for Policy is the principal staff assistant and adviser to the Secretary of Defense for policy matters relating to overall international security policy and political-military affairs and represents the Department at the National Security Council and other external agencies regarding national security policy. Functional areas include homeland defense; NATO affairs; foreign military sales; arms limitation agreements; international trade and technology security; regional security affairs; special operations and low-intensity conflict; stability operations; integration of departmental plans and policies with overall national security objectives; drug control policy, requirements, priorities, systems, resources, and programs; and issuance of policy guidance affecting departmental programs.

Additional Staff In addition, the Secretary and Deputy Secretary of Defense are assisted by a special staff of assistants, including the Assistant Secretary of Defense for Legislative

Affairs; the General Counsel; the Inspector General; the Assistant Secretary of Defense for Public Affairs; the Assistant to the Secretary of Defense (Intelligence Oversight); the Director of Administration and Management; the Under Secretary of Defense (Comptroller)/Chief Financial Officer; the Director of Operational Test and Evaluation; Director, Business Transformation; Director, Net Assessment; Director, Program Analysis and Evaluation; and such other officers as the Secretary of Defense establishes to assist him in carrying out his duties and responsibilities.

Joint Chiefs of Staff

The Joint Chiefs of Staff consist of the Chairman; the Vice Chairman; the Chief of Staff of the Army; the Chief of Naval Operations; the Chief of Staff of the Air Force; and the Commandant of the Marine Corps. The Chairman of the Joint Chiefs of Staff is the principal military adviser to the President, the National Security Council, and the Secretary of Defense. The other members of the Joint Chiefs of Staff are military advisers who may provide additional information upon request from the President, the National Security Council, or the Secretary of Defense. They may also submit their advice when it does not agree with that of the Chairman. Subject to the authority of the President and the Secretary of Defense, the Chairman of the Joint Chiefs of Staff is responsible for assisting the President and the Secretary of Defense in providing strategic direction and planning for the Armed Forces; making recommendations for the assignment of responsibilities within the Armed Forces; comparing the capabilities of American and allied Armed Forces with those of potential adversaries; preparing and reviewing contingency plans that conform to policy guidance; preparing joint logistic and mobility plans; and recommending assignment of logistic and mobility responsibilities.

The Chairman, while so serving, holds the grade of general or admiral and outranks all other officers of the Armed Forces.

The Vice Chairman of the Joint Chiefs performs duties assigned by the Chairman, with the approval of the Secretary of Defense. The Vice Chairman acts as Chairman when there is a vacancy in the office of the Chairman or in the absence or disability of the Chairman. The Vice Chairman, while so serving, holds the grade of general or admiral and outranks all other officers of the Armed Forces except the Chairman of the Joint Chiefs of Staff.

Joint Staff   The Joint Staff, under the Chairman of the Joint Chiefs of Staff, assists the Chairman and the other members of the Joint Chiefs of Staff in carrying out their responsibilities.

The Joint Staff is headed by a Director who is selected by the Chairman in consultation with the other members of the Joint Chiefs of Staff and with the approval of the Secretary of Defense. Officers assigned to serve on the Joint Staff are selected by the Chairman in approximate equal numbers from the Army, Navy, Marine Corps, and Air Force.

Combatant Commands

The combatant commands are military commands with broad continuing missions maintaining the security and defense of the United States against attack; supporting and advancing the national policies and interests of the United States and discharging U.S. military responsibilities in their assigned areas; and preparing plans, conducting operations, and coordinating activities of the forces assigned to them in accordance with the directives of higher authority. The operational chain of command runs from the President to the Secretary of Defense to the commanders of the combatant commands. The Chairman of the Joint Chiefs of Staff serves as the spokesman for the commanders of the combatant commands, especially on the administrative requirements of their commands.

For a complete listing of the combatant commands, including a map of each command's geographic area of responsibility and links to command

Web sites, visit http://www.defense.gov/specials/unifiedcommand/.

Field Activities

Counterintelligence Field Activity The DOD Counterintelligence Field Activity was established in 2002 to build a Defense counterintelligence (CI) system that is informed by national goals and objectives and supports the protection of DOD personnel and critical assets from foreign intelligence services, foreign terrorists, and other clandestine or covert threats. The desired end is a transformed Defense CI system that integrates and synchronizes the counterintelligence activities of the military departments, defense agencies, Joint Staff, and combatant commands.

Defense Technical Information Center The Defense Technical Information Center (DTIC) is a field activity in the Office of the Under Secretary of Defense (Acquisition, Technology, and Logistics). It operates under the authority, direction, and control of the Director, Defense Research and Engineering. DTIC provides defense scientific and technical information, offers controlled access to defense information, and designs and hosts more than 100 DOD Web sites. DTIC's collections include technical reports, summaries of research in progress, independent research and development material, defense technology transfer agreements, and DOD planning documents.

Defense Technology Security Administration The Defense Technology Security Administration (DTSA) is the central DOD point of contact for development and implementation of technology security policies governing defense articles and services and dual-use commodities. DTSA administers the development and implementation of DOD technology security policies on international transfers of defense-related goods, services, and technologies to ensure that critical U.S. military technological advantages are preserved; transfers that could prove detrimental to U.S. security interests are controlled and limited; proliferation of weapons of mass destruction and their means of delivery is prevented; diversion of defense-related goods to terrorists is prevented; legitimate defense cooperation with foreign friends and allies is supported; and the health of the defense industrial base is assured.

Education Activity The Department of Defense Education Activity (DODEA) was established in 1992. It consists of two subordinate organizational entities: the Department of Defense Dependents Schools (DODDS) and the Department of Defense Domestic Dependent Elementary and Secondary Schools (DDESS). DODEA formulates, develops, and implements policies, technical guidance, and standards for the effective management of Defense dependents education activities and programs. It also plans, directs, coordinates, and manages the education programs for eligible dependents of U.S. military and civilian personnel stationed overseas and stateside; evaluates the programmatic and operational policies and procedures for DODDS and DDESS; and provides education activity representation at meetings and deliberations of educational panels and advisory groups.

Human Resources Field Activity The Department of Defense Human Resources Activity (DODHRA) enhances the operational effectiveness and efficiency of a host of dynamic and diverse programs supporting the Office of the Under Secretary of Defense for Personnel and Readiness. The Field Activity supports policy development, performs research and analysis, supports readiness and reengineering efforts, manages the largest automated personnel data repositories in the world, prepares tomorrow's leaders through developmental programs, supports recruiting and retaining talented personnel, and delivers both benefits and critical services to warfighters and their families.

TRICARE Management Activity The TRICARE Management Activity (TMA) was formed in 1998 from the consolidation of the TRICARE Support Office (formerly Civilian Health and Medical Program of the Uniformed Services (CHAMPUS) headquarters), the

Defense Medical Programs Activity, and the integration of health management program functions formerly located in the Office of the Assistant Secretary of Defense for Health Affairs. The mission of TMA is to manage TRICARE; manage the Defense Health Program appropriation; provide operational direction and support to the Uniformed Services in the management and administration of the TRICARE program; and administer CHAMPUS.

Test Resource Management   The Test Resource Management Center (TRMC) is a DOD Field Activity under the authority, direction, and control of the Under Secretary of Defense for Acquisition, Technology, and Logistics. The Center develops policy, plans for, and assesses the adequacy of the major range and test facility base to provide adequate testing in support of development, acquisition, fielding, and sustainment of defense systems. TRMC develops and maintains the test and evaluation resources strategic plan, reviews the proposed DOD test and evaluation budgets, and certifies the adequacy of the proposed budgets and whether they provide balanced support of the strategic plan. TRMC manages the Central Test and Evaluation Investment Program, the Test and Evaluation Science and Technology Program, and the Joint Mission Environment Test Capability Program.

Defense Prisoner of War/Missing Personnel Office   The Defense Prisoner of War/Missing Personnel Office (DPMO) was established in 1993 to provide centralized management of prisoner of war/missing personnel affairs within the DOD. DPMO's primary responsibilities include leadership for and policy oversight over all efforts to account for Americans still missing from past conflicts and the recovery of and accounting for those who may become isolated in hostile territory in future conflicts. The Office also provides administrative and logistical support to the U.S.-Russia Joint Commission on POW/MIAs; conducts research and analysis to help resolve cases of those unaccounted for; examines DOD documents for possible public disclosure; and, through periodic consultations and other appropriate measures, maintains viable channels of communications on POW/MIA matters between DOD and Congress, the families of the missing, and the American public.

Office of Economic Adjustment   The Office of Economic Adjustment (OEA) assists communities that are adversely affected by base closures, expansions, or realignments and Defense contract or program cancellations. OEA provides technical and financial assistance to those communities and coordinates other Federal agencies' involvement through the Defense Economic Adjustment Program.

Washington Headquarters Services
Washington Headquarters Services (WHS), established as a DOD Field Activity on October 1, 1977, is under the authority, direction, and control of the Director of Administration and Management. WHS provides a wide range of administrative and operational services to the Office of the Secretary of Defense, specified DOD components, Federal Government activities, and the general public. This support includes contracting and procurement; Defense facilities management; Pentagon renovation and construction; directives and records management; financial management; library service; human resource services for executive, political, military, and civilian personnel; personnel security services; support for advisory boards and commissions; legal services and advice; information technology and data systems support; enterprise information technology infrastructure services; and planning and evaluation functions.

Defense Media Activity   Defense Media Activity (DMA) gathers and reports Defense news and information from all levels in the Department to the DOD family worldwide through the Armed Forces Radio and Television Network, the Internet, and printed publications. DMA reports news about individual soldiers, sailors, marines, airmen, and Defense civilian employees to the American public through the Hometown News Service. DMA provides World Wide Web infrastructure and services for DOD organizations. It collects, processes, and stores DOD imagery products created by the Department and makes them available to the American public. It trains the Department's public affairs and visual information military and civilian professionals. DMA also operates Stars and Stripes, a news and information organization, free of Government editorial control and censorship for military audiences overseas.

Sources of Information

News Organizations   Official news releases and transcripts of press conferences are available online. Newspapers and radio and television stations may subscribe to receive news releases about individual military members and Defense Department civilian employees at no cost. Phone, 210–925–6541. Email, hometown@dma. mil. Internet, http://www.defense.gov/news/articles.aspx.

Audiovisual Products   Certain Department of Defense productions on film and videotapes, CD–ROMs, and other audiovisual products such as stock footage and still photographs are available to the public. For an up-to-date, full-text, searchable listing of the Department's inventory of photographs and films of operations, exercises, and historical events or for interactive training materials, contact the Defense Imagery Management Center. Phone, 888–743–4662. Email, askdimoc@dma.mil. Internet, http://www.defenseimagery.mil.

Contracts and Small Business Activities   Contact the Director, Small and Disadvantaged Business Utilization, Office of the Secretary of Defense, 3061 Defense Pentagon, Washington, DC 20301–3061. Phone, 703–588–8631.

DOD Directives and Instructions   Contact the Executive Services and Communications Directorate, Washington Headquarters Services, 1155 Defense Pentagon, Washington, DC 20301–1155. Phone, 703–601–4722.

Electronic Access   Information about the following offices is available as listed below:

Office of the Secretary of Defense: Internet, http://www.defense.gov/osd.

Joint Chiefs of Staff: Internet, http://www.jcs.mil.

Central Command: Internet, http://www.centcom.mil.

Combatant Commands: Internet, http://www.defense.gov/specials/unifiedcommand.

European Command: Internet, http://www.eucom.mil.

Joint Forces Command: Internet, http://www.jfcom.mil.

Pacific Command: Internet, http://www.pacom.mil.

Northern Command: Internet, http://www.northcom.mil.

Southern Command: Internet, http://www.southcom.mil.

Strategic Command: Internet, http://www.stratcom.mil.

Transportation Command: Internet, http://www.transcom.mil.

Employment   Positions are filled by a variety of sources. Information concerning current vacancies and how to apply for positions may be found at https://storm.psd.whs.mil. Assistance in applying for positions is also available from our Human Resources Services Center Help Desk at 703–604–6219, 7:30 a.m. to 5:00 p.m. weekdays, or by writing to Washington Headquarters Services, 2521 South Clark Street, Suite 4000, Arlington, VA 22202.

Speakers   Civilian and military officials from the Department of Defense are available to speak to numerous public and private sector groups interested in a variety of defense-related topics, including the global war on terrorism. Requests for speakers should be addressed to the Director for Community Relations and Public Liaison, 1400 Defense Pentagon, Room 2C546, Washington, DC 20310–1400, or by calling 703–695–2733.

Pentagon Tours   For information on guided tours of the Pentagon, send an email using the address below, call 703–697–1776, or write to the Office of the Assistant Secretary of Defense for Public Affairs, 1400 Defense Pentagon, Washington, DC 20301–1400. Email, osd.pentagon.pa.mbx.pentagon-tours-schedule@mail.mil. Internet, https://pentagontours.osd.mil/.

For further information concerning the Department of Defense, contact the Director, Directorate for Public Inquiry and Analysis, Office of the Assistant Secretary of Defense for Public Affairs, 1400 Defense Pentagon, Washington, DC 20301–1400. Phone, 703–428–0711. Internet, http://www.defense.gov.

Department of the Air Force

1690 Air Force Pentagon, Washington, DC 20330–1670
Phone, 703–697–6061. Internet, http://www.af.mil.

Air Force Secretariat

Secretary of the Air Force	DEBORAH LEE JAMES
Under Secretary of the Air Force	ERIC K. FANNING
Deputy Chief Management Officer	DAVID TILLOTSON, III
Deputy Under Secretary, International Affairs	HEIDI H. GRANT
Deputy Under Secretary, Space	TROY E. MEINK
Director, Air Force Small Business Programs	CAROL E. WHITE, *Acting*
Administrative Assistant	PATRICICA J. ZARODKIEWICZ
Auditor General	DANIEL F. MCMILLIN
Assistant Secretary, Acquisition	WILLIAM A. LaPLANTE, JR.
Assistant Secretary, Financial Management and Comptroller	LISA S. DISBROW
General Counsel	GORDON O. TANNER
Assistant Secretary, Installations, Environment and Logistics	MIRANDA A. BALLENTINE
Inspector General	LT. GEN. STEPHEN P. MUELLER
Legislative Liaison	MAJ. GEN. THOMAS W. BERGESON
Assistant Secretary, Manpower and Reserve Affairs	DANIEL R. SITTERLY, *Acting*
Director, Public Affairs	BRIG. GEN. KATHLEEN A. COOK
Information Dominance and Chief Information Officer (SAF/CIO A6)	LT. GEN. MICHAEL J. BASLA

Air Staff

Chief of Staff	GEN. MARK A. WELSH, III
Vice Chief of Staff	GEN. LARRY O. SPENCER
Air Force Sexual Assault Prevention and Response	MAJ. GEN. GINA M. GROSSO
Assistant Vice Chief of Staff	LT. GEN. STEPHEN L. HOOG
Chief Master Sergeant of the Air Force	CMSAF JAMES A. CODY
Deputy Chief of Staff, Manpower, Personnel and Services (A1)	LT. GEN. SAMUEL D. COX
Deputy Chief of Staff, Intelligence, Surveillance and Reconnaissance (A2)	LT. GEN. ROBERT P. OTTO
Deputy Chief of Staff, Operations, Plans and Requirements (A3/5)	LT. GEN. BURTON M. FIELD
Deputy Chief of Staff, Logistics, Installations and Mission Support (A4/7)	LT. GEN. JUDITH A. FEDDER
Deputy Chief of Staff, Strategic Plans and Programs (A8)	LT. GEN. MICHAEL R. MOELLER
Director, Studies and Analyses, Assessments and Lessons Learned (A9)	JACQUELINE R. HENNINGSEN
Assistant Chief of Staff, Strategic Deterrence and Nuclear Integration (A10)	MAJ. GEN. GARRETT HARENCAK
Chief of Chaplains	MAJ. GEN. HOWARD D. STENDAHL

Air Staff

Director, History and Museums Policies and Programs	WALTER GRUDZINSKAS, *Acting*
Judge Advocate General	MAJ. GEN. ROBERT G. KENNEY, *Acting*
Chief of Air Force Reserve	LT. GEN. JAMES F. JACKSON
Scientific Advisory Board	ELIAHU H. NIEWOOD
Chief of Safety	MAJ. GEN. KURT NEUBAUER
Surgeon General	LT. GEN. THOMAS W. TRAVIS
Chief Scientist	MICA R. ENDSLEY-JONES
Test and Evaluation	RANDALL G. WALDER
Director, Air National Guard	LT. GEN. STANLEY E. CLARKE, III

Major Commands

Air Combat Command	GEN. G. MICHAEL HOSTAGE, III
Air Education and Training Command	GEN. ROBIN RAND
Air Force Global Strike Command	LT. GEN. STEPHEN W. WILSON
Air Force Materiel Command	GEN. JANET C. WOLFENBARGER
Air Force Reserve Command	LT. GEN. JAMES F. JACKSON
Air Force Space Command	GEN. WILLIAM L. SHELTON
Air Force Special Operations Command	LT. GEN. ERIC E. FIEL
Air Mobility Command	GEN. PAUL J. SELVA
Pacific Air Forces	GEN. HAWK J. CARLISLE
U.S. Air Forces in Europe	GEN. FRANK GORENC

The Department of the Air Force defends our national interests by retaining air and space superiority; conducting intelligence, surveillance, and reconnaissance; staying rapidly and globally mobile; expanding global strike capabilities; and maintaining command and control systems.

The Department of the Air Force (USAF) was established as part of the National Military Establishment by the National Security Act of 1947 (61 Stat. 502) and came into being on September 18, 1947. The National Security Act Amendments of 1949 redesignated the National Military Establishment as the Department of Defense, established it as an executive department, and made the Department of the Air Force a military department within the Department of Defense (63 Stat. 578). The Department of the Air Force is separately organized under the Secretary of the Air Force. It operates under the authority, direction, and control of the Secretary of Defense (10 U.S.C. 8010). The Department comprises the Office of the Secretary of the Air Force, the Air Staff, and field organizations.

Secretary   The Secretary is responsible for matters pertaining to organization, training, logistical support, maintenance, welfare of personnel, administrative, recruiting, research and development, and other activities prescribed by the President or the Secretary of Defense.

Air Staff   The Air Staff provides professional assistance to the Secretary, the Under Secretary, the Assistant Secretaries, and the Chief of Staff in executing their responsibilities.

Field Organizations   The major commands, field operating agencies, and direct reporting units together represent the field organizations of the Air Force. These are organized primarily on a functional basis in the United States and on a geographic basis overseas. These commands are responsible for accomplishing certain phases of the worldwide activities of the Air Force. They also are responsible for organizing, administering, equipping, and training their subordinate elements for the accomplishment of assigned missions.

Major Commands: Continental U.S. Commands

Air Combat Command   The Air Combat Command operates Air Force bombers and CONUS-based, combat-coded fighter and attack aircraft. It organizes,

DEPARTMENT OF THE AIR FORCE

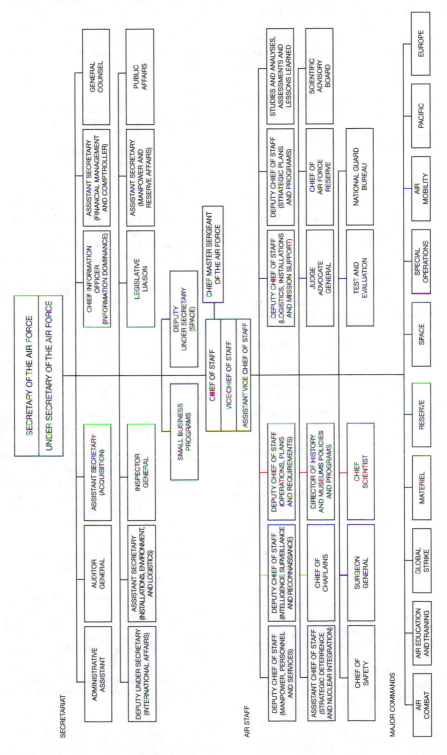

SECRETARIAT

SECRETARY OF THE AIR FORCE

UNDER SECRETARY OF THE AIR FORCE

ADMINISTRATIVE ASSISTANT

AUDITOR GENERAL

ASSISTANT SECRETARY (ACQUISITION)

CHIEF INFORMATION OFFICER (INFORMATION DOMINANCE)

ASSISTANT SECRETARY (FINANCIAL MANAGEMENT AND COMPTROLLER)

GENERAL COUNSEL

DEPUTY UNDER SECRETARY (INTERNATIONAL AFFAIRS)

ASSISTANT SECRETARY (INSTALLATIONS, ENVIRONMENT, AND LOGISTICS)

INSPECTOR GENERAL

LEGISLATIVE LIAISON

ASSISTANT SECRETARY (MANPOWER AND RESERVE AFFAIRS)

PUBLIC AFFAIRS

SMALL BUSINESS PROGRAMS

DEPUTY UNDER SECRETARY (SPACE)

CHIEF MASTER SERGEANT OF THE AIR FORCE

CHIEF OF STAFF

VICE CHIEF OF STAFF

ASSISTANT VICE CHIEF OF STAFF

AIR STAFF

DEPUTY CHIEF OF STAFF (MANPOWER, PERSONNEL, AND SERVICES)

DEPUTY CHIEF OF STAFF (INTELLIGENCE, SURVEILLANCE AND RECONNAISSANCE)

DEPUTY CHIEF OF STAFF (OPERATIONS, PLANS AND REQUIREMENTS)

DEPUTY CHIEF OF STAFF (LOGISTICS, INSTALLATIONS AND MISSION SUPPORT)

DEPUTY CHIEF OF STAFF (STRATEGIC PLANS AND PROGRAMS)

STUDIES AND ANALYSES, ASSESSMENTS AND LESSONS LEARNED

ASSISTANT CHIEF OF STAFF (STRATEGIC DETERRENCE AND NUCLEAR INTEGRATION)

CHIEF OF CHAPLAINS

DIRECTOR OF HISTORY AND MUSEUMS POLICIES AND PROGRAMS

JUDGE ADVOCATE GENERAL

CHIEF OF AIR FORCE RESERVE

SCIENTIFIC ADVISORY BOARD

CHIEF OF SAFETY

SURGEON GENERAL

CHIEF SCIENTIST

TEST AND EVALUATION

NATIONAL GUARD BUREAU

MAJOR COMMANDS

AIR COMBAT

AIR EDUCATION AND TRAINING

GLOBAL STRIKE

MATERIEL

RESERVE

SPACE

SPECIAL OPERATIONS

AIR MOBILITY

PACIFIC

EUROPE

trains, equips, and maintains combat-ready forces for rapid deployment and employment while ensuring strategic air defense forces are ready to meet the challenges of peacetime air sovereignty and wartime air defense.

Internet, http://www.af.mil/AboutUs/FactSheets/Display/tabid/224/Article/104461/air-combat-command.aspx.

Air Education and Training Command The Air Education and Training Command recruits, assesses, commissions, educates, and trains Air Force enlisted and officer personnel. It provides basic military training, initial and advanced technical training, flying training, and professional military and degree-granting professional education. The Command also conducts joint, medical service, readiness, and Air Force security assistance training.

Internet, http://www.af.mil/AboutUs/FactSheets/Display/tabid/224/Article/104471/air-education-and-training-command.aspx.

Air Force Global Strike Command The Air Force Global Strike Command organizes, trains, and equips the Air Force's three intercontinental ballistic missile wings, two B–52 Stratofortress wings, and the only B–2 Spirit wing. These three weapons systems make up two-thirds of the Nation's strategic nuclear triad by providing land-based and airborne nuclear deterrent forces.

Internet, http://www.af.mil/AboutUs/FactSheets/Display/tabid/224/Article/104462/air-force-global-strike-command.aspx.

Air Force Materiel Command The Air Force Materiel Command delivers war-winning expeditionary capabilities through research, development, test, evaluation, acquisition, modernization, and sustainment of aerospace weapon systems throughout their life cycles. Those weapon systems include Air Force fighter, bomber, cargo, and attack fleets and armament. They also include net-centric command and control assets; intelligence, surveillance, and reconnaissance assets; and combat support information systems. In addition, the command oversees basic research and development supporting air, space, and cyberspace capabilities. The command uses an integrated, efficient life cycle management approach in its operations to ensure the best possible support to warfighters while ensuring good stewardship of taxpayer dollars.

Internet, http://www.af.mil/AboutUs/FactSheets/Display/tabid/224/Article/104481/air-force-materiel-command.aspx.

Air Force Reserve Command The Air Force Reserve Command's airmen operate every major Air Force weapons system. The Air Force Reserve provides the Air Force with a surge capacity in times of crisis. Approximately 70,000 citizen airmen from all Air Force specialties are maintained "mission ready" and trained to the same standards as regular Air Force airmen.

Internet, http://www.af.mil/AboutUs/FactSheets/Display/tabid/224/Article/104473/air-force-reserve-command.aspx.

Air Force Space Command The Air Force Space Command provides space and cyberspace capabilities including missile warning, space control, spacelift, satellite operations, and designated cyberspace activities.

Internet, http://www.af.mil/AboutUs/FactSheets/Display/tabid/224/Article/104526/air-force-space-command.aspx.

Air Force Special Operations Command The Air Force Special Operations Command provides the air component of U.S. Special Operations Command, deploying specialized air power and delivering special operations combat power.

Internet, http://www.af.mil/AboutUs/FactSheets/Display/tabid/224/Article/104528/air-force-special-operations-command.aspx.

Air Mobility Command The Air Mobility Command provides airlift, air refueling, special air missions, and aeromedical evacuation for U.S. forces. It also supplies forces to theater commands to support wartime tasking.

Internet, http://www.af.mil/AboutUs/FactSheets/Display/tabid/224/Article/104566/air-mobility-command.aspx.

Major Commands: Overseas Commands

Pacific Air Forces The Pacific Air Forces are responsible for planning, conducting, and coordinating offensive and defensive air operations in the Pacific and Asian theaters.

Internet, http://www.af.mil/AboutUs/FactSheets/Display/tabid/224/Article/104483/pacific-air-forces.aspx.

U.S. Air Forces in Europe The U.S. Air Forces in Europe plan, conduct, control, coordinate, and support air and space operations to achieve United States national and NATO objectives.

Internet, http://www.af.mil/AFSites.aspx?srViewSite=1043.

A list of active Major Commands, Direct Reporting Units, and Field Operating Agencies is available online.

Internet, http://www.af.mil/publicwebsites/index.asp.

Field Operating Agencies

Air National Guard Readiness Center The Air National Guard Readiness Center performs the operational and technical tasks associated with manning, equipping, and training Air National Guard units to required readiness levels.

Internet, http://www.af.mil/AboutUs/FactSheets/Display/tabid/224/Article/104546/air-national-guard.aspx.

Air Force Audit Agency The Air Force Audit Agency provides all levels of Air Force management with independent, objective, and quality audit services that include: reviewing and promoting economy, effectiveness, and efficiency of operations; evaluating programs and activities and assisting management in achieving intended results; and assessing and improving Air Force fiduciary stewardship and the accuracy of financial reporting.

Air Force Civil Engineer Center The Air Force Civil Engineer Center (AFCEC) provides responsive, flexible enterprise-wide installation engineering services, including facility investment planning, design and construction, operations support, real property management, readiness, energy support, environmental compliance and restoration, and audit assertions, acquisition, and program management. AFCEC conducts its operations at more than 75 locations worldwide.

Internet, http://www.af.mil/AboutUs/FactSheets/Display/tabid/224/Article/104487/air-force-civil-engineer-center.aspx.

Air Force Cost Analysis Agency The Air Force Cost Analysis Agency (AFCAA) performs nonadvocate cost analyses for major space, aircraft, and information system programs as required by public law and Department of Defense policy. The agency supports the Air Force-wide cost analysis program by developing and maintaining cost-estimating tools, techniques, and infrastructure. AFCAA provides guidance, analytical support, quantitative risk analyses, and special studies in support of long-range planning, force structure, analysis of alternatives, and lifecycle cost analyses.

Air Force Financial Services Center The Air Force Financial Services Center provides customer service and support to Active Duty and Reserve military and civilian customers throughout the world. The center is responsible for processing temporary and permanent duty travel claims previously performed at base-level Financial Services Offices.

Air Force Flight Standards Agency The Air Force Flight Standards Agency performs worldwide inspection of airfields, navigation systems, and instrument approaches. It provides flight standards to develop Air Force instrument requirements and certifies procedures and directives for cockpit display and navigation systems. It also provides air traffic control and airlift procedures and evaluates air traffic control systems and airspace management procedures.

Air Force Historical Research Agency The Air Force Historical Research Agency serves as a repository for Air Force historical records and provides research facilities for scholars and the general public.

Air Force Intelligence Analysis Agency The Air Force Intelligence Analysis Agency provides national-level intelligence as part of the national intelligence community and tailored intelligence analysis to Air Force headquarters, including authoritative air, air defense, political-military, and strategic products and assessments. The agency is also the Department of Defense's intelligence lead for civilian aviation intelligence analysis. It maintains the HQ USAF Sensitive Compartmented Intelligence Local Wide Area Network components for the National Capital Region, manages physical security requirements, and produces classified media for headquarters staff.

Air Force Intelligence, Surveillance and Reconnaissance Agency   The Air Force Intelligence, Surveillance and Reconnaissance Agency organizes, trains, equips, and presents assigned forces and capabilities to conduct intelligence, surveillance, and reconnaissance for combatant commanders and the Nation through personnel assigned at two wings, two centers, and one intelligence, surveillance and reconnaissance (ISR) group, with locations around the world.

Internet, http://www.af.mil/AboutUs/FactSheets/Display/tabid/224/Article/104553/air-force-isr-agency.aspx.

Air Force Inspection Agency   The Air Force Inspection Agency serves as the primary action arm of the Secretary of the Air Force inspection system. In partnership with the office of Air Force Smart Operations, the agency promotes Air Force Smart Operations for the 21st Century (AFSO21) and provides assistance for process improvement activities.

Internet, http://www.af.mil/AboutUs/FactSheets/Display/tabid/224/Article/104564/air-force-inspection-agency.aspx.

Air Force Installation Contracting Agency   The Air Force Installation Contracting Agency serves as the primary acquisition arm responsible for managing and executing above-wing level operational contracting support activities. It provides responsive enterprise contracting solutions to enable efficient and effective mission and installation operations.

Air Force Legal Operations Agency
The Air Force Legal Operations Agency includes all senior defense counsel,

senior trial counsel, and appellate defense and government counsel in the Air Force, as well as all Air Force civil litigators defending the Air Force against civil law suits claiming damages and seeking other remedies in contracts, environmental, labor, and tort litigation.

Air Force Medical Operations Agency   The Air Force Medical Operations Agency assists the Air Force Surgeon General in developing plans, programs, and policies for the medical service, aerospace medicine, clinical investigations, quality assurance, health promotion, family advocacy, bioenvironmental engineering, military public health, and radioactive material management.

Air Force Medical Support Agency   The Air Force Medical Support Agency provides comprehensive consultative support and policy development for the Air Force Surgeon General in medical force management; and operational support for ground and air expeditionary medical capabilities used in global, homeland security, and force health protection, as well as all aspects of medical and dental services, aerospace medicine operations, and medical support functions.

Air Force Mortuary Affairs Operations
The Air Force Mortuary Affairs Operations is a field operations agency of the Deputy Chief of Staff for Manpower, Personnel and Services that works in support of the entire Department of Defense and other Federal entities. It helps in fulfilling the Nation's commitment of giving dignity, honor, and respect to the fallen and care, service, and support to their families.

Air Force Agency for Modeling and Simulation   The Air Force Agency for Modeling and Simulation implements policies and standards and supports field operations in the areas of modeling and simulation.

Air Force Operations Group   The Air Force Operations Group collects, processes, analyzes, and communicates information, enabling situational awareness of current USAF operations worldwide. This awareness facilitates timely, responsive, and effective decisionmaking by senior USAF leaders and combatant commanders.

Air Force Office of Special Investigations
The Air Force Office of Special Investigations identifies, exploits, and neutralizes criminal, terrorist, and intelligence threats to the U.S. Air Force, Department of Defense and U.S. Government. Its primary responsibilities are criminal investigations and counterintelligence services. The Office protects critical technologies and information; detects and mitigates threats; provides global specialized services; conducts major criminal investigations; and engages foreign adversaries and threats offensively.

Internet, http://www.af.mil/AboutUs/FactSheets/Display/tabid/224/Article/104502/air-force-office-of-special-investigations.aspx.

Air Force Personnel Center The Air Force Personnel Center (AFPC) executes and integrates USAF personnel plans and programs and supervises procedures applicable to the worldwide management and administration of Air Force military and civilian personnel. The center identifies requirements and develops, coordinates, and implements standards, policies, procedures, and actions for assigned personnel and manpower operations. AFPC improves direct combat support and mission effectiveness for Air Force personnel with quality-of-life service programs. The center develops, coordinates, and distributes instructions and procedures that implement policy guidance received from the Deputy Chief of Staff for Manpower, Personnel and Services.

Internet, http://www.af.mil/AboutUs/FactSheets/Display/tabid/224/Article/104554/air-force-personnel-center.aspx.

Air Force Personnel Operations Agency The Air Force Personnel Operations Agency serves as the single Air Force focal point for submission and acceptance of total force human resources information technology requirements.

Air Force Petroleum Agency The Air Force Petroleum Agency is the Air Force service control point for all Defense Logistics Agency fuel-related support issues. The Agency provides a full range of technical and professional services related to fuels, propellants, chemicals, lubricants, gases, and cryogenics for all aerospace vehicles, systems, and equipment.

Internet, http://www.af.mil/AboutUs/FactSheets/Display/tabid/224/Article/104544/air-force-petroleum-agency.aspx.

Air Force Program Executive Offices
The Air Force Program Executive Offices (PEO) are responsible for the execution of a program throughout its lifecycle. While the PEOs are not a specific part of the Air Force headquarters, they have direct reporting responsibilities to the Air Force Service Acquisition Executive and the Assistant Secretary of the Air Force for Acquisition for acquisition- and program-specific issues. The current Air Force PEOs responsible for program execution include areas of aircraft, weapons, command and control, combat support systems, and joint strike fighter.

Air Force Public Affairs Agency The Air Force Public Affairs Agency provides an agile and responsive public affairs capability to the Air Force through three active duty combat camera squadrons, one Reserve combat camera squadron, and four operating locations. It manages the Air Force media center which collects, archives, and distributes Air Force imagery; manages licensing and branding of Air Force trademarks; provides policy guidance and oversight for Air Force public Web site and social media programs; operates the Air Force's official social media program; composes original musical arrangements for Air Force regional bands; and develops training curricula and requirements for the Air Force's nearly 6,000 public affairs practitioners.

Internet, http://www.af.mil/AboutUs/FactSheets/Display/tabid/224/Article/104606/air-force-public-affairs-agency.aspx.

Air Force Review Boards Agency The Air Force Review Boards Agency provides management of various military and civilian appellate processes for the Secretary of the Air Force.

Internet, http://www.af.mil/AboutUs/FactSheets/Display/tabid/224/Article/104511/air-force-review-boards-agency.aspx.

Air Force Safety Center   The Air Force Safety Center's goal is to prevent mishaps and preserve combat readiness by developing, implementing, executing, and evaluating Air Force aviation, ground, weapons, nuclear surety, space, and system programs.

Internet, http://www.af.mil/AboutUs/FactSheets/Display/tabid/224/Article/104488/air-force-safety-center.aspx.

Air Force Security Forces Center   The Air Force Security Forces Center organizes, trains, and equips Air Force security forces worldwide. It develops force protection doctrine, programs, and policies by planning and programming resources to execute the missions of integrated defense operations, nuclear and non-nuclear weapon system security, physical security, combat arms, law enforcement, antiterrorism, resource protection, and corrections.

Air Force Weather Agency   The Air Force Weather Agency provides centralized weather services to the Air Force, Army joint staff, designated unified commands, and other agencies, ensuring standardization of procedures and interoperability within the USAF weather system. It also assesses its technical performance and effectiveness.

Internet, http://www.af.mil/AboutUs/FactSheets/Display/tabid/224/Article/104580/air-force-weather-agency.aspx.

Direct Reporting Units

Air Force District of Washington   The Air Force District of Washington provides support for Headquarters Air Force and other Air Force units in the National Capital Region.

Air Force Operational Test and Evaluation Center   The Air Force Operational Test and Evaluation Center plans and conducts test and evaluation procedures to determine operational effectiveness and suitability of new or modified USAF systems and their capacity to meet mission needs.

Internet, http://www.af.mil/AboutUs/FactSheets/Display/tabid/224/Article/104538/air-force-operational-test-and-evaluation-center.aspx.

U.S. Air Force Academy   The U.S. Air Force Academy provides academic and military instruction and experience to prepare future USAF career officers. The Academy offers Bachelor of Science degrees in 31 academic majors, and upon completion, graduates receive commissions as second lieutenants.

Internet, http://www.usafa.af.mil/.

A list of active direct reporting units and field operating agencies is available online.

Internet, http://www.afhra.af.mil/organizationalrecords/druandfoa.asp.

For further information concerning the Department of the Air Force, contact the Office of the Director of Public Affairs, Department of the Air Force, 1690 Air Force Pentagon, Washington, DC 20330–1670. Phone, 703–697–6061. Internet, http://www.af.mil.

Department of the Army

The Pentagon, Washington, DC 20310
Phone, 703–695–6518. Internet, http://www.army.mil.

Secretary of the Army	JOHN M. MCHUGH
Under Secretary of the Army	BRAD R. CARSON
Assistant Secretary of the Army for Acquisition, Logistics and Technology	HEIDI SHYU
Assistant Secretary of the Army for Civil Works	JO-ELLEN DARCY
Assistant Secretary of the Army for Financial Management and Comptroller	KARL F. SCHNEIDER, *Acting*
Assistant Secretary of the Army for Installations, Energy and Environment	KATHERINE G. HAMMACK

Assistant Secretary of the Army for Manpower and Reserve Affairs	Debra S. Wada
General Counsel	(vacancy)
Administrative Assistant to the Secretary of the Army	Gerald B. O'Keefe
Deputy Under Secretary of the Army	Thomas E. Hawley
Chief Information Officer, G–6	Lt. Gen. Robert S. Ferrell
Inspector General	Lt. Gen. Peter M. Vangjel
Auditor General	Randall L. Exley
Executive Director, Army National Military Cemeteries	Patrick K. Hallinan
Chief of Legislative Liaison	Maj. Gen. William E. Rapp
Director, Small Business Programs	Tracey L. Pinson
Chief of Public Affairs	Brig. Gen. Gary J. Volesky

Office of the Chief of Staff

Chief of Staff, United States Army	Gen. Raymond T. Odierno
Vice Chief of Staff	Gen. John F. Campbell
Director of the Army Staff	Lt. Gen. William T. Grisoli
Vice Director of the Army Staff	Steven J. Redmann

Army Staff

Chief, National Guard Bureau	Gen. Frank J. Grass
Sergeant Major of the Army	SMA Raymond F. Chandler, III
Deputy Chief of Staff, G–1	Lt. Gen. Howard B. Bromberg
Deputy Chief of Staff, G–2	Lt. Gen. Mary A. Legere
Deputy Chief of Staff, G–3/5/7	Lt. Gen. James. L. Huggins, Jr.
Deputy Chief of Staff, G–4	Lt. Gen. Raymond V. Mason
Deputy Chief of Staff, G–8	Lt. Gen. James O. Barclay, III
Chief, Army Reserve	Lt. Gen. Jeffrey W. Talley
Chief of Engineers	Lt. Gen. Thomas P. Bostick
Surgeon General	Lt. Gen. Patricia D. Horoho
Assistant Chief of Staff for Installation Management	Lt. Gen. David D. Halverson
Judge Advocate General	Lt. Gen. Flora D. Darpino
Chief of Chaplains	Maj. Gen. Donald L. Rutherford
Provost Marshal General	Maj. Gen. David E. Quantock
Director, Army National Guard	Maj. Gen. Judd H. Lyons, *Acting*

Commands

Commanding General, U.S. Army Forces Command	Gen. Daniel B. Allyn
Commanding General, U.S. Army Training and Doctrine Command	Gen. David G. Perkins
Commanding General, U.S. Army Materiel Command	Gen. Dennis L. Via

Army Service Component Commands

Commanding General, U.S. Army Pacific	Gen. Vincent K. Brooks
Commanding General, U.S. Army Europe	Lt. Gen. Donald M. Campbell, Jr.
Commanding General, U.S. Army Central	Lt. Gen. James L. Terry
Commanding General, U.S. Army North	Lt. Gen. Perry L. Wiggins
Commanding General, U.S. Army South	Maj. Gen. Joseph P. DiSalvo
Commanding General, U.S. Army Africa/ Southern European Task Force	Maj. Gen. Patrick J. Donahue, II
Commanding General, U.S. Army Special Operations Command	Lt. Gen. Charles T. Cleveland

Army Service Component Commands

Commanding General, U.S. Army Military Surface Deployment and Distribution Command	Maj. Gen. Thomas J. Richardson
Commanding General, U.S. Army Space and Missile Defense Command/Army Strategic Command	Lt. Gen. David L. Mann

Direct Reporting Units

Commanding General, U.S. Army Medical Command	Lt. Gen. Patricia D. Horoho
Commanding General, U.S. Army Intelligence and Security Command	Maj. Gen. Stephen G. Fogarty
Commanding General, U.S. Army Criminal Investigation Command	Maj. Gen. David E. Quantock
Commanding General, U.S. Army Corps of Engineers	Lt. Gen. Thomas P. Bostick
Commanding General, U.S. Army Military District of Washington	Maj. Gen. Jeffrey S. Buchanan
Commanding General, U.S. Army Test and Evaluation Command	Maj. Gen. Peter D. Utley
Commanding General, U.S. Army Installation Management Command	Lt. Gen. David D. Halverson
Superintendent, U.S. Military Academy	Lt. Gen. Robert L. Caslen, Jr.
Director, U.S. Army Acquisition Support Center	Craig A. Spisak
Commanding General, U.S. Army Network Enterprise Technology Command	Maj. Gen. John B. Morrison
Executive Director, Arlington National Cemetery	Patrick K. Hallinan
Commander, U.S. Army Accessions Support Brigade	Col. Brian M. Cavanaugh
Commandant, U.S. Army War College	Maj. Gen. Anthony A. Cucolo, III
Commander, Second Army	Lt. Gen. Edward C. Cardon

The Department of the Army organizes, trains, and equips active duty and reserve forces to preserve peace and security and to defend our Nation. The Army focuses on land operations; its soldiers are trained with modern weaponry and equipment to be ready for rapid response. The Army also administers programs to protect the environment, improve waterway navigation, control floods and beach erosion, and develop water resources. It provides military and natural disaster relief assistance to Federal, State, and local government agencies.

The Continental Congress established the American Continental Army, now called the United States Army, on June 14, 1775, more than a year before the Declaration of Independence. The Department of War was established as an executive department at the seat of government by act approved August 7, 1789 (1 Stat. 49). The Secretary of War was established as its head. The National Security Act of 1947 (50 U.S.C. 401) created the National Military Establishment, and the Department of War was designated the Department

of the Army. The title of its Secretary became Secretary of the Army (5 U.S.C. 171). The National Security Act Amendments of 1949 (63 Stat. 578) provided that the Department of the Army be a military department within the Department of Defense.

Secretary

The Secretary of the Army is the senior official of the Department of the Army. Subject to the direction, authority, and control of the President as Commander

DEPARTMENT OF THE ARMY

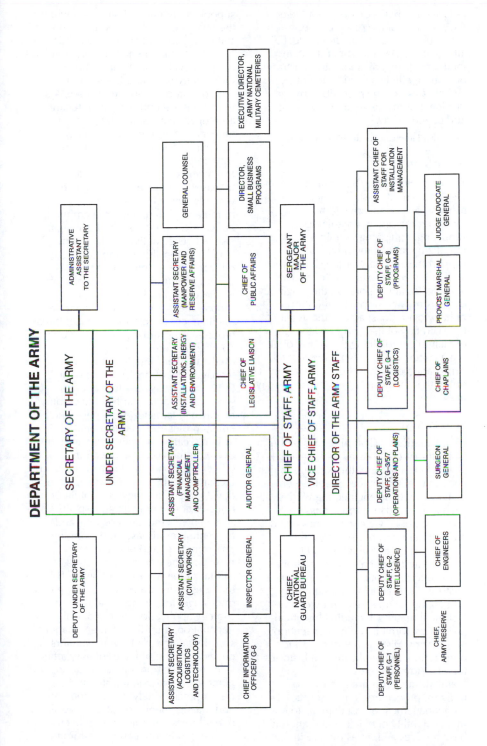

- SECRETARY OF THE ARMY
  - DEPUTY UNDER SECRETARY OF THE ARMY
  - ADMINISTRATIVE ASSISTANT TO THE SECRETARY
- UNDER SECRETARY OF THE ARMY

- ASSISTANT SECRETARY (ACQUISITION, LOGISTICS AND TECHNOLOGY)
- ASSISTANT SECRETARY (FINANCIAL MANAGEMENT AND COMPTROLLER)
- ASSISTANT SECRETARY (CIVIL WORKS)
- ASSISTANT SECRETARY (INSTALLATIONS, ENERGY AND ENVIRONMENT)
- ASSISTANT SECRETARY (MANPOWER AND RESERVE AFFAIRS)
- GENERAL COUNSEL

- CHIEF INFORMATION OFFICER/ G-6
- INSPECTOR GENERAL
- AUDITOR GENERAL
- CHIEF OF LEGISLATIVE LIAISON
- CHIEF OF PUBLIC AFFAIRS
- DIRECTOR, SMALL BUSINESS PROGRAMS
- EXECUTIVE DIRECTOR, ARMY NATIONAL MILITARY CEMETERIES

- CHIEF OF STAFF, ARMY
  - CHIEF NATIONAL GUARD BUREAU
  - SERGEANT MAJOR OF THE ARMY
- VICE CHIEF OF STAFF, ARMY
- DIRECTOR OF THE ARMY STAFF

- DEPUTY CHIEF OF STAFF, G-1 (PERSONNEL)
- DEPUTY CHIEF OF STAFF, G-2 (INTELLIGENCE)
- DEPUTY CHIEF OF STAFF, G-3/5/7 (OPERATIONS AND PLANS)
- DEPUTY CHIEF OF STAFF, G-4 (LOGISTICS)
- DEPUTY CHIEF OF STAFF, G-8 (PROGRAMS)
- ASSISTANT CHIEF OF STAFF FOR INSTALLATION MANAGEMENT

- CHIEF, ARMY RESERVE
- CHIEF OF ENGINEERS
- SURGEON GENERAL
- CHIEF OF CHAPLAINS
- PROVOST MARSHAL GENERAL
- JUDGE ADVOCATE GENERAL

in Chief and of the Secretary of Defense, the Secretary of the Army is responsible for and has the authority to conduct all affairs of the Department of the Army, including its organization, administration, operation, efficiency, and such other activities as may be prescribed by the President or the Secretary of Defense as authorized by law.

For further information, call 703–695–2422.

Army Staff

The Army Staff is the Secretary of the Army's military staff. It makes preparations for deploying the Army, including recruiting, organizing, supplying, equipping, training, mobilizing, and demobilizing it, to support the Secretary or the Chief of Staff in his or her executive capacity; investigates and reports on the efficiency of the Army and its preparation for military operations; acts as the agent of the Secretary of the Army and the Chief of Staff in coordinating the action of all organizations of the Department of the Army; and performs other nonstatutory duties that the Secretary of the Army may prescribe.

Program Areas

Civil Functions   Civil functions of the Department of the Army include the Civil Works Program, the Nation's major Federal water resources development activity involving engineering works such as major dams, reservoirs, levees, harbors, waterways, locks, and many other types of structures; the administration of Arlington and the U.S. Soldiers' and Airmen's Home National Cemeteries; and other related matters.

History   This area includes advisory and coordination service provided on historical matters, including historical properties; formulation and execution of the Army Historical Program; and preparation and publication of histories that the Army requires.

Installations   This area consists of policies, procedures, and resources for the management of installations to ensure the availability of efficient and affordable base services and infrastructure in support of military missions. It includes the review of facilities requirements and stationing, identification and validation of resource requirements, and program and budget development and justification. Other activities include support for base operations; morale, welfare, and recreation; real property maintenance and repair; environmental programs; military construction; housing; base realignment and closure; and competitive sourcing.

Intelligence   This area includes management of Army intelligence with responsibility for policy formulation, planning, programming, budgeting, evaluation, and oversight of intelligence activities. The Army Staff is responsible for monitoring relevant foreign intelligence developments and foreign disclosure; imagery, signals, human, open-source, measurement, and signatures intelligence; counterintelligence; threat models and simulations; and security countermeasures.

Medical   This area includes management of health services for the Army and as directed for other services, agencies, and organizations; health standards for Army personnel; health professional education and training; career management authority over commissioned and warrant officer personnel of the Army Medical Department; medical research, materiel development, testing and evaluation; policies concerning health aspects of Army environmental programs and prevention of disease; and planning, programming, and budgeting for Armywide health services.

Military Operations and Plans   This includes Army forces strategy formation; mid-range, long-range, and regional strategy application; arms control, negotiation, and disarmament; national security affairs; joint service matters; net assessment; politico-military affairs; force mobilization, demobilization, and planning; programming structuring, development, analysis, requirements, and management; operational readiness; overall roles and missions; collective security; individual and unit training;

psychological operations; information operations; unconventional warfare; counterterrorism; operations security; signal security; special plans; equipment development and approval; nuclear and chemical matters; civil affairs; military support of civil defense; civil disturbance; domestic actions; command and control; automation and communications programs and activities; management of the program for law enforcement, correction, and crime prevention for military members of the Army; special operations forces; foreign language and distance learning; and physical security. **Reserve Components** This area includes management of individual and unit readiness and mobilization for Reserve Components, comprising the Army National Guard and U.S. Army Reserve. **Religious** This area includes management of religious and moral leadership and chaplain support activities throughout the Department; religious ministrations, religious education, pastoral care, and counseling for Army military personnel; liaison with ecclesiastical agencies; chapel construction requirements and design approval; and career management of clergymen serving in the Chaplains Corps.

Army Commands

U.S. Army Forces Command
Headquartered at Fort Bragg, NC, U.S. Army Forces Command (FORSCOM) prepares conventional forces to provide a sustained flow of trained and ready land power to combatant commanders in defense of the Nation at home and abroad.

For further information, contact the FORSCOM Public Affairs Office. Phone, 910–570–7225. Internet, http://www.forscom.army.mil.

U.S. Army Training and Doctrine Command
Headquartered in Fort Eustis, VA, U.S. Army Training and Doctrine Command (TRADOC) develops, educates, and trains soldiers, civilians, and leaders; supports unit training; and designs, builds, and integrates a versatile mix of capabilities, formations, and equipment to strengthen the U.S. Army as a force of decisive action.

For further information, contact the TRADOC Public Affairs Office. Phone, 757–501–5876. Internet, http://www.tradoc.army.mil.

U.S. Army Materiel Command U.S. Army Materiel Command (AMC) is the Army's premier provider of materiel readiness—technology, acquisition support, materiel development, logistics power projection, and sustainment—to the total force, across the spectrum of joint military operations. Headquartered at Redstone Arsenal, Alabama, AMC's missions include the development of weapon systems, advanced research on future technologies, and maintenance and distribution of spare parts and equipment. AMC works closely with program executive offices, industry, academia, and other Military Services and Government agencies to develop, test, and acquire equipment that soldiers and units need to accomplish their missions.

For further information, contact the AMC Public Affairs Office. Phone, 256–450–7978. Internet, http://www.army.mil/amc.

Army Service Component Commands

U.S. Army Pacific U.S. Army Pacific (USARPAC) conducts operations to assure, enhance, sustain, and influence military relationships that build partner defense capacity; prepare the force for full spectrum operations; respond to threats; sustain and protect the force; and shape and posture for a stable and secure U.S. Pacific Command area of responsibility. USARPAC carries out a theater security cooperation program of engagement strategy with the 43 Asian and Pacific nations within or bordering its area of responsibility. These countries include the Philippines, Thailand, Vietnam, Japan, Mongolia, Russia, China, South Korea, India, Bangladesh, Australia, New Zealand, Marshall Islands, and Papua New Guinea.

For further information, contact USARPAC. Phone, 808–438–9761. Internet, http://www.usarpac.army.mil.

U.S. Army Europe   U.S. Army Europe (USAREUR) provides the principal land component for U.S. European Command throughout a 51-country area. As the U.S. Army's largest forward-deployed expeditionary force, USAREUR supports NATO and U.S. bilateral, multinational, and unilateral objectives. It supports U.S. Army forces in the European Command area; receives and assists in the reception, staging, and onward movement and integration of U.S. forces; establishes, operates, and expands operational lines of communication; ensures regional security, access, and stability through presence and security cooperation; and supports U.S. combatant commanders and joint and combined commanders.

For further information, contact the USAREUR Public Affairs Office. Phone, 011–49–0611–705–3045 or 3058. Internet, http://www.eur.army.mil.

U.S. Army Central   U.S. Army Central (ARCENT) shapes the U.S. Central Command area of responsibility in 20 countries through forward land power presence and security cooperation engagements that ensure access, build partner capacity, and develop relationships. ARCENT also provides flexible options and strategic depth to the U.S. combatant commander and sets the conditions for improved regional security and stability.

For further information, contact the USARCENT Public Affairs Office. Phone, 803–885–8879. Email, comments@arcent.army.mil. Internet, http://www.arcent.army.mil.

U.S. Army North   U.S. Army North (USARNORTH) supports U.S. Northern Command, the unified command responsible for defending the U.S. homeland and coordinating defense support of civil authorities. USARNORTH helps maintain readiness to support homeland defense, civil support operations, and theater security cooperation activities.

For further information, contact the USARNORTH Public Affairs Office. Phone, 210–221–0015. Email, arnorthpao@conus.army.mil. Internet, http://www.arnorth.army.mil.

U.S. Army South   U.S. Army South (ARSOUTH) is a major subordinate command of U.S. Army Forces Command and is the Army service component command of U.S. Southern Command. ARSOUTH conducts multinational operations and supports security cooperation in the U.S. Southern Command area of responsibility, which encompasses 31 countries and 15 areas of special sovereignty in Central and South America and the Caribbean. These activities counter transnational threats and strengthen regional security in defense of the homeland. ARSOUTH maintains a deployable headquarters at Fort Sam Houston, Texas, where it conducts strategic and operational planning.

For further information, contact the ARSOUTH Public Affairs Office. Phone, 210–216–2497. Email, usarmy.jbsa.arsouth.mbx.pao@mail.mil. Internet, http://www.arsouth.army.mil.

U.S. Army Africa/Southern European Task Force   U.S. Army Africa (USARAF)/Southern European Task Force (SETAF) protects and defends the national security interests of the United States. As the Army Service Component Command for U.S. Africa Command, USARAF/SETAF strengthens land force capabilities of African states and regional organizations, supports U.S. Africa Command operations, and conducts military operations to deter and defeat violent extremist organizations and to create a secure environment in Africa.

For further information, contact the USARAF/SETAF Public Affairs Office. Phone, 011–39–0444–71–7618. Internet, http://www.usaraf.army.mil/.

U.S. Army Special Operations Command   U.S. Army Special Operations Command (USASOC) administers, deploys, educates, equips, funds, mans, mobilizes, organizes, sustains, and trains Army special operations forces to carry out missions worldwide, as directed. These special and diverse military operations support regional combatant commanders, American ambassadors, and other agencies.

For further information, contact the USASOC Public Affairs Office. Phone, 910–432–6005. Email, pao@soc.mil. Internet, http://www.soc.mil.

U.S. Army Military Surface Deployment and Distribution Command   U.S. Army Military Surface Deployment and Distribution Command (SDDC) delivers world-class, origin-to-destination distribution. It is the Army Service Component Command of U.S. Transportation Command and is a subordinate command to Army Materiel Command. SDDC also partners with the commercial transportation industry as the coordinating link between Department of Defense surface transportation requirements and the capability industry provides.

For further information, contact the SDDC Public Affairs Office. Phone, 618–220–6284. Internet, http://www.sddc.army.mil.

U.S. Army Space and Missile Defense Command/Army Strategic Command

U.S. Army Space and Missile Defense Command (SMDC/ARSTRAT) conducts space and missile defense operations and provides planning, integration, control, and coordination of Army forces and capabilities in support of U.S. Strategic Command missions. SMDC/ARSTRAT also supports space, high-altitude, and global missile defense modernization efforts; serves as the Army operational integrator for global missile defense; and conducts mission-related research and development to support Army statutory responsibilities.

For further information, contact the SMDC Public Affairs Office. Phone, 256–955–3887. Internet, http://www.army.mil/info/organization/unitsandcommands/commandstructure/smdc.

Sources of Information

Arlington and Soldiers' and Airmen's Home National Cemeteries For information, write to the Superintendent, Arlington National Cemetery, Arlington, VA 22211. Phone, 703–614–0615. Internet, http://www.arlingtoncemetery. mil/Gallery/Default.aspx?ID=6e883a32-3f06-4e58-b666-55dee37fb6ee.

Army Health Professions Contact the Headquarters U.S. Army Recruiting Command, Health Services Directorate (RCHS–OP), 1307 Third Avenue, Fort Knox, KY 40121. Phone, 502–626–0367. Internet, http://www.goarmy.com/amedd. html.

Army Historical Program For information, write to the U.S. Army

Center of Military History, Collins Hall, 103 Third Avenue, Fort Lesley J. McNair, Washington, DC 20319–5058. Phone, 202–685–2704. Information on the preservation and use of historic buildings is available from the Office of Historic Properties. Phone, 703–692–9892. Email, cmhanswers@conus.army.mil. Internet, http://www.history.army.mil.

Army National Guard Contact the Army National Guard, 1411 Jefferson Davis Highway, Arlington, VA 22202–3231. Phone, 703–627–7273. Internet, http://www.arng.army.mil.

Army Reserve Officers' Training Corps (ROTC) Contact the U.S. Army Cadet Command, Recruiting, Retention and Operations Directorate, ATCC–OP, 55 Patch Road, Fort Monroe, VA 23651. Phone, 757–788–3770. Use the link below to locate a college or university offering the ROTC program in your area. Internet, http://www.goarmy.com/rotc/find-schools.html.

Army Reserve Training Opportunities for Enlisted Personnel and Officers Contact the U.S. Army Human Resources Command, 1600 Spearhead Division Avenue, Fort Knox, KY 40122. Phone, 888–276–9472. Internet, http://goarmyreserve.com. Email, askhrc.army@us.army.mil. Internet, http://www.hrc.army.mil.

Chaplain Recruiting Contact the U.S. Army Recruiting Command, 1307 Third Avenue, Fort Knox, KY 40121–2726. Phone, 502–626–0722 or 866–684–1571. Internet, http://www.goarmy.com/chaplain.

Civilian Employment Contact the civilian personnel advisory center at the desired Army installation or visit the Army civilian personnel Web site. Internet, http://armycivilianservice.com/content/careers.

Contracts For information on contract procurement policies and procedures, contact the Deputy Assistant Secretary of the Army—Procurement, Office of the Assistant Secretary of the Army for Acquisition, Logistics and Technology, 103 Army Pentagon, Washington, DC 20310–0103. Phone, 703–695–2488. Internet, http://www.micc.army.mil/contracting-offices.asp.

Environment Contact the Office of the Deputy Assistant Secretary of the Army for the Environment, Safety and Occupational Health (http://www.asaie. army.mil/Public/ESOH/), or the Army Environmental Policy Institute (http:// www.aepi.army.mil). Use the link below to contact the U.S. Army Environmental Command. Internet, http://www.aec. army.mil.

Films and Videos Address loan requests for Army-produced films to the Visual Information Support Centers of Army installations. Unclassified Army productions are available for sale from the National Audiovisual Center, National Technical Information Service, 5301 Shawnee Road, Alexandria, VA 22312. Phone, 800–553–6847. Email, orders@ ntis.gov. Internet, http://www.ntis.gov/ Index.aspx.

Freedom of Information and Privacy Act Requests Address requests to the Information Management Officer of the Army installation or activity responsible for the desired information. Internet, https://www.rmda.army.mil/.

Judge Advocate General's Corps Contact the Army Judge Advocate Recruiting Office, 9275 Gunston Road, Suite 4440, Fort Belvoir, VA 22060. Phone, 866–276–9524. Internet, http:// www.goarmy.com/jag.

Military Career and Training Opportunities Information on all phases of Army enlistments and specialized training is available from the U.S. Army Recruiting Command, 1307 Third Avenue, Fort Knox, KY 40121–2725. Phone, 877–437–6572. Information on career and training opportunities is available from any of the offices listed in this informational sources section. Internet, http://www.army.mil/join/.

Military Surface Deployment and Distribution Command Information on military transportation news and issues is available online. Internet, http://www. sddc.army.mil/Other/.

Public Affairs and Community Relations For official Army information and community relations information, contact the Office of the Chief of Public Affairs, Department of the Army, 1500 Army Pentagon, Washington, DC 20310–1500.

Phone, 703–697–0050. Automated assistance is also available after normal work hours. Phone, 201–590–6575. Internet, http://www.army.mil/info/ institution/publicAffairs/.

Publications Address requests to either the proponent listed on the title page of the document or the Information Management Officer of the Army activity that publishes the desired publication. Official texts published by Headquarters, Department of the Army, are available from the National Technical Information Service, Department of Commerce, Attn: Order Preprocessing Section, 5301 Shawnee Road, Alexandria, VA 22312. Phone, 800–554–8332. Internet, http:// www.ntis.gov. If the requester does not know which Army activity published the document, contact the Publishing Division, Army Publishing Directorate, Building 1456, 9351 Hall Road, Fort Belvoir, VA 22060–5447. Phone, 703– 693–1557. Internet, http://www.army.mil/ media/publications/.

Research Information on long-range research and development plans concerning future materiel requirements and objectives is available from the Commander, U.S. Army Research, Development and Engineering Command, Attn: AMSRD–PA, 3071 Aberdeen Boulevard, Room 103, Aberdeen Proving Ground, MD 21005. Internet, http://www.army.mil/info/ organization/unitsandcommands/ commandstructure/rdecom/.

Small Business Activities Assistance for small businesses and minority educational institutions to strengthen their participation in the Army contracting program is available through the Office of Small Business Programs, Office of the Secretary of the Army, 106 Army Pentagon, Room 3B514, Washington, DC 20310–0106. Phone, 703–697–2868. Fax, 703–693–3898. Internet, http://www.micc.army.mil/small-business.asp.

Speakers To arrange for an Army speaker to address a civilian organization, contact a nearby Army installation, or write or call the Community Relations Division, Office of the Chief of Public Affairs, 1500 Army Pentagon,

Washington, DC 20310–1500. Address requests for Army Reserve speakers to HQDA (DAAR–PA), Washington, DC 20310–2423, or to the local Army Reserve Center. To arrange for a chaplain to address a civilian organization in the Washington, DC, area, contact the Chief of Chaplains, 2700 Army Pentagon, Washington, DC 20310–2700. Phone, 703–695–1113. Information on speakers is available from the Public Affairs Office, Office of the Chief of Engineers, Washington, DC 20314, or from the nearest Corps of Engineer Division or District Office. Internet, http://www.army. mil/comrel/assetrequests/.

U.S. Military Academy   Contact the Director of Admissions, United States Military Academy, 606 Thayer Road, Building 606, West Point, NY 10996. Phone, 845–938–4041. Email, admissions@usma.edu. Internet, http://www.usma.edu.

For further information concerning the Department of the Army, contact U.S. Army Public Affairs, Community Relations Division, Office of the Chief of Public Affairs, 1500 Army Pentagon, Washington, DC 20310–1500. Internet, http://www.army.mil/info/institution/publicAffairs/.

Department of the Navy
The Pentagon, Washington, DC 20350
Phone, 703–697–7391. Internet, http://www.navy.mil.

Secretary of the Navy	RAYMOND E. MABUS
Under Secretary of the Navy	(VACANCY)
Auditor General	LUTHER BRAGG, *Acting*
Chief of Information	CAPT. DAWN CUTLER, USN, *Acting*
Chief Information Officer	TERRY HALVORSEN
Chief of Legislative Affairs	REAR ADM. MICHAEL T. FRANKEN, USN
General Counsel	PAUL L. OOSTBURG SANZ
Naval Inspector General	VICE ADM. JAMES F. CALDWELL, USN
Judge Advocate General	VICE ADM. NANETTE M. DERENZI, JAGC, USN
Assistant Secretary (Energy, Installations and Environment)	DENNIS V. MCGINN
Assistant Secretary (Financial Management and Comptroller)	SUSAN J. RABERN
Assistant Secretary (Manpower and Reserve Affairs)	JUAN M. GARCIA, III
Assistant Secretary (Research, Development and Acquisition)	SEAN J. STACKLEY
Chief of Naval Research	REAR ADM. MATTHEW L. KLUNDER, USN

Naval Operations

Chief of Naval Operations	ADM. JONATHAN W. GREENERT, USN
Vice Chief of Naval Operations	ADM. MICHELLE J. HOWARD, USN
Master Chief Petty Officer of the Navy	MICHAEL D. STEVENS, USN
Director, Naval Criminal Investigative Service	MARK D. CLOOKIE
Director, Naval Intelligence	VICE ADM. TED N. BRANCH, USN
Director, Naval Nuclear Propulsion Program	ADM. JOHN M. RICHARDSON, USN
Director, Navy Staff	VICE ADM. SCOTT H. SWIFT, USN
Chief of Chaplains of the Navy	REAR ADM. MARK L. TIDD, CHC, USN
Chief of Naval Research/Director, Test and Evaluation and Technology Requirements	REAR ADM. MATTHEW L. KLUNDER, USN
Chief of Naval Reserve	VICE ADM. ROBIN R. BRAUN, USN

Naval Operations

Assistant Chief, Next Generation Enterprise Network System Program Office	VICTOR GAVIN
Deputy Chief of Naval Operations, Integration of Capabilities and Resources	VICE ADM. JOSEPH P. MULLOY, USN
Deputy Chief of Naval Operations, Intelligence Dominance	VICE ADM. TED N. BRANCH, USN
Deputy Chief of Naval Operations, Manpower, Personnel, Education, and Training	VICE ADM. WILLIAM F. MORAN, USN
Deputy Chief of Naval Operations, Fleet Readiness and Logistics	VICE ADM. PHILIP H. CULLOM, USN
Deputy Chief of Naval Operations, Operations, Plans and Strategy	REAR ADM. KEVIN M. DONEGAN, USN, *Acting*
Oceanographer and Navigator of the Navy	REAR ADM. JONATHAN WHITE, USN
Surgeon General of the Navy	VICE ADM. MATTHEW L. NATHAN, MC, USN

Shore Establishment

Chief, Naval Personnel	VICE ADM. WILLIAM F. MORAN, USN
Chief, Bureau of Medicine and Surgery	VICE ADM. MATTHEW L. NATHAN, MC, USN
Commander, Naval Air Systems Command	VICE ADM. DAVID DUNAWAY, USN
Commander, Naval Education and Training Command	REAR ADM. MICHAEL S. WHITE, USN
Commander, Naval Facilities Engineering Command	REAR ADM. KATE L. GREGORY, USN
Commander, Naval Legal Service Command	REAR ADM. JAMES W. CRAWFORD, III, JAGC, USN
Commander, Naval Meteorology and Oceanography	REAR ADM. BRIAN BROWN, USN
Commander, Naval Network Warfare Command	CAPT. JOHN W. CHANDLER, USN
Commander, Naval Sea Systems Command	VICE ADM. WILLIAM H. HILARIDES, USN
Commander, Naval Supply Systems Command	REAR ADM. JONATHAN A. YUEN, SC, USN
Commander, Naval Warfare Development Command	REAR ADM. SCOTT B.J. JERABEK, USNR
Commander, Office of Naval Intelligence	REAR ADM. ELIZABETH L. TRAIN, USN
Commander, Space and Naval Warfare Systems Command	REAR ADM. PATRICK H. BRADY, USN
Director, Strategic Systems Program	REAR ADM. TERRY J. BENEDICT, USN
Superintendent, U.S. Naval Academy	VICE ADM. MICHAEL H. MILLER, USN

Operating Forces

Commander, U.S. Fleet Forces Command	ADM. WILLIAM E. GORTNEY, USN
Commander, Pacific Fleet	ADM. HARRY B. HARRIS, JR., USN
Commander, Military Sealift Command	REAR ADM. THOMAS K. SHANNON, USN
Commander, Naval Forces Central Command	VICE ADM. JOHN W. MILLER, USN
Commander, Naval Forces Europe	ADM. BRUCE W. CLINGAN, USN
Commander, Navy Installations Command	VICE ADM. WILLIAM D. FRENCH, USN
Commander, Naval Reserve Forces Command	REAR ADM. BRYAN CUTCHEN, USN
Commander, Naval Special Warfare Command	REAR ADM. BRIAN L. LOSEY, USN
Commander, Operational Test and Evaluation Force	REAR ADM. JEFFREY R. PENFIELD, USN

[For the Department of the Navy statement of organization, see the Code of Federal Regulations, Title 32, Part 700]

The Department of the Navy protects the United States and its interests by the effective prosecution of war at sea, including the seizure or defense of advanced naval bases with the assistance of its Marine Corps component; supports the forces of all military departments of the United States; and maintains freedom of the seas.

The United States Navy was founded on October 13, 1775, when Congress enacted the first legislation creating the Continental Navy of the American Revolution. The Department of the Navy and the Office of Secretary of the Navy were established by act of April 30, 1798 (10 U.S.C. 5011, 5031). For 9 years prior to that date, by act of August 7, 1789 (1 Stat. 49), the Secretary of War oversaw the conduct of naval affairs.

The National Security Act Amendments of 1949 provided that the Department of the Navy be a military department within the Department of Defense (63 Stat. 578).

The Secretary of the Navy is appointed by the President as the head of the Department of the Navy and is responsible to the Secretary of Defense for the operation and efficiency of the Navy (10 U.S.C. 5031). The Department of the Navy includes the U.S. Coast Guard when it is operating as a Service in the Navy.

Secretary   The Secretary of the Navy is the head of the Department of the Navy, responsible for the policies and control of the Department of the Navy, including its organization, administration, functioning, and efficiency. The members of the Secretary's executive administration assist in the discharge of the responsibilities of the Secretary of the Navy.

Internet, http://www.navy.mil/secnav/.

Legal   The Office of the Judge Advocate General provides all legal advice and related services throughout the Department of the Navy, except for the advice and services provided by the General Counsel. It also provides legal and policy advice to the Secretary of the Navy on military justice, ethics, administrative law, claims, environmental law, operational and international law and treaty interpretation, and litigation involving these issues. The Judge

Advocate General provides technical supervision for the Naval Justice School at Newport, RI.

For further information, contact the Office of the Judge Advocate General, Department of the Navy, Washington Navy Yard, Suite 3000, 1322 Patterson Avenue SE., Washington Navy Yard, DC 20374–5066. Phone, 202–685–5190. Internet, http://www.navy.mil/local/jag/index.asp.

Criminal Investigations   The Naval Criminal Investigative Service provides criminal investigative, counterintelligence, law enforcement, and physical, personnel, and information security support worldwide to Navy and Marine Corps personnel and organizations. The Naval Criminal Investigative Service relies on the professionalism and law enforcement expertise of investigators, crime laboratory technicians, technical investigative specialists, security specialists, and administrative support personnel to carry out its mission.

For further information, contact the Naval Criminal Investigative Service, 27130 Telegraph Road, Quantico, VA 22134. Phone, 877–579–3648. Internet, http://www.ncis.navy.mil.

Research   The Office of Naval Research promotes, plans, initiates, and coordinates naval research, including the coordination of research and development conducted by other agencies and Department of the Navy offices. It also manages and controls activities within or for the Navy relating to patents, inventions, trademarks, copyrights, and royalty payments.

For further information, contact the Public Affairs Office, Office of Naval Research, Ballston Tower One, 800 North Quincy Street, Arlington, VA 22217–5660. Phone, 703–696–5031. Email, onrcsc@onr.navy.mil. Internet, http://www.onr.navy.mil.

Operating Forces   Operating forces carry out operations that enable the Navy to meet its responsibility to uphold and advance the national policies and

DEPARTMENT OF THE NAVY

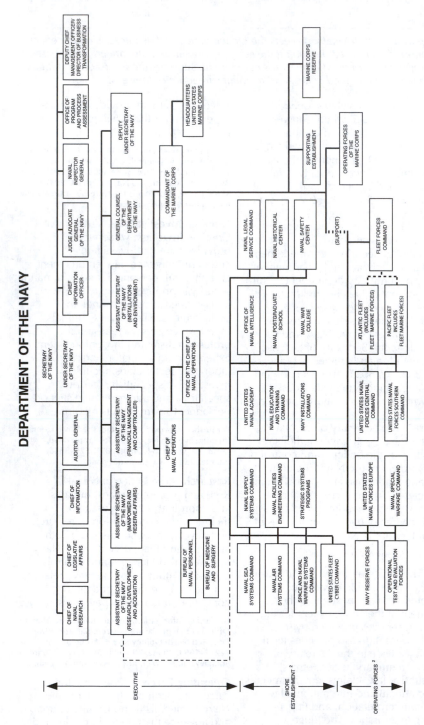

[1] Systems commands and SSP report to ASN (RDA) for acquisition matters only.

[2] Also includes other Echelon 2 commands and subordinate activities under the command or supervision of the designated organizations.

[3] For Interdeployment Training Cycle purposes. Commander, Fleet Forms Command Controls LANFLT and PACFLT assets.

interests of the United States. These forces include the several fleets; seagoing, fleet marine, and other assigned Marine Corps forces; the Military Sealift Command; Naval Reserve forces; and other forces and activities that the President or the Secretary of the Navy may assign. The Chief of Naval Operations administers and commands the operating forces of the Navy.

The Atlantic Fleet is composed of ships, submarines, and aircraft that operate throughout the Atlantic Ocean and Mediterranean Sea.

The Naval Forces Europe includes forces assigned by the Chief of Naval Operations or made available from either the Pacific or Atlantic Fleet to operate in the European theater.

The Pacific Fleet is composed of ships, submarines, and aircraft operating throughout the Pacific and Indian Oceans.

The Military Sealift Command provides ocean transportation for personnel and cargo of all components of the Department of Defense and, as authorized, for other Federal agencies; operates and maintains underway replenishment ships and other vessels providing mobile logistic support to elements of the combatant fleets; and operates ships in support of scientific projects and other programs for Federal agencies.

Other major commands of the operating forces of the Navy are the Naval Forces Central Command, Operational Test and Evaluation Force, Naval Special Warfare Command, and Naval Reserve Force.

Internet, http://www.navy.mil/navydata/organization/orgopfor.asp.

Activities

Air Systems The Naval Air Systems Command provides material support to the Navy and Marine Corps for aircraft, airborne weapons systems, avionics, related photographic and support equipment, ranges, and targets.

For further information, contact the Commander, Naval Air Systems Command, 47123 Buse Road,

Building 2272, Suite 540, Patuxent River, MD 20670–1547. Phone, 301–757–1487. Internet, http://www.navair.navy.mil.

Coast Guard The Commandant of the Coast Guard reports to the Secretary of the Navy and the Chief of Naval Operations when the Coast Guard is operating as a service in the Navy and represents the Coast Guard before the Joint Chiefs of Staff. During such service, Coast Guard operations are integrated and uniform with Department of the Navy operations to the maximum extent possible. The Commandant of the Coast Guard organizes, trains, prepares, and maintains the readiness of the Coast Guard for the performance of national defense missions as directed. The Commandant also maintains a security capability; enforces Federal laws and regulations on and under the high seas and waters subject to the jurisdiction of the United States; and develops, establishes, maintains, and operates aids to maritime navigation, as well as ice-breaking and rescue facilities, with due regard to the requirements of national defense.

Internet, http://www.uscg.mil/.

Computers and Telecommunications
Naval Network Warfare Command operates the Navy's networks to achieve effective command and control through optimal alignment, common architecture, mature processes, and functions and standard terminology. The command enhances the Navy's network security posture and improves IT services through standardized enterprise-level management, network information assurance compliance, enterprise management, and root cause and trend analysis. Naval Network Warfare Command also delivers enhanced space products to operating forces by leveraging Department of Defense, national, commercial, and international space capabilities. The command serves as the Navy's commercial satellite operations manager; it executes tactical-level command and control of Navy networks and leverages Joint Space capabilities for Navy and Joint Operations.

For further information, contact Public Affairs, Naval Network Warfare Command, 112 Lake View Parkway, Suffolk, VA 23435. Phone, 757–203–0205.

Education and Training   The Naval Education and Training Command provides shore-based education and training for Navy, certain Marine Corps, and other personnel; develops specifically designated education and training afloat programs for the fleet; provides voluntary and dependents education; and participates with research and development activities in the development and implementation of the most effective teaching and training systems and devices for optimal education and training.

For further information, contact the NETC Office of Public Affairs, 250 Dallas Street, Pensacola, FL 32508–5220. Phone, 850–452–4858. Email, pnsc. netc.pao@navy.mil. Internet, http://www.navy.mil/ local/cnet/.

Facilities   The Naval Facilities Engineering Command provides material and technical support to the Navy and Marine Corps for shore facilities, real property and utilities, fixed ocean systems and structures, transportation and construction equipment, energy, environmental and natural resources management, and support of the naval construction forces.

For further information, contact the Commander, Naval Facilities Engineering Command and Chief of Civil Engineers, Washington Navy Yard, 1322 Patterson Avenue SE., Suite 1000, Washington, DC 20374–5065. Phone, 202–685–1423. Internet, http://www.navy.mil/local/navfachq/.

Intelligence   The Office of Naval Intelligence ensures the fulfillment of the intelligence requirements and responsibilities of the Department of the Navy.

For further information, contact the Office of Public Affairs, Office of Naval Intelligence, Department of the Navy, 4251 Suitland Road, Washington, DC 20395–5720. Phone, 301–669–5670. Email, pao@ nmic.navy.mil. Internet, http://www.oni.navy.mil.

Manpower   The Bureau of Naval Personnel directs the procurement, distribution, administration, and career motivation of the military personnel of the regular and reserve components of the U.S. Navy to meet the quantitative and qualitative manpower requirements

determined by the Chief of Naval Operations.

For further information, contact the Bureau of Naval Personnel, Department of the Navy, Federal Office Building 2, Washington, DC 20370–5000. Phone, 703–614–2000. Internet, http://www.navy.mil/cnp/ index.asp.

Medicine   The Bureau of Medicine and Surgery directs the medical and dental services for Navy and Marine Corps personnel and their dependents; administers the implementation of contingency support plans and programs to effect medical and dental readiness capability; provides medical and dental services to the fleet, fleet marine force, and shore activities of the Navy; and ensures cooperation with civil authorities in matters of public health disasters and other emergencies.

For further information, contact the Bureau of Medicine and Surgery, Department of the Navy, 2300 E Street NW., Washington, DC 20373–5300. Phone, 202–762–3211. Internet, http://www.med. navy.mil.

Oceanography   The Naval Meteorology and Oceanography Command and the Naval Observatory are responsible for the science, technology, and engineering operations that are essential to explore the ocean and the atmosphere and to provide astronomical data and time for naval and related national objectives. To that end, the naval oceanographic program studies astrometry, hydrography, meteorology, oceanography, and precise time.

For further information, contact the Commander, Naval Meteorology and Oceanography Command, 1100 Balch Boulevard, Stennis Space Center, MS 39529–5005. Phone, 228–688–4384. Internet, http://www.navmetoccom.navy.mil. Contact also the Oceanographer of the Navy, U.S. Naval Observatory, 3450 Massachusetts Avenue NW., Washington, DC 20392–1800. Phone, 202–762– 1026. Internet, http://www.usno.navy.mil/USNO.

Sea Systems   The Naval Sea Systems Command provides material support to the Navy and Marine Corps and to the Departments of Defense and Transportation for ships, submarines, and other sea platforms, shipboard combat systems and components, other surface and undersea warfare and weapons systems, and ordnance expendables not specifically assigned to other system commands.

For further information, contact the Commander, Naval Sea Systems Command, 1333 Isaac Hull Avenue SE., Washington Navy Yard, DC 20376–1010. Phone, 202–781–4123. Email, navsea_publicqueries@navy.mil. Internet, http://www.navsea.navy.mil.

Space and Naval Warfare The Space and Naval Warfare Systems Command provides technical and material support to the Department of the Navy for space systems; command, control, communications, and intelligence systems; and electronic warfare and undersea surveillance.

For further information, contact the Commander, Space and Naval Warfare Systems Command, 4301 Pacific Highway, San Diego, CA 92110–3127. Phone, 619–524–3428. Internet, http://www.spawar.navy.mil.

Strategic Systems The Office of Strategic Systems Programs provides development, production, and material support to the Navy for fleet ballistic missile and strategic weapons systems, security, training of personnel, and the installation and direction of necessary supporting facilities.

For further information, contact the Director, Strategic Systems Programs, Department of the Navy, Nebraska Avenue Complex, 287 Somers Court NW., Suite 10041, Washington, DC 20393–5446. Phone, 202–764–1608. Internet, http://www.ssp.navy.mil.

Supply Systems The Naval Supply Systems Command provides supply management policies and methods and administers related support service systems for the Navy and Marine Corps.

For further information, contact the Commander, Naval Supply Systems Command, 5450 Carlisle Pike, P.O. Box 2050, Mechanicsburg, PA 17055–0791. Phone, 717–605–3565. Email, navsuphqQuestions@navy.mil. Internet, http://www.navy.mil/local/navsup/.

Warfare Development The Navy Warfare Development Command plans and coordinates experiments employing emerging operational concepts; represents the Department of the Navy in joint and other service laboratories and facilities and tactical development commands; and publishes and disseminates naval doctrine.

For further information, contact the Commander, Navy Warfare Development Command, 686 Cushing Road, Sims Hall, Newport, RI 02841. Phone, 401–841–2833. Internet, http://www.navy.mil/local/nwdc/.

Sources of Information

Civilian Employment Information on civilian employment with the Department of the Navy is available from the Office of the Deputy Assistant Secretary of the Navy for Civilian Human Resources. Information on civilian employment opportunities in the Washington, DC, metropolitan area is available from the Secretariat/Headquarters Human Resources Office, Navy Annex, Room 2510, Washington, DC 20370–5240. Phone, 703–693–0888. Internet, http://www.secnav.navy.mil/donhr/Pages/Default.aspx.

Consumer Activities Research programs of the Office of Naval Research cover a broad spectrum of scientific fields. The research is primarily for the needs of the Navy, but some of these programs do research that is relevant to the public. Address inquiries on specific research programs to the Office of Naval Research (Code 10), One Liberty Center 875 N. Randolph Street, Suite 1425, Arlington, VA 22203–1995. Phone, 703–696–5031. Internet, http://www.onr.navy.mil/.

Contracts and Small Business Activities Information on small businesses, minority-owned businesses, and labor surplus activities can be obtained from the Office of Small and Disadvantaged Business Utilization (SADBU), 720 Kennon Avenue SE., Building 36, Room 207, Washington Navy Yard, DC 20374–5015. Phone, 202–685–6485. Email, osbp.info@navy.mil. Internet, http://www.secnav.navy.mil/smallbusiness/pages/index.aspx.

Environment For information on Navy and Marine Corps environmental protection and natural resources management programs, contact the Assistant Secretary of the Navy for Installations and Environment, Environment and Safety, 1000 Navy Pentagon, Room 4A686, Washington, DC 20350–1000. Phone, 703–693–5080. Internet, http://www.secnav.navy.mil/eie/Pages/Environment.aspx.

General Inquiries   Navy recruiting personnel and installation commanders are available to answer general inquiries concerning the Navy, its community, and public information programs. The Office of Information provides accurate and timely information on the Navy so that the general public, the press, and Congress may understand and assess programs, operations, and needs. The Office also coordinates Navy participation in community events and supervises its internal information programs. For general inquiries, contact the Navy Office of Information, 1200 Navy Pentagon, Room 4B463, Washington, DC 20350–1200. Phone, 703–695–0965. Internet, http://www.navy.mil/local/navinfoeast/.

Speakers and Films   For information on speakers, films, and the Naval Recruiting Exhibit Center, contact the Office of Information, Department of the Navy, 1200 Navy Pentagon, Room 4B463, Washington, DC 20350–1200. Phone, 703–695- 0965.

Tours   To broaden the understanding of the mission, functions, and programs of the U.S. Naval Observatory, regular night tours and special day tours for groups are conducted. The night tours require a reservation and are given on alternating Monday nights. For information on observatory activities and public tours, write to the Superintendent, U.S. Naval Observatory, 3450 Massachusetts Avenue NW., Washington, DC 20392–5420. Phone, 202–762–1438. Internet, http://www.usno.navy.mil/USNO/tours-events.

For further information concerning the Navy, contact the Office of Information, Department of the Navy, 1200 Navy Pentagon, Washington, DC 20350–1200. For press inquiries, phone 703–697–7391, or 703–697–5342. Internet, http://www.navy.mil.

United States Marine Corps

Commandant of the Marine Corps, Headquarters, U.S. Marine Corps, 2 Navy Annex (Pentagon 5D773), Washington, DC 20380–1775
Phone, 703–614–1034. Internet, http://www.usmc.mil.

Commandant of the Marine Corps	Gen. James F. Amos, USMC
Assistant Commandant of the Marine Corps	Gen. John M. Paxton, Jr., USMC
Sergeant Major of the Marine Corps	Sgt. Maj. Micheal P. Barrett, USMC
Director, Marine Corps Staff	Maj. Gen. Michael R. Regner, USMC
Director, Command, Control, Communications, and Computers	Brig. Gen. Kevin J. Nally, USMC
Deputy Commandant for Aviation	Lt. Gen. Robert E. Schmidle, USMC
Deputy Commandant for Installations and Logistics	Lt. Gen. William M. Faulkner, USMC
Deputy Commandant for Manpower and Reserve Affairs	Lt. Gen. Robert E. Milstead, Jr., USMC
Deputy Commandant for Plans, Policies, and Operations	Lt. Gen. Ronald L. Bailey, USMC
Deputy Commandant for Programs and Resources	Lt. Gen. Glenn M. Walters, USMC
Counsel for the Commandant	Robert D. Hogue
Staff Judge Advocate for the Commandant	Maj. Gen. Vaughn A. Ary, USMC
Director of Administration and Resource Management	Albert A. Washington
Director of Marine Corps History and Museums	Charles P. Neimeyer
Director of Public Affairs	Brig. Gen. Terry V. Williams, USMC
Director, Special Projects Directorate	Thomas G. Dawson
Legislative Assistant to the Commandant	Brig. Gen. David J. Furness, USMC

Chaplain of the Marine Corps	REAR ADM. MARGARET KIBBEN, CHC, USN
Marine Corps Dental Officer	CAPT. JONATHAN L. HAUN, USMC
Medical Officer of the Marine Corps	REAR ADM. BRIAN PECHA, USN
President, Permanent Marine Corps Uniform Board	COL. TODD S. DESGROSSEILLIERS, USMC
Commanding General, Marine Corps Recruiting Command	MAJ. GEN. MARK A. BRILAKIS, USMC
Commanding General, Marine Corps Combat Development Command	LT. GEN. KENNETH J. GLUECK, JR., USMC
Commander, Marine Corps Systems Commands	BRIG. GEN. FRANCIS L. KELLEY, JR., USMC
Commander, Marine Corps Base Quantico	COL. DAVIS W. MAXWELL, USMC

The Continental Congress established the United States Marine Corps by resolution on November 10, 1775. Marine Corps composition and functions are detailed in 10 U.S.C. 5063.

The Marine Corps, which is part of the Department of the Navy, is the smallest of the Nation's combat forces and is the only service specifically tasked by Congress to be able to fight in the air, on land, and at sea. Although marines fight in each of these dimensions, they are primarily a maritime force, inextricably linked with the Navy to move from the sea to fight on land.

The Marine Corps conducts entry-level training for its enlisted marines at two bases, Marine Corps Recruit Depot, Parris Island, SC, and Marine Corps Recruit Depot, San Diego, CA. Officer candidates are evaluated at Officer Candidate School at Marine Corps Combat Development Command, Quantico, VA. Marines train to be first on the scene to respond to attacks on the United States or its interests, acts of political violence against Americans abroad, disaster relief, humanitarian assistance, or evacuation of Americans from foreign countries.

A complete list of Marine Corps units is available online.

Internet, http://www.marines.mil/Units.aspx.

Sources of Information

General Inquiries Marine Corps recruiting personnel, installation commanders, and Commanding Officers of Marine Corps Districts are available to answer general inquiries concerning the Marine Corps, its community, and public information programs. Internet, http://www.imef.marines.mil/ContactUs.aspx.

Speakers and Films For information on speakers and films, contact the Commandant of the Marine Corps, Headquarters, U.S. Marine Corps (PHC), Room 5E774, The Pentagon, Washington, DC 20380–1775. Phone, 703–614–4309. Internet, http://www.hqmc.marines.mil/cmc/Home.aspx.

Marine Corps Military Career and Training Opportunities The Marine Corps conducts enlisted personnel and officer training programs; provides specialized skill training; participates in the Naval Reserve Officers Training Corps Program for commissioning officers in the Marine Corps; provides the Platoon Leaders Class program for commissioning officers in the Marine Corps Reserve to college freshmen, sophomores, or juniors and the Officer Candidate Class program for college graduates or seniors. Information on these programs is available at most civilian educational institutions and Navy and Marine Corps recruiting stations. Or, write directly to the Marine Corps Recruiting Command, 3280 Russell Road, Quantico, VA 22134–5103. Phone, 703–784–9454. Information on Marine Corps Reserve opportunities can be obtained from local Marine Corps recruiting stations or Marine Corps Reserve drill centers. Or, write directly to the Director, Reserve Affairs, 3280 Russell Road, Suite 507, Quantico, VA 22134–5103. Phone, 703–784–9100. Internet, http://www.marines.com/being-a-marine/marine-corps-careers.

For further information regarding the Marine Corps, contact the Director of Public Affairs, Headquarters, U.S. Marine Corps, 2 Navy Annex (Pentagon 5D773), Washington, DC 20380–1775. Phone, 703–614–1492. Internet, http://www.marines.mil/.

United States Naval Academy

Annapolis, MD 21402–5018
Phone, 410–293–1500. Internet, http://www.usna.edu.

Superintendent	Vice Adm. Michael H. Miller, USN
Commandant of Midshipmen	Capt. Robert E. Clark, II, USN

The U.S. Naval Academy is the undergraduate college of the Naval Service. Through its comprehensive 4-year program, which stresses excellence in academics, physical education, professional training, conduct, and honor, the Academy prepares young men and women morally, mentally, and physically to be professional officers in the Navy and Marine Corps. All graduates receive a bachelor of science degree in 1 of 19 majors.

For further information concerning the U.S. Naval Academy, contact the Superintendent, U.S. Naval Academy, 121 Blake Road, Annapolis, MD 21402–5018. Internet, http://www.usna.edu.

Defense Agencies

Defense Advanced Research Projects Agency

3701 North Fairfax Drive, Arlington, VA 22203–1714
Phone, 703–526–6630. Internet, http://www.darpa.mil.

Director	Arati Prabhakar
Deputy Director	Steven H. Walker

The Defense Advanced Research Projects Agency is a separately organized agency within the Department of Defense and is under the authority, direction, and control of the Under Secretary of Defense (Acquisition, Technology and Logistics). The Agency serves as the central research and development organization of the Department of Defense with a primary responsibility to maintain U.S. technological superiority over potential adversaries. It pursues imaginative and innovative research and development projects, and conducts demonstration projects that represent technology appropriate for joint programs, programs in support of deployed forces, or selected programs of the military departments. To this end, the Agency arranges, manages, and directs the performance of work connected with assigned advanced projects by the military departments, other Government agencies, individuals, private business entities, and educational or research institutions, as appropriate.

For further information, contact the Defense Advanced Research Projects Agency, 3701 North Fairfax Drive, Arlington, VA 22203–1714. Phone, 703–526–6630. Internet, http://www.darpa.mil.

Defense Commissary Agency

1300 E Avenue, Fort Lee, VA 23801
Phone, 804–734–8253. Internet, http://www.commissaries.com.

Director and Chief Executive Officer	Joseph H. Jeu

Deputy Director/Chief Operating Officer	Michael J. Dowling

The Defense Commissary Agency (DeCA) was established in 1990 and is under the authority, direction, and control of the Under Secretary of Defense for Personnel and Readiness and the operational supervision of the Defense Commissary Agency Board of Directors.

DeCA provides an efficient and effective worldwide system of commissaries that sell quality groceries and household supplies at low prices to members of the Armed Services community. This benefit satisfies customer demand for quality products and delivers exceptional savings while enhancing the military community's quality of life. DeCA works closely with its employees, customers, and civilian business partners to satisfy its customers and to promote the commissary benefit. The benefit fosters recruitment, retention, and readiness of skilled and trained personnel.

Sources of Information

Employment information is available at www.commissaries.com or by calling the following telephone numbers: employment (703–603–1600); small business activities (804–734–8000, extension 4–8015/4–8529); contracting for resale items (804–734–8000, extension 4–8884/4–8885); and contracting for operations support and equipment (804–734–8000, extension 4–8391/4–8830).

For further information, contact the Defense Commissary Agency, 1300 E Avenue, Fort Lee, VA 23801–1800. Phone, 800–699–5063, extension 4–8998. Internet, http://www.commissaries.com.

Defense Contract Audit Agency

8725 John J. Kingman Road, Suite 2135, Fort Belvoir, VA 22060–6219
Phone, 703–767–3200. Internet, http://www.dcaa.mil.

Director	Patrick Fitzgerald
Deputy Director	Anita F. Bales

The Defense Contract Audit Agency (DCAA) was established in 1965 and is under the authority, direction, and control of the Under Secretary of Defense (Comptroller)/Chief Financial Officer. DCAA performs all necessary contract audit functions for DOD and provides accounting and financial advisory services to all Defense components responsible for procurement and contract administration. These services are provided in connection with the negotiation, administration, and settlement of contracts and subcontracts to ensure taxpayer dollars are spent on fair and reasonable contract prices. They include evaluating the acceptability of costs claimed or proposed by contractors and reviewing the efficiency and economy of contractor operations. Other Government agencies may request the DCAA's services under appropriate arrangements.

DCAA manages its operations through five regional offices responsible for approximately 104 field audit offices throughout the United States and overseas. Each region is responsible for the contract auditing function in its assigned area. Point of contact information for DCAA regional offices is available at www.dcaa.mil.

For further information, contact the Executive Officer, Defense Contract Audit Agency, 8725 John J. Kingman Road, Suite 2135, Fort Belvoir, VA 22060–6219. Phone, 703–767–3265. Internet, http://www.dcaa.mil.

Defense Contract Management Agency

6350 Walker Lane, Alexandria, VA 22310–3241
Phone, 703–428–1700. Internet, http://www.dcma.mil.

Director	CHARLES E. WILLIAMS, JR.
Deputy Director	JAMES RUSSELL

The Defense Contract Management Agency (DCMA) was established by the Deputy Secretary of Defense in 2000 and is under the authority, direction, and control of the Under Secretary of Defense (Acquisition, Technology, and Logistics). DCMA is responsible for DOD contract management in support of the military departments, other DOD components, the National Aeronautics and Space Administration, other designated Federal and State agencies, foreign governments, and international organizations, as appropriate.

For further information, contact the Public Affairs Office, Defense Contract Management Agency, 6350 Walker Lane, Alexandria, VA 22310–3241. Phone, 703–428–1969. Internet, http://www.dcma.mil.

Defense Finance and Accounting Service

Crystal Mall 3, Room 920, Arlington, VA 22240–5291
Phone, 703–607–2616. Internet, http://www.dfas.mil.

Director	TERESA A. MCKAY
Principal Deputy Director	AUDREY DAVIS

The Defense Finance and Accounting Service (DFAS) was established in 1991 under the authority, direction, and control of the Under Secretary of Defense (Comptroller)/Chief Financial Officer to strengthen and reduce costs of financial management and operations within DOD. DFAS is responsible for all payments to servicemembers, employees, vendors, and contractors. It provides business intelligence and finance and accounting information to DOD decisionmakers. DFAS is also responsible for preparing annual financial statements and the consolidation, standardization, and modernization of finance and accounting requirements, functions, processes, operations, and systems for DOD.

For further information, contact Corporate Communications, Defense Finance and Accounting Service, Crystal Mall 3, Room 924, Arlington, VA 22240–5291. Phone, 703–607–0122. Internet, http://www.dfas.mil.

Defense Information Systems Agency

P.O. Box 4502, Arlington, VA 22204–4502
Phone, 703–607–6900. Internet, http://www.disa.mil.

Director	LT. GEN. RONNIE D. HAWKINS, JR., USAF
Vice Director	REAR ADM. DAVID G. SIMPSON, USN
Chief of Staff	BRIG. GEN. FREDERICK A. HENRY, USA
Senior Enlisted Advisor	SGT. MAJ. ANTONIO N. VIZCARRONDO, JR., USMC

The Defense Information Systems Agency (DISA), established originally as the Defense Communications Agency in 1960, is under the authority, direction, and control of the Assistant Secretary of Defense (Networks and Information Integration). DISA is a combat support agency responsible for planning, engineering, acquiring, fielding, operating, and supporting global net-centric solutions to serve the needs of the President, Vice President, Secretary of Defense, and other DOD components.

For further information, contact the Public Affairs Office, Defense Information Systems Agency, P.O. Box 4502, Arlington, VA 22204–4502. Phone, 703–607–6900. Internet, http://www.disa.mil.

Defense Intelligence Agency

The Pentagon, Washington, DC 20340–5100
Phone, 703–695–0071. Internet, http://www.dia.mil.

Director	Lt. Gen. Michael T. Flynn, USA
Deputy Director	David R. Shedd
Senior Enlisted Advisor	Chief Master Sgt. Roddy D. Hartsook, USAF

The Defense Intelligence Agency (DIA) was established in 1961 and is under the authority, direction, and control of the Under Secretary of Defense for Intelligence. DIA provides timely, objective, and cogent military intelligence to warfighters, force planners, as well as defense and national security policymakers. DIA obtains and reports information through its field sites worldwide and the Defense Attache System; provides timely intelligence analysis; directs Defense Human Intelligence programs; operates the Joint Intelligence Task Force for Combating Terrorism and the Joint Military Intelligence College; coordinates and facilitates Measurement and Signature Intelligence activities; manages and plans collections from specialized technical sources; manages secure DOD intelligence networks; and coordinates required intelligence support for the Secretary of Defense, Joint Chiefs of Staff, Combatant Commanders, and Joint Task Forces.

For further information, contact the Public Affairs Office, Defense Intelligence Agency, Washington, DC 20340–5100. Phone, 703–695–0071. Internet, http://www.dia.mil.

Defense Legal Services Agency

The Pentagon, Washington, DC 20301–1600
Phone, 703–695–3341. Internet, http://www.dod.mil/dodgc.

Director (General Counsel)	Robert S. Taylor, *Acting*
Principal Deputy General Counsel	Robert S. Taylor

The Defense Legal Services Agency (DLSA) was established in 1981 and is under the authority, direction, and control of the General Counsel of the Department of Defense, who also serves as its Director. DLSA provides legal advice and services for specified DOD components and adjudication of personnel security cases for DOD and other assigned Federal agencies and departments. It also provides technical support and assistance for development of the Department's legislative program; coordinates positions on legislation and Presidential Executive orders; provides a centralized legislative and congressional document reference and distribution point for the Department; maintains the Department's historical legislative files; and administers programs governing standards of conduct and alternative dispute resolution.

For further information, contact the Administrative Office, Defense Legal Services Agency, Room 3A734, Washington, DC 20301–1600. Phone, 703–697–8343. Internet, http://www.dod.mil/dodgc.

Defense Logistics Agency
8725 John J. Kingman Road, Fort Belvoir, VA 22060–6221
Phone, 703–767–6200. Internet, http://www.dla.mil.

Director	VICE ADM. MARK D. HARNITCHEK, USN
Vice Director	EDWARD J. CASE
Chief of Staff	RENEE L. ROMAN
Senior Enlisted Advisor	COMMAND SGT. MAJ. SULTAN A. MUHAMMAD, USA

The Defense Logistics Agency (DLA) is under the authority, direction, and control of the Under Secretary of Defense for Acquisition, Technology, and Logistics. DLA supports both the logistics requirements of the military services and their acquisition of weapons and other materiel. It provides logistics support and technical services to all branches of the military and to a number of Federal agencies. DLA supply centers consolidate the requirements of the military services and procure the supplies in sufficient quantities to meet their projected needs. DLA manages supplies in eight commodity areas: fuel, food, clothing, construction material, electronic supplies, general supplies, industrial supplies, and medical supplies. Information on DLA's field activities and regional commands is available at www.dla.mil/ataglance.aspx.

Sources of Information

Employment For the Washington, DC, metropolitan area, all inquiries and applications concerning job recruitment programs should be addressed to Human Resources, Customer Support Office, 3990 East Broad Street, Building 11, Section 3, Columbus, OH, 43213–0919. Phone, 877–352–4762.

Environmental Program For information concerning the environmental program, contact the Staff Director, Environmental and Safety, Defense Logistics Agency, Attn: DSS–E, 8725 John J. Kingman Road, Fort Belvoir, VA 22060–6221. Phone, 703–767–6278.

Procurement and Small Business Activities For information concerning procurement and small business activities, contact the Director, Small and Disadvantaged Business Utilization, Defense Logistics Agency, Attn: DB, 8725 John J. Kingman Road, Fort Belvoir, VA 22060–6221. Phone, 703–767–0192.

Surplus Sales Program Questions concerning this program should be addressed to DOD Surplus Sales, International Sales Office, 74 Washington Avenue North, Battle Creek, MI 49017–3092. Phone, 877–352–2255.

For further information, contact the Defense Logistics Agency, 8725 John J. Kingman Road, Fort Belvoir, VA 22060–6221. Phone, 703–767–5200. Internet, http://www.dla.mil.

Defense Security Cooperation Agency
2800 Defense Pentagon, Washington, DC 20301–2800
Phone, 703–601–3700. Internet, http://www.dsca.mil.

Director	VICE ADM. WILLIAM E. LANDAY, III, USN
Deputy Director	RICHARD A. GENAILLE, JR.

The Defense Security Cooperation Agency (DSCA) was established in 1971 and is under the authority, direction, and control of the Under Secretary of Defense (Policy). DSCA provides traditional security assistance functions such as military assistance, international military education and training, and foreign military sales. DSCA also has program management responsibilities for humanitarian assistance, demining, and other DOD programs.

For further information, contact the Defense Security Cooperation Agency, 2800 Defense Pentagon, Washington, DC 20301–2800. Phone, 703–601–3700. Email, lpa-web@dsca.mil. Internet, http://www.dsca.mil.

Defense Security Service

1340 Braddock Place, Alexandria, VA 22314–1651
Phone, 703–325–9471. Internet, http://www.dss.mil.

Director	STANLEY L. SIMS
Deputy Director	JAMES J. KREN

The Defense Security Service (DSS) is under the authority, direction, and control of the Under Secretary of Defense for Intelligence. DSS ensures the safeguarding of classified information used by contractors on behalf of the DOD and 22 other executive branch agencies under the National Industrial Security Program. It oversees the protection of conventional arms, munitions, and explosives in the custody of DOD contractors; evaluates the protection of selected private sector critical assets and infrastructures (physical and cyber-based systems) and recommends measures needed to maintain operations identified as vital to DOD. DSS makes clearance determinations for industry and provides support services for DOD Central Adjudicative Facilities. It provides security education, training, and proactive awareness programs for military, civilian, and cleared industry to enhance their proficiency and awareness of DOD security policies and procedures. DSS also has a counterintelligence office to integrate counterintelligence principles into security countermeasures missions and to support the national counterintelligence strategy. Information on DSS operating locations and centers is available at http://www.dss.mil/isp/dss_oper_loc.html.

For further information, contact the Defense Security Service, Office of Congressional and Public Affairs, 1340 Braddock Place, Alexandria, VA 22314–1651. Phone, 703–325–9471. Internet, http://www.dss.mil.

Defense Threat Reduction Agency

8725 John J. Kingman Road, MS 6201, Fort Belvoir, VA 22260–5916
Phone, 703–325–2102. Internet, http://www.dtra.mil.

Director	KENNETH A. MEYERS
Deputy Director	MAJ. GEN. JAY G. SANTEE, USAF

The Defense Threat Reduction Agency (DTRA) was established in 1998 and is under the authority, direction, and control of the Under Secretary of Defense for Acquisition, Technology, and Logistics. DTRA's mission is to reduce the threat posed by weapons of mass destruction (WMD). DTRA covers the full range of WMD threats (chemical, biological, nuclear, radiological, and high explosive), bridges the gap between the warfighters and the technical community, sustains the nuclear deterrent, and provides both offensive and defensive technology and operational concepts to warfighters. DTRA reduces the threat of WMD by implementing arms control treaties and executing the Cooperative Threat Reduction Program. It uses combat support, technology development, and chemical-biological defense to deter the use and reduce the impact of such weapons. DTRA also prepares for future threats by developing the technology and concepts needed to counter new WMD threats and adversaries.

For further information, contact the Public Affairs Office, Defense Threat Reduction Agency, 8725 John J. Kingman Road, MS 6201, Fort Belvoir, VA 22060–5916. Phone, 703–767–5870. Internet, http://www.dtra.mil.

Missile Defense Agency

The Pentagon, Washington, DC 20301–7100
Phone, 703–695–6420. Internet, http://www.mda.mil.

Director	Vice Adm. James D. Syring, USN
Deputy Director	Maj. Gen. Samuel A. Greaves, USAF
Executive Director	John H. James, Jr.

[For the Missile Defense Agency statement of organization, see the Code of Federal Regulations, Title 32, Part 388]

The Missile Defense Agency's (MDA) mission is to establish and deploy a layered ballistic missile defense system to intercept missiles in all phases of their flight and against all ranges of threats. This capability will provide a defense of the United States, deployed forces, and allies. MDA is under the authority, direction, and control of the Under Secretary of Defense for Acquisition, Technology, and Logistics. MDA manages and directs DOD's ballistic missile defense acquisition programs and enables the Services to field elements of the overall system as soon as practicable. MDA develops and tests technologies and, if necessary, uses prototype and test assets to provide early capability. Additionally, MDA improves the effectiveness of deployed capabilities by implementing new technologies as they become available or when the threat warrants an accelerated capability.

For further information, contact the Human Resources Directorate, Missile Defense Agency, Washington, DC 20301–7100. Phone, 703–614–8740. Internet, http://www.mda.mil.

National Geospatial-Intelligence Agency

4600 Sangamore Road, Bethesda, MD 20816–5003
Phone, 301–227–7300. Internet, http://www.nga.mil.

Director	Letitia A. Long
Deputy Director	Michael A. Rodrigue
Chief Operating Officer	Ellen E. McCarthy
Military Support Director	Rear Adm. Thomas L. Brown, II, USN

The National Geospatial-Intelligence Agency (NGA), formerly the National Imagery and Mapping Agency, was established in 1996 and is under the authority, direction, and control of the Under Secretary of Defense for Intelligence. NGA is a DOD combat support agency and a member of the national intelligence community. NGA's mission is to provide timely, relevant, and accurate geospatial intelligence in support of our national security. Geospatial intelligence means the use and analysis of imagery to describe, assess, and visually depict physical features and geographically referenced activities on the Earth. Headquartered in Bethesda, MD, NGA has major facilities in the Washington, DC, Northern Virginia, and St. Louis, MO, areas with NGA support teams worldwide.

For further information, contact the Public Affairs Office, National Geospatial-Intelligence Agency, 4600 Sangamore Road, Bethesda, MD 20816–5003. Phone, 301–227–2057. Fax, 301–227–3920. Internet, http://www.nga.mil.

National Security Agency / Central Security Service

Fort George G. Meade, MD 20755–6248
Phone, 301–688–6524. Internet, http://www.nsa.gov.

Director	Gen. Keith B. Alexander, USA
Deputy Director	John C. Inglis

The National Security Agency (NSA) was established in 1952 and the Central Security Service (CSS) was established in 1972. NSA/CSS is under the authority, direction, and control of the Under Secretary of Defense for Intelligence. As the Nation's cryptologic organization, NSA/CSS employs the Nation's premier codemakers and codebreakers. It ensures an informed, alert, and secure environment for U.S. warfighters and policymakers. The cryptologic resources of NSA/CSS unite to provide U.S. policymakers with intelligence information derived from America's adversaries while protecting U.S. Government signals and information systems from exploitation by those same adversaries.

For further information, contact the Public Affairs Office, National Security Agency/Central Security Service, Fort George G. Meade, MD 20755–6248. Phone, 301–688–6524. Internet, http://www.nsa.gov.

Pentagon Force Protection Agency

Washington, DC 20301
Phone, 703–693–3685. Internet, http://www.pfpa.mil.

Director	Steven E. Calvery
Principal Deputy Director	Jonathan H. Cofer
Assistant Director, Law Enforcement	James R. Knodell

The Pentagon Force Protection Agency (PFPA) was established in May 2002 in response to the events of September 11, 2001, and subsequent terrorist threats facing the DOD workforce and facilities in the National Capital Region (NCR). PFPA is under the authority, direction, and control of the Director, Administration and Management, in the Office of the Secretary of Defense. PFPA provides force protection, security, and law enforcement for the people, facilities, infrastructure, and other resources at the Pentagon and for DOD activities and facilities within the NCR that are not under the jurisdiction of a military department. Consistent with the national strategy on combating terrorism, PFPA addresses threats, including chemical, biological, and radiological agents, through a strategy of prevention, preparedness, detection, and response to ensure that the DOD workforce and facilities in the NCR are secure and protected.

For further information, contact the Pentagon Force Protection Agency, Washington, DC 20301. Phone, 703–693–3685. Internet, http://www.pfpa.mil.

Joint Service Schools

Defense Acquisition University

9820 Belvoir Road, Fort Belvoir, VA 22060–5565
Phone, 703–805–2764. Internet, http://www.dau.mil.

President	James P. Woosley

The Defense Acquisition University (DAU), established pursuant to the Defense Acquisition Workforce Improvement Act of 1990 (10 U.S.C. 1701 note), serves as the DOD center for acquisition, technology, and logistics training; performance support; continuous learning; and knowledge sharing. DAU is a unified structure with five regional campuses and the Defense Systems Management College-School of Program Managers, which provides executive and international acquisition training. DAU's mission is to provide the training, career management, and services that enable the acquisition, technology, and logistics community to make smart business decisions and deliver timely and affordable capabilities to warfighters.

For further information, contact the Director, Operations Support Group, Defense Acquisition University, 9820 Belvoir Road, Fort Belvoir, VA 22060–5565. Phone, 800–845–7606. Internet, http://www.dau.mil.

National Intelligence University

Defense Intelligence Analysis Center, Washington, DC 20340–5100
Phone, 202–231–5466. Internet, http://www.ni-u.edu.

President	REAR ADM. DAVID R. ELLISON, USN

The National Intelligence University, formerly the Joint Military Intelligence College, was established in 1962. The College is a joint service interagency educational institution serving the intelligence community and operates under the authority of the Director, Defense Intelligence Agency. Its mission is to educate military and civilian intelligence professionals, conduct and disseminate relevant intelligence research, and perform academic outreach regarding intelligence matters. The College is authorized by Congress to award the bachelor of science in intelligence, master of science and technology intelligence, and master of science of strategic intelligence. Courses are offered to full-time students in a traditional daytime format and for part-time students in the evening, on Saturday, and in an executive format (one weekend per month and a 2-week intensive summer period).

For further information, contact the Admissions Office, National Intelligence University, 200 MacDill Blvd (MCA–2), Washington, DC 20340–5100. Phone, 202–231–5466 or 202–231–3319. Internet, http://www.ni-u.edu.

National Defense University

300 Fifth Avenue, Building 62, Fort McNair, Washington, DC 20319–5066
Phone, 202–685–2649. Internet, http://www.ndu.edu.
The National War College: 300 D Street SW., Building 61, Fort McNair, Washington, DC 20319–5078
Phone, 202–685–3674. Fax, 202–685–6461. Internet, http://www.ndu.edu/nwc/.
Industrial College of the Armed Forces: 408 Fourth Avenue, Building 59, Fort McNair, Washington, DC 20319–5062
Phone, 202–685–4333. Internet, http://www.ndu.edu/icaf/.
Joint Forces Staff College: 7800 Hampton Boulevard, Norfolk, VA 23511–1702
Phone, 757–443–6124. Internet, http://www.jfsc.ndu.edu.
Information Resources Management College: 300 Fifth Avenue, Building 62, Fort McNair, Washington, DC 20319–5066
Phone, 202–685–6300. Internet, http://www.ndu.edu/iCollege/.
College of International Security Affairs: 300 Fifth Avenue, Fort McNair, Washington, DC 20319–5066
Phone, 202–685–7773. Internet, http://www.ndu.edu/cisa.

President, National Defense University	WANDA L. NESBITT, *Acting*
Commandant, National War College	BRIG. GEN. GUY T. COSENTINOUSA
Commandant, Dwight D. Eisenhower School for National Security and Resource Strategy	GEN. THOMAS GORRYUSMC
Commandant, Joint Forces Staff College	REAR ADMIRAL JOHN W. SMITH, JR., USN
Chancellor, Information Resources Management College	MARY S. MCCULLYACTING
Chancellor, College of International Security Affairs	MICHAEL S. BELL

National Defense University

The mission of the National Defense University is to prepare military and civilian leaders from the United States and other countries to evaluate national and international security challenges through multidisciplinary educational and research programs, professional exchanges, and outreach.

The National Defense University was established in 1976 and incorporates the following colleges and programs: the Industrial College of the Armed Forces, the National War College, the Joint Forces Staff College, the Information Resources Management College, the College of International Security Affairs, the Institute for National Strategic Studies, the Center for the Study of Weapons of Mass Destruction, the Center for Technology and National Security Policy, the International Student Management Office, the Joint Reserve Affairs Center, CAPSTONE, the Security of Defense Corporate Fellows Program, the NATO Education Center, the Institute for National Security Ethics and Leadership, the Center for Joint Strategic Logistics Excellence, the Center for Applied Strategic Leaders, and the Center for Complex Operations.

For further information, contact the Human Resources Directorate, National Defense University, 300 Fifth Avenue, Building 62, Fort McNair, Washington, DC 20319–5066. Phone, 202–685–2169. Internet, http://www.ndu.edu.

National War College The National War College provides education in national security policy to selected military officers and career civil service employees of Federal departments and agencies concerned with national security. It is the only senior service college with the primary mission of offering a course of study that emphasizes national security policy formulation and the planning and implementation of national strategy. Its 10-month academic program is an issue-centered study in U.S. national security. The elective program is designed to permit each student to tailor his or her academic experience to meet individual professional development needs.

For further information, contact the Department of Administration, The National War College, 300 D Street SW., Fort McNair, Washington, DC 20319–5078. Phone, 202–685–3674. Internet, http://www.ndu.edu/nwc/.

Dwight D. Eisenhower School for National Security and Resource Strategy
The Industrial College of the Armed Forces is an educational institution that prepares selected military and civilians for strategic leadership and success in developing our national security strategy and in evaluating, marshalling, and managing resources in the execution of that strategy. The College offers an education in the understanding of the importance of industry to our national security strategy, and more importantly the resource component of national security. The rigorous, compressed curriculum, completed in two semesters, leads to a master of science degree in national resource strategy.

For further information, contact the Director of Operations, Industrial College of the Armed Forces, 408 Fourth Avenue, Building 59, Fort McNair, Washington, DC 20319–5062. Phone, 202–685–4333. Internet, http://www.ndu.edu/icaf/.

Joint Forces Staff College The Joint Forces Staff College (JFSC) is an intermediate- and senior-level joint college in the professional military education system dedicated to the study of the principles, perspectives, and techniques of joint operational-level planning and warfare. The mission of JFSC is to educate national security professionals in the planning and execution of joint, multinational, and interagency operations in order to instill a primary commitment to joint, multinational, and interagency teamwork, attitudes, and perspectives. The College accomplishes this mission through four schools: the Joint Advanced Warfighters School, the Joint and Combined Warfighting School, the Joint Continuing and Distance Education School, and the Joint Command, Control, and Information Operations School.

For further information, contact the Public Affairs Officer, Joint Forces Staff College, 7800 Hampton Boulevard, Norfolk, VA 23511–1702. Phone, 757–443–6212. Fax, 757–443–6210. Internet, http://www.jfsc.ndu.edu.

Information Resources Management College The Information Resources Management College provides graduate-level courses in information resources management. The College prepares leaders to direct the information component of national power by leveraging information and information technology for strategic advantage.

The College's primary areas of concentration include policy, strategic planning, leadership/management, process improvement, capital planning and investment, performance- and results-based management, technology assessment, architecture, information assurance and security, acquisition, domestic preparedness, transformation, e-Government, and information operations.

For further information, contact the Office of Student Services, Information Resources Management College, 300 Fifth Avenue, Fort McNair, Washington, DC 20319–5066. Phone, 202–685–6300. Internet, http://www.ndu.edu/irmc.

College of International Security Affairs The College of International Security Affairs (CISA) is one of NDU's five colleges. CISA educates students from across the international, interagency, and interservice communities. CISA's primary areas of concentration include counterterrorism, conflict management of stability of operations, homeland security, and defense and international security studies. CISA is also home to NDU's International Counterterrorism Fellowship Program.

For further information, contact the Office of Academic Affairs, College of International Security Affairs, 300 Fifth Avenue, Fort McNair, Washington, DC 20319–5066. Phone, 202–685–7773. Internet, http://www.ndu.edu/cisa.

Uniformed Services University of the Health Sciences

4301 Jones Bridge Road, Bethesda, MD 20814–4799
Phone, 301–295–3190. Internet, http://www.usuhs.mil.

President   CHARLES L. RICE

Authorized by act of September 21, 1972 (10 U.S.C. 2112), the Uniformed Services University of the Health Sciences was established to educate career-oriented medical officers for the Military Departments and the Public Health Service. The University currently incorporates the F. Edward Hebert School of Medicine (including graduate and continuing education programs) and the Graduate School of Nursing.

Students are selected by procedures recommended by the Board of Regents and prescribed by the Secretary of Defense. The actual selection is carried out by a faculty committee on admissions and is based upon motivation and dedication to a career in the uniformed services and an overall appraisal of the personal and intellectual characteristics of the candidates without regard to sex, race, religion, or national origin. Applicants must be U.S. citizens.

Medical school matriculants will be commissioned officers in one of the uniformed services. They must meet the physical and personal qualifications for such a commission and must give evidence of a strong commitment to serving as a uniformed medical officer. The graduating medical student is required to serve a period of obligation of not less than 7 years, excluding graduate medical education.

Students of the Graduate School of Nursing must be commissioned officers of the Army, Navy, Air Force, or Public Health Service prior to application. Graduate nursing students must serve a commitment determined by their respective service.

For further information, contact the President, Uniformed Services University of the Health Sciences, 4301 Jones Bridge Road, Bethesda, MD 20814–4799. Phone, 301–295–3013. Internet, http://www.usuhs.mil.

DEPARTMENT OF EDUCATION

400 Maryland Avenue SW., Washington, DC 20202
Phone, 202–401–2000. TTY, 800–437–0833. Internet, http://www.ed.gov.

Secretary of Education	ARNE DUNCAN
Deputy Secretary	JAMES H. SHELTON, III
Chief of Staff	EMMA VADEHRA
Assistant Secretary for Communication and Outreach	MASSIE RITSCH
Assistant Secretary for Planning, Evaluation and Policy Development	GABRIELLA GOMEZ, *Acting*
General Counsel	PHILIP ROSENFELT, *Acting*
Inspector General	KATHLEEN S. TIGHE
Director, Institute of Education Sciences	JOHN Q. EASTON
Assistant Secretary for Civil Rights	CATHERINE E. LHAMON
Chief Financial Officer	THOMAS SKELLY, *Acting*
Assistant Secretary for Management	ANDREW JACKSON
Assistant Secretary for Legislation and Congressional Affairs	LLOYD HORWICH, *Acting*
Director, Center for Faith-Based and Neighborhood Partnerships	BRENDA GIRTON-MITCHELL
Assistant Deputy Secretary, Office of Innovation and Improvement	NADYA CHINOY DABBY
Assistant Secretary for Special Education and Rehabilitative Services	MICHAEL K. YUDIN, *Acting*
Assistant Deputy Secretary and Director, Office of English Language Acquisition, Language Enhancement, and Academic Achievement for Limited English Proficient Students	LIBIA GIL, *Acting*
Assistant Secretary for Elementary and Secondary Education	DEBORAH DELISLE
Executive Director, White House Initiative on Educational Excellence for Hispanic Americans	ALEJANDRA CEJA
Under Secretary	THEODORE R. MITCHELL
Chief Operating Officer for Federal Student Aid	JAMES W. RUNCIE
Assistant Secretary for Postsecondary Education	BRENDA DANN-MESSIER, *Acting*
Assistant Secretary for Career, Technical, and Adult Education	BRENDA DANN-MESSIER
Executive Director, White House Initiative on Historically Black Colleges and Universities	GEORGE COOPER
Executive Director, White House Initiative on Tribal Colleges and Universities	WILLIAM MENDOZA
Executive Director, White House Initiative on Asian Americans and Pacific Islanders	KIRAN AHUJA

The Department of Education ensures equal access to education; promotes educational excellence; and makes policy for, administers, and coordinates most

178

Federal assistance to education with the aim of raising student achievement and readiness for the global future.

The Department of Education was created by the Department of Education Organization Act (20 U.S.C. 3411) and is administered under the supervision and direction of the Secretary of Education.

Secretary The Secretary of Education advises the President on education plans, policies, and programs of the Federal Government and serves as the chief executive officer of the Department, supervising all Department activities, providing support to States and localities, and focusing resources to ensure equal access to educational excellence throughout the Nation.

Activities

Institute of Education Sciences The Institute of Education Sciences was formally established by the Education Sciences Reform Act of 2002 (20 U.S.C. 9501 note). The Institute includes national education centers focused on research, special education, statistics, and evaluation and is the mechanism through which the Department supports the research activities needed to improve education policy and practice.

Elementary and Secondary Education The Office of Elementary and Secondary Education directs, coordinates, and formulates policy relating to early childhood, elementary, and secondary education. Included are grants and contracts to State educational agencies and local school districts, postsecondary schools, and nonprofit organizations for disadvantaged, migrant, and Indian children; enhancement of State student achievement assessment systems; improvement of reading instruction; economic impact aid; technology; safe and healthy schools; and after-school learning programs. The Office also focuses on improving K–12 education, providing children with language and cognitive development, early reading, and other readiness skills, and improving the quality of teachers and other instructional staff.

English Language Acquisition The Office of English Language Acquisition, Language Enhancement, and Academic Achievement for Limited English Proficient Students helps children who are limited in their English, including immigrant children and youth, attain English proficiency, develop high levels of academic attainment in English, and meet the same challenging State academic content and student academic achievement standards that all children are expected to meet.

Federal Student Aid Federal Student Aid partners with postsecondary schools and financial institutions to deliver programs and services that help students finance their education beyond high school. This includes administering postsecondary student financial assistance programs authorized under Title IV of the Higher Education Act of 1965, as amended.

Internet, https://studentaid.ed.gov/.

Innovation and Improvement The Office of Innovation and Improvement (OII) oversees competitive grant programs that support innovations in the educational system and disseminates the lessons learned from these innovative practices. OII administers, coordinates, and recommends programs and policy for improving the quality of activities designed to support and test innovations throughout the K–12 system in areas such as parental choice, teacher quality, use of technology in education, and arts in education. OII encourages the establishment of charter schools through planning, start-up funding, and approaches to credit enhancement for charter school facilities. OII also serves as the Department's liaison and resource to the nonpublic education community.

Postsecondary Education The Office of Postsecondary Education (OPE) formulates Federal postsecondary education policy and administers programs that address critical national needs in support of the mission to increase access to quality postsecondary education. OPE develops policy for Federal student financial programs and support programs that reach out to low-

DEPARTMENT OF EDUCATION

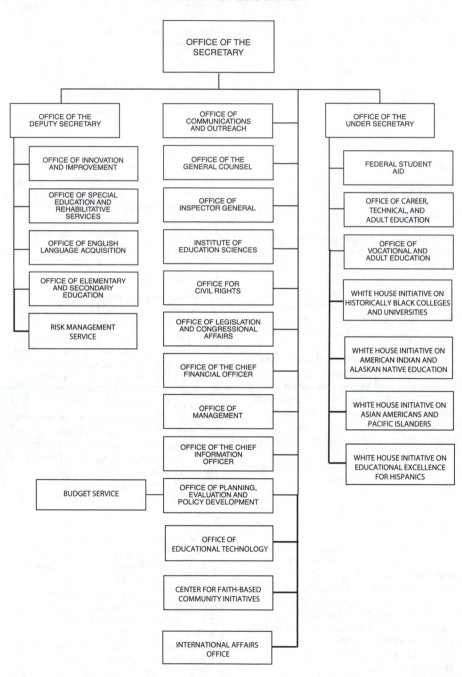

income, first-generation college students and communities. OPE also supports programs that strengthen the capacity of colleges and universities serving a high percentage of disadvantaged students and improve teacher quality. OPE recognizes accrediting agencies that monitor academic quality, promote innovation in higher education, and expand American educational resources for international studies and services.

Internet, http://www2.ed.gov/about/offices/list/ope/index.html.

Special Education and Rehabilitative Services   The Office of Special Education and Rehabilitative Services (OSERS) provides leadership and resources to help ensure that people with disabilities have equal opportunities to learn, work, and live as fully integrated and contributing members of society. OSERS has three components: The Office of Special Education Programs administers the Individuals with Disabilities Education Act legislation, which helps States meet the early intervention and educational needs of infants, toddlers, children, and youth with disabilities. The Rehabilitation Services Administration supports State vocational rehabilitation, independent living, and assistive technology programs that provide people with disabilities the services, technology, and job training and placement assistance they need to gain meaningful employment and lead independent lives. The National Institute on Disability and Rehabilitation Research supports research and development programs that improve the ability of individuals with disabilities to work and live in a barrier-free, inclusive society. OSERS also supports Gallaudet University, the National Technical Institute for the Deaf, the American Printing House for the Blind, and the Helen Keller National Center.

Career, Technical, and Adult Education The Office of Career, Technical, and Adult Education (OCTAE) administers grant, contract, and technical assistance programs for vocational-technical

education and for adult education and literacy. It promotes programs that enable adults to acquire the basic literacy skills necessary to function in today's society. The Office also helps students acquire challenging academic and technical skills and prepare for high-skill, high-wage, and high-demand occupations in the 21st-century global economy. OCTAE provides national leadership and works to strengthen the role of community colleges in expanding access to postsecondary education for youth and adults in advancing workforce development.

Internet, http://www2.ed.gov/about/offices/list/ovae/index.html.

Regional Offices   Each regional office serves as a center for the dissemination of information and provides technical assistance to State and local educational agencies and other institutions and individuals interested in Federal educational activities. Offices are located in Boston, MA; New York, NY; Philadelphia, PA; Atlanta, GA; Chicago, IL; Cleveland, OH; Dallas, TX; Kansas City, MO; Denver, CO; San Francisco, CA; and Seattle, WA.

Internet, http://www2.ed.gov/about/contacts/gen/regions.html.

Sources of Information

Inquiries on the following categories may be directed to the specified office, Department of Education, 400 Maryland Avenue SW., Washington, DC 20202.

Contracts and Small Business Activities Call or write the Office of Small and Disadvantaged Business Utilization. Phone, 202–245–6301. Internet, http://www.ed.gov/fund/contract-opportunities.html.

Employment   Inquiries and applications for employment and inquiries regarding the college recruitment program should be directed to the Human Capital and Client Services. Phone, 202–401–0553. Internet, http://www.ed.gov/jobs.

Organization   Contact the Executive Office, Office of Management. Phone, 202–469–6785.

For further information, contact the Information Resources Center, Department of Education, Room 5E248 (FB–6), 400 Maryland Avenue SW., Washington, DC 20202. Phone, 800 -872-5327. Internet, http://www. ed.gov.

Federally Aided Corporations

American Printing House for the Blind

P.O. Box 6085, Louisville, KY 40206
Phone, 502–895–2405. Internet, http://www.aph.org.

President	Tuck Tinsley, III
Chairman of the Board	Charles Baer

Founded in 1858 as a nonprofit organization, the American Printing House for the Blind (APH) received its Federal charter in 1879 when Congress passed the Act to Promote Education of the Blind. This Act designates APH as the official supplier of educational materials adapted for students who are legally blind and who are enrolled in formal educational programs below the college level. Materials produced and distributed by APH include textbooks in Braille and large type, educational tools such as Braille typewriters and computer software and hardware, teaching aides such as tests and performance measures, and other special supplies. The materials are distributed through allotments to the States to programs serving individuals who are blind.

For further information, contact the American Printing House for the Blind, P.O. Box 6085, Louisville, KY 40206. Phone, 502–895–2405. Internet, http://www.aph.org.

Gallaudet University

800 Florida Avenue NE., Washington, DC 20002
Phone, 202–651–5000. Internet, http://www.gallaudet.edu.

President, Gallaudet University	T. Alan Hurwitz
Chair, Board of Trustees	Benjamin J. Soukup, Jr.

Gallaudet University received its Federal charter in 1864 and is currently authorized by the Education of the Deaf Act of 1986, as amended. Gallaudet is a private, nonprofit educational institution providing elementary, secondary, undergraduate, and continuing education programs for persons who are deaf. The University offers a traditional liberal arts curriculum for students who are deaf and graduate programs in fields related to deafness for students who are deaf and students who are hearing. Gallaudet also conducts a wide variety of basic and applied deafness research and provides public service programs for persons who are deaf and for professionals who work with persons who are deaf.

Gallaudet University is accredited by a number of organizations, among which are the Middle States Association of Colleges and Secondary Schools, the National Council for Accreditation of Teacher Education, and the Conference of Educational Administrators of Schools and Programs for the Deaf.

Laurent Clerc National Deaf Education Center Gallaudet's Laurent Clerc National Deaf Education Center operates elementary and secondary education programs on the main campus of the University. These programs are authorized by the Education of the Deaf Act of 1986 (20 U.S.C. 4304, as amended) for the primary purpose of developing, evaluating, and disseminating model curricula, instructional strategies, and materials in order to serve individuals who are deaf or hard of hearing. The Education of the Deaf Act requires the programs to include students preparing for postsecondary opportunities other than college and students with a broad spectrum of needs, such as students who are academically challenged, come from non-English-speaking homes, have secondary disabilities, are members of minority groups, or are from rural areas.

Model Secondary School for the Deaf The school was established by act of October 15, 1966, which was superseded by the Education of the Deaf Act of 1986. The school provides day and residential facilities for secondary-age students from across the United States from grades 9 to 12, inclusively.

Kendall Demonstration Elementary School The school became the Nation's first demonstration elementary school for the deaf by the act of December 24, 1970 (20 U.S.C. 695), which was also later superseded by the Education of the Deaf Act of 1986. The school is a day program for students from the Washington, DC, metropolitan area from the age of onset of deafness to age 15, inclusively, but not beyond the eighth grade or its equivalent.

For further information, contact the Public Relations Office, Gallaudet University, 800 Florida Avenue NE., Washington, DC 20002. Phone, 202–651–5505. Internet, http://www.gallaudet.edu.

Howard University

2400 Sixth Street NW.,Washington, DC 20059
Phone, 202–806–6100. Internet, http://www.howard.edu.

President	SIDNEY A. RIBEAU

Howard University was established by Congress by the act of March 2, 1867 (14 Stat. 438). It offers instruction in 12 schools and colleges, as follows: the colleges of arts and sciences; dentistry; engineering, architecture, and computer sciences; medicine; pharmacy, nursing, and allied health sciences; the graduate school; the schools of business; communications; divinity; education; law; and social work. In addition, Howard University has research institutes, centers, and special programs in the following areas: cancer, child development, computational science and engineering, international affairs, sickle cell disease, and the national human genome project.

For further information, contact the Office of University Communications, Howard University, 2400 Sixth Street NW., Washington, DC 20059. Phone, 202–806–0970. Internet, http://www.howard.edu.

National Technical Institute for the Deaf / Rochester Institute of Technology

52 Lomb Memorial Drive, Rochester, NY 14623
Phone, 585–475–6317. Internet, http://www.ntid.edu.

President, Rochester Institute of Technology	WILLIAM W. DESTLER
Vice President, National Technical Institute for the Deaf	JAMES J. DeCARO

The National Technical Institute for the Deaf (NTID) was established by act of June 8, 1965 (20 U.S.C. 681) to promote the employment of persons who are deaf by providing technical and professional education. The National Technical Institute for the Deaf Act was superseded by the Education of the Deaf Act of 1986 (20 U.S.C. 4431, as amended). The U.S. Department of Education contracts with the Rochester Institute of Technology (RIT) for the operation of a residential facility for postsecondary technical training and education for individuals who are deaf. The purpose of the special relationship with the host institution is to give NTID's faculty and students access to more facilities, institutional services, and career preparation options than could be provided otherwise by a national technical institute for the deaf operating independently.

NTID offers a variety of technical programs at the certificate, diploma, and associate degree levels. Degree programs include majors in business, engineering, science, and visual communications. In addition, NTID students may participate in approximately 200 educational programs available through RIT.

NTID also conducts applied research in occupational- and employment-related aspects of deafness, communication assessment, demographics of NTID's target population, and learning processes in postsecondary education. In addition, NTID conducts training workshops and seminars related to deafness. These workshops and seminars are offered nationwide to professionals who employ, work with, teach, or serve persons who are deaf.

For further information, contact the Rochester Institute of Technology, National Technical Institute for the Deaf, Department of Recruitment and Admissions, Lyndon Baines Johnson Building, 52 Lomb Memorial Drive, Rochester, NY 14623–5604. Phone, 716–475–6700. Internet, http://www.ntid.edu.

EDITORIAL NOTE: The Department of Energy did not meet the publication deadline for submitting updated information of its activities, functions, and sources of information as required by the automatic disclosure provisions of the Freedom of Information Act (5 U.S.C. 552(a)(1)(A)).

DEPARTMENT OF ENERGY

1000 Independence Avenue SW., Washington, DC 20585
Phone, 202–586–5000. Internet, http://www.energy.gov.

Secretary of Energy	Ernest J. Moniz
Deputy Secretary	Elizabeth Sherwood-Randall
Chief of Staff	Jeffrey Navin, *Acting*
Under Secretary for Nuclear Security and Administrator for National Nuclear Security Administration	Frank G. Klotz
Principal Deputy Administrator for National Nuclear Security Administration	Madelyn Creedon
Deputy Administrator, Defense Programs	Donald L. Cook
Deputy Administrator, Defense Nuclear Nonproliferation	Anne Harrington
Deputy Administrator, Naval Reactors	Adm. John M. Richardson, USN
Deputy Under Secretary, Counterterrorism	Steven Aoki
Associate Administrator, Defense Nuclear Security	Steve Asher, *Acting*
Associate Administrator, Emergency Operations	Joseph J. Krol, Jr.
Associate Administrator, External Affairs	Clarence T. Bishop
Associate Administrator, Acquisition and Project Management	Robert B. Raines
Associate Administrator, Management and Budget	Cynthia Lersten
Associate Administrator, Information Management and Chief Information Officer	Wayne Jones, *Acting*
Associate Administrator, Safety and Health	Don Nichols
Associate Administrator, Infrastructure and Operations	Michael Lempke
Office of General Counsel	Bruce Diamond
Under Secretary of Energy	(vacancy)
Assistant Secretary, Electricity Delivery and Energy Reliability	Patricia A. Hoffman
Assistant Secretary, Energy Efficiency and Renewable Energy	David T. Danielson
Assistant Secretary, Environmental Management	(vacancy)
Principal Deputy Assistant Secretary, Fossil Energy	Christopher A. Smith, *Acting*
Director, Legacy Management	David W. Geiser
Assistant Secretary, Nuclear Energy	Peter B. Lyons
Under Secretary for Science	(vacancy)
Director, Office of Science	William Brinkman
Administrator, Energy Information Administration	Adam E. Sieminski
Loan Program Office	Peter W. Davidson
Indian Energy Policy and Program	Tracey A. LeBeau

Director, Advanced Research Projects Agency-Energy	CHERYL ANN MARTIN, *Acting*
Chief Financial Officer	ALISON DOONE, *Acting*
Chief Human Capital Officer	ROBERT C. GIBBS
Assistant Secretary, Congressional and Intergovernmental Affairs	BRADLEY R. CROWELL
Director, Economic Impact and Diversity	LADORIS G. HARRIS
General Counsel	STEVEN P. CROLEY
Director, Health, Safety and Security	GLENN S. PODONSKY
Director, Hearings and Appeals	POLICARPIO A. MARMOLEJOS
Inspector General	GREGORY H. FRIEDMAN
Director, Intelligence and Counterintelligence	STEVEN K. BLACK
Director, Management	INGRID A.C. KOLB
Assistant Secretary, International Affairs	JONATHAN H. ELKIND, *Acting*
Director, Public Affairs	DANIEL A. LEISTIKOW

The Department of Energy advances the national, economic, and energy security of the United States; promotes scientific and technological innovation to support that advancement; and ensures the environmental cleanup of the national nuclear weapons complex.

The Department of Energy (DOE) was established by the Department of Energy Organization Act (42 U.S.C. 7131), effective October 1, 1977, pursuant to Executive Order 12009 of September 13, 1977. The act consolidated the major Federal energy functions into one Cabinet-level Department.

Secretary   The Secretary decides major energy policy and planning issues; acts as the principal spokesperson for the Department; and ensures effective communication and working relationships with the public and with Federal, State, local, and tribal governments. The Secretary is the principal adviser to the President on energy policies, plans, and programs.

Intelligence and Counterintelligence The Office of Intelligence and Counterintelligence ensures that all departmental intelligence information requirements are met and that the Department's technical, analytical, and research expertise is made available to support U.S. intelligence efforts. The Office develops and implements programs to identify, neutralize, and deter foreign governmental or industrial intelligence activities directed at or involving Department programs, personnel, facilities, technologies, classified information, and sensitive information. The Office ensures effective use of the U.S. Government's intelligence apparatus in support of DOE's need for information on foreign energy situations and potential threats, development and proliferation of global nuclear weapons, and foreign production and consumption of hydrocarbon, nuclear, and other energy sources. The Office formulates all DOE intelligence and counterintelligence policy and coordinates all investigative matters with the Federal Bureau of Investigation.

For further information, contact the Office of Intelligence and Counterintelligence. Phone, 202–586–2610.

Health, Safety and Security The Office of Health, Safety and Security develops policies to protect national security and other critical assets entrusted to the DOE. It also manages security operations for departmental facilities in the national capital area.

For further information, contact the Office of Health, Safety and Security. Phone, 301–903–3777.

Energy Programs

Renewable Energy The Office of Energy Efficiency and Renewable Energy is responsible for formulating and directing programs designed to increase the production and utilization of renewable energy (solar, biomass, wind, geothermal, alcohol fuels, etc.)

DEPARTMENT OF ENERGY

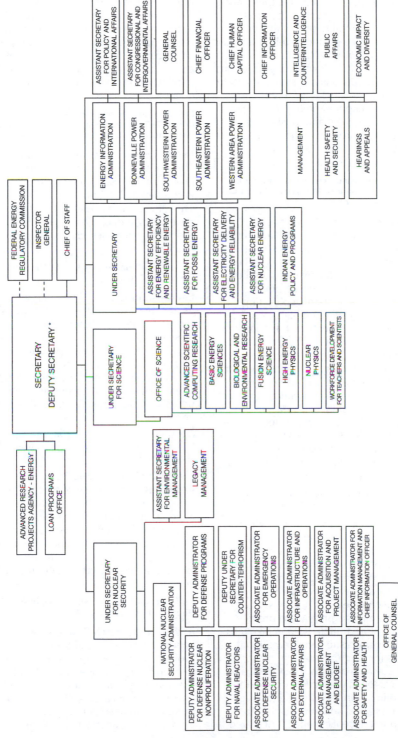

SECRETARY
DEPUTY SECRETARY *

FEDERAL ENERGY REGULATORY COMMISSION
INSPECTOR GENERAL
CHIEF OF STAFF

ADVANCED RESEARCH PROJECTS AGENCY - ENERGY
LOAN PROGRAMS OFFICE

UNDER SECRETARY

ENERGY INFORMATION ADMINISTRATION
BONNEVILLE POWER ADMINISTRATION
SOUTHWESTERN POWER ADMINISTRATION
SOUTHEASTERN POWER ADMINISTRATION
WESTERN AREA POWER ADMINISTRATION

ASSISTANT SECRETARY FOR ENERGY EFFICIENCY AND RENEWABLE ENERGY
ASSISTANT SECRETARY FOR FOSSIL ENERGY
ASSISTANT SECRETARY FOR ELECTRICITY DELIVERY AND ENERGY RELIABILITY
ASSISTANT SECRETARY FOR NUCLEAR ENERGY
INDIAN ENERGY POLICY AND PROGRAMS

ASSISTANT SECRETARY FOR POLICY AND INTERNATIONAL AFFAIRS
ASSISTANT SECRETARY FOR CONGRESSIONAL AND INTERGOVERNMENTAL AFFAIRS
GENERAL COUNSEL
CHIEF FINANCIAL OFFICER
CHIEF HUMAN CAPITAL OFFICER
CHIEF INFORMATION OFFICER
INTELLIGENCE AND COUNTERINTELLIGENCE
PUBLIC AFFAIRS
ECONOMIC IMPACT AND DIVERSITY

MANAGEMENT
HEALTH SAFETY AND SECURITY
HEARINGS AND APPEALS

UNDER SECRETARY FOR SCIENCE

OFFICE OF SCIENCE

ADVANCED SCIENTIFIC COMPUTING RESEARCH
BASIC ENERGY SCIENCES
BIOLOGICAL AND ENVIRONMENTAL RESEARCH
FUSION ENERGY SCIENCE
HIGH ENERGY PHYSICS
NUCLEAR PHYSICS
WORKFORCE DEVELOPMENT FOR TEACHERS AND SCIENTISTS

ASSISTANT SECRETARY FOR ENVIRONMENTAL MANAGEMENT
LEGACY MANAGEMENT

UNDER SECRETARY FOR NUCLEAR SECURITY

NATIONAL NUCLEAR SECURITY ADMINISTRATION

DEPUTY ADMINISTRATOR FOR DEFENSE PROGRAMS
DEPUTY UNDER SECRETARY FOR COUNTER-TERRORISM
ASSOCIATE ADMINISTRATOR FOR EMERGENCY OPERATIONS
ASSOCIATE ADMINISTRATOR FOR INFRASTRUCTURE AND OPERATIONS
ASSOCIATE ADMINISTRATOR FOR ACQUISITION AND PROJECT MANAGEMENT
ASSOCIATE ADMINISTRATOR FOR INFORMATION MANAGEMENT AND CHIEF INFORMATION OFFICER

DEPUTY ADMINISTRATOR FOR DEFENSE NUCLEAR NONPROLIFERATION
DEPUTY ADMINISTRATOR FOR NAVAL REACTORS
ASSOCIATE ADMINISTRATOR FOR DEFENSE NUCLEAR SECURITY
ASSOCIATE ADMINISTRATOR FOR EXTERNAL AFFAIRS
ASSOCIATE ADMINISTRATOR FOR MANAGEMENT AND BUDGET
ASSOCIATE ADMINISTRATOR FOR SAFETY AND HEALTH

OFFICE OF GENERAL COUNSEL

* The Deputy Secretary also serves as the Chief Operating Officer.

and hydrogen and improving the energy efficiency of the transportation, buildings, industrial, and utility sectors through support of research and development and technology transfer activities. It also has responsibility for administering programs that provide financial assistance for State energy planning; weatherizing homes owned by the poor and disadvantaged; implementing State and local energy conservation programs; and promoting energy efficient construction and renovation of Federal facilities.

For further information, contact the Director of Information and Business Management Systems. Phone, 202–586–7241.

Fossil Energy   The Office of Fossil Energy is responsible for research and development of programs involving coal, petroleum, and natural gas. The fossil energy program involves applied research, exploratory development, and limited proof-of-concept testing targeted to high-risk and high-payoff endeavors. The objective of the program is to provide the general technology and knowledge base that the private sector can use to complete development and initiate commercialization of advanced processes and energy systems. The program is principally executed through the National Energy Technology Laboratory. The Office also manages the strategic petroleum reserve, the northeast home heating oil reserve, and the naval petroleum shale reserves.

For further information, contact the Office of Communications. Phone, 202–586–6803.

Nuclear Energy   The Office of Nuclear Energy manages DOE programs involved in the research and development of fission and fusion energy. This includes programs relating to naval and civilian nuclear reactors, the nuclear fuel cycle, and space nuclear applications. The Office manages a program to provide radioactive and stable isotope products to various domestic and international markets for medical research, health care, and industrial research. The Office also conducts technical analyses concerning nonproliferation; assesses alternative nuclear systems and new reactor and fuel cycle concepts; manages depleted

uranium hexafluoride activities, highly enriched uranium downblend, natural uranium sales, and uranium enrichment legacy activities; and evaluates proposed advanced nuclear fission energy concepts and technical improvements for possible application to nuclear powerplant systems.

For further information, contact the Director, Corporate Communications and External Affairs. Phone, 301–903–1636.

Indian Energy Policy and Programs
The Office of Indian Energy Policy and Programs was established by the Energy Policy Act of 2005 (42 U.S.C. 7144e). The Office is responsible for further developing Indian tribal energy by promoting increased energy usage and efficiency.

For further information, contact the Director. Phone, 202–586–1272.

Energy Information   The Energy Information Administration is responsible for collecting, processing, and disseminating data in the areas of energy resource reserves, energy production, demand, consumption, distribution, and technology. It performs analyses of energy data to assist government and nongovernment users in understanding energy trends.

For further information, contact the Director, National Energy Information Center. Phone, 202–586–6537.

Electricity Delivery and Energy Reliability   The Office of Electricity Delivery and Energy Reliability leads a national effort to modernize and expand America's electricity delivery system. The Office works to improve the security and reliability of energy infrastructure and facilitates recovery efforts after major energy supply disruptions.

For further information, contact the Office of the Director. Phone, 202–586–1411.

Advanced Research Projects Agency–Energy   The Advanced Research Projects Agency–Energy (ARPA–E) works to overcome the long-term and high-risk challenges in the development of energy technologies. ARPA–E promotes research and development initiatives. By developing energy technologies that reduce energy imports, improve energy efficiency, and reduce energy-related emissions, the Office enhances the economic security of the United States. Additionally, ARPA–E ensures that the United States maintains global leadership in developing and deploying advanced energy technologies.

For further information, contact the Office of the Director. Phone, 202–287–1004.

Loan Programs Office   The Loan Programs Office is responsible for the domestic and commercial deployment of advanced clean energy technologies furthering national clean energy objectives, including job creation; reducing dependency on foreign oil; improving our environmental legacy; and enhancing American competitiveness in the 21st-century global economy.

For further information, contact Loan Programs Office. Phone, 202–586–8335. Email, lgprogram@hq.doe.gov.

Nuclear Security Programs

Nuclear Security   The National Nuclear Security Administration (NNSA) was created by Congress through the National Defense Authorization Act for Fiscal Year 2000 (113 Stat. 512) to bring focus to the management of the Nation's defense nuclear security programs. Three existing organizations within the Department of Energy—Defense Programs, Defense Nuclear Nonproliferation, and Naval Reactors—were combined into a new, separately managed agency within DOE, headed by an Administrator who reports to the Secretary. NNSA seeks to strengthen national security through military application of nuclear energy and by reducing the global threat from terrorism and weapons of mass destruction.

The Administration's service center and eight site offices provide operations oversight and contract administration for NNSA site activities, acting as the agency's risk acceptance for the site. The site offices are responsible for the safe and secure operation of facilities under the purview of NNSA; supporting NNSA programs to ensure their success in accordance with their expectations; and ensuring the long-term viability of the site to support NNSA programs and projects. More information on the service center and site offices is available online: http://nnsa.energy.gov/aboutus/ourlocations.

For further information, contact the Associate Administrator for Management and Budget. Phone, 202–586–5753.

Defense Programs   The Office of the Deputy Administrator for Defense Programs directs the Nation's nuclear weapons research, development, testing, production, and surveillance program. It is also responsible for the production of the special nuclear materials used by the weapons program within the Department and the management of defense nuclear waste and byproducts. The Office ensures the technology base for the surety, reliability, military effectiveness, and credibility of the nuclear weapons stockpile. It also manages research in inertial confinement fusion.

For further information, contact the Associate Administrator for Management and Budget. Phone, 202–586–5753.

Nuclear Nonproliferation   The Office of the Deputy Administrator for Defense Nuclear Nonproliferation directs the development of the Department's policy, plans, procedures, and research and development activities relating to arms control, nonproliferation, export controls, international nuclear safety and safeguard, and surplus fissile material inventories elimination activities.

For further information, contact the Associate Administrator for Management and Budget. Phone, 202–586–5753.

Naval Reactors   The Office of the Deputy Administrator for Naval Reactors manages and performs research, development, design, acquisition, specification, construction, inspection, installation, certification, testing overhaul, refueling, operations procedures, maintenance, supply support, and ultimate disposition of naval nuclear propulsion plants.

For further information, contact the Deputy Administrator for Naval Reactors. Phone, 202–781–6174.

Environmental Quality Programs

Environmental Management   The Office of the Assistant Secretary for Environmental Management manages safe cleanup and closure of sites and facilities; directs a safe and effective waste management program, including storage and disposal of transuranic and mixed low- and high-level waste; and maintains an applied research program to provide innovative technologies that yield permanent cleanup solutions at reduced costs.

For further information, contact the Director of Communication/External Affairs. Phone, 202–287–5591.

Legacy Management   The Office of Legacy Management manages the Department's post-closure responsibilities and ensures the future protection of the environment and human health. The Office has control and custody of legacy land, structures, and facilities, and is responsible for maintaining them at levels suitable for long-term use.

For further information, contact the Director of Business Operations. Phone, 202–586–7388.

Science Program

The Office of Science supports basic research that underpins DOE missions in national security, energy, and environment; constructs and operates large scientific facilities for the U.S. scientific community; and provides the infrastructure support for 10 national laboratories and an integrated support center. In terms of basic research, the Office of Science provides over 40 percent of Federal support to the physical sciences (including 90 percent of Federal support for high energy and nuclear physics), the sole support to sub-fields of national importance, such as nuclear medicine, heavy element chemistry, and magnetic fusion, and support for the research of scientists and graduate students located in universities throughout the Nation. Office of Science support for major scientific-user facilities, including accelerators, synchrotron light sources, and neutron sources, enables more than 18,000 scientists per year to use these state-of-the-art facilities to conduct research in a wide range of fields, including biology, medicine, and materials. For more information on the 10 national laboratories and support centers, visit http://science.energy.gov.

For further information, contact the Director of Human Resources. Phone, 301–903–5705.

Operations and Field Offices

The vast majority of the Department's energy and physical research and development, environmental restoration, and waste management activities are carried out by contractors who operate Government-owned facilities. Management and administration of Government-owned, contractor-operated facility contracts are the principal responsibility of the Department's five operations offices and three field offices.

Department operations offices provide a formal link between Department headquarters and the field laboratories and other operating facilities. They also manage programs and projects as assigned from lead headquarters program offices. Routine management guidance, coordination, oversight of the operations, field and site offices, and daily specific program direction for the operations offices is provided by the appropriate assistant secretary, office director, or program officer. For more information on the site offices, visit http://nnsa.energy. gov/aboutus/ourlocations.

Power Administrations

The marketing and transmission of electric power produced at Federal hydroelectric projects and reservoirs are carried out by the Department's four Power Administrations. Management oversight of the Power Administrations is the responsibility of the Deputy Secretary.

Bonneville Power Administration   The Administration markets power produced by the Federal Columbia River Power System at the lowest rates, consistent with sound business practices, and gives preference to public entities.

In addition, the Administration is responsible for energy conservation, renewable resource development, and fish and wildlife enhancement under the provisions of the Pacific Northwest Electric Power Planning and Conservation Act of 1980 (16 U.S.C. 839 note).

For further information, contact the Bonneville Power Administration, 905 Eleventh Avenue NE., Portland, OR 97232–4169. Phone, 503–230–3000 or 800–282–3713.

Southeastern Power Administration
The Administration is responsible for the transmission and disposition of surplus electric power and energy generated at reservoir projects in Alabama, Florida, Georgia, Kentucky, Mississippi, North Carolina, South Carolina, Tennessee, Virginia, and West Virginia.

The Administration sets the lowest possible rates for consumers, consistent with sound business principles, and gives preference in the sale of power and energy to public entities.

For further information, contact the Southeastern Power Administration, 1166 Athens Tech Road, Elberton, GA 30635–4578. Phone, 706–213–3800.

Southwestern Power Administration
The Administration is responsible for the sale and disposition of electric power and energy in Arkansas, Kansas, Louisiana, Missouri, Oklahoma, and Texas.

The Administration transmits and disposes of the electric power and energy generated at Federal reservoir projects, supplemented by power purchased from public and private utilities, in such a manner as to encourage the most widespread and economical use. The Administration sets the lowest possible rates to consumers, consistent with sound business principles, and gives preference in the sale of power and energy to public entities.

The Administration also conducts and participates in the comprehensive planning of water resource development in the Southwest.

For further information, contact the Southwestern Power Administration, Suite 1600, Williams Center Tower One, One West Third Street, Tulsa, OK 74103–3532. Phone, 918–595–6600.

Western Area Power Administration
The Administration is responsible for the Federal electric power marketing and transmission functions in 15 Central and Western States, encompassing a geographic area of 1.3 million square miles. The Administration sells power to cooperatives, municipalities, public utility districts, private utilities, Federal and State agencies, and irrigation districts. The wholesale power customers, in turn, provide service to millions of retail consumers in Arizona, California, Colorado, Iowa, Kansas, Minnesota, Montana, Nebraska, Nevada, New Mexico, North Dakota, South Dakota, Texas, Utah, and Wyoming.

The Administration is responsible for the operation and maintenance of transmission lines, substations, and various auxiliary power facilities in the aforementioned geographic area. It also plans, constructs, operates, and maintains additional Federal transmission facilities that may be authorized in the future.

For further information, contact the Western Area Power Administration, 12155 West Alameda Parkway, Lakewood, CO 80228–1213. Phone, 720–962–7000.

Sources of Information

Consumer Information For information on the consumer impact of Department policies and operations and for other DOE consumer information, call 202–586–1908.

Contracts and Small and Disadvantaged Business Utilization Activities Information on business opportunities with the Department and its contractors is available electronically through the Internet at www.pr.doe.gov. For information on existing DOE awards, call 202–586–9051.

Electronic Access Information on the Department of Energy is available online. Internet, http://www.energy.gov.

Employment Most jobs in the Department are in the competitive service. Positions are filled through hiring individuals with Federal civil service status, but may also be filled using lists of competitive eligibles from the Office of Personnel Management or the Department's special examining units. Contact the Office of Human Capital Management. Phone, 202–586–1234.

Freedom of Information Act For administrative and technical support in matters involving the Freedom of

Information, Privacy, and Computer Matching Acts, call 202–586–5955. Email, foia-central@hq.doe.gov.

Inspector General Hotline   To report issues of concern regarding departmental operations, processes, or practices or to report illegal acts or noncriminal violations, use the hotline. Phone, 202–586–4073 or 800–541–1625. Email, ighotmail@hq.doe.gov.

Public Information Issuances, Press Releases, and Publications   For media contacts, call 202–586–5575.

Public Reading Room   For information on Department of Energy materials and public access to the Department's records, call 202–586–3142.

Scientific and Technical Information   The Office manages a system for the centralized collection, announcement, and dissemination of and historical reference to the Department's scientific and technical information and worldwide energy information. Contact the Office of Scientific and Technical Information, 175 Oak Ridge Turnpike, Oak Ridge, TN 37830–7255. Phone, 423–576–1188.

Whistleblower Assistance   Federal or DOE contractor employees wishing to make complaints of alleged wrongdoing against the Department or its contractors should call 202–586–0696.

For further information, contact the Office of Public Affairs, Department of Energy, 1000 Independence Avenue SW., Washington, DC 20585. Phone, 202–586–4940. Internet, http://www.energy.gov.

EDITORIAL NOTE: The Federal Energy Regulatory Commission did not meet the publication deadline for submitting updated information of its activities, functions, and sources of information as required by the automatic disclosure provisions of the Freedom of Information Act (5 U.S.C. 552(a)(1)(A)).

Federal Energy Regulatory Commission

888 First Street NE., Washington, DC 20426
Phone, 202–502–8055. Internet, http://www.ferc.gov.

Chairman	CHERYL A. LAFLEUR
Commissioners	TONY CLARK, PHILIP D. MOELLER, JOHN R. NORRIS, NORMAN C. BAY

The Federal Energy Regulatory Commission (FERC) is an independent agency within the Department of Energy which regulates the interstate transmission of electricity, natural gas, and oil. FERC has retained many of the functions of the Federal Power Commission, such as setting rates and charges for the transportation and sale of natural gas and the transportation of oil by pipelines, as well as the valuation of such pipelines. FERC also reviews proposals to build liquefied natural gas terminals and interstate natural gas pipelines as well as licensing hydropower projects. FERC is composed of five members appointed by the President of the United States with the advice and consent of the Senate. FERC Commissioners serve 5-year terms and have an equal vote on regulatory matters. One member is designated by the President to serve as both Chairman and FERC's administrative head.

For further information, contact the Office of External Affairs. Phone, 202–502–8004 or 866–208–3372. Fax, 202–208–2106. Internet, http://www.ferc.gov.

DEPARTMENT OF HEALTH AND HUMAN SERVICES

200 Independence Avenue SW., Washington, DC 20201
Phone, 202–690–6343. Internet, http://www.hhs.gov.

Secretary of Health and Human Services	SYLVIA MATHEWS BURWELL
Deputy Secretary	WILLIAM CORR
Chief of Staff	ANDREA PALM
Executive Secretary	C'REDA WEEDEN
Director, Office of Intergovernmental and External Affairs	PAUL DIOGUARDI
Assistant Secretary for Health	HOWARD KOH
Surgeon General	BORIS D. LUSHNIAK, *Acting*
Assistant Secretary for Administration	E.J. HOLLAND, JR.
Assistant Secretary for Financial Resources	ELLEN G. MURRAY
Assistant Secretary for Legislation	JIM R. ESQUEA
Assistant Secretary for Planning and Evaluation	RICHARD G. FRANK
Assistant Secretary for Public Affairs	DORI SALCIDO, *Acting*
Assistant Secretary for Preparedness and Response	NICOLE LURIE
Chair, Departmental Appeals Board	CONSTANCE B. TOBIAS
Chief Administrative Law Judge, Office of Medicare Hearings and Appeals	NANCY J. GRISWOLD
Director, Center for Faith-Based and Neighborhood Partnerships	ACACIA BAMBERG SALATTI, *Acting*
Director, Office for Civil Rights	LEON RODRIGUEZ
Director, Office of Global Affairs	NILS DAULAIRE
Director, Office of Health Reform	MICHAEL M. HASH
General Counsel	WILLIAM B. SCHULTZ
Inspector General	DANIEL R. LEVINSON
National Coordinator, Office of the National Coordinator for Health Information Technology	KAREN DESALVO

The Department of Health and Human Services strengthens the public health and welfare of the American people by making affordable and quality health care and childcare accessible, ensuring the safety of food products, preparing for public health emergencies, and advancing the diagnosis, treatment, and curing of life-threatening illnesses.

The Department of Health and Human Services (HHS) was created as the Department of Health, Education, and Welfare on April 11, 1953 (5 U.S.C. app.).

Secretary The Secretary of Health and Human Services advises the President on health, welfare, and income security plans, policies, and programs of the Federal Government and directs Department staff in carrying out the programs and activities of the Department and promotes general public understanding of the Department's goals, programs, and objectives.

For information on HHS regional offices, visit the Department's Web site.
Internet, http://www.hhs.gov/iea/regional/.

194

DEPARTMENT OF HEALTH AND HUMAN SERVICES

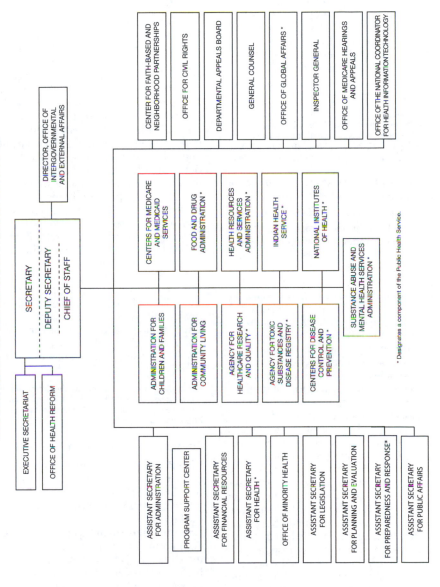

* Designates a component of the Public Health Service.

SECRETARY

DEPUTY SECRETARY

CHIEF OF STAFF

DIRECTOR, OFFICE OF INTERGOVERNMENTAL AND EXTERNAL AFFAIRS

EXECUTIVE SECRETARIAT

OFFICE OF HEALTH REFORM

CENTER FOR FAITH-BASED AND NEIGHBORHOOD PARTNERSHIPS

OFFICE FOR CIVIL RIGHTS

DEPARTMENTAL APPEALS BOARD

GENERAL COUNSEL

OFFICE OF GLOBAL AFFAIRS *

INSPECTOR GENERAL

OFFICE OF MEDICARE HEARINGS AND APPEALS

OFFICE OF THE NATIONAL COORDINATOR FOR HEALTH INFORMATION TECHNOLOGY

CENTERS FOR MEDICARE AND MEDICAID SERVICES

FOOD AND DRUG ADMINISTRATION *

HEALTH RESOURCES AND SERVICES ADMINISTRATION *

INDIAN HEALTH SERVICE *

NATIONAL INSTITUTES OF HEALTH *

ADMINISTRATION FOR CHILDREN AND FAMILIES

ADMINISTRATION FOR COMMUNITY LIVING

AGENCY FOR HEALTHCARE RESEARCH AND QUALITY *

AGENCY FOR TOXIC SUBSTANCES AND DISEASE REGISTRY *

CENTERS FOR DISEASE CONTROL AND PREVENTION *

SUBSTANCE ABUSE AND MENTAL HEALTH SERVICES ADMINISTRATION *

ASSISTANT SECRETARY FOR ADMINISTRATION

PROGRAM SUPPORT CENTER

ASSISTANT SECRETARY FOR FINANCIAL RESOURCES

ASSISTANT SECRETARY FOR HEALTH *

OFFICE OF MINORITY HEALTH

ASSISTANT SECRETARY FOR LEGISLATION

ASSISTANT SECRETARY FOR PLANNING AND EVALUATION

ASSISTANT SECRETARY FOR PREPAREDNESS AND RESPONSE*

ASSISTANT SECRETARY FOR PUBLIC AFFAIRS

Office of Intergovernmental and External Affairs The Office of Intergovernmental and External Affairs (IEA) serves the Secretary as the primary liaison between the Department and State, local, and tribal governments. The mission of the Office is to facilitate communication regarding HHS initiatives as they relate to State, local, and tribal governments. IEA serves the dual role of representing the State and tribal perspective in the Federal policymaking process as well as clarifying the Federal perspective to State and tribal representatives.

For further information, contact the Office of Intergovernmental and External Affairs, 200 Independence Avenue SW., Room 620E, Washington, DC 20201. Phone, 202–690–6060. Internet, http://www.hhs.gov/intergovernmental.

Office of the Assistant Secretary for Preparedness and Response

The Office of the Assistant Secretary for Preparedness and Response (ASPR) was established under the Pandemic and All Hazards Preparedness Act of 2006. ASPR serves as the principal advisor to the Secretary on all matters related to Federal public health and medical preparedness and response for public health emergencies. ASPR's mission is to lead the country in preparing for, responding to, and recovering from the adverse health effects of emergencies and disasters by supporting our communities' ability to withstand adversity, strengthening the Nation's health and response systems, and enhancing national health security. ASPR leads a collaborative policy approach to the Department's preparedness, response, and recovery portfolio and works with partners across Federal, State, local, tribal, and international bodies, in communities, and in the private sector to promote a unified and strategic approach to the challenges of public health and medical preparedness, response, and recovery. In addition, ASPR has operational responsibility for overseeing the advanced research, development, and procurement of medical countermeasures and for coordinating the Federal public health and medical response to incidents.

For further information, contact the Office of the Assistant Secretary for Preparedness and Response, Room 638–G, 200 Independence Avenue SW., Washington, DC 20201. Internet, http://www.phe.gov/preparedness/pages/default.aspx.

Office of the Assistant Secretary for Health

The Office of the Assistant Secretary for Health (ASH) comprises 13 offices and 9 Presidential and secretarial advisory committees. The Assistant Secretary for Health heads the Office and serves as the Secretary's senior public health advisor. ASH provides assistance in implementing and coordinating secretarial decisions for the Public Health Service and coordination of population-based health clinical divisions; provides oversight of research conducted or supported by the Department; implements programs that provide population-based public health services; and provides direction and policy oversight, through the Office of the Surgeon General, for the Public Health Service Commissioned Corps. ASH administers a wide array of interdisciplinary programs related to disease prevention, health promotion, the reduction of health disparities, women's health, HIV/AIDS, vaccine programs, physical fitness and sports, bioethics, population affairs, blood supply, research integrity, and human research protections.

For further information, contact the Office of the Assistant Secretary for Health, 200 Independence Avenue SW., Washington, DC 20201. Internet, http://www.hhs.gov/ash.

Sources of Information

Civil Rights For information on enforcement of civil rights laws, call 800–368–1019. TDD, 800–537–7697. Internet, http://www.hhs.gov/ocr/civilrights.
Contracts and Small Business Activities For information on programs, contact the Director, Office of Small and Disadvantaged Business Utilization. Phone, 202–690–7300. Internet, http://www.hhs.gov/asfr/ogapa/osbdu/.
Departmental Appeals Board For information, call 202–565–0200, or address inquiries to the Departmental

Appeals Board Immediate Office, MS 6127, Wilbur J. Cohen Building, 330 Independence Avenue SW., Room G–644, Washington, DC 20201. Internet, http://www.hhs.gov/dab/.

Inspector General Contact the Office of Inspector General, Wilbur J. Cohen Building, 330 Independence Avenue SW., Washington, DC 20201. Internet, http://oig.hhs.gov/.

Inspector General Hotline To report fraud, waste, or abuse in Department programs, contact the Office of Inspector General, OIG Hotline Operations, P.O. Box 23489, L'Enfant Plaza Station, Washington, DC 20026–3489. TIPS Line, 800–447–8477. OIG Fugitive Line, 888–476–4453. TTY, 800–377–4950. Fax, 800–223–8164. Internet, https://forms.oig.hhs.gov/hotlineoperations/.

Office of the Assistant Secretary for Health Contact the Assistant Secretary for Health, Room 716G, 200 Independence Avenue SW., Washington, DC 20201. Phone, 202–690–7694. Internet, http://www.hhs.gov/ash.

Privacy Rights For information on the HIPAA Privacy Rule or the Patient Safety Act, call 800–368–1019. TDD, 800–537–7697. Internet, http://www.hhs.gov/ocr/privacy.

Public Health Service Commissioned Corps Officer Program Information on the Commissioned Corps Officer programs is available at NIH's Public Health Service Commissioned Corps Officer Web site. Internet, http://www.usphs.gov/.

Support Services (Fee-for-Service Activities) The Program Support Center provides support services to all components of the Department and Federal agencies worldwide. For information on fee-for-service activities in the areas of acquisitions, occupational health, information technology support and security, human resource systems, financial management, and administrative operations, contact the Program Support Center, 5600 Fishers Lane, Rockville, MD 20857. Phone, 301–443–0034. Internet, http://www.psc.gov.

Surgeon General For information on the Surgeon General, visit the Department's Web site. Phone, 301–443–4000. Internet, http://www.surgeongeneral.gov.

For further information, contact the U.S. Department of Health and Human Services, 200 Independence Avenue SW., Washington, DC 20201. Phone, 877–696–6775. Internet, http://www.hhs.gov/contactus.html.

Administration for Children and Families

370 L'Enfant Promenade SW., Washington, DC 20447
Phone, 202–401–9200. Internet, http://www.acf.hhs.gov.

Assistant Secretary for Children and Families | MARK GREENBERG, *Acting*

The Administration for Children and Families administers programs and provides advice to the Secretary on issues relevant to children, youth, and families; child support enforcement; community services; developmental disabilities; family assistance; Native American assistance; and refugee resettlement.

Sources of Information

General Inquiries Address questions to the appropriate office, Administration for Children and Families, 370 L'Enfant Promenade SW., Washington, DC 20447. Phone, 202–401–9215. Internet, http://www.acf.hhs.gov.

For further information, contact the Administration for Children and Families, 370 L'Enfant Promenade SW., Washington, DC 20447. Phone, 202–401–9200. Internet, http://www.acf.hhs.gov.

Administration for Community Living

1 Massachusetts Avenue NW., Suite 5100, Washington, DC 20201
Phone, 202–401–4634. TTY, 800–877–8339. Internet, http://www.acl.gov.

Administrator	KATHY GREENLEE

The Administration for Community Living administers programs and advises the Secretary on issues relevant to people with disabilities, their families and caregivers, and the independence, well-being, and health of older adults.

Sources of Information

Elder Care Services Contact the elder care locator. Phone, 800–677–1116.

Internet, http://www.eldercare.gov/ Eldercare.NET/Public/Index.aspx.

General Inquiries Address questions to the Administration for Community Living, Washington, DC 20201. Phone, 202–619–0724, TTY, 1–800–877–8339. Email, aclinfo@acl.hhs.gov. Internet, http://www.acl.gov/About_ACL/Contact_Us/Index.aspx.

For further information, contact the Administration for Community Living, 1 Massachusetts Avenue NW., Suite 5100, Washington, DC 20201. Phone, 202–401–4634. TTY, 800–877–8339. Internet, http://www.acl.gov.

Agency for Healthcare Research and Quality

540 Gaither Road, Rockville, MD 20850
Phone, 301–427–1364. Internet, http://www.ahrq.gov.

Director	RICHARD KRONICK

The Agency for Healthcare Research and Quality (AHRQ) is charged with improving the quality, safety, efficiency, and effectiveness of health care for all Americans. AHRQ supports research that helps people make more informed decisions and improves the quality of health care services.

Sources of Information

General Inquiries Address questions to the appropriate office at the Agency for Healthcare Research and Quality, 540 Gaither Road, Rockville, MD 20850. Phone, 301–427–1364. Internet, http://www.ahrq.gov.

For further information, contact the Agency for Healthcare Research and Quality, 540 Gaither Road, Rockville, MD 20850. Phone, 301–427–1364. Internet, http://www.ahrq.gov.

Agency for Toxic Substances and Disease Registry

4770 Buford Highway NE., Atlanta, GA 30341
Phone, 770–488–0604. Internet, http://www.atsdr.cdc.gov.

Administrator	THOMAS R. FRIEDEN

The Agency for Toxic Substances and Disease Registry, as part of the Public Health Service, is charged with the prevention of exposure to toxic substances and the prevention of the

adverse health effects and diminished quality of life associated with exposure to hazardous substances from wastesites, unplanned releases, and other sources of pollution present in the environment.

Sources of Information

General Inquiries   Address questions to the Agency for Toxic Substances and Disease Registry. 4770 Buford Highway NE., Atlanta, GA 30341. Phone, 800–232–4636. TTY, (888) 232–6348. Internet, http://www.atsdr.cdc.gov.

For further information, contact the Agency for Toxic Substances and Disease Registry, 4770 Buford Highway NE., Atlanta, GA 30341. Phone, 770–488–0604. Internet, http://www.atsdr.cdc.gov.

Centers for Disease Control and Prevention

1600 Clifton Road, Atlanta, GA 30333
Phone, 800–232–4636. Internet, http://www.cdc.gov.

Director	THOMAS R. FRIEDEN

The Centers for Disease Control and Prevention (CDC), as part of the Public Health Service, is charged with protecting the public health of the Nation by providing leadership and direction in the prevention of and control of diseases and other preventable conditions and responding to public health emergencies. Within the CDC, the following seven centers, institutes, and offices lead prevention, diagnosis, and treatment efforts for public health concerns.

Center for Global Health   The Center leads CDC's global health strategy, working in partnership with foreign governments and international organizations to help countries around the world to effectively plan, manage, and evaluate global health care programs. The Center works to eradicate chronic diseases and life-threatening injuries, expanding global health care programs to address the leading causes of disability, morbidity, and mortality.

Internet, http://www.cdc.gov/globalhealth/index.html.

National Institute for Occupational Safety and Health   The Institute plans, directs, and coordinates a national program to develop and establish recommended occupational safety and health standards and to conduct research, training, technical assistance, and related activities to assure safe and healthy working conditions for every working person.

Internet, http://www.cdc.gov/NIOSH/.

Office of Infectious Diseases   The Office facilitates research, programs, and policies to reduce the national and international burden of infectious diseases. The Office includes the following organizational components: the National Center for HIV/AIDS, Viral Hepatitis, STD and TB Prevention; the National Center for Immunization and Respiratory Diseases; and the National Center for Emerging and Zoonotic Infectious Diseases.

Internet, http://www.cdc.gov/oid/.

Office of Noncommunicable Diseases, Injury, and Environmental Health   The Office provides strategic direction and leadership for the prevention of noncommunicable diseases, injuries, disabilities, and environmental health hazards. The Office includes the following organizational components: the National Center on Birth Defects and Developmental Disabilities; the National Center for Chronic Disease Prevention and Health Promotion; the National Center for Environmental Health; and the National Center for Injury Prevention and Control.

Internet, http://www.cdc.gov/maso/pdf/ONDIEHfs.pdf.

Office of Public Health Preparedness and Response   The Office helps the Nation prepare for and respond to urgent public health threats by providing strategic direction, coordination, and support for CDC's terrorism preparedness and emergency response activities.

Internet, http://www.cdc.gov/phpr/.

Office of Public Health Scientific Services   The Office provides scientific services, knowledge, and resources to promote public health, prepare for potential health threats, and prevent disease, disability, and injury. It includes the following organizational components: the National Center for Health Statistics; the Laboratory Science, Policy and Practice Program Office; the Public Health Informatics and Technology Program Office; the Public Health Surveillance Program Office; the Epidemiology and Analysis Program Office; and the Scientific Education and Professional Development Program Office.

Internet, http://www.cdc.gov/ophss/.

Office of State, Tribal, Local, and Territorial Support The Office provides guidance, strategic direction, oversight, and leadership in support of State, local, territorial, and tribal public health agencies, initiatives, and priorities to improve the capacity and performance of a comprehensive public health system.

Internet, http://www.cdc.gov/stltpublichealth/.

Sources of Information

Employment The majority of scientific and technical positions are filled through the Commissioned Corps of the Public Health Service, a uniformed service of the U.S. Government.

General Inquiries Address questions to the appropriate office at the Centers for Disease Control and Prevention, Department of Health and Human Services, 1600 Clifton Road NE., Atlanta, GA 30333.

For further information, contact the Centers for Disease Control and Prevention, 1600 Clifton Road, Atlanta, GA 30333. Phone, 800–232–4636. TTY, 888–232–6348. Internet, http://www.cdc.gov.

Centers for Medicare and Medicaid Services

7500 Security Boulevard, Baltimore, MD 21244
Phone, 410–786–3000. Internet, http://www.cms.gov.

Administrator   MARILYN TAVENNER

The Centers for Medicare and Medicaid Services, formerly known as the Health Care Financing Administration, administers the Medicare, Medicaid, and related Federal medical care programs.

Sources of Information

General Inquiries Address questions to the appropriate office, Centers for Medicare and Medicaid Services, 7500 Security Boulevard, Baltimore, MD 21244. Internet, http://www.cms.gov.

Medicare Hearings and Appeals For information on Medicare hearings and appeals before administrative law judges, contact the Office of Medicare Hearings and Appeals, 1700 N. Moore Street, Suite 1800, Arlington, Virginia 22209. Phone, 703–235–0635 or 855–556–8475 (toll free). Email, medicare.appeals@hhs.gov. Internet, http://www.hhs.gov/omha.

For further information, contact the Centers for Medicare and Medicaid Services, Department of Health and Human Services, 7500 Security Boulevard, Baltimore, MD 21244. Phone, 410–786–3000. Internet, http://www.cms.gov.

Food and Drug Administration

10903 New Hampshire Avenue, Silver Spring, MD 20993
Phone, 1–888–463–6332. Internet, http://www.fda.gov.

Commissioner   MARGARET A. HAMBURG

The Food and Drug Administration (FDA) protects the public health by ensuring the safety, efficacy, and security of human and veterinary drugs, biological products, medical devices, the Nation's food supply, cosmetics, and products that emit radiation. FDA also advances the public health by accelerating innovations to make medicines more effective and providing the public with accurate, science-based information on medicines and food to improve health. FDA plays a significant role in the Nation's counterterrorism capability by ensuring the security of the food supply.

Sources of Information

Employment FDA uses various civil service examinations and registers in its recruitment for positions. For more information, visit the Department's Web site. Internet, http://www.hhs.gov/careers.

General Inquiries Address questions to the appropriate office, Food and Drug Administration, 10903 New Hampshire Avenue, Silver Spring, MD 20993. Internet, http://answers.hhs.gov/.

For further information contact the Food and Drug Administration, 10903 New Hampshire Avenue, Silver Spring, MD 20993. Phone, 888–463–6332. Internet, http://www.fda.gov.

Health Resources and Services Administration

5600 Fishers Lane, Rockville, MD 20857
Phone, 301–443–3376. Internet, http://www.hrsa.gov.

Administrator	MARY K. WAKEFIELD

The Health Resources and Services Administration (HRSA) improves access to health care services for people who are uninsured, isolated, or medically vulnerable. Comprising 6 bureaus and 10 offices, HRSA provides leadership and financial support to health care providers in every State and U.S. Territory. HRSA grantees provide health care to uninsured people, people living with HIV/AIDS, and pregnant women, mothers, and children. HRSA trains health professionals, improves systems of care in rural communities, and oversees organ, bone marrow, and cord blood donation. HRSA also supports programs that prepare for bioterrorism, compensates individuals harmed by vaccination, and maintains databases that protect against health care malpractice and abuse.

Sources of Information

Employment Most positions are in the Federal civil service. Some health professional positions are filled through the Commissioned Corps of the Public Health Service, a uniformed service of the U.S. Government. Visit USAJOBS, a free web-based job board for Federal job seekers (https://www.usajobs.gov/). Internet, http://www.hrsa.gov/hr/index.html.

General Inquiries Address questions to the appropriate office, Health Resources and Services Administration, 5600 Fishers Lane, Rockville, MD 20857. Internet, http://www.hrsa.gov/index.html.

For further information, contact the Office of Communications, Health Resources and Services Administration, 5600 Fishers Lane, Rockville, MD 20857. Phone, 301–443–3376. Internet, http://www.hrsa.gov/about/contact/.

Indian Health Service

801 Thompson Avenue, Rockville, MD 20852
Phone, 301–443–2650. Internet, http://www.ihs.gov.

Director	Yvette Roubideaux

The Indian Health Service, as part of the Public Health Service, provides a comprehensive health services delivery system for American Indians and Alaska Natives. It assists Native American tribes in developing their health programs; facilitates and assists tribes in coordinating health planning, obtaining, and utilizing health resources available through Federal, State, and local programs, operating comprehensive health programs, and evaluating health programs; and provides comprehensive

health care services, including hospital and ambulatory medical care, preventive and rehabilitative services, and development of community sanitation facilities.

Sources of Information

General Inquiries   Address questions to the appropriate office, Indian Health Service, 801 Thompson Avenue, Rockville, MD 20852. Internet, http://www.ihs.gov/contactus/.

For further information, contact the Management Policy and Internal Control Staff, Indian Health Service, 801 Thompson Avenue, Rockville, MD 20852. Phone, 301–443–2650. Internet, http://www.ihs.gov/contact/.

National Institutes of Health

1 Center Drive, Bethesda, MD 20892
Phone, 301–496–4000. Internet, http://www.nih.gov.

Director	Francis S. Collins

The National Institutes of Health (NIH) supports biomedical and behavioral research domestically and abroad, conducts research in its own laboratories and clinics, trains research scientists, and develops and disseminates credible, science-based health information to the public.

Aging   The Institute conducts and supports research on the aging process, age-related diseases, and other special problems and needs of older Americans. It also provides information about aging to the scientific community, health care providers, and the public.

For further information, contact the National Institute on Aging. Phone, 301–496–1752. Internet, http://www.nia.nih.gov.

Alcohol Abuse and Alcoholism   The Institute leads the national effort to reduce alcohol-related problems by conducting and supporting biomedical and behavioral research into the causes,

consequences, prevention, and treatment of alcohol-use disorders.

For further information, contact the National Institute on Alcohol Abuse and Alcoholism. Phone, 301–443–3885. Internet, http://www.niaaa.nih.gov.

Allergy and Infectious Diseases   The Institute conducts and supports research to study the causes of infectious diseases and immune-mediated diseases and to develop better means of preventing, diagnosing, and treating these diseases.

For further information, contact the National Institute of Allergy and Infectious Diseases. Phone, 866–284–4107 or 301–496–5717. Internet, http://www.niaid.nih.gov.

Arthritis and Musculoskeletal and Skin Diseases   The Institute supports research into the causes, treatment, and prevention of arthritis and musculoskeletal and skin diseases; the training of basic and clinical scientists to carry out this research; and the dissemination of information on research progress in these diseases.

For further information, contact the National Institute of Arthritis and Musculoskeletal and Skin Diseases. Phone, 301–496–8190. Internet, http://www.niams.nih.gov.

Biomedical Imaging and Bioengineering The Institute conducts, coordinates, and supports research, training, dissemination of health information, and other programs with respect to biomedical imaging, biomedical engineering, and associated technologies and modalities with biomedical applications.

For further information, contact the National Institute of Biomedical Imaging and Bioengineering. Phone, 301–451–6768. Internet, http://www.nibib.nih.gov.

Cancer The Institute coordinates the National Cancer Program and conducts and supports research, training, and public education with regard to the cause, diagnosis, prevention, and treatment of cancer.

For further information, contact the Cancer Information Service. Phone, 800–422–6237 or 301–435–3848. Internet, http://www.cancer.gov.

Center for Information Technology The Center provides, coordinates, and manages information technology to advance computational science.

For further information, contact the Center for Information Technology. Phone, 301–496–6203. Internet, http://www.cit.nih.gov.

Child Health and Human Development The Institute conducts and supports basic, translational, clinical, and epidemiological research on the reproductive, rehabilitative, neurobiological, developmental, and behavioral processes that determine, maximize, and maintain the health of children, adults, families, and populations.

For further information, contact the Eunice Kennedy Shriver National Institute of Child Health and Human Development. Phone, 800–370–2943. Internet, http://www.nichd.nih.gov.

Clinical Center The NIH Clinical Center is the clinical research hospital for NIH. By doing clinical research, investigators translate laboratory discoveries into better treatments, therapies, and interventions to improve the Nation's health. The Clinical Center conducts clinical and laboratory research and trains future clinical investigators. Nearly 500,000 volunteers from across the Nation have participated in clinical research studies since the Center opened in 1953. About 1,500 clinical research studies are currently in progress.

For further information, contact the Clinical Center. Phone, 301–496–2563. Internet, http://clinicalcenter.nih.gov.

Complementary and Alternative Medicine The Center's role is to define, through rigorous scientific investigation, the usefulness and safety of complementary health practices that are not generally considered part of conventional care. This scientific research informs decisionmaking by the public, health care professionals, and health policymakers regarding the use and integration of such practices into the health care delivery system in the United States.

For further information, contact the National Center for Complementary and Alternative Medicine. Phone, 888–644–6226. Internet, http://nccam.nih.gov.

Deafness and Other Communication Disorders The Institute conducts and supports biomedical and behavioral research and research training on normal and disordered processes of hearing, balance, smell, taste, voice, speech, and language, and provides health information, based on scientific discovery, to the public. The Institute conducts diverse research performed in its own laboratories and funds a program of research and research grants.

For further information, contact the National Institute on Deafness and Other Communication Disorders. Phone, 301–496–7243. Internet, http://www.nidcd.nih.gov.

Dental and Craniofacial Research The Institute conducts and supports research and research training into the causes, prevention, diagnosis, and treatment of craniofacial, oral, and dental diseases and disorders.

For further information, contact the National Institute of Dental and Craniofacial Research. Phone, 301–496–4261. Internet, http://www.nidcr.nih.gov.

Diabetes and Digestive and Kidney Diseases The Institute conducts, fosters, and supports basic and clinical research into the causes, prevention, diagnosis, and treatment of diabetes, endocrine and metabolic diseases, digestive diseases and nutrition, kidney and urologic diseases, and blood diseases.

For further information, contact the National Institute of Diabetes and Digestive and Kidney Diseases. Phone, 301–496–3583. Internet, http://www2.niddk.nih.gov.

Drug Abuse   The Institute's primary mission is to lead the Nation in bringing the power of science to bear on drug abuse and addiction through the strategic support and conduct of research across a broad range of disciplines and the rapid and effective dissemination and use of the results of that research to significantly improve drug abuse and addiction prevention and treatment and to inform policy.

For further information, contact the National Institute on Drug Abuse. Phone, 301–443–1124. Internet, http://www.nida.nih.gov.

Environmental Health Sciences   The Institute reduces the burden of human illnesses and disability by understanding how the environment influences the development and progression of human disease. To have the greatest impact on preventing disease and improving human health, the Institute focuses on basic science, disease-oriented research, global environmental health, and multidisciplinary training for researchers. NIEHS also houses the National Toxicology Program, a cross-agency organization designed to coordinate toxicity testing across the Federal Government.

For further information, contact the National Institute of Environmental Health Sciences. Phone, 919–541–3345. Internet, http://www.niehs.nih.gov.

Fogarty International Center   The Center addresses global health challenges through innovative and collaborative research and training programs. It also supports and advances the NIH mission through international partnerships.

For further information, contact the Fogarty International Center. Phone, 301–496–2075. Internet, http://www.fic.nih.gov.

General Medical Sciences   The Institute supports basic biomedical research and research training in areas ranging from cell biology, chemistry, and biophysics to genetics, pharmacology, and systemic response to trauma.

For further information, contact the National Institute of General Medical Sciences. Phone, 301–496–7301. Internet, http://www.nigms.nih.gov.

Heart, Lung, and Blood Diseases   The Institute provides leadership for a global program in diseases of the heart, blood vessels, lung, and blood; sleep disorders; and blood resources. It conducts, fosters, and supports an integrated and coordinated program of basic research, clinical investigations and trials, observational studies, and demonstration and education projects.

For further information, contact the National Heart, Lung, and Blood Institute. Phone, 301–496–0554. Internet, http://www.nhlbi.nih.gov.

Human Genome Research   The Institute, which helped lead the Human Genome Project, leads and supports a broad range of initiatives and studies aimed at understanding the structure and function of the human genome and its role in health and disease

For further information, contact the National Human Genome Research Institute. Phone, 301–496–0844. Internet, http://www.genome.gov.

Library of Medicine   The National Library of Medicine is the world's largest biomedical library. It serves as the Nation's chief medical information source, providing medical library services and extensive Web-based information resources, such as PubMed, MedlinePlus, ClinicalTrials.gov, GenBank, and Toxline, to scientists, practitioners, and the general public. It conducts, fosters, and supports research and training in biomedical informatics and supports development and dissemination of clinical terminology standards.

For further information, contact the National Library of Medicine. Phone, 301–496–6308. Internet, http://www.nlm.nih.gov.

Mental Health   The National Institute of Mental Health works to transform the understanding and treatment of mental illnesses through basic and clinical research to further the prevention, recovery, and cure of disabling mental conditions that affect millions of Americans.

For further information, contact the National Institute of Mental Health. Phone, 866–615–6464. Internet, http://www.nimh.nih.gov.

Minority Health and Health Disparities The Institute leads scientific research to improve minority health and eliminate health disparities. To achieve its mission, the Institute plans, reviews, coordinates, and evaluates all minority health and health disparities research and activities of the NIH; conducts and supports research on minority health and health disparities; promotes and supports the training of a diverse research workforce; translates and disseminates research information; and fosters innovative collaborations and partnerships.

For further information, contact the National Institute on Minority Health and Health Disparities. Phone, 301–402–1366. Internet, http://www.nimhd. nih.gov.

Neurological Disorders and Stroke The Institute's mission is to reduce the burden of neurological diseases. It conducts, fosters, coordinates, and guides research and training on the causes, prevention, diagnosis, and treatment of neurological disorders and stroke and supports basic, translational, and clinical research in related scientific areas.

For further information, contact the Brain Resources and Information Network of the National Institute of Neurological Disorders and Stroke, P.O. Box 5801, Bethesda, MD 20824. Phone, 800–352–9424. Internet, http://www.ninds.nih.gov.

Nursing Research The Institute supports clinical and basic research to build the scientific foundation for clinical practice, prevent disease and disability, manage and eliminate symptoms caused by illness, and enhance end-of-life and palliative care. The Institute addresses current workforce challenges by training the next generation of scientists and faculty.

For further information, contact the National Institute of Nursing Research. Phone, 301–496–0207. Internet, http://www.ninr.nih.gov.

Ophthalmological Diseases The Institute conducts, fosters, and supports research on the causes, natural history,

prevention, diagnosis, and treatment of disorders of the eye and visual system. It also directs the National Eye Health Education Program.

For further information, contact the National Eye Institute. Phone, 301–496–5248. Internet, http://www.nei.nih.gov.

Research Resources The National Center for Research Resources supports all aspects of clinical and translational research, connecting researchers, patients, and communities across the Nation. NCRR's matrix of extramural programs enables discoveries made at a molecular and cellular level to move to animal-based studies and then to patient-oriented clinical research. The Center provides thousands of NIH-funded laboratory scientists and clinical researchers with the tools and training they need to understand, detect, treat, and prevent a wide range of diseases.

For further information, contact the National Center for Research Resources. Phone, 301–435–0888. Email, info@ncrr.nih.gov. Internet, http://www.nih. gov/about/almanac/organization/NCRR.htm.

Scientific Review The Center for Scientific Review (CSR) organizes the peer review groups that evaluate the majority of grant applications submitted to NIH. These groups include experienced and respected researchers from across the country and abroad. Since 1946, CSR has ensured that NIH grant applications receive fair, independent, expert, and timely reviews—free from inappropriate influences—so NIH can fund the most promising research. CSR also receives all incoming applications and assigns them to the NIH Institutes and Centers that fund grants.

For further information, contact the Center for Scientific Review. Phone, 301–435–1111. Internet, http://public.csr.nih.gov.

Sources of Information

Employment Information on employment opportunities is available at the "Jobs at NIH" Web page. Internet, http://www.jobs.nih.gov.

General Inquiries Address questions to the appropriate office, National Institutes of Health, 1 Center Drive, Bethesda, MD

20892. Phone, 301–496–4000. Internet, http://www.nih.gov/about/FAQ.htm.

For further information, contact the National Institutes of Health, 1 Center Drive, Bethesda, MD 20892. Phone, 301–496–4000. Internet, http://www.nih.gov.

Substance Abuse and Mental Health Services Administration

1 Choke Cherry Road, Rockville, MD 20857
Phone, 240–276–2130. Internet, http://www.samhsa.gov.

Administrator	PAMELA S. HYDE

The Substance Abuse and Mental Health Services Administration (SAMHSA) reduces the impact of substance abuse and mental illness on America's communities. SAMHSA provides national leadership and a voice for behavioral health; funds State and local service agencies through grants and formulas; collects data and provides surveillance reports on the impact of behavioral health on Americans; leads efforts to provide public education on mental illness and substance abuse prevention, treatment and recovery; regulates and oversees national behavioral health programs; and promotes practice improvement in community-based, primary, and specialty care settings.

Sources of Information

Employment Information is available on SAMHSA's "Jobs and Internships" Web page. Internet, http://beta.samhsa.gov/about-us/jobs-internships.

General Inquiries Address questions to the appropriate office, Substance Abuse and Mental Health Services Administration, 1 Choke Cherry Road, Rockville, MD 20857. Internet, http://beta.samhsa.gov/about-us/contact-us.

For further information, contact the Substance Abuse and Mental Health Services Administration, 1 Choke Cherry Road, Rockville, MD 20857. Phone, 240–276–2130. Internet, http://www.samhsa.gov.

DEPARTMENT OF HOMELAND SECURITY

Washington, DC 20528
Phone, 202–282–8000. Internet, http://www.dhs.gov.

Secretary of Homeland Security	JEH C. JOHNSON
Deputy Secretary	ALEJANDRO N. MAYORKAS
Chief of Staff	CHRISTIAN MARRONE
Executive Secretary	ELISA D. MONTOYA
General Counsel	STEVAN E. BUNNELL
Under Secretary, Management	CHRIS CUMMISKEY, *Acting*
Under Secretary, National Protection and Programs Directorate	SUZANNE E. SPAULDING
Assistant Secretary, Office of Cyber Security and Communications	ROBERTA STEMPLEY, *Acting*
Assistant Secretary, Infrastructure Protection	CAITLIN DURKOVICH
Director, Federal Protective Service	L. ERIC PATTERSON
Under Secretary, Science and Technology	L. REGINALD BROTHERS, JR.
Under Secretary, Office of Intelligence and Analysis	FRANCIS X. TAYLOR
Assistant Secretary, Office of Policy	DAVID HEYMAN
Assistant Secretary, Office of International Affairs	ALAN D. BERSIN
Assistant Secretary, Office of Policy Development	(VACANCY)
Assistant Secretary, Private Sector Office	MICHAEL STROUD, *Acting*
Assistant Secretary, State and Local Law Enforcement	(VACANCY)
Assistant Secretary, Office of Intergovernmental Affairs	PHILIP A. MCNAMARA
Director, U.S. Citizenship and Immigration Services	LEON RODRIGUEZ
Commandant, U.S. Coast Guard	ADM. ROBERT J. PAPP, JR.
Commissioner, U.S. Customs and Border Protection	R. GIL KERLIKOWSKE
Assistant Secretary, U.S. Immigration and Customs Enforcement	THOMAS WINKOWSKI, *Acting*
Administrator, Federal Emergency Management Agency	W. CRAIG FUGATE
Director, U.S. Secret Service	JOSEPH CLANCY, *Acting*
Administrator ,Transportation Security Administration	JOHN S. PISTOLE
Citizenship and Immigration Services Ombudsman	MARIA ODOM, *Acting*
Officer for Civil Rights and Civil Liberties	MEGAN H. MACK, *Acting*
Director, Domestic Nuclear Detection Office	HUBAN GOWADIA, *Acting*
Director, Federal Law Enforcement Training Center	CONNIE L. PATRICK
Assistant Secretary, Office of Health Affairs/ Chief Medical Officer	KATHRYN BRINSFIELD, *Acting*

Inspector General	JOHN ROTH
Assistant Secretary, Office of Legislative Affairs	BRIAN DE VALLANCE, *Acting*
Director, Operations Coordination and Planning	RICHARD CHAVEZ
Chief Privacy Officer	KAREN NEUMAN
Assistant Secretary, Office of Public Affairs	CLARK STEVENS
Chief Financial Officer	CHARLES H. FULGHUM

The Department of Homeland Security enforces and administers our Nation's immigration laws, ensures resilience in the aftermath of disaster, enhances security to prevent terrorism, and safeguards and secures cyberspace.

The Department of Homeland Security (DHS) was established by the Homeland Security Act of 2002 (6 U.S.C. 101 note). The Department came into existence on January 24, 2003, and is administered under the supervision and direction of the Secretary of Homeland Security.

Office of the Secretary

Secretary The Secretary is responsible for developing and coordinating a comprehensive national strategy to protect the United States against terrorist attacks. The Secretary advises the President on how to strengthen U.S. borders, to provide for intelligence analysis and infrastructure protection, to improve the use of science and technology to counter weapons of mass destruction, and to create a comprehensive response and recovery division.

The Office of the Secretary oversees activities in collaboration with other Federal, State, local, and private entities to carry out the Department's overall mission. The Office of the Secretary comprises 10 smaller Offices, which support the Secretary in fulfilling his or her responsibilities.

Privacy Office The Privacy Office protects the collection, use, and disclosure of personally identifiable information and departmental information. It ensures that appropriate access to information is consistent with the vision, strategic mission, and core values of DHS. The Office also implements the policies of the Department to defend and protect the individual rights, liberties, and information interests of our citizens.

The Office has oversight of all privacy and disclosure policy matters, including compliance with the Privacy Act of 1974, the Freedom of Information Act, and the completion of privacy impact statements on all new programs and systems, as required by the E–Government Act of 2002 and Section 222 of the Homeland Security Act.

Office for Civil Rights and Civil Liberties The Office provides legal and policy advice to Department leadership on civil rights and civil liberties issues, investigates and resolves complaints, and provides leadership to DHS Equal Employment Opportunity Programs.

Office of Inspector General The Office of Inspector General (OIG) conducts and supervises audits, investigations, and inspections relating to the Department's programs and operations. The OIG examines, evaluates, and where necessary, critiques these operations and activities, recommending ways for DHS to carry out its responsibilities in the most economical, efficient, and effective manner possible. The OIG also reviews recommendations regarding existing and proposed legislation and regulations relating to the Department's programs and operations.

Citizenship and Immigration Services Ombudsman The Citizenship and Immigration Services Ombudsman (CISOMB) assists individuals and employers in resolving problems connected with pending U.S. Citizenship and Immigration Services (USCIS) cases. In addition, as required by statute, CISOMB identifies common problems experienced by individuals and employers when seeking USCIS services and proposes changes to

DEPARTMENT OF HOMELAND SECURITY

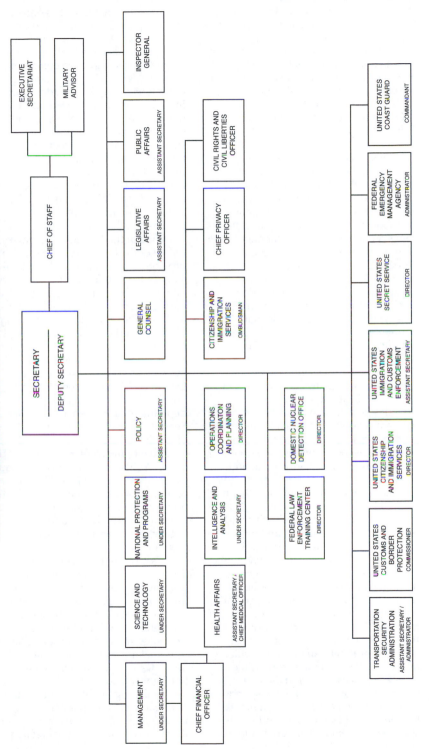

EXECUTIVE SECRETARIAT

MILITARY ADVISOR

CHIEF OF STAFF

SECRETARY
DEPUTY SECRETARY

INSPECTOR GENERAL

PUBLIC AFFAIRS
ASSISTANT SECRETARY

LEGISLATIVE AFFAIRS
ASSISTANT SECRETARY

GENERAL COUNSEL

CIVIL RIGHTS AND CIVIL LIBERTIES OFFICER

CHIEF PRIVACY OFFICER

CITIZENSHIP AND IMMIGRATION SERVICES
OMBUDSMAN

POLICY
ASSISTANT SECRETARY

OPERATIONS COORDINATION AND PLANNING
DIRECTOR

DOMESTIC NUCLEAR DETECTION OFFICE
DIRECTOR

NATIONAL PROTECTION AND PROGRAMS
UNDER SECRETARY

INTELLIGENCE AND ANALYSIS
UNDER SECRETARY

FEDERAL LAW ENFORCEMENT TRAINING CENTER
DIRECTOR

SCIENCE AND TECHNOLOGY
UNDER SECRETARY

HEALTH AFFAIRS
ASSISTANT SECRETARY / CHIEF MEDICAL OFFICER

MANAGEMENT
UNDER SECRETARY

CHIEF FINANCIAL OFFICER

TRANSPORTATION SECURITY ADMINISTRATION
ASSISTANT SECRETARY / ADMINISTRATOR

UNITED STATES CUSTOMS AND BORDER PROTECTION
COMMISSIONER

UNITED STATES CITIZENSHIP AND IMMIGRATION SERVICES
DIRECTOR

UNITED STATES IMMIGRATION AND CUSTOMS ENFORCEMENT
ASSISTANT SECRETARY

UNITED STATES SECRET SERVICE
DIRECTOR

FEDERAL EMERGENCY MANAGEMENT AGENCY
ADMINISTRATOR

UNITED STATES COAST GUARD
COMMANDANT

mitigate such problems and improve the delivery of immigration services. In accomplishing each of these missions, the CISOMB works impartially, soliciting information and feedback from USCIS, other Government agencies, immigration benefits applicants, and the immigration stakeholder community.

Office of Legislative Affairs   The Office of Legislative Affairs (OLA) serves as the Department's primary liaison to Congress. It advocates for the policy interests of the administration and the Secretary. OLA also ensures that all DHS components are actively engaged with Congress in their specific areas of responsibility. The Office articulates views on behalf of DHS components and their legislative initiatives. It responds to requests and inquiries from congressional committees, individual Members of Congress, and their staffs. OLA also participates in the Senate confirmation process for each DHS Presidential nominee.

Office of General Counsel   The Office of General Counsel (OGC) is responsible for ensuring that departmental activities comply with applicable legal requirements. OGC provides legal advice on areas such as national security, immigration, litigation, international law, maritime safety and security, transportation security, border security law, cybersecurity, fiscal and appropriations law, environmental law, and many others. It also ensures that the Department's efforts to secure the Nation are consistent with the civil rights and civil liberties of its citizens and follow the rule of law. OGC also provides legal services in several areas where the law intersects with the achievement of mission goals, such as the coordination of the Department's rulemaking activities, managing interdepartmental clearance of proposed legislation, and providing legal training for law enforcement officers.

Office of Public Affairs   The Office of Public Affairs (OPA) is responsible for managing external and internal communications. The Office responds to national media inquiries, maintains the Department's Web site, and writes speeches for senior Department officials.

The Office manages DHS's organizational identity program, which includes usage of the DHS seal and related guidelines. Also, the Office oversees the Department's employee communication activities, which include coordinating communications for departmentwide initiatives, town hall meetings between management and employees, and the operation and management of an intranet site. Per Presidential directive, OPA's incident communications program guides overall Federal incident communication activity and coordinates with State, local, and international partners to ensure accurate and timely information is provided to the public during a crisis.

Office of the Executive Secretary   The Office of the Executive Secretary (ESEC) provides analytical and administrative support to the Office of the Secretary and the Office of the Deputy Secretary. ESEC manages the Secretary's internal and external correspondence, prepares classified and unclassified briefing materials, and oversees development of departmental testimony, questions for the record, and congressional reports. ESEC also facilitates departmental communications with Federal departments and agencies, the National Security Council, and other White House executive offices.

Office of the Military Advisor   The Senior Military Advisor provides counsel to the Secretary and DHS Components relating to the facilitation, coordination, and execution of policy, procedures, and preparedness activities and operations between DHS and the Department of Defense.

Office of Intergovernmental Affairs   The Office of Intergovernmental Affairs (IGA) is responsible for communicating and coordinating State, local, tribal, and Territorial (SLTT) government interactions throughout the Department. IGA promotes an integrated national approach to homeland security by coordinating and advancing Federal interaction with SLTT governments. IGA is responsible for continuing the homeland security dialogue with SLTT partners, along with the national associations that represent them. IGA serves as the Secretary's primary point of contact for SLTT elected and appointed officials and their associations to ensure there are open lines of communication between the Department and its homeland security partners.

Components

National Protection and Programs Directorate   The Directorate for National Protection and Programs safeguards our critical information systems, borders, seaports, bridges, and highways by working with State, local, and private sector partners to identify threats, determine vulnerabilities, and target resources toward the greatest risks. Its functions include strengthening national risk management efforts for critical infrastructure and defining and advancing homeland security protection initiatives.

Science and Technology Directorate   The Science and Technology Directorate is the primary research and development arm of the Department. The Directorate provides Federal, State, and local officials with the technology and capabilities to protect the homeland. Its strategic objectives are to develop and deploy systems to prevent, detect, and mitigate the consequences of chemical, biological, radiological, nuclear, and explosive attacks; develop equipment, protocols, and training procedures for response to and recovery from those attacks; enhance the Department's and other Federal, State, local, and tribal agencies' technical capabilities to fulfill their homeland security-related functions; and develop technical standards and establish certified laboratories to evaluate homeland security and emergency responder technologies for SAFETY Act certification.

Directorate for Management   The Directorate for Management is responsible for budget, appropriations, expenditure of funds, accounting and finance; procurement; human resources and personnel; information technology systems; facilities, property, equipment, and other material resources; and identification and tracking of

performance measurements relating to the responsibilities of the Department.

The Directorate for Management ensures that the Department's employees have well-defined responsibilities and that managers and their employees have effective means of communicating with one another, with other governmental and nongovernmental bodies, and with the public they serve.

Chief Financial Officer   The Chief Financial Officer oversees all financial management activities relating to the programs and operations of DHS, develops and maintains an integrated accounting and financial management system, and is responsible for financial reporting and internal controls.

Office of Policy   The Office of Policy (PLCY) coordinates departmentwide policies, programs, and planning to ensure consistency. The Office provides a centralized coordination point for developing and communicating policies across the multiple internal and external components of the Homeland Security network. The Office also interacts with other government entities, academia, and includes risk management functions for DHS.

Office of Health Affairs   The Office of Health Affairs (OHA) serves as the principal adviser to the Secretary on medical and public health issues. OHA leads the Department's workforce health protection and medical support activities. The Office also manages and coordinates the Department's biological and chemical defense programs and provides medical and scientific expertise to support DHS preparedness and response efforts.

Office of Intelligence and Analysis   The Office of Intelligence and Analysis, as a member of the U.S. Intelligence Community, is the nexus between the Nation's intelligence apparatus and DHS components and other State, local, and private sector partners. The Office ensures that information is gathered from all relevant DHS field operations and other State, local, and private sector partners and that this information is shared with appropriate stakeholders to produce accurate, timely, and actionable analytical intelligence products and services.

Office of Operations Coordination and Planning   The Office of Operations Coordination and Planning (OPS) provides decision support and enables the Secretary's execution of responsibilities across the homeland security enterprise by promoting situational awareness and information sharing, integrating and synchronizing strategic operations and planning, and administering the DHS continuity program. OPS is responsible for providing a joint operations coordination and planning capability at the strategic level to support DHS operational decisionmaking, Department leadership, and participation in interagency operations throughout the homeland security enterprise and across all mission areas.

Federal Law Enforcement Training Center   The Federal Law Enforcement Training Center (FLETC) serves as an interagency law enforcement training organization for 90 Federal agencies and provides strategically designed training to State, local, rural, tribal, Territorial, and international law enforcement agencies.

Domestic Nuclear Detection Office   The Domestic Nuclear Detection Office (DNDO) is responsible for developing a global nuclear detection architecture and acquiring and supporting the deployment of a domestic nuclear detection system to report any attempt to use nuclear or radiological material against the United States. The Office also works to enhance the nuclear detection efforts of Federal, State, Territorial, tribal, and local governments and the private sector to ensure a coordinated response to such threats.

Transportation Security Administration   The Transportation Security Administration (TSA) protects the Nation's transportation systems to ensure freedom of movement for people and commerce.

United States Customs and Border Protection   U.S. Customs and Border Protection (CBP) is responsible for securing the Nation's borders to protect it against terrorist threats and prevent the illegal entry of inadmissible persons and contraband, while facilitating lawful travel, trade, and immigration.

United States Citizenship and Immigration Services   U.S. Citizenship and Immigration Services (USCIS) ensures that information and decisions on citizenship and immigration benefits are provided to customers in a timely, accurate, consistent, courteous, and professional manner, while also helping to safeguard our national security. USCIS is also responsible for enhancing the integrity of our country's legal immigration system by deterring, detecting, and pursuing immigration-related fraud, combating the unauthorized practice of immigration law, and helping to combat unauthorized employment in the workplace.

United States Immigration and Customs Enforcement   U.S. Immigration and Customs Enforcement (ICE) is the principal investigative arm of DHS. ICE's primary mission is to promote homeland security and public safety through the criminal and civil enforcement of Federal laws governing border control, customs, trade, and immigration.

United States Coast Guard   The U.S. Coast Guard (USCG) protects those on the sea, protects the Nation from seaborne threats, and ensures the safety, security, and stewardship of the Nation's ports, waterways, coasts, and far-reaching maritime regions of economic and national security interest. Coast Guard missions include search and rescue; maritime safety; ports, waterways, and coastal security; drug interdiction; defense readiness; ice operations; aids to navigation; marine environmental protection; living marine resources; and other law enforcement activities.

Federal Emergency Management Agency   Federal Emergency Management Agency (FEMA) manages and coordinates the Federal response to and recovery from major domestic disasters and emergencies of all types. FEMA coordinates programs to improve the effectiveness of emergency response providers at all levels of the government to respond to terrorist attacks, major disasters, and other emergencies. FEMA also initiates proactive mitigation activities, trains first responders, and manages the National Flood Insurance Program and U.S. Fire Administration.

United States Secret Service The U.S. Secret Service (USSS) carries out a unique dual mission of protection and investigation. The Secret Service protects the President, Vice President, visiting heads of state and government, and National Special Security Events; safeguards the Nation's financial infrastructure and payments systems to preserve the integrity of the economy; and protects the White House and other designated buildings within the Washington, DC, area.

Sources of Information

Electronic Access Use the link below to visit the Department of Homeland Security's Web site. Internet, http://www.dhs.gov.

For further information concerning the Department of Homeland Security, contact the Office of Public Affairs, Department of Homeland Security, Washington, DC 20528. Phone, 202–282–8000. Internet, https://www.dhs.gov/about-office-public-affairs.

DEPARTMENT OF HOUSING AND URBAN DEVELOPMENT

451 Seventh Street SW., Washington, DC 20410
Phone, 202–708–1422. Internet, http://www.hud.gov.

Secretary of Housing and Urban Development	JULIÁN CASTRO
Deputy Secretary	HELEN R. KANOVSKY, *Acting*
Senior Advisor to the Secretary	JENNIFER HO
Chief of Staff	NEILAND PARKER
General Counsel	HELEN R. KANOVSKY
Inspector General	DAVID A. MONTOYA
Assistant Secretary for Community Planning and Development	MARK JOHNSTON, *Acting*
Assistant Secretary for Congressional and Intergovernmental Relations	ERIKA L. MORITSUGU
Assistant Secretary for Fair Housing and Equal Opportunity	GUSTAVO F. VELASQUEZ
Assistant Secretary for Housing and Federal Housing Commissioner	CAROL GALANTE
Assistant Secretary for Policy Development and Research	KATHERINE M. O'REGAN
Assistant Secretary for Public and Indian Housing	JEMINE BRYON, *Acting*
Assistant Secretary for Public Affairs	BETSAIDA ALCANTARA
Assistant Deputy Secretary for Field Policy and Management	MARY MCBRIDE
Chief Information Officer	RAFAEL DIAZ
Chief Financial Officer	BRADFORD RAYMOND HUTHER
Chief Procurement Officer	JEMINE BRYON
Chief Human Capital Officer	MICHAEL A. ANDERSON
Director, Office of Healthy Homes and Lead Hazard Control	JON L. GANT
Director, Office of Departmental Equal Employment Opportunity	JOHN P. BENISON
Director, Office of Economic Resilience	HARRIET TREGONING
President, Government National Mortgage Association (Ginnie Mae)	THEODORE TOZER

The Department of Housing and Urban Development oversees our Nation's housing needs, ensures fair housing opportunities, and creates strong, sustainable, and inclusive communities.

The Department of Housing and Urban Development (HUD) was established in 1965 by the Department of Housing and Urban Development Act (42 U.S.C. 3532–3537). It was created to administer the principal programs which provide assistance for housing and for the development of the Nation's communities; to encourage the solution of housing and community development problems through States and localities; and to encourage the maximum contributions that may be made by vigorous private homebuilding and

214

DEPARTMENT OF HOUSING AND URBAN DEVELOPMENT

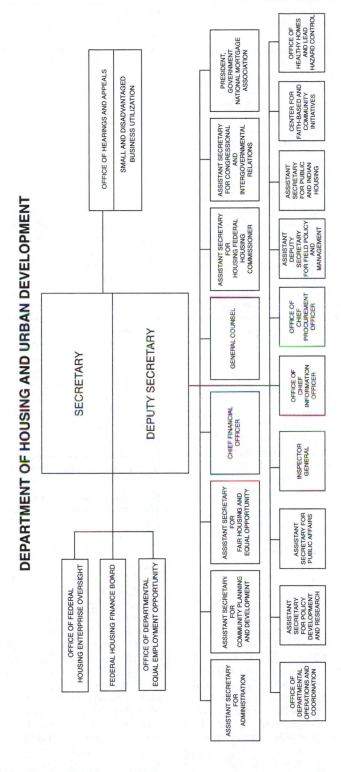

mortgage lending industries to housing, community development, and the national economy.

Although HUD administers many programs, its six major functions are insuring mortgages for single-family and multifamily dwellings and extending loans for home improvement and for the purchasing of mobile homes; channeling funds from investors to the mortgage industry through the Government National Mortgage Association; making direct loans for construction or rehabilitation of housing projects for the elderly and the handicapped; providing Federal housing subsidies for low- and moderate-income families; providing grants to States and communities for community development activities; and promoting and enforcing fair housing and equal housing opportunity.

Secretary   The Secretary formulates recommendations for basic policies in the fields of housing and community development; encourages private enterprise participation in housing and community development; promotes the growth of cities and States and the efficient and effective use of housing and community and economic development resources by stimulating private sector initiatives, public/private sector partnerships, and public entrepreneurship; ensures equal access to housing and affirmatively prevents discrimination in housing; and provides general oversight for the Federal National Mortgage Association.

Program Areas

Community Planning and Development
The Office administers grant programs to help communities plan and finance their growth and development, increase their capacity to govern, and to provide shelter and services for homeless people. The Office is responsible for the implementation of Community Development Block Grant (CDBG) programs for entitlement communities; the State- and HUD-administered Small Cities Program; community development loan guarantees; special purpose grants for insular areas and historically black colleges and universities; Appalachian

Regional Commission grants; the Home Investment in Affordable Housing Program, which provides Federal assistance for housing rehabilitation, tenant-based assistance, first-time homebuyers, and new construction for when a jurisdiction is determined to need new rental housing; the Department's programs to address homelessness; the John Heinz Neighborhood Development Program; community outreach partnerships; the joint community development plan to assist institutions of higher education working in concert with State and local governments to undertake activities under the CDBG program; community adjustment and economic diversification planning grants; the YouthBuild Program, which provides opportunities and assistance to very low income high school dropouts, ages 16 to 24; empowerment zones and enterprise communities; efforts to improve the environment; and community planning and development efforts of other departments and agencies, public and private organizations, private industry, financial markets, and international organizations. More information on community planning and development is available online: http://portal.hud.gov/hudportal/HUD?src=/program_offices/comm_planning.

For further information, contact the Office of Community Planning and Development. Phone, 202–708–2690.

Fair Housing and Equal Opportunity
The Office administers fair housing laws and regulations prohibiting discrimination in public and private housing; equal opportunity laws and regulations prohibiting discrimination in HUD-assisted housing and community development programs; the fair housing assistance grants program to provide financial and technical assistance to State and local government agencies to implement local fair housing laws and ordinances; and the Community Housing Resources Boards program to provide grants for fair housing activities such as outreach and education, identification of institutional barriers to fair housing, and complaint telephone hotlines. More information on fair housing and equal

opportunity is available online: http://portal.hud.gov/hudportal/HUD?src=/program_offices/fair_housing_equal_opp.

For further information, contact the Office of Fair Housing and Equal Opportunity. Phone, 202–708–4252.

Federal Housing Enterprise Oversight

The Office oversees the financial safety and soundness of the Federal National Mortgage Association (Fannie Mae) and the Federal Home Loan Mortgage Corporation (Freddie Mac) to ensure that they are adequately capitalized and operating safely.

For further information, contact the Office of Federal Housing Enterprise Oversight. Phone, 202–414–3800.

Government National Mortgage Association (GNMA)

The mission of this Government corporation, also known as Ginnie Mae, is to support expanded affordable housing by providing an efficient Government-guaranteed secondary market vehicle to link the capital markets with Federal housing markets. Ginnie Mae guarantees mortgage-backed securities composed of FHA-insured or VA-guaranteed mortgage loans that are issued by private lenders and guaranteed by GNMA with the full faith and credit of the United States. Through these programs, Ginnie Mae increases the overall supply of credit available for housing by providing a vehicle for channeling funds from the securities market into the mortgage market. More information on Ginnie Mae is available online: http://www.ginniemae.gov/pages/default.aspx.

For further information, contact the Government National Mortgage Association. Phone, 202–708–0926.

Housing

The Office of Housing is responsible for the Department's housing functions. It oversees aid for construction and financing of new and rehabilitated housing and for preservation of existing housing. The Office underwrites single-family, multifamily, property improvement, and manufactured home loans; administers special purpose programs designed specifically for the elderly, the handicapped, and the chronically mentally ill; administers assisted housing programs for low-income families who are experiencing difficulties affording standard housing; administers grants to fund resident ownership of multifamily house properties; and protects consumers against fraudulent practices of land developers and promoters. More information on housing is available online: http://portal.hud.gov/hudportal/HUD?src=/program_offices/housing.

For further information, contact the Office of Housing. Phone, 202–708–3600.

Healthy Homes and Lead Hazard Control

This Office is responsible for lead hazard control policy development, abatement, training, regulations, and research. Activities of the Office include increasing public and building-industry awareness of the dangers of lead-based paint poisoning and the options for detection, risk reduction, and abatement; encouraging the development of safer, more effective, and less costly methods for detection, risk reduction, and abatement; and encouraging State and local governments to develop lead-based paint programs covering contractor certification, hazard reduction, financing, enforcement, and primary prevention, including public education. More information on healthy homes and lead hazard control is available online: http://portal.hud.gov/hudportal/HUD?src=/program_offices/healthy_homes.

For further information, contact the Office of Healthy Homes and Lead Hazard Control. Phone, 202–755–1785.

Public and Indian Housing

The Office administers public and Indian housing programs; provides technical and financial assistance in planning, developing, and managing low-income projects; provides operating subsidies for public housing agencies (PHAs) and Indian housing authorities (IHAs), including procedures for reviewing the management of public housing agencies; administers the comprehensive improvement assistance and comprehensive grant programs for modernization of low-income housing projects to upgrade living conditions, correct physical deficiencies, and achieve operating efficiency and economy; administers programs for resident participation, resident management, home ownership, economic development and supportive services, and drug-free neighborhood programs; protects tenants from the hazards of lead-based paint poisoning by requiring PHAs and IHAs to comply with HUD regulations for the testing and removal of lead-based paint from low-income housing units; implements and monitors program requirements related to program eligibility and admission of families to public and assisted housing, and tenant income and rent requirements pertaining to continued occupancy; administers the HOPE VI and vacancy reduction programs; administers voucher and certificate programs and the Moderate Rehabilitation Program; coordinates all departmental housing and community development programs for Indian and Alaskan Natives; and awards grants to PHAs and IHAs for the construction, acquisition, and operation of public and Indian housing projects, giving priority to projects for larger families and acquisition of existing units. More information on public and Indian housing is available online: http://portal.hud.gov/hudportal/HUD?src=/program_offices/public_indian_housing.

For further information, contact the Office of Public and Indian Housing. Phone, 202–708–0950.

A complete list of Department of Housing and Urban Development regional offices is available online: http://portal.hud.gov/hudportal/HUD?src=/localoffices/regions.

Sources of Information

Inquiries on the following subjects should be directed to the nearest regional office or to the specified headquarters office, Department of Housing and Urban Development, 451 Seventh Street SW., Washington, DC 20410. Phone, 202–708–0614. TDD, 202–708–1455.
Contracts   Contact the Contracting Division. Phone, 202–708–1290. Directory Locator Phone, 202–708–0614.

TDD, 202–708–1455. Internet, http://portal.hud.gov/hudportal/HUD?src=/program_offices/sdb.
Directory Locator   Phone, 202–708–1112. TDD, 202–708–1455. Internet, http://www5.hud.gov:63001/po/i/netlocator/.
Employment   Inquiries and applications should be directed to the headquarters' Office of Human Resources (phone, 202–708–0408) or to the Personnel Division at the nearest regional office. Internet, http://portal.hud.gov/hudportal/HUD?src=/program_offices/administration/careers.
Freedom of Information Act (FOIA) Requests   Persons interested in inspecting documents or records under the Freedom of Information Act should contact the Freedom of Information Officer. Phone, 202–708–3054. Written requests should be directed to the Director, Executive Secretariat, Department of Housing and Urban Development, Room 10139, 451 Seventh Street SW., Washington, DC 20410. Internet, http://portal.hud.gov/hudportal/HUD?src=/program_offices/administration/foia.
HUD Hotline   The Hotline is maintained by the Office of the Inspector General as a means for individuals to report activities involving fraud, waste, or mismanagement. Phone, 202–708–4200 or 800–347–3735. TDD, 202–708–2451. Internet, http://www.hudoig.gov/hotline.
Program Information Center   The Center provides viewing facilities for information regarding departmental activities, functions, and publications and other literature to headquarters visitors. Phone, 202–708–1420.
Property Disposition   For single-family properties, contact the Property Disposition Division (phone, 202–708–0614) or the Chief Property Officer at the nearest HUD regional office. For multifamily properties, contact the Property Disposition Division (phone, 202–708–0614) or the Regional Housing Director at the nearest HUD regional office. Internet, http://portal.hud.gov/hudportal/HUD?src=/topics/homes_for_sale.

For further information, contact the Office of Public Affairs, Department of Housing and Urban Development, 451 Seventh Street SW., Washington, DC 20410. Phone, 202–708–0980. Internet, http://www.hud.gov.

DEPARTMENT OF THE INTERIOR

1849 C Street NW., Washington, DC 20240
Phone, 202–208–3100. Internet, http://www.doi.gov.

Secretary of the Interior	SARAH M.R. JEWELL
Deputy Secretary	MICHAEL L. CONNOR
Chief Information Officer	SYLVIA BURNS, *Acting*
Deputy Inspector General	MARY L. KENDALL
Solicitor	HILARY C. TOMPKINS
Principal Deputy Special Trustee for American Indians	MICHELE F. SINGER
Assistant Secretary for Fish and Wildlife and Parks	(VACANCY)
Assistant Secretary for Indian Affairs	KEVIN K. WASHBURN
Assistant Secretary for Insular Areas	ESTHER PUAKELA KIA'AINA
Assistant Secretary for Land and Minerals Management	JANICE M. SCHNEIDER
Assistant Secretary for Policy, Management, and Budget	RHEA S. SUH
Assistant Secretary for Water and Science	ANNE J. CASTLE

The Department of the Interior protects America's natural resources and heritage, honors our cultures and tribal communities, and supplies the energy to power our future.

The Department of the Interior was created by act of March 3, 1849 (43 U.S.C. 1451), which transferred to it the General Land Office, the Office of Indian Affairs, the Pension Office, and the Patent Office. It was reorganized by Reorganization Plan No. 3 of 1950, as amended (5 U.S.C. app.).

The Department manages the Nation's public lands and minerals, national parks, national wildlife refuges, and western water resources and upholds Federal trust responsibilities to Indian tribes and Alaska Natives. It is also responsible for migratory wildlife conservation; historic preservation; endangered species conservation; surface-mined lands protection and restoration; mapping geological, hydrological, and biological science for the Nation; and for financial and technical assistance for the insular areas.

Secretary The Secretary of the Interior reports directly to the President and is responsible for the direction and supervision of all operations and activities of the Department. Some areas in which public purposes are broadly applied are detailed below.

Fish and Wildlife and Parks The Office of the Assistant Secretary for Fish and Wildlife and Parks has responsibility for programs associated with the use, management, and conservation of natural resources; lands and cultural facilities associated with the National Park and National Refuge Systems; and the conservation and enhancement of fish, wildlife, and habitat. The Office represents the Department in the coordination and oversight of ecosystems restoration and biological resources programs with other Federal agencies and States and tribes. It also exercises secretarial direction and supervision over the U.S. Fish and Wildlife Service and the National Park Service.

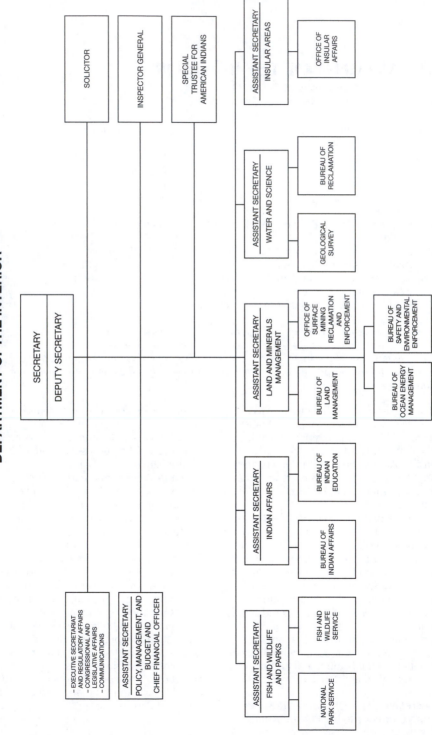

DEPARTMENT OF THE INTERIOR

Indian Affairs The Office of the Assistant Secretary for Indian Affairs is responsible for establishing and implementing Indian policy and programs; maintaining the Federal-tribal Government-to-government relationship; assisting the Secretary of the Interior with carrying out the Department's Federal trust and treaty responsibilities; exercising direction and supervision of the Bureau of Indian Affairs and the Bureau of Indian Education; directly supervising the offices of Federal acknowledgement and self-governance, Indian gaming, economic development, and all administrative and financial resource management activities; and maintaining liaison coordination between the Department and other Federal agencies that provide services or funding to the federally recognized tribes and to the eligible American Indians and Alaska Natives.

The Office of the Special Trustee for American Indians (OST) oversees departmentwide Indian trust reform efforts to provide more effective management of and accountability for the Secretary of the Interior's trust responsibilities to Indians. OST also has programmatic responsibility for the management of financial trust assets, appraisals, and fiduciary trust beneficiary services.

Insular Areas The Office of the Assistant Secretary for Insular Areas (IN) assists the territories of American Samoa, Guam, the U.S. Virgin Islands, and the Commonwealth of the Northern Mariana Islands in developing more efficient and effective government by providing financial and technical assistance and serves as a focal point for the management of relations between the United States and the insular areas by developing and promoting appropriate Federal policies. IN also carries out the Secretary's responsibilities that are related to the three freely associated states (the Federated States of Micronesia, the Republic of the Marshall Islands, and the Republic of Palau), the Palmyra Atoll excluded areas, and Wake Atoll's residual administration.

Land and Minerals Management The Office of the Assistant Secretary for Land and Minerals Management maintains administrative oversight for the Bureau of Land Management, the Bureau of Ocean Energy Management, the Bureau of Safety and Environmental Enforcement, and the Office of Surface Mining Reclamation and Enforcement. These bureaus are responsible for programs associated with public land management; operations management and leasing for conventional and renewable energy resources and minerals on public lands, including the Outer Continental Shelf to the outer limits of U.S. economic jurisdiction; mineral operations management on Indian lands; and surface mining reclamation and enforcement functions.

Water and Science The Office of the Assistant Secretary for Water and Science provides oversight to the U.S. Geological Survey, the Bureau of Reclamation, and the Central Utah Project Completion Act Office. It provides policy direction and oversight in program areas related to water project operations, facility security, and natural resource management, as well as for geologic, hydrologic, cartographic, biologic, and technological research. It provides guidance in developing national water and science policies and environmental improvement.

For further information, contact the Department of the Interior, Washington, DC 20240. Phone, 202–208–3186. Internet, http://www.doi.gov/whatwedo/water/index.cfm.

Sources of Information

Inquiries on the following subjects should be directed to the specified office, Department of the Interior, Washington, DC 20240.

Contracts Contact the Office of Acquisition and Property Management, located at 1849 C Street NW., Rm. 4262, Washington, D.C. 20240. Phone, 202–513–7554.

Electronic Access Information is available online. Use the link below to learn more about the Department's Bureaus and Offices. Internet, http://www.doi.gov/bureaus/index.cfm.

Employment Direct general inquiries to the Human Resources Office for the Office of the Secretary (202–208–6702), the specific bureau or office of interest, or any of the field offices.

Museum   The Interior Museum presents exhibits relevant to the history and mission of the Department. Programs highlight bureau management of cultural and natural resources. The Museum offers tours of the Interior Building's New Deal era art and architecture. For more information, call 202–208–4743. Internet, http://www.doi.gov/interiormuseum/index.cfm.

Library   The Interior Library is a national resource whose holdings support the mission of the Department, its agencies, and bureaus. The Library's collections cover Native American culture and history, American history, national parks, geology, nature, wildlife management, public lands management, and law. In addition, its collection of online subscription databases and other electronic data sources allow departmental personnel and other researchers to access information from Interior Department computers nationwide. The Interior Library maintains an informative Web site that includes access to its catalog of holdings, as well as information about training sessions and other educational programs hosted by the Library. For more information, contact the Interior Library. Phone, (202) 208–5815. Email, library@ios.doi.gov. Internet, http://www.doi.gov/library/index.cfm.

Reading Room   Visit the Department of the Interior Library, Main Interior Building. Phone, 202–208–5815. Internet, http://www.doi.gov/library/about/directions.cfm.

Employee Locator   To locate an employee of the Department of the Interior, call 202–208–3100.

For further information, contact the Department of the Interior, 1849 C Street NW., Washington, DC 20240. Phone, 202–208–3100. Internet, http://www.doi.gov.

Bureau of Indian Affairs
Department of the Interior, Washington, DC 20240
Phone, 202–208–3710. Internet, http://www.bia.gov.

Director   MICHAEL S. BLACK

The Bureau of Indian Affairs (BIA) was created as part of the War Department in 1824 and transferred to the Department of the Interior when the latter was established in 1849. The mission of BIA is to fulfill its trust responsibilities and promote self-determination on behalf of federally recognized tribal governments, American Indians, and Alaska Natives. BIA provides services directly or through contracts, grants, or compacts to approximately 1.9 million American Indians and Alaska Natives, members of 566 federally recognized Indian tribes in the 48 contiguous United States and Alaska.

The scope of BIA's programs is extensive, covering virtually the entire range of State and local governmental services. The programs administered by either tribes or BIA include: management of natural resources on 55 million acres of trust land, fire protection, emergency natural disaster relief, economic development programs in some of the most isolated and economically depressed areas of the United States, law enforcement, administration of tribal courts and detention centers, implementation of legislated land and water claim settlements, building, repair, and maintenance of roads and bridges, repair and maintenance of high-hazard dams, and operation of irrigation systems and agricultural programs on Federal Indian lands.

BIA works with American Indian and Alaska Native tribal governments and organizations, other Federal agencies, State and local governments, and other groups interested in the development and implementation of effective programs.

A complete listing of Bureau of Indian Affairs Regional Offices is available online at www.bia.gov/whoweare/ regionaloffices/index.htm.

Sources of Information

Inquiries regarding Indian Affairs programs, including those of the Bureau of Indian Affairs, may be obtained from the Office of the Assistant Secretary for Indian Affairs, Office of Public Affairs, Department of the Interior, 1849 C Street NW., MS–3658–MIB, Washington, DC 20240. Phone, 202–208–3710.

For further information, contact the Office of the Assistant Secretary for Indian Affairs, Office of Public Affairs, Department of the Interior, MS–3658–MIB, Washington, DC 20240. Phone, 202–208–3710. Internet, http://www.bia.gov.

Bureau of Indian Education

Department of the Interior, Washington, DC 20240
Phone, 202–208–3710. Internet, http://www.bie.edu.

Director	CHARLES M. ROESSEL

The Bureau of Indian Education (BIE) provides quality educational opportunities for eligible American Indian and Alaska Native elementary, secondary, and postsecondary students from federally recognized tribes. BIE is responsible for the direction and management of all education functions, including the formation of policies and procedures, the supervision of all program activities, and the approval of expenditure of funds appropriated for education functions.

BIE is responsible for educating approximately 48,000 American Indian and Alaska Native children at 183 elementary and secondary schools on 64 reservations in 23 States. Of these schools, 126 are tribally operated under the Indian Self-Determination and Education Assistance Act of 1975 (25 U.S.C. 450 et seq.) or the Tribally Controlled Schools Act of 1988 (25 U.S.C. 2501 et seq.), and 57 schools are operated by the Bureau of Indian Education. BIE also oversees two postsecondary schools: Haskell Indian Nations University in Lawrence, KS, and Southwestern Indian Polytechnic Institute in Albuquerque, NM. The Bureau also funds the United Tribes Technical College and Navajo Technical College.

Sources of Information

Inquiries regarding Indian Affairs programs, including those of the Bureau of Indian Education, may be obtained from the Office of the Assistant Secretary for Indian Affairs, Office of Public Affairs, Department of the Interior, 1849 C Street NW., MS–3658–MIB, Washington, DC 20240. Phone, 202–208–3710.

For further information, contact the Office of the Assistant Secretary for Indian Affairs, Office of Public Affairs, Department of the Interior, MS–3658–MIB, Washington, DC 20240. Phone, 202–208–3710. Internet, http://www.bie.edu.

Bureau of Land Management

Department of the Interior, Washington, DC 20240
Phone, 202–912–7400. Internet, http://www.blm.gov.

Deputy Director	NEIL G. KORNZE
Deputy Director for Operations	STEVEN A. ELLIS
Deputy Director for Programs and Policy	LINDA LANCE

The Bureau of Land Management (BLM) was established July 16, 1946, by the consolidation of the General Land Office (created in 1812) and the Grazing Service (formed in 1934).

The BLM manages more land (245 million acres) than any other Federal agency. This land, known as the National System of Public Lands, is primarily located in 12 Western States, including Alaska. The BLM, with a budget of about $1 billion, also administers 700 million acres of subsurface mineral estate throughout the Nation. The BLM's multiple-use mission is to sustain the health and productivity of the public lands for the use and enjoyment of present and future generations. The BLM accomplishes this by managing such activities as outdoor recreation, livestock grazing, mineral development, and energy production, and by conserving natural, historical, cultural, and other resources on public lands.

Resources managed by the BLM include timber, solid minerals, oil and gas, geothermal energy, wildlife habitat, endangered plant and animal species, rangeland vegetation, recreation and cultural values, wild and scenic rivers, designated conservation and wilderness areas, and open space. BLM programs provide for the protection (including fire suppression when appropriate), orderly development, and use of the public lands and resources under principles of multiple use and sustained yield. Land-use plans are developed with public involvement to provide orderly use and development while maintaining and enhancing the quality of the environment. The BLM also manages watersheds to protect soil and enhance water quality; develops recreational opportunities on public lands; administers programs to protect and manage wild horses and burros; and under certain conditions, makes land available for sale to individuals, organizations, local governments, and other Federal agencies when such transfer is in the public interest. Lands may be leased to State and local government agencies and to nonprofit organizations for certain purposes.

The BLM oversees and manages the development of onshore energy and mineral leases and ensures compliance with applicable regulations governing the extraction of these resources. It is responsible for issuing rights-of-way, leases, and permits.

The BLM is also responsible for the survey of Federal lands and establishes and maintains public land records and mining claims records.

A complete list of Bureau of Land Management field offices is available online at http://www.blm.gov.

Sources of Information

Contracts   The BLM and the Department are now acquiring goods and services through the Internet Web site at http://ideasec.nbc.gov. To take advantage of future business opportunities with the BLM, you must: (1) obtain a valid Dun & Bradstreet number from Dun & Bradstreet at www.dnb.com, or by calling them at 800–333–0505, or (2) register your firm on the Central Contractor Registration System at www.ccr.gov. Also, for information about BLM's purchases, how to do business with the BLM, and BLM acquisition offices and contacts, visit the BLM National Acquisition Web site at www.blm.gov/natacq. You may also view BLM's projected purchases of goods and services, known as the Advanced Procurement Plan.

Employment   Inquiries should be directed to the National Operations Center Division of Human Resources Services, any Bureau of Land Management State Office, or the Human Capital Management Directorate, Department of the Interior, Washington, DC. Phone, 202–501–6723. Additional employment information is available online. Internet, http://www.blm.gov/wo/st/en/res/blm_jobs.html.

General Inquiries   For general inquiries, contact any of the State offices or the Bureau of Land Management, Office of Public Affairs, Department of the Interior, Washington, DC 20240. Phone, 202–912–7400. Fax, 202–912–7181. Internet, http://www.blm.gov/wo/st/en/info/directory/WO-610_dir.html.

Publications   The annual publication "Public Land Statistics" is available online. Internet, http://www.blm.gov/public_land_statistics/index.htm.

Reading Rooms   All State offices provide facilities for individuals who wish to examine status records, tract books, or other records relating to the public lands and their resources.

Small Business Activities   The BLM has three major buying offices that provide contacts for small business activities: the Headquarters Office in Washington, DC

(phone, 202–912–7073); the National Operations Center in Lakewood, CO (phone, 303–236–6309); and the Oregon State office (phone, 503–808–6228). The acquisition plan and procurement office contacts are available through the Internet at http://www.blm.gov/wo/st/en/prog/more/procurement.html.

Speakers   Local BLM offices will arrange for speakers to explain BLM programs upon request from organizations within their areas of jurisdiction.

For further information, contact the Office of Public Affairs, Bureau of Land Management, Department of the Interior, MS–2134–LM, Washington, DC 20240. Phone, 202–912–7400. Internet, http://www.blm.gov.

Bureau of Ocean Energy Management
Department of the Interior, Washington, DC 20240
Phone, 202–208–3985. Internet, http://www.boem.gov.

Director   WALTER D. CRUICKSHANK, *Acting*

The Bureau of Ocean Energy Management (BOEM) was created on October 1, 2011, as directed, by Secretarial Order No. 3299, as amended.

BOEM assesses the nature, extent, recoverability, and value of leasable minerals, renewable and other authorized energy, and marine-related activities on the Outer Continental Shelf (OCS). BOEM promotes the exploration, inventory, and responsible development of energy and mineral resources and other authorized energy or marine-related activities; provides a structure to analyze the potential environmental effects of proposed operations related to resource management; develops and implements regulations governing leasing, resource evaluation, resource management, plans, and the economic evaluation of offshore activities; and oversees the financial accountability of lessees, operators, and operating-rights holders to ensure that these responsible parties can meet their financial and contractual commitments.

BOEM promotes cooperative relationships between the Federal Government, States, and tribes and native communities with respect to national, regional, and local issues related to the full scope of its responsibility. The operations of BOEM support a number of national goals and objectives, including energy security, environmental protection, and social and economic development.

A complete list of BOEM regional offices is available online at http://www.boem.gov/BOEM-Regions.

Sources of Information

For more information on the Bureau of Ocean Energy Management, including information on employment, contracts, programs, and activities, contact the Public Affairs Office, Department of the Interior, 1849 C Street NW., Washington, DC 20240–7000. Phone, 202–208–6474. Internet, http://www.boem.gov/BOEM-Newsroom.

For further information, contact the Office of Public Affairs, Bureau of Ocean Energy Management, Department of the Interior, Washington, DC 20240–7000. Phone, 202–208–6474. Email, BOEMPublicAffairs@boem.gov. Internet, http://www.boem.gov.

Bureau of Reclamation

Department of the Interior, Washington, DC 20240
Phone, 202–513–0575. Internet, http://www.usbr.gov.

Commissioner	LOWELL PIMLEY, *Acting*

The Bureau of Reclamation was established pursuant to the Reclamation Act of 1902 (43 U.S.C. 371 et seq.). The Bureau is the largest wholesale water supplier and the second largest producer of hydroelectric power in the United States, with operations and facilities in the 17 Western States. Its facilities also provide substantial flood control, recreation, and fish and wildlife benefits.

A complete list of Bureau of Reclamation offices is available online at http://www.usbr.gov/main/about/addresses.html.

Sources of Information

Contracts   Information on doing business with the Bureau, including information relevant to contractors, manufacturers, and suppliers, is available online and from the Acquisition and Assistance Management Division, Building 67, Denver Federal Center, Denver, CO 80225. Phone, 303–445–2431. Internet, http://www.usbr.gov/mso/aamd/doing-business.html.

Employment   Information on engineering and other positions is available from the nearest regional office or from the Diversity and Human Resources Office, Denver, CO. Phone, 303–445–2684. Internet, http://www.usajobs.gov.

Publications   Publications for sale are available through the National Technical Information Service. Phone, 1–800–553–NTIS (6847). Internet, http://www.ntis.gov.

For further information, contact the Office of Public Affairs, Bureau of Reclamation, Department of the Interior, Washington, DC 20240–0001. Phone, 202–513–0575. Internet, http://www.usbr.gov.

Bureau of Safety and Environmental Enforcement

Department of the Interior, Washington, DC 20240
Phone, 202–208–3985. Internet, http://www.bsee.gov.

Director	JAMES A. WATSON

The Bureau of Safety and Environmental Enforcement (BSEE) was created on May 19, 2010, by Secretarial Order No. 3299, as amended.

BSEE is responsible for regulating and enforcing safety, environment, and conservation compliance during development of the Nation's ocean energy and marine mineral resources on the Outer Continental Shelf (OCS). BSEE is also responsible for field operations, offshore regulatory programs, production and development, training, environmental compliance, the Bureau's aviation program, review and creation of policy, guidance, direction, and oversight of activities related to BSEE's oil spill response program as well as managing and developing area and regional oil spill contingency plans.

Consistent with the Secretary's authorities under the OCS Lands Act, regulations in 30 CFR 250, and cooperation with the Coast Guard, BSEE is responsible for the development, oversight, and enforcement of safety for OCS operations.

For a complete list of BSEE regional offices, go to http://www.bsee.gov/About-BSEE/BSEE–Regions/BSEE–Regions.aspx.

Sources of Information

For further information about Bureau of Safety and Environmental Enforcement employment, contracts, programs, and

activities, contact the Public Affairs
Office, Department of the Interior, 1849
C Street NW., Washington, DC 20240–

7000. Phone, 202–208–3985. Internet,
http://www.bsee.gov/About-BSEE/
Contact-US/Contact-Us.aspx.

For further information, contact the Office of Public Affairs, Bureau of Safety and Environmental Enforcement, Department of the Interior, Washington, DC 20240–7000. Phone, 202–208–3985. Internet, http://www.bsee.gov.

National Park Service
Department of the Interior, Washington, DC 20240
Phone, 202–208–6843. Internet, http://www.nps.gov.

Director	JONATHAN B. JARVIS

The National Park Service was established in the Department of the Interior on August 25, 1916 (16 U.S.C. 1).

The National Park Service is dedicated to protecting the natural and cultural resources and values of the National Park System for the benefit of present and future generations. There are 401 units in the National Park System, including national parks, monuments and memorials, scenic parkways, preserves, reserves, trails, riverways, wild and scenic rivers, seashores, lakeshores, recreation areas, battlefields and battlefield parks and sites, national military parks, international historic sites, and historic sites associated with important movements, events, and personalities of the American past.

The Service is also responsible for managing a great variety of national and international programs designed to help extend the benefits of natural and cultural resource conservation and outdoor recreation throughout this country and the world.

The National Park Service develops and implements park management plans and staffs the areas under its administration. It relates the natural values and historical significance of these areas to the public through talks, tours, films, exhibits, publications, and other interpretive media. It operates campgrounds and other visitor facilities and provides lodging, food, and transportation services in many areas.

The National Park Service also administers the following programs: the State portion of the Land and Water

Conservation Fund, nationwide outdoor recreation coordination and information, State comprehensive outdoor recreation planning, planning and technical assistance for the national wild and scenic rivers system, the national trails system, natural area programs, the National Register of Historic Places, national historic landmarks, historic preservation, technical preservation services, the historic American buildings survey, the historic American engineering record, and interagency archeological services.

A complete list of National Park Service regional offices is available online at www.nps.gov/aboutus/contactinformation.htm.

Sources of Information

Contracts Information on contracts and contracting opportunities is available online. Internet, http://www.nps.gov/aboutus/doingbusinesswithus.htm.

Employment Information on permanent and seasonal job opportunities is available at the USAJobs Web site, the Federal Government's one-stop source for Federal employment. For additional information on permanent careers, seasonal opportunities, and internships with the National Park Service, go online and use the link below. Internet, http://www.nps.gov/aboutus/workwithus.htm.

Grants For information on grants authorized under the Land and Water Conservation Fund, contact the National Park Service, 1849 C Street NW., Washington, DC 20240. Phone, 202–354–6900. For information on grants authorized under the Historic Preservation Fund, contact the National Park Service, 1849 C Street NW., Washington, DC 20240. Phone, 202–354–2067.

Publications National Park Service items are available from the Superintendent of Documents, Government Printing Office, Washington, DC 20401. Phone, 202–512–1800. Items that may be purchased include the National Park System Map and Guide 2011 (Stock No. 024–005–01290–7) and The National Parks: Index 2009–2011 (Stock No. 024–005–01269–9). Contact the Consumer Information Center, Pueblo, CO 81009, for additional publications that are available for purchase. For general park and camping information, visit http://www.nps.gov, or write to the National Park Service, Office of Communications 1849 C Street NW., Washington, DC 20240. Internet, http://www.nps.gov/aboutus/publications.htm.

For further information, contact the Office of Communications, National Park Service, Department of the Interior, Washington, DC 20240. Phone, 202–208–6843. Internet, http://www.nps.gov.

Office of Surface Mining Reclamation and Enforcement

Department of the Interior, Washington, DC 20240
Phone, 202–208–2565. TDD, 202–208–2694. Internet, http://www.osmre.gov.

Director JOSEPH PIZARCHIK

The Office of Surface Mining Reclamation and Enforcement (OSMRE) was established in the Department of the Interior by the Surface Mining Control and Reclamation Act of 1977 (30 U.S.C. 1211).

The Office's primary goal is to assist States and tribes in operating a nationwide program that protects society and the environment from the adverse effects of coal mining, while ensuring that surface coal mining can be done without permanent damage to land and water resources. With most coal mining States responsible for regulating coal mining and reclamation activities within their borders, OSM's main objectives are to oversee State mining regulatory and abandoned-mine reclamation programs, assist States in meeting the objectives of surface mining law, and regulate mining and reclamation activities on Federal and Indian lands, and in those States choosing not to assume primary responsibility.

The Office establishes national policy for the surface mining control and reclamation program provided for in surface mining law, reviews and approves amendments to previously approved State programs, and reviews and recommends approval of new State program submissions. Other activities include: managing the collection, disbursement, and accounting for abandoned-mine land reclamation fees; administering civil penalties programs; establishing technical standards and regulatory policy for reclamation and enforcement efforts; providing guidance for environmental considerations, research, training, and technology transfer for State, tribal, and Federal regulatory and abandoned-mine land reclamation programs; and monitoring and evaluating State and tribal regulatory programs, cooperative agreements, and abandoned-mine land reclamation programs.

Sources of Information

Contracts Contact the Procurement Branch, Office of Surface Mining Reclamation and Enforcement, Department of the Interior, 1951 Constitution Avenue NW., Washington, DC 20240. Phone, 202–208–2902. TDD, 202–208–2737.

Employment Information on career opportunities at OSMRE is available online. Internet, http://www.osmre.gov/employment/Jobs.shtm.

For further information, contact the Office of Communications, Office of Surface Mining Reclamation and Enforcement, Department of the Interior, Washington, DC 20240. Phone, 202–208–2565. TDD, 202–208–2694. Internet, http://www.osmre.gov.

United States Fish and Wildlife Service

Department of the Interior, Washington, DC 20240
Phone, 703–358–4545. Internet, http://www.fws.gov.

Director   Daniel M. Ashe

[For the United States Fish and Wildlife Service statement of organization, see the Code of Federal Regulations, Title 50, Subchapter A, Part 2]

The U.S. Fish and Wildlife Service is the principal Federal agency dedicated to fish and wildlife conservation. The Service's history spans more than 140 years, dating from the establishment of its predecessor agency, the Bureau of Fisheries, in 1871. First created as an independent agency, the Bureau of Fisheries was later placed in the Department of Commerce. A second predecessor agency, the Bureau of Biological Survey, was established in 1885 in the Department of Agriculture. In 1939, the two Bureaus and their functions were transferred to the Department of the Interior. In 1940, they were consolidated into one agency and redesignated the Fish and Wildlife Service by Reorganization Plan No. 3 (5 U.S.C. app.).

The U.S. Fish and Wildlife Service works with others to fulfill its mission: conservation, protection, and enhancement of fish, wildlife, and their habitats for the continuing benefit of the American people. The Service manages the 150-million-acre National Wildlife Refuge System, which comprises 562 refuges and 38 wetland management districts. It also operates 72 national fish hatcheries, a historic national fish hatchery, 65 fishery resource offices, and 81 ecological service field stations. The Service enforces Federal wildlife laws, administers the Endangered Species Act, manages migratory bird populations, restores nationally significant fisheries, conserves and restores wildlife habitat such as wetlands, and assists foreign governments with their conservation efforts. It also oversees the Sport Fish and Wildlife Restoration Programs,

which collect excise taxes on fishing and hunting equipment and distribute the revenues to State fish and wildlife agencies.

The Service is responsible for improving and maintaining fish and wildlife resources by proper management of wildlife and habitat. It also helps meet public demand for wildlife dependent recreational opportunities by maintaining its public lands and restoring native populations of fish and wildlife.

Specific wildlife and fishery resource programs provide wildlife refuge management for public lands, including population control, migration and harvest surveys, and law and gaming enforcement for migratory and nonmigratory birds and mammals. Various programs also monitor hatchery production, stocking, and fishery management and provide technical assistance for coastal anadromous, Great Lakes (in cooperation with Canada), and other inland fisheries.

The Service provides leadership in identifying, protecting, and restoring endangered species of fish, wildlife, and plants. This program develops the Federal Endangered and Threatened Species List, conducts status surveys, prepares recovery plans, and coordinates national and international efforts to operate wildlife refuges.

In the area of resource management, the Service provides leadership for the protection and improvement of land and water environments (habitat preservation) that directly benefit the living natural resources and add quality to human life. The Service administers grant programs benefiting imperiled species, provides technical and financial assistance to private landowners for habitat restoration, completes environmental impact assessments and reviews of potential threats, manages Coastal Barrier Resource System mapping, monitors potential contaminants in wildlife, and studies fish and wildlife population trends.

Public use and information programs include preparing informational brochures and maintaining public Web sites; coordinating environmental studies on Service lands; operating visitor centers, self-guided nature trails, observation towers, and display ponds; and providing recreational activities such as hunting, fishing, and wildlife photography.

The Service's Wildlife and Sport Fish Restoration Program apportions funds for projects designed to conserve and enhance the Nation's fish and wildlife resources. The funds for the projects are generated from excise taxes on sporting arms and fishing equipment.

A complete list of the Service's regional offices is available online at www.fws. gov/.

Sources of Information

Inquiries on the following subjects should be directed to the specified office, U.S. Fish and Wildlife Service, Department of the Interior, 1849 C Street NW., Washington, DC 20240.
Congressional/Legislative Services Congressional staffers and persons seeking information about specific legislation should call the Division of Congressional and Legislative Affairs. Phone, 703–358–2240.
Contracts Contact any of the regional offices or the Washington, DC, headquarters Division of Contracting and Facilities Management. Phone, 703–358–1901.
Electronic Access To access a range of information online, visit the Fish and

Wildlife Service's Web site. Internet, http://www.fws.gov/.
Employment For information regarding employment opportunities with the U.S. Fish and Wildlife Service, contact the regional office in the area where you seek employment or the Headquarters Human Capital Office. Phone, 703–358–1743. Internet, http://www.fws.gov/humancapital/.
Import/Export Permits To obtain CITES permits for importing and exporting wildlife, contact the Office of Management Authority. Phone, 800–358–2104, or 703–358–2104. Internet, http://www.fws.gov/international/permits/do-i-need-a-permit.html.
Law Enforcement To obtain information about the enforcement of wildlife laws or to report an infraction of those laws, contact the nearest regional law enforcement office or the Division of Law Enforcement. Phone, 703–358–1949.
National Wildlife Refuges For general information about the National Wildlife Refuge System, as well as information about specific refuges, contact the nearest national wildlife refuge, the nearest regional refuge office, or the Division of Visitor Services. Phone, 703–358–2029.
News Media Inquiries Specific information on the U.S. Fish and Wildlife Service and its activities is available from the public affairs officer in each of the Service's regional offices or the Division of Public Affairs. Phone, 703–358–2220.
Publications The U.S. Fish and Wildlife Service has publications available on subjects ranging from the National Wildlife Refuge System to endangered species. Some publications are available only as sales items from the Superintendent of Documents, Government Printing Office, Washington, D.C. 20402. Further information is available from the Publications Unit, U.S. Fish and Wildlife Service, 4501 N. Fairfax Drive, MS 3103, Arlington, VA 22203. Phone, 703–358–2196. Internet, http://www.fws.gov/news/.

For further information, contact the Office of Public Affairs, Fish and Wildlife Service, Department of the Interior, Washington, DC 20240. Phone, 703–358–2220. Internet, http://www.fws.gov.

United States Geological Survey

12201 Sunrise Valley Drive, Reston, VA 20192
Phone, 703–648–4000. Internet, http://www.usgs.gov. Email, ASK@usgs.gov.

Director	SUZETTE KIMBALL, *Acting*

The U.S. Geological Survey (USGS) was established by the Organic Act of March 3, 1879 (43 U.S.C. 31). Since March 3, 1879, the U.S. Geological Survey (USGS) has provided the United States with science information needed to make important land use and resource management policy decisions.

The USGS is the Earth and natural science research bureau for the Department of the Interior and the only integrated natural resources research agency in the Federal Government. USGS research and data support the Department's resource and land management information needs and also provide the climate, natural hazards, water, biological, energy, and mineral resources information needed by other Federal, State, tribal, and local government agencies to guide planning, management, and regulatory programs. Emergency response organizations, natural resource managers, land use planners, and other customers use this information to protect lives and property, address environmental health issues, and promote public prosperity for the future well-being of our country.

The USGS conducts research, monitoring, and assessments to contribute to understanding America's lands, water, and biological resources. The USGS provides information to the citizens of the country and to the global community in the form of maps, data, and reports containing analyses and interpretations of water, energy, mineral, and biological resources; land surfaces; marine environments; geologic structures; natural hazards; and dynamic processes of the Earth. USGS data and information are used daily by managers, planners, and citizens to understand, respond to, and plan for changes in the environment.

With more than 130 years of data and experience, USGS employs 8,000 science and science-support staff, in more than 400 science centers across the United States, who work on locally, regionally, and nationally scaled studies, research projects, and sampling and monitoring sites.

Sources of Information

USGS Information on real-time hazards and USGS science programs, publications, news releases, policies, and FAQ's is available online. Explore USGS topics of interest; find out what science is being conducted in your local area; and learn how to be a citizen scientist. Internet, http://www.usgs.gov.

Contracts, Grants, and Cooperative Agreements Information on contracts, grants, and cooperative agreements is available online. It also may be obtained from the USGS Office of Acquisition and Grants, 12201 Sunrise Valley Drive, National Center, MS–205G, Reston, VA 20192. Phone, 703–648–7376. Internet, http://www.usgs.gov/contracts/.

Employment Career information is available online. It is also available from USGS Headquarters Human Resources Office, 12201 Sunrise Valley Drive, Mail Stop 601, Reston, VA 20192 (phone, 703–648–7405); USGS Atlantic Human Resources Office, 12201 Sunrise Valley Drive, Mail Stop 601, Reston, VA 20192 (phone, 703–648–7470); and USGS Pacific Human Resources Office, 3020 East State University Drive, Suite 2001, Sacramento, CA 95819 (phone, 916–278–9394). Internet, http://www.usgs.gov/ohr/.

Communications For news media and congressional inquiries, arranging interviews, and obtaining news releases and other informational products on programs and activities, visit the USGS Newsroom online. The same information is also available from the Office of Communications and Publishing at USGS Headquarters, Office of Communications and Publishing, National Center, MS–119,

Reston, VA 20192 (phone, 703–648–4460); USGS Office of Communications and Publishing, Eastern States Office, National Center, Mail Stop 119, Reston, VA 20192 (phone, 703–648–4356). Internet, http://www.usgs.gov/newsroom/contacts.asp.

General Inquiries   For general inquiries, contact the USGS at 888–ASK–USGS (888–275–8747) or use the link below to visit the Web site. Internet, http://ask.usgs.gov/.

Reports and Maps   The USGS Publications Warehouse (pubs.usgs.gov) is a searchable online resource providing free access to more than 58,000 reports, maps, and other USGS products. The USGS Store (store.usgs.gov) is a searchable, online catalog that allows the user to browse and purchase USGS reports, books, maps, data, educational products, pamphlets, posters, fact sheets, and DVDs.

Water Data   Reliable, impartial, and timely information on the Nation's water resources is available online and by phone at 888–ASK–USGS (888–275–8747). Internet, http://www.usgs.gov/water/.

Natural Hazards   Information on the programs and activities of the natural hazards mission, including information on earthquakes, volcanoes, and landslides, is available online. Internet, http://www.usgs.gov/natural_hazards/.

Maps, Imagery, and Publications   Maps, aerial photographs, and other USGS data sets and publications are accessible online and may be purchased. Internet, http://www.usgs.gov/pubprod/.

Social Media   Visit USGS on Facebook, Twitter, YouTube, and Flickr, and subscribe to our podcast series or RSS and data feeds by using the link below. Internet, http://www.usgs.gov/socialmedia/.

Libraries   Reports, maps, publications, and a variety of Earth and biological information resources and historical documents are available through the USGS library system. A catalog search and information on library locations and directions are available online. Internet, http://library.usgs.gov/.

For additional information, contact the U.S. Geological Survey, Department of the Interior, 12201 Sunrise Valley Drive, Reston, VA 20192. Phone, 703–648–4000. Email, ASK@usgs.gov. Internet, http://www.usgs.gov/ask/.

DEPARTMENT OF JUSTICE

950 Pennsylvania Avenue NW., Washington, DC 20530
Phone, 202–514–2000. Internet, http://www.justice.gov.

Attorney General	ERIC H. HOLDER, JR.
Deputy Attorney General	JAMES M. COLE
Associate Attorney General	TONY WEST
Solicitor General	DONALD B. VERRILLI, JR.
Inspector General	MICHAEL E. HOROWITZ
Assistant Attorney General, Office of Legal Counsel	KARL REMÓN THOMPSON, *Acting*
Assistant Attorney General for Administration, Justice Management Division	LEE J. LOFTHUS
Assistant Attorney General, Antitrust Division	WILLIAM J. BAER
Assistant Attorney General, Civil Division	STUART F. DELERY
Assistant Attorney General, Civil Rights Division	JOCELYN SAMUELS, *Acting*
Assistant Attorney General, Criminal Division	LESLIE RAGON CALDWELL
Assistant Attorney General, National Security Division	JOHN P. CARLIN
Assistant Attorney General, Environment and Natural Resources Division	ROBERT G. DREHER, *Acting*
Assistant Attorney General, Tax Division	KATHRYN KENEALLY
Director, Office of Public Affairs	BRIAN FALLON
Director, Office of Information Policy	MELANIE ANN PUSTAY
Director, Office of Tribal Justice	TRACY TOULOU
Director, Executive Office for U.S. Attorneys	MONTY WILKINSON
Director, Executive Office for U.S. Trustees	CLIFFORD J. WHITE, III
Director, Community Relations Service	GRANDE H. LUM
Counsel, Office of Professional Responsibility	ROBIN C. ASHTON
Director, Professional Responsibility Advisory Office	JERRI U. DUNSTON
Pardon Attorney	RONALD L. RODGERS
Associate Deputy Attorney General and Director, Executive Office for Organized Crime Drug Enforcement Task Forces	JAMES H. DINAN

[For the Department of Justice statement of organization, see the Code of Federal Regulations, Title 28, Chapter I, Part 0]

The Department of Justice serves as counsel for the citizens of the United States and represents them by enforcing the law in the public interest. It fills a key role in deterring criminality and subversion, ensuring healthy business competition, safeguarding consumers, and enforcing drug, immigration, and naturalization laws.

The Department of Justice was established by act of June 22, 1870 (28 U.S.C. 501, 503, 509 note), with the Attorney General as its head. The affairs and activities of the Department of Justice are generally directed by the Attorney General.

Attorney General The Attorney General represents the United States in legal matters generally and gives advice and

DEPARTMENT OF JUSTICE

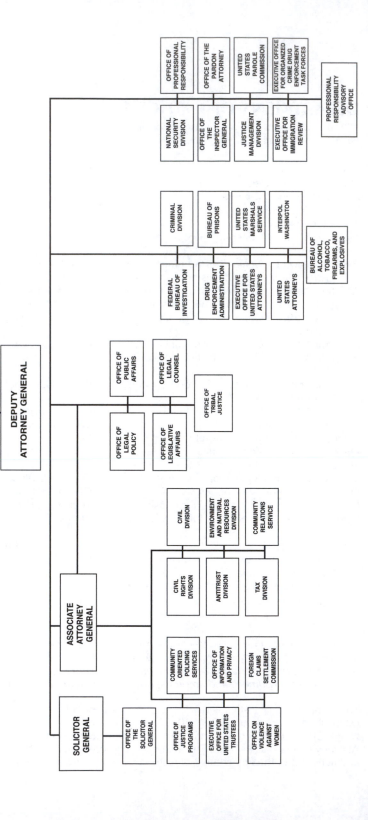

opinions to the President and to the heads of the executive departments of the Government when so requested. The Attorney General appears in person to represent the Government before the U.S. Supreme Court in cases of exceptional gravity or importance.

Community Relations Service The Service offers assistance to communities in resolving disputes relating to race, color, or national origin and facilitates the development of viable agreements as alternatives to coercion, violence, or litigation. It also assists and supports communities in developing local mechanisms as proactive measures to prevent or reduce racial/ethnic tensions.

For a complete list of Community Relations Service Regional Offices, visit www.justice.gov/crs/map.htm.

For further information, contact any regional office or the Director, Community Relations Service, Department of Justice, Suite 2000, 600 E Street NW., Washington, DC 20530. Phone, 202–305–2935. Internet, http://www.justice.gov/crs.

Pardon Attorney The Office of the Pardon Attorney assists the President in the exercise of his pardon power under the Constitution. Generally, all requests for pardon or other forms of executive clemency, including commutation of sentences, are directed to the Pardon Attorney for investigation and review. The Pardon Attorney prepares the Department's recommendation to the President for final disposition of each application.

For further information, contact the Office of the Pardon Attorney, Department of Justice, Suite 11000, 1425 New York Avenue NW., Washington, DC 20530. Phone, 202–616–6070. Internet, http://www.justice.gov/pardon.

Solicitor General The Office of the Solicitor General represents the U.S. Government in cases before the Supreme Court. It decides what cases the Government should ask the Supreme Court to review and what position the Government should take in cases before the Court. It also supervises the preparation of the Government's Supreme Court briefs and other legal documents and the conduct of the oral arguments in the Court. The Solicitor General also decides whether the United States should

appeal in all cases it loses before the lower courts.

For further information, contact the Executive Officer, Office of the Solicitor General, Room 5142, 950 Pennsylvania Avenue NW., RFK Justice Building (Main), Washington, DC 20530–0001. Internet, http://www.justice.gov/osg.

U.S. Attorneys The Executive Office for U.S. Attorneys was created on April 6, 1953, to provide liaison between the Department of Justice in Washington, DC, and the U.S. attorneys. Its mission is to provide general executive assistance to the 94 offices of the U.S. attorneys and to coordinate the relationship between the U.S. attorneys and the organization components of the Department of Justice and other Federal agencies.

For further information, contact the Executive Office for U.S. Attorneys, Department of Justice, Room 2261, 950 Pennsylvania Avenue NW., Washington, DC 20530. Phone, 202–514–1020. Internet, http://www.justice.gov/usao/eousa/.

U.S. Trustee Program The Program was established by the Bankruptcy Reform Act of 1978 (11 U.S.C. 101 et seq.) as a pilot effort in 10 regions encompassing 18 Federal judicial districts to promote the efficiency and protect the integrity of the bankruptcy system by identifying and helping to investigate bankruptcy fraud and abuse. It now operates nationwide except in Alabama and North Carolina. The Bankruptcy Abuse Prevention and Consumer Protection Act of 2005 (11 U.S.C. 101 note) significantly expanded the Program's responsibilities and provided additional tools to combat bankruptcy fraud and abuse. The Executive Office for U.S. Trustees provides day-to-day policy and legal direction, coordination, and control.

For further information, contact the Executive Office for U.S. Trustees, Department of Justice, Suite 6150, 441 G. Street, NW., Washington, DC 20530. Phone, 202–307–1391. Internet, http://www.justice.gov/ust/.

Divisions

Antitrust Division The Assistant Attorney General in charge of the Antitrust Division is responsible for promoting and maintaining competitive markets by enforcing the Federal antitrust laws. This involves investigating possible antitrust violations, conducting grand jury proceedings, reviewing proposed mergers and acquisitions, preparing and trying antitrust cases, prosecuting appeals, and negotiating and enforcing final judgments. The Division prosecutes serious and willful violations of antitrust laws by filing criminal suits that can lead to large fines and jail sentences. Where criminal prosecution is not appropriate, the Division seeks a court order forbidding future violations of the law and requiring steps by the defendant to remedy the anticompetitive effects of past violations.

The Division also is responsible for acting as an advocate of competition within the Federal Government as well as internationally. This involves formal appearances in Federal administrative agency proceedings, development of legislative initiatives to promote deregulation and eliminate unjustifiable exemptions from the antitrust laws, and participation on executive branch policy task forces and in multilateral international organizations. The Division provides formal advice to other agencies on the competitive implications of proposed transactions requiring Federal approval, such as mergers of financial institutions.

For further information, contact the Office of the Assistant Attorney General, Antitrust Division, Department of Justice, 950 Pennsylvania Avenue NW., Washington, DC 20530. Phone, 202–514–2401. Internet, http://www.justice.gov/atr.

Civil Division The Civil Division represents the United States, its departments and agencies, Members of Congress, Cabinet officers, and other Federal employees. Its litigation reflects the diversity of Government activities involving, for example, the defense of challenges to Presidential actions; national security issues; benefit programs; energy policies; commercial issues such as contract disputes, banking, insurance, fraud, and debt collection; all manner of accident and liability claims; and violations of the immigration and consumer protection laws. The Division confronts significant policy issues, which often rise to constitutional dimensions, in defending and enforcing various

Federal programs and actions. Each year, Division attorneys handle thousands of cases that collectively involve billions of dollars in claims and recoveries.

The Division litigates cases in the following areas:

Commercial litigation, litigation associated with the Government's diverse financial involvements including all monetary suits involving contracts, express or implied; actions to foreclose on Government mortgages and liens; bankruptcy and insolvency proceedings; suits against guarantors and sureties; actions involving fraud against the Government, including false or fraudulent claims for Federal insurance, loans, subsidies, and other benefits such as Medicare, false or fraudulent claims for payment under Federal contracts, whistleblower suits, and Government corruption; patent, copyright, and trademark cases and suits arising out of construction, procurement, service contracts, and claims associated with contract terminations; claims for just compensation under the Fifth Amendment; claims for salary or retirement by civilian and military personnel; cases assigned by congressional reference or special legislation; and litigation involving interests of the United States in any foreign court, whether civil or criminal in nature.

Consumer litigation, including civil and criminal litigation and related matters arising under various consumer protection and public health statutes.

Federal programs, including constitutional challenges to statutes, suits to overturn Government policies and programs, challenges to the legality of Government decisions, allegations that the President has violated the Constitution or Federal law, suits to enforce regulatory statutes and to remedy or prevent statutory or regulatory violations.

The areas of litigation include:

Suits against the heads of Federal departments and agencies and other Government officials to enjoin official actions, as well as suits for judicial review of administrative decisions, orders, and regulations; suits involving national security, including suits to protect sensitive intelligence sources and materials; suits to prevent interference with Government operations; litigation concerning the constitutionality of Federal laws; and suits raising employment discrimination claims and Government personnel issues.

Immigration litigation, involving civil litigation under the Immigration and Nationality Act and related laws; district court litigation, habeas corpus review and general advice; petitions for removal order review and immigration-related appellate matters; cases pertaining to the issuance of visas and passports; and litigation arising under the legalization and employer sanction provisions of the immigration laws.

Torts, including the broad range of tort litigation arising from the operation of the Federal Government, constitutional tort claims against Federal Government officials throughout the Government, aviation disasters, environmental and occupational disease, and radiation and toxic substance exposure. It defends petitions filed pursuant to the Vaccine Injury Compensation Program and is responsible for administering the Radiation Exposure Compensation Program. It also handles maritime litigation and suits that seek personal monetary judgments against individual officers or employees.

Appellate, having primary responsibility for the litigation of Civil Division cases in the courts of appeal, and on occasion, State appeal courts. The Appellate Staff prepares Government briefs and presents oral arguments for these cases. Additionally, the Appellate Staff works with the Solicitor General's office to prepare documents filed for these cases in the Supreme Court, including briefs on the merits, petitions for certiorari, and jurisdictional statements. The Appellate Staff also works with the Solicitor General's office to obtain authorization for appellate review.

For further information, contact the Office of the Assistant Attorney General, Civil Division, Department of Justice, Tenth Street and Pennsylvania Avenue NW., Washington, DC 20530.

Phone, 202–514–3301. Internet, http://www.justice. gov/civil.

Civil Rights Division   The Civil Rights Division, headed by an Assistant Attorney General, was established in 1957 to secure effective Federal enforcement of civil rights. The Division is the primary institution within the Federal Government responsible for enforcing Federal statutes prohibiting discrimination on the basis of race, sex, disability, religion, citizenship, and national origin. The Division has responsibilities in the following areas:

Coordination and review of various civil rights statutes that prohibit discrimination on the basis of race, color, national origin, sex, and religion in programs and activities that receive Federal financial assistance by Federal agencies.

Criminal cases involving conspiracies to interfere with federally protected rights; deprivation of rights under color of law; the use of force or threat of force to injure or intimidate someone in their enjoyment of specific rights (such as voting, housing, employment, education, public facilities, and accommodations); interference with the free exercise of religious beliefs or damage to religious property; the holding of a worker in a condition of slavery or involuntary servitude; and interference with persons seeking to obtain or provide reproductive services.

Disability rights cases, achieving equal opportunity for people with disabilities in the United States by implementing the Americans with Disabilities Act (ADA). ADA mandates are carried out through enforcement, certification, regulatory, coordination, and technical assistance activities, combined with an innovative mediation program and a technical assistance grant program. The Division also carries out responsibilities under sections 504 and 508 of the Rehabilitation Act, the Help America Vote Act of 2002, the Small Business Regulatory Enforcement Fairness Act, and Executive Order 12250.

Educational opportunities litigation, involving title IV of the Civil Rights Act of 1964, the Equal Educational Opportunities Act of 1974, and title III of the Americans with Disabilities Act. In addition, the Division is responsible for enforcing other statutes such as title VI of the Civil Rights Act of 1964, title IX of the Education Amendments of 1972, section 504 of the Rehabilitation Act of 1973, title II of the Americans with Disabilities Act, and the Individuals with Disabilities Education Act upon referral from other governmental agencies.

Employment litigation enforcing against State and local government employers the provisions of title VII of the Civil Rights Act of 1964, as amended, and other Federal laws prohibiting employment practices that discriminate on grounds of race, sex, religion, and national origin. The Division also enforces against State and local government and private employers the provisions of the Uniformed Services Employment and Reemployment Rights Act of 1994, which prohibits employers from discriminating or retaliating against an employee or applicant for employment because of such person's past, current, or future military obligation.

Housing and Civil Enforcement statutes enforcing the Fair Housing Act, which prohibits discrimination in housing; the Equal Credit Opportunity Act, which prohibits discrimination in credit; title II of the Civil Rights Act of 1964, which prohibits discrimination in certain places of public accommodation, such as hotels, restaurants, nightclubs and theaters; title III of the Civil Rights Act of 1964, which prohibits discrimination in public facilities; and the Religious Land Use and Institutionalized Persons Act, which prohibits local governments from adopting or enforcing land use regulations that discriminate against religious assemblies and institutions or which unjustifiably burden religious exercise.

Immigration-related unfair employment practices enforcing the antidiscrimination provisions of the Immigration and Nationality Act, which protect U.S. citizens and legal immigrants from employment discrimination based upon citizenship or immigration status and national origin, unfair documentary practices relating to the employment

eligibility verification process, and retaliation.

Special litigation protecting the constitutional and statutory rights of persons confined in certain institutions owned or operated by State or local governments, including facilities for individuals with mental and developmental disabilities, nursing homes, prisons, jails, and juvenile detention facilities where a pattern or practice of violations exist; civil enforcement of statutes prohibiting a pattern or practice of conduct by law enforcement agencies that violates Federal law; and protection against a threat of force and physical obstruction that injures, intimidates, or interferes with a person seeking to obtain or provide reproductive health services, or to exercise the first amendment right of religious freedom at a place of worship.

Voting cases enforcing the Voting Rights Act, the Help America Vote Act of 2002, the National Voter Registration Act, the Voting Accessibility for the Elderly and Handicapped Act, the Uniformed and Overseas Citizens Absentee Voting Act, and other Federal statutes designed to safeguard citizens' rights to vote. This includes racial and language minorities, illiterate persons, individuals with disabilities, overseas citizens, persons who change their residence shortly before a Presidential election, and persons 18 to 20 years of age.

For further information, contact the Executive Officer, Civil Rights Division, Department of Justice, 950 Pennsylvania Avenue NW., Washington, DC 20035. Phone, 202–514–4224. Internet, http://www.justice.gov/crt.

Criminal Division   The Criminal Division develops, enforces, and supervises the application of all Federal criminal laws, except those specifically assigned to other divisions. In addition to its direct litigation responsibilities, the Division formulates and implements criminal enforcement policy and provides advice and assistance, including representing the United States before the United States Courts of Appeal. The Division engages in and coordinates a wide range of criminal investigations and prosecutions, such as those targeting individuals and organizations that engage in international and national drug trafficking and money laundering systems or organizations and organized crime groups. The Division also approves or monitors sensitive areas of law enforcement such as participation in the Witness Security Program and the use of electronic surveillance; advises the Attorney General, Congress, the Office of Management and Budget, and the White House on matters of criminal law; provides legal advice, assistance, and training to Federal, State, and local prosecutors and investigative agencies; provides leadership for coordinating international and national law enforcement matters; and provides training and development assistance to foreign criminal justice systems. Areas of responsibility include the following:

Asset forfeiture and money laundering, including the prosecution of complex, sensitive, multidistrict, and international cases; formulating policy and conducting training in the money laundering and forfeiture areas; developing legislation and regulations; ensuring the uniform application of forfeiture and money laundering statutes; participating in bilateral and multilateral initiatives to develop international forfeiture and money laundering policy and promote international cooperation; adjudicating petitions for remission or mitigation of forfeited assets; distributing forfeited funds and properties to appropriate domestic and foreign law enforcement agencies and community groups within the United States; and ensuring that such agencies comply with proper usage of received funds.

Child exploitation and obscenity, including the prosecution of sexual predators, sex trafficking of children, U.S. citizens and resident aliens who travel abroad to sexually abuse foreign children (sex tourism), and the enforcement of sex offender registration laws; providing forensic assistance to Federal prosecutors and law enforcement agents in investigating and prosecuting child exploitation: coordinating nationwide operations targeting child predators;

and developing policy and legislative proposals related to these issues.

Computer and intellectual property crimes, including cyber attacks on critical information systems (cyberterrorism); strengthening, domestic and international laws prosecute computer crimes; and directing multidistrict and transnational cyber investigations and prosecutions.

Enforcement, including the review of all Federal electronic surveillance requests and requests to apply for court orders permitting the use video surveillance; authorizing or denying the entry of applicants into the Federal Witness Security Program (WSP) and coordinating and administering its program components; reviewing requests for witness immunity ; transfer of prisoners to and from foreign countries to serve the remainder of their prison sentences; attorney and press subpoenas; applications for S-visa status; and disclosure of grand jury information.

Fraud, including the investigation and prosecution of white-collar crimes (corporate, securities, and investment fraud), government program and procurement fraud, and international criminal violations including the bribery of foreign government officials in violation of the Foreign Corrupt Practices Act.

International affairs, including making requests for international extradition and foreign evidence on behalf of Federal, State, and local prosecutors and investigators, fulfilling foreign requests for fugitives and evidence, and negotiating and implementing law enforcement treaties.

Narcotics and dangerous drugs, including domestic and international drug trafficking and narco-terrorism; enforcing laws that criminalize the extraterritorial manufacture or distribution of certain controlled substances; prosecuting drug traffickers who support a person or organization that engages in terrorist activity; and providing targeted intelligence support to the DEA and other law enforcement agencies worldwide.

Organized crime, including combining the resources and expertise of several

Federal agencies in cooperation with the Tax Division, U.S. attorneys offices, and State and local law enforcement to identify, disrupt, and dismantle major drug supply and money laundering organizations through coordinated, nationwide investigations targeting the entire infrastructure of these enterprises.

Assistance to foreign law enforcement institutions, including the creation of new and reforming existing police forces in other countries and international peacekeeping operations; enhancing the capabilities of existing police forces in emerging democracies; and assisting nations that are combating terrorism.

Overseas prosecutorial development, assistance, and training for prosecutors and judicial personnel in other countries to develop and sustain democratic criminal justice institutions.

Policy and legislation, developing legislative proposals and reviewing pending legislation affecting the Federal criminal justice system; reviewing and developing proposed changes to the Federal sentencing guidelines and rules; and analyzing crime policy and program issues.

Public integrity efforts to combat corruption of elected and appointed public officials at all levels of government.

Human rights and special prosecutions, investigating and prosecuting human rights violations, international violent crime, immigration violations, and war crimes.

Appellate work, including drafting briefs and certiorari petitions for the Solicitor General for filing in the U.S. Supreme Court; making recommendations to the Solicitor General as to whether further review is warranted on adverse decisions in the district courts and courts of appeals; and preparing briefs and arguing cases in the courts of appeals.

Counterterrorism, including in conjunction with the National Security Division, investigating and prosecuting terrorist financing and material support cases; establishing and maintaining an essential communication network between the Department of Justice and United States Attorneys' Offices for the rapid transmission of information on terrorism threats and investigative activity; providing and serving as trusted liaisons to the intelligence, defense, and immigration communities as well as to foreign government partners on counterterrorism issues and cases.

For further information, contact the Office of the Assistant Attorney General, Criminal Division, Department of Justice, Tenth Street and Pennsylvania Avenue NW., Washington, DC 20530. Phone, 202–514–2601. Internet, http://www.justice. gov/criminal.

Environment and Natural Resources Division   The Environment and Natural Resources Division is the Nation's environmental lawyer. The Division's responsibilities include enforcing civil and criminal environmental laws that protect America's health and environment. It also defends environmental challenges to Government activities and programs and ensures that environmental laws are implemented in a fair and consistent manner nationwide. It also represents the United States in all matters concerning the protection, use, and development of the Nation's natural resources and public lands, wildlife protection, Indian rights and claims, and the acquisition of Federal property. To carry out this broad mission, the Division litigates in the following areas:

Environmental crimes, prosecuting individuals and corporate entities violating laws designed to protect the environment.

Civil environmental enforcement, on behalf of EPA; claims for damages to natural resources filed on behalf of the Departments of the Interior, Commerce, and Agriculture; claims for contribution against private parties for contamination of public land; and recoupment of money spent to clean up certain oil spills on behalf of the U.S. Coast Guard.

Environmental defense, representing the United States in suits challenging the Government's administration of Federal environmental laws including claims that regulations are too strict or lenient and claims alleging that Federal agencies are not complying with environmental standards.

Wildlife and marine resources protection, including prosecution of smugglers and black-market dealers in protected wildlife.

Use and protection of federally owned public lands and natural resources across a broad spectrum of laws.

Indian resources protection, including establishing water rights, establishing and protecting hunting and fishing rights, collecting damages for trespass on Indian lands, and establishing reservation boundaries and rights to land.

Land acquisition for use by the Federal Government for purposes ranging from establishing public parks to building Federal courthouses.

For further information, contact the Office of the Assistant Attorney General, Environment and Natural Resources Division, Department of Justice, Tenth Street and Pennsylvania Avenue NW., Washington, DC 20530. Phone, 202–514–2701. Internet, http://justice.gov/enrd/.

National Security Division   The National Security Division (NSD) develops, enforces, and supervises the application of all Federal criminal laws related to the national counterterrorism and counterespionage enforcement programs, except those specifically assigned to other divisions. NSD litigates and coordinates a wide range of prosecutions and criminal investigations involving terrorism and violations of the espionage, export control, and foreign agents registration laws. It administers the Foreign Intelligence Surveillance Act and other legal authorities for national security activities; approves and monitors the use of electronic surveillance; provides legal and policy advice regarding the classification of and access to national security information; performs prepublication review of materials written by present and former DOJ employees; trains the law enforcement and intelligence communities; and advises the Department and legislative and executive branches on all areas of national security law. NSD also serves as the Department's representative on interdepartmental boards, committees, and entities dealing with issues related to national security.

NSD also has some additional counterterrorism, counterespionage, and intelligence oversight responsibilities as follows: to promote and oversee national counterterrorism enforcement programs; develop and implement counterterrorism strategies, legislation, and initiatives; facilitate information sharing between and among the Department and other Federal agencies on terrorism threats; share information with international law enforcement officials to assist with international threat information and litigation initiatives; liaison with the intelligence, defense, and immigration communities and foreign governments on counterterrorism issues and cases; supervise the investigation and prosecution of cases involving national security, foreign relations, the export of military and strategic commodities and technology, espionage, sabotage, neutrality, and atomic energy; coordinate cases involving the application for the Classified Information Procedures Act; enforce the Foreign Agents Registration Act of 1938 and related disclosure laws; supervise the preparation of certifications and applications for orders under the Foreign Intelligence Surveillance Act (FISA); represent the United States before the Foreign Intelligence Surveillance Court; participate in the development, implementation, and review of United States intelligence policies; evaluate existing and proposed national security-related activities to determine their consistency with relevant policies and law; monitor intelligence and counterintelligence activities of other agencies to ensure conformity with Department objectives; prepare reports evaluating domestic and foreign intelligence and counterintelligence activities; and process requests to use FISA-derived information in criminal, civil, and immigration proceedings and to disseminate that information to foreign governments.

For further information, contact the Office of the Assistant Attorney General, National Security Division, Department of Justice, Tenth Street and Pennsylvania Avenue NW., Washington, DC 20530. Phone, 202–514–5600. Internet, http://www.justice. gov/nsd

Tax Division   Tax Division ensures the uniform and fair enforcement of Federal tax laws in Federal and State courts. The Division conducts enforcement activities to deter specific taxpayers, as well as the taxpaying public at large, from conduct that deprives the Federal Government of its tax-related revenue. It represents the United States and its officers in all civil and criminal litigation arising under the internal revenue laws, other than proceedings in the U.S. Tax Court. Tax Division attorneys frequently join with assistant U.S. attorneys in prosecuting tax cases. Some criminal tax grand jury investigations and prosecutions are handled solely by Tax Division prosecutors, while others are delegated to assistant U.S. attorneys. Division attorneys evaluate requests by the Internal Revenue Service or U.S. attorneys to initiate grand jury investigations or prosecutions of tax crimes.

The Division handles a wide array of civil tax litigation, including the following: suits to enjoin the promotion of abusive tax shelters and to enjoin activities relating to aiding and abetting the understatement of tax liabilities of others; suits to enforce Internal Revenue Service administrative summonses that seek information essential to determine and collect taxpayers' liabilities, including summonses for records of corporate tax shelters and offshore transactions; suits brought by the United States to set aside fraudulent conveyances and to collect assets held by nominees and egos; tax refund suits challenging the Internal Revenue Service's determination of taxpayers' Federal income, employment, excise, and estate liabilities; bankruptcy litigation raising issues of the validity, dischargeability, and priority of Federal tax claims, and the feasibility of reorganization plans; suits brought by taxpayers challenging determinations made in the collection due process proceedings before the Internal Revenue Service's Office of Appeals; and suits against the United States for damages for the unauthorized disclosure of tax return information or for damages claimed because of alleged injuries caused by Internal Revenue Service employees in the performance of their official duties.

The Division also collects judgments in tax cases. To this end, the Division directs collection efforts and coordinates with, monitors the efforts of, and provides assistance to the various U.S. attorneys' offices in collecting outstanding judgments in tax cases. The Division also works with the Internal Revenue Service, U.S. attorneys, and other Government agencies on policy and legislative proposals to enhance tax administration and handling tax cases assigned to those offices.

For further information, contact the Office of the Assistant Attorney General, Tax Division, Department of Justice, Tenth Street and Pennsylvania Avenue NW., Washington, DC 20530. Phone, 202–514–2901. Internet, http://www.justice. gov/tax/.

Sources of Information

Disability-Related Matters   Contact the Civil Rights Division's ADA Hotline. Phone, 800–514–0301. TDD, 800–514–0383. Internet, http://www.usdoj.gov/crt/ada/adahom1.htm.

Drugs and Crime Clearinghouse   Phone, 800–666–3332 (toll free).

Electronic Access   Information concerning Department of Justice programs and activities is available electronically through the Internet at http://www.justice.gov.

Employment   For general information about employment at the Department of Justice, visit http://www.justice.gov/careers/careers.html.

Attorney and Law Student Employment: The Office of Attorney Recruitment and Management (OARM) administers law student, entry-level and experienced attorney employment opportunities at the Department of Justice. Information about employment opportunities for attorneys and law students is available at http://www.justice.gov/careers/legal/. General information about OARM can be obtained by calling the information line at (202) 514–3397 or by email at AskOARM@usdoj.gov. Email, AskOARM@usdoj.gov. Internet, http://www.justice.gov/careers/legal/.

United States Trustee Program: Room 770, 901 E Street NW., Washington, DC 20530. Phone, 202–616–1000.

Housing Discrimination Matters
Contact the Civil Rights Division's
Housing and Civil Enforcement Section.
Phone, 800–896–7743.

**Immigration-Related Employment
Matters** The Civil Rights Division
maintains a worker hotline. Phone, 800–
255–7688. TDD, 800–237–2515. It also
offers information for employers. Phone,
800–255–8155. TDD, 800–362–2735.

Publications and Films The Annual
Report of the Attorney General of the
United States is published each year by
the Department of Justice and is available
at http://www.justice.gov/ag/publications.
htm. Internet, http://www.justice.gov.

Textbooks on citizenship consisting of
teacher manuals and student textbooks
at various reading levels are distributed
free to public schools for applicants
for citizenship and are on sale to all
others from the Superintendent of
Documents, Government Printing Office,
Washington, DC 20402. Public schools
or organizations under the supervision
of public schools that are entitled to free
textbooks should make their requests
to the appropriate Immigration and
Naturalization Service Regional Office.
For general information, call 202–514–
3946.

The Freedom of Information Act
(FOIA) Guide is updated on a rolling
basis, and the DOJ FOIA Litigation and
Compliance Report is prepared annually,
and both are available at http://www.
justice.gov. The Privacy Act Overview
is prepared biannually and is available
from the Superintendent of Documents,
Government Printing Office, Washington,
DC 20530. It is also available on www.
justice.gov.

Guidelines for Effective Human
Relations Commissions, Annual
Report of the Community Relations
Service, Community Relations Service

Brochure, CRS Hotline Brochure, Police
Use of Deadly Force: A Conciliation
Handbook for Citizens and Police,
Principles of Good Policing: Avoiding
Violence Between Police and Citizens,
Resolving Racial Conflict: A Guide for
Municipalities, and Viewpoints and
Guidelines on Court-Appointed Citizens
Monitoring Commissions in School
Desegregation are available upon
request from the Public Information
Office, Community Relations Service,
Department of Justice, Washington, DC
20530.

A limited number of drug educational
films are available, free of charge, to
civic, educational, private, and religious
groups.

Reading Rooms Reading rooms are
located in Washington, DC, at the
following locations:

Department of Justice, Room 5400,
Tenth Street and Constitution Avenue
NW., Washington, DC 20530. Phone,
202–514–3775.

Board of Immigration Appeals, Suite
2400, 5107 Leesburg Pike, Falls Church,
VA 22041. Phone, 703–305–0168.

National Institute of Justice, 9th Floor,
633 Indiana Avenue NW., Washington,
DC 20531. Phone, 202–307–5883.
Internet, http://www.justice.gov.

**Redress for Wartime Relocation/
Internment** Contact the Civil
Rights Division's Office of Redress
Administration. Helpline phone,
202–219–6900. TDD, 202–219–4710.
Internet, http://www.usdoj.gov.

Small Business Activities Contract
information for small businesses can be
obtained from the Office of Small and
Disadvantaged Business Utilization,
Department of Justice, 2 Constitution
Square, 145 N Street NE., Washington,
DC 20530. Phone, 202–307–1971.

For further information concerning the Department of Justice contact the Office of Public Affairs,
Department of Justice, Tenth Street and Constitution Avenue NW., Washington, DC 20530. Phone, 202–514–
2007. TDD, 202–786–5731. Internet, http://www.justice.gov.

Bureaus

Federal Bureau of Investigation

935 Pennsylvania Avenue NW., Washington, DC 20535
Phone, 202–324–3000. Internet, http://www.fbi.gov.

Director   JAMES B. COMEY

The Federal Bureau of Investigation (FBI) is the principal investigative arm of the United States Department of Justice. It is primarily charged with gathering and reporting facts, locating witnesses, and compiling evidence in cases involving Federal jurisdiction. It also provides law enforcement leadership and assistance to State and international law enforcement agencies.

The FBI was established in 1908 by the Attorney General, who directed that Department of Justice investigations be handled by its own staff. The Bureau is charged with investigating all violations of Federal law except those that have been assigned by legislative enactment or otherwise to another Federal agency. Its jurisdiction includes a wide range of responsibilities in the national security, criminal, and civil fields. Priority has been assigned to areas such as counterterrorism, counterintelligence, cyber crimes, internationally and nationally organized crime/drug matters, and financial crimes.

The FBI also offers cooperative services to local, State, and international law enforcement agencies. These services include fingerprint identification, laboratory examination, police training, the Law Enforcement Online communication and information service for use by the law enforcement community, the National Crime Information Center, and the National Center for the Analysis of Violent Crime.

Sources of Information

Employment   For employment information, contact the Director, Washington, DC 20535, or any of the field offices or resident agencies whose addresses are listed in the front of most local telephone directories.
Publications   The FBI Law Enforcement Bulletin and Uniform Crime Reports— Crime in the United States are available from the Superintendent of Documents, Government Printing Office, Washington, DC 20402.

For further information, contact the Office of Public Affairs, Federal Bureau of Investigation, J. Edgar Hoover FBI Building, 935 Pennsylvania Avenue NW., Washington, DC 20535. Phone, 202–317–2727. Internet, http://www.fbi.gov.

Bureau of Prisons

320 First Street NW., Washington, DC 20534
Phone, 202–307–3198. Internet, http://www.bop.gov.

Director   CHARLES E. SAMUELS, JR.

The BOP was established in 1930 to provide more progressive and humane care for Federal inmates, to professionalize the prison service, and to ensure consistent and centralized administration of the 11 Federal prisons in operation at that time. Today, the Bureau includes more than 100

institutions, and six regional offices. The Bureau has its headquarters, also known as Central Office, in Washington, DC. The Central Office is divided into 10 divisions, including the National Institute of Corrections.

The Correctional Programs Division (CPD) is responsible for inmate classification and programming, including psychology and religious services, substance abuse treatment, case management, and programs for special needs offenders. CPD provides policy direction and daily operational oversight of institution security, emergency preparedness, intelligence gathering, inmate discipline, inmate sentence computations, receiving and discharge, and inmate transportation, as well as coordinating international treaty transfers and overseeing the special security needs of inmates placed in the Federal Witness Protection Program. CPD administers contracts and intergovernmental agreements for the confinement of offenders in community-based programs, community corrections centers, and other facilities including privately managed facilities. CPD staff is also involved in the Bureau's privatization efforts.

The Industries, Education, and Vocational Training Division oversees Federal Prison Industries, or UNICOR, which is a wholly owned Government corporation that provides employment and training opportunities for inmates confined in Federal correctional facilities. Additionally, it is responsible for oversight of educational, occupational, and vocational training and leisure-time programs, as well as those related to inmate release preparation.

The National Institute of Corrections (NIC) provides technical assistance, training, and information to State and local corrections agencies throughout the country, as well as the Bureau. It also provides research assistance and documents through the NIC Information Center.

Sources of Information

Employment   For employment information, contact the Central Office, 320 First Street NW., Washington, DC 20534 (phone, 202–307–3082) or any regional or field office.

Reading Room   The reading room is located at the Bureau of Prisons, 320 First Street NW., Washington, DC 20534. Phone, 202–307–3029.

For further information, contact the Public Information Office, Bureau of Prisons, 320 First Street NW., Washington, DC 20534. Phone, 202–514–6551. Internet, http://www.bop.gov.

United States Marshals Service

Department of Justice, Washington, DC 20530
Phone, 202–307–9000. Internet, http://www.usmarshals.gov.

Director   STACIA HYLTON

The United States Marshals Service is the Nation's oldest Federal law enforcement agency, having served as a vital link between the executive and judicial branches of the Government since 1789. The Marshals Service performs tasks that are essential to the operation of virtually every aspect of the Federal justice system.

The Marshals Service has these responsibilities: providing support and protection for the Federal courts, including security for 800 judicial facilities and nearly 2,000 judges and magistrates, as well as countless other trial participants such as jurors and attorneys; apprehending the majority of Federal fugitives; operating the Federal Witness Security Program and ensuring the safety of endangered Government witnesses; maintaining custody of and transporting thousands of Federal prisoners annually; executing court orders and arrest warrants; managing and selling seized property forfeited to the Government by drug traffickers and other criminals and assisting the Justice Department's asset forfeiture program; responding to emergency circumstances, including civil disturbances, terrorist incidents, and other crisis situations through its Special Operations Group; restoring order in riot and mob-violence situations; providing housing, transportation, and medical care of federal detainees; and operating the U.S. Marshals Service Training Academy.

Sources of Information

Employment For employment information, contact the Field Staffing Branch, United States Marshals Service, Department of Justice, 600 Army Navy Drive, Arlington, VA 22202–4210.

For further information, contact the Office of Public Affairs, U.S. Marshals Service, Department of Justice, Washington, DC 20530. Phone, 202–307–9065. Internet, http://www.usmarshals.gov.

International Criminal Police Organization—United States National Central Bureau

Department of Justice, Washington, DC 20530
Phone, 202–616–9000. Fax, 202–616–8400. Internet, http://www.justice.gov/usncb.

Director	SHAWN A. BRAY

The United States National Central Bureau (USNCB) is the United States representative to INTERPOL, the International Criminal Police Organization. Also known as INTERPOL—Washington. INTERPOL Washington is a separate component under the supervision of the Deputy Attorney General and co-managed with the Department of Homeland Security. It provides an essential communications link between the U.S. police community and their counterparts in the foreign member countries.

INTERPOL is an association of 190 countries dedicated to promoting mutual assistance among law enforcement authorities in the prevention and suppression of international crime. With no police force of its own, INTERPOL has no powers of arrest or search and seizure and therefore relies on the law enforcement authorities of its member countries. Each member country is required to have a national central bureau, such as the USNCB, to act as the primary point of contact for police matters. INTERPOL serves as a channel of communication for its member countries to cooperate in the investigation and prosecution of crime, provides a forum for discussions, working group meetings, and symposia to enable police to focus on specific areas of criminal activity affecting their countries, and issues and maintains information and databases on crime, fugitives, stolen passports and vehicles, missing persons, and humanitarian concerns, which are supplied by and can be used as a source by its member countries.

INTERPOL Washington has permanent staff and detailed special agents from numerous Federal law enforcement agencies. It is organized into the Alien/ Fugitive Division, the Counterterrorism Division, the Drug Division, the Economic Crimes Division, the Human Trafficking and Child Protection Division, the State and Local Police Liaison Division, and the Violent Crimes Division.

For further information, contact the INTERPOL–U.S. National Central Bureau, Department of Justice, Washington, DC 20530. Phone, 202–616–9000. Internet, http://www.justice.gov/interpol-washington.

Drug Enforcement Administration

8701 Morrissette Drive, Springfield, VA 22152
Phone, 202–307–1000. Internet, http://www.justice.gov/dea.

Administrator	MICHELE M. LEONHART

The Drug Enforcement Administration (DEA) is the lead Federal agency in enforcing narcotics and controlled substances laws and regulations. The DEA also enforces the Federal money laundering and bulk currency smuggling statutes when the funds involved in the transactions or smuggling are derived from the sale of narcotics. It was created in July 1973 by Reorganization Plan No. 2 of 1973 (5 U.S.C. app.).

The DEA enforces the provisions of the controlled substances and chemical diversion and trafficking laws and regulations of the United States, and operates on a worldwide basis. It presents cases to the criminal and civil justice systems of the United States—or any other competent jurisdiction—on those significant organizations and their members involved in cultivation, production, smuggling, distribution, laundering of proceeds, or diversion of controlled substances appearing in or destined for illegal traffic in the United States. The DEA disrupts and dismantles these organizations by arresting their members, confiscating their drugs, and seizing their assets; and creates, manages, and supports enforcement-related programs—domestically and internationally—aimed at reducing the availability of and demand for illicit controlled substances.

The DEA's responsibilities include: investigation of major narcotic, chemical, drug-money laundering, and bulk currency smuggling violators who operate at interstate and international levels; seizure and forfeiture of assets derived from, traceable to, or intended to be used for illicit drug trafficking; seizure and forfeiture of assets derived from or traceable to drug-money laundering or the smuggling of bulk currency derived from illegal drugs; enforcement of regulations governing the legal manufacture, distribution, and dispensing of controlled substances; management of an intelligence program that supports drug investigations, initiatives, and operations worldwide; coordination with Federal, State, and local law enforcement

authorities and cooperation with counterpart agencies abroad; assistance to State and local law enforcement agencies in addressing their most significant drug and drug-related violence problems; leadership and influence over international counterdrug and chemical policy and support for institution building in host nations; training, scientific research, and information exchange in support of drug traffic prevention and control; and education and assistance to the public community on the prevention, treatment, and dangers of drugs.

The DEA maintains liaison with the United Nations, INTERPOL, and other organizations on matters relating to international narcotics control programs. It has 222 offices in 21 divisions throughout the United States and 86 foreign offices located in 67 countries.

Sources of Information

Controlled Substances Act Registration Information about registration under the Controlled Substances Act may be obtained from the Office of Diversion Control, 8701 Morrissette Drive, Springfield, VA 22152. Phone: 800–882–9539. Email, DEA.Registration.Help@usdoj.gov Email, DEA.Registration.Help@usdoj.gov.

Employment For employment information, contact the nearest DEA field division recruitment office. Information on other DEA career opportunities is available through the DEA Career Gateway on USAJOBS at https://dea.usajobs.gov.

Publications A limited selection of pamphlets and brochures is available. The most widely requested publication is Drugs of Abuse, an identification manual intended for professional use. Single copies are free.

For further information, contact the Public Affairs Section, Drug Enforcement Administration, 8701 Morrissette Drive Springfield, VA 22152. Phone, 202–307–7977. Internet, http://www.justice.gov/dea.

Office of Justice Programs

Assistant Attorney General	KAROL V. MASON

The Office of Justice Programs (OJP) was established by the Justice

Assistance Act of 1984 (42 U.S.C. 3711) and reauthorized in 1994 and

2005, to provide Federal leadership, coordination, and assistance needed to make the Nation's justice system more efficient and effective in preventing and controlling crime. OJP is responsible for collecting statistical data and conducting analyses; identifying emerging criminal justice issues; developing and testing promising approaches to address these issues; evaluating program results; and disseminating these findings and other information to State and local governments.

The OJP is comprised of the following bureaus and offices: the Bureau of Justice Assistance provides funding, training, and technical assistance to State and local governments to combat violent and drug-related crime and help improve the criminal justice system; the Bureau of Justice Statistics is responsible for collecting and analyzing data on crime, criminal offenders, crime victims, and the operations of justice systems at all levels of government; the National Institute of Justice sponsors research and development programs, conducts demonstrations of innovative approaches to improve criminal justice, and develops new criminal justice technologies; the Office of Juvenile Justice and Delinquency Prevention provides grants and contracts to States to help them improve their juvenile justice systems and sponsors innovative research, demonstration, evaluation, statistics, replication, technical assistance, and training programs to help improve the Nation's understanding of and response to juvenile violence and delinquency; the Office for Victims of Crime administers victim compensation and assistance grant programs and provides funding, training, and technical assistance to victim service organizations, criminal justice agencies, and other professionals to improve the Nation's response to crime victims; and the Office of Sex Offender Sentencing, Monitoring, Apprehending, Registering, and Tracking (SMART) established and maintains the standards of the Sex Offender Registration and Notification Act as defined by the Adam Walsh Act. The SMART Office also provides technical assistance and supports innovative and best practices in the field of sex offender management.

Sources of Information

Employment For employment information, contact the Human Resources Division, 810 Seventh Street, NW., Washington, DC 20531. Phone, 202–307–0730. Internet, http://ojp.gov/about/jobs.htm Internet, http://www.ojp.usdoj.gov/about/jobs.htm.

For further information, contact the Department of Justice Response Center. Phone, 800–421–6770. Internet, http://www.ojp.usdoj.gov. Email, askojp@ojp.usdoj.gov.

Office on Violence Against Women

Director   BEATRICE HANSON, *Acting*

The Office on Violence Against Women (OVW) was established in 2005 to reduce violence against women through the implementation of the Violence Against Women Act. OVW is responsible for administering financial and technical assistance to communities that are developing programs, policies, and practices aimed at ending domestic and dating violence, sexual assault, and stalking.

For further information, contact the Office on Violence Against Women, 145 N Street, NE., Suite 10W.121, Washington, DC, 20530. Phone, 202–307–6026. Internet, http://www.justice.gov/ovw.

Bureau of Alcohol, Tobacco, Firearms and Explosives

Director   B. TODD JONES

The Bureau of Alcohol, Tobacco, Firearms and Explosives (ATF) is responsible for enforcing Federal criminal laws and regulating the firearms and explosives industries. ATF, formerly known as the Bureau of Alcohol, Tobacco, and Firearms, was initially established by Department of Treasury Order No. 221, effective July 1, 1972, which transferred the functions, powers, and duties arising under laws relating to alcohol, tobacco, firearms, and explosives from the Internal Revenue Service to ATF. The Homeland Security Act of 2002 (6 U.S.C. 531) transferred certain functions and authorities of ATF to the Department of Justice and established it under its current name. ATF works, directly and through partnerships, to investigate and reduce violent crime involving firearms and explosives, acts of arson, and illegal trafficking of alcohol and tobacco products. The Bureau provides training and support to its Federal, State, local, and international law enforcement partners and works primarily in 25 field divisions across the 50 States, Puerto Rico, the U.S. Virgin Islands, and Guam. It also has foreign offices in Mexico, Canada, Colombia, and France.

For further information, contact the Office of Public Affairs, Bureau of Alcohol, Tobacco, Firearms and Explosives, Department of Justice, 99 New York Avenue NE., Suite 10W.121, Washington, DC 20530. Phone, 202–648–8500. Internet, http://www.atf.gov.

Offices and Boards

Executive Office for Immigration Review

Director   JUAN P. OSUNA

The Executive Office for Immigration Review, under a delegation of authority from the Attorney General, is charged with adjudicating matters brought under various immigration statutes to its three administrative tribunals: the Board of Immigration Appeals, the Office of the Chief Immigration Judge, and the Office of the Chief Administrative Hearing Officer.

The Board of Immigration Appeals has nationwide jurisdiction to hear appeals from certain decisions made by immigration judges and by district directors of the Department of Homeland Security (DHS). In addition, the Board is responsible for hearing appeals involving disciplinary actions against attorneys and representatives before DHS and the Board.

Decisions of the Board are binding on all DHS officers and immigration judges unless modified or overruled by the Attorney General or a Federal court. All Board decisions are subject to judicial review in Federal court. The majority of appeals reaching the Board involve orders of removal and applications for relief from removal. Other cases before the Board include the removal of aliens applying for admission to the United States, petitions to classify the status of alien relatives for the issuance of preference immigrant visas, fines imposed upon carriers for the violation of the immigration laws, and motions for reopening and reconsideration of decisions previously rendered.

The Office of the Chief Immigration Judge provides overall direction for more than 200 immigration judges located in 53 immigration courts throughout the Nation. Immigration judges are responsible for conducting formal administrative proceedings and act independently in their decisionmaking capacity. Their decisions are administratively final, unless appealed or certified to the Board.

In removal proceedings, an immigration judge determines whether an individual from a foreign country should be admitted or allowed to stay in the United States or be removed. Judges are located throughout the United States, and each judge has jurisdiction to consider various forms of relief available under the law, including applications for asylum.

The Office of the Chief Administrative Hearing Officer is responsible for the general supervision and management of administrative law judges who preside at hearings that are mandated by provisions of immigration law concerning allegations of unlawful employment of aliens, unfair immigration-related employment practices, and immigration document fraud.

For further information, contact the Office of Legislative and Public Affairs, Executive Office for Immigration Review, Department of Justice, 5107 Leesburg Pike, Suite 1902, Falls Church, VA 22041. Phone, 703–305–0289. Internet, http://www.usdoj.gov/eoir.

United States Parole Commission

Chairman   ISAAC FULWOOD, JR.

The United States Parole Commission (USPC) makes parole release decisions for eligible Federal and District of Columbia prisoners; authorizes methods of release and conditions under which release occurs; prescribes, modifies, and monitors compliance with the terms and conditions governing offenders' behavior while on parole or mandatory or supervised release; issues warrants for violation of supervision; determines probable cause for the revocation process; revokes parole, mandatory, or supervised release; releases from supervision those offenders who are no longer a risk to public safety; and promulgates the rules, regulations, and guidelines for the exercise of USPC's

authority and the implementation of a national parole policy.

USPC has sole jurisdiction over the following: Federal offenders who committed offenses before November 1, 1987; D.C. Code offenders who committed offenses before August 5, 2000; D.C. Code offenders sentenced to a term of supervised release; Uniform Code of Military Justice offenders who are in Bureau of Prison's custody; transfer treaty cases; and State probationers and parolees in the Federal Witness Protection Program.

Sources of Information

Reading Rooms   The reading room is located at 90 K Street, NE., Washington, DC 20530. Phone, 202–346–7000.

For further information, contact the U.S. Parole Commission, Department of Justice, 90 K Street, NE., Washington, DC 20530. Phone, 202–346–7000. Internet, http://www.justice.gov/uspc.

Office of Community Oriented Policing Services

Director   RONALD L. DAVIS

The Office of Community Oriented Policing Services (COPS) was established to assist law enforcement agencies in enhancing public safety through the implementation of community policing strategies. COPS does so by providing training to enhance law enforcement officers' problem-solving and community interaction skills assisting law

enforcement and community members to develop initiatives to prevent crime; substantially increasing the number of law enforcement officers directly interacting with the community; and supporting the development of new technologies to shift law enforcement's focus to preventing crime and disorder within their communities.

For further information, contact the Office of Community Oriented Policing Services (COPS), Department of Justice, 935 N Street, NE., Washington, DC 20530. Phone, 202–514–2058. Internet, http://www.cops.usdoj.gov.

Foreign Claims Settlement Commission of the United States

Commissioners	ANUJ C. DESAI, SYLVIA M. BECKER

The Foreign Claims Settlement Commission of the United States is a quasi-judicial, independent agency within the Department of Justice, which adjudicates claims of U.S. nationals against foreign governments, either under specific jurisdiction conferred by Congress or the Department of State or pursuant to international claims settlement agreements. The decisions of the Commission are final and are not reviewable under any standard by any court or other authority. Funds for payment of the Commission's awards are derived from congressional appropriations, international claims settlements, or the liquidation of foreign assets in the United States by the Departments of Justice and the Treasury.

The Commission also has authority to receive, determine the validity and amount, and provide for the payment of claims by members of the U.S. Armed Services and civilians held as prisoners of war or interned by a hostile force in Southeast Asia during the Vietnam conflict or by the survivors of such service members and civilians.

The Commission is also responsible for maintaining records and responding to inquiries related to the various claims programs it has conducted against the Governments of Albania, Bulgaria, China, Cuba, Czechoslovakia, Egypt, Ethiopia, the Federal Republic of Germany, the German Democratic Republic, Hungary, Iran, Italy, Panama, Poland, Romania, the Soviet Union, Vietnam, and Yugoslavia, as well as those authorized under the War Claims Act of 1948 and other statutes.

Sources of Information

Employment For information of attorney positions, contact the Office of the Chief Counsel, Suite 6002, 600 E Street NW., Washington, DC 20579 (phone, 202–616–6975). For all other positions, contact the Chief Administrative Counsel, same address and phone.

Reading Room The reading room is located at 600 E Street NW., Washington, DC 20579. Phone, 202–616–6975.

For further information, contact the Office of the Chairman, Foreign Claims Settlement Commission of the United States, Department of Justice, Suite 6002, 600 E Street NW., Washington, DC 20579. Phone, 202–616–6975. Fax, 202–616–6993.

DEPARTMENT OF LABOR

200 Constitution Avenue NW., Washington, DC 20210
Phone, 202–693–6000. Internet, http://www.dol.gov.

Secretary of Labor	THOMAS E. PEREZ
Deputy Secretary	SETH D. HARRIS
Chief of Staff	ANA M. MA
Chief Administrative Law Judge	STEPHEN L. PURCELL
Chief Administrative Appeals Judge, Administrative Review Board	PAUL IGASAKI
Chief Administrative Appeals Judge, Benefits Review Board	NANCY S. DOLDER
Chairman and Chief Judge, Employees' Compensation Appeals Board	RICHARD DASCHBACH
Director, Center for Faith-Based and Community Initiatives	PHILIP TOM
Executive Secretary	ELIZABETH O. KIM
Ombudsman, Energy Employee Occupational Illness Compensation Program	MALCOLM NELSON
Assistant Secretary for Administration and Management	T. MICHAEL KERR
Assistant Secretary for Congressional and Intergovernmental Affairs	BRIAN KENNEDY
Assistant Secretary of Disability Employment Policy	KATHLEEN MARTINEZ
Assistant Secretary for Policy	(VACANCY)
Chief Economist	JENNIFER HUNT
Chief Financial Officer	JAMES TAYLOR
Director, Office of Federal Contract Compliance Programs	PATRICIA A. SHIU
Director, Office of Labor-Management Standards	(VACANCY)
Director, Office of Workers' Compensation Programs	GARY A. STEINBERG, Acting
Inspector General	(VACANCY)
Senior Advisor for Communications and Public Affairs	CARL FILLICHIO
Solicitor of Labor	M. PATRICIA SMITH
Senior Advisor and Director, Office of Public Engagement	GABRIELA LEMUS

The Department of Labor promotes the welfare of job seekers, wage earners, and retirees by improving working conditions, advancing opportunities for profitable employment, protecting retirement and health care benefits, matching workers to employers, strengthening free collective bargaining, and tracking changes in economic indicators on a national scale.

The Department of Labor (DOL) was created by act of March 4, 1913 (29 U.S.C. 551). Congress first created a Bureau of Labor in the Interior

Department by act of June 24, 1884. The Bureau of Labor later became independent as a Department of Labor without executive rank by act of June 13, 1888. It returned to bureau status in the Department of Commerce and Labor, which was created by act of February 14, 1903 (15 U.S.C. 1501; 29 U.S.C. 1 note).

The Department administers a variety of Federal labor laws to guarantee workers' rights to fair, safe, and healthy working conditions, including minimum hourly wage and overtime pay, protection against employment discrimination, and unemployment insurance.

Office of the Secretary

Secretary The Secretary is the principal adviser to the President on the development and execution of policies and the administration and enforcement of laws relating to wage earners, their working conditions, and their employment opportunities.

Office of the Administrative Law Judges Prior to 1972, the Office of Administrative Law Judges (OALJ) comprised two Administrative Law Judges (referred to as "hearing examiners" until November 7, 1972) who adjudicated a small number of cases arising primarily under Presidential Executive Orders. In 1972, OALJ's role was significantly expanded to include a more diverse range of labor-related cases. It presently employs 42 judges in Washington, DC, and seven district offices located in various cities around the country. OALJ's judges are not political appointees and are guaranteed decisional independence by, and appointed under, the Administrative Procedure Act, 5 U.S.C. 500 et seq. Judges within OALJ preside over trial-type hearings in various matters, including claims for compensation and medical or survivor's benefits under the Longshore and Black Lung statutes; antidiscrimination and retaliation complaints arising under Executive Order 11246 and several whistleblower statutes; enforcement actions brought by other agencies within the Department of Labor such as the Wage and Hour Division and the Employee Benefits Security Administration; and immigration cases

granting or denying employers' requests to hire foreign workers in numerous professional and nonprofessional occupations on either a temporary or permanent basis. Appeals from decisions by OALJ's judges are typically reviewed by either the Administrative Review Board or Benefits Review Board and subsequently by the U.S. Courts of Appeals and U.S. Supreme Court.

Office of the Assistant Secretary for Administration and Management The Office of the Assistant Secretary for Administration and Management is responsible for the development and promulgation of policies, standards, procedures, systems, and materials related to the resource and administrative management of the Department and for the execution of such policies and directives at Headquarters and in the field.

For more information, call 202–693–4040. Internet, http://www.dol.gov/oasam/.

Office of Disability Employment Policy The Office of Disability Employment Policy (ODEP) seeks to increase the number and quality of employment opportunities for people with disabilities by promoting the adoption and implementation of its policy strategies and effective practices and bringing focus to the issue of disability employment. ODEP acts as a facilitator and catalyst among the multiple agencies across the Federal Government that support the education and training needs of people with disabilities, promoting collaboration and realignment of policy based on validated research and emerging successful and innovative practices. ODEP also promotes collaboration, policy and resource alignment, and the adoption and implementation of effective practices by State, local, and nongovernmental entities, including businesses.

For further information, call 202–693–7880. TTY, 202–693–7881. Internet, http://www.dol.gov/odep.

Office of Federal Contract Compliance Programs The Office of Federal Contract Compliance Programs (OFCCP) administers and enforces three equal opportunity mandates:

DEPARTMENT OF LABOR

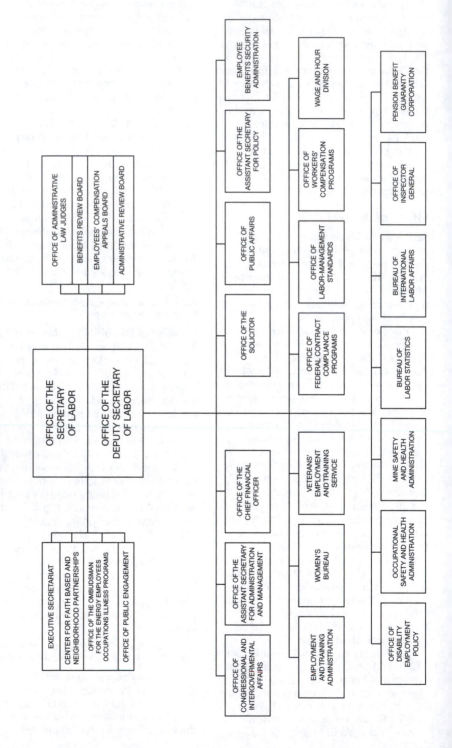

Executive Order 11246, as amended; section 503 of the Rehabilitation Act of 1973, as amended; and the Vietnam Era Veterans' Readjustment Assistance Act of 1974, as amended, 38 U.S.C. 4212. These mandates prohibit Federal contractors and subcontractors from discriminating on the basis of race, color, religion, sex, national origin, disability, or veteran status. They also require Federal contractors and subcontractors to take affirmative steps to ensure equal employment opportunities. OFCCP also shares responsibility with the U.S. Equal Employment Opportunity Commission in enforcing Title I of the Americans with Disabilities Act.

For a complete listing of OFCCP offices across the country, including addresses, telephone numbers, and key officials, visit www.dol.gov/ofccp/contacts/ ofnation2.htm.

For further information, contact the Office of Federal Contract Compliance Programs help desk. Phone, 800–397–6251. Internet, http://www.dol. gov/ofccp/index.htm.

Office of Inspector General The Office of Inspector General conducts audits and investigations to review the effectiveness, efficiency, and integrity of all DOL programs and operations, including those performed by its contractors and grantees. The Office is unique among Inspectors General because it conducts labor racketeering investigations of employee benefit plans, labor-management relations, and internal labor union affairs.

For further information, call 202–693–5100.

Office of Labor-Management Standards The Office of Labor-Management Standards conducts criminal and civil investigations to safeguard the financial integrity of unions and to ensure union democracy. The Office conducts investigative audits of labor unions to uncover and remedy criminal and civil violations of the Labor-Management Reporting and Disclosure Act and related statutes. The Office also publishes the text of the Labor-Management Reporting and Disclosure Act and pamphlets that explain the reporting, election, bonding, and trusteeship provisions of the act. The

pamphlets and reporting forms used by persons covered by the act are available free, in limited quantities, from the OLMS National Office at Room N–5616, 200 Constitution Avenue NW., Washington, DC 20210, and from OLMS field offices.

For a complete listing of Office of Labor-Management Standards regional and district offices, including addresses, telephone numbers, and key officials, visit www.dol.gov/olms/contacts/ lmskeyp.htm.

For Labor-Management Reporting and Disclosure Act assistance, call 202– 693–0123. For electronic forms software technical support, call 866–401–1109. For transit employee protections assistance, call 202–693–0126.

Internet, http://www.dol.gov/olms.

Office of the Ombudsman for the Energy Employees Occupational Illness Compensation Program Act The Office of the Ombudsman for the Energy Employees Occupational Illness Compensation Program Act was established in October 2004 under Part E of the Energy Employees Occupational Illness Compensation Program Act (EEOICPA), as amended, (42 U.S.C. 7385s-15) to administer a system of Federal payments to compensate certain nuclear workers for occupational illnesses caused by exposure to toxic substances. It is a small, independent office, headed by the Ombudsman, who is appointed by the Secretary of Labor. The Office provides information to claimants on the benefits available under Parts E and B of the EEOICPA and issues annual reports to Congress detailing the complaints, grievances, and requests for assistance received by the Office.

For further information, call 202–693–5890.

Office of the Solicitor of Labor The Office of the Solicitor of Labor (SOL) provides comprehensive legal services to help the Department achieve its mission. More specifically, the Solicitor serves dual roles in the Department. First, the Solicitor acts as the Department's chief enforcement officer, pursuing affirmative litigation on behalf of the Secretary before administrative law judges, review boards

and commissions, and in the Federal
district courts and courts of appeals. The
Solicitor also as the Department's general
counsel, assisting in the development
of regulations, standards, and legislative
proposals; providing legal opinions
and advice on all of the Department's
activities; advising the Solicitor General
on Supreme Court litigation involving the
Department's statutes or in other matters
in which we have an institutional interest;
and coordinating with the Department of
Justice (DOJ), as appropriate, to defend
the Department in litigation.

For a complete listing of regional
offices of the Office of the Solicitor,
including addresses, telephone numbers,
and key officials, visit www.dol.gov/sol/
organizations/regions/main.htm.

For a reference to the national
office divisions, visit www.dol.gov/sol/
organizations/divisions/main.htm.

For further information, contact the Office of the
Solicitor, Department of Labor, 200 Constitution
Avenue NW., Washington, DC 20210. Phone,
202–693–5260. Internet, http://www.dol.gov/sol/.

**Office of Workers' Compensation
Programs**   By making timely and
appropriate decisions on claims,
promptly paying benefits, and helping
workers return to their jobs quickly,
the Office of Workers' Compensation
Programs (OWCP) protects the interests
of workers who are injured or become
ill on the job. OWCP serves specific
employee groups that are covered under
four major disability compensation
statutes by mitigating the financial
burden resulting from workplace injury
or illness and promoting return to work
when appropriate. The statutes are the
Federal Employees' Compensation Act,
serving Federal employees; the Longshore
and Harbor Workers' Compensation
Act, serving certain employees engaged
in maritime employment on navigable
waters in the United States; the Black
Lung Benefits Act, serving coal miners
who are totally disabled due to
pneumoconiosis, a respiratory disease
associated with the prolonged inhalation
of coal dust; and the Energy Employees
Occupational Illness Compensation
Act, serving eligible workers who
became ill as a result of work in the

nuclear weapons industry. Dependents
or survivors may also be eligible for
benefits.

For a complete listing of Office of
Workers' Compensation Programs district
offices, including addresses, telephone
numbers, and key officials, visit www.
dol.gov/owcp/owcpkeyp.htm.

For further information, contact the Office of
the Director, Office of Workers' Compensation
Programs, Department of Labor, Room S–3524, 200
Constitution Avenue NW., Washington, DC 20210.
Phone, 202–693–0031. Internet, http://www.dol.
gov/owcp.

Administrative Review Board   The
Administrative Review Board (ARB)
consists of five members appointed
by the Secretary. It issues final agency
decisions for appeals cases under a
wide range of worker protection laws,
including the McNamara O'Hara Service
Contract Act and the Davis Bacon Act.
The appeals cases primarily address
environmental, transportation, and
securities whistleblower protection;
H–1B immigration provisions; child
labor law violations; employment
discrimination; job training; seasonal
and migrant workers; and Federal
construction and service contracts.
The Board's cases generally arise upon
appeal from decisions of Department of
Labor Administrative Law Judges or the
Administrator of the Department's Wage
and Hour Division. Depending upon the
statute at issue, the parties may appeal
the Board's decisions to Federal district
or appellate courts and, ultimately, to the
U.S. Supreme Court.

For further information, call the Administrative
Officer. Phone, 202–693–6234. Internet, http://
www.dol.gov/arb/welcome.html.

Benefits Review Board   The Benefits
Review Board (BRB) consists of five
members appointed by the Secretary.
In 1972, Congress created the Board to
review and issue decisions on appeals
of workers' compensation cases arising
under the Longshore and Harbor
Workers' Compensation Act, and its
extensions, and the Black Lung Benefits
amendments to the Federal Coal Mine
Safety Act of 1969. Board decisions may
be appealed to the U.S. Courts of Appeals
and to the U.S. Supreme Court.

For further information, call the Administrative Officer. Phone, 202–693–6234. Internet, http://www.dol.gov/brb/welcome.html.

Employees' Compensation Appeals Board The Employees' Compensation Appeals Board (ECAB) is a three-member quasi-judicial body appointed by the Secretary and delegated exclusive jurisdiction by Congress to hear and make final decisions on appeals filed by Federal workers arising under the Federal Employees' Compensation Act. The Board was created by Reorganization Plan No. 2 of 1946 (60 Stat. 1095). The Board's decisions are not reviewable and are binding upon the Office of Workers' Compensation Programs (OWCP).

For further information, call the Administrative Officer. Phone, 202–693–6234. Internet, http://www.dol.gov/ecab/welcome.html.

Sources of Information

Contracts General inquiries may be directed to the Procurement Services Center, Room S–4307, 200 Constitution Avenue NW., Washington, DC 20210. Phone, 202–693–4570. Inquiries on doing business with the Job Corps should be directed to the Job Corps Regional Director in the appropriate Department of Labor regional office. Internet, http://www.dol.gov/oasam/boc/ops/index.htm.

Electronic Access Information concerning Department of Labor agencies, programs, and activities is available online. Internet, http://www.dol.gov.

Employment Detailed information about job opportunities with the Department of Labor, including the address and telephone numbers of the personnel offices in the regions and in Washington, DC, is available online. Internet, http://www.dol.gov/dol/jobs.htm.

Inspector General Hotline The Office of the Inspector General works to prevent and detect fraud, waste, and abuse concerning DOL grants, contracts, programs, and operations. It addresses allegations of criminal activity and serious misconduct involving DOL employees. It also investigates allegations of labor racketeering and organized crime influence in the workplace. Contact the Hotline by mail at Office of Inspector General, Department of Labor, 200 Constitution Avenue NW., Room S–5506, Washington, DC 20210, or use the online form. Phone, 202–693–6999 or 800–347–3756 (toll free). Fax, 202–693–7020. Email, hotline@oig.dol.gov. Internet, http://www.oig.dol.gov/hotlineform.htm.

Publications The Office of Public Affairs distributes fact sheets that describe the activities of the major agencies within the Department. Internet, http://www.dol.gov/ebsa/publications/.

Reading Rooms General inquiries may be directed to the Department of Labor Library, Room N–2439, 200 Constitution Avenue NW., Washington, DC 20210. Phone, 202–219–6992. The Office of Labor-Management Standards maintains a Public Disclosure Room at Room N–5616, 200 Constitution Avenue NW., Washington, DC 20210. Reports filed under the Labor-Management Reporting and Disclosure Act may be examined there and purchased for 15 cents per page. Reports also may be obtained by calling the Public Disclosure Room at 202–219–7393, or by contacting a field office.

For further information concerning the Department of Labor, contact the Office of Public Affairs, Department of Labor, Room S–1032, 200 Constitution Avenue NW., Washington, DC 20210. Phone, 202–693–4650. Internet, http://www.dol.gov.

Bureau of International Labor Affairs

Department of Labor, Washington, DC 20210
Phone, 202–693–4770. Internet, http://www.dol.gov/ilab.

Deputy Under Secretary | CAROL PIER, *Acting*
Associate Deputy Undersecretary | MARK MITTELHAUSER

The Bureau of International Labor Affairs improves working conditions, raises living standards, protects workers' rights, and addresses the workplace exploitation of children and other vulnerable populations.

Sources of Information

Contracts and Grants   Information on contracts and grant opportunities is available online. Internet, http://www.dol.gov/ILAB/grants/main.htm.
Employment   Information on career opportunities is available online. Internet, http://www.dol.gov/dol/jobs.htm.

For further information, contact the Bureau of International Affairs, Department of Labor, Room C–4325, Washington, DC 20201. Phone, 202–693–4770. Internet, http://www.dol.gov/ilab.

Bureau of Labor Statistics

2 Massachusetts Avenue NE., Washington, DC 20212
Phone, 202–691–7800; 800–877–8339 (TDD). Internet, http://www.bls.gov.

Commissioner	ERICA GROSHEN
Deputy Commissioner	JOHN GALVIN

The Bureau of Labor Statistics (BLS) was established, in the Department of the Interior, as the Bureau of Labor by the act of June 27, 1884 (23 Stat. 60). It was renamed the Bureau of Labor Statistics by the act of March 4, 1913 (37 Stat. 736). The Bureau of Labor Statistics (BLS) collects, analyzes, and disseminates economic information to support public and private decisionmaking. BLS serves as a statistical resource to the Department of Labor. Data are available relating to employment, unemployment, and other characteristics of the labor force; consumer and producer prices, consumer expenditures, and import and export prices; wages and employee benefits; productivity and technological change; employment projections; occupational illness and injuries; and international comparisons of labor statistics. Most of the data is collected in surveys conducted by the Bureau, the Bureau of the Census (on a contract basis), or on a cooperative basis with State agencies.

The Bureau strives to have its data satisfy a number of criteria, including: relevance to current social and economic issues, timeliness in reflecting today's rapidly changing economic conditions, accuracy and consistently high statistical quality, and impartiality in both subject matter and presentation.

Basic data are issued in monthly, quarterly, and annual news releases; bulletins, reports, and special publications; and periodicals. Regional offices issue additional reports and releases, usually presenting locality or regional detail.

For a complete listing of Bureau of Labor Statistics regional offices, including addresses, telephone numbers, and key officials, visit www.bls.gov/bls/regnhome.htm.

Sources of Information

Electronic Access   Data are available through an electronic news service, magnetic tape, diskettes, and microfiche, as well as online. Internet, http://bls.gov.
Employment   Information on career opportunities is available online. Internet, http://bls.gov/jobs/home.htm.
Mailing Lists   Updates are available by joining the electronic mailing list, which is accessible online. Internet, https://subscriptions.bls.gov/accounts/USDOLBLS/subscriber/new.
Publications   Periodicals include the "Monthly Labor Review," "Consumer Price Index," "Producer Prices and Price Indexes," "Employment and Earnings," "Current Wage Developments," "Occupational Outlook Handbook," and "Occupational Outlook Quarterly." Publications are both free and for sale,

but for-sale items must be obtained from the Superintendent of Documents, Government Printing Office. Inquiries may be directed to the Washington Information Office or to the Bureau's regional offices.

For further information, contact the Bureau of Labor Statistics, Department of Labor, Room 4040, 2 Massachusetts Avenue NE., Washington, DC 20212. Phone, 202–691–7800. Internet, http://www.bls.gov.

Employee Benefits Security Administration

Department of Labor, Washington, DC 20210
Phone, 866–444–3272. Internet, http://www.dol.gov/ebsa.

Assistant Secretary	PHYLLIS C. BORZI
Deputy Assistant Secretary for Policy	(VACANCY)
Deputy Assistant Secretary for Program Operations	ALAN D. LEBOWITZ

The Employee Benefits Security Administration (EBSA) promotes and protects the retirement, health, and other benefits of the over 141 million participants and beneficiaries in over 5 million private sector employee benefit plans. EBSA develops regulations, assists and educates workers, plan sponsors, fiduciaries, and service providers, and enforces the law. The Employee Retirement Income Security Act is enforced through 15 field offices nationwide and a national office in Washington, DC.

For a complete listing of regional and district offices of the Employee Benefits Security Administration, including addresses, telephone numbers, areas served, and key officials, visit www.dol.gov/ebsa/aboutebsa.

Sources of Information

Publications The Employee Benefits Security Administration distributes fact sheets, pamphlets, and booklets on employer obligations and employee rights under the Employee Retirement Income Security Act. A list of publications is available by writing to the Office of Outreach, Education, and Assistance, Employee Benefits Security Administration, Room N–5623, 200 Constitution Avenue NW., Washington, DC 20210. Phone, 866–444–3272. Internet, http://www.dol.gov/ebsa. **Reading Room** The Employee Benefits Security Administration maintains a Public Disclosure Room at Room N–1513, 200 Constitution Avenue NW., Washington, DC 20210. Reports filed under the Employee Retirement Income Security Act may be examined there and purchased for 15 cents per page or by calling the Public Disclosure Room at 202–693–8673.

For further information, contact the Employee Benefits Security Administration, Department of Labor, Room S–2534, Washington, DC 20210. Phone, 866–444–3272. Internet, http://www.dol.gov/ebsa.

Employment and Training Administration

Department of Labor, Washington, DC 20520
Phone, 877–872–5627. Internet, http://www.doleta.gov.

Assistant Secretary	ERIC SELEZNOW, *Acting*
Deputy Assistant Secretarys	GERRI FIALA, ERIC SELEZNOW

The Employment and Training Administration (ETA) provides quality job training, employment, labor market information, and income maintenance services, primarily through State and local workforce development systems. ETA also administers programs to enhance employment opportunities and business prosperity.

For a complete listing of Regional and State Offices of the Employment and Training Administration, including addresses, telephone numbers, areas served, and key officials, visit www.doleta.gov/Regions.

Office of Apprenticeship The Office of Apprenticeship oversees the National Apprenticeship System, sets standards for apprenticeship, and assists States, industry, and labor in developing apprenticeship programs that meet required standards while promoting equal opportunity and safeguarding the welfare of apprentices.

For more information, call 202–693–2796. Internet, http://www.doleta.gov/oa.

Office of Contracts Management The Office of Contracts Management (OCM) provides leadership and direction to ensure acquisition excellence, integrity, accountability, and sound management of procurement resources to support Employment and Training Administration (ETA) and Job Corps goals and guiding principles for the acquisition of goods and services. Job Corps contracts account for 75 percent of the Department's contracting activity. Non-Job Corps contract activity supports ETA grant programs through technical assistance and long-term studies and evaluations.

For further information, contact the Office of Contracts Management, Department of Labor, 200 Constitution Avenue, NW., Suite N–4643, Washington, DC 20210. Phone, 202–693–3701.

Office of Financial Administration The Office of Financial Administration (OFA) is responsible for managing all ETA fiscal resources for programs and activities for which funds are appropriated through its functions of accounting, budget, and financial system oversight. OFA provides critical budgetary, accounting, audit, and internal control management. It coordinates with the Departmental Budget Center and the Office of the Chief Financial Officer to provide financial management supporting the accomplishment of all aspects of ETA's mission.

For further information, call 202–693–3162.

Office of Foreign Labor Certification The Office of Foreign Labor Certification (OFLC) carries out the delegated responsibility of the Secretary of Labor under the Immigration and Nationality Act, as amended, concerning the admission of foreign workers into the United States for employment.

In carrying out this responsibility, OFLC administers temporary nonimmigrant labor certification programs and the permanent labor certification program through ETA's National Processing Centers located, respectively, in Chicago and Atlanta.

OFLC also administers nationally the issuance of employer-requested prevailing wage determinations through ETA's National Prevailing Wage and Helpdesk Center located in Washington, DC. Prevailing wage determinations are issued for use in all nonagricultural temporary labor certification programs and the permanent labor certification program.

For more information, call 202–693–3010. Internet, http://www.foreignlaborcert.doleta.gov.

Office of Job Corps The Office of Job Corps (OJC) teaches young adults relevant skills they need to become employable and independent and helps them secure meaningful jobs or opportunities for further education. OJC has six regional offices responsible for monitoring and oversight of Job Corps centers, outreach and admissions, and career transition services.

For a complete listing of regional offices of the Job Corps, including addresses, telephone numbers, and areas served, visit www.jobcorps.gov/contact.aspx#regional.

For a complete listing of Job Corps centers across the country, including addresses, telephone numbers, and center Web sites, visit www.jobcorps.gov/centers.aspx.

For further information, contact the Office of Job Corps, Department of Labor, 200 Constitution Avenue NW., Room N–4463, Washington, DC 20210. Phone, 202–693–3000. Internet, http://jobcorps.dol.gov.

Office of Management and Administrative Services The Office of Management and Administrative Services (OMAS) is responsible for managing all administrative and grant management programs for ETA. OMAS provides critical grant-making and human resources management, information technology services, controlled correspondence, emergency preparedness, Freedom of Information Act coordination, facilities management, and facilitates communication and coordination of activities providing strategic advice, counsel, and customer service to ETA's six regions. OMAS provides technological infrastructure and administrative support for critical ETA functions.

For further information, call 202–693–2800.

Office of National Response The Office of National Response is responsible for national leadership, oversight, policy guidance, funding allocations, and technical assistance for the National Emergency Grants program for dislocated workers.

For more information, call 202–693–3500. Internet, http://www.doleta.gov/layoff/.

Office of Policy Development and Research The Office of Policy Development and Research (OPDR) supports ETA policies and investments to improve the public workforce system by analyzing, formulating, and recommending legislative changes and options for policy initiatives, including budget justifications. OPDR coordinates ETA legislative and regulatory activities, maintains the ETA portion of the Department's regulatory agenda, and disseminates advisories and publications to the public workforce system. OPDR provides ETA with strategic approaches to improve performance and outcomes through research, demonstrations, and the evaluation of major ETA programs. OPDR manages the Workforce Investment Act performance accountability reporting system; oversees

the maintenance of wage record exchange systems for State and other grantees to verify performance outcomes; coordinates the development of ETA's Operating Plan; and ensures timely dissemination of all workforce program performance results. OPDR coordinates ETA's legislative and regulatory activities and maintains ETA's portion of the Department's regulatory agenda. OPDR coordinates ETA's interactions with international organizations and foreign countries.

For further information, call 202–693–3700.

Office of Trade Adjustment Assistance The Office of Trade Adjustment Assistance is responsible for national leadership, oversight, policy guidance, funding allocations, and technical assistance for dislocated workers seeking to participate in structured training programs.

For further information, call 202–693–3560.

Office of Unemployment Insurance The Office of Unemployment Insurance (OUI) provides national leadership, oversight, policy guidance, and technical assistance to the Federal-State unemployment compensation system. OUI also interprets Federal legislative requirements.

For more information, call 202–693–3029. Internet, http://www.unemploymentinsurance.doleta.gov.

Office of Workforce Investment The Office of Workforce Investment (OWI) provides leadership, oversight, policy guidance, and technical assistance to the Nation's workforce investment system including America's Job Center systems, the youth and adult employment and training programs, and national programs for targeted populations. OWI oversees investments in innovative workforce solutions in high-growth sectors of the economy, including providing training through community colleges. OWI also oversees the development and dissemination of tools and information related to workforce and economic data, career guidance, and workforce skills and competencies.

For further information, call 202–693–3980.

Sources of Information

Publications   The Employment and Training Administration issues periodicals such as "Area Trends in Employment and Unemployment," which are available by subscription through the Superintendent of Documents, Government Printing Office, Washington, DC 20402. Information about publications may be obtained from the Administration's Information Office. Phone, 202–219–6871.

For further information, contact the Employment and Training Administration, Department of Labor, Washington, DC 20210. Phone, 877–872–5627. Internet, http://www.doleta.gov.

Mine Safety and Health Administration

1100 Wilson Boulevard, Arlington, VA 22209
Phone, 202–693–9400. Internet, http://www.msha.gov.

Assistant Secretary	JOSEPH A. MAIN
Deputy Assistant Secretary for Policy	STEPHEN R. WEATHERFORD
Deputy Assistant Secretary for Operations	PATRICIA W. SILVEY

The Administration was established as the Mine Enforcement Safety Administration by the Interior Secretary's Order 2953 of May 7, 1973. It was renamed the Mine Safety and Health Administration by the act of Nov. 9, 1979 (91 Stat. 1319). The Mine Safety and Health Administration (MSHA) seeks to prevent mining-related deaths, diseases, and injuries and promotes safe and healthful workplaces for the Nation's miners. MSHA promulgates and enforces mandatory health and safety standards by thoroughly inspecting each mine once per year; targeting the most common causes of fatal mine accidents and disasters; reducing exposure to health risks from mine dusts and other contaminants; improving training, particularly for inexperienced miners and contractors; strengthening MSHA and the industry's emergency response preparedness; enforcing miners' rights to report hazardous conditions without fear of retaliation; and emphasizing prevention. The Administration also assists States in the development of effective State mine safety and health programs and contributes to the improvement in and expansion of mine safety and health research and development.

For a complete listing of MSHA District and Field Offices, including addresses, telephone numbers, and key officials, visit www.msha.gov/district/disthome.htm.

For further information, contact the Office of Program Education and Outreach Services, Mine Safety and Health Administration, Department of Labor, Room 2317, 1100 Wilson Boulevard, Arlington, VA 22209–3939. Phone, 202–693–9400. Internet, http://www.msha.gov.

Occupational Safety and Health Administration

Department of Labor, Washington, DC 20210
Phone, 800–321–6742. Internet, http://www.osha.gov.

Assistant Secretary	DAVID MICHAELS
Deputy Assistant Secretarys	JORDAN BARAB, GREGORY BAXTER, *Acting*

The Occupational Safety and Health Administration (OSHA), created pursuant to the Occupational Safety and Health Act of 1970 (29 U.S.C. 651 et seq.), assures safe and healthful working conditions for men and women by promulgating common sense, protective health, and safety standards; enforcing workplace safety and health rules; providing training, outreach, education, and assistance to workers and employers in their efforts to control workplace hazards; prevent work-related injuries, illnesses, and fatalities; and partnering with States that run their own OSHA-approved programs.

For a complete listing of OSHA regional and area offices, including addresses, telephone numbers, and key officials, visit www.osha.gov/html/RAmap.html.

For further information, contact the Occupational Safety and Health Administration, Department of Labor, Washington, DC 20210. Phone, 202–693–2000 or 1–800–321–6742. Internet, http://www.osha.gov.

Veterans' Employment and Training Service

Department of Labor, Washington, DC 20210
Phone, 866–487–2365. Internet, http://www.dol.gov/vets.

Assistant Secretary	KEITH KELLY
Deputy Assistant Secretary for Policy	TERESA W. GERTON
Deputy Assistant Secretary for Operations and Management	JOHN K. MORAN

The Veterans' Employment and Training Service (VETS) is responsible for administering veterans' employment and training programs and compliance activities that help veterans and servicemembers succeed in their civilian careers. VETS administers the Jobs for Veterans State Grant program, which provides grants to States to fund personnel dedicated to serving the employment needs of veterans. VETS field staff works closely with and provides technical assistance to State employment workforce agencies to ensure that veterans receive priority of service and gain meaningful employment. VETS also administers three competitive grants programs: the Veterans Workforce Investment Program, the Homeless Veterans Reintegration Program, and the Incarcerated Veterans Transition Program. In addition, VETS prepares separating servicemembers for the civilian labor market through its Transition Assistance Program Employment Workshops.

VETS has three distinct compliance programs: the Federal Contractor Program, Veterans' Preference in Federal hiring and the Uniformed Services Employment and Reemployment Rights Act of 1994 (USERRA). With respect to Federal contractors, VETS promulgates regulations and maintains oversight of the program by assisting contractors to comply with their affirmative action and reporting obligations. Although the Office of Personnel Management is responsible for administering and interpreting statutes and regulations governing veterans' preference in Federal hiring, VETS investigates allegations that veterans' preference rights have been violated. In addition, VETS preserves servicemembers' employment and reemployment rights through its administration and enforcement of the USERRA statute. VETS conducts thorough investigations of alleged violations and conducts an extensive USERRA outreach program.

For a complete listing of Veterans' Employment and Training Service regional and State offices, including addresses, telephone numbers, and key officials, visit www.dol.gov/vets/aboutvets/contacts/main.htm#regionalstatedirectory.

For further information, contact the Assistant Secretary for Veterans' Employment and Training, Department of Labor, Washington, DC 20210. Phone, 202–693–4700. Internet, http://www.dol.gov/vets.

Wage and Hour Division
Department of Labor, Washington, DC 20210
Phone, 866–487–9243. Internet, http://www.dol.gov/whd.

Administrator	(VACANCY)
Deputy Administrator	LAURA A. FORTMAN

The Wage and Hour Division (WHD) enforces Federal minimum wage, overtime pay, recordkeeping, and child labor law requirements of the Fair Labor Standards Act. WHD also enforces the Migrant and Seasonal Agricultural Worker Protection Act, the Employee Polygraph Protection Act, the Family and Medical Leave Act, wage garnishment provisions of the Consumer Credit Protection Act, and a number of employment standards and worker protections as provided in several immigration-related statutes. Additionally, WHD administers and enforces the prevailing wage requirements of the Davis Bacon Act and the Service Contract Act and other statutes applicable to Federal contracts for construction and for the provision of goods and services.

For a complete listing of Wage and Hour Division offices across the country, including addresses, telephone numbers, and key officials, visit www.dol.gov/whd/america2.htm.

Sources of Information

Outreach and Educational Materials WHD provides a wide variety of outreach and educational materials in various languages, such as guides, factsheets, worker rights cards, self-audit assessments, posters, bookmarks, and videos.

For further information, contact the Office of the Administrator, Wage and Hour Division, Department of Labor, Room S–3502, Washington, DC 20210. Phone, 202–693–0051. Internet, http://www.dol.gov/whd.

Women's Bureau
Department of Labor, Washington, DC 20210
Phone, 202–693–6710. Internet, http://www.dol.gov/wb.

Director	LATIFA LYLES, *Acting*
Deputy Director	JOAN HARRIGAN-FARRELLY

The Women's Bureau is responsible for promoting the status of wage-earning women, improving their working conditions, increasing their efficiency, and advancing their opportunities for profitable employment. The Bureau also focuses on the needs of vulnerable women in the workforce.

For a complete listing of regional offices of the Women's Bureau, including addresses, telephone numbers, and key officials, visit www.dol.gov/wb.

For further information, contact the Women's Bureau, Department of Labor, Room S–3002, 200 Constitution Avenue, NW., Washington, DC 20210. Phone, 202–693–6710. Internet, http://www.dol.gov/wb.

DEPARTMENT OF STATE

Secretary of State	JOHN F. KERRY
Deputy Secretary of State	WILLIAM J. BURNS
Deputy Secretary of State for Management and Resources	HEATHER A. HIGGINBOTTOM
Counselor	THOMAS SHANNON
Executive Secretary	JOHN R. BASS
Under Secretary for Arms Control and International Security Affairs	ROSE E. GOTTEMOELLER
Assistant Secretary for International Security and Nonproliferation	THOMAS M. COUNTRYMAN
Assistant Secretary for Political-Military Affairs	PUNEET TALWAR
Assistant Secretary for Arms Control, Verification and Compliance	ANITA FRIEDT, *Acting*
Under Secretary for Civilian Security, Democracy, and Human Rights	SARAH B. SEWALL
Ambassador-at-Large for the Office to Monitor and Combat Trafficking in Persons	LUIS CDEBACA
Assistant Secretary for Democracy, Human Rights, and Labor	TOMASZ P. MALINOWKSI
Assistant Secretary for Population, Refugees, and Migration	ANNE C. RICHARD
Assistant Secretary for Conflict and Stabilization Operations	FREDERICK BARTON
Coordinator and Ambassador-at-Large for Counterterrorism	TINA S. KAIDANOW
Assistant Secretary for International Narcotics and Law Enforcement Affairs	WILLIAM R. BROWNFIELD
Ambassador-at-Large for the Office of Global Criminal Justice	STEPHEN J. RAPP
Under Secretary for Economic Growth, Energy, and the Environment	CATHERINE A. NOVELLI
Assistant Secretary for Economic and Business Affairs	CHARLES H. RIVKIN
Assistant Secretary for Oceans and International Environmental and Scientific Affairs	KERRI-ANN JONES
Assistant Secretary for Energy Resources	CARLOS PASCUAL, *Acting*
Office of the Chief Economist	MARK STONE, *Acting*
Under Secretary for Management	PATRICK F. KENNEDY
Assistant Secretary for Administration	JOYCE A. BARR
Assistant Secretary for Consular Affairs	MICHELE BOND, *Acting*
Assistant Secretary for Diplomatic Security and Foreign Missions	GREGORY B. STARR, *Acting*
Assistant Secretary for Information Resource Management and Chief Information Officer	STEVEN C. TAYLOR
Comptroller, Bureau of the Comptroller and Global Financial Services	CHRISTOPHER H. FLAGGS, *Acting*
Director, Budget and Planning	BARBARA A. RETZLAFF

Director, Office of Management Policy, Rightsizing and Innovation	ALAINA A. TEPLITZ
Director, Foreign Service Institute	NANCY MCELDOWNEY
Director General of the Foreign Service and Director of Human Resources	HANS G. KLEMM, *Acting*
Director, Office of Medical Services	GARY D. PENNER
Director, Overseas Buildings Operations	LYDIA MUNIZ
Under Secretary for Political Affairs	WENDY R. SHERMAN
Assistant Secretary for African Affairs	LINDA THOMAS-GREENFIELD
Assistant Secretary for East Asian and Pacific Affairs	DANIEL R. RUSSEL
Assistant Secretary for European and Eurasian Affairs	VICTORIA NULAND
Assistant Secretary for International Organization Affairs	BATHSHEBA NELL CROCKER
Assistant Secretary for Near Eastern Affairs	ANNE PATTERSON
Assistant Secretary for South and Central Asian Affairs	NISHA DESAI BISWAL
Assistant Secretary for Western Hemisphere Affairs	ROBERTA S. JACOBSON
Under Secretary for Public Diplomacy and Public Affairs	RICHARD A. STENGEL
Assistant Secretary for Educational and Cultural Affairs	EVAN RYAN
Assistant Secretary for Public Affairs	DOUGLAS FRANTZ
Coordinator of International Information Programs	MACON PHILLIPS
Assistant Secretary for Intelligence and Research	DANIEL B. SMITH
Assistant Secretary for Legislative Affairs	JULIE FRIFIELD
Ambassador-at-Large of the Office of Global Women's Issues	CATHERINE M. RUSSELL
Chief of Protocol	NATALIE JONES, *Acting*
Director, Office of Civil Rights	JOHN M. ROBINSON
Director, Office of Policy Planning	DAVID MCKEAN
Director, Office of U.S. Foreign Assistance	ROBERT H. GOLDBERG
Coordinator, Office of U.S. Global AIDS	DEBORAH L. BIRX
Deputy Inspector General	SCOTT LINICK
Legal Adviser	MARY E. MCLEOD, *Acting*

United States Mission to the United Nations

United States Permanent Representative to the United Nations and Representative in the Security Council	SAMANTHA POWER
Deputy United States Representative to the United Nations	ROSEMARY A. DICARLO
United States Alternate Representative for Special Political Affairs in the United Nations	JEFFREY DELAURENTIS
United States Representative to the Economic and Social Council	ELIZABETH M. COUSENS
United States Representative for United Nations Management and Reform	JOSEPH M. TORSELLA

[For the Department of State statement of organization, see the U.S. Code of Federal Regulations, Title 22, Part 5.]

The Department of State advises the President and leads the Nation in foreign policy issues to advance freedom and democracy for the American people and the international community. To this end, the Department compiles research on American overseas interests, disseminates information on foreign policy to the public, negotiates treaties and agreements with foreign nations, and represents the United States in the United Nations and other international organizations and conferences.

The Department of State was established by act of July 27, 1789, as the Department of Foreign Affairs and was renamed Department of State by act of September 15, 1789 (22 U.S.C. 2651 note).

Secretary of State The Secretary of State is responsible for the overall direction, coordination, and supervision of U.S. foreign relations and for the interdepartmental activities of the U.S. Government abroad. The Secretary is the first-ranking member of the Cabinet, is a member of the National Security Council, and is in charge of the operations of the Department, including the Foreign Service.

Regional Bureaus Foreign affairs activities worldwide are handled by the geographic bureaus, which include the Bureaus of African Affairs, European and Eurasian Affairs, East Asian and Pacific Affairs, Near Eastern Affairs, South and Central Asian Affairs, and Western Hemisphere Affairs.

Administration The Bureau of Administration provides support programs and services to Department of State operations worldwide, as well as programs and services to other U.S. Government agencies represented at U.S. Embassies and consulates. These functions include administrative policy, domestic emergency management; management of owned or leased facilities in the United States; procurement, supply, travel, and transportation support; classified pouch, unclassified pouch, and domestic mail distribution; official records, publishing, library, and foreign language interpreting and translating services; and support to the schools abroad that educate dependents of U.S. Government employees assigned to diplomatic and consular missions. Direct services to the public include: authenticating documents used abroad for legal and business purposes;

responding to requests under the Freedom of Information and Privacy Acts; providing the electronic reading room for public reference to State Department records; and determining use of the diplomatic reception rooms of the Harry S. Truman headquarters building in Washington, DC.

For further information, contact the Bureau of Administration. Phone, 703–875–7000. Internet, http://www.state.gov/m/a.

Arms Control, Verification and Compliance The Bureau of Arms Control, Verification and Compliance is responsible for ensuring and verifying compliance with international arms control, nonproliferation, and disarmament agreements and commitments. The Bureau also leads negotiation and implementation efforts with respect to strategic arms control, most recently the new START Treaty and conventional forces in Europe. The Bureau is the principal policy representative to the intelligence community with regard to verification and compliance matters and uses this role to promote, preserve, and enhance key collection and analytic capabilities and to ensure that intelligence verification, compliance, and implementation requirements are met. The Bureau staffs and manages treaty implementation commissions, creates negotiation and implementation policy for agreements and commitments, and develops policy for future arms control, nonproliferation, and disarmament arrangements. It also provides secure government-to-government communication linkages with foreign treaty partners. The Bureau is also responsible for preparing verifiability assessments on proposals and agreements, and reporting these to Congress as required. The Bureau also prepares the "President's Annual Report to Congress on Adherence to

DEPARTMENT OF STATE

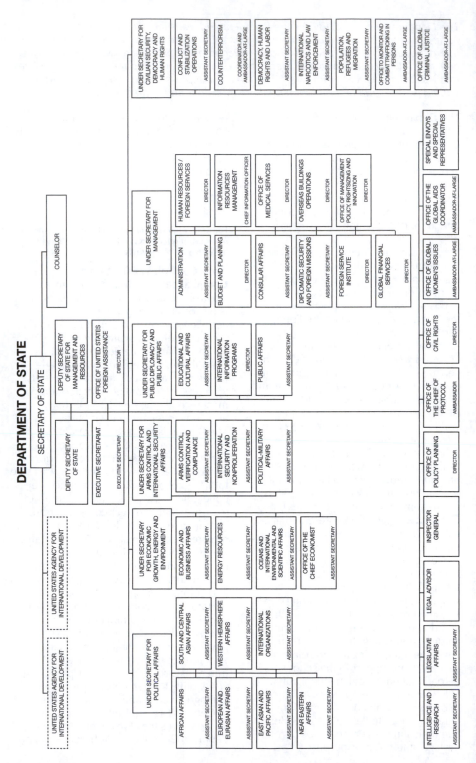

and Compliance With Arms Control, Nonproliferation, and Disarmament Agreements and Commitments," as well as the reports required by the Iran, North Korea, and Syria Nonproliferation Act.

For further information, contact the Bureau of Arms Control, Verification and Compliance. Phone, 202–647–6830. Fax, 202–647–1321. Internet, http://www.state.gov/t/avc/.

Budget and Planning   The Bureau of Budget and Planning manages budgeting and resource management for operation accounts.

For further information, contact the Bureau of Budget and Planning. Phone, 202–647–8515. Internet, http://www.state.gov/s/d/rm/.

Comptroller and Global Financial Services   The Bureau of the Comptroller and Global Financial Services, led by the Chief Financial Officer, integrates strategic planning, budgeting, and performance to secure departmental resources. The Bureau manages all departmental strategic and performance planning; global financial services, including accounting, disbursing, and payroll; issuance of financial statements and oversight of the Department's management control program; coordination of national security resources and remediation of vulnerabilities within the Department's global critical infrastructure; and management of the International Cooperative Administrative Support Services Program.

For further information, contact the Bureau of the Comptroller and Global Financial Services. Phone, 202–647–7490. Internet, http://www.state.gov/m/cgfs/.

Conflict and Stabilization Operations
The Bureau of Conflict and Stabilization Operations advances U.S. national security by driving integrated, civilian-led efforts to prevent, respond to, and stabilize crises in priority states, setting conditions for long-term peace. The Bureau emphasizes sustainable solutions guided by local dynamics and actors and promotes unity of effort, strategic use of scarce resources, and burden-sharing with international partners.

For further information, contact the Bureau of Conflict Stabilization Operations. Phone, 202–663–0323. Internet, http://www.state.gov/g/cso.

Consular Affairs   The Bureau of Consular Affairs is responsible for the protection and welfare of American citizens and interests abroad; the administration and enforcement of the provisions of the immigration and nationality laws insofar as they concern the Department of State and Foreign Service; the issuance of passports and visas; and related services. Approximately 18 million passports a year are issued by the Bureau's Office of Passport Services at the processing centers in Portsmouth, NH, and Charleston, SC, and the regional agencies in Boston, MA; Chicago, IL; Aurora, CO; Honolulu, HI; Houston, TX; Los Angeles, CA; Miami, FL; New Orleans, LA; New York, NY; Philadelphia, PA; San Francisco, CA; Seattle, WA; Norwalk, CT; Detroit, MI; Minneapolis, MN; and Washington, DC. In addition, the Bureau helps secure America's borders against entry by terrorists or narcotraffickers, facilitates international adoptions, and supports parents whose children have been abducted abroad.

More information is available online at the Bureau of Consular Affairs. Internet, http://www.travel.state.gov.

Counterterrorism   The Bureau of Counterterrorism leads the Department in the U.S. Government's effort to counter terrorism abroad and secure the United States against foreign terrorist threats. To carry out its mission, the Bureau develops and implements counterterrorism strategies, promotes international cooperation on counterterrorism issues, serves as the Department's key link on counterterrorism to the Department of Homeland Security, focuses efforts to counter violent extremism, and develops international partner counterterrorism capacity.

For further information, contact CT's Office of Public Affairs. Phone, 202–647–1845. Internet, http://www.state.gov/g/ct.

Democracy, Human Rights, and Labor
The Bureau of Democracy, Human Rights, and Labor (DRL) is responsible for developing and implementing U.S.

policy on democracy, human rights, labor, religious freedom, monitoring and combating anti-Semitism, and advocating for inclusion of people with disabilities. DRL practices diplomatic engagement and advocacy to protect human rights and strengthen democratic institutions. Working with governments, civil society, and multilateral organizations to support democratic governance and human rights, the Bureau also participates in multi-stakeholder initiatives to encourage multinational corporations to adhere to human rights standards of conduct, including the elimination of child labor. DRL fulfills the USG reporting responsibilities on human rights and democracy, producing the annual "Country Reports on Human Rights Practices," the annual "International Religious Freedom" report, and the "Advancing Freedom and Democracy" report. Providing targeted program assistance through the Human Rights and Democracy Fund and other funding streams, the Bureau works to protect human rights and strengthen democratic institutions around the world. DRL programs help prosecute war criminals, promote religious freedom, support workers' rights, encourage accountability in governance, as well as facilitate freedom of expression and freedom to access information on the Internet. The Bureau also has a Congressionally-mandated responsibility to ensure that foreign military assistance and training is not provided to gross violators of human rights. DRL leads the Secretary of State's Task Force on Global Internet Freedom.

For further information, contact the Bureau of Democracy, Human Rights, and Labor. Phone, 202–647–1337. Internet, http://www.state.gov/j/drl.

Diplomatic Security   The Bureau of Diplomatic Security provides a secure environment to promote U.S. interests at home and abroad. The Bureau's mission includes protecting the Secretary of State and other senior Government officials, resident and visiting foreign dignitaries, and foreign missions in the United States; conducting criminal, counterintelligence, and personnel security investigations; ensuring the integrity of international travel documents, sensitive information, classified processing equipment, and management information systems; the physical and technical protection of domestic and overseas facilities of the Department of State; providing professional law enforcement and security training to U.S. and foreign personnel; and a comprehensive, multifaceted overseas security program serving the needs of U.S. missions and resident U.S. citizens and business communities. Through the Office of Foreign Missions, the Bureau regulates the domestic activities of the foreign diplomatic community in the areas of taxation, real property acquisitions, motor vehicle operation, domestic travel, and customs processing.

For further information, contact the Bureau of Diplomatic Security Office of Public Affairs. Phone, 571–345–2502. Internet, http://www.state.gov/m/ds.

Economic and Business Affairs   The Bureau of Economic and Business Affairs (EB) promotes international trade, investment, economic development, and financial stability on behalf of the American people. EB works to build prosperity and economic security at home and abroad by implementing policy related to the promotion of U.S. trade, investment and exports, international development and reconstruction, intellectual property enforcement, terrorism financing and economic sanctions, international communications and information policy, and aviation and maritime affairs. EB formulates and carries out U.S. foreign economic policy and works to sustain a more democratic, secure, and prosperous world.

For further information, contact the Bureau of Economic and Business Affairs. Phone, 202–647–7971. Fax, 202–647–5713. Internet, http://www.state.gov/e/eeb.

Educational and Cultural Affairs   The Bureau of Educational and Cultural Affairs administers the principal provisions of the Mutual Educational and Cultural Exchange Act (the Fulbright-Hays Act), including U.S. international educational and cultural exchange programs. These programs include the prestigious Fulbright Program for students, scholars, and teachers; the International Visitor Leadership Program, which brings leaders and future leaders from other countries to the United States for consultation with their professional colleagues; and professional, youth, sports, and cultural exchanges. Programs are implemented through cooperative relationships with U.S. nongovernmental organizations that support the Bureau's mission.

For further information, contact the Bureau of Educational and Cultural Affairs. Phone, 202–632–6445. Fax, 202–632–2701. Internet, http://exchanges.state.gov/.

Energy Resources   The Bureau of Energy Resources (ENR) leads the State Department in the U.S. Government's promotion of U.S. and international energy policy. ENR works to ensure that international energy markets are secure and predictable in order to mitigate potential disruptions, while also working with international partners to diversify U.S. energy supplies. The Bureau also seeks to encourage the transformation of United States and world production and consumption of energy to confront the limits of a hydrocarbon-based society and rapid increases in energy demand. ENR works to promote good governance, transparency, and reform of energy sectors globally, which will help broaden energy access, further ensure stable energy supplies, and reduce political instability.

For further information, contact the Bureau of Energy Resources. Phone, 202–647–3423. Internet, http://www.state.gov/e/enr.

Foreign Service Institute   The Foreign Service Institute of the Department of State is the Federal Government's primary foreign affairs-related training institution. In addition to the Department of State, the Institute provides training for more than 47 other Government agencies. The Institute has more than 700 courses, including some 70 foreign language courses, ranging in length from 1 day to 2 years. The courses are designed to promote successful performance in each professional assignment, to ease the adjustment to other countries and cultures, and to enhance the leadership

and management capabilities of the foreign affairs community.

For further information, contact the Foreign Service Institute. Phone, 703–302–6729. Fax, 703–302–7227. Internet, http://www.state.gov/m/fsi/.

Information Resource Management
The Bureau of Information Resource Management (IRM) provides the Department with the information technology it needs to carry out U.S. diplomacy in the information age. The IRM Bureau is led by the Department's Chief Information Officer. IRM establishes effective information resource management planning and policies; ensures availability of information technology systems and operations, including information technology contingency planning, to support the Department's diplomatic, consular, and management operations; exercises management responsibility to ensure the Department's information resources meet the business requirements of the Department and provide an effective basis for knowledge sharing and collaboration within the Department and with other foreign affairs agencies and partners; exercises delegated approving authority for the Secretary of State for the development and administration of the Department's computer and information security programs and policies.

For further information, contact the Bureau of Information Resource Management. Phone, 202–647–2977. Internet, http://www.state.gov/m/irm/.

Inspector General   The Office of Inspector General (OIG) conducts independent audits, inspections, and investigations to promote effective management, accountability, and positive change in the Department of State, the Broadcasting Board of Governors (BBG), and the foreign affairs community. OIG provides leadership to promote integrity, efficiency, effectiveness, and economy; prevents and detects waste, fraud, abuse, and mismanagement; identifies vulnerabilities and recommends constructive solutions; offers expert assistance to improve Department and BBG operations; communicates timely, useful information that facilitates decision-making and achieves measurable gains; and keeps the Department, BBG, and Congress informed.

For further information, contact the Office of Inspector General. Phone, 202–663–0340. Internet, http://www.oig.state.gov.

Intelligence and Research   The primary mission of the Bureau of Intelligence and Research (INR) is to harness intelligence to serve U.S. diplomacy. Drawing on all-source intelligence, INR provides value-added independent analysis of events to Department policymakers, ensures that intelligence activities support foreign policy and national security purposes, and serves as the focal point in the Department for ensuring policy review of sensitive counterintelligence and law enforcement activities. The Bureau also analyzes geographical and international boundary issues. INR is a member of the U.S. Intelligence Community and serves as the Community's Executive Agent for Analytical Outreach.

For further information, contact the Bureau of Intelligence and Research. Phone, 202–647–1080. Internet, http://www.state.gov/s/inr.

International Information Programs
The Bureau of International Information Programs (IIP) informs, engages, and influences international audiences about U.S. policy and society to advance America's interests. IIP is a leader in developing and implementing public diplomacy strategies that measurably influence international audiences through quality programs and cutting-edge technologies. IIP provides localized contact for U.S. policies and messages, reaching millions worldwide in English, Arabic, Chinese, French, Persian, Russian, and Spanish. IIP delivers America's message to the world through a number of key products and services. These programs reach, and are created strictly for, key international audiences, such as U.S. diplomatic missions abroad, the media, government officials, opinion leaders, and the general public in more than 140 countries around the world. They include Web and print publications, in-person and telecommunications-based speaker programs, and information resource services. IIP orchestrates the State Department's efforts to counter anti-American disinformation/propaganda and serves as the Department's chief link with other agencies in coordinating international public diplomacy programs.

For further information, contact the Bureau of International Information Programs. Phone, 202–632–9942. Fax, 202–632–9901. Internet, http://www.state.gov/r/iip/.

International Narcotics and Law Enforcement   The Bureau of International Narcotics and Law Enforcement Affairs (INL) is responsible for developing policies and managing programs to combat and counter international narcotics production and trafficking, and for strengthening law enforcement and other rule of law institutional capabilities outside the United States. The Bureau also directs narcotics control coordinators at posts abroad and provides guidance on narcotics control, justice sector reform, and anticrime matters to the chiefs of missions. It supports the development of strong, sustainable criminal justice systems as well as training for police force and judicial officials. INL works closely with a broad range of other U.S. Government agencies.

For further information, contact the Bureau of International Narcotics and Law Enforcement Affairs. Phone, 202–647–2842. Fax, 202–736–4045. Internet, http://www.state.gov/j/inl.

International Organizations   The Bureau of International Organization Affairs provides guidance and support for U.S. participation in international organizations and conferences and formulates and implements U.S. policy toward international organizations, with particular emphasis on those organizations which make up the United Nations system. It provides direction in the development, coordination, and implementation of U.S. multilateral policy.

For further information, contact the Bureau of International Organization Affairs. Phone, 202–647–9600. Fax, 202–647–2175. Internet, http://www.state.gov/p/io/.

International Security and Nonproliferation   The Bureau of International Security and

Nonproliferation (ISN), is responsible for managing a broad range of nonproliferation, counterproliferation, and arms control functions. ISN leads U.S. efforts to prevent the spread of weapons of mass destruction (nuclear, radiological, chemical, and biological weapons) related materials, and their delivery systems. It is responsible for spearheading efforts to promote international consensus on weapons of mass destruction proliferation through bilateral and multilateral diplomacy; addressing weapons of mass destruction proliferation threats posed by nonstate actors and terrorist groups by improving physical security, using interdiction and sanctions, and actively participating in the Proliferation Security Initiative; coordinating the implementation of key international treaties and arrangements, working to make them relevant to today's security challenges; working closely with the U.N., the G–8, NATO, the Organization for the Prohibition of Chemical Weapons, the International Atomic Energy Agency, and other international institutions and organizations to reduce and eliminate the threat posed by weapons of mass destruction; and supporting efforts of foreign partners to prevent, protect against, and respond to the threat or use of weapons of mass destruction by terrorists.

For further information, contact the Bureau of International Security and Nonproliferation. Phone, 202–647–9868. Fax, 202–736–4863. Internet, http://www.state.gov/t/isn.

Legal Adviser   The Office of the Legal Adviser advises the Secretary of State and other Department officials on all domestic and international legal matters relating to the Department of State, Foreign Service, and diplomatic and consular posts abroad. The Office's lawyers draft, negotiate, and interpret treaties, international agreements, domestic statutes, departmental regulations, Executive orders, and other legal documents; provide guidance on international and domestic law; represent the United States in international organization, negotiation, and treaty commission meetings; work on domestic

and foreign litigation affecting the Department's interests; and represent the United States before international tribunals, including the International Court of Justice.

For further information, contact the Office of the Legal Adviser. Phone, 202–647–9598. Fax, 202–647–7096. Internet, http://www.state.gov/s/l/.

Legislative Affairs   The Bureau of Legislative Affairs coordinates legislative activity for the Department of State and advises the Secretary, the Deputy, as well as the Under Secretaries and Assistant Secretaries on legislative strategy. The Bureau facilitates effective communication between State Department officials and the Members of Congress and their staffs. Legislative Affairs works closely with the authorizing, appropriations, and oversight committees of the House and Senate, as well as with individual Members that have an interest in State Department or foreign policy issues. The Bureau also manages Department testimony before House and Senate hearings, organizes Member and staff briefings, facilitates congressional travel to overseas posts for Members and staff throughout the year, reviews proposed legislation, and coordinates Statements of Administration Policy on legislation affecting the conduct of U.S. foreign policy. The Legislative Affairs staff advises individual Bureaus of the Department on legislative and outreach strategies and coordinates those strategies with the Secretary's priorities.

For further information, contact the Bureau of Legislative Affairs. Phone, 202–647–1714. Internet, http://www.state.gov/s/h/.

Medical Services   The Office of Medical Services (MED) develops, manages, and staffs a worldwide primary health care system for U.S. Government employees and their eligible dependents residing overseas. In support of its overseas operations, MED approves and monitors the medical evacuation of patients, conducts pre-employment and in-service physical clearance examinations, and provides clinical referral and advisory services. MED also provides for emergency medical response in the event of a crisis at an overseas post.

For further information, contact the Office of Medical Services. Phone, 202–663–1649. Fax, 202–663–1613. Internet, http://www.state.gov/m/med.

Oceans and International Environmental and Scientific Affairs   The Bureau of Oceans and International Environmental and Scientific Affairs (OES) serves as the foreign policy focal point for international oceans, as well as environmental and scientific efforts. OES projects, protects, and promotes U.S. global interests in these areas by articulating U.S. foreign policy, encouraging international cooperation, and negotiating treaties and other instruments of international law. The Bureau serves as the principal adviser to the Secretary of State on international environment, science, and technology matters and takes the lead in coordinating and brokering diverse interests in the interagency process, where the development of international policies or the negotiation and implementation of relevant international agreements are concerned. The Bureau seeks to promote the peaceful exploitation of outer space, develop and coordinate policy on international health issues, encourage government-to-government scientific cooperation, and prevent the destruction and degradation of the planet's natural resources and the global environment.

For further information, contact the Bureau of Oceans and International Environmental and Scientific Affairs. Phone, 202–647–6961. Fax, 202–647–0217. Internet, http://www.state.gov/e/oes/.

Overseas Buildings Operations   The Bureau of Overseas Buildings Operations (OBO) directs the worldwide overseas buildings program for the Department of State and the U.S. Government community serving abroad under the authority of the chiefs of mission. Along with the input and support of other State Department bureaus, foreign affairs agencies, and Congress, OBO sets worldwide priorities for the design, construction, acquisition, maintenance, use, and sale of real properties and the use of sales proceeds. OBO also serves as the Single Real Property Manager of all overseas facilities under the authority of the chiefs of mission.

For further information, contact the Bureau of Overseas Buildings Operations. Phone, 703–875–4131. Fax, 703–875–5043. Internet, http://www.state.gov/obo.

Political-Military Affairs   The Bureau of Political-Military Affairs is the principal link between the Departments of State and Defense and is the Department of State's lead on operational military matters. The Bureau provides policy direction in the areas of international security, security assistance, military operations, defense strategy and policy, counterpiracy measures, and defense trade. Its responsibilities include coordinating the U.S. Government's response to piracy in the waters off the Horn of Africa, securing base access to support the deployment of U.S. military forces overseas, negotiating status of forces agreements, coordinating participation in coalition combat and stabilization forces, regulating arms transfers, directing military assistance to U.S. allies, combating illegal trafficking in small arms and light weapons, facilitating the education and training of international peacekeepers and foreign military personnel, managing humanitarian mine action programs, and assisting other countries in reducing the availability of man-portable air defense systems.

For further information, contact the Bureau of Political-Military Affairs. Phone, 202–647–9022. Fax, 202–736–4413. Internet, http://www.state.gov/t/pm.

Population, Refugees, and Migration   The Bureau of Population, Refugees, and Migration directs the Department's population, refugee, and migration policy development. It administers U.S. contributions to international organizations and nongovernmental organizations for humanitarian assistance- and protection-related programs on behalf of refugees, conflict victims, and internally displaced persons. The Bureau oversees the annual admissions of refugees to the United States for permanent resettlement, working closely with the Department of Homeland Security, the Department of Health and Human Services, and various State and private voluntary agencies. It coordinates U.S. international population policy and promotes its goals through bilateral and multilateral cooperation. It works closely with the U.S. Agency for International Development, which administers U.S. international population programs. The Bureau also coordinates the Department's international migration policy through bilateral and multilateral diplomacy. The Bureau oversees efforts to encourage greater participation in humanitarian assistance and refugee resettlement on the part of foreign governments and uses humanitarian diplomacy to increase access and assistance to those in need in the absence of political solutions.

For further information, contact the Bureau of Population, Refugees, and Migration. Phone, 202–453–9339. Fax, 202–453–9394. Internet, http://www.state.gov/g/prm.

Public Affairs   The Bureau of Public Affairs (PA) supports U.S. foreign policy goals and objectives, advances national interests, and enhances National security by informing and influencing domestic and global public opinion about American interaction with the rest of the world. In addition, PA works to help Americans understand the importance of foreign affairs by conducting press briefings for the domestic and foreign press, pursuing media outreach by other means, arranging townhall meetings and community speakers, and preparing historical studies on U.S. diplomacy and foreign affairs matters.

For further information, contact the Bureau of Public Affairs. Phone, 202–647–6575. Internet, http://www.state.gov/r/pa.

Protocol   The Chief of Protocol is the principal adviser to the U.S. Government, the President, the Vice President, and the Secretary of State on matters of diplomatic procedure governed by law or international custom and practice. The Office is responsible for arranging visits of foreign chiefs of state, heads of government, and other high officials to the United States; organizing credential presentations of newly arrived Ambassadors, as presented to the President and to the Secretary of State; operating the President's

guest house, Blair House; organizing delegations representing the President at official ceremonies abroad; conducting official ceremonial functions and public events; interpreting the official order of precedence; conducting outreach programs of cultural enrichment and substantive briefings of the Diplomatic Corps; accrediting of over 118,000 embassy, consular, international organization, and other foreign government personnel, members of their families, and domestics throughout the United States; determining entitlement to diplomatic or consular immunity; publishing of diplomatic and consular lists; resolving problems arising out of diplomatic or consular immunity, such as legal and police matters; and approving the opening of embassy and consular offices in conjunction with the Office of Foreign Missions.

For further information, contact the Office of the Chief of Protocol. Phone, 202–647–1735. Fax, 202–647–1560. Internet, http://www.state.gov/s/cpr/.

Foreign Service   To a great extent the future of our country depends on the relations we have with other countries, and those relations are conducted principally by the U.S. Foreign Service. Trained representatives stationed worldwide provide the President and the Secretary of State with much of the raw material from which foreign policy is made and with the recommendations that help shape it.

Ambassadors are the personal representatives of the President and report to the President through the Secretary of State. Ambassadors have full responsibility for implementation of U.S. foreign policy by any and all U.S. Government personnel within their country of assignment, except those under military commands. Their responsibilities include negotiating agreements between the United States and the host country, explaining and disseminating official U.S. policy, and maintaining cordial relations with that country's government and people.

For a complete listing of Foreign Service posts, including addresses, telephone numbers, and key officials, use the link below.

Internet, http://www.usembassy.gov/.

The Bureau of Verification, Compliance, and Implementation is responsible for ensuring and verifying compliance with international arms control, nonproliferation, and disarmament agreements and commitments. The Bureau also leads negotiation and implementation efforts with respect to strategic arms control, most recently the new START Treaty, and conventional forces in Europe. The Bureau is the principal policy representative to the intelligence community with regard to verification and compliance matters, and uses this role to promote, preserve, and enhance key collection and analytic capabilities and to ensure that intelligence verification, compliance, and implementation requirements are met. The Bureau staffs and manages treaty implementation commissions, creating negotiation and implementation policy for agreements and commitments, and developing policy for future arms control, nonproliferation, and disarmament arrangements. It also provides support to arms control, nonproliferation, and disarmament policymaking, including information technology support and secure government-to-government communication linkages with foreign treaty partners. The Bureau is also responsible for preparing verifiability assessments on proposals and agreements, and reporting these to Congress as required. The Bureau also prepares the President's Annual Report to Congress on Adherence to and Compliance With Arms Control, Nonproliferation, and Disarmament Agreements and Commitments, as well as the reports required by the Iran, North Korea, and Syria Nonproliferation Act.

For further information, contact the Bureau of Verification, Compliance, and Implementation. Phone, 202–647–5315. Fax, 202–647–1321.

Sources of Information

Contracts General inquiries may be directed to the Office of Acquisitions Management (A/LM/AQM), Department of State, P.O. Box 9115, Arlington, VA 22219. Phone, 703–516–1706. Fax, 703–875–6085. Internet, http://www.state.gov/m/a/c8020.htm.

Diplomatic and Official Passports Inquirers for these types of passports should contact their respective travel offices. The U.S. Government only issues these types of passports to individuals traveling abroad in connection with official employment. Additional information is available online at Consular Affairs. Internet, http://travel.state.gov.

Electronic Access The Department's Bureau of Public Affairs, Office of Public Communication, coordinates the online dissemination of public information. The Department's main Web site and the Secretary's Web site (www.state.gov/secretary/) provide comprehensive, up-to-date information on foreign policy, support for U.S. businesses and careers, the counterterrorism rewards program, and much more. The Bureau of Consular Affairs Web site (travel.state.gov) provides travel warnings and other information designed to help Americans travel safely abroad, as well as information on U.S. passports, visas, and downloadable applications. The State Department's Virtual Reading Room (http://foia.state.gov/#0) uses new information technologies to enable access to unique historical records of international significance, which have been made available to the public under the Freedom of Information Act or as a special collection. Internet, http://www.state.gov/r/pa/.

Employment Inquiries about employment in the Foreign Service should be directed to HR/REE, Room H–518, 2401 E Street NW., Washington, DC 20522. Phone, 202–261–8888. Information on civil service positions in the Department of State and copies of civil service job announcements can be accessed online. Individual questions may be directed to cspapps@state.gov. Job information staff is also available to answer questions from 8:30 a.m. to 4:30 p.m. eastern time on Federal workdays. Phone, 202–663–2176. Internet, http://www.careers.state.gov.

Freedom of Information Act and Privacy Act Requests Requests from the public for Department of State records should be addressed to the Director, Office of Information Programs and Services, A/GIS/IPS/RL, Department of State, SA–2, Washington, DC 20522–8100. Additional information is available online at the Virtual Reading Room or by contacting the FOIA Requester Service Center at 202–261–8484. Internet, http://foia.state.gov/Search/Search.aspx.

International Adoptions Inquiries regarding adoption of foreign children by private U.S. citizens should be directed to the Office of Children's Issues, Bureau of Consular Affairs, Department of State, SA–29, 2201 C Street NW., Washington, DC 20520–4818. Phone, 888–407–4747 or 202–501–4444 (international). Internet, http://adoption.state.gov.

Missing Persons, Emergencies, and Deaths of Americans Abroad For information concerning missing persons, emergencies, travel warnings, overseas voting, judicial assistance, and arrests or deaths of Americans abroad, contact the Office of American Citizens Services and Crisis Management, Department of State. Phone, 888–407–4747 or 202–501–4444 (international). Correspondence should be directed to this address: Overseas Citizens Services, Bureau of Consular Affairs, Department of State, SA–29, 2201 C Street NW., Washington, DC 20520. Inquiries regarding international parental child abduction should be directed to the Office of Children's Issues, Bureau of Consular Affairs, Department of State, SA–29, 2201 C Street NW., Washington, DC 20520–4818. Phone, 888–407–4747 or 202–501–4444 (international). Internet, http://travel.state.gov/content/passports/english/emergencies.html.

Passports Passport information, including where to apply, is available online at the Bureau of Consular Affairs. For passport questions, travel emergencies, or to make an appointment at any regional passport agency, call the National Passport Information Center at 887–4–USA–PPT (887–487–2778)

(TDD/TTY: 888–874–7793). Passport information is available 24 hours, 7 days a week; customer service representatives are available weekdays, 8 a.m. to 10 p.m., eastern standard time, excluding Federal holidays. Correspondence can be submitted electronically at http://travel.state.gov/passport/about or can be directed to the appropriate regional agency (http://travel.state.gov/passport/) or the Correspondence Branch, Passport Services, Room 510, 1111 Nineteenth Street NW., Washington, DC 20524. Internet, http://travel.state.gov/content/travel/english.html.

Publications Publications that are produced on a regular basis include "Background Notes" and the "Foreign Relations" series. The Bureau of Public Affairs also occasionally publishes brochures and other publications to inform the public of U.S. diplomatic efforts. Internet, http://www.state.gov/r/pa/ei/rls/dos/221.htm.

Small Business Information Information on doing business with the Department of State is available from the Office of Small and Disadvantaged Business Utilization. The publication, "A Guide to Doing Business With the Department of State," the current "Forecast of Contracting Opportunities," and small business links are available online. Phone, 703–875–6822. Internet, http://www.state.gov/s/dmr/sdbu/.

Telephone Directory The Department's telephone directory can be accessed online. Internet, http://www.state.gov/m/a/gps/directory/.

Tips for U.S. Travelers Abroad Information for Americans on traveling abroad, including a traveler's checklist and tips on destinations, personal safety, health, and other topics, is available online at the Bureau of Consular Affairs. Internet, http://travel.state.gov/content/passports/english/go.html.

Visas For information on visas for foreigners wishing to enter the United States, visit the Bureau of Consular Affairs online or call 202–663–1225. Internet, http://travel.state.gov/content/visas/english.html.

For further information, contact the Office of Public Communication, Public Information Service, Bureau of Public Affairs, Department of State, Washington, DC 20520. Phone, 202–647–6575. Internet, http://www.state.gov.

EDITORIAL NOTE: The Department of Transportation did not meet the publication deadline for submitting updated information of its activities, functions, and sources of information as required by the automatic disclosure provisions of the Freedom of Information Act (5 U.S.C. 552(a)(1)(A)).

DEPARTMENT OF TRANSPORTATION

1200 New Jersey Avenue SE., Washington, DC 20590
Phone, 202–366–4000. Internet, http://www.dot.gov.

Secretary of Transportation	ANTHONY R. FOXX
Deputy Secretary	VICTOR M. MENDEZ
Under Secretary for Policy	PETER M. ROGOFF
General Counsel	KATHRYN B. THOMSON
Assistant Secretary for Administration	BRODI FONTENOT
Assistant Secretary for Aviation and International Affairs	SUSAN L. KURLAND
Assistant Secretary for Budget and Programs and Chief Financial Officer	SYLVIA I. GARCIA
Assistant Secretary for Governmental Affairs	DANA G. GRESHAM
Assistant Secretary for Transportation Policy	(VACANCY)
Chief of Staff	JOAN DEBOER
Chief Information Officer	RICHARD MCKINNEY
White House Liaison	NATE TURNBULL
Director, Civil Rights	CAMILLE M. HAZEUR
Director, Drug and Alcohol Policy and Compliance	PATRICE M. KELLY
Director, Executive Secretariat	CAROL C. DARR
Director, Public Affairs	SASHA J. JOHNSON
Director, Small and Disadvantaged Business Utilization	BRANDON NEAL
Director, Intelligence, Security, and Emergency Response	MICHAEL W. LOWDER
Inspector General	CALVIN L. SCOVEL, III

[For the Department of Transportation statement of organization, see the Code of Federal Regulations, Title 49, Part 1, Subpart A]

The Department of Transportation establishes national transportation policy for highway planning and construction, motor carrier safety, urban mass transit, railroads, aviation, and the safety of waterways, ports, highways, and pipelines.

The Department of Transportation (DOT) was established by act of October 15, 1966, as amended (49 U.S.C. 102 and 102 note), "to assure the coordinated, effective administration of the transportation programs of the Federal Government" and to develop "national transportation policies and programs conducive to the provision of fast, safe, efficient, and convenient transportation at the lowest cost consistent therewith." It became operational in April 1967 and was comprised of elements transferred from eight other major departments and agencies.

Secretary The Department of Transportation is administered by the Secretary of Transportation, who is the principal adviser to the President in all matters relating to Federal transportation programs.

Under Secretary The Under Secretary for Policy serves as a principal policy adviser to the Secretary and provides leadership in policy development for the Department.

278

DEPARTMENT OF TRANSPORTATION

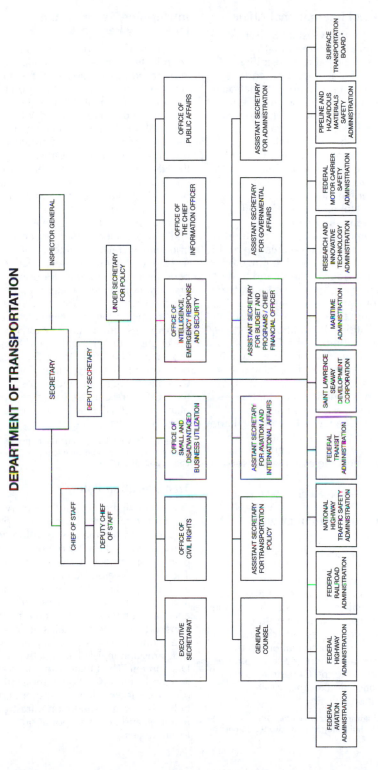

* The Surface Transportation Board is administratively affiliated with the Department of Transportation.

Aviation and International Affairs

The Office of the Assistant Secretary for Aviation and International Affairs has principal responsibility for the development, review, and coordination of policy for international transportation, and for development, coordination, and implementation of policy relating to economic regulation of the airline industry. The Office licenses U.S. and foreign carriers to serve in international air transportation and conducts carrier fitness determinations for carriers serving the United States. The Office also participates in negotiations with foreign governments to develop multilateral and bilateral aviation and maritime policies on a wide range of international transportation and trade matters and to coordinate cooperative agreements for the exchange of scientific and technical information between nations. In addition to these responsibilities, the Office resolves complaints concerning unfair competitive practices in domestic and international air transportation, establishes international and intra-Alaska mail rates, determines the disposition of requests for approval and immunization from the antitrust laws of international aviation agreements, and administers the essential air service program.

For further information, call 202–366–8822.

Drug and Alcohol Policy and Compliance

The Office ensures that the national and international drug and alcohol policies and goals of the Secretary are developed and carried out in a consistent, efficient, and effective manner within the transportation industries. The Office provides expert advice, counsel, and recommendations to the Secretary regarding drugs and alcohol as they pertain to the Department of Transportation and testing within the transportation industry.

For further information, contact the Office of Drug and Alcohol Policy and Compliance. Phone, 202–366–3784.

Intelligence, Security, and Emergency Response

The Office ensures development, coordination, and execution of plans and procedures for the Department of Transportation to balance transportation security requirements with safety, mobility, and economic needs of the Nation through effective intelligence, security, preparedness, and emergency response programs. The Office monitors the Nation's transportation network on a continuous basis; advises the Secretary on incidents affecting transportation systems; provides leadership on national preparedness, response, and transportation security matters; briefs the Secretary on intelligence relevant to the transportation sector; performs DOT's National Response Framework Emergency Support Function responsibilities; coordinates DOT participation in emergency preparedness and response exercises under the National Training and Exercise Program; administers DOT's Continuity of Government and Continuity of Operations programs; and serves as the DOT representative for emergency planning for civil aviation support to NATO and other allies.

For further information, contact the Office of Intelligence, Security, and Emergency Response. Phone, 202–366–6525.

Transportation Policy

The Office of the Assistant Secretary for Transportation Policy has principal responsibility for analysis, development, articulation, and review of policies and plans for all modes of transportation. The Office develops, coordinates, and evaluates public policy on safety, energy, and environmental initiatives which affect air, surface, marine, and pipeline transportation and maintains policy and economic oversight of regulatory programs and legislative initiatives of the Department. The Office also analyzes the economic and institutional implications of current and emerging transportation policy issues, transportation infrastructure finances, and new transportation technologies.

For further information, contact the Office of Transportation Policy. Phone, 202–366–4416.

Sources of Information

Inquiries for information on the following subjects should be directed to the specified office, Department of Transportation, Washington, DC 20590, or to the address indicated.

Civil Rights For information on equal employment opportunity, nondiscrimination in DOT employment and transportation services, or DOT's Disadvantaged Business Enterprise certification appeals program, contact the Director, Departmental Office of Civil Rights. Phone, 202–366–4648. Internet, http://www.dot.gov/ost/docr.

Consumer Activities For information about air travelers' rights or for assistance in resolving consumer problems with providers of commercial air transportation services, contact the Consumer Affairs Division (phone, 202–366–2220). To report vehicle safety problems, obtain information on motor vehicle and highway safety, or to request consumer information publications, call the National Highway Traffic Safety Administration's 24-hour auto safety hotline. Phone, 202–366–0123 or 800–424–9393.

Contracts Contact the Office of the Senior Procurement Executive. Phone, 202–366–4263.

Employment The principal occupations in the Department are air traffic controller, aviation safety specialist, electronics maintenance technician, engineer (civil, aeronautical, automotive, electrical, highway, and general), administrative/management, and clerical. For further information, contact the Transportation Administrative Service Center DOT Connection, Room PL–402, 1200 New Jersey Avenue SE., Washington, DC 20590. Phone, 202–366–9391 or 800–525–2878.

Environment Inquiries on environmental activities and programs should be directed to the Assistant Secretary for Transportation Policy, Office of Transportation Policy Development, Washington, DC 20590. Phone, 202–366–4416.

Films Many films on transportation subjects are available for use by educational institutions, community groups, private organizations, etc. Requests for specific films relating to a particular mode of transportation may be directed to the appropriate operating administration.

Fraud, Waste, and Abuse To report, contact the Office of Inspector General hotline, P.O. Box 23178, Washington, DC 20026–0178. Phone, 202–366–1461 or 800–424–9071.

Publications The Department and its operating agencies issue publications on a wide variety of subjects. Many of these publications are available from the issuing agency or for sale from the Government Printing Office and the National Technical Information Service, 5285 Port Royal Road, Springfield, VA 22151. Contact the Department or the specific agency at the addresses indicated in the text.

Reading Rooms Contact the Department of Transportation Dockets, W12–140, 1200 New Jersey, SE., Washington, DC 20590. Phone, 800–647–5527. Administrations and their regional offices maintain reading rooms for public use. Contact the specific administration at the address indicated in the text. Other reading rooms include: Department of Transportation Library, Room 2200, 1200 New Jersey Avenue SE., Washington, DC 20590. Phone, 202–366–0745. Department of Transportation Law Library, Room W12–300, 1200 New Jersey Avenue SE., Washington, DC 20590. Phone, 202–366–0746.

Speakers The Department of Transportation and its operating administrations and regional offices make speakers available for civic, labor, and community groups. Contact the specific agency or the nearest regional office at the address indicated in the text.

Surface Transportation Board Proceedings and Public Records Requests for public assistance with pending or potential proceedings of the Board should be addressed to the Office of Public Assistance, Governmental Affairs, and Compliance, Surface Transportation Board, 395 E Street SW.,

Washington, DC 20423–0001. Phone, 202–245–0238. Requests for access to the Board's public records should be made to the Office of the Secretary, Surface Transportation Board, 395 E Street SW., Washington, DC 20423–0001. Phone, 202–245–0232.

Telephone Directory The Department of Transportation telephone directory is available for sale by the Superintendent of Documents, Government Printing Office, Washington, DC 20402.

For further information concerning the Department of Transportation, contact the Office of Public Affairs, Department of Transportation, 1200 New Jersey Avenue SE., Washington, DC 20590. Phone, 202–366–5580. Internet, http://www.dot.gov.

Federal Aviation Administration

800 Independence Avenue SW., Washington, DC 20591
Phone, 202–366–4000; 866–835–5322. Internet, http://www.faa.gov.

Administrator	MICHAEL P. HUERTA
Deputy Administrator	MICHAEL G. WHITAKER
Chief of Staff	SASHA J. JOHNSON
Chief Counsel	(VACANCY)
Chief Operating Officer, Air Traffic Organization	TERI BRISTOL
Assistant Administrator for Civil Rights	MAMIE MALLORY AND WILBUR BARHAM
Assistant Administrator for Finance and Management	VICTORIA B. WASSMER
Assistant Administrator for Government and Industry	RODERICK D. HALL
Assistant Administrator for Human Resource Management	CARROLYN J. BOSTICK
Assistant Administrator for Policy, International Affairs and Environment	CARL BURLESON
Assistant Administrator for Communications	KRISTIE M. GRECO
Assistant Administrator for Security and Hazardous Materials	CLAUDIO MANNO
Associate Administrator for Airports	(VACANCY)
Associate Administrator for Aviation Safety	MARGARET M. GILLIGAN
Associate Administrator for Commercial Space Transportation	GEORGE C. NIELD

The Federal Aviation Administration (FAA), formerly the Federal Aviation Agency, was established by the Federal Aviation Act of 1958 (72 Stat. 731). The agency became a component of the Department of Transportation in 1967 pursuant to the Department of Transportation Act (49 U.S.C. 106). The mission of the FAA is to regulate civil aviation and U.S. commercial space transportation, maintain and operate air traffic control and navigation systems for both civil and military aircraft, and develop and administer programs relating to aviation safety and the National Airspace System.

Activities

Air Navigation Facilities The agency is responsible for the location, construction or installation, maintenance, operation, and quality assurance of Federal visual and electronic aids to air navigation. The agency operates and maintains voice/data communications equipment, radar facilities, computer systems, and visual display equipment at flight service stations, airport traffic control towers, and air route traffic control centers.

Airport Programs The agency maintains a national plan of airport requirements, administers a grant program for development of public use airports to assure and improve safety and to meet current and future airport capacity needs, evaluates the environmental impacts of airport development, and administers an airport noise compatibility program with the goal of reducing noncompatible uses around airports. It also develops standards and technical guidance on airport planning, design, safety, and operations and provides grants to assist public agencies in airport system and master planning and airport development and improvement.

Airspace and Air Traffic Management The safe and efficient utilization of the navigable airspace is a primary objective of the agency. To meet this objective, it operates a network of airport traffic control towers, air route traffic control centers, and flight service stations. It develops air traffic rules and regulations and allocates the use of the airspace. It also provides for the security control of air traffic to meet national defense requirements.

Civil Aviation Abroad Under the Federal Aviation Act of 1958 and the International Aviation Facilities Act (49 U.S.C. app. 1151), the agency encourages aviation safety and civil aviation abroad by exchanging aeronautical information with foreign aviation authorities; certifying foreign repair stations, airmen, and mechanics; negotiating bilateral airworthiness agreements to facilitate the import and export of aircraft and components; and providing technical assistance and training in all areas of the agency's expertise. It provides technical representation at international conferences, including participation in the International Civil Aviation Organization and other international organizations.

Commercial Space Transportation The agency regulates and encourages the U.S. commercial space transportation industry. It licenses the private sector launching of space payloads on expendable launch vehicles and commercial space launch facilities. It also sets insurance requirements for the protection of persons and property and ensures that space transportation activities comply with U.S. domestic and foreign policy.

Registration The agency provides a system for registering aircraft and recording documents affecting title or interest in the aircraft, aircraft engines, propellers, appliances, and spare parts.

Research, Engineering, and Development The research, engineering, and development activities of the agency are directed toward providing the systems, procedures, facilities, and devices needed for a safe and efficient system of air navigation and air traffic control to meet the needs of civil aviation and the air defense system. The agency also performs an aeromedical research function to apply knowledge gained from its research program and the work of others to the safety and promotion of civil aviation and the health, safety, and efficiency of agency employees. The agency also supports development and testing of improved aircraft, engines, propellers, and appliances.

Safety Regulation The Administration issues and enforces rules, regulations, and minimum standards relating to the manufacture, operation, and maintenance of aircraft, as well as the rating and certification (including medical) of airmen and the certification of airports serving air carriers. It performs flight inspection of air navigation facilities in the United States and, as required, abroad.

Test and Evaluation The agency conducts tests and evaluations of specified items such as aviation systems, subsystems, equipment, devices, materials, concepts, or procedures at any phase in the cycle of their development from conception to acceptance and implementation, as well as assigned independent testing at key decision points.

Other Programs The agency administers the aviation insurance program under the defense materials system with respect to priorities and allocation for civil aircraft and civil aviation operations. The agency develops specifications for the preparation of aeronautical charts. It publishes current information on airways and airport service and issues technical publications for the improvement of safety in flight, airport planning and design, and other aeronautical activities. It serves as the executive administration for the operation and maintenance of the Department of Transportation automated payroll and personnel systems.

For a complete list of Federal Aviation Administration field offices, go to www.faa.gov.

For further information, contact the Office of Communications, Federal Aviation Administration, Department of Transportation, 800 Independence Avenue SW., Washington, DC 20591. Phone, 202–267–3883. Fax, 202–267–5039. Internet, http://www.faa.gov.

Federal Highway Administration

1200 New Jersey Avenue SE., Washington, DC 20590
Phone, 202–366–0650. Internet, http://www.fhwa.dot.gov.

Administrator	Victor M. Mendez
Deputy Administrator	Gregory G. Nadeau
Executive Director	Jeffrey F. Paniati
Chief Counsel	(vacancy)
Chief Financial Officer	Elissa K. Konove
Associate Administrator for Administration	Sarah J. Shores
Associate Administrator for Civil Rights	Warren S. Whitlock
Associate Administrator for Federal Lands Highway	Joyce A. Curtis
Associate Administrator for Infrastructure	Walter C. "Butch" Waidelich, Jr.
Associate Administrator for Operations	Jeffrey A. Lindley
Associate Administrator for Planning, Environment, and Realty	Gloria M. Shepherd
Associate Administrator for Policy and Governmental Affairs	David Kim
Associate Administrator for Public Affairs	(vacancy)
Associate Administrator for Research, Development, and Technology	Michael F. Trentacoste
Associate Administrator for Safety	Anthony T. Furst

The Federal Highway Administration (FHWA) was established as an agency of the Department of Transportation by the Department of Transportation Act (49 U.S.C. 104). Title 23 of the United States Code and other supporting legislation authorize the Administration's various activities.

FHWA's mission is to improve mobility on our Nation's highways through national leadership, innovation, and program delivery. The Administration works with Federal, State, and local agencies as well as other stakeholders and partners to preserve and improve the National Highway System, which includes the Interstate System and other roads of importance for national defense and mobility. The FHWA works to improve highway safety and minimize traffic congestion on these and other key facilities. The FHWA bears the responsibility of ensuring that America's roads and highways remain safe, technologically up-to-date, and environmentally friendly.

Through surface transportation programs, innovative and traditional financing mechanisms, and new types of pavement and operational technology, FHWA increases the efficiency by which people and goods move throughout the Nation. The Administration also works to improve the efficiency of highway and road connections to other modes of transportation. The Federal-aid Highway

Program's budget is primarily divided between Federal-aid funding and the Federal Lands Highway Program.

Programs

Federal-aid Highway Program FHWA manages the Federal-aid Highway Program, which provides financial and technical assistance to States for constructing and improving the Nation's transportation infrastructure. The program includes the provision of engineering standards and policies, technical expertise, and other assistance related to the maintenance of highways, rural and urban roads, bridges, tunnels, hydraulic/geotechnical structures, and other engineering activities. Projects associated with the Federal-aid highway program include the National Highway System, Surface Transportation Program, Highway Bridge Program, Congestion Mitigation and Air Quality Improvement Program, Intelligent Transportation Systems Program, Transportation Infrastructure Finance and Innovation Act Program, the Emergency Relief Program, and the Federal Lands Highway Program.

Federal Lands Highway Program The Federal Lands Highway Program (FLHP) funds and gives technical assistance to a coordinated program of public roads servicing the transportation needs of Federal and Indian lands. The Program provides funding for public roads and highways on Federal and tribal lands that are not a State or local government responsibility. The planning, construction, and improvement of highways and bridges in national forests and parks, other federally owned land, and tribal lands benefit from FLHP funding.

Field and Division Offices

The FHWA consists of a Headquarters office in Washington, DC; a Federal-aid division office in each State, the District of Columbia, and Puerto Rico; four metropolitan offices in New York City, Philadelphia, Chicago, and Los Angeles serving as extensions of the corresponding Federal-aid division offices; and three Federal Lands Highway division offices.

A complete list of FHWA field and division offices is available online.

Internet, http://www.fhwa.dot.gov/about/field.cfm.

For further information, contact the Department of Transportation, Federal Highway Administration, Office of Information and Management Services, 1200 New Jersey Avenue, SE., Washington, DC 20590. Phone, 202–366–0534. Internet, http://www.fhwa.dot.gov.

Federal Railroad Administration

1200 New Jersey Avenue, SE., West Bldg., Washington, DC 20590
Phone, 202–493–6014. Internet, http://www.fra.dot.gov.

Administrator	JOSEPH C. SZABO
Deputy Administrator	KAREN J. HEDLUND
Chief Counsel	MELISSA L. PORTER
Executive Director	STACY CUMMINGS
Chief Financial Officer	REBECCA PENNINGTON
Associate Administrator for Administration	MICHAEL LOGUE
Associate Administrator for Railroad Policy and Development	PAUL NISSENBAUM
Associate Administrator for Railroad Safety/ Chief Safety Officer	ROBERT C. LAUBY
Associate Administrator for Communications and Legislative Affairs	KEVIN F. THOMPSON
Associate Director of Congressional Affairs	NATHAN J. ROBINSON
Director, Public Engagement	TIMOTHY BARKLEY
Director, Office of Civil Rights	CALVIN GIBSON

The Federal Railroad Administration was created pursuant to section 3(e)(1) of the Department of Transportation Act of 1966 (49 U.S.C. 103). The purpose of the Administration is to promulgate and enforce rail safety regulations, administer railroad financial assistance programs, conduct research and development in support of improved railroad safety and national rail transportation policy, provide for the rehabilitation of Northeast Corridor rail passenger service, and consolidate government support of rail transportation activities.

Activities

Passenger and Freight Services The Administration oversees and provides financial assistance to Amtrak and administers financial assistance programs to demonstrate high-speed rail technology, to reduce grade crossing hazards in high-speed rail corridors, to provide for investments in small freight railroads and other rail projects, to plan for high-speed rail projects, and to plan and deploy magnetic levitation technology.

Railroad Safety The Administration administers and enforces the Federal laws and related regulations designed to promote safety on railroads; exercises jurisdiction over all areas of rail safety under the Rail Safety Act of 1970, such as track maintenance, inspection standards, equipment standards, and operating practices. Railroad and related industry

equipment, facilities, and records are inspected and required reports reviewed. In addition, the Administration educates the public about safety at highway-rail grade crossings and the danger of trespassing on rail property.

Research and Development The Administration's ground transportation research and development program seeks to advance all aspects of intercity ground transportation and railroad safety pertaining to the physical sciences and engineering, in order to improve railroad safety and ensure that railroads continue to be a viable national transportation resource.

Transportation Test Center The Administration tests and evaluates conventional and advanced railroad systems and components at the Transportation Test Center near Pueblo, CO. Private sector companies and the Governments of the United States, Canada, and Japan use the facility to explore the operation of conventional and advanced systems under controlled conditions. It is used by Amtrak for the testing of new high-speed locomotives and trains and by the Federal Transit Administration for testing urban rapid transit vehicles.

For further information, contact the Transportation Technology Center, Pueblo, CO 81001. Phone, 719–584–0507.

For a complete list of Federal Railroad Administration regional offices, go to http://www.fra.dot.gov.

For further information, contact the Office of Public Affairs, Federal Railroad Administration, Department of Transportation, 1200 New Jersey Avenue SE., Washington, DC 20590. Phone, 202–493–6024. Internet, http://www.fra.dot.gov.

National Highway Traffic Safety Administration

1200 New Jersey Avenue SE., Washington, DC 20590
Phone, 202–366–9550; 888–327–4236. Internet, http://www.nhtsa.gov.

Administrator	(VACANCY)
Deputy Administrator	DAVID J. FRIEDMAN
Director of Communications	NATHAN TAYLOR
Chief Counsel	O. KEVIN VINCENT
Director, Office of Civil Rights	REGINA MORGAN
Director, Office of Governmental Affairs, Policy and Strategic Planning	(VACANCY)

Senior Associate Administrator for Policy and Operations	(VACANCY)
Supervisor, Executive Secretariat	JULIE KORKOR
Director, Office of Human Resources	DARLENE PEOPLES
Associate Administrator for Planning, Administrative, and Financial Management	MARY SPRAGUE
Associate Administrator, Communications and Consumer Information	SUSAN GORCOWSKI
Chief Information Officer	COLLEEN COGGINS
Senior Associate Administrator for Traffic Injury Control	BRIAN M. MCLAUGHLIN
Associate Administrator for Research and Program Development	JEFFREY P. MICHAEL
Associate Administrator for Regional Operations and Program Delivery	MAGGI D. GUNNELS
Senior Associate Administrator for Vehicle Safety	DANIEL C. SMITH
Associate Administrator for Rulemaking	(VACANCY)
Associate Administrator for Enforcement	NANCY L. LEWIS
Associate Administrator for Vehicle Safety Research	NATHANIEL BEUSE
Associate Administrator, National Center for Statistics and Analysis	TERRY T. SHELTON

[For the National Highway Traffic Safety Administration statement of organization, see the Code of Federal Regulations, Title 49, Part 501]

The National Highway Traffic Safety Administration (NHTSA) was established by the Highway Safety Act of 1970 (23 U.S.C. 401 note) to help reduce the number of deaths, injuries, and economic losses resulting from motor vehicle crashes on the Nation's highways.

The Administration carries out programs relating to the safety performance of motor vehicles and related equipment; administers the State and community highway safety program with the FHWA; regulates the Corporate Average Fuel Economy program; issues Federal Motor Vehicle Safety Standards (FMVSS) that prescribe safety features and levels of safety-related performance for vehicles and vehicular equipment; rates the safety of passenger vehicles in the New Car Assessment Program; monitors and participates in international vehicle safety forums to harmonize the FMVSS where appropriate; investigates and prosecutes odometer fraud; carries out the National Driver Register Program to facilitate the exchange of State records on problem drivers; conducts studies and operates programs aimed at reducing economic losses in motor vehicle crashes and repairs; performs studies, conducts demonstration projects, issues regulations requiring manufacturers to provide motor vehicle consumer information to vehicle purchasers and promotes programs to reduce impaired driving, increase seat belt use, and reduce risky driver behaviors; and issues theft prevention standards for passenger motor vehicles.

Activities

Research and Program Development

The Administration provides a foundation for the development of motor vehicle and highway safety program standards by analyzing data and researching, developing, testing, and evaluating motor vehicles, motor vehicle equipment, and advanced technologies, and collecting and analyzing crash data. The research program covers numerous areas affecting safety and includes laboratory-testing facilities to obtain necessary basic data. NHTSA strives to encourage industry to adopt advanced motor vehicle safety designs, elevate public awareness of safety potentials, and provide a base for vehicle safety information.

Regional Operations and Program Delivery The Administration administers State highway safety grant programs, authorized by the Safe, Accountable, Flexible, Efficient Transportation Equity Act: A Legacy for Users. The Highway Safety formula grant program provides funds to the States, Indian nations, and the territories each year to support safety programs, particularly in the following national priority areas: occupant protection, impaired driving, police traffic services, emergency medical services, data/traffic records, motorcycle safety, pedestrian and bicycle safety, speed control, and roadway safety. Incentive grants are also used to encourage States to implement effective impaired driving, occupant protection, motorcycle safety, and data improvement programs.

Rulemaking The Administration issues Federal Motor Vehicle Safety Standards that prescribe safety features and levels of safety-related performance for vehicles and vehicular equipment. The Administration participates in the United Nations World Forum for the Harmonization of Vehicle Regulations (WP.29) to improve, update, and harmonize its standards. It also conducts the New Car Assessment Program and the Governments Five Star Safety Rating Program, under which child seats, passenger cars, light trucks, and vans are subjected to a variety of assessments to evaluate their safety performance. These assessments are highly publicized and the vehicle star ratings are required to be placed on a new vehicles price label. Consumers use this information to make more informed decisions about how vehicles can keep them from getting in a crash and how well they would be protected if they were in a crash. The Administration educates consumers on topics such as distracted driving, as well as the proper use of vehicle safety features and child seats. To promote maximum feasible fuel economy, it manages a program establishing and revising fleet average fuel economy standards for passenger car and light

truck manufacturers. The Administration also carries out an antitheft program, which includes issuing rules requiring that certain passenger motor vehicles meet parts-marking requirements, the designation of likely high-theft truck lines and calculating and publishing annual motor vehicle theft rates.

Enforcement NHTSA's Office of Enforcement assures that all new vehicles sold in the U.S. meet applicable Federal Motor Vehicle Safety Standards (FMVSS). Under its compliance program, the Office conducts random tests and collects consumer complaints to identify and investigate problems with motor vehicles and vehicular equipment. If a vehicle or equipment suffers from a safety-related defect or does not meet all applicable FMVSS, the Office seeks a recall under which manufacturers must notify owners and remedy the defect free of charge. The Office then monitors recalls to ensure that owners are notified in a timely manner and that the scope of the recall and the remedy are adequate to correct the defect. The Office also assures that all motor vehicles subject to the CAFE regulations meet their respective CAFE targets, and it enforces violations of Federal odometer fraud regulations through criminal prosecution of offenders.

National Center for Statistics and Analysis The Administration maintains a collection of scientific and technical information related to motor vehicle safety and operates the National Center for Statistics and Analysis, whose activities include the development and maintenance of national highway-crash data collection systems and related statistical and economic analysis efforts. These comprehensive motor vehicle safety information resources serve as documentary reference points for Federal, State, and local agencies, as well as industry, universities, and the public.

Communications and Consumer Information The Administration develops, directs, and implements communication strategies based on NHTSA policy and programs, including campaigns to support high visibility enforcement efforts such as "Click It or

Ticket" and "Drive Sober or Get Pulled Over." It also promotes safety messages for NHTSA vehicle-related issues. The Office also manages all NHTSA Web sites and the toll-free Motor Vehicle Auto Safety Hotline to identify safety problems in motor vehicles and equipment. Consumers can call the hotline (phone, 888–327–4236; TDD, 800–424–9153 or 202–366–7800 in the Washington, DC, area) to report safety-related problems. English- and Spanish-speaking representatives are available between 8 a.m. and 10 p.m. eastern standard time, Monday through Friday, except Federal holidays. Consumers can also reach the hotline via the Internet at www.nhtsa.dot. gov/hotline. These calls form the basis for investigations and, ultimately, recalls if safety-related defects are identified. The hotline and the Web sites provide information to consumers about vehicle and child seat recalls, crash test results, and a variety of other highway safety information.

For a complete list of National Highway Traffic Safety Administration Regional Offices, go to www.nhtsa.dot. gov/nhtsa/whatis/regions.

For further information, contact the Office of Communications and Consumer Information, National Highway Traffic Safety Administration, Department of Transportation, 1200 New Jersey Avenue SE., Washington, DC 20590. Phone, 202–366–9550. Internet, http://www.nhtsa.dot.gov.

Federal Transit Administration

1200 New Jersey Avenue SE., Washington, DC 20590
Phone, 202–366–4043. Internet, http://www.fta.dot.gov.

Administrator	PETER M. ROGOFF
Deputy Administrator	THERESE M. MCMILLAN
Executive Director	MATTHEW J. WELBES
Associate Administrator for Administration	MATTHEW M. CROUCH
Associate Administrator for Budget and Policy	ROBERT J. TUCCILLO
Associate Administrator for Communications and Congressional Affairs	BRIAN D. FARBER
Associate Administrator for Planning	LUCY GARLIAUSKAS
Associate Administrator for Program Management	HENRIKA BUCHANAN-SMITH
Associate Administrator for Research, Demonstration, and Innovation	VINCENT VALDES
Chief Counsel	DORVAL R. CARTER, JR.
Director, Office of Civil Rights	LINDA C. FORD, *Acting*

[For the Federal Transit Administration statement of organization, see the Code of Federal Regulations, Title 49, Part 601]

The Federal Transit Administration (FTA) (formerly the Urban Mass Transportation Administration) was established as an operating administration of the U.S. Department of Transportation by section 1 of Reorganization Plan No. 2 of 1968 (5 U.S.C. app. 1), effective July 1, 1968. FTA's mission is to improve public transportation for America's communities by assisting in developing improved public transportation and providing financial assistance to State and local governments to finance public transportation systems and carry out national transit goals and policy.

Programs

Alternatives Analysis This program provides grants to assist identifying public transportation needs and the costs and benefits of various transportation strategies for a defined travel corridor. The results of such studies may be the selection of a locally preferred transportation alternative, which is the first step in the process of developing viable projects for possible future funding under the New Starts and Small Starts program.

For further information, call 202–366–2053. Internet, http://www.fta.dot.gov/grants/13094_7395.html.

Capital Investment   This program assists in financing the acquisition, construction, reconstruction, and improvement of facilities and equipment for use in public transportation service in urban areas. There are three categories of funds available under the Capital Investment program: Fixed Guideway Modernization funds for rolling stock renewal, safety-related improvements, and signal and power modernization; New Starts and Small Starts funds for construction of new fixed guideway systems or extensions to existing fixed guideway systems or corridor based rapid bus systems; and Bus and Bus Facilities funds for the acquisition of buses and rolling stock, ancillary equipment, and the construction of bus facilities.

For further information, call 202–366–2053. Internet, http://www.fta.dot.gov/grants/13093_3558.html (Fixed Guideway Modernization grants), http://www.fta.dot.gov/grants/13094_3559.html (New Starts and Small Starts), and http://www.fta.dot.gov/grants/13094_3557.html (Bus and Bus Facilities).

Clean Fuels Grant Program   This program was developed to assist nonattainment and maintenance areas in achieving or maintaining the National Ambient Air Quality Standards for ozone and carbon monoxide (CO), and it supports emerging clean fuel and advanced propulsion technologies for transit buses and markets for those technologies. Program funding is used for purchasing or leasing clean fuel buses, including buses that employ a lightweight composite primary structure and vans for use in revenue service; constructing or leasing clean fuel bus facilities (including electrical recharging facilities and related equipment); and projects relating to clean fuel, biodiesel, hybrid electric, or zero emissions technology buses.

For more information, call 202–366–2053. Internet, http://www.fta.dot.gov/cleanfuels.

Elderly and Persons With Disabilities
The program provides financial assistance to private nonprofit agencies to meet the transportation needs of elderly persons and persons with disabilities where services provided by public operators are unavailable, insufficient, or inappropriate; to public bodies approved by the State to coordinate services for elderly persons or persons with disabilities; or to public bodies which certify to the Governor that no nonprofit corporation or association is readily available in an area to provide the service. Funds are allocated by formula to the States. Local organizations apply for funding through a designated State agency.

For further information, call 202–366–2053. Internet, http://www.fta.dot.gov/grants/13093_3556.html.

Job Access and Reverse Commute Grants   This program makes funding available to public agencies and nonprofit organizations to pay the capital and operating costs of delivering new or expanded job access or reverse commute services and to promote the use of transit during nontraditional work hours, as well as encourage employer-based transportation strategies. The program provides funding for job access projects implementing new or expanded transportation services for transporting welfare recipients and low-income persons to and from jobs and needed employment support services such as child care and reverse commute projects implementing new or expanded general purpose public transportation services to transport residents of urban, rural, and suburban areas to suburban employment centers.

For further information, call 202–366–0176. Internet, http://www.fta.dot.gov/funding/grants.

New Freedom   This program makes capital and operating funding available to support new public transportation services that go beyond the requirements of the Americans with Disabilities Act (ADA) of 1990. Funding is available for private nonprofit organizations, State and local governmental authorities, and operators of public transportation services including private operators of public transportation services. Eligible projects must be targeted toward individuals with disabilities and meet the intent of the program by removing barriers to transportation and assisting persons with disabilities with transportation, including transportation to and from jobs and employment services.

For further information, call 202–366–2053. Internet, http://www.fta.dot.gov/grants/13093_3549.html.

Non-Urbanized Area Assistance   This program provides funds for public transportation in areas outside urbanized areas by formula to the States. Funding may be used for capital, operating, and administrative expenses for public transportation projects that meet the needs of rural communities, and 15 percent of annual funds may be used for intercity bus service.

For further information, call 202–366–2053. Internet, http://www.fta.dot.gov/grants/13093_3555.html.

Over-the-Road Bus Program   This program makes funds available to private operators of over-the-road buses to finance the incremental capital and training costs of complying with DOT's over-the-road bus accessibility regulation. Accessibility projects improve mobility for individuals with disabilities by providing financial assistance to help make vehicles accessible and provide sensitivity and equipment training to drivers and other personnel.

For further information, call 202–366–2053. Internet, http://www.fta.dot.gov/grants/13094_11856.html.

Planning   This program provides financial assistance in meeting the transportation planning needs of metropolitan planning organizations by allocating funds to States, which, in turn, are allocated to the metropolitan planning organizations. Assistance is available for transportation planning, technical assistance studies, demonstrations, management training, and cooperative research.

For further information, call 202–366–4033. Internet, http://www.fta.dot.gov/12347_4160.html.

Paul S. Sarbanes Transit in Parks
This program provides funding for alternative transportation projects in and around National Parks and other Federal recreation areas. Alternative transportation includes visitor shuttle bus systems, bicycle and pedestrian trails, ferries, and other forms of public or nonmotorized transportation. Projects funded through this program reduce congestion, protect sensitive natural and cultural treasures, and enhance the visitor experience. Funding is awarded through a competitive process to units of Federal land management agencies and to State, local and tribal government agencies.

For further information, call 202–366–2053. Internet, http://www.fta.dot.gov/transitinparks.

Research and Technology   This program seeks to improve public transportation for America's communities by delivering research products and services that assist transit agencies to improve their systems. Under this program, FTA partners with the transportation industry to undertake research, development, and demonstration projects that will improve the safety, quality, efficiency, reliability, cost-effectiveness, and environmental performance of public transportation in America and that leads to increases in transit ridership.

Transit research and technology efforts are undertaken with both public and private research organizations, universities, transit providers, and industry suppliers and manufacturers. Projects include: research on the state of the transit industry; public transportation services, management, and operational practices; asset management and maintenance research; advanced technologies that improve bus and rail services; standards development; bus rapid transit research; advanced propulsion systems, including fuel-cell-powered transit buses; research to improve energy efficiency and reduce emissions; and international activities that promote American transit products and services overseas.

For further information, call 202–366–4052. Internet, http://www.fta.dot.gov/research.

Rural Transportation Assistance   This program allocates funds annually to the States to provide assistance for transit research, technical assistance, training, and related support activities for transit providers serving nonurbanized areas. Additional funds are used at the national level to develop training materials, develop and maintain a national clearinghouse on rural transit activities and information, and provide technical assistance through peer practitioners to promote exemplary techniques and practices.

For further information, call 202–366–2053. Internet, http://www.fta.dot.gov/grants/13093_3554.html.

Safety   FTA's safety program supports State and local agencies in fulfilling their responsibility for the safety of public transportation facilities and services, through the encouragement and sponsorship of safety and security planning, training, information collection and analysis, drug control programs, system/safety assurance reviews, generic research, and other cooperative government/industry activities.

For further information, call 202–366–4020. Internet, http://www.fta.dot.gov/about/12419.html.

Training and Technical Assistance Through the National Transit Institute (NTI), FTA develops and offers training courses for improving transit planning, operations, workforce performance, and productivity. NTI courses are conducted at sites across the United States on a wide variety of subjects, ranging from multimodal planning to management development, third-party contracting, safety, and security. Current NTI course offerings are available online at www. ntionline.com.

For further information, call 202–366–6635.

For further information, contact the Office of Communications and Congressional Affairs, Federal Transit Administration, Department of Transportation, 1200 New Jersey Avenue SE., Washington, DC 20590. Phone, 202–366–4043. Internet, http://www.fta.dot.gov.

Maritime Administration

1200 New Jersey Avenue SE., Washington, DC 20590
Phone, 202–366–5807; 800–996–2723. Internet, http://www.marad.dot.gov.

Administrator	PAUL N. JAENICHEN
Deputy Administrator	PAUL N. JAENICHEN
Executive Director	JOEL SZABAT
Assistant Administrator	(VACANCY)
Associate Administrator for Administration/ Chief Information Officer	KEITH WASHINGTON, *Acting*
Associate Administrator for National Security	KEVIN M. TOKARSKI
Associate Administrator for Intermodal Systems Development	H. KEITH LESNICK
Associate Administrator for Environment and Compliance	JOHN P. QUINN
Associate Administrator for Business and Workforce Development	GEORGE M. ZOUKEE
Associate Administrator for Budget and Programs/Chief Financial Officer	LYDIA MOSCHKIN
Chief Counsel	FRANKLIN R. PARKER
Director of Congressional and Public Affairs	MICHAEL NOVAK
Director of Civil Rights	PATTIE TOM
Secretary, Maritime Subsidy Board	JULIE P. AGARWAL
Superintendent, United States Merchant Marine Academy	JAMES A. HELIS, USMS

The Maritime Administration was established by Reorganization Plan No. 21 of 1950 (5 U.S.C. app.). The Maritime Act of 1981 (46 U.S.C. 1601) transferred the Maritime Administration to the Department of Transportation. The Administration manages programs to aid in the development, promotion, and operation of the U.S. merchant marine. It is also charged with organizing and directing emergency merchant ship operations.

The Maritime Administration administers subsidy programs to pay the difference between certain costs of operating ships under the U.S. flag and foreign competitive flags on essential services, and the difference between the costs of constructing ships in U.S. and foreign shipyards. It provides financing guarantees for the construction, reconstruction, and reconditioning of ships; and enters into capital construction fund agreements that grant tax deferrals on moneys to be used for the acquisition, construction, or reconstruction of ships.

The Administration constructs or supervises the construction of merchant-type ships for the Federal Government. It helps industry generate increased business for U.S. ships and conducts programs to develop ports, facilities, and intermodal transport, and to promote domestic shipping.

It conducts program and technical studies and administers a war risk insurance program that insures operators and seamen against losses caused by hostile action if domestic commercial insurance is not available.

Under emergency conditions the Maritime Administration charters Government-owned ships to U.S. operators, requisitions or procures ships owned by U.S. citizens, and allocates them to meet defense needs.

It maintains a national defense reserve fleet of Government-owned ships that it operates through ship managers and general agents when required in national defense interests. An element of this activity is the Ready Reserve force consisting of a number of ships available for quick-response activation.

The Administration regulates sales to aliens and transfers to foreign registry of ships that are fully or partially owned by U.S. citizens. It also disposes of Government-owned ships found nonessential for national defense.

The Administration operates the U.S. Merchant Marine Academy, Kings Point, NY, where young people are trained to become merchant marine officers, and conducts training in shipboard firefighting at Toledo, OH. It also administers a Federal assistance program for the maritime academies operated by the States of California, Maine, Massachusetts, Michigan, New York, and Texas.

For a complete list of Maritime Administration offices, go to www.marad. dot.gov/about_us_landing_page/gateway_ offices/Gateway_Presence.htm.

For further information, contact the Office of Congressional and Public Affairs, Maritime Administration, Department of Transportation, 1200 New Jersey Avenue SE., Washington, DC 20590. Phone, 202–366–5807 or 800–996–2723. Internet, http://www.marad.dot.gov.

Saint Lawrence Seaway Development Corporation

55 M Street, SE., Suite 930, Washington, DC 20003.
Phone, 202–366–0091; 800–785–2779. Fax, 202–366–7147. Internet, http://www.seaway.dot.gov.
Mailing address, 1200 New Jersey Avenue, SE., Washington, DC 20590.
Operations address, 180 Andrews Street, Massena, NY 13662
Phone, 315–764–3200. Fax, 315–764–3235.

Washington, DC

Administrator	CRAIG H. MIDDLEBROOK, *Acting*
Deputy Administrator	CRAIG H. MIDDLEBROOK
Senior Advisor to the Administrator	ANITA K. BLACKMAN

Washington, DC

Chief Counsel	CARRIE MANN-LAVIGNE
Director of Budget and Programs	KEVIN P. O'MALLEY
Director of Congressional Affairs and Public Relations	NANCY T. ALCALDE
Director of Trade Development	REBECCA A. SPRUILL

Massena, NY

Associate Administrator	SALVATORE L. PISANI
Deputy Associate Administrator	CAROL A. FENTON
Chief Counsel	CARRIE MANN-LAVIGNE
Chief Financial Officer	MARSHA S. SIENKIEWICZ
Human Resources Officer	JULIE A. KUENZLER
Director of Engineering and Maintenance	THOMAS A. LAVIGNE
Director of Lock Operations and Marine Services	LORI K. CURRAN

The Saint Lawrence Seaway Development Corporation was established by the Saint Lawrence Seaway Act of May 13, 1954 (33 U.S.C. 981–990) and became an operating administration of the Department of Transportation in 1966.

The Corporation, working cooperatively with the Saint Lawrence Seaway Management Corporation (SLSMC) of Canada, is dedicated to operating and maintaining a safe, reliable, and efficient deep draft waterway between the Great Lakes and the Atlantic Ocean. It ensures the safe transit of commercial and noncommercial vessels through the two U.S. locks and the navigation channels of the Saint Lawrence Seaway System. The Corporation works jointly with SLSMC on all matters related to rules and regulations, overall operations, vessel inspections, traffic control, navigation aids, safety, operating dates, and trade development programs.

The Great Lakes/Saint Lawrence Seaway System extends from the Atlantic Ocean to the Lake Superior ports of Duluth/Superior, a distance of 2,342 miles. The Corporation's main customers are vessel owners and operators, Midwest States and Canadian provinces, Great Lakes port communities, shippers and receivers of domestic and international cargo, and the Great Lakes/Saint Lawrence Seaway Systems maritime and related service industries. International and domestic commerce through the Seaway contributes to the economic prosperity of the entire Great Lakes region.

For further information, contact the Director of Congressional and Public Relations, Saint Lawrence Seaway Development Corporation, U.S. Department of Transportation, 1200 New Jersey Avenue SE., Washington, DC 20590. Phone, 202–366–0091. Fax, 202–366–7147. Internet, http://www.seaway.dot.gov and http://www.greatlakes-seaway.com.

Pipeline and Hazardous Materials Safety Administration

1200 New Jersey Avenue SE., Washington, DC 20590
Phone, 202–366–4433. Internet, http://www.phmsa.dot.gov.

Administrator	CYNTHIA L. QUARTERMAN
Deputy Administrator	TIMOTHY P. BUTTERS
Assistant Administrator/Chief Safety Officer	STEPHEN L. DOMOTOR
Chief Counsel	VANESSA L. ALLEN SUTHERLAND

Associate Administrator for Management and Administration	SCOTT POYER
Associate Administrator for Pipeline Safety	JEFFREY D. WIESE
Associate Administrator for Hazardous Materials Safety	MAGDY EL-SIBAIE
Director, Office of Civil Rights	ROSANNE GOODWILL, *Acting*
Director, Office of Governmental, International, and Public Affairs	PATRICIA KLINGER, *Acting*

The Pipeline and Hazardous Materials Safety Administration was established on February 20, 2005. It is responsible for hazardous materials transportation and pipeline safety.

Hazardous Materials

The Office of Hazardous Materials Safety develops and issues regulations for the safe and secure transportation of hazardous materials by all modes, excluding bulk transportation by water. The regulations cover shipper and carrier operations, packaging and container specifications, and hazardous materials definitions. The Office provides training and outreach to help shippers and carriers meet the requirements of the hazardous material regulations. The Office is also responsible for the enforcement of regulations other than those applicable to a single mode of transportation. The Office manages a fee-funded grant program to assist States in planning for hazardous materials emergencies and to assist States and Indian tribes with training for hazardous materials emergencies. Additionally, the Office maintains a national safety program to safeguard food and certain other products from contamination during motor or rail transportation.

For further information, call 202–366–0656. Internet, hazmat.dot.gov.

For a complete listing of Office of Hazardous Materials Safety offices, go to www.phmsa.dot.gov/hazmat/about/org.

Pipelines

The Office of Pipeline Safety's (OPS) mission is to ensure the safety, security, and environmental protection of the Nation's pipeline transportation system. The Office establishes and enforces safety and environmental standards for transportation of gas and hazardous liquids by pipeline. OPS also analyzes data, conducts education and training, promotes damage prevention, and conducts research and development for pipeline safety. Through OPS-administered grants-in-aid, States that voluntarily assume regulatory jurisdiction of pipelines can receive funding for up to 50 percent of the costs for their intrastate pipeline safety programs. OPS engineers inspect most interstate pipelines and other facilities not covered by the State programs. The Office also implements the Oil Pollution Act of 1990 by providing approval for and testing of oil pipeline spill response plans.

For further information, call 202–366–4595.

For a complete list of Office of Pipeline Safety's regional offices, go to www. phmsa.dot.gov/public/contact.

For further information, contact the Office of Governmental, International and Public Affairs, Pipeline and Hazardous Materials Safety Administration, Department of Transportation, Suite 8406, 1200 New Jersey Avenue SE., Washington, DC 20590. Phone, 202–366–4831. Internet, http://www.phmsa.dot.gov.

Research and Innovative Technology Administration

1200 New Jersey Avenue SE., Washington, DC 20590
Phone, 202–366–7582. Internet, http://www.rita.dot.gov. Email, info.rita@dot.gov.

Administrator	GREGORY D. WINFREE, *Acting*
Deputy Administrator	(VACANCY)

Chief Counsel	ELLEN PARTRIDGE
Chief Financial Officer	ANDREW JULIAN
Associate Administrator for Administration	AUDREY FARLEY
Associate Administrator for Intelligent Transportation Systems Joint Program Office	KENNETH LEONARD
Associate Administrator for Research, Development and Technology	KEVIN WOMACK
Director, Bureau of Transportation Statistics	PATRICIA S. HU
Director, Office of Civil Rights	DARYL HART
Director, Office of Government, International, and Public Affairs	JANE MELLOW
Director, Volpe National Transportation Systems Center	ROBERT C. JOHNS
Director, Transportation Safety Institute	CHRISTINE LAWRENCE
Public Affairs Contact	NANCY WILOCKHA

The Research and Innovative Technology Administration (RITA) was created under the Norman Y. Mineta Research and Special Programs Improvement Act (49 U.S.C. 101 note). RITA coordinates, facilitates, and reviews the Department's research and development programs and activities; performs comprehensive transportation statistics research, analysis, and reporting; and promotes the use of innovative technologies to improve our Nation's transportation system.

RITA brings together important DOT data, research, and technology transfer assets and provides strategic direction and oversight of DOT's Intelligent Transportation Systems Program.

RITA is composed of the staff from the Office of Research, Development, and Technology; the Volpe National Transportation Systems Center; the Transportation Safety Institute; and the Bureau of Transportation Statistics.

For further information, contact the Research and Innovative Technology Administration, Department of Transportation, 1200 New Jersey Avenue SE., Washington, DC 20590. Phone, 202–366–4180. Email, info. rita@dot.gov. Internet, http://www.rita.dot.gov.

Federal Motor Carrier Safety Administration

1200 New Jersey Avenue SE., Washington, DC 20590
Phone, 202–366–2519. Internet, http://www.fmcsa.dot.gov.

Administrator	ANNE S. FERRO
Deputy Administrator	WILLIAM A. BRONROTT
Assistant Administrator/Chief Safety Officer	JACK VAN STEENBURG
Regulatory Ombudsman	STEVEN LAFRENIERE
Associate Administrator for Administration	DAPHNE JEFFERSON
Chief Financial Officer	PAMELA REED
Associate Administrator for Enforcement and Program Delivery	WILLIAM A. QUADE
Associate Administrator for Research and Information Technology/Chief Information Officer	G. KELLY LEONE
Associate Administrator of Field Operations	ANNE L. COLLINS
Associate Administrator for Policy and Program Development	LARRY MINOR
Chief Counsel	SCOTT DARLING, III
Director, Office of Civil Rights	KENNETH D. MAY

Director, Office of Communications	MARISSA PADILLA
Associate Director for Governmental Affairs	JOHN DRAKE

The Federal Motor Carrier Safety Administration was established within the Department of Transportation on January 1, 2000, pursuant to the Motor Carrier Safety Improvement Act of 1999 (49 U.S.C. 113).

Formerly a part of the Federal Highway Administration, the Federal Motor Carrier Safety Administration's primary mission is to prevent commercial motor vehicle-related fatalities and injuries. Activities of the Administration contribute to ensuring safety in motor carrier operations through strong enforcement of safety regulations, targeting high-risk carriers and commercial motor vehicle drivers; improving safety information systems and commercial motor vehicle technologies; strengthening commercial motor vehicle equipment and operating standards; and increasing safety awareness. To accomplish these activities, the Administration works with Federal, State, and local enforcement agencies, the motor carrier industry, labor safety interest groups, and others.

Activities

Commercial Drivers' Licenses   The Administration develops standards to test and license commercial motor vehicle drivers.

Data and Analysis   The Administration collects and disseminates data on motor carrier safety and directs resources to improve motor carrier safety.

Regulatory Compliance and Enforcement The Administration operates a program to improve safety performance and remove high-risk carriers from the Nation's highways.

Research and Technology   The Administration coordinates research and development to improve the safety of motor carrier operations and commercial motor vehicles and drivers.

Safety Assistance   The Administration provides States with financial assistance for roadside inspections and other commercial motor vehicle safety programs. It promotes motor vehicle and motor carrier safety.

Other Activities   The Administration supports the development of unified motor carrier safety requirements and procedures throughout North America. It participates in international technical organizations and committees to help share the best practices in motor carrier safety throughout North America and the rest of the world. It enforces regulations ensuring safe highway transportation of hazardous materials and has established a task force to identify and investigate those carriers of household goods that have exhibited a substantial pattern of consumer abuse.

For a complete list of Federal Motor Carrier Safety Administration field offices, go to www.fmcsa.dot.gov/about/aboutus.htm

For further information, contact the Federal Motor Carrier Safety Administration, 1200 New Jersey Avenue SE., Washington, DC 20590. Phone, 202–366–2519. Internet, http://www.fmcsa.dot.gov.

Surface Transportation Board

395 E Street SW., Washington, DC 20423
Phone, 202–245–0245. Internet, http://www.stb.dot.gov.

Chairman	DANIEL R. ELLIOTT, III
Vice Chairman	DEBRA L. MILLER
Commissioner	ANN D. BEGEMAN
Director, Office of Public Assistance, Governmental Affairs and Compliance	LUCILLE L. MARVIN
Managing Director	LELAND L. GARDNER

Director, Office of Economics   WILLIAM F. HUNEKE
Director, Office of Environmental Analysis   VICTORIA J. RUTSON
Director, Office of Proceedings   RACHEL D. CAMPBELL
General Counsel   CRAIG KEATS

The Surface Transportation Board was established in 1996 by the Interstate Commerce Commission (ICC) Termination Act of 1995 (49 U.S.C. 10101 et seq.) as an independent adjudicatory body organizationally housed within the Department of Transportation with jurisdiction over certain surface transportation economic regulatory matters formerly under ICC jurisdiction. The Board consists of three members, appointed by the President with the advice and consent of the Senate for 5-year terms.

The Board adjudicates disputes and regulates interstate surface transportation through various laws pertaining to the different modes of surface transportation. The Board's general responsibilities include the oversight of firms engaged in transportation in interstate and foreign commerce to the extent that it takes place within the United States, or between or among points in the contiguous United States and points in Alaska, Hawaii, or U.S. Territories or possessions. Surface transportation matters under the Board's jurisdiction in general include railroad rate and service issues, rail restructuring transactions (mergers, line sales, line construction, and line abandonments), and labor matters related thereto; certain trucking company, moving van, and noncontiguous ocean shipping company rate matters; certain intercity passenger bus company structure, financial, and operational matters; and certain pipeline matters not regulated by the Federal Energy Regulatory Commission.

In performing its functions, the Board is charged with promoting, where appropriate, substantive and procedural regulatory reform and providing an efficient and effective forum for the resolution of disputes. Through the granting of exemptions from regulations where warranted, the streamlining of its decisionmaking process and the regulations applicable thereto, and the consistent and fair application of legal and equitable principles, the Board seeks to provide an effective forum for efficient dispute resolution and facilitation of appropriate market-based business transactions. Through rulemakings and case disposition, it strives to develop new and better ways to analyze unique and complex problems, to reach fully justified decisions more quickly, to reduce the costs associated with regulatory oversight, and to encourage private sector negotiations and resolutions to problems, where appropriate.

For further information, contact the Office of Public Assistance, Governmental Affairs, and Compliance, Surface Transportation Board, 395 E Street SW., Washington, DC, 20423. Phone, 202–245–0230. Internet, http://www.stb.dot.gov.

DEPARTMENT OF THE TREASURY

Secretary of the Treasury	JACOB J. LEW
Deputy Secretary of the Treasury	SARAH BLOOM RASKIN
Treasurer of the United States	ROSIE RIOS
Chief of Staff	CHRISTIAN A. WEIDEMAN
Counselor to the Secretarys	RANDY DEVALK, MICHAEL STEGMAN
Inspector General	ERIC THORSON
Treasury Inspector General for Tax Administration	J. RUSSELL GEORGE
Treasury Special Inspector General for the Troubled Asset Relief Program	CHRISTY ROMERO
Under Secretary for Domestic Finance	MARY MILLER
Assistant Secretary for Financial Institutions	AMIAS GERETY
Assistant Secretary for Financial Markets	MATTHEW S. RUTHERFORD
Assistant Secretary for Financial Stability	TIMOTHY J. BOWLER
Fiscal Assistant Secretary	DAVID A. LEBRYK
Assistant Secretary for Economic Policy	KAREN DYNAN
General Counsel	CHRISTOPHER J. MEADE
Under Secretary for International Affairs	D. NATHAN SHEETS
Assistant Secretary for International Finance	(VACANCY)
Assistant Secretary for International Markets and Development	MARISA LAGO
Assistant Secretary for Legislative Affairs	ALASTAIR FITZPAYNE
Assistant Secretary for Management	NANI A. COLORETTI
Assistant Secretary for Public Affairs	NATALIE WYETH EARNEST
Assistant Secretary for Tax Policy	MARK J. MAZUR
Under Secretary for Terrorism and Financial Intelligence	DAVID COHEN
Assistant Secretary for Intelligence and Analysis	LESLIE IRELAND
Assistant Secretary for Terrorist Financing	DANIEL GLASER

As financial agent for the U.S. Government, the Department of the Treasury manufactures coins and currency, enforces financial laws, and recommends economic, tax, and fiscal policies.

The Treasury Department was created by act of September 2, 1789 (31 U.S.C. 301 and 301 note). Many subsequent acts have figured in the development of the Department, delegating new duties to its charge and establishing the numerous bureaus and divisions that now constitute the Treasury.

Secretary   As a major policy adviser to the President, the Secretary recommends domestic and international financial, economic, and tax policy; formulates broad fiscal policies that have general significance for the economy; and manages the public debt. The Secretary also oversees the activities of the Department in carrying out its major law enforcement responsibility; in serving as the financial agent for the U.S. Government; and in manufacturing coins, currency, and other products for customer agencies. The Secretary also acts as the Government's chief financial officer.

299

DEPARTMENT OF THE TREASURY

SECRETARY

DEPUTY SECRETARY

OFFICE OF THE CHIEF OF STAFF

INSPECTOR GENERAL

TREASURY INSPECTOR GENERAL FOR TAX ADMINISTRATION

SPECIAL INSPECTOR GENERAL FOR THE TROUBLED ASSET RELIEF PROGRAM

UNDER SECRETARY INTERNATIONAL AFFAIRS

ASSISTANT SECRETARY TAX POLICY

ALCOHOL AND TOBACCO TAX AND TRADE BUREAU

ASSISTANT SECRETARY ECONOMIC POLICY

ASSISTANT SECRETARY PUBLIC AFFAIRS

ASSISTANT SECRETARY LEGISLATIVE AFFAIRS

ASSISTANT SECRETARY MANAGEMENT / CHIEF FINANCIAL OFFICER

GENERAL COUNSEL

LEGAL DIVISION

TREASURER

ASSISTANT SECRETARY INTERNATIONAL FINANCE

ASSISTANT SECRETARY INTERNATIONAL MARKETS AND DEVELOPMENT

UNITED STATES MINT

BUREAU OF ENGRAVING AND PRINTING

UNDER SECRETARY TERRORISM AND FINANCIAL INTELLIGENCE

ASSISTANT SECRETARY TERRORIST FINANCING

ASSISTANT SECRETARY INTELLIGENCE AND ANALYSIS

FINANCIAL CRIMES ENFORCEMENT NETWORK

OFFICE OF FINANCIAL ASSETS CONTROL

UNDER SECRETARY DOMESTIC FINANCE

ASSISTANT SECRETARY FINANCIAL MARKETS

ASSISTANT SECRETARY FINANCIAL STABILITY

ASSISTANT SECRETARY FINANCIAL INSTITUTIONS

COMMUNITY DEVELOPMENT FINANCIAL INSTITUTIONS FUND

FEDERAL INSURANCE OFFICE

ASSISTANT SECRETARY FISCAL

BUREAU OF THE FISCAL SERVICE

OFFICE OF FINANCIAL RESEARCH

INTERNAL REVENUE SERVICE

OFFICE OF THE COMPTROLLER OF THE CURRENCY

Activities

Economic Policy The Office of the Assistant Secretary for Economic Policy helps policymakers determine economic policies. The Office analyzes domestic and international economic issues and developments in the financial markets, assists in forming official economic projections, and works closely with Federal Government agencies to make economic forecasts supporting the yearly budget process.

Enforcement The Office of the Assistant Secretary for Enforcement coordinates Treasury law enforcement matters, including the formulation of policies for Treasury enforcement activities, and cooperates on law enforcement matters with other Federal agencies. It oversees the Alcohol and Tobacco Tax and Trade Bureau, charged with collecting excise taxes on alcoholic beverages and tobacco products; the Office of Financial Enforcement, assisting in implementing the Bank Secrecy Act and administering related Treasury regulations; and the Office of Foreign Assets Control, controlling assets in the United States of "blocked" countries and the flow of funds and trade to them.

Domestic Finance The Office of Domestic Finance works to preserve confidence in the U.S. Treasury market, manage Federal fiscal operations, and strengthen financial institutions and markets; to promote access to credit; and to improve financial access and education in service of America's long-term economic strength and stability.

Financial Institutions The Office of Financial Institutions coordinates the Department's efforts regarding financial institutions legislation and regulation, legislation affecting Federal agencies that regulate or insure financial institutions, and securities markets legislation and regulation. The Office also coordinates the Department's effort on financial education policy and ensures the resiliency of the financial services sector.

Financial Markets The Office of Financial Markets serves to formulate policy on Federal debt management, State and local finance (including the Federal debt), Federal Government credit policies, and lending and privatization. This Office also oversees the Federal Financing Bank, and the Assistant Secretary serves as the senior member of the Treasury Financing Group and coordinates the President's Working Group on Financial Markets.

Fiscal Affairs The Office of the Fiscal Assistant Secretary provides policy oversight of the Fiscal Service bureaus and develops policy on payments, collections, debt financing operations, electronic commerce, Governmentwide accounting, Government investment fund management, and other related issues. The Office also performs two critical functions for the Department: It manages the daily cash position of the Government, and it produces the cash and debt forecasts used to determine the size and timing of the Government's financing operations.

Financial Stability The Office of Financial Stability (OFS) within the U.S. Treasury was created by the Emergency Economic Stabilization Act of 2008 (12 U.S. C. 5201 et seq.) to administer the Troubled Asset Relief Program (TARP). The purpose of the TARP was to help restore the liquidity and stability to the U.S. financial system following the 2008 financial crisis. Treasury's authority to make financial commitments under TARP ended on October 3, 2010. Today, OFS is focused on winding down the TARP investments in a manner that balances speed of exit with maximizing taxpayer returns as well as continuing to help homeowners prevent avoidable foreclosures.

International Development and Markets The Office of the Assistant Secretary for Development and Markets manages the work of the Committee on Foreign Investment in the United States and Treasury's Office of Technical Assistance. The Office also advises and assists the Under Secretary for International Affairs and other policymakers on financial and economic policies surrounding major bilateral and multilateral engagements. It plays a similar role in the formulation and execution of policies affecting export finance, financial services, trade, and multilateral development, including the World Bank, the regional development banks, and emerging global issues like food security and climate finance.

International Finance   The Office of the Assistant Secretary for International Finance conducts macroeconomic analyses on global, regional, country-specific bases to advise and assist the Under Secretary for International Affairs and other policymakers in the formulation and execution of financial and economic policy towards and through the International Monetary Fund and other major multilateral and bilateral engagements like the U.S.-China Strategic and Economic Dialogue and the G–20.

Tax Policy   The Office of the Assistant Secretary for Tax Policy advises and assists the Secretary and the Deputy Secretary in the formulation and execution of domestic and international tax policies and programs. These functions include analysis of proposed tax legislation and tax programs; projections of economic trends affecting tax bases; studies of effects of alternative tax measures; preparation of official estimates of Government receipts for the President's annual budget messages; legal advice and analysis on domestic and international tax matters; assistance in the development and review of tax legislation and domestic and international tax regulations and rulings; and participation in international tax treaty negotiations and in maintenance of relations with international organizations on tax matters.

Treasurer of the United States   The Office of the Treasurer of the United States was established on September 6, 1777. The Treasurer was originally charged with the receipt and custody of Government funds, but many of these functions have been assumed by different bureaus of the Department. In 1981, the Treasurer was assigned responsibility for oversight of the Bureau of Engraving and Printing and the United States Mint. The Treasurer reports to the Secretary through the Assistant Secretary for Management/Chief Financial Officer.

Treasury Inspector General for Tax Administration   The Treasury Inspector

General for Tax Administration (TIGTA) was established in January 1999, in accordance with the Internal Revenue Service Restructuring and Reform Act of 1998 (26 U.S.C. 1 note), to provide independent oversight of the Internal Revenue Service programs and activities. TIGTA is charged with monitoring the Nation's tax laws to ensure that the Internal Revenue Service (IRS) acts with efficiency, economy, and effectiveness toward program accomplishment; ensuring compliance with applicable laws and regulations, preventing, detecting, and deterring fraud, waste, and abuse; investigating activities or allegations related to fraud, waste, and abuse by IRS personnel; and protecting the IRS against attempts to corrupt or threaten its employees.

Sources of Information

Contracts   Write to the Director, Office of Procurement, Suite 400–W, 1310 G Street NW., Washington, DC 20220. Phone, 202–622–0203.

Environment   Environmental statements prepared by the Department are available for review in the Departmental Library. Information on Treasury environmental matters may be obtained from the Office of the Assistant Secretary of the Treasury for Management and Chief Financial Officer, Treasury Department, Washington, DC 20220. Phone, 202–622–0043.

General Inquiries   For general information about the Treasury Department, including copies of news releases and texts of speeches by high-level Treasury officials, write to the Office of the Assistant Secretary (Public Affairs and Public Liaison), Room 3430, Departmental Offices, Treasury Department, Washington, DC 20220. Phone, 202–622–2920.

Inspector General   For general information, contact the Assistant Inspector General for Management at 202–927–5200 or visit the Office of Inspector General (OIG) Web site. To report the possible existence of a Treasury activity constituting mismanagement, gross waste of funds, abuse of authority, a substantial and specific danger to the public health and safety, or a violation of law, rules, or regulations (not including the Internal Revenue Service, which reports to the Treasury Inspector General for Tax Administration), contact the OIG by email or phone at 800–359–3898; or write to Treasury OIG Hotline, Office of Inspector General, 1500 Pennsylvania Avenue NW., Washington, DC 20220. For Freedom of Information Act/Privacy Act requests, write to Freedom of Information Act Request, Treasury OIG, Office of Counsel, Suite 510, 740 15th Street NW., Washington, DC 20220. Email, hotline@oig.treas.gov. Internet, http://www.treas.gov/inspector-general.

Reading Room The Reading Room is located in the Treasury Library, Room 1428, Main Treasury Building, 1500 Pennsylvania Avenue NW., Washington, DC 20220. Phone, 202–622–0990.

Small and Disadvantaged Business Activities Write to the Director, Office of Small and Disadvantaged Business Utilization, Suite 400–W, 1310 G Street NW., Washington, DC 20220. Phone, 202–622–0530.

Tax Legislation Information on tax legislation may be obtained from the Assistant Secretary (Tax Policy), Departmental Offices, Treasury Department, Washington, DC 20220. Phone, 202–622–0050.

Telephone Directory The Treasury Department telephone directory is available for sale by the Superintendent of Documents, Government Printing Office, Washington, DC 20402.

Treasury Inspector General for Tax Administration Individuals wishing to report fraud, waste, or abuse against or by IRS employees should write to the Treasury Inspector General for Tax Administration, P.O. Box 589, Ben Franklin Station, Washington, DC 20044–0589. Phone, 800–366–4484. Email, complaints@tigta.treas.gov.

For further information, contact the Public Affairs Office, Department of the Treasury, 1500 Pennsylvania Avenue NW., Washington, DC 20220. Phone, 202–622–2960. Internet, http://www.treasury.gov.

Alcohol and Tobacco Tax and Trade Bureau

Administrator	JOHN J. MANFREDA
Deputy Administrator	MARY G. RYAN
Assistant Administrator (Field Operations)	THOMAS R. CRONE
Assistant Administrator (Headquarters Operations)	THERESA M. MCCARTHY
Assistant Administrator for Information Resources and Chief Information Officer	ROBERT J. HUGHES
Assistant Administrator for Management and Chief Financial Officer	CHERI D. MITCHELL
Chief Counsel	ANTHONY P. GLEDHILL

The Alcohol and Tobacco Tax and Trade Bureau (TTB) was established on January 24, 2003, by the Homeland Security Act of 2002 (6 U.S.C. 531). TTB collects Federal alcohol, tobacco, firearms, and ammunition excise taxes; regulates the production, labeling, and advertising of alcohol beverages; and investigates unfair or unlawful trade in alcohol and tobacco products. TTB regulates alcohol and tobacco producers, importers, and wholesalers. Regulation of retailers takes place on a State and local level.

Sources of Information

General Inquiries For general information about TTB, please visit the Frequently Asked Questions section of TTB's web page. You may also write to the Administrator's Office, 1310 G Street NW., Box 12, Washington, DC 20005. Phone, 202–453–2000. Email, TTBInternetQuestions@ttb.gov.

Advertising, Labeling, and Formulation Customer Service Desk Direct inquiries about the advertising, labeling, and formulation of alcohol beverages to

202–453–2250 or 866–927–2533. Email, alfd@ttb.treas.gov. Internet, http://www. ttb.gov/alfd/index.shtml.

Electronic Reading Room The TTB Electronic Reading Room contains materials specifically required to be maintained by the Freedom of Information Act. To view these materials, visit http://www.ttb.gov/foia/err.shtml. Some records are also available by appointment in the TTB Public Reading Room located at 1310 G Street NW., Washington, DC 20005. To make an appointment, call 202–882–9904.

Consumer Complaints Information on filing a complaint is available online.

Internet, http://www.ttb.gov/consumer/ filing_complaint.shtml.

Fraud Tipline To report fraud, diversion, and illegal activity by producers, importers, or wholesalers of alcohol and tobacco, please contact the TTB Tipline. Phone, 1–855–882–8477. TTD, 202–882–9914. Email, tips@ttb.gov.

National Revenue Center Information on permits, applications, claims, filing excise tax returns, and other tax collection activities is available online and from the National Revenue Center, 550 Main Street, Suite 8002, Cincinnati, Ohio 45202. Phone, 513–684–3334 or 877–882–3277. Internet, http://www.ttb. gov/nrc/index.shtml.

For further information, contact the Administrator's Office, Alcohol and Tobacco Tax and Trade Bureau. Phone, 202–453–2000. Internet, http://www.ttb.gov.

Office of the Comptroller of the Currency

Comptroller	THOMAS J. CURRY
Senior Deputy Comptroller and Chief of Staff	PAUL M. NASH
Chief Information Officer	EDWARD J. DORRIS
Deputy to the Chief of Staff and Liaison to the Federal Deposit Insurance Corporation	WILLIAM A. ROWE, III
Executive Director for the Office of Minority and Women Inclusion	JOYCE COFIELD
Senior Deputy Comptroller for Enterprise Governance and Ombudsman	LARRY L. HATTIX
First Senior Deputy Comptroller and Chief Counsel	AMY S. FRIEND
Senior Deputy Comptroller for the Office of Management and Chief Financial Officer	KATHY K. MURPHY, *Acting*
Senior Deputy Comptroller for Bank Supervision Policy and Chief National Bank Examiners	JENNIFER C. KELLY, JOHN C. LYONS
Senior Deputy Comptroller for Economics	DAVID NEBHUT
Senior Deputy Comptroller for Large Bank Supervision	MARTIN PFINSGRAFF

[For the Office of the Comptroller of the Currency statement of organization, see the Code of Federal Regulations, Title 12, Part 4]

The Office of the Comptroller of the Currency (OCC) was created February 25, 1863 (12 Stat. 665), as a bureau of the Department of the Treasury. Its primary mission is to regulate national banks. The Office is headed by the Comptroller, who is appointed for a 5-year term by the President with the advice and consent of the Senate. In July

2011, the Office of Thrift Supervision was integrated into the OCC, along with the responsibility for the supervision of Federal savings associations.

The OCC regulates national banks and Federal savings associations through its power to examine banks; approve or deny applications for new bank charters, branches, or mergers; take enforcement actions—such as bank closures—against banks that are not in compliance with laws and regulations; and issue rules, regulations, and interpretations on banking practices.

The OCC supervises approximately 1,900 national banks, Federal savings associations, and Federal branches, including their trust activities and overseas operations. Each bank is examined by a nationwide staff of approximately 2,500 bank examiners who are supervised by four district offices. The OCC is independently funded through assessments of bank assets.

Sources of Information

Freedom of Information Act Requests
For Freedom of Information Act requests, contact the Manager, Disclosure

Services and Administrative Operations, Communications Division. Phone, 202–649–6758. Fax, 202–649–6160.
Contracts For information about contracts, contact the Acquisition Management Division. Phone, 202–649–6597. Fax, 571–293–4356.
Employment For information regarding national bank examiner employment opportunities (generally hired at the entry level through a college recruitment program), contact the Director for Human Resources Operations. Phone, 202–649–6590. Fax, 202–649–5998.
Publications OCC publications are available online. Copies of certain publications are available in print from the Communications Division. Phone, 202–649–6759. Fax, 202–649–6168. Internet, http://www.occ.gov/publications/index-publications.html.

For further information, contact the Communications Division, Office of the Comptroller of the Currency, 400 7th Street SW., Washington, DC 20219. Phone, 202–649–6700. Internet, http://www.occ.gov.

Bureau of Engraving and Printing

Director	LARRY R. FELIX
Deputy Director	LEONARD R. OLIJAR
Associate Director (Chief Financial Officer)	DEBRA H. RICHARDSON
Associate Director (Chief Information Officer)	HARRY SINGH, *Acting*
Associate Director for Eastern Currency Facility	JON J. CAMERON
Associate Director for Western Currency Facility	CHARLENE WILLIAMS
Associate Director for Management	WILL LEVY, III
Associate Director for Product and Technology Development	JUDITH DIAZ MYERS
Associate Director for Corporate Planning and Strategic Analysis	ANDREW BRUNHART
Chief Counsel	SIDNEY ROCKE

The Bureau of Engraving and Printing operates on basic authorities conferred by act of July 11, 1862 (31 U.S.C. 303), and additional authorities contained in past appropriations made to the Bureau that are still in force. Operations are financed by a revolving fund established in 1950 in accordance with Public Law 81–656. The Bureau is headed by a Director who is selected by the Secretary of the Treasury.

The Bureau designs, prints, and finishes all of the Nation's paper currency

and many other security documents, including White House invitations and military identification cards. It also is responsible for advising and assisting Federal agencies in the design and production of other Government documents that, because of their innate value or for other reasons, require security or counterfeit-deterrence characteristics.

The Bureau also operates a second currency manufacturing plant in Fort

Worth, TX (9000 Blue Mound Road, 76131). Phone, 817–231–4000.

Sources of Information

Address questions on the following subjects to the appropriate office, Bureau of Engraving and Printing.

Contracts and Small Business Activities Information relating to contracts and small business activities may be obtained by contacting the Office of Acquisition. Phone, 202–874–2065.

Employment Information regarding employment opportunities and required qualifications is available from the Office of Human Resources. Phone, 202–874–2633.

Freedom of Information Act Requests Inquiries should be directed to 202–874–3733.

General Inquiries Requests for information about the Bureau, its products, or numismatic and philatelic interests should be directed to 202–874–3019.

Mail Order Sales Uncut sheets of currency, engraved Presidential portraits, historical engravings of national landmarks, and other souvenirs and mementos are available for purchase online and by phone at 800–456–3408. Internet, http://www.moneyfactory.com/.

Tours Tours of the Bureau's facilities are provided year-round according to the schedules listed below. Up-to-the-minute tour information is available online. Internet, http://www.moneyfactory.com/tours.html.

Washington, DC During peak season, March through August, 9 a.m. until 10:45 a.m. and 12:30 p.m. until 2 p.m., tickets are required for all tours. Tours begin every 15 minutes, with the last tour beginning at 2 p.m. The times between 11 a.m. and 12:15 p.m. are reserved for school and other groups. The ticket booth is located on Raoul Wallenberg Place (formerly Fifteenth Street) and opens at 8 a.m. Tour tickets are free. The ticket booth remains open for the morning and evening tours until all tickets have been distributed. Lines form early, and tickets go quickly, typically by 9 a.m. during peak season. Tickets are distributed on a first-come, first-served basis. Lines form on Raoul Wallenberg Place. Evening tours, running from April through August, 5 p.m. until 7 p.m., are offered every 15 minutes. During nonpeak season, September through February, 9 a.m. until 2 p.m, tickets are not necessary for tours. Lines form on Fourteenth Street. No tours are given on weekends, Federal holidays, or between Christmas and New Year's Day. For information on the Washington, DC, Tour and Visitor Center, call 202–874–2330 or 866–874–2330. Internet, http://www.moneyfactory.gov/tours/washingtondctours.html.

Fort Worth, TX During peak season, June and July, 11 a.m. until 5 p.m, a new tour starts every 30 minutes. The Tour and Visitor Center opens at 10:30 a.m. and closes at 6:30 p.m. During nonpeak season, August through May, 9 a.m. until 2 p.m., the Visitor Center opens at 8:30 a.m. and closes at 3:30 p.m. No tours are given on weekends, Federal holidays, or between Christmas and New Year's Day. For information on the Fort Worth Tour and Visitor Center, call 817–231–4000 or 866–865–1194. Internet, http://www.moneyfactory.gov/tours/fortworthtxtours.html.

For further information, contact the Office of External Relations, Bureau of Engraving and Printing, Department of the Treasury, Room 533–M, Fourteenth and C Streets SW., Washington, DC 20228. Phone, 202–874–3019. Fax, 202–874–3177. Internet, http://www.moneyfactory.com.

Bureau of the Fiscal Service

Commissioner	SHERYL R. MORROW
Deputy Commissioner, Financial Services and Operations	WANDA J. ROGERS
Deputy Commissioner, Finance and Administration	KIMBERLY MCCOY

Deputy Commissioner, Accounting and Shared Services	Cynthia Z. Springer
Director, Legislative and Public Affairs	Joyce Harris
Chief Counsel	Margaret Marquette
Assistant Commissioner, Debt Management Services	Jeffrey Schramek
Assistant Commissioner, Revenue Collections Management	Corvelli McDaniel, *Acting*
Assistant Commissioner, Governmentwide Accounting	Christina Ho
Assistant Commissioner, Information and Security Services (Chief Information Officer)	(vacancy)
Assistant Commissioner, Management (Chief Financial Officer)	Patricia M. Greiner
Assistant Commissioner, Payment Management	John Hill
Executive Director, Government Securities Regulations	Lori Santamorena
Assistant Commissioner, Office of Administrative Services	Douglas Anderson
Assistant Commissioner, Public Debt Accounting	Matthew Miller
Assistant Commissioner, Treasury Securities Services	Dara Seaman

The Bureau of the Fiscal Service provides central payment services to Federal program agencies, operates the Federal Government's collections and deposit systems, provides Governmentwide accounting and reporting services, manages the collection of delinquent debt owed to the Federal Government, borrows the money needed to operate the Federal Government, accounts for the resulting public debt, and provides reimbursable support to Federal agencies.

Payments Each year, the Fiscal Service disburses more than one billion non-Defense payments to a wide variety of recipients, such as those individuals who receive Social Security, IRS tax refunds, and veterans' benefits. In Fiscal Year 2012, the Fiscal Service issued more than $2.4 trillion in payments, 88 percent of which were issued electronically.

Collections Fiscal Service administers the world's largest collection system, processing more than 400 million transactions through the support of six Federal Reserve Banks and a network of over 100 financial institutions. In Fiscal Year 2012, the Fiscal Service collected over $3.16 trillion in Federal revenues from individual and corporate income tax deposits, customs duties, loan repayments, fines, proceeds from leases, as well as other sources of revenue.

Fiscal Service and IRS manage the Electronic Federal Tax Payment System (www.eftps.gov), which allows individuals and businesses to pay Federal taxes through the Internet. EFTPS–Online also provides such features as an instant, printable acknowledgment for documenting each transaction, the ability to schedule advance payments, and access to payment history.

The Treasury Offset Program is one of the methods used to collect delinquent debt. Fiscal Service uses the program to withhold Federal payments, such as Federal income tax refunds, Federal salary payments, and Social Security benefits, to recipients with delinquent debts, including past-due child support obligations and State and Federal income tax debt.

Do Not Pay The Fiscal Service Do Not Pay Business Center has a two-part vision for programs administered or funded by the Federal Government: to help prevent and stop improper payments from being made, and to identify and to mitigate fraud, waste and abuse. The goal of the program is to integrate Do Not Pay into existing business processes by providing agencies access to current and relevant data to help make an award or payment decision.

Debt Financing   The Bureau auctions and issues Treasury bills, notes, and bonds and manages the sales and redemption of savings bonds. It provides daily and other periodic reports to account for the composition and size of the debt. In addition, the Bureau implements the regulations for the Government securities market. These regulations provide for investor protection while maintaining a fair and liquid market for Government securities.

Accounting   Fiscal Service gathers and publishes Governmentwide financial information that is used by the public and private sectors to monitor the Government's financial status and establish fiscal and monetary policies. These publications include the "Daily Treasury Statement," "Monthly Treasury Statement," "Treasury Bulletin," "U.S. Government Annual Report," and "Financial Report of the U.S. Government."

Electronic Commerce   Through its electronic money programs, Fiscal Service offers new payment and collection technologies using the Internet and card technologies to help Federal agencies modernize their cash management activities. Examples include stored-value cards used on military bases, point-of-sale check conversion, and Internet credit card collection programs.

Shared Services   The Administrative Resource Center (ARC) delivers franchise services on a reimbursable basis to more than 85 Treasury and Federal Government agencies. ARC provides services in six areas: financial management, investment accounting, human resources, information technology, procurement, and travel.

Sources of Information

Inquiries on the following subjects should be directed to the appropriate office, Bureau of the Fiscal Service, 401 Fourteenth Street SW., Washington, DC 20227. Fax, 202–874–7016.

Do Not Pay   The Do Not Pay Business Center supports Federal agencies in their efforts to reduce the number of improper payments. For more information, use the link below. Internet, http://www. donotpay.treas.gov/.

Electronic Access   Information on the public debt; on U.S. Savings Bonds; and on Treasury bills, notes, bonds, and other Treasury securities is available online. Forms and publications may be ordered electronically using the same Web site. Internet, http://www.treasurydirect.gov/.

Employment   General Employment inquiries should be addressed to the Bureau of the Fiscal Service, Division of Human Resources, PO Box 1328, Recruitment and Classification Branch, Parkersburg, WV 26106–1328. Phone, 304–480–6144.

Savings Bonds   Savings bonds may be purchased and held in an online account. Current rate information is available online or by calling 800–487–2663. Requests for information about all series of savings bonds, savings notes, and retirement plans or individual retirement bonds should be addressed to the Bureau of the Fiscal Service, Division of Customer Assistance, PO Box 7012, Parkersburg, WV 26106–7012. Phone, 304–480–7711. Internet, https://www. treasurydirect.gov/indiv/products/prod_ eebonds_glance.htm.

Shared Services   Information on services offered to other Government agencies is available online. Internet, http://arc. publicdebt.treas.gov/fshome.htm.

Treasury Securities   Information inquiries regarding the purchase of Treasury bills, bonds, and notes should be addressed to the Bureau of the Fiscal Service, Division of Customer Assistance, PO Box 7015, Parkersburg, WV 26106– 7015. Phone, 800–722–2678.

For further information, contact the Office of Legislative and Public Affairs, Bureau of the Fiscal Service, Department of the Treasury, 401 Fourteenth Street SW., Washington, DC 20227. Phone, 202–874–6750. Internet, http://www.fiscal.treasury.gov.

Internal Revenue Service

Commissioner of Internal Revenue	DANIEL I. WERFEL, *Acting*
Deputy Commissioner for Operations Support	BETH TUCKER
Deputy Commissioner for Services and Enforcement	(VACANCY)
Chief Counsel	WILLIAM J. WILKINS
Commissioner, Large Business and International Division	HEATHER C. MALOY
Commissioner, Small Business and Self-Employed Division	FARIS FINK
Commissioner, Tax Exempt and Government Entities Division	MICHAEL JULAINELLE, *Acting*
Commissioner, Wage and Investment Division	PEGGY BOGADI
Chief Financial Officer	PAMELA LARUE
Chief, Agency-Wide Shared Services	DAVID GRANT
Chief, Appeals	SHELLY KAY
Chief, Communications and Liaison	TERRY LEMONS, *Acting*
Chief, Criminal Investigation	RICHARD WEBER
Chief Technology Officer	TERRY V. MILHOLLAND
National Taxpayer Advocate	NINA E. OLSON
Director, Office of Research, Analysis and Statistics	ROSEMARY MARCUSS
Chief Human Capital Officer	DAVID KRIEG
Director, Office of Privacy, Information Protection and Data Security	REBECCA A. CHIARAMIDA
Director, Office of Professional Responsibility	KAREN L. HAWKINS
Director, Whistleblower Office	STEVE A. WHITLOCK
Executive Director, Office of Equity, Diversity and Inclusion	MONICA DAVY
Senior Advisor to the Commissioner for Compliance Analytics	DEAN R. SILVERMAN
Director, Return Preparer Office	CAROL A. CAMPBELL
Director, Online Services	RAJIVE MATHUR
Director, Affordable Care Act Office	SARAH HALL INGRAM

The Office of the Commissioner of Internal Revenue was established by act of July 1, 1862 (26 U.S.C. 7802). The Internal Revenue Service (IRS) administers and enforces the internal revenue laws and related statutes, except those relating to alcohol, tobacco, firearms, and explosives. It collects the proper amount of tax revenue, at the least cost to the public, by efficiently applying the tax law with integrity and fairness. The IRS aims for the highest possible degree of voluntary compliance in accordance with the tax laws and regulations; advises the public of their rights and responsibilities; determines the extent of compliance and the causes of noncompliance; properly administers and enforces the tax laws; and continually searches for and implements new, more efficient ways of accomplishing its mission. The IRS ensures satisfactory resolution of taxpayer complaints; provides taxpayer service and education; determines, assesses, and collects internal revenue taxes; determines pension plan qualifications and exempt organization status; and prepares and issues rulings and regulations to supplement the provisions of the Internal Revenue Code.

Most of the collected revenues depend on the individual income tax and the social insurance and retirement taxes. Other major revenue sources are corporate income, excise, estate, and gift taxes. The 16th Amendment of the

Constitution, ratified on February 3, 1913, gave Congress the authority to levy taxes on the income of individuals and corporations.

Sources of Information

Audiovisual Materials   Films providing information on the American tax system, examination and appeal rights, and the tax responsibilities of running a small business are available. Some of the films are also available in Spanish. The films can be obtained by contacting any territory office. Also available are audio and video cassette tapes that provide step-by-step instructions for preparing basic individual income tax forms. These tapes are available in many local libraries.

Contracts   Write to the Internal Revenue Service (OS:A:P), 1111 Constitution Avenue NW., Washington, DC 20224. Phone, 202–283–1710.

Customer Service   The Internal Revenue Service provides year-round tax information and assistance to taxpayers, primarily through its Web site and toll-free telephone system, which also includes telephone assistance to deaf and hearing-impaired taxpayers who have access to a teletypewriter or television/ phone. The toll-free numbers are listed in local telephone directories and in the annual tax form packages. Taxpayers may also visit agency offices for help with their tax problems. Individual preparation is available for handicapped or other individuals unable to use the group preparation method. Foreign language tax assistance is also available at many locations. The IRS encourages taxpayers to use the resources available at www.irs. gov for assistance with their tax questions or to locate electronic filing sources.

Educational Programs   The Service provides, free of charge, general tax information publications and booklets on specific tax topics. Taxpayer information materials also are distributed to major television networks and many radio and television stations, daily and weekly newspapers, magazines, and specialized publications. Special educational materials and films are provided for use in high schools and colleges. Individuals starting a new business are given specialized materials and information at small business workshops, and community colleges provide classes based on material provided by the Service. The community outreach tax assistance program provides assistance to community groups. Through the volunteer income tax assistance program and the tax counseling for the elderly program, the Service recruits, trains, and supports volunteers who offer free tax assistance to low-income, elderly, military, and non-English-speaking taxpayers. Materials, films, and information on the educational programs can be obtained by contacting any territory office.

Employment   For information, write to the recruitment coordinator at any of the territory offices.

Publications   "The Annual Report— Commissioner of Internal Revenue," the "Internal Revenue Service Data Book," and periodic reports of statistics of income are available from the Superintendent of Documents, Government Printing Office, Washington, DC 20402. "Examination of Returns, Appeal Rights, and Claims for Refund," "Your Federal Income Tax," "Farmer's Tax Guide," "Tax Guide for Small Business," and other publications are available at Internal Revenue Service offices free of charge.

Reading Rooms   Public reading rooms are located in the national office and in each territory office.

Speakers   Arrangements for speakers on provisions of the tax law and operations of the Internal Revenue Service for professional and community groups may be made by writing to the Senior Commissioner's Representative. For national organizations, write to the Communications Division at the IRS National Headquarters in Washington, DC.

Taxpayer Advocate   Each district has a problem resolution staff to address taxpayer complaints that cannot be resolved through regular channels. Internet, http://www.irs.gov/Advocate.

For further information, contact the Internal Revenue Service, Department of the Treasury, 1111 Constitution Avenue NW., Washington, DC 20224. Phone, 202–622–5000.

United States Mint

Director	(VACANCY)
Deputy Director	RICHARD A. PETERSON
Chief Counsel	DANIEL P. SHAVER
Chief Administrative Officer	BEVERLY ORTEGA BABERS
Associate Director, Workforce Solutions	ANNIE D. BROWN
Associate Director, Information Technology	LAUREN BUSCHOR
Associate Director, Manufacturing	DAVID M. CROFT, *Acting*
Associate Director, Sales and Marketing	J. MARC LANDRY, *Acting*
Associate Director, Finance	DAVID A. MOTL
Chief of U.S. Mint Police	DENNIS P. O'CONNOR

The establishment of a mint was authorized by act of April 2, 1792 (1 Stat. 246). The Bureau of the Mint was established by act of February 12, 1873 (17 Stat. 424), and recodified on September 13, 1982 (31 U.S.C. 304, 5131). The name was changed to United States Mint by Secretarial order dated January 9, 1984.

The primary mission of the Mint is to produce an adequate volume of circulating coinage for the Nation to conduct its trade and commerce. The Mint also produces and sells numismatic coins, American Eagle gold and silver bullion coins, and national medals. In addition, the Fort Knox Bullion Depository is the primary storage facility for the Nation's gold bullion.

The U.S. Mint maintains sales centers at the Philadelphia and Denver Mints and at Union Station in Washington, DC. Public tours are conducted, with free admission, at the Philadelphia and Denver Mints.

For a complete list of U.S. Mint field facilities, visit www.usmint.gov/about_ the_mint.

Sources of Information

Contracts and Employment Inquiries should be directed to the facility head of the appropriate field office or to the Director of the Mint.

Numismatic Services The United States Mint maintains public exhibit and sales areas at the Philadelphia and Denver Mints and at Union Station in Washington, DC. Brochures and order forms for official coins, medals, and other numismatic items are available online. Internet, http://www.usmint.gov/.

Publications The "CFO Annual Financial Report" is available from the United States Mint, Department of the Treasury, 801 Ninth Street NW., Washington, DC 20220. Phone, 202–354–7800.

For further information, contact the United States Mint, Department of the Treasury, 801 Ninth Street NW., Washington, DC 20220. Phone, 202–354–7200.

EDITORIAL NOTE: The Department of Veterans Affairs did not meet the publication deadline for submitting updated information of its activities, functions, and sources of information as required by the automatic disclosure provisions of the Freedom of Information Act (5 U.S.C. 552(a)(1)(A)).

DEPARTMENT OF VETERANS AFFAIRS

810 Vermont Avenue NW., Washington, DC 20420
Phone, 202–461–4800. Internet, http://www.va.gov.

Secretary of Veterans Affairs	ROBERT A. MCDONALD
Deputy Secretary	SLOAN D. GIBSON
Chief of Staff	JOSE D. RIOJAS, *Acting*
General Counsel	WILLIAM A. GUNN
Chairman, Board of Veterans' Appeals	STEVEN L. KELLER, *Acting*
Inspector General	RICHARD J. GRIFFIN, *Acting*
Executive Director, Office of Acquisition, Logistics, and Construction	GLENN D. HAGGSTROM
Executive Director, Office of Small and Veteran Business Programs	THOMAS J. LENEY
Director, Office of Employment Discrimination Complaint Adjudication	MAXANNE R. WITKIN
Director, Center for Women Veterans	IRENE TROWELL-HARRIS
Director, Center for Minority Veterans	BARBARA WARD
Advisory Committee Management Officer	VIVIAN DRAKE, *Acting*
Director, Center for Faith-Based and Neighborhood Partnerships	E. TERRI LAVELLE
Special Assistant, Nongovernmental Organization Gateway Initiative Office	DOUG CARMON
Director, Federal Recovery Coordination Office	CAROL WEESE, *Acting*
Veterans' Service Organizations Liaison	KEVIN SECOR
Director, Office of Survivors Assistance	DEBRA A. WALKER
Executive in Charge, Office of Management, and Chief Financial Officer	W. TODD GRAMS
Assistant Secretary for Information and Technology	STEPHEN W. WARREN
Assistant Secretary for Policy and Planning	ROBERT D. SNYDER, *Acting*
Assistant Secretary for Operations, Security, and Preparedness	KEVIN T. HANRETTA
Assistant Secretary for Human Resources and Administration	GINA S. FARRISEE
Assistant Secretary for Public and Intergovernmental Affairs	JOSHUA TAYLOR, *Acting*
Assistant Secretary for Congressional and Legislative Affairs	CHRISTOPHER E. O'CONNOR, *Acting*
Under Secretary for Benefits, Veterans Benefits Administration	ALLISON A. HICKEY
Under Secretary for Health, Veterans Health Administration	ROBERT L. JESSE
Under Secretary for Memorial Affairs, National Cemetery Administration	STEVE L. MURO

The Department of Veterans Affairs operates programs to benefit veterans and members of their families. Benefits include compensation payments for disabilities or

312

death related to military service; pensions; education and rehabilitation; home loan guaranty; burial; and a medical care program incorporating nursing homes, clinics, and medical centers.

The Department of Veterans Affairs (VA) was established as an executive department by the Department of Veterans Affairs Act (38 U.S.C. 201 note). It is comprised of three organizations that administer veterans programs: the Veterans Health Administration, the Veterans Benefits Administration, and the National Cemetery Administration. Each organization has field facilities and a central office component. Staff offices support the overall function of the Department and its Administrations.

Activities

Advisory Committee Management Office The Advisory Committee Management Office serves as the coordinating office for the Department's 25 Federal advisory committees. It is responsible for establishing clear and uniform goals, standards, and procedures for advisory committee activities. It is also responsible for ensuring that VA advisory committee operations are in compliance with the provisions of the Federal Advisory Committee Act.

Office of Acquisition, Logistics, and Construction The Office of Acquisition, Logistics, and Construction (OALC) is a multifunctional organization responsible for directing the acquisition, logistics, construction, and leasing functions within the VA. The Executive Director, OALC, is also the Chief Acquisition Officer for the VA.

Cemeteries The National Cemetery Administration (NCA) is responsible for the management and oversight of 131 national cemeteries in the United States and Puerto Rico, as well as 33 soldiers' lots, Confederate cemeteries, and monument sites. Burial in a national cemetery is available to eligible veterans and their spouses and dependent children. At no cost to the family, a national cemetery burial includes the gravesite, graveliner, opening and closing of the grave, headstone or marker, and perpetual care as part of a national shrine. If a veteran is buried in an unmarked grave in a private cemetery anywhere in the world, NCA will provide a headstone or marker. If a veteran died on or after November 1, 1990, and is buried in a grave marked with a privately purchased headstone, NCA will provide a headstone or marker to supplement the grave or a medallion to be affixed to the permanent headstone. NCA's State Cemetery Grants Program provides funds to State and tribal governments to establish, expand, or improve veterans' cemeteries. NCA issues Presidential Memorial Certificates to recognize the service of honorably discharged servicemembers or veterans.

Center for Minority Veterans The Center for Minority Veterans (CMV), established by the Veterans' Benefits Improvement Act of 1984 (38 U.S.C. 101 note), promotes the use of VA benefits, programs, and services by minority veterans. The CMV focuses on the unique and special needs of African Americans, Hispanics, Asian Americans, Pacific Islanders, and Native Americans, which include American Indians, Native Hawaiians, and Alaska Natives.

Center for Women Veterans The Center for Women Veterans (CWV), established by the Veterans' Benefits Improvement Act of 1984 (38 U.S.C. 101 note), reports to the Secretary's Office and oversees the Department's programs for women veterans. The CWV Director serves as the primary advisor to the Secretary on all matters related to policies, legislation, programs, issues, and initiatives affecting women veterans. The CWV ensures that women veterans receive benefits and services on par with male veterans; VA programs are responsive to gender-specific needs of women veterans; outreach is performed to improve women veterans' awareness of services, benefits, and eligibility criteria; and women veterans are treated with dignity and respect.

Health Services The Veterans Health Administration (VHA) is home to the largest integrated health care system in

DEPARTMENT OF VETERANS AFFAIRS

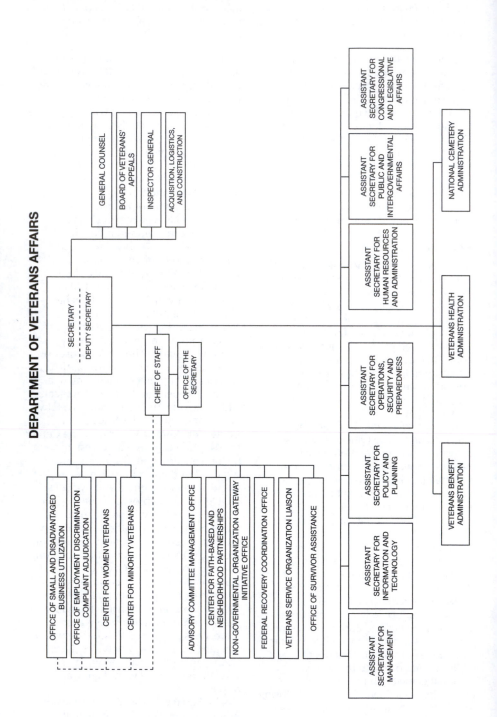

the United States. It provides hospital, nursing home, domiciliary, and outpatient medical and dental care to eligible veterans of military service in the Armed Forces. VHA conducts both individual medical and health care delivery research projects and multihospital research programs, to include assisting in the education of physicians, dentists, and the training of many other health care professionals through affiliations with educational institutions and organizations. VHA treated over 6 million patients in 2010, and has over 1,600 sites of care which include: 152 hospitals, 965 outpatient clinics, 133 community living centers, and 293 Vet Centers. In 2010, VA hospitals also had approximately 680,000 inpatient admissions and more than 75 million outpatient visits. The number of women veterans using VA health care doubled from 160,000 in 2000 to 315, 000 in 2010. VA hospitals provide more public data about quality and safety than any health care system in the world and held academic affiliations with more than 1,200 educational institutions. More than 100,000 health care students receive clinical training from VA each year.

Historically, VHA has been at the forefront in developing new devices, treatments, and tools for various conditions and diseases, including the first electronic health record, cardiac pacemaker, bionic ankle, and successful liver transplant. It has also developed new drugs and treatments for acquired immune deficiency syndrome/human immunodeficiency virus, diabetes, Alzheimer's disease, and osteoporosis. Currently, VHA medical centers provide a wide range of services including traditional hospital-based services such as critical care, mental health, orthopedics, pharmacy, radiology, and physical therapy. Furthermore, most VA medical centers offer additional medical and surgical specialties services including pathology, dermatology, dental, geriatrics, neurology, oncology, prosthetics, urology, and vision care. Some medical centers also offer advanced services such as organ transplants and plastic surgery. VHA also distinguishes itself as the Nation's largest provider of graduate medical education and major contributor to medical research.

Operations, Security, and Preparedness The Assistant Secretary for Operations, Security, and Preparedness (OSP) coordinates VA's emergency management, preparedness, personal identity verification, physical security, personnel security and suitability, police services, law enforcement activities, and ensures compliance and resource management in the OSP, so the Department can continue to perform the mission-essential functions under all circumstances across the spectrum of threats. OSP directs and provides oversight for the VA's overall operations for planning, response, and security and law enforcement programs in support of the National Response Framework, Homeland Security Presidential Directive 12, and other related Executive orders and Federal regulations.

Veterans Benefits The Veterans Benefits Administration provides information, advice, and assistance to veterans, their dependents, beneficiaries, representatives, and others applying for VA benefits. It also cooperates with the Department of Labor and other Federal, State, and local agencies in developing employment opportunities for veterans and referral for assistance in resolving socioeconomic, housing, and other related problems.

The Compensation and Pension Service is responsible for claims for disability compensation and pension, specially adapted housing, accrued benefits, adjusted compensation in death cases, and reimbursement for headstone or marker; allowances for automobiles and special adaptive equipment; special clothing allowances; emergency officers' retirement pay; survivors' claims for death compensation, dependency and indemnity compensation, death pension, and burial and plot allowance claims; forfeiture determinations; and a benefits protection program for minors and incompetent adult beneficiaries.

The Education Service administers the Montgomery GI Bill program and other programs which provide education benefits to qualified active-duty members, veterans, certain dependents of veterans, and members of the Selected and Ready Reserve. The Service also checks school records to ensure that they comply with the pertinent law, approves courses for the payment of educational benefits, and administers a work-study program. Additional details are available at www.gibill.va.gov.

The Insurance Service's operations for the benefit of servicemembers, veterans, and their beneficiaries are available through the regional office and insurance center (phone, 800–669–8477) in Philadelphia, PA, which provides the full range of activities necessary for a national life insurance program. Activities include the complete maintenance of individual accounts, underwriting functions, life and death insurance claims awards, and any other insurance-related transactions. The Service also administers the Veterans Mortgage Life Insurance Program for those disabled veterans who receive a VA grant for specially adapted housing and supervises the Servicemembers' Group Life Insurance Program and the Veterans' Group Life Insurance Program.

The Loan Guaranty Service is responsible for operations that include appraising properties to establish their values; approving grants for specially adapted housing; supervising the construction of new residential properties; establishing the eligibility of veterans for the program; evaluating the ability of a veteran to repay a loan and the credit risk; making direct loans to Native American veterans to acquire a home on trust land; servicing and liquidating defaulted loans; and disposing of real estate acquired as the consequence of defaulted loans.

The Vocational Rehabilitation and Employment Service provides outreach, motivation, evaluation, counseling, training, employment, and other rehabilitation services to service-connected disabled veterans. Vocational and educational counseling, as well as the evaluation of abilities, aptitudes, and interests are provided to veterans and servicepersons. Counseling, assessment, education programs, and in some cases, rehabilitation services are available

to spouses and children of totally and permanently disabled veterans as well as surviving orphans, widows, and widowers of certain deceased veterans.

Vocational training and rehabilitation services are available to children with spina bifida having one or both parents who served in the Republic of Vietnam during the Vietnam era, or served in certain military units in or near the demilitarized zone in Korea, between September 1, 1967 and August 31, 1971.

Veterans' Appeals The Board of Veterans' Appeals (BVA) renders final decisions on behalf of the Secretary on appeals from decisions of local VA offices. The Board reviews all appeals for entitlement to veterans' benefits, including claims for service connection, increased disability ratings, total disability ratings, pension, insurance benefits, educational benefits, home loan guarantees, vocational rehabilitation, dependency and indemnity compensation, health care delivery, and fiduciary matters. The Board has jurisdiction over appeals arising from the VA regional offices, VA medical centers, the National Cemetery Administration, and the Office of General Counsel. The Board's mission is to conduct hearings and issue timely, understandable, and quality decisions for veterans and other appellants in compliance with the requirements of law. Final BVA decisions are appealable to the U.S. Court of Appeals for Veterans Claims.

Field Facilities The Department's operations are handled through the following field facilities: cemeteries, domiciliaries, medical centers, outpatient clinics, and regional offices. Cemeteries provide burial services to veterans, their spouses, and dependent children. Domiciliaries provide the least intensive level of inpatient medical care, including necessary ambulatory medical treatment, rehabilitation, and support services, in a structured environment to veterans who are unable because of their disabilities to provide adequately for themselves in the community. Medical centers provide eligible beneficiaries with medical and other health care services equivalent to those provided by private sector institutions, augmented in many instances by services to meet the special requirements of veterans. Outpatient clinics provide eligible beneficiaries with ambulatory care. Regional offices grant benefits and services provided by law for veterans, their dependents, and beneficiaries within an assigned territory; furnish information regarding VA benefits and services; adjudicate claims and make awards for disability compensation and pension; conduct outreach and information dissemination; provide support and assistance to various segments of the veteran population to include former prisoners of war, minority, homeless, women, and elderly veterans; supervise payment of VA benefits to incompetent beneficiaries; provide vocational rehabilitation and employment training; administer educational benefits; guarantee loans for purchase, construction, or alteration of homes; process grants for specially adapted housing; process death claims; and assist veterans in exercising rights to benefits and services.

For a storehouse of key staff and facility information within 1,811 VA facilities, use the link below.

Internet, http://www.va.gov/directory/guide/home.asp?isflash=1.

Sources of Information

Audiovisuals Persons interested in the availability of VA video productions or exhibits for showing outside of VA may write to the Chief, Media Services Division (032B), Department of Veterans Affairs, 810 Vermont Avenue NW., Washington, DC 20420. Phone, 202–461–5282. Email, vacomedia-photoservices@va.gov.

Contracts Information on business opportunities with the VA can be found at www1.va.gov/oamm/oa/dbwva/index.cfm. Additional information is available at the Office of Acquisition and Material Management Web site at www1.va.gov/oamm. Information on solicitations issued by VA is available at www.va.gov/oamm/busopp/index.htm.

Small Business Programs Persons seeking information on VA's small and veteran-owned business programs may

call 800–949–8387 or 202–461–4300. More information on these programs is available online at the Office of Small and Disadvantaged Business Utilization Web site. Internet, http://www.va.gov/osdbu/.

Veterans Business Ownership Services The Center for Veterans Enterprise qualifies veteran-owned small businesses to participate in VA VOSB set-asides. This Center is a component of the Office of Small and Disadvantaged Business Utilization. Phone, 866–584–2344 or 202–303–3260 Option #6. Internet, www.vetbiz.gov. Email, vacve@va.gov.

Employment The VA employs physicians, dentists, podiatrists, optometrists, nurses, nurse anesthetists, physician assistants, expanded-function dental auxiliaries, registered respiratory therapists, certified respiratory technicians, licensed physical therapists, occupational therapists, pharmacists, and licensed practical or vocational nurses under VA's excepted merit system. This system does not require civil service eligibility. Other professional, technical, administrative, and clerical occupations, such as veterans claims examiners, secretaries, and management analysts, exist in VA that do require civil service eligibility. Persons interested in employment should contact the human resources services office at the nearest VA facility, or use the link below to start building a career with the VA's online resources. All qualified applicants will receive consideration for appointments without regard to race, religion, color, national origin, sex, political affiliation, or any nonmerit factor. Internet, http://www.va.gov/jobs/.

Freedom of Information Act Requests The VA has a decentralized system for handling FOIA requests. All FOIA requests should be addressed directly to any of the approximately 400 geographically dispersed components that may maintain the records you are seeking. Requests can be sent by mail, email, or facsimile. To see the list of VA offices authorized to receive requests, visit http://www.FOIA_Offices.asp.

If you are unsure which office is the custodian of the records being sought, send your request to: Director, FOIA Service, (005R1C), 810 Vermont Avenue NW., Washington, DC 20420. Phone, 877–750–3642. Fax 202–273–0487.

Inspector General Inquiries and Hotline Publicly available documents and information on the VA Office of Inspector General are available at www.va.gov/ oig. Complaints may be sent by mail to the VA Inspector General (53E), P.O. Box 50410, Washington, DC 20091–0410. Hotline phone, 800–488–8244. Email, vaoighotline@va.gov.

Medical Center (Hospital) Design, Construction, and Related Services Construction projects for VA medical centers and other facilities in excess of $4 million are managed and controlled at the VA central office, located in Washington, DC. Projects requiring design, construction, and other related services are advertised on the FirstGov Web site at www.usa.gov. Submit project-specific qualifications (SF 254 and SF 255) to the Director, A/E Evaluation and Program Support Team (181A), 810 Vermont Avenue NW., Washington, DC 20420.

Additional information regarding the selection process can be found on the VA Office of Facilities Management Web site at www.cfm.va.gov. Construction projects for VA medical centers and other facilities which are less than $4 million are managed and controlled at the individual medical centers. For information regarding these specific projects, contact the Acquisition and Materiel Management Office at each individual VA medical center. Addresses and additional information on VA medical centers can be found on the VA Web site at www.va.gov/facilities.

News Media Representatives may contact VA through the nearest regional Office of Public Affairs: Atlanta (404–929–5880); Chicago (312–980–4235); Dallas (817–385–3720); Denver (303–914–5855); Los Angeles (310–268–4207); New York (212–807–3429); Washington, DC (202–530–9360). National media may contact the Office of Public Affairs in the VA Central Office, 810 Vermont Avenue NW., Washington, DC 20420. Phone, (202) 461–7400.

Publications The "Annual Performance and Accountability Report" may be obtained online at http://www.va.gov/ budget/report/.

The 2010 VA pamphlet, "Federal Benefits for Veterans, Dependents and Survivors" (80–98–1), is available for sale by the Superintendent of Documents, Government Printing Office, Washington, DC 20402. This publication is also available at http://www.va.gov/opa/ publication.

The "Board of Veterans Appeals Index" (I–01–1), an index to appellate decisions, is available on microfiche in annual accumulation from July 1977 through December 1994. The quarterly indexes may be purchased for $7 and annual cumulative indexes for $22.50. The "VADEX/CITATOR of Appellate Research Materials" is a complete printed quarterly looseleaf accumulation of research material which may be purchased for $175 with binder and for $160 without binder. The Vadex Infobase, a computer-searchable version of the VADEX, is also available on diskettes for $100 per copy. These publications may be obtained by contacting Promisel and Korn, Inc. Phone, 301–986–0650. Archived BVA decisions are available at www.va.gov.

An April 2002 pamphlet entitled "How Do I Appeal" (01–02–02A) is available at www.bva.va.gov. Printed copies can be obtained at Mail Processing Section (014), Board of Veterans' Appeals, 810 Vermont Avenue, NW., Washington, DC 20420. There is no charge for individual copies. A large quantity of pamphlets may be purchased from the Superintendent of Documents, Government Printing Office, Washington, DC 20402. Call 202–512–1800 or visit www.gpoacess.gov/index. html for more information.

The VA pamphlet, "A Summary of Department of Veteran Affairs Benefits" (27–82–2), may be obtained without charge from any VA regional office.

"Interments in VA National Cemeteries", VA NCA–IS–1, details eligibility information and contains a list of both national and State veterans cemeteries. Copies may be obtained without charge from the National Cemetery Administration (41C1), 810

Vermont Avenue NW., Washington, DC 20420. Call 800–827–1000 or visit www.cem.va.gov for more information.

VA's annual budget submission may be obtained online at http://www.va.gov/budget.

For further information, contact the Office of Public and Intergovernmental Affairs, Department of Veterans Affairs, 810 Vermont Avenue NW., Washington, DC 20420. Phone, 202–273–6000. Internet, http://www.va.gov/opa.

EXECUTIVE BRANCH: INDEPENDENT AGENCIES AND GOVERNMENT CORPORATIONS

ADMINISTRATIVE CONFERENCE OF THE UNITED STATES

1120 Twentieth Street NW., Suite 706 South, Washington, DC 20036
Phone, 202–480–2080. Fax, 202–386–7190. Internet, http://www.acus.gov.

Chairman	Paul R. Verkuil
Executive Director	Matthew L. Wiener
Research Director	Gretchen E. Jacobs
General Counsel	Shawne C. McGibbon
Deputy General Counsel	David M. Pritzker
Chief Financial and Operations Officer	Harry M. Seidman
Communications Director	Megan C. Kindelan
Council	
Vice Chair	Thomasina V. Rogers
Members	Preeta D. Bansal, Ronald A. Cass, Steven P. Croley, Mariano-Florentino Cuéllar, Theodore B. Olson, Edith Ramirez, Jane C. Sherburne, Geovette E. Washington, (vacancy)

The Administrative Conference develops recommendations for improving the fairness and effectiveness of procedures by which Federal agencies administer regulatory, benefit, and other Government programs.

The Administrative Conference of the United States was established as a permanent independent agency by the Administrative Conference Act (5 U.S.C. 591–596) enacted in 1964. The Conference was the successor to two temporary Administrative Conferences during the Eisenhower and Kennedy administrations.

The Conference ceased operations on October 31, 1995, due to termination of funding by Congress. Congress reauthorized the Conference in 2004 and again in 2008. The 2004 legislation expanded its responsibilities to include specific attention to achieving more effective public participation and efficiency, reducing unnecessary litigation, and improving the use of science in the rulemaking process. Funding was approved in 2009, and the

ADMINISTRATIVE CONFERENCE OF THE UNITED STATES

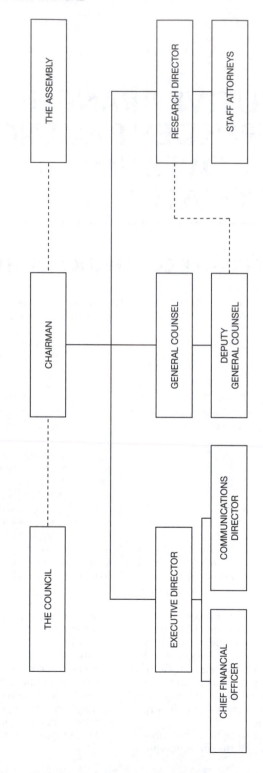

Conference was officially re-established in March 2010.

By statute the Administrative Conference has no fewer than 75 and no more than 101 members, a majority of whom are Government officials. The Chairman of the Conference is appointed by the President with the advice and consent of the Senate for a 5-year term. The Council, which acts as the executive board, consists of the Chairman and 10 other members appointed by the President for 3-year terms. Federal officials named to the Council may constitute no more than half of the total Council membership. The Chairman is the only full-time, compensated member of the Conference. Members representing the private sector are appointed by the Chairman, with the approval of the Council, for 2-year terms.

The entire membership is divided into committees, each assigned a broad area of interest such as adjudication, administration, collaborative governance, judicial review, regulation, or rulemaking. The membership meeting in plenary session constitutes the Assembly of the Conference, which by statute must meet at least once, and customarily meets twice, each year.

Activities

Subjects for inquiry are developed by the Chairman and approved by the Council, often based on input from government and nongovernment experts in administrative procedure. The committees conduct thorough studies of these subjects and propose recommendations, based on supporting reports, ordinarily prepared for the Conference by expert consultants. Recommendations are evaluated by the Council and, if ready for Assembly consideration, are distributed to the membership with the supporting reports and placed on the agenda of the next plenary session for discussion and a final vote. The deliberations of the committees and Assembly are open to the public.

Recommendations adopted by the Conference may be addressed to administrative agencies, Congress, the President, or the Judicial Conference. Most recommendations call for action on the part of affected agencies or for new legislation. A substantial number of recommendations were implemented prior to the termination of Conference activities in 1995, and implementation activities are underway for the newer recommendations.

The Chairman may make independent inquiries into procedural matters, including matters proposed by individuals inside or outside the Government. The purpose of such inquiries is to determine whether the problems should be made the subject of Conference study in the interest of developing fairer and more effective or efficient procedures.

Upon the request of the head of a department or agency, the Chairman is authorized to furnish advice and assistance on matters of administrative procedure. The Conference may collect information and statistics from departments and agencies and publish such reports as it considers useful for evaluating and improving administrative processes. The Conference also serves as a forum for the interchange among departments and agencies of information that may be useful in improving administrative practices and procedures.

Sources of Information

The Conference makes available copies of its recommendations and reports, news on work currently in progress, and the Chairman's annual report. Most of this information, including documents, publications, and recommendations, is available online.

For further information, contact the Office of the Chairman, Administrative Conference of the United States, 1120 Twentieth Street NW., Suite 706 South, Washington, DC 20036. Phone, 202–480–2080. Fax, 202–386–7190. Email, info@acus.gov. Internet, http://www.acus.gov.

AFRICAN DEVELOPMENT FOUNDATION

1400 I Street NW., Suite 1000, Washington, DC 20005
Phone, 202–673–3916. Fax, 202–673–3810. Internet, http://www.usadf.gov.

Board of Directors

Chairman	JOHN W. LESLIE, JR.
Vice Chairman	JOHN O. AGWUNOBI
Board Members	MIMI ALEMAYEHOU, WARD BREHM, MORGAN M. DAVIS, IQBAL PAROO, (VACANCY)

Staff

President	SHARI BERENBACH
General Counsel	DORIS MASON MARTIN
Chief Financial Officer and Director for Strategic Planning	WILLIAM E. SCHUERCH

[For the African Development Foundation statement of organization, see the Code of Federal Regulations, Title 22, Part 1501]

The African Development Foundation promotes development and empowerment in Africa and enhances and strengthens U.S. relations with Africa through effective development assistance.

The African Development Foundation was established by the African Development Foundation Act (22 U.S.C. 290h) as a Government corporation to support the self-help efforts of the poor in Africa. The Foundation is led by a Board of Directors, consisting of a Chairman, a Vice Chairman, and five Board Members, nominated by the President with the advice and consent on the Senate.

The Foundation invests in private and nongovernmental organizations in Africa to promote and support innovative enterprise development, generate jobs, and increase incomes of the poor. It seeks to expand local institutional and financial capacities to foster entrepreneurship, ownership, and community-based economic development among marginalized and underserved populations in sub-Saharan Africa.

For further information, contact the Office of the President, African Development Foundation, 1400 I Street NW., Suite 1000, Washington, DC 20005–2248. Phone, 202–673–3916. Fax, 202–673–3810. Email, info@usadf.gov. Internet, http://www.usadf.gov.

BROADCASTING BOARD OF GOVERNORS

330 Independence Avenue SW., Washington, DC 20237
Phone, 202–203–4545. Internet, http://www.bbg.gov.

Chairman	JEFFREY SHELL
Board Members	MATTHEW C. ARMSTRONG, RYAN C. CROCKER, SUSAN MCCUE, MICHAEL P. MEEHAN, KENNETH WEINSTEIN, (2 VACANCIES)
Secretary of State (ex officio)	JOHN F. KERRY
General Counsel	PAUL KOLLMER-DORSEY
Chief Financial Officer	LESLIE HYLAND
Director, Global Strategy	ROBERT BOLE
Director, Global Communications	SUZIE CARROLL

Director, Global Operations	ANDRÉ MENDES
Deputy Director, International Broadcasting Bureau	JEFFREY N. TRIMBLE
Director, Office of Communications and External Affairs	LYNNE WEIL
Director, Office of Strategy and Development Planning and Performance Measurement	BRUCE SHERMAN
Director, Office of Digital and Design Innovation	ADAM MARTIN, *Acting*
Director, Office of Marketing and Program Placement	DOUG BOYNTON
Director, Office of Performance Review	JOHN LIPPMAN, *Acting*
Director, Office of Civil Rights	DELIA L. JOHNSON
Director, Office of Contracts	CHERYLYNN PETERS, *Acting*
Director, Office of Human Resources	DONNA GRACE
Director, Office of Security	FRED LANG, *Acting*
Director, Office of Policy	CHARLES GOOLSBY
Director, Office of Technology, Services and Innovation, and Chief Information Officer	TERRY BALAZS, *Acting*
Director, Voice of America	DAVID ENSOR
Director, Office of Cuba Broadcasting	CARLOS A. GARCÍA-PÉREZ
President, Radio Free Europe/Radio Libertys	JOHN GIAMBALVO, *Acting*, NENAD PEJIC, *Acting*
President, Radio Free Asia	LIBBY LIU
President, Middle East Broadcasting Networks	BRIAN T. CONNIFF

The Broadcasting Board of Governors informs, engages, and connects people around the world in support of freedom and democracy.

The Broadcasting Board of Governors (BBG) became an independent agency on October 1, 1999, by authority of the Foreign Affairs Reform and Restructuring Act of 1998 (22 U.S.C. 6501 note). It is composed of nine members. Eight members are appointed by the President and confirmed by the Senate; the ninth, an ex officio member, is the Secretary of State.

The BBG serves as the governing body for all civilian U.S. international media and provides programming in 61 languages via radio, television, and the Internet. The BBG broadcast services include the Voice of America, the Office of Cuba Broadcasting, Radio Free Europe/ Radio Liberty, Radio Free Asia, and the Middle East Broadcasting Networks. The BBG relies on the International Broadcasting Bureau for transmission and technical support of its broadcast services.

All BBG broadcast services adhere to the broadcasting standards and principles of the International Broadcasting Act of 1994, which include reliable, accurate, and comprehensive news; balanced and comprehensive presentations of U.S. thought, institutions, and policies, as well as discussions about those policies; information about developments throughout the world; and a variety of opinions from nations around the world.

Activities

International Broadcasting Bureau The International Broadcasting Bureau (IBB) provides program delivery and essential support services for U.S. international media. The IBB is responsible for the BBG's strategic planning and for integrating activities across the Federal and grantee broadcasters for greater organizational efficiency. The IBB manages a global network of transmitting sites, an extensive system of leased satellite and fiber optic circuits, and an increasing variety of rapidly growing Internet and mobile audience platforms and services. The IBB is responsible

BROADCASTING BOARD OF GOVERNORS

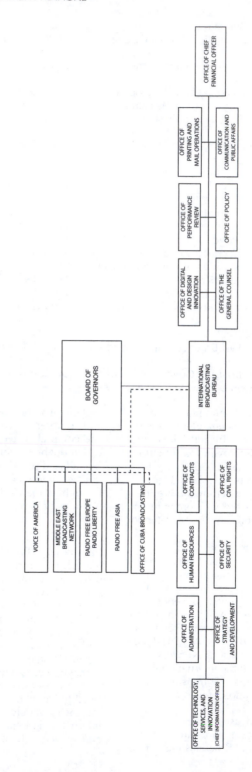

for program placement services and marketing for all BBG broadcast organizations. It provides research and evaluations of broadcasts. The IBB manages the BBG's financial operations, legal support, and communications. It also provides information technology, human resources, Equal Employment Opportunity, procurement, security, and other administrative support for the agency.

Internet, http://www.bbg.gov.

Voice of America   The Voice of America (VOA) is a multimedia international broadcasting service funded by the U.S. Government through the Broadcasting Board of Governors. VOA began broadcasting in 1942 and now reaches more than 164 million people worldwide. VOA provides accurate, comprehensive, and trustworthy news and information, as well as informed discussion about the United States and the world. It strives to engage audiences in regions deemed critical to the U.S. through the preferred medium—radio, television, Internet, or digital media— of the people in those regions. VOA broadcasts approximately 1,800 hours of news, information, educational, and cultural programming every week to a global audience. Programs are produced in 45 languages.

Internet, http://www.voanews.com.

Radio Free Europe/Radio Liberty
Radio Free Europe/Radio Liberty (RFE/RL) is a private nonprofit corporation reaching more than 19 million people in 28 languages and in 21 countries, including Afghanistan, Iran, Iraq, Pakistan, and Russia. RFE/RL journalists provide what many people cannot get locally: uncensored news, responsible discussion, and open debate. RFE/RL uses the latest digital technologies—the Internet, SMS text messaging, online video, satellite radio, and popular social media networks—and trusted broadcast radio to reach people in some of the most closed societies on Earth. With more than 60 years of surrogate broadcasting experience, RFE/RL continues to bring audiences the rich, immediate, and

interactive content they seek. RFE/RL is funded by a grant from the BBG.

Internet, http://www.rferl.org.

Radio Free Asia   Radio Free Asia (RFA) is a private, nonprofit news organization, operating under a grant from the BBG. Broadcasting daily in nine languages to listeners in Asia whose governments restrict media, RFA delivers award-winning, reliable news and information, along with a range of voices and opinions from within Asia, to demonstrate freedom of expression over the airwaves, on television, and online. Through shortwave, medium wave, satellite and transmission television, social media, and the Internet, RFA broadcasts in Mandarin, Cantonese, Uyghur, three Tibetan dialects, Burmese, Vietnamese, Korean, Lao, and Khmer. Headquartered in Washington, DC, RFA has seven overseas bureaus and a vast network of correspondents around the world.

Internet, http://www.rfa.org.

Middle East Broadcasting Networks
The Middle East Broadcasting Networks, Inc. (MBN) is the nonprofit news organization that operates Alhurra Television, Radio Sawa, and MBN Digital under a grant from the BBG. Alhurra, Radio Sawa, and MBN Digital provide an open line of communication between the people of the Middle East and the United States. MBN's networks deliver accurate information on the United States, its policies, and its people with a broad range of perspectives and an exchange of ideas on relevant issues. MBN networks have an audience of more than 30 million people in 21 countries in the Middle East and North Africa.

Internet, http://www.alhurra.com/.

Office of Cuba Broadcasting   The Office of Cuba Broadcasting conducts the operations of the Martís at its headquarters in Miami, FL. The Martís are a multimedia hub of news, information, and analysis that provides the people of Cuba with interactive programs 7 days a week through television (satellite and transmission), shortwave and medium wave radio, as well as flash drives, emails, DVDs, and SMS text. Combined with the online platform, martinoticias. com, they are a one-of-kind service that brings objective information to all Cubans.

Internet, http://www.martinoticias.com.

For further information, contact the Office of Public Affairs, Broadcasting Board of Governors, 330 Independence Avenue SW., Washington, DC 20237. Phone, 202–203–4400. Fax, 202–203–4961. Email, publicaffairs@bbg.gov. Internet, http://www.bbg.gov.

CENTRAL INTELLIGENCE AGENCY

Washington, DC 20505
Phone, 703–482–0623. Internet, http://www.cia.gov.

Director	JOHN O. BRENNAN
Deputy Director	AVRIL D. HAINES

[For the Central Intelligence Agency statement of organization, see the Code of Federal Regulations, Title 32, Part 1900]

The Central Intelligence Agency collects, evaluates, and disseminates vital information on political, military, economic, scientific, and other developments abroad needed to safeguard national security.

The Central Intelligence Agency was established by the National Security Act of 1947, as amended (50 U.S.C. 401 et seq.). It now functions under that statute, Executive Order 12333 of December 4, 1981, the Intelligence Reform and Terrorism Prevention Act of 2004 (50 U.S.C. 401 note), and other laws, Executive orders, regulations, and directives.

The Central Intelligence Agency is headed by the Director, whom the President appoints with the advice and consent of the Senate.

The Central Intelligence Agency uses human source collection and other appropriate means to gather intelligence; however, it neither carries out internal security functions nor exercises police, subpoena, or other law enforcement powers. The Agency correlates, evaluates, and disseminates national security intelligence. It also directs and coordinates intelligence collecting outside the United States by U.S. Intelligence Community elements authorized to engage in human source collection.

In coordination with other departments, agencies, and authorized elements of the United States Government, the Agency ensures that resources are used effectively and that adequate consideration is given to the risks, both to the United States and to those involved in collecting intelligence abroad. The Agency carries out other intelligence-related tasks that are necessary for safeguarding national security, as the President or the Director of National Intelligence (DNI) may indicate. Under the direction of the DNI and consistent with section 207 of the Foreign Service Act of 1980, the Agency coordinates relationships between elements of the U.S. Intelligence Community and the security or intelligence services of foreign governments or international organizations in matters of national security and clandestine intelligence.

For further information, contact the Central Intelligence Agency, Office of Public Affairs, Washington, DC 20505. Phone, 703–482–0623. Fax, 571–204–3800. Internet, https://www.cia.gov.

COMMODITY FUTURES TRADING COMMISSION

1155 Twenty-first Street NW, Washington, DC 20581
Phone, 202–418–5000. Fax, 202–418–5521. Internet, http://www.cftc.gov.

Chairman	TIMOTHY G. MASSAD
Commissioners	SHARON Y. BOWEN, J. CHRISTOPHER
	GIANCARLO, SCOTT D. O'MALIA,
	(VACANCY)
General Counsel	JONATHAN L. MARCUS
Executive Director	ANTHONY C. THOMPSON
Director, Division of Market Oversight	VINCE A. MCGONAGLE
Director, Division of Clearing and Risk	ANANDA RADHAKRISHNAN
Director, Division of Swap Dealer and	GARY BARNETT
Intermediary Oversight	
Director, Division of Enforcement	GRETCHEN LOWE
Director, Office of International Affairs	SARAH JOSEPHSON
Chief Economist	SAYEE SRINIVASAN
Chief Information Officer	JOHN ROGERS

[For the Commodity Futures Trading Commission statement of organization, see the Code of Federal Regulations, Title 17, Part 140]

The Commodity Futures Trading Commission fosters open, competitive, and financially sound markets by protecting market users and the public from fraud, manipulation, abusive practices, and systemic risk related to derivatives subject to the Commodity Exchange Act.

The Commodity Futures Trading Commission was established by the Commodity Futures Trading Commission Act of 1974 (7 U.S.C. 2). The Commission began operation in April 1975, and its authority to regulate futures trading was renewed by Congress in 1978, 1982, 1986, 1992, 1995, 2000, and 2008. In 2010, the Dodd-Frank Wall Street Reform and Consumer Protection Act (12 U.S.C. 5301 et seq.) gave the Commission new and expanded responsibilities and authorities for regulation of the swaps marketplace.

The Commission consists of five Commissioners who are appointed by the President, with the advice and consent of the Senate. One Commissioner is designated by the President to serve as Chairman. The Commissioners serve staggered 5-year terms, and by law no more than three Commissioners can belong to the same political party. The Commission has nine major operating components: the Divisions of Market Oversight, Clearing and Risk, Swap Dealer and Intermediary Oversight, Enforcement, and the Offices of the Executive Director, the General Counsel, the Chief Economist, International Affairs, and Data and Technology.

Activities

The Commission regulates trading on the U.S. futures and options markets, which offer commodity futures and options contracts, as well as the swaps marketplace in the United States. This oversight of the derivatives marketplace is carried out through the various activities of the Commission.

The Commission oversees derivatives clearing organizations and other market participants in the clearing process, including futures commission merchants, swap dealers, major swap participants, and large traders. In addition, the Commission oversees the registration and compliance of intermediaries and futures industry self-regulatory organizations, including U.S. derivatives exchanges and the National Futures Association. The Commission also oversees trade execution facilities and data repositories, conducts surveillance, reviews new exchange applications, and examines

COMMODITY FUTURES TRADING COMMISSION

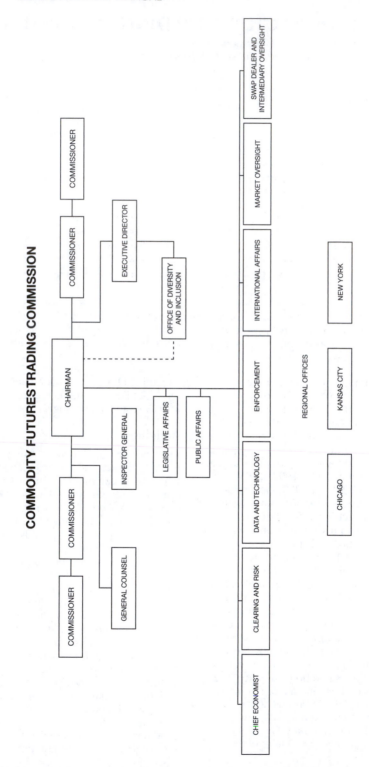

COMMISSIONER

COMMISSIONER

COMMISSIONER

COMMISSIONER

CHAIRMAN

EXECUTIVE DIRECTOR

OFFICE OF DIVERSITY AND INCLUSION

GENERAL COUNSEL

INSPECTOR GENERAL

LEGISLATIVE AFFAIRS

PUBLIC AFFAIRS

CHIEF ECONOMIST

CLEARING AND RISK

DATA AND TECHNOLOGY

ENFORCEMENT

INTERNATIONAL AFFAIRS

MARKET OVERSIGHT

SWAP DEALER AND INTERMEDIARY OVERSIGHT

REGIONAL OFFICES

CHICAGO

KANSAS CITY

NEW YORK

existing exchanges to ensure compliance with applicable core principles. Under the Dodd-Frank Act, the Commission is also responsible for developing and monitoring compliance with regulations addressing registration, business conduct standards, capital adequacy, and margin requirements for swap dealers and major swap participants.

Exercising the Commission's authority, its staff also investigates and prosecutes alleged violations of the Commodity Exchange Act and Commission

regulations. Potential violations include fraud, manipulation, and other abuses concerning commodity derivatives and swaps that threaten market integrity, market participants, and the general public.

The Commission maintains regional offices in Chicago, IL, and New York, NY, where many of the Nation's designated contract markets are located. An additional regional office is located in Kansas City, MO.

For further information, contact the Office of Public Affairs, Commodity Futures Trading Commission, 1155 Twenty-first Street NW., Washington, DC 20581. Phone, 202–418–5080. Internet, http://www.cftc.gov.

CONSUMER FINANCIAL PROTECTION BUREAU

1700 G Street NW., Washington, DC 20552
Phone, 202–435–7000. Internet, http://www.consumerfinance.gov.

Director	RICHARD CORDRAY
Deputy Director	STEVEN ANTONAKES
Chief of Staff, Office of the Director	CHRISTOPHER D'ANGELO
Ombudsman	WENDY KAMENSHINE
Administrative Law Judge	(VACANCY)
Chief Operating Officer	SARTAJ ALAG
Chief Administrative Officer	SUZANNE TOSINI
Chief Financial Officer	STEPHEN AGOSTINI
Chief Human Capital Officer	DENNIS SLAGTER
Chief Information Officer	ASHWIN VASAN
Assistant Director, Office of Consumer Response	SCOTT PLUTA
Director, Office of Minority and Women Inclusion	STUART ISHIMARU
Chief Procurement Officer	DAVID GRAGAN
Assistant Director, Office of Equal Opportunity Employment	M. STACEY BACH
Associate Director, Consumer Education and Engagement	GAIL HILLEBRAND
Assistant Director, Consumer Engagement	PETER JACKSON
Assistant Director, Financial Education	CAMILLE BUSETTE
Assistant Director, Financial Empowerment	DANIEL DODD-RAMIREZ
Assistant Director, Older Americans	NORA EISENHOWER
Assistant Director, Servicemember Affairs	HOLLISTER PETRAEUS
Assistant Director, Students	ROHIT CHOPRA
Associate Director, Supervision, Enforcement, and Fair Lending	STEVEN ANTONAKES
Assistant Director, Enforcement	KENT MARKUS
Assistant Director, Fair Lending and Equal Opportunity	PATRICE FICKLIN
Assistant Director, Office of Supervision Examinations	PAUL SANFORD

Assistant Director, Office of Supervision Policy	PEGGY TWOHIG
Associate Director, Markets and Regulations	DAVID SILBERMAN
Assistant Director, Card Markets	WILLIAM WADE-GERY, *Acting*
Assistant Director, Credit Information, Collections, and Deposits Markets	BAYARD STONE, JR.
Assistant Director, Installment and Liquidity Lending Markets	JEFFREY LANGER
Assistant Director, Mortgage Markets	ABHISHEK AGARWAL, *Acting*
Assistant Director, Regulations	KELLY COCHRAN
Assistant Director, Research	CHRISTOPHER CARROLL
Associate Director, External Affairs	ZIXTA MARTINEZ
Assistant Director, Communications	JENNIFER HOWARD
Assistant Director, Community Affairs	CHRIS VAETH
Assistant Director, Office of Financial Institutions and Business Liaisons	DANIEL SMITH
Staff Director, Consumer Advisory Board and Councils	DELICIA HAND
Assistant Director, Intergovernmental Affairs	CHERYL PARKER-ROSE
Assistant Director, Legislative Affairs	CATHERINE GALICIA
General Counsel	MEREDITH FUCHS
Principal Deputy General Counsel	(VACANCY)
Deputy General Counsel, General Law and Ethics	RICHARD LEPLEY
Deputy General Counsel, Oversight, Litigation and Enforcement Support	TO-QUYEN TRUONG
Deputy General Counsel, Law and Policy	STEPHEN VAN METER

The Consumer Financial Protection Bureau educates consumers to recognize predatory practices; enforces Federal consumer financial laws and supervises banks, credit unions, and other financial companies; and studies consumer financial markets, financial services providers, and consumers.

The Consumer Financial Protection Bureau (CFPB) is an independent Federal agency established by title X of the Dodd-Frank Wall Street Reform and Consumer Protection Act of 2012 (12 U.S.C. 5491). CFPB is headed by a Director, whom the President appoints and the Senate confirms.

The Bureau regulates the offering and provision of consumer financial products and services under Federal consumer financial laws. It works to give consumers the information they need to understand the terms of their agreements with financial companies. It also works to make regulations and guidance as clear and streamlined as possible so providers of consumer financial products and services can understand and follow the rules without assistance.

CFPB's principal activities center on writing rules, supervising companies, and enforcing Federal consumer financial

protection laws; restricting unfair, deceptive, or abusive acts or practices; taking consumer complaints; promoting financial education; researching consumer behavior; monitoring financial markets for new risks to consumers; and enforcing laws that prohibit discrimination and other unfair treatment in consumer finance.

Sources of Information

Consumer Help For consumer help, call 855–411–2372, 8 a.m. to 8 p.m. eastern standard time, weekdays. TTY/TDD, 855–729–2372. Information is also available by writing to the Consumer Financial Protection Bureau, P.O. Box 4503, Iowa City, IA 52244. Email, info@ consumerfinance.gov. Internet, http://www.consumerfinance.gov/askcfpb/.

Publications Bulk orders of CFPB publications, in both English and Spanish,

CONSUMER FINANCIAL PROTECTION BUREAU

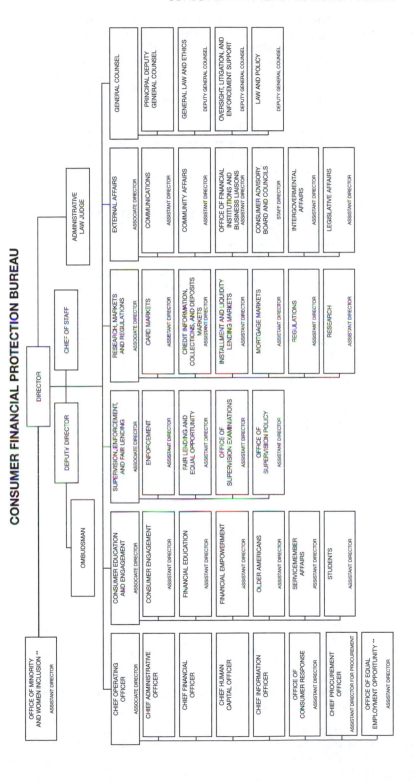

DIRECTOR

ADMINISTRATIVE LAW JUDGE

CHIEF OF STAFF

DEPUTY DIRECTOR

OMBUDSMAN

OFFICE OF MINORITY AND WOMEN INCLUSION **
ASSISTANT DIRECTOR

GENERAL COUNSEL
PRINCIPAL DEPUTY GENERAL COUNSEL
GENERAL LAW AND ETHICS
DEPUTY GENERAL COUNSEL
OVERSIGHT, LITIGATION, AND ENFORCEMENT SUPPORT
DEPUTY GENERAL COUNSEL
LAW AND POLICY
DEPUTY GENERAL COUNSEL

EXTERNAL AFFAIRS
ASSOCIATE DIRECTOR
COMMUNICATIONS
ASSISTANT DIRECTOR
COMMUNITY AFFAIRS
ASSISTANT DIRECTOR
OFFICE OF FINANCIAL INSTITUTIONS AND BUSINESS LIAISONS
ASSISTANT DIRECTOR
CONSUMER ADVISORY BOARD AND COUNCILS
STAFF DIRECTOR
INTERGOVERNMENTAL AFFAIRS
ASSISTANT DIRECTOR
LEGISLATIVE AFFAIRS
ASSISTANT DIRECTOR

RESEARCH, MARKETS AND REGULATIONS
ASSOCIATE DIRECTOR
CARD MARKETS
ASSISTANT DIRECTOR
CREDIT INFORMATION, COLLECTIONS, AND DEPOSITS MARKETS
ASSISTANT DIRECTOR
INSTALLMENT AND LIQUIDITY LENDING MARKETS
ASSISTANT DIRECTOR
MORTGAGE MARKETS
ASSISTANT DIRECTOR
REGULATIONS
ASSISTANT DIRECTOR
RESEARCH
ASSISTANT DIRECTOR

SUPERVISION, ENFORCEMENT, AND FAIR LENDING
ASSOCIATE DIRECTOR
ENFORCEMENT
ASSISTANT DIRECTOR
FAIR LENDING AND EQUAL OPPORTUNITY
ASSISTANT DIRECTOR
OFFICE OF SUPERVISION EXAMINATIONS
ASSISTANT DIRECTOR
OFFICE OF SUPERVISION POLICY
ASSISTANT DIRECTOR

CONSUMER EDUCATION AND ENGAGEMENT
ASSOCIATE DIRECTOR
CONSUMER ENGAGEMENT
ASSISTANT DIRECTOR
FINANCIAL EDUCATION
ASSISTANT DIRECTOR
FINANCIAL EMPOWERMENT
ASSISTANT DIRECTOR
OLDER AMERICANS
ASSISTANT DIRECTOR
SERVICEMEMBER AFFAIRS
ASSISTANT DIRECTOR
STUDENTS
ASSISTANT DIRECTOR

CHIEF OPERATING OFFICER
ASSOCIATE DIRECTOR
CHIEF ADMINISTRATIVE OFFICER
CHIEF FINANCIAL OFFICER
CHIEF HUMAN CAPITAL OFFICER
CHIEF INFORMATION OFFICER
OFFICE OF CONSUMER RESPONSE
ASSISTANT DIRECTOR
CHIEF PROCUREMENT OFFICER
ASSISTANT DIRECTOR FOR PROCUREMENT
OFFICE OF EQUAL EMPLOYMENT OPPORTUNITY **
ASSISTANT DIRECTOR

** Position has direct reporting responsibilities to the Director.

can be ordered online. Internet, http://promotions.usa.gov/cfpbpubs.html.
Whistleblowers   The Bureau welcomes tips from people who know of potential Federal consumer financial law violations. Whistleblowers and law enforcement tipsters, including current or former employees of potential

violators, contractors, vendors, or industry competitors, should call 855–695–7974 or send an email to whistleblower@cfpb.gov. Internet, http://www.consumerfinance.gov/blog/the-cfpb-wants-you-to-blow-the-whistle-on-lawbreakers/.

For further information, contact the Consumer Financial Protection Bureau, 1700 G Street NW., Washington, DC 20552. Phone, 202–435–7000. Email, info@consumerfinance.gov. Internet, http://www.consumerfinance. gov.

CONSUMER PRODUCT SAFETY COMMISSION

4330 East-West Highway, Bethesda, MD 20814
Phone, 301–504–7923. Internet, http://www.cpsc.gov.

Chair	ROBERT S. ADLER, *Acting*
Commissioners	ANN M. BUERKLE, MARIETTA ROBINSON, JOSEPH P. MOHOROVIC, ELLIOT F. KAYE
General Counsel	STEPHANIE TSACOUMIS
Director, Office of Legislative Affairs	JENILEE KEEFE SINGER, *Acting*
Director, the Secretariat	TODD A. STEVENSON
Director, Office of Equal Employment Opportunity and Minority Enterprise	KATHLEEN V. BUTTREY
Executive Director	ELLIOT KAYE
Deputy Executive Director, Operations Support	DEWANE RAY
Deputy Executive Director, Safety Operations	JAY HOWELL
Assistant Executive Director, Office of Hazard Identification and Reduction	GEORGE BORLASE
Inspector General	CHRISTOPHER W. DENTEL
Director, Office of Human Resources Management	DONNA M. SIMPSON
Director, Office of Global Outreach, Education, and Small Business Ombudsman	JAY HOWELL
Assistant Executive Director, Office of Information and Technology Services	PATRICK D. WEDDLE
Director, Office of Communications	SCOTT J. WOLFSON
Director, Office of Financial Management, Planning and Evaluation	JAY HOFFMAN
Director, Office of Compliance and Field Operations	MARC J. SCHOEM
Director, Office of Import Survelliance	CAROL CAVE
Director, Office of Facilities	DOUGLAS BROWN

[For the Consumer Product Safety Commission statement of organization, see the Code of Federal Regulations, Title 16, Part 1000]

The Consumer Product Safety Commission protects the public by reducing the risk of injuries and deaths from consumer products.

The Consumer Product Safety Commission was established as an

independent regulatory agency by the Consumer Product Safety Act

CONSUMER PRODUCT SAFETY COMMISSION

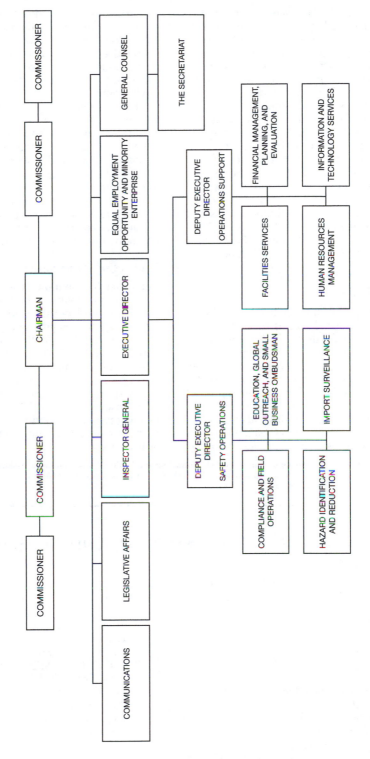

(15 U.S.C. 2051 et seq.) in 1973 and reauthorized by the Consumer Product Safety Improvement Act of 2008. The Commission consists of up to five members, who are appointed by the President with the advice and consent of the Senate, for 7-year terms.

The Commission implements provisions of the Flammable Fabrics Act (15 U.S.C. 1191); Poison Prevention Packaging Act of 1970 (15 U.S.C. 1471); Federal Hazardous Substances Act (15 U.S.C. 1261); act of August 2, 1956 (15 U.S.C. 1211), prohibiting the transportation of refrigerators without door safety devices; Children's Gasoline Burn Prevention Act (15 U.S.C. 2056 note); and Virginia Graeme Baker Pool and Spa Safety Act (15 U.S.C. 8001 et seq.).

Activities

To help protect the public from risks of injury and deaths associated with consumer products, the Commission requires manufacturers to report defects in products that could present substantial hazards and carry out consumer recalls to address hazards in consumer products; collects information on consumer product-related injuries and maintains an Injury Information Clearinghouse; conducts research on consumer product hazards; assists in the development of voluntary safety standards; establishes mandatory consumer product standards; bans hazardous consumer products; and conducts outreach programs for consumers, industry, and local governments.

CPSC operates SaferProducts.gov, where consumers can view and report on unsafe consumer products. The Commission also has a special project to reach underserved Americans. The Neighborhood Safety Network is an effort to disseminate safety information to hard-to-reach populations by partnering with organizations within these populations. Organizations may register for this program at www.cpsc.gov/nsn.

Sources of Information

Consumer Information   The Commission operates a toll-free Consumer Product Safety Hotline, 800–638–2772 (English and Spanish), and a teletypewriter for the hearing-impaired, 800–595–7054. Additional safety information may be obtained from www.Recalls.gov, www.PoolSafely.gov, and www.ATVSafety.gov. Internet, http://www.cpsc.gov.
Reading Room   A public information room is maintained at the Commission's headquarters.

For further information, contact the Office of Information and Public Affairs, Consumer Product Safety Commission, 4330 East-West Highway, Bethesda, MD 20814. Phone, 301–504–7908. Email, info@cpsc.gov. Internet, http://www.cpsc.gov.

CORPORATION FOR NATIONAL AND COMMUNITY SERVICE

1201 New York Avenue NW., Washington, DC 20525
Phone, 202–606–5000. Internet, http://www.nationalservice.gov.

Chair	LISA GARCÍA QUIROZ
Vice Chair	(VACANCY)
Members	JANET HARTLEY, HYEPIN IM, MATTHEW F. MCCABE, PHYLLIS N. SEGAL, (9 VACANCIES)
Chief Executive Officer	WENDY SPENCER
Chief of Staff	ASIM MISHRA
Inspector General	DEBORAH J. JEFFREY
Chief Financial Officer	DAVID REBICH

The Corporation for National and Community Service fosters civic engagement through service and volunteering.

The Corporation for National and Community Service (CNCS) was established on October 1, 1993, by the National and Community Service Trust Act of 1993 (42 U.S.C. 12651 et seq.). CNCS is a Federal corporation governed by a 15-member bipartisan Board of Directors, appointed by the President and with the advice and consent of the Senate. The Board has responsibility for overall policy direction of the Corporation's activities and has the power to make all final grant decisions, approve the strategic plan and annual budget, and advise and make recommendations to the President and the Congress regarding changes in the national service laws.

As the nation's largest grantmaker for service and volunteering, CNCS engages more than 5 million Americans in service through its core programs—AmeriCorps, Senior Corps, the Social Innovation Fund, and the Volunteer Generation Fund—and leads President Obama's national call to service initiative, United We Serve. CNCS harnesses America's most powerful resource: the energy and talents of our citizens. From grade school through retirement, CNCS empowers Americans and fosters a lifetime of service to improve lives, strengthen communities, and foster civic engagement.

AmeriCorps AmeriCorps provides intensive opportunities for more than 75,000 Americans each year to serve their communities. AmeriCorps members recruit, train, and supervise community volunteers, tutor and mentor youth, build affordable housing, teach computer skills, clean parks and streams, run afterschool programs, and help communities respond to disasters and nonprofit groups to become self-sustaining. In exchange for a year of full-time service, AmeriCorps members earn an education award that can be used to pay for college or graduate school, or to pay back qualified student loans. Since 1994 more than 800,000 Americans have served in AmeriCorps. AmeriCorps has three main programs: AmeriCorps*State and National, AmeriCorps*NCCC, and AmeriCorps*VISTA.

AmeriCorps*State and National supports a wide range of local service programs that engage thousands of Americans in intensive community service each year, providing grants to a network of local and national organizations and agencies committed to using national service to address critical community needs in education, public safety, health, and the environment. Each of these organizations and agencies, in turn, uses their AmeriCorps funding to recruit, place, and supervise AmeriCorps members nationwide.

AmeriCorps*State and National operates through national and local nonprofit organizations, public agencies, and faith-based and community groups. More than three-quarters of AmeriCorps grant funding goes to Governor-appointed State Service commissions, which in turn award grants

CORPORATION FOR NATIONAL AND COMMUNITY SERVICE

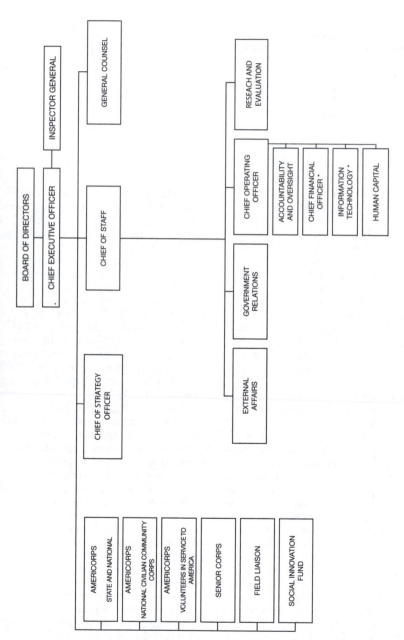

* Denotes staff that also have reporting line to the Chief Executive Officer.

to nonprofit groups to respond to local needs. AmeriCorps*NCCC (National Civilian Community Corps) is a team-based, residential program for men and women from age 18 to 24 that combines the best practices of civilian service, including leadership and team building. AmeriCorps*VISTA (Volunteers in Service to America) members serve full-time, for 1 year, in nonprofits, public agencies, and faith-based organizations to fight poverty, improve health services, increase housing opportunities, and bridge the digital divide.

Senior Corps   Senior Corps taps the skills, talents, and experience of more than 330,000 Americans age 55 and older to meet a wide range of community challenges through three programs: Retired and Senior Volunteers Program (RSVP), Foster Grandparents, and Senior Companions. RSVP volunteers help local police departments conduct safety patrols, participate in environmental projects, provide intensive educational services to children and adults, respond to natural disasters, and recruit other volunteers. Foster Grandparents serve as tutors and mentors to young people with special needs. Senior Companions help homebound seniors and other adults maintain independence in their own homes. Senior Corps volunteers served 1.5 million Americans, including 560,000 veterans and 300,000 children.

Social Innovation Fund   The Social Innovation Fund (SIF) is an approach to transforming lives and communities that positions the Federal Government to be a catalyst for promoting community solutions with evidence of strong results. A key White House initiative and program of CNCS, the Fund seeks to identify solutions that work and to make them work for more people. SIF combines public and private resources to foster innovative community-based solutions that have produced results in low-income communities in three priority areas: economic opportunity, health, and youth development.

Other Initiatives   As the Federal agency for service and volunteerism, CNCS carries out the Call to Service authority in multiple ways. CNCS's initiatives include:

the Martin Luther King, Jr. National Day of Service, the September 11th National Day of Service and Remembrance, National Mentoring Month, the President's Higher Education Community Service Honor Roll, and United We Serve, a nationwide effort launched with the White House in 2009 to engage Americans in service to meet community needs. As a result of United We Serve, hundreds of thousands of Americans have joined with friends and neighbors to replenish food banks, provide health services, support veterans and military families, restore public lands, and more. CNCS has also partnered with other agencies and nonprofit organizations on the "Let's Read!" initiative to reduce summer reading loss and the "Let's Move!" initiative to combat childhood obesity, and "Joining Forces," an effort led by First Lady Michelle Obama and Dr. Jill Biden to engage Americans in supporting veterans and military families.

The Corporation and its programs work with the USA Freedom Corps, established on January 29, 2002, by Executive Order 13254. USA Freedom Corps is a White House initiative to foster a culture of citizenship, service, and responsibility, and help all Americans answer the President's call to service.

Sources of Information

Electronic Access   For information on programs and activities, visit CNCS's Web site. For information on joining AmeriCorps, visit www.nationalservice. gov/AmeriCorps. Internet, http://www. nationalservice.gov.

General Information   For information on AmeriCorps, call 800–942–2677. For information on Senior Corps programs, call 800–424–8867. TDD, 202–565–2799.

Grants   To find discretionary funding opportunities that Federal agencies have posted, use the Grants.gov Web site. State program offices and commissions on national and community service are located in most States. They are the best sources of information on programs in specific States or communities. Contact information for CNCS State offices and State service commissions is listed on

CNCS's Web site. Internet, http://www.
grants.gov/web/grants/home.html.

For further information, contact the Corporation for National and Community Service, 1201 New York Avenue NW., Washington, DC 20525. Phone, 202–606–5000. Internet, http://www.nationalservice.gov.

DEFENSE NUCLEAR FACILITIES SAFETY BOARD

625 Indiana Avenue NW., Suite 700, Washington, DC 20004
Phone, 202–694–7000. Fax, 202–208–6518. Internet, http://www.dnfsb.gov.

Chairman	PETER S. WINOKUR
Vice Chair	JESSIE H. ROBERSON
Members	JOSEPH F. BADER, SEAN SULLIVAN,
	(VACANCY)
General Counsel	RICHARD N. REBACK, *Acting*
General Manager	MARK T. WELCH, *Acting*
Technical Director	STEVEN STOKES

The Defense Nuclear Facilities Safety Board reviews and evaluates the content and implementation of standards relating to the design, construction, operation, and decommissioning of the Department of Energy's defense nuclear facilities.

The Defense Nuclear Facilities Safety Board was established as an independent agency on September 29, 1988, by the Atomic Energy Act of 1954, as amended (42 U.S.C. 2286–2286i).

The Board is composed of five members appointed by the President with the advice and consent of the Senate. Members of the Board are appointed from among United States citizens who are respected experts in the field of nuclear safety.

Activities

The Defense Nuclear Facilities Safety Board reviews and evaluates the content and implementation of standards for defense nuclear facilities of the Department of Energy (DOE); investigates any event or practice at these facilities which may adversely affect public health and safety; and reviews and monitors the design, construction, and operation of facilities. The Board makes recommendations to the Secretary of Energy concerning DOE defense nuclear facilities to ensure adequate protection of public health and safety. In the event that any aspect of operations, practices, or occurrences reviewed by the Board is determined to present an imminent or severe threat to public health and safety, the Board transmits its recommendations directly to the President.

For further information, contact the Defense Nuclear Facilities Safety Board, 625 Indiana Avenue NW., Suite 700, Washington, DC 20004. Phone, 202–694–7000. Internet, http://www.dnfsb.gov.

ENVIRONMENTAL PROTECTION AGENCY

1200 Pennsylvania Avenue NW., Washington, DC 20460
Phone, 202–272–0167. Internet, http://www.epa.gov.

Administrator	REGINA MCCARTHY
Deputy Administrator	ROBERT PERCIASEPE
Associate Administrator for External Affairs and Environmental Education	THOMAS REYNOLDS

DEFENSE NUCLEAR FACILITIES SAFETY BOARD

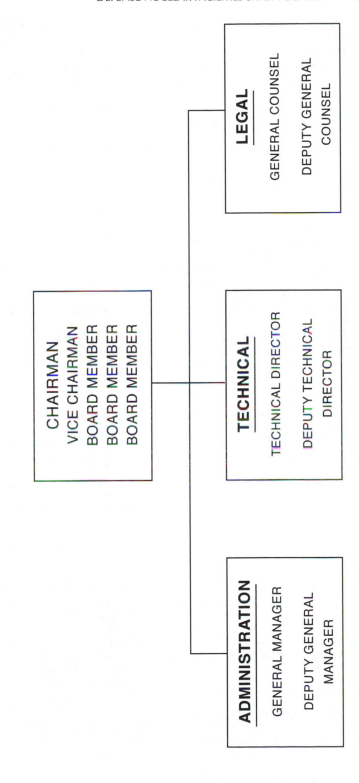

CHAIRMAN
VICE CHAIRMAN
BOARD MEMBER
BOARD MEMBER
BOARD MEMBER

ADMINISTRATION

GENERAL MANAGER

DEPUTY GENERAL
MANAGER

TECHNICAL

TECHNICAL DIRECTOR

DEPUTY TECHNICAL
DIRECTOR

LEGAL

GENERAL COUNSEL

DEPUTY GENERAL
COUNSEL

Associate Administrator for Congressional and Intergovernmental Relations	LAURA VAUGHT
Associate Administrator for Policy	JOEL BEAUVAIS
Associate Administrator for Homeland Security	PETER JUTRO, *Acting*
Chief Judge, Office of Administrative Law Judges	SUSAN L. BIRO
Director, Executive Secretariat	ERIC WACHTER
Director, Office of Children's Health Protection	JACQUELINE MOSBY, *Acting*
Director, Office of Civil Rights	VELVETA GOLIGHTLY-HOWELL
Director, Office of Federal Advisory Committee Management and Outreach	CYNTHIA JONES-JACKSON, *Acting*
Director, Office of Executive Services	DIANE N. BAZZLE
Director, Office of Small Business Programs	JEANETTE L. BROWN
Director, Science Advisory Board	CHRISTOPHER ZARBA
Lead Environmental Appeals Judge, Environmental Appeals Board	LESSYE FRASER
Assistant Administrator for Administration and Resources Management	CRAIG E. HOOKS
Assistant Administrator for Air and Radiation	JANET MCCABE, *Acting*
Assistant Administrator for Enforcement and Compliance Assurance	CYNTHIA GILES
Assistant Administrator for Environmental Information	RENEE WYNN, *Acting*
Assistant Administrator for International and Tribal Affairs	JANE NISHIDA, *Acting*
Assistant Administrator for Chemical Safety and Pollution Prevention	JAMES J. JONES
Assistant Administrator for Research and Development	LEK KADELI, *Acting*
Assistant Administrator for Solid Waste and Emergency Response	MATHY V. STANISLAUS
Assistant Administrator for Water	NANCY STONER, *Acting*
Chief Financial Officer	MARYANN FROELICH, *Acting*
General Counsel	AVI S. GARBOW
Inspector General	ARTHUR A. ELKINS, JR.

The Environmental Protection Agency protects human health and safeguards the environment.

The Environmental Protection Agency (EPA) was established in the executive branch as an independent agency pursuant to Reorganization Plan No. 3 of 1970 (5 U.S.C. app.), effective December 2, 1970. The Agency facilitates coordinated and effective governmental action to protect the environment. It also serves as the public's advocate for a livable environment.

Core Functions

Air and Radiation   The Office of Air and Radiation develops air quality policies, programs, regulations, and

standards, including emission standards for stationary sources, for mobile sources, and for hazardous air pollutants. It also conducts research and disseminates information on indoor air pollutants. This Office provides technical direction, support, and evaluation of regional air activities; offers training in the field of air pollution control; gives technical assistance to States and agencies operating radiation protection programs; and provides technical support and policy direction to international efforts to reduce global and transboundary air pollution and its effects.

For further information, call 202–564–7400.

ENVIRONMENTAL PROTECTION AGENCY

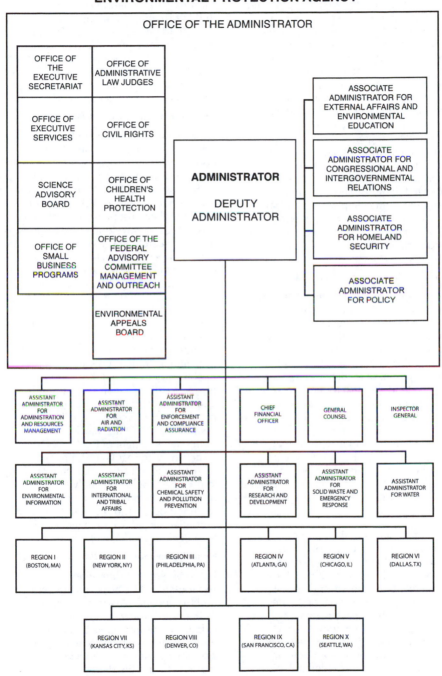

OFFICE OF THE ADMINISTRATOR

OFFICE OF THE EXECUTIVE SECRETARIAT	OFFICE OF ADMINISTRATIVE LAW JUDGES
OFFICE OF EXECUTIVE SERVICES	OFFICE OF CIVIL RIGHTS
SCIENCE ADVISORY BOARD	OFFICE OF CHILDREN'S HEALTH PROTECTION
OFFICE OF SMALL BUSINESS PROGRAMS	OFFICE OF THE FEDERAL ADVISORY COMMITTEE MANAGEMENT AND OUTREACH
	ENVIRONMENTAL APPEALS BOARD

ADMINISTRATOR

DEPUTY ADMINISTRATOR

ASSOCIATE ADMINISTRATOR FOR EXTERNAL AFFAIRS AND ENVIRONMENTAL EDUCATION

ASSOCIATE ADMINISTRATOR FOR CONGRESSIONAL AND INTERGOVERNMENTAL RELATIONS

ASSOCIATE ADMINISTRATOR FOR HOMELAND SECURITY

ASSOCIATE ADMINISTRATOR FOR POLICY

ASSISTANT ADMINISTRATOR FOR ADMINISTRATION AND RESOURCES MANAGEMENT

ASSISTANT ADMINISTRATOR FOR AIR AND RADIATION

ASSISTANT ADMINISTRATOR FOR ENFORCEMENT AND COMPLIANCE ASSURANCE

CHIEF FINANCIAL OFFICER

GENERAL COUNSEL

INSPECTOR GENERAL

ASSISTANT ADMINISTRATOR FOR ENVIRONMENTAL INFORMATION

ASSISTANT ADMINISTRATOR FOR INTERNATIONAL AND TRIBAL AFFAIRS

ASSISTANT ADMINISTRATOR FOR CHEMICAL SAFETY AND POLLUTION PREVENTION

ASSISTANT ADMINISTRATOR FOR RESEARCH AND DEVELOPMENT

ASSISTANT ADMINISTRATOR FOR SOLID WASTE AND EMERGENCY RESPONSE

ASSISTANT ADMINISTRATOR FOR WATER

REGION I (BOSTON, MA)

REGION II (NEW YORK, NY)

REGION III (PHILADELPHIA, PA)

REGION IV (ATLANTA, GA)

REGION V (CHICAGO, IL)

REGION VI (DALLAS, TX)

REGION VII (KANSAS CITY, KS)

REGION VIII (DENVER, CO)

REGION IX (SAN FRANCISCO, CA)

REGION X (SEATTLE, WA)

Water   The Office of Water provides agencywide policy, guidance and direction for EPA's water quality, drinking water, groundwater, wetlands protection, marine and estuarine protection, and other related programs. The Office's responsibilities include: program policy development and evaluation; environmental and pollution source standards development; program policy guidance and overview, technical support, and evaluation of regional activities as they relate to drinking water and water programs; development and implementation of programs for education, technical assistance and technology transfer; development of selected demonstration programs; long-term strategic planning and special studies; economic and long-term environmental analysis; and development and implementation of pollution prevention strategies.

For further information, call 202–564–5700.

Solid Waste and Emergency Response   The Office of Solid Waste and Emergency Response provides agencywide policy, guidance, and direction for EPA's solid waste and emergency response programs. The Office's responsibilities include: development of guidelines and standards for the land disposal of hazardous wastes and for underground storage tanks; technical assistance in the development, management, and operation of solid waste management activities; analyses on the recovery of useful energy from solid waste; and development and implementation of a program to respond to hazardous waste sites and spills.

For further information, call 202–566–0200.

Chemical Safety and Pollution Prevention   The Office of Chemical Safety and Pollution Prevention is responsible for EPA's strategies for implementation and integration of the pollution prevention, pesticides, and toxic substances programs and developing and operating Agency programs and policies for assessment and control of pesticides and toxic substances as well as recommending policies and developing operating programs for implementing the Pollution Prevention Act. The Office develops recommendations for EPA's priorities for research, monitoring regulatory and information gathering activities relating to implementing the Pollution Prevention Act, pesticides, and toxic substances; and monitoring and assessing pollution prevention, pesticides and toxic substances program operations in EPA headquarters and regional offices.

For further information, call 202–564–2902.

Research and Development   The Office of Research and Development conducts leading-edge research and fosters the sound use of science and technology to fulfill EPA's mission to protect human health and safeguard the natural environment. The Office of Research and Development is responsible for the research and development needs of EPA's operating programs and the conduct of an integrated research and development program for the Agency. The Assistant Administrator serves as the Agency's principal science adviser and is responsible for the development, direction, and conduct of a national environmental research, development, and demonstration program in health risk assessment, health effects, engineering and technology, processes and effects, acid rain deposition, monitoring systems, and quality assurance. The Office participates in the development of EPA's policy, standards, and regulations; provides for dissemination of scientific and technical knowledge, including analytical methods, monitoring techniques, and modeling methodologies; and provides technical and scientific advice on agencywide technical program issues.

For further information, call 202–564–6620.

Enforcement and Compliance Assurance   The Office of Enforcement and Compliance Assurance serves as the primary adviser to the Administrator in matters concerning enforcement, compliance assurance, and environmental-equity efforts. It also provides the direction and review of all administrative, civil and criminal enforcement, and compliance monitoring and assurance activities. The Office manages the national criminal enforcement program as well as regulatory, site remediation, and Federal facilities enforcement and compliance assurance programs. The Office manages both administrative and judicial activities in the enforcement and compliance programs and provides case preparation and investigative expertise for enforcement activities through the National Enforcement Investigations Center.

For further information, call 202–564–2440.

Regional Offices

EPA's 10 regional offices are committed to the development of strong local programs for pollution abatement. The regional administrators are responsible for accomplishing, within their regions, the Agency's national program objectives. They develop, propose, and implement an approved regional program for comprehensive and integrated environmental protection activities.

Internet, http://www2.epa.gov/aboutepa.

Sources of Information

Requests for information on the following subjects should be directed to the appropriate organization listed below. EPA's postal address is 1200 Pennsylvania Avenue NW., Washington, DC 20460. Internet, http://www.epa.gov/.

Contracts and Procurement   Office of Acquisition Management. Phone, 202–564–4310. Internet, http://www2. epa.gov/home/contracting-epa.

Directory Assistance   Phone, 202–272–0167. EPA's staff directory is available online. Internet, http://cfpub.epa.gov/locator/index.cfm.

Employment   Office of Human Resources. Phone, 202–564–4606. Internet, http://www.epa.gov/careers/.

Freedom of Information Act Requests National Freedom of Information Officer. Phone, 202–566–1667. Email, hq.foia@ epa.gov. Internet, http://www.epa.gov/foia/.

Grants and Fellowships   Office of Grants and Debarment. Phone, 202–564–5315. Internet, http://www2.epa. gov/home/grants-and-other-funding-opportunities.

Telephone Directory   Directories may be purchased by calling the Superintendent of Documents, Government Printing Office. Phone 202–512–0000.

For further information, contact the Office of External Affairs and Environmental Education, Environmental Protection Agency, 1200 Pennsylvania Avenue NW., Washington, DC 20460–0001. Phone, 202–272–0167. Internet, http://www.epa.gov.

EDITORIAL NOTE: The Equal Employment Opportunity Commission did not meet the publication deadline for submitting updated information of its activities, functions, and sources of information as required by the automatic disclosure provisions of the Freedom of Information Act (5 U.S.C. 552(a)(1)(A)).

EQUAL EMPLOYMENT OPPORTUNITY COMMISSION

131 M Street NE., Washington, DC 20507
Phone, 202–663–4900. TTY, 202–663–4444. Internet, http://www.eeoc.gov.

Chair	JACQUELINE A. BERRIEN
Vice Chair	JENNY R. YANG
Commissioners	CONSTANCE S. BARKER, CHAI R. FELDBLUM, VICTORIA A. LIPNIC
Executive Officer	BERNADETTE WILSON, *Acting*
Chief Operating Officer	CLAUDIA WITHERS
General Counsel	P. DAVID LOPEZ
Inspector General	MILTON A. MAYO, JR.
Director, Office of Communications and Legislative Affairs	TODD COX
Director, Office of Equal Opportunity	MATTHEW MURPHY
Director, Office of Federal Operations	CARLTON M. HADDEN
Director, Legal Counsel	PEGGY R. MASTROIANNI
Director, Office of Field Programs	NICHOLAS INZEO
Chief Financial Officer	GERMAINE ROSEBORO
Director, Office of Human Resources	LISA WILLIAMS
Director, Office of Information Technology	KIMBERLY HANCHER
Director, Office of Research, Information, and Planning	DEIDRE FLIPPEN

The Equal Employment Opportunity Commission enforces laws prohibiting employment discrimination based on race, color, gender, religion, national origin, age, disability, or genetic information.

The Equal Employment Opportunity Commission (EEOC) was created by Title VII of the Civil Rights Act of 1964 (42 U.S.C. 2000e-4), and became operational July 2, 1965. Laws enforced by EEOC include Title VII of the Civil Rights Act of 1964 (42 U.S.C. 2000e et seq.), the Age Discrimination in Employment Act of 1967 (29 U.S.C. 621 et seq.), sections of the Rehabilitation Act of 1973 (29 U.S.C. 791 et seq.) and the Civil Rights Act of 1991 (105 Stat. 1071), the Equal Pay Act of 1963 (29 U.S.C. 206), Title I of the Americans with Disabilities Act of 1990 (42 U.S.C. 12101 et seq.), and Title II of the Genetic Information Non-

Discrimination Act of 2008 (42 U.S.C. 2000ff et seq.).

The EEOC is a bipartisan commission comprising five members appointed by the President, with the advice and consent of the Senate, for staggered 5-year terms. The President designates a Chairman and Vice Chairman. In addition to the members of the Commission, the President appoints a General Counsel, with the advice and consent of the Senate, to support the Commission and provide direction, coordination, and supervision of the EEOC's litigation program. The General Counsel serves for a term of 4 years.

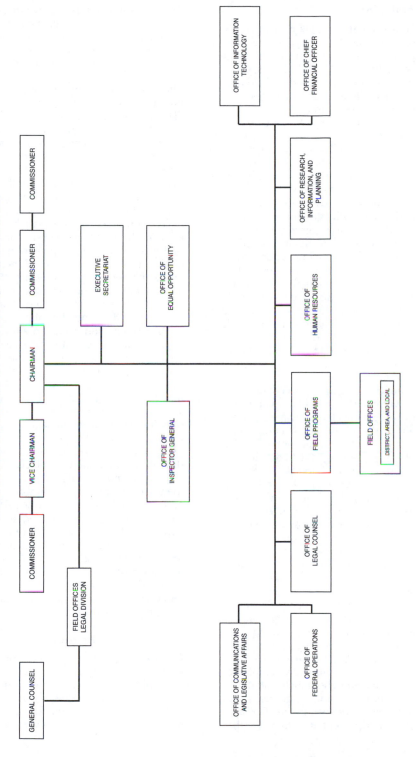

Activities

Enforcement   The EEOC enforces its
statutory, regulatory, policy, and program
responsibilities through its headquarters-
based Office of Field Programs, Office
of General Counsel, and 53 field offices.
The field offices receive charges of
discrimination from the public and
use a variety of resolution methods,
tailored to each charge, from voluntary
mediation to full-scale investigation and
conciliation. The field staff is responsible
for achieving a wide range of objectives
that focus on the quality, timeliness,
and appropriateness of individual, class,
and systemic charges; for securing
relief for victims of discrimination in
accordance with Commission policies;
for counseling individuals about their
rights under the laws enforced by the
EEOC; and for conducting outreach
and technical assistance programs. The
Office of General Counsel conducts the
Commission's litigation in U.S. District
Courts and Courts of Appeal.

Information on the nearest field office
is available online: http://www.eeoc.gov/
field/index.cfm.

**Complaints Against the Federal
Government**   The EEOC establishes
the procedures for Federal employees
and job applicants to file complaints of
employment discrimination or retaliation.
The agency charged with discrimination
is responsible for informal counseling
and, if a complaint is filed and accepted,
investigating the claims raised therein.
At the conclusion of the investigation,
complainants may request a hearing
before an EEOC administrative judge or
that the agency issue a final decision on
the matter. The agency's final decision
or final action after a hearing may be
appealed to the Commission.

In addition, the Office of Federal
Operations provides oversight and
technical assistance concerning
equal employment opportunity (EEO)
complaint adjudication and the
maintenance of affirmative employment
programs throughout the Federal
Government. Using the guidance and
principles contained in the EEOC's
EEO Management Directive 715, the
Commission monitors and evaluates
Federal agencies' affirmative employment
programs under Title VII and section 501
of the Rehabilitation Act and ensures that
all Federal employees compete on a fair
and level playing field.

Other Activities   The Commission
promotes voluntary compliance with
EEO statutes through a variety of
educational and technical assistance
activities. The Commission's outreach
and education programs provide general
information about the EEOC, its mission,
rights and responsibilities under the
statutes enforced by the Commission,
and the charge/complaint process.
EEOC representatives are available, on
a limited basis and at no cost, to make
presentations and participate in meetings,
conferences, and seminars with employee
and employer groups, professional
associations, students, nonprofit entities,
community organizations, and other
members of the general public.

The Commission offers more in-
depth training tailored to employers
for a fee. This training is available to
private employers and State, local, and
Federal government personnel through
the EEOC Training Institute. The EEOC
Training Institute provides a wide variety
of training to educate managers and
employees on the laws enforced by the
EEOC and how to prevent and eliminate
discrimination in the workplace.

The Commission publishes data on
the employment status of minorities
and women through six employment
surveys covering private employers,
apprenticeship programs, labor unions,
State and local governments, elementary
and secondary schools, and colleges
and universities. This collection of data
is shared with selected Federal agencies
and is made available, in appropriate
form, for public use.

Sources of Information

Electronic Access   Information on the
Commission's programs and activities is
available online. EEOC's most popular
publications may be downloaded from
its Web site in PDF format for easy
reproduction. Internet, http://www.eeoc.
gov/.

Employment The Commission hires in various job categories, including attorneys, information intake representatives, investigators, mediators, office automation assistants, paralegals, program analysts, and social scientists. Opportunities for employment are posted online: https://www.usajobs.gov/. Address questions to the appropriate district office or to the Office of Human Resources, Equal Employment Opportunity Commission, 131 M Street NE., Washington, DC 20507. Phone, 202–663–4306. Internet, http://www.eeoc.gov/eeoc/jobs/index.cfm.

General Inquiries A nationwide toll-free telephone number links callers with the appropriate field office where charges may be filed. Phone, 800–669–4000. TTY, 800–669–6820. Internet, https://eeoc.custhelp.com/app/answers/list.

Media Inquiries Representatives of the media should address their questions to the Office of Communications, Office of Communications and Legislative Affairs, 131 M Street NE., Washington, DC 20507. Phone, 202–663–4191. TTY, 202–663–4494. Email, newsroom@eeoc.gov. Internet, http://www.eeoc.gov/eeoc/newsroom/index.cfm.

Information About Survey Forms For information on EEO reports and survey forms, contact the Office of Research, Information, and Planning, 131 M Street NE., Washington, DC 20507. Phone, 202–663–4947. Internet, http://www.eeoc.gov/employers/reporting.cfm.

Publications Publications unavailable online may be obtained by phone or fax. Phone, 800–669–3362. TTY, 800–800–3302. Fax, 513–489–8692. Internet, http://www.eeoc.gov/eeoc/publications/index.cfm.

Reading Room EEOC Library, 131 M Street NE., Washington, DC 20507. Phone, 202–663–4630.

Speakers Office of the Executive Secretariat, 131 M Street NE., Washington, DC 20507. Phone, 202–663–4070. TTY, 202–663–4494.

For further information, contact the Equal Employment Opportunity Commission, 131 M Street NE., Washington, DC 20507. Phone, 202–663–4191. Internet, http://www.eeoc.gov.

EDITORIAL NOTE: The Export-Import Bank of the United States did not meet the publication deadline for submitting updated information of its activities, functions, and sources of information as required by the automatic disclosure provisions of the Freedom of Information Act (5 U.S.C. 552(a)(1)(A)).

EXPORT-IMPORT BANK OF THE UNITED STATES

811 Vermont Avenue NW., Washington, DC 20571
Phone, 202–565–3946; 800–565–3946. Internet, http://www.exim.gov.

President/Chairman	FRED P. HOCHBERG
First Vice President/Vice Chair	WANDA FELTON
Directors	SEAN R. MULVANEY, PATRICIA LOUI, (VACANCY)
Executive Vice President/Chief Operating Officer	JOHN A. MCADAMS, *Acting*
Senior Vice President, Export Finance	JOHN A. MCADAMS
Senior Vice President/Chief Financial Officer	DAVID M. SENA
Vice President, Treasurer	NATHALIE HERMAN
Vice President, Controller	JOSEPH SORBERA
Vice President, Asset Management	JESSICA FARMER
Senior Vice President, Small Business	JAMES BURROWS
Vice President, Transportation Portfolio Management	B. MICHELE DIXEY
Senior Vice President/General Counsel	ANGELA MARIANA FREYRE
Vice President, Trade Finance Division	ANNETTE B. MARESH
Vice President, Business Credit	PAMELA S. BOWERS
Vice President, Global Business Development	RAYMOND J. ELLIS
Vice President, Office of Industry Sector Development	C. MICHAEL FORGIONE
Vice President, International Relations	ISABEL GALDIZ
Vice President, Structured Finance	JOHN SCHUSTER
Vice President, Short-Term Trade Finance	WALTER KOSCIOW
Senior Vice President, Credit and Risk Management	KENNETH M. TINSLEY
Senior Vice President, Business and Product Development	ROBERT A. MORIN
Vice President, Credit Review and Compliance	WALTER HILL, JR.
Vice President, Engineering and Environment	JAMES A. MAHONEY, JR.
Vice President, Credit Underwriting	DAVID W. CARTER
Vice President, Country Risk and Economic Analysis	WILLIAM A. MARSTELLER
Chief Banking officer and Senior Vice President	CLAUDIA SLACIK
Senior Vice President and Chief of Staff	SCOTT MULHAUSER
Senior Vice President, Resource Management	MICHAEL CUSHING
Executive Vice President, Chief Risk Officer	CHARLES J. HALL
Chief Information Officer	(VACANCY)
Senior Vice President, Policy and Planning	JAMES C. CRUSE
Vice President, Customer Experience	STEPHANIE THUM
Vice President, Policy Analysis	HELENE WALSH
Vice President, Operations and Data Quality	NICOLE M.B. VALTOS
Senior Vice President, Communications	BRADLEY CARROLL
Vice President, Communications	DOLLINE HATCHETT

Vice President, Public Affairs	CATRELL BROWN
Senior Vice President, Strategy	(VACANCY)
Senior Vice President, Congressional Affairs	SCOTT P. SCHLOEGEL
Vice President, Congressional Affairs	STEPHEN RUBRIGHT
Vice President, Business Processes, Total Enterprise Modernization	MICHELE A. KUESTER
Inspector General	OSVALDO GRATACOS

The Export-Import Bank assists in financing the export of U.S. goods and services to international markets.

The Export-Import Bank of the United States (Ex-Im Bank), established in 1934, operates as an independent agency of the U.S. Government under the authority of the Export-Import Bank Act of 1945, as amended (12 U.S.C. 635 et seq.). Its Board of Directors consists of a President and Chairman, a First Vice President and Vice Chair, and three other Directors. All are appointed by the President with the advice and consent of the Senate.

Ex-Im Bank helps American exporters adjust to government-supported financing competition from other countries, so that U.S. exports can compete for overseas business on the basis of price, performance, and service, and in doing so, preserve U.S. jobs. The Bank also fills gaps in the availability of commercial financing for creditworthy export transactions by providing a variety of financing mechanisms, including working capital guarantees, export-credit insurance, and financing to help foreign buyers purchase U.S. goods and services.

Ex-Im Bank is required to find a reasonable assurance of repayment for each transaction it supports. Its legislation requires it to meet the financing terms of competitor export credit agencies, but not to compete with commercial lenders. Legislation restricts the Bank's operation in some countries and its support for military goods and services.

Ex-Im Bank operates at no cost to the U.S. taxpayer and has earned nearly $1.6 billion above its operating costs since fiscal year 2008. Its total authorizations support an estimated $50 billion in U.S. export sales and approximately 255,000 American jobs in communities across the country.

Activities

Ex-Im Bank is authorized to have loans, guarantees, and insurance outstanding at any one time in aggregate amount not in excess of $120 billion. It supports U.S. exporters through a range of diverse programs. These programs are offered under four broad categories of export financing: working capital guarantees, export credit insurance, loan guarantees, and direct loans.

Ex-Im Bank initiated several changes to enhance its support to small business. The Bank's regional offices are now dedicated exclusively to small business outreach and support. The Bank also established a Small Business Committee to coordinate, evaluate, and make recommendations on Bank functions necessary for a successful small business strategy, and the small business division is led by a senior vice president.

Regional Offices

The Export-Import Bank operates export finance centers and field offices across the country. A complete listing with contact information is available at www.exim.gov/about/contact/.

For further information, contact the Business Development Office, Export-Import Bank, 811 Vermont Avenue NW., Washington, DC 20571. Phone, 202–565–3946 or 800–565–3946. Internet, http://www.exim.gov.

FARM CREDIT ADMINISTRATION

1501 Farm Credit Drive, McLean, VA 22102–5090
Phone, 703–883–4000. Fax, 703–734–5784. Internet, http://www.fca.gov.

Chair/Chief Executive Officer	JILL LONG THOMPSON
Member of the Boards	KENNETH A. SPEARMAN, LELAND A. STROM
Secretary to the Board	DALE L. AULTMAN
Chief Operating Officer	WILLIAM J. HOFFMAN
Director, Office of Congressional and Public Affairs	MICHAEL A. STOKKE
General Counsel	CHARLES R. RAWLS
Inspector General	ELIZABETH DEAN
Director, Office of Examination and Chief Examiner	S. ROBERT COLEMAN
Director, Office of Regulatory Policy	GARY K. VAN METER
Director, Office of Secondary Market Oversight	LAURIE A. REA
Director, Office of Management Services	STEPHEN G. SMITH
Director, Equal Employment and Inclusion	THAIS BURLEW
Designated Agency Ethics Official	WENDY R. LAGUARDA

[For the Farm Credit Administration statement of organization, see the Code of Federal Regulations, Title 12, Parts 600 and 611]

The Farm Credit Administration ensures the safe and sound operation of the banks, associations, affiliated service organizations, and other entities of the Farm Credit System, and protects the interests of the public and those who borrow from Farm Credit institutions or invest in Farm Credit securities.

The Farm Credit Administration (FCA) was established as an independent financial regulatory agency in the executive branch of the Federal Government by Executive Order 6084 on March 27, 1933. FCA carries out its responsibilities by conducting examinations of the various Farm Credit lending institutions, which are Farm Credit Banks, the Agricultural Credit Bank, Agricultural Credit Associations, and Federal Land Credit Associations.

FCA also examines the service organizations owned by the Farm Credit lending institutions, as well as the National Consumer Cooperative Bank.

FCA policymaking is vested in the Farm Credit Administration Board, whose three full-time members are appointed to 6-year terms by the President, with the advice and consent of the Senate. One member of the Board is designated by the President as Chairman and serves as the Administration's chief executive officer. The Board is responsible for approving rules and regulations, providing for

the examination and regulation of and reporting by Farm Credit institutions, and establishing the policies under which the Administration operates. Board meetings are regularly held on the second Thursday of the month and are subject to the Government in the Sunshine Act. Public announcements of these meetings are published in the Federal Register.

The lending institutions of the Farm Credit System were established to provide adequate and dependable credit and closely related services to farmers, ranchers, and producers or harvesters of aquatic products; persons engaged in providing on-the-farm services; rural homeowners; and associations of farmers, ranchers, and producers or harvesters of aquatic products, or federations of such associations that operate on a cooperative basis and are engaged in marketing, processing, supply, or business service functions for the benefit of their members. Initially capitalized by the United States Government, the Farm Credit lending institutions are

FARM CREDIT ADMINISTRATION

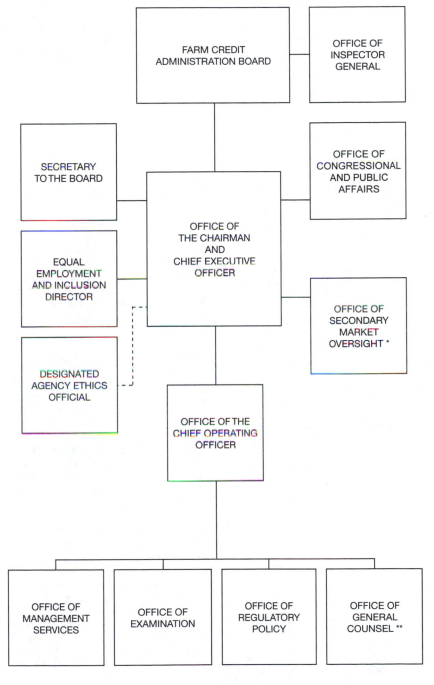

* Reports to the Board for policy and to the Chief Executive Officer for administration.
** Maintains a confidential advisory relationship with each of the Board members.

organized as cooperatives and are completely owned by their borrowers. The loan funds provided to borrowers by these institutions are obtained primarily through the sale of securities to investors in the Nation's capital markets.

The Agricultural Credit Act of 1987, as amended (12 U.S.C. 2279aa-1), established the Federal Agricultural Mortgage Corporation (commonly known as Farmer Mac). The Corporation, designated as part of the Farm Credit System, is a federally chartered instrumentality of the United States and promotes the development of a secondary market for agricultural real estate and rural housing loans. Farmer Mac also provides guarantees for the timely payment of principal and interest on securities representing interests in or obligations backed by pools of agricultural real estate loans. The Administration is responsible for the examination and regulation of Farmer Mac to ensure the safety and soundness of its operations.

The Administration manages regulations under which Farm Credit institutions operate. These regulations implement the Farm Credit Act of 1971, as amended (12 U.S.C. 2001), and have the force and effect of law. Similar to the authorities of other Federal regulators of financial institutions, the Administration's authorities include the power to issue cease-and-desist orders, to levy civil monetary penalties, to remove officers and directors of Farm Credit institutions, and to establish financial and operating reporting requirements. Although it is prohibited from participation in routine management or operations of Farm Credit institutions, the Administration is authorized to become involved in these institutions' management and operations when the Farm Credit Act or its regulations have been violated, when taking an action to correct an unsafe or unsound practice, or when assuming a formal conservatorship over an institution.

The Administration does not operate on funds appropriated by Congress;

it derives income from assessments collected from the institutions that it regulates and examines. In addition to its headquarters in McLean, VA, the Administration maintains four field offices located in Aurora, CO; Bloomington, MN; Irving, TX; and Sacramento, CA.

Authority for the organization and activities of the Farm Credit System may be found in the Farm Credit Act of 1971, as amended.

Sources of Information

Inquiries for information on the following subjects may be directed to the specified office, Farm Credit Administration, 1501 Farm Credit Drive, McLean, VA 22102–5090.

Contracts and Procurement   Inquiries regarding the Administration's procurement and contracting activities should be directed in writing to the Office of Management Services. Phone, 703–883–4378. TTY, 703–883–4056. Requests for proposals, invitations for bids, and requests for quotations are posted online at www.fca.gov/about/procurement.html.

Employment   Inquiries regarding employment should be directed to the Office of Management Services. Phone, 703–883–4135. TTY, 703–883–4056. Vacancy announcements are posted online at www.fca.gov/about/careers.html.

Freedom of Information Requests   Requests for agency records must be submitted in writing, clearly labeled "FOIA Request" and addressed to the Freedom of Information Act Officer. Phone, 703–883–4020 TTY, 703–883–4056. Requests may be submitted online at www.fca.gov/home/submit_foia.html.

Publications   Publications and information on the Farm Credit Administration and the Farm Credit System may be obtained by writing to the Office of Congressional and Public Affairs. Phone, 703–883–4056 (voice and TTY). Fax, 703–790–3260. They are also posted online at www.fca.gov/reports/index.html. Email, info-line@fca.gov.

For further information, contact the Office of Congressional and Public Affairs, Farm Credit Administration, 1501 Farm Credit Drive, McLean, VA 22102–5090. Phone, 703–883–4056. Email, info-line@fca.gov. Internet, http://www.fca.gov.

FEDERAL COMMUNICATIONS COMMISSION

445 Twelfth Street SW., Washington, DC 20554
Phone, 888–225–5322. TTY, 888–835–5322. Internet, http://www.fcc.gov.

Chairman	TOM WHEELER
Commissioners	MIGNON CLYBURN, MICHAEL O'REILLY, AJIT PAI, JESSICA ROSENWORCEL
Managing Director	JON WILKINS, *Acting*
General Counsel	JONATHAN SALLET, *Acting*
Inspector General	DAVID L. HUNT
Chief, Consumer and Governmental Affairs Bureau	KRIS MONTEITH, *Acting*
Chief, Enforcement Bureau	TRAVIS LEBLANC, *Acting*
Chief, International Bureau	MINDEL DE LA TORRE
Chief, Media Bureau	WILLIAM T. LAKE
Chief, Office of Administrative Law Judges	RICHARD L. SIPPEL
Chief, Office of Engineering and Technology	JULIUS KNAPP
Chief, Office of Strategic Planning and Policy Analysis	JONATHAN CHAMBERS, *Acting*
Chief, Public Safety and Homeland Security Bureau	DAVID G. SIMPSON
Chief, Wireless Telecommunications Bureau	ROGER SHERMAN, *Acting*
Chief, Wireline Competition Bureau	JULIE VEACH
Director, Office of Communications Business Opportunities	THOMAS REED
Director, Office of Legislative Affairs	SARA MORRIS, *Acting*
Director, Office of Media Relations	SHANNON GILSON
Director, Office of Workplace Diversity	THOMAS WYATT

[For the Federal Communications Commission statement of organization, see the Code of Federal Regulations, Title 47, Part 0]

The Federal Communications Commission regulates interstate and foreign communications by radio, television, wire, satellite, and cable.

The Federal Communications Commission (FCC) was established by the Communications Act of 1934 (47 U.S.C. 151 et seq.) and is charged with regulating interstate and foreign communications by wire and radio in the public interest. The scope of FCC regulation includes radio and television broadcasting; telephone, and cable television operation; two-way radio and radio operators; and satellite communication.

The Commission comprises five members, who are appointed by the President with the advice and consent of the Senate. One of the members is designated by the President as Chairman.

Activities

Media Bureau The Media Bureau develops, recommends, and administers policy and licensing programs relating to electronic media, including cable television, multichannel video programming distribution, broadcast television and radio, and satellite services in the United States and its territories. The Bureau also conducts rulemaking

FEDERAL COMMUNICATIONS COMMISSION

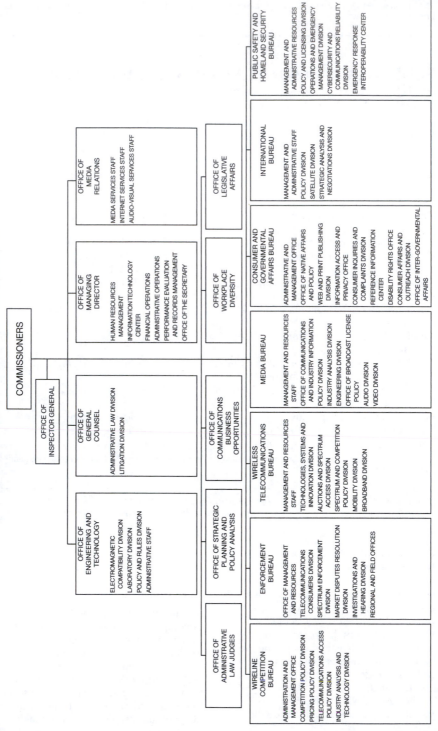

proceedings, studies and analyzes electronic media services; resolves waiver petitions, declaratory rulings, and adjudications related to electronic media services; and processes applications for authorization, assignment, transfer, and renewal of media services, including AM, FM, TV, the cable television relay service, and related matters.

For further information, contact the Media Bureau. Phone, 202–418–7200, or 888–225–5322.

Wireline Competition Bureau The
Wireline Competition Bureau advises and makes recommendations to the FCC on policies concerning telephone landlines and fixed, as opposed to mobile, broadband. The Bureau ensures choice, opportunity, and fairness in the development of wireline communications; assesses the present and future wireline communication needs of the Nation; encourages the development and widespread availability of wireline communication services; promotes investment in wireline communication infrastructure; and reviews and coordinates orders, programs, and actions initiated by other bureaus and offices in matters affecting wireline communications to ensure consistency with overall FCC policy.

For further information, contact the Wireline Competition Bureau. Phone, 202–418–1500, or 888–225–5322.

Consumer and Governmental
Affairs Bureau The Consumer and Governmental Affairs Bureau develops and administers the FCC's consumer and governmental affairs policies and initiatives. The Bureau facilitates public participation in the Commission's decisionmaking process; represents the Commission on consumer and Government committees, working groups, task forces, and conferences; works with public, Federal, State, local, and tribal agencies to develop and coordinate policies; oversees the Consumer Advisory Committee and the Intergovernmental Advisory Committee; provides expert advice and assistance regarding compliance with applicable disability and accessibility requirements, rules, and regulations; resolves informal complaints through mediation; and conducts consumer outreach and education programs.

For further information, contact the Consumer and Governmental Affairs Bureau. Phone, 202–418–1400, or 888–225–5322.

Enforcement Bureau The Enforcement
Bureau serves as the FCC's primary agency for enforcing the Communications Act, other communications statutes, and the FCC's rules. The Bureau investigates and resolves complaints regarding common carriers (wireline, wireless, and international) and noncommon carriers subject to the Commission's jurisdiction under Title II of the Communications Act; radio frequency interference, equipment, and devices; accessibility to communications services and equipment for persons with disabilities; noncompliance with the lighting and marking of radio transmitting towers and pole attachment regulations; and unauthorized construction and operation of communication facilities and false distress signals.

For further information, contact the Enforcement Bureau. Phone, 202–418–7450, or 888–225–5322.

International Bureau The International
Bureau serves as the FCC's principal representative in international conferences and negotiations. The Bureau promotes procompetitive policies abroad, coordinating the FCC's global spectrum activities and advocating U.S. interests in international communications and competition. It provides advice and technical assistance to U.S. trade officials in the negotiation and implementation of telecommunications trade agreements; and promotes the international coordination of spectrum allocation and frequency and orbital assignments in order to minimize cases of international radio interference involving U.S. licenses.

For further information, contact the International Bureau. Phone, 202–418–0437, or 888–225–5322.

Wireless Telecommunications Bureau
The Wireless Telecommunications Bureau administers all domestic commercial and private wireless communication programs and rules. It addresses present and future wireless communication

and spectrum needs; promotes access, efficiency, and innovation in the allocation, licensing, and use of electromagnetic spectrum; ensures choice, opportunity, and fairness in the development of wireless communication services and markets; and promotes the development and widespread availability of wireless broadband, mobile, and other wireless communication services, devices, and facilities, including through open networks. The Bureau also develops, recommends, administers, and coordinates policy for wireless communication services, including rulemaking, interpretations, and equipment standards; advises the public on FCC rules; serves as the FCC's principal policy and administrative resource for all spectrum auctions; and processes wireless service and facility authorization applications.

For further information, contact the Wireless Telecommunications Bureau. Phone, 202–418–0600, or 888–225–5322.

Public Safety and Homeland Security Bureau   The Public Safety and Homeland Security Bureau develops, recommends, and administers FCC's policies pertaining to public safety communication. This includes 911 and E911; operability and interoperability of public safety communications; communications infrastructure protection and disaster response; and network security and reliability. The Bureau also serves as a clearinghouse for public safety communication information, which encompasses priority emergency communication programs; alert and warning of U.S. citizens; continuity of government operations and operational planning; public safety outreach (e.g. first-responder organizations and hospitals); disaster management coordination and outreach; and studies and reports of public safety, homeland security, and disaster management issues.

For further information, contact the Public Safety and Homeland Security Bureau. Phone, 202–418–1300, or 888–225–5322. Email, pshsbinfo@fcc.gov.

Sources of Information

Consumer Assistance   For general information on FCC operations, contact the FCC Consumer Center, 445 Twelfth Street SW., Washington, DC 20554. Phone, 888–225–5322. TTY, 888–835–5322.

Contracts and Procurement   Direct inquiries to the Contracts and Purchasing Center may be sent electronically using the email address below. Email, CPCHelp@fcc.gov.

Electronic Access   Information is available online from the FCC's Web site. Internet, http://www.fcc.gov/.

Employment and Recruitment   Requests for employment information may be directed to the Recruitment and Staffing Service Center. Phone, 202–418–0130. To view or apply for job vacancies online, use the link below. Internet, http://www.fcc.gov/jobs.

Equal Employment Practices by Industry   Direct inquiries to the FCC Consumer Center may be made by calling 888–225–5322.

Ex-Parte Presentations   Inquiries concerning ex-parte presentations may be directed to the Commission's Office of General Counsel. Phone, 202–418–1720.

Federal Advisory Committee Management   Direct inquiries may be made to the Office of the Managing Director. Phone, 202–418–2178.

Fees   Information concerning the FCC's fee programs is available online or by contacting the Registration System/Fee Filer Help Desk at 1–877–480–3201 (option 4) or ARINQUIRIES@fcc.gov. Internet, http://www.fcc.gov/fees.

Freedom of Information Act Requests   Contact the FOIA Requester Service Center. Phone, 202–418–1379. Email, foia@fcc.gov.

Internal Equal Employment Practices   Direct inquiries may be made to the Office of Workplace Diversity. Phone, 202–418–1799.

Licensing   Information concerning the FCC's licensing systems is available online. Internet, http://www.fcc.gov/encyclopedia/licensing.

Public Inspection   Records available for public inspection are maintained online at www.fcc.gov. Some reports are held

confidentially by law. Additionally, each broadcasting station makes publicly available certain information about the station's operation, a current copy of the application filed for license, and nonconfidential FCC reports.
Publications The Office of Media Relations distributes public notices and press releases. Public notices and press releases are available at www.fcc.gov. The Consumer and Governmental Affairs Bureau maintains an online consumer publications library. Internet, http://www.fcc.gov/encyclopedia/consumer-publications-library.

For further information, contact the Consumer Center, Federal Communications Commission, 445 Twelfth Street SW., Washington, DC 20554. Phone, 888–225–5322. TTY, 888–835–5322. Internet, http://www.fcc.gov.

FEDERAL DEPOSIT INSURANCE CORPORATION

550 Seventeenth Street NW., Washington, DC 20429
Phone, 703–562–2222. Internet, http://www.fdic.gov.

Board of Directors

Chairman	MARTIN J. GRUENBERG
Vice Chairman	THOMAS J. HOENIG
Director (Director, Consumer Financial Protection Bureau)	RICHARD CORDRAY
Director (Comptroller of the Currency)	THOMAS J. CURRY
Director	JEREMIAH O. NORTON

Washington Office

Senior Advisor to the Chairman	(VACANCY)
Deputy to the Chairman	KYMBERLY K. COPA
Senior Advisor, International Resolution Policy	DAVID S. HOELSCHER
Deputy to the Chairman and Chief Financial Officer	STEVEN O. APP
Deputy to the Chairman for Communications	ANDREW S. GRAY
Deputy to the Chairman and Chief Operating Officer	BARBARA A. RYAN
Chief of Staff	BARBARA A. RYAN
General Counsel	RICHARD J. OSTERMAN, JR., *Acting*
Deputy to the Vice Chairman	KATHY KALSER, *Acting*
Director, Division of Administration	ARLEAS U. KEA
Director, Division of Finance	CRAIG JARVILL
Director, Division of Information Technology	RUSSELL G. PITTMAN
Chief Information Officer and Chief Privacy Officer	MARTIN D. HENNING, *Acting*
Director, Division of Insurance and Research	DIANE ELLIS
Director, Division of Resolutions and Receiverships	BRET D. EDWARDS
Director, Division of Risk Management Supervision	DOREEN R. EBERLEY
Chief Risk Officer	STEPHEN A. QUICK
Director, Office of Complex Financial Institutions	ARTHUR J. MURTON
Director, Office of Minority and Women Inclusion	MELODEE BROOKS, *Acting*
Director, Division of Depositor and Consumer Protection	MARK PEARCE

Washington Office

Director, Office of International Affairs	FRED S. CARNS
Director, Office of Legislative Affairs	ERIC SPITLER
Chief Learning Officer, Corporate University	SUZANNAH SUSSER, Acting
Inspector General	FRED W. GIBSON, Acting
Ombudsman	COTTRELL L. WEBSTER

The Federal Deposit Insurance Corporation preserves and promotes public confidence in U.S. financial institutions by insuring bank and thrift deposits, periodically examining State-chartered banks, and liquidating assets of failed institutions.

The Federal Deposit Insurance Corporation (FDIC) was established under the Banking Act of 1933 after numerous banks failed during the Great Depression. FDIC began insuring banks on January 1, 1934. The basic insurance coverage per depositor at each insured bank and savings association is $250,000.

The FDIC is managed by a five-member Board of Directors, all of whom the President appoints and the Senate confirms. No more than three of the Directors can be affiliated with the same political party.

FDIC receives no congressional appropriations. Its funding comes from insurance premiums on deposits held by insured banks and savings associations and from interest on the investment of those premiums in U.S. Government securities. FDIC has authority to borrow up to $100 billion from the Treasury for insurance purposes.

Activities

The FDIC insures about $11 trillion of U.S. bank and thrift deposits. As required by law, the fund relies on two sources of income: premiums paid by banks and savings associations, and the interest on the investment of those premiums in U.S. Government securities. An institution's level of capitalization and potential risk to the insurance fund determines its premiums.

The FDIC examines about 3,800 State-chartered commercial and savings banks that are not members of the Federal Reserve System, called State nonmember banks. The FDIC also has authority to examine other types of FDIC-insured institutions for deposit insurance purposes. The two types of examinations conducted are for safety and soundness and for compliance with applicable consumer laws such as the Truth in Lending Act, the Home Mortgage Disclosure Act, the Equal Credit Opportunity Act, the Fair Housing Act, and the Community Reinvestment Act. FDIC examiners work on site at the institution, and they analyze computer data offsite.

A failed bank or savings association is generally closed by its chartering authority, and the FDIC is named receiver. The FDIC is required to resolve the closure in a manner that is least costly to the FDIC. Ordinarily, the FDIC attempts to locate a healthy institution to acquire the failed entity. If such an entity cannot be found, the FDIC pays depositors the amount of their insured funds, usually by the next business day following the closure. Depositors with funds that exceed the insurance limit often receive an advance dividend, which is a portion of their uninsured funds that is determined by an estimate of the future proceeds from liquidating the failed institution's remaining assets. Depositors with funds in a failed institution that exceed the insurance limit receive a receivership certificate for those funds and partial payments of their uninsured funds as asset disposition permits.

As part of its insurance, supervisory, and receivership responsibilities, the FDIC approves or disapproves of mergers, consolidations, and acquisitions where the resulting bank is an insured State nonmember; approves or disapproves of proposals by banks to establish and operate a new branch, close an existing branch, or move its main office from one location to another; and approves

FEDERAL DEPOSIT INSURANCE CORPORATION

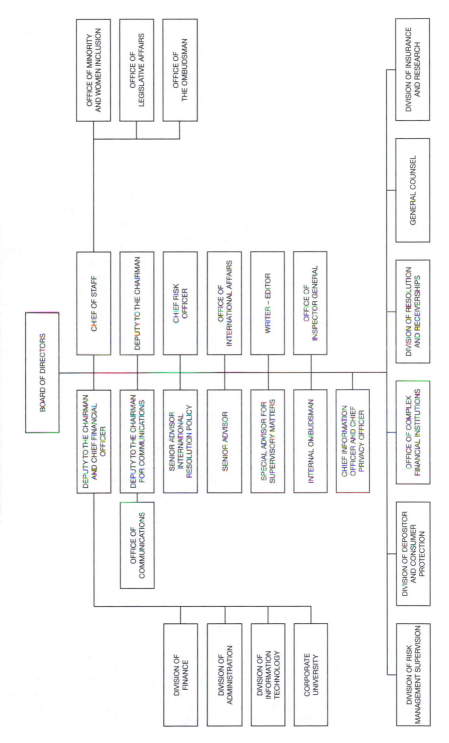

- BOARD OF DIRECTORS
- OFFICE OF MINORITY AND WOMEN INCLUSION
- OFFICE OF LEGISLATIVE AFFAIRS
- OFFICE OF THE OMBUDSMAN
- CHIEF OF STAFF
- DEPUTY TO THE CHAIRMAN
- CHIEF RISK OFFICER
- OFFICE OF INTERNATIONAL AFFAIRS
- WRITER – EDITOR
- OFFICE OF INSPECTOR GENERAL
- DEPUTY TO THE CHAIRMAN AND CHIEF FINANCIAL OFFICER
- DEPUTY TO THE CHAIRMAN FOR COMMUNICATIONS
- SENIOR ADVISOR INTERNATIONAL RESOLUTION POLICY
- SENIOR ADVISOR
- SPECIAL ADVISOR FOR SUPERVISORY MATTERS
- INTERNAL OMBUDSMAN
- CHIEF INFORMATION OFFICER AND CHIEF PRIVACY OFFICER
- OFFICE OF COMMUNICATIONS
- DIVISION OF FINANCE
- DIVISION OF ADMINISTRATION
- DIVISION OF INFORMATION TECHNOLOGY
- CORPORATE UNIVERSITY
- DIVISION OF RISK MANAGEMENT SUPERVISION
- DIVISION OF DEPOSITOR AND CONSUMER PROTECTION
- OFFICE OF COMPLEX FINANCIAL INSTITUTIONS
- DIVISION OF RESOLUTION AND RECEIVERSHIPS
- GENERAL COUNSEL
- DIVISION OF INSURANCE AND RESEARCH

or disapproves of requests to engage as principal in activities and investments that are not permissible for a national bank. It also issues enforcement actions, including cease-and-desist orders, for specific violations or practices requiring corrective action and reviews changes in ownership or control of a bank.

Sources of Information

Consumer Information   For consumer information inquiries or to submit a complaint against State nonmember banks, call the Consumer Response Center at 1–877–275–3342 (TTY 1–800–925–4618), weekdays between 8:00 a.m. and 8:00 p.m., eastern time, or write to the Federal Deposit Insurance Corporation, Consumer Response Center, 1100 Walnut Street, Box 11, Kansas City, MO 64106. Internet, http://www.fdic.gov/consumers/consumer/ccc/.

General Inquiries   Written requests for general information may be sent to the FDIC's Public Information Center, 3501 Fairfax Drive, Room E–1002, Arlington, VA 22226. Phone, 703–562–2200 or 877–275–3342. Internet, http://www.fdic.gov/about/contact/ask/.

Public Records   FDIC records are available on the Agency's Web site. Inquiries about other types of records available to the public, including records available under the Freedom of Information Act, should be directed to the Chief, FOIA/PA Group 550 17th Street NW., Washington, DC 20429, or to a regional office. Internet, http://www.fdic.gov/about/freedom/.

Publications   Publications, press releases, congressional testimony, directives to financial institutions, and other documents are available through the Public Information Center. Phone, 877–275–3342 (press 1, then press 5). Email, publicinfo@fdic.gov. Internet, http://www.fdic.gov/news/publications/PIChardcopies.html.

For further information and media inquiries, contact the Office of Communications, Federal Deposit Insurance Corporation, 550 Seventeenth Street NW., Washington, DC 20429. Phone, 202–898–6993. Email, communications@fdic.gov. Internet, http://www.fdic.gov.

FEDERAL ELECTION COMMISSION

999 E Street NW., Washington, DC 20463
Phone, 202–694–1100; 800–424–9530. Internet, http://www.fec.gov.

Chairman	LEE E. GOODMAN
Vice Chair	ANN M. RAVEL
Commissioners	CAROLINE C. HUNTER, MATTHEW S. PETERSEN, STEVEN T. WALTHER, ELLEN L. WEINTRAUB
Staff Director	ALEC PALMER
General Counsel	(VACANCY)
Inspector General	LYNNE A. MCFARLAND
Chief Financial Officer	JUDY BERNING, *Acting*

The Federal Election Commission provides public disclosure of campaign finance activities and ensures compliance with campaign finance laws and regulations.

The Federal Election Commission is an independent agency established by section 309 of the Federal Election Campaign Act of 1971, as amended (2 U.S.C. 437c). It comprises six Commissioners, whom the President appoints with the advice and consent of the Senate. The act also provides for three statutory officers—the Staff Director, the General Counsel, and the Inspector General—whom the Commission appoints.

FEDERAL ELECTION COMMISSION

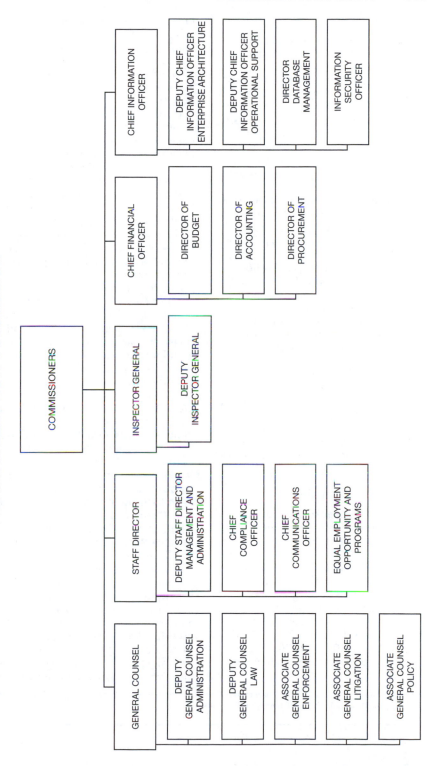

COMMISSIONERS

- CHIEF INFORMATION OFFICER
  - DEPUTY CHIEF INFORMATION OFFICER ENTERPRISE ARCHITECTURE
  - DEPUTY CHIEF INFORMATION OFFICER OPERATIONAL SUPPORT
  - DIRECTOR DATABASE MANAGEMENT
  - INFORMATION SECURITY OFFICER
- CHIEF FINANCIAL OFFICER
  - DIRECTOR OF BUDGET
  - DIRECTOR OF ACCOUNTING
  - DIRECTOR OF PROCUREMENT
- INSPECTOR GENERAL
  - DEPUTY INSPECTOR GENERAL
- STAFF DIRECTOR
  - DEPUTY STAFF DIRECTOR MANAGEMENT AND ADMINISTRATION
  - CHIEF COMPLIANCE OFFICER
  - CHIEF COMMUNICATIONS OFFICER
  - EQUAL EMPLOYMENT OPPORTUNITY AND PROGRAMS
- GENERAL COUNSEL
  - DEPUTY GENERAL COUNSEL ADMINISTRATION
  - DEPUTY GENERAL COUNSEL LAW
  - ASSOCIATE GENERAL COUNSEL ENFORCEMENT
  - ASSOCIATE GENERAL COUNSEL LITIGATION
  - ASSOCIATE GENERAL COUNSEL POLICY

Activities

The Commission administers and enforces the Federal Election Campaign Act of 1971, as amended (2 U.S.C. 431 et seq.), and the Revenue Act, as amended (26 U.S.C. 1 et seq.). These laws provide for the public funding of Presidential elections, public disclosure of the financial activities of political committees involved in Federal elections, and limitations and prohibitions on contributions and expenditures made to influence Federal elections.

Public Funding of Presidential Elections The Commission oversees the public financing of Presidential elections by certifying Federal payments to primary candidates, general election nominees, and national nominating conventions. It also audits recipients of Federal funds and may require repayments to the U.S. Treasury if a committee makes nonqualified campaign expenditures.

Disclosure The Commission ensures public disclosure of the campaign finance activities reported by political committees supporting Federal candidates. Committee reports, filed regularly, disclose the sources of campaign money and how that money is spent. The Commission places reports on the public record within 48 hours after they are received and digitizes the data contained in them.

Sources of Information

Congressional, Legislative, and Intergovernmental Affairs The Office of Congressional, Legislative and Intergovernmental Affairs serves as the Commission's primary congressional and executive branch liaison. It informs Members of Congress about Commission decisions, and it also informs the Commission about legislative developments. Phone, 202–694–1006 or 800–424–9530 (ext. 1006). Email, congress@fec.gov. Internet, http://www. fec.gov/about/offices/cong_affairs/cong_affairs.shtml.

Employment Inquiries regarding employment opportunities should be directed to the Director, Office of Human Resources. Phone, 202–694–1080 or 800–424–9530 (ext. 1080). Email, personnel@fec.gov. Internet, http://www. fec.gov/pages/jobs/jobs.shtml.

General Inquiries The Information Division provides information and assistance to Federal candidates, political committees, and the general public. It answers questions on campaign finance laws, conducts workshops and seminars on the law, and provides publications and forms. Phone, 202–694–1100 or 800–424–9530. Email, info@fec.gov. Internet, http://www.fec.gov/pages/contact.shtml.

Media Inquiries The Press Office answers inquiries from print and broadcast media sources, issues press releases on Commission actions and statistical data, responds to requests for information, and distributes other materials. Representatives of the media should contact the Press Office. Phone, 202–694–1220 or 800–424–9530. Email, press@fec.gov. Internet, http://www.fec. gov/press/index.shtml.

Public Records The Public Disclosure Division, located at 999 E Street NW., Washington, DC, provides space for public inspection of all campaign finance reports and statements since 1972. It is open to the public weekdays, 9 a.m. to 5 p.m. Phone, 202–694–1120 or 800–424–9530. Email, pubrec@fec.gov.

Reading Room The library contains a collection of basic legal research resources on political campaign financing, corporate and labor political activity, and campaign finance reform. It is open to the public weekdays, 9 a.m. to 5 p.m. Phone, 202–694–1600 or 800–424–9530. FEC publications and forms are available from the Agency's Web site on its "Library" page. Internet, http://www.fec.gov/general/library.shtml.

For further information, contact the Information Division, Federal Election Commission, 999 E Street NW., Washington, DC 20463. Phone, 202–694–1100 or 800–424–9530.

FEDERAL HOUSING FINANCE AGENCY

400 7th Street SW., Washington, DC 20024
Phone, 202–649–3800. Internet, http://www.fhfa.gov.

Director	MELVIN L. WATT
Chief Operating Officer	RICHARD B. HORNSBY
Deputy Director, Conservatorship	WANDA DELEO
Deputy Director, Federal Home Loan Bank Regulation	FRED C. GRAHAM
Deputy Director, Enterprise Regulation	NINA NICHOLS, *Acting*
Deputy Director, Supervision Policy and Support	NINA NICHOLS
Deputy Director, Housing Mission and Goals	SANDRA THOMPSON
Inspector General	LAURA S. WERTHEIMER
General Counsel	ALFRED M. POLLARD

The Federal Housing and Finance Agency ensures that Fannie Mae, Freddie Mac, and the Federal Home Loan Bank System serve as a reliable source of liquidity and funding for housing finance and community investment. It provides research and data, supervision, and policies for strengthening and securing the United States secondary mortgage markets.

The Federal Housing and Finance Agency (FHFA) was established by the Housing and Economic Recovery Act of 2008 (42 USC 4501 note) as an independent agency in the executive branch. The merger of the Federal Housing Finance Board and the Office of Federal Housing Enterprise Oversight, combined with the transfer of the Department of Housing and Urban Development's Government-sponsored enterprise mission team, formed the FHFA.

FHFA is managed by a Director whom the President appoints and the Senate confirms. FHFA's Director also serves as the Chairman of the Federal Housing Oversight Board. The Secretary of the Treasury, the Secretary of Housing and Urban Development, and the Chairman of the Securities and Exchange Commission are also members of the Board.

FHFA was created to oversee Fannie Mae, Freddie Mac, the 12 Federal Home Loan Banks (FHLB), and the Office of Finance, which issues and services all debt securities for the FHL Banks. The Agency's increased regulatory powers and affordable housing goals were designed to enable the 14 Government-sponsored loan enterprises (Fannie Mae, Freddie Mac, and the FHL Banks) to assist troubled mortgage markets more effectively.

Internet, http://www.fhfa.gov/AboutUs.

Activities

FHFA oversight strengthens vital components of the Nation's secondary mortgage markets. It oversees maintenance of adequate capital and internal controls; operations that foster efficient, competitive, and resilient national housing finance markets; and compliance with the rules, regulations, guidelines, and orders issued by authorizing statutes and FHFA.

Sources of Information

Employment The Agency's mission-critical occupations include examiners, accountants, economists, financial analysts, information technology specialists, and attorneys. FHFA regularly recruits for support positions: budget, procurement, and human resource specialists; facilities and space management professionals; and student interns. It advertises opportunities for employment on its Web site and on USAJOBS, the Federal Government's free web-based job board (https://www.usajobs.gov/). Questions and applications

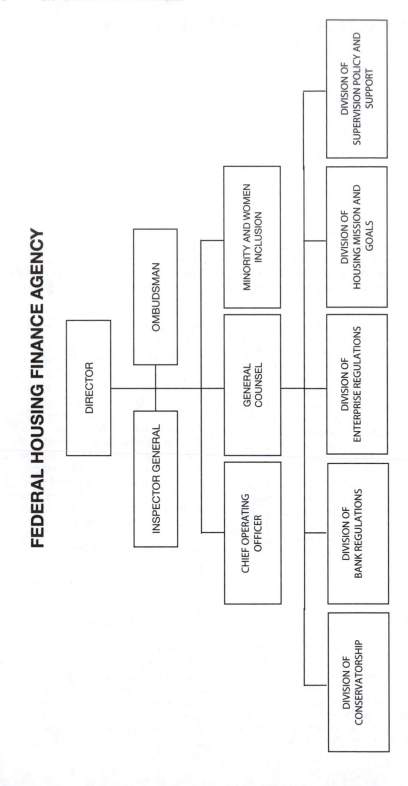

FEDERAL HOUSING FINANCE AGENCY

DIRECTOR

OMBUDSMAN

INSPECTOR GENERAL

CHIEF OPERATING OFFICER

GENERAL COUNSEL

MINORITY AND WOMEN INCLUSION

DIVISION OF CONSERVATORSHIP

DIVISION OF BANK REGULATIONS

DIVISION OF ENTERPRISE REGULATIONS

DIVISION OF HOUSING MISSION AND GOALS

DIVISION OF SUPERVISION POLICY AND SUPPORT

may be sent to the Office of Human Resources Management, FHFA, 400 7th Street SW., Washington, DC 20024. Internet, http://www.fhfa.gov/AboutUs/ Careers.

General Inquiries Contact the Office of Congressional Affairs and Communications, Federal Housing Finance Agency, 400 7th Street SW., Washington, DC 20024. Phone, 202–649–3800. Send consumer inquiries to the following email address: consumerhelp@fhfa.gov. Email, fhfainfo@ fhfa.gov. Internet, http://www.fhfa.gov.

Media Inquiries The Office of Congressional Affairs and Communications answers questions from print, Internet, and broadcast media sources; issues press releases; responds to requests for information; and distributes other materials. Media representatives should call 202–649–3700. Email, mediainquiries@fhfa.gov. Internet, https:// www.fhfa.gov/AboutUs/Contact.

Office of Congressional Affairs and Communications The Office of Congressional Affairs and Communications provides liaison with Congress, the public, the media, and other Federal agencies. The Office keeps Congress informed about Agency policies and decisions; handles consumer contact and complaints; interacts with the public, industry, and media outlets; and manages and maintains the Agency's Web site portal and internal communications. For more information, call 202–649–3802.

Publications FHFA posts its publications online for download. The Agency generally does not mail hard copies, but all requests are considered. Written requests for copies of publications may be addressed to the Office of Congressional Affairs and Communications, FHFA, 400 7th Street SW., Washington, DC 20024. Email, fhfainfo@fhfa.gov. Internet, http://www. fhfa.gov/AboutUs/reportsplans.

Public Records FHFA public records are published online. Questions about other publicly accessible records, including those covered under the Freedom of Information Act, should be directed to the Chief FOIA Officer. Email, foia@fhfa.gov. Internet, http://www.fhfa.gov/AboutUs/ FOIAPrivacy/Pages/FOIA.aspx.

For further information, contact the Office of Congressional Affairs and Communications, Federal Housing Finance Agency, 400 7th Street SW., Washington, DC 20024. Phone, 866–796–5595. Email, fhfainfo@fhfa. gov. Internet, https://www.fhfa.gov/AboutUs/Contact.

FEDERAL LABOR RELATIONS AUTHORITY

1400 K Street NW., Washington, DC 20005
Phone, 202–218–7770. Internet, http://www.flra.gov.

Chair	Carol W. Pope
Members	Ernest DuBester, Patrick Pizzella
Executive Director	Sarah W. Spooner
Chief Counsel	William R. Tobey
Chief, Case Intake and Publication	Gina K. Grippando
Solicitor	William R. Tobey, *Acting*
Inspector General	Dana Rooney-Fisher
Chief Administrative Law Judge	Charles Center
General Counsel	Julia A. Clark
Federal Service Impasses Panel	
Chair	Mary E. Jacksteit
Members	Barbara B. Franklin, Edward F. Hartfield, Martin H. Malin, H. Joseph Schimansky, Donald S. Wasserman, (vacancy)
Executive Director	(vacancy)

Foreign Service Labor Relations Board
Chair   CAROL W. POPE
Members   EARL W. HOCKENBERRY, JR., STEPHEN R.
                                                 LEDFORD

Foreign Service Impasse Disputes Panel
Chair   MARY E. JACKSTEIT
Members   BETTY BOLDEN, DIANE T. McFADGEN,
                                                 ALEXANDRIA L. PANEHAL, JONITA
                                                 WHITAKER

The Federal Labor Relations Authority oversees labor-management relations between the Federal Government and its employees.

The Federal Labor Relations Authority was created as an independent establishment by Reorganization Plan No. 2 of 1978 (5 U.S.C. app.), effective January 1, 1979, pursuant to Executive Order 12107 of December 28, 1978, to consolidate the central policymaking functions in Federal labor-management relations. Its duties and authority are specified in Title VII (Federal Service Labor-Management Relations) of the Civil Service Reform Act of 1978 (5 U.S.C. 7101–7135).

The Authority comprises three members, whom the President nominates and the Senate confirms to a 5-year term. The Chairman of the Authority serves as the chief executive and administrative officer. The Chairman also chairs the Foreign Service Labor Relations Board. The General Counsel of the Authority investigates alleged unfair labor practices, files and prosecutes unfair labor practice complaints before the Authority, and exercises such other powers as the Authority may prescribe.

Activities

The Authority adjudicates disputes arising under the Federal Labor-Management Relations Program, deciding cases concerning the negotiability of collective bargaining agreement proposals, appeals concerning unfair labor practices and representation petitions, and exceptions to grievance arbitration awards. It also assists Federal agencies and unions in understanding their rights and responsibilities under the program.

The Federal Service Impasses Panel, an entity within the Authority, assists in resolving negotiation impasses between agencies and unions. After investigating an impasse, the Panel can either recommend procedures to the parties for the resolution of the impasse or assist the parties in resolving the impasse through whatever methods and procedures it considers appropriate, including factfinding and recommendations. If the parties do not arrive at a settlement after receiving assistance from the Panel, the Panel may hold hearings and take whatever action is necessary to resolve the impasse.

The Foreign Service Labor Relations Board and the Foreign Service Impasse Disputes Panel administer provisions of chapter 2 of the Foreign Service Act of 1980 (22 U.S.C. 3921) concerning labor-management relations. This chapter establishes a statutory labor-management relations program for Foreign Service employees of the U.S. Government. Administrative and staff support is provided by the Federal Labor Relations Authority and the Federal Service Impasses Panel.

Sources of Information

Employment   Contact the Human Resources Division. Phone, 202–218–7979. Internet, http://www.flra.gov/jobs.
Public Information and Publications   The Authority assists in the reproduction of documents and ordering of transcripts of hearings. Requests for publications should be submitted to the Chief, Case Intake and Publication. Phone, 202–218–7740. Internet, http://www.flra.gov/CIP.

FEDERAL LABOR RELATIONS AUTHORITY

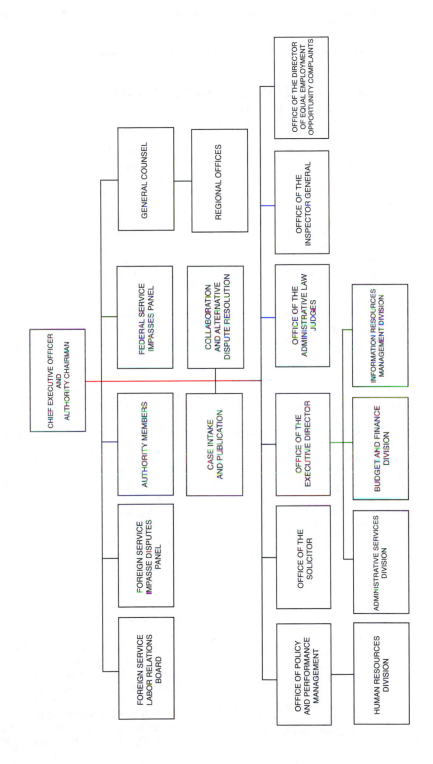

For further information, contact the Office of the Executive Director, Federal Labor Relations Authority, 1400 K Street NW., Washington, DC 20005. Phone, 202–218–7791. Email, flraexecutivedirector@flra.gov. Internet, http://www.flra.gov/oed.

FEDERAL MARITIME COMMISSION

800 North Capitol Street NW., Washington, DC 20573
Phone, 202–523–5707. Internet, http://www.fmc.gov.

Chairman	MARIO CORDERO
Commissioners	WILLIAM P. DOYLE, REBECCA F. DYE, MICHAEL A. KHOURI, RICHARD A. LIDINSKY, JR.
General Counsel	(VACANCY)
Secretary	KAREN V. GREGORY
Director, Consumer Affairs and Dispute Resolution Services	REBECCA A. FENNEMAN
Chief, Administrative Law Judge	CLAY G. GUTHRIDGE
Director, Office of Equal Employment Opportunity	KEITH I. GILMORE
Inspector General	(VACANCY)
Director, Office of Managing Director	VERN W. HILL
Director, Bureau of Certification and Licensing	SANDRA L. KUSUMOTO
Director, Bureau of Enforcement	PETER J. KING
Director, Bureau of Trade Analysis	FLORENCE A. CARR

The Federal Maritime Commission regulates the waterborne foreign commerce of the United States. It ensures that U.S. oceanborne trades are open to all on fair and equitable terms and protects against concerted activities and unlawful practices.

The Federal Maritime Commission was established by Reorganization Plan No. 7 of 1961 (46 U.S.C. 301–307), effective August 12, 1961. It is an independent agency that regulates shipping under the following statutes: the Shipping Act of 1984, as amended (46 U.S.C. 40101–41309); Section 19 of the Merchant Marine Act, 1920 (46 U.S.C. 42101–42109); the Foreign Shipping Practices Act of 1988 (46 U.S.C. 42301–42307); and the act of November 6, 1966 (46 U.S.C. 44101–44106).

Activities

Agreements The Commission reviews agreements by and among ocean common carriers and/or marine terminal operators, filed under section 5 of the Shipping Act of 1984, for statutory compliance as well as for likely impact on competition. It also monitors activities under all effective agreements for

compliance with the provisions of law and its rules, orders, and regulations.
Tariffs The Commission monitors and prescribes requirements to ensure accessibility and accuracy of electronic tariff publications of common carriers engaged in the foreign commerce of the United States. Special permission applications may be submitted for relief from statutory and/or Commission tariff requirements.
Service Contracts The Commission receives and reviews filings of confidential service contracts between shippers and ocean common carriers. The Commission also monitors publication of certain essential terms of those service contracts.
Non-Vessel-Operating Common Carrier Service Arrangements The Commission receives and reviews service arrangements entered into by non-vessel-operating common carriers and their customers. Cargo moving under these

FEDERAL MARITIME COMMISSION

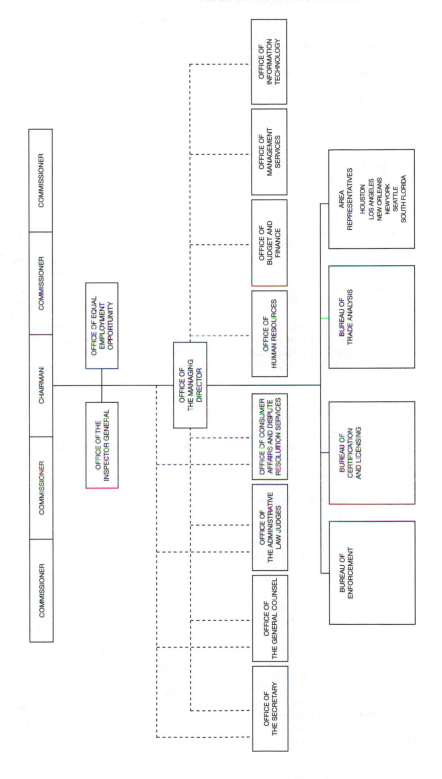

COMMISSIONER | COMMISSIONER | CHAIRMAN | COMMISSIONER | COMMISSIONER

OFFICE OF THE INSPECTOR GENERAL

OFFICE OF EQUAL EMPLOYMENT OPPORTUNITY

OFFICE OF THE MANAGING DIRECTOR

OFFICE OF THE SECRETARY

OFFICE OF THE GENERAL COUNSEL

OFFICE OF THE ADMINISTRATIVE LAW JUDGES

OFFICE OF CONSUMER AFFAIRS AND DISPUTE RESOLUTION SERVICES

OFFICE OF HUMAN RESOURCES

OFFICE OF BUDGET AND FINANCE

OFFICE OF MANAGEMENT SERVICES

OFFICE OF INFORMATION TECHNOLOGY

BUREAU OF ENFORCEMENT

BUREAU OF CERTIFICATION AND LICENSING

BUREAU OF TRADE ANALYSIS

AREA REPRESENTATIVES
HOUSTON
LOS ANGELES
NEW ORLEANS
NEW YORK
SEATTLE
SOUTH FLORIDA

service arrangements is exempt from the tariff publication and adherence requirements of the Shipping Act, on the condition that the service arrangements must be filed with the Commission.

Licenses The Commission issues licenses to those persons and entities in the United States who wish to carry out the business of providing freight forwarding services and non-vessel-operating common carrier services.

Passenger Indemnity The Commission administers the passenger indemnity provisions of the act of November 6, 1966, which require shipowners and operators to obtain certificates of financial responsibility to pay judgments for personal injury or death or to refund fares in the event of nonperformance of voyages.

Complaints The Commission reviews alleged or suspected violations of the shipping statutes and rules and regulations of the Commission and may take administrative action to institute formal proceedings, to refer matters to other governmental agencies, or to bring about voluntary agreement between the parties.

Formal Adjudicatory Procedures The Commission conducts formal investigations and hearings on its own motion and adjudicates formal complaints in accordance with the Administrative Procedure Act (5 U.S.C. note prec. 551).

Alternative Dispute Resolution The Commission reviews informal complaints and assists parties in resolving disputes. Mediation and other dispute resolution services are available to assist parties in achieving a more acceptable resolution to a dispute at less cost than may be possible in litigation. These services are available before and after the commencement of litigation. The Commission also provides an informal process to adjudicate certain complaints involving less than $50,000 in damages.

Rulemaking The Commission promulgates rules and regulations to interpret, enforce, and ensure compliance with shipping and related statutes by common carriers and other persons subject to the Commission's jurisdiction.

Investigation and Economic Analyses The Commission prescribes and administers programs to ensure compliance with the provisions of the shipping statutes. These programs include: education and outreach activities; the collection of information relating to field investigation of activities and practices of ocean common carriers, terminal operators, agreements among ocean common carriers and/or marine terminal operators, ocean transportation intermediaries, passenger vessel operators, and other persons subject to the shipping statutes; and rate analyses, studies, and economic reviews of current and prospective trade conditions, including the extent and nature of competition in various trade areas.

International Affairs The Commission conducts investigations of foreign governmental and carrier practices that adversely affect the U.S. shipping trade. In consultation with other executive agencies, the Commission takes action to effect the elimination of discriminatory practices on the part of foreign governments against shipping in the United States foreign trade and to achieve comity between the United States and its trading partners.

Sources of Information

Electronic Access Information on the Federal Maritime Commission is available online. Internet, http://www.fmc.gov/about/contact_us.aspx.

Electronic Reading Room Decisions issued from July 1987 to the present and logs of all documents filed or issued in formal proceedings are available on the Commission's Web site. Internet, http://www.fmc.gov/electronic_reading_room/default1.aspx.

Employment Contact the Office of Human Resources, Federal Maritime Commission, 800 North Capitol Street NW., Washington, DC 20573–0001. Phone, 202–523–5773. Internet, http://www.fmc.gov/about/employment_opportunities.aspx.

Consumer Affairs and Dispute Resolution Services Contact the Office of Consumer Affairs and Dispute Resolution Services. Phone, 202–523–5807. Email, complaints@fmc.gov. Internet, http:// www.fmc.gov/bureaus_offices/consumer_

affairs_and_dispute_resolution_services. aspx.

For further information, contact the Office of the Secretary, Federal Maritime Commission, 800 North Capitol Street NW., Washington, DC 20573–0001. Phone, 202–523–5725. Fax, 202–523–0014. Email, secretary@fmc.gov. Internet, http://www.fmc.gov.

FEDERAL MEDIATION AND CONCILIATION SERVICE

2100 K Street NW., Washington, DC 20427
Phone, 202–606–8100. Internet, http://www.fmcs.gov.

Director   Scot L. Beckenbaugh, *Acting*

The Federal Mediation and Conciliation Service helps labor and management resolve disputes in collective bargaining contract negotiation, provides training to unions and management in cooperative processes, and provides alternative dispute resolution services and training to Government agencies.

The Federal Mediation and Conciliation Service (FMCS) was created by the Labor Management Relations Act, 1947 (29 U.S.C. 172). The President, with the advice and consent of the Senate, appoints the Director.

Activities

By providing mediators to assist labor and management resolve their differences, FMCS reduces interstate commerce flow disruptions that stem from disputes. Mediators have no law enforcement authority and rely wholly on persuasive techniques.

With the exception of airlines and railroads, FMCS offers its services to any industry that affects interstate commerce and whose employees have union representation. When FMCS deems that a dispute may interrupt the flow of commerce substantially, it becomes involved, either on its own initiative or at the request of one or more of the disputants. The Labor Management Relations Act requires that parties to a labor contract must file a dispute notice if agreement is not reached 30 days in advance of a contract termination or reopening date. The notice must be filed

with FMCS and the appropriate State or local mediation agency. If State or other conciliation services are available to the parties, FMCS avoids mediating disputes that may affect, only lightly, interstate commerce.

Mediation   FMCS mediators focus on establishing sound, stable, and enduring labor-management relations. Their efforts help to reduce the incidence of work stoppages. The mediator's basic function is to encourage and promote better day-to-day relations between labor and management so that problematic issues arising in negotiations may be settled through cooperation and compromise rather than dispute. To locate a mediator online, use the link below.

Internet, http://www.fmcs.gov/internet/ findMediator.asp?categoryID=72.

Arbitration   At the joint request of employers and unions, FMCS does provide its roster of arbitrators, who are private practitioners and qualified as neutrals, to adjudicate matters in dispute. For further information, contact the Office of Arbitration Services. Phone, 202–606–5111.

Internet, http://www.fmcs.gov/internet/categoryList. asp?categoryID=24.

For further information, contact the Public Affairs Office, Federal Mediation and Conciliation Service, 2100 K Street NW., Washington, DC 20427. Phone, 202–606–8100. Internet, http://www.fmcs.gov.

FEDERAL MINE SAFETY AND HEALTH REVIEW COMMISSION

1331 Pennsylvania Avenue NW., Suite 520N, Washington, DC 20004–1710
Phone, 202–434–9900. Internet, http://www.fmshrc.gov.

Chairman	MARY LUCILLE JORDAN
Commissioners	WILLIAM I. ALTHEN, ROBERT F. COHEN, JR., PATRICK NAKAMURA, MICHAEL G. YOUNG
Chief Administrative Law Judge	ROBERT J. LESNICK
General Counsel	MICHAEL A. MCCORD
Executive Director	LISA M. BOYD

The Federal Mine Safety and Health Review Commission ensures compliance with occupational safety and health standards in the Nation's surface and underground coal, metal, and nonmetal mines.

The Federal Mine Safety and Health Review Commission is an independent, adjudicative agency established by the Federal Mine Safety and Health Act of 1977 (30 U.S.C. 801 et seq.), as amended. It provides administrative trial and appellate review of legal disputes arising from enforcement actions taken by the Department of Labor.

The Commission comprises five members who are appointed by the President with the advice and consent of the Senate. Each member serves a 6-year term, and all the terms are staggered. The President appoints one of the Commissioners to serve as the Chairman.

The Commission and its Office of Administrative Law Judges are charged with deciding cases brought before it by the Mine Safety and Health Administration, mine operators, and miners or their representatives. These cases generally involve review of the Administration's enforcement actions, including citations, mine-closure orders, and proposals for civil penalties issued for violations of the act or the mandatory safety and health standards promulgated by the Secretary of Labor. The Commission also has jurisdiction over discrimination complaints filed by miners or their representatives in connection with their safety and health, complaints for compensation filed on behalf of miners idled as a result of mine closure orders issued by the Administration, and disputes over mine emergency response plans.

Cases brought before the Commission are assigned to the Office of Administrative Law Judges, and hearings are conducted pursuant to the requirements of the Administrative Procedure Act (5 U.S.C. 554, 556) and the Commission's procedural rules (29 CFR 2700).

A judge's decision becomes a final, but nonprecedential order of the Commission 40 days after issuance unless the Commission has directed the case for review in response to a petition or on its own motion. If a review is conducted, a decision of the Commission becomes final 30 days after issuance unless a party adversely affected seeks review in the U.S. Circuit Court of Appeals for the District of Columbia or the Circuit within which the mine subject to the litigation is located.

As far as practicable, hearings are held at locations convenient to the affected mines. In addition to its Washington, DC, offices, the Office of Administrative Law Judges maintains an office in the Colonnade Center, Room 280, 1244 Speer Boulevard, Denver, CO 80204.

Sources of Information

Commission decisions are published bimonthly and are available through the Superintendent of Documents, U.S. Government Printing Office, Washington, DC 20402. The Commission's Web site

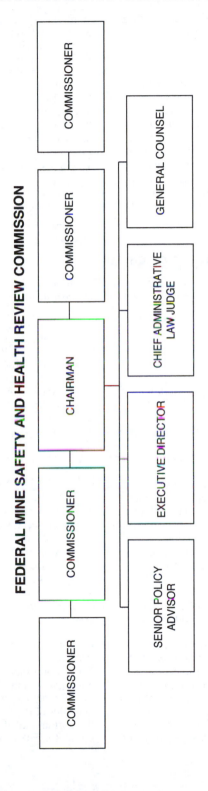

FEDERAL MINE SAFETY AND HEALTH REVIEW COMMISSION

COMMISSIONER

COMMISSIONER

CHAIRMAN

COMMISSIONER

COMMISSIONER

GENERAL COUNSEL

CHIEF ADMINISTRATIVE LAW JUDGE

EXECUTIVE DIRECTOR

SENIOR POLICY ADVISOR

includes recent decisions, a searchable database of previous decisions, procedural rules, audio recordings of recent public meetings, and other pertinent information.

Requests for Commission records should be submitted in accordance with the Commission's Freedom of Information Act regulations. Other information, including Commission rules of procedure and brochures explaining the Commission's functions, is available

from the Executive Director, Federal Mine Safety and Health Review Commission, 1331 Pennsylvania Avenue NW., Suite 520N, Washington, DC 20004–1710.

For information on filing requirements, the status of cases before the Commission, or docket information, contact the Office of General Counsel or the Docket Office, Federal Mine Safety and Health Review Commission, 1331 Pennsylvania Avenue NW., Suite 520N, Washington, DC 20004–1710.

For further information, contact the Executive Director, Federal Mine Safety and Health Review Commission, 1331 Pennsylvania Avenue NW., Suite 520N, Washington DC 20004–1710. Phone, 202–434–9905. Fax, 202–434–9906. Email, fmshrc@fmshrc.gov. Internet, http://www.fmshrc.gov.

FEDERAL RESERVE SYSTEM

Twentieth Street and Constitution Avenue NW., Washington, DC 20551
Phone, 202–452–3000. Internet, http://www.federalreserve.gov.

Chairman	JANET L. YELLEN
Vice Chair	STANLEY FISCHER
Members	JEROME H. POWELL, JEREMY C. STEIN, DANIEL K. TARULLO, LAEL BRAINARD, (VACANCY)
Director, Division of Board Members	MICHELLE A. SMITH
General Counsel	SCOTT G. ALVAREZ
Secretary	ROBERT DE V. FRIERSON
Director, Division of Banking Supervision and Regulation	MICHAEL S. GIBSON
Director, Division of Consumer and Community Affairs	TONDA PRICE, *Acting*
Director, Division of Federal Reserve Bank Operations and Payment Systems	LOUISE L. ROSEMAN
Director, Division of Information Technology	SHARON L. MOWRY
Director, Division of International Finance	STEVEN B. KAMIN
Director, Management Division	MICHELL C. CLARK
Director, Division of Monetary Affairs	WILLIAM B. ENGLISH
Director, Division of Research and Statistics	DAVID W. WILCOX
Inspector General	MARK BIALEK

The Federal Reserve System, the central bank of the United States, administers and formulates the Nation's credit and monetary policy.

The Federal Reserve System (FRS) was established by the Federal Reserve Act (12 U.S.C. 221), approved December 23, 1913. Its major responsibility is in the execution of monetary policy. It also performs other functions, such as the transfer of funds, handling Government deposits and debt issues, supervising and

regulating banks, and acting as lender of last resort.

FRS contributes to the strength and vitality of the U.S. economy. By influencing the lending and investing activities of depository institutions and the cost and availability of money and credit, the FRS promotes the full use of human and capital resources, the growth of productivity, relatively stable prices, and equilibrium in the Nation's international balance of payments. Through its supervisory and regulatory banking functions, FRS helps maintain a commercial banking system that is responsive to the Nation's financial needs and objectives.

FRS comprises the Board of Governors; the 12 Federal Reserve Banks and their 25 branches and other facilities; the Federal Open Market Committee; the Federal Advisory Council; the Consumer Advisory Council; the Thrift Institutions Advisory Council; and the Nation's financial institutions, including commercial banks, savings and loan associations, mutual savings banks, and credit unions.

Board of Governors The Board comprises seven members appointed by the President with the advice and consent of the Senate. The Chairman of the Board of Governors is a member of the National Advisory Council on International Monetary and Financial Policies. The Board determines general monetary, credit, and operating policies for the System as a whole and formulates the rules and regulations necessary to carry out the purposes of the Federal Reserve Act. The Board's principal duties consist of monitoring credit conditions; supervising the Federal Reserve Banks, member banks, and bank holding companies; and regulating the implementation of certain consumer credit protection laws.

The Board has the power, within statutory limitations, to fix the requirements for reserves to be maintained by depository institutions on transaction accounts or nonpersonal time deposits. The Board reviews and determines the discount rate charged by the Federal Reserve Banks. For the purpose of preventing excessive use of credit for the purchase or carrying of securities, the Board is authorized to regulate the amount of credit that may be initially extended and subsequently maintained on any security (with certain exceptions).

Supervision of Federal Reserve Banks
The Board is authorized to make examinations of the Federal Reserve Banks, to require statements and reports from such Banks, to supervise the issue and retirement of Federal Reserve notes, to require the establishment or discontinuance of branches of Reserve Banks, and to exercise supervision over all relationships and transactions of those Banks with foreign branches.

Supervision of Bank Holding Companies
The Federal Reserve supervises and regulates bank holding companies. Its objective is to maintain the separation between banking and commerce by controlling the expansion of bank holding companies, preventing the formation of banking monopolies, restraining certain trade practices in banking, and limiting the nonbanking activities of bank holding companies. A company that seeks to become a bank holding company must obtain the prior approval of the Federal Reserve. Any company that qualifies as a bank holding company must register and file reports with the FRS.

Supervision of Banking Organizations
The Federal Reserve supervises and regulates domestic and international activities of U.S. banking organizations. It supervises State-chartered banks that are members of the System, all bank holding companies, and Edge Act and agreement corporations (corporations chartered to engage in international banking).

The Board has jurisdiction over the admission of State banks and trust companies to membership in the FRS, membership termination for these banks, the establishment of branches by these banks, and the approval of bank mergers and consolidations where the resulting institution will be a State member bank. It receives copies of condition reports submitted to the Federal Reserve Banks. It has power to examine all member banks and the affiliates of member banks and to require condition reports from them. It has authority to require periodic and other public disclosure of information with respect to an equity security of a State member bank that is held by 500 or more persons. It establishes minimum standards with respect to installation, maintenance, and operation of security devices and procedures by State member banks. It can issue cease-and-desist orders in connection with violations of law or unsafe or unsound banking practices by State member banks and to remove directors or officers of such banks in certain circumstances. It also can suspend member banks from use of the Federal Reserve System's credit facilities for using bank credit for speculation or other purposes inconsistent with the maintenance of sound credit conditions.

The Board may grant authority to member banks to establish branches in foreign countries or dependencies or insular possessions of the United States, to invest in the stocks of banks or corporations engaged in international or foreign banking, or to invest in foreign banks. It also charters, regulates, and supervises certain corporations that engage in foreign or international banking and financial activities.

The Board is authorized to issue general regulations permitting interlocking relationships in certain circumstances between member banks and organizations dealing in securities or between member banks and other banks.

The Board prescribes regulations to ensure a meaningful disclosure by lenders of credit terms so that consumers will be able to compare more readily the various credit terms available and will be informed about rules governing credit cards, including their potential liability for unauthorized use.

The Board has authority to impose reserve requirements and interest rate ceilings on branches and agencies of foreign banks in the United States, to grant loans to them, to provide them access to Federal Reserve services, and to limit their interstate banking activities.

Federal Open Market Committee   The Federal Open Market Committee comprises the Board of Governors and five of the presidents of the Reserve Banks. The Chairman of the Board of Governors is traditionally the Chairman of the Committee. The president of the Federal Reserve Bank of New York serves as a permanent member of the Committee. Four of the twelve Reserve Bank presidents rotate annually as members of the Committee.

Open market operations of the Reserve Banks are conducted under regulations adopted by the Committee and pursuant to specific policy directives issued by the Committee, which meets in Washington, DC, at frequent intervals. Purchases and sales of securities in the open market are undertaken to supply bank reserves to support the credit and money needed for long-term economic growth, to offset cyclical economic swings, and to accommodate seasonal demands of businesses and consumers for money and credit. These operations are carried out principally in U.S. Government obligations, but they also include purchases and sales of Federal agency obligations. All operations are conducted in New York, where the primary markets for these securities are located; the Federal Reserve Bank of New York executes transactions for the Federal Reserve System Open Market Account in carrying out these operations.

Under the Committee's direction, the Federal Reserve Bank of New York also undertakes transactions in foreign currencies for the Federal Reserve System Open Market Account. The purposes of these operations include helping to safeguard the value of the dollar in international exchange markets and facilitating growth in international liquidity in accordance with the needs of an expanding world economy.

Federal Reserve Banks   The 12 Federal Reserve Banks are located in Atlanta, GA; Boston, MA; Chicago, IL; Cleveland, OH; Dallas, TX; Kansas City, MO; Minneapolis, MN; New York, NY; Philadelphia, PA; Richmond, VA; San Francisco, CA; and St. Louis, MO. Branch banks are located in Baltimore, MD; Birmingham, AL; Buffalo, NY; Charlotte, NC; Cincinnati, OH; Denver, CO; Detroit, MI; El Paso, TX; Helena, MT; Houston, TX; Jacksonville, FL; Little Rock, AR; Los Angeles, CA; Louisville, KY; Memphis, TN; Miami, FL; Nashville, TN; New Orleans, LA; Oklahoma City, OK; Omaha, NE; Pittsburgh, PA; Portland, OR; Salt Lake City, UT; San Antonio, TX; and Seattle, WA.

Reserves on Deposit The Reserve Banks receive and hold on deposit the reserve or clearing account deposits of depository institutions. These banks are permitted to count their vault cash as part of their required reserve.

Extensions of Credit The Federal Reserve is required to open its discount window to any depository institution that is subject to its reserve requirements on transaction accounts or nonpersonal time deposits. Discount window credit provides for Federal Reserve lending to eligible depository institutions under two basic programs. One is the adjustment credit program; the other supplies more extended credit for certain limited purposes.

Short-term adjustment credit is the primary type of Federal Reserve credit. It is available to help borrowers meet temporary requirements for funds. Borrowers are not permitted to use adjustment credit to take advantage of any spread between the discount rate and market rates.

Extended credit is provided through three programs designed to assist depository institutions in meeting longer term needs for funds. One provides seasonal credit—for periods running up to 9 months—to smaller depository institutions that lack access to market funds. A second program assists institutions that experience special difficulties arising from exceptional circumstances or practices involving only that institution. Finally, in cases where more general liquidity strains are affecting a broad range of depository institutions— such as those whose portfolios consist primarily of longer term assets—credit may be provided to address the problems of particular institutions being affected by the general situation.

Currency Issue The Reserve Banks issue Federal Reserve notes, which constitute the bulk of money in circulation. These notes are obligations of the United States and are a prior lien upon the assets of the issuing Federal Reserve Bank. They are issued against a pledge by the Reserve Bank with the Federal Reserve agent of collateral security including gold certificates, paper discounted or purchased by the Bank, and direct obligations of the United States.

Other Powers The Reserve Banks are empowered to act as clearinghouses and as collecting agents for depository institutions in the collection of checks and other instruments. They are also authorized to act as depositories and fiscal agents of the United States and to exercise other banking functions specified in the Federal Reserve Act. They perform a number of important functions in connection with the issue and redemption of United States Government securities.

Sources of Information

Employment Written inquiries regarding employment should be addressed to the Director, Division of Personnel, Board of Governors of the Federal Reserve System, Washington, DC 20551.

Procurement Firms seeking business with the Board should address their inquiries to the Director, Division of Support Services, Board of Governors of the Federal Reserve System, Washington, DC 20551.

Publications Among the publications issued by the Board are "The Federal Reserve System: Purposes and Functions" and a series of pamphlets, including "Guide to Business Credit and the Equal Credit Opportunity Act"; "Consumer Handbook"; "Making Deposits: When Will Your Money Be Available"; and "When Your Home Is On the Line: What You Should Know About Home Equity Lines of Credit." Copies of these pamphlets are available free of charge. Information regarding publications may be obtained in Room MP–510 (Martin Building) of the Board's headquarters. Phone, 202–452–3244.

Reading Room A reading room where persons may inspect public records is located in Room B–1122 at the Board's headquarters, Twentieth Street and Constitution Avenue NW., Washington, DC 20551. Information regarding the availability of records may be obtained by calling 202–452–3684.

For further information, contact the Office of Public Affairs, Board of Governors, Federal Reserve System, Washington, DC 20551. Phone, 202–452–3204 or 202–452–3215. Internet, http://www.federalreserve.gov.

FEDERAL RETIREMENT THRIFT INVESTMENT BOARD

77 K Street NE., Washington, DC 20002
Phone, 202–942–1600. Fax, 202–942–1676. Internet, http://www.frtib.gov/Home.html.

Chairman	MICHAEL D. KENNEDY
Members	DANA K. BILYEU, WILLIAM S. JASIEN, DAVID A. JONES, RONALD D. McCRAY
Executive Director	GREGORY T. LONG
Chief Investment Officer	TRACEY A. RAY
Director of Participant Services	THOMAS K. EMSWILER
Director of External Affairs	KIMBERLY A. WEAVER
General Counsel	JAMES B. PETRICK
Chief Technology Officer	MARK WALTHER
Chief Financial Officer	SUSAN C. CROWDER
Director of Enterprise Planning	RENEE WILDER
Director, Resource Management	GISILE GOETHE, *Acting*
Director of Enterprise Risk Management	JAY AHUJA
Director, Office of Communications and Education	JAMES COURTNEY

The Federal Retirement Thrift Investment Board administers the Thrift Savings Plan, which provides Federal employees the opportunity to save for additional retirement security.

The Federal Retirement Thrift Investment Board was established as an independent agency by the Federal Employees' Retirement System Act of 1986 (5 U.S.C. 8351 and 8401–79). The act vests responsibility for the agency in six named fiduciaries: the five Board members and the Executive Director. The President, with the advice and consent of the Senate, appoints the five members of the Board, one of whom is designated as Chairman. The members serve on a part-time basis, and they appoint the Executive Director, who is responsible for the management of the agency and the Plan.

Activities

The Thrift Savings Plan is a tax-deferred, defined contribution plan that was established as one of the three parts of the Federal Employees' Retirement System. For employees covered under the System, savings accumulated through the Plan make an important addition to Social Security retirement benefits and the System's Basic Annuity. Civil Service Retirement System employees and members of the Uniformed Services may also take advantage of the Plan to supplement their annuities.

The Board operates the Thrift Savings Plan and manages the investments of the Thrift Savings Fund solely for the benefit of participants and their beneficiaries. As part of these responsibilities, the Board maintains an account for each Plan participant, makes loans, purchases annuity contracts, and provides for the payment of benefits.

Internet, https://www.tsp.gov/index.shtml.

For further information, contact the Director of External Affairs, Federal Retirement Thrift Investment Board, 77 K Street NE., Washington, DC 20002. Phone, 202–942–1640. Internet, http://www.frtib.gov/Home.html.

FEDERAL TRADE COMMISSION

600 Pennsylvania Avenue NW., Washington, DC 20580
Phone, 202–326–2222. Internet, http://www.ftc.gov.

Chair	EDITH RAMIREZ
Commissioners	JULIE BRILL, TERRELL McSWEENY, MAUREEN K. OHLHAUSEN, JOSHUA D. WRIGHT
Chief of Staff	HEATHER HIPPSLEY
Executive Director	DAVID ROBBINS
Chief Administrative Law Judge	D. MICHAEL CHAPPELL
Director, Bureau of Competition	DEBORAH L. FEINSTEIN
Director, Bureau of Consumer Protection	JESSICA RICH
Director, Bureau of Economics	MARTIN S. GAYNOR
Director, Office of Congressional Relations	JEANNE BUMPUS
Director, Office of International Affairs	RANDOLPH W. TRITELL
Director, Office of Policy Planning	ANDREW I. GAVIL
Director, Office of Public Affairs	JUSTIN COLE
Director, Equal Employment Opportunity	KEVIN WILLIAMS
General Counsel	JONATHAN E. NUECHTERLEIN
Inspector General	SCOTT WILSON
Secretary of the Commission	DONALD S. CLARK

[For the Federal Trade Commission statement of organization, see the Code of Federal Regulations, Title 16, Part 0]

The Federal Trade Commission protects America's consumers and enforces laws that prohibit anticompetitive, deceptive, or unfair business practices.

The Federal Trade Commission (FTC) was established in 1914 by the Federal Trade Commission Act (15 U.S.C. 41–58). The Commission comprises five members, whom the President appoints, with the advice and consent of the Senate, for a term of 7 years. No more than three of the Commissioners may be members of the same political party. The President designates one of them as Chair of the Commission to oversee its administrative management.

Activities

The FTC protects consumers and promotes competition in broad sectors of the economy. Its work centers on safeguarding and strengthening free and open markets and helping consumers make informed choices. The FTC performs its mission by using a variety of tools: law enforcement, rulemaking, research, studies of marketplace trends and legal developments, and consumer and business education. The FTC envisions a U.S. economy that is vigourously competive and offers accessible and accurate information to consumers, an econonmy that yields high-quality products at competitive prices and fosters efficiency, innovation, and consumer choice.

Competition   The FTC prevents anticompetitive mergers and assures that the marketplace is free from anticompetitive business practices. To achieve its goal of promoting competition, the FTC engages in six law enforcement-related activities: premerger notification, merger and joint venture enforcement, merger and joint venture compliance, nonmerger enforcement, nonmerger compliance, and antitrust policy. Policy initiatives, research, and business guidance and education also play a role in promoting competition.

Consumer Protection   The FTC brings a variety of consumer protection cases and works with State attorneys general and other State and local consumer protection officials. To achieve its goal of protecting consumers, the FTC relies on five law

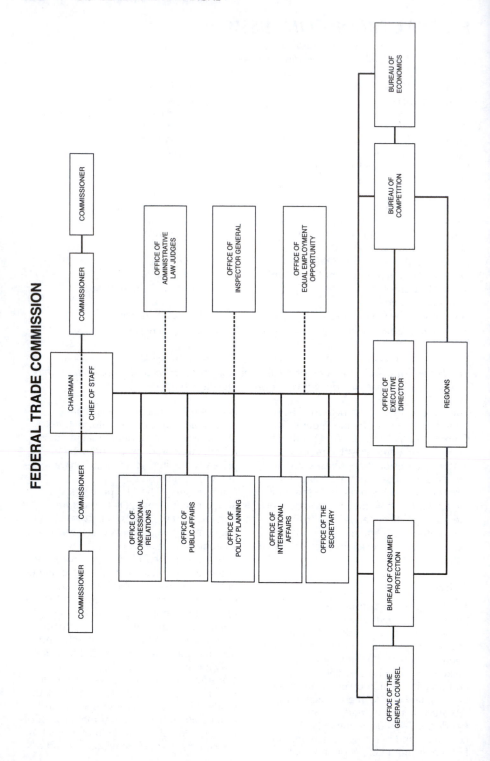

FEDERAL TRADE COMMISSION

enforcement functions: privacy and identity protection, financial practices, marketing practices, advertising practices, and enforcement. Policy initiatives, research, and business and consumer education also enhance protection.

Enforcement The FTC's law enforcement work covers actions to foster voluntary compliance with the law and formal administrative or Federal court litigation leading to mandatory orders against offenders.

The FTC issues an administrative complaint or authorizes the filing of a Federal district court complaint charging a person, partnership, or corporation with violating one or more of the statutes enforced by the FTC. If the charges are not contested, settled by consent of the parties, or are found to be true after an administrative hearing or a Federal court trial, an administrative law judge or Federal court judge issues an order requiring discontinuance of the unlawful practices. Also, the FTC may request that a U.S. district court issue preliminary relief to halt allegedly unfair or deceptive practices, to prevent an anticompetitive merger or unfair methods of competition from taking place, or to prevent violations of any statute enforced by the FTC, pending the full adjudication of the matter. In Federal court, the FTC may obtain other relief, including monetary redress. An order issued after an administrative or Federal court proceeding that requires the respondent to cease and desist or take other corrective action may be appealed.

International Affairs The FTC works with other nations and international organizations to promote sound competition and consumer protection policies and provide technical assistance to enable developing competition and consumer protection agencies to perform their missions.

Regional Offices A list of Federal Trade Commission regional offices is available online.

Internet, http://www.ftc.gov/ro/index.shtml.

Sources of Information

Complaints To file a complaint in English or Spanish, use the link below or call 1–877–FTC–HELP (1–877–382–4357). The FTC enters complaints into Consumer Sentinel, a secure, online database available to more than 2,000 civil and criminal law enforcement agencies in the U.S. and abroad. To inform the Competition Bureau about particular business practices, call 202–326–3300, send an e-mail to antitrust@ftc.gov, or write to the Office of Policy and Coordination, Bureau of Competition, Federal Trade Commission, 600 Pennsylvania Avenue, NW., Washington, DC 20580. Internet, https://www.ftccomplaintassistant. gov/#crnt&panel1-1.

Contracts and Procurement For information on contracts and procurement, contact the Assistant Chief Financial Officer for Acquisitions, Federal Trade Commission, Washington, DC 20580. Phone, 202–326–2339. Fax, 202–326–3529. Internet, http://www.ftc. gov/ftc/oed/fmo/procure/procure.shtm.

Employment Job seekers must apply for most positions online, through the Office of Personnel Management's application system, USAJOBS (https:// my.usajobs.gov/). For employment-related information, contact the Human Capital Management Office. Phone, 202–326–2021. TTY, 202–326–3422. Internet, http://www.ftc.gov/about-ftc/ careers-ftc.

General Inquiries To obtain general information or reach a variety of offices, contact the Federal Trade Commission at 202–326–2222. Internet, http://www.ftc. gov/about-ftc/bureaus-offices.

Publications Free consumer and business education publications are available from the Consumer Response Center, Federal Trade Commission, Washington, DC 20580. Phone, 877–382–4357. TTY, 866–653–4261. Internet, https://bulkorder.ftc.gov/.

Workshops Information on conferences and workshops that are open to the public is available online. Internet, http://www.ftc.gov/news-events/events-calendar/all.

For further information, contact the Office of Public Affairs, Federal Trade Commission, 600 Pennsylvania Avenue NW., Washington, DC 20580. Phone, 202–326–2180. Fax, 202–326–3366. Internet, http://www.ftc. gov/about-ftc/bureaus-offices/office-public-affairs.

GENERAL SERVICES ADMINISTRATION

1275 First Street NE., Washington, DC 20417
Internet, http://www.gsa.gov.

Administrator	DANIEL M. TANGHERLINI
Deputy Administrator	DENISE TURNER-ROTH
Chief of Staff	ADAM NEUFELD
White House Liaison	REGINALD H. CARDOZO, JR.
Chairman, Civilian Board of Contract Appeals	STEPHEN M. DANIELS
Inspector General	BRIAN D. MILLER
General Counsel	KRIS E. DURMER
Associate Administrator, Office of Civil Rights	MADELINE C. CALIENDO
Associate Administrator, Office of Government-wide Policy	ANNE E. RUNG
Associate Administrator, Office of Citizen Services and Innovative Technologies	DAVID L. MCCLURE
Associate Administrator, Office of Communications and Marketing	BETSAIDA ALCANTARA
Associate Administrator, Office of Congressional and Intergovernmental Affairs	LISA A. AUSTIN
Associate Administrator, Office of Small Business Utilization	KAREN POOLE, *Acting*
Associate Administrator, Office of Emergency Response and Recovery	ROBERT CARTER, *Acting*
Chief Financial Officer	MICHAEL CASELLA
Chief Human Capital Officer	ANTHONY E. COSTA
Chief Information Officer	SONNY HASHMI, *Acting*
Chief Administrative Services Officer	CYNTHIA A. METZLER
Chief Acquisition Officer	ANNE E. RUNG
Commissioner, Federal Acquisition Service	THOMAS A. SHARPE
Commissioner, Public Buildings Service	NORMAN DONG
Regional Administrator, New England	ROBERT ZARNETSKE
Regional Administrator, Northeast and Caribbean	DENISE L. PEASE
Regional Administrator, Mid-Atlantic	SARA MANZANO-DIAZ
Regional Administrator, Southeast Sunbelt	ERVILLE KOEHLER
Regional Administrator, Great Lakes	ANN P. KALAYIL
Regional Administrator, Heartland	JASON O. KLUMB
Regional Administrator, Greater Southwest	SYLVIA HERNANDEZ, *Acting*
Regional Administrator, Rocky Mountain	SUSAN B. DAMOUR
Regional Administrator, Pacific Rim	RUTH F. COX
Regional Administrator, Northwest/Arctic	GEORGE E. NORTHCROFT
Regional Administrator, National Capital	JULIA E. HUDSON

[For the General Services Administration statement of organization, see the Code of Federal Regulations, Title 41, Part 105–53]

The General Services Administration makes policy for and provides management of Government property and records, including construction and operation of buildings; procurement and distribution of supplies; utilization and disposal of real and personal property; transportation, travel, fleet, and communications management; and the Governmentwide automatic data processing resources program.

The General Services Administration (GSA) was established by section 101 of the Federal Property and Administrative Services Act of 1949 (40 U.S.C. 751).

Civilian Board of Contract Appeals
The Civilian Board of Contract Appeals resolves disputes between contractors and executive agencies, excluding the Postal Service, Postal Rate Commission, National Aeronautics and Space Administration, and Tennessee Valley Authority. The Board also hears and decides requests for review of transportation audit rate determinations; claims by Federal civilian employees, including Department of Defense employees, regarding travel and relocation expenses; claims for the proceeds of the sale of property of certain Federal civilian employees; cases involving the Indian Self-Determination and Education Assistance Act and the Federal Crop Insurance Corporation; and arbitration requests to resolve disputes between applicants and the Federal Emergency Management Agency over funding for public assistance applications arising from the damage caused by Hurricanes Katrina and Rita and applications by prevailing parties for fees under the Equal Access to Justice Act.

The Board also provides alternative dispute resolution services to executive agencies in contract-related disputes. Although it is located within the Administration, the Board functions as an independent tribunal.

For further information, contact the Civilian Board of Contract Appeals, General Services Administration, Washington, DC 20405. Phone, 202–606–8800. Internet, http://www.cbca.gsa.gov/.

Office of Government-wide Policy The Office of Government-wide Policy (OGP) collaborates with the Federal community to develop policies and guidelines for the management and efficient use of Government property, technology, and administrative services.

OGP's policymaking authority and policy support activities cover the following areas: electronic government and information technology, acquisition, real property and the workplace, travel, transportation, personal property, aircraft, the Federal motor vehicle fleet, mail, regulatory information, energy efficiency, and the use of Federal Advisory Committees. OGP also provides leadership to interagency groups and promotes Governmentwide management reform. OGP's six business lines are the Office of Acquisition Policy; the Office of Asset and Transportation Policy; the Office Committee and Regulatory Management; the Office of Information, Integrity, and Access; the Office of Federal High-Performance Green Buildings; the Office of Executive Councils. For further information on OGP, call 202–501–8880.

The Office of Acquisition Policy (OAP) leads positive change in acquisition policy through its role on the Federal Acquisition Regulation (FAR) Council as well as through GSA acquisition policy, guidance, and reporting to stakeholders. OAP, in conjunction with the Department of Defense and NASA, writes the FAR, which serves as the rule book for all Federal agency procurements and governs the billions of dollars spent by the Federal Government every year. OAP also hosts the Federal Acquisition Institute (FAI), which is charged with fostering and promoting the development of the Federal acquisition workforce, along with its training, certification, and warrant needs. OAP also oversees acquisition integrity functions for GSA. The Regulatory Secretariat Division staff prepares, compiles, and processes regulatory and general notices for publication in the "Federal Register." The OAP is headed by the Deputy Chief Acquisition Officer/Senior Procurement Executive and includes the Office of Government-wide Acquisition Policy; the

GENERAL SERVICES ADMINISTRATION

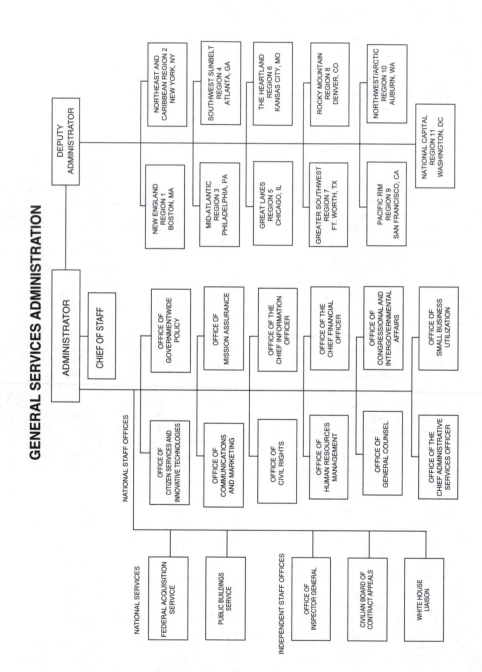

Office of General Services Acquisition Policy, Integrity and Workforce; and the Federal Acquisition Institute. For further information, call 202–501–1777.

The Office of Asset and Transportation Policy supports Federal agencies in the economic and efficient management of assets and specific services. It develops effective policies and guidance for travel, employee relocation allowances and entitlements, personal and real property, motor vehicles, aircraft, transportation, and mail. The Office maintains liaisons with State and local governments, industry, and professional organizations, and it participates in the work of boards, committees, and groups related to asset and transportation management. The Office also provides advice, guidance, and formal classroom training and consultation to agencies regarding establishing and managing Federal advisory committees, as mandated by the Federal Advisory Committee Act. The Office of Asset and Transportation Policy's divisions include: policy performance, aviation, transportation and mail, personal property, real property, travel and relocation, motor vehicle, and the Committee Management Secretariat. For further information, call 202–501–1777.

The Office of Committee and Regulatory Management develops Governmentwide policies, guidance, performance measures, regulations, and training on the management and operation of the Federal advisory committees. It also gathers and publishes information about Federal regulations and their effect on society.

The Office of Information, Integrity, and Access develops, coordinates, and defines information technology business strategies that allow Federal agencies to improve services to American citizens. The Office also provides assistance for and develops policy in the following areas: data and acquisition management, identity credentialing and access management, information management and improvements of analysis capability and architecture development efforts on cross-agency priorities and enterprise data management strategies, Dot Gov domain registration and management, and Section 508 accessibility management. For further information, call 202–501–0202.

The Office of Federal High-Performance Green Buildings helps the Federal Government operate more efficiently and effectively by minimizing the Federal footprint through efficient use of energy, water, and resources. It also helps create healthy and productive workspaces for Federal employees. Congress authorized this Office to increase Federal leadership in sustainable real property portfolio management and operations. The Office works to promote, coordinate, and stimulate environmentally friendly construction and building management practices across the entire Federal Government, which has over 400,000 owned or leased buildings containing over 3 billion square feet of space. The Office has three principal categories of activity: leading and coordinating the greening of the Federal real estate portfolio, supporting innovation and collaboration on the development of new technologies, and supplying the market with information and best practices. To accomplish its goals, the Office relies on an interdisciplinary team of energy, water, air quality, sustainable design, facilities management, budgeting, human behavior, organizational effectiveness, and communications experts. For further information, call 202–219–1522.

The Office of Executive Councils coordinates with the Office of Management and Budget and Federal management councils to identify performance improvement initiatives to pursue Governmentwide, to lead working groups to drive these initiatives, to establish performance goals, and to facilitate the adoption of new processes by Federal agencies. The Office analyzes data, diagnoses challenges, identifies best practices, and documents the benefits delivered by the initiatives. This Office also provides technical and management services to the following Federal management councils: the Chief Acquisition Officers Council, the Chief Financial Officers Council, the

Chief Information Officers Council, the Performance Improvement Council, and the President's Management Council. For further information, call 202–273–4925.

For further information, contact the Office of Government-wide Policy. Phone, 202–501–8880. Internet, http://www.gsa.gov/portal/category/21396.

Citizen Services and Innovative Technologies The Office of Citizen Services and Innovative Technologies (OCSIT) is the Nation's focal point for information and services offered by the Federal Government to the public. The Office provides tools, practices, and templates to facilitate the Government's adoption of new technologies to enhance customer service and improve operational efficiency and effectiveness. OCSIT also creates products and services that help Federal agencies innovate, enhance public services and engagement, and improve resource management.

For 40-years, the Office has been using multiple delivery channels to provide consumer information and services to the public. The Office works closely with other Federal agencies to ensure that

Government information is available and accessible to the public. OCSIT manages the U.S. Government's official Web portal USA.Gov, where online visitors can find information on any aspect of the Federal Government, and GobiernoUSA.gov, the Spanish language version of the portal.

OCSIT manages the Federal Citizen Information Center (FCIC), which helps Federal agencies and departments develop, promote, and distribute useful consumer information to the public. Citizens can get the access they need in a variety of ways: consulting FCIC's print publications, calling 1–800–333–4636, sending an e-mail, or accessing one of FCIC's Web sites, which are listed below. The FCIC also maintains the National Contact Center and publishes the "Consumer Information Catalog" and the "Consumer Action Handbook." For information on these two publications, use the following link: http://www.gsa. gov/portal/content/103355.

For further information, contact the Federal Citizen Information Center's National Contact Center. Phone, 1–800–333–4636. Internet, http://www.gsa. gov/portal/category/101011.

The FCIC maintains the following Government information Web sites.

Web Site	Resources
http://www.usa.gov/	General Government information
http://kids.usa.gov/	Government information for kids
http://www.publications.usa.gov/	Government informational publications
http://www.howto.gov/	Information to help Government agencies enhance customer experience
https://www.challenge.gov/	Government challenges that are posted for the public to help solve and win prizes
http://www.data.gov/	Accessible and readable Government datasets
http://www.usa.gov/gobiernousa/	General Government information in Spanish

Small Business Utilization The Office of Small Business Utilization (OSBU) promotes increased access to GSA's nationwide procurement opportunities for small, HUBZone, and minority-, veteran-, and women-owned businesses. OSBU engages in activities that make it possible for the small business community to meet key contracting experts and be counseled on the procurement process. OSBU monitors and implements small business policies and manages a range of programs mandated by law.

For further information, contact the Office of Small Business Utilization. Phone, 202–501–1021. Internet, http://www.gsa.gov/portal/category/21015.

Federal Acquisition Service

The Federal Acquisition Service (FAS) provides acquisition and procurement support services for Federal agencies to increase overall Government efficiency. FAS programs include tools and resources that aid in the acquisition of products, services, and full-service programs in information technology, telecommunications, professional services, supplies, motor vehicles, travel and transportation, charge cards, and personal property utilization and disposal. For further information, contact the Office of the Commissioner, Federal Acquisition Service. Phone, 703–605–5400.

FAS offers customers a variety of ways to acquire the products, services, and solutions they seek. Key acquisition programs include multiple awards schedules and Governmentwide acquisition contracts that provide customers easy access to information technology, telecommunications, and professional products and services. These products, services, and tools are accessible on GSA's Web site: GSA Advantage!; eBuy and eOffer/eMod; Schedule Sales Query; GSA eLibrary; GSA Xcess, Transportation Management Services Solutions, and other electronic tools.

For further information, contact the Office of the Commissioner, Federal Acquisition Service. Phone, 703–605–5400. Internet, http://www.gsa.gov/portal/content/105080?utm_source=FAS&utm_medium=print-radio&utm_term=fas&utm_campaign=shortcuts.

Public Buildings Service

The Public Buildings Service (PBS) is the landlord for the civilian Federal Government, providing workspace solutions to more than one million Federal employees in 2,100 communities across the Nation, stimulating local economies by designing, building, managing, and maintaining public buildings, as well as leasing from the private sector. PBS is a leader in sustainable design, energy conservation, and green building technologies. Its portfolio consists of 378 million square feet in over 9,000 assets across all 50 States, 6 U.S. Territories, and the District of Columbia. The Service preserves and maintains 471 historic properties and commissions the country's most talented artists to produce works of art for Federal buildings, as well as preserves artwork commissioned under the Works Progress Administration. PBS collects rent from

Federal tenants, which is deposited into the Federal Buildings Fund, the principal funding mechanism for PBS.

For further information, contact the Office of the Commissioner, Public Buildings Service. Phone, 202–501–1100. Internet, http://www.gsa.gov/portal/content/104444?utm_source=PBS&utm_medium=print-radio&utm_term=pbs&utm_campaign=shortcuts.

Regional Offices

GSA operates 11 regional offices. A complete list of these offices is available online.

Internet, http://www.gsa.gov/regions.

Sources of Information

Contracts Individuals seeking to do business with the General Services Administration may access information online. Internet, http://www.gsa.gov/portal/content/105344?utm_source=FAS&utm_medium=print-radio&utm_term=howtosell&utm_campaign=shortcuts.

Electronic Access Information on the Civilian Board of Contract Appeals is available on its Web page. Internet, http://www.cbca.gsa.gov/.

Information on the GSA Inspector General is available on its Web page. Internet, http://www.gsaig.gov/.

Employment Federal employment opportunities, including openings at GSA, are posted online at https://www.usajobs.gov/. For more information on careers at the Agency, use the link below. Internet, http://www.gsa.gov/portal/content/105311?utm_source=CPO&utm_medium=print-radio&utm_term=HDR_0_careers&utm_campaign=shortcuts.

Fraud and Waste Use the Inspector General's FraudNet hotline to report fraud or waste. Phone, 202–501–1780, or 1–800–424–5210. Email, fraudnet@gsa.gov. Internet, http://www.gsa.gov/portal/content/101741.

Freedom of Information Act Requests Freedom of Information Act requests should be addressed to the GSA FOIA Office, General Services Administration, 1800 F Street NW., Room 7308, Washington, DC 20405. Phone, 1–855–675–3642. Fax, 202–501–2727. Email, gsa.foia@gsa.gov. Internet, http://www.

gsa.gov/portal/content/105305?utm_
source=OAS&utm_medium=print-
radio&utm_term=foia&utm_
campaign=shortcuts.

Privacy Act Requests   Privacy Act
requests should be addressed to the GSA
Privacy Act Officer, Office of the Chief
Information Security Officer, Policy and
Compliance Division, (ISP), General
Services Administration, 1800 F Street,
NW., Washington, DC 20405. Phone,
202–208–1317. Email, GSA.privacyact@
gsa.gov. Internet, http://www.gsa.gov/
portal/content/105034.

Property Disposal   Inquiries about the
redistribution or competitive sale of
surplus real property should be directed
to the Office of Real Property Disposal,
Public Buildings Service, 1800 F Street
NW., Washington, DC 20405. Phone,
202–501–0084. Internet, http://www.gsa.
gov/portal/content/105035.

Public and News Media Inquiries
Inquiries from both the general public
and news media should be directed
to the Office of Communications
and Marketing, General Services
Administration, 1800 F Street NW.,
Washington, DC 20405. Phone, 202–
501–1231. Internet, http://www.gsa.gov/
portal/category/25728.

Publications   GSA publications are
available online from the Government
Printing Office bookstore at http://
bookstore.gpo.gov. Orders and questions
about publications and paid subscriptions
should be directed to the Superintendent
of Documents, Government Printing
Office, Washington, DC 20401. Some
subscriptions may be obtained free of
charge or at cost from a Small Business
Center or GSA's Centralized Mailing List
Service (phone, 1–817–334–5215). If a
publication is not available from these
sources, contact a specific GSA staff
office, regional office, or service. The
relevant addresses and phone numbers
are available on GSA's Web site. For a
free copy of the Federal Government TTY
Directory, contact the Federal Citizen

Information Center, Department TTY,
Pueblo, CO 81009. Phone, 888–878–
3256. The directory is also available
online. Internet, http://www.federalrelay.
us/tty.

For a free copy of the quarterly
"Consumer Information Catalog,"
which contains information on food,
nutrition, employment, Federal benefits,
the environment, fraud, privacy and
Internet issues, investing and credit,
and education, write to the Federal
Citizen Information Center, Pueblo, CO
81009. Phone, 888–878–3256. Internet,
http://publications.usa.gov/USAPubs.
php?NavCode=K.

For information on Federal programs
and services, call the Federal Citizen
Information Center's National Contact
Center at 800–333–4636, weekdays, 8
a.m. to 8 p.m. eastern standard time. For
a free copy of the Federal Relay Service
Brochure, call 877–387–2001. TTY,
1–877–387–8339. Internet, http://www.
gsa.gov/portal/category/101011?utm_
source=OCSIT&utm_medium=print-
radio&utm_term=FCIC&utm_
campaign=shortcuts.

For a free copy of the Federal Relay
Service Brochure, call 877–387–2001.
TTY, 1–877–387–8339.

Small Business Activities   Questions
concerning programs to assist small
businesses should be directed to the
Office of Small Business Utilization.
Phone, 1–855–672–8472. For business
tools and resources and information
on business opportunities and small
business training, use the link below.
Internet, http://www.gsa.gov/portal/
content/105221.

Speakers   Requests for speakers should
be directed to the nearest regional
office or the Office of Communications
and Marketing, General Services
Administration, 1800 F Street NW.,
Washington, DC 20405. Phone, 202–
501–1231. Internet, http://www.gsa.gov/
portal/category/25728.

**For further information concerning the General Services Administration, contact the Office of
Communications and Marketing, General Services Administration, Washington, DC 20417. Phone, 202–501–
1231. Internet, http://www.gsa.gov/portal/category/25728.**

INTER-AMERICAN FOUNDATION

1331 Pennsylvania Avenue, NW., Suite 1200 North, Washington, DC 20004
Phone, 202–360–4530. Internet, http://www.iaf.gov.

Chair	EDUARDO ARRIOLA
Vice Chair	THOMAS J. DODD
Directors	JOHN P. SALAZAR, JACK C. VAUGHN, JR., ROGER W. WALLACE, J. KELLY RYAN, (2 VACANCIES)
President	ROBERT N. KAPLAN
General Counsel	PAUL ZIMMERMAN
Vice President for Programs	STEPHEN COX
Chief Operating Officer	LESLEY DUNCAN
Director for External and Government Affairs	MANUEL NUÑEZ
Director of Evaluations	EMILIA RODRIGUEZ-STEIN

The Inter-American Foundation supports social and economic development in Latin America and the Caribbean.

The Inter-American Foundation (IAF) was created in 1969 (22 U.S.C. 290f) as an experimental U.S. foreign assistance program. The IAF is governed by a nine-person Board of Directors appointed by the President with the advice and consent of the Senate. Six members are drawn from the private sector and three from the Federal Government. The Board of Directors appoints the President of the Foundation.

The IAF works in Latin America and the Caribbean to promote equitable, participatory, and sustainable self-help development by awarding grants directly to local organizations throughout the region. It also partners with the public and private sectors to build support and to mobilize local, national, and international resources for grassroots development.

For further information, contact the Office of the President, Inter-American Foundation, 1331 Pennsylvania Avenue, NW., Suite 1200 North, Washington, DC 20004. Phone, 202–360–4530. Internet, http://www.iaf. gov.

MERIT SYSTEMS PROTECTION BOARD

1615 M Street NW., Fifth Floor, Washington, DC 20419
Phone, 202–653–7200; 800–209–8960. Fax, 202–653–7130. Internet, http://www.mspb.gov.

Chairman	SUSAN TSUI GRUNDMANN
Vice Chairman	ANNE WAGNER
Member	MARK A. ROBBINS
Executive Director	JAMES M. EISENMANN
Clerk of the Board	WILLIAM D. SPENCER
Director, Financial and Administrative Management	KEVIN NASH
Director, Information Resources Management	TOMMY HWANG
Director, Office of Appeals Counsel	SUSAN M. SWAFFORD
Director, Office of Equal Employment Opportunity	JERRY BEAT
Director, Office of Policy and Evaluation	JAMES M. READ
Director, Office of Regional Operations	DEBORAH MIRON

General Counsel   BRYAN G. POLISUK
Legislative Counsel   ROSALYN L. COATES

[For the Merit Systems Protection Board statement of organization, see the Code of Federal Regulations, Title 5, Part 1200]

The Merit Systems Protection Board protects the integrity of the Federal personnel merit systems and the rights of Federal employees.

The Merit Systems Protection Board is a successor agency to the United States Civil Service Commission, established by act of January 16, 1883 (22 Stat. 403). Reorganization Plan No. 2 of 1978 (5 U.S.C. app.) redesignated part of the Commission as the Merit Systems Protection Board. The Board is comprised of three members appointed by the President with the advice and consent of the Senate.

Activities

The Board has responsibility for hearing and adjudicating appeals by Federal employees of adverse personnel actions, such as removals, suspensions, and demotions. It also resolves cases involving reemployment rights, denial of periodic step increases in pay, actions against administrative law judges, and charges of prohibited personnel practices, including charges in connection with whistleblowing.

The Board has the authority to enforce its decisions and to order corrective and disciplinary actions. An employee or applicant for employment involved in an appealable action that also involves an allegation of discrimination may ask the Equal Employment Opportunity Commission to review a Board decision. Final decisions and orders of the Board can be appealed to the U.S. Court of Appeals for the Federal Circuit.

The Board reviews regulations issued by the Office of Personnel Management and has the authority to require agencies to cease compliance with any regulation that could constitute a prohibited personnel practice. It also conducts special studies of the civil service and other executive branch merit systems and reports to the President and the Congress on whether the Federal workforce is being adequately protected against political abuses and prohibited personnel practices.

For a complete list of Merit Systems Protection Board offices, use the Quick Link below.

Internet, http://www.mspb.gov/contact/contact.htm.

For further information, contact the Merit Systems Protection Board, 1615 M Street NW., Washington, DC 20419. Phone, 202–653–7200 or 800–209–8960. TDD, 800–877–8339. Fax, 202–653–7130. Email, mspb@mspb.gov. Internet, http://www.mspb.gov.

NATIONAL AERONAUTICS AND SPACE ADMINISTRATION

300 E Street SW., Washington, DC 20546
Phone, 202–358–0000. Internet, http://www.nasa.gov.

Administrator   CHARLES F. BOLDEN, JR.
Deputy Administrator   (VACANCY)
Associate Administrator   ROBERT M. LIGHTFOOT
Associate Deputy Administrator   RICHARD KEEGAN
Associate Deputy Administrator for Strategy and   REBECCA SPYKE KEISER
    Policy
Chief of Staff   DAVID P. RADZANOWSKI

MERIT SYSTEMS PROTECTION BOARD

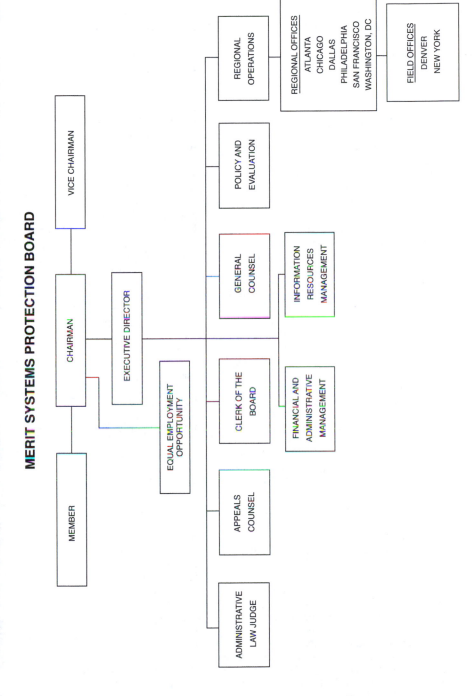

Director, Office of Evaluation	HELEN GRANT, *Acting*
Director, Council Staff	(VACANCY)
Deputy Chief of Staff	MIKE FRENCH
White House Liaison	JONATHAN A. HERCZEG
Assistant Associate Administrator	ARTHUR MAPLES, *Acting*
Chief Financial Officer	DAVID RADZANOWSKI
Chief Information Officer	LARRY N. SWEET
Chief Scientist	ELLEN R. STOFAN
Chief Technologist	DAVID MILLER
Inspector General	PAUL K. MARTIN
Chief Engineer	RALPH R. ROE
Chief Health and Medical Officer	RICHARD S. WILLIAMS
Chief Safety and Mission Assurance Officer	TERRENCE W. WILCUTT
Associate Administrator, Diversity and Equal Opportunity	BRENDA R. MANUEL
Associate Administrator, Education	ROOSEVELT Y. JOHNSON
Associate Administrator, International and Interagency Relations	MICHAEL F. O'BRIEN
General Counsel	MICHAEL C. WHOLLEY
Associate Administrator, Legislative and Intergovernmental Affairs	L. SETH STATLER
Associate Administrator, Communications	DAVID S. WEAVER
Associate Administrator, Small Business Programs	GLENN A. DELGADO
Associate Administrator, Aeronautics Research Mission Directorate	JAIWON SHIN
Associate Administrator, Human Exploration and Operations Mission Directorate	WILLIAM H. GERSTENMAIER
Associate Administrator, Science Mission Directorate	JOHN M. GRUNSFELD
Associate Administrator for Space Technology Mission Directorate	MICHAEL GAZARIK
Associate Administrator, Mission Support Directorate	RICHARD J. KEEGAN
Assistant Administrator, Human Capital Management	JERI L. BUCHHOLZ
Assistant Administrator, Strategic Infrastructure	CALVIN WILLIAMS
Executive Director, Headquarters Operations	JAY M. HENN
Executive Director, NASA Shared Services Center	MARK V. GLORIOSO
Director, Internal Controls and Management Systems	NANCY A. BAUGHER
Assistant Administrator, Procurement	BILL MCNALLY
Assistant Administrator, Protective Services	JOSEPH S. MAHALEY
Director, NASA Management Office	RICHARD J. KEEGAN, *Acting*
Director, Ames Research Center	S. PETE WORDEN
Director, Dryden Flight Research Center	DAVID D. MCBRIDE
Director, Glenn Research Center	JAMES M. FREE, *Acting*
Director, Goddard Space Flight Center	CHRISTOPHER J. SCOLESE
Director, Johnson Space Center	ELLEN OCHOA
Director, Kennedy Space Center	ROBERT D. CABANA
Director, Langley Research Center	STEPHEN G. JURCZYK
Director, Marshall Space Flight Center	PATRICK E. SCHEUERMANN
Director, Stennis Space Center	RICHARD J. GILBRECH
Director, Jet Propulsion Laboratory	CHARLES ELACHI

[For the National Aeronautics and Space Administration statement of organization, see the Code of Federal Regulations, Title 14, Part 1201]

The National Aeronautics and Space Administration reaches for the future in space exploration, scientific discovery, and aeronautics research to benefit all humankind.

The National Aeronautics and Space Administration (NASA) was established by the National Aeronautics and Space Act of 1958, as amended (42 U.S.C. 2451 et seq.).

Activities

Aeronautics Research Mission Directorate   The Aeronautics Research Mission Directorate (ARMD) conducts high-quality, cutting-edge research that generates innovative concepts, tools, and technologies to enable revolutionary advances in our Nation's future aircraft as well as in the airspace in which they will fly. ARMD programs will facilitate a safer, more environmentally friendly, and more efficient national air transportation system. In addition, NASA's aeronautics research will continue to play a vital role in supporting NASA's human and robotic space exploration activities.

For further information, call 202–358–2047.

Human Exploration and Operations Mission Directorate   The Human Exploration and Operations Mission Directorate is responsible for NASA space operations in and beyond low Earth orbit, developing new exploration and transportation systems, and performing scientific research to enable sustained and affordable human exploration. It manages launch services, space communications and navigation, and works with the Mission Support Directorate to ensure the availability of appropriate rocket propulsion test capabilities that support human and robotic exploration requirements.

For further information, call 202–358–1562.

Science Mission Directorate   The Science Mission Directorate carries out the scientific exploration of Earth and space to expand the frontiers of Earth science, heliophysics, planetary science, and astrophysics. By sponsoring research and exploiting robotic observatory and explorer spacecraft, the directorate provides virtual human access to the most distant reaches of space and time, as well as more practical information relevant to changes on Earth.

For further information, call 202–358–3889. Internet, http://science.nasa.gov/about-us/organization-and-leadership/division-bios/.

Space Technology Mission Directorate   The Space Technology Mission Directorate develops, demonstrates, and infuses revolutionary, high-payoff technologies by pushing the boundaries of aerospace science. It employs a portfolio approach spanning a range of disciplines and technology readiness levels to advance technologies for the benefit of NASA, the aerospace industry, and other Government agencies and to address national needs. Research and technology development takes place in NASA Centers, academia, and industry, and it benefits from leveraged partnerships with other Government agencies and international partners. The directorate invests in technologies that have high potential for offsetting mission risk, reducing cost, and advancing existing capabilities, thereby enabling the Nation to pursue more challenging missions.

For further information, call 202–358–0454.

Mission Support Directorate   The Mission Support Directorate provides effective and efficient institutional support to enable the Agency to accomplish its missions successfully. It focuses on reducing institutional risk to NASA's current and future missions by improving processes, stimulating efficiency, and providing consistency and uniformity across institutional capabilities and services.

For further information, call 202–358–2789.

NATIONAL AERONAUTICS AND SPACE ADMINISTRATION

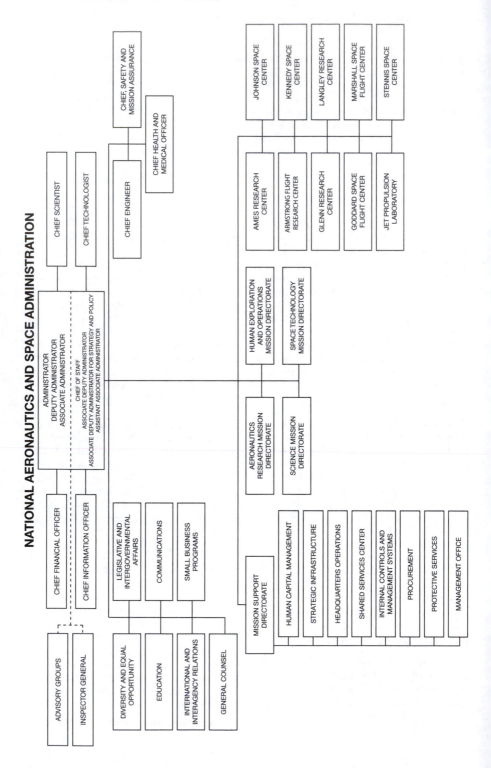

NASA Centers

Ames Research Center Located in California's Silicon Valley, the Center enables exploration through selected developments, innovative technologies, and interdisciplinary scientific discovery. It provides leadership in Astrobiology; small satellites; technologies for CEV, CLV, and HLV; the search for habitable planets; supercomputing; intelligent-adaptive systems; advanced thermal protection; and airborne astronomy. The Center also develops tools for a safer, more efficient national airspace, and it cultivates partnerships that benefit NASA's mission.

For further information, use the link below. Internet, http://www.nasa.gov/centers/ames/home/index.html#.U7RoFZRdUwA.

Armstrong Flight Research Center Located at Edwards Air Force Base, California, the Center carries out flight research and technology integration; validates space exploration concepts; conducts airborne remote sensing and science missions; enables airborne astrophysics observation missions to discover the origin, structure, evolution, and destiny of the universe; and supports space shuttle and International Space Station operations. It also supports activities in all four of NASA's Mission Directorates.

For further information, use the link below. Internet, http://www.nasa.gov/centers/armstrong/home/index.html#.U7Rsn5RdUwB.

Glenn Research Center Located at Lewis Field, next to Cleveland Hopkins International Airport, the Center develops critical space flight systems and technologies to advance the exploration of our solar system and beyond. In partnership with U.S. companies, universities, and other Government institutions, the Center's research and development efforts focus on advancements in propulsion, power, communications, nuclear, and human-related aerospace systems. Its scientists and engineers also develop new technologies for making airplanes quieter, safer, and less harmful to the environment.

For further information, use the link below. Internet, http://www.nasa.gov/centers/glenn/home/index.html#.U7R0kpRdUwA.

Goddard Space Flight Center Located in Greenbelt, MD, the Center expands our knowledge of Earth and its environment, the solar system, and the universe by observing them from space. It also conducts scientific investigations, develops and operates space systems, and advances essential technologies.

For further information, use the link below. Internet, http://www.nasa.gov/centers/goddard/home/index.html#.U7R3kpRdUwA.

Johnson Space Center Located in Houston, TX, the Center specializes in human space flight. It hosts and staffs program and project offices; selects and trains astronauts; manages and conducts projects that build, test, and integrate human-rated systems for transportation, habitation, and working in space; and plans and operates human space flight missions. This work requires a comprehensive understanding of space and planetary environments, as well as research into the effects of those environments on human physiology. It also requires development of technology to sustain and preserve life; maintenance of a supply chain to design, manufacture, and test flight products; selection, training, and provision of medical care to those who fly space missions; and ongoing administrative mission support services. The Center is currently hosting the International Space Station Program, the Multi-Purpose Crew Vehicle Program, and the Human Research Program. It plays a lead role in developing, operating, and integrating human exploration missions that include commercial, academic, international, and U.S. Government partners.

For further information, use the link below. Internet, http://www.nasa.gov/centers/johnson/home/index.html#.U7R6vJRdUwA.

Kennedy Space Center Located on Florida's east coast, the Center is responsible for NASA's space launch operations and spaceport and range technologies. Home to NASA's Launch Services Program, it manages the processing and launching of astronaut crews and associated payloads. Its management activities include the International Space Station segments, research experiments and supplies, and NASA's scientific and research spacecraft. These scientific and research spacecraft range from robotic landers to Earth observation satellites and space-based telescopes on a variety of launch vehicles.

Innovative technology experts at the Center support NASA's current programs and future exploration missions by developing new products and processes that benefit the Agency and consumers. The Center remains a leader in cutting-edge research and development in the areas of physics, chemistry, technology, prototype designing, engineering, environmental conservation, and renewable energy.

For further information, use the link below. Internet, http://www.nasa.gov/centers/kennedy/home/index. html#.U7SAWJRdUwA.

Langley Research Center Located in Hampton, VA, the Center is renowned for its scientific and technological expertise in aerospace research, systems integration, and atmospheric science. Established in 1917 as an aeronautics lab, it has a rich heritage in space and science technologies. Its engineers conduct critical research in materials and structures; aerodynamics; and hypersonic, supersonic, and subsonic flight. Langley researchers and engineers also have developed and validated technologies to improve the effectiveness, safety, environmental compatibility, and efficiency of the Nation's air transportation system. The Center supports the space exploration program and space operations with systems analysis and engineering, aerosciences, materials and structures, and technology and systems development and testing. It continues to play a principal role in understanding and protecting our planet through atmospheric measurement, instruments, missions, and prediction algorithms. By determining appropriate preventative and corrective action for problems, trends, or issues across NASA programs and projects, its Engineering

and Safety Center personnel have improved mission safety.

For further information, use the link below. Internet, http://www.nasa.gov/centers/langley/home/index. html#.U7SEs5RdUwA.

Marshall Space Flight Center Located in Huntsville, AL, the Center provides unique expertise in development and integration of space transportation and propulsion systems; space systems and technologies; and scientific research, instruments, and experiments required for space exploration and space operations. It manages the following programs and projects: the space launch system, International Space Station (ISS) environmental control and life support systems, ISS payload operations, numerous ISS facilities and experiments, the Chandra X-ray Observatory, the Discovery and New Frontiers Programs, space technology demonstration missions, and the Michoud Assembly Facility, a space vehicle manufacturing and assembly complex located in New Orleans, LA.

For further information, use the link below. Internet, http://www.nasa.gov/centers/marshall/home/index. html#.U7SMnpRdUwA.

Stennis Space Center Located near Bay St. Louis, MS, the Center serves as NASA's rocket propulsion testing ground. It provides test services not only for America's space program, but also for the Department of Defense and private sector. Its unique rocket propulsion test capabilities will be used extensively in developing NASA's new space launch system. The Applied Science and Technology Project Office supports NASA's science and technology goals through project management. The Office also supports NASA's Applied Sciences Program.

For further information, use the link below. Internet, http://www.nasa.gov/centers/stennis/home/index. html#.U7SRVZRdUwA.

Jet Propulsion Laboratory The Laboratory is a Federally Funded Research and Development Center (FFRDC) managed under contract by the California Institute of Technology (Caltech) in Pasadena, CA. The FFRDC is a unique nongovernment entity sponsored and funded by NASA to meet specific long-term technical needs that cannot be met by other organizations within NASA. As part of this special relationship, the Laboratory must operate in the public interest with objectivity and independence, avoid organizational conflicts of interest, and fully disclose its affairs to NASA. The Laboratory develops and maintains technical and managerial competencies to perform the following missions in support of NASA's strategic goals: to explore our solar system to understand its formation and evolution; to establish a continuous and permanent robotic presence on Mars to discover its history and habitability; to make critical measurements and models to understand the global and regional integrated Earth system; to conduct observations to search for neighboring solar systems and Earth-like planets and help understand formation, evolution, and composition of the Universe; to conduct communications and navigation for deep space missions; to provide support, particularly in robotic infrastructures and precursors, that enables human exploration of the Moon, Mars, and beyond; and, under Caltech's initiative, to collaborate with other Federal and State government agencies and commercial endeavors in areas synergistic with the Laboratory's work performed for NASA.

For further information, use the link below. Internet, http://www.nasa.gov/centers/jpl/about/index.html#.U7VzS5RdUwA.

Sources of Information

Contracts and Small Business Activities Direct inquiries regarding contracting for small businesses to the Associate Administrator for Small Business Programs, Room 2K39, NASA Headquarters, 300 E Street SW., Washington, DC 20546. Phone, 202–358–2088. Internet, http://www.osbp.nasa.gov/.

Employment Direct questions to the NASA Shared Services Center, Stennis, MS 39529. Phone, 877–677–2123. Email, nssc-contactcenter@nasa.gov. Internet, http://nasajobs.nasa.gov/.

Library NASA Headquarters Library, Room 1W55, 300 E Street SW., Washington, DC 20546. Phone, 202–358–0168. Email, library@hq.nasa.gov. Internet, http://www.hq.nasa.gov/office/hqlibrary.

Office of Inspector General Hotline Report crimes, fraud, waste, and abuse in NASA programs and operations by calling the OIG Hotline (800–424–9183); by writing to the NASA Inspector General (P.O. Box 23089, L'Enfant Plaza Station, Washington, DC 20026); or by using the link below and sending a message. Internet, http://oig.nasa.gov/cyberhotline.html.

Publications The NASA Scientific and Technical Information (STI) Program provides access to a wide variety of research papers. For more information, contact NASA STI by email (nasa-dl-sti-id@mail.nasa.gov), or visit the Web site (http://www.sti.nasa.gov).

The NASA History Program Office supports research in agency history and on the history of aeronautics and space research. Books, monographs, and exhibits funded by the History Office may be accessed for free online (http://www.history.nasa.gov). Print copies may be purchased from the Headquarters Information Center or the Government Printing Office. For further information, contact the History Office online (histinfo@nasa.gov) or by phone (202–358–0384).

Additional publications are available onsite at the NASA Headquarters Library in Washington, DC, and online. Use the link below to access the "Find Publications" menu on the NASA HQ Library Web page. Internet, http://www.hq.nasa.gov/office/hqlibrary/.

For further information, contact the Headquarters Information Center, National Aeronautics and Space Administration, Washington, DC 20546. Phone, 202–358–0000. Internet, http://www.nasa.gov.

NATIONAL ARCHIVES AND RECORDS ADMINISTRATION

700 Pennsylvania Avenue NW., Washington, DC, 20408–0001
Phone, 866–272–6272. Internet, http://www.archives.gov.

Archivist of the United States	DAVID S. FERRIERO
Deputy Archivist of the United States	DEBRA STEIDEL WALL
Director, Congressional Affairs	JOHN HAMILTON
Director, Equal Employment Opportunity Office	ISMAEL MARTINEZ
General Counsel	GARY M. STERN
Executive Director, National Historical Publications and Records Commission	KATHLEEN M. WILLIAMS
Inspector General	JAMES E. SPRINGS, *Acting*
Chief Strategy and Communications Officer	DONNA M. GARLAND
Chief Operating Officer	WILLIAM J. BOSANKO
Chief Human Capital Officer	SEAN M. CLAYTON
Director, Office of the Federal Register	CHARLES A. BARTH
Executive for Agency Services	JAY A. TRAINER
Chief Records Officer for the U.S. Government	PAUL M. WESTER, JR.
Director, Federal Records Centers Program	DAVID M. WEINBERG
Director, Information Security Oversight Office	JOHN P. FITZPATRICK
Director, National Declassification Center	SHERYL SHENBERGER
Director, Office of Government Information Services	MIRIAM NISBET
Executive for Research Services	WILLIAM A. MAYER
Executive for Legislative Archives, Presidential Libraries, and Museum Services	JAMES B. GARDNER
Executive for Information Services	SWAMALI HALDAR, *Acting*
Executive for Business Support Services	CHARLES K. PIERCY
Public Affairs Officer	CHRIS ISLEIB

[For the National Archives and Records Administration statement of organization, see the Federal Register of June 25, 1985, 50 FR 26278]

The National Archives and Records Administration safeguards and preserves the records of the U.S. Government, ensuring that the American people can discover, use, and learn from their documentary heritage. It establishes policies and procedures for managing Federal records; oversees the Presidential Libraries system; promotes civic education; and publishes the laws, regulations, Presidential papers, and other public documents.

The National Archives and Records Administration (NARA) is the successor agency to the National Archives Establishment, which was created in 1934 and later, in 1949, incorporated into the General Services Administration as the National Archives and Records Service. NARA was established as an independent agency in the Federal Government's executive branch by act of October 19, 1984 (44 U.S.C. 2101 et seq.), effective April 1, 1985.

Archival Program NARA maintains the U.S. Government's most historically valuable records, ranging from the Revolutionary War era to the recent past; arranges and preserves records and prepares finding aids to facilitate their use; makes records publicly accessible online and in its research rooms; answers requests for information contained in its holdings; and provides, for a fee, copies of records. NARA holdings include the records of the U.S. House of Representatives and Senate, which are preserved and administered by the Center for Legislative Archives. Many important records are available in microfilm and

NATIONAL ARCHIVES AND RECORDS ADMINISTRATION

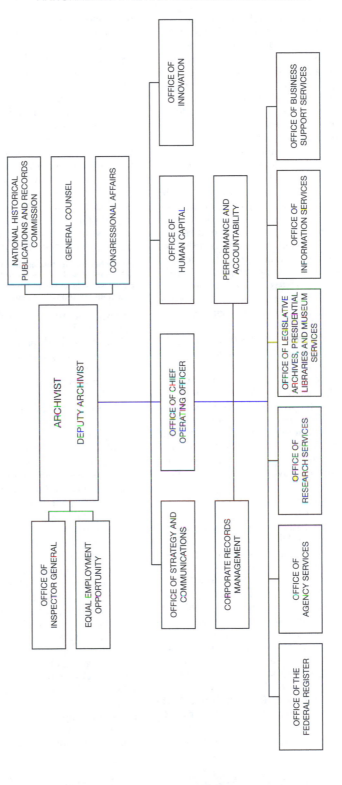

ARCHIVIST
DEPUTY ARCHIVIST

NATIONAL HISTORICAL PUBLICATIONS AND RECORDS COMMISSION

GENERAL COUNSEL

CONGRESSIONAL AFFAIRS

OFFICE OF INSPECTOR GENERAL

EQUAL EMPLOYMENT OPPORTUNITY

OFFICE OF INNOVATION

OFFICE OF HUMAN CAPITAL

PERFORMANCE AND ACCOUNTABILITY

OFFICE OF CHIEF OPERATING OFFICER

OFFICE OF STRATEGY AND COMMUNICATIONS

CORPORATE RECORDS MANAGEMENT

OFFICE OF BUSINESS SUPPORT SERVICES

OFFICE OF INFORMATION SERVICES

OFFICE OF LEGISLATIVE ARCHIVES, PRESIDENTIAL LIBRARIES AND MUSEUM SERVICES

OFFICE OF RESEARCH SERVICES

OFFICE OF AGENCY SERVICES

OFFICE OF THE FEDERAL REGISTER

accessible online. Archival records are maintained in NARA facilities in the Washington, DC, area. Records of exceptional local or regional interest are maintained in NARA archives located in other parts of the country. There are also nine NARA-affiliated archives holding NARA-owned records and making them available to the public.

Records Management   To ensure proper documentation of the organization, policies, and activities of the Government, NARA develops standards and guidelines for nationwide management and disposition of recorded information. It appraises Federal records and approves disposition schedules. NARA also inspects agency records and management practices, develops records management training programs, provides guidance and assistance on records management, and stores inactive records.

Agency Services   Agency Services leads NARA's efforts to meet the ongoing records management needs of the Federal Government and to represent the public interest in the accountability and transparency of this management. Its components include the Office of the Chief Records Officer; the Federal Records Centers Program, including the National Personnel Records Center; the Information Security Oversight Office; the National Declassification Center; and the Office of Government Information Services.

Office of Innovation   The Office of Innovation creates innovative ways to serve its customers and to increase access to and delivery of records through all forms of media. Its mission includes demonstrating leadership in the archival and information access field. The Office coordinates NARA's efforts for Open Government and the National Digital Strategy. It comprises several divisions: digitization; digital engagement, including Internet, social media, and NARA's online catalog; business architecture, standards and authorities; and the Innovation Hub.

Office of the Chief Records Officer   The Office of the Chief Records Officer assists Government agencies with their records management programs and the lifecycle

management of Federal records. The Office formulates recommendations for Governmentwide policies, procedures, regulations, and guidance on the creation, management, and disposition of records in various media. It conducts inspections, evaluations, and surveys of records and records management programs in agencies; reports its findings; and recommends improvements or necessary corrective actions. The Office also provides records management services. These services include appraisal and scheduling, technical assistance, training, consultation, and analysis regarding policy matters, as well as identifying permanent records eligible for transfer to the National Archives.

For further information on the duties and programs of the Office of the Chief Records Officer, send a request to the email address above. Email, rm.communications@nara.gov.

Federal Records Centers Program
NARA's Federal Records Centers Program (FRCP) stores and services active and inactive records for Federal agencies. A national network of 17 facilities, the FRCP system currently stores more than 27 million cubic feet of records. Since 1999, the FRCP system has operated as a reimbursable program that provides the Federal community with services on a fee-for-service basis. These services include storage of textual and special media records; management of classified and nonclassified records; retrieval of records needed by customers to conduct daily business or fulfill statutory requirements; expedited responses to congressional inquiries, litigation, and urgent business needs; disposition services, including the disposal of temporary records that have reached the end of their required retention period and the transfer of permanent records to the legal custody of the National Archives; and a variety of special projects based on customer needs.

The National Personnel Records Center (NPRC) in St. Louis, MO, is the largest facility in the FRCP system. This facility stores and services the civilian personnel, medical, and pay records of former U.S. Civil Service employees and the personnel, medical, and related records of discharged military personnel. The NPRC maintains research rooms in which Federal agency personnel and the public can review official military and civilian personnel folders and other related records. It also provides services and technical advice relating to records disposition, filing and classification schemes, document conversion, and the protection of vital civilian and military records to Federal agencies.

To request military records, visit www.archives. gov/veterans/. For further information on the Federal Records Centers, visit www.archives.gov/ frc/ or contact the FRCP. Phone, 314–801–9300. Email, frc@nara.gov. For further information on the National Personnel Records Center, visit www. archives.gov/st-louis or contact the NPRC. Phone, 314–801–0800. Fax, 301–801–9195.

Information Security Oversight Office

The Information Security Oversight Office (ISOO) oversees programs for Classified National Security Information and Controlled Unclassified Information in both Government and industry and reports to the President annually on their status. ISOO receives policy and program guidance from the National Security Council and operates under the authority of Executive Orders 12829, 13549, 13587, 13526, and 13556. As an organizational component of the National Archives and Records Administration, ISOO's goals are to hold classification activities to the minimum necessary standard in order to protect national security, promote consistency and transparency in the handling of Controlled Unclassified Information, safeguard Classified National Security Information in both Government and industry efficiently and cost-effectively, and promote declassification and public access to information as soon as security considerations permit.

ISOO is responsible for implementing and monitoring the National Industrial Security Program (NISP). The Director of ISOO also serves as the Chair of the NISP Policy Advisory Committee, a forum used to discuss policy issues in dispute and to recommend changes to those policies. ISOO acts as a consultant for policy guidance to the Executive Agent for Safeguarding Classified Information on Computer Networks. It also serves as the Chair of the State, Local, Tribal, and Private Sector Entities Policy Advisory Committee to discuss program-related policy issues, facilitate the resolution of disputes, and recommend policy and procedural changes to remove undue impediments to the sharing of information under the program. As a member of the Senior Information Sharing and Safeguarding Steering Committee and the Insider Threat Task Force, ISOO plays a leading role in the development, coordination, oversight, and promulgation of policies, objectives, and priorities for establishing and integrating security, counterintelligence, user audits and monitoring, and other safeguarding capabilities and practices within agencies.

The Office was also named the Executive Agent for administering Executive Order 13556, "Controlled Unclassified Information" (CUI). CUI establishes consistent information sharing and protection practices by replacing the ad hoc, agency-specific policies and procedures with an executive branchwide program to manage all unclassified information that requires safeguarding and/or dissemination controls pursuant to and consistent with applicable law, regulations, and Governmentwide policies.

For further information, contact the Information Security Oversight Office. Phone, 202–357–5250. Email, isoo@nara.gov. Internet, http://www.archives. gov/isoo.

National Declassification Center

The National Declassification Center (NDC) was established by Executive Order 13526 and began operations in early January 2010. The Center is responsible for the timely and appropriate processing of referrals between agencies for accessioned Federal records and transferred Presidential records; general interagency declassification activities necessary to fulfill the requirements of sections 3.3 and 3.4 of the Order; the exchange among agencies of detailed declassification guidance to support equity recognition; the development of effective, transparent, and standard declassification work processes, training, and quality assurance measures;

the development of solutions to declassification challenges posed by electronic records, special media, and emerging technologies; and the linkage and effective utilization of existing agency databases and the use of new technologies to support declassification activities under the purview of the Center.

For further information, contact the National Declassification Center. Phone, 301–837–1719. Email, ndc@nara.gov. Internet, http://www.archives. gov/declassification.

Office of Government Information Services   Established under the OPEN Government Act of 2007 (5 U.S.C. 101 note), the Office of Government Information Services (OGIS) reviews Freedom of Information Act (FOIA) activities throughout the Government. OGIS serves as liaison between individuals making FOIA requests and administrative agencies, providing mediation services and resolving disputes as necessary. OGIS reviews policies and procedures of administrative agencies under FOIA. OGIS also reviews agency compliance with FOIA and recommends policy changes to Congress and the President.

For further information, contact the Office of Government Information Services. Phone, 202–741–5770. Email, ogis@nara.gov. Internet, http://ogis. archives.gov/.

Research Services   Research Services provides world-class services to customers who wish to access NARA's accessioned Federal records. Records are available for research purposes in reading rooms at the National Archives Building (Archives I) in Washington, DC; the National Archives (Archives II) in College Park, MD; and various regional facilities throughout the Nation.

For a listing of Records Services facilities, visit the Locations Nationwide section on NARA's Web site. Internet, http://www.archives.gov/locations/.

Presidential Libraries   Through the Presidential Libraries, which are located at sites selected by the Presidents and built with private funds, NARA preserves and makes available the records, personal papers, and artifacts of a President's administration. Each Library operates a research room and provides reference

services for Presidential papers and other historical materials. The Libraries display artifacts and other holdings in museum exhibits illustrating the life and times of a President. The Presidential Libraries also provide programming for students of all ages promoting citizen engagement. NARA operates the Libraries of Presidents Herbert Hoover through George W. Bush. While such records were once considered personal papers, all Presidential records created on or after January 20, 1981, are declared by law to be owned and controlled by the United States and are required to be transferred to NARA at the end of the administration, pursuant to the Presidential Records Act of 1978 (44 U.S.C. 2201 et seq.). The Office of Presidential Libraries within the National Archives oversees the archival, museum, and education programs of the 13 Presidential Libraries.

For further information, contact the Office of Presidential Libraries. Phone, 301–837–3250. Fax, 301–837–3199. Internet, http://www.archives.gov/ presidential-libraries.

Office of the Federal Register   The Office of the Federal Register (OFR) prepares and publishes a variety of public documents.

Upon passage by Congress and approval by the President, the OFR assigns each new act of Congress a public or private law number and publishes the text of the new law in slip law (pamphlet) form. This slip law serves as the official publication of the law and is admissible as legal evidence of the law's provisions. The OFR also publishes the "United States Statutes at Large," an annual compilation of all the laws passed during a congressional session.

Each Federal workday, the OFR publishes the "Federal Register," which contains current Presidential proclamations and Executive orders, Federal agency regulations having general applicability and legal effect, proposed agency rules, and documents required by statute to be published. All Federal regulations in force are codified annually in the "Code of Federal Regulations."

Presidential speeches, news conferences, messages, and other materials released by the White House Office of the Press Secretary are published online in the "Daily Compilation of Presidential Documents" and annually in the "Public Papers of the Presidents." The "Daily Compilation of Presidential Documents," as well as electronic versions of the previous "Weekly Compilation of Presidential Documents," from 1993 onward, can be accessed at www.presidentialdocuments. gov.

"The United States Government Manual," published annually, serves as the official handbook of the Federal Government, providing extensive information on the legislative, judicial, and executive branches. The Manual can be accessed at http://www. usgovernmentmanual.gov/.

OFR publications are available online and in paper editions.

For further information, contact Information Services and Technology, Office of the Federal Register. Phone, 202–741–6000. TTY, 202–741– 6086. Fax, 202–741–6012. Email, fedreg.info@nara. gov. Internet, http://www.ofr.gov.

National Historical Publications and Records Commission
The National Historical Publications and Records Commission (NHPRC) is NARA's grant-making affiliate. NHPRC promotes the preservation and use of America's documentary heritage essential to understanding our democracy, history, and culture. NHPRC grants help State and local archives, universities, historical societies, and other nonprofit organizations preserve and manage electronic records, improve training and techniques, strengthen archival programs, preserve and process records collections, and provide access to them through the publication of finding aids and documentary editions of the papers of the Founding Era and other themes and historical figures in American history. NHPRC works in partnership with a national network of State historical records advisory boards. It also provides Federal leadership in public policy for the preservation of, and access to, America's documentary heritage.

For further information, contact the National Historical Publications and Records Commission.

Phone, 202–357–5010. Email, nhprc@archives.gov. Internet, http://www.archives.gov/nhprc.

National Archives Trust Fund Board
The National Archives Trust Fund Board receives funds from the sale of reproductions of historic documents and publications about the records, as well as from gifts and bequests. The Board invests these funds and uses income to support archival functions such as the preparation of publications that make historic records information more widely available. Members of the Board are the Archivist of the United States, the Secretary of the Treasury, and the Chairman of the National Endowment for the Humanities.

For further information, contact the Secretary, National Archives Trust Fund Board. Phone, 301–837–3165.

Sources of Information

Calendar of Events To be added to the mailing list for the monthly National Archives Calendar of Events or for a recorded announcement of events at National Archives locations in Washington, DC, and College Park, MD, call 202–357–5000. TDD, 301– 837–0482. Or, using the link below, go to Calendar of Events on NARA's Web site. Internet, http://www.archives.gov/ calendar/.

Congressional Affairs The Congressional Affairs staff maintains contact with and responds to inquiries from congressional offices. Phone, 202–357–5100. Fax, 202–357–5959.

Contracts Information on business opportunities with NARA is available online. Internet, http://www.fbo.gov.

Communications The Communications staff responds to inquiries from the media and maintains contact with them; issues press releases and other material online, in print, and through social media; produces the agency's magazine, "Prologue"; and serves as the liaison with organizations representing the archival profession, scholarly organizations, and other groups served by NARA. Phone, 202–357–5300.

Modern Archives Institute For information, contact the Modern Archives Institute, Room 307, National Archives

Building, 700 Pennsylvania Avenue NW., Washington, DC 20408–0001. Phone, 202–357–5259. Internet, http://www.archives.gov/preservation/modern-archives-institute/.

Know Your Records Program   For information, contact the Customer Service Center, Room G–13, National Archives Building, 700 Pennsylvania Avenue, NW., Washington, DC 20408–0001. Phone, 202–357–5260. Email, kyr@nara.gov. Internet, http://www.archives.gov/dc-metro/know-your-records.

Records Management Workshops   For information on workshops, contact the National Records Management Training Program. Email, NARA.RecordsMgtTraining@nara.gov. Internet, http://www.archives.gov/records-mgmt/training/index.html.

Federal Register Workshop   For information on the monthly workshop, "The Federal Register: What It Is and How To Use It," call 202–741–6008.

Institute for the Editing of Historical Documents/Archives Leadership Institute   For information on the Institute for the Editing of Historical Documents or the Archives Leadership Institute, contact NHPRC, National Archives and Records Administration, 700 Pennsylvania Avenue NW., Washington, DC 20408–0001. Phone, 202–357–5010. Email, nhprc@archives.gov. Internet, http://www.archives.gov/nhprc.

Electronic Access   Information on NARA, its holdings and publications, and links to its social media sites are available online. Email, inquire@nara.gov. Internet, http://www.archives.gov.

Employment   For job opportunities, contact the nearest NARA facility or the Office of Human Capital, Talent Management Division, Staffing and Recruitment Branch, Room 370, 1 Archives Drive, St. Louis, MO 63138. Phone, 800–827–4898. TDD, 314–801–0886. Internet, http://www.archives.gov/careers/jobs.

Freedom of Information Act/Privacy Act Requests   For operational records of the National Archives and Records Administration, contact the NARA Freedom of Information Act/Privacy Act

Officer, General Counsel Staff, National Archives and Records Administration, 8601 Adelphi Road, College Park, MD 20740–6001. Phone, 301–837–3642. Fax, 301–837–0293. For archival records in the custody of Research Services in the Washington, DC, area, contact the Special Access/FOIA Staff, National Archives and Records Administration, 8601 Adelphi Road, College Park, MD 20740–6001. Phone, 301–837–3190. Fax, 301–837–1864. For archival records located at a NARA archives location outside the Washington, DC, metropolitan area, contact the facility holding the records. To determine the location of records, search NARA's online Archival Research Catalog at www.archives.gov/research/arc. For archival records in the custody of a Presidential Library, contact the Library that has custody of the records. For records in the physical custody of the Washington National Records Center or the regional Records Centers, contact the Federal agency that transferred the records to the facility. Records stored in the Records Centers remain in the legal custody of the agency that created them. Visit our Web site for a listing of NARA archival facilities. Internet, http://www.archives.gov/locations.

Grants   For NHPRC grants, contact NHPRC, National Archives and Records Administration, 700 Pennsylvania Avenue NW., Washington, DC 20408–0001. Phone, 202–357–5010. Email, nhprc@archives.gov. Internet, http://www.archives.gov/nhprc.

Museum Shops   Publications, document facsimiles, and document-related souvenirs are available for sale at the National Archives in Washington, DC, and at each Presidential Library. Phone, 202–357–5271. Internet, http://www.myarchivesstore.org.

Exhibits   There are permanent and temporary exhibits at the National Archives in Washington, DC (home of the Declaration of Independence, Constitution, and Bill of Rights) and as part of the museum facilities of the Presidential Libraries. Several of NARA's regional facilities regularly host exhibits, and the Agency has traveling exhibits that bring National Archives records to communities across the Nation. For information on Presidential Library exhibits, please contact 301–837–3250; for information on programs and their hours at the National Archives, please call 202–357–5000; for information on traveling and regional exhibits and exhibit loans, please contact the Exhibits Office at 202–357–5210. Email, National_Archives_Exhibits_Staff@nara. gov. Internet, http://www.archives.gov/exhibits.

Center for Legislative Archives The Center for Legislative Archives houses the official records of the U.S. House of Representatives and U.S. Senate from 1789 to the present. House and Senate records remain in the permanent legal custody of the House and Senate and are governed by House and Senate rules, respectively. The Center responds to requests from congressional committees for the timely delivery of records to support the current business needs of the Congress. The Center is a full-service archive, providing records management guidance to the House and Senate Archivists, processing and providing public access to congressional and legislative branch records, and creating exhibits, public programs, and educational materials and workshops on the history of Congress and representative government. The Center reports to the Advisory Committee on the Records of Congress on its programs, activities, and resources. For further information, contact the Center for Legislative Archives. Phone, 202–357–5350. Fax, 202–357–5911. Email, legislative. archives@nara.gov. Internet, http://www. archives.gov/legislative.

Agency Publications Free brochures, pamphlets, and agency finding aids to records are available from the Customer Service Center (RD–DC), Room G–13, National Archives and Records Administration, 700 Pennsylvania Avenue NW., Washington, DC 20408–0001. Phone, 866–325–7208. Fax, 202–501–7170. To purchase other NARA publications, go to http://estore.archives. gov/ or phone, toll free, 1–800–234–8861, press 5, then press 4; or 301–837–

3163. Internet, http://www.archives.gov/publications.

Records Management Publications Most records management publications are available on the NARA Web site. Limited quantities of some records management publications and posters are available in hardcopy from the National Records Management Training Program, National Archives and Records Administration, 8601 Adelphi Road, College Park, MD 20740–6001. Email, NARA.RecordsMgtTraining@nara. gov. Internet, http://www.archives.gov/publications/records-mgmt.html.

Laws, Regulations, and Presidential Documents Information on laws, regulations, and Presidential documents is available from the Office of the Federal Register, National Archives and Records Administration, Washington, DC 20408. Phone, 202–741–6000. Email, fedreg. info@nara.gov. Internet, www.archives. gov/federal-register or www.ofr.gov. To subscribe to the "Federal Register" table of contents electronic mailing list, go to listserv.access.gpo.gov and select online mailing list archives, FEDREGTOC–L. To receive email notification of new public laws, subscribe to PENS (Public Laws Electronic Notification Service) at www.archives.gov/federal-register, "New Public Laws."

NHPRC Guidelines NHPRC guidelines are available online and from the NHPRC, National Archives and Records Administration, 700 Pennsylvania Avenue NW., Washington, DC 20408–0001. Phone, 202–357–5010. Email, nhprc@ archives.gov. Internet, http://www. archives.gov/nhprc.

Newsletter for Research at the National Archives "Researcher News" offers the most important and up-to-date information for conducting research at the National Archives. The newsletter is accessible online. Join the "Researcher News" mailing list by sending a request to the email address below. Email, kyr@ nara.gov. Internet, www.archives.gov/researcher/newsletter.

Research Facilities Records are available for research purposes in reading rooms at the National Archives Building, 700 Pennsylvania Avenue NW.,

Washington, DC (phone, 202–357–5400); at the National Archives at College Park, 8601 Adelphi Road, College Park, MD (phone, 866–272–6272); and at each Presidential Library, the National Personnel Records Center, and at NARA's 13 archives locations throughout the country. Written requests for information may be sent to any of these units, or they may be addressed to the Customer Services Division, National Archives at College Park, Room 1000, 8601 Adelphi Road, College Park, MD 20740–6001. Phone, 866–272–6272. Email, inquire@nara.gov.

Federal Register Public Inspection Desk   The Public Inspection Desk of the Office of the Federal Register is open every Federal business day for public inspection of documents scheduled for publication in the next day's "Federal Register." The Office is located at Suite 700, 800 North Capitol Street NW., Washington, DC. Phone, 202–741–6000. Documents currently on public inspection also may be viewed online. Internet, http://www.ofr.gov.

Public Programs   The National Archives conducts regular public programs at its public facilities. Many of these programs support genealogy and other common uses of our records. Frequent "Know Your Records" programs and an annual genealogy fair are held in Washington, DC. For more information on the National Archives and its genealogy programs, visit the Web site. The William G. McGowan Theater of the National Archives Experience also offers programs each month featuring authors, films, and expert panels speaking on topics related to and often drawn from National Archives holdings. For more information on National Archives Experience programs, call 202–357–5000. To obtain a calendar of events, send an email request. Email, public.program@nara.gov.

Teacher Workshops and Teaching Materials   The National Archives education specialists have developed programs to train teachers in the use of primary source material as a teaching aid. They also provide information on how teachers can obtain documentary materials to incorporate into their lessons and for display in the classroom. For further information, contact the Education Team. Phone, 202–357–5235. Email, edteam@nara.gov.

Reserved Visits and Tours   Advance reservations for entry to the National Archives Experience are available through our partners at www.recreation.gov. The convenience fee for online reservations is $1.50 per person, and admission to all of the National Archives Experience exhibits is free. Individuals and groups may reserve up to 15 spaces for the guided tour conducted by a volunteer docent (available only at 9:45 a.m., weekdays). Individuals may reserve up to 20 spaces and groups may reserve up to 100 spaces for a timed visit entry. Visitors with advance reservations enter through the Special Events door at Constitution Avenue and 7th Street and must be in line at the entrance at least 10 minutes prior to the start time of their visit. Security screening will be conducted upon entry. There are no refunds on any ticket orders. For more details on tours, contact the Tour Office at 202–357–5450. Advanced reservations for guided tours of the National Archives at College Park, MD, are available only Monday through Thursday between 10:30 a.m. and 2:30 p.m. Group size is limited to 20 people. For more information and reservations, contact the Volunteer Program staff. Phone, 301–837–3002. Email, volunteercp@nara.gov.

Volunteer Service   Volunteer service opportunities are available at the National Archives Building and the National Archives at College Park, MD. Volunteers conduct tours, provide information in the exhibit halls, work with staff archivists in processing historic documents, and serve as research aides in the genealogical orientation room. For more information and a volunteer application, visit our Web site by using the link below. Volunteer Program staff may be reached in Washington, DC: Phone, 202–357–5272. Fax, 202–357–5925. In College Park, MD: Phone, 301–837–3002. Fax, 301–837–3603. Presidential Libraries and NARA's regional locations offer similar opportunities. Contact the facility closest to you for information on volunteer opportunities. Internet, http://www. archives.gov/careers/volunteering/.

For further information, write or visit the National Archives and Records Administration, 700 Pennsylvania Avenue NW., Washington, DC 20408–0001. Phone, 202–357–5400. Email, inquire@nara.gov. Internet, http:// www.archives.gov.

NATIONAL CAPITAL PLANNING COMMISSION

401 Ninth Street NW., Suite 500, Washington, DC 20004
Phone, 202–482–7200. Internet, http://www.ncpc.gov.

Chairman	L. Preston Bryant, Jr.
Members	Arrington Dixon, John M. Hart, Robert E. Miller, Elizabeth White
Secretary of the Interior (ex officio)	Sarah M.R. Jewell
Secretary of Defense (ex officio)	Charles T. Hagel
Chairman, Senate Committee on Homeland Security and Governmental Affairs (ex officio)	Thomas R. Carper
Chairman, House Committee on Oversight and Government Reform (ex officio)	Darrell Issa
Mayor of the District of Columbia (ex officio)	Vincent C. Gray
Chairman, Council of the District of Columbia (ex officio)	Philip Mendelson
Staff	
Executive Director	Marcel C. Acosta
Chief Operating Officer	Barry S. Socks
General Counsel	Anne R. Schuyler
Director, Office of Public Engagement	Julia A. Koster
Director, Physical Planning	Elizabeth Miller
Director, Policy and Research	Michael A. Sherman
Director, Urban Design and Plan Review	Christine Saum
Secretary to the Commission and Director, Office of Administration	Deborah B. Young

[For the National Capital Planning Commission statement of organization, see the Code of Federal Regulations, Title 1, Part 456.2]

The National Capital Planning Commission is the central agency for conducting planning and development activities for Federal lands and facilities in the National Capital Region. The region includes the District of Columbia and all land areas within the boundaries of Montgomery and Prince George's Counties in Maryland and Fairfax, Loudoun, Prince William, and Arlington Counties and the City of Alexandria in Virginia.

The National Capital Planning Commission was established as a park planning agency by act of June 6, 1924, as amended (40 U.S.C. 8701 et seq.). Two years later its role was expanded to include comprehensive planning. In 1952, under the National Capital Planning Act, the Commission was designated the central planning agency for the Federal and District of Columbia governments.

In 1973, the National Capital Planning Act was amended by the District of Columbia Home Rule Act, which made the mayor of the District of Columbia the chief planner for the District and gave the Commission specific authority for reviewing certain District decisions. The

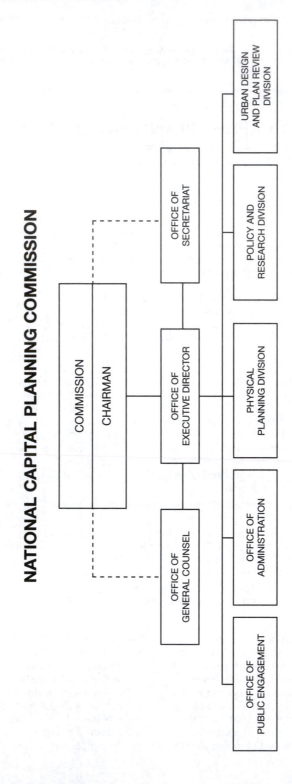

NATIONAL CAPITAL PLANNING COMMISSION

Commission continues to serve as the central planning agency for the Federal Government in the National Capital Region.

The Commission is composed of five appointed and seven ex officio members. Three citizen members, including the Chairman, are appointed by the President, with the remaining two appointed by the mayor of the District of Columbia. Presidential appointees include one resident each from Maryland and Virginia and one from anywhere else in the United States. The two mayoral appointees must be District of Columbia residents.

For further information, contact the National Capital Planning Commission, 401 Ninth Street NW., Suite 500, Washington, DC 20004. Phone, 202–482–7200. Fax, 202–482–7272. Email, info@ncpc.gov. Internet, http://www.ncpc.gov.

NATIONAL CREDIT UNION ADMINISTRATION

1775 Duke Street, Alexandria, VA 22314
Phone, 703–518–6300. Internet, http://www.ncua.gov.

Chairman	DEBBIE MATZ
Members	MICHAEL E. FRYZEL, RICHARD T. METSGER
Executive Director	MARK A. TREICHEL
General Counsel	MICHAEL MCKENNA
Inspector General	JAMES W. HAGEN
Director, Office of Examination and Insurance	LARRY FAZIO
Director, Office of National Examinations and Supervision	SCOTT HUNT
Chief Financial Officer	MARY ANN WOODSON
Chief Information Officer	RONNIE LEVINE
Director, Office of Small Credit Union Initiatives	WILLIAM MYERS
Director, Office of Human Resources	CHERYL EYRE
Director, Public and Congressional Affairs	TODD M. HARPER
Director, Office of Consumer Protection	GAIL LASTER

[For the National Credit Union Administration statement of organization, see the Code of Federal Regulations, Title 12, Part 720]

The National Credit Union Administration is responsible for chartering, insuring, supervising, and examining Federal credit unions and administering the National Credit Union Share Insurance Fund.

The National Credit Union Administration (NCUA) was established by act of March 10, 1970 (12 U.S.C. 1752), and reorganized by act of November 10, 1978 (12 U.S.C. 226), as an independent agency in the executive branch of the Federal Government. It regulates and insures all Federal credit unions and insures State-chartered credit unions that apply and qualify for share insurance.

Activities

Chartering NCUA grants Federal credit union charters to groups sharing a common bond of occupation or association or groups within a well-defined neighborhood, community, or rural district. A preliminary investigation is made to determine if certain standards are met before granting a Federal charter.

Examinations The Administration regularly examines Federal credit unions to determine their solvency and compliance with laws and regulations and to assist credit union management and operations.

For further information, contact the Director, Office of Examination and Insurance. Phone, 703–518–6360.

Share Insurance   The act of October 19, 1970 (12 U.S.C. 1781 et seq.), provides for a program of share insurance. The insurance is mandatory for Federal credit unions. State-chartered credit unions in many States are required to have Federal share insurance, and it is optional for other State-chartered credit unions. Credit union members' accounts are insured up to $250,000. The National Credit Union Share Insurance Fund requires each insured credit union to place and maintain a 1-percent deposit of its insured savings with the Fund.

For further information, contact the Director, Office of Examination and Insurance. Phone, 703–518–6360.

Supervision   Supervisory activities are carried out through regular examiner contacts and through periodic policy and regulatory releases from the Administration. NCUA also identifies emerging problems and monitors operations between examinations.

For a complete list of NCUA regional offices, visit http://www.ncua.gov/about/pages/Contact.aspx .

Sources of Information

Consumer Assistance   Questions about credit union insurance and other consumer matters can be directed to NCUA's Consumer Assistance Center at 800–755–1030, from 9 a.m. to 5 p.m.,

eastern standard time, Monday through Friday. After business hours, consumers may leave a recorded message.

Consumer Complaints   NCUA investigates the complaints of members unable to resolve problems with their Federal credit unions. Complaints should be sent to the regional office in the State where the credit union is located.

Employment   Inquiries and applications for employment should be directed to the Office of Human Resources, National Credit Union Administration, 1775 Duke Street, Alexandria, VA 22314–3428.

Federally Insured Credit Unions   A directory of federally insured credit unions, their addresses, asset levels, and membership numbers is available for review at NCUA's central and regional offices. Copies of the directory are available at a nominal fee from NCUA, Publications, 1775 Duke Street, Alexandria, VA 22314–3428. Phone, 703–518–6340. The directory is also available online. Internet, http://www.ncua.gov/Legal/GuidesEtc/Pages/CUDirectory.aspx.

Publications   A listing and copies of NCUA publications are available from NCUA, Publications, 1775 Duke Street, Alexandria, VA 22314–3428. Phone, 703–518–6340. Publications are also available online. Internet, http://www.ncua.gov/Legal/GuidesEtc/Pages/default.aspx.

Starting a Federal Credit Union   Groups interested in forming a Federal credit union may obtain free information by writing to the appropriate regional office.

For further information, contact the Office of Public and Congressional Affairs, National Credit Union Administration, 1775 Duke Street, Alexandria, VA 22314–3428. Phone, 703–518–6330. Internet, http://www.ncua.gov.

NATIONAL FOUNDATION ON THE ARTS AND THE HUMANITIES

National Endowment for the Arts

400 7th Street SW., Washington, DC 20506
Phone, 202–682–5400. TDD, 202–682–5496. Internet, http://www.arts.gov.

Chairman	R. Jane Chu
Senior Deputy Chairman	Joan Shigekawa
Deputy Chairman, Management and Budget	Winona Varnon

Deputy Chairman, Programs and Partnerships	PATRICE WALKER POWELL
Chief of Staff and White House Liaison	MIKE GRIFFIN
Budget Officer	JOHN SOTELO
Chief Information Officer	MICHAEL BURKE
Director, Accessibility	BETH BIENVENU
Director, Administrative Services	KATHY DAUM
Director, Artist Communities and Presenting and Multidisciplinary Works and Coordinator of International Activities	MICHAEL ORLOVE
Director, Arts Education	AYANNA N. HUDSON
Director, Civil Rights, Equal Employment Opportunity	MARISA E. MARINOS
Director, Dance	DOUGLAS SONNTAG
Director, Design	JASON SCHUPBACH
Director, Folk and Traditional Arts	BARRY BERGEY
Director, Guidelines and Panel Operations	JILLIAN L. MILLER
Director, Human Resources	CRAIG M. MCCORD, SR.
Director, Literature	AMY STOLLS, *Acting*
Director, Media Arts	MARY SMITH, *Acting*
Director, Museums and Visual Arts	WENDY CLARK, *Acting*
Director, Music and Opera	DOUGLAS SONNTAG, *Acting*
Director, Public Affairs	JESSAMYN SARMIENTO
Director, Research and Analysis	SUNIL IYENGAR
Director, State and Regional Partnerships	LAURA SCANLAN
Director, Strategic Partnerships	DAN LURIE
Director, Theater and Musical Theater	DOUGLAS SONNTAG, *Acting*
Federal Partnerships Coordinator	TONY TIGHE
Finance Officer	SANDRA STUECKLER
General Counsel	INDIA PINKNEY
Grants and Contracts Officer	NICKI JACOBS
Inspector General	AUVONETT JONES

The National Endowment for the Arts advances artistic excellence, creativity, and innovation for the benefit of individuals and communities.

Through its grants and programs, the Arts Endowment brings great art to all 50 States and 6 U.S. jurisdictions, including rural areas, inner cities, and military bases. The Arts Endowment awards competitive matching grants to nonprofit organizations, to units of State or local government, and to federally recognized tribal communities or tribes for projects, programs, or activities in the fields of artist communities, arts education, dance, design, folk and traditional arts, literature, local arts agencies, media arts, museums, music, musical theater, opera, presenting, theater, and visual arts. In addition, it awards competitive nonmatching individual fellowships in literature and honorary fellowships in jazz, folk and traditional arts, and opera. Forty percent of the Arts Endowment's grant funds go to the 56 State and jurisdictional arts agencies and their 6 regional arts organizations in support of arts projects in thousands of communities across the country.

Sources of Information

Grants   For information about Arts Endowment funding opportunities, contact the Public Affairs Office. Phone, 202–682–5400. TDD, 202–682–5496. Internet, http://www.arts.gov/grants. **Publications**   To obtain a copy of the "Annual Report for the National Endowment for the Arts," funding guidelines, or other publications, contact the Public Affairs Office. Phone, 202–682–5400. TDD, 202–682–5496. Internet, http://arts.gov/publications.

For further information, contact the Public Affairs Office, National Endowment for the Arts, 400 7th Street SW., Washington, DC 20506–0001. Phone, 202–682–5400. TDD, 202–682–5496. Internet, http://www.arts.gov.

National Endowment for the Humanities

1100 Pennsylvania Avenue NW., Washington, DC 20506
Phone, 202–606–8400; 800–634–1121. Internet, http://www.neh.gov. Email, info@neh.gov.

Chairman	WILLIAM D. ADAMS
Deputy Chairman	CAROLE WATSON
Chief Information Officer	BRETT BOBLEY
General Counsel	MICHAEL MCDONALD
Inspector General	LAURA M.H. DAVIS
White House Liaison and Director of Congressional Affairs	COURTNEY CHAPIN
Director, Communications	JUDY HAVEMANN
Assistant Chairman for Partnership and Strategic Initiatives	EVAGREN O. CALDERA
Assistant Chairman for Planning and Operations	JEFFREY THOMAS
Assistant Chairman for Programs	ADAM WOLFSON
Director, Accounting	JOHN GLEASON
Director, Administrative Services	BARRY MAYNES
Director, Division of Education Programs	WILLIAM C. RICE
Director, Division of Preservation and Access	NADINA GARDNER
Director, Division of Public Programs	KAREN MITTELMAN
Director, Division of Research Programs	JANE AIKIN
Director, EDSITEment Partnership	CAROL PETERS
Director, Federal/State Partnership	EDYTHE MANZA
Director, Information Resource Management	TANYA PELTZ
Director, Office of Challenge Grants	ANDREA ANDERSON, *Acting*
Director, Office of Digital Humanities	BRETT BOBLEY
Director, Office of Grant Management	ROBERT STRAUGHTER, *Acting*
Director, Office of Human Resources	ANTHONY MITCHELL
Director, Office of Planning and Budget	LARRY MYERS
Director, Office of Publications	DAVID SKINNER
Director, We the People Program	CAROLE WATSON

The National Endowment for the Humanities supports research, education, preservation, and public programs in the humanities.

According to the agency's authorizing legislation, the term "humanities" includes, but is not limited to, the study of the following: language, both modern and classical; linguistics; literature; history; jurisprudence; philosophy; archeology; comparative religion; ethics; the history, criticism, and theory of the arts; and those aspects of the social sciences that employ historical or philosophical approaches.

To increase understanding and appreciation of the humanities, the Endowment makes grants to individuals,

groups, or institutions: schools, colleges, universities, museums, public television stations, libraries, public agencies, and nonprofit private groups.

Bridging Cultures Initiative This initiative encourages projects that explore the ways in which cultures around the globe, as well as the many subcultures within America's borders, have influenced American society.

For further information, call 202–606–8337.

Challenge Grants Nonprofit institutions interested in developing new sources of long-term support for educational,

NATIONAL ENDOWMENT FOR THE HUMANITIES

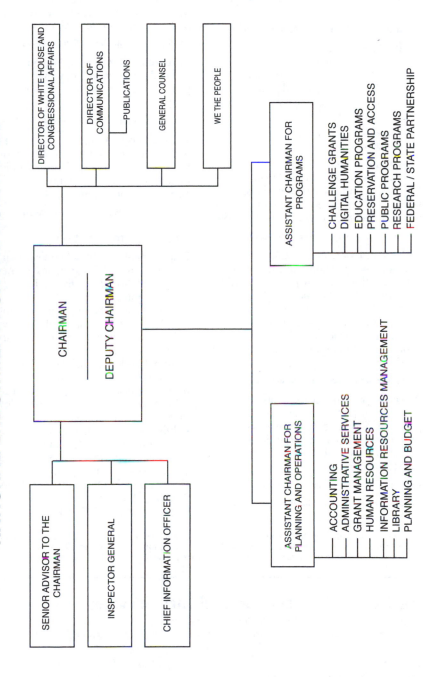

CHAIRMAN
DEPUTY CHAIRMAN

DIRECTOR OF WHITE HOUSE AND CONGRESSIONAL AFFAIRS
DIRECTOR OF COMMUNICATIONS
└ PUBLICATIONS
GENERAL COUNSEL
WE THE PEOPLE

SENIOR ADVISOR TO THE CHAIRMAN
INSPECTOR GENERAL
CHIEF INFORMATION OFFICER

ASSISTANT CHAIRMAN FOR PROGRAMS
- CHALLENGE GRANTS
- DIGITAL HUMANITIES
- EDUCATION PROGRAMS
- PRESERVATION AND ACCESS
- PUBLIC PROGRAMS
- RESEARCH PROGRAMS
- FEDERAL / STATE PARTNERSHIP

ASSISTANT CHAIRMAN FOR PLANNING AND OPERATIONS
- ACCOUNTING
- ADMINISTRATIVE SERVICES
- GRANT MANAGEMENT
- HUMAN RESOURCES
- INFORMATION RESOURCES MANAGEMENT
- LIBRARY
- PLANNING AND BUDGET

scholarly, preservation, and public programs in the humanities may be assisted in these efforts by a challenge grant.

For further information, call 202–606–8309.

Digital Humanities The Office of Digital Humanities encourages and supports projects that use or study the impact of digital technology on education, preservation, public programming, and research in the humanities.

For further information, call 202–606–8401. Email, odh@neh.gov.

Education Through grants to educational institutions and fellowships to scholars and teachers, this division strengthens sustained thoughtful study of the humanities at all levels of education.

For further information, call 202–606–8500.

Federal and State Partnership Humanities committees in each of the 50 States, the Virgin Islands, Puerto Rico, the District of Columbia, the Northern Mariana Islands, American Samoa, and Guam receive grants from the Endowment, which they in turn grant to support humanities programs at the local level.

For further information, call 202–606–8254.

Preservation and Access This division supports projects that will create, preserve, and increase the availability of resources important for research, education, and public programming in the humanities.

For further information, call 202–606–8570.

Public Programs This division strives to fulfill the Endowment's mandate "to increase public understanding of the humanities" by supporting those institutions and organizations that develop and present humanities programming for general audiences.

For further information, call 202–606–8268.

Research This division promotes original research in the humanities by providing grants for significant research projects.

For further information, call 202–606–8389.

We the People Program This program is designed to encourage and enhance the teaching, study, and understanding of American history, culture, and democratic principles.

For further information, call 202–606–8235.

Sources of Information

Employment National Endowment for the Humanities job vacancies are posted online at USAJOBS. Internet, https://www.usajobs.gov/.

Grants Those interested in applying for a humanities grant should visit www.neh.gov for information and guidelines related to grant programs offered by the National Endowment for the Humanities. For further information, call 202–606–8400. Applications for grants must be submitted online using the link below. Internet, http://www.grants.gov.

Publications The Endowment's bimonthly review, "Humanities", is available by subscription ($24 domestic, $33.60 foreign) through the U.S. Government Printing Office, P.O. Box 979050, St. Louis, MO 63197–9000, or by phone at 202–512–1800.

For further information, contact the Office of Communications, National Endowment for the Humanities, Room 510, 1100 Pennsylvania Avenue NW., Washington, DC 20506. Phone, 202–606–8400 or 800–634–1121. TDD, 202–606–8282 or 866–372–2930. Email, info@neh.gov. Internet, http://www.neh.gov.

Institute of Museum and Library Services

1800 M Street NW., Ninth Floor, Washington, DC 20036
Phone, 202–653–4657. Internet, http://www.imls.gov. Email, imlsinfo@imls.gov.

Director	SUSAN HILDRETH
Deputy Director for Library Services	MAURA MARX
Deputy Director for Museum Services	CLAUDIA FRENCH

Director of Communications and Government Affairs	MAMIE BITTNER
General Counsel	NANCY E. WEISS
Chief Operating Officer	MICHAEL D. JERGER
Chief Financial Officer	CHRIS CATIGNANI
Chief Information Officer	STEPHANIE BURWELL
Grants Management Officer	MARY E. KENNELLY
Associate Deputy Director for Library Services, State Programs	(VACANCY)
Associate Deputy Director for Library Services, Discretionary Programs	ROBERT HORTON
Director of Planning, Research, and Evaluation	CARLOS A. MANJARREZ

The Institute of Museum and Library Services creates strong libraries and museums that connect people to information and ideas.

The Institute of Museum and Library Services (IMLS) was established within the National Foundation on the Arts and the Humanities by the Museum and Library Services Act of September 30, 1996 (110 Stat. 3009), which amended the Museum Services Act (20 U.S.C. 961 et seq.). The Institute combines the administration of Federal museum programs, which the Institute of Museum Services formerly managed, and Federal library programs, which the Department of Education formerly managed. The Institute's Director is appointed by the President with the advice and consent of the Senate and is authorized to make grants to museums and libraries. The Director receives policy advice on museum and library programs from the National Museum and Library Services Board, a 20-member board appointed by the President, and from the Director, Deputy Director for the Office of Museum Services, and Deputy Director for the Office of Library Services.

IMLS is the primary source of Federal support for the Nation's 123,000 libraries and 17,500 museums. It helps libraries and museums improve innovation, learning, and cultural and civic engagement. Through grantmaking, policy development, and research, IMLS helps libraries and museums deliver more and better services to individuals and their communities. IMLS awards grants to art, history, general, children's, natural history, science, and technology museums, as well as to historic houses, zoos, aquariums, botanical gardens,

arboretums, nature centers, and planetariums. It also awards grants to public, school, academic, research, and special libraries. The Institute makes grants that improve electronic sharing of information and expand public access to information and services.

African American History and Culture Museum Grants These grants provide professional training, technical assistance, internships, and outside expertise for African American museums to increase their institutional capacity and sustainability.

Internet, http://www.imls.gov/applicants/name.aspx.

Conservation Assessment Program IMLS helps support the cost of the program through a cooperative agreement with Heritage Preservation. The program supports conservation and research projects that include Professional conservators making onsite visits to identify conservation priorities.

Internet, http://www.imls.gov/applicants/name.aspx.

Laura Bush 21st Century Librarian Program This program supports projects to recruit and educate future librarians, faculty, and library leaders; to promote early career research; and to assist in the professional development of librarians and library staff.

Internet, http://www.imls.gov/applicants/name.aspx.

Museum Assessment Program IMLS helps support the cost of the program through a cooperative agreement with the American Alliance of Museums. The program helps museums assess their strengths, assess their weaknesses, and plan for the future.

Internet, http://www.imls.gov/applicants/name.aspx.

Museums for America   This program supports projects designed to help an individual museum better serve its public.

Internet, http://www.imls.gov/applicants/name.aspx.

National Arts and Humanities Youth Program Awards   This program is a project of the President's Committee on the Arts and the Humanities in partnership with IMLS, the National Endowment for the Arts, and the National Endowment for the Humanities. These awards acknowledge museums and libraries for their afterschool and out-of-school arts and humanities programming for young Americans.

Internet, http://www.imls.gov/applicants/name.aspx.

National Leadership Grants   These grants enhance the quality of archive, library, and museum services nationwide. They support projects intended to advance professional practice in these fields.

Internet, http://www.imls.gov/applicants/name.aspx.

National Medal for Museum and Library Service   This award honors outstanding institutions that provide exceptional and meaningful public service for communities that they serve.

Internet, http://www.imls.gov/applicants/name.aspx.

Native American Library Services   This program provides small grants to tribes and Alaska Native villages to maintain core library operations and support technical assistance. Enhancement grants help implement new library services and promote innovative practices.

Internet, http://www.imls.gov/applicants/name.aspx.

Native American/Native Hawaiian Museum Services Program   This program strengthens museum services to Native American tribes and Native Hawaiian organizations in the areas of programming and professional development.

Internet, http://www.imls.gov/applicants/name.aspx.

Sparks! Ignition Grants   These grants help archives, museums, and libraries innovate and enhance the way they operate and provide services.

Internet, http://www.imls.gov/applicants/name.aspx.

State Program Grants   IMLS, through the Library Services and Technology Act, provides annual grants to support library services in each State using a population-based formula. For more information, contact your State librarian or use the link below.

Internet, http://www.imls.gov/programs/default.aspx.

Sources of Information

Electronic Access   Information on IMLS programs, application guidelines, and lists of grantees is available online. Email, imlsinfo@imls.gov. Internet, http://www.imls.gov.

Grants, Contracts, and Cooperative Agreements   For information on applying for IMLS funding, contact the appropriate program office. Museum representatives should contact the Office of Museum Services, Institute of Museum and Library Services, 1800 M Street NW., Ninth Floor, Washington, DC 20036. Phone, 202–653–4798. Library representatives should contact the Office of Library Services, Institute of Museum and Library Services, 1800 M Street NW., Washington, DC 20036. Phone, 202–653–4700.

For further information, contact the Office of Communications and Government Affairs, Institute of Museum and Library Services, 1800 M Street NW., Washington, DC 20036. Phone, 202–653–4757. Email, imlsinfo@imls.gov. Internet, http://www.imls.gov.

NATIONAL LABOR RELATIONS BOARD

1099 Fourteenth Street NW., Washington, DC 20570
Phone, 202–273–1000. TDD, 202–273–4300. Internet, http://www.nlrb.gov.

Chairman	MARK G. PEARCE
Members	KENT Y. HIROZAWA, HARRY I. JOHNSON, III, PHILIP A. MISCIMARRA, NANCY J. SCHIFFER
Executive Secretary	GARY W. SHINNERS
Director, Representation Appeals	(VACANCY)
Solicitor	WILLIAM B. COWEN
Chief Administrative Law Judge	ROBERT A. GIANNASI
Director, Office of Public Affairs	GREGORY J. KING
Inspector General	DAVID P. BERRY
General Counsel	RICHARD F. GRIFFIN, JR.
Deputy General Counsel	JENNIFER ABRUZZO
Director, Equal Employment Opportunity	BRENDA V. HARRIS
Director, Employee Development	THOMAS J. CHRISTMAN, JR.
Chief Information Officer	BRYAN BURNETT
Director, Division of Administration	VENTRIS C. GIBSON
Associate General Counsel, Division of Operations-Management	ANNE G. PURCELL
Associate General Counsel, Division of Enforcement Litigation	JOHN H. FERGUSON
Associate General Counsel, Division of Advice	BARRY J. KEARNEY

[For the National Labor Relations Board statement of organization, see the Federal Register of June 14, 1979, 44 FR 34215]

The National Labor Relations Board prevents and remedies unfair labor practices committed by private sector employers and unions. It safeguards employees' rights to organize and determine whether to have unions as their bargaining representative.

The National Labor Relations Board (NLRB) is an independent agency created by Congress to administer the National Labor Relations Act of 1935 (Wagner Act; 29 U.S.C. 167). The Board is authorized to designate appropriate units for collective bargaining and to conduct secret ballot elections to determine whether employees desire representation by a labor organization.

Activities

In addition to preventing and remedying unfair labor practices, the NLRB conducts secret ballot elections among employees in appropriate collective-bargaining units to determine whether or not they desire to be represented by a labor organization in bargaining with employers over wages, hours, and working conditions. It also conducts secret ballot elections among employees who have been covered by a union-security agreement to determine whether or not they wish to revoke their union's authority to make such agreements. In jurisdictional disputes between two or more unions, the Board determines which competing group of workers is entitled to perform the work involved.

The regional directors and their staffs process representation, unfair labor practice, and jurisdictional dispute cases. They issue complaints in unfair labor practice cases, seek settlement of unfair labor practice charges, obtain compliance with Board orders and court judgments, and petition district courts for injunctions to prevent or remedy unfair labor practices. The regional directors conduct hearings in representation cases, hold elections pursuant to the agreement of the parties or the decisionmaking authority delegated to them by the Board

NATIONAL LABOR RELATIONS BOARD

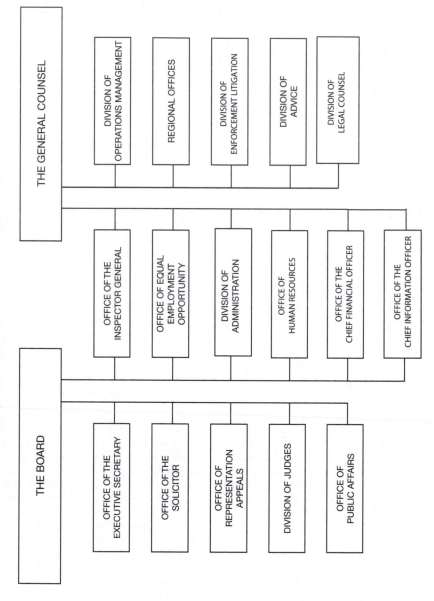

THE GENERAL COUNSEL

- DIVISION OF OPERATIONS MANAGEMENT
- REGIONAL OFFICES
- DIVISION OF ENFORCEMENT LITIGATION
- DIVISION OF ADVICE
- DIVISION OF LEGAL COUNSEL

- OFFICE OF THE INSPECTOR GENERAL
- OFFICE OF EQUAL EMPLOYMENT OPPORTUNITY
- DIVISION OF ADMINISTRATION
- OFFICE OF HUMAN RESOURCES
- OFFICE OF THE CHIEF FINANCIAL OFFICER
- OFFICE OF THE CHIEF INFORMATION OFFICER

THE BOARD

- OFFICE OF THE EXECUTIVE SECRETARY
- OFFICE OF THE SOLICITOR
- OFFICE OF REPRESENTATION APPEALS
- DIVISION OF JUDGES
- OFFICE OF PUBLIC AFFAIRS

or pursuant to Board directions, and issue certifications of representatives when unions win or certify the results when they lose employee elections. The regional directors process petitions for bargaining unit clarification, for amendment of certification, and for rescission of a labor organization's authority to make a union-shop agreement. They also conduct national emergency employee referendums.

Administrative law judges conduct hearings in unfair labor practice cases, make findings of fact and conclusions of law, and recommend remedies for violations found. Their decisions can be appealed to the Board for a final agency determination. The Board's decisions are subject to review in the U.S. courts of appeals.

To find contact information for National Labor Relations Board regional and resident offices, use the link below.

Internet, http://www.nlrb.gov/who-we-are/regional-offices.

Sources of Information

Contracts Prospective suppliers of goods and services may inquire about agency procurement and contracting practices by writing to the Chief, Acquisitions Management Branch, National Labor Relations Board, Washington, DC 20570. Phone, 202–273–4047.

Employment The Board appoints administrative law judges from a register established by the Office of Personnel Management. The agency hires attorneys

for all its offices, field examiners for its resident offices, and administrative personnel for its Washington and resident offices. Inquiries regarding college and law school recruiting programs should be directed to the appropriate regional or Headquarters office. Employment inquiries and applications may be sent to any regional office or the Washington Human Resources Office. Internet, http://www.nlrb.gov/who-we-are/careers.

Programs and Activities Information on programs and activities is available on NLRB's Web site. Internet, http://www.nlrb.gov/what-we-do.

Publications To inspect formal case documents or read agency publications, visit the Washington or field offices. Case documents and agency publications are also available on NLRB's Web site. The Board's offices offer free informational leaflets in limited quantities. Internet, http://www.nlrb.gov/cases-decisions.

Speakers To provide a better understanding of the National Labor Relations Act and the Board's policies, procedures, and services, Washington and regional office personnel are available to serve as speakers for labor and civic organizations, educational institutions, management organizations, bar associations, and other similar groups. Requests for speakers or panelists may be made to Washington officials or to the appropriate regional director. Requests also may be made by using the link below and filling out the online form. Internet, http://www.nlrb.gov/news-outreach/request-speaker.

For further information, contact the Office of Public Affairs, National Labor Relations Board, 1099 Fourteenth Street NW., Suite 11550, Washington, DC 20570. Phone, 202–273–1991. Internet, http://www.nlrb.gov.

NATIONAL MEDIATION BOARD

1301 K Street NW., Suite 250 East, Washington, DC 20005
Phone, 202–692–5000. Internet, http://www.nmb.gov.

Chairman	LINDA A. PUCHALA
Members	NICHOLAS C. GEALE, HARRY R. HOGLANDER
Chief of Staff	DANIEL RAINEY
General Counsel, Office of Legal Affairs	MARY JOHNSON

Director, Administration	(VACANCY)
Director, Arbitration Services	ROLAND WATKINS
Director, Mediation and Alternative Dispute Resolution Services	(VACANCY)

The National Mediation Board facilitates labor-management relations within the railroads and the airlines.

The National Mediation Board (NMB) is an independent agency established by the 1934 amendments to the Railway Labor Act of 1926 (45 U.S.C. 151–158, 160–162, 1181–1188). The Board is composed of three members, appointed by the President and confirmed by the Senate. The Board designates a Chairman on a yearly basis.

The Agency's dispute-resolution processes are designed to resolve disputes over the negotiation of new or revised collective bargaining agreements and the interpretation or application of existing agreements. It also effectuates employee rights of self-organization where a representation dispute exists.

Activities

Mediation and Alternative Dispute Resolution Following receipt of an application for mediation, the NMB assigns a mediator to assist the parties in reaching an agreement. The NMB is obligated to use its best efforts to bring about a peaceful resolution to the dispute. If such efforts do not settle the dispute, the NMB advises the parties and offers interest arbitration as an alternative approach to resolve the remaining issues. If either party rejects this offer, the NMB releases the parties from formal mediation. This release triggers a 30-day cooling off period. During this period, NMB continues to work with the parties to achieve a consensual resolution. If, however, an agreement is not reached by the end of the 30-day period, the parties are free to exercise lawful self-help, such as carrier-imposed working conditions or a strike by the union/organization.

In addition to traditional mediation services, NMB also provides voluntary Alternative Dispute Resolution (ADR) services. ADR services include facilitation, training, grievance mediation,

and an Online Dispute Resolution component, which applies technology to the dispute resolution process. The purpose of the ADR program is to assist the parties in learning and applying more effective, less confrontational methods for resolving their disputes, and to help them resolve more of their own disputes without outside intervention.

Presidential Emergency Board If NMB determines that a dispute threatens to substantially deprive any section of the country of essential transportation service, it notifies the President. The President may, at his discretion, establish a Presidential Emergency Board (PEB) to investigate and report back within 30 days. After the PEB has been created and for 30 days after it has made its report to the President, neither party to the dispute may exercise self-help.

There are also special emergency procedures for unresolved disputes affecting publicly funded and operated commuter railroads and their employees. If the mediation procedures are exhausted, the parties to the dispute, or the Governor of any State where the railroad operates, may request that the President establish a PEB. The President is required to establish such a board if requested. If no settlement is reached within 60 days following the creation of the PEB, NMB is required to conduct a public hearing on the dispute. If there is no settlement within 120 days after the creation of the PEB, any party, or the Governor of any affected state, may request a second, final-offer PEB. No self-help is permitted pending the exhaustion of these emergency procedures.

Representation When a labor organization or individual files an application with NMB to represent employees, the Agency assigns an investigator to conduct a representation investigation. Should the applicant

NATIONAL MEDIATION BOARD

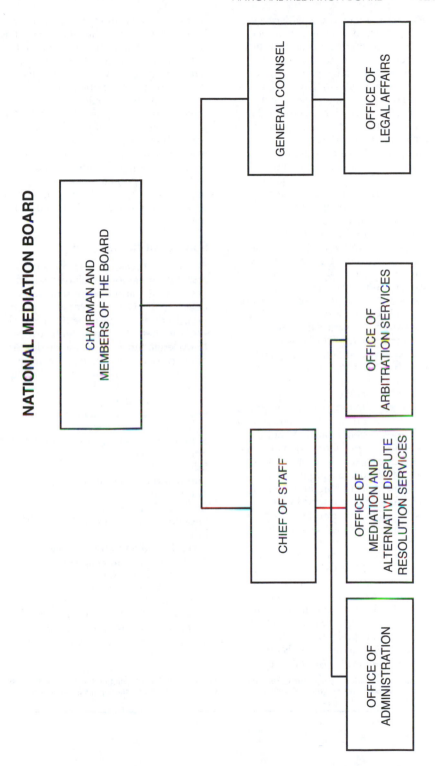

meet the requirements, NMB continues the investigation, usually with a secret telephone or Internet election. NMB is responsible for ensuring that the requirements for a fair election process have been maintained. If the employees vote to be represented, NMB issues a certification which commences the carrier's statutory duty to bargain with the certified representative.

Arbitration   NMB provides both grievance arbitration and interest arbitration. Grievance arbitration is a process for resolving disputes regarding the interpretation or application of an existing collective bargaining agreement. Grievances must be handled through grievance arbitration if not otherwise resolved, and cannot be used by the parties to trigger self-help actions. NMB has significant administrative responsibilities for grievance arbitration in the railroad industry, which includes those before the National Railroad Adjustment Board (NRAB), as well as the two types of arbitration panels established by the labor-management parties at each railroad: public law boards (PLBs) and special boards of adjustment (SBAs). Grievance arbitration in the airline industry is accomplished at the various system boards of adjustment created jointly by labor and management at the parties' expense. NMB furnishes panels of prospective arbitrators for the parties' selection in both the airline and railroad industries. NMB also pays the salary and travel expenses of the arbitrators for railroad arbitration proceedings. Grievance arbitration decisions are final and binding with very limited grounds for judicial review.

Interest arbitration is a process to establish the terms of a new or modified collective bargaining agreement through arbitration, rather than through negotiations. Unlike grievance arbitration, its use is not statutorily required. NMB offers the parties the opportunity to use binding interest arbitration when the agency has determined that further mediation efforts will not be successful. In addition, the parties may directly agree to resolve their collective bargaining dispute or portions of their dispute through interest arbitration. NMB generally provides the parties with panels of potential arbitrators from which they choose an individual to resolve their dispute. In some instances, however, the parties agree to allow NMB to directly appoint an arbitrator. Interest arbitration decisions are final and binding with very narrow grounds for judicial appeal.

Sources of Information

Electronic Access   For information on NMB operations, including weekly case activity reports, representation determinations, press releases, and the Board's directory, visit the Board's Web site. Internet, http://www.nmb.gov/.

Knowledge Store   The Knowledge Store contains over 100,000 documents in an easily searchable format, including arbitration awards, representation decisions, annual reports, PEB reports, industry contracts, and union constitutions and bylaws. To access the Store online, use the link below. Internet, http://knowledgestore.nmb.gov/ks/search/index.html.

Publications   The Annual Reports of the NMB are available online in the Knowledge Store. Internet, http://knowledgestore.nmb.gov/ks/search/index.html.

Virtual Reading Room   Copies of collective-bargaining agreements between labor and management of various rail and air carriers and NMB Determinations (back to at least October 1, 1998) are available online in the Knowledge Store. Internet, http://knowledgestore.nmb.gov/ks/search/index.html.

For further information, contact the Public Information Officer, National Mediation Board, Suite 250 East, 1301 K Street NW., Washington, DC 20005–7011. Phone, 202–692–5050. Internet, http://www.nmb.gov.

NATIONAL RAILROAD PASSENGER CORPORATION (AMTRAK)

60 Massachusetts Avenue NE., Washington, DC 20002
Phone, 202–906–3000. Internet, http://www.amtrak.com.

Board of Directors

Chairman	ANTHONY R. COSCIA
Vice Chairman	JEFFREY R. MORELAND
Directors	CHRISTOPHER R. BEALL, YVONNE B. BURKE, THOMAS C. CARPER, ALBERT DICLEMENTE, JOSEPH SZABO
President and Chief Executive Officer, AMTRAK (ex officio)	JOSEPH H. BOARDMAN
Secretary of Transportation (ex officio)	ANTHONY R. FOXX

Officers

President and Chief Executive Officer	JOSEPH H. BOARDMAN
Vice President, General Counsel and Corporate Secretary	ELEANOR D. ACHESON
Vice President, Government Affairs and Corporate Communications	JOSEPH H. MCHUGH
Chief Human Capital Officer	BARRY MELNKOVIC
Vice President, Operations	D. J. STADTLER
Chief Officer, Marketing and Sales	MATTHEW H. HARDISON
Chief of Police	POLLY HANSON
Vice President, Northeast Corridor Infrastructure and Investment Development	STEPHEN J. GARDNER
Chief Financial Officer	GERALD SOKOL, JR.
Chief Information Officer	JASON MOLFETAS
Chief, Emergency Management and Corporate Security	SUSAN K. REINERTSON
Chief, Corporate Research and Strategy	MARK YACHMETZ
Inspector General	THOMAS HOWARD

[For the National Railroad Passenger Corporation statement of organization, see the Code of Federal Regulations, Title 49, Part 700]

The National Railroad Passenger Corporation provides intercity rail passenger service in the United States.

The National Railroad Passenger Corporation (Amtrak) was created by the Rail Passenger Service Act of 1970, as amended (49 U.S.C. 241), and was incorporated under the laws of the District of Columbia. By developing, operating, and improving U.S. intercity rail passenger service, Amtrak provides a balanced nationwide transportation system.

Amtrak operates approximately 300 trains per day, serving over 500 stations in 46 States, over a system of 22,000 route miles. Of this route system, Amtrak owns about 530 route miles in the Northeast and several other small track segments elsewhere in the country.

Amtrak owns or leases its stations and owns its own repair and maintenance facilities. The Corporation employs a total workforce of approximately 20,000 and provides all reservation, station, and onboard service staffs, as well as train and engine operating crews. Outside the Northeast Corridor, Amtrak may enter into contracts with privately or publicly owned railroads to operate on their track. These railroads are responsible for the condition of the roadbed and for coordinating the flow of traffic.

In fiscal year 2013, Amtrak transported over 31 million people, 86,000 passengers traveling per day. Amtrak also runs commuter trains under contract with several commuter agencies.

Although Amtrak's basic route system was originally designated by the Secretary of Transportation in 1971, modifications have been made to the Amtrak system and to individual routes that have resulted in more efficient and cost-effective operations. Capital funding has increased in recent years, allowing Amtrak to make progress in bringing its network to a state of good repair and in reducing debt load.

For further information, contact the Government Affairs Department, Amtrak, 60 Massachusetts Avenue NE., Washington, DC 20002. Phone, 202–906–3918. Internet, http://www.amtrak.com.

NATIONAL SCIENCE FOUNDATION

4201 Wilson Boulevard, Arlington, VA 22230
Phone, 703–292–5111. TDD, 800–281–8749. Internet, http://www.nsf.gov. Email, info@nsf.gov.

National Science Board

Chair	DAN E. ARVIZU
Vice Chair	KELVIN K. DROEGEMEIER
Members	DEBORAH L. BALL, BONNIE BASSLER, ARTHUR BIENENSTOCK, RAY M. BOWEN, VINTON G. CERF, RUTH DAVID, INEZ FUNG, ESIN GULARI, G. PETER LEPAGE, ALAN I. LESHNER, W. CARL LINEBERGER, STEPHEN MAYO, GEORGE P. PETERSON, DOUGLAS D. RANDALL, GERALDINE RICHMOND, ANNEILA I. SARGENT, DIANE L. SOUVAINE, ARNOLD F. STANCELL, CLAUDE M. STEELE, ROBERT J. ZIMMER, MARIA T. ZUBER
Member (ex officio)	FRANCE A. CÓRDOVA

National Science Foundation

Director	FRANCE A. CÓRDOVA
Deputy Director	CORA B. MARRETT
Executive Officer	MICHAEL L. VAN WOERT
General Counsel	LAWRENCE RUDOLPH
Office Head, Office of International and Integrative Activities	WANDA WARD
Office Head, Office of Legislative and Public Affairs	JUDY GAN
Office Head, Office of Diversity and Inclusion	CLAUDIA J. POSTELL
Inspector General	ALLISON C. LERNER
Assistant Director for Biological Sciences	JOHN C. WINGFIELD
Assistant Director for Computer and Information Science and Engineering	FARNAM JAHANIAN
Assistant Director for Education and Human Resources	JOAN FERRINI-MUNDY
Assistant Director for Engineering	PRAMOD P. KHARGONEKAR
Assistant Director for Geosciences	ROGER WAKIMOTO
Assistant Director for Mathematical and Physical Sciences	FLEMING CRIM

National Science Foundation

Assistant Director for Social, Behavioral, and Economic Sciences	JOANNE S. TORNOW, *Acting*
Chief Financial Officer and Office Head, Office of Budget, Finance, and Award Management	MARTHA A. RUBENSTEIN
Chief Human Capital Officer and Office Head, Office of Information and Resource Management	(VACANCY)
Chief Information Officer	AMY NORTHCUTT
Chief Technology Officer	JOSE MUNOZ

[For the National Science Foundation statement of organization, see the Federal Register of February 8, 1993, 58 FR 7587–7595; May 27, 1993, 58 FR 30819; May 2, 1994, 59 FR 22690; and October 6, 1995, 60 FR 52431]

The National Science Foundation promotes the progress of science and engineering by supporting research and education.

The National Science Foundation (NSF) is an independent agency created by the National Science Foundation Act of 1950, as amended (42 U.S.C. 1861–1875).

NSF purposes are to increase the Nation's base of scientific and engineering knowledge; to strengthen its ability to conduct research in all areas of science and engineering; to develop and help implement science and engineering education programs that can better prepare the Nation for meeting the challenges of the future; and to promote international cooperation through science and engineering. In its role as a leading Federal supporter of science and engineering, the agency also has an important role in national policy planning.

The Director and the Deputy Director are appointed by the President, with the advice and consent of the Senate, to a 6-year term and an unspecified term, respectively. The Foundation's activities are guided by the National Science Board (NSB). NSB comprises a chair, a vice chair, 24 board members, and the Director ex officio. Members are appointed by the President with the advice and consent of the Senate for 6-year terms, with one-third appointed every 2 years. They are selected because of their records of distinguished service in science, engineering, education, research management, or public affairs to be broadly representative of the views

of national science and engineering leadership. The Board also has a broad national policy responsibility to monitor and make recommendations to promote the health of U.S. science and engineering research and education.

The Foundation's Office of Inspector General is responsible for conducting and supervising audits, inspections, and investigations relating to the programs and operations of the Foundation, including allegations of misconduct in science.

Activities

NSF initiates and supports fundamental, long-term, merit-selected research in all the scientific and engineering disciplines. This support is made through grants, contracts, and other agreements awarded to universities, colleges, academic consortia, and nonprofit and small business institutions. Most of this research is directed toward the resolution of scientific and engineering questions concerning fundamental life processes, natural laws and phenomena, fundamental processes influencing the human environment, and the forces affecting people as members of society as well as the behavior of society as a whole.

The Foundation encourages cooperative efforts by universities, industries, and government. It also promotes the application of research

NATIONAL SCIENCE FOUNDATION

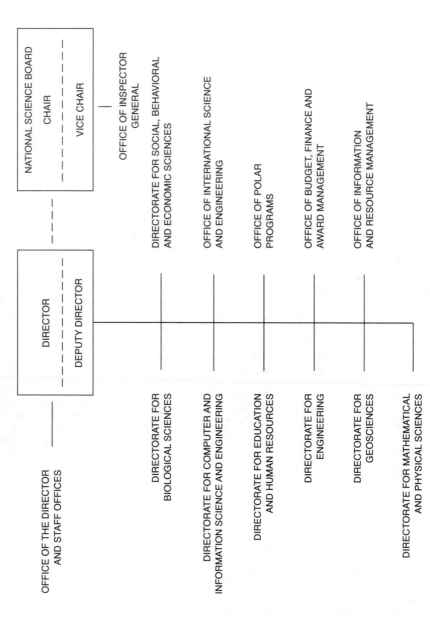

and development for better products and services that improve the quality of life and stimulate economic growth.

The Foundation promotes the development of research talent through support of undergraduate and graduate students, as well as postdoctoral researchers. It administers special programs to identify and encourage participation by groups underrepresented in science and technology and to strengthen research capability at smaller institutions, small businesses, undergraduate colleges, and universities.

The Foundation supports major national and international science and engineering activities, including the U.S. Antarctic Program, the Ocean Drilling Program, global geoscience studies, and others. Cooperative scientific and engineering research activities support exchange programs for American and foreign scientists and engineers, execution of jointly designed research projects, participation in the activities of international science and engineering organizations, and travel to international conferences.

Support is provided through contracts and cooperative agreements with national centers where large facilities are made available for use by qualified scientists and engineers. Among the types of centers supported by the Foundation are astronomy and atmospheric sciences, biological and engineering research, science and technology, supercomputers, and long-term ecological research sites.

The Foundation's science and engineering education activities include grants for research and development activities directed to model instructional materials for students and teachers and the application of advanced technologies to education. Grants also are available for teacher preparation and enhancement and informal science education activities. Funding is also provided for college science instrumentation, course and curriculum improvement, faculty and student activities, and minority resource centers. In addition, studies of the status of math, science, and engineering education are supported.

NSF presents the Vannevar Bush Award annually to a person who, through public service activities in science and technology, has made an outstanding contribution toward the welfare of mankind and the Nation. It also presents the Public Service Award to one individual who and to one company, corporation, or organization that have increased the public understanding of science or engineering by serving the public in areas other than research. NSF annually presents the Alan T. Waterman Award to an outstanding young scientist or engineer for support of research and study. The Foundation also provides administrative support for the President's Committee on the National Medal of Science.

Information on awards is available on the agency's Web site.

Internet, http://www.nsf.gov/awards/about.jsp.

Sources of Information

Board and Committee Minutes Summary minutes of the open meetings of the National Science Board may be obtained from its Office. Phone, 703–292–7000. Information on NSB meetings, minutes, and reports is available online. Summary minutes of the Foundation's advisory groups may be obtained from the contacts listed in the notice of meetings published in the "Federal Register" or under "News and Media" on the Foundation's Web site. General information about the Foundation's advisory groups may be obtained from the Division of Human Resource Management, Room 315, Arlington, VA 22230. Phone, 703–292–8180. Internet, http://www.nsf.gov/nsb/meetings/.

Contracts The Foundation publicizes contracting and subcontracting opportunities in the "Commerce Business Daily" and other appropriate publications. Organizations seeking to undertake contract work for the Foundation should contact either the Division of Contracts, Policy, and Oversight (phone, 703–292–8240) or the Division of Administrative Services (phone, 703–292–8190), National Science Foundation, Arlington, VA

22230. Internet, http://www.nsf.gov/bfa/dcca/index.jsp.

Employment Inquiries may be directed to the Division of Human Resource Management, National Science Foundation, Room 315, Arlington, VA 22230. Phone, 703–292–8180. TDD, 703–292–8044. Internet, http://www.nsf.gov/careers/.

Fellowships Consult the NSF "Guide to Programs" and appropriate announcements and brochures for postdoctoral fellowship opportunities that may be available through some Foundation divisions. Beginning graduate and minority graduate students wanting to apply for fellowships should contact the Directorate for Education and Human Resources. Phone, 703–292–8601. Internet, http://www.nsf.gov/funding/pgm_summ.jsp?pims_id=6201.

Freedom of Information Act Requests Requests for agency records should be submitted in accordance with the Foundation's FOIA regulation at 45 CFR 612. Such requests should be clearly identified with "FOIA REQUEST" and be addressed to the FOIA Officer, Office of General Counsel, National Science Foundation, Room 1265, Arlington, VA 22230. Phone, 703–292–8060. Fax, 703–292–9041. Email, foia@nsf.gov. Internet, http://www.nsf.gov/policies/foia.jsp.

Grants Individuals or organizations planning to submit grant proposals should refer to the NSF "Guide to Programs," "Grant Proposal Guide" (NSF–01–2), and appropriate program brochures and announcements that may be obtained as indicated in the Publications section. Internet, http://www.nsf.gov/publications/pub_summ.jsp?ods_key=gpg.

Office of Inspector General For more information, contact the Office of Inspector General, National Science Foundation, Room 1135, Arlington, VA 22230. Phone, 703–292–7100. Internet, http://www.nsf.gov/oig/index.jsp.

Privacy Act Requests Requests for personal records should be submitted in accordance with the Foundation's Privacy Act regulation at 45 CFR 613. Such requests should be clearly identified with "PRIVACY ACT REQUEST" and be addressed to the Privacy Act Officer, National Science Foundation, Room 1265, Arlington, VA 22230. Phone, 703–292–8060. Internet, http://www.nsf.gov/policies/foia.jsp.

Publications The National Science Board assesses the status and health of science and its various disciplines, including such matters as human and material resources, in reports submitted to the President for submission to the Congress. The National Science Foundation issues publications that announce and describe new programs, critical dates, and application procedures for competitions. Single copies of these publications can be ordered by writing to NSF Clearinghouse, P.O. Box 218, Jessup, MD 20794–0218. Phone, 301–947–2722. Email, pubinfo@nsf.gov. Internet, http://www.nsf.gov/publications/.

Reading Room A collection of Foundation policy documents and staff instructions, as well as current indexes, are available to the public for inspection and copying during regular business hours, 8:30 a.m. to 5 p.m., weekdays, in the National Science Foundation Library, Room 225, Arlington, VA 22230. Phone, 703–292–7830.

Small Business Activities The Office of Small Business Research and Development provides information on opportunities for Foundation support to small businesses with strong research capabilities in science and technology. Phone, 703–292–8330. The Office of Small and Disadvantaged Business Utilization oversees agency compliance with the provisions of the Small Business Act and the Small Business Investment Act of 1958, as amended (15 U.S.C. 631, 661, 683). Phone, 703–292–8330. Internet, http://www.nsf.gov/div/index.jsp?org=IIP.

For further information, contact the National Science Foundation Information Center, 4201 Wilson Boulevard, Arlington, VA 22230. Phone, 703–292–5111. TDD, 800–281–8749. Email, info@nsf.gov. Internet, http://www.nsf.gov.

NATIONAL TRANSPORTATION SAFETY BOARD

490 L'Enfant Plaza East, SW., Washington, DC 20594
Phone, 202–314–6000. Fax, 202–314–6110. Internet, http://www.ntsb.gov.

Chairman	DEBORAH A.P. HERSMAN
Vice Chairman	CHRISTOPHER A. HART
Members	MARK R. ROSEKIND, ROBERT L. SUMWALT, EARL R. WEENER
Chief Financial Officer	EDWARD BENTHALL, *Acting*
General Counsel	DAVID K. TOCHEN
Chief Administrative Law Judge	ALFONSO MONTANO
Chief Information Officer	ROBERT P. SCHERER
Managing Director	DAVID L. MAYER
Director, Office of Communications	THOMAS E. ZOELLER
Director, Office of Equal Employment Opportunity, Diversity, and Inclusion	FARA D. GUEST
Director, Office of Administration	LOLA A. WARD
Director, Office of Aviation Safety	JOHN DELISI
Director, Office of Highway Safety	DONALD F. KAROL
Director, Office of Marine Safety	TRACY MURRELL
Director, Office of Railroad, Pipeline, and Hazardous Materials Investigations	ROBERT HALL
Director, Office of Research and Engineering	JOSEPH M. KOLLY

[For the National Transportation Safety Board statement of organization, see the Code of Federal Regulations, Title 49, Part 800]

The National Transportation Safety Board investigates accidents, conducts studies, and makes recommendations to Government agencies, the transportation industry, and others on safety measures and practices.

The National Transportation Safety Board (NTSB) was established in 1967. On April 1, 1975, the Independent Safety Board Act of 1974 (49 U.S.C. 1111) reestablished the NTSB an independent agency outside the Department of Transportation.

NTSB consists of five Members appointed for 5-year terms by the President with the advice and consent of the Senate. The President designates two of these Members as Chairman and Vice Chairman of the Board for 2-year terms. The designation of the Chairman is made with the advice and consent of the Senate.

Activities

Accident Investigation   NTSB is responsible for investigating, determining probable cause, making safety recommendations, and reporting the facts and circumstances of incidents in the following areas: U.S. civil aviation and certain public-use aircraft accidents; railroad accidents in which there is a fatality, substantial property damage, or that involve a passenger train; pipeline accidents in which there is a fatality, substantial property damage, or significant injury to the environment; highway accidents, including railroad grade-crossing accidents, that the Board selects in cooperation with the States; major marine casualties and marine accidents involving a public vessel and a nonpublic vessel, in accordance with regulations prescribed jointly by the Board and the U.S. Coast Guard; certain accidents involving hazardous materials; and other transportation accidents that are catastrophic, involve problems of a recurring character, or otherwise should be investigated in the judgment of the Board.

Safety Problem Identification   NTSB makes recommendations on matters pertaining to transportation safety and

NATIONAL TRANSPORTATION SAFETY BOARD

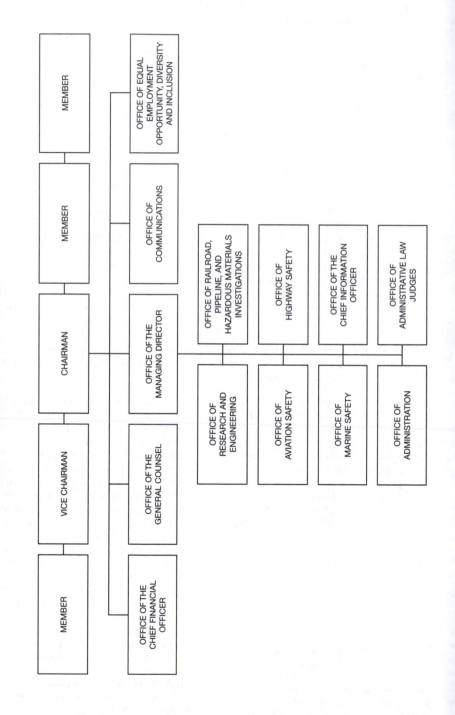

is a catalyst for transportation accident prevention by conducting safety studies and special investigations; assessing techniques of accident investigation and publishing recommended procedures; establishing regulatory requirements for reporting accidents; evaluating the transportation safety consciousness and efficacy of other Government agencies in the prevention of accidents; evaluating the adequacy of safeguards and procedures concerning the transportation of hazardous materials and the performance of other Government agencies charged with ensuring the safe transportation of such materials; and reporting annually to the Congress on its activities.

Family Assistance for Aviation Disasters NTSB coordinates the resources of the Federal Government and other organizations to support the efforts of local and State governments and airlines to meet the needs of aviation disaster victims and their families. It assists in making Federal resources available to local authorities and airlines.

Certificate, Civil Penalty, and License Appeal On appeal, NTSB reviews the suspension, amendment, modification, revocation, or denial of certain certificates, licenses, and assessments of civil penalties issued by the Secretary of Transportation. NTSB also reviews on appeal from the orders of any administrative law judge decisions of the Commandant of the Coast Guard that revoke, suspend, or deny certain licenses, certificates, documents, and registers.

For contact information on NTSB aviation, highway, and railroad safety regional offices, use the link below.

Internet, http://www.ntsb.gov/about/contact.html.

Sources of Information

Contracts and Procurement Inquiries regarding NTSB's procurement and contracting activities should be addressed to the Contracting Officer, National Transportation Safety Board, Washington, DC 20594. Phone, 202–314–6102.

Electronic Access Agency information, including aircraft accident data, synopses of aircraft accidents, speeches and congressional testimony given by Board Members and staff, press releases, job vacancy announcements, and notices of Board meetings, public hearings, and other agency events, is available online. Internet, http://www.ntsb.gov/.

Employment Send applications for employment to the Human Resources Division, National Transportation Safety Board, Washington, DC 20594. Phone, 202–314–6230. Internet, http://www. ntsb.gov/about/employment.html.

Publications Publications are provided free of charge to the following categories of subscribers: Federal, State, or local transportation agencies; international transportation organizations or foreign governments; educational institutions or public libraries; nonprofit public safety organizations; and the news media. Persons in these categories who are interested in receiving copies of Board publications should contact the Records Management Division, National Transportation Safety Board, Washington, DC 20594. Phone, 202– 314–6551. All other persons interested in receiving publications must purchase them from the National Technical Information Service, 5285 Port Royal Road, Springfield, VA 22161. Orders may be placed by telephone to the Subscription Unit at 703–487–4630 or to the sales desk at 703–487–4768. See also "Publications" online at the bottom of NTSB's home page. Internet, http://www. ntsb.gov/index.html.

Reading Room The Board's Public Reference Room is available for record inspection or photocopying. It is located on the 6th Floor at the Board's Washington, DC, headquarters and is open from 8:45 a.m. to 4:45 p.m., weekdays. Requests for access to public records should be made in person at the guards desk or by calling 202–314–6551 or 1–800–877–6799.

For further information, contact the Office of Public Affairs, National Transportation Safety Board, 490 L'Enfant Plaza East, SW., Washington, DC 20594. Phone, 202–314–6100. Fax, 202–314–6110. Internet, http://www.ntsb.gov.

NUCLEAR REGULATORY COMMISSION

Washington, DC 20555
Phone, 301–415–7000. Internet, http://www.nrc.gov. Email, opa.resource@nrc.gov.

Chairman	ALLISON M. MACFARLANE
Commissioners	STEPHEN G. BURNS, JEFFREY MARTIN BARAN, WILLIAM C. OSTENDORFF, KRISTINE L. SVINICKI
Executive Director, Advisory Committee on Reactor Safeguards	EDWIN M. HACKETT
Chief Administrative Judge, Atomic Safety and Licensing Board Panel	E. ROY HAWKENS
Director, Office of Commission Appellate Adjudication	BROOKE D. POOLE
Director, Office of Congressional Affairs	V. RENEE SIMPSON
Director, Office of Public Affairs	ELIOT B. BRENNER
Inspector General	HUBERT T. BELL, JR.
Chief Financial Officer	JAMES E. DYER
General Counsel	MARGARET M. DOANE
Director, Office of International Programs	NADER L. MAMISH
Secretary of the Commission	ANNETTE L. VIETTI-COOK
Executive Director for Operations	MARK A. SATORIUS
Deputy Executive Director for Reactor and Preparedness Programs	MICHAEL R. JOHNSON
Deputy Executive Director for Materials, Waste, Research, State, Tribal and Compliance Programs	MICHAEL F. WEBER
Deputy Executive Director for Corporate Management	DARREN B. ASH

[For the Nuclear Regulatory Commission statement of organization, see the Code of Federal Regulations, Title 10, Part I]

The Nuclear Regulatory Commission licenses and regulates civilian use of nuclear energy to protect public health and safety and the environment.

The Nuclear Regulatory Commission (NRC) was established as an independent regulatory agency under the provisions of the Energy Reorganization Act of 1974 (42 U.S.C. 5801 et seq.) and Executive Order 11834 of January 15, 1975. All licensing and related regulatory functions formerly assigned to the Atomic Energy Commission were transferred to the Nuclear Regulatory Commission.

The Commission's major program components are the Office of Nuclear Reactor Regulation, the Office of New Reactors, the Office of Nuclear Material Safety and Safeguards, the Office of Federal and State Materials and Environmental Management Programs, and the Office of Nuclear Regulatory Research. Its headquarters are located in Rockville, Maryland, and there are four regional offices.

The Commission ensures that nuclear materials and facilities for civilian use are managed in a manner consistent with public health and safety, environmental quality, national security, and antitrust laws. Most of the Commission's effort is focused on regulating the use of nuclear energy to generate electric power.

Activities

NRC is primarily responsible for the following functions: licensing the construction, operation, and closure of nuclear reactors and other nuclear facilities, such as nuclear fuel cycle facilities, low-level radioactive waste disposal sites under NRC jurisdiction,

NUCLEAR REGULATORY COMMISSION

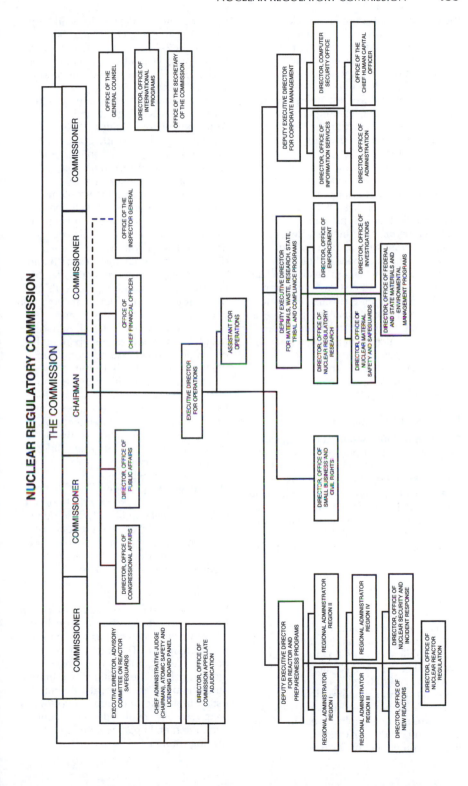

THE COMMISSION

COMMISSIONER · COMMISSIONER · CHAIRMAN · COMMISSIONER · COMMISSIONER

OFFICE OF THE GENERAL COUNSEL

DIRECTOR, OFFICE OF INTERNATIONAL PROGRAMS

OFFICE OF THE SECRETARY OF THE COMMISSION

OFFICE OF THE INSPECTOR GENERAL

OFFICE OF CHIEF FINANCIAL OFFICER

DIRECTOR, OFFICE OF PUBLIC AFFAIRS

DIRECTOR, OFFICE OF CONGRESSIONAL AFFAIRS

EXECUTIVE DIRECTOR, ADVISORY COMMITTEE ON REACTOR SAFEGUARDS

CHIEF ADMINISTRATIVE JUDGE (CHAIRMAN), ATOMIC SAFETY AND LICENSING BOARD PANEL

DIRECTOR, OFFICE OF COMMISSION APPELLATE ADJUDICATION

EXECUTIVE DIRECTOR FOR OPERATIONS

ASSISTANT FOR OPERATIONS

DEPUTY EXECUTIVE DIRECTOR FOR CORPORATE MANAGEMENT

DIRECTOR, COMPUTER SECURITY OFFICE

OFFICE OF THE CHIEF HUMAN CAPITAL OFFICER

DIRECTOR, OFFICE OF INFORMATION SERVICES

DIRECTOR, OFFICE OF ADMINISTRATION

DEPUTY EXECUTIVE DIRECTOR FOR MATERIALS, WASTE, RESEARCH, STATE, TRIBAL AND COMPLIANCE PROGRAMS

DIRECTOR, OFFICE OF NUCLEAR REGULATORY RESEARCH

DIRECTOR, OFFICE OF NUCLEAR MATERIAL SAFETY AND SAFEGUARDS

DIRECTOR, OFFICE OF ENFORCEMENT

DIRECTOR, OFFICE OF INVESTIGATIONS

DIRECTOR, OFFICE OF FEDERAL AND STATE MATERIALS AND ENVIRONMENTAL MANAGEMENT PROGRAMS

DIRECTOR, OFFICE OF SMALL BUSINESS AND CIVIL RIGHTS

DEPUTY EXECUTIVE DIRECTOR FOR REACTOR AND PREPAREDNESS PROGRAMS

REGIONAL ADMINISTRATOR REGION I

REGIONAL ADMINISTRATOR REGION II

REGIONAL ADMINISTRATOR REGION III

REGIONAL ADMINISTRATOR REGION IV

DIRECTOR, OFFICE OF NEW REACTORS

DIRECTOR, OFFICE OF NUCLEAR SECURITY AND INCIDENT RESPONSE

DIRECTOR, OFFICE OF NUCLEAR REACTOR REGULATION

the geologic repository for high-level radioactive waste, and nonpower test and research reactors; licensing the possession, use, processing, handling, and export of nuclear material; licensing the operators of nuclear power and nonpower test and research reactors; inspecting licensed facilities and activities; conducting the U.S. Government research program on light-water reactor safety; developing and implementing rules and regulations that govern licensed nuclear activities; investigating nuclear incidents and allegations concerning any matter regulated by the Commission; maintaining the NRC Incident Response Program; collecting, analyzing, and disseminating information about the operational safety of commercial nuclear power reactors and certain nonreactor activities; developing effective working relationships with the States regarding reactor operations and the regulation of nuclear material; and assuring that adequate regulatory programs are maintained by those States that exercise regulatory control over certain nuclear materials in the State.

Sources of Information

Freedom of Information Act Requests Requests for copies of records should be directed to the FOIA or Privacy Act Officer, Mail Stop T–5 F09, Nuclear Regulatory Commission, Washington, DC 20555–0001. Phone, 301–415–7169. Fax, 301–415–5130. Requests may also be made by using the link below and completing the "FOIA Request Submittal Form." Internet, http://www.nrc.gov/reading-rm/foia/foia-submittal-form.html.

Publications NRC publishes scientific, technical, and administrative information on licensing and regulation of civilian nuclear facilities and materials, as well as periodic and annual reports. Some publications and documents are available on NRC's Web site. The U.S. Government Printing Office and the National Technical Information Service sell single copies of, or subscriptions to, the Commission's publications. To obtain prices and order publications, contact the Superintendent of Documents,

Government Printing Office, Mail Stop SSOP, Washington, DC 20402–0001 (phone, 202–512–1800; Internet, http://www.gpo.gov/about/bookstore.htm) or NTIS, 5301 Shawnee Road, Alexandria, VA 22312 (phone, 703–605–6050; Internet, www.ntis.gov). Internet, http://www.nrc.gov/reading-rm.html.

Active Regulatory Guides NRC regulatory guides provide guidance to licensees and applicants on implementing specific parts of the Commission's regulations, techniques used by its staff in evaluating specific problems or postulated accidents, and data needed by the staff in its review of applications for permits or licenses. Regulatory guides are issued in the following 10 broad divisions: power reactors, research and test reactors, fuels and materials facilities, environmental and siting, materials and plant protection, products, transportation, occupational health, antitrust and financial review, and general. Active Regulatory Guides may be obtained free of charge by downloading them from the Nuclear Regulatory Commission's online library. In addition, those who are interested may examine and copy, for a fee, publicly accessible documents at the Commission's Public Document Room, O1–F21, One White Flint North, 11555 Rockville Pike, Rockville, MD 20852. Internet, http://www.nrc.gov/reading-rm/doc-collections/reg-guides/.

Draft Regulatory Guides NRC issues regulatory guides in draft form to solicit public comment and involve the public in developing the agency's regulatory positions. Some draft guides are proposed revisions of existing guides. Draft regulatory guides have not received complete staff review and, therefore, they do not represent official Nuclear Regulatory Commission staff positions. In finalizing the guides, the staff considers all comments received during the public comment period. These drafts may be downloaded from the online library using the link below. The public may comment on draft guides and other documents issued in draft form online at http://www.nrc.gov/public-involve/doc-comment.html. Internet, http://www.nrc.gov/reading-rm.html.

Reading Rooms   The Public Document Room in Rockville, Maryland, maintains an extensive collection of documents related to Nuclear Regulatory Commission licensing proceedings and other significant actions. Documents issued prior to October 1999 are available in paper or microfiche. Documents issued after October 1999 are available from the Commission's full-text document management system, which can be accessed using the link below. The headquarters' Public Document Room is located on the first floor at One White Flint North, 11555 Rockville Pike, Rockville, MD, and is open weekdays, from 7:45 a.m. to 4:15 p.m., except on Federal holidays. Internet, http://www. nrc.gov/reading-rm/adams.html. **Documents**   Documents from the collection may be reproduced, with some exceptions, on paper, microfiche, or CD–ROM for a nominal fee. For additional information regarding the Public Document Room, contact the Nuclear Regulatory Commission, Public Document Room, Washington, DC 20555–0001. Phone, 301–415–4737 or 800–397–4209. Fax, 301–415–3548. Email, pdr.resource@nrc.gov. Internet, http://www.nrc.gov/reading-rm/pdr.html. **Microfiche Collections**   Selected regional libraries of the Government Printing Office Federal Depository Library Program maintain permanent microfiche collections of Nuclear Regulatory Commission documents released between January 1981 and October 1999. Contact the Public Document Room at 301–415–4737 or 800–397–4209.

For further information, contact the Office of Public Affairs, Nuclear Regulatory Commission, Washington, DC 20555–0001. Phone, 301–415–8200. Email, opa.resource@nrc.gov. Internet, http://www.nrc.gov.

OCCUPATIONAL SAFETY AND HEALTH REVIEW COMMISSION

1120 Twentieth Street NW., Washington, DC 20036–3457
Phone, 202–606–5380. Fax, 202–418–3017. Internet, http://www.oshrc.gov.

Chairman	THOMASINA V. ROGERS
Commissioners	CYNTHIA L. ATTWOOD, HEATHER L. MACDOUGALL
General Counsel	NADINE N. MANCINI
Chief Administrative Law Judge	COVETTE ROONEY
Executive Director	DEBRA A. HALL
Executive Secretary	JOHN X. CERVENY, *Acting*

The Occupational Safety and Health Review Commission ensures the timely and fair resolution of cases involving the alleged exposure of American workers to unsafe or unhealthy working conditions.

The Occupational Safety and Health Review Commission is an independent, quasi-judicial agency established by the Occupational Safety and Health Act of 1970 (29 U.S.C. 651–678).

The Commission rules on cases when disagreements arise over the results of safety and health inspections performed by the Department of Labor's Occupational Safety and Health Administration (OSHA). Employers have the right to dispute alleged job safety or health violations that OSHA inspectors find, the penalties that OSHA proposes, and the time given to correct a hazardous situation.

The Occupational Safety and Health Act covers virtually every employer in the country. Its purpose is to reduce personal injuries, illness, and deaths of working men and women in the United States that result from their employment.

OCCUPATIONAL SAFETY AND HEALTH REVIEW COMMISSION

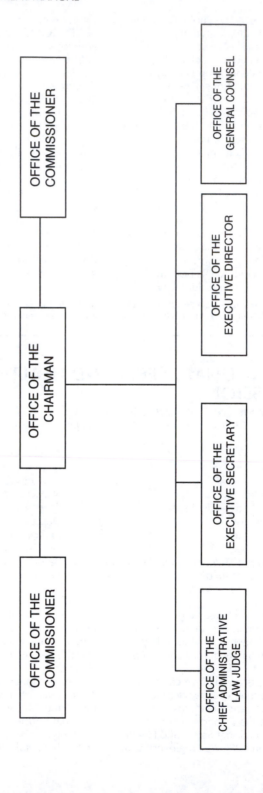

It requires employers to provide a work environment free from recognized hazards that cause or are likely to cause death or serious physical harm to their employees. It also requires employers to comply with occupational safety and health standards promulgated under the act.

Activities

The Commission was created to adjudicate enforcement actions initiated under the act when they are contested by employers, employees, or representatives of employees. A case arises when a citation, issued to an employer as the result of an OSHA inspection, is contested within 15 working days of receipt of the report.

There are two levels of adjudication within the Commission. All cases are first assigned to an administrative law judge. A hearing is generally held in the community or as close as possible to where the alleged violation occurred. After the hearing, the judge issues a decision, based on findings of fact and conclusions of law.

A substantial number of the judge's decisions become final orders of the Commission. Commission members, however, will issue the final order if a party petitions the Commission members for review of the judge's decision and the petition is granted.

After a final order is issued, any party to the case may seek a review of the decision in the United States courts of appeals.

The Commission's principal office is in Washington, DC. Administrative law judges are also located in Atlanta and Denver regional offices.

Sources of Information

Publications   The Commission's publications are available online. Copies of its publications and decisions are also available from the Office of the Executive Secretary. Phone, 202–606–5400. Fax, 202–606–5050. Internet, http://www.oshrc.gov/publications/index.html.

For further information, contact the Office of the Executive Director, Occupational Safety and Health Review Commission, 1120 Twentieth Street NW., Washington, DC 20036–3457. Phone, 202–606–5380. Fax, 202–418–3017. Internet, http://www.oshrc.gov.

OFFICE OF THE DIRECTOR OF NATIONAL INTELLIGENCE

Washington, DC 20511
Phone, 703–733–8600. Internet, http://www.dni.gov.

Director	JAMES R. CLAPPER
Principal Deputy Director	STEPHANIE O'SULLIVAN
Deputy Director for Intelligence Integration	ROBERT CARDILLO
Director, National Counterterrorism Center	MATTHEW OLSEN
Director, National Counterproliferation Center	MAJA LEHNUS
National Counterintelligence Executive	FRANK MONTOYA
Assistant Director for Policy and Strategy	CORIN STONE
Assistant Deputy Director for Acquisition, Technology and Facilities	KEVIN MEINERS
Associate Director for Systems and Resource Analyses	TROY MEINK
Chief Information Officer	AL TARASIUK
Chief Financial Officer	RICHARD FRAVEL
Chief Human Capital Officer	DEBORAH KIRCHER
Program Manager, Information Sharing Environment	KSHEMENDRA PAUL

General Counsel	ROBERT S. LITT
Director, Public Affairs	SHAWN S. TURNER
Civil Liberties Protection Officer	ALEXANDER W. JOEL
Inspector General	CHARLES MCCULLOUGH, III
Chief, Equal Employment Opportunity and Diversity	RITA SAMPSON

The Office of the Director of National Intelligence oversees and coordinates the foreign and domestic activities of the Intelligence Community across the Federal Government.

The Office of the Director of National Intelligence (ODNI) was established by the Intelligence Reform and Terrorism Prevention Act of 2004 (50 U.S.C. 403). The Office began operation on April 21, 2005.

The Office is headed by the Director of National Intelligence, who is appointed by the President with the advice and consent of the Senate. The Director reports directly to the President and is the principal intelligence adviser.

ODNI ensures that the President, the heads of departments and agencies of the executive branch, the Chairman of the Joint Chiefs of Staff and senior military commanders, and the Congress receive timely and objective national intelligence. It also establishes objectives and priorities for collection, analysis, production, and dissemination of national intelligence; ensures the availability of and access to intelligence information within the Intelligence Community; develops the annual budget for the National Intelligence Program; oversees coordination of relationships with the intelligence or security services of foreign governments and international organizations; ensures that accurate analysis of intelligence information is derived from all sources to support national security needs; develops personnel policies and programs to enhance the capacity for joint operations and to facilitate staffing of community management functions; and jointly oversees the development and implementation of an acquisition program management plan with the Secretary of Defense.

For further information, contact the Office of the Director of National Intelligence, Washington, DC 20511. Phone, 703–733–8600. Internet, http://www.dni.gov.

OFFICE OF GOVERNMENT ETHICS

1201 New York Avenue NW., Suite 500, Washington, DC 20005–3917
Phone, 202–482–9300. TTY, 800–877–8339. Fax, 202–482–9237. Internet, http://www.oge.gov.

Director	WALTER M. SHAUB, JR.
General Counsel	DAVID J. APOL
Program Counsel	SHELLEY K. FINLAYSON
Deputy Director for Compliance	JOSEPH E. GANGLOFF
Assistant Director for Compliance	BARBARA A. MULLEN-ROTH

[For the Office of Government Ethics statement of organization, see the Code of Federal Regulations, Title 5, Part 2600]

The Office of Government Ethics directs executive branch policies related to preventing conflicts of interest on the part of Government employees and resolving those conflicts of interest that do occur.

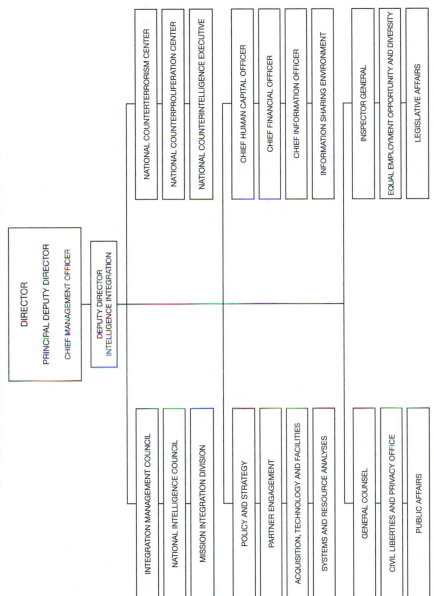

OFFICE OF THE DIRECTOR OF NATIONAL INTELLIGENCE

DIRECTOR
PRINCIPAL DEPUTY DIRECTOR
CHIEF MANAGEMENT OFFICER

DEPUTY DIRECTOR
INTELLIGENCE INTEGRATION

NATIONAL COUNTERTERRORISM CENTER
NATIONAL COUNTERPROLIFERATION CENTER
NATIONAL COUNTERINTELLIGENCE EXECUTIVE

CHIEF HUMAN CAPITAL OFFICER
CHIEF FINANCIAL OFFICER
CHIEF INFORMATION OFFICER
INFORMATION SHARING ENVIRONMENT

INSPECTOR GENERAL
EQUAL EMPLOYMENT OPPORTUNITY AND DIVERSITY
LEGISLATIVE AFFAIRS

INTEGRATION MANAGEMENT COUNCIL
NATIONAL INTELLIGENCE COUNCIL
MISSION INTEGRATION DIVISION

POLICY AND STRATEGY
PARTNER ENGAGEMENT
ACQUISITION, TECHNOLOGY AND FACILITIES
SYSTEMS AND RESOURCE ANALYSES

GENERAL COUNSEL
CIVIL LIBERTIES AND PRIVACY OFFICE
PUBLIC AFFAIRS

442   U.S. GOVERNMENT MANUAL

The Office of Government Ethics (OGE) is an executive branch agency established under the Ethics in Government Act of 1978, as amended (5 U.S.C. app. 401).

The Director of OGE is appointed by the President with the advice and consent of the Senate for a 5-year term.

Activities

The Office of Government Ethics develops appropriate ethics policies for the executive branch through the promulgation of regulations on standards of ethical conduct, public and confidential financial disclosure of executive branch officials, and ethics training programs. By reviewing the financial disclosure reports submitted by nominees for, incumbents of, and those leaving executive branch positions requiring Presidential appointment with Senate confirmation, OGE also identifies and resolves actual and potential conflicts of interest. These financial disclosure reports are available for public inspection.

The Office also provides education and training to 6,000 ethics officials through instructor-led and Web-based training programs; assesses the effectiveness of public and confidential financial disclosure systems maintained by executive branch agencies; maintains an extensive program to provide advice on standards of ethical conduct and conflict of interest laws; conducts onsite reviews of agency ethics programs; orders corrective action on the part of agencies and employees; evaluates the effectiveness of the Ethics in Government Act, the conflict of interest laws, and other related statutes and recommends appropriate changes; and provides technical assistance in support of U.S. international anticorruption and good governance initiatives.

Sources of Information

Electronic Access Information on OGE's services and programs is available online.
Publications The Office of Government Ethics periodically updates its publication "The Informal Advisory Letters and Memoranda and Formal Opinions of the United States Office of Government Ethics," which is available from the Government Printing Office. In addition, OGE has ethics publications and instructional resources available. Upon request, OGE also provides copies of executive branch public financial disclosure reports in accordance with the Ethics in Government Act and OGE's regulations.

For further information, contact the Office of Government Ethics, Suite 500, 1201 New York Avenue NW., Washington, DC 20005–3917. Phone, 202–482–9300. TTY, 800–877–8339. Fax, 202–482–9237. Email, contactoge@oge.gov. Internet, http://www.oge.gov.

OFFICE OF PERSONNEL MANAGEMENT

1900 E Street NW., Washington, DC 20415–0001
Phone, 202–606–1800. TTY, 202–606–2532. Internet, http://www.opm.gov.

Director	KATHERINE ARCHULETA
Chief of Staff and Director of External Affairs	ANN MARIE HABERSHAW
Inspector General	PATRICK E. MCFARLAND
General Counsel	KAMALA VASAGAM
Chief Financial Officer	DENNIS D. COLEMAN
Associate Director, Employee Services and Chief Human Capital Officer	MARK REINHOLD, *Acting*
Associate Director, Merit System Accountability and Compliance	MARK W. LAMBERT
Associate Director, Retirement Services	KENNETH ZAWONDY, JR.
Associate Director, Federal Investigative Services	MERTON MILLER

Associate Director, Human Resources Solutions	JOSEPH KENNEDY
Director, Combined Federal Campaign	KEITH WILLINGHAM
Director, Congressional and Legislative Affairs	ANGELA KOUTERS
Director, Communications	JACKIE KOSZCZUK
Director, Planning and Policy Analysis	JONATHAN FOLEY
Director, Executive Secretariat	JOZETTA ROBINSON
Director, Facilities, Security, and Contracting	WILLIAM N. PATTERSON
Director, Federal Executive Institute	SUZANNE LOGAN
Director, Equal Employment Opportunity	LASHONN WOODLAND, *Acting*
Director, Internal Oversight and Compliance	JANET BARNES
Chief Information Officer	DONNA SEYMOUR
Executive Director, Chief Human Capital Officers Council	JUSTIN R. JOHNSON
Director, Diversity and Inclusion	VERONICA E. VILLALOBOS
Chair, Federal Prevailing Rate Advisory Committee	SHELDON I. FRIEDMAN
Actuary	STEVEN M. NIU
Director, Healthcare and Insurance	JOHN O'BRIEN
Chief Operating Officer	ANGELA BAILEY

[For the Office of Personnel Management statement of organization, see the Federal Register of Jan. 5, 1979, 44 FR 1501]

The Office of Personnel Management administers a merit system to ensure compliance with personnel laws and regulations and assists agencies in recruiting, examining, and promoting people on the basis of their knowledge and skills, regardless of their race, religion, sex, political influence, or other nonmerit factors.

The Office of Personnel Management (OPM) was created as an independent establishment by Reorganization Plan No. 2 of 1978 (5 U.S.C. app.), pursuant to Executive Order 12107 of December 28, 1978. Many of the functions of the former United States Civil Service Commission were transferred to OPM.

Activities

Employee Benefits   OPM manages numerous activities that directly affect the well-being of the Federal employee and indirectly enhance employee effectiveness. These include health benefits, life insurance, and retirement benefits.

Examining and Staffing   The Office of Personnel Management is responsible for providing departments and agencies with technical assistance and guidance in examining competitive positions in the Federal civil service for General Schedule grades 1 through 15 and Federal Wage system positions. In addition, OPM is responsible for the following duties: providing testing and examination

services, at the request of an agency, on a reimbursable basis; establishing basic qualification standards for all occupations; certifying agency delegated examining units to conduct examining; providing employment information for competitive service positions; and providing policy direction and guidance on promotions, reassignments, appointments in the excepted and competitive services, reinstatements, temporary and term employment, veterans preference, workforce planning and reshaping, organizational design, career transition, and other staffing provisions.

Executive Resources   OPM leads in the selection, management, and development of Federal executives. OPM provides policy guidance, consulting services, and technical support on Senior Executive Service (SES) recruitment, selection, succession planning, mobility performance, awards, and removals. It reviews agency nominations for SES career appointments and administers the Qualifications Review Boards that certify candidates' executive qualifications.

OFFICE OF PERSONNEL MANAGEMENT

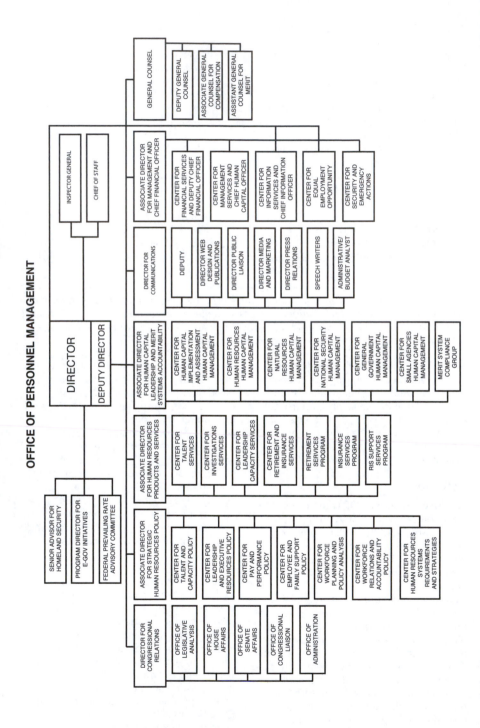

It manages SES, senior-level, and scientific and professional space allocations to agencies, administers the Presidential Rank Awards program, and conducts orientation sessions for newly appointed executives. In addition, OPM manages three interagency residential development and training centers for executives and managers.

Investigations   The Office of the Inspector General conducts comprehensive and independent audits, investigations, and evaluations relating to OPM programs and operations. It is responsible for administrative actions against health care providers who commit sanctionable offenses with respect to the Federal Employees' Health Benefits Program or other Federal programs.

For further information, contact the Office of the Inspector General. Phone, 202–606–1200.

Personnel Systems   OPM provides leadership and guidance to agencies on systems to support the manager's personnel management responsibilities. These include the following: white- and blue-collar pay systems, including SES and special occupational pay systems; geographical adjustments and locality payments; special rates to address recruitment and retention problems; allowances and differentials, including recruitment and relocation bonuses, retention allowances, and hazardous duty/environmental pay; and premium pay; annual and sick leave, court leave, military leave, leave transfer and leave bank programs, family and medical leave, excused absence, holidays, and scheduling of work, including flexible and compressed work schedules; performance management, covering appraisal systems, performance pay and awards, and incentive awards for suggestions, inventions, and special acts; classification policy and standards for agencies to determine the series and grades for Federal jobs; labor-management relations, including collective bargaining, negotiability, unfair labor practices, labor-management cooperation, and consulting with unions on Governmentwide issues; systems and techniques for resolving disputes with employees; quality of worklife initiatives, such as employee health and fitness, work and family, AIDS in the workplace, and employee assistance programs; human resources development, including leadership and administration of the Human Resources Development Council and the Government Performance and Results Act interest group; the Training and Management Assistance program, to help agencies develop training and human resources management solutions, including workforce planning and succession management strategies, e-learning applications, traditional classroom training materials, compensation and performance management systems, and other customized products; information systems to support and improve Federal personnel management decisionmaking; and Governmentwide instructions for personnel processing and recordkeeping and for release of personnel data under the Freedom of Information Act and the Privacy Act.

OPM also provides administrative support to special advisory bodies, including the Federal Prevailing Rate Advisory Committee, the Federal Salary Council, and the Presidential Advisory Committee on Expanding Training Opportunities.

Oversight   OPM assesses human capital management Governmentwide and within agencies to gather information for policy development and program refinement, ensure compliance with law and regulation, and enhance agency capability for human resources management accountability. Agency accountability systems help ensure that human capital decisions are consistent with merit principles and that human capital strategies are aligned with mission accomplishment. OPM also works with agencies to find better and more strategic ways to manage Federal human capital.

Workforce Diversity   OPM provides leadership, direction, and policy for Governmentwide affirmative recruiting programs for women, minorities, individuals with disabilities, and veterans. It also provides leadership, guidance, and technical assistance to promote merit and equality in systemic workforce recruitment, employment, training, and retention. In addition, OPM gathers, analyzes, and maintains statistical data on the diversity of the Federal workforce and prepares evaluation reports for Congress and others on individual agency and Governmentwide progress toward full workforce representation for all Americans in the Federal sector.

Other Personnel Programs OPM coordinates the temporary assignment of employees between Federal agencies and State, local, and Indian tribal governments, institutions of higher education, and other eligible nonprofit organizations for up to 2 years, for work of mutual benefit to the participating organizations. It administers the Presidential Management Intern Program, which provides 2-year, excepted appointments with Federal agencies to recipients of graduate degrees in appropriate disciplines. In addition, the Office of Personnel Management administers the Federal Merit System Standards, which apply to certain grant-aided State and local programs.

Federal Executive Boards Federal Executive Boards (FEBs) were established by Presidential memorandum on November 10, 1961, to improve internal Federal management practices and to provide a central focus for Federal participation in civic affairs in major metropolitan centers of Federal activity. They carry out their functions under OPM supervision and control.

FEBs serve as a means for disseminating information within the Federal Government and for promoting discussion of Federal policies and activities of importance to all Federal executives in the field. Each Board is composed of heads of Federal field offices in the metropolitan area. A chairman is elected annually from among the membership to provide overall leadership to the Board's operations. Committees and task forces carry out interagency projects consistent with the Board's mission.

Federal Executive Boards are located in 28 metropolitan areas that are important centers of Federal activity. These areas are as follows: Albuquerque-Santa Fe, NM; Atlanta, GA; Baltimore, MD; Boston, MA; Buffalo, NY; Chicago, IL; Cincinnati, OH; Cleveland, OH; Dallas-Fort Worth, TX; Denver, CO; Detroit, MI; Honolulu, HI; Houston, TX; Kansas City, MO; Los Angeles, CA; Miami, FL; Minneapolis-St. Paul, MN; New Orleans, LA; New York, NY; Newark, NJ; Oklahoma City, OK; Philadelphia, PA; Pittsburgh, PA; Portland, OR; St. Louis, MO; San Antonio, TX; San Francisco, CA; and Seattle, WA.

Federal Executive Associations or Councils have been locally organized in approximately 65 other metropolitan areas to perform functions similar to the Federal Executive Boards but on a lesser scale of organization and activity.

For further information, contact the Director for Federal Executive Board Operations, Office of Personnel Management, Room 5524, 1900 E Street NW., Washington, DC 20415–0001. Phone, 202–606–1000.

Sources of Information

Contracts For information, contact the Chief, Contracting Division, Office of Personnel Management, Washington, DC 20415–0071. Phone, 202–606–2240. Internet, http://www.opm.gov/about-us/doing-business-with-opm/contracting-opportunities/.

Employment Information on Federal employment and current job openings Governmentwide is available on OPM's home page. Select "Job Seekers" from the list to access the Federal Government's largest online jobs portal. For information on employment opportunities within OPM, contact the Director of Human Resources. Phone, 202–606–2400. Internet, http://www.opm.gov/.

Publications The Chief, Publications Services Division, can provide information on Federal personnel management publications. Phone, 202–606–1822. Internet, http://www.opm.gov/news/reports-publications/publications-database/.

For further information, contact the Office of Communications, Office of Personnel Management, 1900 E Street NW., Washington, DC 20415–0001. Phone, 202–606–1800. TTY, 202–606–2532. Internet, http://www. opm.gov.

OFFICE OF SPECIAL COUNSEL

1730 M Street NW., Suite 218, Washington, DC 20036–4505
Phone, 202–254–3600; 800–872–9855. Fax, 202–653–5151. Internet, http://www.osc.gov.

Special Counsel	Carolyn N. Lerner
Principal Deputy Special Counsel	Mark P. Cohen
Deputy Special Counsel, Policy and Congressional Affairs	Adam Miles
Deputy Special Counsel, Litigation and Legal Affairs	Eric Bachman
Senior Communications Specialist	Nicholas Schwellenbach
Associate Special Counsel, Investigation and Prosecution Division/Field	Bruce D. Fong
Associate Special Counsel, Investigation and Prosecution Division/HQ	Louis Lopez
Chief Administrative Officer	(Vacancy)
Associate Special Counsel, Special Projects	(Vacancy)
Chief, Alternative Dispute Resolution	Jane Juliano
General Counsel	Lisa V. Terry
Chief, Complaints Examining Unit	Barbara J. Wheeler
Chief, Disclosure Unit	Catherine A. McMullen
Chief, Hatch Act Unit	Ana Galindo-Marrone
Chief, Uniformed Services Employment and Reemployment Rights Act Unit	Patrick H. Boulay
Chief Financial Officer	Karl P. Kammann
Chief Human Capital Officer	James J. Wilson
Chief Information Officer	Wing W. Leung
Chief, Dallas Field Office	Anne Gullick
Chief, San Francisco Field Office	Joseph Siegelman
Chief, Detroit Field Office	Christopher Tall

The Office of Special Counsel investigates allegations of certain activities prohibited by civil service laws, rules, or regulations and litigates before the Merit Systems Protection Board.

The Office of Special Counsel (OSC) was established on January 1, 1979, by Reorganization Plan No. 2 of 1978 (5 U.S.C. app.). The Civil Service Reform Act of 1978 (5 U.S.C. 1101 note), which became effective on January 11, 1979, enlarged its functions and powers. Pursuant to provisions of the Whistleblower Protection Act of 1989 (5 U.S.C. 1211 et seq.), OSC functions as an independent investigative and prosecutorial agency within the executive branch that litigates before the Merit Systems Protection Board.

Activities

The Office of Special Counsel safeguards the merit system in Federal employment by protecting employees and applicants from prohibited personnel practices, especially reprisal for whistleblowing. The Office also operates a secure channel for Federal whistleblower disclosures of violations of laws, rules, or regulations; gross mismanagement; gross waste of funds; abuse of authority; and substantial and specific danger to public health and safety. In addition, OSC issues advice on

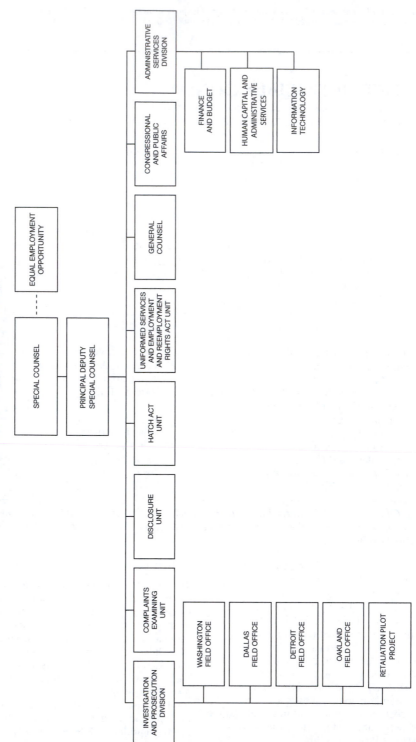

OFFICE OF SPECIAL COUNSEL

SPECIAL COUNSEL

EQUAL EMPLOYMENT OPPORTUNITY

PRINCIPAL DEPUTY SPECIAL COUNSEL

INVESTIGATION AND PROSECUTION DIVISION

COMPLAINTS EXAMINING UNIT

DISCLOSURE UNIT

HATCH ACT UNIT

UNIFORMED SERVICES AND EMPLOYMENT AND REEMPLOYMENT RIGHTS ACT UNIT

GENERAL COUNSEL

CONGRESSIONAL AND PUBLIC AFFAIRS

ADMINISTRATIVE SERVICES DIVISION

FINANCE AND BUDGET

HUMAN CAPITAL AND ADMINISTRATIVE SERVICES

INFORMATION TECHNOLOGY

WASHINGTON FIELD OFFICE

DALLAS FIELD OFFICE

DETROIT FIELD OFFICE

OAKLAND FIELD OFFICE

RETALIATION PILOT PROJECT

the Hatch Act and enforces its restrictions on political activity by Government employees. Finally, OSC protects the civilian employment and reemployment rights of military servicemembers under the Uniformed Services Employment and Reemployment Act. OSC enhances Government accountability and performance by the realization of a diverse, inclusive Federal workplace where employees embrace excellence in service, uphold merit system principles, are encouraged to disclose wrongdoing, and are protected against reprisals and other unlawful employment practices.

Sources of Information

A complete listing of OSC contacts, including field offices, media inquiries, and the whistleblower disclosure hotline, is available online. Internet, http://www. osc.gov/contacts.htm.

For further information, contact the Office of Special Counsel, 1730 M Street NW., Suite 218, Washington, DC 20036–4505. Phone, 202–254–3600 or 800–872–9855. Fax, 202–254–3711. Internet, http://www.osc. gov.

OVERSEAS PRIVATE INVESTMENT CORPORATION

1100 New York Avenue NW., Washington, DC 20527
Phone, 202–336–8400. Fax, 202–336–7949. Internet, http://www.opic.gov.

President and Chief Executive Officer	ELIZABETH L. LITTLEFIELD
Executive Vice President	MIMI ALEMAYEHOU
Chief of Staff	JOHN E. MORTON
Deputy Chief of Staff	PAULA TUFRO
Senior Advisor to the President and Chief Executive Officer for Policy and Operations	PAVNEET SINGH
Chief Financial Officer	ALLAN VILLABROZA
Vice President and General Counsel	KIMBERLY HEIMERT
Vice President, Investment Policy	MARGARET L. KUHLOW
Vice President, Office of Administrative Services and Chief Information Officer	DENNIS LAUER
Vice President, Insurance	JOHN F. MORAN
Vice President, Human Resources	RITA MOSS
Vice President, Small and Medium Enterprise Finance	JAMES C. POLAN
Vice President, External Affairs	JUDITH PRYOR
Vice President, Structured Finance	MICHAEL WHALEN
Head of Investment Funds and Chief Investment Strategist	WILLIAM R. PEARCE

[For the Overseas Private Investment Corporation statement of organization, see the Code of Federal Regulations, Title 22, Chapter VII]

The Overseas Private Investment Corporation promotes economic growth and job opportunities both at home and abroad by encouraging U.S. private investment in developing countries and emerging markets.

The Overseas Private Investment Corporation (OPIC) was established in 1971 as an independent agency by the Foreign Affairs Reform and Restructuring Act (112 Stat. 2681–790). OPIC helps U.S. businesses invest overseas, fosters economic development in new and emerging markets, complements the private sector in managing risks associated with foreign direct investment, and supports U.S. foreign policy. OPIC charges market-based fees for its products, and it operates on a self-sustaining basis at no net cost to taxpayers.

Activities

OPIC is the U.S. Government's development finance institution. It mobilizes private capital to help solve critical development challenges and in doing so, advances U.S. foreign policy. Because OPIC works with the U.S. private sector, it helps U.S. businesses gain footholds in emerging markets, catalyzing revenues, jobs, and growth opportunities both at home and abroad. OPIC achieves its mission by providing investors with financing, guarantees, political risk insurance, and support for private equity investment funds.

OPIC financing provides medium- to long-term funding through direct loans and loan guaranties to eligible investment projects. Small- and medium-enterprise financing is available for businesses with annual revenues of less than $400 million, while OPIC's structured financing focuses on larger U.S. businesses and supports large-scale projects that require great amounts of capital. For businesses with annual revenues less than $35 million, OPIC's Small Business Center (SBC) offers qualified small businesses the opportunity to utilize OPIC's streamlined approval process.

Loans and guarantees range from a minimum $350,000 to a maximum of $250 million on projects sponsored by U.S. businesses. If a project requires more than OPIC's maximum per-project lending capacity, OPIC is experienced in working with colenders to bring sufficient resources to a project. In most cases, the U.S. sponsor is expected to contribute at least 25 percent of the project equity,

have a proven record in the industry, and have the means to contribute to the financial successes of the project.

In response to the shortfall of private equity capital in developing countries, OPIC provides support for the creation of privately owned and managed investment funds. OPIC is one of the largest private equity fund sponsors in developing nations and is typically one of the first to enter an unproven market in that capacity. These funds make direct equity and equity-related investments in new, expanding, or privatizing emerging market companies. OPIC-supported funds help emerging economies access long-term growth capital, management skills, and financial expertise, all of which are key factors in expanding economic development and creating new opportunities for people in low-income and developing nations.

Sources of Information

General Inquiries   Contact the Information Officer, Office of External Affairs, Overseas Private Investment Corporation, 1100 New York Avenue, NW., Washington, DC 20527. Phone, 202–336–8799 (InfoLine) or 202–336–8400 (Operator). Email, info@opic.gov. Internet, http://www.opic.gov/doing-business-us/contact-us.

Publications   OPIC programs are detailed in the "Annual Report" and the "Program Handbook." Both publications are available free of charge. To access the "Program Handbook," go to http://www.opic.gov/sites/default/files/docs/OPIC_Handbook.pdf. Use the link below to see the annual reports. Internet, http://www.opic.gov/media-connections/annual-reports.

For further information, contact the Overseas Private Investment Corporation, 1100 New York Avenue NW., Washington, DC 20527. Phone, 202–336–8400. Fax, 202–336–7949. Internet, http://www.opic.gov.

PEACE CORPS

1111 Twentieth Street NW., Washington, DC 20526
Phone, 202–692–2000; 855–855–1961. Fax, 202–692–2231. Internet, http://www.peacecorps.gov.

Director	CAROLYN HESSLER-RADELET
Deputy Director	(VACANCY)

Chief of Staff	LAURA CHAMBERS
White House Liaison	JACKLYN DAO
Associate Director for Global Operations	CARLOS TORRES
Director of Congressional Relations	KATHLEEN BEALE
General Counsel	M. WILLIAM RUBIN
Executive Secretariat	MELANIE WILHELM
Director of Communications	MAUREEN KNIGHTLY
Director of Office of Strategic Information, Research, and Planning	CATHRYN THORUP
Director of Civil Rights and Diversity	DAVID KING
Inspector General	KATHY A. BULLER
Director of Peace Corps Response	SARAH MORGENTHAU
Regional Director, Africa	RICHARD DAY
Regional Director, Europe, Mediterranean and Asia	KERI LOWRY
Regional Director, Inter-America and the Pacific	NINA FAVOR, *Acting*
Director of Overseas Programming and Training Support	SONIA STINES DERENONCOURT
Chief Financial Officer	JOSEPH HEPP
Associate Director for Management	(VACANCY)
Associate Director for Health Services	PAUL JUNG
Director of Victim Advocacy	KELLIE GREENE
Chief Information Officer	DORINE ANDREWS
Associate Director for Volunteer Recruitment and Selection	HELEN LOWMAN
Associate Director for Safety and Security	(VACANCY)
Chief Acquisition Officer	LINDA BRAINARD
Chief Compliance Officer	DALJIT BAINS
Director of Global Health and HIV	MARIE MCLEOD
Associate Director for Strategic Partnerships	COREY GRIFFIN
Director of Third Goal and Returned Volunteer Services	(VACANCY)
Director of Innovation	PATRICK CHOQUETTE

The Peace Corps helps people of interested countries meet their need for trained men and women and promotes mutual understanding between Americans and citizens of other countries.

The Peace Corps was established by the Peace Corps Act of 1961, as amended (22 U.S.C. 2501), and was made an independent agency by title VI of the International Security and Development Cooperation Act of 1981 (22 U.S.C. 2501–1).

Activities

The Peace Corps consists of a Washington, DC, headquarters, eight area offices, and overseas operations in 65 countries, relying on more than 7,200 volunteers.

To fulfill the Peace Corps mandate, men and women are trained for a 9- to 14-week period in the appropriate local language, the technical skills necessary for their particular jobs, and the cross-cultural skills needed to adjust to a society with traditions and attitudes different from their own. Volunteers serve for a period of 2 years, living among the people with whom they work. Volunteers are expected to become a part of the community through their service.

Thousands of volunteers serve worldwide and work in six program areas: agriculture, business development, education, environment, health and HIV/AIDS, and youth development. Community-level projects are designed to match the skills of volunteers with

PEACE CORPS

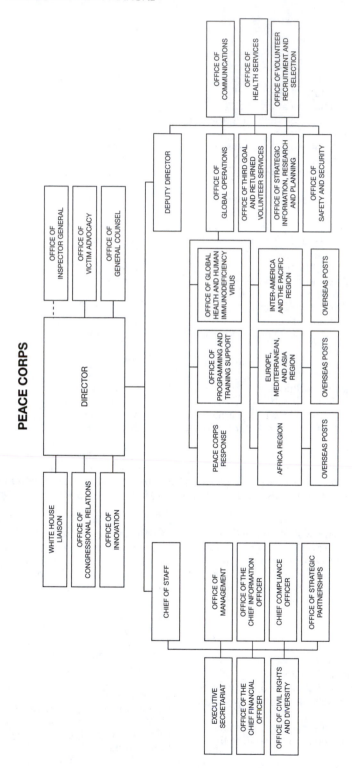

the resources of host-country agencies and other international assistance organizations to help solve specific development problems, often in conjunction with private volunteer organizations.

In the United States, the Peace Corps is working to promote an understanding of people in other countries. Through its World Wise Schools program, volunteers partner with elementary and junior high school students in the United States to encourage an exchange of letters, pictures, music, and artifacts. Participating students increase their knowledge of geography, languages, and different cultures, while gaining an appreciation for voluntarism.

The Peace Corps offers other domestic programs that rely on former volunteers. Working together with universities, local public school systems, and private businesses and foundations, these former volunteers help solve some of

our Nation's most pressing domestic problems.

A complete listing of Peace Corps area offices, including addresses, telephone numbers, and areas served, is available online.

Internet, http://www.peacecorps.gov.

Sources of Information

Becoming a Peace Corps Volunteer
Contact the nearest area office, or use the link below. An "Application Portal" is available online. Internet, http://www.peacecorps.gov/volunteer/.

Employment   Contact the Peace Corps, Office of Human Resource Management, Washington, DC 20526. Phone, 202–692–1200. Peace Corps vacancy announcements are available online. Internet, http://www.peacecorps.gov/about/jobs/.

General Inquiries   Contact the Peace Corps Washington, DC, headquarters or one of its area offices.

For further information, contact the Press Office, Peace Corps, 1111 Twentieth Street NW., Washington, DC 20526. Phone, 202–692–2230 or 855–855–1961. Fax, 202–692–2201. Internet, http://www.peacecorps.gov.

EDITORIAL NOTE: The Pension Benefit Guaranty Corporation did not meet the publication deadline for submitting updated information of its activities, functions, and sources of information as required by the automatic disclosure provisions of the Freedom of Information Act (5 U.S.C. 552(a)(1)(A)).

PENSION BENEFIT GUARANTY CORPORATION

1200 K Street NW., Washington, DC 20005
Phone, 202–326–4000; 800–400–7242. Internet, http://www.pbgc.gov.

Board of Directors

Chairman (Secretary of Labor)	THOMAS E. PEREZ
Member (Secretary of the Treasury)	JACOB J. LEW
Member (Secretary of Commerce)	PENNY S. PRITZKER

Officials

Director	JOSHUA GOTBAUM
Deputy Director, Operations	(VACANCY)
General Counsel	JUDITH STARR
Inspector General	DEBORAH STOVER-SPRINGER, *Acting*
Chief of Staff	ANN ORR
Chief Counsel	ISRAEL GOLDOWITZ
Chief Financial Officer	PATRICIA KELLY
Chief Information Officer	BARRY C. WEST
Chief Investment Officer	JOHN GREENBERG
Chief Management Officer	ALICE C. MARONI
Chief, Negotiations and Restructuring	SANDY RICH
Chief Policy Officer	J. JIONI PALMER, *Acting*
Director, Benefits Administration and Payment	PHILIP R. LANGHAM
Director, Budget and Organizational Performance Department	EDGAR BENNETT
Director, Corporate Finance and Restructuring	KRISTINA ARCHEVAL
Director, Facilities and Services	CATHLEEN KRONOPOLUS
Director, Human Resources	ARRIE ETHERIDGE
Director, Legislative and Regulatory	JOHN HANLEY
Director, Policy, Research, and Analysis	NEELA RANADE, *Acting*
Director, Procurement	STEVE BLOCK

The Pension Benefit Guaranty Corporation protects the retirement incomes of American workers in private-sector defined benefit pension plans.

The Pension Benefit Guaranty Corporation (PBGC) is a self-financing, wholly owned Government corporation subject to the Government Corporation Control Act (31 U.S.C. 9101–9109). The Corporation, established by title IV of the Employee Retirement Income Security Act of 1974 (29 U.S.C. 1301–1461), operates in accordance with policies established by its Board of Directors, which consists of the Secretaries of Labor, Commerce, and the Treasury. The Secretary of Labor is Chairman of

the Board. A seven-member Advisory Committee, composed of two labor, two business, and three public members appointed by the President, advises the agency on investment issues.

Activities

Coverage The Corporation insures most private sector defined-benefit pension plans, which provide a pension benefit based on factors such as age, years of service, and salary.

PENSION BENEFIT GUARANTY CORPORATION

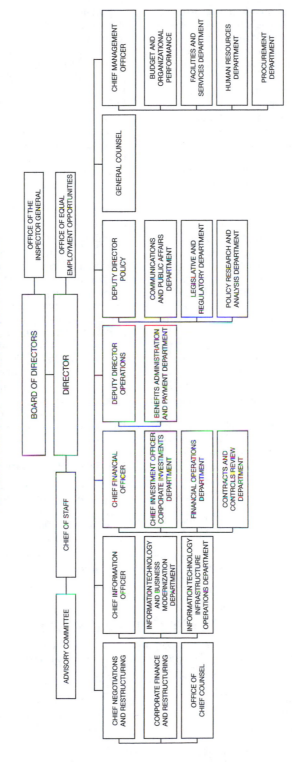

The Corporation administers two insurance programs, separately covering single-employer and multiemployer plans. More than 40 million workers and retirees participate in nearly 26, 000 covered plans

Single-Employer Insurance   Under the single-employer program, the Corporation guarantees payment of basic pension benefits if an insured plan terminates without sufficient assets to pay those benefits. However, the law limits the total monthly benefit that the agency may guarantee for one individual to $4,789.77 per month for a 65-year-old individual in a pension plan that terminates in 2013. The law also sets other restrictions on PBGC's guarantee, including limits on the insured amount of recent benefit increases. In certain cases, the Corporation may also pay some benefits above the guaranteed amount depending on the funding level of the plan and amounts recovered from employers.

A plan sponsor may terminate a single-employer plan in a standard termination if the plan has sufficient assets to purchase private annuities to cover all benefit liabilities. If a plan does not have sufficient assets, the sponsor may seek to transfer the pension liabilities to the PBGC by demonstrating that it meets the legal criteria for a distress termination. In either termination, the plan administrator must inform participants in writing at least 60 days prior to the date the administrator proposes to terminate the plan. Only a plan that has sufficient assets to pay all benefit liabilities may terminate in a standard termination. The Corporation also may institute termination of underfunded plans in certain specified circumstances.

Multiemployer Insurance   Under title IV, as revised in 1980 by the Multiemployer Pension Plan Amendments Act (29 U.S.C. 1001 note), which changed the insurable event from plan termination to plan insolvency, the Corporation provides financial assistance to multiemployer plans that are unable to pay nonforfeitable benefits. The plans are obligated to repay such assistance. The act also made employers withdrawing from a plan liable to the plan for a portion of its unfunded vested benefits.

Premium Collections   All defined-benefit pension plans insured by PBGC are required to pay premiums to the Corporation according to rates set by Congress. The per-participant flat-rate premium for plan years beginning in 2013 is $42.00 for single-employer plans and $12.00 for multiemployer plans. Underfunded single-employer plans must also pay an additional premium equal to $9 per $1,000 of unfunded vested benefits. A termination premium of $1,250 per participant per year applies to certain distress and involuntary plan terminations, payable for 3 years after the termination.

Sources of Information

Access to the Pension Benefit Guaranty Corporation is available online. TTY/TDD users may call the Federal Relay Service toll free at 1–800–877–8339 and ask to be connected to 1–800–400–7242.

For further information, contact the Pension Benefit Guaranty Corporation, 1200 K Street NW., Washington, DC 20005–4026. Phone, 202–326–4000 or 1–800–400–7242 . Internet, http://www.pbgc.gov.

POSTAL REGULATORY COMMISSION

901 New York Avenue NW., Suite 200, Washington, DC 20268–0001
Phone, 202–789–6800. Fax, 202–789–6861. Internet, http://www.prc.gov.

Chairman	Ruth Y. Goldway
Vice Chairman	Mark Acton
Commissioners	Robert G. Taub, (2 vacancies)
General Counsel	David A. Trissell

Director, Office of Accountability and Compliance	MARGARET CIGNO
Director, Office of Public Affairs and Government Relations	ANN FISHER
Director, Office of Secretary and Administration	SHOSHANA M. GROVE
Inspector General	JOHN F. CALLENDER

[For the Postal Regulatory Commission statement of organization, see the Code of Federal Regulations, Title 39, Part 3002]

The Postal Regulatory Commission develops and implements a modern system of postal rate regulation.

The Postal Regulatory Commission is the successor agency to the Postal Rate Commission, which was created by the Postal Reorganization Act, as amended (39 U.S.C. 101 et seq.). The Commission was established as an independent agency in the executive branch of Government by the Postal Accountability and Enhancement Act (39 U.S.C. 501). It is composed of five Commissioners, appointed by the President with the advice and consent of the Senate, one of whom is designated as Chairman.

The Commission promulgates rules and regulations, establishes procedures, and takes other actions necessary to carry out its obligations. It considers complaints received from interested persons relating to United States Postal Service rates, regulations, and services. The Commission also has certain reporting obligations, including a report on universal postal service and the postal monopoly.

Sources of Information

Employment The Commission's programs require attorneys, economists, statisticians, accountants, industrial engineers, marketing specialists, and administrative and clerical personnel to fulfill its responsibilities. Requests for employment information should be directed to the Personnel Officer.

Electronic Access Current docketed case materials are available online. Email may be sent to the Commission at prc-admin@prc.gov or prc-dockets@prc.gov. Internet, http://www.prc.gov/prc-pages/dockets-search/default.aspx.

Reading Room Facilities for inspection and copying of records, viewing automated daily lists of docketed materials, and accessing the Commission's Internet site are located at Suite 200, 901 New York Avenue NW., Washington, DC. The room is open from 8 a.m. to 4:30 p.m., Monday through Friday, except legal holidays.

Rules of Practice and Procedure The Postal Regulatory Commission's Rules of Practice and Procedure governing the conduct of proceedings before the Commission may be found in parts 3001, 3010, 3015, 3020, 3025, 3030, 3031, 3050, and 3060 of title 39 of the "Code of Federal Regulations."

For further information, contact the Secretary, Postal Regulatory Commission, 901 New York Avenue NW., Suite 200, Washington, DC 20268–0001. Phone, 202–789–6840. Internet, http://www.prc.gov.

RAILROAD RETIREMENT BOARD

844 North Rush Street, Chicago, IL 60611–2092
Phone, 312–751–4777. Fax, 312–751–7154. Internet, http://www.rrb.gov. Email, opa@rrb.gov.

Chairman	MICHAEL S. SCHWARTZ
Labor Member	WALTER A. BARROWS
Management Member	STEVEN J. ANTHONY

Inspector General	Martin J. Dickman
Director, Administration	Keith B. Earley
Director, Equal Opportunity	Lynn E. Cousins
Director, Human Resources	Marguerite V. Daniels
Director, Public Affairs	Michael P. Freeman
Chief, Acquisition Management	Paul T. Ahern
Facility Manager	Scott L. Rush
General Counsel	Karl T. Blank
Director, Legislative Affairs	Margaret S. Lindsley
Director, Hearings and Appeals	Rachel L. Simmons
Secretary to the Board	Martha P. Rico
Chief Actuary	Frank J. Buzzi
Chief Information Officer	Ram Murthy
Chief Financial Officer and Senior Executive Officer	George V. Govan
Director, Field Service	Daniel J. Fadden
Director, Programs	Martha M. Barringer
Director, Policy and Systems	Ronald Russo
Director, Program Evaluation and Management Services	Janet M. Hallman
Director, Retirement Benefits	Cecilia A. Freeman
Director, Survivor Benefits	Valerie F. Allen
Director, Disability Benefits	John R. Coleman
Director, Unemployment and Programs Support	Micheal T. Pawlak

[For the Railroad Retirement Board statement of organization, see the Code of Federal Regulations, Title 20, Part 200]

The Railroad Retirement Board administers comprehensive retirement-survivor and unemployment-sickness benefit programs for the Nation's railroad workers and their families.

The Railroad Retirement Board (RRB) was originally established by the Railroad Retirement Act of 1934, as amended (45 U.S.C. 201–228z-1).

The RRB derives statutory authority from the Railroad Retirement Act of 1974 (45 U.S.C. 231–231u) and the Railroad Unemployment Insurance Act (45 U.S.C. 351–369). It administers these acts and participates in the administration of the Social Security Act and the Health Insurance for the Aged Act insofar as they affect railroad retirement beneficiaries.

The RRB is composed of three members appointed by the President with the advice and consent of the Senate: one upon recommendations of representatives of railroad employees; one upon recommendations of railroad employers; and one, the Chairman, as a public member.

Activities   The Railroad Retirement Act provides for the payment of annuities to individuals who have completed at least 10 years of creditable railroad service, or 5 years if performed after 1995, and have ceased compensated service upon their attainment of specified ages, or at any age if permanently disabled for all employment. In some circumstances occupational disability annuities or supplemental annuities are provided for career employees.

A spouse's annuity is provided, under certain conditions, for the wife or husband of an employee annuitant. Divorced spouses may also qualify.

Survivor annuities are awarded to the qualified spouses, children, and parents of deceased career employees, and various lump-sum benefits are also available under certain conditions.

Benefits based upon qualifying railroad earnings in a preceding 1-year period are provided under the Railroad Unemployment Insurance Act to individuals who are unemployed in a benefit year, but who are ready and

RAILROAD RETIREMENT BOARD

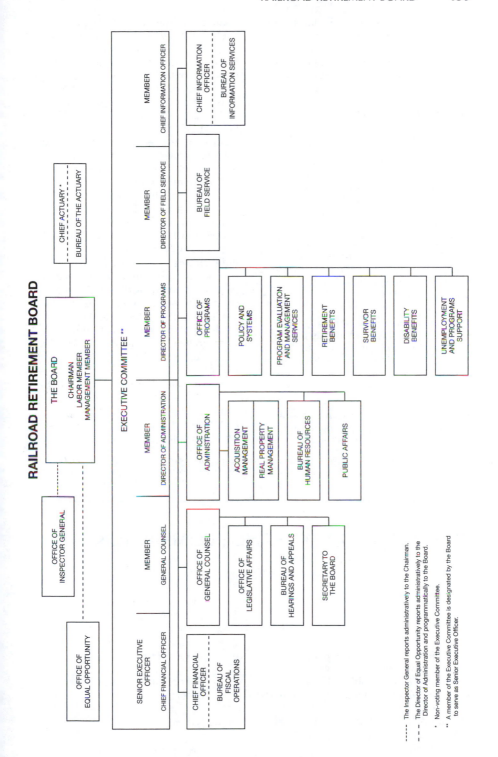

EXECUTIVE COMMITTEE **

THE BOARD
CHAIRMAN
LABOR MEMBER
MANAGEMENT MEMBER

OFFICE OF INSPECTOR GENERAL

CHIEF ACTUARY *
BUREAU OF THE ACTUARY

OFFICE OF EQUAL OPPORTUNITY

SENIOR EXECUTIVE OFFICER

MEMBER
GENERAL COUNSEL

MEMBER
DIRECTOR OF ADMINISTRATION

MEMBER
DIRECTOR OF PROGRAMS

MEMBER
DIRECTOR OF FIELD SERVICE

MEMBER
CHIEF INFORMATION OFFICER

CHIEF FINANCIAL OFFICER
BUREAU OF FISCAL OPERATIONS

OFFICE OF GENERAL COUNSEL

OFFICE OF ADMINISTRATION

OFFICE OF PROGRAMS

BUREAU OF FIELD SERVICE

CHIEF INFORMATION OFFICER
BUREAU OF INFORMATION SERVICES

OFFICE OF LEGISLATIVE AFFAIRS

BUREAU OF HEARINGS AND APPEALS

SECRETARY TO THE BOARD

ACQUISITION MANAGEMENT

REAL PROPERTY MANAGEMENT

BUREAU OF HUMAN RESOURCES

PUBLIC AFFAIRS

POLICY AND SYSTEMS

PROGRAM EVALUATION AND MANAGEMENT SERVICES

RETIREMENT BENEFITS

SURVIVOR BENEFITS

DISABILITY BENEFITS

UNEMPLOYMENT AND PROGRAMS SUPPORT

- - - - - The Inspector General reports administratively to the Chairman.

- - - The Director of Equal Opportunity reports administratively to the Director of Administration and programmatically to the Board.

* Non-voting member of the Executive Committee.

** A member of the Executive Committee is designated by the Board to serve as Senior Executive Officer.

willing to work, and to individuals who are unable to work because of sickness or injury.

The RRB maintains, through its field offices, a placement service for unemployed railroad personnel.

Sources of Information

Benefit Inquiries   The RRB maintains direct contact with railroad employees and railroad retirement beneficiaries through its field offices located across the country. Field personnel explain benefit rights and responsibilities on an individual basis, assist employees in applying for benefits, and answer questions related to the benefit programs. The RRB also relies on railroad labor groups and employers for assistance in keeping railroad personnel informed about its benefit programs. To locate the nearest field office, individuals should check with their rail employer or local union official. Information may also be obtained by calling the RRB at 877–772–5772 or by visiting the agency's Web site at www.rrb.gov. Most offices are open to the public from 9 a.m. to 3:30 p.m., Monday through Friday.

Congressional and Legislative Assistance   Congressional offices making inquiries regarding constituents' claims should contact the Congressional Inquiry Section. Phone, 312–751–4970. Fax, 312–751–7154. Email, opa@rrb.gov. For information regarding legislative matters, contact the Office of Legislative Affairs, Suite 500, 1310 G Street NW., Washington, DC 20005–3004. Phone, 202–272–7742. Fax, 202–272–7728. Email, ola@rrb.gov.

Electronic Access   Railroad Retirement Board information is available online. Internet, https://secure.rrb.gov/.

Employment   Employment inquiries should be directed to the Bureau of Human Resources, Railroad Retirement Board, 844 North Rush Street, Chicago, IL 60611–2092. Phone, 312–751–4580. Email, recruit@rrb.gov.

Publications   General information pamphlets on benefit programs may be obtained from the RRB's field offices or Chicago headquarters. Requests for annual reports or statistical data should be directed to Public Affairs at the Chicago headquarters. Phone, 312–751–4777. Fax, 312–751–7154. Email, opa@rrb.gov.

Telecommunications Devices for the Deaf (TDD)   The RRB provides TDD services. Phone 312–751–4701 for beneficiary inquiries or 312–751–4334 for equal opportunity inquiries.

For further information, contact Public Affairs, Railroad Retirement Board, 844 North Rush Street, Chicago, IL 60611–2092. Phone, 312–751–4777. Fax, 312–751–7154. Email, opa@rrb.gov. Internet, http://www.rrb.gov.

SECURITIES AND EXCHANGE COMMISSION

100 F Street NE., Washington, DC 20549
Phone, 202–551–7500. Internet, http://www.sec.gov.

Chair	MARY JO WHITE
Commissioners	LUIS A. AGUILAR, DANIEL M. GALLAGHER, MICHAEL S. PIWOWAR, KARA M. STEIN
Director, Office of Legislative and Intergovernmental Affairs	TIMOTHY HENSELER
Director, Office of Public Affairs	JOHN NESTER
Director, Office of Investor Education and Advocacy	LORI J. SCHOCK
Investor Advocate, Office of the Investor Advocate	RICK A. FLEMING
Secretary	(VACANCY)

Chief Operating Officer	JEFFERY HESLOP
Associate Executive Director, Office of Human Resources	LACEY DINGMAN
Director, Office of Support Operations	BARRY D. WALTERS
Chief Financial Officer	KENNETH JOHNSON
General Counsel	ANNE K. SMALL
Ethics Counsel	SHIRA P. MINTON
Director, Division of Corporation Finance	KEITH HIGGINS
Director, Division of Enforcement	ANDREW CERESNEY
Director, Division of Investment Management	NORMAN B. CHAMP, III
Director, Division of Trading and Markets	STEPHEN LUPARELLO
Director, Office of Compliance Inspections and Examinations	ANDREW BOWDEN
Director, Office of Credit Ratings	THOMAS BUTLER
Chief Accountant	PAUL BESWICK
Chief Administrative Law Judge	BRENDA P. MURRAY
Director and Chief Economist, Division of Economic and Risk Analysis	CRAIG LEWIS
Chief Information Officer, Office of Information Technology	THOMAS BAYER
Director, Office of International Affairs	PAUL LEDER
Director, Office of Equal Employment Opportunity	ALTA RODRIGUEZ
Director, Office of Minority and Women Inclusion	PAMELA GIBBS
Director, Office of Support Operations and Chief FOIA Officer	BARRY D. WALTERS
Inspector General	CARL W. HOECKER

[For the Securities and Exchange Commission statement of organization, see the Code of Federal Regulations, Title 17, Part 200]

The Securities and Exchange Commission protects investors, facilitates capital formation, and maintains efficient, fair, and orderly markets.

The Securities and Exchange Commission (SEC) was created under authority of the Securities Exchange Act of 1934 (15 U.S.C. 78a–78jj) and was organized on July 2, 1934. The Commission serves as adviser to United States district courts in reorganization proceedings for debtor corporations in which a substantial public interest is involved. The Commission also has certain responsibilities under section 15 of the Bretton Woods Agreements Act of 1945 (22 U.S.C. 286k-1) and section 851(e) of the Internal Revenue Code of 1954 (26 U.S.C. 851(e)).

The Commission is vested with quasi-judicial functions. Persons aggrieved by its decisions in the exercise of those functions have a right of review by the United States courts of appeals.

A complete listing of SEC regional offices, including addresses, telephone numbers, and key officials, is available online.

Internet, http://www.sec.gov/contact/addresses.htm.

Activities

Full and Fair Disclosure The Securities Act of 1933 (15 U.S.C. 77a) requires issuers of securities and their controlling persons making public offerings of securities in interstate commerce or via mail to file registration statements containing financial and other pertinent data about the issuer and the securities being offered with the SEC. There are limited exemptions, such as government securities, nonpublic offerings, and intrastate offerings, as well as certain offerings not exceeding $1.5 million. The effectiveness of a registration statement may be refused or suspended after a

SECURITIES AND EXCHANGE COMMISSION

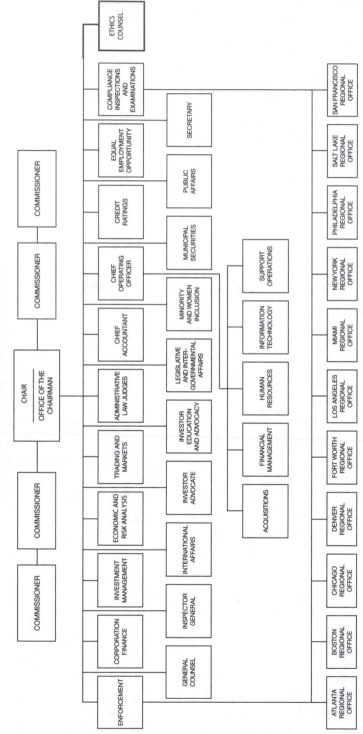

public hearing if the statement contains material misstatements or omissions, thus barring sale of the securities until it is appropriately amended.

Regulation of Investment Advisers Persons who, for compensation, engage in the business of advising others with respect to securities must register with the Commission. The Commission is authorized to define what practices are considered fraudulent or deceptive and to prescribe means to prevent those practices.

Regulation of Mutual Funds and Other Investment Companies The Commission registers investment companies and regulates their activities to protect investors. The regulation covers sales load, management contracts, composition of boards of directors, and capital structure. The Commission must also determine the fairness of various transactions of investment companies before they actually occur.

The Commission may institute court action to enjoin the consummation of mergers and other plans of reorganization of investment companies if such plans are unfair to securities holders. It may impose sanctions by administrative proceedings against investment company management for violations of the act and other Federal securities laws. It also may file court actions to enjoin acts and practices of management officials involving breaches of fiduciary duty and personal misconduct and to disqualify such officials from office.

Regulation of Securities Markets The Securities Exchange Act of 1934 assigns to the Commission broad regulatory responsibilities over the securities markets, the self-regulatory organizations within the securities industry, and persons conducting a business in securities. Persons who execute transactions in securities generally are required to register with the Commission as broker-dealers. Securities exchanges and certain clearing agencies are required to register with the Commission, and associations of brokers or dealers are permitted to register with the Commission. The act also provides for the establishment of the Municipal Securities Rulemaking Board

to formulate rules for the municipal securities industry.

The Commission oversees the self-regulatory activities of the national securities exchanges and associations, registered clearing agencies, and the Municipal Securities Rulemaking Board. In addition, the Commission regulates industry professionals, such as securities brokers and dealers, certain municipal securities professionals, Government securities brokers and dealers, and transfer agents.

Rehabilitation of Failing Corporations In cases of corporate reorganization proceedings administered in Federal courts, the Commission may participate as a statutory party. The principal functions of the Commission are to protect the interests of public investors involved in such cases through efforts to ensure their adequate representation and to participate in legal and policy issues that are of concern to public investors generally.

Representation of Debt Securities Holders The Commission safeguards the interests of purchasers of publicly offered debt securities issued pursuant to trust indentures.

Enforcement Activities The Commission's enforcement activities are designed to secure compliance with the Federal securities laws administered by the Commission and the rules and regulations adopted thereunder. These activities include measures to do the following: compel compliance with the disclosure requirements of the registration and other provisions of the relevant acts; prevent fraud and deception in the purchase and sale of securities; obtain court orders enjoining acts and practices that operate as a fraud upon investors or otherwise violate the laws; suspend or revoke the registrations of brokers, dealers, investment companies, and investment advisers who willfully engage in such acts and practices; suspend or bar from association persons associated with brokers, dealers, investment companies, and investment advisers who have violated any provision of the Federal securities laws; and prosecute persons who have engaged in fraudulent activities or other willful violations of those laws.

In addition, attorneys, accountants, and other professionals who violate the securities laws face possible loss of their privilege to practice before the Commission.

To this end, private investigations are conducted into complaints or other indications of securities violations. Established evidence of law violations is used in appropriate administrative proceedings to revoke registration or in actions instituted in Federal courts to restrain or enjoin such activities. Where the evidence tends to establish criminal fraud or other willful violation of the securities laws, the facts are referred to the Attorney General for criminal prosecution of the offenders. The Commission may assist in such prosecutions.

Sources of Information

Inquiries regarding the following matters should be directed to the appropriate office, Securities and Exchange Commission, 100 F Street NE., Washington, DC 20549. Internet, http://www.sec.gov.

Contracts Information on SEC procurement and contracting activities is available from the Office of Administrative Services. Phone, 202–551–7300. Internet, http://www.sec.gov/about/offices/oas.htm.

Employment Applicants must apply for a particular vacancy and complete a process of competitive selection. This process does not apply, however, to attorney vacancies. The Commission runs a college and law school recruitment program, which relies on campus visits and student interviews. Inquiries should be directed to the Office of Human Resources. Phone, 202–551–7500. Fax, 202–777–1028. Internet, http://www.sec.gov/careers#.U6m2tpRdUwA.

Investor Assistance and Complaints The Office of Investor Education and Advocacy answers investors' questions, assists them with specific problems regarding their relations with broker-dealers and companies, and advises the Commission and other offices and divisions regarding problems frequently encountered by investors and possible regulatory solutions. Phone, 202–551–6551. Consumer information line, 800–732–0330. Fax, 202–772–9295. Complaints and inquiries may also be directed to any regional or district office. Internet, http://www.sec.gov/investor#.U6m0RJRdUwB.

Publications SEC forms are available on the agency's Web site. Other publications, including publications for investors (http://www.sec.gov/investor/pubs.shtml), are also available online. For more information, contact the Publications Unit. Phone, 202–551–4040. Internet, http://www.sec.gov/edgar.shtml#.U6my35RdUwC.

Reading Rooms Registration statements and other public documents filed with the Commission are available for public inspection in the Commission's public reference room in Washington, DC. It is open weekdays, except on holidays, between the hours of 10:00 a.m. and 3:00 p.m. Phone, 202–551–5850. The Commission maintains a library that is open during the same hours as the public reference room. Phone, 202–551–5450. Fax, 202–772–9326.

Small Business Activities Information for small businesses, including information on legal obligations when they sell securities and on financial and other reporting obligations when their securities are traded publicly, is available online. Contact the Office of Small Business Policy for more information. Phone, 202–551–3460. Internet, http://www.sec.gov/info/smallbus.shtml.

For further information, contact the Office of Public Affairs, Securities and Exchange Commission, 100 F Street NE., Washington, DC 20549. Phone, 202–551–4120. Fax, 202–777–1026. Internet, http://www.sec.gov.

SELECTIVE SERVICE SYSTEM

National Headquarters, Arlington, VA 22209–2425
Phone, 703–605–4100. Internet, http://www.sss.gov.

Director	LAWRENCE G. ROMO
Deputy Director	EDWARD T. ALLARD, III
Chief of Staff	JOEL C. SPANGENBERG
General Counsel	RUDY G. SANCHEZ, JR.
Associate Director for Operations	MARIANO C. CAMPOS, JR.
Associate Director for Public and Intergovernmental Affairs	RICHARD S. FLAHAVAN
Associate Director for Financial Management/ Chief Financial Officer	RODERICK R. HUBBARD
Chief Information Officer	JERRY KLOTZ

[For the Selective Service System statement of organization, see the Code of Federal Regulations, Title 32, Part 1605]

The Selective Service System supplies the Armed Forces with manpower in an emergency and operates an Alternative Service Program for men classified as conscientious objectors.

The Selective Service System was established by the Military Selective Service Act (50 U.S.C. app. 451–471a). The act requires the registration of male citizens of the United States and all other male persons who are in the United States and who are ages 18 to 25. The act exempts members of the active Armed Forces and nonimmigrant aliens. Proclamation 4771 of July 20, 1980, requires male persons born on or after January 1, 1960, and who have attained age 18, but have not attained age 26 to register. Registration is conducted at post offices within the United States, at U.S. embassies and consulates outside the United States, and online at the Selective Service System's Web site.

The act imposes liability for training and service in the Armed Forces upon registrants who are ages 18 to 26, except those who are exempt or deferred. Persons who have been deferred remain liable for training and service until age 35. Aliens are not liable for training and service until they have remained in the United States for more than 1 year. Conscientious objectors who are found to be opposed to all service in the Armed Forces are required to perform civilian work in lieu of induction into the Armed Forces.

The authority to induct registrants, including doctors and allied medical specialists, expired July 1, 1973.

A complete listing of the Selective Service System's regional offices is available online.

Internet, https://www.sss.gov/struct.htm.

Sources of Information

Employment Inquiries should be sent to the Director, Selective Service System, Attn: SPT/HR, Arlington, VA 22209–2425. Phone, 703–605–4040. Search the Federal Government's free web-based job board using the link below. Internet, https://www.usajobs.gov/.

Procurement Inquiries should be sent to the Director, Selective Service System, Attn: STP/LO, Arlington, VA 22209–2425. Phone, 703–605–4038.

Publications Selective Service regulations appear in chapter XVI of title 32 of the "Code of Federal Regulations." Internet, https://www.sss.gov/public.htm.

Requirements of Law Persons seeking information concerning the requirements of the Military Selective Service Act should contact the National Headquarters of the Selective Service System. Phone, 703–605–4100. Internet, https://www.sss.gov/regist%20information.htm.

SELECTIVE SERVICE SYSTEM

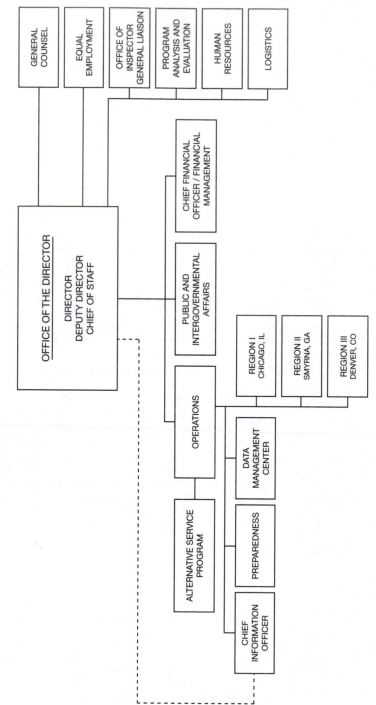

- - - Chief Information Officer with direct access to the Director

For further information, contact the Office of Public and Intergovernmental Affairs, Selective Service System, Arlington, VA 22209–2425. Phone, 703–605–4100. Email, information@sss.gov. Internet, https://www.sss. gov/contact.htm.

SMALL BUSINESS ADMINISTRATION

409 Third Street SW., Washington, DC 20416
Phone, 202–205–6600. Fax, 202–205–7064. Internet, http://www.sba.gov.

Administrator	MARIA CONTRERAS-SWEET
Deputy Administrator	(VACANCY)
Chief Counsel for Advocacy	WINSLOW SARGENT
Chief Financial Officer	(VACANCY)
Chief Information Officer	RENEE MACKLIN
Chief Operating Officer	PAUL CHRISTY
Chief of Staff	(VACANCY)
General Counsel	SARA LIPSCOMB
Inspector General	PEGGY E. GUSTAFSON
Associate Administrator for Business Development	DARRYL K. HAIRSTON
Associate Administrator for Capital Access	ANN MARIE MEHLUM
Associate Administrator for Disaster Assistance	JAMES RIVERA
Associate Administrator for Entrepreneurial Development	TAMEKA MONTGOMERY
Associate Administrator for Field Operations	ROBERT S. HILL
Associate Administrator for Government Contracting and Business Development	JOHN SHORAKA
Associate Administrator for International Trade	JAVIER SAADE
Associate Administrator for Small Business Development Centers	CARROLL A. THOMAS
Assistant Administrator for Communications and Public Liaison	FREDERICK BALDASSARO
Assistant Administrator for Faith Based and Neighborhood Partnerships	SARAH BARD
Assistant Administrator for Hearings and Appeals	DELORICE P. FORD
Assistant Administrator for Native American Affairs	CHRISTOPHER L. JAMES
Assistant Administrator for Veterans Business Development	RHETT JEPPSON
Assistant Administrator for Women's Business Ownership	ANA R. HARVEY
Director of Credit Risk Management	BRENT M. CIURLINO
Director of HUBZone Program	MARIANA PARDO

[For the Small Business Administration statement of organization, see the Code of Federal Regulations, Title 13, Part 101]

The Small Business Administration aids, counsels, assists, and protects the interests of small business; ensures that small-business concerns receive a fair portion of Government purchases, contracts and subcontracts, and sales of Government property; makes loans to small-business concerns, State and local development companies, and the victims of natural disasters or of certain types of economic injury; and licenses, regulates, and makes loans to small-business investment companies.

SMALL BUSINESS ADMINISTRATION

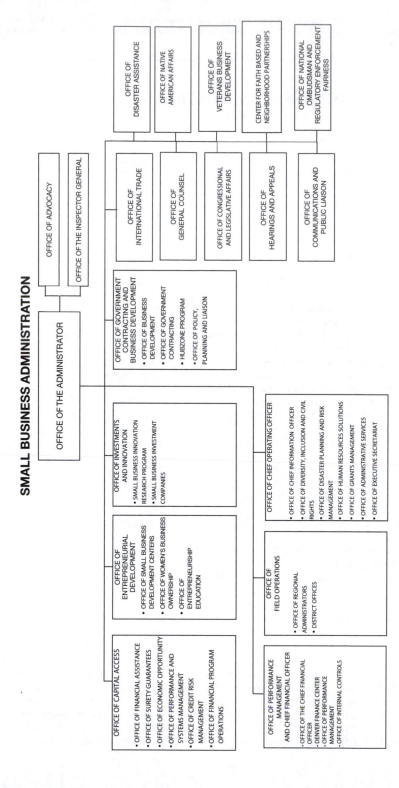

The Small Business Administration (SBA) was created by the Small Business Act of 1953 and derives its present existence and authority from the Small Business Act (15 U.S.C. 631 et seq.) and the Small Business Investment Act of 1958 (15 U.S.C. 661).

Activities

Advocacy   The Office of Advocacy is mandated by Congress to serve as an independent voice within the Federal Government for the approximately 27.2 million small businesses throughout the country. The Office is headed by the Chief Counsel for Advocacy, appointed by the President from the private sector with the advice and consent of the Senate, who advances the views, concerns, and interests of small business before the Congress, the White House, and Federal and State regulatory agencies.

The Office monitors and reports annually on Federal agency compliance with the Regulatory Flexibility Act (RFA), which requires agencies to analyze the impact of their regulations on small businesses and consider less burdensome alternatives. Small entities include small businesses, nonprofit organizations, and governmental jurisdictions. Executive Order 13272 requires Federal agencies to take the Office's comments into consideration before proposed regulations are finalized and requires the Office to train Federal agencies on RFA compliance.

The Office is one of the leading national sources for information on the state of small business and the issues that affect small-business success and growth. It conducts economic and statistical research into matters affecting the competitive strength of small business, jobs created by small businesses, and the impact of Federal laws, regulations, and programs on small businesses, making recommendations to policymakers for appropriate adjustments to meet the special needs of small business.

Additionally, regional advocates enhance communication between the small-business community and the Chief Counsel. As the Chief Counsel's direct link to local business owners, State and local government agencies, State legislatures, and small-business organizations, they help identify new issues and problems of small business by monitoring the effect of Federal and State regulations and policies on the local business communities within their regions.

For further information, contact the Office of Advocacy. Phone, 202–205–6533. Email, advocacy@sba.gov.

Business and Community Initiatives

The Office of Business and Community Initiatives (OBCI) develops and cosponsors counseling, education, training, and information resources for small businesses. It has partnered with the private sector to promote entrepreneurial development. OBCI directs the national program of the Service Corps of Retired Executives (SCORE), a resource partner of SBA. SCORE provides free counseling, mentoring, training seminars, and specialized assistance to veterans and active military personnel. For more information, visit www.score.org. OBCI also offers young entrepreneurs a teen-business site at www.sba.gov/teens.

The Office of International Visitors briefs foreign delegations, business organizations, and international nongovernmental organizations (NGOs) on the SBA model.

In addition to education and training events, SBA offers an online management series on business growth and sustainability at www.sba.gov/library/pubs.

For further information, contact the Office of Business and Community Initiatives. Phone, 202–205–6665.

Capital Access   The Office of the Associate Administrator for Capital Access provides overall direction for SBA's financial programs. It offers a comprehensive array of debt and equity programs for startup and expanding businesses. In addition to lending to businesses that sell their products and services domestically, the Office provides financial assistance programs for small-business exporters in the form of loan programs and technical assistance.

The Office also oversees a surety bond guarantee program for small-business contractors and SBA's lender oversight programs.

For further information, contact the Office of Capital Access. Phone, 202–205–6657.

Disaster Assistance   SBA serves as the Federal disaster bank for nonfarm, private sector losses. It lends money to help the victims of disasters repair or replace most disaster-damaged property. Direct loans with subsidized interest rates are made to assist individuals, homeowners, businesses of all sizes, and nonprofit organizations.

For further information, contact the Office of Disaster Assistance. Phone, 202–205–6734.

Financial Assistance   SBA provides its guarantee to lending institutions and certified development companies that make loans to small-business concerns, which in turn use the loans for working capital and financing the acquisition of land and buildings; the construction, conversion, or expansion of facilities; and the purchase of machinery and equipment.

The Administration also provides small-scale financial and technical assistance to very small businesses through loans and grants to nonprofit organizations that act as intermediaries under SBA's microloan program.

For further information, contact the nearest Small Business Administration district office (see Field Operations below).

Government Contracting   SBA helps small businesses, including small disadvantaged businesses, women-owned small businesses, HUBZone-certified firms, and service-disabled veteran-owned small businesses obtain a fair share of Government procurement through a variety of programs and services. The contracting liaison helps small businesses secure an equitable share of natural resources sold by the Federal Government. It works closely with Federal agencies and the Office of Management and Budget to establish policy and regulations concerning small-business access to Government contracts. It assists in the formulation of

small-business procurement policies as they relate to size standards, the Small Business Innovation Research Program, and the Small Business Technology Transfer Program.

For further information, contact the nearest Office of Government Contracting. Phone, 202–205–6459. Internet, http://www.sba.gov/GC/indexcontacts. html.

International Trade   The Office of International Trade (OIT) supports small-business access to export markets and participates in broader U.S. Government activities related to trade policy and international commercial affairs to encourage an environment of trade and international economic policies favorable to small businesses. These activities are designed to facilitate both entrance and growth into the international marketplace, including educational initiatives, technical assistance programs and services, and risk management and trade finance products.

SBA's export promotion activities for small business combine financial and technical assistance through a nationwide delivery system. Export-finance products include long-term, short-term, and revolving lines of credit through SBA's 7(a) Loan Program, administered by a staff of field-based export specialists located in U.S. Export Assistance Centers (USEACs). They work with the U.S. Department of Commerce and the Export-Import Bank of the United States, and the effort is leveraged through close collaboration with commercial lenders, Small Business Development Centers, and local business development organizations.

Available financial assistance can provide a business with up to $1.25 million, with terms up to 25 years for real estate and 15 years for equipment. Export Working Capital Program loans generally provide 12 months of renewable financing. For smaller loan amounts, SBA Export Express has a streamlined, quick approval process for businesses needing up to $250,000. Technical assistance includes making available to current and potential small-business exporters export training, export legal assistance, and collaboration with the 30 Small Business

Development Centers with international trade expertise and the Government's USA Trade Information Center.

SBA is required to work with the Government's international trade agencies to ensure that small business is adequately represented in bilateral and multilateral trade negotiations. OIT represents SBA and the Government on two official U.S. Government-sponsored multilateral organizations concerned with small business: the Organization for Economic Cooperation and Development and Asia-Pacific Economic Cooperation. SBA's trade policy involvement is carried out with the U.S. Trade Representative and the Commerce Department's International Trade Administration. Private sector input on trade policy is achieved through participation with the small-business Industry Sector Advisory Committee on international trade. OIT also lends support to the Government's key trade initiatives, such as Trade Promotion Authority, the Central American Free Trade Area, and the Free Trade Area of the Americas. The Commerce and State Departments, the Agency for International Development, and the U.S. Trade Representative look to the SBA to share ideas and provide small-business technical expertise to certain countries.

OIT's office in Washington, DC, coordinates SBA's participation/operation of USEACs, including budget, policy, and administration. It participates in a variety of interagency trade efforts and financial programs. OIT provides representations to the Cabinet-level Trade Promotion Coordinating Committee concerning trade and international economic policy. It also participates on the Industry Sector Advisory Council on Small Business International Trade and the congressionally sponsored Task Force on Small Business International Trade. SBA's Administrator is also a sitting member of the President's Export Council.

OIT's field offices provide a nationwide network of service delivery for small-business exporters. Full-time SBA export specialists staff 16 USEACs. Their outreach efforts are supplemented by the 68 SBA district offices staffed by employees with collateral duties as international trade officers.

For further information, contact the Office of International Trade. Phone, 202–205–6720. Internet, http://www.sba.gov/oit.

Venture Capital   The Small Business Investment Company (SBIC) program was created in 1958 to fill the gap between the availability of venture capital and the needs of small businesses in startup and growth situations. The structure of the program is unique in that SBICs are privately owned and managed venture capital funds, licensed and regulated by the SBA, that use their own capital plus funds borrowed with an SBA guarantee to make equity and debt investments in qualifying small businesses. The New Markets Venture Capital (NMVC) program is a sister program focused on low-income areas, which augments the contribution made by SBICs to small businesses in the United States. In addition, NMVC companies may make technical assistance grants to potential portfolio companies.

The Government itself does not make direct investments or target specific industries in the SBIC program. Fund portfolio management and investment decisions are left to qualified private fund managers. To obtain an SBIC license, an experienced team of private equity managers must secure minimum commitments from private investors. SBICs may only invest in small businesses having net worth of less than $18 million and average aftertax income for the previous 2 years of less than $6 million.

For further information, contact the Investment Division. Phone, 202–205–6510. Internet, http://www.sba.gov/inv.

HUBZone Program   The HUBZone Program provides Federal contracting assistance for qualified small businesses located in historically underutilized business zones in an effort to increase employment, capital investment, and economic development in these areas, including Indian reservations. The Office coordinates efforts with other Federal agencies and local municipal governments to leverage resources to assist qualified small businesses located in HUBZone areas. The program provides for set-asides, sole source awards, and price evaluation preferences for HUBZone small businesses and establishes goals for awards to such firms.

For further information on the HUBZone Program, call 202–205–6731. Email, hubzone@sba.gov. Internet, http://www.sba.gov/hubzone.

Business Development   The Office of Business Development is responsible for the 8(a) Business Development Program. The Office assists small businesses by providing access to capital and credit, business counseling, training workshops, technical guidance, and assistance with contracts and loans. Its primary business development tools are the Mentor-Protégé Program and the 7(j) Management and Technical Assistance Program.

For further information, call the Office of Business Development. Phone, 202–205–5852. Internet, http://www.sba.gov/about-offices-content/1/2896.

Native American Affairs   The Office of Native American Affairs was established to assist and encourage the creation, development, and expansion of Native American-owned small businesses by developing and implementing initiatives designed to address those difficulties encountered by Native Americans as they start, develop, and expand small businesses. In addition, in an effort to address the unique conditions encountered by reservation-based entrepreneurs, the Office is developing a web-based resource entitled the "Tribal Self Assessment Tool." It is intended to allow tribal nations to assess their vision and goals relative to their governance structure, culture, capabilities, and resources. The tool is free and will be available online.

For further information, contact the Office of Native American Affairs. Phone, 202–205–7364. Internet, http://www.sba.gov/naa.

Regulatory Fairness Program   Congress established the National Ombudsman and 10 Regulatory Fairness Boards in 1996 as part of the Small Business Regulatory Enforcement Fairness Act (SBREFA). The National Ombudsman's primary mission is to assist small businesses when they experience excessive or unfair federal regulatory enforcement actions, such as repetitive audits or investigations, excessive fines, penalties, threats, retaliation or other unfair enforcement action by a Federal agency. The National Ombudsman receives comments from small-business concerns and acts as a liaison between them and Federal agencies. Comments received from small businesses are forwarded to Federal agencies for review and Federal agencies are requested to consider the fairness of their enforcement action. A copy of the agency's response is sent to the small business owner by the Office of the National Ombudsman. In some cases, fines have been lowered or eliminated and decisions changed in favor of the small-business owner.

Each of the Regulatory Fairness Boards (RegFair) has five volunteer members who are owners, operators, or officers of small-business concerns that are appointed by the SBA Administrator for 3-year terms. Each RegFair Board meets at least annually with the Ombudsman on matters of concern to small businesses relating to the enforcement or compliance activities of Federal agencies; reports to the Ombudsman on substantiated instances of excessive enforcement; and, prior to publication, provides comment on the annual report to Congress.

For further information, contact the Office of the National Ombudsman. Phone, 202–205–2417 or 888–734–3247. Internet, http://www.sba.gov/ombudsman.

Small Business Development Centers   The Office of Small Business Development Centers (OSBDC) provides counseling and training to existing and prospective small-business owners at more than 950 service locations in every State, Puerto Rico, the U.S. Virgin Islands, Guam, and American Samoa. OSBDC develops national policies and goals, establishes standards for the selection and performance of its Small Business Development Centers (SBDCs), monitors compliance with applicable Office of Management and Budget circulars and laws, and implements new approaches to improve existing centers. OSBDC also oversees 63 lead centers and maintains liaison with other Federal, State, and local agencies and private organizations whose activities relate to its centers. It also assesses how the program is affected by substantive developments and policies in other SBA areas, Government agencies, and the private sector.

The Small Business Development Center Program is a cooperative effort of the private sector, the educational community, and Federal, State, and local governments. The program enhances local economic development by providing small businesses with the management and technical assistance they need to succeed. It also provides services such as development of business plans, manufacturing assistance, financial packages, procurement contracts, and international trade assistance. Special areas include ecommerce; technology transfer; IRS, EPA, and OSHA regulatory compliance; research and development; defense economic transition assistance; disaster recovery assistance; and market research. Based on client need assessments, business trends, and individual business requirements, SBDCs modify their services to meet the evolving needs of the small-business community.

For further information, contact the Office of Small Business Development Centers. Phone, 202–205–6766. Internet, http://www.sba.gov/about-offices-content/1/700.

Surety Bonds   Through its Surety Bond Guarantee Program, SBA helps small and emerging contractors to obtain the bonding necessary for them to bid on and receive contracts up to $5 million. SBA guarantees bonds that are issued by participating surety companies and reimburses between 70 percent and 90 percent of losses and expenses incurred should a small business default on the contract. Construction, service, or supply contractors are eligible for the program if they, together with their affiliates, meet the size standard for the primary industry in which the small business is engaged, as defined by the North American Industry Classification System (NAICS).

For further information, contact the Office of Surety Guarantees. Phone, 202–205–6540. Internet, http://www.sba.gov/osg.

Technology   The Office of Technology has authority and responsibility for directing and monitoring the Governmentwide activities of the Small Business Innovation Research Program (SBIR) and the Small Business Technology Transfer Program (STTR). The Office develops and issues policy directives for the general conduct of the programs within the Federal Government and maintains a source file and information program to provide each interested and qualified small-business concern with information on opportunities to compete for SBIR and STTR program awards. The Office also coordinates with each participating Federal agency in developing a master release schedule of all program solicitations; publishes the Presolicitation Announcement quarterly online, which contains pertinent facts on upcoming solicitations; and surveys and monitors program operations within the Federal Government and reports on the progress of the programs each year to Congress.

The Office has four main objectives: to expand and improve SBIR and STTR; to increase private sector commercialization of technology developed through Federal research and development; to increase small-business participation in Federal research and development; and to improve the dissemination of information concerning SBIR and STTR, particularly with regard to participation by women-owned small-business concerns and by socially and economically disadvantaged small-business concerns.

For further information, contact the Office of Technology. Phone, 202–205–6450. Email, technology@sba.gov.

Veterans Affairs   The Office of Veterans Business Development (OVBD) is responsible for the formulation, execution, and promotion of policies and programs that provide assistance to small-business concerns owned and controlled by veterans and service-disabled veterans, which includes reserve component members of the U.S. military. Additionally, OVBD serves as an ombudsman for the full consideration of veterans in all programs of the Administration.

OVBD provides counseling and works with every SBA program to ensure that veterans receive special consideration in the operation of that program. OVBD also provides numerous tools, such as the Vet Gazette newsletter, Reserve and Guard business assistance kits, program design assistance, and training events. Additionally, OVBD manages five Veterans Business Outreach Centers to provide outreach, directed referrals, and tailored entrepreneurial development services such as business training, counseling, and mentoring to veterans, including service-disabled veterans, and reservists. These Centers provide an in-depth resource for existing and potential veteran entrepreneurs. The Office also coordinates SBA collaborative efforts with veterans service organizations; the Departments of Defense, Labor, and Veterans Affairs; the National Veterans Business Development Corporation; State departments of veterans affairs; the National Committee for Employer Support of the Guard and Reserve; the Department of Defense Yellow Ribbon Reintegration Program; and other public, civic, and private organizations to ensure that the entrepreneurial needs of veterans, service-disabled veterans, and self-employed members of the Reserve and National Guard are being met.

For further information, contact the Office of Veterans Business Development. Phone, 202–205–6773. Internet, http://www.sba.gov/vets.

Women's Business Ownership   The Office of Women's Business Ownership (OWBO) provides assistance to current and potential women business owners and acts as their advocate in the public and private sectors. OWBO assists women in becoming full partners in economic development by providing business training, counseling, mentoring, and other assistance through representatives in local SBA offices, Women's Business Centers (WBCs), and mentoring roundtables. Each WBC is tailored to meet the needs of its individual community and places a special emphasis on helping women who are socially and economically

disadvantaged. Assistance covers every stage of business, from startup to going public. There are WBCs in almost every State and U.S. Territory.

OWBO works with other SBA programs, Federal agencies, and private sector organizations to leverage its resources and improve opportunities for women-owned businesses to access Federal procurement and international trade opportunities. OWBO also works with the National Women's Business Council and the Department of Labor to maintain the most current research on women's business ownership.

SBA has loan guaranty programs to help women access the credit and capital they need to start and grow successful businesses. The 7(a) Loan Guaranty Program offers a number of effective ways to finance business needs, including unsecured smaller loans and revolving lines of credit. The 504 Program provides long-term, fixed-rate financing for major fixed assets, such as land and buildings, through certified development programs. Equity financing is available through the Small Business Investment Company Program. The Microloan Program offers direct small loans, combined with business assistance, through SBA-licensed intermediaries nationwide. The SBA does not offer grants for small businesses.

For further information, contact the Women's Business Ownership representative in your SBA district office. Phone, 202–205–6673. Email, owbo@sba.gov. Internet, http://www.sba.gov/aboutsba/sbaprograms/onlinewbc/index.html.

Field Operations   The Office of Field Operations provides management direction and oversight to SBA's 10 regional and 68 district offices. It serves as the liaison between the district offices, the Administration's program delivery system, and the headquarters administrative and program offices.

A complete listing of the regional, district, and disaster field offices of the SBA, including addresses, telephone numbers, and key officials, is available online.

For further information, contact the Office of Field Operations. Phone, 202–205–6808. Internet, http://www.sba.gov/about-offices-content/1/37.

Sources of Information

Electronic Access The U.S. Business Adviser is available online at http://business.usa.gov/. To access the Administration's electronic bulletin board by using a modem, use one of the following phone numbers: 800–697–4636 (limited access), 900–463–4636 (full access), or 202–401–9600 (Washington, DC, metropolitan area). To access general information on the Small Business Administration online, use the link below. Internet, http://ftp.sbaonline.sba.gov/.

General Information Contact the nearest Small Business Administration field office, or call the SBA answer desk.

Phone, 800–827–5722. Fax, 202–205–7064. TDD, 704–344–6640. Email, answerdesk@sba.gov. Internet, http://www.sba.gov/about-sba/what_we_do/contact_sba.

Public Affairs For public inquiries and small-business advocacy affairs, contact the Office of Public Communications and Public Liaison, 409 Third Street SW., Washington, DC 20416. Phone, 202–205–6740. Internet, http://www.sba.gov/about-sba/sba_newsroom.

Publications A free copy of "The Resource Directory for Small Business Management," a listing of for-sale publications and videotapes, is available from local SBA offices or the SBA answer desk.

For further information, contact the Office of Public Communications and Public Liaison, Small Business Administration, 409 Third Street SW., Washington, DC 20416. Phone, 202–205–6740. Email, answerdesk@sba.gov. Internet, http://www.sba.gov/.

SOCIAL SECURITY ADMINISTRATION

6401 Security Boulevard, Baltimore, MD 21235
Phone, 410–965–1234. Internet, http://www.socialsecurity.gov.

Commissioner	CAROLYN W. COLVIN, *Acting*
Deputy Commissioner	CAROLYN W. COLVIN
Chief of Staff	JAMES A. KISSKO
Deputy Chief of Staff	KATHERINE A. THORNTON
Executive Secretary	KARENA L. KILGORE
Chief Actuary	STEPHEN C. GOSS
Deputy Commissioner for Communications	DOUGLAS K. WALKER
Deputy Commissioner for Budget, Finance, and Management	PETER D. SPENCER
Deputy Commissioner for Disability Adjudication and Review	GLENN E. SKLAR
Deputy Commissioner for Human Resources	REGINALD F. WELLS
Deputy Commissioner for Legislation and Congressional Affairs	SCOTT L. FREY
Deputy Commissioner for Operations	NANCY A. BERRYHILL
Deputy Commissioner for Retirement and Disability Policy	MARIANNA LACANFORA, *Acting*
Deputy Commissioner for Systems and Chief Information Officer	WILLIAM B. ZIELINSKI
General Counsel	DAVID F. BLACK
Inspector General	PATRICK P. O'CARROLL
Chief Strategic Officer	RUBY D. BURRELL

[For the Social Security Administration statement of organization, see the Code of Federal Regulations, Title 20, Part 422]

The Social Security Administration manages the retirement, survivors, and disability insurance programs that are known as Social Security; it administers the Supplemental Security Income program for the aged, blind, and disabled; and it assigns Social Security numbers to U.S. citizens and maintains earnings records based on those numbers.

The Social Security Administration (SSA) was established by Reorganization Plan No. 2 of 1946 (5 U.S.C. app.), effective July 16, 1946. It became an independent agency in the executive branch by the Social Security Independence and Program Improvements Act of 1994 (42 U.S.C. 901), effective March 31, 1995.

The SSA is headed by a Commissioner, whom the President appoints with the advice and consent of the Senate.

By law, the Deputy Commissioner assists in administering the programs necessary to accomplish the Administration's mission. The Deputy Commissioner performs duties that the Commissioner, Chief Financial Officer, Chief Information Officer, General Counsel, Chief Actuary, and Inspector General assign or delegate to him or her.

Programs and Activities

Old-Age, Survivors, and Disability Insurance   The agency administers social insurance programs that provide monthly benefits to retired and disabled workers, to their spouses and children, and to survivors of insured workers. Financing is under a system of contributory social insurance, whereby employees, employers, and the self-employed pay contributions that are pooled in special trust funds. When earnings stop or decrease because the worker retires, dies, or becomes disabled, monthly cash benefits are paid to supplement the family's reduced income.

Supplemental Security Income   The SSA administers this needs-based program for the aged, blind, and disabled. A basic Federal monthly payment is financed by general revenue, rather than from a special trust fund. Some States, choosing to provide payments to supplement the benefits, have agreements with the Administration under which it administers the supplemental payments for those States.

Internet, http://www.socialsecurity.gov/disabilityssi/ssi.html.

Medicare   While the administration of Medicare is the responsibility of the Centers for Medicare and Medicaid Services, SSA provides Medicare assistance to the public through SSA field offices and call centers. It adjudicates requests for hearings and appeals of Medicare claims.

Internet, http://www.socialsecurity.gov/medicare/.

Black Lung   By agreement with the Department of Labor, the SSA assists in the administration of the black lung benefits provisions of the Federal Coal Mine Health and Safety Act of 1969, as amended (30 U.S.C. 901).

Regional Offices   The Administration's operations are decentralized to provide services at the local level. Each of the 10 SSA regions, under the overall direction of its regional commissioner, contains a network of field offices and call centers. These offices and centers provide liaison between the SSA and public. The Administration operates over 1,250 field offices, 35 Teleservice centers, 14 Social Security card centers, 6 processing centers, and its Office of Central Operations. These centers are responsible for informing the public of the purposes and provisions of Social Security programs and their rights and responsibilities; assisting with claims filed for retirement, survivors, disability, or health insurance benefits, black lung benefits, or Supplemental Security Income; developing and adjudicating claims; assisting certain beneficiaries in claiming reimbursement for medical expenses; developing cases involving earnings records, coverage, and fraud-related questions; making rehabilitation service referrals; and assisting claimants in filing appeals on SSA determinations of benefit entitlement or amount.

Internet, http://www.socialsecurity.gov/agency/contact/.

SOCIAL SECURITY ADMINISTRATION

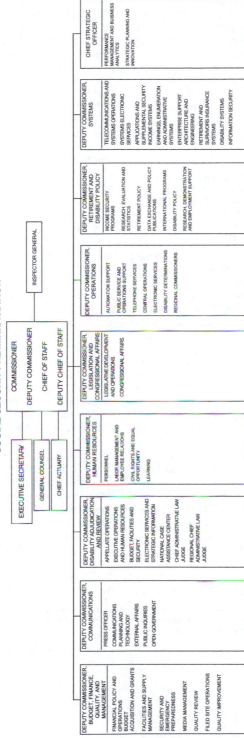

COMMISSIONER
DEPUTY COMMISSIONER
CHIEF OF STAFF
DEPUTY CHIEF OF STAFF

INSPECTOR GENERAL

EXECUTIVE SECRETARY
GENERAL COUNSEL
CHIEF ACTUARY

DEPUTY COMMISSIONER, BUDGET, FINANCE, QUALITY, AND MANAGEMENT
FINANCIAL POLICY AND OPERATIONS
BUDGET
ACQUISITION AND GRANTS
FACILITIES AND SUPPLY MANAGEMENT
SECURITY AND EMERGENCY PREPAREDNESS
MEDIA MANAGEMENT
QUALITY REVIEW
FILED SITE OPERATIONS
QUALITY IMPROVEMENT

DEPUTY COMMISSIONER, COMMUNICATIONS
PRESS OFFICER
COMMUNICATIONS PLANNING AND TECHNOLOGY
EXTERNAL AFFAIRS
PUBLIC INQUIRIES
OPEN GOVERNMENT

DEPUTY COMMISSIONER, DISABILITY ADJUDICATION AND REVIEW
APPELLATE OPERATIONS
EXECUTIVE OPERATIONS AND HUMAN RESOURCES
BUDGET, FACILITIES AND SECURITY
ELECTRONIC SERVICES AND STRATEGIC INFORMATION
NATIONAL CASE ASSISTANCE CENTER
CHIEF ADMINISTRATIVE LAW JUDGE
REGIONAL CHIEF ADMINISTRATIVE LAW JUDGE

DEPUTY COMMISSIONER, HUMAN RESOURCES
PERSONNEL
LABOR MANAGEMENT AND EMPLOYEE RELATIONS
CIVIL RIGHTS AND EQUAL OPPORTUNITY
LEARNING

DEPUTY COMMISSIONER, LEGISLATION AND CONGRESSIONAL AFFAIRS
LEGISLATIVE DEVELOPMENT AND OPERATIONS
CONGRESSIONAL AFFAIRS

DEPUTY COMMISSIONER, OPERATIONS
AUTOMATION SUPPORT
PUBLIC SERVICE AND OPERATIONS SUPPORT
TELEPHONE SERVICES
CENTRAL OPERATIONS
ELECTRONIC SERVICES
DISABILITY DETERMINATIONS
REGIONAL COMMISSIONERS

DEPUTY COMMISSIONER, RETIREMENT AND DISABILITY POLICY
INCOME SECURITY PROGRAMS
RESEARCH, EVALUATION AND STATISTICS
RETIREMENT POLICY
DATA EXCHANGE AND POLICY PUBLICATIONS
INTERNATIONAL PROGRAMS
DISABILITY POLICY
RESEARCH, DEMONSTRATION AND EMPLOYMENT SUPPORT

DEPUTY COMMISSIONER, SYSTEMS
TELECOMMUNICATIONS AND SYSTEMS OPERATIONS
SYSTEMS ELECTRONIC SERVICES
APPLICATIONS AND SUPPLEMENTAL SECURITY INCOME SYSTEMS
EARNINGS, ENUMERATION AND ADMINISTRATIVE SYSTEMS
ENTERPRISE SUPPORT ARCHITECTURE AND ENGINEERING
RETIREMENT AND SURVIVORS INSURANCE SYSTEMS
DISABILITY SYSTEMS
INFORMATION SECURITY

CHIEF STRATEGIC OFFICER
PERFORMANCE MANAGEMENT AND BUSINESS ANALYTICS
STRATEGIC PLANNING AND INNOVATION

Hearing Offices   SSA also administers a nationwide hearings and appeals program that provides a mechanism for individuals dissatisfied with determinations affecting their rights to and amounts of benefits or their participation in programs under the Social Security Act. The act allows for administrative appeals of these determinations in accordance with the requirements of the Administrative Procedure and Social Security Acts. SSA has approximately 168 hearing offices located in the 10 SSA regions.

For further information, contact the Social Security Administration. Phone, 800–772–1213. TTY, 800–325–0778. Internet, http://www.socialsecurity. gov/appeals/about_odar.html.

Sources of Information

Address correspondence on the following subjects to the appropriate office, Social Security Administration, 6401 Security Boulevard, Baltimore, MD 21235.
Contracts and Small Business Activities Contact the Office of Acquisitions and Grants. Phone, 410–965–7467. Internet, http://www.socialsecurity.gov/oag/.
Electronic Access   Information regarding the Social Security Administration may be obtained through the Internet at www. socialsecurity.gov.
Employment   Current job openings are posted on the Federal Government's free web-based job board at https://www. usajobs.gov/. For information on careers with the Social Security Administration, use the link below. Internet, http://www. socialsecurity.gov/careers/.
General Information   The Office of the Deputy Commissioner for Operations manages SSA's toll-free public service telephone. Phone, 800–772–1213. TTY, 800–325–0778.
Inspector General   The Office of the Inspector General has a toll-free hotline

for reporting abuse, fraud, and waste. The hotline operates between 10 a.m. and 4 p.m. eastern standard time (phone, 800–269–0271; TTY, 866–501–2101). Persons may submit allegations by fax at 410–597–0118, or by mail to Social Security Fraud Hotline, P.O. Box 17785, Baltimore, MD 21235–7768. An online form is also available for reporting allegations. Internet, https://www. socialsecurity.gov/fraudreport/oig/public_ fraud_reporting/.
Publications   The Office of the Deputy Commissioner for Budget, Finance, Quality, and Management and the Office of Media Management, publish numerous pamphlets on SSA programs. The Administration also collects a large volume of economic, demographic, and other data in furtherance of its program mission. Basic data on employment, payments, and other items of program interest are published regularly in the "Social Security Bulletin," its "Annual Statistical Supplement," and in special releases and reports on selected topics of public interest. Single copies may be obtained at any local office or by calling 800–772–1213. Requests for bulk orders of publications should be sent to the Social Security Administration, Center for Forms, Publications and Postal Policy, 1300 Annex Building, 6401 Security Boulevard, Baltimore, MD 21235–6401. Over 150 publications in English, Spanish, and other languages are available on the SSA's Web site. Internet, http://www.socialsecurity.gov/pubs/.
Speakers and Films   Public or private groups and organizations can request SSA speakers, films, and exhibits. These resources are available nationwide, and requests should be directed to a local Social Security office. Internet, https:// secure.ssa.gov/ICON/main.jsp.

For further information, contact the Office of Public Inquiries, Social Security Administration, 6401 Security Boulevard, Windsor Park Building, Baltimore, MD 21235. Phone, 410–965–0707. Internet, http://www. socialsecurity.gov/agency/contact/mail.html.

TENNESSEE VALLEY AUTHORITY
400 West Summit Hill Drive, Knoxville, TN 37902
Phone, 865–632–2101. Internet, http://www.tva.com.

Chairman	JOSEPH H. RITCH
Directors	MARILYN A. BROWN, V. LYNN EVANS, BARBARA S. HASKEW, RICHARD C. HOWORTH, PETER MAHURIN, MICHAEL R. MCWHERTER, WILLIAM B. SANSOM, (VACANCY)
President and Chief Executive Officer	WILLIAM D. JOHNSON
Executive Vice President and Chief External Relations Officer	ROBIN E. MANNING
Executive Vice President and Chief Financial Officer	JOHN M. THOMAS, III
Executive Vice President and Chief Nuclear Officer	JOSEPH P. GRIMES
Executive Vice President and Chief Operating Officer	CHARLES G. PARDEE
Executive Vice President and General Counsel	RALPH E. RODGERS
Senior Vice President, Human Resources and Communications	KATHERINE J. BLACK
Senior Vice President, Nuclear Construction	MICHAEL D. SKAGGS
Senior Vice President, Shared Services	ROBIN E. MANNING

The Tennessee Valley Authority conducts a unified program of resource development for the advancement of economic growth in the Tennessee Valley region.

The Tennessee Valley Authority (TVA) is a wholly owned Government corporation created by the act of May 18, 1933 (16 U.S.C. 831–831dd). All functions of the Authority are vested in its nine-member Board of Directors, the members of which are appointed by the President with the advice and consent of the Senate. The Board designates one member as Chairman.

Programs and Activities

TVA's programs and activities include flood control, navigation, electric power production and transmission, recreation improvement, water supply and water quality management, environmental stewardship, and economic development.

TVA's electric power program is financially self-supporting and operates as part of an independent system with TVA's system of dams on the Tennessee River and its larger tributaries. These dams provide flood regulation on the Tennessee River and contribute to regulation of the lower Ohio and Mississippi Rivers. The system maintains a continuous 9-foot-draft navigation channel for the length of the 650-mile Tennessee River main stream, from Paducah, KY, to Knoxville, TN. The dams harness the power of the rivers to produce electricity. They also provide other benefits, notably outdoor recreation and water supply.

TVA operates the river management system and provides assistance to State and local governments in reducing local flood problems. It also works with other agencies to encourage full and effective use of the navigable waterway by industry and commerce.

TVA is the wholesale power supplier for 155 local municipal and cooperative electric systems serving customers in parts of 7 States. It supplies power to 56 industries and Federal installations whose power requirements are large or unusual. Power to meet these demands is supplied from dams, coal-fired powerplants, nuclear powerplants, combustion turbine and diesel installations, solar energy sites, wind turbines, a methane gas facility, and a pumped-storage hydroelectric plant; U.S. Corps of Engineers dams in the Cumberland Valley; and Aluminum Company of America dams, whose operation is coordinated with TVA's system.

Economic development is at the heart of TVA's mission of making the Tennessee Valley a better place to live. A healthy economy means quality jobs, more investment in the region, sustainable growth, and opportunities for residents in the southeastern region to build more prosperous lives. TVA Economic Development takes a regional approach to economic growth by partnering with power distributors and both public and private organizations to attract new investments and quality jobs, supporting retention and growth of existing businesses and industries, preparing communities for leadership and economic growth, and providing financial and technical services.

Sources of Information

Citizen Participation   TVA Communications, 400 West Summit Hill Drive, Knoxville, TN 37902–1499. Phone, 865–632–2101.
Contracts   Purchasing, WT 3A, 400 West Summit Hill Drive, Knoxville, TN 37902–1499. Phone, 865–632–4796. This office will direct inquiries to the appropriate procurement officer.
Economic Development   OCP 2A–NST, One Century Place, 26 Century

Boulevard, Suite 100, Nashville, TN 37214. Mailing address: P.O. Box 292409, Nashville, TN 37229–2409. Phone, 615–232–6051. For information on economic development, visit TVA's Economic Development Web page using the link below. Internet, http://www.tva.com/econdev/index.htm.
Electric Power Supply   1101 Market Street, Chattanooga, TN 37402. Phone, 423–751–6000.
Electric Rates   One Century Plaza, 26 Century Boulevard, Suite 100, Nashville, TN 37214–3685.
Employment   For information on employment opportunities, visit TVA's Employment Web page using the link below. Internet, http://www.tva.com/employment/index.htm.
Library Services   TVA Research Library, 400 West Summit Hill Drive, Knoxville, TN 37902–1499. Phone, 865–632–3464. Chattanooga Office Complex, LP4A–C, 1101 Market Street, Chattanooga, TN 37402–2791. Phone, 423–751–4913. P.O. Box 1010, CTR 1E–M, Muscle Shoals, AL 35662. Phone, 256–386–2872.
Maps   Maps Information and Photo Records, HV 1C–C, 2837 Hickory Valley Road, Chattanooga, TN 37421. Phone, 423–499–6285 or 800–627–7882.
Publications   TVA Communications, WT 7D, 400 West Summit Hill Drive, Knoxville, TN 37902–1499. Phone, 865–632–6000.

For further information, contact the Tennessee Valley Authority at either 400 West Summit Hill Drive, Knoxville, TN 37902–1499. Phone, 865–632–3199. One Massachusetts Avenue NW., Washington, DC 20044. Phone, 202–898–2999. Internet, http://www.tva.gov.

TRADE AND DEVELOPMENT AGENCY

1000 Wilson Boulevard, Suite 1600, Arlington, VA 22209–3901
Phone, 703–875–4357. Fax, 703–875–4009. Internet, http://www.ustda.gov.

Director	LEOCADIA I. ZAK
Deputy Director	PEGGY PHILBIN
General Counsel	ENOH T. EBONG
Chief of Staff	CLARK JENNINGS
Resource Advisor	MICHAEL HILLIER
Director, Congressional Affairs and Public Relations	THOMAS R. HARDY

Evaluation Officer	DIANA ROSSITER
Chief Financial Officer	LIZ GUSTAFSON
Chief, Office of Acquisition Management	GARTH HIBBERT
Administrative Officer	CAROLYN HUM
Grants Administrator	PATRICIA DAUGHETEE
Regional Directors	
East Asia	CARL B. KRESS
Latin America and Caribbean	NATHAN YOUNGE
Middle East, North Africa, Europe and Eurasia	CARL B. KRESS
South and Southeast Asia	HENRY D. STEINGASS
Sub-Saharan Africa	LIDA FITTS, *Acting*
Director for Global Programs-Worldwide	ANDREA LUPO

The Trade and Development Agency advances economic development and U.S. commercial interest in developing and middle-income countries.

The Trade and Development Program was established on July 1, 1980, as a component organization of the International Development Cooperation Agency. Section 2204 of the Omnibus Trade and Competitiveness Act of 1988 (22 U.S.C. 2421) made it a separate component agency. The organization was renamed the Trade and Development Agency (USTDA) and made an independent agency within the executive branch of the Federal Government on October 28, 1992, by the Jobs Through Exports Act of 1992 (22 U.S.C. 2421).

USTDA is a foreign assistance agency that delivers its program commitments through overseas grants and contracts with U.S. firms. The agency helps companies create U.S. jobs through the export of U.S. goods and services for priority development projects in emerging economies. USTDA links U.S. businesses to export opportunities by funding project planning activities, pilot projects, and reverse trade missions while creating sustainable infrastructure and economic growth in partner countries.

USTDA provides grant funding to overseas project sponsors for the planning of projects that support the development of modern infrastructure and an open trading system. The hallmark of USTDA development assistance has always involved building partnerships between U.S. companies and overseas project sponsors to bring proven private sector solutions to developmental challenges.

USTDA works with other U.S. Government agencies to bring their particular expertise and resources to a development objective. These agencies include the Departments of State, the Treasury, Commerce, Transportation, and Energy; the Office of the U.S. Trade Representative; the Export-Import Bank of the United States; and the Overseas Private Investment Corporation.

Activities   USTDA funds various forms of technical assistance, training, early investment analysis, reverse trade missions, and business workshops that support the development of a modern infrastructure and a fair and open trading environment. Working closely with a foreign project sponsor, USTDA makes its funds available on the condition that the foreign entity contract with a U.S. firm to perform the activity funded. This affords American firms market entry, exposure, and information, thus helping them to establish a position in markets that are otherwise difficult to penetrate. USTDA is involved in many sectors, including transportation, energy, and information and communications technologies.

USTDA-funded studies evaluate the technical, economic, and financial aspects of a development project. They also advise the host nation about the availability of U.S. goods and services and can be used by financial institutions in assessing the creditworthiness of an undertaking. Grants are based on an official request for assistance made by the sponsoring government or private sector organization of a developing or middle-income nation.

TRADE AND DEVELOPMENT AGENCY

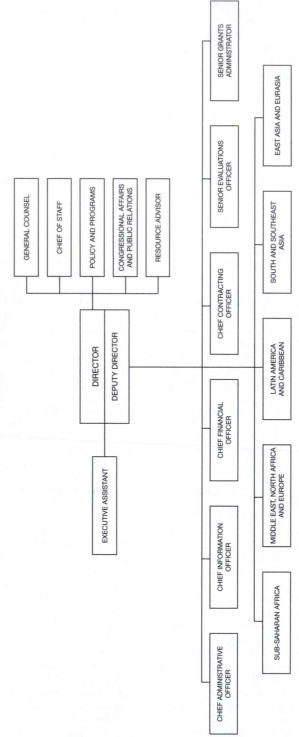

Sources of Information

Requests for proposals to conduct USTDA-funded technical assistance and feasibility studies or definitional missions involving review of projects under consideration for USTDA support are listed on the Federal Business Opportunities (FBO) Web site. Links to the FBO postings can be found at www.ustda.gov. In an effort to provide timely information on Agency-supported activities, USTDA sends out an electronic newsletter with current business opportunities and a calendar of events on a biweekly basis. A free email subscription is available online. Agency news, reports, and lists of current business opportunities and upcoming events are also available online. USTDA's library maintains final reports on the Agency's activities. The reports are available for public review on weekdays, from 8:30 a.m. to 5:30 p.m. Regional program inquiries should be directed to the assigned Regional Director or Country Manager. Phone, 703–875–4357.

For further information, contact the U.S. Trade and Development Agency, 1000 Wilson Boulevard, Suite 1600, Arlington, VA 22209–3901. Phone, 703–875–4357. Fax, 703–875–4009. Email, info@ustda.gov. Internet, http://www.ustda.gov.

UNITED STATES AGENCY FOR INTERNATIONAL DEVELOPMENT

1300 Pennsylvania Avenue NW., Washington, DC 20523
Phone, 202–712–0000. Internet, http://www.usaid.gov.

Administrator	RAJIV SHAH
Deputy Administrator	ALFONSO E. LENHARDT
Counselor	SUSAN REICHLE
Chief of Staff	MARGART C. SULLIVAN
Associate Administrator	MARK FEIERSTEIN
Assistant Administrator for Africa	EARL W. GAST
Assistant Administrator for Asia	DENISE ROLLINS
Assistant Administrator for Europe and Eurasia	PAIGE ALEXANDER
Assistant Administrator for Middle East	ALINA L. ROMANOWSKI, *Acting*
Assistant Administrator for Global Health	ARIEL PABLOS-MENDEZ
Assistant Administrator for Economic Growth, Education and Environment	ERIC G. POSTEL
Assistant Administrator for Democracy, Conflict and Humanitarian Assistance	NANCY E. LINDBORG
Assistant to the Administrator, Bureau for Food Security	TJADA D'OYEN MCKENNA, *Acting*
Senior Deputy Assistant Administrator, Bureau for Management	ANGELIQUE CRUMBLY
Assistant Administrator for Legislative and Public Affairs	T. CHARLES COOPER
Assistant to the Administrator, Policy, Planning and Learning	J. ALEX THIER

[For the Agency for International Development statement of organization, see the Federal Register of Aug. 26, 1987, 52 FR 32174]

The United States Agency for International Development works to eradicate extreme global poverty and to enable resilient and democratic societies realize their potential.

The United States Agency for International Development (USAID) is an independent Federal agency established by 22 U.S.C. 6563. Its principal statutory authority is the Foreign Assistance Act of 1961, as amended (22 U.S.C. 2151 et seq.). USAID serves as the focal point within the Government for economic matters affecting U.S. relations with developing countries. It administers international economic and humanitarian assistance programs. The Administrator is under the direct authority and foreign policy guidance of the Secretary of State.

Programs

USAID works in over 100 countries to promote broadly shared economic prosperity, strengthen democracy and good governance, protect human rights, improve global health, advance food security and agriculture, improve environmental sustainability, further education, help societies prevent and recover from conflicts, and provide humanitarian assistance in the wake of natural and manmade disasters.

Democracy   USAID promotes the transition to and consolidation of democratic regimes throughout the world. Programs focus on such problems as human rights abuses; misperceptions of democracy and free-market capitalism; lack of experience with democratic institutions; the absence or weakness of intermediary organizations; nonexistent, ineffectual, or undemocratic political parties; disenfranchisement of women, indigenous peoples, and minorities; failure to implement national charter documents; powerless or poorly defined democratic institutions; tainted elections; and inability to resolve conflicts peacefully.

Economic Growth   The Agency promotes broad-based economic growth by addressing factors that enhance the capacity for growth and by working to remove obstacles that obstruct individual opportunity. Programs concentrate on strengthening market economies, expanding economic opportunities for the disadvantaged in developing countries, and building human skills and capacities to facilitate broad-based participation.

Environment   Environmental programs support two strategic goals: 1) reducing long-term threats to the biosphere, particularly loss of biodiversity and change in climate; 2) promoting sustainable economic growth locally, nationally, and regionally by addressing shortsighted environmental, economic, and developmental practices. Globally, USAID programs focus on reducing sources and enhancing sinks of greenhouse gas emissions and on promoting innovative approaches to the conservation and sustainable use of the planet's biological diversity. The approach adopted to address national environmental problems differs from county to country, depending on its environmental priorities. Strategies may include improving agricultural, industrial, and natural resource management practices; strengthening public policies and institutions; dialoguing with country governments and international agencies; and environmental research and education.

Global Health and Population   The Agency improves access and quality of services for maternal and child health, nutrition, voluntary family planning, and reproductive health. It prevents and treats HIV/AIDS, malaria, and tuberculosis. It assists countries in the design and implementation of state-of-the-art public health approaches to end preventable child-maternal deaths and achieve an AIDS-free generation. The Agency takes advantage of economies of scale in procurement, technical services, and commodities. To promote sustainability, the Agency helps expand health systems and the health workforce by adopting and scaling-up proven health interventions across programs and countries. USAID also contributes to a cooperative global effort to stabilize world population growth and support women's reproductive rights. The types of population and health programs supported vary with the particular needs of individual countries and the kinds of approaches that local communities initiate and support.

UNITED STATES AGENCY FOR INTERNATIONAL DEVELOPMENT

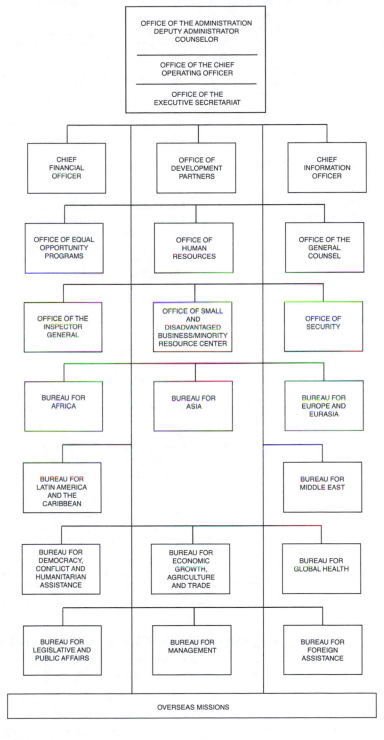

Humanitarian Assistance and Post-Crisis Transitions   The Agency gives humanitarian assistance to save lives, reduce suffering, help victims return to self-sufficiency, and reinforce democracy. Programs focus on disaster prevention, preparedness, and mitigation; timely delivery of disaster relief and short-term rehabilitation supplies and services; preservation of basic institutions of civil governance during a disaster crisis; support for democratic institutions during periods of national transition; and building and reinforcement of local capacity to anticipate and handle disasters and their aftermath.

Overseas Organizations   USAID country organizations are located in countries where a bilateral program is being implemented. The in-country organizations are subject to the direction and guidance of the chief U.S. diplomatic representative in the country, usually the Ambassador. The organizations report to the Agency's assistant administrators for the following geographic bureaus: Africa, Asia and the Near East, Europe and the New Independent States, and Latin America and the Caribbean.

The overseas program activities that involve more than one country are administered by regional offices. These offices may also have country organizational responsibilities for assigned countries. Generally, the offices are headed by a regional development officer.

Development Assistance Coordination and Representative Offices provide liaison with various international organizations and represent U.S. interests in development assistance matters. These Offices may be only partially staffed by USAID personnel and may be headed by employees of other U.S. Government agencies.

For information on and a complete list of USAID overseas missions, use the link below. Internet, http://www.usaid.gov/where-we-work.

Sources of Information

Congressional Affairs   Congressional inquiries may be directed to the Bureau for Legislative and Public Affairs, USAID/LPA, Washington, DC 20523–0001. Phone, 202–712–4340. Internet, http://www.usaid.gov/who-we-are/organization/bureaus/bureau-legislative-and-public-affairs.

Contracting and Small Business Inquiries   For information on contracting opportunities, contact the Office of Small and Disadvantaged Business Utilization, U.S. Agency for International Development, Washington, DC 20523–0001. Phone, 202–567–4730. Fax, 202–567–4740. Internet, http://www.usaid.gov/partnership-opportunities/respond-solicitation.

Employment   For information on employment opportunities, contact the Workforce Planning, Recruitment, and Personnel Systems Division, Office of Human Resources, U.S. Agency for International Development, Washington, DC 20523–0001. Internet, http://www.usaid.gov/careers.

General Inquiries   Send questions to the Bureau for Legislative and Public Affairs, USAID/LPA, Washington, DC 20523–0001. Phone, 202–712–4810. Fax, 202–216–3524. Comments, questions, and recommendations also may be sent online by using the link below and completing the form. Internet, http://www.usaid.gov/comment.

For further information, contact the United States Agency for International Development, 1300 Pennsylvania Avenue NW., Washington, DC 20523–0001. Phone, 202–712–0000. Internet, http://www.usaid.gov.

UNITED STATES COMMISSION ON CIVIL RIGHTS

1331 Pennsylvania Avenue NW., Suite 1150, Washington, DC 20425
Phone, 202–376–8128. TTY, 202–376–8116. Internet, http://www.usccr.gov.

Chairman   Martin R. Castro
Vice Chair   (VACANCY)

Commissioners

Staff Director

ROBERTA ACHTENBERG, GAIL HERIOT,
PETER N. KIRSANOW, DAVID
KLADNEY, MICHAEL YAKI, (VACANCY)
MARLENE SALLO

[For the Commission on Civil Rights statement of organization, see the Code of Federal Regulations, Title 45, Part 701]

The Commission on Civil Rights collects and studies information on discrimination or denials of equal protection of the laws because of race, color, religion, sex, age, disability, national origin, or in the administration of justice in such areas as voting rights, enforcement of Federal civil rights laws, and equal opportunity in education, employment, and housing.

The Commission on Civil Rights was first created by the Civil Rights Act of 1957, as amended, and reestablished by the United States Commission on Civil Rights Act of 1994, as amended (42 U.S.C. 1975).

Activities

The Commission conducts hearings on important civil rights issues, including issuing subpoenas for the production of documents and the attendance of witnesses; publishes studies and reports on a wide range of civil rights issues to inform and advise policymakers; holds public briefings, issues press releases, makes information publicly available online, and provides a complaint referral service to promote greater public awareness of civil rights issues, protections, and enforcement; and sustains advisory committee involvement in the national program planning to strengthen factfinding.

Regional Programs The Commission maintains 51 State Advisory Committees (SACs), one for each State and the District of Columbia. Each SAC is composed of citizen volunteers who are familiar with local and State civil rights issues. SAC members assist the Commission with factfinding, investigating, and disseminating information. The Commission seeks to ensure that advisory committees are diverse and represent a variety of backgrounds, skills, experiences, and perspectives. This diversity promotes debate and full exploration of the issues. All appointments are made in a nondiscriminatory manner. For a complete listing of the regional divisions of the U.S. Commission on Civil Rights, including addresses, telephone numbers, and areas served, use the link below.

Internet, http://www.usccr.gov/contact/regional. php.

Sources of Information

Complaints Complaints alleging denials of civil rights may be reported to Complaints Referral, 1331 Pennsylvania Avenue NW., Suite 1150 Washington, DC 20425. Phone, 202–376–8513 or 800–552–6843. Internet, http://www. usccr.gov/filing/index.php.

Employment Information is available on the "Careers" Web page. Or, contact the Human Resources Office, 1331 Pennsylvania Avenue NW., Suite 1150, Washington, DC 20425. Phone, 202–376–8364. Internet, http://www.usccr. gov/about/careers.php.

Publications A publication catalog may be obtained from the Administrative Services and Clearinghouse Division. Publications are available upon request. Contact the Administrative Services and Clearinghouse Division, 1331 Pennsylvania Avenue NW., Suite 1150, Washington, DC 20425. Phone, 202–376–8105. Internet, http:// www.dmssearch.gpo.gov/Highlighter. aspx?DocId=477&Index=D%3a%5c Websites%5cUseIndex%5cUSCCR&Hit Count=11&hits=2+5+7+19+54+56+5c+ 8b+4d8+4f0+4f4+&q1=publications.

Reading Room The National Civil Rights Clearinghouse Library is located at 1331 Pennsylvania Avenue NW., Washington, DC 20425. Phone, 202–376–8110.

UNITED STATES COMMISSION ON CIVIL RIGHTS

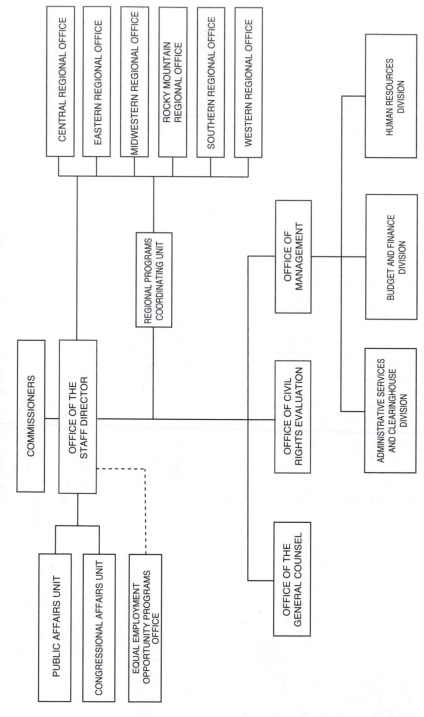

For further information, contact the Office of the Staff Director, United States Commission on Civil Rights, 1331 Pennsylvania Avenue NW., Suite 1150, Washington, DC 20425. Phone, 202–376–7700. TTY, 202–376–8116. Internet, http://www.usccr.gov.

UNITED STATES INTERNATIONAL TRADE COMMISSION

500 E Street SW., Washington, DC 20436
Phone, 202–205–2000. Internet, http://www.usitc.gov.

Chairman	IRVING A. WILLIAMSON
Vice Chairman	(VACANCY)
Commissioners	MEREDITH M. BROADBENT, DAVID S. JOHANSON, F. SCOTT KIEFF, DEAN A. PINKERT, RHONDA K. SCHMIDTLEIN
Chief Administrative Law Judge	CHARLES E. BULLOCK
Director of Operations	ROBERT B. KOOPMAN
Director, Office of Economics	(VACANCY)
Director, Office of Industries	KAREN LANEY
Director, Office of Investigations	CATHERINE B. DEFILIPPO
Director, Office of Tariff Affairs and Trade Agreements	JAMES R. HOLBEIN
Director, Office of Unfair Import Investigations	MARGARET D. MACDONALD
Director, Office of Analysis and Research Services	JAMES KENNEDY
General Counsel	DOMINIC L. BIANCHI
Director, Office of External Relations	LYN M. SCHLITT
Chief Information Officer	ROBERT N. RIESS, *Acting*
Director, Office of Information Technology Services	(VACANCY)
Director, Office of Enterprise Security Management	(VACANCY)
Chief Administrative Officer	STEPHEN MCLAUGHLIN
Director, Office of Human Resources	PATRICIA R. CONNELLY
Director, Office of Security and Support Services	ROBERT N. RIESS
Chief Financial Officer	JOHN M. ASCIENZO, *Acting*
Director, Office of Procurement	(VACANCY)
Director, Office of Finance	JOHN M. ASCIENZO
Director, Office of Budget	CHRIS SWETZ
Secretary	LISA R. BARTON, *Acting*
Inspector General	PHILIP M. HENEGHAN
Director, Office of Equal Employment Opportunity	ALTIVIA JACKSON

The United States International Trade Commission produces studies, reports, and recommendations on international trade and tariffs for the President, the U.S. Trade Representative, and congressional committees. It also conducts international trade relief investigations.

The United States International Trade Commission (USITC) is an independent agency created by the Revenue Act (39 Stat. 795) and originally named the United States Tariff Commission. The name was changed to the United States

UNITED STATES INTERNATIONAL TRADE COMMISSION

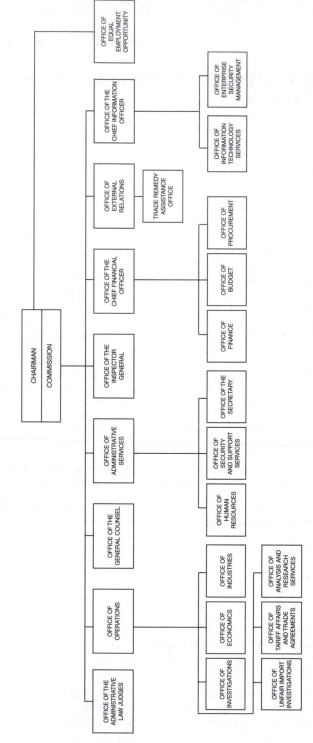

International Trade Commission by section 171 of the Trade Act of 1974 (19 U.S.C. 2231).

The President, with the advice and consent of the Senate, appoints six commissioners for 9-year terms, unless the appointment is made to fill an unexpired term. The Chairman and Vice Chairman are designated by the President for 2-year terms, and succeeding Chairmen may not be of the same political party. The Chairman generally is responsible for the administration of the Commission. Not more than three Commissioners may be members of the same political party (19 U.S.C. 1330).

Activities

The Commission performs a number of functions pursuant to the statutes referred to above. Under the Tariff Act of 1930, the Commission has broad powers of investigation relating to the customs laws of the United States and foreign countries; the volume of importation in comparison with domestic production and consumption; the conditions, causes, and effects of foreign industrial competition with United States industries; and all other factors affecting competition between articles of the United States and imported articles. The Commission is required, whenever requested, to convey its available information to the President, the House Committee on Ways and Means, and the Senate Committee on Finance. The President, Congress, or the two committees mentioned can direct the Commission to undertake investigations and studies.

To carry out these responsibilities, the Commission engages in extensive research, conducts specialized studies, and maintains a high degree of expertise in all matters relating to the commercial and international trade policies of the United States.

Imported Articles Subsidized or Sold at Less Than Fair Value   The Commission conducts preliminary-phase investigations to determine whether imports of foreign merchandise allegedly being subsidized or sold at less than fair value injure or threaten to injure an industry in the United States. If the Commission's

determination is affirmative and the Secretary of Commerce determines there is reason to believe or suspect such unfair practices are occurring, then the Commission conducts final-phase investigations to determine the injury or threat of injury to an industry.

Under the Uruguay Round Agreements Act, the Commission also conducts sunset reviews. In these reviews, the Commission evaluates whether material injury to a U.S. industry would continue or recur if the antidumping duty or countervailing duty order under review were revoked. Such injury reviews must be conducted on all antidumping duty and countervailing duty orders every 5 years for as long as the orders remain in effect.

Unfair Practices in Import Trade   The Commission applies U.S. statutory and common law of unfair competition to the importation of products into the United States and their sale. If the Commission determines that there is a violation of law, it will direct that the articles involved be excluded from entry into the United States, or it may issue cease-and-desist orders directing the person engaged in such violation to stop.

Trade Negotiations   The Commission advises the President as to the probable economic effect on the domestic industry and on consumers of modification of duties and other barriers to trade that may be considered for inclusion in any proposed trade agreement with foreign countries.

Generalized System of Preferences   With respect to articles that may be considered for preferential removal of the duty on imports from designated developing countries, the Commission advises the President as to the probable economic effect such removal will have on the domestic industry and on consumers.

Industry Adjustment to Import Competition (Global Safeguard Actions)   The Commission conducts investigations upon petition on behalf of an industry, a firm, a group of workers, or other entity representative of an industry to determine whether an article is being imported in such increased quantities as to injure or threaten to injure the domestic industry producing an article like or directly competitive with the imported article. If the Commission's finding is affirmative, it recommends to the President the action that would address such a threat and be most effective in facilitating positive adjustment by the industry to import competition. The President determines if import relief is appropriate.

The Commission reports on developments within an industry that has been granted import relief and advises the President of the probable economic effect of the reduction or elimination of the tariff increase that has been granted. The President may continue, modify, or terminate the import relief previously granted.

Imports From NAFTA Countries (Bilateral Safeguard Actions)   The Commission investigates whether, as a result of the reduction or elimination of a duty provided for under the North American Free Trade Agreement (NAFTA), a Canadian article or a Mexican article, is being imported in such increased quantities and under such conditions that imports of the article cause serious injury or (except in the case of a Canadian article) a threat of serious injury to the domestic industry producing an article that is like or directly competitive with the imported article. If the Commission's determination is in the affirmative, the Commission recommends to the President the relief that is necessary to prevent or remedy serious injury. Commission investigations under these provisions are similar procedurally to those conducted under the global safeguard action provisions.

Market Disruption From Communist Countries   The Commission conducts investigations to determine whether increased imports of an article produced in a Communist country are causing market disruption in the United States. If the Commission's determination is in the affirmative, the President may take the same action as in the case of serious injury to an industry, except that the action would apply only to imports of the article from the Communist country. Commission investigations conducted

under this provision are similar procedurally to those conducted under the global safeguard action provisions.

Import Interference With Agricultural Programs   The Commission conducts investigations, at the direction of the President, to determine whether imports or potential imports may interfere with the Department of Agriculture's agricultural programs or reduce the amount of any product processed in the United States. After investigating, the Commission discloses findings and makes recommendations. The President may then restrict the imports in question by imposing import fees or quotas. Such fees or quotas may be applied only against countries that are not members of the World Trade Organization.

Uniform Statistical Data   The Commission, in cooperation with the Secretary of the Treasury and the Secretary of Commerce, for statistical purposes, enumerates articles imported into and exported from the United States and seeks to compare such data with domestic production statistical programs.

Harmonized Tariff Schedule of the United States, Annotated   The Commission issues a publication containing the U.S. tariff schedules and related matters and considers questions concerning the arrangement of such schedules and the classification of articles.

International Trade Studies   The Commission conducts studies, investigations, and research projects on a broad range of topics relating to international trade, pursuant to requests of the President, the House Ways and Means Committee, the Senate Finance Committee, either branch of the Congress, or on its own motion. Public reports of these studies, investigations, and research projects are issued in most cases.

The Commission also keeps informed of the operation and effect of provisions relating to duties or other import restrictions of the United States contained in various trade agreements. Occasionally, the Commission is required by statute to perform specific trade-related studies.

Sources of Information

Inquiries should be directed to the relevant office or to the Secretary, United States International Trade Commission, 500 E Street SW., Washington, DC 20436. Phone, 202–205–2000.

Contracts Contact the Director, Office of Procurement. Phone, 202–205–2252. Internet, http://www.usitc.gov/procurement/.

Electronic Access Commission publications, news releases, "Federal Register" notices, scheduling information, the Commission's interactive Trade and Tariff DataWeb, and general information on USITC are available online. Investigation-related public inspection files are available through the Electronic Document Imaging System (EDIS). Internet, http://www.usitc.gov/press_room/.

Employment The Commission employs international economists, attorneys, accountants, commodity and industry specialists and analysts, and clerical and other support personnel. For more information, contact the Director, Office of Human Resources. Phone, 202–205–2651. Email, hr@usitc.gov. Internet, http://www.usitc.gov/employment/positions.htm.

Publications The Commission publishes results of investigations on various commodities and subjects. Other publications include an annual report to the Congress on the operation of the trade agreements program and an annual review of Commission activities. Specific information on these publications can be obtained from the Office of the Secretary. Internet, http://www.usitc.gov/secretary/.

Reading Rooms Reading rooms are open to the public in the Office of the Secretary and the USITC Main Library. The USITC Law Library is publicly accessible by prior arrangement. Call 202–205–3287 to schedule a visit. Internet, http://www.usitc.gov/secretary/.

For further information, contact the Secretary, United States International Trade Commission, 500 E Street SW., Washington, DC 20436. Phone, 202–205–2000. Internet, http://www.usitc.gov/secretary/.

UNITED STATES POSTAL SERVICE

475 L'Enfant Plaza SW., Washington, DC 20260
Phone, 202–268–2000. Internet, http://www.usps.gov.

Board of Governors

Chairman	MICKEY D. BARNETT
Vice Chairman	JAMES H. BILBRAY
Governors	LOUIS J. GIULIANO, DENNIS J. TONER, ELLEN C. WILLIAMS, (4 VACANCIES)
Postmaster General, Chief Executive Officer	PATRICK R. DONAHOE
Deputy Postmaster General	RONALD A. STROMAN
Secretary	JULIE S. MOORE
Inspector General	DAVID C. WILLIAMS

Officers

Postmaster General, Chief Executive Officer	PATRICK R. DONAHOE
Deputy Postmaster General	RONALD A. STROMAN
Consumer and Industry Affairs Vice President	JAMES NEMEC
Corporate Communications Vice President	WILLIAM WHITMAN, JR.
Government Relations and Public Policy Vice President	SHEILA MEYERS, *Acting*
Judicial Officer	WILLIAM CAMPBELL
Chief Marketing and Sales Officer, Executive Vice President	NAGISA MANABE
New Products and Innovation Vice President	GARY REBLIN

Officers

Global Business Vice President	GISELLE E. VALERA
Pricing Vice President	CYNTHIA SANCHEZ-HERNANDEZ
Sales Vice President	CLIFF RUCKER
Secure Digital Solutions Vice President	RANDY S. MISKANIC
Chief Operating Officer, Executive Vice President	MEGAN J. BRENNAN
Delivery and Post Office Operations Vice President	EDWARD F. PHELAN, JR.
Facilities Vice President	TOM SAMRA
Network Operations Vice President	DAVID E. WILLIAMS
Retail Channel Vice President	KELLY M. SIGMON
Capital Metro Area Operations Vice President	KRISTIN SEAVER
Eastern Area Operations Vice President	JOSHUA COLIN
Great Lakes Area Operations Vice President	JACQUELINE KRAGE STRAKO
Northeast Area Operations Vice President	RICHARD P. ULUSKI
Pacific Area Operations Vice President	DEAN GRANHOLM
Southwest Area Operations Vice President	JO ANN FEINDT
Western Area Operations Vice President	DREW ALIPERTO
Chief Financial Officer, Executive Vice President	JOSEPH CORBETT
Controller Vice President	SCOTT DAVIS, *Acting*
Finance and Planning Vice President	SHAWN E. MOSSMAN
Supply Management Vice President	SUSAN M. BROWNELL
Chief Human Relations Officer, Executive Vice President	JEFFREY WILLIAMSON
Employee Resource Management Vice President	ROSEMARIE FERNANDEZ
Labor Relations Vice President	DOUG TULINO
Chief Information Officer, Executive Vice President	JAMES COCHRANE
Engineering Systems Vice President	MICHAEL J. AMATO
Information Technology Vice President	JOHN EDGAR
Mail Entry and Payment Technology Vice President	PRITHA MEHRA
Product Information Vice President	ROBERT CINTRON
General Counsel, Executive Vice President	THOMAS J. MARSHALL
Chief Postal Inspector	GUY COTTRELL

[For the United States Postal Service statement of organization, see the Code of Federal Regulations, Title 39, Part 221]

The United States Postal Service provides mail processing and delivery services to individuals and businesses within the United States.

The Postal Service was created as an independent establishment of the executive branch by the Postal Reorganization Act (39 U.S.C. 101 et seq.), approved August 12, 1970. The present United States Postal Service commenced operations on July 1, 1971.

In FY 2013, the Postal Service had approximately 491,000 career employees and handled over 158 billion pieces of mail. The chief executive officer of the Postal Service, the Postmaster General, is appointed by the nine Governors of the Postal Service, who are appointed by the President with the advice and consent of the Senate. The Governors and the Postmaster General appoint the Deputy Postmaster General, and these 11 people constitute the Board of Governors.

In addition to the national headquarters, there are area and district offices supervising more than 35,000 post offices, branches, stations, contract postal

UNITED STATES POSTAL SERVICE

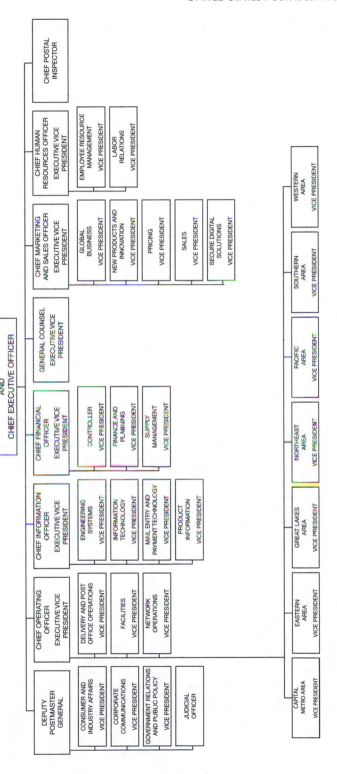

units, village post offices, and community post offices throughout the United States.

Activities

In order to expand and improve service to the public, the Postal Service is engaged in customer cooperation activities, including the development of programs for both the general public and major customers. The Consumer Advocate, a postal ombudsman, represents the interest of the individual mail customer in matters involving the Postal Service by bringing complaints and suggestions to the attention of top postal management and solving the problems of individual customers. To provide services responsive to public needs, the Postal Service operates its own planning, research, engineering, real estate, and procurement programs and maintains close ties with international postal organizations.

The Postal Service is the only Federal agency whose employment policies are governed by a process of collective bargaining under the National Labor Relations Act. Labor contract negotiations, affecting all bargaining unit personnel, as well as personnel matters involving employees not covered by collective bargaining agreements, are administered by Labor Relations or Human Resources.

The U.S. Postal Inspection Service is the Federal law enforcement agency that has jurisdiction in criminal matters affecting the integrity and security of the mail. Postal Inspectors enforce more than 200 Federal statutes involving mail fraud, mail bombs, child pornography, illegal drugs, mail theft, and other postal crimes, as well as being responsible for the protection of all postal employees.

Postal Service customers and employees can file mail fraud complaints, find local Postal Inspection Service offices, and receive information on common fraud schemes by calling 1–877–876–2455 or using the link below. To report fraudulent mail activity, call the Mail Fraud Hotline (1–800–372–8347).

Internet, http://www.uspsoig.gov/hotline.

Sources of Information

Consumer Information   For general information 24 hours a day, call 1–800–ASK–USPS (1–800–275–8777). To find shipping rates, buy stamps, print postage, track packages, locate ZIP Codes, shop at the Postal Store, change addresses, and learn answers to frequently asked questions, use the link below. Internet, http://www.usps.com.

Contracts and Small Business Activities For comprehensive supply management information, use the link below. Internet, http://about.usps.com/doing-business/welcome.htm.

Employment   General information on jobs, including information on programs for veterans, may be accessed by contacting the nearest post office or using the link below. Information on U.S. Postal Inspector Service employment opportunities is available at https://postalinspectors.uspis.gov/employment. Internet, http://about.usps.com/careers/welcome.htm.

Inspector General   The Office of Inspector General maintains a toll-free hotline for reporting fraud, waste, or mismanagement: 1–888–USPS–OIG (1–888–877–7644); for the hearing impaired, 1–866–OIG TEXT (1–866–644–8398). Reports also may be emailed (hotline@uspsoig.gov) or sent to the United States Postal Service, Office of Inspector General Hotline, 10th Floor, 1735 N. Lynn Street, Arlington, VA 22209–2020. Information on the Office of Inspector General, on publicly available documents, and on certain Freedom of Information Act documents is available online. Internet, http://www.uspsoig.gov.

Philatelic Sales   For information on currently available stamps, philatelic items, and collectibles, use the link below. Internet, http://uspsstamps.com/.

Publications   Information on mailability, on postage rates and fees, and on other topics is available from the nearest post office. Most postal regulations affecting domestic and international mail, purchasing, and employee and labor relations can be found in Postal Service manuals. A wide range of publications, including Postal Service manuals and periodicals, are available online. Internet, http://about.usps.com/periodicals-publications/welcome.htm.

Reading Rooms Reading rooms are maintained at the library, which is located at USPS Headquarters on the 11th Floor. Its holdings include historic, legal, regulatory, and other documents. Phone, 202–268–2900.

For further information, contact the United States Postal Service, 475 L'Enfant Plaza SW., Washington, DC 20260. Phone, 202–268–2000. Internet, http://www.usps.gov.

Boards, Commissions, and Committees

Below is a list of Federal boards, commissions, councils, etc., not listed elsewhere in the Manual, which were established by congressional or Presidential action, whose functions are not strictly limited to the internal operations of a parent department or agency and which are authorized to publish documents in the Federal Register. While the editors have attempted to compile a complete and accurate listing, suggestions for improving coverage of this guide are welcome. Please address your comments to the Office of the Federal Register, National Archives and Records Administration, Washington, DC 20408. Phone, 202–741–6040. E-mail, fedreg.info@nara.gov. Internet, www.ofr.gov.

Federal advisory committees, as defined by the Federal Advisory Committee Act, as amended (5 U.S.C. app.), have not been included here. Information on Federal advisory committees may be obtained from the Committee Management Secretariat, General Services Administration, General Services Building (MC), Room G–230, Washington, DC 20405. Phone, 202–273–3556. Internet, www.gsa.gov/committeemanagement.

Administrative Committee of the Federal Register

Office of the Federal Register, National Archives and Records Administration, 8601 Adelphi Road, College Park, MD 20740–6001. Phone, 202–741–6000. E-mail, fedreg.info@nara.gov. Internet, www.ofr.gov.

Advisory Council on Historic Preservation

401 F. Street NW., Suite 308, Washington, DC 20001–2637. Phone, 202–517–0200. E-mail, achp@achp.gov. Internet, www.achp.gov.

American Battle Monuments Commission

2300 Clarendon Boulevard, Court House Plaza 2, Suite 500, Arlington, VA 22201. Phone, 703–696–6900. E-mail, info@abmc.gov. Internet, www.abmc.gov.

Appalachian Regional Commission

1666 Connecticut Avenue NW., Suite 700, Washington, DC 20009–1068. Phone, 202–884–7700. E-mail, info@arc.gov. Internet, www.arc.gov.

Architectural and Transportation Barriers Compliance Board[1]

1331 F Street NW., Suite 1000, Washington, DC 20004–1111. Phone, 202–272–0080, toll free, 800–872–2253 or TTY, 202–272–0082, toll free, 800–993–2822. Fax, 202–272–0081. E-mail, info@access-board.gov. Internet, www.access-board.gov.

Arctic Research Commission

4350 North Fairfax Drive, Suite 510, Arlington, VA 22203. Phone, 703–525–0111. Fax, 703–525–0114. E-mail, info@arctic.gov. Internet, www.arctic.gov.

---

[1] Also known as the Access Board.

Arthritis and Musculoskeletal Interagency Coordinating Committee

National Institutes of Health/NIAMS, Building 31—MSC 2350, Room 4C02, 31 Center Drive, Bethesda, MD 20892–2350. Phone, 301–496–8190. Fax, 301–480–2814. E-mail, NIAMSInfo@mail.nih.gov. Internet, www.niams.nih.gov.

Barry M. Goldwater Scholarship and Excellence in Education Program

Phone, 319–688–4335. Internet, www.act.org/goldwater.

Chemical Safety and Hazard Investigation Board

2175 K Street NW., Suite 400, Washington, DC 20037–1809. Phone, 202–261–7600. Fax, 202–261–7650. Internet, www.csb.gov.

Citizens' Stamp Advisory Committee

United States Postal Service c/o Stamp Development, 475 L'Enfant Plaza SW., Room 3300, Washington, DC 20260–3501. Internet, http://about.usps.com/who-we-are/csac.

U.S. Commission of Fine Arts

National Building Museum, 401 F Street NW., Suite 312, Washington, DC 20001–2728. Phone, 202–504–2200. Fax, 202–504–2195. E-mail, cfastaff@cfa.gov. Internet, www.cfa.gov.

Committee on Foreign Investment in the United States

Department of the Treasury, 1500 Pennsylvania Avenue NW., Washington, DC 20220. Phone, 202–622–1860. E-mail, CFIUS@treasury.gov. Internet, http://www.treasury.gov/resource-center/international/Pages/Committee-on-Foreign-Investment-in-US.aspx

Committee for the Implementation of Textile Agreements

Office of Textiles and Apparel, U.S. Department of Commerce, Washington, DC 20230. Phone, 202–482–5078. Fax, 202–482–2331. E-mail, OTEXA@trade.gov. Internet, otexa.ita.doc.gov/cita.htm.

Committee for Purchase From People Who Are Blind or Severely Disabled

1401 S. Clark Street, Suite 10800, Arlington, VA 22202–3259. Phone, 703–603–7740. Fax, 703–608–0655. E-mail, info@abilityone.gov. Internet, www.abilityone.gov.

Coordinating Council on Juvenile Justice and Delinquency Prevention

Department of Justice, Office of Juvenile Justice and Delinquency Prevention, 810 7th Street NW., Washington, DC 20531. Phone, 202–616–7567. Fax, 202–307–2819. E-mail, ddunston@aeioonline.com. Internet, www.juvenilecouncil.gov.

Delaware River Basin Commission

25 State Police Drive, P.O. Box 7360, West Trenton, NJ 08628–0360. Phone, 609–883–9500. Fax, 609–883–9522. E-mail, clarke.rupert@drbc.state.nj.us. Internet, www.nj.gov/drbc.

Endangered Species Program

4401 N. Fairfax Drive, Room 420, Arlington, VA 22203. Phone, 703–358–2171. Internet, www.fws.gov/endangered.

Export Administration Operating Committee

Department of Commerce, Bureau of Industry and Security, 14th Street and Constitution Avenue, NW., Washington, DC 20230. Phone, 202–482–4811. Internet, www.bis.doc.gov/index.htm.

Federal Financial Institutions Examination Council

3501 Fairfax Drive, D8073a, Arlington, VA 22226. Phone, 703–516–5590. Internet, www.ffiec.gov.

Federal Financing Bank

Department of the Treasury, 1500 Pennsylvania Avenue NW., Washington, DC 20220. Phone, 202–622–2470. Fax, 202–622–0707. E-mail, ffb@do.treas.gov. Internet, www.treasury.gov/ffb.

Federal Interagency Committee on Education

Department of Education, 400 Maryland Avenue SW., Washington, DC 20202. Phone, 202–401–3673. Internet, ed.gov/about/bdscomm/list/com.html.

Federal Laboratory Consortium for Technology Transfer

Washington, DC Liaison Office. Phone, 240–444–1383. E-mail, gkjones. ctr@federallabs.org. Internet, www. federallabs.org.

Federal Library and Information Center Committee

Library of Congress, 101 Independence Avenue SE., Washington, DC 20540–4935. Phone, 202–707–4800. Internet, www.loc.gov/flicc/.

Harry S. Truman Scholarship Foundation

712 Jackson Place NW., Washington, DC 20006. Phone, 202–395–4831. Fax, 202–395–6995. E-mail, office@truman. gov. Internet, www.truman.gov.

Indian Arts and Crafts Board

U.S. Department of the Interior, Room MS 2528–MIB, 1849 C Street NW., Washington, DC 20240. Phone, 202–208–3773. E-mail, iacb@ios.doi.gov. Internet, www.iacb.doi.gov.

J. William Fulbright Foreign Scholarship Board

Department of State, Bureau of Educational and Cultural Affairs, 2200 C Street NW., Washington, DC 20522–0500. Phone, 202–203–7010. E-mail, fulbright@state.gov. Internet, fulbright. state.gov.

James Madison Memorial Fellowship Foundation

1613 Duke Street Alexandria, VA 22314. Phone, 800–525–6928. Internet, www. jamesmadison.com.

Japan-US Conference on Cultural and Educational Interchange (CULCON)

1201 15th Street NW., Suite 330, Washington, DC 20005. Phone, 202–653–9800. Fax, 202–653–9802. E-mail, culcon@jusfc.gov. Internet, culcon.jusfc. gov.

Joint Board for the Enrollment of Actuaries

Internal Revenue Service, SE: RPO, REFM, 1111 Constitution Avenue, NW, Park 4, Floor 4, Washington, DC 20224. Fax, 703–414–2225. E-mail, nhqjbea@irs.gov. Internet, www.irs.gov/taxpros/actuaries/index.html.

Marine Mammal Commission

4340 East-West Highway, Suite 700, Bethesda, MD 20814. Phone, 301–504–0087. Fax, 301–504–0099. E-mail, mmc@mmc.gov. Internet, www.mmc.gov.

Medicare Payment Advisory Commission

425 Eye St., N.W. Suite 701 Washington, DC 20001. Phone, 202–220–3700. Fax, 202–220–3759. Internet, www.medpac. gov.

Migratory Bird Conservation Commission

Secretary, Migration Bird Conservation Commission, Mail Code: ARLSQ–622, 4401 North Fairfax Drive, Arlington, VA 22203–1610. Phone, 703–358–1713. Fax, 703–358–2223. Email, realty@fws. gov. Internet, www.fws.gov/refuges/realty/mbcc.html.

Mississippi River Commission

Mississippi River Commission, 1400 Walnut Street, Vicksburg, MS 39180–0080. Phone, 601–634–5757. E-mail, cemvd-pa@usace.army.mil. Internet, www.mvd.usace.army.mil/

Morris K. and Stewart L. Udall Foundation

130 South Scott Avenue, Tucson, AZ 85701–1922. Phone, 520–901–8500. Fax, 520–670–5530. Internet, www.udall. gov.

National Council on Disability

1331 F Street NW., Suite 850, Washington, DC 20004. Phone, 202–272–2004. TTY, 202–272–2074. Fax, 202–272–2022. E-mail, ncd@ncd.gov. Internet, www.ncd.gov.

National Indian Gaming Commission

90 K Street NE., Suite 200, Washington, DC 20002. Phone, 202–632–7003. Fax, 202–632–7066. E-mail, contactus@nigc. gov. Internet, www.nigc.gov.

National Park Foundation

1201 Eye Street NW., Suite 550B, Washington, DC 20005. Phone, 202–354–6460. Fax, 202–371–2066. E-mail, ask-npf@nationalparks.org. Internet, www.nationalparks.org.

Northwest Power and Conservation Council

851 SW. Sixth Avenue, Suite 1100, Portland, OR 97204. Phone, 503–222–5161 or 800–452–5161. Fax, 503–820–2370. E-mail, info@nwcouncil.org. Internet, www.nwcouncil.org.

Office of Navajo and Hopi Indian Relocation

201 East Birch Avenue, Flagstaff, AZ 86001. Phone, 928–779–2721. TTY, 800–877–8339. Fax, 928–774–1977. E-mail, webmaster@onhir.gov. Internet, http://onhir.gov

Permanent Committee for the Oliver Wendell Holmes Devise

Library of Congress, Manuscript Division, Washington, DC 20540–4680. Phone, 202–707–1082.

President's Intelligence Advisory Board

New Executive Office Building, Room 5020, Washington, DC 20502. Phone, 202–456–2352. Fax, 202–395–3403. Internet, www.whitehouse.gov/administration/eop/piab.

Presidio Trust

103 Montgomery Street, P.O. Box 29052, San Francisco, CA 94129–0052. Phone, 415–561–5300. TTY, 415–561–5301. Fax, 415–561–5315. E-mail, presidio@presidiotrust.gov. Internet, www.presidio. gov.

Social Security Advisory Board

400 Virginia Avenue SW., Suite 625, Washington, DC 20024. Phone, 202–475–7700. Fax, 202–475–7715. E-mail, ssab@ssab.gov. Internet, www. ssab.gov.

Susquehanna River Basin Commission

4423 North Front Street, Harrisburg, PA 17110. Phone, 717–238–0423. Fax, 717–238–2436. E-mail, srbc@srbc.net. Internet, www.srbc.net.

Trade Policy Staff Committee

Office of the United States Trade Representative, 600 17th Street NW.,Washington, DC 20508. Phone, 202–395–3475. Fax, 202–395–4549. Internet, www.ustr.gov.

United States Nuclear Waste Technical Review Board

2300 Clarendon Boulevard, Suite 1300, Arlington, VA 22201. Phone, 703–235–4473. Fax, 703–235–4495. Internet, www.nwtrb.gov.

Veterans Day National Committee

Department of Veterans Affairs, 810 Vermont Avenue NW., Mail Code 002C, Washington, DC 20420. Phone, 202–461–5386. E-mail, vetsday@va.gov. Internet, www1.va.gov/opa/vetsday.

White House Commission on Presidential Scholars

Department of Education, 400 Maryland Avenue SW., Washington, DC 20202–8173. Phone, 202–401–0961. Fax, 202–260–7464. E-mail, presidential.scholars@ed.gov. Internet, www.ed.gov/programs/psp/index.html.

QUASI-OFFICIAL AGENCIES

LEGAL SERVICES CORPORATION

3333 K Street NW., Washington, DC 20007
Phone, 202–295–1500. Fax, 202–337–6797. Internet, http://www.lsc.gov.

President	JAMES J. SANDMAN
General Counsel, Corporate Secretary and Vice President for Legal Affairs	RONALD S. FLAGG
Vice President for Grants Management	LYNN A. JENNINGS
Chief Information Officer	PETER S. CAMPBELL
Director, Office of Compliance and Enforcement	LORA RATH
Director, Office of Information Management	JOHN MEYER
Director, Office of Program Performance	JANET LABELLA
Treasurer and Comptroller	DAVID L. RICHARDSON
Director, Office of Human Resources	TRACI HIGGINS
Director, Government Relations and Public Affairs	CAROL A. BERGMAN
Director, Media Relations	CARL RAUSCHER
Inspector General	JEFFREY E. SCHANZ

[For the Legal Services Corporation statement of organization, see the Code of Federal Regulations, Title 45, Part 1601]

The Legal Services Corporation promotes equal access to justice and provides civil legal assistance to low-income persons.

The Legal Services Corporation (LSC) is a private, nonprofit corporation established by the Legal Services Act of 1974, as amended (42 U.S.C. 2996), to promote equal access to justice under the law for all Americans.

LSC is headed by an 11-member Board of Directors, appointed by the President and confirmed by the Senate. By law, the Board is bipartisan and no more than six members may be of the same political party.

LSC is funded by congressional appropriations and provides legal services through grants to independent local legal services provider programs selected through a system of competition. In 2013, LSC funded 134 programs. Together, they serve every county and congressional district in the Nation, as well as the U.S. territories. Programs are also funded to address the needs of Native Americans and migrant farmworkers.

The legal services delivery system is based on several principles: local priorities, national accountability, competition for grants, and a strong public-private partnership. Local programs are governed by their own boards of directors, which set priorities and determine the types of cases that will be handled subject to restrictions set by Congress. A majority of each local board is appointed by local bar associations, and one-third of each local board is composed of client representatives

505

LEGAL SERVICES CORPORATION

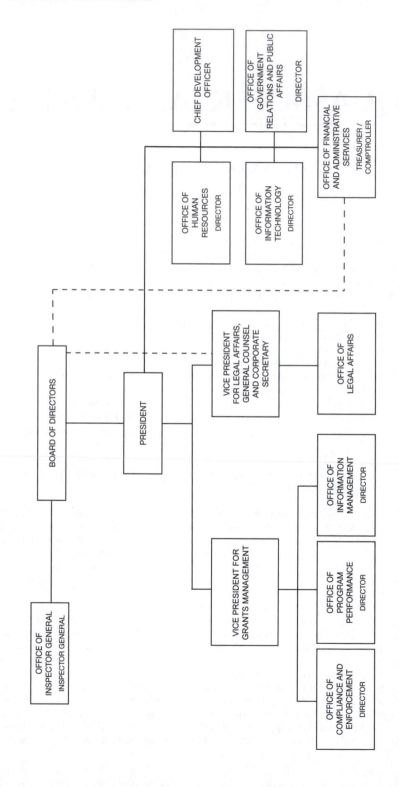

appointed by client groups. Each board hires its own executive director. Programs may supplement their LSC grants with additional funds from State and local governments and other sources. They further leverage Federal funds by involving private attorneys in the delivery of legal services for the poor, mostly through volunteer pro bono work.

Programs that LSC funds do not handle criminal cases, nor do they accept fee-generating cases that private attorneys are willing to accept on a contingency basis. In addition, in 1996 a series of new limitations were placed upon activities in which LSC-funded programs may engage on behalf of their clients, even with non-LSC funds. All programs must comply with laws enacted by Congress and the implementing regulations promulgated by LSC.

For further information, contact the Office of Government Relations and Public Affairs, Legal Services Corporation, 3333 K Street NW., Washington, DC 20007–3522. Phone, 202–295–1500. Fax, 202–337–6797. Internet, http://www.lsc.gov.

SMITHSONIAN INSTITUTION

1000 Jefferson Drive SW., Washington, DC 20560
Phone, 202–633–1000. Internet, http://www.si.edu.

Board of Regents

The Chief Justice of the United States (Chancellor)	JOHN G. ROBERTS, JR.
The Vice President of the United States	JOSEPH R. BIDEN, JR.
Member of the Senates	THAD COCHRAN, PATRICK J. LEAHY, JACK REED
Member of the House of Representatives	XAVIER BECERRA, THOMAS J. COLE, SAMUEL JOHNSON
Citizen Members	BARBARA BARRETT, STEVE M. CASE, JOHN FAHEY, SHIRLEY ANN JACKSON, ROBERT P. KOGOD, RISA LAVIZZO-MOUREY, JOHN W. McCARTER, JR., DAVID M. RUBENSTEIN, (VACANCY)

Officials

Secretary	G. WAYNE CLOUGH
Inspector General	EPIN CHRISTENSEN
Director, Communications and External Affairs	EVELYN LIEBERMAN
Director, Equal Employment and Minority Affairs	ERA L. MARSHALL
Director, Advancement and Philanthropic Giving	VIRGINIA B. CLARK
Director, Government Relations	NELL PAYNE
General Counsel	JUDITH E. LEONARD
Under Secretary for Finance and Administration and Chief Financial Officer	AL HORVATH
Chief Information Officer	DERON BURBA
Director, Accessibility Program	ELIZABETH ZIEBARTH
Director, Facilities Engineering and Operations	NANCY BECHTOL
Director, Human Resources	JAMES DOUGLAS
Director, Investments	AMY CHEN
Deputy Under Secretary for Collections and Interdisciplinary Support	SCOTT MILLER
Director, Policy and Analysis	H. WHITNEY WATRISS, *Acting*

Officials

Director, Smithsonian Institution Archives	ANNE VAN CAMP
Director, Special Events and Protocol	KAREN KELLER
Undersecretary for History, Art, and Culture	RICHARD KURIN
Director, Anacostia Community Museum	CAMILE AKEJU
Director, Archives of American Art	KATE HAW
Director, Asian Pacific American Program	KONRAD NG
Director, Center for Folklife and Cultural Heritage	MICHAEL MASON
Director, Cooper-Hewitt National Design Museum	CAROLINE BAUMANN
Director, Freer Gallery of Art and Arthur M. Sackler Gallery	JULIAN RABY
Director, Hirshhorn Museum and Sculpture Garden	KERRY BROUGHER, *Acting*
Director, National Museum of African American History and Culture	LONNIE BUNCH
Director, National Museum of African Art	JOHNNETTA B. COLE
Director, National Museum of American History	JOHN GRAY
Director, National Museum of the American Indian	KEVIN GOVER
Director, National Portrait Gallery	KIM SAJET
Director, National Postal Museum	ALLEN KANE
Director, Smithsonian Affiliations	HAROLD CLOSTER
Director, Smithsonian Associates	FREDIE ADELMAN, *Acting*
Director, Smithsonian American Art Museum and Renwick Gallery	ELIZABETH BROUN
Director, Smithsonian Center for Learning and Digital Access	STEPHANIE NORBY
Director, Smithsonian Latino Center	EDUARDO DIAZ
Director, Smithsonian Institution Traveling Exhibition Service	MYRIAM SPRINGUEL, *Acting*
Under Secretary for Science	JOHN KRESS, *Acting*
Director, National Air and Space Museum	JOHN R. DAILEY
Director, National Museum of Natural History	KIRK JOHNSON
Director, National Science Resources Center	THOMAS EMRICK, *Acting*
Director, Fellowships and Internships	ERIC WOODARD
Director, National Zoological Park	DENNIS KELLY
Director, Smithsonian Astrophysical Observatory	CHARLES ALCOCK
Director, Smithsonian Environmental Research Center	ANSON H. HINES
Director, Smithsonian Libraries	NANCY E. GWINN
Director, Smithsonian Marine Station	VALERIE PAUL
Director, Smithsonian Museum Conservation Institute	ROBERT KOESTLER
Director, Smithsonian Tropical Research Institute	WILLIAM WCISLO, *Acting*
President, Smithsonian Enterprises / Director, Smithsonian Media	CHRIS LIEDEL
Editor-in-Chief, Smithsonian Magazine	MICHAEL CARUSO
Assistant Secretary for Education and Access	CLAUDINE K. BROWN

The Smithsonian Institution is an independent trust instrumentality of the United States which comprises the world's largest museum and research complex; includes 19 museums and galleries, the National Zoo, and research facilities in several States and the Republic of Panama; and is dedicated to public education, national service, and scholarship in the arts, sciences, history, and culture.

The Smithsonian Institution was created by an act of Congress on August 10, 1846 (20 U.S.C. 41 et seq.), to carry out the terms of the will of British scientist James Smithson (1765–1829), who in 1826 had bequeathed his entire estate to the United States "to found at Washington, under the name of the Smithsonian Institution, an establishment for the increase and diffusion of knowledge among men." On July 1, 1836, Congress accepted the legacy and pledged the faith of the United States to the charitable trust.

In September 1838, Smithson's legacy, which amounted to more than 100,000 gold sovereigns, was delivered to the mint at Philadelphia. Congress vested responsibility for administering the trust in the Secretary of the Smithsonian and the Smithsonian Board of Regents, composed of the Chief Justice, the Vice President, three Members of the Senate, three Members of the House of Representatives, and nine citizen members appointed by joint resolution of Congress. To carry out Smithson's mandate, the Institution executes the following functions: conducts scientific and scholarly research; publishes the results of studies, explorations, and investigations; preserves for study and reference more than 137 million artifacts, works of art, and scientific specimens; organizes exhibits representative of the arts, the sciences, American history, and world culture; shares Smithsonian resources and collections with communities throughout the Nation; and engages in educational programming and national and international cooperative research.

Smithsonian activities are supported by its trust endowments and revenues; gifts, grants, and contracts; and funds appropriated to it by Congress. Admission to the museums in Washington, DC, is free.

Activities

Anacostia Community Museum   The Museum, located in the historic Fort Stanton neighborhood of Southeast Washington, serves as a national resource for exhibitions, historical documentation, and interpretive and educational programs relating to the impact of history and contemporary social issues on urban communities.

For further information, contact the Anacostia Community Museum, 1901 Fort Place SE., Washington, DC 20020. Phone, 202–633–1000. Internet, http://anacostia.si.edu.

Archives of American Art   The Archives contains the Nation's largest collection of documentary materials reflecting the history of visual arts in the United States. On the subject of art in America, it is the largest archives in the world, holding more than 16 million documents. The Archives gathers, preserves, and microfilms the papers of artists, craftsmen, collectors, dealers, critics, and art societies. These papers include manuscripts, letters, diaries, notebooks, sketchbooks, business records, clippings, exhibition catalogs, transcripts of tape-recorded interviews, and photographs of artists and their work.

For further information, contact the Archives of American Art, Suite 2200, 750 Ninth Street NW., Washington, DC 20001. Phone, 202–633–7940. Internet, http://www.aaa.si.edu.

Cooper-Hewitt National Design Museum The Museum is the only museum in the country devoted exclusively to historical and contemporary design. Collections include objects in such areas as applied arts and industrial design, drawings and prints, glass, metalwork, wallcoverings, and textiles. Changing exhibits and public programs seek to educate by exploring the role of design in daily life. The Museum is closed until November 2014. Programming will be offered offsite and online.

For further information, contact Cooper-Hewitt National Design Museum, 2 East Ninety-First Street, New York, NY 10128. Phone, 212–849–8400. Internet, http://cooperhewitt.org.

Freer Gallery of Art   The building, the original collection, and an endowment were the gift of Charles Lang Freer

SMITHSONIAN INSTITUTION

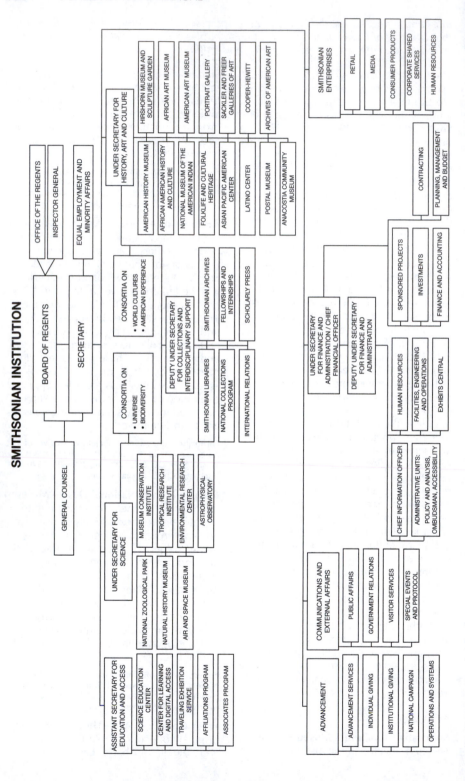

(1854–1919). The Gallery houses one of the world's most renowned collections of Asian art, an important group of ancient Egyptian glass, early Christian manuscripts, and works by 19th- and early 20th-century American artists. The objects in the Asian collection represent the arts of East Asia, the Near East, and South and Southeast Asia, including paintings, manuscripts, scrolls, screens, ceramics, metalwork, glass, jade, lacquer, and sculpture. Members of the staff conduct research on objects in the collection and publish results in scholarly journals and books for general and scholarly audiences.

For further information, contact the Freer Gallery of Art, Jefferson Drive at Twelfth Street SW., Washington, DC 20560. Phone, 202–633–1000. Internet, http://www.asia.si.edu.

Hirshhorn Museum and Sculpture Garden   From cubism to minimalism, the Museum houses major collections of modern and contemporary art. The nucleus of the collection is the gift and bequest of Joseph H. Hirshhorn (1899–1981). Supplementing the permanent collection are loan exhibitions. The Museum houses a collection research facility, a specialized art library, and a photographic archive, available for consultation by prior appointment. The outdoor sculpture garden is located nearby on the National Mall. There is an active program of public service and education, including docent tours, lectures on contemporary art and artists, and films of historic and artistic interest.

For further information, contact the Hirshhorn Museum and Sculpture Garden, Seventh Street and Independence Avenue SW., Washington, DC 20560. Phone, 202–633–1000. Internet, http://www.hirshhorn.si.edu.

National Air and Space Museum   Created to memorialize the development and achievements of aviation and spaceflight, the Museum collects, displays, and preserves aeronautical and space flight artifacts of historical significance as well as documentary and artistic materials related to air and space. Among its artifacts are full-size planes, models, and instruments. Highlights of the collection include the Wright brothers' Flyer, Charles Lindbergh's Spirit

of St. Louis, a Moon rock, and Apollo spacecraft. The exhibitions and study collections record the human conquest of the air from its beginnings to recent achievements. The principal areas in which work is concentrated include flight craft of all types, spaceflight vehicles, and propulsion systems. The Museum's IMAX Theater and the 70-foot domed Einstein Planetarium are popular attractions. The Museum's Steven F. Udvar-Hazy Center, at Washington Dulles International Airport, opened in December 2003. Its featured artifacts include a space shuttle and the Enola Gay B–29 World War II bomber.

For further information, contact the National Air and Space Museum, Sixth Street and Independence Avenue SW., Washington, DC 20560. Phone, 202–633–1000. Internet, http://airandspace.si.edu.

National Museum of African Art   This is the only art museum in the United States dedicated exclusively to portraying the creative visual traditions of Africa. Its research components, collection, exhibitions, and public programs establish the Museum as a primary source for the examination and discovery of the arts and culture of Africa. The collection includes works in wood, metal, fired clay, ivory, and fiber. The Eliot Elisofon Photographic Archives includes slides, photos, and film segments on Africa. There is also a specialized library.

For further information, contact the National Museum of African Art, 950 Independence Avenue SW., Washington, DC 20560. Phone, 202–633–1000. Internet, http://africa.si.edu.

National Museum of African American History and Culture   The Museum was established in 2003 and will be the only national museum devoted exclusively to the documentation of African American life, art, history, and culture. Scheduled for completion in 2016, the Museum will be built on the National Mall on a 5-acre tract adjacent to the Washington Monument. In the meantime, the Museum has exhibition space on the second floor of the National Museum of American History.

For further information, contact the National Museum of African American History and Culture, Capital Gallery, Suite 7001, 600 Maryland Avenue

SW., Washington, DC 20024. Phone, 202–633–1000. Internet, http://www.nmaahc.si.edu.

Smithsonian American Art Museum

The Museum's art collection spans centuries of American painting, sculpture, folk art, photography, and graphic art. A major center for research in American art, the Museum has contributed to such resources as the Inventory of American Paintings Executed Before 1914, the Smithsonian Art Index, and the Inventory of American Sculpture. The library, shared with the National Portrait Gallery, contains volumes on art, history, and biography, with special emphasis on the United States. The Donald W. Reynolds Center for American Art and Portraiture is home to the Smithsonian American Art Museum, the National Portrait Gallery, and the Archives of American Art. Hundreds of images from the collection and extensive information on its collections, publications, and activities are available electronically on the Museum's Web site.

For further information, contact the Smithsonian American Art Museum, Eighth and F Streets NW., Washington, DC 20006. Phone, 202–633–1000. Internet, http://www.americanart.si.edu.

Renwick Gallery   The Gallery, a branch of the Smithsonian American Art Museum, is dedicated to exhibiting crafts of all periods and to collecting 20th-century American crafts. It offers changing exhibitions of American crafts and decorative arts, both historical and contemporary, and a rotating selection from its permanent collection. The Gallery's grand salon is elegantly furnished in the Victorian style of the 1860s and 1870s. The Gallery closes for a 2-year renovation beginning in early 2014.

For further information, contact the Renwick Gallery, Seventeenth Street and Pennsylvania Avenue NW., Washington, DC 20006. Phone, 202–633–1000. Internet, http://www.americanart.si.edu/renwick.

National Museum of American History

In pursuit of its fundamental mission to inspire a broader understanding of the United States and its people, the Museum provides learning opportunities, stimulates the imagination of visitors, and presents challenging ideas about the Nation's past. The Museum's exhibits provide a unique view of the American experience. Emphasis is placed upon innovative individuals representing a wide range of cultures, who have shaped our heritage, and upon science and the remaking of our world through technology. Exhibits draw upon strong collections in the sciences and engineering, agriculture, manufacturing, transportation, political memorabilia, costumes, musical instruments, coins, Armed Forces history, photography, computers, ceramics, and glass. Classic cars, icons of the American Presidency, First Ladies' gowns, the Star-Spangled Banner flag, Whitney's cotton gin, Morse's telegraph, the John Bull locomotive, Dorothy's ruby slippers from "The Wizard of Oz," and other American icons are highlights of the collection. The West Wing of the Museum is closed for renovation until 2015.

For further information, contact the National Museum of American History, Fourteenth Street and Constitution Avenue NW., Washington, DC 20560. Phone, 202–633–1000. Internet, http://www. americanhistory.si.edu.

National Museum of the American Indian

The Museum was established in 1989, and the building on the National Mall opened September 2004. Much of the collection of the Museum is comprised of the collection of the former Heye Foundation in New York City. It is an institution of living cultures dedicated to the collection, preservation, study, and exhibition of the life, languages, literature, history, and arts of the Native peoples of the Americas. Highlights include Northwest Coast carvings; dance masks; pottery and weaving from the Southwest; painted hides and garments from the North American Plains; goldwork of the Aztecs, Incas, and Maya; and Amazonian featherwork. The National Museum of the American Indian also operates the George Gustav Heye Center at the Alexander Hamilton U.S. Custom House in New York City.

For further information, contact the National Museum of the American Indian, Fourth Street and Independence Avenue SW., Washington, DC 20560. Phone, 202–633–1000. Internet, http:// americanindian.si.edu.

National Museum of Natural History

Dedicated to understanding the natural world and the place of humans in it, the Museum's permanent exhibitions focus on human cultures, Earth sciences, biology, and anthropology, with the most popular displays featuring gem stones such as the Hope Diamond, dinosaurs, insects, marine ecosystems, birds, and mammals. In 2010, the Museum celebrated its 100th anniversary with the opening of a new permanent exhibition, the David H. Koch Hall of Human Origins. An IMAX theater offers large-format films. The Museum's encyclopedic collections comprise more than 126 million specimens, making the Museum one of the world's foremost facilities for natural history research. The Museum's seven departments are anthropology, botany, entomology, invertebrate zoology, mineral sciences, paleobiology, and vertebrate zoology. Doctorate-level staff researchers ensure the continued growth and value of the collection by conducting studies in the field and laboratory.

For further information, contact the National Museum of Natural History, Tenth Street and Constitution Avenue NW., Washington, DC 20560. Phone, 202–633–1000. Internet, http://www.mnh.si.edu.

National Portrait Gallery

The Gallery was established in 1962 for the exhibition and study of portraiture depicting men and women who have made significant contributions to the history, development, and culture of the United States. The Gallery contains more than 19,000 works, including photographs and glass negatives. The first floor of the Gallery is devoted to changing exhibitions from the Gallery's collection of paintings, sculpture, prints, photographs, and drawings as well as to special portrait collections. Featured on the second floor are the permanent collection of portraits of eminent Americans and the Hall of Presidents, including the famous Gilbert Stuart portrait-from-life of George Washington. The two-story American Victorian Renaissance Great Hall on the third floor of the Gallery houses and exhibit of 20th century Americans and is used for special events and public programs. The Gallery shares a large library with the Smithsonian American Art Museum and the Archives of American Art. The education department offers public programs; outreach programs for adult groups; and walk-in and group tours.

For further information, contact the National Portrait Gallery, Eighth and F Streets NW., Washington, DC 20001. Phone, 202–633–1000. Internet, http://www.npg.si.edu.

National Postal Museum

The Museum houses the Nation's postal history and philatelic collection, the largest of its kind in the world, with more than 13 million objects. The Museum is devoted to the history of America's mail service, and major galleries include exhibits on mail service in colonial times and during the Civil War, the Pony Express, modern mail service, automation, mail transportation, and the art of letters, as well as displays of the Museum's priceless stamp collection. Highlights include three mail planes, a replica of a railway mail car, displays of historic letters, handcrafted mail boxes, and rare U.S. and foreign-issue stamps and covers. The Museum opened its newest permanent gallery, the William H. Gross Stamp Gallery, in September 2013.

For further information, contact the National Postal Museum, 2 Massachusetts Avenue NE., Washington, DC 20001. Phone, 202–633–1000. Internet, http://postalmuseum.si.edu.

National Zoological Park

The National Zoo is an international leader in wildlife conservation, education, and research. Home to more than 2,000 animals, the Zoo encompasses 163 acres along Rock Creek Park in Northwest Washington. Exhibits include the David M. Rubenstein Family Giant Panda Habitat, where the giant pandas Mei Xiang and Tian Tian reside with their cub Bao Bao. Built to mimic the animals' natural habitat in China, it is part of the Zoo's Asia Trail, which also takes visitors through the habitats of red pandas, Asian small-clawed otters, fishing cats, sloth bears, and clouded leopards. Other highlights include the Elephant Trails, home to the Asian elephant Kandula, who was born at the Zoo in 2001; Amazonia, a 15,000-square-foot rain forest habitat;

the Reptile Discovery Center, featuring African pancake tortoises and the world's largest lizards, Komodo dragons; and the Great Ape House, home to gorillas, orangutans, and other primates.

For further information, contact the National Zoo, 3001 Connecticut Avenue NW., Washington, DC 20008. Phone, 202- 633–4888. Internet, http:// nationalzoo.si.edu.

Center for Folklife and Cultural Heritage The Center is responsible for research, documentation, and presentation of grassroots cultural traditions. It maintains a documentary collection and produces Smithsonian Folkways Recordings, educational materials, documentary films, publications, and traveling exhibits, as well as the annual Smithsonian Folklife Festival on the National Mall. Recent Folklife festivals have featured a range of American music styles, a number of State tributes, and performers from around the world. Admission to the festival is free. The 2-week program includes Fourth of July activities on the National Mall.

For further information, contact the Center for Folklife and Cultural Heritage, Capital Gallery, Suite 2001, 600 Maryland Avenue SW., Washington, DC 20024. Phone, 202–633–1000. Internet, http://www. folklife.si.edu.

Arthur M. Sackler Gallery This Asian art museum opened in 1987 on the National Mall. Changing exhibitions drawn from major collections in the United States and abroad, as well as from the permanent holdings of the Sackler Gallery, are displayed in the distinctive below-ground museum. The Gallery's growing permanent collection is founded on a group of art objects from China, South and Southeast Asia, and the ancient Near East that were given to the Smithsonian by Arthur M. Sackler (1913– 1987). The Museum's current collection features Persian manuscripts; Japanese paintings; ceramics, prints, and textiles; sculptures from India; and paintings and metalware from China, Korea, Japan, and Southeast Asia. The Sackler Gallery is connected by an underground exhibition space to the neighboring Freer Gallery.

For further information, contact the Arthur M. Sackler Gallery, 1050 Independence Avenue SW., Washington, DC 20560. Phone, 202–633–1000. Internet, http://www.asia.si.edu.

Smithsonian Institution Archives The Smithsonian Institution Archives acquires, preserves, and makes available for research the official records of the Smithsonian Institution and the papers of individuals and organizations associated with the Institution or with its work. These holdings document the growth of the Smithsonian and the development of American science, history, and art.

For further information, contact the Smithsonian Institution Archives, Capital Gallery, Suite 3000, 600 Maryland Avenue SW., Washington, DC 20024. Phone, 202–633–5870. Internet, http://siarchives. si.edu/.

Smithsonian Astrophysical Observatory The Smithsonian Astrophysical Observatory and the Harvard College Observatory have coordinated research activities under a single director in a cooperative venture, Harvard-Smithsonian Center for Astrophysics. The Center's research activities are organized in the following areas of study: atomic and molecular physics, radio and geoastronomy, high-energy astrophysics, optical and infrared astronomy, planetary sciences, solar and stellar physics, and theoretical astrophysics. Research results are published in the Center Preprint Series and other technical and nontechnical bulletins and distributed to scientific and educational institutions around the world.

For more information, contact the Smithsonian Astrophysical Observatory, 60 Garden Street, Cambridge, MA 02138. Phone, 617–495–7463. Internet, http://www.cfa.harvard.edu/sao.

Smithsonian Museum Conservation Institute The Institute researches preservation, conservation, and technical study and analysis of collection materials. Its researchers investigate the chemical and physical processes that are involved in the care of art, artifacts, and specimens and attempt to formulate conditions and procedures for storage, exhibit, and stabilization that optimize the preservation of these objects. In interdisciplinary collaborations with archeologists, anthropologists, and art historians, natural and physical scientists study and analyze objects from the collections and related materials to expand knowledge and understanding of their historical and scientific context.

For further information, contact the Museum Conservation Institute, Museum Support Center, Suitland, MD 20746. Phone, 301–238–1240. Internet, http://www.si.edu/mci.

Smithsonian Environmental Research Center (SERC)   The Center is the leading national research center for understanding environmental issues in the coastal zone. SERC is dedicated to increasing knowledge of the biological and physical processes that sustain life on Earth. The Center, located near the Chesapeake Bay, trains future generations of scientists to address ecological questions of the Nation and the globe.

For further information, contact the Smithsonian Environmental Research Center, 647 Contees Wharf Road, Edgewater, MD 21037. Phone, 443–482–2200. Internet, http://www.serc.si.edu.

Smithsonian Libraries   The Smithsonian Institution Libraries include more than 1 million volumes (among them, 40,000 rare books) with strengths in natural history, art, science, humanities, and museology. Many volumes are available through interlibrary loan.

For further information, contact the Smithsonian Institution Libraries, Tenth Street and Constitution Avenue NW., Washington, DC 20560. Phone, 202–633–2240. Internet, http://library.si.edu.

Smithsonian Institution Traveling Exhibition Service (SITES)   Since 1952, SITES has been committed to making Smithsonian exhibitions available to millions of people who cannot view them firsthand at the Smithsonian museums. Exhibitions on art, history, and science travel to more than 250 locations each year.

For further information, contact the Smithsonian Institution Traveling Exhibition Service, Suite 7103, 470 L'Enfant Plaza SW., Washington, DC 20024. Phone, 202–633–1000. Internet, http://www.sites.si.edu.

Smithsonian Marine Station at Fort Pierce   The research institute features a state-of-the-art laboratory where Station scientists catalog species and study marine plants and animals. Among the most important projects being pursued at the site is the search for possible causes of fishkills, including Pfiesteria and other organisms.

For further information, contact the Smithsonian Marine Station at Fort Pierce, 701 Seaway Drive, Fort Pierce, FL 34949. Phone, 772–462–6220. Internet, http://www.sms.si.edu.

Smithsonian Tropical Research Institute (STRI)   The Institute is a research organization for advanced studies of tropical ecosystems. Headquartered in the Republic of Panama, STRI maintains extensive facilities in the Western Hemisphere tropics. It is the base of a corps of tropical researchers who study the evolution, behavior, ecology, and history of tropical species of systems ranging from coral reefs to rain forests.

For further information, contact the Smithsonian Tropical Research Institute, 1100 Jefferson Drive SW., Suite 3123, Washington, DC 20560. Phone, 202–633–4700. Phone (Panama), 011–507–212–8000. Internet, http://www.stri.org.

Sources of Information

Contracts and Small Business Activities Information regarding procurement of supplies, property management and utilization services for Smithsonian Institution organizations, and contracts for construction, services, etc., may be obtained from the Director, Office of Contracting, Smithsonian Institution, 2011 Crystal Drive, Suite 350, Arlington, VA 22202. Phone, 202–633–7290

Education and Research Write to the Directors of the following offices at the Smithsonian Institution, Washington, DC 20560: Office of Fellowships and Internships (www.si.edu/ofg), Center for Folklife and Cultural Heritage (www.folklife.si.edu), National Science Resources Center (www.nsrconline. org), and Smithsonian Center for Learning and Digital Access (http:// smithsonianeducation.org).

Electronic Access Information about the Smithsonian Institution is available online at www.si.edu.

Employment Employment information for the Smithsonian is available from the Office of Human Resources, Smithsonian Institution, Capital Gallery, Suite 5060, 600 Maryland Avenue SW., Washington, DC 20560. Phone, 202–633–6370. Internet, http://www.sihr.si.edu.

Media Affairs Members of the press may contact the Smithsonian Office of Public Affairs, 1000 Jefferson Drive SW., Washington, DC 20560. Phone, 202–633–2400. Internet, http://newsdesk. si.edu.

Memberships For information about the Friends of the Smithsonian, write to PO Box 37012, MRC 712 Washington, DC 20013–7012. Phone, 202–633–6300. Email, membership@si.edu. Internet, http://smithsonianmembership.com.

For information about the Resident Associate Program, write to Smithsonian Associates, PO Box 23293, Washington, DC 20026–3293. Phone, 202–633–3030. Internet, http://residentassociates.org.

For information about the Smithsonian National Associate Program, call 800–766–2149. Internet, http://www. smithsonianmag.com/member-services.

For information about the National Air and Space Society, call 202–633–2603. Email, MembershipNASM@si.edu. Internet, http://www.nasm.si.edu/ getinvolved/membership.

For information about the Friends of the National Zoo, call 202–633–3038. Internet, http://nationalzoo.si.edu/ Audiences/Members.

For information about National Museum of the American Indian membership, call 800–242–6624. Email, NMAImember@si.edu. Internet, http:// americanindian.si.edu.

Photographs Photographs and slides from the Smithsonian photographic archives are available to researchers, publishers, Government agencies, and the general public. A searchable database of images is available through the Internet. Purchase or use of images may require permission from the Smithsonian curatorial unit that holds copyright. For assistance, contact Smithsonian Photographic Services at 202–633–1933.

Publications To download the Smithsonian Institution's annual reports, visit www.si.edu/About/Annual-Report. To receive a hardcopy, call 202–633– 1000 or send an email to info@si.edu. http://www.smithsonianbooks.com Smithsonian Books, in collaboration with the Smithsonian Institution, publishes narrative nonfiction books on history,

culture, science and technology, and the arts, as well as signature illustrated books based on our museums and collections. Titles are distributed by Random House Publisher Services. http:// www.scholarlypress.si.edu Smithsonian Institution Scholarly Press, in conjunction with Rowman & Littlefield Publishing Group, Inc., publishes the research and other scholarly contributions of Smithsonian authors. A free brochure providing a brief guide to the Smithsonian Institution is published in several languages. For a copy, call Visitor Information at 202–633–1000 or send an email to info@si.edu. Copies are also available at museum information desks.

Smithsonian Books, in collaboration with the Smithsonian Institution, publishes narrative nonfiction books on history, culture, science and technology, and the arts, as well as signature illustrated books based on our museums and collections. Titles are distributed by Random House Publisher Services. Internet, http://www.smithsonianbooks. com.

Smithsonian Institution Scholarly Press, in conjunction with Rowman & Littlefield Publishing Group, Inc., publishes the research and other scholarly contributions of Smithsonian authors. Internet, http://www.scholarlypress. si.edu.

The goSmithsonian visitors guide may be purchased at museum information desks for $2 or obtained online at www. gosmithsonian.com.

A free brochure providing a brief guide to the Smithsonian Institution is published in English and several foreign languages. For a copy, call Visitor Information at 202–633–1000 or send an email to info@si.edu. Copies are also available at museum information desks.

Telephone Office of Visitor Services, 202–633–1000, provides a taped message with weekly announcements on hours of operation and events.

Tours For information about museum and gallery tours, contact the Smithsonian Information Center, 1000 Jefferson Drive SW., Washington, DC 20560. Phone, 202–633–1000. School groups are welcome. Special behind-the-scenes tours are offered through the various memberships.

Visitor Information   The Smithsonian Information Center, located in the original Smithsonian building, commonly known as The Castle, provides general orientation through films, computer interactive programs, and visitor information specialists to help members and the public learn about the national collections, museum events, exhibitions, and special programs. Write to the

Smithsonian Information Center, 1000 Jefferson Drive SW., Washington, DC 20560. Phone, 202–633–1000.

Volunteer Service Opportunities   The Smithsonian Institution welcomes volunteers and offers a variety of interesting service opportunities. For information, write to Office of Visitor Services, 1000 Jefferson Drive SW., Washington, DC 20560. Phone, 202–633–1000.

For further information, contact the Smithsonian Information Center, 1000 Jefferson Drive SW., Washington, DC 20560. Phone, 202–633–1000. TDD, 202–357–1729. Internet, http://www.si.edu.

John F. Kennedy Center for the Performing Arts

John F. Kennedy Center for the Performing Arts, Washington, DC 20566
Phone, 202–467–4600. Internet, http://www.kennedy-center.org.

Chairman	DAVID M. RUBENSTEIN
President	MICHAEL M. KAISER

The Kennedy Center is the only official memorial to President Kennedy in Washington, DC. Since its opening in 1971, the Center has presented a year-round program of the finest in music, dance, opera, and drama from the United States and abroad. The Kennedy Center box office is open daily, and general information and tickets may be obtained online or by calling 202–467–4600 or 202–416–8524 (TTY). The Friends of the Kennedy Center volunteers provide visitor services. Tours are available free of charge between 10 a.m. and 5 p.m. on weekdays and between 10 a.m. and 1 p.m. on weekends. Free performances are given every day at 6 p.m. on the Millennium Stage in the Grand Foyer.

Sources of Information

Contracts and Small Business Activities Use the link below to search and monitor opportunities posted on the Federal Business Opportunities Web site. For more information, contact the John F. Kennedy Center for the Performing Arts, Washington, DC 20566. Internet, https:// www.fbo.gov/.

Education and Research   For information on education programs, contact the John F. Kennedy Center

for the Performing Arts, Washington, DC 20566. Phone, 202–416–8000. Internet, http://www.kennedy-center.org/ education/.

Electronic Access   Information on the John F. Kennedy Center for the Performing Arts is available online. Internet, http://www.kennedy-center.org/ index.cfm.

Employment   For information on employment opportunities, write to the John F. Kennedy Center for the Performing Arts, Human Resources Department, Washington, DC 20566. Phone, 202–416–8604. Internet, http:// ch.tbe.taleo.net/CH07/ats/careers/ jobSearch.jsp?org=THEKENNC&cws=1.

Memberships   Information on national and local activities, including the bimonthly Kennedy Center News for members, is available at information desks inside the John F. Kennedy Center or by writing to Memberships Services, John F. Kennedy Center for the Performing Arts, Washington, DC 20566. Phone, 202–416–8310. Internet, http://www.kennedy-center.org/support/ membership/kcmembership.html.

Special Functions   For information on using the facilities for special functions, contact the Office of Special Events, John

F. Kennedy Center for the Performing Arts, Washington, DC 20566. Phone, 202–416–8000. Internet, http://www.kennedy-center.org/eventplanning/.

Theater Operations   For information on using the John F. Kennedy Center's theaters, contact the Booking Coordinator, John F. Kennedy Center for the Performing Arts, Washington, DC 20566. Phone, 202–416–8032. Internet, http://www.kennedy-center.org/theaterrental/.

Volunteer Service Opportunities   For information on volunteer opportunities, write to Friends of the Kennedy Center, Washington, DC 20566. Phone, 202–416–8000. Internet, http://www.kennedy-center.org/support/volunteers/.

For further information, contact the John F. Kennedy Center for the Performing Arts. Phone, 202–467–4600. Internet, http://www.kennedy-center.org.

EDITORIAL NOTE: The National Gallery of Art did not meet the publication deadline for submitting updated information of its activities, functions, and sources of information as required by the automatic disclosure provisions of the Freedom of Information Act (5 U.S.C. 552(a)(1)(A)).

National Gallery of Art

4th and Constitution Avenue NW., Washington, DC 20565
Phone, 202–737–4215. Internet, http://www.nga.gov.

President	VICTORIA P. SANT
Director	SHARON PERCY ROCKEFELLER

Activities

The National Gallery of Art houses one of the finest collections in the world, illustrating Western man's achievements in painting, sculpture, and the graphic arts. The West Building includes European (13th through early 20th century) and American (18th through early 20th century) works. An extensive survey of Italian painting and sculpture, including the only painting by Leonardo da Vinci in the Americas, is on display in the Gallery. Rich in Dutch masters and French impressionists, the collection offers superb surveys of American, British, Flemish, Spanish, and 15th- and 16th-century German art, as well as Renaissance medals and bronzes, Chinese porcelains, and about 97,000 works of graphic art from the 12th to the 20th centuries. The East Building collections and Sculpture Garden contain important works by major 20th-century artists. The Gallery relies on public and private resources. Federal appropriations support its operations and maintenance, and its acquisitions of artwork, as well as numerous special programs, are made possible through private donations and funds. A fellowship program promotes graduate and postgraduate research; programs to educate schoolchildren and the general public operate daily; and an extension service provides education resources free of charge to millions of people each year.

Sources of Information

Calendar of Events The events calendar is available online. To receive the calendar, call the calendar of events message line (Phone, 202–842–6662), or visit the "Calendar of Events Subscription" Web page (http://www.nga.gov/content/ngaweb/contact-us/calendar-subscription.html). Email, calendar@nga.gov. Internet, http://www.nga.gov/content/ngaweb/calendar.html?chosendate=08%2F28%2F2014&pageNumber=1.

Concerts Concerts by world-renowned musicians are open to the public, and admission is free. Seating is on a first-come, first-seated basis. The entrance at 6th Street and Constitution Avenue remains open on Sunday until 6:30 p.m. There are special areas for families with small children. Late entry or reentry of the West Building after 6:30 p.m. is not permitted. Phone, 202–842–6941. Internet, http://www.nga.gov/content/ngaweb/calendar/concerts.html?category=Concerts&pageNumber=1.

Contracts and Small Business Activities For more information, contact the National Gallery of Art, Office of Procurement and Contracts, 2000–B South Club Drive, Landover, MD 20785. Phone, 202–842–6745. Fax, 202–312–2792. Internet, https://www.fbo.gov/index?s=agency&mode=list&tab=list&tabmode=list&_so_list_fromda5df66D9f809a53b1563b95a6dce8e3=80&_so_list_fromda5df66d9f809a53b1563b95a6dce8e3_page=5.

Educational Resources The National Gallery of Art provides slide teaching and multimedia programs, videocassettes, CD–ROMs, DVDs, and videodiscs at no charge to individuals, schools, and civic organizations nationwide.

For more information, including the free catalog of education resources, contact the Department of Education Resources, National Gallery of Art, 2000–B South Club Drive, Landover, MD 20785. Phone, 202–842–6273. Email, edresources@nga.gov. Internet, http://www.nga.gov/content/ngaweb/education/learningresources.html.

Electronic Access   Information on the National Gallery of Art is available online. NGAkids (http://www.nga.gov/content/ngaweb/education/kids.html) offers interactive activities and adventures with works of art from the Gallery's collection and an animated tale set in the Gallery's Sculpture Garden. Internet, http://www.nga.gov/content/ngaweb/about.html.

Employment   For information on employment opportunities at the National Gallery of Art, contact the Personnel Office, National Gallery of Art, 601 Pennsylvania Avenue South NW., Second Floor, Washington, DC 20004. Phone, 202–842–6282. TDD, 202–842–6176. Email, staffing@nga.gov. Internet, http://www.nga.gov/content/ngaweb/opportunities/employment-opportunities.html.

Family Programs   The Gallery offers a range of free family programs suitable for children ages 4 and up, including workshops, children's films, music performances, and storytelling. Phone, 202–789–3030. Email, family@nga.gov. Internet, http://www.nga.gov/content/ngaweb/education/families.html.

Fellowships   For information on research fellowship programs, contact the Center for Advanced Study in the Visual Arts. Phone, 202–842–6480. Fax, 202–842–6733. Email, casva@nga.gov. Internet, http://www.nga.gov/content/ngaweb/research/casva/fellowships.html.

Films   An ongoing program of classic cinema, documentary, avant-garde, and area premieres takes place each weekend. Seating is on a first-come, first-seated basis, and there is no admission fee to attend. Doors open approximately 30 minutes before each show. Visiting filmmakers and scholars discuss films with the audiences following some screenings. The auditorium is equipped with an FM wireless listening system for the hearing impaired. Receivers,

earphones, and neckloops are available at the art information desk near the main entrance in the East Building. Please note: While the East Building is undergoing renovations, screenings take place in alternate locations. Phone, 202–842–6799. Email, film_department@nga.gov. Internet, http://www.nga.gov/film.

Internships   For information on internship programs for college graduates and graduate students, contact the Department of Academic Programs, National Gallery of Art, 2000–B South Club Drive, Landover, MD 20785. Phone, 202–842–6257. Fax, 202–842–6935. Email, intern@nga.gov. Internet, http://www.nga.gov/content/ngaweb/education/interns-fellows.html.

Lectures   Lecture events are free and open to the public. Seating is available on a first-come, first-seated basis. Internet, http://www.nga.gov/content/ngaweb/education/adults.html.

Library   The National Gallery of Art Library maintains a collection of more than 400,000 books and periodicals on the history, theory, and criticism of art and architecture. The collection's holdings center on Western art from the Middle Ages to the present and on American art from the colonial era to the present. The library is open by appointment on Mondays from noon to 4:30 p.m. and Tuesday through Friday from 10 a.m. to 4:30 p.m. It is closed on Federal holidays. To make an appointment, call 202–842–6511. Internet, http://www.nga.gov/content/ngaweb/research/library/About.html.

Library Image Collections   The Department of Image Collections is the National Gallery of Art's study and research center for images of Western art and architecture. The collection now contains nearly 13 million photographs, slides, negatives, and microform images, making this resource one of the largest of its kind. The Department serves the Gallery's staff, members of the Center for Advanced Study in the Visual Arts, visiting scholars, and serious adult researchers. The library is open by appointment on Mondays from noon to 4:30 p.m. and Tuesday through Friday from 10 a.m. to 4:30 p.m. It is closed on all Federal holidays. Phone, 202–842–6026. Internet, http://www.nga.gov/resources/dlidesc.shtm.

Memberships The Circle of the National Gallery of Art is a membership program that supports special projects for which Federal funds are not available. For information on The Circle of the National Gallery of Art, write to The Circle, National Gallery of Art, 2000–B South Club Drive, Landover, MD 20785. Phone, 202–842–6450. Internet, http://www.nga.gov/content/ngaweb/support/membership.html.

Publications The Gallery Shops sell publications on the Gallery's collections and quality reproductions of artwork. Make an online purchase using The Gallery Shops Web site (https://shop.nga.gov/). Or, place an order by calling 800–697–9350. The Office of Press and Public Information offers a free, bimonthly calendar of events. To subscribe to the calendar, call the calendar of events message line (Phone, 202–842–6662), or visit the "Calendar of Events Subscription" Web page (http://www.nga.gov/content/ngaweb/contact-us/calendar-subscription.html). Art information desks and the Visitor Services Office also distribute the calendar and "Brief Guide to the National Gallery of Art". Internet, http://www.nga.gov/content/ngaweb/research/publications.html.

Tours The education division offers gallery talks and lectures. Phone, 202–842–6247. Internet, http://www.nga.gov/content/ngaweb/visit/tours-and-guides.html.

Visitor Services The Visitor Services Office of the National Gallery of Art assists those with special needs, responds to written and telephone requests, and provides information on planning a visit to the Washington, DC, area. For more information, write to the National Gallery of Art, Office of Visitor Services, 2000–B South Club Drive, Landover, MD 20785. Phone, 202–842–6691. Internet, http://www.nga.gov/content/ngaweb/visit.html.

Volunteer Opportunities For information on volunteering at an art information desk or as a docent, contact Volunteer Opportunities. Phone, 202–789–3013. Internet, http://www.nga.gov/content/ngaweb/opportunities/volunteer-opportunities.html.

Library Volunteering For information on volunteer opportunities in the National Gallery of Art Library, send a résumé to the Head of Reader Services, National Gallery of Art Library, 2000–B South Club Drive, Landover, MD 20785. Phone, 202–842–6510. Internet, http://www.nga.gov/content/ngaweb/opportunities/volunteer-opportunities.html.

Horticulture Volunteers The horticulture division recruits volunteers to work indoors and outside. Volunteers may start at any time of year and are encouraged to commit for 12 months to experience the different seasons of horticulture. Phone, 202–842–6844. Email, gardens@nga.gov. Internet, http://www.nga.gov/content/ngaweb/opportunities/volunteer-opportunities/horticulture-volunteers.html.

Works on Paper Works of art on paper that are not on display may be viewed by appointment on weekdays by calling 202–842–6380. The Matisse cutouts are on display in the East Building Concourse from 10 a.m. to 3 p.m., Monday through Saturday, and from 11 a.m. to 4 p.m., Sunday. Internet, http://www.nga.gov/content/ngaweb/research/make-an-appointment.html.

For further information, contact the National Gallery of Art. Phone, 202–737–4215. TTY, 202–842–6176. Internet, http://www.nga.gov.

Woodrow Wilson International Center for Scholars

Scholar Administration Office, Woodrow Wilson Center, One Woodrow Wilson Plaza, 1300 Pennsylvania Avenue NW., Washington, DC 20004–3027
Phone, 202–691–4000. Fax, 202–691–4001. Internet, http://www.wilsoncenter.org.

Director	JANE HARMAN
Executive Vice President	ANDREW S. SELEE

Activities

Created by an Act of Congress in 1968, the Woodrow Wilson International Center for Scholars is a national, living memorial honoring the legacy of President Woodrow Wilson. The Wilson Center, headquartered in Washington, DC, and supported by both public and private funds, provides a strictly nonpartisan space for scholars and policymakers to interact. By conducting relevant, timely research and promoting dialogue from all perspectives, the Center works to address critical current and emerging challenges confronting the United States and the world.

Sources of Information

Electronic Access   Information on the Woodrow Wilson Center is available online. Internet, www.wilsoncenter.org.
Employment   For information on employment opportunities at the Woodrow Wilson Center, contact the Office of Human Resources, One Woodrow Wilson Plaza, 1300 Pennsylvania Avenue NW., Washington, DC 20004–3027. Job announcements are posted online. Internet, http://www.wilsoncenter.org/opportunities/Job.
Fellowships and Internship   The Woodrow Wilson Center offers residential fellowships that allow academics, public officials, journalists, business professionals, and others to pursue their research and writing at the Center while interacting with policymakers in Washington. The Center also invites public policy scholars and senior scholars from a variety of disciplines to conduct research for varying lengths of time in residence. For more information, call 202–691–4000. The Center also has a year-round need for interns to assist the program and projects staff and to act as research assistants for scholars and fellows. For more information, call 202–691–4053. Internet, http://www.wilsoncenter.org/fellowships-grants.
Media Affairs   Members of the press may contact the Woodrow Wilson Center at 202–691–4217.
Presidential Memorial Exhibit   The Woodrow Wilson Center houses the Woodrow Wilson Presidential Memorial Exhibit which includes memorabilia, historical information, photographs, several short films, and a memorial hall with quotations. The exhibit is open weekdays, 8:30 a.m. to 5 p.m. Admission is free.
Publications   The Woodrow Wilson Center publishes policy briefs and research reports, as well as books written by staff and visiting scholars and fellows, through the Wilson Center Press. It also produces "Dialogue," a weekly radio and television program about national and international affairs, history, and culture. For more information, call 202–691–4000.
Visitor Services   Events, unless otherwise noted, are free and open to the public, and photo identification is required for entry. A listing of events at the Woodrow Wilson Center is available online. Internet, http://www.wilsoncenter.org/events.

For further information, contact the Woodrow Wilson International Center for Scholars, One Woodrow Wilson Plaza, 1300 Pennsylvania Avenue NW., Washington, DC 20004–3027. Phone, 202–691–4000. Fax, 202–691–4001. Internet, http://www.wilsoncenter.org.

STATE JUSTICE INSTITUTE

11951 Freedom Drive, Suite 1020, Reston, VA 20190
Phone, 571–313–8843. Internet, http://www.sji.gov.

Board of Directors

Chairman	JAMES R. HANNAH
Vice Chairman	DANIEL J. BECKER
Secretary	GAYLE A. NACHTIGAL
Treasurer	HERNÁN D. VERA
Members	DAVID V. BREWER, ISABEL FRAMER, JONATHAN LIPPMAN, WILFREDO MARTINEZ, JOHN B. NALBANDIAN, MARSHA J. RABITEAU, CHASE T. ROGERS

Officers

Executive Director	JONATHAN D. MATTIELLO

The State Justice Institute awards grants to improve the administration of justice in the State courts of the United States.

State Justice Institue (SJI) was established by the State Justice Institute Authorization Act of 1984 (42 U.S.C. 10701 et seq.) as a private, nonprofit corporation to further the development and improvement of judicial administration in the State courts.

SJI is supervised by a Board of Directors consisting of 11 members appointed by the President with the advice and consent of the Senate. The Board is statutorily composed of six judges, a State court administrator, and four members of the public, of whom no more than two can be of the same political party.

In carrying out its mission, SJI develops solutions to common issues faced by State courts; provides practical products to judges and court staff; ensures that effective approaches in one State are quickly and economically shared with other courts nationwide; and supports national, regional, and in-State educational programs to speed the transfer of solutions.

To accomplish these broad objectives, SJI is authorized to provide funds, through grants, cooperative agreements, and contracts, to State courts and organizations that can assist in the improvement of judicial administration in the State courts.

Sources of Information

Inquiries concerning grants, publications, speakers, or Privacy Act/Freedom of Information Act requests should be directed to the Executive Director, State Justice Institute, 11951 Freedom Drive, Suite 1020, Reston, VA 20190. Phone, 571–313–8843.

Additional information is available on the SJI Web site: www.sji.gov.

For further information, contact the State Justice Institute, 11951 Freedom Drive, Suite 1020, Reston, VA 20190. Phone, 571–313–8843. Internet, http://www.sji.gov.

UNITED STATES HOLOCAUST MEMORIAL MUSEUM

100 Raoul Wallenberg Place, SW., Washington, DC 20024–2126
Phone, 202–488–0400. TTY, 202–488–0406. Internet, http://www.ushmm.org.

United States Holocaust Memorial Council

Chairman	TOM A. BERNSTEIN
Vice Chairman	JOSHUA B. BOLTEN

United States Holocaust Memorial Council

Museum Director	SARA J. BLOOMFIELD
Members	ELLIOTT ABRAMS, MATTHEW L. ADLER, ELISA SPUNGEN BILDNER, LEE T. BYCEL, MICHAEL CHERTOFF, DIANA SHAW CLARK, WILLIAM J. DANHOF, SHEFALI RAZDAN DUGGAL, KITTY DUKAKIS, JOHN FARAHI, TODD A. FISHER, JONATHAN SAFRAN FOER, AMY R. FRIEDKIN, K. CHAYA FRIEDMAN, NANCY B. GILBERT, MARK D. GOODMAN, SAMUEL N. GORDON, SANFORD L. GOTTESMAN, JOSEPH D. GUTMAN, CHERYL F. HALPERN, S. FITZGERALD HANEY, BETH HEIFETZ, J. DAVID HELLER, ALLAN M. HOLT, JANE H. JELENKO, AMY KASLOW, ROMAN R. KENT, HOWARD KONAR, M. RONALD KRONGOLD, ALAN B. LAZOWSKI, DEBORAH E. LIPSTADT, SUSAN E. LOWENBERG, LESLIE MEYERS, MICHAEL B. MUKASEY, DEBORAH A. OPPENHEIMER, CHERYL PEISACH, DANA PERLMAN, RICHARD S. PRICE, RONALD RATNER, GREG A. ROSENBAUM, MENACHEM Z. ROSENSAFT, MICHAEL P. ROSS, KIRK A. RUDY, ELLIOT J. SCHRAGE, MAUREEN SCHULMAN, DANIEL J. SILVA, ANDREA LAVIN SOLOW, MARC R. STANLEY, MICHAEL ASHLEY STEIN, MICHELE TAYLOR, HOWARD D. UNGER, CLEMANTINE WAMARIYA, ELIE WIESEL
Member of the House of Representatives	MICHAEL GRIMM, STEVE ISRAEL, PATRICK MEEHAN, HENRY A. WAXMAN, (VACANCY)
Member of the Senates	ALAN S. FRANKEN, ORRIN G. HATCH, BERNARD SANDERS, (2 VACANCIES)
Department of Education (ex officio)	PHILIP H. ROSENFELT
Department of the Interior (ex officio)	SARAH GREENBERGER
Department of State (ex officio)	(VACANCY)
General Counsel (ex officio)	GERARD LEVAL
Internal Auditor (ex officio)	MEL SCHWARTZ
Secretary (ex officio)	JANE M. MILLER

United States Holocaust Memorial Museum

Director	SARA J. BLOOMFIELD
Chief of Staff	WILLIAM PARSONS
General Counsel	RONALD F. CUFFE
Chief Development Officer	JORDAN TANNENBAUM
Chief Financial Officer	MINNIE CARMICHAEL
Chief Information Officer	JOSEPH KRAUS
Chief Marketing Officer	LORNA MILES
Chief Program Officer	SARAH OGILVIE

United States Holocaust Memorial Museum

Director, Center for Advanced Holocaust Studies	PAUL SHAPIRO
Director, Center for the Prevention of Genocide	CAMERON HUDSON, *Acting*
Director, Collections	MICHAEL GRUNBERGER
Director, Museum Operations and Administration	TANELL COLEMAN
Director, National Institute for Holocaust Education	MICHAEL ABRAMOWITZ
Director, Planning	DARA GOLDBERG
Senior Program Advisor for Institutional Projects	ARNOLD KRAMER

The United States Holocaust Memorial Museum maintains a permanent living memorial to the victims of the Holocaust and provides ways to document, study, and interpret the Holocaust.

The United States Holocaust Memorial Museum (USHMM) was established by the act of October 7, 1980 (36 U.S.C. 1401–1408). It received permanent authorization as an independent establishment by the act of October 12, 2000 (36 U.S.C. 2301 et seq.).

USHMM is governed by a council, which serves as the board of trustees. The council comprises 55 members appointed by the President, for staggered 5-year terms. Five members each are appointed from both the House of Representatives and Senate. There are also three nonvoting ex-officio members from the Departments of Education, Interior, and State.

USHMM operates as a public-private partnership. Its activities and programs are supported by planned giving, endowments, and revenues; gifts, grants, and contracts; and Federal funding. The Museum is open every day, except on Yom Kippur and Christmas, and admission is free.

Activities

Jack, Joseph and Morton Mandel Center for Advanced Holocaust Studies   The Center works with the United States Holocaust Memorial Council's Academic Committee to support research projects and publications on the Holocaust, provide access to Holocaust-related archival materials for study and new research, sponsor fellowship opportunities for pre- and postdoctoral researchers, and offer seminars, summer research workshops, conferences, lectures, and symposia.

For further information, contact the Jack, Joseph, and Morton Mandel Center for Advanced Holocaust Studies. Phone, 202–488–0400. TTY, 202–488–0406. Internet, http://www.ushmm.org/research/the-center-for-advanced-holocaust-studies/about-the-center-for-advanced-holocaust-studies.

Center for the Prevention of Genocide   The Center, guided by the Council's Committee on Conscience, raises awareness of genocide, influences policymaking on genocide prevention, and stimulates worldwide action to prevent genocide and related mass atrocities. It seeks to make genocide prevention a national and international priority by increasing public awareness and mobilizing worldwide support to avert these crimes against humanity.

For further information, contact the Center for the Prevention of Genocide. Internet, http://www.ushmm.org/confront-genocide/about. Email, genocideprevention@ushmm.org.

National Institute for Holocaust Education   The Institute promotes a variety of resources and programs to help educators, professionals, and students increase their knowledge of Holocaust history and understand its relevance today. Educational outreach programs provide teachers with classroom strategies and resources for teaching students about the Holocaust.

For further information, contact the National Institute for Holocaust Education. Internet, http://www.ushmm.org/educators/teaching-about-the-holocaust.

UNITED STATES HOLOCAUST MEMORIAL MUSEUM

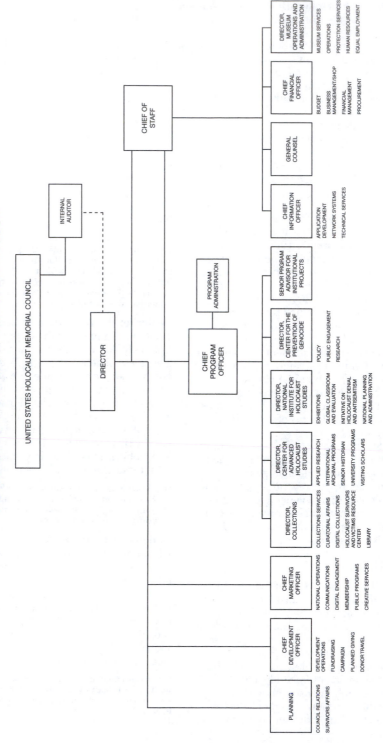

Programs

Law, Justice, and the Holocaust Program This program examines the decisions German jurists made and the pressures they faced under the Nazi regime. This is a one-day program for judges, prosecutors, and court administrators.

For further information, contact the Law, Justice, and the Holocaust Program. Internet, http://www. ushmm.org/professionals-and-student-leaders/ judiciary.

Civic and Defense Initiatives Program This program explores the ways in which the military can work to prevent genocide today.

Lessons of the Holocaust Program This program examines the role that law enforcement professionals played in the Holocaust. It also challenges them to reflect on their professional and personal responsibilities in a democracy today.

For further information, contact the Lessons of the Holocaust Program. Internet, http://www. ushmm.org/professionals-and-student-leaders/law-enforcement.

Programs on Ethics, Religion, and the Holocaust These programs focus on the response of churches to the Holocaust and the ways in which religious institutions, leaders, and theologians have addressed this history and its legacy.

For further information, contact the Programs on Ethics, Religion, and the Holocaust. Internet, http:// www.ushmm.org/research/the-center-for-advanced-holocaust-studies/programs-ethics-religion-the-holocaust.

Youth and Community Initiatives Program This program introduces students to Holocaust history and helps them develop leadership skills for confronting hatred and promoting human dignity.

For further information, contact the Student Leaders Program. Internet, http://www.ushmm.org/ professionals-and-student-leaders/student-leaders.

Sources of Information

Calendar of Events For information on upcoming events, visit the Museum's online calendar. Internet, http://www. ushmm.org/online/calendar..

Exhibitions and Collections The Museum's holdings include art, books, pamphlets, advertisements, maps, film and video historical footage, audio and video oral testimonies, music and sound recordings, furnishings, architectural fragments, models, machinery, tools, microfilm and microfiche of government documents and other official records, personal effects, personal papers, photographs, photo albums, and textiles. The self-guided Permanent Exhibition spans three floors and presents a narrative history of the Holocaust with historical artifacts, photographs, and film footage. Special exhibitions include Remember the Children: Daniel's Story (for children 8 and up) and Some Were Neighbors: Collaboration and Complicity in the Holocaust. The Museum's traveling exhibitions have appeared in numerous cities, states, and countries. These exhibitions extend the history of the Holocaust beyond the Museum's walls. For more information, the Museum's website. Internet, http://www.ushmm.org/ information/exhibitions.

Reserved Visits and Tours Admission to the Museum is free. From March through August, timed passes are required to enter the Permanent Exhibition. No passes are required for any other Museum exhibitions. Advance passes for entry to the Museum's Permanent Exhibition are available at https://tix.extremetix.com/ Online/USHMM. The convenience fee for advance passes is $1.00 per person. Advanced group reservations are also available at https://secure.ushmm.org/ online/group-reservation. For more information on reserved visits and tours, visit the Museum's website. Internet, http://www.ushmm.org/information/plan-a-visit..

Volunteer Opportunities The Museum welcomes volunteers and offers a variety of service opportunities. Unpaid internship opportunities are also available. For internship information, go to http://www.ushmm.org/information/ career-volunteer-opportunities/ internships. Internet, http://www.ushmm. org/information/career-volunteer-opportunities/volunteering.

For further information, contact the United States Holocaust Memorial Museum, 100 Raoul Wallenberg Place, SW., Washington, DC 20024–2126. Phone, 202–488–0400. TTY, 202–488–0406. Internet, http://www. ushmm.org.

UNITED STATES INSTITUTE OF PEACE

2301 Constitution Avenue NW., Washington, DC 20037
Phone, 202–457–1700. Fax, 202–429–6063. Internet, http://www.usip.org.

Board of Directors

Chairman	STEPHEN J. HADLEY
Vice Chairman	GEORGE E. MOOSE
Members	JUDY ANSLEY, ERIC S. EDELMAN, JOSEPH ELDRIDGE, KERRY KENNEDY, IKRAM U. KHAN, STEPHEN D. KRASNER, JOHN A. LANCASTER, JEREMY A. RABKIN, NANCY ZIRKIN
Secretary of State (ex officio)	JOHN F. KERRY
Secretary of Defense (ex officio)	CHARLES T. HAGEL
President, National Defense University (ex officio)	MAJ. GEN. GREGG F. MARTIN, USA
President, U.S. Institute of Peace (ex officio)	KRISTIN LORD, *Acting*

Officials

President	KRISTIN LORD, *Acting*
Executive Vice President	KRISTIN LORD
Director, Congressional Relations	LAURIE SCHULTZ-HEIM
Director, Intergovernmental Affairs	LINWOOD Q. HAM
Director, Public Affairs and Communication	(VACANCY)

The United States Institute of Peace prevents, mitigates, and resolves violent conflicts around the world by direct engagement in conflict zones and providing analysis, education, and resources to those working for peace.

The United States Institute of Peace (USIP) is an independent quasi-Federal institution established by Congress pursuant to title XVII of the Defense Authorization Act of 1985, as amended (22 U.S.C. 4601–4611), to develop, apply, and foster cost-effective strategies and tools to prevent, mitigate, and resolve violent international conflicts, particularly those that threaten or harm America's strategic and security interests. The USIP Act defines the organization's mission "to serve the people and the government through the widest possible range of education and training, basic and applied research opportunities, and peace information services on the means to promote international peace and the resolution of conflicts among nations and peoples of the world without

recourse to violence." A bipartisan Board of Directors, appointed by the President and confirmed by the Senate, governs the Institute. The Board comprises members from outside the Federal service, the Secretary of State, the Secretary of Defense, and the President of the National Defense University. The Board appoints the President of the Institute.

Programs and Activities

The Institute supports U.S. national security and foreign affairs through conflict management and peacebuilding operations; training in conflict management and peacebuilding tradecraft and best practices; and conflict research and analysis. In carrying out its mission, USIP operates on the ground in conflict zones, providing services that include facilitating dialogue among parties in conflict; building conflict management skills and capacity; indentifying and disseminating best practices in conflict management; promoting the rule of law; reforming and strengthening education systems; strengthening civil society; and educating the public through media and other outreach activities. USIP works in partnership with the State and Defense Departments, the U.S. Agency for International Development, nongovernmental organizations, higher and secondary educational institutions, foreign governments, and international organizations to promote collaborative problemsolving through conflict management operations, training and analysis, facilitated dialogue, Track 1.5 diplomacy, and special events. The Institute conducts practitioner training in conflict management, including mediation and negotiating skills for government and military personnel, civil society leaders, and staff of nongovernmental and international organizations. The Institute extends its reach through grants, fellowships, and scholarships to nonprofit organizations in the United States and overseas.

Sources of Information

More information is available online at the Institute's Web site. For further information, contact the Office of Public Affairs and Communications, United States Institute of Peace, 2301 Constitution Avenue NW., Washington, DC 20037. Phone, 202–457–1700. Fax, 202–429–6063. Internet, http://www. usip.org/newsroom.

INTERNATIONAL ORGANIZATIONS

AFRICAN DEVELOPMENT BANK

Avenue Jean-Paul II, 01 BP 1387, Abidjan 01, Côte d'Ivoire
Phone, +225 20 26 10 20. Internet, http://www.afdb.org. Email, afdb@afdb.org.

President   DONALD KABERUKA

The African Development Bank (AFDB) was established in 1964 and, by charter amendment, opened its membership to non-African countries in 1982. Its mandate is to contribute to the economic development and social progress of its regional members. Bank membership totals 78, including 53 African countries and 25 nonregional countries. With the September 1999 ratification of the agreement on the fifth general capital increase, Bank ownership is 60 percent African and 40 percent nonregional.

The African Development Fund (AFDF), the concessional lending affiliate, was established in 1972 to complement AFDB operations by providing concessional financing for high-priority development projects in the poorest African countries. The Fund's membership consists of 27 nonregional member countries, South Africa, and AFDB, which represents its African members and is allocated half of the votes.

In February 2003, security concerns resulted in AFDB headquarters temporarily relocating to Tunis, Tunisia. On September 8, 2014, the AFDB returned to its headquarters in Abidjan, Côte d'Ivoire.

ASIAN DEVELOPMENT BANK

Headquarters: 6 ADB Avenue, Mandaluyong City, 1550 Metro Manila, Philippines
Phone, +632 632–4444. Fax, +632 636–2444. Internet, http://www.adb.org. Email, information@adb.org.
ADB North American Representative Office: 900 17th Street NW., Suite 900, Washington DC 20006
Phone, 202–728–1500. Fax, 202 728 1505.

President   TAKEHIKO NAKAO

The Asian Development Bank (ADB) commenced operations on December 19, 1966. It now has 67 member countries: 48 from Asia and 19 from outside the region.

The purpose of the ADB is to foster sustainable economic development, poverty alleviation, and cooperation among its developing member countries in the Asia-Pacific region. The ADB invests in infrastructure, health care services, financial and public administration systems, and helps nations prepare for the impact of climate change and better manage their natural resources. The ADB is committed to helping developing member countries evolve into thriving, modern economies that are well integrated with each other and the world. Its primary vehicles for assistance are loans, grants, policy dialogue, technical assistance, and equity investments.

EUROPEAN BANK FOR RECONSTRUCTION AND DEVELOPMENT

One Exchange Square, London EC2A 2JN, United Kingdom
Phone, +44 20 7338 6000. Internet, http://www.ebrd.com.

President	SUMA CHAKRABARTI

The European Bank for Reconstruction and Development (EBRD) is a multilateral development bank that supports economic development projects in 34 countries from central Europe to central Asia. Investing primarily in private sector clients whose needs cannot be fully met by commercial credit and equity markets, the EBRD promotes entrepreneurship and fosters transition towards open and democratic market economies.

The Bank, which is owned by 64 countries and two intergovernmental institutions, is based in London.

INTER-AMERICAN DEFENSE BOARD

2600 Sixteenth Street NW., Washington, DC 20441
Phone, 202–939–6041. Internet, http://www.jid.org. Email, protocol@jid.org.

Chairman	LT. GEN. WERTHER ARAYA MENGHINI

The Inter-American Defense Board is the oldest permanently constituted, international military organization in the world. It was founded by Resolution XXXIX of the Meeting of Foreign Ministers at Rio de Janeiro in January 1942. The Board is governed according to Statutes that the General Assembly of the Organization of American States approved in March 2006. Senior armed forces officers from the member nations staff the various agencies of the Board. Its three major components are the Council of Delegates, the Secretariat, and the Inter-American Defense College.

The Board studies and recommends to member governments measures it deems necessary for the safety and security of the hemisphere. It also acts as a technical military adviser for the Organization of American States and is involved in projects such as disaster preparedness and humanitarian demining programs in Central and South America.

The Inter-American Defense College, founded in 1962, prepares senior military officers and civilian functionaries for positions in their respective governments. The College provides an 11-month, professionally-oriented, multidisciplinary, graduate-level course of study focusing on the Western Hemisphere's most pressing defense and security issues.

INTER-AMERICAN DEVELOPMENT BANK

Headquarters: 1300 New York Avenue NW., Washington, DC 20577
Phone, 202–623–1000. Fax, 202–623–3096. Internet, http://www.iadb.org.

President	LUIS ALBERTO MORENO

The Inter-American Development Bank (IDB) was established in 1959 to help accelerate economic and social development in Latin America and the Caribbean. It is based in Washington, DC.

The Bank has 48 member countries, 26 of which are borrowing members in Latin America and the Caribbean.

INTERNATIONAL MONETARY FUND

700 Nineteenth Street NW., Washington, DC 20431
Phone, 202–623–7000. Fax, 202–623–4661. Internet, http://www.imf.org.

Managing Director and Chairman of the Executive Board	CHRISTINE LAGARDE
First Deputy Managing Director	DAVID LIPTON
Deputy Managing Directors	NAOYUKI SHINOHARA, MIN ZHU, (VACANCY)

The Final Act of the United Nations Monetary and Financial Conference, signed at Bretton Woods, NH, on July 22, 1944, set forth the original Articles of Agreement of the International Monetary Fund (IMF). The Agreement became effective on December 27, 1945, when the President, authorized by the Bretton Woods Agreements Act (22 U.S.C. 286), accepted membership for the United States in IMF, the Agreement having thus been accepted by countries whose combined financial commitments (quotas) equaled approximately 80 percent of IMF's original quotas. The inaugural meeting of the Board of Governors was held in March 1946, and the first meeting of the Executive Directors was held May 6, 1946.

On May 31, 1968, the Board of Governors approved an amendment to the Articles of Agreement for the establishment of a facility based on Special Drawing Rights (SDR) in IMF and for modification of certain IMF rules and practices. The amendment became effective on July 28, 1969, and the Special Drawing Account became operative on August 6, 1969. United States acceptance of the amendment and participation in the Special Drawing Account were authorized by the Special Drawing Rights Act (22 U.S.C. 286 et seq.).

On April 30, 1976, the Board of Governors approved a second amendment to the Articles of Agreement, which entered into force on April 1, 1978. This amendment gave members the right to adopt exchange arrangements of their choice while placing certain obligations on them regarding their exchange rate policies, over which IMF was to exercise firm surveillance. The official price of gold was abolished, and the SDR account was promoted as the principal reserve asset of the international monetary system. United States acceptance of this amendment was authorized by the Bretton Woods Agreements Act Amendments (22 U.S.C. 286e–5).

On June 28, 1990, the Board of Governors approved a third amendment to the Articles of Agreement, which became effective on November 11, 1992. Under this amendment, a member's voting rights and certain related rights may be suspended by a 70-percent majority of the executive board if the member, having been declared ineligible to use the general resources of the Fund, persists in its failure to fulfill any of its obligations under the Articles.

The IMF has 188 member countries. It promotes international monetary cooperation through a permanent forum for consultation and collaboration on international monetary problems; facilitates the expansion and balanced growth of international trade; promotes exchange rate stability; assists in the establishment of an open multilateral system of payments for current transactions among members; and gives confidence to members by making IMF resources temporarily available to them under adequate safeguards.

IMF helps its members correct imbalances in their international balances of payments. It periodically examines the economic developments and policies of its member countries, offers policy advice, and at member's request and upon executive board approval, provides financial assistance through a variety of financial facilities designed to address specific problems. These financing mechanisms provide access to the Fund's general resources to offer short-term assistance during crises of market confidence, compensatory financing to countries suffering declines in export earnings, emergency assistance for countries recovering from natural disasters or armed conflict, and low-interest rate resources to support structural adjustment and promote growth in the poorest countries. IMF also provides technical assistance and training to its members.

For further information, contact the Chief, Public Affairs Division, External Relations Department, International Monetary Fund, 700 Nineteenth Street NW., Washington, DC 20431. Phone, 202–623–7300. Fax, 202–623–6278. Email, publicaffairs@imf.org. Internet, http://www.imf.org.

INTER-AMERICAN INVESTMENT CORPORATION

Headquarters: 1350 New York Avenue NW., Washington, DC 20577
Phone, 202–623–3901. Internet, http://www.iic.int.

Chairman, Board of Directors	LUIS ALBERTO MORENO
General Manager	CARL MUÑANA

The Inter-American Investment Corporation (IIC), an affiliate of the Inter-American Development Bank based in Washington, DC, was established in 1985 to promote the economic development of its Latin American and Caribbean members by financing small- and medium-size private enterprises. IIC provides project financing in the form of direct loans and equity investments, lines of credit to local financial intermediaries, and investments in local and regional investment funds.

IIC has 44 member countries, of which 27 are in the Western Hemisphere, including the United States, and 17 are outside the region.

INTERNATIONAL ORGANIZATION FOR MIGRATION

Headquarters: 17 Route des Morillons, C.P. 17, CH–1211 Geneva 19, Switzerland. Mailing address, P.O. Box 71, CH–1211, Geneva 19, Switzerland
Phone, 011–41–22–717–9111. Fax, 011–41–22–798–6150. Internet, http://www.iom.int.

Email, hq@iom.int.

Washington Office: Suite 700, 1752 N Street NW., Washington, DC 20036
Phone, 202–862–1826. Fax, 202–862–1879. Email, IOMWashington@iom.int.
New York Office: 122 E. 42d Street, 48th Floor, New York, NY 10168
Phone, 212–681–7000. Fax, 212–867–5887. Email, newyork@iom.int.

Director General	WILLIAM LACY SWING
Deputy Director General	LAURA THOMPSON
Chief of Mission (Washington, DC)	LUCA DALL' OGLIO
Permanent Observer to the United Nations	MICHELE KLEIN SOLOMON

Established in 1951, the International Organization for Migration (IOM) is the leading intergovernmental organization in the field of migration. With 155 member states, an additional 11 states holding observer status, and offices in over 100 countries, IOM is dedicated to promoting humane and orderly migration for the benefit of all. It does so by providing services and advice to migrants and governments, while working in close cooperation with governmental, intergovernmental, and non-governmental partners. IOM has observer status at the United Nations.

IOM works with its partners to meet the growing operational challenges of migration management; advance understanding of migration issues; encourage social and economic development through migration; and uphold the human dignity and well-being of migrants.

IOM has been at the forefront of emergency response to ensure assistance and protection to stranded migrants and displaced persons. IOM has a lead role under the UN Cluster Approach in Camp Co-coordination and Camp Management in Natural Disasters and is a key partner in Emergency Shelter, Logistics, Health, Protection and Early Recovery.

IOM's expertise and services also include: providing secure, reliable, and cost-effective services for persons requiring migration assistance; promoting humane and orderly management of migration and the effective respect for the human rights of migrants; providing expert advice, technical cooperation, and operational assistance to build national capacities and facilitate cooperation on migration matters; assisting states to facilitate the integration of migrants in their new environment and to engage diasporas, including as development partners; advising states in the development and delivery of programs and technical expertise to combat migrant smuggling and human trafficking; working with national health systems to reduce mortality, morbidity, and disabilities and to enhance access to rights-based health and well-being services throughout the migration cycle; and working with states in the area of labor migration, amongst others.

ORGANIZATION OF AMERICAN STATES

Seventeenth Street and Constitution Avenue NW., Washington, DC 20006
Phone, 202–370–5000. Fax, 202–458–3967. Internet, http://www.oas.org.

Secretary General	JOSÉ M. INSULZA
Assistant Secretary General	ALBERT R. RAMDIN

The Organization of American States (OAS) brings together the countries of the Western Hemisphere to strengthen cooperation and advance common interests. At the core of the OAS mission is a commitment to democracy. Building on this foundation, OAS works to promote good governance, strengthen human rights, foster peace and security, expand trade, and address the complex problems caused by poverty, drugs, and corruption. Through decisions made by its political bodies and programs carried out by its General Secretariat, OAS promotes greater inter-American cooperation and understanding.

OAS member states have intensified their cooperation since the end of the cold war, taking on new and important challenges. In 1994, the region's 34 democratically elected presidents and prime ministers met in Miami for the First Summit of the Americas, where they established broad political, economic, and social development goals. They have continued to meet periodically since then to examine common interests and priorities. Through the ongoing Summits of the Americas process, the region's leaders have entrusted the OAS with a growing number of responsibilities to help advance the countries' shared vision.

With four official languages—English, Spanish, Portuguese, and French— the OAS reflects the rich diversity of peoples and cultures across the Americas. The OAS has 35 member states: the independent nations of North, Central, and South America, and of the Caribbean. Since 1962, Cuba has been barred from participation by resolution of the Eighth Meeting of Consultation of Ministers of Foreign Affairs. Countries from all around the world are permanent observers, closely following the issues that are critical to the Americas and often providing key financial support for OAS programs.

Member states set major policies and goals through the General Assembly, which gathers the hemisphere's foreign ministers once a year in regular session. The Permanent Council, made up of ambassadors appointed by member states, meets regularly at OAS headquarters in Washington, DC, to guide ongoing policies and actions. The chairmanship of the Permanent Council rotates every 3 months, in alphabetical order of countries. Each member state has an equal voice, and most decisions are made through consensus.

Also under the OAS umbrella are several specialized agencies that have considerable autonomy: the Pan American Health Organization in Washington, DC; the Inter-American Children's Institute in Montevideo, Uruguay; the Inter-American Institute for Cooperation on Agriculture in San Jose, Costa Rica; and the Pan American Institute of Geography and History and the Inter-American Indian Institute, both in Mexico City.

In 1948, 21 nations of the hemisphere signed the OAS Charter at the Ninth International Conference of American States. They were Argentina, Bolivia, Brazil, Chile, Colombia, Costa Rica, Cuba (barred from participation), Dominican Republic, Ecuador, El Salvador, Guatemala, Haiti, Honduras, Mexico, Nicaragua, Panama, Paraguay, Peru, United States of America, Uruguay, and Venezuela.

Subsequently, 14 other countries joined the OAS by signing and ratifying the Charter. They were Barbados, Trinidad and Tobago, Jamaica, Grenada, Suriname, Dominica, Saint Lucia, Antigua and Barbuda, Saint Vincent and the Grenadines, the Bahamas, Saint Kitts and Nevis, Canada, Belize, and Guyana. This brings the number of member states to 35.

For further information, contact the Organization of American States, Seventeenth Street and Constitution Avenue NW., Washington, DC 20006. Phone, 202–370–5000. Fax, 202–458–3967.

UNITED NATIONS

United Nations, New York, NY 10017
Phone, 212–963–1234. Internet, http://www.un.org.
United Nations Office at Geneva: Palais des Nations, 1211 Geneva 10, Switzerland
United Nations Office at Vienna: Vienna International Centre, P.O. Box 500, A–1400, Vienna,

Austria

Washington, DC: U.N. Information Centre, Suite 400, 1775 K Street NW., Washington, DC 20006

Phone, 202-331-8670. Fax, 202-331-9191. Internet, http://www.unicwash.org. Email, unicdc@ unic.org.

Secretary-General	BAN KI-MOON
Director-General, U.N. Office at Geneva	KASSYM-JOMART TOKAYEV
Director-General, U.N. Office at Vienna	YURY FEDOTOV
Director, Washington DC Information Centre	RODNEY BENT

The United Nations is an international organization that was set up in accordance with the Charter drafted by governments represented at the Conference on International Organization meeting at San Francisco. The Charter was signed on June 26, 1945, and came into force on October 24, 1945, when the required number of ratifications and accessions had been made by the signatories. Amendments increasing membership of the Security Council and the Economic and Social Council came into effect on August 31, 1965.

The United Nations now consists of 193 member states, of which 51 are founding members.

The purposes of the United Nations set out in the Charter are to maintain international peace and security; to develop friendly relations among nations; to achieve international cooperation in solving international problems of an economic, social, cultural, or humanitarian character and in promoting respect for human rights; and to be a center for harmonizing the actions of nations in the attainment of these common ends.

The principal organs of the United Nations are as follows:

General Assembly   All states that are members of the United Nations are members of the General Assembly. Its functions are to consider and discuss any matter within the scope of the Charter of the United Nations and to make recommendations to the members of the United Nations and other organs. It approves the budget of the organization, the expenses of which are borne by the members as apportioned by the General Assembly.

The General Assembly may call the attention of the Security Council to situations likely to endanger international peace and security, may initiate studies, and may receive and consider reports from other organs of the United Nations. Under the "Uniting for Peace" resolution adopted by the General Assembly in November 1950, if the Security Council fails to act on an apparent threat to or breach of the peace or act of aggression because of lack of unanimity of its five permanent members, the Assembly itself may take up the matter within 24 hours—in emergency special session— and recommend collective measures, including, in case of a breach of the peace or act of aggression, use of armed force when necessary to maintain or restore international peace and security.

The General Assembly normally meets in regular annual session from September through December. It also has met in special sessions and emergency special sessions.

Security Council   The Security Council consists of 15 members, of which 5—the People's Republic of China, France, Russia, the United Kingdom, and the United States of America—are permanent members. The 10 nonpermanent members are elected for 2-year terms by the General Assembly. The primary responsibility of the Security Council is to act on behalf of the members of the United Nations in maintenance of international peace and security. Measures that may be employed by the Security Council are outlined in the Charter.

The Security Council, together with the General Assembly, also elects the judges of the International Court of Justice and makes a recommendation to the General

Assembly on the appointment of the Secretary-General of the organization.

The Security Council first met in London on January 17, 1946, and is so organized as to be able to function continuously.

Economic and Social Council This organ is responsible, under the authority of the General Assembly, for the economic and social programs of the United Nations. Its functions include making or initiating studies, reports, and recommendations on international economic, social, cultural, educational, health, and related matters; promoting respect for and observance of human rights and fundamental freedoms for all; calling international conferences and preparing draft conventions for submission to the General Assembly on matters within its competence; negotiating agreements with the specialized agencies and defining their relationship with the United Nations; coordinating the activities of the specialized agencies; and consulting with nongovernmental organizations concerned with matters within its competence. The Council consists of 54 members of the United Nations elected by the General Assembly for 3-year terms; 18 are elected each year.

The Council usually holds two regular sessions a year. It has also held a number of special sessions.

Trusteeship Council The Trusteeship Council was initially established to consist of any member states that administered trust territories, permanent members of the Security Council that did not administer trust territories, and enough other nonadministering countries elected by the General Assembly for 3-year terms to ensure that membership would be equally divided between administering and nonadministering members. Under authority of the General Assembly, the Council considered reports from members administering trust territories, examined petitions from trust territory inhabitants, and provided for periodic inspection visits to trust territories.

With the independence of Palau, the last remaining U.N. trust territory, the Trusteeship Council formally suspended operations after nearly half a century. The Council will henceforth meet only on an extraordinary basis, as the need may arise.

International Court of Justice The International Court of Justice is the principal judicial organ of the United Nations. It has its seat at The Hague, the Netherlands. All members of the United Nations are ipso facto parties to the Statute of the Court. Nonmembers of the United Nations may become parties to the Statute of the Court on conditions prescribed by the General Assembly on the recommendation of the Security Council.

The jurisdiction of the Court comprises all cases that the parties refer to it and all matters specially provided for in the Charter of the United Nations or in treaties and conventions in force.

The Court consists of 15 judges known as members of the Court. They are elected for 9-year terms by the General Assembly and the Security Council, voting independently, and may be reelected.

Secretariat The Secretariat consists of a Secretary-General and "such staff as the Organization may require." The Secretary-General, who is appointed by the General Assembly on the recommendation of the Security Council, is the chief administrative officer of the United Nations. He acts in that capacity for the General Assembly, the Security Council, the Economic and Social Council, and the Trusteeship Council. Under the Charter, the Secretary-General "may bring to the attention of the Security Council any matter that in his opinion may threaten the maintenance of international peace and security."

WORLD BANK GROUP

Headquarters: 1818 H Street NW., Washington, DC 20433
Phone, 202–473–1000. Fax, 202–477–6391. Internet, http://www.worldbank.org.

President	JIM YONG KIM

The World Bank Group consists of five institutions: the International Bank for Reconstruction and Development (IBRD), the International Development Association (IDA), the International Finance Corporation (IFC), Multilateral Investment Guarantee Agency (MIGA), and the International Centre for the Settlement of Investment Disputes (ICSID). The two primary economic and social development institutions are the IBRD and the IDA. Donor countries and countries with borrowing rights—188 in total—support and benefit from these two development banks. The other three institutions complement the activities of the IBRD and the IDA.

International Bank for Reconstruction and Development

The International Bank for Reconstruction and Development (IBRD) officially came into existence in 1944.

The Bank's purpose is to promote economic, social, and environmental progress in developing nations by reducing poverty so that their people may live better and fuller lives. The Bank lends funds at market-determined interest rates, provides advice, and serves as a catalyst to stimulate outside investments. Its resources come primarily from funds raised in the world capital markets, its retained earnings, and repayments on its loans.

International Development Association

The International Development Association (IDA) came into existence in 1960, as an institution of the World Bank Group. The Association's resources consist of subscriptions and supplementary resources in the form of general replenishments on a three year revolving cycle, mostly from its more industrialized and developed members; special contributions by its richer members; repayments on earlier credits; and transfers from IBRD's net earnings.

The Association promotes economic development, reduces poverty, and raises the standard of living in the least developed areas of the world. It does this by financing their developmental requirements on concessionary terms, which are more flexible and bear less heavily on the balance of payments than those of conventional loans, thereby furthering the objectives of IBRD and supplementing its activities.

International Finance Corporation

Headquarters: 2121 Pennsylvania Avenue NW., Washington, DC 20433
Phone, 202–473–7711. Fax, 202–974–4384. Internet, http://www.ifc.org.

President	JIM YONG KIM
Executive Vice President and Chief Executive Officer	JIN-YONG CAI

The International Finance Corporation (IFC), an institution of the World Bank Group, was established in 1956 to promote productive private enterprise in developing member countries.

The Corporation pursues its objective principally through direct debt and equity investments in projects that establish new businesses or expand, modify, or diversify existing businesses. It also encourages co-financing by other investors and lenders.

Additionally, advisory services and technical assistance are provided by IFC to developing member countries in areas such as capital market development, privatization, corporate restructuring, and foreign investment.

Multilateral Investment Guarantee Agency

Headquarters: 1818 H Street NW., Washington, DC 20433
Phone, 202–458–2538. Fax, 202–522–0316. Internet, http://www.miga.org.

President	JIM YONG KIM
Executive Vice President and Chief Executive Officer	KEIKO HONDA

The Multilateral Investment Guarantee Agency (MIGA), an institution of the World Bank Group, was formally constituted in 1988.

Its basic purpose is to facilitate the flow of foreign private investment for productive purposes to developing member countries by offering long-term political risk insurance in the areas of expropriation, transfer restriction, breach of contract, and war and civil disturbance; and by providing advisory and consultative services. The Agency cooperates with national investment insurance schemes, such as OPIC, and with private insurers.

International Centre for the Settlement of Investment Disputes

Headquarters: 1818 H Street NW., MSN J2–200, Washington, DC 20433
Phone, 202–458–1534. Fax, 202–522–2615. Internet, http://icsid.worldbank.org/ICSID/. Email, ICSIDsecretariat@worldbank.org.

President	JIM YONG KIM
Secretary-General	MEG KINNEAR

The International Centre for the Settlement of Investment Disputes (ICSID) is an autonomous international institution affiliated with the World Bank Group established under the Convention on the Settlement of Investment Disputes between States and Nationals of Other States. The Convention sets forth ICSID's mandate, organization, and core functions. The primary purpose of ICSID is to provide facilities for conciliation and arbitration of international investment disputes.

The ICSID Convention is a multilateral treaty formulated by the Executive Directors of the International Bank for Reconstruction and Development (the World Bank). The treaty entered into force in 1966. There are currently 159 signatory states to the ICSID Convention of which 150 countries also deposited their instruments of ratification, acceptance, or approval of the Convention.

OTHER INTERNATIONAL ORGANIZATIONS

Below is a list of other international organizations that do not have separate entries elsewhere in the Manual. The United States participates in these organizations in accordance with the provisions of treaties, other international agreements, congressional legislation, or executive arrangements. In some cases, no financial contribution is involved.

Various commissions, councils, or committees subsidiary to the organizations listed here are not named separately on this list. These include the international bodies for drugs and crime, which are subsidiary to the United Nations.

This listing is provided for reference purposes and should not be considered exhaustive. For more information on international organizations and United States participation in them, contact the State Department's Bureau of International Organization Affairs. Phone, 202–647–9600. Internet, http://go.usa.gov/UjzR.

I. Specialized Agencies of the United Nations and Related Organizations

Food and Agricultural Organization
International Atomic Energy Agency
International Civil Aviation Organization
International Fund for Agriculture Development
International Labor Organization
International Maritime Organization
International Telecommunication Union
United Nations Educational, Scientific and Cultural Organization (UNESCO)
Universal Postal Union
World Health Organization
World Intellectual Property Organization
World Meteorological Organization

II. Peacekeeping and Political Missions Administered by the United Nations Department of Peacekeeping Operations

Africa

United Nations Hybrid Operation in Darfur (UNAMID)
United Nations Integrated Stabilization Mission in Mali (MINUSMA)
United Nations Interim Security Force for Abyei (UNISFA)
United Nations Mission for the Referendum in Western Sahara (MINURSO)
United Nations Mission in Liberia (UNMIL)
United Nations Mission in the Republic of South Sudan (UNMISS)
United Nations Operation in Côte d'Ivoire (UNOCI)
United Nations Organization Stabilization Mission in the Democratic Republic of the Congo (MONUSCO)
United Nations Stabilization Mission in the Central African Republic (MINUSCA)

Americas

United Nations Stabilization Mission in Haiti (MINUSTAH)

Middle East

United Nations Assistance Mission in Afghanistan (UNAMA)
United Nations Disengagement Observer Force (UNDOF)

United Nations Interim Force in Lebanon (UNIFIL)
United Nations Military Observer Group in India and Pakistan (UNMOGIP)
United Nations Truce Supervision Organization (UNTSO)

Europe

United Nations Interim Administration Mission in Kosovo (UNMIK)
United Nations Peacekeeping Force in Cyprus (UNFICYP)

III. Inter-American Organizations

Border Environment Cooperation Commission
Caribbean Postal Union
Inter-American Center of Tax Administrators
Inter-American Children's Institute
Inter-American Commission of Human Rights
Inter-American Commission of Women
Inter-American Committee Against Terrorism
Inter-American Committee on Natural Disaster Reduction
Inter-American Council for Integral Development
Inter-American Drug Abuse Control Commission
Inter-American Indian Institute
Inter-American Institute for Cooperation in Agriculture
Inter-American Institute for Global Change Research
Inter-American Investment Corporation
Inter-American Telecommunications Commission
Inter-American Tropical Tuna Commission
Pan American Health Organization
Pan American Institute of Geography and History
Pan American Railway Congress Association
Postal Union of the Americas, Spain and Portugal

IV. Regional Organizations

Antarctic Treaty System
Arctic Council
Asia-Pacific Economic Cooperation
Asia Pacific Energy Research Center

Colombo Plan for Cooperative Economic and Social Development in Asia and the Pacific
Commission for Environmental Cooperation
Commission for Labor Cooperation
International Commission for the Conservation of Atlantic Tunas
North Atlantic Assembly
North Atlantic Treaty Organization
North Atlantic Salmon Conservation Organization
North Pacific Anadromous Fish Commission
North Pacific Coast Guard Forum
North Pacific Marine Science Organization
Northwest Atlantic Fisheries Organization
Secretariat of the Pacific Community
South Pacific Regional Environment Program
Western and Central Pacific Fisheries Commission

V. Other International Organizations

Bioversity International
Center for International Forestry Research (CIFOR)
Commission for the Conservation of Antarctic Marine Living Resources
Community of Democracies
Comprehensive Nuclear Test Ban Treaty Organization
Consultative Group on International Agricultural Research (CGIAR)
COPAS–SARSAT (Search and Rescue Satellite System)
Global Biodiversity Information Facility
Global Environment Facility
Hague Conference on Private International Law
Human Frontier Science Program Organization
Integrated Ocean Drilling Program Council
International Agency for Research on Cancer (IARC)
International Bureau for the Permanent Court of Arbitration
International Bureau of Weights and Measures
International Center for Agricultural Research in the Dry Areas
International Center for the Study of the Preservation and the Restoration of Cultural Property

International Coffee Organization

International Committee of the Red Cross (ICRC)

International Cotton Advisory Committee

International Council for the Exploration of the Seas

International Court of Justice

International Criminal Police Organization (INTERPOL)

International Customs Tariffs Bureau

International Development Law Organization

International Energy Agency

International Energy Forum Secretariat

International Fertilizer Development Center

International Grains Council

International Hydrographic Organization

International Institute for Applied Systems Analysis

International Institute for Cotton

International Institute for the Unification of Private Law

International Mobile Satellite Organization

International Organization for Legal Metrology

International Organization of Supreme Audit Institutions

International Research and Training Institute for the Advancement of Women

International Rubber Study Group

International Science and Technology Center

International Seed Testing Association

International Sugar Council

International Telecommunications Satellite Organization

International Tropical Timber Organization

International Union of Credit and Investment Insurers (Berne Union)

International Whaling Commission

Inter-Parliamentary Union

Iran-United States Claims Tribunal

Multinational Force and Observers

Nuclear Energy Agency

Organization for Economic Cooperation and Development

Organization for the Prohibition of Chemical Weapons

Organization for Security and Cooperation in Europe

Permanent International Association of Navigation Congresses

Preparatory Commission for the Comprehensive Nuclear Test-Ban Treaty

Regional Environmental Center for Central and Eastern Europe

Science and Technology Center in Ukraine

Standards and Trade Development Facility

Wassenaar Arrangement

World Association of Investment Promotion Agencies

World Customs Organization

World Heritage Fund

World Organization for Animal Health

World Trade Organization

VI. Special Voluntary Programs

Asian Vegetable Research and Development Center

Convention on International Trade in Endangered Species of Wild Fauna and Flora (CITES)

Global Fund to Fight HIV/AIDS, Tuberculosis, and Malaria

International Council for Science

International Crop Research Institute for Semi-Arid Tropics

International Federation of the Red Cross and Red Crescent Societies

International Food Policy Research Institute

International Fund for Agricultural Development

International Institute of Tropical Agriculture

International Strategy for Disaster Reduction

Joint United Nations Program on HIV/AIDS (UNAIDS)

Korean Peninsula Energy Development Organization

Multilateral Fund for the Implementation of the Montreal Protocol

Ramsar Convention on Wetlands

United Nations Capital Development Fund

United Nations Children's Fund (UNICEF)

United Nations Conference on Trade and Development

United Nations Democracy Fund

United Nations Development Fund for Women (UNIFEM)

United Nations Development Program

United Nations Economic Commission for Europe

United Nations Environment Program

United Nations Framework Convention on Climate Change
United Nations Convention to Combat Desertification
United Nations High Commissioner for Human Rights Programs
United Nations High Commissioner for Refugees Programs
United Nations Human Settlements Program (UN HABITAT)

United Nations Population Fund (UNFPA)
United Nations Relief and Works Agency for Palestine Refugees (UNRWA)
United Nations Voluntary Fund for Technical Cooperation in the Field of Human Rights
United Nations Voluntary Fund for the Victims of Torture
United Nations World Food Program
World Agroforestry Center

SELECTED BILATERAL ORGANIZATIONS

Below is a list of bilateral organizations in which the United States participates with its two neighbors, Mexico and Canada. This listing is for reference purposes only and should not be considered exhaustive.

Border Environment Cooperation Commission

United States Section: P.O. Box 221648, El Paso, TX 79913. Phone, 877–277–1703. Fax, 915–975–8280. E-mail, becc@cocef.org. Internet, www.becc.org.

Mexican Section: Bulevar Tomas Fernadez 8069, Ciudad Juarez, Chihuahua, 32470. Phone, 011–52–656–688–4600. Fax, 011–52–656–625–6180. Internet, www.cocef.org.

Great Lakes Fishery Commission

2100 Commonwealth Boulevard, Suite 100, Ann Arbor, MI 48105. Telephone, 734–662–3209. Fax, 734–741–2010. Email, info@glfc.org. Internet, www.glfc.org.

International Boundary Commission, United States and Canada

United States Section: 2000 L Street NW., Suite 615, Washington, DC 20036. Phone, 202–736–9102. Fax, 202–632–2008. E-mail, hipsleyk@ibcusca.org. Internet, www.internationalboundarycommission.org.

Canadian Section: 575–615 Booth Street, Ottawa, Ontario K1A 0E9 Canada. Phone, (613) 944–4515. Fax, (613) 992–1122. E-mail, ibc-cfi@nrcan.gc.ca. Internet, www.internationalboundarycommission.org.

International Boundary and Water Commission, United States and Mexico

United States Section: Suite C–100, 4171 North Mesa Street, El Paso, TX 79902. Phone, 800–262–8857. Internet, www.ibwc.state.gov.

Mexican Section: Avenue Universidad 2180, Zona Chamizal, C.P. 32310, Ciudad Juarez, Chihuahua, 32310. Phone, 011–52–656–639–7951 or 011–52–656–613–7311. Fax, 011–52–656–613–9943. E-mail, cilamex@cila.gob.mx. Internet, www.sre.gob.mx/cila.

International Joint Commission—United States and Canada

United States Section: 2000 L Street NW., Suite 615, Washington, DC 20440. Phone, 202–736–9009. Fax, 202–632–2007. E-mail: commission@washington.ijc.org. Internet, www.ijc.org.

Canadian Section: 234 Laurier Avenue West, 22d Floor, Ottawa, Ontario K1P 6K6. Phone, 613–995–2984. Fax, 613–993–5583. E-mail: commission@ottawa.ijc.org. Internet, www.ijc.org.

Great Lakes Regional Office: 100 Ouellette Avenue, 8th Floor, Windsor, Ontario N9A 6T3. Phone, 519–257–6700. Fax, 519–257–6740. E-mail: nevinj@windsor.ijc.org. Internet, www.ijc.org.

International Pacific Halibut Commission

2320 W. Commodore Way, Suite 300, Seattle, WA 98199–1287. Phone, 206–634–1838. Fax, 206–632–2983. Internet, www.iphc.int.

Joint Mexican-United States Defense Commission

United States Section: Room 2E773, The Pentagon, Washington, DC 20318. Phone, 703–695–8164.

Mexican Section: 6th Floor, 1911 Pennsylvania Avenue NW., Mexican Embassy, Washington, DC 20006. Phone, 202–728–1748.

Permanent Joint Board on Defense— United States and Canada

United States Section: Room 2E773, The Pentagon, Washington, DC 20318. Phone, 703–695–8164.

Canadian Section: Director of Western Hemisphere, 101 Colonel By Drive, Ottawa, ON K1A 0K2. Phone, 613–992–4423.

COMMONLY USED AGENCY ACRONYMS

ABMC AMERICAN BATTLE MONUMENTS COMMISSION
ACF ADMINISTRATION OF CHILDREN AND FAMILIES
ACFR ADMINISTRATIVE COMMITTEE OF THE FEDERAL REGISTER
ADF AFRICAN DEVELOPMENT FOUNDATION
AFRH ARMED FORCES RETIREMENT HOME
AHRQ AGENCY FOR HEALTHCARE RESEARCH AND QUALITY
AMS AGRICULTURAL MARKETING SERVICE
AMTRAK NATIONAL RAILROAD PASSENGER CORPORATION
AOA ADMINISTRATION ON AGING
APHIS ANIMAL AND PLANT HEALTH INSPECTION SERVICE
APPAL APPALACHIAN STATES LOW LEVEL RADIOACTIVE WASTE COMMISSION
ARCTIC ARCTIC RESEARCH COMMISSION
ARS AGRICULTURAL RESEARCH SERVICE
ARTS NATIONAL FOUNDATION ON THE ARTS AND THE HUMANITIES
ATBCB ARCHITECTURAL AND TRANSPORTATION BARRIERS COMPLIANCE BOARD

ATF ALCOHOL, TOBACCO, FIREARMS, AND EXPLOSIVES BUREAU
ATSDR AGENCY FOR TOXIC SUBSTANCES AND DISEASE REGISTRY
BBG BROADCASTING BOARD OF GOVERNORS
BEA BUREAU OF ECONOMIC ANALYSIS
BGSEEF BARRY M. GOLDWATER SCHOLARSHIP AND EXCELLENCE IN EDUCATION FOUNDATION
BIA BUREAU OF INDIAN AFFAIRS
BIS BUREAU OF INDUSTRY AND SECURITY
BLM BUREAU OF LAND MANAGEMENT
BLS BUREAU OF LABOR STATISTICS
BOP FEDERAL PRISONS BUREAU
BOR BUREAU OF RECLAMATION
BPA BONNEVILLE POWER ADMINISTRATION
BPD BUREAU OF PUBLIC DEBT
CBO CONGRESSIONAL BUDGET OFFICE
CCC COMMODITY CREDIT CORPORATION
CCJJDP COORDINATING COUNCIL ON JUVENILE JUSTICE AND DELINQUENCY PREVENTION

CDC	CENTERS FOR DISEASE CONTROL AND PREVENTION	CSREES	COOPERATIVE STATE RESEARCH, EDUCATION, AND EXTENSION SERVICE
CDFI	COMMUNITY DEVELOPMENT FINANCIAL INSTITUTIONS FUND	DARPA	DEFENSE ADVANCED RESEARCH PROJECTS AGENCY
CEQ	COUNCIL ON ENVIRONMENTAL QUALITY	DARS	DEFENSE ACQUISITION REGULATIONS SYSTEM
CFTC	COMMODITY FUTURES TRADING COMMISSION	DC	DENALI COMMISSION
CFPB	CONSUMER FINANCIAL PROTECTION BUREAU	DCAA	DEFENSE CONTRACT AUDIT AGENCY
CIA	CENTRAL INTELLIGENCE AGENCY	DEA	DRUG ENFORCEMENT ADMINISTRATION
CITA	COMMITTEE FOR THE IMPLEMENTATION OF TEXTILE AGREEMENTS	DEPO	DISABILITY EMPLOYMENT POLICY OFFICE
CMS	CENTERS FOR MEDICARE & MEDICAID SERVICES	DFAS	DEFENSE FINANCE AND ACCOUNTING SERVICES
CNCS	CORPORATION FOR NATIONAL AND COMMUNITY SERVICE	DHS	DEPARTMENT OF HOMELAND SECURITY
COE	CORPS OF ENGINEERS	DIA	DEFENSE INTELLIGENCE AGENCY
COFA	COMMISSION OF FINE ARTS	DISA	DEFENSE INFORMATION SYSTEMS AGENCY
COLC	COPYRIGHT OFFICE, LIBRARY OF CONGRESS	DLA	DEFENSE LOGISTICS AGENCY
COPS	COMMUNITY ORIENTED POLICING SERVICES	DNFSB	DEFENSE NUCLEAR FACILITIES SAFETY BOARD
CORP	CORPORATION FOR NATIONAL AND COMMUNITY SERVICE	DOC	DEPARTMENT OF COMMERCE
CPPBSD	COMMITTEE FOR PURCHASE FROM PEOPLE WHO ARE BLIND OR SEVERELY DISABLED	DOD	DEPARTMENT OF DEFENSE
		DOE	DEPARTMENT OF ENERGY
		DOI	DEPARTMENT OF THE INTERIOR
		DOJ	DEPARTMENT OF JUSTICE
CPSC	CONSUMER PRODUCT SAFETY COMMISSION	DOL	DEPARTMENT OF LABOR
		DOS	DEPARTMENT OF STATE
CRB	COPYRIGHT ROYALTY BOARD, LIBRARY OF CONGRESS	DOT	DEPARTMENT OF TRANSPORTATION
CRC	CIVIL RIGHTS COMMISSION	DRBC	DELAWARE RIVER BASIN COMMISSION
CSB	CHEMICAL SAFETY AND HAZARD INVESTIGATION BOARD	DSCA	DEFENSE SECURITY COOPERATION AGENCY
		DSS	DEFENSE SECURITY SERVICE
CSEO	CHILD SUPPORT ENFORCEMENT OFFICE	DTRA	DEFENSE THREAT REDUCTION AGENCY
CSOSA	COURT SERVICES AND OFFENDER SUPERVISION AGENCY FOR THE DISTRICT OF COLUMBIA	EAB	BUREAU OF ECONOMIC ANALYSIS
		EAC	ELECTION ASSISTANCE COMMISSION

EBSA	EMPLOYEE BENEFITS SECURITY ADMINISTRATION	FCC	FEDERAL COMMUNICATIONS COMMISSION
ECAB	EMPLOYEES' COMPENSATION APPEALS BOARD	FCIC	FEDERAL CROP INSURANCE CORPORATION
ECSA	ECONOMICS AND STATISTICS ADMINISTRATION	FCSIC	FARM CREDIT SYSTEM INSURANCE CORPORATION
ED	DEPARTMENT OF EDUCATION	FDA	FOOD AND DRUG ADMINISTRATION
EDA	ECONOMIC DEVELOPMENT ADMINISTRATION	FDIC	FEDERAL DEPOSIT INSURANCE CORPORATION
EEOC	EQUAL EMPLOYMENT OPPORTUNITY COMMISSION	FEC	FEDERAL ELECTION COMMISSION
EERE	ENERGY EFFICIENCY AND RENEWABLE ENERGY OFFICE	FEMA	FEDERAL EMERGENCY MANAGEMENT AGENCY
EIA	ENERGY INFORMATION ADMINISTRATION	FERC	FEDERAL ENERGY REGULATORY COMMISSION
EIB	EXPORT IMPORT BANK OF THE UNITED STATES	FFIEC	FEDERAL FINANCIAL INSTITUTIONS EXAMINATION COUNCIL
EOA	ENERGY OFFICE, AGRICULTURE DEPARTMENT	FHEO	FAIR HOUSING AND EQUAL OPPORTUNITY
EOIR	EXECUTIVE OFFICE FOR IMMIGRATION REVIEW	FHFA	FEDERAL HOUSING FINANCE AGENCY
		FHFB	FEDERAL HOUSING FINANCE BOARD
EOP	EXECUTIVE OFFICE OF THE PRESIDENT	FHWA	FEDERAL HIGHWAY ADMINISTRATION
EPA	ENVIRONMENTAL PROTECTION AGENCY	FINCEN	FINANCIAL CRIMES ENFORCEMENT NETWORK
ERS	ECONOMIC RESEARCH SERVICE	FINCIC	FINANCIAL CRISIS INQUIRY COMMISSION
ESA	EMPLOYMENT STANDARDS ADMINISTRATION	FISCAL	FISCAL SERVICE
		FLETC	FEDERAL LAW ENFORCEMENT TRAINING CENTER
ETA	EMPLOYMENT AND TRAINING ADMINISTRATION	FLRA	FEDERAL LABOR RELATIONS AUTHORITY
FAA	FEDERAL AVIATION ADMINISTRATION	FMC	FEDERAL MARITIME COMMISSION
FAR	FEDERAL ACQUISITION REGULATION	FMCS	FEDERAL MEDIATION AND CONCILIATION SERVICE
FAS	FOREIGN AGRICULTURAL SERVICE		
FASAB	FEDERAL ACCOUNTING STANDARDS ADVISORY BOARD	FMCSA	FEDERAL MOTOR CARRIER SAFETY ADMINISTRATION
FBI	FEDERAL BUREAU OF INVESTIGATION	FNS	FOOD AND NUTRITION SERVICE
FCA	FARM CREDIT ADMINISTRATION	FPPO	FEDERAL PROCUREMENT POLICY OFFICE

FR	OFFICE OF THE FEDERAL REGISTER	ICEB	IMMIGRATION AND CUSTOMS ENFORCEMENT BUREAU
FRA	FEDERAL RAILROAD ADMINISTRATION		
FRS	FEDERAL RESERVE SYSTEM	IHS	INDIAN HEALTH SERVICE
FRTIB	FEDERAL RETIREMENT THRIFT INVESTMENT BOARD	IIO	INTERNATIONAL INVESTMENT OFFICE
		IRS	INTERNAL REVENUE SERVICE
FS	FOREST SERVICE	ISOO	INFORMATION SECURITY OVERSIGHT OFFICE
FSA	FARM SERVICE AGENCY		
FSIS	FOOD SAFETY AND INSPECTION SERVICE	ITA	INTERNATIONAL TRADE ADMINISTRATION
FTA	FEDERAL TRANSIT ADMINISTRATION	ITC	INTERNATIONAL TRADE COMMISSION
FTC	FEDERAL TRADE COMMISSION	JBEA	JOINT BOARD FOR ENROLLMENT OF ACTUARIES
FTZB	FOREIGN TRADE ZONES BOARD		
		LMSO	LABOR MANAGEMENT STANDARDS OFFICE
FWS	FISH AND WILDLIFE SERVICE	LOC	LIBRARY OF CONGRESS
GAO	GOVERNMENT ACCOUNTABILITY OFFICE	LSC	LEGAL SERVICES CORPORATION
GEO	GOVERNMENT ETHICS OFFICE	MARAD	MARITIME ADMINISTRATION
GIPSA	GRAIN INSPECTION, PACKERS AND STOCKYARDS ADMINISTRATION	MBDA	MINORITY BUSINESS DEVELOPMENT AGENCY
		MCC	MILLENNIUM CHALLENGE CORPORATION
GPO	GOVERNMENT PRINTING OFFICE	MDA	MISSILE DEFENSE AGENCY
GSA	GENERAL SERVICES ADMINISTRATION	MISS	MISSISSIPPI RIVER COMMISSION
HHS	DEPARTMENT OF HEALTH AND HUMAN SERVICES	MKU	MORRIS K. UDALL SCHOLARSHIP AND EXCELLENCE IN NATIONAL ENVIRONMENTAL POLICY FOUNDATION
HHSIG	INSPECTOR GENERAL OFFICE, HEALTH AND HUMAN SERVICES DEPARTMENT		
HOPE	BOARD OF DIRECTORS OF THE HOPE FOR HOMEOWNERS PROGRAM	MMC	MARINE MAMMALCOMMISSION
HPAC	HISTORIC PRESERVATION, ADVISORY COUNCIL	MMS	MINERALS MANAGEMENT SERVICE
HRSA	HEALTH RESOURCES AND SERVICES ADMINISTRATION	MSHA	MINE SAFETY AND HEALTH ADMINISTRATION
HST	HARRY S. TRUMAN SCHOLARSHIP FOUNDATION	MSHFRC	FEDERAL MINE SAFETY AND HEALTH REVIEW COMMISSION
HUD	DEPARTMENT OF HOUSING AND URBAN DEVELOPMENT	MSPB	MERIT SYSTEMS PROTECTION BOARD
IAF	INTER AMERICAN FOUNDATION	NARA	NATIONAL ARCHIVES AND RECORDS ADMINISTRATION

NASA	NATIONAL AERONAUTICS AND SPACE ADMINISTRATION		NPREC	NATIONAL PRISON RAPE ELIMINATION COMMISSION
NASS	NATIONAL AGRICULTURAL STATISTICS SERVICE		NPS	NATIONAL PARK SERVICE
			NRC	NUCLEAR REGULATORY COMMISSION
NCA	NATIONAL CEMETERY ADMINISTRATION		NRCS	NATURAL RESOURCES CONSERVATION SERVICE
NCD	NATIONAL COUNCIL ON DISABILITY		NSA	NATIONAL SECURITY AGENCY/CENTRAL SECURITY SERVICE
NCLIS	NATIONAL COMMISSION ON LIBRARIES AND INFORMATION SCIENCE		NSF	NATIONAL SCIENCE FOUNDATION
			NTIA	NATIONAL TELECOMMUNICATIONS AND INFORMATION ADMINISTRATION
NCPPCC	NATIONAL CRIME PREVENTION AND PRIVACY COMPACT COUNCIL		NTSB	NATIONAL TRANSPORTATION SAFETY BOARD
NCS	NATIONAL COMMUNICATIONS SYSTEM		NWTRB	NUCLEAR WASTE TECHNICAL REVIEW BOARD
NCUA	NATIONAL CREDIT UNION ADMINISTRATION		OCC	COMPTROLLER OF THE CURRENCY
NEC	NATIONAL ECONOMIC COUNCIL		ODNI	OFFICE OF THE DIRECTOR OF NATIONAL INTELLIGENCE
NEIGHBOR	NEIGHBORHOOD REINVESTMENT CORPORATION		OEPNU	OFFICE OF ENERGY POLICY AND NEW USES
NHTSA	NATIONAL HIGHWAY TRAFFIC SAFETY ADMINISTRATION		OFAC	OFFICE OF FOREIGN ASSETS CONTROL
			OFCCP	OFFICE OF FEDERAL CONTRACT COMPLIANCE PROGRAMS
NIFA	NATIONAL INSTITUTE OF FOOD AND AGRICULTURE		OFHEO	FEDERAL HOUSING ENTERPRISE OVERSIGHT OFFICE
NIGC	NATIONAL INDIAN GAMING COMMISSION			
NIH	NATIONAL INSTITUTES OF HEALTH		OFPP	OFFICE OF FEDERAL PROCUREMENT POLICY
NIL	NATIONAL INSTITUTE FOR LITERACY		OJJDP	JUVENILE JUSTICE AND DELINQUENCY PREVENTION OFFICE
NIST	NATIONAL INSTITUTE OF STANDARDS AND TECHNOLOGY		OJP	JUSTICE PROGRAMS OFFICE
NLRB	NATIONAL LABOR RELATIONS BOARD		OMB	OFFICE OF MANAGEMENT AND BUDGET
NMB	NATIONAL MEDIATION BOARD		ONDCP	OFFICE OF NATIONAL DRUG CONTROL POLICY
NNSA	NATIONAL NUCLEAR SECURITY ADMINISTRATION		ONHIR	OFFICE OF NAVAJO AND HOPI INDIAN RELOCATION
NOAA	NATIONAL OCEANIC AND ATMOSPHERIC ADMINISTRATION		OPIC	OVERSEAS PRIVATE INVESTMENT CORPORATION

OPM	OFFICE OF PERSONNEL MANAGEMENT	RMA	RISK MANAGEMENT AGENCY
OPPM	OFFICE OF PROCUREMENT AND POLICY MANAGEMENT	RRB	RAILROAD RETIREMENT BOARD
OSC	OFFICE OF SPECIAL COUNSEL	RTB	RURAL TELEPHONE BANK
		RUS	RURAL UTILITIES SERVICE
OSHA	OCCUPATIONAL SAFETY AND HEALTH ADMINISTRATION	SAMHSA	SUBSTANCE ABUSE AND MENTAL HEALTH SERVICES ADMINISTRATION
OSHRC	OCCUPATIONAL SAFETY AND HEALTH REVIEW COMMISSION	SBA	SMALL BUSINESS ADMINISTRATION
OSM	OFFICE OF SURFACE MINING RECLAMATION AND ENFORCEMENT	SEC	SECURITIES AND EXCHANGE COMMISSION
		SIGIR	SPECIAL INSPECTOR GENERAL FOR IRAQ RECONSTRUCTION
OSTP	OFFICE OF SCIENCE AND TECHNOLOGY POLICY		
OTS	OFFICE OF THRIFT SUPERVISION	SJI	STATE JUSTICE INSTITUTE
		SLSDC	SAINT LAWRENCE SEAWAY DEVELOPMENT CORPORATION
PACIFIC	PACIFIC NORTHWEST ELECTRIC POWER AND CONSERVATION PLANNING COUNCIL	SRBC	SUSQUEHANNA RIVER BASIN COMMISSION
PBGC	PENSION BENEFIT GUARANTY CORPORATION	SSA	SOCIAL SECURITY ADMINISTRATION
		SSS	SELECTIVE SERVICE SYSTEM
PC	PEACE CORPS		
PHMSA	PIPELINE AND HAZARDOUS MATERIALS SAFETY ADMINISTRATION	STB	SURFACE TRANSPORTATION BOARD
		SWPA	SOUTHWESTERN POWER ADMINISTRATION
PHS	PUBLIC HEALTH SERVICE	TA	TECHNOLOGY ADMINISTRATION
PRC	POSTAL REGULATORY COMMISSION	TREAS	DEPARTMENT OF THE TREASURY
PRES	PRESIDENTIAL DOCUMENTS	TSA	TRANSPORTATION SECURITY ADMINISTRATION
PT	PRESIDIO TRUST		
PTO	PATENT AND TRADEMARK OFFICE	TTB	ALCOHOL AND TOBACCO TAX AND TRADE BUREAU
RATB	RECOVERY ACCOUNTABILITY AND TRANSPARENCY BOARD	TVA	TENNESSEE VALLEY AUTHORITY
RBS	RURAL BUSINESS COOPERATIVE SERVICE	URMCC	UTAH RECLAMATION MITIGATION AND CONSERVATION COMMISSION
RHS	RURAL HOUSING SERVICE		
RISC	REGULATORY INFORMATION SERVICE CENTER	USA	ARMY DEPARTMENT
		USAF	AIR FORCE DEPARTMENT
RITA	RESEARCH AND INNOVATIVE TECHNOLOGY ADMINISTRATION	USAID	UNITED STATES AGENCY FOR INTERNATIONAL DEVELOPMENT
		USBC	BUREAU OF THE CENSUS

USCBP	CUSTOMS AND BORDER PROTECTION BUREAU		USPC	PAROLE COMMISSION
USCC	U.S. CHINA ECONOMIC AND SECURITY REVIEW COMMISSION		USPS	POSTAL SERVICE
			USSC	UNITED STATES SENTENCING COMMISSION
USCERT	UNITED STATES COMPUTER EMERGENCY READINESS TEAM		USSS	SECRET SERVICE
			USTR	OFFICE OF UNITED STATES TRADE REPRESENTATIVE
USCG	COAST GUARD			
USCIS	U.S. CITIZENSHIP AND IMMIGRATION SERVICES		USUHS	UNIFORMED SERVICES UNIVERSITY OF THE HEALTH SCIENCES
USDA	DEPARTMENT OF AGRICULTURE		VA	DEPARTMENT OF VETERANS AFFAIRS
USEIB	EXPORT IMPORT BANK			
USGS	U.S. GEOLOGICAL SERVICE		VCNP	VALLES CALDERA TRUST
			VETS	VETERANS EMPLOYMENT AND TRAINING SERVICE
USHMM	UNITED STATES HOLOCAUST MEMORIAL MUSEUM		WAPA	WESTERN AREA POWER ADMINISTRATION
USIP	UNITED STATES INSTITUTE OF PEACE		WCPO	WORKERS COMPENSATION PROGRAMS OFFICE
USJC	JUDICIAL CONFERENCE OF THE UNITED STATES		WHD	WAGE AND HOUR DIVISION
USMINT	UNITED STATES MINT			
USN	NAVY DEPARTMENT			

HISTORY OF AGENCY ORGANIZATIONAL CHANGES

NOTE: Italicized terms indicate obsolete agencies, organizations, and programs. Refer to the name of the obsolete entity in this index for more explanation. Some dates prior to March 4, 1933 are included to provide additional information.

Entries are indexed using the most significant term in their titles, or when there is more than one significant term, the entry uses the first significant term. Thus, **Bureau of the Budget** is found at **Budget, Bureau of the,** and **Annual Assay Commission** is found at **Assay Commission, Annual.**

Accounting Office, General   Established by act of June 10, 1921 (42 Stat. 20). Renamed Government Accountability Office by act of July 7, 2004 (118 Stat. 814).

ACTION   Established by Reorg. Plan No. 1 of 1971 (5 U.S.C. app.), effective July 1, 1971. Reorganized by act of Oct. 1, 1973 (87 Stat. 405). Functions relating to SCORE and ACT programs transferred to Small Business Administration by EO 11871 of July 18, 1975 (40 FR 30915). Functions exercised by the Director of ACTION prior to Mar. 31, 1995, transferred to the Corporation for National and Community Service (107 Stat. 888 and Proclamation 6662 of Apr. 4, 1994 (57 FR 16507)).

Acts of Congress   *See* **State, Department of**

Administrative Conference of the United States   Established by act of Aug. 30, 1964 (78 Stat. 615). Terminated by act of Nov. 19, 1995 (109 Stat. 480). Reauthorized in 2004, 2008, and 2009 by acts of Oct. 30, 2004 (118 Stat. 2255), July 30, 2008 (122 Stat. 2914), and March 11, 2009 (123 Stat. 656). Reestablished by Congress on Mar. 3, 2010 upon confirmation of chairman.

Advanced Research Projects Agency   *See* **Defense Advanced Research Projects Agency**

Advisory Board.   *See other part of title*

Advisory Committee.   *See other part of title*

Advisory Council.   *See other part of title*

Aeronautical Board   Organized in 1916 by agreement of *War* and Navy Secretaries. Placed under supervision of President by military order of July 5, 1939. Dissolved by Secretary of Defense letter of July 27, 1948, and functions transferred to *Munitions Board* and *Research and Development*

Board. Military order of July 5, 1939, revoked by military order of Oct. 18, 1948.

Aeronautics, Bureau of   Established in the Department of the Navy by act of July 12, 1921 (42 Stat. 140). Abolished by act of Aug. 18, 1959 (73 Stat. 395) and functions transferred to *Bureau of Naval Weapons*.

Aeronautics, National Advisory Committee for   Established by act of Mar. 3, 1915 (38 Stat. 930). Terminated by act of July 29, 1958 (72 Stat. 432), and functions transferred to National Aeronautics and Space Administration, established by same act.

Aeronautics Administration, Civil   *See* **Aeronautics Authority, Civil**

Aeronautics Authority, Civil   Established under act of June 23, 1938 (52 Stat. 973). Renamed *Civil Aeronautics Board* and Administrator transferred to the Department of Commerce by Reorg. Plan Nos. III and IV of 1940, effective June 30, 1940. Office of Administrator designated *Civil Aeronautics Administration* by Department Order 52 of Aug. 29, 1940. *Administration* transferred to *Federal Aviation Agency* by act of Aug. 23, 1958 (72 Stat. 810). Functions of *Board* under act of Aug. 23, 1958 (72 Stat. 775), transferred to National Transportation Safety Board by act of Oct. 15, 1966 (80 Stat. 931). Functions of *Board* terminated or transferred—effective in part Dec. 31, 1981; in part Jan. 1, 1983; and in part Jan. 1, 1985—by act of Aug. 23, 1958 (92 Stat. 1744). Most remaining functions transferred to Secretary of Transportation, remainder to U.S. Postal Service. Termination of *Board* finalized by act of Oct. 4, 1984 (98 Stat. 1703).

Aeronautics Board, Civil   *See* **Aeronautics Authority, Civil**

Aeronautics Branch   Established in the Department of Commerce to carry out provisions of act of May

20, 1926 (44 Stat. 568). Renamed *Bureau of Air Commerce* by Secretary's administrative order of July 1, 1934. Personnel and property transferred to *Civil Aeronautics Authority* by EO 7959 of Aug. 22, 1938.

Aeronautics and Space Council, National   Established by act of July 29, 1958 (72 Stat. 427). Abolished by Reorg. Plan No. 1 of 1973, effective June 30, 1973.

Aging, Administration on   Established by *Secretary of Health, Education, and Welfare* on Oct. 1, 1965, to carry out provisions of act of July 14, 1965 (79 Stat. 218). Reassigned to *Social and Rehabilitation Service* by Department reorganization of Aug. 15, 1967. Transferred to Office of Assistant Secretary for Human Development by Secretary's order of June 15, 1973. Transferred to the Office of the Secretary of Health and Human Services by Secretary's reorganization notice dated Apr. 15, 1991. Transferred to the Administration for Community Living by Department's notice of April 18, 2012 (77 FR 23250).

Aging, Federal Council on   Established by Presidential memorandum of Apr. 2, 1956. Reconstituted at Federal level by Presidential letter of Mar. 7, 1959, to *Secretary of Health, Education, and Welfare.* Abolished by EO 11022 of May 15, 1962, which established *President's Council on Aging.*

Aging, Office of   Established by *Secretary of Health, Education, and Welfare* June 2, 1955, as *Special Staff on Aging.* Terminated Sept. 30, 1965, and functions assumed by Administration on Aging.

Aging, President's Council on   Established by EO 11022 of May 14, 1962. Terminated by EO 11022, which was revoked by EO 12379 of Aug. 17, 1982.

Agricultural Adjustment Administration   Established by act of May 12, 1933 (48 Stat. 31). Consolidated into *Agricultural Conservation and Adjustment Administration* as *Agricultural Adjustment Agency,* Department of Agriculture, by EO 9069 of Feb. 23, 1942. Grouped with other agencies to form *Food Production Administration* by EO 9280 of Dec. 5, 1942. Transferred to *War Food Administration* by EO 9322 of Mar. 26, 1943. Administration terminated by EO 9577 of June 29, 1945, and functions transferred to Secretary of Agriculture. Transfer made permanent by Reorg. Plan No. 3 of 1946, effective July 16, 1946. Functions of *Agricultural Adjustment Agency* consolidated with *Production and Marketing Administration* by Secretary's Memorandum 1118 of Aug. 18, 1945.

Agricultural Adjustment Agency   *See* **Agricultural Adjustment Administration**

Agricultural Advisory Commission, National   Established by EO 10472 of July 20, 1953. Terminated Feb. 4, 1965, on resignation of members.

Agricultural Chemistry and Engineering, Bureau of   *See* **Agricultural Engineering, Bureau of**

Agricultural Conservation and Adjustment Administration   Established by EO 9069 of Feb. 23,

1942, consolidating *Agricultural Adjustment Agency, Sugar Agency, Federal Crop Insurance Corporation,* and *Soil Conservation Service.* Consolidated into *Food Production Administration* by EO 9280 of Dec. 5, 1942.

Agricultural Conservation Program Service   Established by Secretary of Agriculture Jan. 21, 1953, from part of *Production and Marketing Administration.* Merged with *Commodity Stabilization Service* by Secretary's Memorandum 1446, supp. 2, of Apr. 19, 1961.

Agricultural Developmental Service, International   Established by Secretary of Agriculture memorandum of July 12, 1963. Functions and delegations of authority transferred to Foreign Agricultural Service by Secretary's memorandum of Mar. 28, 1969. Functions transferred by Secretary to *Foreign Economic Development Service* Nov. 8, 1969.

Agricultural Economics, Bureau of   Established by act of May 11, 1931 (42 Stat. 532). Functions transferred to other units of the Department of Agriculture, including *Consumer and Marketing Service* and Agricultural Research Service, under Secretary's Memorandum 1320, supp. 4, of Nov. 2, 1953.

Agricultural Engineering, Bureau of   Established by act of Feb. 23, 1931 (46 Stat. 1266). Merged with *Bureau of Chemistry and Soils* by Secretarial order of Oct. 16, 1938, to form *Bureau of Agricultural Chemistry and Engineering.*

Agricultural and Industrial Chemistry, Bureau of   *Bureau of Chemistry* and *Bureau of Soils,* created in 1901, combined into *Bureau of Chemistry and Soils* by act of Jan. 18, 1927 (44 Stat. 976). Soils units transferred to other agencies of the Department of Agriculture and remaining units of *Bureau of Chemistry and Soils* and *Bureau of Agricultural Engineering* consolidated with *Bureau of Agricultural Chemistry and Engineering* by Secretary's order of Oct. 16, 1938. In February 1943 agricultural engineering research made part of *Bureau of Plant Industry, Soils, and Agricultural Engineering,* and organization for continuing agricultural chemistry research relating to crop utilization named *Bureau of Agricultural and Industrial Chemistry,* in accordance with *Research Administration* Memorandum 5 issued pursuant to EO 9069 of Feb. 23, 1942, and in conformity with Secretary's Memorandums 960 and 986. Functions transferred to *Agricultural Research Service* under Secretary's Memorandum 1320, supp. 4, of Nov. 2, 1953.

Agricultural Library, National   Established by Secretary of Agriculture Memorandum 1496 of Mar. 23, 1962. Consolidated into *Science and Education Administration* by Secretary's order of Jan. 24, 1978. Reestablished as National Agricultural Library by Secretary's order of June 16, 1981. Became part of Agricultural Research Service in 1994 under Department of Agriculture reorganization.

Agricultural Marketing Administration   Established by EO 9069 of Feb. 23, 1942, consolidating *Surplus*

Marketing Administration, Agricultural Marketing Service, and *Commodity Exchange Administration. Division of Consumers' Counsel* transferred to *Administration* by Secretary's memorandum of Feb. 28, 1942. Consolidated into *Food Distribution Administration* in the Department of Agriculture by EO 9280 of Dec. 5, 1942.

Agricultural Marketing Service Established by the Secretary of Agriculture pursuant to act of June 30, 1939 (53 Stat. 939). Merged into *Agricultural Marketing Administration* by EO 9069 of Feb. 23, 1942. Renamed *Consumer and Marketing Service* by Secretary's Memorandum 1567, supp. 1, of Feb. 8, 1965. Reestablished as Agricultural Marketing Service by the Secretary of Agriculture on Apr. 2, 1972, under authority of Reorg. Plan No. 2 of 1953 (67 Stat. 633).

Agricultural Relations, Office of Foreign *See* **Agricultural Service, Foreign**

Agricultural Research Administration Established by EO 9069 of Feb. 23, 1942. Superseded by Agricultural Research Service.

Agricultural Research Service Established by Secretary of Agriculture Memorandum 1320, supp. 4, of Nov. 2, 1953. Consolidated into *Science and Education Administration* by Secretary's order of Jan. 24, 1978. Reestablished as Agricultural Research Service by Secretarial order of June 16, 1981.

Agricultural Service, Foreign Established by act of June 5, 1930 (46 Stat. 497). Economic research and agricultural attaché activities administered by *Foreign Agricultural Service Division, Bureau of Agricultural Economics,* until June 29, 1939. Transferred by Reorg. Plan No. II of 1939, effective July 1, 1939, from the Department of Agriculture to the Department of State. Economic research functions of *Division* transferred to *Office of Foreign Agricultural Relations* June 30, 1939. Functions of *Office* transferred to Foreign Agricultural Service Mar. 10, 1953. Agricultural attaché's placed in the Department of Agriculture by act of Aug. 28, 1954 (68 Stat. 908).

Agricultural Stabilization and Conservation Service Established June 5, 1961, by the Secretary of Agriculture under authority of revised statutes (5 U.S.C. 301) and Reorg. Plan No. 2 of 1953 (5 U.S.C. app.). Abolished and functions assumed by the *Farm Service Agency* by Secretary's Memorandum 1010–1 dated Oct. 20, 1994 (59 FR 60297, 60299).

Agricultural Statistics Division Transferred to *Bureau of Agricultural Economics* by EO 9069 of Feb. 23, 1942.

Agriculture, Division of *See* **Farm Products, Division of**

Air Commerce, Bureau of *See* **Aeronautics Branch**

Air Coordinating Committee Established Mar. 27, 1945, by interdepartmental memorandum; formally established by EO 9781 of Sept. 19, 1946. Terminated by EO 10883 of Aug. 11, 1960, and

functions transferred for liquidation to *Federal Aviation Agency.*

Air Force, National Commission on the Structure of the Established by act of January 2, 2013 (126 Stat. 1703). Terminated 90 days after submission of final report to President on May 1, 2014.

Air Force Management Engineering Agency Established in 1975 in Air Force as separate operating unit. Made subordinate unit of Air Force Military Personnel Center (formerly Air Force Manpower and Personnel Center) in 1978. Reestablished as separate operating unit of Air Force, effective Mar. 1, 1985, by Secretarial order.

Air Force Manpower and Personnel Center Certain functions transferred on activation of Air Force Management Engineering Agency, which was made separate operating unit from Air Force Manpower and Personnel Center (later Air Force Military Personnel Center) in April 1985 by general order of Chief of Staff.

Air Force Medical Service Center Renamed Air Force Office of Medical Support by Program Action Directive 85–1 of Mar. 6, 1985, approved by Air Force Vice Chief of Staff.

Air Mail, Bureau of Established in Interstate Commerce Commission to carry out provisions of act of June 12, 1934 (48 Stat. 933). Personnel and property transferred to *Civil Aeronautics Authority* by EO 7959 of Aug. 22, 1938.

Air Patrol, Civil Established in *Civilian Defense Office* by Administrative Order 9 of Dec. 8, 1941. Transferred to *Department of War* as auxiliary of Army Air Forces by EO 9339 of Apr. 29, 1943. Transferred to the Department of the Air Force by Secretary of Defense order of May 21, 1948. Established as civilian auxiliary of U.S. Air Force by act of May 26, 1948 (62 Stat. 274).

Air Safety Board Established by act of June 23, 1938 (52 Stat. 973). Functions transferred to *Civil Aeronautics Board* by Reorg. Plan No. IV of 1940, effective June 30, 1940.

Airways Modernization Board Established by act of Aug. 14, 1957 (71 Stat. 349). Transferred to *Federal Aviation Agency* by EO 10786 of Nov. 1, 1958.

Alaska, Board of Road Commissioners for Established in *Department of War* by act of Jan. 27, 1905 (33 Stat. 616). Functions transferred to the Department of Interior by act of June 30, 1932 (47 Stat. 446), and delegated to *Alaska Road Commission.* Functions transferred to the Department of Commerce by act of June 29, 1956 (70 Stat. 377), and terminated by act of June 25, 1959 (73 Stat. 145).

Alaska, Federal Field Committee for Development Planning in Established by EO 11182 of Oct. 2, 1964. Abolished by EO 11608 of July 19, 1971.

Alaska, Federal Reconstruction and Development Planning Commission for Established by EO 11150 of Apr. 2, 1964. Abolished by EO 11182 of

Oct. 2, 1964, which established *President's Review Committee for Development Planning in Alaska* and *Federal Field Committee for Development Planning in Alaska.*

Alaska, President's Review Committee for Development Planning in   Established by EO 11182 of Oct. 2, 1964. Superseded by *Federal Advisory Council on Regional Economic Development* established by EO 11386 of Dec. 28, 1967. EO 11386 revoked by EO 12553 f Feb. 25, 1986.

Alaska Communication System   Operational responsibility vested in Secretary of the Army by act of May 26, 1900 (31 Stat. 206). Transferred to Secretary of the Air Force by Secretary of Defense reorganization order of May 24, 1962.

Alaska Engineering Commission   *See* **Alaska Railroad**

Alaska Game Commission   Established by act of Jan. 13, 1925 (43 Stat. 740). Expired Dec. 31, 1959, pursuant to act of July 7, 1958 (72 Stat. 339).

Alaska International Rail and Highway Commission   Established by act of Aug. 1, 1956 (70 Stat. 888). Terminated June 30, 1961, under terms of act.

Alaska Natural Gas Transportation System, Office of Federal Inspector of Construction for the   Established by Reorg. Plan No. 1 of 1979 (5 U.S.C. app.), effective July 1, 1979. Abolished by act of Oct. 24, 1992 (106 Stat. 3128) and functions and authority vested in the Inspector transferred to the Secretary of Energy. Functions vested in the Secretary of Energy transferred to the Federal Coordinator, Office of the Federal Coordinator for Alaska Natural Gas Transportation Projects by act of Oct. 13, 2004 (118 Stat. 1261).

Alaska Power Administration   Established by the Secretary of the Interior in 1967. Transferred to the Department of Energy by act of Aug. 4, 1977 (91 Stat. 578).

Alaska Railroad   Built pursuant to act of Mar. 12, 1914 (38 Stat. 305), which created *Alaska Engineering Commission.* Placed under the Secretary of the Interior by EO 2129 of Jan. 26, 1915, and renamed Alaska Railroad by EO 3861 of June 8, 1923. Authority to regulate tariffs granted to Interstate Commerce Commission by EO 11107 of Apr. 25, 1963. Authority to operate Railroad transferred to the Secretary of Transportation by act of Oct. 15, 1966 (80 Stat. 941), effective Apr. 1, 1967. Railroad purchased by State of Alaska, effective Jan. 5, 1985.

Alaska Road Commission   *See* **Alaska, Board of Road Commissioners for**

Alcohol, Bureau of Industrial   Established by act of May 27, 1930 (46 Stat. 427). Consolidated into *Bureau of Internal Revenue* by EO 6166 of June 10, 1933. Consolidation deferred until May 11, 1934, by EO 6639 of Mar. 10, 1934. Order also transferred to Internal Revenue Commissioner certain functions imposed on Attorney General by act of May 27,

1930, with relation to enforcement of criminal laws concerning intoxicating liquors remaining in effect after repeal of 18th amendment; personnel of, and appropriations for, *Bureau of Industrial Alcohol;* and necessary personnel and appropriations of *Bureau of Prohibition,* Department of Justice.

Alcohol, Drug Abuse, and Mental Health Administration   Established by the *Secretary of Health, Education, and Welfare* by act of May 21, 1972 (88 Stat. 134). Redesignated as an agency of the Public Health Service from the *National Institute of Mental Health* Sept. 25, 1973, by the Secretary of Health, Education, and Welfare. Functions transferred to the Department of Health and Human Services by act of Oct. 17, 1979 (93 Stat. 695). Established as an agency of the Public Health Service by act of Oct. 27, 1986 (100 Stat. 3207– 106). Renamed Substance Abuse and Mental Health Services Administration by act of July 10, 1992 (106 Stat. 325).

Alcohol Abuse and Alcoholism, National Institute on   Established within the National Institute of Mental Health, *Department of Health, Education, and Welfare* by act of Dec. 31, 1970 (84 Stat. 1848). Removed from within the National Institute of Mental Health and made an entity within the Alcohol, Drug Abuse, and Mental Health Administration by act of May 14, 1974 (88 Stat. 1356). Functions transferred to the Department of Health and Human Services by act of Oct. 17, 1979 (93 Stat. 695). (*See also* act of Oct. 27, 1986; 100 Stat. 3207–106.) Abolished by act of July 10, 1992 (106 Stat. 331). Reestablished by act of July 10, 1992 (106 Stat. 359).

Alcohol Administration, Federal   *See* **Alcohol Control Administration, Federal**

Alcohol Control Administration, Federal   Established by EO 6474 of Dec. 4, 1933. Abolished Sept. 24, 1935, on induction into office of Administrator, *Federal Alcohol Administration,* as provided in act of Aug. 29, 1935 (49 Stat. 977). Abolished by Reorg. Plan No. III of 1940, effective June 30, 1940, and functions consolidated with activities of Internal Revenue Service.

Alcohol, Tobacco, and Firearms, Bureau of   Established within Treasury Department by Treasury Order No. 221, eff. July 1, 1972. Transferred to Bureau of Alcohol, Tobacco, Firearms, and Explosives in Justice Department by act of Nov. 25, 2002, except some authorities, functions, personnel, and assets relating to administration and enforcement of certain provisions of the Internal Revenue Code of 1986 and title 27 of the U.S. Code (116 Stat. 2275).

Alexander Hamilton Bicentennial Commission   Established by act of Aug. 20, 1954 (68 Stat. 746). Terminated Apr. 30, 1958.

Alien Property Custodian   Appointed by President Oct. 22, 1917, under authority of act of Oct. 6, 1917 (40 Stat. 415). Office transferred to *Alien Property Division,* Department of Justice, by EO 6694 of May 1, 1934. Powers vested in President by act delegated to Attorney General by EO 8136 of May 15, 1939. Authority vested in Attorney General by EO's 6694 and 8136 transferred by EO 9142 of Apr. 21, 1942, to *Office of Alien Property Custodian, Office for Emergency Management,* as provided for by EO 9095 of Mar. 11, 1942.

American Forces Information Service Established by Secretary of Defense Directive 5122.10 of March 13, 1989. Dissolved by Secretary's Directive 5105.74 of Dec. 18, 2007 and functions transferred to Defense Media Activity effective Oct. 1, 2008.

American Republics, Office for Coordination of Commercial and Cultural Relations between the Established by *Council of National Defense* order approved by President Aug. 16, 1940. Succeeded by *Office of the Coordinator of Inter-American Affairs, Office for Emergency Management,* established by EO 8840 of July 30, 1941. Renamed *Office of Inter-American Affairs* by EO 9532 of Mar. 23, 1945. Information functions transferred to the Department of State by EO 9608 of Aug. 31, 1945. Terminated by EO 9710 of Apr. 10, 1946, and functions transferred to the Department of State, functioning as *Institute of Inter-American Affairs.* Transferred to *Foreign Operations Administration* by Reorg. Plan No. 7, effective Aug. 1, 1953.

American Revolution Bicentennial Administration *See* **American Revolution Bicentennial Commission**

American Revolution Bicentennial Commission Established by act of July 4, 1966 (80 Stat. 259). *American Revolution Bicentennial Administration* established by act of Dec. 11, 1973 (87 Stat. 697), to replace *Commission. Administration* terminated June 30, 1977, pursuant to terms of act. Certain continuing functions transferred to the Secretary of the Interior by EO 12001 of June 29, 1977.

Anacostia Neighborhood Museum Renamed Anacostia Museum by Smithsonian Institution announcement of Apr. 3, 1987.

Animal Industry, Bureau of Established in the Department of Agriculture by act of May 29, 1884 (23 Stat. 31). Functions transferred to Agricultural Research Service by Secretary's Memorandum 1320, supp. 4, of Nov. 2, 1953.

Apprenticeship, Federal Committee on Previously known as *Federal Committee on Apprentice Training,* established by EO 6750–C of June 27, 1934. Functioned as part of *Division of Labor Standards,* Department of Labor, pursuant to act of Aug. 16, 1937 (50 Stat. 664). Transferred to *Office of Administrator, Federal Security Agency,* by EO 9139 of Apr. 18, 1942. Transferred to *Bureau of Training, War Manpower Commission,* by EO 9247 of Sept. 17, 1942. Returned to the Department of Labor by EO 9617 of Sept. 19, 1945.

Archive of Folksong Renamed Archive of Folk Culture by administrative order of Deputy Librarian of Congress, effective Sept. 21, 1981.

Archives Council, National Established by act of June 19, 1934 (48 Stat. 1122). Transferred to General Services Administration by act of June 30, 1949 (63 Stat. 378). Terminated on establishment of Federal Records Council by act of Sept. 5, 1950 (64 Stat. 583).

Archives Establishment, National *Office of Archivist of the U.S.* and *National Archives* created by act of June 19, 1934 (48 Stat. 1122). Transferred to General Services Administration by act of June 30, 1949 (63 Stat. 381), and incorporated as *National Archives and Records Service* by order of General Services Administrator, together with functions of *Division of the Federal Register, National Archives Council, National Historical Publications Commission,* National Archives Trust Fund Board, *Trustees of the Franklin D. Roosevelt Library,* and Administrative Committee of the Federal Register. Transferred from General Services Administration to National Archives and Records Administration by act of Oct. 19, 1984 (98 Stat. 2283), along with certain functions of Administrator of General Services transferred to Archivist of the United States, effective Apr. 1, 1985.

Archives and Records Service, National *See* **Archives Establishment, National**

Archives Trust Fund Board, National *See* **Archives Establishment, National**

Area Redevelopment Administration Established May 8, 1961, by the Secretary of Commerce pursuant to act of May 1, 1961 (75 Stat. 47) and Reorg. Plan No. 5 of 1950, effective May 24, 1950. Terminated Aug. 31, 1965, by act of June 30, 1965 (79 Stat. 195). Functions transferred to Economic Development Administration in the Department of Commerce by Department Order 4–A, effective Sept. 1, 1965.

Arlington Memorial Amphitheater Commission Established by act of Mar. 4, 1921 (41 Stat. 1440). Abolished by act of Sept. 2, 1960 (74 Stat. 739), and functions transferred to the Secretary of Defense.

Arlington Memorial Bridge Commission Established by act of Mar. 4, 1913 (37 Stat. 885; D.C. Code (1951 ed.) 8–158). Abolished by EO 6166 of June 10, 1933, and functions transferred to *Office of National Parks, Buildings, and Reservations.*

Armed Forces, U.S. Court of Appeals for the *See* **Military Appeals, United States Court of**

Armed Forces, Industrial College of the Renamed Dwight D. Eisenhower School for National Security and Resource Strategy by act of Dec. 31, 2011 (125 Stat. 1701).

Armed Forces Medical Library Founded in 1836 as *Library of the Surgeon General's Office,* U.S. Army. Later known as *Army Medical Library,* then *Armed Forces Medical Library* in 1952. Personnel and property transferred to National Library of Medicine established in Public Health Service by act of Aug. 3, 1956 (70 Stat. 960).

Armed Forces Museum Advisory Board, National Established by act of Aug. 30, 1961 (75

Stat. 414). Functions discontinued due to lack of funding.

Armed Forces Staff College Renamed Joint Forces Staff College by act of Oct. 30, 2000 (144 Stat. 165A–230).

Armed Services Renegotiation Board Established by Secretary of Defense directive of July 19, 1948. Abolished by Secretary's letter of Jan. 18, 1952, and functions transferred to *Renegotiation Board.*

Arms Control and Disarmament Agency, U.S. Established by act of Sept. 26, 1961 (75 Stat. 631). Abolished by act of Oct. 21, 1998 (112 Stat. 2681– 767) and functions transferred to the Secretary of State.

Army Communications Command, U.S. Renamed U.S. Army Information Systems Command by Department General Order No. 26 of July 25, 1984.

Army Industrial College Established in *Department of War* by General Order No. 7 of February 25, 1924. Renamed The Industrial College of the Armed Forces by *Department of War* memorandum of April 11, 1946.

Army Materiel Development and Readiness Command, U.S. Renamed U.S. Army Materiel Command by Department General Order No. 28 of Aug. 15, 1984.

Army and Navy, Joint Board Placed under direction of President by military order of July 5, 1939. Abolished Sept. 1, 1947, by joint letter of Aug. 20, 1947, to President from Secretaries of *War* and Navy.

Army and Navy Staff College Established Apr. 23, 1943, and operated under Joint Chiefs of Staff. Redesignated the National War College, effective July 1, 1946.

Army Specialist Corps Established in *Department of War* by EO 9078 of Feb. 26, 1942. Abolished by the *Secretary of War* Oct. 31, 1942, and functions merged into central *Officer Procurement Service.*

Arts, National Collection of Fine Established within Smithsonian Institution by act of Mar. 24, 1937 (50 Stat. 51). Renamed *National Museum of American Art* in Smithsonian Institution by act of Oct. 13, 1980 (94 Stat. 1884).

Arthritis, Diabetes, and Digestive and Kidney Diseases, National Institute of See **Arthritis, Metabolism, and Digestive Diseases, National Institute of**

Arthritis, Metabolism, and Digestive Diseases, National Institute of Renamed *National Institute of Arthritis, Diabetes, and Digestive and Kidney Diseases* by Secretary's order of June 15, 1981, pursuant to act of Dec. 19, 1980 (94 Stat. 3184). Renamed National Institute of Diabetes and Digestive and Kidney Diseases and National Institute of Arthritis and Musculoskeletal and Skin Diseases by act of Nov. 20, 1985 (99 Stat. 820).

Arts, Advisory Committee on the Established under authority of act of Sept. 20, 1961 (75 Stat. 527). Terminated July 1973 by act of Oct. 6, 1972. Formally abolished by Reorg. Plan No. 2 of 1977, effective Apr. 1, 1978.

Arts, National Council on the Established in Executive Office of the President by act of Sept. 3, 1964 (78 Stat. 905). Transferred to National Foundation on the Arts and the Humanities by act of Sept. 29, 1965 (79 Stat. 845).

Assay Commission, Annual Established initially by act of Apr. 2, 1792 (1 Stat. 250) and by act of Feb. 12, 1873 (Revised Statute sec. 3647; 17 Stat. 432). Terminated and functions transferred to the Secretary of the Treasury by act of Mar. 14, 1980 (94 Stat. 98).

Assistance, Bureau of Public Renamed *Bureau of Family Services* by order of the *Secretary of Health, Education, and Welfare,* effective Jan. 1, 1962. Functions redelegated to *Social and Rehabilitation Service* by Secretary's reorganization of Aug. 15, 1967.

Assistance Coordinating Committee, Adjustment Established by act of Jan. 3, 1975 (88 Stat. 2040). Inactive since 1981.

Assistance Payments Administration Established by *Secretary of Health, Education, and Welfare* reorganization of Aug. 15, 1967. Transferred by *Secretary's* reorganization of Mar. 8, 1977 (42 FR 13262), from *Social and Rehabilitation Service* to Social Security Administration.

Athletics, Interagency Committee on International Established by EO 11117 of Aug. 13, 1963. Terminated by EO 11515 of Mar. 13, 1970.

Atlantic-Pacific Interoceanic Canal Study Commission Established by act of Sept. 22, 1964 (78 Stat. 990). Terminated Dec. 1, 1970, pursuant to terms of act.

Atomic Energy Commission Established by act of Aug. 1, 1946 (60 Stat. 755). Abolished by act of Oct. 11, 1974 (88 Stat. 1237) and functions transferred to *Energy Research and Development Administration* and Nuclear Regulatory Commission.

Aviation, Interdepartmental Committee on Civil International Established by Presidential letter of June 20, 1935. Terminated on organization of *Civil Aeronautics Authority.*

Aviation Agency, Federal Established by act of Aug. 23, 1958 (72 Stat. 731). Transferred to Secretary of Transportation by act of Oct. 15, 1966 (80 Stat. 931). *Agency* reestablished as Federal Aviation Administration by act of Jan 12, 1983 (96 Stat. 2416).

Aviation Commission, Federal Established by act of June 12, 1934 (48 Stat. 938). Terminated Feb. 1, 1935, under provisions of act.

Beltsville Research Center Established to operate with other agencies of the Department of Agriculture under *Agricultural Research Administration.*

Consolidated into *Agricultural Research Administration*, the Department of Agriculture, by EO 9069 of Feb. 23, 1942.

Bilingual Education and Minority Languages Affairs, Office of Renamed Office of English Language Acquisition, Language Enhancement, and Academic Achievement for Limited English Proficient Students by act of Jan. 8, 2002 (115 Stat. 2089).

Biobased Products and Bioenergy, Advisory Committee on Established by EO 13134 of June 3, 1999. Abolished by EO 13423 of Jan. 24, 2007.

Biobased Products and Bioenergy, Interagency Council on Established by EO 13134 of June 3, 1999. Abolished by EO 13423 of Jan. 24, 2007.

Biobased Products and Bioenergy Coordination Office, National Established by EO 13134 of June 3, 1999. Abolished by EO 13423 of Jan. 24, 2007.

Biological Service, National Established in the Department of the Interior in 1995 by Secretarial order. Transferred to U.S. Geological Survey as new Biological Resources Division by Secretarial Order No. 3202, Sept. 30, 1996.

Biological Survey, Bureau of Established by Secretary's order July 1, 1885, as part of *Division of Entomology*, Department of Agriculture. Made separate bureau by act of Apr. 23, 1904 (33 Stat. 276). Transferred to the Department of the Interior by Reorg. Plan No. II of 1939, effective July 1, 1939. Consolidated with *Bureau of Fisheries* into *Fish and Wildlife Service* by Reorg. Plan No. III of 1940, effective June 30, 1940.

Biological Survey, National Established in the Department of the Interior by Secretarial Order 3173 of Sept. 29, 1993. Renamed *National Biological Service* by Secretarial order in 1995.

Blind, Inc., American Printing House for the Established in 1858 as privately owned institution in Louisville, KY. Functions of the Secretary of the Treasury, except that relating to perpetual trust funds, transferred to *Federal Security Agency* by Reorg. Plan No. II of 1939, effective July 1, 1939. Functions performed by *Department of Health, Education, and Welfare* transferred to the Department of Education.

Blind-made Products, Committee on Purchases of Established by act of June 25, 1938 (52 Stat. 1196). Renamed *Committee for Purchase of Products and Services of the Blind and Other Severely Handicapped* by act of June 23, 1971 (85 Stat. 77). Renamed *Committee for Purchase from the Blind and Other Severely Handicapped* by act of July 25, 1974 (88 Stat. 392). Renamed Committee for Purchase From People Who Are Blind or Severely Disabled by act of Oct. 29, 1992 (106 Stat. 4486).

Blind and Other Severely Handicapped, Committee for Purchase of Products and Services of the *See* **Blind-made Products, Committee on Purchases of**

Board. *See other part of title*

Bond and Spirits Division Established as *Taxes and Penalties Unit*, as announced by Assistant to Attorney General in departmental circular of May 25, 1934, pursuant to EO 6639 of May 10, 1934. Abolished by administrative order of October 1942, and functions transferred to Tax, Claims, and Criminal Divisions, Department of Justice.

Bonneville Power Administration Established by the Secretary of the Interior pursuant to act of Aug. 20, 1937 (50 Stat. 731). Transferred to the Department of Energy by act of Aug. 4, 1977 (91 Stat. 578).

Boston National Historic Sites Commission Established by joint resolution of June 16, 1955 (69 Stat. 137). Terminated June 16, 1960, by act of Feb. 19, 1957 (71 Stat. 4).

Brazil-U.S. Defense Commission, Joint Established in May 1942 by agreement between the U.S. and Brazil. Terminated in September 1977 at direction of Brazilian Government.

Broadcast Bureau Merged with *Cable Television Bureau* to form Mass Media Bureau by Federal Communications Commission order, effective Nov. 30, 1982.

Broadcast Intelligence Service, Foreign *See* **Broadcast Monitoring Service, Foreign**

Broadcast Monitoring Service, Foreign Established in Federal Communications Commission by Presidential directive of Feb. 26, 1941. Renamed *Foreign Broadcast Intelligence Service* by FCC order of July 28, 1942. Transferred to *Department of War* by Secretarial order of Dec. 30, 1945. Act of May 3, 1945 (59 Stat. 110), provided for liquidation 60 days after Japanese armistice. Transferred to *Central Intelligence Group* Aug. 5, 1946, and renamed *Foreign Broadcast Information Service.*

Budget, Bureau of the Established by act of June 10, 1921 (42 Stat. 20), in the Department of the Treasury under immediate direction of President. Transferred to Executive Office of the President by Reorg. Plan No. I of 1939, effective July 1, 1939. Reorganized by Reorg. Plan No. 2 of 1970, effective July 1, 1970, and renamed Office of Management and Budget.

Buildings Administration, Public Established as part of *Federal Works Agency* by Reorg. Plan No. I of 1939, effective July 1, 1939. Abolished by act of June 30, 1949 (63 Stat. 380), and functions transferred to General Services Administration.

Buildings Branch, Public Organized in *Procurement Division*, established in the Department of the Treasury by EO 6166 of June 10, 1933. Consolidated with *Branch of Buildings Management*, National Park Service, to form *Public Buildings Administration, Federal Works Agency*, under Reorg. Plan No. I of 1939, effective July 1, 1939.

Buildings Commission, Public Established by act of July 1, 1916 (39 Stat. 328). Abolished by EO 6166 of June 10, 1933, and functions transferred to *Office of National Parks, Buildings, and Reservations*, Department of the Interior. Functions transferred to *Public Buildings Administration, Federal Works Agency,* under Reorg. Plan No. I of 1939, effective July 1, 1939.

Buildings Management, Branch of Functions of National Park Service (except those relating to monuments and memorials) consolidated with *Public Buildings Branch, Procurement Division,* Department of the Treasury, to form *Public Buildings Administration, Federal Works Agency,* in accordance with Reorg. Plan No. I of 1939, effective July 1, 1939.

Buildings and Public Parks of the National Capital, Office of Public Established by act of Feb. 26, 1925 (43 Stat. 983), by consolidation of *Office of Public Buildings and Grounds* under Chief of Engineers, U.S. Army, and *Office of Superintendent of State, War, and Navy Department Buildings.* Abolished by EO 6166 of June 10, 1933, and functions transferred to *Office of National Parks, Buildings, and Reservations,* Department of the Interior.

Bureau. *See other part of title*

Business, Cabinet Committee on Small Established by Presidential letter of May 31, 1956. Dissolved January 1961.

Business Administration, Domestic and International *See* **Business and Defense Services Administration**

Business and Defense Services Administration Established by the Secretary of Commerce Oct. 1, 1953, and operated under Department Organization Order 40–1. Abolished by Department Organization Order 40–1A of Sept. 15, 1970, and functions transferred to *Bureau of Domestic Commerce.* Functions transferred to *Domestic and International Business Administration,* effective Nov. 17, 1972. *Administration* terminated by Secretary's order of Dec. 4, 1977, and functions assumed by *Industry and Trade Administration.*

Business Economics, Office of Established by the Secretary of Commerce Jan. 17, 1946. Renamed *Office of Economic Analysis* Dec. 1, 1953. Transferred to the *Administration of Social and Economic Statistics* along with Bureau of the Census and renamed Bureau of Economic Analysis on Jan. 1, 1972.

Business Operations, Bureau of International Established by the Secretary of Commerce Aug. 8, 1961, by Departmental Orders 173 and 174. Abolished by Departmental Order 182 of Feb. 1, 1963, which established *Bureau of International Commerce.* Functions transferred to *Domestic and International Business Administration,* effective Nov. 17, 1972.

Cable Television Bureau Merged with *Broadcast Bureau* by Federal Communications Commission order to form Mass Media Bureau, effective Nov. 30, 1982.

California Debris Commission Established by act of Mar. 1, 1893 (27 Stat. 507). Abolished by act of Nov.

17, 1986 (100 Stat. 4229), and functions transferred to the Secretary of the Interior.

Canal Zone Government Established by act of Aug. 24, 1912 (37 Stat. 561). Abolished by act of Sept. 27, 1979 (93 Stat. 454).

Capital Housing Authority, National Established by act of June 12, 1934 (48 Stat. 930). Made agency of District of Columbia government by act of Dec. 24, 1973 (87 Stat. 779), effective July 1, 1974.

Capital Park Commission, National Established by act of June 6, 1924 (43 Stat. 463). *National Capital Park and Planning Commission* named successor by act of Apr. 30, 1926 (44 Stat. 374). Functions transferred to National Capital Planning Commission by act of July 19, 1952 (66 Stat. 781).

Capital Park and Planning Commission, National *See* **Capital Park Commission, National**

Capital Regional Planning Council, National Established by act of July 19, 1952 (66 Stat. 785). Terminated by Reorg. Plan No. 5 of 1966, effective Sept. 8, 1966.

Capital Transportation Agency, National Established by act of July 14, 1960 (74 Stat 537). Authorized to establish rapid rail transit system by act of Sept. 8, 1965 (79 Stat. 663). Functions transferred to Washington Metropolitan Area Transit Authority by EO 11373 of Sept. 20, 1967.

Career Executive Board Established by EO 10758 of Mar. 4, 1958. Terminated July 1, 1959, and EO 10758 revoked by EO 10859 of Feb. 5, 1960.

Caribbean Organization Act of June 30, 1961 (75 Stat. 194), provided for acceptance by President of Agreement for the Establishment of the Caribbean Organization, signed at Washington, June 21, 1960. Article III of Agreement provided for termination of *Caribbean Commission,* authorized by Agreement signed Oct. 30, 1946, on first meeting of Caribbean Council, governing body of *Organization.* Terminated, effective Dec. 31, 1965, by resolution adopted by Council.

Cemeteries and Memorials in Europe, National Supervision transferred from *Department of War* to American Battle Monuments Commission by EO 6614 of Feb. 26, 1934, which transfer was deferred to May 21, 1934, by EO 6690 of Apr. 25, 1934.

Cemeteries and Parks, National *Department of War* functions regarding National Cemeteries and Parks located in continental U.S. transferred to *Office of National Parks, Buildings, and Reservations,* Department of the Interior, by EO 6166 of June 10, 1933.

Cemetery System, National Established in the *Veterans' Administration* by act of June 18, 1973 (87 Stat. 75). Redesignated as the National Cemetery Administration by act of Nov. 11, 1998 (112 Stat. 3337).

Censorship, Office of Established by EO 8985 of Dec. 19, 1941. Terminated by EO 9631 of Sept. 28, 1945.

Censorship Policy Board Established by EO 8985 of Dec. 19, 1941. Terminated by EO 9631 of Sept. 28, 1945.

Census, Bureau of the *See* **Census Office**

Census Office Established temporarily within the Department of the Interior in accordance with act of Mar. 3, 1899. Established as a permanent office by act of Mar. 6, 1902. Transferred from the Department of the Interior to *Department of Commerce and Labor* by act of Feb. 14, 1903. Remained in the Department of Commerce under provisions of Reorganization Plan No. 5 of May 24, 1950, effective May 24, 1950.

Center. *See other part of title*

Central. *See other part of title*

Chemistry and Soils, Bureau of *See* **Agricultural and Industrial Chemistry, Bureau of**

Chesapeake Bay Center for Environmental Studies Established in 1965 in Annapolis, MD, as part of Smithsonian Institution by Secretarial order. Merged with *Radiation Biology Laboratory* by Secretarial Order July 1, 1983, to form Smithsonian Environmental Research Center.

Chief Information Officers Council Established by EO 13011 of July 16, 1996. Abolished by EO 13403 of May 12, 2006.

Chief People Officer, Office of the Renamed Office of the Chief Human Capital Officer by administrative order 5440.597 of June 16, 2006.

Chief Strategic Officer, Office of the Established by the Commissioner of Social Security Dec. 20, 2002. Abolished by Commissioner's memorandum of Jan. 14, 2008, and functions transferred to the Office of the Deputy Commissioner for Budget, Finance, and Management.

Child Development, Office of *See* **Children's Bureau**

Children's Bureau Established by act of Apr. 9, 1912 (37 Stat. 79). Placed in the Department of Labor by act of Mar. 4, 1913 (37 Stat. 737). Transferred, with exception of child labor functions, to *Social Security Administration, Federal Security Agency,* by Reorg. Plan No. 2 of 1946, effective July 16, 1946. Continued under *Administration* when *Agency* functions assumed by the *Department of Health, Education, and Welfare.* Reassigned to *Welfare Administration* by Department reorganization of Jan. 28, 1963. Reassigned to *Social and Rehabilitation Service* by Department reorganization of Aug. 15, 1967. Reassigned to *Office of Child Development* by Department reorganization order of Sept. 17, 1969.

Child Health and Human Development, National Institute of Established by act of Oct. 17, 1962 (76 Stat. 1072). Renamed Eunice Kennedy Shriver National Institute of Child Health and Human Development by act of Dec. 21, 2007 (121 Stat. 1826).

China, U.S. Court for Established by act of June 30, 1906 (34 Stat. 814). Transferred to the Department of Justice by EO 6166 of June 10, 1933, effective Mar. 2, 1934. Act of June 30, 1906, repealed effective Sept. 1, 1948 (62 Stat. 992).

Christopher Columbus Quincentenary Jubilee Commission Established by act of Aug. 7, 1984 (98 Stat. 1257). Terminated pursuant to terms of act.

Civil defense. *See* **Defense**

Civil Rights, Commission on Established by act of Sept. 9, 1957 (71 Stat. 634). Terminated in 1983 and reestablished by act of Nov. 30, 1983 (97 Stat. 1301). Renamed United States Commission on Civil Rights by act of Nov. 2, 1994 (108 Stat. 4683).

Civil Service Commission, U.S. Established by act of Jan. 16, 1883 (22 Stat. 403). Redesignated as Merit Systems Protection Board and functions transferred to Board and Office of Personnel Management by Reorg. Plan No. 2 of 1978, effective Jan. 1, 1979.

Civil War Centennial Commission Established by act of Sept. 7, 1957 (71 Stat. 626). Terminated May 1, 1966, pursuant to terms of act.

Civilian Conservation Corps Established by act of June 28, 1937 (50 Stat. 319). Made part of *Federal Security Agency* by Reorg. Plan No. I of 1939, effective July 1, 1939. Liquidation provided for by act of July 2, 1942 (56 Stat. 569), not later than June 30, 1943.

Civilian Health and Medical Program of the United States, Office of Established as field activity in the Department of Defense in 1974. Functions consolidated into the TRICARE Management Activity in November 1997 by Defense Reform Initiative.

Civilian Production Administration Established by EO 9638 of Oct. 4, 1945. Consolidated with other agencies to form *Office of Temporary Controls, Office for Emergency Management,* by EO 9809 of Dec. 12, 1946.

Civilian Service Awards Board, Distinguished Established by EO 10717 of June 27, 1957. Terminated by EO 12014 of Oct. 19, 1977, and functions transferred to *U.S. Civil Service Commission.*

Claims, U.S. Court of Established Feb. 25, 1855 (10 Stat. 612). Abolished by act of Apr. 2, 1982 (96 Stat. 26) and trial jurisdiction transferred to *U.S. Claims Court* and appellate functions merged with those of *U.S. Court of Customs and Patent Appeals* to form U.S. Court of Appeals for the Federal Circuit. *U.S. Claims Court* renamed U.S. Court of Federal Claims by act of Oct. 29, 1992 (106 Stat. 4516).

Claims Commission of the United States, International Established in the Department of State by act of Mar. 10, 1950 (64 Stat. 12). Abolished by

Reorg. Plan No. 1 of 1954, effective July 1, 1954, and functions transferred to Foreign Claims Settlement Commission of the United States.

Claims Settlement Commission of the United States, Foreign   Established by Reorg. Plan No. 1 of 1954, effective July 1, 1954. Transferred to the Department of Justice by act of Mar. 14, 1980 (94 Stat. 96).

Clark Sesquicentennial Commission, George Rogers   Established by Public Resolution 51 (45 Stat. 723). Expenditures ordered administered by the Department of the Interior by EO 6166 of June 10, 1933.

Classification Review Committee, Interagency   Established by EO 11652 of Mar. 8, 1972. Abolished by EO 12065 of June 28, 1978.

Clemency Board, Presidential   Established in Executive Office of the President by EO 11803 of Sept. 16, 1974. Final recommendations submitted to President Sept. 15, 1975, and *Board* terminated by EO 11878 of Sept. 10, 1975.

Coal Commission, National Bituminous   Established under authority of act of Aug. 30, 1935 (49 Stat. 992). Abolished by Reorg. Plan No. II of 1939, effective July 1, 1939, and functions transferred to *Bituminous Coal Division,* Department of the Interior.

Coal Consumers' Counsel, Office of the Bituminous   Established by act of Apr. 11, 1941 (55 Stat. 134), renewing provisions of act of Apr. 23, 1937 (50 Stat. 72) for 2 years to continue functions of *Consumers' Counsel Division,* Department of the Interior. Functions continued by acts of Apr. 24, 1943 (57 Stat. 68), and May 21, 1943 (57 Stat. 82). Terminated Aug. 24, 1943.

Coal Division, Bituminous   Established July 1, 1939, by Secretary of the Interior Order 1394 of June 16, 1939, as amended by Order 1399, of July 5, 1939, pursuant to act of Apr. 3, 1939 (53 Stat. 562) and Reorg. Plan No. II of 1939, effective July 1, 1939. Administered functions vested in *National Bituminous Coal Commission* by act of Apr. 23, 1937 (50 Stat. 72). Act extended to Aug. 24, 1943, on which date it expired.

Coal Labor Board, Bituminous   Established by act of July 12, 1921 (42 Stat. 140). Abolished as result of U.S. Supreme Court decision, May 18, 1936, in case of *Carter* v. *Carter Coal Company et al.*

Coal Mine Safety Board of Review, Federal   Established by act of July 16, 1952 (66 Stat. 697). Inactive after Mar. 30, 1970, pursuant to act of Dec. 30, 1969 (83 Stat. 803).

Coal Mines Administration   Established by the Secretary of the Interior July 1, 1943. Abolished by Secretary's Order 1977 of Aug. 16, 1944, as amended by Order 1982 of Aug. 31, 1944, and functions assumed by *Solid Fuels Administration for War.* Administration reestablished in the Department of the Interior by EO 9728 of May 21, 1946. Terminated June 30, 1947, by act of Mar. 27, 1942 (56 Stat. 176).

Coal Research, Office of   Established in the Department of the Interior by act of July 7, 1960 (74 Stat. 336). Functions transferred to *Energy Research and Development Administration* by act of Oct. 11, 1974 (88 Stat. 1237).

Coalition Provisional Authority, Inspector General of the   Established by act of Nov. 6, 2003 (117 Stat. 1234). Renamed Special Inspector General for Iraq Reconstruction by act of Oct. 28, 2004 (118 Stat. 2078.)

Coalition Provisional Authority, Office of the Inspector General of the   Established by act of Nov. 6, 2003 (117 Stat. 1234). Renamed Office of the Special Inspector General for Iraq Reconstruction by act of Oct. 28, 2004 (118 Stat. 2078).

Coast and Geodetic Survey   *See* **Coast Survey**

Coast Guard, U.S.   Established by act of Jan. 28, 1915 (38 Stat. 800) as a military service and branch of the U.S. Armed Forces at all times and as a service in Treasury Department, except when operating as a service in the Navy. Transferred from the Department of the Treasury to the Department of the Navy by EO 8929 of Nov. 1, 1941. Returned to the Department of the Treasury by EO 9666 of Dec. 28, 1945. Transferred to the Department of Transportation by act of Oct. 15, 1966 (80 Stat. 931). Transferred to Homeland Security Department by act of Nov. 25, 2002 (116 Stat. 2249) with related authorities and functions of the Secretary of Transportation.

Coast Survey   Established by act of Feb. 10, 1807 (2 Stat. 413). Redesignated as *Coast and Geodetic Survey* by act of June 20, 1878 (20 Stat. 206). Transferred to *Environmental Science Services Administration* by Reorg. Plan No. 2 of 1965, effective July 13, 1965.

Codification Board   Established by act of June 19, 1937 (50 Stat. 304). Abolished by Reorg. Plan No. II of 1939, effective July 1, 1939, and functions transferred to *Division of the Federal Register.*

Coinage, Joint Commission on the   Established by act of July 23, 1965 (79 Stat. 258). Expired Jan. 4, 1975, pursuant to act of Oct. 6, 1972 (88 Stat. 776).

Columbia Institution for the Instruction of the Deaf and Dumb, and the Blind   Established by act of Feb. 16, 1857 (11 Stat. 161). Renamed *Columbia Institution for the Instruction of the Deaf and Dumb* by act of Feb. 23, 1865 (13 Stat. 436). Renamed *Columbia Institution for the Instruction of the Deaf* by act of Mar. 4, 1911 (36 Stat. 1422). Renamed *Gallaudet College* by act of June 18, 1954 (68 Stat. 265). Functions of the *Department of Health, Education, and Welfare* transferred to the Department of Education by act of Oct. 17, 1979 (93 Stat. 695). Renamed Gallaudet University by act of Aug. 4, 1986 (100 Stat. 781).

Commander in Chief, U.S. Fleet, and Chief of Naval Operations   Duties of two positions prescribed by EO 8984 of Dec. 18, 1941. Combined under one officer by EO 9096 of Mar. 12, 1942.

Commerce, Bureau of Domestic *See* **Business and Defense Services Administration**

Commerce, Bureau of Foreign Established by the Secretary of Commerce Oct. 12, 1953, by Reorg. Plan No. 5 of 1950, effective May 24, 1950. Abolished by department order of Aug. 7, 1961, and functions vested in *Bureau of International Programs* and *Bureau of International Business Operations.*

Commerce, Bureau of Foreign and Domestic Established by act of Aug. 23, 1912 (37 Stat. 407). Functions reassigned to other offices of the Department of Commerce due to internal reorganizations.

Commerce, Bureau of International*See* **Business Operations, Bureau of International**

Commerce Service, Foreign Established in *Bureau of Foreign and Domestic Commerce,* Department of Commerce, by act of Mar. 3, 1927 (44 Stat. 1394). Transferred to the Department of State as part of Foreign Service by Reorg. Plan No. II of 1939, effective July 1, 1939.

Commercial Company, U.S. Established Mar. 27, 1942, as subsidiary of *Reconstruction Finance Corporation.* Transferred to *Office of Economic Warfare* by EO 9361 of July 15, 1943. *Office* consolidated into *Foreign Economic Administration* by EO 9380 of Sept. 25, 1943. Functions returned to *Corporation* by EO 9630 of Sept. 27, 1945, until June 30, 1948.

Commercial Policy, Executive Committee on Established by Presidential letter of Nov. 11, 1933, to Secretary of State. Abolished by EO 9461 of Aug. 7, 1944.

Commercial Standards Division Transferred with *Division of Simplified Trade Practice* from *National Bureau of Standards* to the Secretary of Commerce by Reorg. Plan No. 3 of 1946, effective July 16, 1946, to permit reassignment to *Office of Domestic Commerce.* Functions transferred to *National Bureau of Standards* by the Department of Commerce Order 90, June 7, 1963, pursuant to Reorg. Plan No. 5 of 1950, effective May 24, 1950.

Commission. *See other part of title*

Committee. *See also other part of title*

Committee Management Secretariat Established in the Office of Management and Budget Jan. 5, 1973, by act of Oct. 6, 1972 (86 Stat. 772). Functions transferred to General Services Administrator by Reorg. Plan No. 1 of 1977, effective Apr. 1, 1978. Reassigned to the *National Archives and Records Service* by GSA order of Feb. 22, 1979. Transferred in Archives to Office of the Federal Register by GSA order of Oct. 14, 1980. Transferred to Office of the Archivist of the United States by GSA order of Sept. 24, 1982. Reassigned to Office of Program Initiatives, GSA, by GSA order of May 18, 1984. Transferred to Office of Management Services, GSA, by GSA order of Apr. 7, 1986.

Commodities Corporation, Federal Surplus *See* **Relief Corporation, Federal Surplus**

Commodity Credit Corporation Organized by EO 6340 of Oct. 16, 1933, and managed in close affiliation with *Reconstruction Finance Corporation.* Transferred to the Department of Agriculture by Reorg. Plan No. I of 1939, effective July 1, 1939.

Commodity Exchange Administration *See* **Grain Futures Administration**

Commodity Exchange Authority *See* **Grain Futures Administration**

Commodity Exchange Commission Established by act of Sept. 21, 1922 (42 Stat. 998). Functions transferred to Commodity Futures Trading Commission by act of Oct. 23, 1974 (88 Stat. 1414).

Commodity Stabilization Service Established in the Department of Agriculture Nov. 2, 1953, by Secretary's Memorandum 1320, supp. 4. Renamed Agricultural Stabilization and Conservation Service by Secretary's Memorandum 1458 of June 14, 1961, effective June 5, 1961.

Communication Agency, International *See* *Information Agency, U.S.*

Communications Program, Joint Tactical Combined with *Joint Interoperability of the Tactical Command and Control Systems Programs* to form Joint Tactical Command, Control, and Communications Agency in July 1984, pursuant to DOD Directive 5154.28.

Community Development Corporation Established in the Department of Housing and Urban Development by act of Dec. 31, 1970 (84 Stat. 1791). Renamed *New Community Development Corporation* by act of Aug. 22, 1974 (88 Stat. 725). Abolished Nov. 30, 1983, by act of Nov. 30, 1983 (97 Stat. 1238), and functions transferred to Assistant Secretary for Community Planning and Development, Department of Housing and Urban Development.

Community Development Corporation, New *See* **Community Development Corporation**

Community Facilities, Bureau of Established in 1945 by *Federal Works Administrator.* Transferred by act of June 30, 1949 (63 Stat. 380), to General Services Administration, functioning as *Community Facilities Service.* Certain functions transferred to various agencies, including the Department of the Interior, *Housing and Home Finance Agency,* and *Federal Security Agency* by Reorg. Plans Nos. 15, 16, and 17 of 1950, effective May 24, 1950.

Community Facilities Administration Established in *Housing and Home Finance Agency* by Administrator's Organizational Order 1 of Dec. 23, 1954. Terminated by act of Sept. 9, 1965 (79 Stat. 667), and functions transferred to the Department of Housing and Urban Development.

Community Organization, Committee on Established in *Office of Defense Health and Welfare Services* Sept. 10, 1941. Functions transferred to *Federal Security Agency* by EO 9338 of Apr. 29, 1943.

Community Relations Service   Established in the Department of Commerce by act of July 2, 1964 (78 Stat. 241). Transferred to the Department of Justice by Reorg. Plan No. 1 of 1966, effective Apr. 22, 1966.

Community Service, Commission on National and   Established by act of Nov. 16, 1990 (104 Stat. 3168). Abolished by act of Sept. 21, 1993, and functions vested in the Board of Directors or the Executive Director prior to Oct. 1, 1993, transferred to the Corporation for National and Community Service (107 Stat. 873, 888).

Community Services Administration   Established by act of Jan. 4, 1975 (88 Stat. 2291) as successor to *Office of Economic Opportunity.* Abolished as independent agency through repeal of act of Aug. 20, 1964 (except titles VIII and X of such act) by act of Aug. 13, 1981 (95 Stat. 519).

Community Services Administration   Functions concerning Legal Services Program transferred to Legal Services Corporation by act of July 25, 1974 (88 Stat. 389). Renamed *Public Services Administration* by *Health, Education, and Welfare* departmental notice of Nov. 3, 1976. Transferred to *Office of Human Development* by Secretary's reorganization of Mar. 8, 1977 (42 FR 13262).

Community War Services   Established in *Office of the Administrator* under EO 9338 of Apr. 29, 1943, and *Federal Security Agency* order. Terminated Dec. 31, 1946, by act of July 26, 1946 (60 Stat. 695).

Conciliation Service, U.S.   Established by act of Mar. 4, 1913 (37 Stat. 738). Functions transferred to Federal Mediation and Conciliation Service, established by act of June 23, 1947 (61 Stat. 153).

Conference on Security and Cooperation in Europe   Renamed Organization for Security and Cooperation in Europe by EO 13029, Dec. 3, 1996 (61 FR 64591).

Consolidated Farm Service Agency   Established by act of Oct. 13, 1994 (108 Stat. 3214). Renamed Farm Service Agency (61 FR 1109), effective Jan. 16, 1996.

Constitution, Commission on the Bicentennial of the United States   Established by act of Sept. 29, 1983, as amended (97 Stat. 722). Terminated by act of Dec. 3, 1991 (105 Stat. 1232).

Constitution, transfer of functions   *See* **Statutes at Large and other matters**

Construction, Collective Bargaining Committee in   Established by EO 11849 of Apr. 1, 1975. Inactive since Jan. 7, 1976. Formally abolished by EO 12110 of Dec. 28, 1978.

Construction, Equipment and Repairs, Bureau of   Established in the Department of the Navy by act of Aug. 31, 1842 (5 Stat. 579). Abolished by act of July 5, 1862 (12 Stat. 510), and functions distributed among *Bureau of Equipment and Recruiting, Bureau*

of Construction and Repair, and *Bureau of Steam Engineering.*

Construction Branch   Established in the Department of the Treasury in 1853 and designated *Bureau of Construction* under control of *Office of Supervising Architect* by Sept. 30, 1855. *Office* incorporated into *Public Buildings Branch, Procurement Division,* by EO 6166 of June 10, 1933. Transferred to *Federal Works Agency* by Reorg. Plan No. I of 1939, effective July 1, 1939, when *Public Buildings Branch* of *Procurement Division, Bureau of Buildings Management,* National Park Service, Department of the Interior—so far as latter concerned with operation of public buildings for other departments or agencies—and *U.S. Housing Corporation* consolidated with *Public Buildings Administration, Federal Works Agency.*

Construction Industry Stabilization Committee   Established by EO 11588 of Mar. 29, 1971. Abolished by EO 11788 of June 18, 1974.

Construction and Repair, Bureau of   Established by act of July 5, 1862 (12 Stat. 510), replacing *Bureau of Construction, Equipment and Repairs.* Abolished by act of June 20, 1940 (54 Stat. 492), and functions transferred to *Bureau of Ships.*

Consumer Advisory Council   Established by EO 11136 of Jan. 3, 1964. *Office of Consumer Affairs* established in Executive Office of the President by EO 11583 of Feb. 24, 1971, and Council reestablished in *Office.*

Consumer Affairs, Office of   Established by EO 11583 of Feb. 24, 1971. Transferred to the *Department of Health, Education, and Welfare* by EO 11702 of Jan. 25, 1973.

Consumer Affairs Staff, National Business Council for   Established in the Department of Commerce by departmental organization order of Dec. 16, 1971. Terminated by departmental order of Dec. 6, 1973, due to lack of funding.

Consumer agencies   Consumer agencies of *National Emergency Council* and *National Recovery Administration* reorganized and functions transferred, together with those of *Consumers' Advisory Board, NRA,* and *Cabinet Committee on Price Policy,* to *Consumers' Division, NRA,* by EO 7120 of July 30, 1935. *Division* transferred to the Department of Labor by EO 7252 of Dec. 21, 1935. Transferred to *Division of Consumers' Counsel, Agricultural Adjustment Administration,* Department of Agriculture, by Secretary of Labor letter of Aug. 30, 1938, to the Secretary of Agriculture. Continued as *Consumer Standards Project* until June 30, 1941. Research on consumer standards continued by *Consumer Standards Section, Consumers' Counsel Division,* transferred to *Agricultural Marketing Administration* by administrative order of Feb. 28, 1942. Other project activities discontinued.

Consumer Cooperative Bank, National   Established by act of Aug. 20, 1978 (92 Stat. 499). Removed from mixed-ownership, Government corporation status by acts of Sept. 13, 1982 (96 Stat. 1062) and Jan. 12, 1983 (96 Stat. 2478).

Consumer Information and Insurance Oversight, Office of Established by Health and Human Services Secretary's notice of April 19, 2010 (75 FR 20364). Abolished by Centers for Medicare & Medicaid's notice of Jan. 26, 2011 (76 FR 4703).

Consumer Interests, President's Committee on Established by EO 11136 of Jan. 3, 1964. Abolished by EO 11583 of Feb. 24, 1971.

Consumer and Marketing Service Established by the Secretary of Agriculture Feb. 2, 1965. Renamed Agricultural Marketing Service Apr. 2, 1972, by Secretary's order and certain functions transferred to Animal and Plant Health Inspection Service.

Consumers' Counsel Established in *National Bituminous Coal Commission* by act of Aug. 30, 1935 (49 Stat. 993). Office abolished by Reorg. Plan No. II of 1939, effective July 1, 1939, and functions transferred to Office of Solicitor, Department of the Interior, to function as *Consumers' Counsel Division* under direction of the Secretary of the Interior. Functions transferred to *Office of the Bituminous Coal Consumers' Counsel* June 1941 by act of Apr. 11, 1941 (55 Stat. 134).

Consumers' Counsel Division *See* **Consumers' Counsel**

Consumers' Counsel, Division of Established by act of May 12, 1933 (48 Stat. 31). Transferred by order of the Secretary of Agriculture from *Agricultural Adjustment Administration* to supervision of *Director of Marketing,* effective Feb. 1, 1940. Transferred to *Agricultural Marketing Administration* by administrative order of Feb. 28, 1942.

Consumers' Problems, Adviser on *See* **Consumer agencies**

Contract Committee Government *See* **Contract Compliance, Committee on Government**

Contract Compliance, Committee on Government Established by EO 10308 of Dec. 3, 1951. Abolished by EO 10479 of Aug. 13, 1953, which established successor *Government Contract Committee.* Abolished by EO 10925 of Mar. 6, 1961, and records and property transferred to *President's Committee on Equal Employment Opportunity.*

Contract Settlement, Office of Established by act of July 1, 1944 (58 Stat. 651). Transferred to *Office of War Mobilization and Reconversion* by act of Oct. 3, 1944 (58 Stat. 785). Terminated by EO 9809 of Dec. 12, 1946, and Reorg. Plan No. 1 of 1947, effective July 1, 1947, and functions transferred to the Department of the Treasury. Functions transferred to General Services Administration by act of June 30, 1949 (63 Stat. 380).

Contract Settlement Advisory Board Established by act of July 1, 1944 (58 Stat. 651). Transferred to the Department of the Treasury by EO 9809 of Dec. 12, 1946, and by Reorg. Plan No. 1 of 1947,

effective July 1, 1947. Transferred to General Services Administration by act of June 30, 1949 (63 Stat. 380) and established as *Contract Review Board.* Renamed Board of Contract Appeals in 1961 by Administrator's order. Board established as independent entity within General Services Administration Feb. 27, 1979, pursuant to act of Nov. 1, 1978 (92 Stat. 2383).

Contract Settlement Appeal Board, Office of Established by act of July 1, 1944 (58 Stat. 651). Transferred to the Department of the Treasury by EO 9809 of Dec. 12, 1946, and by Reorg. Plan No. 1 of 1947, effective July 1, 1947. Functions transferred to General Services Administration by act of June 30, 1949 (63 Stat. 380). Abolished by act of July 14, 1952 (66 Stat. 627).

Contract Termination Board, Joint Established Nov. 12, 1943, by *Director of War Mobilization.* Functions assumed by *Office of Contract Settlement.*

Contracts Division, Public Established in the Department of Labor to administer act of June 30, 1936 (49 Stat. 2036). Consolidated with Wage and Hour Division by Secretarial order of Aug. 21, 1942. Absorbed by Wage and Hour Division by Secretarial order of May 1971.

Cooperation Administration, International Established by Department of State Delegation of Authority 85 of June 30, 1955, pursuant to EO 10610 of May 9, 1955. Abolished by act of Sept. 4, 1961 (75 Stat. 446), and functions redelegated to Agency for International Development pursuant to Presidential letter of Sept. 30, 1961, and EO 10973 of Nov. 3, 1961.

Cooperative State Research, Education, and Extension Service Established by act of Oct. 13, 1994 (108 Stat. 3178). Reorganized into the National Institute of Food and Agriculture by Secretary's Memorandum 1062–001 of Sept. 17, 2009.

Cooperative State Research Service Established in the Department of Agriculture. Incorporated into Cooperative State, Research, Education, and Extension Service under Department of Agriculture reorganization in 1995.

Coordinating Council for Comparative Effectiveness Research, Federal Established by act of Feb. 17, 2009 (123 Stat 187). Terminated by act of Mar. 23, 2010 (124 Stat. 747).

Coordinating Service, Federal *Office of Chief Coordinator* created by Executive order promulgated in *Bureau of the Budget* Circular 15, July 27, 1921, and duties enlarged by other *Bureau* circulars. Abolished by EO 6166 of June 10, 1933. Contract form, Federal traffic, and surplus property functions transferred to *Procurement Division* by order of the Secretary of the Treasury, approved by President Oct. 9, 1933, issued pursuant to EO's 6166 of June 10, 1933, and 6224 of July 27, 1933.

Copyright Arbitration Royalty Panels Established by act of Dec. 17, 1993 (107 Stat. 2304). Replaced by Copyright Royalty Judges under act of Nov. 30, 2004 (118 Stat. 2351).

Copyright Royalty Tribunal   Established as an independent entity within the legislative branch by act of Oct. 19, 1976 (90 Stat. 2594). Abolished by act of Dec. 17, 1993 (107 Stat. 2304), and functions transferred to copyright arbitration royalty panels.

Copyrighted Works, National Commission on New Technological Uses of   Established by act of Dec. 31, 1974 (88 Stat. 1873). Terminated Sept. 29, 1978, pursuant to terms of act.

Corporate Payments Abroad, Task Force on Questionable   Established by Presidential memorandum of Mar. 31, 1976. Terminated Dec. 31, 1976, pursuant to terms of memorandum.

Corporation, Federal Facilities   Established in the Department of the Treasury by EO 10539 of June 22, 1954. Placed under supervision of Director appointed by General Services Administrator by EO 10720 of July 11, 1957. Dissolved by act of Aug. 30, 1961 (75 Stat. 418), and functions transferred to Administrator of General Services.

Corregidor-Bataan Memorial Commission   Established by act of Aug. 5, 1953 (67 Stat. 366). Terminated May 6, 1967, by act of Dec. 23, 1963 (77 Stat. 477).

Cost Accounting Standards Board   Established by act of Aug. 15, 1970 (84 Stat. 796). Terminated Sept. 30, 1980, due to lack of funding. Reestablished by act of Nov. 17, 1988 (102 Stat. 4059).

Cost of Living Council   Established by EO 11615 of Aug. 15, 1971. Abolished by EO 11788 of June 18, 1974.

Cotton Stabilization Corporation   Organized June 1930 under laws of Delaware by *Federal Farm Board* pursuant to act of June 15, 1929 (46 Stat. 11). Certificate of dissolution filed with Corporation Commission of Delaware Dec. 27, 1934.

Cotton Textile Industry, Board of Inquiry for the   Established by EO 6840 of Sept. 5, 1934. Abolished by EO 6858 of Sept. 26, 1934.

Council.   *See other part of title*

Counterespionage Section   Transferred from the Criminal Division to the National Security Division by act of Mar. 9, 2006 (120 Stat. 249).

Counterintelligence, Office of   Established within the Department of Energy by Public Law 106–65 of Oct. 5, 1999 (113 Stat. 955). Merged with *Office of Intelligence* to form *Office of Intelligence and Counterintelligence* by memorandum of March 9, 2006 of the Secretary of Energy.

Counterterrorism Section   Transferred from the Criminal Division to the National Security Division by act of Mar. 9, 2006 (120 Stat. 249).

Courts   Under act of Aug. 7, 1939 (53 Stat. 1223), and revised June 25, 1948 (62 Stat. 913), to provide for administration of U.S. courts, administrative jurisdiction over all continental and territorial courts

transferred to Administrative Office of the U.S. Courts, including U.S. courts of appeals and district courts, District Court for the Territory of Alaska, U.S. District Court for the District of the Canal Zone, District Court of Guam, District Court of the Virgin Islands, Court of Claims, Court of Customs and Patent Appeals, and Customs Courts.

Credit Unions, Bureau of Federal   *See* **Credit Union System, Federal**

Credit Union System, Federal   Established by act of June 26, 1934 (48 Stat. 1216), to be administered by *Farm Credit Administration.* Transferred to Federal Deposit Insurance Corporation by EO 9148 of Apr. 27, 1942, and Reorg. Plan No. 1 of 1947, effective July 1, 1947. Functions transferred to *Bureau of Federal Credit Unions, Federal Security Agency,* established by act of June 29, 1948 (62 Stat. 1091). Functions transferred to the *Department of Health, Education, and Welfare* by Reorg. Plan No. 1 of 1953, effective Apr. 11, 1953. Functions transferred to National Credit Union Administration by act of Mar. 10, 1970 (84 Stat. 49).

Crime, National Council on Organized   Established by EO 11534 of June 4, 1970. Terminated by EO 12110 of Dec. 28, 1978.

Critical Materials Council, National   Established within Executive Office of the President by act of July 31, 1984 (98 Stat. 1250). *Office* abolished in September 1993 due to lack of funding and functions transferred to the Office of Science and Technology Policy.

Crop Insurance Corporation, Federal   Established by act of Feb. 16, 1938. Consolidated with the *Agricultural Stabilization and Conservation Service* and *Farmers' Home Administration* in 1995 to form the *Farm Service Agency* pursuant to act of Oct. 13, 1994 (108 Stat. 3178).

Crop Production Loan Office   Authorized by Presidential letters of July 26, 1918, and July 26, 1919, to the Secretary of Agriculture. Further authorized by act of Mar. 3, 1921 (41 Stat. 1347). Transferred to Farm Credit Administration by EO 6084 of Mar. 27, 1933.

Cultural Center, National   Established in Smithsonian Institution by act of Sept. 2, 1958 (72 Stat. 1698). Renamed John F. Kennedy Center for the Performing Arts by act of Jan. 23, 1964 (78 Stat. 4).

Customs, Bureau of   Established under sec. 1 of act of Mar. 3, 1927 (19 U.S.C. 2071) in Treasury Department. Functions relating to award of numbers to undocumented vessels, vested in *Collectors of Customs,* transferred to Commandant of Coast Guard by EO 9083 of Feb. 27, 1942. Transfer made permanent by Reorg. Plan No. 3 of 1946, effective July 16, 1946. Redesignated U.S. Customs Service by the Department of the Treasury Order 165–23 of Apr. 4, 1973. Functions transferred to and agency established within Homeland Security Department by act of Nov. 25, 2002 (116 Stat. 2178).

Customs Court, U.S. Formerly established as Board of General Appraisers by act of June 10, 1890 (26 Stat. 136). Renamed *U.S. Customs Court* by act of May 26, 1926 (44 Stat. 669). Renamed U.S. Court of International Trade by act of Oct. 10, 1980 (94 Stat. 1727).

Customs and Patent Appeals, U.S. Court of Established by act of Mar. 2, 1929 (45 Stat. 1475). Abolished by act of Apr. 2, 1982 (96 Stat. 28) and functions merged with appellate functions of *U.S. Court of Claims* to form U.S. Court of Appeals for the Federal Circuit.

Dairy Industry, Bureau of *Bureau of Dairying* established in the Department of Agriculture by act of May 29, 1924 (43 Stat. 243). *Bureau of Dairy Industry* designation first appeared in act of May 11, 1926 (44 Stat. 499). Functions transferred to Agricultural Research Service by Secretary's Memorandum 1320, supp. 4, of Nov. 2, 1953.

Deepwater Horizon Oil Spill and Offshore Drilling, The National Commission on the Established by EO 13543 of May 21, 2010. Terminated March 11, 2011 pursuant to terms of order.

Defense, Advisory Commission to the Council of National *See* **Defense, Council of National**

Defense, Council of National Established by act of Aug. 29, 1916 (39 Stat. 649). *Advisory Commission*—composed of Advisers on Industrial Production, Industrial Materials, Employment, Farm Products, Price Stabilization, Transportation, and Consumer Protection—established by *Council* pursuant to act and approved by President May 29, 1940. *Commission* decentralized by merging divisions with newly created national defense units. Agencies evolved from *Commission*, except *Office of Agricultural War Relations* and *Office of Price Administration*, made units of *Office for Emergency Management. Council* inactive.

Defense, Office of Civilian Established in *Office for Emergency Management* by EO 8757 of May 20, 1941. Terminated by EO 9562 of June 4, 1945.

Defense Administration, Federal Civil Established in *Office for Emergency Management* by EO 10186 of Dec. 1, 1950; subsequently established as independent agency by act of Jan. 12, 1951 (64 Stat. 1245). Functions transferred to *Office of Defense and Civilian Mobilization* by Reorg. Plan No. 1 of 1958, effective July 1, 1958.

Defense Advanced Research Projects Agency Established as a separate agency of the Department of Defense by DOD Directive 5105.41 dated July 25, 1978. Renamed *Advanced Research Projects Agency* by order of the Secretary of Defense dated July 13, 1993. Reestablished by act of Feb. 10, 1996 (110 Stat. 406).

Defense Advisory Council, Civil Established by act of Jan. 12, 1951 (64 Stat. 1245). Transferred to *Office of Defense and Civilian Mobilization* by Reorg. Plan No. 1 of 1958, effective July 1, 1958.

Defense Aid Reports, Division of Established in *Office for Emergency Management* by EO 8751 of May 2, 1941. Abolished by EO 8926 of Oct. 28, 1941, which created *Office of Lend-Lease Administration.*

Defense Air Transportation Administration Established Nov. 12, 1951, by Department of Commerce Order 137. Abolished by Amendment 3 of Sept. 13, 1962, to Department Order 128 (revised) and functions transferred to *Office of the Under Secretary of Commerce for Transportation.*

Defense Atomic Support Agency Renamed *Defense Nuclear Agency* by General Order No. 1 of July 1, 1971.

Defense Audiovisual Agency Established by DOD Directive 5040.1 of June 12, 1979. Abolished by Secretary's memorandum of Apr. 19, 1985, and functions assigned to the military departments.

Defense Audit Service Established by DOD Directive of Oct. 14, 1976. Abolished by Deputy Secretary's memorandum of Nov. 2, 1982, and functions transferred to Office of the Inspector General.

Defense Civil Preparedness Agency Functions transferred from the Department of Defense to the Federal Emergency Management Agency by EO 12148 of July 20, 1979.

Defense and Civilian Mobilization Board Established by EO 10773 of July 1, 1938. Redesignated *Civil and Defense Mobilization Board* by act of Aug. 26, 1958 (72 Stat. 861). Abolished by *Office of Emergency Preparedness* Circular 1200.1 of Oct. 31, 1962.

Defense Communications Agency Established by direction of the Secretary of Defense on May 12, 1960. Renamed Defense Information Systems Agency by DOD Directive 5105.19 dated June 25, 1991.

Defense Communications Board Established by EO 8546 of Sept. 24, 1940. Renamed *Board of War Communications* by EO 9183 of June 15, 1942. Abolished by EO 9831 of Feb. 24, 1947, and property transferred to Federal Communications Commission.

Defense Coordinating Board, Civil Established by EO 10611 of May 11, 1955. EO 10611 revoked by EO 10773 of July 1, 1958.

Defense Electric Power Administration Established by Order 2605 of Dec. 4, 1950 of the Secretary of the Interior. Abolished June 30, 1953, by Secretary's Order 2721 of May 7, 1953. Reestablished by Departmental Manual Release No. 253 of Aug. 6, 1959. Terminated by Departmental Manual Release No. 1050 of Jan. 10, 1977.

Defense Fisheries Administration Established by Order 2605 of Dec. 4, 1950 of the Secretary of the Interior. Abolished June 30, 1953, by Secretary's Order 2722 of May 13, 1953.

Defense Health and Welfare Services, Office of Established by EO 8890 of Sept. 3, 1941. Terminated by EO 9338 of Apr. 29, 1943, and functions transferred to *Federal Security Agency.*

Defense Homes Corporation Incorporated pursuant to President's letter to the Secretary of the Treasury of Oct. 18, 1940. Transferred to *Federal Public Housing Authority* by EO 9070 of Feb. 24, 1942.

Defense Housing Coordinator Office established July 21, 1940, by *Advisory Commission to Council of National Defense.* Functions transferred to *Division of Defense Housing Coordination, Office for Emergency Management,* by EO 8632 of Jan. 11, 1941.

Defense Housing Division, Mutual Ownership Established by Administrator of *Federal Works Agency* under provisions of act of June 28, 1941 (55 Stat. 361). Functions transferred to *Federal Public Housing Authority, National Housing Agency,* by EO 9070 of Feb. 24, 1942.

Defense Intelligence College Established by DOD Directive 3305.1 of January 28, 1983. Renamed Joint Military Intelligence College by DOD Directive 3305.1 of January 14, 1998. *See also Defense Intelligence School.*

Defense Intelligence School Established by DOD Directive 5105.25 of November 2, 1962. Renamed Defense Intelligence College by DOD Directive 3305.1 of January 28, 1983.

Defense Investigative Service Established by the Secretary of Defense Jan. 1, 1972. Renamed Defense Security Service in November 1997 by Defense Reform Initiative.

Defense Manpower Administration Established by the Secretary of Labor by General Order 48, pursuant to EO 10161 of Sept. 9, 1950, and Reorg. Plan No. 6 of 1950, effective May 24, 1950. General Order 48 revoked by General Order 63 of Aug. 25, 1953, which established *Office of Manpower Administration* in Department.

Defense Mapping Agency Established as a the Department of Defense agency in 1972. Functions transferred to the National Imagery and Mapping Agency by act of Sept. 23, 1996 (110 Stat. 2677).

Defense Materials Procurement Agency Established by EO 10281 of Aug. 28, 1951. Abolished by EO 10480 of Aug. 14, 1953, and functions transferred to General Services Administration.

Defense Materials Service *See* **Emergency Procurement Service**

Defense Materiel Readiness Board Established by act of Jan. 28, 2008 (122 Stat. 260). Abolished by act of Jan. 2, 2013 (126 Stat. 2362).

Defense Mediation Board, National Established by EO 8716 of Mar. 19, 1941. Terminated on creation of *National War Labor Board, Office for Emergency Management* by EO 9017 of Jan. 12, 1942. Transferred to the Department of Labor by EO

9617 of Sept. 19, 1945. *Board* terminated by EO 9672 of Dec. 31, 1945, which established *National Wage Stabilization Board* in the Department of Labor. Terminated by EO 9809 of Dec. 12, 1946, and functions transferred to the Secretary of Labor and the Department of the Treasury, effective Feb. 24, 1947.

Defense Medical Programs Activity Functions consolidated into the TRICARE Management Activity in November 1997 by Defense Reform Initiative.

Defense Minerals Administration Established by Order 2605 of Dec. 4, 1950 of the Secretary of the Interior. Functions assigned to *Defense Materials Procurement Agency.* Functions of exploration for critical and strategic minerals redelegated to the Secretary of the Interior and administered by *Defense Minerals Exploration Administration* by Secretary's Order 2726 of June 30, 1953. Termination of program announced by Secretary June 6, 1958. Certain activities continued in *Office of Minerals Exploration,* Department of the Interior.

Defense Minerals Exploration Administration *See* **Defense Minerals Administration**

Defense Mobilization, Office of Established in Executive Office of the President by EO 10193 of Dec. 16, 1950. Superseded by *Office of Defense Mobilization* established by Reorg. Plan No. 3 of 1953, effective June 12, 1953, which assumed functions of former *Office, National Security Resources Board,* and critical materials stockpiling functions of Army, Navy, Air Force, and Interior Secretaries and of *Army and Navy Munitions Board.* Consolidated with *Federal Civil Defense Administration* into *Office of Defense and Civilian Mobilization* by Reorg. Plan No. 1 of 1958, effective July 1, 1958, and offices of Director and Deputy Director terminated.

Defense Mobilization Board Established by EO 10200 of Jan. 3, 1951, and restated in EO 10480 of Aug. 14, 1953. Terminated by EO 10773 of July 1, 1958.

Defense Nuclear Agency Established in 1971. Renamed *Defense Special Weapons Agency* by DOD Directive 5105.31 of June 14, 1995.

Defense Nuclear Counterintelligence, Office of Established by act of Oct. 5, 1999 (113 Stat. 960). Abolished by act of Oct. 17, 2006 (120 Stat. 2507) and functions transferred to the Secretary of Energy.

Defense Plant Corporation Established by act of June 25, 1940 (54 Stat. 572). Transferred from *Federal Loan Agency* to the Department of Commerce by EO 9071 of Feb. 24, 1942. Returned to *Federal Loan Agency* pursuant to act of Feb. 24, 1945 (59 Stat. 5). Dissolved by act of June 30, 1945 (59 Stat. 310), and functions transferred to *Reconstruction Finance Corporation.*

Defense Plants Administration, Small Established by act of July 31, 1951 (65 Stat. 131). Terminated July 31, 1953, by act of June 30, 1953 (67 Stat. 131). Functions relating to liquidation transferred to Small

Business Administration by EO 10504 of Dec. 1, 1953.

Defense Production Administration Established by EO 10200 of Jan. 3, 1951. Terminated by EO 10433 of Feb. 4, 1953, and functions transferred to *Office of Defense Mobilization.*

Defense Property Disposal Service Renamed Defense Reutilization and Marketing Service by Defense Logistics Agency General Order 10–85, effective July 1, 1985.

Defense Prisoner of War/Missing in Action Office. Established by DOD Directive 5110.10, July 16, 1993. Renamed Defense Prisoner of War/Missing Personnel Office by Secretary of Defense memorandum of May 30, 1996.

Defense Public Works Division Established in *Public Works Administration.* Transferred to *Office of Federal Works Administrator* by administrative order of July 16, 1941. Abolished by administrative order of Mar. 6, 1942, and functions transferred to *Office of Chief Engineer, Federal Works Agency.*

Defense Purchases, Office for the Coordination of National Established by order of *Council of National Defense,* approved June 27, 1940. Order revoked Jan. 7, 1941, and records transferred to Executive Office of the President.

Defense Research Committee, National Established June 27, 1940, by order of *Council of National Defense.* Abolished by order of *Council* June 28, 1941, and reestablished in *Office of Scientific Research and Development* by EO 8807 of June 28, 1941. *Office* terminated by EO 9913 of Dec. 26, 1947, and property and records transferred to *National Military Establishment.*

Defense Resources Committee Established by Administrative Order 1496 of June 15, 1940. Replaced by *War Resources Council* by Administrative Order 1636 of Jan. 14, 1942. Inactive.

Defense Security Assistance Agency Established on Sept. 1, 1971. Renamed the Defense Security Cooperation Agency by DOD Directive 5105.38.

Defense Solid Fuels Administration Established by Order 2605 of Dec. 4, 1950 of the Secretary of the Interior. Abolished June 29, 1954, by Secretary's Order 2764.

Defense Special Weapons Agency Established by General Order No. 1 of July 1, 1971. Functions transferred to the Defense Threat Reduction Agency by DOD Directive 5105.62 of Sept. 30, 1998.

Defense Stockpile Manager, National Established by act of Nov. 14, 1986 (100 Stat. 4067). Functions transferred from the Administrator of General Services to the Secretary of Defense by EO 12626 of Feb. 25, 1988.

Defense Supplies Corporation Established under act of June 25, 1940 (54 Stat. 572). Transferred from *Federal Loan Agency* to the Department of

Commerce by EO 9071 of Feb. 24, 1942. Returned to *Federal Loan Agency* by act of Feb. 24, 1945 (59 Stat. 5). Dissolved by act of June 30, 1945 (59 Stat. 310), and functions transferred to *Reconstruction Finance Corporation.*

Defense Supply Agency Renamed Defense Logistics Agency by DOD Directive 5105.22 of Jan. 22, 1977.

Defense Supply Management Agency Established in the Department of Defense by act of July 1, 1952 (66 Stat. 318). Abolished by Reorg. Plan No. 6 of 1953, effective June 30, 1953, and functions transferred to the Secretary of Defense.

Defense Technology Security Administration Established on May 10, 1985. Functions transferred to the Defense Threat Reduction Agency by DOD Directive 5105.62 of Sept. 30, 1998.

Defense Transport Administration Established Oct. 4, 1950, by order of Commissioner of *Interstate Commerce Commission* in charge of *Bureau of Service,* pursuant to EO 10161 of Sept. 9, 1950. Terminated by DTA Commissioner's order, effective July 1, 1955, and functions transferred to *Bureau of Safety and Service, Interstate Commerce Commission.*

Defense Transportation, Office of Established in *Office for Emergency Management* by EO 8989 of Dec. 18, 1941. Terminated by EO 10065 of July 6, 1949.

Deficit Reduction, Joint Select Committee on Established by act of Aug. 2, 2011 (125 Stat. 259). Terminated January 31, 2012, pursuant to the act (125 Stat. 263).

Director. *See other part of title*

Disarmament Administration, U.S. Established in the Department of State. Functions transferred to *U.S. Arms Control and Disarmament Agency* by act of Sept. 26, 1961 (75 Stat. 638).

Disarmament Problems, President's Special Committee on Established by President Aug. 5, 1955. Dissolved in February 1958.

Disaster Assistance Administration, Federal Functions transferred from the Department of Housing and Urban Development to the Federal Emergency Management Agency by EO 12148 of July 20, 1979.

Disaster Loan Corporation Grouped with other agencies to form *Federal Loan Agency* by Reorg. Plan No. I of 1939, effective July 1, 1939. Transferred to the Department of Commerce by EO 9071 of Feb. 24, 1942. Returned to *Federal Loan Agency* by act of Feb. 24, 1945 (59 Stat. 5). Dissolved by act of June 30, 1945 (59 Stat. 310), and functions transferred to *Reconstruction Finance Corporation.*

Disease Control, Center for Established within the Public Health Service by the *Secretary of Health, Education, and Welfare* on July 1, 1973. Renamed *Centers for Disease Control* by Health and Human

Services Secretary's notice of Oct. 1, 1980 (45 FR 67772). Renamed Centers for Disease Control and Prevention by act of Oct. 27, 1992 (106 Stat. 3504).

Displaced Persons Commission   Established by act of June 25, 1948 (62 Stat. 1009). Terminated Aug. 31, 1952, pursuant to terms of act.

District of Columbia   Established by acts of July 16, 1790 (1 Stat. 130), and Mar. 3, 1791. *Corporations of Washington and Georgetown* and *levy court of Washington County* abolished in favor of territorial form of government in 1871. Permanent commission government established July 1, 1878. District Government created as municipal corporation by act of June 11, 1878 (20 Stat. 102). Treated as branch of U.S. Government by various statutory enactments of Congress. District Government altered by Reorg. Plan No. 3 of 1967, effective Nov. 3, 1967. Charter for local government in District of Columbia provided by act of Dec. 24, 1973 (87 Stat. 774).

District of Columbia, Highway Commission of the   Established by act of Mar. 2, 1893 (27 Stat 532). *National Capital Park and Planning Commission* named successor by act of Apr. 30, 1926 (44 Stat. 374). Functions transferred to National Capital Planning Commission by act of July 19, 1952 (66 Stat. 781).

District of Columbia, Reform-School of the   Established by act of May 3, 1876 (19 Stat. 49). Renamed *National Training School for Boys* by act of May 27, 1908 (35 Stat. 380). Transferred to the Department of Justice by Reorg. Plan No. II of 1939, effective July 1, 1939, to be administered by Director of Bureau of Prisons.

District of Columbia Auditorium Commission   Established by act of July 1, 1955 (69 Stat. 243). Final report submitted to Congress Jan. 31, 1957, pursuant to act of Apr. 27, 1956 (70 Stat. 115).

District of Columbia Redevelopment Land Agency   Established by act of Aug. 2, 1946 (60 Stat. 790). Agency established as instrumentality of District Government by act of Dec. 24, 1973 (87 Stat. 774), effective July 1, 1974.

District of Columbia-Virginia Boundary Commission   Established by act of Mar. 21, 1934 (48 Stat. 453). Terminated Dec. 1, 1935, to which date it had been extended by Public Resolution 9 (49 Stat. 67).

Division.   *See other part of title*

Domestic Council   Established in Executive Office of the President by Reorg. Plan No. 2 of 1970, effective July 1, 1970. Abolished by Reorg. Plan No. 1 of 1977, effective Mar. 26, 1978, and functions transferred to President and staff designated as *Domestic Policy Staff.* Pursuant to EO 12045 of Mar. 27, 1978, *Staff* assisted President in performance of transferred functions. Renamed Office of Policy Development in 1981. Abolished in February 1992 by President's reorganizational statement, effective May 1992.

Domestic Policy Staff   *See* **Domestic Council**

Dominican Customs Receivership   Transferred from *Division of Territories and Island Possessions,* Department of the Interior, to the Department of State by Reorg. Plan No. IV of 1940, effective June 30, 1940.

Drug Abuse, National Institute on   Established within the National Institute of Mental Health, *Department of Health, Education, and Welfare* by act of Mar. 21, 1972 (86 Stat. 85). Removed from within the National Institute of Mental Health and made an entity within the Alcohol, Drug Abuse, and Mental Health Administration by act of May 14, 1974 (88 Stat. 136). Functions transferred to the Department of Health and Human Services by act of Oct. 17, 1979 (93 Stat. 695). (*See also* act of Oct. 27, 1986; 100 Stat. 3207–106.) Abolished by act of July 10, 1992 (106 Stat. 331). Reestablished by act of July 10, 1992 (106 Stat. 361).

Drug Abuse, President's Advisory Commission on Narcotic and   Established by EO 11076 of Jan. 15, 1963. Terminated November 1963 under terms of order.

Drug Abuse Control, Bureau of   Established in Food and Drug Administration, Department of Health and Human Services, to carry out functions of act of July 15, 1965 (79 Stat. 226). Functions transferred to *Bureau of Narcotics and Dangerous Drugs,* Department of Justice, by Reorg. Plan No. 1 of 1968, effective Apr. 8, 1968. Abolished by Reorg. Plan No. 2 of 1973, effective July 1, 1973, and functions transferred to Drug Enforcement Administration.

Drug Abuse Law Enforcement, Office of   Established by EO 11641 of Jan. 28, 1972. Terminated by EO 11727 of July 6, 1973, and functions transferred to Drug Enforcement Administration.

Drug Abuse Policy, Office of   Established in Executive Office of the President by act of Mar. 19, 1976 (90 Stat. 242). Abolished by Reorg. Plan No. 1 of 1977, effective Mar. 26, 1978, and functions transferred to President.

Drug-Free Schools, Office of Safe   Abolished by the Secretary of Education on Sept. 25, 2011. Programs transferred to *Office of Safe and Healthy Students* within the Office of Elementary and Secondary Education.

Drug Abuse Prevention, Treatment, and Rehabilitation, Cabinet Committee on   Established Apr. 27, 1976, by Presidential announcement. Terminated by Presidential memorandum of Mar. 14, 1977.

Drug Law Enforcement, Cabinet Committee for   Established Apr. 27, 1976, pursuant to Presidential message to Congress of Apr. 27, 1976. Abolished by Presidential memorandum of Mar. 14, 1977.

Drug Law Enforcement, Cabinet Committee for   Established Apr. 27, 1976, pursuant to

Presidential message to Congress of Apr. 27, 1976. Abolished by Presidential memorandum of Mar. 14, 1977.

Drugs, Bureau of Narcotics and Dangerous *See* **Drug Abuse Control, Bureau of**

Drugs and Biologics, National Center for Renamed *Center for Drugs and Biologics* by Food and Drug Administration notice of Mar. 9, 1984 (49 FR 10166). Reestablished as Center for Drug Evaluation and Research and Center for Biologics Evaluation and Research by Secretary's notice of Oct. 6, 1987 (52 FR 38275).

Drunk Driving, Presidential Commission on Established by EO 12358 of Apr. 14, 1982. Terminated Dec. 31, 1983, by EO 12415 of Apr. 5, 1983.

Dryden Research Center, Hugh L. Formerly separate field installation of National Aeronautics and Space Administration. Made component of Ames Research Center by NASA Management Instruction 1107.5A of Sept. 3, 1981.

Economic Administration, Foreign Established in *Office for Emergency Management* by EO 9380 of Sept. 25, 1943. Functions of *Office of Lend-Lease Administration, Office of Foreign Relief and Rehabilitation Operations, Office of Economic Warfare* (together with *U.S. Commercial Company, Rubber Development Corporation, Petroleum Reserves Corporation,* and *Export-Import Bank of Washington* and functions transferred thereto by EO 9361 of July 15, 1943), and foreign economic operations of *Office of Foreign Economic Coordination* transferred to *Administration.* Foreign procurement activities of *War Food Administration* and Commodity Credit Corporation transferred by EO 9385 of Oct. 6, 1943. Terminated by EO 9630 of Sept. 27, 1945, and functions redistributed to the Departments of State, Commerce, and Agriculture and the *Reconstruction Finance Corporation.*

Economic Analysis, Office of *See* **Business Economics, Office of**

Economic Cooperation Administration Established by act of Apr. 3, 1948 (62 Stat. 138). Abolished by act of Oct. 10, 1951 (65 Stat. 373), and functions transferred to *Mutual Security Agency* pursuant to EO 10300 of Nov. 1, 1951.

Economic Coordination, Office of Foreign *See* **Board of Economic Operations**

Economic Defense Board Established by EO 8839 of July 30, 1941. Renamed *Board of Economic Warfare* by EO 8982 of Dec. 17, 1941. *Board* terminated by EO 9361 of July 15, 1943, and *Office of Economic Warfare* established in *Office for Emergency Management. Office of Economic Warfare* consolidated with *Foreign Economic Administration* by EO 9380 of Sept. 25, 1943.

Economic Development, Office of Regional Established by the Secretary of Commerce Jan. 6, 1966, pursuant to act of Aug. 26, 1965 (79

Stat. 552). Abolished by Department Order 5A, Dec. 22, 1966, and functions vested in Economic Development Administration.

Economic Development Service, Foreign Established by order of the Secretary of Agriculture Nov. 8, 1969. Abolished by order of Secretary Feb. 6, 1972, and functions transferred to Economic Research Service.

Economic Growth and Stability, Advisory Board on Established by Presidential letter to Congress of June 1, 1953. Superseded by *National Advisory Board on Economic Policy* by Presidential direction Mar. 12, 1961. *Cabinet Committee on Economic Growth* established by President Aug. 21, 1962, to succeed *Board.*

Economic Management Support Center Established by Secretary of Agriculture Memorandum 1836 of Jan. 9, 1974. Consolidated with other Department units into *Economics, Statistics, and Cooperatives Service* by Secretary's Memorandum 1927, effective Dec. 23, 1977.

Economic Operations, Board of Established by Department of State order of Oct. 7, 1941. Abolished by departmental order of June 24, 1943, and functions transferred to *Office of Foreign Economic Coordination* established by same order. *Office* abolished by departmental order of Nov. 6, 1943, pursuant to EO 9380 of Sept. 25, 1943.

Economic Opportunity, Office of Established in Executive Office of the President by act of Aug. 20, 1964 (78 Stat. 508). All OEO programs except three transferred by administrative action to the Departments of *Health, Education, and Welfare, Labor,* and *Housing and Urban Development* July 6, 1973. Community Action, Economic Development, and Legal Services Programs transferred to *Community Services Administration* by act of Jan. 4, 1975 (88 Stat. 2310).

Economic Policy, Council on Established by Presidential memorandum of Feb. 2, 1973. Functions absorbed by *Economic Policy Board* Sept. 30, 1974.

Economic Policy, Council on Foreign Established Dec. 22, 1954, by Presidential letter of Dec. 11, 1954. Abolished by President Mar. 12, 1961, and functions transferred to Secretary of State.

Economic Policy, Council on International Established in Executive Office of the President by Presidential memorandum of January 1971. Reestablished by act of Aug. 29, 1972 (86 Stat. 646). Terminated Sept. 30, 1977, on expiration of statutory authority.

Economic Policy, National Advisory Board on *See* **Economic Growth and Stability, Advisory Board on**

Economic Policy Board, President's Established by EO 11808 of Sept. 30, 1974. Terminated by EO 11975 of Mar. 7, 1977.

Economic Recovery Advisory Board, President's Established by EO 13501 of February

6, 2009. Terminated February 12, 2011 pursuant to terms of order.

Economic Research Service   Established by Secretary of Agriculture Memorandum 1446, supp. 1, of Apr. 3, 1961. Consolidated with other Department of Agriculture units into *Economics, Statistics, and Cooperatives Service* by Secretary's Memorandum 1927, effective Dec. 23, 1977. Redesignated as Economic Research Service by Secretarial order of Oct. 1, 1981.

Economic Security, Advisory Council on   Established by EO 6757 of June 29, 1934. Terminated on approval of act of Aug. 14, 1935 (49 Stat. 620) Aug. 14, 1935.

Economic Security, Committee on   Established by EO 6757 of June 29, 1934. Terminated as formal agency in April 1936, as provided in act, but continued informally for some time thereafter.

Economic Stabilization, Office of   Established in *Office for Emergency Management* by EO 9250 of Oct. 3, 1942. Terminated by EO 9620 of Sept. 20, 1945, and functions transferred to *Office of War Mobilization and Reconversion*. Reestablished in *Office for Emergency Management* by EO 9699 of Feb. 21, 1946. Transferred by EO 9762 of July 25, 1946, to *Office of War Mobilization and Reconversion*. Consolidated with other agencies to form *Office of Temporary Controls* by EO 9809 of Dec. 12, 1946.

Economic Stabilization Agency   Established by EO 10161 of Sept. 9, 1950, and EO 10276 of July 31, 1951. Terminated, except for liquidation purposes, by EO 10434 of Feb. 6, 1953. Liquidation completed Oct. 31, 1953, pursuant to EO 10480 of Aug. 14, 1953.

Economic Stabilization Board   Established by EO 9250 of Oct. 3, 1942. Transferred to *Office of War Mobilization and Reconversion* by EO 9620 of Sept. 20, 1945. Returned to *Office of Economic Stabilization* on reestablishment by EO 9699 of Feb. 21, 1946. *Board* returned to *Office of War Mobilization and Reconversion* by EO 9762 of July 25, 1946. Functions terminated by EO 9809 of Dec. 12, 1946.

Economic Warfare, Board of   *See* **Economic Defense Board**

Economic Warfare, Office of   *See* **Economic Defense Board**

Economics, Bureau of Industrial   Established by the Secretary of Commerce Jan. 2, 1980, in conjunction with Reorg. Plan No. 3 of 1979, effective Oct. 1, 1980, and operated under Department Organization Order 35–5B. Abolished at bureau level by Secretarial order, effective Jan. 22, 1984 (49 FR 4538). Industry-related functions realigned and transferred from Under Secretary for Economic Affairs to Under Secretary for International Trade. Under Secretary for Economic Affairs retained units to support domestic macroeconomic policy functions.

Economics, Statistics, and Cooperatives Service   Renamed *Economics and Statistics Service* by Secretary of Agriculture Memorandum 2025 of Sept. 17, 1980. Redesignated as Economic Research Service and *Statistical Reporting Service* by Secretarial order of Oct. 1, 1981.

Economy Board, Joint   Placed under direction of President by military order of July 5, 1939. Abolished Sept. 1, 1947, by joint letter of Aug. 20, 1947, from Secretaries of *War* and Navy to President.

Education, Federal Board for Vocational   Established by act of Feb. 23, 1917 (39 Stat. 929). Functions transferred to the Department of the Interior by EO 6166 of June 10, 1933. Functions assigned to *Commissioner of Education* Oct. 10, 1933. *Office of Education* transferred from the Department of the Interior to the *Federal Security Agency* by Reorg. Plan No. I of 1939, effective July 1, 1939. *Board* abolished by Reorg. Plan No. 2 of 1946, effective July 16, 1946.

Education, National Institute of   Established by act of June 23, 1972 (86 Stat. 327). Transferred to Office of Educational Research and Improvement, Department of Education, by act of Oct. 17, 1979 (93 Stat. 678), effective May 4, 1980.

Education, Office of   Established as independent agency by act of Mar. 2, 1867 (14 Stat. 434). Transferred to the Department of the Interior by act of July 20, 1868 (15 Stat. 106). Transferred to *Federal Security Agency* by Reorg. Plan No. I of 1939, effective July 1, 1939. Functions of *Federal Security Administrator* administered by *Office of Education* relating to student loans and defense-related education transferred to *War Manpower Commission* by EO 9247 of Sept. 17, 1942.

Education, Office of Bilingual   Abolished by act of Oct. 17, 1979 (93 Stat. 675), and functions transferred to Office of Bilingual Education and Minority Languages Affairs, Department of Education.

Education Beyond the High School, President's Committee on   Established by act of July 26, 1956 (70 Stat. 676). Terminated Dec. 31, 1957. Certain activities continued by *Bureau of Higher Education, Office of Education.*

Education Division   Established in the *Department of Health, Education, and Welfare* by act of June 23, 1972 (86 Stat. 327). Functions transferred to the Department of Education by act of Oct. 17, 1979 (93 Stat. 677).

Education Goals Panel, National Terminated by Congressional mandate, March 15, 2002.

Education Statistics, National Center for   Established in the Office of the Assistant Secretary, Department of Health and Human Services, by act of Aug. 21, 1974 (88 Stat. 556). Transferred to the Office of Educational Research and Improvement, Department of Education, by act of Oct. 17, 1979 (93 Stat. 678), effective May 4, 1980. Renamed *Center for Education Statistics* by act of Oct. 17, 1986 (100 Stat. 1579). Renamed National

Center for Education Statistics by act of Apr. 28, 1988 (102 Stat. 331).

Educational and Cultural Affairs, Bureau of Established by Secretary of State in 1960. Terminated by Reorg. Plan No. 2 of 1977, effective July 1, 1978, and functions transferred to *International Communication Agency,* effective Apr. 1, 1978.

Educational and Cultural Affairs, Interagency Council on International Established Jan. 20, 1964, by Foreign Affairs Manual Circular, under authority of act of Sept. 21, 1961 (75 Stat. 527). Terminated Oct. 1973 following creation of Subcommittee on International Exchanges by National Security Council directive.

Educational Exchange, U.S. Advisory Commission on Established by act of Jan. 27, 1948 (62 Stat. 10). Abolished by act of Sept. 21, 1961 (75 Stat. 538), and superseded by U.S. Advisory Commission on International Educational and Cultural Affairs.

Efficiency, Bureau of Organized under act of Feb. 28, 1916 (39 Stat. 15). Abolished by act of Mar. 3, 1933 (47 Stat. 1519), and records transferred to *Bureau of the Budget.*

Elderly, Committee on Mental Health and Illness of the Established by act of July 29, 1975 (89 Stat. 347). Terminated Sept. 30, 1977.

Electoral votes for President and Vice President, transfer of functions *See* **State, Department of**

Electric Home and Farm Authority Incorporated Aug. 1, 1935, under laws of District of Columbia. Designated as U.S. agency by EO 7139 of Aug. 12, 1935. Continued by act of June 10, 1941 (55 Stat. 248). Grouped with other agencies in *Federal Loan Agency* by Reorg. Plan. No. I of 1939, effective July 1, 1939. Functions transferred to the Department of Commerce by EO 9071 of Feb. 24, 1942. Terminated by EO 9256 of Oct. 13, 1942.

Electric Home and Farm Authority, Inc. Organized Jan. 17, 1934, under laws of State of Delaware by EO 6514 of Dec. 19, 1933. Dissolved Aug. 1, 1935, and succeeded by *Electric Home and Farm Authority.*

Electricity Delivery and Energy Reliability, Office of Established by Secretary of Energy announcement of June 9, 2005. Position of director elevated to Assistant Secretary of Electricity Delivery and Energy Reliability by Secretary's memorandum EXEC–2007–010607 of Oct. 24, 2007.

Electricity Transmission and Distribution, Office of Renamed *Office of Electricity Delivery and Energy Reliability* by the Secretary of Energy's memo of Feb. 15, 2005.

Emergency Administration of Public Works, Federal Established by act of June 16, 1933 (48 Stat. 200). Operation continued by subsequent legislation, including act of June 21, 1938 (52 Stat. 816). Consolidated with *Federal Works Agency* as *Public Works Administration* by Reorg. Plan No. I of

1939, effective July 1, 1939. Functions transferred to *Office of Federal Works Administrator* by EO 9357 of June 30, 1943.

Emergency Conservation Work Established by EO 6101 of Apr. 5, 1933. Succeeded by *Civilian Conservation Corps.*

Emergency Council, National Established by EO 6433–A of Nov. 17, 1933. Consolidated with *Executive Council* by EO 6889–A of Oct. 29, 1934. Abolished by Reorg. Plan No. II of 1939, effective July 1, 1939, and functions (except those relating to *Radio Division* and *Film Service*) transferred to Executive Office of the President.

Emergency Council, Office of Economic Adviser to National Established by EO 6240 of Aug. 3, 1933, in connection with *Executive Council,* which later consolidated with *National Emergency Council.* Records and property used in preparation of statistical and economic summaries transferred to *Central Statistical Board* by EO 7003 of Apr. 8, 1935.

Emergency Management, Office for Established in Executive Office of the President by administrative order of May 25, 1940, in accordance with EO 8248 of Sept. 8, 1939. Inactive.

Emergency Management Agency, Federal Established in EO 12127 of Mar. 31, 1979. Functions transferred to Department of Homeland Security by act of Nov. 25, 2002 (116 Stat. 2213). Established as a distinct entity with the Department of Homeland Security by act of Oct. 4, 2006 (120 Stat. 1400).

Emergency Mobilization Preparedness Board Established Dec. 17, 1981, by the President. Abolished by Presidential directive of Sept. 16, 1985.

Emergency Planning, Office of Established as successor to *Office of Civil and Defense Mobilization* by act of Sept. 22, 1961 (75 Stat. 630). Renamed *Office of Emergency Preparedness* by act of Oct. 21, 1968 (82 Stat. 1194). Terminated by Reorg. Plan No. 2 of 1973, effective July 1, 1973, and functions transferred to the Departments of the Treasury and Housing and Urban Development and the General Services Administration.

Emergency Preparedness, Office of *See* **Emergency Planning, Office of**

Emergency Procurement Service Established Sept. 1, 1950, by Administrator of General Services. Renamed *Defense Materials Service* Sept. 7, 1956. Functions transferred to *Property Management and Disposal Service* July 29, 1966. *Service* abolished July 1, 1973, and functions transferred to Federal Supply Service, Public Buildings Service, and Federal Property Resources Service.

Emergency Relief Administration, Federal Established by act of May 12, 1933 (48 Stat. 55). Expired June 30, 1938, having been liquidated by *Works Progress Administrator* pursuant to act of May 28, 1937 (50 Stat. 352).

Employee-Management Relations Program, President's Committee on the Implementation of the Federal   Established by EO 10988 of Jan. 17, 1962. Terminated upon submission of report to President June 21, 1963.

Employees' Compensation, Bureau of   Transferred from *Federal Security Agency* to the Department of Labor by Reorg. Plan No. 19 of 1950, effective May 24, 1950. Functions absorbed by Employment Standards Administration Mar. 13, 1972.

Employees' Compensation Appeals Board   Transferred from *Federal Security Agency* to the Department of Labor by Reorg. Plan No. 19 of 1950, effective May 24, 1950.

Employees' Compensation Commission, U.S.   Established by act of Sept. 7, 1916 (39 Stat. 742). Abolished by Reorg. Plan No. 2 of 1946, effective July 16, 1946, and functions transferred to *Federal Security Administrator.*

Employment Board, Fair   Established by *U.S. Civil Service Commission* pursuant to EO 9980 of July 26, 1948. Abolished by EO 10590 of Jan. 18, 1955.

Employment of People With Disabilities, President's Committee on   Created by EO 12640 of May 10, 1988. Duties subsumed by the Office of Disability Employment within the Department of Labor as directed by Public Law 106–554 of Dec. 21, 2000.

Employment of the Physically Handicapped, President's Committee on   Established by EO 10640 of Oct. 10, 1955, continuing *Committee* established by act of July 11, 1949 (63 Stat. 409). Superseded by President's Committee on Employment of the Handicapped established by EO 10994 of Feb. 14, 1962.

Employment Policy, President's Committee on Government   Established by EO 10590 of Jan. 18, 1955. Abolished by EO 10925 of Mar. 6, 1961, and functions transferred to *President's Committee on Equal Employment Opportunity.*

Employment Practice, Committee on Fair   Established in *Office of Production Management* by EO 8802 of June 25, 1941. Transferred to *War Manpower Commission* by Presidential letter effective July 30, 1942. Committee terminated on establishment of *Committee on Fair Employment Practice, Office for Emergency Management,* by EO 9346 of May 27, 1943. Terminated June 30, 1946, by act of July 17, 1945 (59 Stat. 743).

Employment Security, Bureau of   Transferred from *Federal Security Agency* to the Department of Labor by Reorg. Plan No. 2 of 1949, effective Aug. 20, 1949. Abolished by order of Mar. 14, 1969 of the Secretary of Labor, and functions transferred to *Manpower Administration.*

Employment Service, U.S.   Established in the Department of Labor in 1918 by departmental order. Abolished by act of June 6, 1933 (48 Stat. 113), and created as bureau with same name. Functions

consolidated with unemployment compensation functions of *Social Security Board, Bureau of Employment Security,* and transferred to *Federal Security Agency* by Reorg. Plan No. I of 1939, effective July 1, 1939. *Service* transferred to *Bureau of Placement, War Manpower Commission,* by EO 9247 of Sept. 17, 1942. Returned to the Department of Labor by EO 9617 of Sept. 19, 1945. Transferred to *Federal Security Agency* by act of June 16, 1948 (62 Stat. 443), to function as part of *Bureau of Employment Security,* Social Security Administration. *Bureau,* including *U.S. Employment Service,* transferred to the Department of Labor by Reorg. Plan No. 2 of 1949, effective Aug. 20, 1949. Abolished by reorganization of *Manpower Administration,* effective Mar. 17, 1969, and functions assigned to *U.S. Training and Employment Service.*

Employment Stabilization Board, Federal   Established by act of Feb. 10, 1931 (46 Stat. 1085). Abolished by EO 6166 of June 10, 1933. Abolition deferred by EO 6623 of Mar. 1, 1934, until functions of *Board* transferred to *Federal Employment Stabilization Office,* established in the Department of Commerce by same order. *Office* abolished by Reorg. Plan No. I of 1939, effective July 1, 1939, and functions transferred from the Department of Commerce to *National Resources Planning Board,* Executive Office of the President.

Employment Stabilization Office, Federal.   *See* **Employment Stabilization Board, Federal**

Employment and Training, Office of Comprehensive   Established in the Department of Labor. Terminated due to expiration of authority for appropriations after fiscal year 1982. Replaced by *Office of Employment and Training Programs.*

Employment and Training Programs, Office of   Renamed Office of Job Training Programs by Employment and Training Administration reorganization in the Department of Labor, effective June 1984.

Endangered Species Scientific Authority   Established by EO 11911 of Apr. 13, 1976. Terminated by act of Dec. 28, 1979 (93 Stat. 1228), and functions transferred to the Secretary of the Interior.

Energy Administration, Federal   Established by act of May 7, 1974 (88 Stat. 96). Assigned additional responsibilities by acts of June 22, 1974 (88 Stat. 246), Dec. 22, 1975 (89 Stat. 871), and Aug. 14, 1976 (90 Stat. 1125). Terminated by act of Aug. 4, 1977 (91 Stat. 577), and functions transferred to the Department of Energy.

Energy Advisory Support Office, Secretary of   Abolished by secretarial decision of Feb. 6, 2006.

Energy Assurance, Office of   Abolished pursuant to Conference Report No. 108–729 on H.R. 4818, Consolidated Appropriations Act. Functions merged with *Office of Electricity Delivery and Energy Reliability.*

Energy Conservation, Office of   Established by Interior Secretarial Order 2953 May 7, 1973. Functions transferred to *Federal Energy Administration* by act of May 7, 1974 (88 Stat. 100).

Energy Data and Analysis, Office of   Established by Interior Secretarial Order 2953 of May 7, 1973. Functions transferred to *Federal Energy Administration* by act of May 7, 1974 (88 Stat. 100).

Energy Policy Office   Established in Executive Office of the President by EO 11726 of June 29, 1973. Abolished by EO 11775 of Mar. 26, 1974.

Energy Programs, Office of   Established by Department of Commerce Organization Order 25–7A, effective Sept. 24, 1975. Terminated by act of Aug. 4, 1977 (91 Stat. 581), and functions transferred to the Department of Energy.

Energy Research and Development Administration   Established by act of Oct. 11, 1974 (88 Stat. 1234). Assigned responsibilities by acts of Sept. 3, 1974 (88 Stat. 1069, 1079), Oct. 26, 1974 (88 Stat. 1431), and Dec. 31, 1974 (88 Stat. 1887). Terminated by act of Aug. 4, 1977 (91 Stat. 577), and functions transferred to the Department of Energy.

Energy Resources Council   Established in Executive Office of the President by act of Oct. 11, 1974 (88 Stat. 1233). Establishing authority repealed by act of Aug. 4, 1977 (91 Stat. 608), and *Council* terminated.

Energy Supplies and Resources Policy, Presidential Advisory Committee on   Established July 30, 1954, by President. Abolished Mar. 12, 1961, by President and functions transferred to the Secretary of the Interior.

Enforcement Commission, National   Established by General Order 18 of *Economic Stabilization Administrator*, effective July 30, 1952. Functions transferred to Director, *Office of Defense Mobilization*, and Attorney General by EO 10494 of Oct. 14, 1953.

Engineering, Bureau of   *See* **Steam Engineering, Bureau of**

Entomology, Bureau of   *See* **Entomology and Plant Quarantine, Bureau of**

Entomology and Plant Quarantine, Bureau of   *Bureau of Entomology* and *Bureau of Plant Quarantine* created by acts of Apr. 23, 1904 (33 Stat. 276), and July 7, 1932 (47 Stat. 640), respectively. Consolidated with disease control and eradication functions of *Bureau of Plant Industry* into *Bureau of Entomology and Plant Quarantine* by act of Mar. 23, 1934 (48 Stat. 467). Functions transferred to Agricultural Research Service by Secretary's Memorandum 1320, supp. 4, of Nov. 2, 1953.

Environment, Cabinet Committee on the   *See* **Environmental Quality Council**

Environmental Financing Authority   Established by act of Oct. 18, 1972 (86 Stat. 899). Expired June 30, 1975, pursuant to terms of act.

Environmental Quality Council   Established by EO 11472 of May 29, 1969. Renamed *Cabinet Committee on the Environment* by EO 11514 of Mar. 5, 1970. EO 11514 terminated by EO 11541 of July 1, 1970.

Environment, Safety, and Health, Office of   Established by act of Aug. 4, 1977 (91 Stat. 570). Abolished by Secretary of Energy memorandum 2006–007929 of Aug. 30, 2006, and functions transferred to Office of Health, Safety, and Security.

Environmental Science Services Administration   Established in the Department of Commerce by Reorg. Plan No. 2 of 1965, effective July 13, 1965, by consolidating *Weather Bureau* and *Coast and Geodetic Survey.* Abolished by Reorg. Plan No. 4 of 1970, effective Oct. 3, 1970, and functions transferred to National Oceanic and Atmospheric Administration.

Equal Employment Opportunity, President's Committee on   Established by EO 10925 of Mar. 6, 1961. Abolished by EO 11246 of Sept. 24, 1965, and functions transferred to the Department of Labor and *U.S. Civil Service Commission.*

Equal Opportunity, President's Council on   Established by EO 11197 of Feb. 5, 1965. Abolished by EO 11247 of Sept. 24, 1965, and functions transferred to the Department of Justice.

Equipment, Bureau of   Established as *Bureau of Equipment and Recruiting* by act of July 5, 1862 (12 Stat. 510), replacing *Bureau of Construction, Equipment and Repairs.* Designated as *Bureau of Equipment* in annual appropriation acts commencing with fiscal year 1892 (26 Stat. 192) after cognizance over enlisted personnel matters transferred, effective July 1, 1889, to *Bureau of Navigation.* Functions distributed among bureaus and offices in the Department of the Navy by act of June 24, 1910 (61 Stat. 613). Abolished by act of June 30, 1914 (38 Stat. 408).

Ethics, Office of Government   Established in the Office of Personnel Management by act of Oct. 26, 1978 (92 Stat. 1862). Became a separate executive agency status by act of Nov. 3, 1988 (102 Stat. 3031).

European Migration, Intergovernmental Committee for   Renamed Intergovernmental Committee for Migration by Resolution 624, passed by Intergovernmental Committee for European Migration Council, effective Nov. 11, 1980.

Evacuation, Joint Committee on   *See* **Health and Welfare Aspects of Evacuation of Civilians, Joint Committee on**

Exchange Service, International   Established in 1849 in Smithsonian Institution. Renamed Office of Publications Exchange by Secretary's internal directive of Jan. 11, 1985.

Executive Branch of the Government, Commission on Organization of the   Established by act of July 7, 1947 (61 Stat. 246). Terminated June 12, 1949, pursuant to terms of act. Second *Commission* *on Organization of the Executive Branch of the Government* established by act of July 10, 1953 (67 Stat. 142). Terminated June 30, 1955, pursuant to terms of act.

Executive Council   Established by EO 6202–A of July 11, 1933. Consolidated with *National Emergency Council* by EO 6889–A of Oct. 29, 1934.

Executive Exchange, President's Commission on   *See* **Personnel Interchange, President's Commission on**

Executive orders   *See* **State, Department of**

Executive Organization, President's Advisory Council on   Established by President Apr. 5, 1969. Terminated May 7, 1971.

Executive Protective Service   *See* **Secret Service Division**

Executives, Active Corps of   Established in ACTION by act of Oct. 1, 1973 (87 Stat. 404). Transferred to Small Business Administration by EO 11871 of July 18, 1975.

Export Administration, Bureau of   Established as a separate agency within the Department of Commerce on Oct. 1, 1987 (50 USC app. 2401 *et seq.*). Renamed Bureau of Industry and Security by Department of Commerce internal organization order of Apr. 18, 2002 (67 FR 20630).

Export Control, Administrator of   Functions delegated to Administrator by Proc. 2413 of July 2, 1940, transferred to *Office of Export Control, Economic Defense Board,* by EO 8900 of Sept. 15, 1941. Renamed *Board of Economic Warfare* by EO 8982 of Dec. 17, 1941. *Board* terminated by EO 9361 of July 15, 1943.

Export Control, Office of   *See* **Export Control, Administrator of**

Export-Import Bank of Washington   Organization of District of Columbia banking corporation directed by EO 6581 of Feb. 2, 1934. Certificate of incorporation filed Feb. 12, 1934. Grouped with other agencies to form *Federal Loan Agency* by Reorg. Plan No. I of 1939, effective July 1, 1939. Transferred to the Department of Commerce by EO 9071 of Feb. 24, 1942. Functions transferred to *Office of Economic Warfare* by EO 9361 of July 15, 1943. Established as permanent independent agency by act of July 31, 1945 (59 Stat. 526). Renamed Export-Import Bank of the U.S. by act of Mar. 13, 1968 (82 Stat. 47).

Export-Import Bank of Washington, DC, Second   Authorized by EO 6638 of Mar. 9, 1934. Abolished by EO 7365 of May 7, 1936, and records transferred to *Export-Import Bank of Washington,* effective June 30, 1936.

Export Marketing Service   Established by the Secretary of Agriculture Mar. 28, 1969. Merged with Foreign Agricultural Service by Secretary's memorandum of Dec. 7, 1973, effective Feb. 3, 1974.

Exports and Requirements, Division of   Established in *Office of Foreign Economic Coordination* by the Department of State order of Feb. 1, 1943. Abolished by departmental order of Nov. 6, 1943, pursuant to EO 9380 of Sept. 25, 1943.

Extension Service   Established by act of May 14, 1914 (38 Stat. 372). Consolidated into *Science and Education Administration* by Secretary's order of Jan. 24, 1978. Reestablished as *Extension Service* by Secretarial order of June 16, 1981. Became part of Cooperative State, Research, Education, and Extension Service under Department of Agriculture's reorganization in 1995.

Facts and Figures, Office of   Established in *Office for Emergency Management* by EO 8922 of Oct. 24, 1941. Consolidated with *Office of War Information* in *Office for Emergency Management* by EO 9182 of June 13, 1942.

Family Security Committee   Established in *Office of Defense Health and Welfare Services* Feb. 12, 1941, by administrative order. Terminated Dec. 17, 1942.

Family Services, Bureau of   *See* **Assistance, Bureau of Public**

Family Support Administration   Established on Apr. 4, 1986, in the Department of Health and Human Services under authority of section 6 of Reorganization Plan No. 1 of 1953, effective Apr. 11, 1953 (*see also* 51 FR 11641). Merged into Administration for Children and Families by Secretary's reorganization notice dated Apr. 15, 1991.

Farm Board, Federal   Established by act of June 15, 1929 (46 Stat. 11). Renamed Farm Credit Administration and certain functions abolished by EO 6084 of Mar. 27, 1933. Administration placed under the Department of Agriculture by Reorg. Plan No. I of 1939, effective July 1, 1939. Made independent agency in the executive branch of the Government, to be housed in the Department of Agriculture, by act of Aug. 6, 1953 (67 Stat. 390). Removed from the Department of Agriculture by act of Dec. 10, 1971 (85 Stat. 617).

Farm Credit Administration   *See* **Farm Board, Federal**

Farm Loan Board, Federal   Established in the Department of the Treasury to administer act of July 17, 1916 (39 Stat. 360). Offices of appointed members of *Board,* except member designated as *Farm Loan Commissioner,* abolished by EO 6084 of Mar. 27, 1933, and *Board* functions transferred to *Farm Loan Commissioner,* subject to jurisdiction and control of Farm Credit Administration. Title changed to *Land Bank Commissioner* by act of June 16, 1933. Abolished by act of Aug. 6, 1953 (67 Stat. 393).

Farm Loan Bureau, Federal   Established in the Department of the Treasury under supervision of *Federal Farm Loan Board* and charged with execution of act of July 17, 1916 (39 Stat. 360). Transferred to *Farm Credit Administration* by EO 6084 of Mar. 27, 1933.

Farm Loan Commissioner   *See* **Farm Loan Board, Federal**

Farm Mortgage Corporation, Federal   Established by act of Jan. 31, 1934 (48 Stat. 344). Transferred to the Department of Agriculture by Reorg. Plan No. I of 1939, effective July 1, 1939, to operate under supervision of Farm Credit Administration. Abolished by act of Oct. 4, 1961 (75 Stat. 773).

Farm Products, Division of (Also known as *Division of Agriculture*)

Established by *Advisory Commission to Council of National Defense* pursuant to act of Aug. 29, 1916 (39 Stat. 649). *Office of Agricultural Defense Relations* (later known as *Office for Agricultural War Relations*) established in the Department of Agriculture by Presidential letter of May 5, 1941, which transferred to the Secretary of Agriculture functions previously assigned to *Division of Agriculture*. Functions concerned with food production transferred to *Food Production Administration* and functions concerned with food distribution transferred to *Food Distribution Administration* by EO 9280 of Dec. 5, 1942.

Farm Security Administration   *See* **Resettlement Administration**

Farm Service Agency   Established by Secretary's Memorandum 1010–1 dated Oct. 20, 1994, under authority of the act of Oct. 13, 1994 (7 U.S.C. 6901), and assumed certain functions of the *Agricultural Stabilization and Conservation Service*, the *Farmers' Home Administration*, and the *Federal Crop Insurance Corporation*. Renamed *Consolidated Farm Service Agency* by Acting Administrator on Dec. 19, 1994.

Farmer Cooperative Service   Established by Secretary of Agriculture Memorandum 1320, supp. 4, of Dec. 4, 1953. Consolidated with other Department of Agriculture units into *Economics, Statistics, and Cooperatives Service* by Secretary's Memorandum 1927, effective Dec. 23, 1977.

Farmers' Home Administration.   *See* **Resettlement Administration**

Federal.   *See also other part of title*

Federal Advisory Council   Established in *Federal Security Agency* by act of June 6, 1933 (48 Stat. 116). Transferred to the Department of Labor by Reorg. Plan No. 2 of 1949, effective Aug. 20, 1949.

Federal Register, Administrative Committee of the   *See* **Archives Establishment, National**

Federal Register, Division of the   Established by act of July 26, 1935 (49 Stat. 500). Transferred to General Services Administration as part of *National Archives and Records Service* by act of June 30, 1949 (63 Stat. 381). Renamed Office of the Federal Register by order of General Services Administrator, Feb. 6, 1959. Transferred to National Archives and Records Administration by act of Oct. 19, 1984 (98 Stat. 2283).

Federal Register, Office of the   *See* **Federal Register, Division of the**

Federal Reserve Board   Renamed Board of Governors of the Federal Reserve System, and Governor and Vice Governor designated as Chairman and Vice Chairman, respectively, of Board by act of Aug. 23, 1935 (49 Stat. 704).

Federal Tax Reform, President's Advisory Panel on   Established by EO 13369 of Jan. 7, 2005. Abolished by EO 13446 of Sept. 28, 2007.

Field Services, Office of   Established by the Secretary of Commerce Feb. 1, 1963, by Department Organization Order 40–3. Terminated by Department Organization Order 40–1A of Sept. 15, 1970, and functions transferred to *Bureau of Domestic Commerce*.

Filipino Rehabilitation Commission   Established by act of June 29, 1944 (58 Stat. 626). Inactive pursuant to terms of act.

Film Service, U.S.   Established by *National Emergency Council* in September 1938. Transferred to *Office of Education, Federal Security Agency*, by Reorg. Plan No. II of 1939, effective July 1, 1939. Terminated June 30, 1940.

Films, Coordinator of Government   Director of *Office of Government Reports* designated *Coordinator of Government Films* by Presidential letter of Dec. 18, 1941. Functions transferred to *Office of War Information* by EO 9182 of June 13, 1942.

Financial Capability, President's Advisory Council on   Established by EO 13530 of January 29, 2010. Terminated on January 29, 2013 by sec. 3 of EO 13591 of November 11, 2011.

Financial Operations, Bureau of Government   Renamed Financial Management Service by Order 145–21 of the Secretary of the Treasury, effective Oct. 10, 1984.

Fire Administration, U.S.   *See* **Fire Prevention and Control Administration, National**

Fire Council, Federal   Established by EO 7397 of June 20, 1936. Transferred July 1, 1939, to *Federal Works Agency* by EO 8194 of July 6, 1939, with functions under direction of *Federal Works Administrator*. Transferred with *Federal Works Agency* to General Services Administration by act of June 30, 1949 (63 Stat. 380). Transferred to the Department of Commerce by EO 11654 of Mar. 13, 1972.

Fire Prevention and Control, National Academy for   Established in the Department of Commerce by act of Oct. 29, 1974 (88 Stat. 1537). Transferred to Federal Emergency Management Agency by Reorg. Plan No. 3 of 1978, effective Apr. 1, 1979.

Fire Prevention and Control Administration, National   Renamed U.S. Fire Administration by act of Oct. 5, 1978 (92 Stat. 932). Transferred to Federal

Emergency Management Agency by Reorg. Plan No. 3 of 1978, effective Apr. 1, 1979

Fiscal Responsibility and Reform, National Commission on   Established by EO 13531 of Feb. 18, 2010. Terminated 30 days after submission of final report to President on January 31, 2011.

Fish Commission, U.S.   *Commissioner of Fish and Fisheries* established as head of *U.S. Fish Commission* by joint resolution of Feb. 9, 1871 (16 Stat. 594). *Commission* established as *Bureau of Fisheries* in *Department of Commerce and Labor* by act of Feb. 14, 1903 (32 Stat. 827). Department of Labor created by act of Mar. 4, 1913 (37 Stat. 736), and *Bureau* remained in the Department of Commerce. Transferred to the Department of the Interior by Reorg. Plan No. II of 1939, effective July 1, 1939. Consolidated with *Bureau of Biological Survey* into *Fish and Wildlife Service* by Reorg. Plan No. III of 1940, effective June 30, 1940.

Fish and Wildlife Service   Established by Reorg. Plan No. III of 1940, effective June 30, 1940, consolidating *Bureau of Fisheries* and *Bureau of Biological Survey.* Succeeded by U.S. Fish and Wildlife Service.

Fisheries, Bureau of   *See* **Fish Commission, U.S.**

Fisheries, Bureau of Commercial   Organized in 1959 under U.S. Fish and Wildlife Service, the Department of the Interior. Abolished by Reorg. Plan No. 4 of 1970, effective Oct. 3, 1970, and functions transferred to National Oceanic and Atmospheric Administration.

Fishery Coordination, Office of   Established in the Department of the Interior by EO 9204 of July 21, 1942. Terminated by EO 9649 of Oct. 29, 1945.

Flood Indemnity Administration, Federal   Established in *Housing and Home Finance Agency* by Administrator's Organizational Order 1, effective Sept. 28, 1956, redesignated as Administrator's Organizational Order 2 on Dec. 7, 1956, pursuant to act of Aug. 7, 1956 (70 Stat. 1078). Abolished by Administrator's Organizational Order 3, effective July 1, 1957, due to lack of funding.

Flood Protection Structure Accreditation Task Force   Established by act of July 6, 2012 (126 Stat. 942). Terminated upon submission of final report not later than July 6, 2013.

Food, Cost of Living Council Committee on   Established by EO 11695 of Jan. 11, 1973. Abolished by EO 11788 of June 18, 1974.

Food, Drug, and Insecticide Administration   Established by act of Jan. 18, 1927 (44 Stat. 1002). Renamed Food and Drug Administration by act of May 27, 1930 (46 Stat. 422). Transferred from the Department of Agriculture to *Federal Security Agency* by Reorg. Plan No. IV of 1940, effective June 30, 1940. Transferred to *Department of Health, Education, and Welfare* by Reorg. Plan No. 1 of 1953, effective Apr. 11, 1953.

Food Distribution Administration   Established in the Department of Agriculture by EO 9280 of Dec. 5, 1942, consolidating *Agricultural Marketing Administration, Sugar Agency,* distribution functions of *Office for Agricultural War Relations,* regulatory work of *Bureau of Animal Industry,* and food units of *War Production Board.* Consolidated with other agencies by EO 9322 of Mar. 26, 1943, to form *Administration of Food Production and Distribution.*

Food and Drug Administration   *See* **Food, Drug, and Insecticide Administration**

Food Industry Advisory Committee   Established by EO 11627 of Oct. 15, 1971. Abolished by EO 11781 of May 1, 1974.

Food and Nutrition Service   Established Aug. 8, 1969, by Secretary of Agriculture under authority of 5 U.S.C. 301 and Reorg. Plan No. 2 of 1953 (5 U.S.C. app.). Abolished by Secretary's Memorandum 1010–1 dated Oct. 20, 1994. Functions assumed by Food and Consumer Service.

Food Production Administration   Established in the Department of Agriculture by EO 9280 of Dec. 5, 1942, which consolidated *Agricultural Adjustment Agency,* Farm Credit Administration, *Farm Security Administration,* Federal Crop Insurance Corporation, Soil Conservation Service, and food production activities of *War Production Board, Office of Agricultural War Relations,* and *Division of Farm Management and Costs, Bureau of Agricultural Economics.* Consolidated with other agencies by EO 9322 of Mar. 26, 1943, to form *Administration of Food Production and Distribution.*

Food Production and Distribution, Administration of   Established by consolidation of *Food Production Administration, Food Distribution Administration,* Commodity Credit Corporation, and Extension Service, Department of Agriculture, by EO 9322 of Mar. 26, 1943, under direction of Administrator, directly responsible to President. Renamed *War Food Administration* by EO 9334 of Apr. 19, 1943. Terminated by EO 9577 of June 29, 1945, and functions transferred to the Secretary of Agriculture. Transfer made permanent by Reorg. Plan No. 3 of 1946, effective July 16, 1946.

Food Safety and Quality Service   Renamed Food Safety and Inspection Service by Agriculture Secretary's memorandum of June 19, 1981.

Foods, Bureau of   Renamed Center for Food Safety and Applied Nutrition by Food and Drug Administration notice of Mar. 9, 1984 (49 FR 10166).

Foreign.   *See also other part of title*

Foreign Aid, Advisory Committee on Voluntary   Established by President May 14, 1946. Transferred from the Department of State to the Director of the *Mutual Security Agency,* and later to Director of the *Foreign Operations Administration,* by Presidential letter of June 1, 1953.

Foreign Intelligence Advisory Board, President's Established by EO 12863 of Sept. 13, 1993. Abolished by EO 13462 of Feb. 29, 2008.

Foreign Operations Administration Established by Reorg. Plan No. 7 of 1953, effective Aug. 1, 1953, and functions transferred from *Office of Director of Mutual Security, Mutual Security Agency, Technical Cooperation Administration, Institute of Inter-American Affairs.* Abolished by EO 10610 of May 9, 1955, and functions and offices transferred to the Departments of State and Defense.

Foreign Scholarships, Board of Renamed J. William Fulbright Foreign Scholarship Board by act of Feb. 16, 1990 (104 Stat. 49).

Forest Reservation Commission, National Established by act of Mar. 1, 1911 (36 Stat. 962). Terminated by act of Oct. 22, 1976 (90 Stat. 2961), and functions transferred to the Secretary of Agriculture.

Forests, Director of Established by Administrative Order 1283 of May 18, 1938. Made part of *Office of Land Utilization,* Department of the Interior, by Administrative Order 1466 of Apr. 15, 1940.

Freedmen's Hospital Established by act of Mar. 3, 1871 (16 Stat. 506; T. 32 of D.C. Code). Transferred from the Department of the Interior to *Federal Security Agency* by Reorg. Plan No. IV of 1940, effective June 30, 1940.

Fuel Yards Established by act of July 1, 1918 (40 Stat. 672). Transferred from *Bureau of Mines,* Department of Commerce, to *Procurement Division,* Department of the Treasury, by EO 6166 of June 10, 1933, effective Mar. 2, 1934.

Fuels Coordinator for War, Office of Solid *See* **Fuels Administration for War, Solid**

Fuels Corporation, U.S. Synthetic Established by act of June 30, 1980 (94 Stat. 636). Terminated Apr. 18, 1986, by act of Dec. 19, 1985 (99 Stat. 1249), and functions transferred to the Secretary of the Treasury.

Fund-Raising Within the Federal Service, President's Committee on Established by EO 10728 of Sept. 6, 1957. Abolished by EO 10927 of Mar. 18, 1961, and functions transferred to *U.S. Civil Service Commission.*

Gallaudet College *See* **Columbia Institution for the Instruction of the Deaf and Dumb, and the Blind**

General Programs, Office of Renamed Office of Public Programs by the Chairman, National Endowment for the Humanities, in January 1991.

Geographic Board, U.S. Established by EO 27–A of Sept. 4, 1890. Abolished by EO 6680 of Apr. 17, 1935, and duties transferred to *U.S. Board on Geographical Names,* Department of the Interior, effective June 17, 1934. *Board* abolished by act of July 25, 1947 (61 Stat. 457), and duties assumed by *Board on Geographic Names.*

Geographical Names, U.S. Board on *See* **Geographic Board, U.S.**

Geography, Office of Function of standardizing foreign place names placed in the Department of the Interior conjointly with the *Board on Geographic Names* by act of July 25, 1947 (61 Stat. 456). Functions transferred to the Department of Defense by memorandum of understanding by the Departments of the Interior and Defense and the *Bureau of the Budget* Mar. 9, 1968.

Geological Survey Established in the Department of the Interior by act of Mar. 3, 1879 (20 Stat. 394). Renamed United States Geological Survey by acts of Nov. 13, 1991 (105 Stat. 1000) and May 18, 1992 (106 Stat. 172).

Germany, Mixed Claims Commission, U.S. and Established by agreement of Aug. 10, 1922, between U.S. and Germany. Duties extended by agreement of Dec. 31, 1928. Time limit for filing claims expired June 30, 1928. All claims disposed of by Oct. 30, 1939. Terminated June 30, 1941.

Global Communications, Office of Established within the White House Office by EO 13283 of Jan. 21, 2003. Abolished by EO 13385 of Sept. 29, 2005

Global Health Affairs, Office of Renamed Office of Global Affairs by Secretary of Health and Human Services notice of June 22, 2011 (76 FR 36539).

Goethals Memorial Commission Established by act of Aug. 4, 1935 (49 Stat. 743). Placed under jurisdiction of *Department of War* by EO 8191 of July 5, 1939.

Government. *See other part of title*

Grain Futures Administration Established in the Department of Agriculture under provisions of act of Sept. 21, 1922 (42 Stat. 998). Superseded by *Commodity Exchange Administration* by order of Secretary, effective July 1, 1936. Consolidated with other agencies into *Commodity Exchange Branch, Agricultural Marketing Administration,* by EO 9069 of Feb. 23, 1942. Functions transferred to the Secretary of Agriculture by EO 9577 of June 29, 1945. Transfer made permanent by Reorg. Plan No. 3 of 1946, effective July 16, 1946. Functions transferred to *Commodity Exchange Authority* by Secretary's Memorandum 1185 of Jan. 21, 1947. Functions transferred to Commodity Futures Trading Commission by act of Oct. 23, 1974 (88 Stat. 1414).

Grain Inspection Service, Federal Established in the Department of Agriculture by act of Oct. 21, 1976 (90 Stat. 2868). Abolished by Secretary's Memorandum 1010–1 dated Oct. 20, 1994, and program authority and functions transferred to the Grain Inspection, Packers and Stockyards Administration.

Grain Stabilization Corporation Organized as Delaware corporation to operate in connection with *Federal Farm Board* pursuant to act of June 15, 1929 (46 Stat. 11). Terminated by filing of certificate of dissolution with Corporation Commission of State of Delaware Dec. 14, 1935.

Grant Administration, Office of   Transferred from the Office of the General Council to the Deputy Director, U.S. Trade and Development Agency by administrative order of Apr. 25, 2007.

Grants and Program Systems, Office of   Abolished and functions transferred to Cooperative State Research Service, Department of Agriculture, by Secretarial Memorandum 1020–26 of July 1, 1986.

Grazing Service   Consolidated with *General Land Office* into Bureau of Land Management, Department of the Interior, by Reorg. Plan No. 3 of 1946, effective July 16, 1946.

Great Lakes Basin Commission   Established by EO 11345 of Apr. 20, 1967. Terminated by EO 12319 of Sept. 9, 1981.

Great Lakes Pilotage Administration   Established in the Department of Commerce to administer act of June 30, 1960 (74 Stat. 259). Administration of act transferred to the Secretary of Transportation by act of Oct. 15, 1966 (80 Stat. 931).

Greening the Government through Waste Prevention and Recycling, Steering Committee   Established by EO 13101 of Sept. 14, 1998. Abolished by EO 13423 of Jan. 24, 2007.

Gulf Coast Ecosystem Restoration Council Task Force   Established by EO 13554 of Oct. 5, 2010. Terminated by EO 13626 of Sept. 10, 2012.

Handicapped, National Center on Education Media and Materials for the   Established by agreement between the *Secretary of Health, Education, and Welfare* and Ohio State University, pursuant to acts of Aug. 20, 1969 (83 Stat. 102) and Apr. 13, 1970 (84 Stat. 187). Authorization deleted by act of Nov. 29, 1975 (89 Stat. 795), and the Secretary was authorized to enter into agreements with non-Federal organizations to establish and operate centers for handicapped.

Handicapped, National Council on the   Established in the *Department of Health, Education, and Welfare* by act of Nov. 6, 1978 (92 Stat. 2977). Transferred to the Department of Education by act of Oct. 17, 1979 (93 Stat. 677). Reorganized as independent agency by act of Feb. 22, 1984 (98 Stat. 26).

Handicapped Employees, Interagency Committee on   Alternately renamed Interagency Committee on Employment of People with Disabilities by EO 12704 of Feb. 26, 1990.

Handicapped Individuals, White House Conference on   Established by act of Dec. 7, 1974 (88 Stat. 1617). Terminated Dec. 30, 1977, pursuant to terms of act.

Handicapped Research, National Institute of   Renamed National Institute on Disability and Rehabilitation Research by act of Oct. 21, 1986 (100 Stat. 1820).

Health, Cost of Living Council Committee on   Established by EO 11695 of Jan. 11, 1973. Abolished by EO 11788 of June 18, 1974.

Health, Education, and Welfare, Department of   Established by Reorganization Plan No. 1 of 1953 (5 U.S.C. app.), effective Apr. 11, 1953. Renamed Department of Health and Human Services by act of Oct. 17, 1979 (93 Stat. 695).

Health, Welfare, and Related Defense Activities, Office of the Coordinator of   *Federal Security Administrator* designated as Coordinator of health, welfare, and related fields of activity affecting national defense, including aspects of education under *Federal Security Agency,* by *Council of National Defense,* with approval of President, Nov. 28, 1940. Office of Coordinator superseded by *Office of Defense Health and Welfare Services,* established in *Office for Emergency Services* by EO 8890 of Sept. 3, 1941.

Health Care Technology, National Council on   Established by act of July 1, 1944, as amended (92 Stat. 3447). Renamed *Council on Health Care Technology* by act of Oct. 30, 1984 (98 Stat. 2820). Name lowercased by act of Oct. 7, 1985 (99 Stat. 493). Terminated by act of Dec. 19, 1989 (103 Stat. 2205).

Health Facilities, Financing, Compliance, and Conversion, Bureau of   Renamed Bureau of Health Facilities by Department of Health and Human Services Secretarial order of Mar. 12, 1980 (45 FR 17207).

Health Industry Advisory Committee   Established by EO 11695 of Jan. 11, 1973. Abolished by EO 11781 of May 1, 1974.

Health Manpower, Bureau of   Renamed Bureau of Health Professions by Department of Health and Human Services Secretarial order of Mar. 12, 1980 (45 FR 17207).

Health and Medical Committee   Established by *Council of National Defense* order of Sept. 19, 1940. Transferred to *Federal Security Agency Council* order approved by President Nov. 28, 1940. Reestablished in *Office of Defense Health and Welfare Services, Office for Emergency Management,* by EO 8890 of Sept. 3, 1941. *Committee* transferred to *Federal Security Agency* by EO 9338 of Apr. 29, 1943.

Health Reform, White House Office of   Established by EO 13507 of April 8, 2009. Revoked by EO 13569 of April 5, 2011.

Health Resources Administration   Established in Public Health Service. Abolished by Department of Health and Human Services Secretarial reorganization of Aug. 20, 1982 (47 FR 38409), and functions transferred to Health Resources and Services Administration.

Health Service, Public   Originated by act of July 16, 1798 (1 Stat. 605). Transferred from the Department of the Treasury to the *Federal Security Agency* by Reorg. Plan No. I of 1939, effective July 1, 1939.

Health Services Administration   Established in Public Health Service. Abolished by Department of Health and Human Services Secretarial reorganization of Aug. 20, 1982 (47 FR 38409), and functions transferred to Health Resources and Services Administration.

Health Services Industry, Committee on the   Established by EO 11627 of Oct. 15, 1971. Abolished by EO 11695 of Jan. 11, 1973.

Health Services and Mental Health Administration   Established in Public Health Service Apr. 1, 1968. Abolished by *Department of Health, Education, and Welfare* reorganization order and functions transferred to *Centers for Disease Control, Health Resources Administration,* and *Health Services Administration,* effective July 1, 1973.

Health Services Research, National Center for   Established by act of July 23, 1974 (88 Stat. 363). Transferred from *Health Resources Administration* to Office of the Assistant Secretary for Health by *Department of Health, Education, and Welfare* reorganization, effective Dec. 2, 1977. Renamed *National Center for Health Services Research and Health Care Technology Assessment* by Secretary's order, pursuant to act of Oct. 30, 1984 (98 Stat. 2817). Terminated by act of Dec. 19, 1989 (103 Stat. 2205).

Health Statistics, National Center for   Established by act of July 23, 1974 (88 Stat. 363). Transferred from *Health Resources Administration* to Office of the Assistant Secretary for Health by the *Department of Health, Education, and Welfare* reorganization, effective Dec. 2, 1977. Transferred to *Centers for Disease Control* by Secretary's notice of Apr. 2, 1987 (52 FR 13318).

Health and Welfare Activities, Interdepartmental Committee to Coordinate   Appointed by President Aug. 15, 1935, and reestablished by EO 7481 of Oct. 27, 1936. Terminated in 1939.

Health and Welfare Aspects of Evacuation of Civilians, Joint Committee on   Established August 1941 as joint committee of *Office of Defense Health and Welfare Services* and *Office of Civilian Defense.* Reorganized in June 1942 and renamed *Joint Committee on Evacuation. Office of Defense Health and Welfare Services* abolished by EO 9388 of Apr. 29, 1943, and functions transferred to *Federal Security Agency. Committee* terminated.

Heart and Lung Institute, National   Renamed National Heart, Lung, and Blood Institute by act of Apr. 22, 1976 (90 Stat. 402).

Heritage Conservation and Recreation Service   Established by the Secretary of the Interior Jan. 25, 1978. Abolished by Secretarial Order 3060 of Feb. 19, 1981, and functions transferred to National Park Service.

Hemispheric Defense Studies, Center for   Established by Department of Defense Directive 3200.12 of Sept. 3, 1997. Abolished by act of Oct. 17, 2006 (120 Stat. 2353).

Highway Safety Agency, National   Established in the Department of Commerce by act of Sept. 9, 1966 (80 Stat. 731). Functions transferred to the Department of Transportation by act of Oct. 15, 1966 (80 Stat. 931). Functions transferred to *National Highway Safety Bureau* by EO 11357 of June 6, 1967. *Bureau* renamed National Highway Traffic Safety Administration by act of Dec. 31, 1970 (84 Stat. 1739).

Highway Safety Bureau, National   *See* **Highway Safety Agency, National**

Home Economics, Bureau of Human Nutrition and   *See* **Home Economics, Office of**

Home Economics, Office of   Renamed *Bureau of Home Economics* by Secretary's Memorandum 436, effective July 1, 1923, pursuant to act of Feb. 26, 1923 (42 Stat. 1289). Redesignated *Bureau of Human Nutrition and Home Economics* February 1943 in accordance with *Research Administration* Memorandum 5 issued pursuant to EO 9069 of Feb. 23, 1942, and in conformity with Secretary's Memorandums 960 and 986. Functions transferred to Agricultural Research Service by Secretary's Memorandum 1320, supp. 4, of Nov. 2, 1953.

Home Loan Bank Administration, Federal   *See* **Home Loan Bank Board, Federal**

Home Loan Bank Board   *See* **Home Loan Bank Board, Federal**

Home Loan Bank Board, Federal   Established by acts of July 22, 1932 (47 Stat. 725), June 13, 1933 (48 Stat. 128), and June 27, 1934 (48 Stat. 1246). Grouped with other agencies to form *Federal Loan Agency* by Reorg. Plan No. I of 1939, effective July 1, 1939. Functions transferred to *Federal Home Loan Bank Administration, National Housing Agency,* by EO 9070 of Feb. 24, 1942. Abolished by Reorg. Plan No. 3, effective July 27, 1947, and functions transferred to *Home Loan Bank Board, Housing and Home Finance Agency.* Renamed *Federal Home Loan Bank Board* and made independent agency by act of Aug. 11, 1955 (69 Stat. 640). Abolished by act of Aug. 9, 1989 (103 Stat. 354, 415), and functions transferred to Office of Thrift Supervision, Resolution Trust Corporation, Federal Deposit Insurance Corporation, and Federal Housing Finance Board. (*See also* **Thrift Supervision, Office of**).

Home Loan Bank System, Federal   Grouped with other agencies to form *Federal Loan Agency* by Reorg. Plan No. I of 1939, effective July 1, 1939. Functions transferred to *Federal Home Loan Bank Administration, National Housing Agency,* by EO 9070 of Feb. 24, 1942. Transferred to *Housing and Home Finance Agency* by Reorg. Plan No. 3 of 1947, effective July 27, 1947.

Home Mortgage Credit Extension Committee, National Voluntary   Established by act of Aug.

2, 1954 (68 Stat 638). Terminated Oct. 1, 1965, pursuant to terms of act.

Home Owners' Loan Corporation   Established by act of June 13, 1933 (48 Stat. 128), under supervision of *Federal Home Loan Bank Board.* Grouped with other agencies to form *Federal Loan Agency* by Reorg. Plan No. I of 1939, effective July 1, 1939. Transferred to *Federal Home Loan Bank Administration, National Housing Agency,* by EO 9070 of Feb. 24, 1942. Board of Directors abolished by Reorg. Plan No. 3 of 1947, effective July 27, 1947, and functions transferred, for liquidation of assets, to *Home Loan Bank Board, Housing and Home Finance Agency.* Terminated by order of *Secretary of the Home Loan Bank Board,* effective Feb. 3, 1954, pursuant to act of June 30, 1953 (67 Stat. 121).

Homesteads, Division of Subsistence   Established by act of June 16, 1933 (48 Stat. 205). Secretary of the Interior authorized to administer section 208 of act by EO 6209 of July 21, 1933. *Federal Subsistence Homesteads Corporation* created by Secretary's order of Dec. 2, 1933, and organization incorporated under laws of Delaware. Transferred to *Resettlement Administration* by EO 7041 of May 15, 1935.

Homesteads Corporation, Federal Subsistence   See **Homesteads, Division of Subsistence**

Hospitalization, Board of Federal   Organized Nov. 1, 1921. Designated as advisory agency to *Bureau of the Budget* May 7, 1943. Terminated June 30, 1948, by Director's letter of May 28, 1948.

Housing, President's Committee on Equal Opportunity in   Established by EO 11063 of Nov. 20, 1962. Inactive as of June 30, 1968.

Housing Administration, Federal   Established by act of June 27, 1934 (48 Stat. 1246). Grouped with other agencies to form *Federal Loan Agency* by Reorg. Plan No. I of 1939, effective July 1, 1939. Functions transferred to *Federal Housing Administration, National Housing Agency,* by EO 9070 of Feb. 24, 1942. Transferred to *Housing and Home Finance Agency* by Reorg. Plan No. 3, effective July 27, 1947. Functions transferred to the Department of Housing and Urban Development by act of Sept. 9, 1965 (79 Stat. 667).

Housing Administration, Public   Established as constituent agency of *Housing and Home Finance Agency* by Reorg. Plan No. 3 of 1947, effective July 27, 1947. Functions transferred to the Department of Housing and Urban Development by act of Sept. 9, 1965 (79 Stat. 667).

Housing Agency, National   Established by EO 9070 of Feb. 24, 1942, to consolidate housing functions relating to *Federal Home Loan Bank Board, Federal Home Loan Bank System, Federal Savings and Loan Insurance Corporation, Home Owners' Loan Corporation, U.S. Housing Corporation, Federal Housing Administration, U.S. Housing Authority, Defense Homes Corporation, Division of Defense Housing Coordination, Central Housing Committee, Farm Security Administration* with respect to nonfarm housing, *Public Buildings Administration, Division*

of Defense Housing, Mutual Ownership Defense Housing Division, Office of Administrator of Federal Works Agency, and the Departments of *War* and the Navy with respect to housing located off military installations. Agency dissolved on creation of *Housing and Home Finance Agency* by Reorg. Plan No. 3 of 1947, effective July 27, 1947.

Housing Authority, Federal Public   Established by EO 9070 of Feb. 24, 1942. Public housing functions of *Federal Works Agency, the Departments of War* and the Navy (except housing located on military installations), and *Farm Security Administration* (nonfarm housing) transferred to *Authority,* and *Defense Homes Corporation* administered by the Commissioner of the *Authority'.* Functions transferred to *Public Housing Administration, Housing and Home Finance Agency,* by Reorg. Plan No. 3 of 1947, effective July 27, 1947.

Housing Authority, U.S.   Established in the Department of the Interior by act of Sept. 1, 1937 (50 Stat. 888). Transferred to *Federal Works Agency* by Reorg. Plan No. I of 1939, effective July 1, 1939. Transferred to *Federal Public Housing Authority, National Housing Agency,* by EO 9070 of Feb. 24, 1942. Office of Administrator abolished by Reorg. Plan No. 3 of 1947, effective July 27, 1947, and functions transferred to *Public Housing Administration, Housing and Home Finance Agency.*

Housing Corporation, U.S.   Incorporated July 10, 1918, under laws of New York. Transferred from the Department of Labor to the Department of the Treasury by EO 7641 of June 22, 1937. Transferred from the Department of the Treasury to the *Public Buildings Administration, Federal Works Agency,* by EO 8186 of June 29, 1939. Functions transferred for liquidation to *Federal Home Loan Bank Administration, National Housing Agency,* by EO 9070 of Feb. 24, 1942. Terminated Sept. 8, 1952, by the *Secretary of the Home Loan Bank Board.*

Housing Council, National   Established in *Housing and Home Finance Agency* by Reorg. Plan No. 3 of 1947, effective July 27, 1947. Terminated by Reorg. Plan No. 4 of 1965, effective July 27, 1965, and functions transferred to President.

Housing Division   Established in *Public Works Administration* by act of June 16, 1933 (48 Stat. 195). Functions transferred to *U.S. Housing Authority* by EO 7732 of Oct. 27, 1937.

Housing Enterprise Oversight, Office of Federal   Office and positions of Director and Deputy Director established within the Department of Housing and Urban Development by the act of October 28, 1992 (106 Stat. 3944). Abolished by the act of July 30, 2008 (122 Stat. 2794), and functions, personnel, and property transferred to Federal Housing Finance Agency.

Housing Expediter, Office of the   Established in *Office of War Mobilization and Reconversion* by Presidential letter of Dec. 12, 1945, to *Housing Expediter.* Functions of *Housing Expediter* defined by EO 9686 of Jan. 26, 1946. *Housing Expediter* confirmed in position of *National Housing*

Administrator Feb. 6, 1946. *Office of the Housing Expediter* established by act of May 22, 1946 (60 Stat. 208). Functions of *Office* and *National Housing Administrator* segregated by EO 9820 of Jan. 11, 1947. Housing functions of *Civilian Production Administration* transferred to *Office* by EO 9836 of Mar. 22, 1947, effective Apr. 1, 1947. Rent control functions of *Office of Temporary Controls* transferred to *Office* by EO 9841 of Apr. 23, 1947. *Office* terminated by EO 10276 of July 31, 1951, and functions transferred to *Economic Stabilization Agency.*

Housing Finance Board, Federal Established by the act of August 9, 1989 (103 Stat. 354, 415), and certain functions transferred from Federal Home Loan Bank Board. Abolished by the act of July 30, 2008 (122 Stat. 2797), and functions, personnel, and property transferred to Federal Housing Finance Agency.

Housing and Home Finance Agency Established by Reorg. Plan No. 3 of 1947, effective July 27, 1947. Terminated by act of Sept. 9, 1965 (79 Stat. 667), and functions transferred to the Department of Housing and Urban Development.

Howard University Established by act of Mar. 2, 1867 (14 Stat. 438). Functions of the Department of the Interior transferred to *Federal Security Agency* by Reorg. Plan No. IV of 1940, effective June 30, 1940. Functions of the *Department of Health, Education, and Welfare* transferred to the Department of Education by act of Oct. 17, 1979 (93 Stat. 678).

Human Development, Office of Established in *Department of Health, Education, and Welfare.* Renamed Office of Human Development Services and component units transferred to or reorganized under new administrations in Office by Secretary's reorganization order of July 26, 1977. Merged into the Administration for Children and Families by Secretary of Health and Human Services reorganization notice dated Apr. 15, 1991.

Human Development Services, Office of *See* **Human Development, Office of**

Human Embryo Stem Cell Registry Approved by Presidential announcement of Aug. 9, 2001 and established through National Institute of Health's Departmental Notice NOT–OD–01–058 of Aug. 27, 2001. Renamed Human Pluripotent Stem Cell Registry by EO 13435 of June 20, 2007.

Hydrographic Office Jurisdiction transferred from *Bureau of Navigation* to Chief of Naval Operations by EO 9126 of Apr. 8, 1942, and by Reorg. Plan No. 3 of 1946, effective July 16, 1946. Renamed U.S. Naval Oceanographic Office by act of July 10, 1962 (76 Stat. 154).

Imagery and Mapping Agency, National Established by act of Sept. 23, 1996 (110 Stat. 2677). Renamed National Geospatial-Intelligence Agency by act of Nov. 24, 2003 (117 Stat. 1568).

Imagery Office, Central Established as a Department of Defense agency on May 6, 1992.

Functions transferred to National Imagery and Mapping Agency by act of Sept. 23, 1996 (110 Stat. 2677).

Immigration, Bureau of Established as branch of the Department of the Treasury by act of Mar. 3, 1891 (26 Stat. 1085). Transferred to *Department of Commerce and Labor* by act of Feb. 14, 1903 (34 Stat. 596). Made *Bureau of Immigration and Naturalization* by act of June 29, 1906 (37 Stat. 736). Made separate division after the Department of Labor created by act of Mar. 4, 1913 (37 Stat. 736). Consolidated into Immigration and Naturalization Service, Department of Labor, by EO 6166 of June 10, 1933. Transferred to the Department of Justice by Reorg. Plan No. V of 1940, effective June 14, 1940. Abolished by act of Nov. 25, 2002 (116 Stat. 2205) and functions transferred to Homeland Security Department.

Immigration, Commissioners of Offices of commissioners of immigration of the several ports created by act of Aug. 18, 1894 (28 Stat. 391). Abolished by Reorg. Plan No. III of 1940, effective June 30, 1940, and functions transferred to *Bureau of Immigration and Naturalization,* Department of Labor.

Immigration and Naturalization, Bureau of *See* **Immigration, Bureau of**

Immigration and Naturalization, District Commissioner of Created by act of Aug. 18, 1894 (28 Stat. 391). Abolished by Reorg. Plan No. III of 1940, effective June 30, 1940. Functions administered by the Commissioner of Immigration and Naturalization, Department of Justice, through district immigration and naturalization directors.

Immigration and Naturalization Service *See* **Immigration, Bureau of**

Import Programs, Office of Established by the Secretary of Commerce Feb. 14, 1971. Functions transferred to *Domestic and International Business Administration,* effective Nov. 17, 1972.

Indian Claims Commission Established by act of Aug. 13, 1946 (60 Stat. 1049). Terminated by act of Oct. 8, 1976 (90 Stat. 1990), and pending cases transferred to *U.S. Court of Claims* Sept. 30, 1978.

Indian Commissioners, Board of Established by section 2039, Revised Statutes. Abolished by EO 6145 of May 25, 1933.

Indian Education Programs, Office of Established within the Bureau of Indian Affairs, Department of the Interior, by act of June 23, 1972 (86 Stat. 343). Renamed Bureau of Indian Education by Departmental Manual Release No. 3721 of Aug. 29, 2006.

Indian Medical Facilities Functions transferred from the Department of the Interior to the *Department of Health, Education, and Welfare,* to be administered by the Surgeon General of Public Health Service, by act of Aug. 5, 1954 (68 Stat. 674).

Indian Opportunity, National Council on Established by EO 11399 of Mar. 6, 1968. Terminated Nov. 26, 1974, by act of Nov. 26, 1969 (83 Stat. 220).

Indian Policy Review Commission, American Established by act of Jan. 2, 1975 (88 Stat. 1910). Terminated June 30, 1977, pursuant to terms of act.

Industrial Analysis, Committee of Established by EO 7323 of Mar. 21, 1936. Terminated Feb. 17, 1937.

Industrial Cooperation, Coordinator for Established by EO 7193 of Sept. 26, 1935. Continued by EO 7324 of Mar. 30, 1936. Terminated June 30, 1937.

Industrial Emergency Committee Established by EO 6770 of June 30, 1934. Consolidated with *National Emergency Council* by EO 6889–A of Oct. 29, 1934.

Industrial Pollution Control Council Staff, National Established by Department of Commerce Organization Order 35–3 of June 17, 1970. *Staff* abolished by departmental organization order of Sept. 10, 1973. Council inactive.

Industrial Recovery Board, National Established by EO 6859 of Sept. 27, 1934. Terminated by EO 7075 of June 15, 1935.

Industrial Recovery Board, Special Established by EO 6173 of June 16, 1933. Functions absorbed by *National Emergency Council* under terms of EO 6513 of Dec. 18, 1933.

Industrial Relations, Office of Activated in the Department of the Navy Sept. 14, 1945. Superseded June 22, 1966, by creation of *Office of Civilian Manpower Management.*

Industry and Trade Administration *See* **Business and Defense Services Administration**

Information, Committee for Reciprocity Established by EO 6750 of June 27, 1934; reestablished by EO 10004 of Oct. 5, 1948, which revoked EO 6750. Superseded by EO 10082 of Oct. 5, 1949; abolished by EO 11075 of Jan. 15, 1963, which revoked EO 10082.

Information, Coordinator of Established by Presidential order of July 11, 1941. Functions exclusive of foreign information activities transferred by military order of June 13, 1942, to jurisdiction of Joint Chiefs of Staff, *War Department,* as *Office of Strategic Services.* Foreign information functions transferred to *Office of War Information* by EO 9182 of June 13, 1942.

Information, Division of Established pursuant to Presidential letter of Feb. 28, 1941, to *Liaison Officer, Office of Emergency Management.* Abolished by EO 9182 of June 13, 1942. Functions relating to public information on war effort transferred and consolidated with *Office of War Information,* and publication services relating to specific agencies of OEM transferred to those agencies.

Information, Office of Coordinator of Transferred, exclusive of foreign information activities, to *Office of War Information* by EO 9182 of June 13, 1942. Designated *Office of Strategic Services* and transferred to jurisdiction of Joint Chiefs of Staff by military order of June 13, 1942. Terminated by EO 9621 of Sept. 20, 1945, and functions distributed to the Departments of State and *War.*

Information Administration, International Transferred from the Department of State to the *U.S. Information Agency* by Reorg. Plan No. 8 of 1953, effective Aug. 1, 1953.

Information Agency, U.S. Established by Reorg. Plan No. 8 of 1953, effective Aug. 1, 1953. Abolished by Reorg. Plan No. 2 of 1977, effective Apr. 1, 1978; replaced by and functions transferred to *International Communication Agency.* Redesignated *U.S. Information Agency* by act of Aug. 24, 1982 (96 Stat. 291). Abolished by act of Oct. 21, 1998 (112 Stat. 2681–761), and functions transferred to the Department of State, effective Oct. 1, 1999.

Information and Public Affairs, Office of Merged with *Office of Intergovernmental Affairs* to form Office of Public and Intergovernmental Affairs by Order 1–85 of June 5, 1985 of the Secretary of Labor.

Information Resources Management, Office of *See* **Telecommunications Service, Automated Data**

Information Resources Management Service Established in the General Services Administration. Renamed Information Technology Service in 1995.

Information Security Committee, Interagency Established by EO 12065 of June 28, 1978. Abolished by EO 12356 of Apr. 2, 1982.

Information Security Oversight Office Established in General Services Administration by EO 12065 of June 28, 1978. EO 12065 revoked by EO 12356 of Apr. 2, 1982, which provided for continuation of Office.

Information Service, Government *See* **Information Service, U.S.**

Information Service, Interim International Established in the Department of State by EO 9608 of Aug. 31, 1945. Abolished Dec. 31, 1945, pursuant to terms of order.

Information Service, U.S. Established in March 1934 as division of *National Emergency Council.* Transferred to *Office of Government Reports* by Reorg. Plan No. II of 1939, effective July 1, 1939. Consolidated, along with other functions of *Office,* into *Division of Public Inquiries, Bureau of Special Services, Office of War Information,* by EO 9182 of June 13, 1942. *Bureau of Special Services* renamed *Government Information Service* and transferred to *Bureau of the Budget* by EO 9608 of Aug. 31, 1945. *Service* transferred to *Office of Government Reports* by EO 9809 of Dec. 12, 1946.

Information Systems Council Established by EO 13356 of Aug. 27, 2004. Abolished by EO 13388 of Oct. 25, 2005 (70 FR 62025).

Information Technology Service Established in General Services Administration. Abolished by General Services Administrative Order No. 5440.492, Aug. 21, 1996, and functions transferred to Federal Telecommunications Service.

Insane, Government Hospital for the Established by act of Mar. 3, 1855 (10 Stat. 682). Renamed Saint Elizabeth's Hospital by act of July 1, 1916 (39 Stat. 309). Transferred from the Department of the Interior to *Federal Security Agency* by Reorg. Plan No. IV of 1940, effective June 30, 1940. Transferred to *Department of Health, Education, and Welfare* by Reorg. Plan No. 1 of 1953, effective Apr. 11, 1953. Functions redelegated to National Institute of Mental Health by Secretary's reorganization order of Aug. 9, 1967. Property and administration transferred to District of Columbia Government by act of Nov. 8, 1984 (98 Stat. 3369).

Installations, Director of Established in the Department of Defense by act of July 14, 1952 (66 Stat. 625). Abolished by Reorg. Plan No. 6 of 1953, effective June 30, 1953, and functions transferred to the Secretary of Defense.

Insular Affairs, Bureau of Transferred from *Department of War* to *Division of Territories and Island Possessions,* the Department of the Interior, by Reorg. Plan No. II of 1939, effective July 1, 1939.

Insurance Administrator, Federal Established by act of Aug. 1, 1968 (82 Stat. 567). Functions transferred to Federal Emergency Management Agency by Reorg. Plan No. 3 of 1978, effective Apr. 1, 1979.

Integrity and Efficiency, President's Council on Established by EO 12301 of Mar. 26, 1981 (46 FR 19211). Abolished and reestablished by EO 12625 of Jan 27, 1988 (53 FR 2812). Abolished and reestablished by EO 12805 of May 11, 1992 (57 FR 20627).

Intelligence, Office of Established within the Department of Energy by Public Law 106–65 of Oct. 5, 1999 (113 Stat. 955). Merged with *Office of Counterintelligence* to form Office of Intelligence and Counterintelligence by memorandum of March 9, 2006 of the Secretary of Energy.

Intelligence Activities, President's Board of Consultants on Foreign Established by EO 10656 of Feb. 6, 1956. EO 10656 revoked by EO 10938 of May 4, 1961, and *Board* terminated. Functions transferred to President's Foreign Intelligence Advisory Board.

Intelligence Advisory Board, President's Foreign Established by EO 11460 of Mar. 20, 1969. Abolished by EO 11984 of May 4, 1977. Reestablished by EO 12331 of Oct. 20, 1981.

Intelligence Authority, National Established by Presidential directive of Jan. 22, 1946. Terminated on creation of Central Intelligence Agency under National Security Council by act of July 26, 1947 (61 Stat. 497).

Intelligence Group, Central Terminated on creation of Central Intelligence Agency by act of July 26, 1947 (61 Stat. 497).

Intelligence Policy and Review, Office of Transferred from the Criminal Division to the National Security Division by act of Mar. 9, 2006 (120 Stat. 249).

Inter-American Affairs, Institute of *See* **American Republics, Office for Coordination of Commercial and Cultural Relations between the**

Inter-American Affairs, Office of *See* **American Republics, Office for Coordination of Commercial and Cultural Relations between the**

Inter-American Affairs, Office of the Coordinator of *See* **American Republics, Office for Coordination of Commercial and Cultural Relations between the**

Interagency. *See other part of title*

Interdepartmental. *See also other part of title*

Interdepartmental Advisory Council Established January 1941 to advise *Coordinator of Health, Welfare, and Related Defense Activities.* Terminated on creation of *Office of Defense Health and Welfare Service* Sept. 3, 1941.

Interest and Dividends, Committee on Established by EO 11695 of Jan. 11, 1973. Abolished by EO 11781 of May 1, 1974.

Intergovernmental Affairs, Office of Merged with *Office of Information and Public Affairs* to form Office of Public and Intergovernmental Affairs by Order 1–85 of June 5, 1985 of the Secretary of Labor. Renamed Office of Intergovernmental and External Affairs by Secretary of Health and Human Services notice of July 19, 2011 (76 FR 42710).

Intergovernmental and Interagency Affairs, Office of Abolished by decision of March 21, 2005 of the Secretary of Education under authority of section 413 of the Department of Education Organization Act.

Intergovernmental Relations, Advisory Commission on Established by act of Sept. 24, 1959 (73 Stat. 703). Terminated pursuant to act of Nov. 19, 1995 (109 Stat. 480). Continued in existence by act of Oct. 19, 1996 (110 Stat. 4004).

Intergovernmental Relations, Commission on Established by act of July 10, 1953 (67 Stat. 145). Final report submitted to Congress by June 30, 1955, pursuant to act of Feb. 7, 1955 (69 Stat. 7).

Intergovernmental Relations, Office of Established by EO 11455 of Feb. 14, 1969. Functions transferred to *Domestic Council* by EO 11690 of Dec. 14, 1972.

Interim Compliance Panel Established by Dec. 30, 1969 (83 Stat. 774). Terminated June 30, 1976, pursuant to terms of act.

Internal Revenue Service Functions relating to alcohol, tobacco, firearms, and explosives transferred to Bureau of Alcohol, Tobacco, and Firearms by Department of Treasury order of July 1, 1972.

Internal Security Division Established July 9, 1945, by transfer of functions from Criminal Division. Abolished Mar. 22, 1973, and functions transferred to Criminal Division, Department of Justice.

International *See also other part of title*

International Activities, Office of Renamed *Office of Service and Protocol* by Secretary of the Smithsonian Institution internal directive of Jan. 11, 1985.

International Development, Agency for Transferred from the Department of State to *U.S. International Development Cooperation Agency* by Reorg. Plan No. 2 of 1979, effective Oct. 1, 1979. Continued as agency within *IDCA* by IDCA Delegation of Authority No. 1 of Oct. 1, 1979. By act of Oct. 21, 1998 (112 Stat. 2681–790), became independent agency.

International Development Cooperation Agency, U.S. Established by Reorg. Plan No. 2 of 1979, effective Oct. 1, 1979. Abolished by act of Oct. 21, 1998 (112 Stat. 2681–790) and functions transferred to the Department of State, U.S. Agency for International Development, and Overseas Private Investment Corporation.

Interstate Commerce Commission Created by act of Feb. 4, 1887 (24 Stat. 379). Certain functions as cited in act of Oct. 15, 1966 (80 Stat. 931) transferred to the Secretary of Commerce. Functions relating to railroad and pipeline safety transferred to Federal Railroad Administrator and motor carrier safety to Federal Highway Administrator by act. Abolished by act of Dec. 29, 1995 (109 Stat. 932) and many functions transferred to the newly created Surface Transportation Board within the Department of Transportation.

Investigation, Bureau of Established by act of May 22, 1908 (35 Stat. 235). Functions consolidated with investigative functions of *Bureau of Prohibition, Division of Investigation,* Department of Justice, by EO 6166 of June 10, 1933, effective Mar. 2, 1934.

Investigation, Division of Designated as Federal Bureau of Investigation in the Department of Justice by act of Mar. 22, 1935 (49 Stat. 77).

Investigation and Research, Board of Established by act of Sept. 18, 1940 (54 Stat. 952). Extended to Sept. 18, 1944, by Proc. 2559 of June 26, 1942.

Investigations, Division of Established by administrative order of Apr. 27, 1933. Abolished Jan. 17, 1942, by administrative order and functions transferred to *Branch of Field Examination, General Land Office,* Department of the Interior.

Investments, Office of Foreign Direct Established in the Department of Commerce Jan. 2, 1968, by Departmental Organization Order 25–3 to carry out provisions of EO 11387 of Jan. 1, 1968. Controls on foreign investments terminated Jan. 29, 1974.

Iraq Reconstruction, Office of the Inspector General for Established by act of Nov. 6, 2003 (117 Stat. 1234). Abolished by act of Oct. 17, 2006 (120 Stat. 2397).

Iraq Transition Assistance Office Established by EO 13431 of May 8, 2007 (72 FR 26709). Personnel and administration transferred to Iraq Strategic Partnership Office by EO 13541 of May 7, 2010 (75 FR 26879).

Jamestown-Williamsburg-Yorktown National Celebration Commission Established by act of Aug. 13, 1953 (67 Stat. 576). Terminated upon submission of final report to Congress Mar. 1, 1958.

Job Corps, Office of Transferred from the Employment and Training Administration to the Office of the Secretary, U.S. Department of Labor by act of Dec. 30, 2005 (119 Stat. 2842). Transferred from the Office of the Secretary, U.S. Department of Labor to the Employment and Training Administration by act of Dec. 16, 2009 (123 Stat. 3238).

Joint. *See also other part of title*

Joint Resolutions of Congress *See* **State, Department of**

Judicial Procedure, Commission on International Rules of Established by act of Sept. 2, 1958 (72 Stat. 1743). Terminated Dec. 31, 1966, by act of Aug. 30, 1964 (78 Stat. 700).

Justice Assistance, Research, and Statistics, Office of Established in the Department of Justice by act of Dec. 27, 1979 (93 Stat. 1201). Abolished by act of Oct. 12, 1984 (98 Stat. 2091).

Kennedy, Commission To Report Upon the Assassination of President John F. Established by EO 11130 of Nov. 29, 1963. Report submitted Sept. 24, 1964, and *Commission* discharged by Presidential letter of same date.

Labor, President's Committee on Migratory Appointed by Presidential letter of Aug. 26, 1954. Formally established by EO 10894 of Nov. 15, 1960. Terminated Jan. 6, 1964, by the Secretary of Labor in letter to members, with approval of President.

Labor and Commerce, Department of Established by act of Feb. 14, 1903 (32 Stat. 825). Reorganized into separate Departments of Labor and Commerce by act of Mar. 4, 1913 (37 Stat. 736).

Labor Department, Solicitor for Transferred from the Department of Justice to the Department of Labor by EO 6166 of June 10, 1933.

Labor-Management Advisory Committee Established by EO 11695 of Jan. 11, 1973. Abolished by EO 11788 of June 18, 1974.

Labor-Management Policy, President's Advisory Committee on Established by EO 10918 of Feb. 16, 1961. Abolished by EO 11710 of Apr. 4, 1973.

Labor-Management Relations Services, Office of Established by Order 3–84 of May 3, 1984 of the Secretary of Labor. Renamed Bureau of Labor-Management Relations and Cooperative Programs by Secretarial Order 7–84 of Sept. 20, 1984 (49 FR 38374).

Labor-Management Services Administration *Office of Pension and Welfare Benefit Programs* transferred from *Administration* and constituted as separate unit by Order 1–84 of Jan. 20, 1984 of the Secretary of Labor (49 FR 4269). Remaining labor-management relations functions reassigned by Secretarial Order 3–84 of May 3, 1984.

Labor Organization, International Established in 1919 by Treaty of Versailles with U.S. joining in 1934. U.S. membership terminated Nov. 1, 1977, at President's direction. The U.S. rejoined the organization in February 1980.

Labor Relations Council, Federal Established by EO 11491 of Oct. 29, 1969. Abolished by Reorg. Plan No. 2 of 1978, effective Jan. 1, 1979, and functions transferred to Federal Labor Relations Authority.

Labor Standards, Apprenticeship Section, Division of Transferred to *Federal Security Agency* by EO 9139 of Apr. 18, 1942, functioning as *Apprentice Training Service.* Transferred to *War Manpower Commission* by EO 9247 of Sept. 17, 1942, functioning in *Bureau of Training.* Returned to the Department of Labor by EO 9617 of Sept. 19, 1945.

Labor Standards, Bureau of Established by Labor departmental order in 1934. Functions absorbed by Occupational Safety and Health Administration in May 1971.

Land Bank Commissioner *See* **Farm Loan Board, Federal**

Land Law Review Commission, Public Established by act of Sept. 19, 1964 (78 Stat. 982). Terminated Dec. 31, 1970, pursuant to terms of act.

Land Office, General Consolidated with *Grazing Service* into Bureau of Land Management, Department of the Interior, by Reorg. Plan No. 3 of 1946, effective July 16, 1946.

Land Office, Office of Recorder of the General Created in the Department of the Interior by act of July 4, 1836 (5 Stat. 111). Abolished by Reorg. Plan No. III of 1940, effective June 30, 1940, and functions transferred to *General Land Office.*

Land Policy Section Established in 1934 as part of *Program Planning Division, Agricultural Adjustment Administration.* Personnel taken over by *Resettlement Administration* in 1935.

Land Problems, Committee on National Established by EO 6693 of Apr. 28, 1934. Abolished by EO 6777 of June 30, 1934.

Land Program, Director of Basis of program found in act of June 16, 1933 (48 Stat. 200). *Special Board of Public Works* established by EO 6174 of June 16, 1933. Land Program established by *Board* by resolution passed Dec. 28, 1933, and amended July 18, 1934. *Federal Emergency Relief Administration* designated to administer program Feb. 28, 1934. Land Program transferred to *Resettlement Administration* by EO 7028 of Apr. 30, 1935. Functions of *Administration* transferred to the Secretary of Agriculture by EO 7530 of Dec. 31, 1936. Land conservation and land-utilization programs administered by *Administration* transferred to *Bureau of Agricultural Economics* by Secretary's Memorandum 733. Administration of land programs placed under Soil Conservation Service by Secretary's Memorandum 785 of Oct. 6, 1938.

Land Use Coordination, Office of Established by Secretary of Agriculture Memorandum 725 of July 12, 1937. Abolished Jan. 1, 1944, by General Departmental Circular 21 and functions administered by *Land Use Coordinator.*

Land Use and Water Planning, Office of Established in the Department of the Interior by Secretarial Order No. 2953 of May 7, 1973. Abolished by Secretarial Order No. 2988 of Mar. 11, 1976.

Law Enforcement Assistance Administration Established by act of June 19, 1968 (82 Stat. 197). Operations closed out by the Department of Justice due to lack of appropriations and remaining functions transferred to *Office of Justice Assistance, Research, and Statistics.*

Law Enforcement Training Center, Federal *See* **Law Enforcement Training Center, Consolidated Federal**

Law Enforcement Training Center, Consolidated Federal Established by Treasury Order No. 217, Mar. 2, 1970. Renamed Federal Law Enforcement Training Center by Amendment No. 1 to Treasury Order No. 217 on Aug. 14, 1975. Transferred to Department of Homeland Security by act of Nov. 25, 2002 (116 Stat. 2178).

Legislative Affairs, Office of Renamed Office of Intergovernmental and Legislative Affairs Feb. 24, 1984, by Attorney General's Order 1054–84 (49 FR 10177).

Lend-Lease Administration, Office of Established by EO 8926 of Oct. 28, 1941, to replace *Division of Defense Aid Reports.* Consolidated with *Foreign Economic Administration* by EO 9380 of Sept. 25, 1943.

Lewis and Clark Trail Commission Established by act of Oct. 6, 1964 (78 Stat. 1005). Terminated October 1969 by terms of act.

Libraries and Information Science, National Commission on Established by act of July 20, 1970 (84 Stat. 440). As per close out activities, the Commission was abolished by act of Dec. 26, 2007 (121 Stat. 2204), and functions transferred to the Institute of Museum and Library Services pursuant to instructions set forth in House Report 110–231 and Senate Report 110–107.

Library of Congress Police   Established by act of Aug. 4, 1950 (64 Stat. 411). Personnel transferred to United States Capitol Police by acts of Dec. 26, 2007 (121 Stat. 2228) and Jan. 7, 2008 (121 Stat. 2546).

Lighthouses, Bureau of   Established in the Department of Commerce by act of Aug. 7, 1789 (1 Stat. 53). Consolidated with U.S. Coast Guard by Reorg. Plan No. II of 1939, effective July 1, 1939.

Lincoln Sesquicentennial Commission   Established by joint resolution of Sept. 2, 1957 (71 Stat. 587). Terminated Mar. 1, 1960, pursuant to terms of joint resolution.

Liquidation, Director of   Established in *Office for Emergency Management* by EO 9674 of Jan. 4, 1946. Terminated by EO 9744 of June 27, 1946.

Liquidation Advisory Committee   Established by EO 9674 of Jan. 4, 1946. Terminated by EO 9744 of June 27, 1946.

Literacy, National Institute for   Established by act of July 25, 1991 (105 Stat. 333). Abolished by act of Dec. 16, 2009 (123 Stat. 3267).

Loan Agency, Federal   Established by Reorg. Plan No. I of 1939, effective July 1, 1939, by consolidating *Reconstruction Finance Corporation*—including subordinate units of *RFC Mortgage Company, Disaster Loan Corporation, Federal National Mortgage Association, Defense Plant Corporation, Defense Homes Corporation, Defense Supplies Corporation, Rubber Reserve Company, Metals Reserve Company,* and *War Insurance Corporation* (later known as *War Damage Corporation*)— with *Federal Home Loan Bank Board, Home Owners' Loan Corporation, Federal Savings and Loan Insurance Corporation, Federal Housing Administration, Electric Home and Farm Authority,* and *Export-Import Bank of Washington. Federal Home Loan Bank Board, Federal Savings and Loan Insurance Corporation, Home Owners' Loan Corporation, Federal Housing Administration,* and *Defense Homes Corporation* transferred to *National Housing Agency* by EO 9070 of Feb. 24, 1942. *Reconstruction Finance Corporation* and its units (except *Defense Homes Corporation*), *Electric Home and Farm Authority,* and *Export-Import Bank of Washington* transferred to the Department of Commerce by EO 9071 of Feb. 24, 1942. *RFC* and units returned to *Federal Loan Agency* by act of Feb. 24, 1945 (59 Stat. 5). *Agency* abolished by act of June 30, 1947 (61 Stat. 202), and all property and records transferred to *Reconstruction Finance Corporation.*

Loan Fund, Development   Established in *International Cooperation Administration* by act of Aug. 14, 1957 (71 Stat. 355). Created as independent corporate agency by act of June 30, 1958 (72 Stat. 261). Abolished by act of Sept. 4, 1961 (75 Stat. 445), and functions redelegated to Agency for International Development.

Loan Policy Board   Established by act of July 18, 1958 (72 Stat. 385). Abolished by Reorg. Plan No. 4 of 1965, effective July 27, 1965, and functions transferred to Small Business Administration.

Longshoremen's Labor Board, National   Established in the Department of Labor by EO 6748 of June 26, 1934. Terminated by Proc. 2120 of Mar. 11, 1935.

Low-Emission Vehicle Certification Board   Established by act of Dec. 31, 1970 (84 Stat. 1701). Terminated by act of Mar. 14, 1980 (94 Stat. 98).

Lowell Historic Canal District Commission   Established by act of Jan. 4, 1975 (88 Stat. 2330). Expired January 1977 pursuant to terms of act.

Loyalty Review Board   Established Nov. 10, 1947, by *U.S. Civil Service Commission,* pursuant to EO 9835 of Mar. 21, 1947. Abolished by EO 10450 of Apr. 27, 1953.

Management, Budget and Evaluation, Office of   Established within the Department of Energy pursuant to the Conference Report No. 107–258 on H.R. 2311, Energy and Water Development Appropriations Act, 2002. Abolished by memorandum of July 28, 2005 of the Secretary of Energy, and various functions transferred within the Department of Energy to the *Office of Management, Office of Chief Financial Officer,* and *Office of Human Capital Management.*

Management Improvement, Advisory Committee on   Established by EO 10072 of July 29, 1949. Abolished by EO 10917 of Feb. 10, 1961, and functions transferred to *Bureau of the Budget.*

Management Improvement, President's Advisory Council on   Established by EO 11509 of Feb. 11, 1970. Inactive as of June 30, 1973.

Manpower, President's Committee on   Established by EO 11152 of Apr. 15, 1964. Terminated by EO 11515 of Mar. 13, 1970.

Manpower Administration   Renamed Employment and Training Administration by Order 14–75 of Nov. 12, 1975 of the Secretary of Labor.

Manpower Management, Office of Civilian   Renamed Office of Civilian Personnel by Notice 5430 of Oct. 1, 1976 of the Secretary of the Navy.

Marine Affairs, Office of   Established by the Secretary of the Interior Apr. 30, 1970, to replace *Office of Marine Resources,* created by Secretary Oct. 22, 1968. Abolished by Secretary Dec. 4, 1970.

Marine Corps Memorial Commission, U.S.   Established by act of Aug. 24, 1947 (61 Stat. 724). Terminated by act of Mar. 14, 1980 (94 Stat. 98).

Marine Debris Coordinating Committee   Renamed Interagency Marine Debris Coordinating Committee by act of Dec. 22, 2006 (120 Stat. 3337).

Marine Inspection and Navigation, Bureau of   See *Navigation and Steamboat Inspection, Bureau of*

Marine Resources and Engineering Development, National Council on   Established in Executive Office of the President by act of June 17, 1966 (80 Stat. 203). Terminated Apr. 30, 1971, due to lack of funding.

Maritime Administration   Established in the Department of Commerce by Reorg. Plan No. 21 of 1950, effective May 24, 1950. Transferred to the Department of Transportation by act of Aug. 6, 1981 (95 Stat. 151).

Maritime Advisory Committee   Established by EO 11156 of June 17, 1964. Terminated by EO 11427 of Sept. 4, 1968.

Maritime Board, Federal   *See* **Maritime Commission, U.S.**

Maritime Commission, U.S.   Established by act of June 29, 1936 (49 Stat. 1985), as successor agency to *U.S. Shipping Board* and *U.S. Shipping Board Merchant Fleet Corporation.* Training functions transferred to Commandant of Coast Guard by EO 9083 of Feb. 27, 1942. Functions further transferred to *War Shipping Administration* by EO 9198 of July 11, 1942. Abolished by Reorg. Plan No. 21 of 1950, effective May 24, 1950, which established *Federal Maritime Board* and *Maritime Administration* as successor agencies. *Board* abolished, regulatory functions transferred to Federal Maritime Commission, and functions relating to subsidization of merchant marine transferred to the Secretary of Commerce by Reorg. Plan No. 7 of 1961, effective Aug. 12, 1961.

Maritime Labor Board   Authorized by act of June 23, 1938 (52 Stat. 968). Mediatory duties abolished by act of June 23, 1941 (55 Stat. 259); title expired June 22, 1942.

Marketing Administration, Surplus   Established by Reorg. Plan No. III of 1940, effective June 30, 1940, consolidating functions vested in *Federal Surplus Commodities Corporation* and *Division of Marketing and Marketing Agreements, Agricultural Adjustment Administration.* Consolidated with other agencies into *Agricultural Marketing Administration* by EO 9069 of Feb. 23, 1942.

Marketing and Marketing Agreements, Division of   Established in the Department of Agriculture by act of June 3, 1937 (50 Stat. 246). Consolidated with *Federal Surplus Commodities Corporation* into *Surplus Marketing Administration* by Reorg. Plan No. III of 1940, effective June 30, 1940.

Mediation, U.S. Board of   Established by act of May 20, 1926 (44 Stat. 577). Abolished by act of June 21, 1934 (48 Stat. 1193), and superseded by National Mediation Board, July 21, 1934.

Medical Information Systems Program Office, Tri-Service   Renamed Defense Medical Systems Support Center by memorandum of the Assistant Secretary of Defense (Health Affairs) May 3, 1985.

Medical Services Administration   Established by the *Secretary of Health, Education, and Welfare* reorganization of Aug. 15, 1967. Transferred from *Social and Rehabilitation Service* to Health Care Financing Administration by Secretary's reorganization of Mar. 8, 1977 (42 FR 13262).

Medicine and Surgery, Department of   Established in the *Veterans Administration* by act of Sept. 2, 1958 (72 Stat. 1243). Renamed *Veterans Health Services and Research Administration* in the Department of Veterans Affairs by act of Oct. 25, 1988 (102 Stat. 2640). Renamed Veterans Health Administration by act of May 7, 1991 (105 Stat. 187).

Memorial Commission, National   Established by Public Resolution 107 of Mar. 4, 1929 (45 Stat. 1699). Terminated by EO 6166 of June 10, 1933, and functions transferred to *Office of National Parks, Buildings, and Reservations,* Department of the Interior.

Mental Health, National Institute of   Established by act of July 3, 1946 (60 Stat. 425). Made entity within the Alcohol, Drug Abuse, and Mental Health Administration by act of May 14, 1974 (88 Stat. 135). Functions transferred to the Department of Health and Human Services by act of Oct. 17, 1979 (93 Stat. 695). (*See also* act of Oct. 27, 1986; 100 Stat. 3207–106.) Abolished by act of July 10, 1992 (106 Stat. 331). Reestablished by act of July 10, 1992 (106 Stat. 364).

Metals Reserve Company   Established June 28, 1940, by act of Jan. 22, 1932 (47 Stat. 5). Transferred from *Federal Loan Agency* to the Department of Commerce by EO 9071 of Feb. 24, 1942. Returned to *Federal Loan Agency* by act of Feb. 24, 1945 (59 Stat. 5). Dissolved by act of June 30, 1945 (59 Stat. 310), and functions transferred to *Reconstruction Finance Corporation.*

Metric Board, U.S.   Established by act of Dec. 23, 1975 (89 Stat. 1007). Terminated Oct. 1, 1982, due to lack of funding.

Mexican-American Affairs, Interagency Committee on   Established by Presidential memorandum of June 9, 1967. Renamed *Cabinet Committee on Opportunities for Spanish-Speaking People* by act of Dec. 30, 1969 (83 Stat. 838). Terminated Dec. 30, 1974, pursuant to terms of act.

Mexican Claims Commission, American   Established by act of Dec. 18, 1942 (56 Stat. 1058). Terminated Apr. 4, 1947, by act of Apr. 3, 1945 (59 Stat. 59).

Mexican Claims Commission, Special   Established by act of Apr. 10, 1935 (49 Stat. 149). Terminated by EO 7909 of June 15, 1938.

Mexico Commission for Border Development and Friendship, U.S.   Established through exchange of notes of Nov. 30 and Dec. 3, 1966, between U.S. and Mexico. Terminated Nov. 5, 1969.

Micronesian Claims Commission   Established by act of July 1, 1971 (85 Stat. 92). Terminated Aug. 3, 1976, pursuant to terms of act.

Migration, Intergovernmental Committee for European   Renamed Intergovernmental Committee for Migration by Resolution 624, passed by *Intergovernmental Committee for European Migration Council,* effective Nov. 11, 1980.

Migration, International Committee for   Created in 1951. Renamed International Organization for Migration pursuant to article 29, paragraph 2, of the ICM constitution, effective Nov. 14, 1989.

Migratory Bird Conservation Commission   Chairmanship transferred from the Secretary of Agriculture to the Secretary of the Interior by Reorg. Plan No. II of 1939, effective July 1, 1939.

Military Air Transport Service   Renamed *Military Airlift Command* in U.S. Air Force by HQ MATS/MAC Special Order G–164 of Jan. 1, 1966.

Military Airlift Command   Inactivated June 1, 1992.

Military Appeals, United States Court of   Established under Article I of the Constitution of the United States pursuant to act of May 5, 1950, as amended. Renamed United States Court of Appeals for the Armed Forces by act of Oct. 5, 1994 (108 Stat. 2831).

Military Establishment, National   Established as executive department of the Government by act of July 26, 1947 (61 Stat. 495). Designated Department of Defense by act of Aug. 10, 1949 (63 Stat. 579).

Military Intelligence College, Joint   Established by DoD Directive 3305.1 of January 14, 1998. Renamed *National Defense Intelligence College by DOD Instruction 3305.01 of Dec. 22, 2006. See also* Defense Intelligence College.

Military Purchases, Interdepartmental Committee for Coordination of Foreign and Domestic   Informal liaison committee created on Presidential notification of Dec. 6, 1939, to the Secretaries of the Treasury and War and the Acting Secretary of the Navy. Committee dissolved in accordance with Presidential letter to the Secretary of the Treasury Apr. 14, 1941, following approval of act of Mar. 11, 1941 (55 Stat. 31).

Military Renegotiation Policy and Review Board   Established by directive of the Secretary of Defense July 19, 1948. Abolished by Secretary's letter of Jan. 18, 1952, which transferred functions to *Renegotiation Board.*

Military Sea Transportation Service   Renamed Military Sealift Command in U.S. Navy by COMSC notice of Aug. 1, 1970.

Militia Bureau   Established in 1908 as *Division of Militia Affairs, Office of the Secretary of War.* Superseded in 1933 by National Guard Bureau.

Mine Health and Safety Academy, National   Transferred from the Department of the Interior to the Department of Labor by act of July 25, 1979 (93 Stat. 111).

Minerals Exploration, Office of   Established by act of Aug. 21, 1958 (72 Stat. 700). Functions transferred to *Geological Survey* by Order 2886 of Feb. 26, 1965 of the Secretary of the Interior.

Minerals Management Service   Established on Jan. 19, 1982 by Secretarial order. Renamed as the *Bureau of Ocean Energy Management, Regulation and Enforcement* on June 18, 2010 by Secretarial order 3302. Reorganized into the Bureau of Ocean Energy Management and the Bureau of Safety and Environmental Enforcement by Secretarial order 3299 of May 19, 2010.

Minerals Mobilization, Office of   Established by the Secretary of the Interior pursuant to act of Sept. 8, 1950 (64 Stat. 798) and EO 10574 of Nov. 5, 1954, and by order of *Office of Defense Mobilization.* Succeeded by *Office of Minerals and Solid Fuels* Nov. 2, 1962. *Office of Minerals Policy Development* combined with *Office of Research and Development* in the Department of the Interior May 21, 1976, under authority of Reorg. Plan No. 3 of 1950, to form *Office of Minerals Policy and Research Analysis.* Abolished Sept. 30, 1981, by Secretarial Order 3070 and functions transferred to Bureau of Mines.

Minerals Policy and Research Analysis, Office of   *See* **Minerals Mobilization, Office of**

Minerals and Solid Fuels, Office of   Established by the Secretary of the Interior Oct. 26, 1962. Abolished and functions assigned to Deputy Assistant Secretary—Minerals and Energy Policy, Office of the Assistant Secretary—Mineral Resources, effective Oct. 22, 1971.

Mines, Bureau of   Established in the Department of the Interior by act of May 16, 1910 (36 Stat. 369). Transferred to the Department of Commerce by EO 4239 of June 4, 1925. Transferred to the Department of the Interior by EO 6611 of Feb. 22, 1934. Renamed United States Bureau of Mines by act of May 18, 1992 (106 Stat. 172). Terminated pursuant to act of Jan. 26, 1996 (110 Stat. 32). Certain functions transferred to Secretary of Energy by act of Apr. 26, 1996 (110 Stat. 1321–167).

Mining Enforcement and Safety Administration   Established by Order 2953 of May 7, 1973 of the Secretary of the Interior. Terminated by departmental directive Mar. 9, 1978, and functions transferred to Mine Safety and Health Administration, Department of Labor, established by act of Nov. 9, 1977 (91 Stat. 1319).

Minority Business Enterprise, Office of   Renamed Minority Business Development Agency by Commerce Secretarial Order DOO–254A of Nov. 1, 1979.

Minority Health and Health Disparities, National Center on   Established by act of act of Nov. 22, 2000 (114 Stat. 2501). Renamed National Institute on

Minority Health and Health Disparities by act of Mar. 23, 2010 (124 Stat. 973).

Mint, Bureau of the   Renamed U.S. Mint by Treasury Secretarial order of Jan. 9, 1984 (49 FR 5020).

Missile Sites Labor Commission   Established by EO 10946 of May 26, 1961. Abolished by EO 11374 of Oct. 11, 1967, and functions transferred to Federal Mediation and Conciliation Service.

Missouri Basin Survey Commission   Established by EO 10318 of Jan. 3, 1952. Final report of *Commission* submitted to President Jan. 12, 1953, pursuant to EO 10329 of Feb. 25, 1952.

Missouri River Basin Commission   Established by EO 11658 of Mar. 22, 1972. Terminated by EO 12319 of Sept. 9, 1981.

Mobilization, Office of Civil and Defense   *See* **Mobilization, Office of Defense and Civilian**

Mobilization, Office of Defense and Civilian   Established by Reorg. Plan No. 1 of 1958, effective July 1, 1958. Redesignated as *Office of Civil and Defense Mobilization* by act of Aug. 26, 1958 (72 Stat. 861), consolidating functions of *Office of Defense Mobilization* and *Federal Civil Defense Administration*. Civil defense functions transferred to the Secretary of Defense by EO 10952 of July 20, 1961, and remaining organization redesignated *Office of Emergency Planning* by act of Sept. 22, 1961 (75 Stat. 630).

Mobilization Policy, National Advisory Board on   Established by EO 10224 of Mar. 15, 1951. EO 10224 revoked by EO 10773 of July 1, 1958.

Monetary and Financial Problems, National Advisory Council on International   Established by act of July 31, 1945 (59 Stat. 512). Abolished by Reorg. Plan No. 4 of 1965, effective July 27, 1965, and functions transferred to President. Functions assumed by National Advisory Council on International Monetary and Financial Policies, established by EO 11269 of Feb. 14, 1966.

Monument Commission, National   Established by act of Aug. 31, 1954 (68 Stat. 1029). Final report submitted in 1957, and audit of business completed September 1964.

Monuments in War Areas, American Commission for the Protection and Salvage of Artistic and Historic   Established by President June 23, 1943; announced by Secretary of State Aug. 20, 1943. Activities assumed by the Department of State Aug. 16, 1946.

Morris K. Udall Foundation   Established by act of Mar. 19, 1992 (106 Stat 79). Renamed Morris K. Udall and Stewart L. Udall Foundation by act of Nov. 3, 2009 (123 Stat. 2977).

Mortgage Association, Federal National   Chartered Feb. 10, 1938, by act of June 27, 1934 (48 Stat. 1246). Grouped with other agencies to form *Federal Loan Agency* by Reorg. Plan No. I of 1939, effective July 1, 1939. Transferred to the Department of

Commerce by EO 9071 of Feb. 24, 1942. Returned to *Federal Loan Agency* by act of Feb. 24, 1945 (59 Stat. 5). Transferred to *Housing and Home Finance Agency* by Reorg. Plan No. 22 of 1950, effective July 10, 1950. Rechartered by act of Aug. 2, 1954 (68 Stat. 590) and made constituent agency of *Housing and Home Finance Agency*. Transferred with functions of *Housing and Home Finance Agency* to the Department of Housing and Urban Development by act of Sept. 9, 1965 (79 Stat. 667). Made Government-sponsored, private corporation by act of Aug. 1, 1968 (82 Stat. 536).

Motor Carrier Claims Commission   Established by act of July 2, 1948 (62 Stat. 1222). Terminated Dec. 31, 1952, by acts of July 11, 1951 (65 Stat. 116), and Mar. 14, 1952 (66 Stat. 25).

Mount Rushmore National Memorial Commission   Established by act of Feb. 25, 1929 (45 Stat. 1300). Expenditures ordered administered by the Department of the Interior by EO 6166 of June 10, 1933. Transferred to National Park Service, Department of the Interior, by Reorg. Plan No. II of 1939, effective July 1, 1939.

Mounted Horse Unit   Transferred from the United States Capitol Police to the United States Park Police by Public Law 109–55 of Aug. 2, 2005 (119 Stat. 572).

Munitions Board   Established in the Department of Defense by act of July 26, 1947 (61 Stat. 499). Abolished by Reorg. Plan No. 6 of 1953, effective June 30, 1953, and functions vested in the Secretary of Defense.

Munitions Board, Joint Army and Navy   Organized in 1922. Placed under direction of President by military order of July 5, 1939. Reconstituted Aug. 18, 1945, by order approved by President. Terminated on establishment of *Munitions Board* by act of July 26, 1947 (61 Stat. 505).

Museum of American Art, National   Renamed Smithsonian American Art Museum by Act of October 27, 2000 (114 Stat. 1463).

Museum of History and Technology, National   Renamed National Museum of American History in Smithsonian Institution by act of Oct. 13, 1980 (94 Stat. 1884).

Museum Services, Institute of   Established by act of June 23, 1972 (86 Stat. 327). Transferred to Office of Educational Research and Improvement, Department of Education, by act of Oct. 17, 1979 (93 Stat. 678), effective May 4, 1980. Transferred to National Foundation on the Arts and the Humanities by act of Dec. 23, 1981 (95 Stat. 1414). Functions transferred to the Institute of Museum and Library Services by act of Sept. 30, 1996 (110 Stat. 3009– 307).

Narcotics, Bureau of   Established in the Department of the Treasury by act of June 14, 1930 (46 Stat. 585). Abolished by Reorg. Plan No. 1 of 1968, effective Apr. 8, 1968, and functions transferred to *Bureau of Narcotics and Dangerous Drugs,* Department of Justice.

**Narcotics, President's Council on
Counter-**   Renamed President's Drug Policy Council
by EO 13023, Nov. 6, 1996 (61 FR 57767).

**Narcotics Control, Cabinet Committee on
International**   Established by Presidential
memorandum of Aug. 17, 1971. Terminated by
Presidential memorandum of Mar. 14, 1977.

National.   *See other part of title*

Naval Material, Office of   Established by act of Mar.
5, 1948 (62 Stat. 68). Abolished by the Department of
Defense reorg. order of Mar. 9, 1966, and functions
transferred to the Secretary of the Navy (31 FR 7188).

Naval Material Command   *See* **Naval Material
Support Establishment**

Naval Material Support Establishment   Established
by Department of the Navy General Order 5 of July
1, 1963 (28 FR 7037). Replaced by *Naval Material
Command* pursuant to General Order 5 of Apr. 29,
1966 (31 FR 7188). Functions realigned to form
Office of Naval Acquisition Support, and termination
of *Command* effective May 6, 1985.

Naval Observatory   Jurisdiction transferred from
Bureau of Navigation to Chief of Naval Operations
by EO 9126 of Apr. 8, 1942, and by Reorg. Plan No.
3 of 1946, effective July 16, 1946.

Naval Oceanography Command   Renamed Naval
Meteorology and Oceanography Command in 1995.

**Naval Petroleum and Oil Shale Reserves, Office
of**   Established by the Secretary of the Navy,
as required by law (70A Stat. 457). Jurisdiction
transferred to the Department of Energy by act of
Aug. 4, 1977 (91 Stat. 581).

Naval Reserve   Established by act of Mar. 3, 1915
(38 Stat. 940). Redesignated Navy Reserve by Public
Law 109–163 of Jan. 6, 2006 (119 Stat. 3233).

Naval Weapons, Bureau of   Established by act of
Aug. 18, 1959 (73 Stat. 395), to replace *Bureau
of Ordnance and Aeronautics*. Abolished by
Department of Defense reorg. order of Mar. 9, 1966,
and functions transferred to the Secretary of the Navy
(31 FR 7188), effective May 1, 1966.

Navigation, Bureau of   Created by act of July 5,
1884 (23 Stat. 118), as special service under the
Department of the Treasury. Transferred to the
Department of Commerce and Labor by act of Feb.
4, 1903 (32 Stat. 825). Consolidated with *Bureau of
Navigation and Steamboat Inspection* by act of June
30, 1932 (47 Stat. 415).

Navigation, Bureau of   Renamed Bureau of Naval
Personnel by act of May 13, 1942 (56 Stat. 276).

**Navigation and Steamboat Inspection, Bureau
of**   Renamed *Bureau of Marine Inspection and
Navigation* by act of May 27, 1936 (49 Stat.
1380). Functions transferred to *Bureau of Customs*,
Department of the Treasury, and U.S. Coast Guard by
EO 9083 of Feb. 28, 1942. Transfer made permanent

and *Bureau* abolished by Reorg. Plan. No. 3 of 1946,
effective July 16, 1946.

Navy, Department of   Defense housing functions
transferred to *Federal Public Housing Authority,
National Housing Agency,* by EO 9070 of Feb. 24,
1942.

**Navy Bureau of Medicine and Surgery, Dental
Division of**   Renamed Dental Corps of the Navy
Bureau of Medicine and Surgery by act of Oct. 17,
2006 (120 Stat. 2234).

Navy Commissioners, Board of   Established by act
of Feb. 7, 1815 (3 Stat. 202). Abolished by act of Aug.
31, 1842 (5 Stat. 579).

**Neighborhoods, National Commission
on**   Established by act of Apr. 30, 1977 (91 Stat. 56).
Terminated May 4, 1979, pursuant to terms of act.

**Neighborhoods, Voluntary Associations and
Consumer Protection, Office of**   Abolished
and certain functions transferred to Office of the
Assistant Secretary for Housing—Federal Housing
Commissioner and Office of the Assistant Secretary
for Community Planning and Development. Primary
enabling legislation, act of Oct. 31, 1978 (92 Stat.
2119), repealed by act of Aug. 13, 1981 (95 Stat.
398). Abolishment of *Office* and transfer of functions
carried out by Housing and Urban Development
Secretarial order.

New England River Basins Commission   Established
by EO 11371 of Sept. 6, 1967. Terminated by EO
12319 of Sept. 9, 1981.

Nicaro Project   Responsibility for management
of Nicaro nickel producing facilities in Oriente
Province, Cuba, transferred from *Office of Special
Assistant to the Administrator (Nicaro Project)* to
Defense Materials Service by General Services
Administrator, effective July 7, 1959. Facilities
expropriated by Cuban Government and nationalized
Oct. 26, 1960.

Noble Training Center   Transferred from Public
Health Service to the Center for Domestic
Preparedness, Department of Homeland Security by
act of Oct. 4, 2006 (120 Stat. 1433).

**Northern Mariana Islands Commission on Federal
Laws**   Created by joint resolution of Mar. 24, 1976
(90 Stat. 263). Terminated upon submission of final
report in August 1985.

Nursing Research, National Center for   Renamed
National Institute of Nursing Research by act of June
10, 1993 (107 Stat. 178).

Nutrition Division   Functions transferred from
Department of Health, Education, and Welfare to
the Department of Agriculture by EO 9310 of Mar.
3, 1943.

Ocean Mining Administration   Established by
Interior Secretarial Order 2971 of Feb. 24, 1975.
Abolished by Department Manual Release 2273 of
June 13, 1980.

Oceanography, Interagency Committee on   Established by *Federal Council for Science and Technology* pursuant to EO 10807 of Mar. 13, 1959. Absorbed by *National Council on Marine Resources and Engineering Development* pursuant to Vice Presidential letter of July 21, 1967.

Office   *See also other part of title*

Office Space, President's Advisory Commission on Presidential   Established by act of Aug. 3, 1956 (70 Stat. 979). Terminated June 30, 1957, by act of Jan. 25, 1957 (71 Stat. 4).

Official Register   Function of preparing *Official Register* vested in Director of the Census by act of Mar. 3, 1925 (43 Stat. 1105). Function transferred to *U.S. Civil Service Commission* by EO 6166 of June 10, 1933. Yearly compilation and publication required by act of Aug. 28, 1935 (49 Stat. 956). Act repealed by act of July 12, 1960 (74 Stat. 427), and last *Register* published in 1959.

Ohio River Basin Commission   Established by EO 11578 of Jan. 13, 1971. Terminated by EO 12319 of Sept. 9, 1981.

Oil and Gas, Office of   Established by the Secretary of the Interior May 6, 1946, in response to Presidential letter of May 3, 1946. Transferred to *Federal Energy Administration* by act of May 7, 1974 (88 Stat. 100).

Oil Import Administration   Established in the Department of the Interior by Proc. 3279 of Mar. 10, 1959. Merged into *Office of Oil and Gas* Oct. 22, 1971.

Oil Import Appeals Board   Established by the Secretary of Commerce Mar. 13, 1959, and made part of Office of Hearings and Appeals Dec. 23, 1971.

On-Site Inspection Agency   Established on Jan. 26, 1988. Functions transferred to the Defense Threat Reduction Agency by DOD Directive 5105.62 of Sept. 30, 1998.

Operations Advisory Group   Established by EO 11905 of Feb. 18, 1976. Abolished by Presidential Directive No. 2 of Jan. 20, 1977.

Operations Coordinating Board   Established by EO 10483 of Sept. 2, 1953, which was superseded by EO 10700 of Feb. 25, 1957. EO 10700 revoked by EO 10920 of Feb. 18, 1961, and *Board* terminated.

Ordnance, Bureau of   *See* **Ordnance and Hydrography, Bureau of**

Ordnance and Hydrography, Bureau of   Established in the Department of the Navy by act of Aug. 31, 1842 (5 Stat. 579). Replaced under act of July 5, 1862 (12 Stat. 510), by *Bureau of Ordnance* and *Bureau of Navigation*. Abolished by act of Aug. 18, 1959 (73 Stat. 395), and functions transferred to *Bureau of Naval Weapons*.

Organization, President's Advisory Committee on Government   Established by EO 10432 of Jan. 24, 1953. Abolished by EO 10917 of Feb. 10, 1961, and functions transferred to *Bureau of the Budget* for termination.

Organizations Staff, International   Functions merged with Foreign Agricultural Service by memorandum of Dec. 7, 1973 of, effective Feb. 3, 1974.

Overseas Private Investment Corporation   Transferred as separate agency to *U.S. International Development Cooperation Agency* by Reorg. Plan No. 2 of 1979, effective Oct. 1, 1979. Became an independent agency following the abolition of *IDCA* by act of Oct. 21, 1998 (112 Stat. 2681–790).

Oversight Board (for the Resolution Trust Corporation)   Established by act of Aug. 9, 1989 (103 Stat. 363). Renamed *Thrift Depositor Protection Oversight Board* by act of Dec. 12, 1991 (105 Stat. 1767). Abolished by act of July 29, 1998 (112 Stat. 908). Authority and duties transferred to the Secretary of the Treasury.

Pacific Northwest River Basins Commission   Established by EO 11331 of Mar. 6, 1967. Terminated by EO 12319 of Sept. 9, 1981.

Packers and Stockyards Administration   Established by Memorandum 1613, supp. 1, of May 8, 1967 of the Secretary of Agriculture. Certain functions consolidated into Agricultural Marketing Service by Secretary's Memorandum 1927 of Jan. 15, 1978. Remaining functions incorporated into the Grain Inspection, Packers and Stockyards Administration by Secretary's Memorandum 1010–1 dated Oct. 20, 1994.

Panama Canal   Operation of piers at Atlantic and Pacific terminals transferred to *Panama Railroad Company* by EO 7021 of Apr. 19, 1935. Panama Canal reestablished as *Canal Zone Government* by act of Sept. 26, 1950 (64 Stat. 1038).

Panama Canal Commission   Established by act of Oct. 1, 1979, as amended (22 U.S.C. 3611). U.S. responsibility terminated by stipulation of the Panama Canal Treaty of 1977, which transferred responsibility for the Panama Canal to the Republic of Panama, effective Dec. 31, 1999. Commission terminated by act of Sept. 30, 2004 (118 Stat. 1140).

Panama Canal Company   Established by act of June 29, 1948 (62 Stat. 1076). Abolished and superseded by *Panama Canal Commission* (93 Stat. 454).

Panama Railroad Company   Incorporated Apr. 7, 1849, by New York State Legislature. Operated under private control until 1881, when original *French Canal Company* acquired most of its stock. *Company* and its successor, *New Panama Canal Company,* operated railroad as common carrier and also as adjunct in attempts to construct canal. In 1904 their shares of stock in *Panama Railroad Company* passed to ownership of U.S. as part of assets of *New Panama Canal Company* purchased under act of June 28,

1902 (34 Stat. 481). Remaining shares purchased from private owners in 1905. *Panama Railroad Company* reincorporated by act of June 29, 1948 (62 Stat. 1075) pursuant to requirements of act of Dec. 6, 1945 (59 Stat. 597). Reestablished as *Panama Canal Company* by act of Sept. 26, 1950 (64 Stat. 1038). The Secretary of the Army was directed to discontinue commercial operations of *Company* by Presidential letter of Mar. 29, 1961.

Paperwork, Commission on Federal Established by act of Dec. 27, 1974 (88 Stat. 1789). Terminated January 1978 pursuant to terms of act.

Park Service, National Functions in District of Columbia relating to space assignment, site selection for public buildings, and determination of priority in construction transferred to *Public Buildings Administration, Federal Works Agency,* under Reorg. Plan No. I of 1939, effective July 1, 1939.

Park Trust Fund Board, National Established by act of July 10, 1935 (49 Stat. 477). Terminated by act of Dec. 18, 1967 (81 Stat. 656), and functions transferred to National Park Foundation.

Parks, Buildings, and Reservations, Office of National Established in the Department of the Interior by EO 6166 of June 10, 1933. Renamed National Park Service by act of Mar. 2, 1934 (48 Stat. 362).

Parole, Board of Established by act of June 25, 1948 (62 Stat. 854). Abolished by act of Mar. 15, 1976 (90 Stat. 219), and functions transferred to U.S. Parole Commission.

Patent Office Provisions of first patent act administered by the Department of State, with authority for granting patents vested in board comprising Secretaries of State and *War* and Attorney General. Board abolished, authority transferred to Secretary of State, and registration system established by act of Feb. 21, 1793 (1 Stat. 318). *Office* made bureau in the Department of State in October 1802, headed by *Superintendent of Patents. Office* reorganized in 1836 by act of June 4, 1836 (5 Stat. 117) under *Commissioner of Patents. Office* transferred to the Department of the Interior in 1849. *Office* transferred to the Department of Commerce by EO 4175 of Mar. 17, 1925.

Patents Board, Government Established by EO 10096 of Jan. 23, 1950. Abolished by EO 10930 of Mar. 24, 1961, and functions transferred to the Secretary of Commerce.

Pay Board Established by EO 11627 of Oct. 15, 1971. Abolished by EO 11695 of Jan. 11, 1973.

Payment Limitations, Commission on Application of Established by act of May 13, 2002 (116 Stat. 216). Abolished by acts of May 22, 2008 (122 Stat. 1025) and June 18, 2008 (122 Stat. 1753).

Peace Corps Established in the Department of State by EO 10924 of Mar. 1, 1961, and continued by act of Sept. 22, 1961 (75 Stat. 612), and EO 11041 of Aug. 6, 1962. Functions transferred to ACTION by

Reorg. Plan No. 1 of 1971, effective July 1, 1971. Made independent agency in executive branch by act of Dec. 29, 1981 (95 Stat. 1540).

Pennsylvania Avenue, Temporary Commission on Established by EO 11210 of Mar. 25, 1956. Inactive as of Nov. 15, 1969, due to lack of funding.

Pennsylvania Avenue Development Corporation Established by act of Oct. 27, 1972 (86 Stat. 1266). Terminated pursuant to act of Jan. 26, 1996 (110 Stat. 32) and act of Apr. 26, 1996 (110 Stat. 1321– 198). Functions transferred to General Services Administration, National Capital Planning Commission, and National Park Service (61 FR 11308), effective Apr. 1, 1996.

Pension and Welfare Benefit Programs, Office of *See* **Labor-Management Services Administration**

Pensions, Commissioner of Provided for by act of Mar. 2, 1833 (4 Stat. 668). Continued by act of Mar. 3, 1835 (4 Stat. 779), and other acts as *Office of the Commissioner of Pensions.* Transferred to the Department of the Interior as bureau by act of Mar. 3, 1849 (9 Stat. 395). Consolidated with other bureaus and agencies into *Veterans Administration* by EO 5398 of July 21, 1930.

Pensions, Office of the Commissioner of *See* **Pensions, Commissioner of**

Perry's Victory Memorial Commission Created by act of Mar. 3, 1919 (40 Stat. 1322). Administration of Memorial transferred to National Park Service by act of June 2, 1936 (49 Stat. 1393). *Commission* terminated by terms of act and membership reconstituted as advisory board to the Secretary of Interior

Perry's Victory Memorial Commission Created by act of Mar. 3, 1919 (40 Stat. 1322). Administration of Memorial transferred to National Park Service by act of June 2, 1936 (49 Stat. 1393). *Commission* terminated by terms of act and membership reconstituted as advisory board to the Secretary of Interior.

Personal Property, Office of *See* **Supply Service, Federal**

Personnel, National Roster of Scientific and Specialized Established by *National Resources Planning Board* pursuant to Presidential letter of June 18, 1940, to the Secretary of the Treasury. After Aug. 15, 1940, administered jointly by *Board* and *U.S. Civil Service Commission.* Transferred to *War Manpower Commission* by EO 9139 of Apr. 18, 1942. Transferred to the Department of Labor by EO 9617 of Sept. 19, 1945. Transferred with *Bureau of Employment Security* to *Federal Security Agency* by act of June 16, 1948 (62 Stat. 443). Transferred to the Department of Labor by Reorg. Plan No. 2 of 1949, effective Aug. 20, 1949, and became inactive. Roster functions transferred to National Science Foundation by act of May 10, 1950 (64 Stat. 154). Reactivated in 1950 as *National Scientific Register* by *Office of Education, Federal Security Agency,* through *National Security Resources Board* grant of funds, and continued by National Science Foundation funds until December 1952, when *Register* integrated into Foundation's National Register of Scientific and Technical Personnel project in Division of Scientific Personnel and Education.

Personnel Administration, Council of Established by EO 7916 of June 24, 1938, effective Feb. 1, 1939. Made unit in *U.S. Civil Service Commission* by EO 8467 of July 1, 1940. Renamed *Federal Personnel Council* by EO 9830 of Feb. 24, 1947. Abolished by act of July 31, 1953 (67 Stat. 300), and personnel and records transferred to *Office of Executive Director, U.S. Civil Service Commission.*

Personnel Council, Federal *See* **Personnel Administration, Council of**

Personnel Interchange, President's Commission on Established by EO 11451 of Jan. 19, 1969. Continued by EO 12136 of May 15, 1979, and renamed *President's Commission on Executive Exchange.* Continued by EO 12493 of Dec. 5, 1984. Abolished by EO 12760 of May 2, 1991.

Personnel Management, Liaison Office for Established by EO 8248 of Sept. 8, 1939. Abolished by EO 10452 of May 1, 1953, and functions transferred to *U.S. Civil Service Commission.*

Petroleum Administration for Defense Established under act of Sept. 8, 1950 (64 Stat. 798) by Order 2591 of Oct. 3, 1950 of the Secretary of the Interior, pursuant to EO 10161 of Sept. 9, 1950. Continued by Secretary's Order 2614 of Jan. 25, 1951, pursuant to EO 10200 of Jan. 3, 1951, and PAD Delegation 1 of Jan. 24, 1951. Abolished by Secretary's Order 2755 of Apr. 23, 1954.

Petroleum Administration for War *See* **Petroleum Coordinator for War, Office of**

Petroleum Administrative Board Established Sept. 11, 1933, by the Secretary of the Interior. Terminated Mar. 31, 1936, by EO 7076 of June 15, 1935. The Secretary of the Interior was authorized to execute functions vested in President by act of Feb. 22, 1935 (49 Stat. 30) by EO 7756 of Dec. 1, 1937. Secretary also authorized to establish *Petroleum Conservation Division* to assist in administering act. Records of *Petroleum Administrative Board* and *Petroleum Labor Policy Board* housed with *Petroleum Conservation Division, Office of Oil and Gas,* acting as custodian for the Secretary of the Interior.

Petroleum Coordinator for War, Office of Secretary of the Interior designated *Petroleum Coordinator for National Defense* pursuant to Presidential letter of May 28, 1941, and approved *Petroleum Coordinator for War* pursuant to Presidential letter of Apr. 20, 1942. *Office* abolished by EO 9276 of Dec. 2, 1942, and functions transferred to *Petroleum Administration for War,* established by same EO. *Administration* terminated by EO 9718 of May 3, 1946.

Petroleum Labor Policy Board Established by the Secretary of the Interior, as *Administrator of Code of Fair Competition for Petroleum Industry,*

on recommendation of Planning and Coordination Committee Oct. 10, 1933. Reorganized by Secretary Dec. 19, 1933, and reorganization confirmed by order of Mar. 8, 1935. Terminated Mar. 31, 1936, when *Petroleum Administrative Board* abolished by EO 7076 of June 15, 1935.

Petroleum Reserves Corporation Established June 30, 1943, by *Reconstruction Finance Corporation.* Transferred to *Office of Economic Warfare* by EO 9360 of July 15, 1943. *Office* consolidated into *Foreign Economic Administration* by EO 9380 of Sept. 25, 1943. Functions transferred to *Reconstruction Finance Corporation* by EO 9630 of Sept. 27, 1945. *RFC's* charter amended Nov. 9, 1945, to change name to *War Assets Corporation. Corporation* designated by *Surplus Property Administrator* as disposal agency for all types of property for which *Reconstruction Finance Corporation* formerly disposal agency. Domestic surplus property functions of *Corporation* transferred to *War Assets Administration* by EO 9689 of Jan. 31, 1946. *Reconstruction Finance Corporation Board of Directors* ordered by President to dissolve *War Assets Corporation* as soon after Mar. 25, 1946, as practicable.

Philippine Alien Property Administration Established in *Office for Emergency Management* by EO 9789 of Oct. 14, 1946. Abolished by EO 10254 of June 15, 1951, and functions transferred to the Department of Justice.

Philippine War Damage Commission Established by act of Apr. 30, 1946 (60 Stat. 128). Terminated Mar. 31, 1951, by act of Sept. 6, 1950 (64 Stat. 712).

Photographic Interpretation Center, National Functions transferred to the National Imagery and Mapping Agency by act of Sept. 23, 1996 (110 Stat. 2677).

Physical Fitness, Committee on Established in *Office of Federal Security Administrator* by EO 9338 of Apr. 29, 1943. Terminated June 30, 1945.

Physical Fitness, President's Council on *See* **Youth Fitness, President's Council on**

Physician Payment Review Commission Established by act of Apr. 7, 1986 (100 Stat. 190). Terminated by act of Aug. 5, 1997 (111 Stat. 354). Assets, staff, and continuing responsibility for reports transferred to Medicare Payment Advisory Commission.

Planning Board, National Established by *Administrator of Public Works* July 30, 1933. Terminated by EO 6777 of June 30, 1934.

Plant Industry, Bureau of Established by act of Mar. 2, 1902 (31 Stat. 922). Soil fertility and soil microbiology work of *Bureau of Chemistry and Soils* transferred to *Bureau* by act of May 17, 1935. Soil chemistry and physics and soil survey work of *Bureau of Chemistry and Soils* transferred to *Bureau* by Secretary's Memorandum 784 of Oct. 6, 1938. In February 1943 engineering research of *Bureau of Agricultural Chemistry and Engineering* transferred to *Bureau of Plant Industry, Soils, and*

Agricultural Engineering by Research Administration Memorandum 5 issued pursuant to EO 9069 of Feb. 23, 1942, and in conformity with Secretary's Memorandums 960 and 986. Functions transferred to Agricultural Research Service by Secretary's Memorandum 1320, supp. 4, of Nov. 2, 1953.

Plant Industry, Soils, and Agricultural Engineering, Bureau of   See **Plant Industry, Bureau of**

Plant Quarantine, Bureau of   See **Entomology and Plant Quarantine, Bureau of**

Policy Development, Office of   See **Domestic Council**

Post Office, Department of   See **Postal Service**

Postal Rate Commission   Renamed Postal Regulatory Commission by act of Dec. 20, 2006 (120 Stat. 3241).

Postal Savings System   Established by act of June 25, 1910 (36 Stat. 814). System closed by act of Mar. 28, 1966 (80 Stat. 92).

Postal Service   Created July 26, 1775, by Continental Congress. Temporarily established by Congress by act of Sept. 22, 1789 (1 Stat. 70), and continued by subsequent acts. *Department of Post Office* made executive department under act of June 8, 1872 (17 Stat. 283). Offices of First, Second, Third, and Fourth Assistant Postmasters General abolished and Deputy Postmaster General and four Assistant Postmasters General established by Reorg. Plan No. 3 of 1949, effective Aug. 20, 1949. Reorganized as U.S. Postal Service in executive branch by act of Aug. 12, 1970 (84 Stat. 719), effective July 1, 1971.

Power Commission, Federal   Established by act of June 10, 1920 (41 Stat. 1063). Terminated by act of Aug. 4, 1977 (91 Stat. 578), and functions transferred to the Department of Energy.

Preparedness, Office of   Renamed *Federal Preparedness Agency* by General Services Administrator's order of June 26, 1975.

Preparedness Agency, Federal   Functions transferred from General Services Administration to Federal Emergency Management Agency by EO 12148 of July 20, 1979.

President's.   *See other part of title*

Presidential.   *See other part of title*

Press Intelligence, Division of   Established in August 1933. Made division of *National Emergency Council* July 10, 1935. Continued in *Office of Government Reports* by Reorg. Plan No. II of 1939, effective July 1, 1939. Transferred to *Office of War Information* by EO 9182 of June 13, 1942, functioning in *Bureau of Special Services*. *Office* abolished by EO 9608 of Aug. 31, 1945, and *Bureau* transferred to *Bureau of the Budget*. Upon reestablishment of *Office of Government Reports*, by EO 9809 of Dec. 12, 1946, *Division of Press Intelligence* made unit of *Office*.

Price Administration, Office of   Established by EO 8734 of Apr. 11, 1941, combining *Price Division* and *Consumer Division* of *National Defense Advisory Commission*. Renamed *Office of Price Administration* by EO 8875 of Aug. 28, 1941, which transferred *Civilian Allocation Division* to *Office of Production Management*. Consolidated with other agencies into *Office of Temporary Controls* by EO 9809 of Dec. 12, 1946, except *Financial Reporting Division*, transferred to Federal Trade Commission.

Price Commission   Established by EO 11627 of Oct. 15, 1971. Abolished by EO 11695 of Jan. 11, 1973.

Price Decontrol Board   Established by act of July 25, 1946 (60 Stat. 669). Effective period of act of Jan. 30, 1942 (56 Stat. 23), extended to June 30, 1947, by joint resolution of June 25, 1946 (60 Stat. 664).

Price Stability for Economic Growth, Cabinet Committee on   Established by Presidential letter of Jan. 28, 1959. Abolished by Presidential direction Mar. 12, 1961.

Price Stabilization, Office of   Established by General Order 2 of *Economic Stabilization Administrator* Jan. 24, 1951. *Director of Price Stabilization* provided for in EO 10161 of Sept. 9, 1950. Terminated Apr. 30, 1953, by EO 10434 of Feb. 6, 1953, and provisions of acts of June 30, 1952 (66 Stat. 296) and June 30, 1953 (67 Stat. 131).

Prices and Costs, Committee on Government Activities Affecting   Established by EO 10802 of Jan. 23, 1959. Abolished by EO 10928 of Mar. 23, 1961.

Priorities Board   Established by order of *Council of National Defense*, approved Oct. 18, 1940, and by EO 8572 of Oct. 21, 1940. EO 8572 revoked by EO 8629 of Jan. 7, 1941.

Prison Industries, Inc., Federal   Established by EO 6917 of Dec. 11, 1934. Transferred to the Department of Justice by Reorg. Plan No. II of 1939, effective July 1, 1939.

Prison Industries Reorganization Administration   Functioned from Sept. 26, 1935, to Sept. 30, 1940, under authority of act of Apr. 8, 1935 (49 Stat. 115), and of EO's 7194 of Sept. 26, 1935, 7202 of Sept. 28, 1935, and 7649 of June 29, 1937. Terminated due to lack of funding.

Private Sector Programs, Office of   Functions transferred to the Office of Citizen Exchanges within the Bureau of Educational and Cultural Affairs, USIA, by act of Feb. 16, 1990 (104 Stat. 56).

Processing tax   *Agricultural Adjustment Administration's* function of collecting taxes declared unconstitutional by U.S. Supreme Court Jan. 6, 1936. Functions under acts of June 28, 1934 (48 Stat. 1275), Apr. 21, 1934 (48 Stat. 598), and Aug. 24, 1935 (49 Stat. 750) discontinued by repeal of these laws by act of Feb. 10, 1936 (49 Stat. 1106).

Processing Tax Board of Review   Established in the Department of the Treasury by act of June 22, (49

Stat. 1652). Abolished by act of Oct. 21, 1942 (56 Stat. 967).

Proclamations   See **State, Department of**

Procurement, Commission on Government   Established by act of Nov. 26, 1969 (83 Stat. 269). Terminated Apr. 30, 1973, due to expiration of statutory authority.

Procurement and Assignment Service   Established by President Oct. 30, 1941. Transferred from *Office of Defense Health and Welfare Services* to *War Manpower Commission* by EO 9139 of Apr. 18, 1942. Transferred to *Federal Security Agency* by EO 9617 of Sept. 19, 1945, which terminated *Commission.*

Procurement Division   Established in the Department of the Treasury by EO 6166 of June 10, 1933. Renamed *Bureau of Federal Supply* by Department of the Treasury Order 73 of Nov. 19, 1946, effective Jan. 1, 1947. Transferred to General Services Administration as Federal Supply Service by act of June 30, 1949 (63 Stat. 380).

Procurement Policy, Office of Federal   Established within Office of Management and Budget by act of Aug. 30, 1974 (88 Stat. 97). Abolished due to lack of funding and functions transferred to Office of Management and Budget by act of Oct 28, 1993 (107 Stat. 1236).

Product Standards Policy, Office of   Formerly separate operating unit under Assistant Secretary for Productivity, Technology, and Innovation, Department of Commerce. Transferred to *National Bureau of*

Production Areas, Committee for Congested   Established in Executive Office of the President by EO 9327 of Apr. 7, 1943. Terminated Dec. 31, 1944, by act of June 28, 1944 (58 Stat. 535).

Production Authority, National   Established in the Department of Commerce Sept. 11, 1950, by EO's 10161 of Sept. 9, 1950, 10193 of Dec. 16, 1950, and 10200 of Jan. 3, 1951. Abolished by order of Oct. 1, 1953 of the Secretary of Commerce, and functions merged into *Business and Defense Services Administration.*

Production Management, Office of   Established in *Office for Emergency Management* by EO 8629 of Jan. 7, 1941. Abolished by EO 9040 of Jan. 24, 1942, and personnel and property transferred to *War Production Board.*

Production and Marketing Administration   Established by Secretary of Agriculture Memorandum 1118 of Aug. 18, 1945. Functions transferred under Department reorganization by Secretary's Memorandum 1320, supp. 4, of Nov. 2, 1953.

Productivity Council, National   Established by EO 12089 of Oct. 23, 1978. EO 12089 revoked by EO 12379 of Aug. 17, 1982.

Programs, Bureau of International   Established by the Secretary of Commerce Aug. 8, 1961, by Departmental Orders 173 and 174. Abolished by Departmental Order 182 of Feb. 1, 1963, which established *Bureau of International Commerce.* Functions transferred to *Domestic and International Business Administration,* effective Nov. 17, 1972.

Programs, Office of Public   Established in the National Archives and Records Administration. Reorganized by Archivist under Notice 96–260, Sept. 23, 1996, effective Jan. 6, 1997. Functions restructured and transferred to Office of Records Services—Washington, DC.

Prohibition, Bureau of   Established by act of May 27, 1930 (46 Stat. 427). Investigative functions consolidated with functions of *Bureau of Investigation* into *Division of Investigation,* Department of Justice. by EO 6166 of June 10, 1933, which set as effective date Mar. 2, 1934, or such later date as fixed by President. All other functions performed by *Bureau of Prohibition* ordered transferred to such division in the Department of Justice as deemed desirable by Attorney General.

Property, Office of Surplus   Established in *Procurement Division,* Department of the Treasury, by EO 9425 of Feb. 19, 1944, and act of Oct. 3, 1944 (58 Stat. 765), under general direction of *Surplus Property Board* established by same legislation. Transferred to the Department of Commerce by EO 9541 of Apr. 19, 1945. Terminated by EO 9643 of Oct. 19, 1945, and activities and personnel transferred to *Reconstruction Finance Corporation.*

Property Administration, Surplus   See **War Property Administration, Surplus**

Property Board, Surplus   See **War Property Administration, Surplus**

Property Council, Federal   Established by EO 11724 of June 25, 1973, and reconstituted by FO 11954 of Jan. 7, 1977. Terminated by EO 12030 of Dec. 15, 1977.

Property Management and Disposal Service   See **Emergency Procurement Service**

Property Office, Surplus   Established in *Division of Territories and Island Possessions,* Department of the Interior, under Regulation 1 of *Surplus Property Board,* Apr. 2, 1945. Transferred to *War Assets Administration* by EO 9828 of Feb. 21, 1947.

Property Review Board   Established by EO 12348 of Feb. 25, 1982. EO 12348 revoked by EO 12512 of Apr. 29, 1985.

Protective Service, Federal   Functions established in the *Federal Works* Agency by act of June 1, 1948 (62 Stat. 281). Functions transferred to General Services Administrator by act of June 30, 1949 (63 Stat. 380). Established as an agency within General Services Administration by GSA Administrator on Jan. 11, 1971 (ADM. 5440.46). Transferred to Homeland Security Department by act of Nov. 25, 2002 (116 Stat. 2178).

**Prospective Payment Assessment
Commission**   Established by act of Apr. 20, 1983 (97 Stat. 159). Terminated by act of Aug. 5, 1997 (111 Stat. 354). Assets, staff, and continuing responsibility for reports transferred to the Medicare Payment Advisory Commission.

Provisions and Clothing, Bureau of   Established by acts of Aug. 31, 1842 (5 Stat. 579), and July 5, 1862 (12 Stat. 510). Designated *Bureau of Supplies and Accounts* by act of July 19, 1892 (27 Stat. 243). Abolished by Department of Defense reorg. order of Mar. 9, 1966, and functions transferred to the Secretary of the Navy (31 FR 7188).

Public   *See other part of title*

**Publications Commission, National
Historical**   Established by act of Oct. 22, 1968 (82 Stat. 1293). Renamed National Historical Publications and Records Commission by act of Dec. 22, 1974 (88 Stat. 1734).

**Puerto Rican Hurricane Relief
Commission**   Established by act of Dec. 21, 1928 (45 Stat. 1067). No loans made after June 30, 1934, and *Commission* abolished June 3, 1935, by Public Resolution 22 (49 Stat. 320). Functions transferred to *Division of Territories and Island Possessions,* Department of the Interior. After June 30, 1946, collection work performed in *Puerto Rico Reconstruction Administration.* Following termination of *Administration,* remaining collection functions transferred to the Secretary of Agriculture by act of July 11, 1956 (70 Stat. 525).

Puerto Rico, U.S.-Puerto Rico Commission on the Status of   Established by act of Feb. 20, 1964 (78 Stat. 17). Terminated by terms of act.

**Puerto Rico Reconstruction
Administration**   Established in the Department of the Interior by EO 7057 of May 28, 1935. Terminated Feb. 15, 1955, by act of Aug. 15, 1953 (67 Stat. 584).

Radiation Biology Laboratory   *See* **Radiation and Organisms, Division of**

Radiation Council, Federal   Established by EO 10831 of Aug. 14, 1959, and act of Sept. 23, 1959 (73 Stat. 688). Abolished by Reorg. Plan No. 3 of 1970, effective Dec. 2, 1970, and functions transferred to Environmental Protection Agency.

Radiation and Organisms, Division of   Established by Secretarial order of May 1, 1929, as part of Smithsonian Astrophysical Observatory. Renamed *Radiation Biology Laboratory* by Secretarial order of Feb. 16, 1965. Merged with *Chesapeake Center for Environmental Studies* by Secretarial order of July 1, 1983, to form Smithsonian Environmental Research Center.

Radio Commission, Federal   Established by act of Feb. 23, 1927 (44 Stat. 1162). Abolished by act of June 19, 1934 (48 Stat. 1102), and functions transferred to Federal Communications Commission.

Radio Division   Established by *National Emergency Council* July 1, 1938. Transferred to *Office of Education, Federal Security Agency,* by Reorg. Plan No. II of 1939, effective July 1, 1939. Terminated June 30, 1940, by terms of act of June 30, 1939 (53 Stat. 927).

Radio Propagation Laboratory, Central   Transferred from *National Bureau of Standards* to *Environmental Science Services Administration* by the Department of Commerce Order 2–A, effective July 13, 1965.

Radiological Health, National Center for Devices and   Renamed Center for Devices and Radiological Health by Food and Drug Administration notice of Mar. 9, 1984 (49 FR 10166).

Rail Public Counsel, Office of   Established by act of Feb. 5, 1976 (90 Stat. 51). Terminated Dec. 1, 1979, due to lack of funding.

Railroad Administration, U.S.   *See* **Railroads, Director General of**

Railroad and Airline Wage Board   Established by *Economic Stabilization Administrator's* General Order 7 of Sept. 27, 1951, pursuant to act of Sept. 8, 1950 (64 Stat. 816). Terminated Apr. 30, 1953, by EO 10434 of Feb. 6, 1953, and acts of June 30, 1952 (66 Stat. 296), and June 30, 1953 (67 Stat. 131).

Railroads, Director General of   Established under authority of act of Aug. 29, 1916 (39 Stat. 645). Organization of *U.S. Railroad Administration* announced Feb. 9, 1918. Office abolished by Reorg. Plan No. II of 1939, effective July 1, 1939, and functions transferred to the Secretary of the Treasury.

Railway Association, U.S.   Established by act of Jan. 2, 1974 (87 Stat. 985). Terminated Apr. 1, 1987, by act of Oct. 21, 1986 (100 Stat. 1906).

Railway Labor Panel, National   Established by EO 9172 of May 22, 1942. EO 9172 revoked by EO 9883 of Aug. 11, 1947.

Reagan Centennial Commission, Ronald   Established by act of June 2, 2009 (123 Stat. 1767). Terminated May 31, 2011, by act of May 12, 2011 (125 Stat. 215).

Real Estate Board, Federal   Established by EO 8034 of Jan. 14, 1939. Abolished by EO 10287 of Sept. 6, 1951.

Reclamation, Bureau of   *See* **Reclamation Service**

Reclamation Service   Established July 1902 in *Geological Survey* by the Secretary of the Interior, pursuant to act of June 17, 1902 (32 Stat. 388). Separated from Survey in 1907 and renamed *Bureau of Reclamation* June 1923. Power marketing functions transferred to the Department of Energy by act of Aug. 4, 1977 (91 Stat. 578). *Bureau* renamed *Water and Power Resources Service* by Secretarial Order 3042 of Nov. 6, 1979. Renamed Bureau of Reclamation by Secretarial Order 3064 of May 18, 1981.

Reconciliation Service Established by Director of Selective Service pursuant to EO 11804 of Sept. 16, 1974. Program terminated Apr. 2, 1980.

Reconstruction Finance Corporation Established Feb. 2, 1932, by act of Jan. 22, 1932 (47 Stat. 5). Grouped with other agencies to form *Federal Loan Agency* by Reorg. Plan No. I of 1939, effective July 1, 1939. Transferred to the Department of Commerce by EO 9071 of Feb. 24, 1942. Returned to *Federal Loan Agency* by act of Feb. 24, 1945 (59 Stat. 5). *Agency* abolished by act of June 30, 1947 (61 Stat. 202), and functions assumed by *Corporation*. Functions relating to financing houses or site improvements, authorized by act of Aug. 10, 1948 (61 Stat. 1275), transferred to *Housing and Home Finance Agency* by Reorg. Plan No. 23 of 1950, effective July 10, 1950. *Corporation* Board of Directors, established by act of Jan. 22, 1932 (47 Stat. 5), abolished by Reorg. Plan No. 1 of 1951, effective May 1, 1951, and functions transferred to Administrator and *Loan Policy Board* established by same plan, effective Apr. 30, 1951. Act of July 30, 1953 (67 Stat. 230), provided for *RFC* succession until June 30, 1954, and for termination of its lending powers Sept. 28, 1953. Certain functions assigned to appropriate agencies for liquidation by Reorg. Plan No. 2 of 1954, effective July 1, 1954. *Corporation* abolished by Reorg. Plan No. 1 of 1957, effective June 30, 1957, and functions transferred to *Housing and Home Finance Agency*, General Services Administration, Small Business Administration, and the Department of the Treasury.

Records Administration, Office of Established in the National Archives and Records Administration. Reorganized by Archivist under Notice 96–260, Sept. 23, 1996, effective Jan. 6, 1997. Functions restructured and transferred to Office of Records Services—Washington, DC.

Records Centers, Office of Federal Established in the National Archives and Records Administration. Reorganized by Archivist under Notice 96–260, Sept. 23, 1996, effective Jan. 6, 1997. Functions restructured and transferred to Office of Regional Records Services.

Records and Information Management, Office of Functions transferred from *National Archives and Records Service* to *Automated Data and Telecommunications Service* by General Services Administrator's decision, effective Jan. 10, 1982, regionally and Apr. 1, 1982, in Washington, DC.

Recovery Administration, Advisory Council, National Established by EO 7075 of June 15, 1935. Transferred to the Department of Commerce by EO 7252 of Dec. 21, 1935, and functions ordered terminated not later than Apr. 1, 1936, by same order. *Committee of Industrial Analysis* created by EO 7323 of Mar. 21, 1936, to complete work of *Council*.

Recovery Administration, National Established by President pursuant to act of June 16, 1933 (48 Stat. 194). Provisions of title I of act repealed by Public Resolution 26 of June 14, 1935 (49 Stat. 375), and extension of *Administration* in skeletonized form authorized until Apr. 1, 1936. *Office of Administrator, National Recovery Administration,* created by EO 7075 of June 15, 1935. *Administration* terminated by EO 7252 of Dec. 21, 1935, which transferred *Division of Review, Division of Business Corporation,* and *Advisory Council* to the Department of Commerce for termination of functions by Apr. 1, 1936. *Consumers' Division* transferred to the Department of Labor by same order.

Recovery Review Board, National Established by EO 6632 of Mar. 7, 1934. Abolished by EO 6771 of June 30, 1934.

Recreation, Bureau of Outdoor Established in the Department of the Interior by act of May 28, 1963 (77 Stat. 49). Terminated by Secretary's order of Jan. 25, 1978, and functions assumed by *Heritage Conservation and Recreation Service.*

Recreation and Natural Beauty, Citizens' Advisory Committee on Established by EO 11278 of May 4, 1966. Terminated by EO 11472 of May 29, 1969.

Recreation and Natural Beauty, President's Council on Established by EO 11278 of May 4, 1966. Terminated by EO 11472 of May 29, 1969.

Recreation Resources Review Commission, Outdoor Established by act of June 28, 1958 (72 Stat. 238). Final report submitted to President January 1962 and terminated Sept. 1, 1962.

Regional Action Planning Commissions Authorized by act of Aug. 26, 1965 (79 Stat. 552). Federal role abolished through repeal by act of Aug. 13, 1981 (95 Stat. 766). At time of repeal, eight commissions—Coastal Plains, Four Corners, New England, Old West Ozarks, Pacific Northwest, Southwest Border, Southwest Border Region, and Upper Great Lakes—affected.

Regional Archives, Office of Special and Established in the National Archives and Records Administration. Reorganized by Archivist under Notice 96–260, Sept. 23, 1996, effective Jan. 6, 1997. Functions restructured and transferred between Office of Records Services—Washington, DC and Office of Regional Records Services.

Regional Councils, Federal Established by EO 12314 of July 22, 1981. Abolished by EO 12407 of Feb. 22, 1983.

Regional Operations, Executive Director of Established in Food and Drug Administration by order of May 20, 1971 of the *Secretary of Health, Education, and Welfare.* Merged into Office of Regulatory Affairs by order of Nov. 5, 1984 of the Secretary of Health and Human Services.

Regulations and Rulings, Office of Established in the U.S. Customs and Border Protection. Abolished by act of Oct. 13, 2006 (120 Stat. 1924) and functions transferred to the Office of International Trade.

Regulatory Council, U.S. Disbanded by Vice Presidential memorandum of Mar. 25, 1981. Certain functions continued in Regulatory Information Service Center.

Regulatory Relief, Presidential Task Force on Establishment announced in President's remarks Jan. 22, 1981. Disbanded and functions transferred to Office of Management and Budget in August 1983.

Rehabilitation Services Administration Functions transferred from *Department of Health, Education, and Welfare* to Office of Special Education and Rehabilitative Services, Department of Education, by act of Oct. 17, 1979 (93 Stat. 678), effective May 4, 1980.

Relief Corporation, Federal Surplus Organized under powers granted to President by act of June 16, 1933 (48 Stat. 195). Charter granted by State of Delaware Oct. 4, 1933, and amended Nov. 18, 1935, changing name to *Federal Surplus Commodities Corporation* and naming the Secretary of Agriculture, *Administrator of Agricultural Adjustment Administration,* and *Governor of Farm Credit Administration* as Board of Directors. Continued as agency under the Secretary of Agriculture by acts of June 28, 1937 (50 Stat. 323) and Feb. 16, 1938 (52 Stat. 38). Consolidated with *Division of Marketing and Marketing Agreements* into *Surplus Marketing Administration* by Reorg. Plan No. III of 1940, effective June 30, 1940. Merged into *Agricultural Marketing Administration* by EO 9069 of Feb. 23, 1942.

Relief and Rehabilitation Operations, Office of Foreign Established in the Department of State as announced by White House Nov. 21, 1942. Consolidated with *Foreign Economic Administration* by EO 9380 of Sept. 25, 1943.

Renegotiation Board Established by act of Mar. 23, 1951 (65 Stat. 7). Terminated Mar. 31, 1979, by act of Oct. 10, 1978 (92 Stat. 1043).

Rent Advisory Board Established by EO 11632 of Nov. 22, 1971. Abolished by EO 11695 of Jan. 11, 1973.

Rent Stabilization, Office of Established by General Order 9 of *Economic Stabilization Administrator* July 31, 1951, pursuant to act of June 30, 1947 (61 Stat. 193), and EO' s 10161 of Sept. 9, 1950, and 10276 of July 31, 1951. Abolished by EO 10475 of July 31, 1953, and functions transferred to *Office of Defense Mobilization. Office of Research and Development* combined with *Office of Minerals Policy Development* in the Department of the Interior May 21, 1976, under authority of Reorg. Plan No. 3 of 1950, effective May 24, 1950, to form *Office of Minerals Policy and Research Analysis.* Abolished Sept. 30, 1981, by Secretarial Order 3070 and functions transferred to *Bureau of Mines.*

Reports, Office of Government Established July 1, 1939, to perform functions of *National Emergency Council* abolished by Reorg. Plan No. II of 1939, effective July 1, 1939. Established as administrative unit of Executive Office of the President by EO 8248 of Sept. 8, 1939. Consolidated with *Office of War Information, Office for Emergency Management,* by EO 9182 of June 13, 1942. Reestablished in Executive Office of the President by EO 9809 of Dec. 12, 1946, which transferred to it functions of *Media*

Programming Division and *Motion Picture Division, Office of War Mobilization and Reconversion,* and functions transferred from *Bureau of Special Services, Office of War Information,* to *Bureau of the Budget* by EO 9608 of Aug. 31, 1945. Subsequent to enactment of act of July 30, 1947 (61 Stat. 588), functions of *Office* restricted to advertising and motion picture liaison and operation of library. Terminated June 30, 1948.

Research, Office of University Transferred from *Office of Program Management and Administration,* Research and Special Programs Administration, to Office of Economics, Office of the Assistant Secretary for Policy and International Affairs, under authority of the Department of Transportation appropriation request for FY 1985, effective Oct. 1, 1984.

Research and Development Board Established in the Department of Defense by act of July 26, 1947 (61 Stat. 499). Abolished by Reorg. Plan No. 6 of 1953, effective June 30, 1953, and functions vested in the Secretary of Defense.

Research and Development Board, Joint Established June 6, 1946, by charter of Secretaries of *War* and Navy. Terminated on creation of *Research and Development Board* by act of July 26, 1947 (61 Stat. 506).

Research and Intelligence Service, Interim Established in the Department of State by EO 9621 of Sept. 20, 1945. Abolished Dec. 31, 1945, pursuant to terms of order.

Research and Special Programs Administration Established by act of Oct. 24, 1992 (106 Stat. 3310). Abolished and certain duties and powers transferred to both the Pipeline Hazardous Materials Safety Administration and the Administrator of the Research and Innovative Technology Administration, Department of Transportation, by act of Nov. 30, 2004 (118 Stat. 2424–2426).

Research Resources, Division of Established in National Institutes of Health, Department of Health and Human Services. Renamed National Center for Research Resources by Secretarial notice of Feb. 23, 1990 (55 FR 6455) and act of June 10, 1993 (107 Stat. 178).

Research Service, Cooperative State Established by Secretary of Agriculture Memorandum 1462, supp. 1, of Aug. 31, 1961. Consolidated into *Science and Education Administration* by Secretary's order of Jan. 24, 1978. Reestablished as Cooperative State Research Service by Secretarial order of June 16, 1981.

Research and Service Division, Cooperative Functions transferred to the Secretary of Agriculture in *Farmer Cooperative Service* by act of Aug. 6, 1953 (67 Stat. 390).

Resettlement Administration Established by EO 7027 of Apr. 30, 1935. Functions transferred to the Department of Agriculture by EO 7530 of Dec. 31, 1936. Renamed *Farm Security Administration* by Secretary's Memorandum 732 of Sept. 1, 1937.

Abolished by act of Aug. 14, 1946 (60 Stat. 1062) and functions incorporated into the *Farmers' Home Administration,* effective Jan. 1, 1947. *Farmers' Home Administration* abolished, effective Dec. 27, 1994, under authority of Secretary's Memorandum 1010–1 dated Oct. 20, 1994 (59 FR 66441). Functions assumed by the *Consolidated Farm Service Agency* and the *Rural Housing and Community Development Service.*

Resolution Trust Corporation   Established by act of Aug. 9, 1989 (103 Stat. 369). Board of Directors of the Corporation abolished by act of Dec. 12, 1991 (105 Stat. 1769). Corporation functions terminated pursuant to act of Dec. 17, 1993 (107 Stat. 2369).

Resources Board and Advisory Committee, National   Established by EO 6777 of June 30, 1934. Abolished by EO 7065 of June 7, 1935, and functions transferred to *National Resources Committee.*

Resources Committee, National   Established by EO 7065 of June 7, 1935. Abolished by Reorg. Plan No. I of 1939, effective July 1, 1939, and functions transferred to *National Resources Planning Board* in Executive Office of the President. *Board* terminated by act of June 26, 1943 (57 Stat. 169).

Resources Planning Board, National   *See* **Resources Committee, National**

Retired Executives, Service Corps of   Established in ACTION by act of Oct. 1, 1973 (87 Stat. 404). Transferred to Small Business Administration by EO 11871 of July 18, 1975.

Retraining and Reemployment Administration   Established by EO 9427 of Feb. 24, 1944, and act of Oct. 3, 1944 (58 Stat. 788). Transferred from *Office of War Mobilization and Reconversion* to the Department of Labor by EO 9617 of Sept. 19, 1945. Terminated pursuant to terms of act.

Revenue Sharing, Office of   Established by the Secretary of the Treasury to administer programs authorized by acts of Oct. 20, 1972 (86 Stat. 919), and July 22, 1976 (90 Stat. 999). Transferred from the Office of the Secretary to Assistant Secretary (Domestic Finance) by Department of the Treasury Order 242, rev. 1, of May 17, 1976.

Review, Division of   Established in *National Recovery Administration* by EO 7075 of June 15, 1935. Transferred to the Department of Commerce by EO 7252 of Dec. 21, 1935, and functions terminated Apr. 1, 1936. *Committee of Industrial Analysis* created by EO 7323 of Mar. 21, 1936, to complete work of *Division.*

RFC Mortgage Company   Organized under laws of Maryland Mar. 14, 1935, pursuant to act of Jan. 22, 1932 (47 Stat. 5). Grouped with other agencies to form *Federal Loan Agency* by Reorg. Plan No. I of 1939, effective July 1, 1939. Transferred to the Department of Commerce by EO 9071 of Feb. 24, 1942. Returned to *Federal Loan Agency* by act of Feb. 24, 1945 (59 Stat. 5). Assets and liabilities

transferred to *Reconstruction Finance Corporation* by act of June 30, 1947 (61 Stat. 207).

River Basins, Neches, Trinity, Brazos, Colorado, Guadalupe, San Antonio, Nueces, and San Jacinto, and Intervening Areas, U.S. Study Commission on   Established by act of Aug. 28, 1958 (72 Stat. 1058). Terminated June 30, 1962.

River Basins, Savannah, Altamaha, Saint Mary's, Apalachicola-Chattahoochee, and Perdido-Escambia, and Intervening Areas, U.S. Study Commission on   Established by act of Aug. 28, 1958 (72 Stat. 1090). Terminated Dec. 23, 1962.

Road Inquiry, Office of   Established by the Secretary of Agriculture under authority of act of Aug. 8, 1894 (28 Stat. 264). Federal aid for highways to be administered by the Secretary of Agriculture through *Office of Public Roads and Rural Engineering* authorized by act of July 11, 1916 (39 Stat. 355), known as *Bureau of Public Roads* after July 1918. Transferred to *Federal Works Agency* by Reorg. Plan No. I of 1939, effective July 1, 1939, and renamed *Public Roads Administration.* Transferred to General Services Administration as *Bureau of Public Roads* by act of June 30, 1949 (63 Stat. 380). Transferred to the Department of Commerce by Reorg. Plan No. 7 of 1949, effective Aug. 20, 1949. Transferred to the Secretary of Transportation by act of Oct. 15, 1966 (80 Stat. 931), and functions assigned to Federal Highway Administration.

Roads, Bureau of Public   *See* **Road Inquiry, Office of**

Roads Administration, Public   *See* **Road Inquiry, Office of**

Roads and Rural Engineering, Office of Public   *See* **Road Inquiry, Office of**

Rock Creek and Potomac Parkway Commission   Established by act of Mar. 14, 1913 (37 Stat. 885). Abolished by EO 6166 of June 10, 1933, and functions transferred to *Office of National Parks, Buildings, and Reservations,* Department of the Interior.

Roosevelt Centennial Commission, Theodore   Established by joint resolution of July 28, 1955 (69 Stat. 383). Terminated Oct. 27, 1959, pursuant to terms of act.

Roosevelt Library, Franklin D.   Functions assigned to National Park Service by Reorg. Plan No. 3 of 1946, effective July 16, 1946, transferred to General Services Administration by Reorg. Plan No. 1 of 1963, effective July 27, 1963.

Roosevelt Library, Trustees of the Franklin D.   Established by joint resolution of July 18, 1939 (53 Stat. 1063). Transferred to General Services Administration by act of June 30, 1949 (63 Stat. 381). Abolished by act of Mar. 5, 1958 (72 Stat. 34), and Library operated by *National Archives and Records Service,* General Services Administration.

Roosevelt Memorial Commission, Franklin Delano   Established by joint resolution of Aug. 11, 1955 (69 Stat. 694). Terminated by act of Nov. 14, 1997 (111 Stat. 1601).

Rubber Development Corporation   Establishment announced Feb. 20, 1943, by the Secretary of Commerce. Organized under laws of Delaware as subsidiary of *Reconstruction Finance Corporation.* Assumed all activities of *Rubber Reserve Company* relating to development of foreign rubber sources and procurement of rubber therefrom. Functions transferred to *Office of Economic Warfare* by EO 9361 of July 15, 1943. *Office* consolidated into *Foreign Economic Administration* by EO 9380 of Sept. 25, 1943. *Office* returned to *Reconstruction Finance Corporation* by EO 9630 of Sept. 27, 1945. Certificate of incorporation expired June 30, 1947.

Rubber Producing Facilities Disposal Commission   Established by act of Aug. 7, 1953 (67 Stat. 408). Functions transferred to *Federal Facilities Corporation* by EO 10678 of Sept. 20, 1956.

Rubber Reserve Company   Established June 28, 1940, under act of Jan. 22, 1932 (47 Stat. 5). Transferred from *Federal Loan Agency* to the Department of Commerce by EO 9071 of Feb. 24, 1942. Returned to *Federal Loan Agency* by act of Feb. 24, 1945 (59 Stat. 5). Dissolved by act of June 30, 1945 (59 Stat. 310), and functions transferred to *Reconstruction Finance Corporation.*

Rural Areas Development, Office of   Established by Secretary of Agriculture memorandum in 1961 (revised Sept. 21, 1962). Renamed *Rural Community Development Service* by Secretary's Memorandum 1570 of Feb. 24, 1965.

Rural Business and Cooperative Development Service   Established within the Department of Agriculture by Secretary's Memorandum 1020–34 dated Dec. 31, 1991. Renamed Rural Business-Cooperative Service (61 FR 2899), effective Jan. 30, 1996.

Rural Community Development Service   Established by Secretary of Agriculture Memorandum 1570 of Feb. 25, 1965, to supersede *Office of Rural Areas Development.* Abolished Feb. 2, 1970, by Secretary's Memorandum 1670 of Jan. 30, 1970, and functions transferred to other agencies in the Department of Agriculture.

Rural Development Administration   Established within the Department of Agriculture by Secretary's Memorandum 1020–34 dated Dec. 31, 1991. Abolished Dec. 27, 1994 (59 FR 66441) under authority of Secretary's Memorandum 1010–1 dated Oct. 20, 1994. Functions assumed by the Rural Business and Cooperative Development Service.

Rural Development Committee   *See* **Rural Development Program, Committee for**

Rural Development Policy, Office of   Established initially as *Office of Rural Development Policy Management and Coordination,* Farmers Home Administration, by Secretary of Agriculture

Memorandum 1020–3 of Oct. 26, 1981. Abolished in 1986 due to lack of funding.

Rural Development Program, Committee for   Established by EO 10847 of Oct. 12, 1959. Abolished by EO 11122 of Oct. 16, 1963, which established *Rural Development Committee. Committee* superseded by EO 11307 of Sept. 30, 1966, and functions assumed by the Secretary of Agriculture.

Rural Development Service   Established by Agriculture Secretarial order in 1973. Functions transferred to *Office of Rural Development Coordination and Planning, Farmers Home Administration,* by Secretarial order in 1978.

Rural Electrification Administration   Established by EO 7037 of May 11, 1935. Functions transferred by EO 7458 of Sept. 26, 1936, to *Rural Electrification Administration* established by act of May 20, 1936 (49 Stat. 1363). Transferred to the Department of Agriculture by Reorg. Plan No. II of 1939, effective July 1, 1939. Abolished by Secretary's Memorandum 1010–1 dated Oct. 20, 1994, and functions assumed by Rural Utilities Service.

Rural Housing and Community Development Service   Established by act of Oct. 13, 1994 (108 Stat. 3219). Renamed Rural Housing Service (61 FR 2899), effective Jan. 30, 1996.

Rural Rehabilitation Division   Established April 1934 by act of May 12, 1933 (48 Stat. 55). Functions transferred to *Resettlement Administration* by *Federal Emergency Relief Administrator's* order of June 19, 1935.

Saint Elizabeth's Hospital   *See* **Insane, Government Hospital for the**

Saint Lawrence Seaway Development Corporation   Established by act of May 13, 1954 (68 Stat. 92). Secretary of Commerce given direction of general policies of *Corporation* by EO 10771 of June 20, 1958. Transferred to the Department of Transportation by act of Oct. 15, 1966 (80 Stat. 931).

Salary Stabilization, Office of   *See* **Salary Stabilization Board**

Salary Stabilization Board   Established May 10, 1951, by *Economic Stabilization Administrator's* General Order 8. Stabilization program administered by *Office of Salary Stabilization.* Terminated Apr. 30, 1953, by EO 10434 of Feb. 6, 1953, and acts of June 30, 1952 (66 Stat. 296), and June 30, 1953 (67 Stat. 131).

Sales Manager, Office of the General   Established by the Secretary of Agriculture Feb. 29, 1976. Consolidated with Foreign Agricultural Service by Secretary's Memorandum 2001 of Nov. 29, 1979.

Savings Bonds, Interdepartmental Committee for the Voluntary Payroll Savings Plan for the Purchase of U.S.   Established by EO 11532 of June 2, 1970. Superseded by EO 11981 of Mar. 29, 1977, which established Interagency Committee for the Purchase of U.S. Savings Bonds.

Savings and Loan Advisory Council, Federal Established by act of Oct. 6, 1972 (86 Stat. 770). Continued by act of Dec. 26, 1974 (88 Stat. 1739). Terminated by act of Aug. 9, 1989 (103 Stat. 422).

Savings and Loan Insurance Corporation, Federal Established by act of June 27, 1934 (48 Stat. 1246). Grouped with other agencies to form *Federal Loan Agency* by Reorg. Plan No. I of 1939, effective July 1, 1939. Transferred to *Federal Home Loan Bank Administration, National Housing Agency,* by EO 9070 of Feb. 24, 1942. Board of Trustees abolished by Reorg. Plan No. 3 of 1947, effective July 27, 1947, and functions transferred to *Home Loan Bank Board.* Abolished by act of Aug. 9, 1989 (103 Stat. 354).

Savings Bonds Division, United States Established by Departmental Order 62 of Dec. 26, 1945, as successor to the War and Finance Division, War Savings Staff, and Defense Savings Staff. Functions transferred to Bureau of Public Debt by Departmental Order 101–05 of May 11, 1994, and *Division* renamed Savings Bond Marketing Office.

Science, Engineering, and Technology, Federal Coordinating Council for Established by act of May 11, 1976 (90 Stat. 471). Abolished by Reorg. Plan No. 1 of 1977, effective Feb. 26, 1978, and functions transferred to President. Functions redelegated to Director of the Office of Science and Technology Policy and Federal Coordinating Council for Science, Engineering, and Technology, established by EO 12039 of Feb. 24, 1978.

Science, Engineering, and Technology Panel, Intergovernmental Established by act of May 11, 1976 (90 Stat. 465). Abolished by Reorg. Plan No. 1 of 1977, effective Feb. 26, 1978, and functions transferred to President. Functions redelegated to Director of Office of Science and Technology Policy by EO 12039 of Feb. 24, 1978, which established Intergovernmental Science, Engineering, and Technology Advisory Panel.

Science Advisory Committee, President's Established by President Apr. 20, 1951, and reconstituted Nov. 22, 1957. Terminated with *Office of Science and Technology,* effective July 1, 1973.

Science Exhibit-Century 21 Exposition, U.S. Established Jan. 20, 1960, by Department of Commerce Order 167. Abolished by revocation of order on June 5, 1963.

Science and Technology, Federal Council for *See* **Scientific Research and Development, Interdepartmental Committee on**

Science and Technology, Office of Established by Reorg. Plan No. 2 of 1962, effective June 8, 1962. *Office* abolished by Reorg. Plan No. 1 of 1973, effective June 30, 1973, and functions transferred to National Science Foundation.

Science and Technology, President's Committee on Established by act of May 11, 1976 (90 Stat. 468). Abolished by Reorg. Plan No. 1 of 1977, effective Feb. 26, 1978, and functions transferred to President.

Scientific and Policy Advisory Committee Established by act of Sept. 26, 1961 (75 Stat. 631). Terminated Apr. 30, 1996 under terms of act.

Scientific Research and Development, Interdepartmental Committee on Established by EO 9912 of Dec. 24, 1947. EO 9912 revoked by EO 10807 of Mar. 13, 1959, which established *Federal Council for Science and Technology.* Abolished by act of May 11, 1976 (90 Stat. 472).

Scientific Research and Development, Office of Established in *Office for Emergency Management* by EO 8807 of June 28, 1941. Terminated by EO 9913 of Dec. 26, 1947, and property transferred to *National Military Establishment* for liquidation.

Scientists and Engineers, National Committee for the Development of Established by President Apr. 3, 1956. Renamed *President's Committee on Scientists and Engineers* May 7, 1957. Final report submitted Dec. 17, 1958, and expired Dec. 31, 1958.

Scientists and Engineers, President's Committee on *See* **Scientists and Engineers, National Committee for the Development of**

Screw Thread Commission, National Established by act of July 18, 1918 (40 Stat. 912). Terminated by EO 6166 of June 10, 1933, and records transferred to the Department of Commerce, effective Mar. 2, 1934. Informal Interdepartmental Screw Thread Committee established on Sept. 14, 1939, consisting of representatives of the Departments of *War,* the Navy, and Commerce.

Sea Grant Review Panel, National Established by act of Oct. 8, 1976 (90 Stat. 1967). Renamed National Sea Grant Advisory Board by act of Oct. 13, 2008 (122 Stat. 4207.

Secret Service, United States *See* **Secret Service Division**

Secret Service Division Established July 5, 1865, as a Bureau under Treasury Department. Acknowledged as distinct agency within Treasury Department in 1883. *White House Police Force* created on October 1, 1922, and placed under supervision of *Secret Service Division* in 1930. *White House Police Force* renamed *Executive Protective Service* by act of June 30, 1970 (84 Stat. 358). *Executive Protective Service* renamed U.S. Secret Service Uniformed Division by act of Nov. 15, 1977 (91 Stat. 1371). *Treasury Police Force* merged into Secret Service on Oct. 5, 1986. U.S. Secret Service transferred to Homeland Security Department by act of Nov. 25, 2002 (116 Stat. 2224).

Security and Safety Performance Assurance, Office of Established by Secretary of Energy memorandum of December 2, 2003. Abolished by Secretary's Memorandum 2006–007929 of Aug. 30, 2006 and functions transferred to the Office of Health, Safety and Security.

Security, Commission on Government   Established by act of Aug. 9, 1955 (69 Stat. 595). Terminated Sept. 22, 1957, pursuant to terms of act.

Security, Office of the Director for Mutual   *See* Security Agency, Mutual

Security Agency, Federal   Established by Reorg. Plan No. I of 1939, effective July 1, 1939, grouping under one administration *Office of Education, Public Health Service, Social Security Board, U.S. Employment Service, Civilian Conservation Corps,* and *National Youth Administration.* Abolished by Reorg. Plan No. 1 of 1953, effective Apr. 11, 1953, and functions and units transferred to *Department of Health, Education, and Welfare.*

Security Agency, Mutual   Established and continued by acts of Oct. 10, 1951 (65 Stat. 373) and June 20, 1952 (66 Stat. 141). *Agency* and *Office of Director for Mutual Security* abolished by Reorg. Plan No. 7 of 1953, effective Aug. 1, 1953, and functions transferred to *Foreign Operations Administration,* established by same plan.

Security and Individual Rights, President's Commission on Internal   Established by EO 10207 of Jan. 23, 1951. Terminated by EO 10305 of Nov. 14, 1951.

Security Resources Board, National   Established by act of July 26, 1947 (61 Stat. 499). Transferred to Executive Office of the President by Reorg. Plan No. 4 of 1949, effective Aug. 20, 1949. Functions of *Board* transferred to Chairman and *Board* made advisory to him by Reorg. Plan No. 25 of 1950, effective July 10, 1950. Functions delegated by Executive order transferred to *Office of Defense Mobilization* by EO 10438 of Mar. 13, 1953. *Board* abolished by Reorg. Plan No. 3 of 1953, effective June 12, 1953, and remaining functions transferred to *Office of Defense Mobilization.*

Security Training Commission, National   Established by act of June 19, 1951 (65 Stat. 75). Expired June 30, 1957, pursuant to Presidential letter of Mar. 25, 1957.

Seed Loan Office   Authorized by Presidential letters of July 26, 1918, and July 26, 1919, to the Secretary of Agriculture. Further authorized by act of Mar. 3, 1921 (41 Stat. 1347). Office transferred to Farm Credit Administration by EO 6084 of Mar. 27, 1933.

Selective Service Appeal Board, National   Established by EO 9988 of Aug. 20, 1948. Inactive as of Apr. 11, 1975.

Selective Service Records, Office of   *See* Selective Service System

Selective Service System   Established by act of Sept. 16, 1940 (54 Stat. 885). Placed under jurisdiction of *War Manpower Commission* by EO 9279 of Dec. 5, 1942, and designated *Bureau of Selective Service.* Designated Selective Service System, separate agency, by EO 9410 of Dec. 23, 1943. Transferred

for liquidation to *Office of Selective Service Records* established by act of Mar. 31, 1947 (61 Stat. 31). Transferred to Selective Service System by act of June 24, 1948 (62 Stat. 604).

Self-Help Development and Technical Development, Office of   Established in *National Consumer Cooperative Bank* by act of Aug. 20, 1978 (92 Stat. 499). Abolished by act of Aug. 13, 1981 (95 Stat. 437), and assets transferred to Consumer Cooperative Development Corporation, Department of Commerce, Dec. 30, 1982.

Services, Bureau of Special   *See* Office of War Information

Services, Division of Central Administrative   Established by *Liaison Officer for Emergency Management* pursuant to Presidential letter of Feb. 28, 1941. Terminated by EO 9471 of Aug. 25, 1944, and functions discontinued or transferred to constituent agencies of *Office for Emergency Management* and other agencies.

Shipbuilding Stabilization Committee   Originally organized by *National Defense Advisory Commission* in 1940. Established August 1942 by *War Production Board.* Transferred to the Department of Labor from *Civilian Production Administration,* successor agency to *Board,* by EO 9656 of Nov. 15, 1945. Terminated June 30, 1947.

Shipping Board, U.S.   Established by act of Sept. 7, 1916 (39 Stat. 729). Abolished by EO 6166 of June 10, 1933, and functions, including those with respect to *U.S. Shipping Board Merchant Fleet Corporation,* transferred to *U.S. Shipping Board Bureau,* Department of Commerce, effective Mar. 2, 1934. Separation of employees deferred until Sept. 30, 1933, by EO 6245 of Aug. 9, 1933. Functions assumed by *U.S. Maritime Commission* Oct. 26, 1936, pursuant to act of June 29, 1936 (49 Stat. 1985).

Shipping Board Bureau, U.S.   *See* Shipping Board, U.S.

Shipping Board Emergency Fleet Corporation, U.S.   Established Apr. 16, 1917, under authority of act of Sept. 7, 1916 (39 Stat. 729). Renamed *U.S. Shipping Board Merchant Fleet Corporation* by act of Feb. 11, 1927 (44 Stat. 1083). Terminated Oct. 26, 1936, under provisions of act of June 29, 1936 (49 Stat. 1985), and functions transferred to *U.S. Maritime Commission.*

Shipping Board Merchant Fleet Corporation, U.S.   *See* Shipping Board Emergency Fleet Corporation, U.S.

Ships, Bureau of   Established by act of June 20, 1940 (54 Stat. 493), to replace *Bureau of Engineering* and *Bureau of Construction and Repair.* Abolished by Department of Defense reorg. order of Mar. 9, 1966, and functions transferred to the Secretary of the Navy (31 FR 7188).

Simpson Historical Research Center, Albert F.   Renamed Headquarters USAF Historical Research

Center by special order of Dec. 16, 1983 of the Secretary of Defense.

Small and Disadvantaged Business Utilization, Office of Established within certain Defense Departments by act of Oct. 24, 1978 (92 Stat. 1770). Renamed Office of Small Business Programs by Public Law 109–163 of Jan. 6, 2006 (119 Stat. 3399).

Smithsonian Symposia and Seminars, Office of Renamed Office of Interdisciplinary Studies by Smithsonian Institution announcement of Mar. 16, 1987.

Social Development Institute, Inter-American Established by act of Dec. 30, 1969 (83 Stat. 821). Renamed Inter-American Foundation by act of Feb. 7, 1972 (86 Stat. 34).

Social Protection, Committee on Established in *Office of Defense Health and Welfare Services* by administrative order June 14, 1941. Functions transferred to *Federal Security Agency* by EO 9338 of Apr. 29, 1943.

Social and Rehabilitation Service Established by the *Secretary of Health, Education, and Welfare* reorganization of Aug. 15, 1967. Abolished by Secretary's reorganization of Mar. 8, 1977 (42 FR 13262), and constituent units—*Medical Services Administration, Assistance Payments Administration, Office of Child Support Enforcement, and Public Services Administration*—transferred.

Social Security Administration *See* **Social Security Board**

Social Security Board Established by act of Aug. 14, 1935 (49 Stat. 620). Incorporated into *Federal Security Agency* by Reorg. Plan No. I of 1939, effective July 1, 1939. *Social Security Board* abolished and Social Security Administration established by Reorg. Plan No. 2 of 1946 (5 U.S.C. app.), effective July 16, 1946, and functions of the *Board* transferred to *Federal Security Administrator.* Social Security Administration transferred from the *Federal Security Agency* by Reorganization Plan No. 1 of 1953 (5 U.S.C. app.), effective Apr. 11, 1953, to the *Department of Health, Education, and Welfare.* Social Security Administration became an independent agency in the executive branch by act of Aug. 15, 1994 (108 Stat. 1464), effective Mar. 31, 1995.

Soil Conservation Service *See* **Soil Erosion Service**

Soil Erosion Service Established in the Department of the Interior following allotment made Aug. 25, 1933. Transferred to the Department of Agriculture by Secretary of Interior administrative order of Mar. 25, 1935. Made *Soil Conservation Service* by order of the Secretary of Agriculture, Apr. 27, 1935, pursuant to provisions of act of Apr. 27, 1935 (49 Stat. 163). Certain functions of *Soil Conservation Service* under jurisdiction of the Department of the Interior transferred from the Department of Agriculture to the Department of the Interior by Reorg. Plan No. IV of 1940, effective June 30, 1940. *Soil Conservation Service* abolished by act of Oct. 13, 1994 (108

Stat. 3225) and functions assumed by the Natural Resources Conservation Service.

Soils, Bureau of *See* **Agricultural and Industrial Chemistry, Bureau of** and **Plant Industry, Bureau of**

Solicitor General, Office of Assistant Established in the Department of Justice by act of June 16, 1933 (48 Stat. 307). Terminated by Reorg. Plan No. 2 of 1950, effective May 24, 1950.

Southeastern Power Administration Established by the Secretary of the Interior in 1943 to carry out functions under act of Dec. 22, 1944 (58 Stat. 890). Transferred to the Department of Energy by act of Aug. 4, 1977 (91 Stat. 578).

Southwestern Power Administration Established by the Secretary of the Interior in 1943 to carry out functions under act of Dec. 22, 1944 (58 Stat. 890). Transferred to the Department of Energy by act of Aug. 4, 1977 (91 Stat. 578).

Space Access and Technology, Office of Established in the National Aeronautics and Space Administration. Abolished by Administrator's order of Feb. 24, 1997.

Space Communications, Office of Established in the National Aeronautics and Space Administration. Abolished by Administrator's order of Feb. 24, 1997.

Space Payload Technology Organization, Joint Operationally Responsive Established by act of Jan. 6, 2006 (119 Stat. 3408). Abolished by acts of Oct. 17, 2006 (120 Stat. 2358) and Dec. 20, 2006 (120 Stat. 3286).

Space Science, Office of *See* **Space and Terrestrial Applications, Office of**

Space Science Board Renamed Space Studies Board by authority of the National Research Council, National Academy of Sciences, effective May 8, 1989.

Space Station, Office of Established in the National Aeronautics and Space Administration. Abolished in 1990 and remaining functions transferred to the Office of Space Flight.

Space Technology Laboratories, National Renamed John C. Stennis Space Center by EO 12641 of May 20, 1988.

Space and Terrestrial Applications, Office of Combined with *Office of Space Science* to form Office of Space Science and Applications by National Aeronautics and Space Administrator's announcement of Sept. 29, 1981.

Space Tracking and Data Systems, Office of Renamed Office of Space Operations by National Aeronautics and Space Administrator's announcement of Jan. 9, 1987.

Space Transportation Operations, Office of Combined with *Office of Space Transportation Systems* to form Office of Space Transportation

Systems, National Aeronautics and Space Administration, effective July 1982.

Space Transportation Systems, Office of See **Space Transportation Operations, Office of**

Spanish-Speaking People, Cabinet Committee on Opportunities for See **Mexican-American Affairs, Interagency Committee on**

Special. See other part of title

Specifications Board, Federal Established by *Bureau of the Budget* Circular 42 of Oct. 10, 1921. Transferred from *Federal Coordinating Service* to *Procurement Division* by order of Oct. 9, 1933 of the Secretary of the Treasury. *Board* superseded by *Federal Specifications Executive Committee*, set up by *Director of Procurement* under Circular Letter 106 of July 16, 1935.

Sport Fisheries and Wildlife, Bureau of Established in the Department of the Interior by act of Aug. 8, 1956 (70 Stat. 1119). *Bureau* replaced by U.S. Fish and Wildlife Service pursuant to act of Apr. 22, 1974 (88 Stat. 92).

Standards, National Bureau of See **Weights and Measures, Office of Standard**

State, Department of Duty of Secretary of State of procuring copies of all statutes of the States, as provided for in act of Sept. 28, 1789 (R.S. 206), abolished by Reorg. Plan No. 20 of 1950, effective May 24, 1950. Functions of numbering, editing, and distributing proclamations and Executive orders transferred from the Department of State to the *Division of the Federal Register, National Archives,* by EO 7298 of Feb. 18, 1936. Duty of Secretary of State of publishing Executive proclamations and treaties in newspapers in District of Columbia, provided for in act of July 31, 1876 (19 Stat. 105), abolished by Reorg. Plan No. 20 of 1950, effective May 24, 1950. Functions concerning publication of U.S. Statutes at Large, acts and joint resolutions in pamphlet form known as slip laws, and amendments to the Constitution; electoral votes for President and Vice President; and Territorial papers transferred from the Department of State to the Administrator of the General Services Administration by Reorg. Plan No. 20 of 1950. (*See also* **Archives Establishment, National**)

State and Local Cooperation, Division of Established by *Advisory Commission to Council of National Defense* Aug. 5, 1940. Transferred to *Office of Civilian Defense.*

State and Local Government Cooperation, Committee on Established by EO 11627 of Oct 15, 1971. Abolished by EO 11695 of Jan. 11, 1973.

State Technical Services, Office of Established by the Secretary of Commerce Nov. 19, 1965, pursuant to act of Sept. 14, 1965 (79 Stat. 697). Abolished by Secretary, effective June 30, 1970.

Statistical Board, Central Organized Aug. 9, 1933, by EO 6225 of July 27, 1933. Transferred to *Bureau*

of the Budget by Reorg. Plan No. I of 1939, effective July 1, 1939. Expired July 25, 1940, and functions taken over by *Division of Statistical Standards, Bureau of the Budget.*

Statistical Committee, Central Established by act of July 25, 1935 (49 Stat. 498). Abolished by Reorg. Plan No. I of 1939, effective July 1, 1939, and functions transferred to *Bureau of the Budget.*

Statistical Policy Coordination Committee Established by EO 12013 of Oct. 7, 1977. Abolished by EO 12318 of Aug. 21, 1981.

Statistical Reporting Service Established by Memorandum 1446, supp. 1, part 3, of 1961 of the Secretary of Agriculture. Consolidated with other departmental units into *Economics, Statistics, and Cooperatives Service* by Secretary's Memorandum 1927, effective Dec. 23, 1977. Redesignated as *Statistical Reporting Service* by Secretary's order of Oct. 1, 1981. Renamed National Agricultural Statistics Service.

Statistics Administration, Social and Economic Established Jan. 1, 1972, by the Secretary of Commerce. Terminated by Department of Commerce Organization Order 10–2, effective Aug. 4, 1975 (40 FR 42765). Bureau of Economic Analysis and Bureau of the Census restored as primary operating units of the Department of Commerce by Organization Orders 35–1A and 2A, effective Aug. 4, 1975.

Statutes at Large See **State, Department of**

Statutes of the States See **State, Department of**

Steam Engineering, Bureau of Established in the Department of the Navy by act of July 5, 1862 (12 Stat. 510). Redesignated as *Bureau of Engineering* by act of June 4, 1920 (41 Stat. 828). Abolished by act of June 20, 1940 (54 Stat. 492), and functions transferred to *Bureau of Ships.*

Steamboat Inspection Service President authorized to appoint *Service* by act of June 28, 1838 (5 Stat. 252). Secretary of Treasury authorized to establish boards of local inspectors at enumerated ports throughout the U.S. by act of Feb. 28, 1871 (16 Stat. 440). Authority to appoint boards of local inspectors delegated to *Secretary of Commerce and Labor* by act of Mar. 4, 1905 (33 Stat. 1026). Consolidated with *Bureau of Navigation and Steamboat Inspection* by act of June 30, 1932 (47 Stat. 415).

Stock Catalog Board, Federal Standard Originated by act of Mar. 2, 1929 (45 Stat. 1461). Transferred from *Federal Coordinating Service* to *Procurement Division* by order of Oct. 9, 1933 of the Secretary of the Treasury.

Strategic Defense Initiative Organization Established in 1986 as a separate agency of the Department of Defense. Renamed Ballistic Missile Defense Organization by Deputy Secretary's memorandum in May 1993.

Strategic Posture of the United States, Commission on the Implementation of the New   Established by act of Jan. 6, 2006 (119 Stat. 3431). Terminated by act of Jan. 28, 2009 (122 Stat. 328)

Strategic Services, Office of   *See* **Information, Office of Coordinator of**

Strategic Trade, Office of   Established in the U.S. Customs and Border Protection pursuant to Customs Service Reorganization plan, effective Sept. 30, 1995. Abolished by act of Oct. 13, 2006 (120 Stat. 1924) and functions transferred to the Office of International Trade.

Subversive Activities Control Board   Established by act of Sept. 23, 1950 (64 Stat. 987). Terminated June 30, 1973, due to lack of funding.

Sugar Division   Created by act of May 12, 1933 (48 Stat. 31), authorized by act of Sept. 1, 1937 (50 Stat. 903). Taken from *Agricultural Adjustment Administration* and made independent division of the Department of Agriculture by Secretary's Memorandum 783, effective Oct. 16, 1938. Placed under *Agricultural Conservation and Adjustment Administration* by EO 9069 of Feb. 23, 1942, functioning as *Sugar Agency*. Functions transferred to *Food Distribution Administration* by EO 9280 of Dec. 5, 1942.

Sugar Rationing Administration   Established by Memorandum 1190 of Mar. 31, 1947, of the Secretary of Agriculture under authority of act of Mar. 31, 1947 (61 Stat. 35). Terminated Mar. 31, 1948, on expiration of authority.

Supplies and Accounts, Bureau of   *See* **Provisions and Clothing, Bureau of**

Supplies and Shortages, National Commission on   Established by act of Sept. 30, 1974 (88 Stat. 1168). Terminated Mar. 31, 1977, pursuant to terms of act.

Supply, Bureau of Federal   *See* **Procurement Division**

Supply, Office of   Renamed Office of Procurement and Property by Smithsonian Institution announcement of Nov. 4, 1986.

Supply Committee, General   Established by act of June 17, 1910 (36 Stat. 531). Abolished by EO 6166 of June 10, 1933, effective Mar. 2, 1934, and functions transferred to *Procurement Division,* the Department of the Treasury.

Supply Priorities and Allocations Board   Established in *Office for Emergency Management* by EO 8875 of Aug. 28, 1941. Abolished by EO 9024 of Jan. 16, 1942, and functions transferred to *War Production Board.*

Supply Service, Federal   Renamed *Office of Personal Property* by General Services Administration (GSA) order, effective Sept. 28, 1982; later renamed *Office of Federal Supply and Services* by GSA order of Jan. 22, 1983; then redesignated *Federal Supply Service.* Merged with *Federal Technology Service* to form Federal Acquisition Service by GSA Order No. 5440.591 of Sept. 9, 2005. *See also* act of Oct. 6, 2006 (120 Stat. 1735).

Surveys and Maps, Federal Board of   *See* **Surveys and Maps of the Federal Government, Board of**

Surveys and Maps of the Federal Government, Board of   Established by EO 3206 of Dec. 30, 1919. Renamed *Federal Board of Surveys and Maps* by EO 7262 of Jan. 4, 1936. Abolished by EO 9094 of Mar. 10, 1942, and functions transferred to Director, *Bureau of the Budget.*

Space System Development, Office of   Established in the National Aeronautics and Space Administration. Renamed Office of Space Access and Technology in 1995.

Tariff Commission, U.S.   Established by act of Sept. 8, 1916 (39 Stat. 795). Renamed U.S. International Trade Commission by act of Jan. 3, 1975 (88 Stat. 2009).

Tax Appeals, Board of   Established as an independent agency within the executive branch by act of June 2, 1924 (43 Stat. 336). Continued by acts of Feb. 26, 1926 (44 Stat. 105) and Feb. 10, 1939 (53 Stat. 158). Renamed *Tax Court of the United States* by act of Aug. 16, 1954 (68A Stat. 879). Renamed United States Tax Court by act of Dec. 30, 1969 (83 Stat. 730).

Technical Advisory Board for First Responder Interoperability   Established by act of Feb. 22, 2012 (126 Stat. 208). Terminated on July 6, 2012 by operation of law.

Technical Cooperation Administration   Transferred from the Department of State to *Mutual Security Agency* by EO 10458 of June 1, 1953. Transferred to *Foreign Operations Administration* by Reorg. Plan No. 7 of 1953, effective Aug. 1, 1953.

Technical Services, Office of   Designated unit of Office of the Secretary of Commerce by Department Order 179, July 23, 1962. Functions transferred to *National Bureau of Standards* by Order 90 of Jan. 30, 1964.

Technology Administration   Established by act of Oct. 24, 1988 (102 Stat. 2593). Abolished by act of Aug. 9, 2007 (121 Stat. 587) and functions absorbed by National Institute of Standards and Technology, Department of Commerce.

Technology Assessment, Office of   Created by act of Oct. 13, 1972 (86 Stat. 797). Office inactive as of Sept. 30, 1995.

Technology, Automation, and Economic Progress, National Commission on   Established by act of Aug. 19, 1964 (78 Stat. 463). Terminated January 1966 pursuant to terms of act.

Technology Service, Federal   Merged with *Federal Supply Service* to form Federal Acquisition Service by General Services Administration Order No. 5440.591

of Sept. 9, 2005. *See also* act of Oct. 6, 2006 (120 Stat. 1735).

Telecommunications Adviser to the President   Established in Executive Office of the President by EO 10297 of Oct. 9, 1951. EO 10297 revoked by EO 10460 of June 16, 1953, and functions transferred to Director of *Office of Defense Mobilization.*

Telecommunications Management, Director of   Established in *Office of Emergency Planning* by EO 10995 of Feb. 16, 1962. Assignment of radio frequencies delegated to Government agencies and foreign diplomatic establishments by EO 11084 of Feb. 16, 1963. Abolished by Reorg. Plan No. 1 of 1970, effective Apr. 20, 1970.

Telecommunications Policy, Office of   Established in Executive Office of the President by Reorg. Plan No. 1 of 1970, effective Apr. 20, 1970. Abolished by Reorg. Plan No. 1 of 1977, effective Mar. 26, 1978, and certain functions transferred to President with all other functions transferred to the Department of Commerce.

Telecommunications Service, Automated Data   Renamed *Office of Information Resources Management* by General Services Administration order of Aug. 17, 1982. Later renamed Information Resources Management Service.

Temporary Controls, Office of   Established in *Office for Emergency Management* by EO 9809 of Dec. 12, 1946, consolidating *Office of War Mobilization and Reconversion, Office of Economic Stabilization, Office of Price Administration,* and *Civilian Production Administration.* Functions with respect to Veterans' Emergency Housing Program transferred to *Housing Expediter* by EO 9836 of Mar. 22, 1947. Functions with respect to distribution and price of sugar products transferred to the Secretary of Agriculture by act of Mar. 31, 1947 (61 Stat. 36). Office terminated by EO 9841 of Apr. 23, 1947, and remaining functions redistributed.

Temporary Emergency Court of Appeals   Established by act of Dec. 22, 1971 (85 Stat. 749). Abolished by act of Oct. 29, 1992, effective Apr. 30, 1993 (106 Stat. 4507). Court's jurisdiction and pending cases transferred to the United States Court of Appeals for the Federal Circuit.

Territorial Affairs, Office of   Established by Interior Secretarial Order 2951 of Feb. 6, 1973. Abolished by Departmental Manual Release 2270 of June 6, 1980, and functions transferred to Office of Assistant Secretary for Territorial and International Affairs.

Territorial papers   *See* **State, Department of**

Territories, Office of   Established by the Secretary of the Interior July 28, 1950. Functions reassigned to *Deputy Assistant Secretary for Territorial Affairs* in *Office of the Assistant Secretary—Public Land Management,* Department of the Interior, by Secretarial Order 2942, effective July 1, 1971.

Terrorism, Cabinet Committee To Combat   Established by Presidential memorandum of Sept. 25, 1972. Terminated by National Security Council memorandum of Sept. 16, 1977.

Terrorist Threat Integration Center   Established on May 1, 2003, pursuant to Presidential initiative. Transferred to the National Counterterrorism Center by act of Dec. 17, 2004 (118 Stat. 3697).

Textile National Industrial Relations Board   Established by administrative order of June 28, 1934. Abolished by EO 6858 of Sept. 26, 1934, which created *Textile Labor Relations Board* in connection with the Department of Labor. *Board* terminated July 1, 1937, and functions absorbed by *U.S. Conciliation Service,* Department of Labor.

Textile National Industrial Relations Board, Cotton   Established by original Code of Fair Competition for the Cotton Textile Industry, as amended July 10, 1934. Abolished by EO 6858 of Sept. 26, 1934.

Textile Work Assignment Board, Cotton   Amendments to Code of Fair Competition for Cotton Textile Industry approved by EO 6876 of Oct. 16, 1934, and *Cotton Textile Work Assignment Board* appointed by *Textile Labor Relations Board. Board* expired June 15, 1935.

Textile Work Assignment Board, Silk   Appointed by *Textile Labor Relations Board* following President's approval of amendments to Code of Fair Competition for Silk Textile Industry by EO 6875 of Oct. 16, 1934. Terminated June 15, 1935.

Textile Work Assignment Board, Wool   Established by EO 6877 of Oct. 16, 1934. Terminated June 15, 1935.

Textiles, Office of   Established by the Secretary of Commerce Feb. 14, 1971. Functions transferred to *Domestic and International Business Administration,* effective Nov. 17, 1972.

Thrift Depositor Protection Oversight Board.   *See* **Oversight Board (of the Resolution Trust Corporation).**

Thrift Supervision, Office of   Established by act of August 9, 1989 (103 Stat. 352). Abolished by act of July 21. 2010, (124 Stat. 1522), and functions transferred to Office of the Comptroller of the Currency, Federal Deposit Insurance Corporation, Federal Reserve Board of Governors, and Consumer Financial Protection Bureau.

Trade, Special Adviser to the President on Foreign   Established by EO 6651 of Mar. 23, 1934. Terminated on expiration of *National Recovery Administration.*

Trade Administration, International   *See* **Business and Defense Services Administration**

Trade Agreements, Interdepartmental Committee on   Established by Secretary of State in 1934 and reestablished by EO 9832 of Feb. 25, 1947. Abolished by EO 11075 of Jan. 15, 1963.

Trade and Development Program Established by act of Sept. 4, 1961, as amended (88 Stat. 1804). Designated separate entity within the *U.S. International Development Cooperation Agency* by act of Sept. 4, 1961, as amended (102 Stat. 1329). Renamed Trade and Development Agency by act of Oct. 28, 1992 (106 Stat. 3657).

Trade Expansion Act Advisory Committee Established by EO 11075 of Jan. 15, 1963. Abolished by EO 11846 of Mar. 27, 1975, and records transferred to Trade Policy Committee established by same EO.

Trade Negotiations, Office of the Special Representative for Renamed Office of the U.S. Trade Representative by EO 12188 of Jan. 4, 1980.

Trade Policy Committee Established by EO 10741 of Nov. 25, 1957. Abolished by EO 11075 of Jan. 15, 1963.

Traffic Safety, President's Committee for Established by Presidential letter of Apr. 14, 1954. Continued by EO 10858 of Jan. 13, 1960. Abolished by EO 11382 of Nov. 28, 1967.

Traffic Safety Agency, National Established in the Department of Commerce by act of Sept. 9, 1966 (80 Stat. 718). Activity transferred to the Department of Transportation by act of Oct. 15, 1966 (80 Stat. 931). Responsibility placed in *National Highway Safety Bureau* by EO 11357 of June 6, 1967.

Training and Employment Service, U.S. Established in *Manpower Administration,* Department of Labor, Mar. 17, 1969. Abolished by Secretary's letter of Dec. 6, 1971, and functions assigned to *Office of Employment Development Programs* and *U.S. Employment Service.*

Training School for Boys, National *See* **District of Columbia, Reform-School of the**

Transportation, Federal Coordinator of Established by act of June 16, 1933 (48 Stat. 211). Expired June 16, 1936, under provisions of Public Resolution 27 (49 Stat. 376).

Transportation, Office of Established in the Department of Agriculture by Secretary's Memorandum 1966 dated Dec. 12, 1978. Abolished by Secretary's Memorandum 1030–25 dated Dec. 28, 1990.

Transportation and Communications Service Established by General Services Administrator Oct. 19, 1961. Abolished by Administrator's order, effective July 15, 1972. Motor equipment, transportation, and public utilities responsibilities assigned to Federal Supply Service; telecommunications function assigned to *Automated Data Telecommunications Service.*

Transportation and Public Utilities Service Abolished by General Services

Administration order of Aug. 17, 1982. Functions transferred to various GSA organizations.

Transportation Safety Board, National Established in the Department of Transportation by act of Oct. 15, 1966 (80 Stat. 935). Abolished by act of Jan. 3, 1975 (88 Stat. 2156), which established independent National Transportation Safety Board.

Transportation Security Administration Established by act of Nov. 19, 2001 (115 Stat. 597). Functions transferred from Department of Transportation to Department of Homeland Security by act of Nov. 25, 2002 (116 Stat. 2178).

Transportation Statistics, Bureau of Established by act of Dec. 18, 1991 (105 Stat. 2172). Transferred to Research and Innovative Technology Administration, Transportation Department, by act of Nov. 30, 2004 (118 Stat. 2424).

Travel Service, U.S. Replaced by *U.S. Travel and Tourism Administration,* Department of Commerce, pursuant to act of Oct. 16, 1981 (95 Stat. 1014).

Travel and Tourism Administration, U.S. Established by act of Oct. 16, 1981 (95 Stat. 1014). Abolished by act of Oct. 11, 1996 (110 Stat. 3407).

Travel and Tourism Advisory Board Established by act of Oct. 16, 1981 (95 Stat. 1017). Abolished by act of Oct. 11, 1996 (110 Stat. 3407).

Treasury, Office of the Assistant Secretary of the— Electronics and Information Technology Established by Secretary's Order 114–1 of Mar. 14, 1983. Abolished by Secretary's Order 114–3 of May 17, 1985, and functions transferred to Office of the Assistant Secretary for Management. Certain provisions effective Aug. 31, 1985 (50 FR 23573).

Treasury, Solicitor of the Position established when certain functions of *Solicitor of the Treasury* transferred to the Department of Justice by EO 6166 of June 10, 1933. *Solicitor of the Treasury* transferred from the Department of Justice to the Department of the Treasury by same order. *Office of Solicitor of the Treasury* abolished by act of May 10, 1934 (48 Stat. 758), and functions transferred to General Counsel, the Department of the Treasury.

Treasury Police Force *See* **Secret Service Division**

Treasury Secretary, Assistant Office abolished by Reorg. Plan No. III of 1940, effective June 30, 1940, and functions transferred to Fiscal Assistant Secretary, Department of the Treasury.

Treasury Under Secretary for Enforcement, Office of Established by act of Oct. 28, 1993 (107 Stat. 1234). Office abolished by act of Dec. 8, 2004 (118 Stat. 3245), and functions transferred to the Office of the Under Secretary for Terrorism and Financial Crimes, Department of the Treasury.

Treaties *See* **State, Department of**

Typhus Commission, U.S. of America Established in *Department of War* by EO 9285 of Dec. 24, 1942. Abolished June 30, 1946, by EO 9680 of Jan. 17, 1946.

U.S. *See other part of title*

Uniformed Services University of the Health Sciences, School of Medicine of the Renamed F. Edward He'bert School of Medicine by act of Sept. 24, 1983 (97 Stat. 704).

United Nations Educational, Scientific and Cultural Organization U.S. membership in UNESCO authorized by act of July 30, 1946 (60 Stat. 712). Announcement of U.S. intention to withdraw made Dec. 28, 1983, in accordance with UNESCO constitution. Official U.S. withdrawal effective Dec. 31, 1984, by Secretary of State's letter of Dec. 19, 1984. The U.S. maintained status as an observer mission in UNESCO from 1984–2003, and rejoined the organization in October 2003.

Upper Mississippi River Basin Commission Established by EO 11659 of Mar. 22, 1972. Terminated by EO 12319 of Sept. 9, 1981.

Urban Affairs, Council for Established in Executive Office of the President by EO 11452 of Jan. 23, 1969. Terminated by EO 11541 of July 1, 1970.

Urban Mass Transportation Administration Functions regarding urban mass transportation established in the Department of Housing and Urban Development by act of July 9, 1964 (78 Stat. 302). Most functions transferred to the Department of Transportation by Reorg. Plan No. 2 of 1968, effective June 30, 1968 (82 Stat. 1369), and joint responsibility assigned to the Departments of Transportation and Housing and Urban Development for functions relating to research, technical studies, and training. Transportation and Housing and Urban Development Under Secretaries agreed in November 1969 that the Department of Transportation should be focal point for urban mass transportation grant administration; at which time functions transferred to the Department of Transportation. Renamed Federal Transit Administration by act of Dec. 18, 1991 (105 Stat. 2088).

Urban Renewal Administration Established in *Housing and Home Finance Agency* by Administrator's Organizational Order 1 of Dec. 23, 1954. Functions transferred to the Department of Housing and Urban Development by act of Sept. 9, 1965 (78 Stat. 667), and *Administration* terminated.

Utilization and Disposal Service Established July 1, 1961, by Administrator of General Services and assigned functions of Federal Supply Service and Public Buildings Service. Functions transferred to *Property Management and Disposal Service* July 29, 1966.

Veterans Administration Legal work in defense of suits against the U.S. arising under act of June 7, 1924 (43 Stat. 607), transferred to the Department of Justice by EO 6166 of June 10, 1933. Transfer deferred to Sept. 10, 1933, by EO 6222 of July 27,

1933. Established as an independent agency under the President by Executive Order 5398 of July 21, 1930, in accordance with the act of July 3, 1930 (46 Stat. 1016) and the act of Sept. 2, 1958 (72 Stat. 1114). Made an executive department in the executive branch and redesignated the Department of Veterans Affairs by act of Oct. 25, 1988 (102 Stat. 2635).

Veterans Appeals, U.S. Court of Established by act of Nov. 18, 1988 (102 Stat. 4113). Renamed U.S. Court of Appeals for Veterans Claims by act of Nov. 11, 1998 (112 Stat. 3341).

Veterans Education Appeals Board *See* **Veterans Tuition Appeals Board**

Veterans Employment and Training, Advisory Committee on Renamed Advisory Committee on Veterans Employment, Training, and Employer Outreach by act of June 15, 2006 (120 Stat. 403).

Veterans Employment Service Renamed Veterans' Employment and Training Service by Order 4–83 of Mar. 24, 1983 of the Secretary of Labor (48 FR 14092).

Veterans Health Administration *See* **Medicine and Surgery, Department of**

Veterans Health Services and Research Administration *See* **Medicine and Surgery, Department of**

Veterans Placement Service Board Established by act of June 22, 1944 (58 Stat. 293). Abolished by Reorg. Plan No. 2 of 1949, effective Aug. 20, 1949, and functions transferred to the Secretary of Labor.

Veterans Tuition Appeals Board Established by act of Aug. 24, 1949 (63 Stat. 654). Functions assumed by *Veterans Education Appeals Board* established by act of July 13, 1950 (64 Stat. 336). *Board* terminated by act of Aug. 28, 1957 (71 Stat. 474).

Veterinary Medicine, Bureau of Established in Food and Drug Administration, *Department of Health, Education, and Welfare.* Renamed Center for Veterinary Medicine by FDA notice of Mar. 9, 1984 (49 FR 10166).

Virgin Islands Public works programs under act of Dec. 20, 1944 (58 Stat. 827), transferred from General Services Administrator to the Secretary of the Interior by Reorg. Plan No. 15 of 1950, effective May 24, 1950.

Virgin Islands Company Established in 1934. Reincorporated as Government corporation by act of June 30, 1949 (63 Stat. 350). Program terminated June 30, 1965, and *Corporation* dissolved July 1, 1966.

Virgin Islands Corporation *See* **Virgin Islands Company**

Visitor Facilities Advisory Commission, National Established by act of Mar. 12, 1968 (82

Stat. 45). Expired Jan. 5, 1975, pursuant to act of Oct. 6, 1972 (86 Stat. 776).

Vocational Rehabilitation, Office of Established to administer provisions of act of July 6, 1943 (57 Stat. 374). Other duties delegated by acts of Aug. 3, 1954 (68 Stat. 652), Nov. 8, 1965 (79 Stat. 1282), July 12, 1960 (74 Stat. 364), and July 10, 1954 (68 Stat. 454). Redesignated *Vocational Rehabilitation Administration* Jan. 28, 1963. Made component of newly created *Social and Rehabilitation Service* as *Rehabilitation Services Administration* by *Department of Health, Education, and Welfare* reorganization of Aug. 15, 1967.

Vocational Rehabilitation Administration *See* **Vocational Rehabilitation, Office of**

Voluntary Citizen Participation, State Office of Renamed State Office of Volunteerism in ACTION by notice of Apr. 18, 1986 (51 FR 13265), effective May 18, 1986.

Volunteer Service, International, Secretariat for Established in 1962 by International Conference on Middle Level Manpower called by President. Terminated Mar. 31, 1976, due to insufficient funding.

Volunteers in Service to America Established by act of Nov. 8, 1966 (80 Stat. 1472). Service administered by *Office of Economic Opportunity* and functions transferred to ACTION by Reorg. Plan No. 1 of 1971, effective July 1, 1971.

Wage Adjustment Board Established May 29, 1942, by the Secretary of Labor at Presidential direction of May 14, 1942, to accomplish purpose of act of Mar. 3, 1931 (46 Stat. 1494), as amended by acts of Aug. 30, 1935 (49 Stat. 1011), and Jan. 30, 1942 (56 Stat. 23). Disbanded on termination of *National Wage Stabilization Board.*

Wage and Price Stability, Council on Established in Executive Office of the President by act of Aug. 24, 1974 (88 Stat. 750). Abolished by EO 12288 of Jan. 29, 1981. Funding ceased beyond June 5, 1981, by act of June 5, 1981 (95 Stat. 74), and authorization for appropriations repealed by act of Aug. 13, 1981 (95 Stat. 432).

Wage and Price Stability Program *See* **Wage and Price Stability, Council on**

Wage Stabilization Board Established by EO 10161 of Sept. 9, 1950. Reconstituted by EO 10377 of July 25, 1952. Terminated Apr. 30, 1953, by EO 10434 of Feb. 6, 1953, and acts of June 30, 1952 (66 Stat. 296), and June 30, 1953 (67 Stat. 131).

Wage Stabilization Board, National *See* **Defense Mediation Board, National**

Wallops Flight Center, Wallops Island, VA Formerly separate field installation of National Aeronautics and Space Administration. Made component of Goddard Space Flight Center by NASA Management Instruction 1107.10A of Sept. 3, 1981.

War, Solid Fuels Administration for Established in the Department of the Interior by EO 9332 of Apr. 19, 1943. Absorbed *Office of Solid Fuels Coordinator for War* (originally established as *Office of Solid Fuels Coordinator for National Defense*) pursuant to Presidential letter of Nov. 5, 1941; later changed by Presidential letter of May 25, 1942. Terminated by EO 9847 of May 6, 1947.

War Assets Administration Established in *Office for Emergency Management* by EO 9689 of Jan. 31, 1946. Functions transferred to *Surplus Property Administration* by Reorg. Plan No. 1 of 1947, effective July 1, 1947, and agency renamed *War Assets Administration*. Abolished by act of June 30, 1949 (63 Stat. 738), and functions transferred for liquidation to General Services Administration.

War Assets Corporation *See* **Petroleum Reserves Corporation**

War Claims Commission Established by act of July 3, 1948 (62 Stat. 1240). Abolished by Reorg. Plan No. 1 of 1954, effective July 1, 1954, and functions transferred to Foreign Claims Settlement Commission of the U.S.

War Commodities Division Established in *Office of Foreign Economic Coordination* by Department of State Order of Aug. 27, 1943. *Office* abolished by departmental order of Nov. 6, 1943, pursuant to EO 9380 of Sept. 25, 1943, which established *Foreign Economic Administration* in *Office for Emergency Management.*

War Communications, Board of *See* **Defense Communications Board**

War Contracts Price Adjustment Board Established by act of Feb. 25, 1944 (58 Stat. 85). Abolished by act of Mar. 23, 1951 (65 Stat. 7), and functions transferred to *Renegotiation Board,* established by same act, and General Services Administrator.

War Damage Corporation *See* **War Insurance Corporation**

War, Department of Established by act of Aug. 7, 1789 (1 Stat. 49), succeeding similar department established prior to adoption of the Constitution. Three military departments—Army; Navy, including naval aviation and U.S. Marine Corps; and Air Force—reorganized under *National Military Establishment* by act of July 26, 1947 (61 Stat. 495).

War Finance Corporation Established by act of Apr. 5, 1918 (40 Stat. 506). Functions and obligations transferred by Reorg. Plan No. II of 1939, effective July 1, 1939, to the Secretary of the Treasury for liquidation not later than Dec. 31, 1939.

War Food Administration *See* **Food Production and Distribution, Administration of**

War Information, Office of Established in *Office of Emergency Management* by EO 9182 of June 13, 1942, consolidating *Office of Facts and Figures; Office of Government Reports; Division of Information, Office for Emergency Management;* and

Foreign Information Service—Outpost, Publications, and Pictorial Branches, Coordinator of Information. Abolished by EO 9608 of Aug. 31, 1945. *Bureau of Special Services* and functions with respect to review of publications of Federal agencies transferred to *Bureau of the Budget.* Foreign information activities transferred to the Department of State.

War Insurance Corporation   Established Dec. 13, 1941, by act of June 10, 1941 (55 Stat. 249). Charter filed Mar. 31, 1942. Renamed *War Damage Corporation* by act of Mar. 27, 1942 (56 Stat. 175). Transferred from *Federal Loan Agency* to the Department of Commerce by EO 9071 of Feb. 24, 1942. Returned to *Federal Loan Agency* by act of Feb. 24, 1945 (59 Stat. 5). *Agency* abolished by act of June 30, 1947 (61 Stat. 202), and functions assumed by *Reconstruction Finance Corporation.* Powers of *War Damage Corporation,* except for purposes of liquidation, terminated as of Jan. 22, 1947.

War Labor Board, National   See **Defense Mediation Board, National**

War Manpower Commission   Established in *Office for Emergency Management* by EO 9139 of Apr. 18, 1942. Terminated by EO 9617 of Sept. 19, 1945, and functions, except *Procurement and Assignment Service,* transferred to the Department of Labor.

War Mobilization, Office of   Established by EO 9347 of May 27, 1943. Transferred to *Office of War Mobilization and Reconversion* by EO 9488 of Oct. 3, 1944.

War Mobilization and Reconversion, Office of   Established by act of Oct. 3, 1944 (58 Stat. 785). Consolidated with other agencies by EO 9809 of Dec. 12, 1946, to form *Office of Temporary Controls. Media Programming Division* and *Motion Picture Division* transferred to *Office of Government Reports,* reestablished by same order. Certain other functions transferred to President and the Secretary of Commerce.

War Mobilization and Reconversion Advisory Board, Office of   Established by act of Oct. 3, 1944 (58 Stat. 788). Transferred to *Office of Temporary Controls* by EO 9809 of Dec. 12, 1946.

War Plants Corporation, Smaller   Established by act of June 11, 1942 (56 Stat. 351). Functions transferred by EO 9665 of Dec. 27, 1945, to *Reconstruction Finance Corporation* and the Department of Commerce. Abolished by act of June 30, 1947 (61 Stat. 202), and functions transferred for liquidation to General Services Administration by Reorg. Plan No. 1 of 1957, effective July 1, 1957.

War and Post War Adjustment Policies, Advisory Unit on   Established in *Office of War Mobilization* by Presidential direction Nov. 6, 1943. Report submitted Feb. 15, 1944, and Unit Director and Assistant Director submitted letter to Director of *War Mobilization* ending their work May 12, 1944.

War Production Board   Established in *Office for Emergency Management* by EO 9024 of Jan. 16, 1942. *Board* terminated and successor agency,

Civilian Production Administration, established by EO 9638 of Oct. 4, 1945.

War Property Administration, Surplus   Established in *Office of War Mobilization* by EO 9425 of Feb. 19, 1944. Terminated on establishment of *Surplus Property Board* by act of Oct. 3, 1944 (58 Stat. 768). *Surplus Property Administration* established in *Office of War Mobilization and Reconversion* by act of Sept. 18, 1945 (59 Stat. 533), and *Board* abolished. Domestic functions of *Administration* merged into *War Assets Corporation, Reconstruction Finance Corporation,* by EO 9689 of Jan. 31, 1946. Foreign functions transferred to the Department of State by same order. Transfers made permanent by Reorg. Plan No. 1 of 1947, effective July 1, 1947.

War Refugee Board   Established in Executive Office of the President by EO 9417 of Jan. 22, 1944. Terminated by EO 9614 of Sept. 14, 1945.

War Relations, Agricultural, Office for   See **Farm Products, Division of**

War Relief Agencies, President's Committee on   Established by Presidential letter of Mar. 13, 1941. *President's War Relief Control Board* established by EO 9205 of July 25, 1942, to succeed *Committee. Board* terminated by EO 9723 of May 14, 1946, and functions transferred to the Department of State.

War Relief Control Board, President's   See **President's Committee on War Relief Agencies**

War Relocation Authority   Established in *Office for Emergency Management* by EO 9102 of Mar. 18, 1942. Transferred to the Department of the Interior by EO 9423 of Feb. 16, 1944. Terminated by EO 9742 of June 25, 1946.

War Resources Board   Established in August 1939 as advisory committee to work with *Joint Army and Navy Munitions Board.* Terminated by President Nov. 24, 1939.

War Resources Council   See **Defense Resources Committee**

War Shipping Administration   Established in *Office for Emergency Management* by EO 9054 Feb. 7, 1942. Terminated by act of July 8, 1946 (60 Stat. 501), and functions transferred to *U.S. Maritime Commission,* effective Sept. 1, 1946.

Water, Office of Saline   Established to perform functions vested in the Secretary of the Interior by act of July 29, 1971 (85 Stat. 159). Merged with *Office of Water Resources Research* to form *Office of Water Research and Technology* by Secretary's Order 2966 of July 26, 1974.

Water Commission, National   Established by act of Sept. 26, 1968 (82 Stat. 868). Terminated Sept. 25, 1973, pursuant to terms of act.

Water Policy, Office of   Established by Department of the Interior Manual Release 2374 of Dec. 29, 1981, under authority of Assistant Secretary.

Abolished by Secretarial Order No. 3096 of Oct. 19, 1983, and functions transferred to *Geological Survey* and *Office of Policy Analysis*.

Water Pollution Control Administration, Federal Established under the *Secretary of Health, Education, and Welfare* by act of Oct. 2, 1965 (79 Stat. 903). Transferred to the Department of the Interior by Reorg. Plan No. 2 of 1966, effective May 10, 1966. Renamed *Federal Water Quality Administration* by act of Apr. 3, 1970. Abolished by Reorg. Plan No. 3 of 1970, effective Dec. 2, 1970, and functions transferred to Environmental Protection Agency.

Water and Power Resources Service Renamed Bureau of Reclamation May 18, 1981, by Interior Secretarial Order 3064.

Water Quality Administration, Federal *See* **Water Pollution Control Administration, Federal Water**

Research and Technology, Office of Established by Interior Secretarial Order 2966 of July 26, 1974. Abolished by Secretarial order of Aug. 25, 1982, and functions transferred to Bureau of Reclamation, Geological Survey, and *Office of Water Policy*.

Water Resources Council Established by act of July 22, 1965 (89 Stat 575). Inactive as of Oct. 1, 1982.

Water Resources Research, Office of Established to perform functions vested in the Secretary of the Interior by act of July 17, 1964 (78 Stat. 329). Merged with *Office of Saline Water* to form *Office of Water Research and Technology* by Secretary's Order 2966 of July 26, 1974.

Watergate Special Prosecution Force Established by Attorney General order, effective May 25, 1973. Terminated by Attorney General order, effective June 20, 1977.

Waterways Corporation, Inland Incorporated under act of June 3, 1924 (43 Stat. 360). Transferred from the *Department of War* to the Department of Commerce by Reorg. Plan No. II of 1939, effective July 1, 1939. *Corporation* sold to *Federal Waterways Corporation* under contract of July 24, 1953. Renamed *Federal Barge Lines, Inc.* Liquidated by act of July 19, 1963 (77 Stat. 81).

Weather Bureau Established in the Department of Agriculture by act of Oct. 1, 1890 (26 Stat. 653). Transferred to the Department of Commerce by Reorg. Plan No. IV of 1940, effective June 30, 1940. Functions transferred to *Environmental Science Services Administration* by Reorg. Plan No. 2 of 1965, effective July 13, 1965.

Weather Control, Advisory Committee on Established by act of Aug. 13, 1953 (67 Stat. 559). Act of Aug. 28, 1957 (71 Stat. 426), provided for termination by Dec. 31, 1957.

Weed and Seed, Executive Office of Abolished by Public Law 109–162 of Jan. 5, 2006 (119 Stat. 3107). Functions transferred to Office of Weed and

Seed Strategies, Office of Justice Programs, within the Department of Justice.

Weights and Measures, Office of Standard Renamed *National Bureau of Standards* by act of Mar. 3, 1901 (31 Stat. 1449). *Bureau* transferred from the Department of the Treasury to the *Department of Commerce and Labor* by act of Feb. 14, 1903 (32 Stat. 825). *Bureau* established within the Department of Commerce by act of Mar. 4, 1913 (37 Stat. 736). Renamed National Institute of Standards and Technology by act of Aug. 23, 1988 (102 Stat. 1827).

Welfare Administration Established by the *Secretary of Health, Education, and Welfare* reorganization of Jan. 28, 1963. Components consisted of *Bureau of Family Services, Children's Bureau, Office of Juvenile Delinquency and Youth Development,* and *Cuban Refugee Staff.* These functions reassigned to *Social and Rehabilitation Service* by Department reorganization of Aug. 15, 1967.

White House Police Force *See* **Secret Service Division**

Wilson Memorial Commission, Woodrow Established by act of Oct. 4, 1961 (75 Stat. 783). Terminated on submittal of final report to President and Congress Sept. 29, 1966.

Women, Interdepartmental Committee on the Status of Established by EO 11126 of Nov. 1, 1963. Terminated by EO 12050 of Apr. 4, 1978.

Women, President's Commission on the Status of Established by EO 10980 of Dec. 14, 1961. Submitted final report to President Oct. 11, 1963.

Women's Army Auxiliary Corps Established by act of May 14, 1942 (56 Stat. 278). Repealed in part and superseded by act of July 1, 1943 (57 Stat. 371), which established *Women's Army Corps. Corps* abolished by the Secretary of Defense Apr. 24, 1978, pursuant to provisions of 10 U.S.C. 125A.

Women's Business Enterprise Division Renamed *Office of Women's Business Enterprise* by Small Business Administrator's reorganization, effective Aug. 19, 1981. Renamed Office of Women's Business Ownership Aug. 19, 1982.

Women's Reserve Established in U.S. Coast Guard by act of Nov. 23, 1942 (56 Stat. 1020).

Women's Year, 1975, National Commission on the Observance of International Established by EO 11832 of Jan. 9, 1975. Continued by act of Dec. 23, 1975 (89 Stat. 1003). Terminated Mar. 31, 1978, pursuant to terms of act.

Wood Utilization, National Committee on Established by Presidential direction in 1925. Abolished by EO 6179–B of June 16, 1933.

Work Projects Administration *See* **Works Progress Administration**

Work-Training Programs, Bureau of Abolished by reorganization of *Manpower Administration* and functions assigned to *U.S. Training and Employment Service,* effective Mar. 17, 1969.

Working Group on Streamlining Paperwork for Executive Nominations Established by act of Aug. 10, 2012 (126 Stat. 1292). Terminated July 7, 2013, pursuant to terms of act.

Working Life, Productivity and Quality of, National Center for Established by act of Nov. 28, 1975 (89 Stat. 935). Authorized appropriations expired Sept. 30, 1978, and functions assumed by *National Productivity Council.*

Works, Advisory Committee on Federal Public Established by President Oct. 5, 1955. Abolished by President Mar. 12, 1961, and functions assigned to *Bureau of the Budget.*

Works Administration, Federal Civil Established by EO 6420–B of Nov. 9, 1933. Function of employment expired March 1934. Function of settling claims continued under *Works Progress Administration.*

Works Administration, Public *See* **Emergency Administration of Public Works, Federal**

Works Agency, Federal Established by Reorg. Plan No. I of 1939, effective July 1, 1939. Functions relating to defense housing transferred to *Federal Public Housing Authority, National Housing Agency,* by EO 9070 of Feb. 24, 1942. Abolished by act of June 30, 1949 (63 Stat. 380), and functions transferred to General Services Administration.

Works Emergency Housing Corporation, Public Established by EO 6470 of Nov. 29, 1933. Incorporated under laws of State of Delaware. Abolished and liquidated as of Aug. 14, 1935, by filing of certificate of surrender of corporate rights.

Works Emergency Leasing Corporation, Public Incorporated Jan. 3, 1934, under laws of Delaware by direction of Administrator of Public Works. Terminated with filed certificate of dissolution with secretary of state of Delaware Jan. 2, 1935.

Works Progress Administration Established by EO 7034 of May 6, 1935, and continued by subsequent yearly emergency relief appropriation acts. Renamed *Work Projects Administration* by Reorg. Plan No. I of 1939, effective July 1, 1939, which provided for consolidation of *Works Progress Administration* into *Federal Works Agency.* Transferred by President to *Federal Works Administrator* Dec. 4, 1942.

Works, Special Board of Public *See* **Land Program, Director of**

Yards and Docks, Bureau of Established by acts of Aug. 31, 1842 (5 Stat. 579), and July 5, 1862 (12 Stat. 510). Abolished by Department of Defense reorg. order of Mar. 9, 1966, and functions transferred to the Secretary of the Navy (31 FR 7188).

Youth Administration, National Established in *Works Progress Administration* by EO 7086 of June 26, 1935. Transferred to *Federal Security Agency* by Reorg. Plan No. I of 1939, effective July 1, 1939. Transferred to *Bureau of Training, War Manpower Commission,* by EO 9247 of Sept. 17, 1942. Terminated by act of July 12, 1943 (57 Stat. 539).

Youth Crime, President's Committee on Juvenile Delinquency and Established by EO 10940 of May 11, 1961. Terminated by EO 11529 of Apr. 24, 1970.

Youth Fitness, President's Council on Established by EO 10673 of July 16, 1956. Renamed *President's Council on Physical Fitness* by EO 11074 of Jan. 8, 1963. Renamed President's Council on Physical Fitness and Sports by EO 11398 of Mar. 4, 1968. Abolished and reestablished by EO 13265 of June 6, 2002. Renamed President's Council on Fitness, Sports, and Nutrition by EO 13545 of June 22, 2010.

Youth Opportunity, President's Council on Established by EO 11330 of Mar. 5, 1967. Inactive as of June 30, 1971; EO 11330 revoked by EO 12379 of Aug. 17, 1982.

Youth Programs, Office of Established in the Department of the Interior by Secretarial Order No. 2985 of Jan. 7, 1965. Functions moved to Office of Historically Black College and University Programs and Job Corps, Office of the Secretary, by Departmental Manual Release 2788 of Mar. 22, 1988.